Microsoft

Core Reference

Sixth Edition

PROGRAMMING WITH MICROSOFT® VISUAL C++® .NET

George Shepherd
with David Kruglinski

PUBLISHED BY
Microsoft Press
A Division of Microsoft Corporation
One Microsoft Way
Redmond, Washington 98052-6399

Library of Congress Cataloging-in-Publication Data
Shepherd, George
Programming with Microsoft Visual C++ .NET, Sixth Edition (Core Reference) / George Shepherd.
p. cm.
Includes index.
ISBN 0-7356-1549-7

2002

Printed and bound in the United States of America.

1 2 3 4 5 6 7 8 9 QWT 7 6 5 4 3 2

Distributed in Canada by H.B. Fenn and Company Ltd.

A CIP catalogue record for this book is available from the British Library.

Microsoft Press books are available through booksellers and distributors worldwide. For further information about international editions, contact your local Microsoft Corporation office or contact Microsoft Press International directly at fax (425) 936-7329. Visit our Web site at www.microsoft.com/mspress. Send comments to: *mspinput@microsoft.com.*

Acquisitions Editors: Juliana Aldous and Danielle Bird
Project Editor: Denise Bankaitis
Technical Editor: Julie Xiao

Body Part No. X08-68165

Dedicated to Sandy Daston and Ted Shepherd

Table of Contents

Acknowledgments

This part of book writing is always the best— everybody involved is nearly done with the manuscript and all that's left to do is to thank everybody. Because the author's name appears on the cover, it's sometimes easy to forget all the other folks involved in a project as large as this. Many other folks gave their time and energy to this project, and I wish to thank you.

Thank you Sandy Daston and Ted Shepherd—my family, for your support while I wrote this book.

Thank you, Denise Bankaitis. As the project editor, you kept me going by reminding me of the importance of this project (a key C++ reference for .NET) and by coordinating the efforts of the rest of the team, which includes Julie Xiao, Ina Chang, Danielle Bird, Juliana Aldous, Joel Panchot, Carl Diltz, and Gina Cassill.

Thank you, Julie Xiao, for keeping the manuscript accurate.

Thank you, Ina Chang, for making my sentences readable.

Thank you, Danielle Bird and Juliana Aldous. As acquisition editors, you got this project rolling and kept it on track.

Thank you, Joel Panchot, for making sure the art in this book looks good.

Thank you, Carl Diltz and Gina Cassill, for composing the manuscript and making it look great.

I would also like to thank the folks at DevelopMentor, for providing a wonderful environment and community for thinking and learning about modern computing. You guys are wonderful.

Introduction

The release of the Microsoft Visual Studio .NET (and Visual C++ .NET in particular) has underscored Microsoft's increasing focus on Internet technologies, which are at the heart of the Microsoft .NET architecture. In addition to supporting the .NET initiative, Visual C++ .NET keeps all the productivity-boosting features you're familiar with, such as Edit And Continue, IntelliSense, AutoComplete, and code tips. Visual C++ .NET also includes many new features such as managed code extensions for .NET programming, support for attributed code, and a more consistent development environment. These features take Visual C++ .NET to a new level. This book will get you up to speed on the latest technologies introduced into Visual C++.

.NET, MFC, and ATL

The technology churn we face these days is pretty impressive. We went from no computers on our office desktops to nearly everyone having a computer running MS-DOS in the 1980s to nearly everyone running Microsoft Windows by the mid-1990s. The technology wheel is about to turn again. In the late 1990s, everyone was developing Web sites by hand using tools such as raw Hypertext Markup Language (HTML), Common Gateway Interface (CGI), Internet Server Application Programming Interface (ISAPI) DLLs, Java, and Active Server Pages (ASP). In July 2000, Microsoft announced to the world that it would change all that by betting the company on a new technology direction named .NET.

The current thrust of Microsoft is indeed .NET. For a number of years, it's been possible to build a Web site by setting up a server somewhere, getting an IP address, and putting up some content. Anyone with the URL of your site can surf there and check it out. Commercial enterprises have been taking advantage of the Web by posting information that's useful to customers. The Web has also become an invaluable research tool and efficient news broadcast medium.

The computing world of the near future will involve the Web heavily. However, rather than just having human eyeballs look at Web sites, computers themselves will look at Web sites. That is, Web sites will be programmable through Web services. The .NET vision also pushes the responsibility of providing a rich user interface out to the server.

With so much emphasis on Web services and server-based user interfaces, it might seem that standalone applications and client-side user interface scenarios—normally the realm of tools such as the Microsoft Foundation Class Library (MFC)—will be left in the dust. But the need for rich client-side user interfaces is unlikely to go away. Many thought that the advent of the PC and distribution technologies would spell the end of centralized processing on mainframes and minicomputers. It turns out that PCs and distribution technologies only added to the available computing arsenal. The .NET vision of Web services and rich user interfaces provided by the server only adds to the options available to software developers. Rich client-side user interfaces will continue to be viable for many types of applications, running alongside other applications that use other kinds of user interfaces (such as server-generated user interfaces).

MFC is a mature and well-understood technology that's accompanied by a host of third-party extensions. For at least a little while longer, MFC represents the most effective way to write full-featured standalone applications. A good portion of this book will focus on MFC-style development, but we'll also cover Windows Forms—the .NET way to write client-side user interfaces.

Of course, the next question is: Where does this leave COM? COM has solved many problems related to distributed processing, but it has some serious shortcomings—mostly centered around component versioning and type information. Microsoft's .NET vision is based on the common language runtime. The runtime takes the place of COM as the interoperability standard within .NET. We'll cover .NET and the common language runtime in depth in Part VI of this book.

COM and the common language runtime represent different approaches to component architecture, but Microsoft has taken great care to ensure a seamless coexistence. The interoperability path between COM and the runtime is smooth in most cases. Within the .NET world, you probably won't find yourself using COM as a component architecture. However, you might find yourself using Active Template Library (ATL) Server, which is a high-performance means of writing Web sites.

I've updated the coverage of ATL and MFC in this edition of the book because you'll still find it very useful. More important, I'll show you how to leverage your heritage code (sounds better than "legacy code," doesn't it?) as you move into the .NET world.

Managed C++ vs. C#

The .NET platform has introduced a new C++-like language named C#. C# is a curly-brace-oriented language without all the headaches of C++. Much of C#'s appeal is due to the fact that it's missing some of the more problematic elements of C++ (such as raw pointer management) while maintaining the useful features (such as virtual functions). The C# compiler eventually emits managed code—the kind that runs under the common language runtime.

However, the entire world isn't going to switch over to C# overnight. There's just too much C++ code out there to convert. Also, it will take a bit of time for developers to become fully comfortable with C#. In the meantime, .NET has introduced extensions to C++ for producing managed code (code that runs under the common language runtime). Managed Extensions for C++ will help ease the burden of developing software for the .NET platform because they allow you to quickly update existing C++ code to work with .NET. Getting the managed code features in C++ means sprinkling your code with various keywords. In the end, C# and managed C++ boil down to the same executable code once the compilers are done with it. In the .NET world, you'll probably find yourself writing new components using C# while using managed C++ to add .NET features to your existing code base.

.NET vs. the Java Platform

In recent years, we've seen a great deal of interest in the Java programming language and platform. Java became a great boon for Internet developers by providing a useful means of distributing client user interfaces (through Java applets) and by providing enterprise solutions through Java Enterprise Edition. Now, .NET has become the best Internet development platform available today. Unlike the Java platform, which requires that you write all your code using the Java syntax, .NET often lets you use multiple syntaxes to arrive at the same machine instruction set. You can use C++ (the main focus of this book) and its managed extensions, Visual Basic .NET, C#, and even a host of third-party .NET languages to write your programs. Once you develop your source code, it is compiled to intermediate language and then eventually machine code before it runs. Because .NET code is managed by a runtime, you get benefits such as garbage collection and better code security.

Who This Book Is For

Visual C++ .NET, with its sophisticated application framework and support for .NET, is for professional programmers, and so is this book. I'll assume that you're proficient in the C language—you can write an if statement without consulting the manual. And I'll assume that you've been exposed to the C++ language—you've at least taken a course or read a book even if you haven't written much code. You might compare learning C++ to learning French. You can study French in school, but you won't be able to speak fluently unless you go to a French-speaking country and start talking to people.

The Visual C++ wizards save you time and improve accuracy, but programmers must understand the code that the wizards generate and, ultimately, they must understand the structure of the MFC and ATL libraries, the inner workings of the Windows operating system, and how .NET works. I won't assume, however, that you already know Windows and .NET programming. I'm sure that proficient C programmers can learn Windows the MFC way and the .NET way. It's more important to know C++ than it is to know the Win32 application programming interface (API). You should, however, know how to run Windows and Windows-based applications.

If you're already experienced with the Win32 API or with the MFC library, there's something in this book for you, too. You'll learn about new features such as the Multiple Top-Level Interface (MTI) and the Visual C++ .NET wizards. If you haven't already figured out the Component Object Model (COM), this book presents some important theory that will get you started on understanding ActiveX controls. You'll also learn about ATL Server and OLE DB templates. And you'll learn about C++ programming for the Internet (including Dynamic HTML). Finally, this book includes hard-to-find coverage of the new managed C++ extensions.

What's Not Covered

It's impossible to cover every aspect of Windows and .NET programming in a single book. I've excluded topics that depend on special-purpose hardware and software, such as MAPI, TAPI, and communications port access. I'll cover using ActiveX controls in an application and writing ActiveX controls using ATL, but I'll defer the in-depth coverage to Adam Denning and his *ActiveX Controls Inside Out* (Microsoft Press, 1997). I'll get you started with 32-bit memory management, DLL theory, multi-threaded programming techniques, and .NET programming, but you need to get the third edition of Jeffrey Richter's Programming Applications for Microsoft Windows (Microsoft Press, 1997) if you're serious about these subjects. Another useful book is MFC Internals by George Shepherd and Scot Wingo (Addison-Wesley, 1996). I'll also give you a head start into the .NET space, but I'll leave the hardcore runtime issues to Jeffrey Richter's Applied .NET Programming (Microsoft Press, 2002).

How to Use This Book

When you're starting with Visual C++ .NET, you can use this book as a tutorial by going through it sequentially. Later, you can use it as a reference by looking up topics in the table of contents or in the index. Because of the tight interrelationships among many application framework elements, it wasn't possible to cleanly isolate each concept in its own chapter, so the book isn't organized as an encyclopedia. When you use this book, you'll definitely want to keep the online help available for looking up classes and member functions.

If you're experienced with earlier versions of Visual C++, scan Part I for an overview of new features. Then skip the basic MFC coverage in Part II but read the more advanced coverage. Also, be sure to read the .NET coverage. Much of the software development community's efforts are heading in this direction, and Visual C++ .NET fully supports the .NET programming model.

How This Book Is Organized

As the table of contents shows, this book has six parts and an appendix section.

Part I: Windows, Visual C++ .NET, and Application Framework Fundamentals

This part tries to strike a balance between abstract theory and practical application. After a quick review of Win32 and the Visual C++ .NET components, you'll be introduced to the MFC application framework and the document-view architecture. You'll look at a simple "Hello, world!" program built with the MFC library classes that requires only 30 lines of code.

Part II: MFC Essentials

The MFC library documentation presents all the application framework elements in quick succession, with the assumption that you're at least familiar with the original Windows API. In Part II of this book, you're confined to one major application framework component—the view, which is really a window. You'll learn what experienced Windows programmers know already, but in the context of C++ and the MFC library classes. You'll use the Visual C++ .NET tools that eliminate much of the coding drudgery that early Windows programmers had to endure.

This part covers a lot of territory, including graphics programming with bitmaps, dialog data exchange, ActiveX control usage, 32-bit memory management, and multi-threaded programming. The exercises will help you to write reasonably sophisticated Windows-based programs, but those programs won't take advantage of the advanced application framework features.

Part III: MFC's Document-View Architecture

This part introduces the real core of application framework programming—the document-view architecture. You'll learn what a document is (something much more general than a word processing document), and you'll see how to connect the document to the view that you studied in Part II. You'll be amazed, once you've written a document class, at how the MFC library simplifies file I/O and printing.

Along the way, you'll learn about command message processing, toolbars and status bars, splitter frames, and context-sensitive help. You'll also be introduced to the Single Document Interface (SDI), the Multiple Document Interface (MDI), and the Multiple Top-Level Interface (MTI), which is the current standard for Windows-based applications such as Microsoft Word.

Part III also discusses dynamic link libraries (DLLs) written with the MFC library. You'll learn the distinction between an extension DLL and a regular DLL.

Part IV: COM, Automation, ActiveX, and OLE

COM itself deserves more than one book. Part IV will get you started in learning fundamental COM theory from the MFC point of view. You'll progress to Automation, which is the link between C++ and Visual Basic for Applications (VBA). You'll also become familiar with uniform data transfer, and you'll learn the basics of compound documents and embedded objects. You'll learn about the ATL class library support for OLE DB.

Part V: Programming for the Internet

This part starts with a technical Internet tutorial that covers the TCP/IP protocol and the fundamentals of Internet programming. You'll learn how to develop servers using ATL Server, and you'll learn how to program for Dynamic HTML.

Part VI: .NET and Beyond

The Internet is evolving as the next frontier for software development. The Internet is no longer just about building Web sites for people to simply look at—it's about Web sites that people can program. The wire's in place, but until the advent of XML, no one was been able to agree on how to send method calls across the Internet. Two main thrusts of .NET include Web services and server-based user interfaces. .NET fully supports both these notions, along with a new way to write client user interfaces: Windows Forms. Part VI covers what .NET is all about and what you can do with it as a platform. Included here are chapters on the common language runtime and managed code, programming managed components using C++, ASP.NET, and ADO.NET.

Appendixes

Appendix A contains a list of message map macros and their corresponding handler function prototypes. The code wizards available from Class View usually generate this code for you, but sometimes you must make manual entries.

Appendix B offers a description of the MFC application framework's runtime class information and dynamic creation system. This is independent of the runtime type information (RTTI) feature that is now a part of ANSI C++.

Win32 vs. Win16

A few old computers out there are still running Windows 3.1. However, there's not much point in spending money writing new programs for obsolete technology. This edition of Programming with Microsoft Visual C++ .NET is about 32-bit programming for Windows 98/Me and Windows NT/2000/XP using the Win32 API. If you really need to do 16-bit programming, I suggest that you find an old copy of the second edition of this book.

System Requirements

To use this book, you'll need to have Visual C++ .NET or Visual Studio .NET installed on your computer. Any computer that satisfies the minimum requirements for Visual C++ .NET will work effectively with most of the examples in this book. Be aware that Windows XP Home Edition and Windows NT 4.0 don't support the hosting of ASP.NET Web applications with the .NET Framework. You can build these projects on these operating systems, but you'll need to upload the projects to a properly configured host to execute them.

Sample Files

You can find the sample files on the book's companion CD, along with other supplemental content. To access the files on the CD, insert the disc in your computer's CD drive and make a selection from the menu that appears. If the AutoRun feature is not enabled on your system (if a menu doesn't appear when you insert the CD into the drive), run StartCD.exe in the root folder of the companion CD. Installing the sample files on your hard disk requires approximately 60 MB of disk space. If you have trouble running any of these files, refer to the text in the book that describes these programs.

With a conventional C-language program using the Windows API, the source code files tell the whole story. With the MFC library application framework, things are not so simple. The MFC Application Wizard generates much of the C++ code, and the resources originate in the resource editors. The examples in the early chapters of this book include step-by-step instructions for using the tools to generate and customize the source code files. You'd be well advised to walk through those instructions for the first few examples—there's very little code to type. For the middle chapters, use the code from the sample files but read through the steps to appreciate the role of the resource editors and the wizards. For the final chapters, not all the source code is listed. You'll need to examine the sample files for those examples.

Aside from the sample files, the book's supplemental content includes two eBook installations: a standalone eBook installation and a Visual Studio Help eBook installation. The standalone eBook installation allows you to access an electronic version of the print book directly from your desktop. The Visual Studio Help eBook installation allows you to access the second electronic version of the print book directly from the Visual Studio .NET help system.

Visual Studio .NET Professional Trial Version

In addition to the companion CD, this book also includes a DVD with an evaluation copy of Visual Studio .NET Professional. This evaluation copy can help you follow the examples in this book and get you started learning Visual C++ .NET, but the software will expire and stop working 60 days after you install it.

You can learn more about this evaluation copy and its system requirements at *http://msdn.microsoft.com/vstudio/productinfo/trial.asp*. Note that no product support is available for the trial version.

Windows Forms Library Extensions

One of the biggest selling points behind MFC during the 1990s was the great class libraries available for extending the framework. With Windows Forms on the horizon, it's time to keep an eye out for class libraries that extend Windows Forms.

MFC and its extensions were confined to the C++ language, but the .NET common language runtime offers a variety of syntaxes for writing Windows Forms, including C#, Visual Basic .NET, and Managed C++. Syncfusion, a company based in Cary, North Carolina, provides a wide variety of .NET tools to make programming for .NET easier. Syncfusion's Essential Suite includes components to make your .NET Windows Forms applications more solid and polished. You can download a fully functional 15-day trial version from *http://www.syncfusion.com*, as well as the Essential Suite Interactive Showcase, an application that shows several Syncfusion components in action. The components run under the common language runtime, so they work with Managed C++ as well as with C# and Visual Basic .NET.

Microsoft Press Support Information

Every effort has been made to ensure the accuracy of this book and the contents of the companion CD. Microsoft Press provides corrections for books at *http://www.microsoft.com/mspress/support/*.

To connect directly to the Microsoft Press Knowledge Base and submit a query, go to: *http://www.microsoft.com/mspress/support/search.asp*.

If you have comments, questions, or ideas regarding this book or the companion content or questions that are not answered by querying the Knowledge Base, please send them to Microsoft Press using postal mail or e-mail:

Microsoft Press
Attn: Programming with Microsoft Visual C++ .NET Editor
One Microsoft Way
Redmond, WA 98052-6399
mspinput@microsoft.com

Note that product support is not offered through the above mail addresses. For Microsoft Visual C++ .NET support information, please visit the Microsoft Support Web site at: *http://support.microsoft.com*.

Part I

Windows, Visual C++ .NET, and Application Framework Fundamentals

1

Windows and Visual C++ .NET

In the early nineties, the battle was for the desktop operating system. Now that battle is over, and Microsoft Windows runs on the vast majority of personal computer systems. This chapter summarizes the low-level Windows programming model (Win32, in particular) and shows you how the Microsoft Visual C++ .NET components work together to help you write applications for Windows. Along the way, you might learn some new things about Windows as well.

The Windows Programming Model

No matter which development tools you use, programming for Windows is different from old-style batch-oriented or transaction-oriented programming. To get started, you need to know some Windows fundamentals. As a frame of reference, we'll use the well-known MS-DOS programming model. Even if you don't currently program for plain MS-DOS, you're probably familiar with it.

Message Processing

When you write an MS-DOS–based application in C, the only absolute requirement is a function named *main*. The operating system calls *main* when the user runs the program, and from that point on, you can use any programming structure you want. If your program needs to get user keystrokes or otherwise use operating system services, it calls an appropriate function, such as *getchar*, or perhaps uses a character-based windowing library.

When the Windows operating system launches a program, it calls the program's *WinMain* function. Somewhere your application must have *WinMain*, which performs some specific tasks. Its most important task is creating the application's main window, which must have its own code to process messages that Windows sends it. An essential difference between a program written for MS-DOS and a program written for Windows is that an MS-DOS–based program calls the operating system to get user input but a Windows-based program processes user input via messages from the operating system.

> **Note** Many development environments for Windows, including Visual C++ .NET with Microsoft Foundation Class (MFC) library version 7.0, simplify programming by hiding the *WinMain* function and structuring the message-handling process. When you use the MFC library, you need not write a *WinMain* function, but it is essential that you understand the link between the operating system and your programs.

Most messages in Windows are strictly defined and apply to all programs. For example, a *WM_CREATE* message is sent when a window is being created, a *WM_LBUTTONDOWN* message is sent when the user presses the left mouse button, a *WM_CHAR* message is sent when the user types a character, and a *WM_CLOSE* message is sent when the user closes a window. All messages have two 32-bit parameters that convey information such as cursor coordinates, key code, and so forth. Windows sends *WM_COMMAND* messages to the appropriate window in response to user menu choices, dialog box button clicks, and so on. Command message parameters vary depending on the window's menu layout. You can define your own messages, which your program can send to any window on the desktop. These user-defined messages actually make C++ look a little like Smalltalk.

Don't worry yet about how these messages are connected to your code. That's the job of the application framework. Be aware, though, that the Windows message processing requirement imposes a lot of structure on your program. Don't try to force your Windows-based programs to look like your old MS-DOS programs. Study the examples in this book, and then be prepared to start fresh.

The Windows Graphics Device Interface

Many MS-DOS programs write directly to the video memory and the printer port. The disadvantage of this technique is the need to supply driver software for every video board and every printer model. Windows introduced a layer of abstraction called the Graphics Device Interface (GDI). Windows provides the video and printer drivers, so your program doesn't need to know the type of video board and printer attached to the system. Instead of addressing the hardware, your program calls GDI functions that reference a data structure called a *device context*. Windows maps the device context structure to a physical device and issues the appropriate input/output instructions. The GDI is almost as fast as direct video access, and it allows different applications written for Windows to share the display.

Later in the book, we'll look at GDI+. As you might guess, GDI+ is the successor to GDI. The services of GDI+ are exposed through a set of C++ classes deployed as managed code—that is, code running under the common language runtime. GDI+ introduces several enhancements over classic GDI, including gradient brushes, cardinal splines, independent path objects, scalable regions, alpha blending, and multiple image formats.

Resource-Based Programming

To do data-driven programming in MS-DOS, you must either code the data as initialization constants or provide separate data files for your program to read. When you program for Windows, you store data in a resource file using a number of established formats. The linker combines this binary resource file with the C++ compiler's output to generate an executable program. Resource files can include bitmaps, icons, menu definitions, dialog box layouts, and strings. They can even include custom resource formats that you define.

You use a text editor to edit a program, but you generally use WYSIWYG (what you see is what you get) tools to edit resources. If you're laying out a dialog box, for example, you select elements (buttons, list boxes, and so forth) from an array of icons called a *control palette*, and you position and size the elements with the mouse. Visual C++ .NET has graphics resource editors for all standard resource formats.

Memory Management

With each new version of Windows, memory management gets easier. If you've heard horror stories about locking memory handles, thunks, and burgermasters, don't worry. That's all in the past. Today you simply allocate the memory you need, and Windows takes care of the details. Chapter 10 describes current memory management techniques for Win32, including virtual memory and memory-mapped files.

Dynamic-Link Libraries

In the MS-DOS environment, all of a program's object modules are statically linked during the build process. Windows allows dynamic linking, which means that specially constructed libraries can be loaded and linked at run time. Multiple applications can share dynamic-link libraries (DLLs), which saves memory and disk space. Dynamic linking increases program modularity because you can compile and test DLLs separately.

Designers originally created DLLs for use with the C language, and C++ has added some complications. The MFC library developers succeeded in combining all the application framework classes into a few ready-built DLLs. This means that you can statically or dynamically link the application framework classes into your application. In addition, you can create your own extension DLLs that build on the MFC DLLs. Chapter 22 includes information about creating MFC extension DLLs and regular DLLs.

The Win32 Application Programming Interface

Early Windows programmers wrote applications in C for the Win16 application programming interface (API). Of course, today few folks write 16-bit applications. Most developers write applications using the Win32 API. The main difference between the Win16 functions and the Win32 functions is that in the latter, many of the parameters have been widened. So while the Windows API has changed over the years (and continues to change), developers using the MFC library have remained insulated from these changes because the MFC standard was designed to work with either Win16 or Win32 underneath.

Visual C++ .NET Components

Visual C++ .NET consists of several complete Windows application development systems in one product. If you want, you can develop C-language Windows-based programs using only the Win32 API. C-language Win32 programming is described in Charles Petzold's book *Programming Windows*, Fifth Edition (Microsoft Press, 1998). (Petzold has a new book on Windows-based programming from Microsoft Press, called *Programming Microsoft Windows with C#*, which covers programming Windows using C# and Windows Forms. We'll take a look at programming Windows using Windows Forms and C++ later in this book.) You can use many Visual C++ .NET tools, including the resource editors, to make low-level Win32 programming easier. You can also use application framework libraries such as the MFC library and Windows Forms in the managed library to further speed your Windows-based application development.

Finally, Visual C++ .NET includes the Active Template Library (ATL), which you can use to develop ActiveX controls. ATL programming is neither Win32 C-language programming nor MFC programming, and it's complex enough to deserve its own book. However, we'll touch on ATL development in this book. ATL will probably find itself most at home within the high-performance Web server environment.

The first section of this book is about C++ programming within the MFC library application framework that's part of Visual C++ .NET. You'll be using the C++ classes documented in the Microsoft Visual C++ MFC Library Reference included in the Visual Studio .NET documentation, and you'll also be using application framework–specific Visual C++ .NET tools such as Class View.

> **Note** Use of the MFC library programming interface doesn't cut you off from the Win32 functions. In fact, you'll almost always need some direct Win32 calls in your MFC library programs.

A quick run-through of the Visual C++ .NET components will help you get your bearings before you zero in on the application framework. Figure 1-1 shows an overview of the Visual C++ MFC application build process.

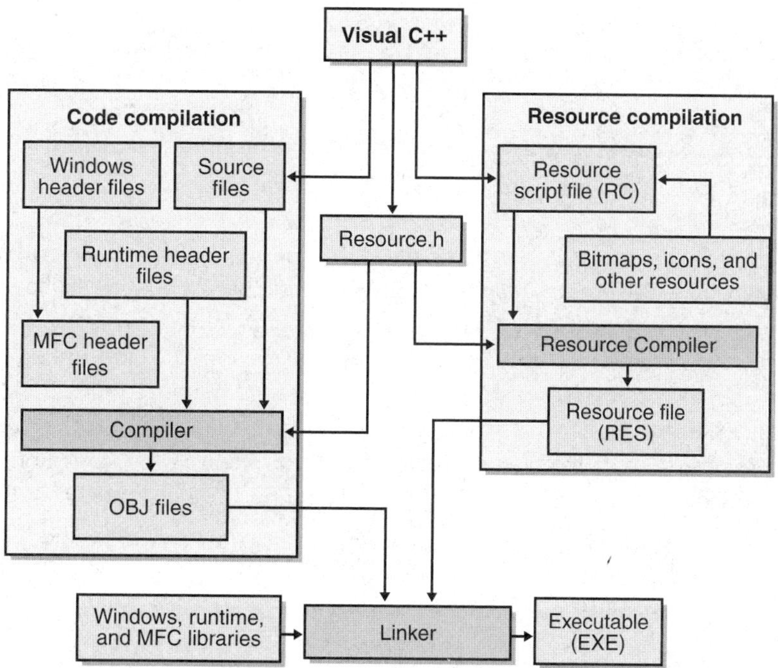

Figure 1-1 The Visual C++ MFC application build process.

Visual C++ .NET and the Build Process

Visual Studio .NET is a suite of developer tools that includes Visual C++ .NET. The Visual Studio .NET integrated development environment (IDE) is shared by several tools, including Visual C++ .NET, Microsoft Visual C#, and Microsoft Visual Basic .NET. The IDE has come a long way from the original Visual Workbench, which was based on QuickC for Windows. Docking windows, configurable toolbars, and a customizable editor that runs macros are now part of Visual Studio .NET. The online help system (now integrated with the MSDN Library viewer) works like a Web browser. Figure 1-2 shows Visual C++ .NET in action.

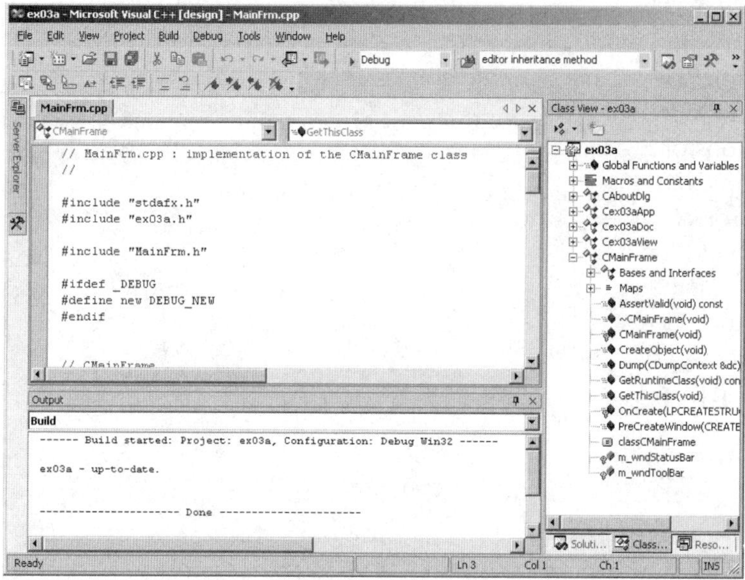

Figure 1-2 Visual C++ .NET windows.

If you've used earlier versions of Visual C++, you already understand how Visual C++ .NET operates (although some of the menus might have changed). But if you're new to IDEs, you'll need to know what a *project* is. A project is a collection of interrelated source files that are compiled and linked to make up an executable Windows-based program or a DLL. Source files for each project are generally stored in a separate subdirectory. A project also depends on many files outside the project subdirectory, such as include files and library files.

Visual Studio .NET also supports building projects outside of the development environment. Within Visual Studio .NET, makefiles are still supported. (A *makefile* stores compiler and linker options and expresses all the interrelationships among source files.) That is, you can still type up a makefile by hand and run it though NMAKE.EXE. (A source code file needs specific include files, an executable file requires certain object modules and libraries, and so forth.) NMAKE reads the makefile and then invokes the compiler, assembler, resource compiler, and linker to produce the final output, which is generally an executable file. NMAKE uses built-in inference rules that tell it, for example, to invoke the compiler to generate an OBJ file from a specified CPP file. Note that Visual C++ .NET no longer supports the ability to export a makefile for the active project from the development environment. Use *Devenv* command line switches to build Visual Studio .NET projects at the command line.

In a Visual C++ .NET project, a text-format project file (with a VCPROJ extension) maintains the dependencies between project parts. A separate text-format solution file (with an SLN extension) has an entry for each project in the solution. The solution file organizes projects, project items, and solution items into a single solution by providing the environment with references to their locations on disk. It's possible to have multiple projects in a solution, but all the examples in this book have just one project per solution. To work on an existing project, you tell Visual C++ .NET to open the SLN file, and then you can edit and build the project.

Visual C++ .NET creates some intermediate files too. Table 1-1 lists the files that Visual C++ .NET generates in the solution.

Table 1-1 File Types Generated in Visual C++ .NET Projects

Filename extension	Description
APS	Supports Resource View
BSC	Browser information file
IDL	Interface Definition Language file
NCB	Supports Class View
SLN	Solution file*
SUO	Holds solution options and configuration
VCPROJ	Project file*

* Do not delete or edit in a text editor.

The Resource View Window and the Resource Editors

When you open the Resource View window (choose Resource View from the View menu) in the Visual C++ .NET IDE, you can select a resource for editing. The main window hosts a resource editor appropriate for the resource type. The window can also host a WYSIWYG editor for menus and a powerful graphical editor for dialog boxes, and it includes tools for editing icons, bitmaps, and strings. The dialog editor allows you to insert ActiveX controls in addition to standard Windows controls and the Windows common controls.

Each project usually has one text-format resource script (RC) file that describes the project's menu, dialog box, string, and accelerator resources. The RC file also has *#include* statements to bring in resources from other subdirectories. These resources include project-specific items, such as bitmap (BMP) and icon (ICO) files, and resources common to all Visual C++ .NET programs, such as error message strings. Editing the RC file outside the resource editors is not recommended. The resource editors can also process EXE and DLL files, so you can use the Clipboard to "steal" resources, such as bitmaps and icons, from other Windows-based applications.

The C/C++ Compiler

The Visual C++ .NET compiler can process both C source code and C++ source code. It determines the language by looking at the source code's filename extension. The C extension indicates C source code, and the CPP or CXX extension indicates C++ source code. The compiler is compliant with all ANSI (American National Standards Institute) standards, including the latest recommendations of a working group on C++ libraries, and has additional Microsoft extensions. Templates, exceptions, and runtime type information (RTTI) are fully supported in Visual C++ .NET. The C++ Standard Template Library (STL) is also included, although it is not integrated into the MFC library.

The Source Code Editor

Visual C++ .NET includes a sophisticated source code editor that supports many features such as dynamic syntax coloring, auto-tabbing, keyboard bindings for a variety of popular editors (such as VI and EMACS), and pretty printing. Starting with Visual C++ 6, the environment includes a feature named AutoComplete. If you have used any of the Microsoft Office products or Visual Basic, you might already be familiar with this technology. Using the Visual Studio .NET AutoComplete feature, all you have to do is type the beginning of a programming statement and the editor will provide you with a list of possible completions to choose from. This feature is extremely handy when you are working with C++ objects and have forgotten an exact member function or data member name—they're all there in the list for you. Thanks to this feature, you no longer have to memorize thousands of Win32 APIs or rely heavily on the online help system.

The Resource Compiler

The Visual C++ resource compiler reads an ASCII RC file from the resource editors and writes a binary RES file for the linker.

The Linker

The linker reads the OBJ and RES files produced by the C/C++ compiler and the resource compiler, and it accesses LIB files for MFC code, runtime library code, and Windows code. It then writes the project's EXE file. An incremental link option minimizes the execution time when only minor changes have been made to the source files. The MFC header files contain *#pragma* statements (special compiler directives) that specify the required library files, so you don't have to tell the linker explicitly which libraries to read.

The Debugger

If your program works the first time, you don't need a debugger. The rest of us might need one from time to time. Visual Studio .NET provides an integrated debugger by combining features of the earlier versions of Visual C++ and Visual Basic debuggers and adding many new features. These new features include the following:

- **Cross-language debugging** Visual Studio .NET lets you debug projects that are part of the same solution even if they're written in different languages.
- **Attachment to a running program** Visual Studio .NET lets you attach to and debug a program that is running outside of Visual Studio .NET.
- **Remote debugging** Visual Studio .NET supports remote debugging. That is, you can attach to a program that's running on another server.
- **Debugging of ASP.NET Web applications** ASP.NET files are compiled, so they get the same treatment during debugging that other languages get. This makes it much easier than before to debug Web applications.
- **.NET Framework classes for debugging and code tracing** The .NET Framework classes make it easy to instrument and put trace statements in your code. Because these classes are managed code, you can run them within managed C++ code.

Figure 1-3 shows the integrated debugger in action.

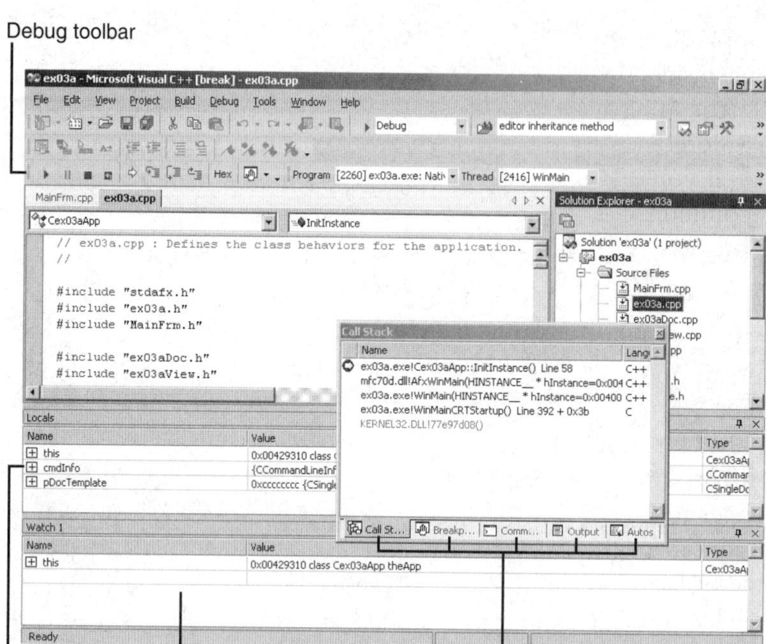

Figure 1-3 The Visual C++ .NET debugger window.

Note that the Variables and Watch windows can expand an object pointer to show all data members of the derived class and base classes. If you position the cursor on a simple variable, the debugger will show you its value in a little window. To debug a program, you must build the program with the compiler and linker options set to generate debugging information.

Visual C++ .NET includes an Edit And Continue feature. Edit And Continue lets you debug an application, change the application, and then continue debugging with the new code. This feature dramatically reduces the amount of time you spend debugging because you no longer have to manually leave the debugger, recompile, and then debug again. To use this feature, you simply edit any code while you're in the debugger and then hit the Continue button. Visual C++ .NET will compile the changes and restart the debugger for you.

The MFC Application Wizard

The MFC Application Wizard is a code generator that creates a working skeleton of a Windows-based application with features, class names, and source code filenames that you specify using dialog boxes. You'll use the MFC Application Wizard extensively as you work through the examples in this book. Don't confuse the MFC Application Wizard with older code generators that generate all the code for an application. The MFC Application Wizard code is minimalist code; the functionality is inside the application framework base classes.

The MFC Application Wizard gets you started quickly with a new application. Moreover, the wizard is extensible—you can write your own code generators. If you discover that your team needs to develop multiple projects with a telecommunications interface, you can build a special wizard that automates the process.

Class View

You can open the Class View window by choosing Class View from the View menu. You get a tree view of all the classes in your project, which displays member functions and data members, as shown in Figure 1-2. Double-click an element, and you will see the source code immediately. When you make changes to your code, Class View will reflect the changes by updating its content automatically. Earlier versions of Visual C++ included a single component named ClassWizard that handled almost all tasks involved in managing Visual C++ class code. The ClassWizard functionality has been replaced with several new wizards that individually perform such tasks as adding whole new classes, adding virtual functions to a class, and adding message-handler functions. For example, adding classes and functions has been replaced by functionality found in Class View.

Solution Explorer

Solution Explorer represents an organized view of your entire project. An entire Visual Studio .NET application might include many items—including many projects. Solution Explorer allows you to manage all aspects of a solution.

Solution Explorer includes a tree view listing the items in your project. Solution Explorer allows you to open the items for modification or perform other management tasks. The tree view of the items shows the logical relationship of the solution to projects and solution items. The view does not necessarily represent a physical storage relationship. You can associate files with the solution but not a specific project by adding them directly to the solution.

The Object Browser

If you write an application from scratch, you probably have a good mental picture of your source code files, classes, and member functions. If you take over someone else's application, however, you'll generally need some assistance.

The Visual C++ .NET Object Browser (the browser, for short) lets you examine (and edit) an application from the class or function viewpoint instead of from the file viewpoint. It's a little like the "inspector" tools available with object-oriented libraries such as Smalltalk.

To invoke the browser, you choose Other Windows, Object Browser from the View menu. The browser has the following viewing modes:

- **Definitions and References** You select any function, variable, type, macro, or class and then see where it's defined and used in your project.
- **Sorting** You can sort objects and members alphabetically, by type, and by access.
- **Derived Classes and Members/Base Classes and Members** These are graphical class hierarchy diagrams. For a selected class, you see the derived classes or the base classes plus members. You can control the hierarchy expansion with the mouse.

A typical browser window is shown in Chapter 3.

> **Note** If you rearrange the lines in any source code file, Visual C++ .NET will regenerate the browser database when you rebuild the project. This increases the build time.

Unified Modeling Language Tools

Visual C++ .NET now includes Unified Modeling Language (UML) tools. UML is a set of diagramming and program description conventions for describing a system. The diagram types contained in UML include class diagrams, object diagrams, activity diagrams, and state diagrams. Many organizations are standardizing on UML as the way to document their systems.

Visual C++ .NET includes a command on the Project menu for reverse-engineering a project into a UML diagram. To reverse-engineer a Visual C++ .NET project into a set of UML diagrams, you first generate browser information for the project. Then you choose Visio UML, Reverse Engineer from the Project menu. Visual C++ .NET will generate a UML package (collection of diagrams) of your project and will fire up a copy of Visio and display the package. (The UML diagrams are generated in Visio format.)

Note To view the online help for a Visio UML solution, you must keep Visio active and running. At the end of the Visual Studio .NET Enterprise Architect installation, you will see an option to install Visio.

Online Help

Starting with Visual C++ 6, the help system has been moved to a separate application named the MSDN Library Viewer. This help system is based on HTML. Each topic is covered in an individual HTML document, and then all are combined into indexed files. The MSDN Library Viewer uses code from Microsoft Internet Explorer 4, so it works like the Web browser you already know. The MSDN Library can access the help files from the Visual Studio .NET CDs or from your hard disk, depending upon your choices during the install process, and it can access HTML files on the Internet.

Visual C++ .NET allows you to access help in different ways:

- **By book** When you choose Contents from Visual Studio .NET's Help menu, the Contents window opens and displays Visual Studio .NET documentation and the MSDN Library. Here you'll find Visual Studio .NET, the .NET Framework SDK, Platform SDK documentation, and more, all organized hierarchically by book and chapter. The scope of contents displayed depends on the filter you choose.
- **By topic** When you choose Index from Visual Studio .NET's Help menu, the Index window opens. You type a keyword in this window to see the topics and articles included for that keyword. The scope of topics displayed depends on the filter you choose.
- **By word** When you choose Search from Visual Studio .NET's Help menu, the Search window opens. You can use this window to perform a full-text search for a combination of words to view articles that contain those words. The scope of the search results depends on the filter you apply.
- **Dynamic help** Dynamic help helps you run Visual Studio .NET by providing pointers to information specific to the current area you're using or to the task you're trying to complete within the IDE.
- **F1 help** This is the programmer's best friend. Just move the cursor inside a function, macro, or class name and then press the F1 key, and the help system will go to work. If the name is found in several places—in the MFC and Win32 help files, for example—the Index window displays a list of topics, where you can choose the help topic you want.

However you access online help, you can copy any help text to the Clipboard for inclusion in your program.

Windows Diagnostic Tools

Visual C++ .NET contains a number of useful diagnostic tools. SPY++ gives you a tree view of your system's processes, threads, and windows. It also lets you view messages and examine the windows of running applications. Visual C++ .NET also includes a whole suite of ActiveX utilities, an ActiveX control test program, and other utilities.

The MFC Library Version 7

The MFC library version 7 is one of the main subjects of this book. It defines the application framework that you'll be learning intimately. Chapter 2 will get you started with actual code and will introduce some important concepts.

The ATL Library Version 7.0

The ATL is separate from the MFC library and is used for building ActiveX controls. You can build ActiveX controls with either the MFC or ATL library, but ATL controls are much smaller and are quicker to load on the Internet. Chapter 27 and Chapter 28 provide a brief overview of ATL and creating ActiveX controls with ATL. We'll also take a look at ATL Server in this book.

.NET Support

Visual Studio .NET fully supports the .NET Framework. While DLLs, C++, the MFC library, COM, and ATL can all work together to create Windows applications, the whole system does have a couple of warts. Once in a while, it seems that some parts are stuck together with bandages. One of the primary goals of .NET is to unify the programming model so the Windows platform is more solid. For example, the common language runtime functions to give all programming syntaxes a consistent set of data types. ASP.NET also runs under the runtime, making Web application programming much more consistent.

In addition to Visual Basic .NET, Microsoft is updating C++ to run under the new environment by adding managed extensions. You use managed extensions to tell the Visual C++ .NET compiler to emit code that runs under the runtime. There's a lot of heritage C++ code out there, and using managed extensions promises to make moving over to .NET much easier. I'll cover .NET and Visual C++ .NET's role in building .NET applications in detail in the second half of the book.

2

The Microsoft Foundation Class Library Application Framework

This chapter introduces the Microsoft Foundation Class (MFC) library 7.0 application framework and explains its benefits. It includes a stripped-down but fully operational MFC library program for Microsoft Windows that should help you understand what application framework programming is all about. I'm keeping theory to a minimum here, but I've included sections on message mapping and on documents and views to help you understand the examples in later chapters.

Why Use This Application Framework?

If you're going to develop applications for Windows, you've got to choose a development environment. Assuming that you've already rejected non-C options such as Microsoft Visual Basic and Borland Delphi, here are some of your remaining options:

- Program in C with the Win32 API.
- Write your own C++ Windows class library that uses Win32.
- Use the MFC library application framework.
- Use another Windows-based application framework. (Most of them are defunct, however—such as Borland's Object Windows Library [OWL].)

> **Note** We'll cover .NET Windows Forms in Part VI of this book.

If you're starting from scratch, any option will involve a big learning curve. If you're already a Win32 programmer, you'll still have a learning curve with the MFC library. Since its release, the MFC library has become the dominant Windows class library. But even if you're familiar with it, it's still a good idea to step through the features of this programming choice.

The MFC library is the low-level C++ interface to the Windows API C++ has been a standard for many developers for a number of years. It's turned into a mature, well-understood framework with great third-party support. If you need the highest-performance applications, your applications must live as closely to the Windows API as possible. C++ and MFC are as close as you can get without writing *WndProc* methods by hand.

Application framework applications use a standard structure Any programmer starting on a large project develops some kind of structure for the code. The problem is that each programmer's structure is different, and it's difficult for a new team member to learn the structure and conform to it. The MFC library application framework includes its own application structure—one that's been proven in many software environments and in many projects. If you write a program for Windows that uses the MFC library, you can safely retire to a Caribbean island, knowing that your minions can easily maintain and enhance your code back home.

Don't think that the MFC library's structure makes your programs inflexible. With the MFC library, your program can call Win32 functions at any time, so you can take maximum advantage of Windows.

Application framework applications are small and fast Back in the 16-bit days, you could build a self-contained Windows EXE file that was less than 20 KB in size. Today, Windows-based programs are larger. One reason is that 32-bit code is fatter. Even with the large memory model, a Win16 program uses 16-bit addresses for stack variables and many globals. Win32 programs use 32-bit addresses for everything and often use 32-bit integers because they're more efficient than 16-bit integers. In addition, the C++ exception-handling code consumes a lot of memory.

That old 20 KB program didn't have a docking toolbar, splitter windows, print preview capabilities, or control container support—features that users now expect. MFC programs are bigger because they do more and look better.

Fortunately, it's now easy to build applications that dynamically link to the MFC code (and to C run-time code), so the size goes back down again—from 192 KB to about 20 KB! Of course, you'll need some big support DLLs in the background, but those are a fact of life these days.

As far as speed is concerned, you're working with machine code produced by an optimizing compiler. Execution is fast, but you might notice a startup delay as the support DLLs are loaded.

The Visual C++ .NET tools reduce coding drudgery The Visual C++ .NET resource editors, the MFC Application Wizard, and the code wizards available from Class View significantly reduce the time needed to write code that's specific to your application. For example, the resource editor creates a header file that contains assigned values for *#define* constants. The MFC Application Wizard generates skeleton code for your entire application, and you can use the Properties window to add message handlers and map messages to them.

The MFC library application framework is feature rich The MFC library 1.0 classes, introduced with C/C++ 7.0, included the following features:

- A C++ interface to the Windows API
- General-purpose (non-Windows-specific) classes, including:
  - Collection classes for lists, arrays, and maps
  - A useful and efficient string class
  - Time, time span, and date classes
  - File access classes for operating system independence
  - Support for systematic object storage and retrieval to and from disk
- A "common root object" class hierarchy
- Streamlined Multiple Document Interface (MDI) application support
- Some support for OLE 1.0

The MFC library 2.0 classes (in Visual C++ 1.0) picked up where the version 1.0 classes left off by supporting many user interface features that are found in current Windows-based applications, plus they introduced the application framework architecture. Here's a summary of the important new features:

- Full support for File Open, Save, and Save As commands and the most recently used file list
- Print preview and printer support

- Support for scrolling windows and splitter windows
- Support for toolbars and status bars
- Access to Visual Basic controls
- Support for context-sensitive help
- Support for automatic processing of data entered in a dialog box
- An improved interface to OLE 1.0
- DLL support

The MFC library 2.5 classes (in Visual C++ 1.5) contributed the following:

- Open Database Connectivity (ODBC) support that allows your application to access and update data stored in many popular databases such as Microsoft Access, Microsoft FoxPro, and Microsoft SQL Server
- An interface to OLE 2.01, with support for in-place editing, linking, drag and drop, and OLE Automation

Visual C++ 2.0 was the first 32-bit version of the product. It included support for Microsoft Windows NT version 3.5. It also contained the MFC library 3.0, which had the following new features:

- Tab dialog box (property sheet) support (which was also added to Visual C++ 1.51, included on the same CD)
- Docking control bars that were implemented within MFC
- Support for thin-frame windows
- A separate Control Development Kit (CDK) for building 16-bit and 32-bit OLE controls, although no OLE control container support was provided

A subscription release, Visual C++ 2.1 with the MFC library 3.1, added the following:

- Support for the new Windows 95 (beta) common controls
- A new ODBC Level 2 driver integrated with the Access Jet database engine
- Winsock classes for TCP/IP data communication

Microsoft decided to skip Visual C++ 3.0 and proceeded directly to 4.0 in order to synchronize the product version with the MFC library. The MFC library 4.0 contains these additional features:

- New OLE-based Data Access Objects (DAO) classes for use with the Jet engine
- Use of the Windows 95 docking control bars instead of the MFC control bars
- Full support for the common controls in the released version of Windows 95, with new tree view and rich-edit view classes
- New classes for thread synchronization
- OLE control container support

Visual C++ 4.2 was an important subscription release that included the MFC library 4.2. The following new features were included:

- WinInet classes
- ActiveX Documents server classes
- ActiveX synchronous and asynchronous moniker classes
- Enhanced MFC ActiveX Control classes, with features such as windowless activation, optimized drawing code, and so forth
- Improved MFC ODBC support, including recordset bulk fetches and data transfer without binding

Visual C++ 5.0 included the MFC library 4.21, which fixed some 4.2 bugs. Visual C++ 5.0 introduced some worthwhile features of its own as well:

- A redesigned IDE, Microsoft Developer Studio 97, which included an HTML-based online help system and integration with other languages, including Java
- The Active Template Library (ATL) for efficient ActiveX control construction for the Internet
- C++ language support for COM (Component Object Model) client programs with the new *#import* statement for type libraries, as described in Chapter 25.

  Visual C++ 6.0 includes the MFC library 6.0. (Notice that the versions are synchronized again.) Many of the features in the MFC library 6.0 enabled developers to support the modern platform at the time, the Microsoft Active Platform, including the following:

- MFC classes that encapsulate the new Windows common controls introduced as part of Microsoft Internet Explorer 4.0
- Support for Dynamic HTML (DHTML), which allows MFC programmers to create applications that can dynamically manipulate and generate HTML pages

- Active Document Containment, which allows MFC-based applications to contain Active Documents
- OLE DB Consumers and Providers Template support and ActiveX Data Objects (ADO) data binding, which help database developers who use the MFC library or ATL

The latest edition of Visual C++, Visual C++ .NET, includes the MFC library 7.0. Many of the features in the MFC library 7.0 support Internet programming (and the new Microsoft .NET platform) and also improve the Windows development environment. The new features include the following:

- Enhanced support for HTML help within MFC applications
- Support for windowless controls
- DHTML dialog boxes and editing components
- HTTP argument management classes
- Windows 2000 Print dialog box
- Stricter message-handler type checking
- Date support beyond the year 2038

The Learning Curve

All the benefits sound great, don't they? But you're probably thinking, "You don't get something for nothing." Yes, that's true. To use the application framework effectively, you have to learn it thoroughly, and that takes time. If you had to learn C++, Windows, and the MFC library (without OLE) all at the same time, it would take at least six months before you were really productive. Interestingly, that's close to the learning time for the Win32 API alone.

How can that be if the MFC library offers so much more? For one thing, you can avoid many programming details that C-language Win32 programmers are forced to learn. From my own experience, I can say that an object-oriented application framework makes programming for Windows easier to learn—that is, once you understand object-oriented programming.

The MFC library won't bring real Windows-based programming to the masses. Programmers of applications for Windows have usually commanded higher salaries than other programmers, and that situation will continue. The MFC library's learning curve, together with the application framework's power, should ensure that MFC library programmers will continue to be in strong demand.

What's an Application Framework?

One definition of *application framework* is "an integrated collection of object-oriented software components that offers all that's needed for a generic application." That isn't a very useful definition, is it? If you really want to know what an application framework is, you'll have to read the rest of this book. The application framework example that you'll look at later in this chapter is a good starting point.

An Application Framework vs. a Class Library

One reason that C++ is a popular language is that it can be "extended" with class libraries. Some class libraries are delivered with C++ compilers, others are sold by third-party software firms, and still others are developed in-house. A class library is a set of related C++ classes that can be used in an application. A mathematics class library, for example, might perform common mathematics operations, and a communications class library might support the transfer of data over a serial link. Sometimes you construct objects of the supplied classes, sometimes you derive your own classes—it all depends on the design of the particular class library.

An application framework is a superset of a class library. An ordinary library is an isolated set of classes designed to be incorporated into any program, but an application framework defines the structure of the program itself. Microsoft didn't invent the application framework concept. It first appeared in the academic world, and the first commercial version was MacApp for the Apple Macintosh. Since the MFC library 2.0 was introduced, other companies, including Borland, have released similar products.

An Application Framework Example

Enough generalizations. It's time to look at some code—not pseudocode but real code that actually compiles and runs with the MFC library. Guess what? It's the good old "Hello, world!" application, with a few additions. (If you've used version 1.0 of the MFC library, this code will be familiar except for the frame window base class.) It's about the minimum amount of code for a working MFC library application for Windows. (Contrast it with an equivalent pure Win32 application such as you would see in a Petzold book!) You don't have to understand every line now. Don't bother to type it in and test it, because EX21B on the companion CD is quite similar. Wait for the next chapter, where you'll start using the "real" application framework.

> **Note** By convention, MFC library class names begin with the letter C.

Following is the source code for the header and implementation files for our MYAPP application. The classes *CMyApp* and *CMyFrame* are each derived from MFC library base classes. First, here is the MyApp.h header file for the MYAPP application:

```
// application class
class CMyApp : public CWinApp
{
public:
    virtual BOOL InitInstance();
};

// frame window class
class CMyFrame : public CFrameWnd
{
public:
    CMyFrame();
protected:
    // "afx_msg" indicates that the next two functions are part
    //  of the MFC library message dispatch system
    afx_msg void OnLButtonDown(UINT nFlags, CPoint point);
    afx_msg void OnPaint();
    DECLARE_MESSAGE_MAP()
};
```

And here is the MyApp.cpp implementation file for the MYAPP application:

```
#include <afxwin.h> // MFC library header file declares base classes
#include "myapp.h"

CMyApp theApp; // the one and only CMyApp object

BOOL CMyApp::InitInstance()
{
    m_pMainWnd = new CMyFrame();
    m_pMainWnd->ShowWindow(m_nCmdShow);

    m_pMainWnd->UpdateWindow();
    return TRUE;
}
```

```
BEGIN_MESSAGE_MAP(CMyFrame, CFrameWnd)
    ON_WM_LBUTTONDOWN()
    ON_WM_PAINT()
END_MESSAGE_MAP()

CMyFrame::CMyFrame()
{
    Create(NULL, "MYAPP Application");
}

void CMyFrame::OnLButtonDown(UINT nFlags, CPoint point)
{
    TRACE("Entering CMyFrame::OnLButtonDown - %lx, %d, %d\n",
          (long) nFlags, point.x, point.y);
}

void CMyFrame::OnPaint()
{
    CPaintDC dc(this);
    dc.TextOut(0, 0, "Hello, world!");
}
```

Here are some of the program elements:

- **The *WinMain* function** Windows requires your application to have a *WinMain* function. You don't see *WinMain* here because it's hidden inside the application framework.
- **The *CMyApp* class** An object of class *CMyApp* represents an application. The program defines a single global *CMyApp* object, *theApp*. The *CWinApp* base class determines most of the *theApp* object's behavior.
- **Application startup** When the user starts the application, Windows calls the application framework's built-in *WinMain* function, and *WinMain* looks for your globally constructed application object of a class derived from *CWinApp*. Don't forget that in a C++ program global objects are constructed before the main program is executed.
- **The *CMyApp::InitInstance* member function** When the *WinMain* function finds the application object, it calls the virtual *InitInstance* member function, which makes the calls needed to construct and display the application's main frame window. You must override *InitInstance* in your derived application class because the *CWinApp* base class doesn't know what kind of main frame window you want.
- **The *CWinApp::Run* member function** The *Run* function is hidden in the base class, but it dispatches the application's messages to its windows, thus keeping the application running. *WinMain* calls *Run* after it calls *InitInstance*.

- **The *CMyFrame* class** An object of class *CMyFrame* represents the application's main frame window. When the constructor calls the *Create* member function of the base class *CFrameWnd*, Windows creates the actual window structure and the application framework links it to the C++ object. You must call the *ShowWindow* and *UpdateWindow* functions, also member functions of the base class, in order to display the window.

- **The *CMyFrame::OnLButtonDown* function** This function is a sneak preview of the MFC library's message-handling capability. I've elected to "map" the left mouse button down event to a *CMyFrame* member function. You'll learn the details of the MFC library's message mapping in Chapter 5. For the time being, accept that this function gets called when the user presses the left mouse button. The function invokes the MFC library TRACE macro to display a message in the debugging window.

- **The *CMyFrame::OnPaint* function** The application framework calls this important mapped member function of class *CMyFrame* every time it's necessary to repaint the window: at the start of the program, when the user resizes the window, and when all or part of the window is newly exposed. The *CPaintDC* statement relates to the classic Graphics Device Interface (GDI) and is explained in later chapters. The *TextOut* function displays "Hello, world!" (We'll look at GDI+ when we discuss .NET).

- **Application shutdown** The user shuts down the application by closing the main frame window. This action initiates a sequence of events, which ends with the destruction of the *CMyFrame* object, the exit from *Run*, the exit from *WinMain*, and the destruction of the *CMyApp* object.

Look at the code example again. This time try to get the big picture. Most of the application's functionality is in the MFC library base classes *CWinApp* and *CFrameWnd*. In writing MYAPP, I've followed a few simple structure rules and have written key functions in my derived classes. C++ lets you "borrow" a lot of code without copying it. Think of it as a partnership between you and the application framework. The application framework provides the structure, and you provide the code that makes the application unique.

Now you're beginning to see why the application framework is more than just a class library. Not only does the application framework define the application structure, but it also encompasses more than C++ base classes. You've already seen the hidden *WinMain* function at work. Other elements support message processing, diagnostics, DLLs, and so forth.

MFC Library Message Mapping

Take a look at the *OnLButtonDown* member function in the previous example. You might think that it would be an ideal candidate for a virtual function. A window base class would define virtual functions for mouse event messages and other standard messages, and derived window classes could override the functions as necessary. Some Windows class libraries do work this way.

However, the MFC library application framework doesn't use virtual functions for Windows messages. Instead, it uses macros to "map" specified messages to derived class member functions. Why the rejection of virtual functions? Suppose the MFC library used virtual functions for messages. The *CWnd* class would declare virtual functions for more than 100 messages. C++ requires a virtual function dispatch table, called a *vtable*, for each derived class used in a program. Each vtable needs one 4-byte entry for each virtual function, regardless of whether the functions are actually overridden in the derived class. Thus, for each distinct type of window or control, the application would need a table consisting of over 400 bytes to support virtual message handlers.

What about message handlers for menu command messages and messages from button clicks? You couldn't define these as virtual functions in a window base class because each application might have a different set of menu commands and buttons. The MFC library message map system avoids large vtables, and it accommodates application-specific command messages in parallel with ordinary Windows messages. It also allows selected nonwindow classes, such as document classes and the application class, to handle command messages. The MFC library uses macros to connect (or map) Windows messages to C++ member functions. No extensions to the C++ language are necessary.

An MFC message handler requires a function prototype, a function body, and an entry (macro invocation) in the message map. The Properties window helps you add message handlers to your classes. You select a Windows message ID from a list box, and the wizard generates the code with the correct function parameters and return values.

Documents and Views

The previous example used an application object and a frame window object. Most of your MFC library applications will be more complex. Typically, they'll contain application and frame classes plus two other classes that represent the "document" and the "view." This document-view architecture is the core of the application framework and is loosely based on the *Model/View/Controller* classes from the Smalltalk world.

In simple terms, the document-view architecture separates data from the user's view of the data. One obvious benefit is multiple views of the same data. Consider a document that consists of a month's worth of stock quotes stored on disk. Suppose a table view and a chart view of the data are both available. The user updates values through the table view window, and the chart view window changes because both windows display the same information (but in different views).

In an MFC library application, documents and views are represented by instances of C++ classes. Figure 2-1 shows three objects of class *CStockDoc* corresponding to three companies: AT&T, IBM, and GM. All three documents have a table view attached, and one document also has a chart view. As you can see, there are four view objects—three objects of class *CStockTableView* and one of class *CStockChartView*.

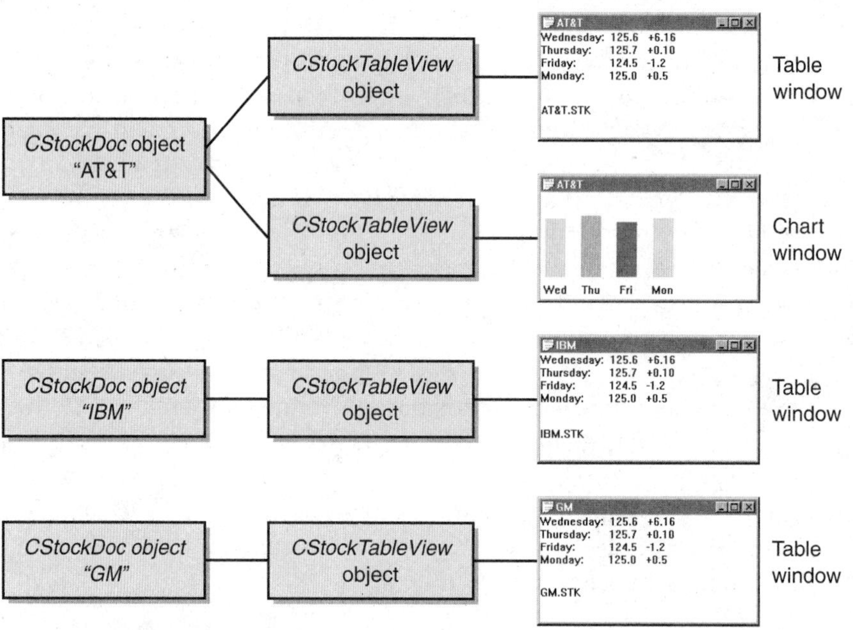

Figure 2-1 The document-view relationship.

The document base class code interacts with the File Open and File Save commands; the derived document class does the actual reading and writing of the document object's data. (The application framework does most of the work of displaying the File Open and File Save dialog boxes and opening, closing, reading, and writing files.) The view base class represents a window contained inside a frame window; the derived view class interacts with its associated document class and does the application's display and printer I/O. The derived view class and its base classes handle Windows messages. The MFC library orchestrates all interactions among documents, views, frame windows, and the application object, mostly through virtual functions.

Don't think that a document object must be associated with a disk file that is read entirely into memory. If a "document" were really a database, for example, you could override selected document class member functions and the File Open command would bring up a list of databases instead of a list of files.

Part II

MFC Essentials

3

Getting Started with the MFC Application Wizard

Chapter 2 introduced the MFC library's document-view architecture. This hands-on chapter will show you how to build a functioning MFC library application while insulating you from the complexities of the class hierarchy and object interrelationships. You'll work with only one document-view program element: the view class that is closely associated with a window. For the time being, you can ignore elements such as the application class, the frame window, and the document. Of course, your application won't be able to save its data to disk and won't support multiple views, but Part III of this book will give you plenty of opportunity to explore using those features.

Because resources are so important in Microsoft Windows–based applications, you'll use Resource View in this chapter to visually explore the resources of your new program. The chapter will also give you some hints on setting up your Windows environment for maximum build speed and optimal debugging output.

> **Note** To compile and run the examples presented in this chapter and in the following chapters, you must have Microsoft Windows NT 4.0, Windows 2000, or Windows XP installed, plus all the Microsoft Visual C++ .NET components. Be sure that Visual C++ .NET's executable, include, and library directories are set correctly. (You can change the directories by choosing Options from the Tools menu and clicking the Projects folder.) If you have any problems with the steps presented, please refer to your Visual C++ .NET documentation and Readme files for troubleshooting instructions.

What's a View?

From a user's standpoint, a *view* is an ordinary window that the user can size, move, and close in the same way as any other Windows-based application window. From the programmer's perspective, a view is a C++ object of a class derived from the MFC library *CView* class. Like any C++ object, the view object's behavior is determined by the member functions (and data members) of the class—both the application-specific functions in the derived class and the standard functions inherited from the base classes.

With Visual C++ .NET, you can produce interesting applications for Windows by simply adding code to the derived view class that the MFC Application Wizard code generator produces. When your program runs, the MFC library application framework constructs an object of the derived view class and displays a window that is tightly linked to the C++ view object. As is customary in C++ programming, the view class code is divided into two source modules—the header file (H) and the implementation file (CPP).

MFC Library Application Types

The MFC library supports three application types: Single Document Interface (SDI), Multiple Document Interface (MDI), and Multiple Top-Level Windows Interface (MTI). An SDI application has, from the user's point of view, only one window. If the application depends on disk-file "documents," only one document can be loaded at a time. The original Windows Notepad is an example of an SDI application. An MDI application has multiple child windows, each of which corresponds to an individual document. Earlier versions of Microsoft Office applications (before Office 2000) such as Microsoft Word are examples of MDI applications. An MTI application is a single instance of an application running several of the top-level windows. Modern versions of the Office applications use this model.

When you run the MFC Application Wizard to create a new project, MDI is the default application type. For the early examples in this book, you'll be generating SDI applications because fewer classes and features are involved. Be sure to select the Single Document option (on the Application Type page of the MFC Application Wizard) for these examples. Starting with Chapter 18, you'll be generating MDI applications. The MFC library application framework architecture ensures that most SDI examples can be upgraded easily to MDI applications.

MFC Library User Interfaces

In addition to providing options for SDI, MDI, and MTI-style application interfaces, the MFC library gives you a choice between a standard application user interface (UI) and a Windows Explorer–style UI. Examples of the classic-style UI include Microsoft Word and Microsoft Paintbrush. The Windows Explorer–style UI features two panes separated by a splitter. The left pane usually includes a TreeView with expandable nodes, and the right pane usually includes a ListView. Windows Explorer is an example of this style of UI.

Ex03a: The "Do-Nothing" Application

The MFC Application Wizard generates the code for a functioning MFC library application. This working application simply brings up an empty window with a menu attached. Later, you add code that draws inside the window. You take the following steps to build an application:

1. **Run the MFC Application Wizard to generate SDI application source code.** Choose New Project from Visual C++'s File menu. Select Visual C++ Projects, and then select MFC Application from the list of templates, as shown here.

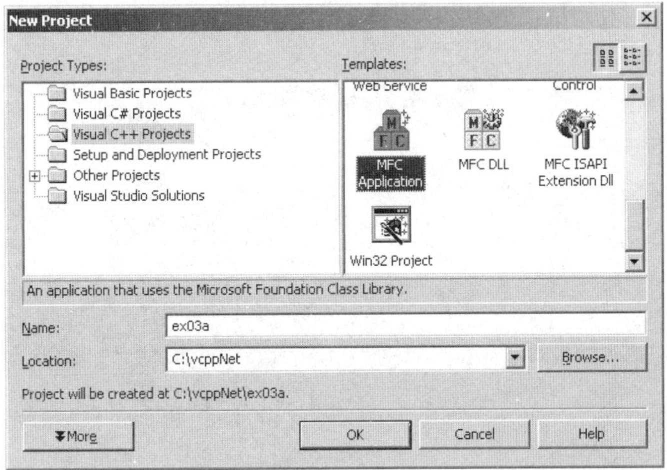

Type **C:\vcppnet** in the Location box. Type **Ex03a** in the Name box, and then click OK. Use the links on the left side of the dialog box to move through the various Application Wizard pages to set up project options.

On the Application Type page, select the Single Document option and accept the defaults for the rest of the application, as shown here:

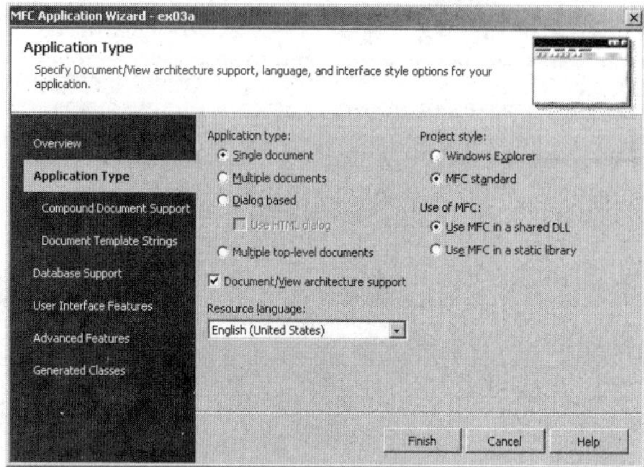

On the Generated Classes page, shown below, notice that the class names and source-file names have been generated based on the project name Ex03a. You can make changes to these names at this point if you want to. Click Finish. The wizard will create your application's subdirectory (Ex03a under \vcppnet) and a series of files in that subdirectory. When the wizard is finished, look in the application's subdirectory.

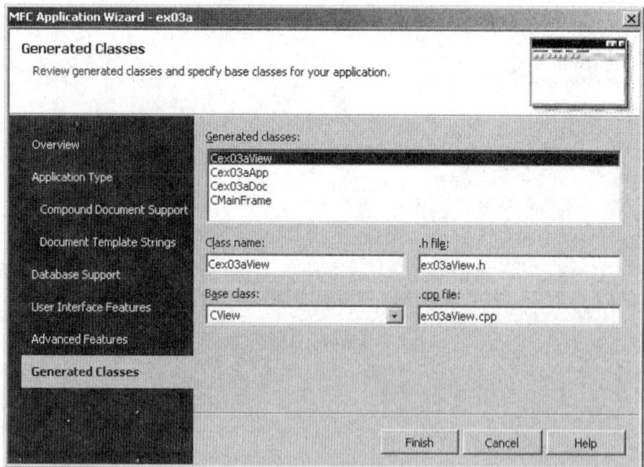

Table 3-1 lists the files that are of interest (for now).

Table 3-1 Important Files in the Application's Subdirectory

File	Description
Ex03a.vcproj	A project file that allows Visual C++ .NET to build your application
Ex03a.sln	A solution file that contains a single entry for ex03a.vcproj
Ex03a.rc	An ASCII resource script file
Ex03aView.cpp	A view class implementation file that contains *CEx03aView* class member functions
Ex03aView.h	A view class header file that contains the *CEx03aView* class declaration
ReadMe.txt	A text file that explains the purpose of the generated files
resource.h	A header file that contains *#define* constant definitions

Open the ex03aView.cpp and ex03aView.h files and look at the source code. Together, these files define the *CEx03aView* class, which is central to the application. An object of class *CEx03aView* corresponds to the application's view window, where all the "action" takes place.

2. **Compile and link the generated code.** In addition to generating code, the MFC Application Wizard creates custom project and workspace files for your application. The project file, ex03a.vcproj, specifies all the file dependencies along with the compile and link option flags. Because the new project becomes Visual C++ .NET's current project, you can now build the application by choosing Build from the Build menu or by clicking the Build toolbar button, shown here:

If the build is successful, an executable program named Ex03a.exe will be created in a new Debug subdirectory underneath \vcppnet\Ex03a. The OBJ files and other intermediate files are also stored in Debug. Compare the file structure on disk with the structure in Solution Explorer, shown on the next page.

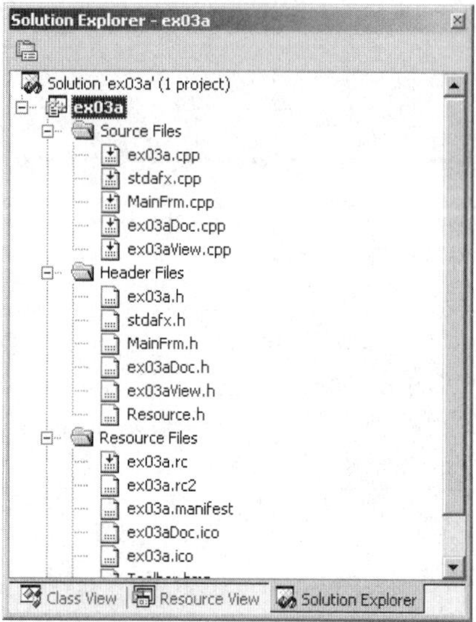

Solution Explorer contains a logical view of your project. The header files show up under Header Files, even though they are in the same subdirectory as the CPP files. The resource files are stored in the \res subdirectory.

3. **Test the resulting application.** Choose Start Without Debugging from the Debug menu. Experiment with the program. It doesn't do much, does it? (What do you expect with no coding?) Actually, as you might guess, the program has a lot of features—you simply haven't activated them yet. Close the program window when you've finished experimenting.

4. **Browse the application.** Press CTRL+ALT+J to bring up the Object Browser. If your project settings don't specify browser database creation, Visual C++ .NET will offer to change the settings and recompile the program for you. (To change the settings yourself, choose Properties from the Project menu. Open the C/C++ folder, click on the Browse Information property page, and change the Enable Browse Information property to Include All Browse Information (/FR).)

After you expand the hierarchy, you should see output similar to this:

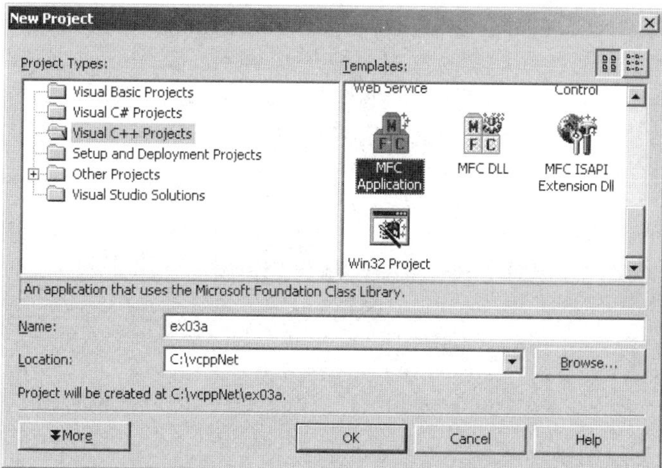

Compare the browser output to Class View:

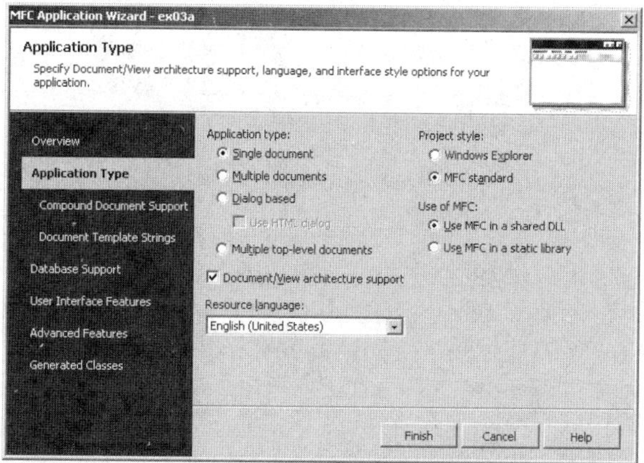

Class View shows the class hierarchy, much like the Object Browser does. But the Object Browser shows all the functions available on a class, and Class View shows only those that have been overridden. If Class View is sufficient for you, don't bother building the browser database.

The *CEx03aView* View Class

The MFC Application Wizard generated the *CEx03aView* view class, which is specific to the Ex03a application. (The wizard generates classes based on the project name you entered in the New Project dialog box.) *CEx03aView* is at the bottom of a long inheritance chain of MFC library classes, as shown previously in the Object Browser window. The class picks up member functions and data members all along the chain. You can learn about these classes in the *Microsoft Foundation Class Reference* (online or printed version), but be sure to look at the descriptions for every base class because the descriptions of inherited member functions aren't generally repeated for derived classes.

The most important *CEx03aView* base classes are *CWnd* and *CView*. *CWnd* provides the *CEx03aView* view class's "windowness," and *CView* provides the hooks to the rest of the application framework, particularly to the document and to the frame window, as you'll see in Chapter 12 of this book.

Drawing Inside the View Window: The Windows GDI

Now you're ready to write code to draw inside the view window. You'll be making a few changes directly to the Ex03a source code. Specifically, you'll be fleshing out the *OnDraw* member function in ex03aView.cpp and working with the device context and the Graphics Device Interface (GDI).

The *OnDraw* Member Function

OnDraw is a virtual member function of the *CView* class that the application framework calls every time the view window needs to be repainted. A window needs to be repainted if the user resizes the window or reveals a previously hidden part of the window, or if the application changes the window's data. If the user resizes the window or reveals a hidden area, the application framework calls *OnDraw*, but if a function in your program changes the data, it must inform Windows of the change by calling the view's inherited *Invalidate* (or *InvalidateRect*) member function. This call to *Invalidate* triggers a later call to *OnDraw*.

Even though you can draw inside a window at any time, it's better to let window changes accumulate and then process them all together in the *OnDraw* function. That way, your program can respond both to program-generated events and to Windows-generated events such as size changes.

The Windows Device Context

Recall from Chapter 1 that Windows doesn't allow direct access to the display hardware but communicates through an abstraction called a *device context* that is associated with the window. In the MFC library, the device context is a C++ object of class *CDC* that is passed (by pointer) as a parameter to *OnDraw*. After you have the device context pointer, you can call the many *CDC* member functions that do the work of drawing.

Adding Draw Code to the Ex03a Program

Now let's write the code to draw some text and a circle inside the view window. Be sure that the project Ex03a is open in Visual C++ .NET. You can use Class View to locate the code for the function (double-click *OnDraw*), or you can open the source code file ex03aView.cpp from Solution Explorer and locate the function yourself.

1. **Edit the *OnDraw* function in ex03aView.cpp.** Find the Application Wizard–generated *OnDraw* function in ex03aView.cpp:

```
void CEx03aView::OnDraw(CDC* /* pDC */)
{
    CEx03aDoc* pDoc = GetDocument();
    ASSERT_VALID(pDoc);

    // TODO: add draw code for native data here
}
```

Uncomment the pointer to the device context and add the following boldface code (which you type in) to replace the previous code:

```
void CEx03aView::OnDraw(CDC* pDC)
{
    pDC->TextOut(0, 0, "Hello, world!");  // prints in default font
                                          // & size, top left corner
    pDC->SelectStockObject(GRAY_BRUSH);   // selects a brush for the
                                          //  circle interior
    pDC->Ellipse(CRect(0, 20, 100, 120)); // draws a gray circle
                                          //  100 units in diameter
}
```

You can safely remove the call to *GetDocument* because we're not dealing with documents yet. The functions *TextOut*, *SelectStockObject*, and *Ellipse* are all member functions of the application framework's device context class CDC. The *Ellipse* function draws a circle if the bounding rectangle's length is equal to its width.

The MFC library provides a handy utility class, *CRect*, for Windows rectangles. A temporary *CRect* object serves as the bounding rectangle argument for the ellipse drawing function. You'll see more of the *CRect* class in quite a few of the examples in this book.

2. **Recompile and test Ex03a.** Choose Build from the Build menu, and if there are no compile errors, test the application again. Now you have a program that visibly does something!

For Win32 Programmers

Rest assured that the standard Windows *WinMain* and window procedure functions are hidden away inside the application framework. You'll see those functions later in this book, when we examine the MFC library frame and application classes. In the meantime, you're probably wondering what happened to the *WM_PAINT* message. You'd expect to do your window drawing in response to this Windows message, and you'd expect to get your device context handle from a *PAINTSTRUCT* structure returned by the Windows *BeginPaint* function.

It so happens that the application framework has done all the dirty work for you and served up a device context (in object pointer form) in the virtual function *OnDraw*. As explained in Chapter 2, true virtual functions in window classes are an MFC library rarity. MFC library message map functions dispatched by the application framework handle most Windows messages. MFC 1.0 programmers always defined an *OnPaint* message map function for their derived window classes. Beginning with version 2.5, however, *OnPaint* was mapped in the *CView* class, and that function made a polymorphic call to *OnDraw*. Why? Because *OnDraw* needs to support the printer as well as the display. Both *OnPaint* and *OnPrint* call *OnDraw*, thus enabling the same drawing code to accommodate both the printer and the display.

A Preview of the Resource Editors

Now that you have a complete application program, it's a good time for a quick look at the resource editors. Although the application's resource script, Ex03a.rc, is an ASCII file, modifying it with a text editor is not a good idea. That's the resource editors' job.

The Contents of Ex03a.rc

The resource file determines much of the Ex03a application's "look and feel." The file Ex03a.rc contains (or points to) the Windows resources listed in Table 3-2.

Table 3-2 Windows Resources Contained in MFC Applications

Resource	Description
Accelerator	Includes definitions for keys that simulate menu and toolbar selections.
Dialog	Includes layout and contents of dialog boxes. Ex03a has only the About dialog box.
Icon	Represents icons (16-by-16-pixel and 32-by-32-pixel versions), such as the application icon you see in Windows Explorer and in the application's About dialog box. Ex03a uses the MFC logo for its application icon.
Manifest	Contains the run-time type information for the application.
Menu	Represents the application's top-level menu and associated shortcut menus.
String table	Includes strings that are not part of the C++ source code.
Toolbar	Represents the row of buttons immediately below the menu.
Version	Includes program description, version number, language, and so on.

In addition to the resources listed above, ex03a.rc contains these statements

```
#include "afxres.h"
```

and further in the file contains this statement

```
#include "afxres.rc"
```

which bring in some MFC library resources common to all applications. These resources include strings, graphical buttons, and elements needed for printing and for OLE.

> **Note** If you're using the shared DLL version of the MFC library, the common resources are stored inside the MFC DLL.

The Ex03a.rc file also contains this statement:

```
#include "resource.h"
```

This statement brings in some *#define* constants, including *IDR_MAINFRAME* (which identifies the menu, icon, string list, and accelerator table), *IDR_EX03ATYPE* (which identifies the default document icon, which we won't use in this program), and *IDD_ABOUTBOX* (which identifies the About dialog box). This same resource.h file is included indirectly by the application's source code files. If you use a resource editor to add more constants (symbols), the definitions will ultimately show up in resource.h. Be careful if you edit this file in text mode because your changes might be removed the next time you use a resource editor.

Running the Dialog Resource Editor

The Dialog resource editor allows you to create or edit dialog box resources. To run the editor, follow these steps:

1. **Open the project's RC file.** Choose Resource View from the View menu. If you expand each item, you'll see the following in the Resource View window:

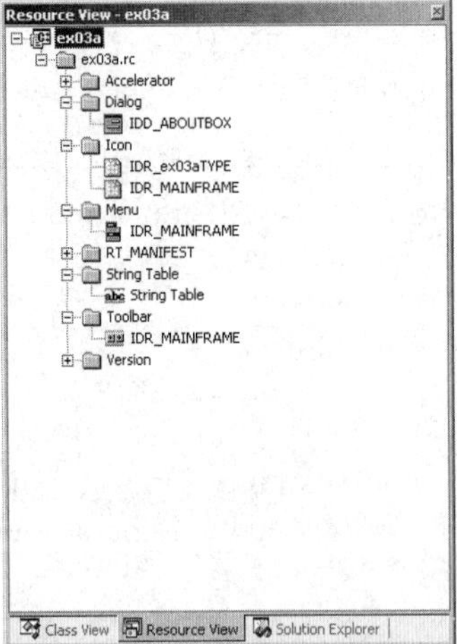

2. **Examine the application's resources.** Now take some time to explore the individual resources. When you select a resource by double-clicking on it, another window opens with tools appropriate for the selected resource. If you open a dialog resource, the control palette should appear. If it doesn't, click the Toolbox button on the left side of Visual Studio .NET.

3. **Modify the IDD_ABOUTBOX dialog box.** Make some changes to the About Ex03a dialog box.

   You can change the size of the window by dragging the right and bottom borders, move the OK button, change the text, and so forth. Simply click on an element to select it, and then right-click to change its properties.

4. **Rebuild the project with the modified resource file.** In Visual C++ .NET, choose Build from the Build menu. Notice that no actual C++ recompilation is necessary. Visual C++ .NET saves the edited resource file, and then the Resource Compiler (rc.exe) processes Ex03a.rc to produce a compiled version, Ex03a.res, which is fed to the linker. The linker runs quickly because it can link the project incrementally.

5. **Test the new version of the application.** Run the Ex03a program again, and then choose About from the application's Help menu to confirm that your dialog box was changed as expected.

Win32 Debug Target vs. Win32 Release Target

When you build your application, you can choose one of two targets: debug and release. These are the two default targets generated by the MFC Application Wizard. The default project settings are summarized in Table 3-4.

Table 3-4 MFC Application Wizard Default Project Settings

Option	Release Build	Debug Build
Source Code Debugging	Disabled	Enabled for both compiler and linker
MFC Diagnostic Macros	Disabled (*NDEBUG* defined)	Enabled (*_DEBUG* defined)
Library Linkage	MFC Release library	MFC Debug libraries
Compiler Optimization	Speed optimization (not available in Learning Edition)	No optimization (faster compile)

You develop your application in Debug mode, and then you rebuild in Release mode before delivery. The Release build EXE will be smaller and faster, assuming you've fixed all the bugs. You select the configuration from the build target window in the toolbar, as shown in Figure 1-2 in Chapter 1. By default, the Debug output files and intermediate files are stored in the project's Debug subdirectory and the Release files are stored in the Release subdirectory. You can change these directories on the General property page in the Configuration Properties folder, which you can access in the project's Property Pages dialog box.

You can create your own custom configurations if you need to, by choosing Configuration Manager from Visual C++ .NET's Build menu.

Understanding Precompiled Headers

When the MFC Application Wizard generates a project, it generates switch settings and files for precompiled headers. You must understand how the make system processes precompiled headers in order to manage your projects effectively.

> **Note** Visual C++ .NET has two precompiled header "systems": automatic and manual. Automatic precompiled headers, which are activated by the /Yx compiler switch, store compiler output in a "database" file. Manual precompiled headers are activated by the /Yc and /Yu switch settings and are central to all the MFC Application Wizard–generated projects.

Precompiled headers represent compiler "snapshots" taken at a particular line of source code. In MFC library programs, the snapshot is generally taken immediately after the following statement:

```
#include  "StdAfx.h"
```

The file StdAfx.h contains *#include* statements for the MFC library header files. The file's contents depend on the options you select when you run the MFC Application Wizard, but the file always contain these statements:

```
#include <afxwin.h>
#include <afxext.h>
```

If you're using compound documents, StdAfx.h also contains this statement:

```
#include <afxole.h>
```

And if you're using Automation or ActiveX controls, it contains:

```
#include <afxdisp.h>
```

If you're using Internet Explorer 4.0 Common Controls, StdAfx.h contains this statement:

```
#include <afxdtctl.h>
```

Occasionally, you'll need other header files—for example, the header for template-based collection classes that is accessed by this statement:

```
#include <afxtempl.h>
```

The source file StdAfx.cpp contains only this statement:

```
#include  "StdAfx.h"
```

This statement is used to generate the precompiled header file in the project directory. The MFC library headers included by StdAfx.h never change, but they do take a long time to compile. The compiler switch */Yc*, used only with StdAfx.cpp, causes the creation of the precompiled header (PCH) file. The switch */Yu*, used with all the other source code files, causes the use of an existing PCH file. The switch */Fp* specifies the PCH filename that would otherwise default to the project name (with the PCH extension) in the target's output files subdirectory. Figure 3-1 illustrates the whole process.

The MFC Application Wizard sets the */Yc* and */Yu* switches for you, but you can make changes if you need to. It's possible to define compiler switch settings for individual source files. If you select only StdAfx.cpp in the C/C++ folder in the project's Property Pages dialog box, you'll see the */Yc* setting on the Precompiled Headers property page. This overrides the */Yu* setting that is defined for the target.

Be aware that PCH files are big—10 MB is typical. If you're not careful, you'll fill up your hard disk. You can keep things under control by periodically cleaning out your projects' Debug directories, or you can use the */Fp* compiler option to reroute PCH files to a common directory.

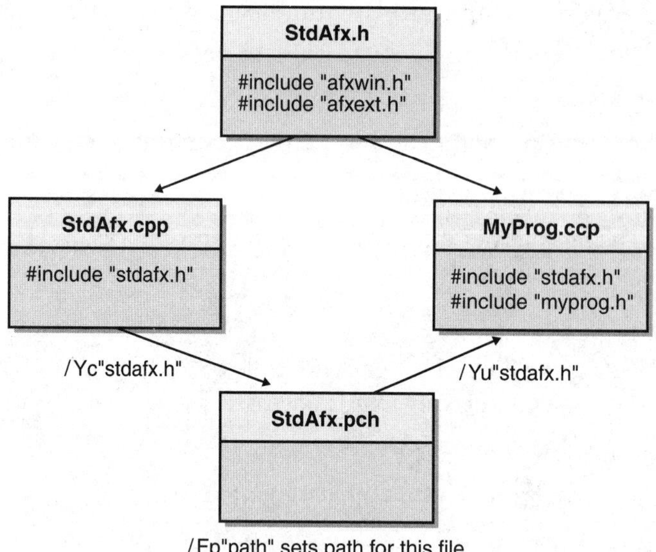

Figure 3-1 The Visual C++ .NET precompiled header process.

Two Ways to Run a Program

Visual C++ .NET lets you run your program directly (by pressing CTRL+F5) or through the debugger (by pressing F5). Running your program directly is much faster because Visual C++ .NET doesn't have to load the debugger first. If you know you don't want to see diagnostic messages or use breakpoints, start your program by pressing CTRL+F5.

4

Visual C++ .NET Wizards

Developing for the Microsoft platform involves a lot of boilerplate coding. Back in the early days of Windows development, most developers started a Windows-based project armed with only a copy of Charles Petzold's *Programming Windows* and the Windows Software Development Kit (SDK). Even the Windows SDK documentation recommended the editor inheritance method of application development.

To understand the fundamental underpinnings of any technology, you have to write all the code for an application. But there comes a time when writing the same boilerplate again and again becomes merely a drill and a waste of time. To address this issue, the Microsoft Visual Studio .NET environment provides a set of code generators to start you off on all types of projects. The available project templates appear in the New Project window when you choose New, Project from the File menu. You select the project template you want, run through the dialog boxes to configure the project, and click Finish. *Voilà*—you've got a working application.

But that's not the end of the story. The wizard technology is extensible—you can write your own wizards. This chapter gives you a rundown of Visual Studio .NET's wizards and explains how to write your own.

Wizard Types

Visual Studio .NET supports two types of wizards: those with a user interface and those without. Depending on the complexity of your wizard, you might want to include a user interface. Most of the wizards you'll see in this book include one. For example, the MFC Application Wizard includes several pages that provide such options as type of document interface (SDI or MDI), whether to support printing and print preview, and whether to use ActiveX controls. For simple application types, you might not need a user interface.

Wizards without user interfaces simply take a project name you supply and generate project files based on templates you provide. Wizards with user interfaces tend to be a little more involved and can include several pages of application options.

In fact, the source code for all the Visual C++ .NET wizards is available. You can find the Wizard source code files in the \Program Files\Microsoft Visual Studio .NET\VC7\VCWizards directory.

How Wizards Work

Before we create a wizard, let's look at how wizards work. We'll look at the three main parts of a wizard: the original boilerplate code, the user interface, and the code it generates.

The general idea behind a code generator is to create a basic project for you to relieve you from having to type all the boilerplate code. That basically means a bare-bones application or library that works and compiles. However, you want the code to reflect the nature of the project. For example, if you're writing a payroll application, you want the classes in the application to have names like *CPayrollDoc*, *CPayrollView*, and *CPayrollFrame*. It's the wizard's job to substitute the plain vanilla names of the basic application with the names the developer types in.

The wizard is also responsible for adding or leaving out certain parts of code, depending on the developer's selections. For example, if you select the About dialog box from a list of options, the wizard will add the correct code for the dialog box to the finished application.

The wizard presents these choices through a user interface. The heart of the wizard's interface is an HTML control named *IVCWizCtrlUI*. The Visual Studio .NET wizards use HTML to drive the user interface. When you execute the wizard, the *IVCWizCtrlUI* interface looks for the list of files representing the user interface and displays those pages within the wizard. The wizard is responsible for managing navigation through each of the pages as well as generating the code when the developer clicks the Finish button.

A wizard can contain any number of pages, each driven by a separate HTML file. The wizard provides navigation functionality through the Next and Back buttons (or any other format you specify). The HTML files that implement the wizard interface contain the *SYMBOL* tag, which identifies the default for developer-defined options.

The wizard maintains a symbol table during the lifetime of its execution. The symbol table is just a dictionary lookup mechanism for making substitutions. The symbols declared in the HTML file are written into the symbol table when the user clicks Finish. For example, examine the following HTML in a wizard user interface:

```
<SYMBOL NAME='SOURCE_FILE' VALUE='MySource.cpp' TYPE=text></SYMBOL>
```

In the wizard user interface, the text box represents an input box for the user to type into. The text box is identified using the symbol *SOURCE_FILE*. This is the key the wizard will look for when it makes substitutions for source files. We'll look at how that works in just a minute. Basically, each HTML file used by the wizard is responsible for recording user selections to the symbols table.

Logic within the wizards is usually implemented using JScript. If you need to provide customized behavior from within the wizard, you can use JScript functions to access the Visual C++ Wizard Model. These functions are in the HTML page section headed *<SCRIPT LANGUAGE='JSCRIPT'>*.

> **Note** For more information about the Visual C++ Wizard Model and other object models that make up the Visual C++ Extensibility Object Model, refer to the MSDN Library.

Creating a Wizard

The first step in creating a wizard is to write and debug a boilerplate application. Once you've done that, you can use Visual Studio .NET to generate a blank wizard for you. Visual Studio .NET includes a wizard named the Custom Wizard for creating wizards. This wizard generates all the files necessary to implement a wizard.

To create a wizard, choose New, Project from the File menu, select Visual C++ Projects, and then select the Custom Wizard template. Type a name for the wizard in the Project Name text box. The Custom Wizard includes only two pages: an overview page and the Application Settings page. The Application Settings page lets you specify a wizard-friendly name, whether to include a user interface, and the number of pages in the wizard. The files created by the Custom Wizard are listed in Table 4-1.

Table 4-1 Files Generated by the Custom Wizard

Files	Description
Project.vsz	A text file that identifies the wizard engine and provides context and optional custom parameters.
Project.vsdir	A text file that provides a routing service between the Visual Studio shell and the items in the wizard project.
HTML files (optional)	Files for wizards that implement a user interface. The wizard user interface is implemented as HTML. Wizards without a user interface do not contain HTML files. The Default.htm file specifies the user interface features. Wizards with more than one page specified in the Application Settings page of the Custom Wizard include additional files; these files are named Page_*PageNum*.htm.
Script files	Wizard logic code is executed as script. A wizard includes a JScript file named Default.js for each project. A wizard also includes Common.js. These files contain JScript functions that access the Visual C++ Wizard, Code, Project, and Resource Editor Models to customize a wizard. You can customize and add functions in the wizard project's Default.js file.
Template files	A collection of text files in the Templates directory that contain directives. These files are parsed and inserted into the symbol table based on the user's selections. The template text files are rendered according to the user input and added to the project. The appropriate information is obtained by directly accessing the wizard control's symbol table.
Templates.inf	A text file that lists all templates associated with the project.
Default.vcproj	An XML file that contains the information on the project type.
Sample.txt	A template file that shows how your wizard directives are used.
ReadMe.txt	A template file that contains a summary of each file created by the Custom Wizard.
Images file (optional)	A file of images, such as icons, GIFs, BMPs, and other HTML-supported image formats, to enhance your wizard's user interface. Of course, a wizard that has no user interface does not need images.

(continued)

Table 4-1 Files Generated by the Custom Wizard *(continued)*

Files	Description
Styles.css (optional)	A file that defines the styles for the user interface. Again, if your wizard has no user interface, the Custom Wizard does not create a CSS file.
Common.js	Common JScript functionality used by all wizards. This file isn't actually generated by the Custom Wizard—it's included in the source code that's generated.

Creating a Wizard for Developing Web Applications Using Managed C++

In this section, we'll look at how to create a custom application wizard that generates a Web application using ASP.NET and managed C++. We'll look at the details involved in writing a Web Forms applications using ASP.NET and managed C++ in the second half of the book. For now, we'll create an application wizard that can generate Web Forms applications. A Web Forms application involves several different kinds of files to be generated. In addition, we can add several options such as tracing/debugging options and include several kinds of controls to see how the application wizard works. The files included in the Web Forms application include source code for a Managed C++ DLL, an ASP.NET (ASPX) file, a Web.Config file, and a Visual Studio Solution file. Each of these files will need to contain a couple of different substitutions made by the application wizard.

We'll create our wizard using the Custom Wizard. As mentioned, the Custom Wizard is a canned Visual Studio .NET wizard that creates a custom wizard. The name of the sample wizard for this chapter will be *ManagedCWebFormWizard*. The wizard will have a user interface consisting of one page. You can have as many pages as you want in your wizard. We're keeping it to one page in this example to make the sample more digestible.

The user interface itself will include check boxes for adding controls to the page and for turning on debugging and tracing options. Solution Explorer lets you get to the HTML page representing the wizard user interface. Editing this page is much like editing normal dialog boxes. You can select a control from the Toolbox on the left side of the Visual Studio .NET's IDE, place the control on the page, and set its properties using the Properties window. The wizard has six check boxes on the interface page. Three of the check boxes will manage the controls on the Web Form—one each for adding a *CheckBox* control to the Web Form, for adding a *Label* control, and for adding a *TextBox* control. You can use the Properties window to provide IDs for each of the controls. The *TextBox* check box has an ID of *UseTextBox*, the *Label* check box has an ID of *UseLabel*, and the *CheckBox* check box an ID of *UseCheckBox*. When the wizard generates the code, it looks for these symbols to add code to the ASPX page and the code page.

The three other check boxes are for managing debug options: one for page tracing, one for request tracing, and one to turn on debugging. The check boxes have IDs of *UsePageTracing*, *UseRequestTracing*, and *UsePageDebugging*. As with the user interface page, the wizard will look for these symbols to add the right code to the generated project.

Figure 4-1 shows default.htm, the user interface page, as it will appear in the finished wizard.

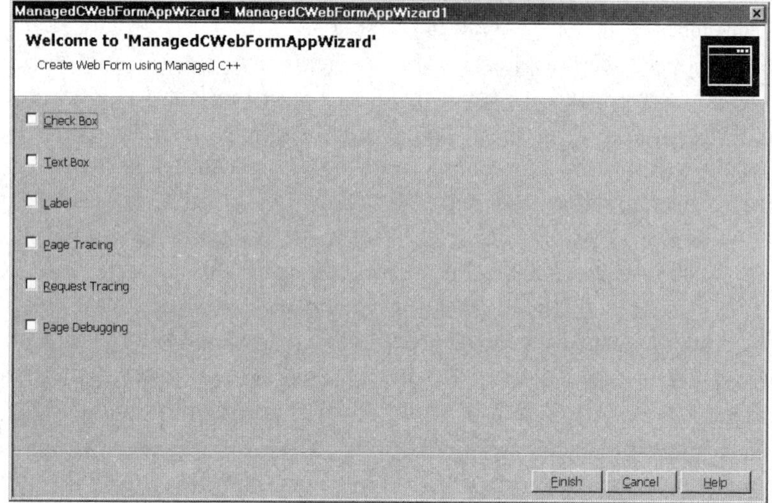

Figure 4-1 Default.htm of the ManagedCWebFormWizard application in the finished wizard.

Once the controls are on the page, they need to be associated with symbols that the wizard can use to make substitutions. The wizard's default user interface page (default.htm) has a block of symbol entries. You then modify the symbols for the Web application wizard, as shown here:

```
<SYMBOL NAME="UseCheckBox" TYPE="checkbox" VALUE="false"></SYMBOL>
<SYMBOL NAME="UseTextBox" TYPE="checkbox" VALUE="false"></SYMBOL>
<SYMBOL NAME="UseLabel" TYPE="checkbox" VALUE="false"></SYMBOL>
<SYMBOL NAME="UsePageTracing" TYPE="checkbox" VALUE="false"></SYMBOL>
<SYMBOL NAME="UseRequestTracing" TYPE="checkbox" VALUE="false"></SYMBOL>
<SYMBOL NAME="UsePageDebugging" TYPE="checkbox" VALUE="false"></SYMBOL>
```

Notice that each of these symbols is associated with a check box on the wizard user interface page.

The next step is to take the original source code and insert annotations where you want the wizard to add replacement code. Once we have the original boilerplate code, all the original boilerplate source code for the wizard will live under the Templates directory for that wizard. The final ManagedCWebForm will need to include three files: the header file containing the C++ class, the ASPX file containing the Web page layout information, and the Web.Config file containing the configuration settings. The boilerplate code for these files will be included in the Template directory for the wizard. Let's take a look at the boilerplate code the wizard will use to generate the applications. Here's the code for the C++ header file:

```
// ManagedCWebForm.h

#pragma once

using namespace System;
#using <System.Dll>
#using <System.Web.dll>

using namespace System;
using namespace System::Web;
using namespace System::Web::UI;
using namespace System::Web::UI::WebControls;
using namespace System::Collections;
using namespace System::ComponentModel;

namespace ProgVSNET_ManagedCWebForm
{
    public __gc class ManagedCWebPage : public Page
    {
        public:
            Button* m_button;

[!if UseLabel]
            Label* m_label;
[!endif]
[!if UseTextBox]
            TextBox* m_text;
[!endif]
[!if UseCheckBox]
            CheckBox* m_check;
[!endif]
```

(continued)

```
        ManagedCWebPage()
        {
            // To do: Construction code here...
        }

        void SubmitEntry(Object* o, EventArgs* e)
        {
            // Called when Submit button pressed
            // To do: insert Page Loading code here...
            String* str;

            str = new String("Hello ");
            str = str->Concat(str, m_text->get_Text());
            str = str->Concat(str, new String(" you pushed Submit"));
[!if UseLabel]
            m_label->set_Text(str);
[!if UseLabel]
        }

        void Page_Load(Object* o, EventArgs* e)
        {
            // To do: insert Page Loading code here...
[!if UsePageTracing]
            Trace->Write("Custom", "Inside Page_Load");
[!endif]
            if(!IsPostBack) {
            }
        }
    };
}
```

When the wizard generates the final code, it looks for the key symbol contained in the square brace to see whether it is in the symbol table. In our example, the expressions are simply Boolean tests. If the check boxes are selected, the controls or debugging features are turned on. Otherwise, they're turned off, and the specific code will be omitted from the generated source code. The same principle applies to every file that needs to be generated. For example, the wizard will take the following boilerplate code for the ASP.NET page and examine the *UseRequestTracing*, *UseTextBox*, *UseLabel*, and *UseCheckBox* symbols to figure out what code to include:

```
<%@ Page Language="C#"
[!if UseRequestTracing]
    Trace=true
[!endif]
    Inherits="ProgVSNET_ManagedCWebForm.ManagedCWebPage"
%>
```

```
<html>
<body>
<form runat=server>
<h2>ASP.NET Web Form</h2>

<br><br><br>

    <asp:Button Text="Sumit Entry" id="m_button"
        OnClick="SubmitEntry" runat=server /><br/>

    <asp:Label Text="Type your name here" runat=server />


[!if UseTextBox]
    <asp:TextBox id="m_text" runat=server /><br/>
[!endif]

[!if UseCheckBox]
    <asp:CheckBox id="m_check" runat=server /> <br/>
[!end]

[!if UseLabel]
    <asp:Label id="m_label" runat=server />
[!endif]

</form>
</body>
</html>
```

The last file that needs to be created is the Web.Config file—an XML file that ASP.NET looks for to learn how to configure the Web application. In this case, page-level tracing and page debugging are turned on or off depending on the state of the check boxes, as shown in the following code:

```
<configuration>
    <system.web>
[!if UsePageDebugging]
    <compilation debug='true'></compilation>
[!endif]
[!if UsePageTracing]
    <trace enabled='true'></trace>
[!endif]
    </system.web>
</configuration>
```

In addition to the code boilerplate, the wizard also needs to know which files to include when it generates the application. The Templates directory for the wizards includes a file named Templates.inf that includes a list of files to generate when it produces the application. Templates.inf tells the wizard which files to include in the final project. For our example, we'll add ManagedCWebForm.cpp, ManagedCWebForm.h, ManagedCWebForm.aspx, and Web.config to this file. This file works the same way as the other files described earlier—the wizard checks for symbols in the symbol table and generates the application based on selections made within the user interface. As the script code generates the project, the script code calls the *GetTargetName* function to change the name of the core files (ManagedCWebForm.aspx, ManagedCWebForm.cpp, and ManagedWebForm.h) to reflect the name of the project typed in by the developer when he or she runs the wizard. Here's the *GetTargetName* method modified to make the file name substitutions.

```
function GetTargetName(strName, strProjectName)
{
    try
    {
        var strTarget = strName;

        if (strName.substr(0, 15) == "ManagedCWebForm")
        {
            var strlen = strName.length;
            strTarget = strProjectName + strName.substr(15, strlen - 15);
        }
        return strTarget;
    }
    catch(e)
    {
        throw e;
    }
}
```

After the wizard generates the files, it creates a project out of those files. The scripts for creating the project are found in the scripts subdirectory for the wizard project. The default scripts generated by the Custom Wizard include a method named *AddConfig*. Visual Studio .NET includes a project object model that lets you change the project configuration of the generated project. Following is the source code that flips the DLL switch on and generates a managed assembly. (We'll cover managed code in the last part of the book.)

```
function AddConfig(proj, strProjectName)
{
    try
    {
        var config = proj.Object.Configurations('Debug');
        config.IntermediateDirectory = 'Debug';
        config.OutputDirectory = 'Debug';
```

```
        config.ConfigurationType = typeDynamicLibrary;

        var CLTool = config.Tools('VCCLCompilerTool');
        // TODO: Add compiler settings
        CLTool.CompileAsManaged = managedAssembly;

        var LinkTool = config.Tools('VCLinkerTool');
        // TODO: Add linker settings

        config = proj.Object.Configurations('Release');
        config.IntermediateDirectory = 'Release';
        config.OutputDirectory = 'Release';

        var CLTool = config.Tools('VCCLCompilerTool');
        // TODO: Add compiler settings
        CLTool.CompileAsManaged = managedAssembly;

        var LinkTool = config.Tools('VCLinkerTool');
        // TODO: Add linker settings
    }
    catch(e)
    {
        throw e;
    }
}
```

Once the wizard has been created, you need to let Visual Studio .NET know of its existence. In order for Visual Studio .NET to pick up on the wizard, the wizard needs its own directory under \Program Files\Microsoft Visual Studio .NET\VC7\VCWizards. The user interface files go into the HTML directory underneath the wizard directory, the template files (boilerplate code) go into the Templates directory underneath the wizard directory, the images go in the Images directory under the wizard directory, and the scripts go under the Scripts directory underneath the wizard directory. Both the user interface files and the template files can be localized. The VSDIR file, the VSZ file, and the icon file go under \Program Files\Microsoft Visual Studio .NET\VC7\VCProjects. As mentioned earlier, the VSDIR and VSZ files are generated by the Custom Wizard.

The application wizard model within Visual Studio .NET is rich and flexible. We only looked at substitutions that use the state of a check box to determine whether to include code. There are many other ways to set up the application wizard to generate any kind of application. In fact, this wizard architecture is also how Visual Studio .NET implements its other wizards—including the ATL Simple Object Wizard, the Generic C++ Class Wizard, and the Add Member Variable Wizard.

Each of these wizards can reach into Visual Studio .NET and access the entire Visual Studio object model, which is how the environment seems to understand the classes and other code within your application.

Be sure to check out \Program Files\Microsoft Visual Studio .NET\VC7\VCWizards for more examples—you'll find all of Visual Studio .NET's wizards there.

5

Windows Message Mapping

In Chapter 3, you saw how the MFC library application framework calls the view class's virtual *OnDraw* function. In the online help for the MFC library, where it documents the *CView* class and its base class, *CWnd*, you'll see several hundred member functions. Functions whose names begin with *On*—such as *OnKeyDown* and *OnLButtonUp*—are member functions that the application framework calls in response to various Windows "events" such as keystrokes and mouse clicks.

Most of these functions that are called by the application framework aren't virtual functions and thus require more programming steps. This chapter explains how to use the Microsoft Visual C++ .NET Class View's Properties window to set up the message map structure necessary for connecting the application framework to your functions' code.

This chapter includes sample applications of message map functions. The first two applications use an ordinary *CView* class. The Ex05a example shows the interaction between user-driven events and the *OnDraw* function. The Ex05b example shows the effects of different Windows mapping modes.

More often than not, however, you'll want a scrolling view. The last example, Ex05c, uses *CScrollView* in place of the *CView* base class. This allows the MFC library application framework to insert scroll bars and connect them to the view.

Getting User Input: Message Map Functions

The Ex03a application from Chapter 3 does not accept user input (other than the standard Microsoft Windows resizing and window close commands). The window contains menus and a toolbar, but these are not "connected" to the view code. I won't discuss the menus and the toolbar until Part III of this book because they depend on the frame class, but plenty of other Windows input sources will keep you busy until then. However, before you can process any Windows event, even a mouse click, you must learn how to use the MFC library message map system.

The Message Map

When the user clicks the left mouse button in a view window, Windows sends a message—specifically, *WM_LBUTTONDOWN*—to that window. If your program needs to take action in response to *WM_LBUTTONDOWN*, your view class must have a member function that looks like this:

```
void CMyView::OnLButtonDown(UINT nFlags, CPoint point)
{
    // event processing code here
}
```

Your class header file must also have the corresponding prototype:

```
afx_msg void OnLButtonDown(UINT nFlags, CPoint point);
```

The *afx_msg* notation is a "no-op" that alerts you that this is a prototype for a message map function.

Next, your code file needs a message map macro that connects your *OnLButtonDown* function to the application framework:

```
BEGIN_MESSAGE_MAP(CMyView, CView)
    ON_WM_LBUTTONDOWN() // entry specifically for OnLButtonDown
    // other message map entries
END_MESSAGE_MAP()
```

Finally, your class header file needs this statement:

```
DECLARE_MESSAGE_MAP()
```

How do you know which function goes with which Windows message? Chapter Appendix A (and the MFC library online documentation) includes a table that lists all standard Windows messages and corresponding member function prototypes. You can manually code the message-handling functions—indeed, you still have to do that for certain messages. But fortunately, the code wizards available from Class View's Properties window automate the coding of most message map functions.

Saving the View's State: Class Data Members

If your program accepts user input, you'll want the user to get some visual feedback. The view's *OnDraw* function draws an image based on the view's current state, and user actions can alter that state. In a full-blown MFC library application, the document object holds the state of the application, but you're not to that point yet. For now, we'll use two view class data members, *m_rectEllipse* and *m_nColor*. The first is an object of class *CRect*, which holds the current bounding rectangle of an ellipse, and the second is an integer that holds the current ellipse color value.

> **Note** By convention, MFC library nonstatic class data member names begin with *m_*.

We'll make a message-mapped member function toggle the ellipse color (the view's state) between gray and white. (The toggle is activated by a click of the left mouse button.) The initial values of *m_rectEllipse* and *m_nColor* are set in the view's constructor, and the color is changed in the *OnLButtonDown* member function.

> **Note** Why not use a global variable for the view's state? Because if you do, you'll be in trouble if your application has multiple views. Besides, encapsulating data in objects is a big part of what object-oriented programming is all about.

Initializing a View Class Data Member

The most efficient place to initialize a class data member is in the constructor, as shown here:

```
CMyView::CMyView() : m_rectEllipse(0, 0, 200, 200) {...}
```

You can initialize *m_nColor* with the same syntax. We're using a built-in type (integer), so the generated code is the same if you use an assignment statement in the constructor body.

Invalid Rectangle Theory

The *OnLButtonDown* function can toggle the value of *m_nColor* all day, but if that's all it did, the *OnDraw* function wouldn't get called (unless, for example, the user resized the view window). The *OnLButtonDown* function must call the *InvalidateRect* function (a member function that the view class inherits from *CWnd*). *InvalidateRect* triggers a Windows *WM_PAINT* message, which is mapped in the *CView* class to call to the virtual *OnDraw* function. If necessary, *OnDraw* can access the "invalid rectangle" parameter that was passed to *InvalidateRect*.

You can optimize painting in Windows in two ways. First, you must be aware that Windows updates only those pixels that are inside the invalid rectangle. Thus, the smaller you make the invalid rectangle (in the *OnLButtonDown* handler, for instance), the more quickly it can be repainted. Second, it's a waste of time to execute drawing instructions outside the invalid rectangle. Your *OnDraw* function can call the *CDC* member function *GetClipBox* to determine the invalid rectangle, and then it can avoid drawing objects outside it. Remember that *OnDraw* is being called not only in response to your *InvalidateRect* call but also when the user resizes or exposes the window. Thus, *OnDraw* is responsible for all drawing in a window, and it has to adapt to whatever invalid rectangle it gets.

For Win32 Programmers

The MFC library makes it easy to attach your own state variables to a window through C++ class data members. In Win32 programming, the *WNDCLASS* members *cbClsExtra* and *cbWndExtra* are available for this purpose, but the code for using this mechanism is so complex that developers tend to use global variables instead.

The Window's Client Area

A window has a rectangular client area that excludes the border, caption bar, menu bar, and any docking toolbars. The *CWnd* member function *GetClientRect* supplies you with the client-area dimensions. Normally, you're not allowed to draw outside the client area, and most mouse messages are received only when the cursor is in the client area.

CRect, *CPoint*, and *CSize* Arithmetic

The *CRect*, *CPoint*, and *CSize* classes are derived from the Windows *RECT*, *POINT*, and *SIZE* structures, and thus they inherit public integer data members, as follows:

CRect	*left, top, right, bottom*
CPoint	*x, y*
CSize	*cx, cy*

If you look in the *MFC Library Reference*, you'll see that these three classes have a number of overloaded operators. You can, among other things, do the following:

- Add a *CSize* object to a *CPoint* object
- Subtract a *CSize* object from a *CPoint* object
- Subtract one *CPoint* object from another, yielding a *CSize* object
- Add a *CPoint* or *CSize* object to a *CRect* object
- Subtract a *CPoint* or *CSize* object from a *CRect* object

The *CRect* class has member functions that relate to the *CSize* and *CPoint* classes. For example, the *TopLeft* member function returns a *CPoint* object, and the *Size* member function returns a *CSize* object. From this, you can begin to see that a *CSize* object is the "difference between two *CPoint* objects" and that you can "bias" a *CRect* object by a *CPoint* object.

Determining Whether a Point Is Inside a Rectangle

The *CRect* class has a member function, *PtInRect*, that tests a point to see whether it falls inside a rectangle. The second *OnLButtonDown* parameter, *point*, is an object of class *CPoint* that represents the cursor location in the client area of the window. If you want to know whether that point is inside the *m_rectEllipse* rectangle, you can use *PtInRect* in this way:

```
if (m_rectEllipse.PtInRect(point)) {
    // point is inside rectangle
}
```

As you'll soon see, however, this simple logic applies only if you're working in device coordinates (which you are at this stage).

The *CRect LPCRECT* Operator

If you read the *MFC Library Reference* carefully, you'll notice that *CWnd::InvalidateRect* takes an *LPCRECT* parameter (a pointer to a *RECT* structure), not a *CRect* parameter. A *CRect* parameter is allowed because the *CRect* class defines an overloaded operator, *LPCRECT()*, that returns the address of a *CRect* object, which is equivalent to the address of a *RECT* object. Thus, the compiler converts *CRect* arguments to *LPCRECT* arguments when necessary. You call functions as if they have *CRect* reference parameters.

The following view member function code retrieves the client rectangle coordinates and stores them in *rectClient*:

```
CRect rectClient;
GetClientRect(rectClient);
```

Determining Whether a Point Is Inside an Ellipse

The Ex05a code determines whether the mouse hit is inside the rectangle. If you want to make a better test, you can find out whether the hit is inside the ellipse. To do this, you construct an object of class *CRgn* that corresponds to the ellipse and then use the *PtInRegion* function instead of *PtInRect*. Here's the code:

```
CRgn rgn;
rgn.CreateEllipticRgnIndirect(m_rectEllipse);
if (rgn.PtInRegion(point)) {
    // point is inside ellipse
}
```

Note that the *CreateEllipticRgnIndirect* function is another function that takes an *LPCRECT* parameter. It builds a special region structure within Windows that represents an elliptical region inside a window. That structure is then attached to the C++ *CRgn* object in your program. (The same type of structure can also represent a polygon.)

The Ex05a Example

In the Ex05a example, an ellipse (which happens to be a circle) changes color when the user clicks the left mouse button while the mouse cursor is inside the rectangle that bounds the ellipse. You'll use the view class data members to hold the view's state, and you'll use the *InvalidateRect* function to cause the view to be redrawn.

In the Chapter 3 example, drawing in the window depends on only one function, *OnDraw*. The Ex05a example requires three customized functions (including the constructor) and two data members. The complete *CEx05aView* header and source code files are shown below. (The steps for creating the program are listed after the code.) All changes to the original MFC Application Wizard output and *OnLButtonDown* are shown in boldface.

Ex05aView.H

```
// Ex05aView.h : interface of the Cex05aView class
//

#pragma once

class CEx05aView : public CView
{
protected: // create from serialization only
    CEx05aView();
    DECLARE_DYNCREATE(CEx05aView)

// Attributes
public:
    CEx05aDoc* GetDocument() const


// Operations
public:

// Overrides
    public:
    virtual void OnDraw(CDC* pDC);  // overridden to draw this view
    virtual BOOL PreCreateWindow(CREATESTRUCT& cs);
    protected:
    virtual BOOL OnPreparePrinting(CPrintInfo* pInfo);
    virtual void OnBeginPrinting(CDC* pDC, CPrintInfo* pInfo);
    virtual void OnEndPrinting(CDC* pDC, CPrintInfo* pInfo);

// Implementation
public:
    virtual ~CEx05aView();
#ifdef _DEBUG
    virtual void AssertValid() const;
    virtual void Dump(CDumpContext& dc) const;
#endif

protected:

// Generated message map functions
protected:
    afx_msg void OnLButtonDown(UINT nFlags, CPoint point);
    DECLARE_MESSAGE_MAP()
```

(continued)

```
private:
    int m_nColor;
    CRect m_rectEllipse;
#ifndef _DEBUG  // debug version in Ex05aView.cpp
inline CEx05aDoc* CEx05aView::GetDocument() const
   { return reinterpret_cast<CEx05aDoc*>(m_pDocument); }
#endif

};
```

Ex05aView.cpp

```
// Ex05aView.cpp : implementation of the CEx05aView class
//

#include "stdafx.h"
#include "Ex05a.h"

#include "Ex05aDoc.h"
#include "Ex05aView.h"

#ifdef _DEBUG
#define new DEBUG_NEW

#endif

///////////////////////////////////////////////////////////////////////////
// CEx05aView

IMPLEMENT_DYNCREATE(CEx05aView, CView)

BEGIN_MESSAGE_MAP(CEx05aView, CView)
    ON_WM_LBUTTONDOWN()
    // Standard printing commands
    ON_COMMAND(ID_FILE_PRINT, CView::OnFilePrint)
    ON_COMMAND(ID_FILE_PRINT_DIRECT, CView::OnFilePrint)
    ON_COMMAND(ID_FILE_PRINT_PREVIEW, CView::OnFilePrintPreview)
END_MESSAGE_MAP()
///////////////////////////////////////////////////////////////////////////
// CEx05aView construction/destruction

CEx05aView::CEx05aView() : m_rectEllipse(0, 0, 200, 200)
{
    m_nColor = GRAY_BRUSH;
}

CEx05aView::~CEx05aView()
{
}
```

(continued)

```
BOOL CEx05aView::PreCreateWindow(CREATESTRUCT& cs)
{
    // TODO: Modify the Window class or styles here by modifying
    //  the CREATESTRUCT cs

    return CView::PreCreateWindow(cs);
}

///////////////////////////////////////////////////////////////////////
// CEx05aView drawing

void CEx05aView::OnDraw(CDC* pDC)
{
    pDC->SelectStockObject(m_nColor);
    pDC->Ellipse(m_rectEllipse);
}

///////////////////////////////////////////////////////////////////////
// CEx05aView printing

BOOL CEx05aView::OnPreparePrinting(CPrintInfo* pInfo)
{
    // default preparation
    return DoPreparePrinting(pInfo);
}

void CEx05aView::OnBeginPrinting(CDC* /*pDC*/, CPrintInfo* /*pInfo*/)
{
    // TODO: add extra initialization before printing
}

void CEx05aView::OnEndPrinting(CDC* /*pDC*/, CPrintInfo* /*pInfo*/)
{
    // TODO: add cleanup after printing
}

///////////////////////////////////////////////////////////////////////
// CEx05aView diagnostics

#ifdef _DEBUG
void CEx05aView::AssertValid() const
{
    CView::AssertValid();
}

void CEx05aView::Dump(CDumpContext& dc) const
{
    CView::Dump(dc);
}
```

(continued)

```
CEx05aDoc* CEx05aView::GetDocument() // non-debug version is inline
{
    ASSERT(m_pDocument->IsKindOf(RUNTIME_CLASS(CEx05aDoc)));
    return (CEx05aDoc*)m_pDocument;
}
#endif //_DEBUG

/////////////////////////////////////////////////////////////////////////////
// CEx05aView message handlers

void CEx05aView::OnLButtonDown(UINT nFlags, CPoint point)
{
    if (m_rectEllipse.PtInRect(point)) {
        if (m_nColor == GRAY_BRUSH) {
            m_nColor = WHITE_BRUSH;
        }
        else {
            m_nColor = GRAY_BRUSH;
        }
        InvalidateRect(m_rectEllipse);
    }
}
```

Using Class View with Ex05a

Look at the following Ex05aView.h source code:

```
afx_msg void OnLButtonDown(UINT nFlags, Cpoint point);
```

Now look at the following Ex05aView.cpp source code:

```
ON_WM_LBUTTONDOWN()
```

The MFC Application Wizard used to generate comment lines for the benefit of the Class Wizard. Fortunately, these comments are no longer needed. Visual C++ .NET keeps track of the entire state of your code at all times, including mapping functions and maps to specific lines in your code. The code wizards available from the Class View's Properties window add message handler prototypes based on this internal information. In addition, the code wizards generate a skeleton *OnLButtonDown* member function in Ex05aView.cpp, complete with the correct parameter declarations and return type.

Notice how the combination of the MFC Application Wizard and code wizards is different from a conventional code generator. You run a conventional code generator only once and then edit the resulting code. You run the MFC Application Wizard to generate the application only once, but you can run the code wizards as many times as necessary, and you can edit the code at any time.

Using the MFC Application Wizard and the Code Wizards Together

The following steps show how you use the MFC Application Wizard and the code wizards available from Class View's Properties window to create this application:

1. **Run the MFC Application Wizard to create Ex05a.** Use the wizard to generate an SDI project named Ex05a in the \vcppnet subdirectory. The default class names are shown here.

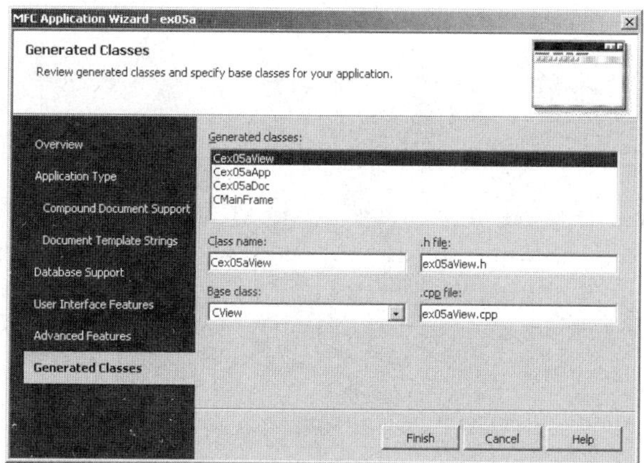

2. **Add the *m_rectEllipse* and *m_nColor* data members to CEx05aView.** Choose Class View from the View menu in Visual C++ .NET and right-click the *CEx05aView* class. Choose Add Variable and then insert the following two data members:

```
private:
    CRect m_rectEllipse;
    int m_nColor;
```

   If you prefer, you can type the above code inside the class declaration in the file ex05aView.h.

3. **Use the Class View's Properties window to add a *CEx05aView* class message handler.** Select the *CEx05aView* class within Class View, as shown in the following illustration. Next, right-click on CEx05aView and choose Properties. Click the Messages button on the Properties window's toolbar. Scroll down and click on the *WM_LBUTTONDOWN* entry. You'll see a drop-down combo box appear next to the entry. Select <Add> OnLButtonDown. The *OnLButtonDown* function will be written into the code and will appear inside the Code Editor.

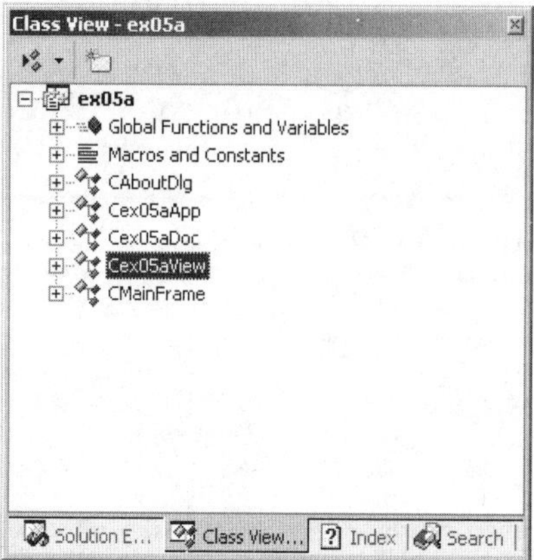

4. **Edit the *OnLButtonDown* code in Ex05aView.cpp.** Once you add the message handler, the file Ex05aView.cpp will open in the Code Editor and the cursor will be positioned to the newly generated *OnLButtonDown* member function. The following boldface code (that you type in) replaces the previous code:

```
void CEx05aView::OnLButtonDown(UINT nFlags, CPoint point)
{
    if (m_rectEllipse.PtInRect(point)) {
        if (m_nColor == GRAY_BRUSH) {
            m_nColor = WHITE_BRUSH;
        }
        else {
            m_nColor = GRAY_BRUSH;
        }
        InvalidateRect(m_rectEllipse);
    }
}
```

5. **Edit the constructor and the *OnDraw* function in Ex05aView.cpp.** The following boldface code (that you type in) replaces the previous code:

```
CEx05aView::CEx05aView() : m_rectEllipse(0, 0, 200, 200)
{
    m_nColor = GRAY_BRUSH;
}
:
void CEx05aView::OnDraw(CDC* pDC)
{
    pDC->SelectStockObject(m_nColor);
    pDC->Ellipse(m_rectEllipse);
}
```

6. **Build and run the Ex05a program.** Choose Build from the Build menu or, on the Build toolbar, click the button shown here.

Next, choose Start Without Debugging from the Debug menu. The resulting program will respond to clicks of the left mouse button by changing the color of the circle in the view window. (Don't click the mouse's left button quickly in succession; Windows will interpret this as a double-click rather than two single clicks.)

For Win32 Programmers

A conventional Windows-based application registers a series of window classes (not the same as C++ classes) and, in the process, assigns a unique function, known as a *window procedure*, to each class. Each time the application calls *CreateWindow* to create a window, it specifies a window class as a parameter and thus links the newly created window to a window procedure function. This function, which is called each time Windows sends a message to the window, tests the message code that is passed as a parameter and then executes the appropriate code to handle the message.

The MFC application framework has a single window class and window procedure function for most window types. This window procedure function looks up the window handle (passed as a parameter) in the MFC handle map to get the corresponding C++ window object pointer. The window procedure function then uses the MFC runtime class system to determine the C++ class of the window object. Next, it locates the handler function in static tables created by the dispatch map functions, and finally it calls the handler function with the correct window object selected.

Using Windows Mapping Modes

Up to now, your drawing units have been display pixels, also known as *device coordinates*. The Ex05a drawing units are pixels because the device context has the default mapping mode, *MM_TEXT*, assigned to it. The following statement draws a square of 200 by 200 pixels, with its top left corner at the top left of the window's client area. (Positive *y* values increase as you move down the window.)

```
pDC->Rectangle(CRect(0, 0, 200, 200));
```

This square will look smaller on a high-resolution display of 1024-by-768 pixels than on a standard VGA display that is 640-by-480 pixels, and it will look tiny if printed on a laser printer with 600-dpi resolution. (Try EX05A's Print Preview feature to see for yourself.)

What if you want the square to be 4-by-4 centimeters (cm), regardless of the display device? Windows provides a number of other mapping modes, or coordinate systems, that you can associate with the device context. Coordinates in the current mapping mode are called *logical coordinates*. If you assign the *MM_HIMETRIC* mapping mode, for example, a logical unit is $^{1}/_{100}$ millimeter (mm) instead of 1 pixel. In the *MM_HIMETRIC* mapping mode, the *y* axis runs in the opposite direction to that in the *MM_TEXT* mode: *y* values decrease as you move down. Thus, a 4-by-4-cm square is drawn in logical coordinates this way:

```
pDC->Rectangle(CRect(0, 0, 4000, -4000));
```

Looks easy, doesn't it? Well, it isn't, because you can't work only in logical coordinates. Your program is always switching between device coordinates and logical coordinates, and you need to know when to convert between them. This section gives you a few rules that can make your programming life easier. First, you need to know what mapping modes Windows gives you.

The *MM_TEXT* Mapping Mode

At first glance, *MM_TEXT* appears to be no mapping mode at all, but rather another name for device coordinates. Almost. In *MM_TEXT*, coordinates map to pixels, values of *x* increase as you move right, and values of *y* increase as you move down, but you're allowed to change the origin through calls to the *CDC* functions *SetViewportOrg* and *SetWindowOrg*.

Here's some code that sets the window origin to (100, 100) in logical coordinate space and then draws a 200-by-200-pixel square offset by (100, 100). (An illustration of the output is shown in Figure 5-1.) The logical point (100, 100) maps to the device point (0, 0). A scrolling window uses this kind of transformation.

```
void CMyView::OnDraw(CDC* pDC)
{
    pDC->SetMapMode(MM_TEXT);
    pDC->SetWindowOrg(CPoint(100, 100));
    pDC->Rectangle(CRect(100, 100, 300, 300));
}
```

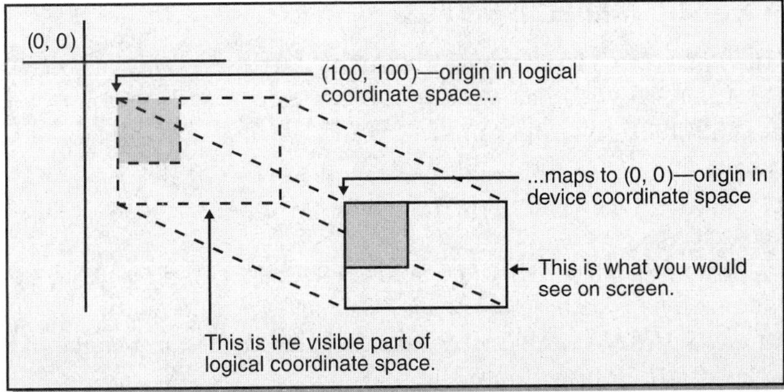

Figure 5-1 A square drawn after the origin has been moved to (100, 100).

The Fixed-Scale Mapping Modes

One important group of Windows mapping modes provides fixed scaling. You've already seen that, in the *MM_HIMETRIC* mapping mode, *x* values increase as you move right and *y* values decrease as you move down. All fixed mapping modes follow this convention, and you can't change it. The only difference among the fixed mapping modes is the actual scale factor, as shown in Table 5-1.

Table 5-1. The Scale Factor for Mapping Modes

Mapping Mode	Logical Unit
MM_LOENGLISH	0.01 inch
MM_HIENGLISH	0.001 inch
MM_LOMETRIC	0.1 mm
MM_HIMETRIC	0.01 mm
MM_TWIPS	1/1440 inch

The last mapping mode, *MM_TWIPS*, is most often used with printers. One *twip* is $^1/_{20}$ point. (A *point* is a type measurement unit that equals exactly $^1/_{72}$ inch in Windows.) If the mapping mode is *MM_TWIPS* and you want, for example, 12-point type, you set the character height to 12 × 20, or 240, twips.

The Variable-Scale Mapping Modes

Windows provides two mapping modes, *MM_ISOTROPIC* and *MM_ANISOTROPIC*, that allow you to change the scale factor as well as the origin. With these mapping modes, your drawing can change size as the user changes the size of the window. Also, if you invert the scale of one axis, you can "flip" an image about the other axis and you can define your own arbitrary fixed-scale factors.

With the *MM_ISOTROPIC* mode, a 1:1 aspect ratio is always preserved. In other words, a circle is always a circle as the scale factor changes. With the *MM_ANISOTROPIC* mode, the *x* and *y* scale factors can change independently. Circles can be squished into ellipses.

Here's an *OnDraw* function that draws an ellipse that fits exactly in its window:

```
void CMyView::OnDraw(CDC* pDC)
{
    CRect rectClient;

     GetClientRect(rectClient);
    pDC->SetMapMode(MM_ANISOTROPIC);
    pDC->SetWindowExt(1000, 1000);
    pDC->SetViewportExt(rectClient.right, -rectClient.bottom);
    pDC->SetViewportOrg(rectClient.right / 2, rectClient.bottom / 2);

    pDC->Ellipse(CRect(-500, -500, 500, 500));
}
```

What's going on here? The functions *SetWindowExt* and *SetViewportExt* work together to set the scale, based on the window's current client rectangle returned by the *GetClientRect* function. The resulting window size is exactly 1000-by-1000 logical units. The *SetViewportOrg* function sets the origin to the center of the window. Thus, a centered ellipse with a radius of 500 logical units fills the window exactly, as illustrated in Figure 5-2.

Here are the formulas for converting logical units to device units:

- *x* scale factor = *x* viewport extent / *x* window extent
- *y* scale factor = *y* viewport extent / *y* window extent
- device *x* = logical *x* × *x* scale factor + *x* origin offset
- device *y* = logical *y* × *y* scale factor + *y* origin offset

Suppose the window is 448 pixels wide (*rectClient.right*). The right edge of the ellipse's client rectangle is 500 logical units from the origin. The *x* scale factor is $^{448}/_{1000}$, and the *x* origin offset is $^{448}/_{2}$ device units. If you use the formulas shown above, the right edge of the ellipse's client rectangle comes out to 448 device units, the right edge of the window. The *x* scale factor is expressed as a ratio (viewport extent/window extent) because Windows device coordinates are integers, not floating-point values. The extent values are meaningless by themselves.

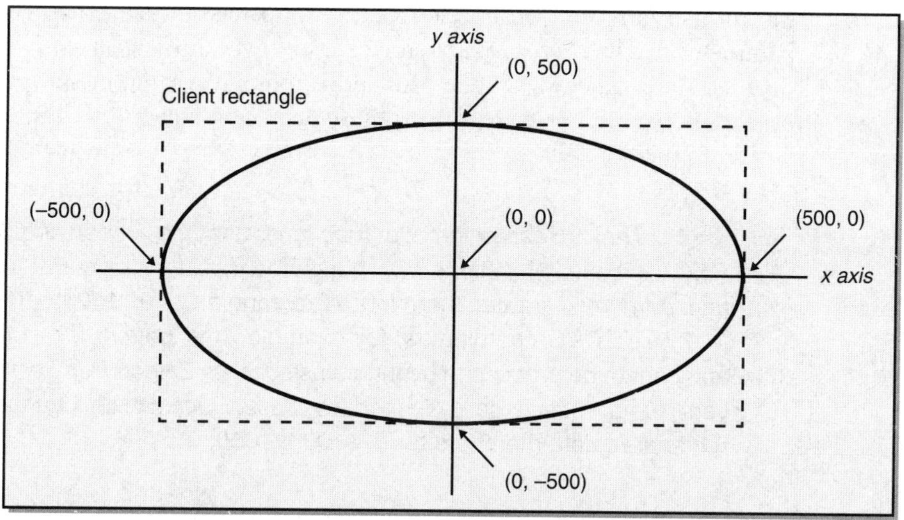

Figure 5-2 A centered ellipse drawn in the *MM_ANISOTROPIC* mapping mode.

If you substitute *MM_ISOTROPIC* for *MM_ANISOTROPIC* in the preceding example, the "ellipse" is always a circle, as shown in Figure 5-3. It expands to fit the smallest dimension of the window rectangle.

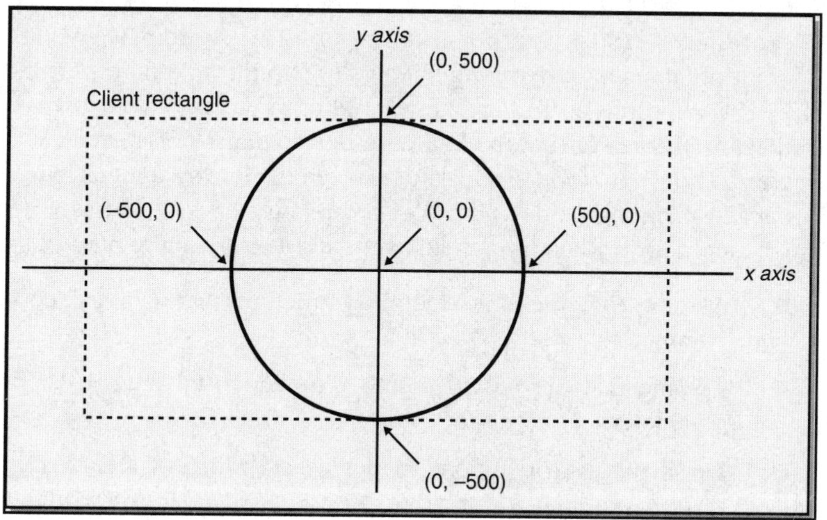

Figure 5-3 A centered ellipse drawn in the *MM_ISOTROPIC* mapping mode.

Coordinate Conversion

Once you set the mapping mode (plus the origin) of a device context, you can use logical coordinate parameters for most *CDC* member functions. If you get the mouse cursor coordinates from a Windows mouse message (the *point* parameter in *OnLButtonDown*), for example, you're dealing with device coordinates. Many other MFC library functions, particularly the member functions of class *CRect*, work correctly only with device coordinates.

> **Note** The *CRect* arithmetic functions use the underlying Win32 *RECT* arithmetic functions, which assume that *right* is greater than *left* and *bottom* is greater than *top*. A rectangle (0, 0, 1000, –1000) in *MM_HIMETRIC* coordinates, for example, has *bottom* less than *top* and cannot be processed by functions such as *CRect::PtInRect* unless your program first calls *CRect::NormalizeRect*, which changes the rectangle's data members to (0, –1000, 1000, 0).

Furthermore, you're likely to need a third set of coordinates that we'll call *physical coordinates*. Why do you need another set? Suppose you're using the *MM_LOENGLISH* mapping mode in which a logical unit is 0.01 inch, but an inch on the screen represents a foot (12 inches) in the real world. Now suppose the user works in inches and decimal fractions. A measurement of 26.75 inches translates to 223 logical units, which must ultimately be translated to device coordinates. You'll want to store the physical coordinates as either floating-point numbers or scaled long integers to avoid rounding-off errors.

For the physical-to-logical translation, you're on your own, but the Windows GDI takes care of the logical-to-device translation for you. The *CDC* functions *LPtoDP* and *DPtoLP* translate between the two systems as long as the device context mapping mode and associated parameters have already been set. Your job is to decide when to use each system. Here are a few rules of thumb:

- Assume that the *CDC* member functions take logical coordinate parameters.
- Assume that the *CWnd* member functions take device coordinate parameters.
- Do all hit-test operations in device coordinates. Define regions in device coordinates. Functions such as *CRect::PtInRect* work best with device coordinates.

- Store long-term values in logical or physical coordinates. If you store a point in device coordinates and the user scrolls through a window, that point is no longer valid.

Suppose you need to know whether the mouse cursor is inside a rectangle when the user clicks the left mouse button. The code is shown here:

```
// m_rect is CRect data member of the derived view class with MM_LOENGLISH
//  logical coordinates

void CMyView::OnLButtonDown(UINT nFlags, CPoint point)
{
    CRect rect = m_rect; // rect is a temporary copy of m_rect.
    CClientDC dc(this);  // This is how we get a device context
                         //  for SetMapMode and LPtoDP
                         //  -- more in next chapter
    dc.SetMapMode(MM_LOENGLISH);
    dc.LPtoDP(rect);     // rect is now in device coordinates
    if (rect.PtInRect(point)) {
        TRACE("Mouse cursor is inside the rectangle.\n");
    }
}
```

Notice the use of the *TRACE* macro (covered in Chapter 2).

> **Note** As you'll soon see, it's better to set the mapping mode in the virtual *CView* function *OnPrepareDC* instead of in the *OnDraw* function.

The Ex05b Example: Converting to the *MM_HIMETRIC* Mapping Mode

Ex05b is Ex05a converted to *MM_HIMETRIC* coordinates. The Ex05b project on the companion CD uses new class names and filenames, but the following instructions take you through modifying the Ex05a code. Like Ex05a, Ex05b performs a hit-test so that the ellipse changes color only when you click inside the bounding rectangle.

1. **Use the Class View's Properties window to override the virtual *OnPrepareDC* function.** You can override virtual functions for selected MFC library base classes, including *CView* in the Properties window. The code wizards available from the Properties window generate the correct function prototype in the class's header file and a skeleton function in the CPP file. Select the class name *CEx05aView*

in Class View, right-click on it, and then choose Properties. Click the Overrides button on the Properties window toolbar and select the *OnPrepareDC* function in the list. Add the function. Visual C++ .NET will load the implementation file so you can edit the function as shown here:

```
void CEx05aView::OnPrepareDC(CDC* pDC, CPrintInfo* pInfo)
{
    pDC->SetMapMode(MM_HIMETRIC);
    CView::OnPrepareDC(pDC, pInfo);
}
```

The application framework calls the virtual *OnPrepareDC* function just before it calls *OnDraw*.

2. **Edit the view class constructor.** You must change the coordinate values for the ellipse rectangle. That rectangle is now 4-by-4 centimeters instead of 200-by-200 pixels. Note that the *y* value must be negative; otherwise, the ellipse will be drawn on the "virtual screen" right above your monitor! Change the values as shown here:

```
CEx05aView::CEx05aView() : m_rectEllipse(0, 0, 4000, -4000)
{
    m_nColor = GRAY_BRUSH;
}
```

3. **Edit the *OnLButtonDown* function.** This function must convert the ellipse rectangle to device coordinates in order to do the hit-test. Change the function as shown in the following code:

```
void CEx05aView::OnLButtonDown(UINT nFlags, CPoint point)
{
    CClientDC dc(this);
    OnPrepareDC(&dc);
    CRect rectDevice = m_rectEllipse;
    dc.LPtoDP(rectDevice);
    if (rectDevice.PtInRect(point)) {
        if (m_nColor == GRAY_BRUSH) {
            m_nColor = WHITE_BRUSH;
        }
        else {
            m_nColor = GRAY_BRUSH;
        }
        InvalidateRect(rectDevice);
    }
}
```

4. **Build and run the Ex05b program.** The output should look similar to the output from Ex05a, except that the ellipse size will be different. If you try using Print Preview again, the ellipse should appear much larger than it did in Ex05a.

Creating a Scrolling View Window

As the lack of scroll bars in Ex05a and Ex05b indicates, the MFC library *CView* class, the base class of *CEx05bView*, doesn't directly support scrolling. Another MFC library class, *CScrollView*, does support scrolling. *CScrollView* is derived from *CView*. We'll create a new program, Ex05c, that uses *CScrollView* in place of *CView*. All the coordinate conversion code you added in Ex05b sets you up for scrolling.

The *CScrollView* class supports scrolling from the scroll bars but not from the keyboard. It's easy enough to add keyboard scrolling, so we'll do it.

A Window Is Larger Than What You See

If you use the mouse to shrink the size of an ordinary window, the contents of the window will remain anchored at the top left of the window and items at the bottom and/or on the right of the window will disappear. When you expand the window, the items will reappear. You can correctly conclude that a window is larger than the viewport that you see on the screen. The viewport doesn't have to be anchored at the top left of the window area, however. Through the use of the *CWnd* functions *ScrollWindow* and *SetWindowOrg*, the *CScrollView* class allows you to move the viewport anywhere within the window, including areas above and to the left of the origin.

Scroll Bars

Windows makes it easy to display scroll bars at the edges of a window, but Windows by itself doesn't make any attempt to connect those scroll bars to their window. That's where the *CScrollView* class fits in. *CScrollView* member functions process the *WM_HSCROLL* and *WM_VSCROLL* messages sent by the scroll bars to the view. Those functions move the viewport within the window and do all the necessary housekeeping.

Scrolling Alternatives

The *CScrollView* class supports a particular kind of scrolling that involves one big window and a small viewport. Each item is assigned a unique position in this big window. If, for example, you have 10,000 address lines to display, instead of having a window 10,000 lines long, you probably want a smaller window with scrolling logic that selects only as many lines as the screen can display. In that case, you should write your own scrolling view class derived from *CView*.

The *OnInitialUpdate* Function

You'll be seeing more of the *OnInitialUpdate* function when you study the document-view architecture, starting in Chapter 15. The virtual *OnInitialUpdate* function is important here because it is the first function called by the framework after your view window is fully created. The framework calls *OnInitialUpdate* before it calls *OnDraw* for the first time, so *OnInitialUpdate* is the natural place for setting the logical size and mapping mode for a scrolling view. You set these parameters with a call to the *CScrollView::SetScrollSizes* function.

Accepting Keyboard Input

Keyboard input is really a two-step process. Windows sends *WM_KEYDOWN* and *WM_KEYUP* messages, with virtual key codes, to a window, but before they get to the window they are translated. If an ANSI character is typed (resulting in a *WM_KEYDOWN* message), the translation function checks the keyboard shift status and then sends a *WM_CHAR* message with the proper code, either uppercase or lowercase. Cursor keys and function keys don't have codes, so there's no translation to do. The window gets only the *WM_KEYDOWN* and *WM_KEYUP* messages.

You can use the Class View's Properties window to map all these messages to your view. If you're expecting characters, map *WM_CHAR*; if you're expecting other keystrokes, map *WM_KEYDOWN*. The MFC library neatly supplies the character code or virtual key code as a handler function parameter.

The Ex05c Example: Scrolling

The goal of Ex05c is to make a logical window 20 centimeters wide by 30 centimeters high. The program draws the same ellipse that it drew in the Ex05b project. You could edit the Ex05b source files to convert the *CView* base class to a *CScrollView* base class, but it's easier to start over with the MFC Application Wizard. The wizard generates the *OnInitialUpdate* override function for you. Here are the steps:

1. **Run the MFC Application Wizard to create Ex05c.** Use the wizard to generate an SDI program named Ex05c in the \vcppnet subdirectory. Set the *CEx05cView* base class to *CScrollView*, as shown here.

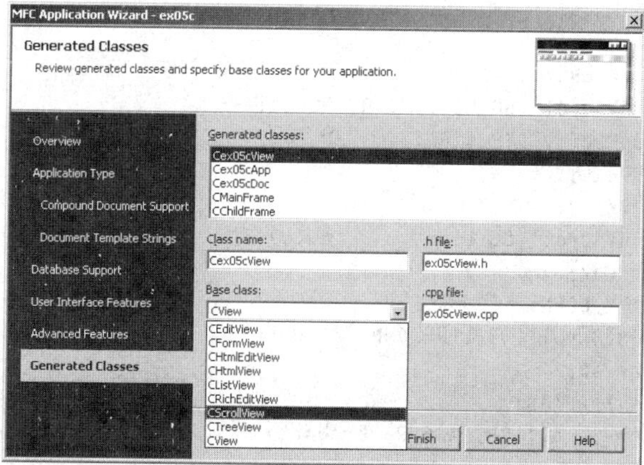

2. **Add the *m_rectEllipse* and *m_nColor* data members in Ex05cView.h.** Insert the following code using the Add Member Variable Wizard available from the Class View's Properties window or by typing inside the *CEx05cView* class declaration:

```
private:
    CRect m_rectEllipse;
    int m_nColor;
```

   These are the same data members that were added in the Ex05a and Ex05b projects.

3. **Modify the MFC Application Wizard–generated *OnInitialUpdate* function.** Edit *OnInitialUpdate* in Ex05cView.cpp as shown here:

```
void CEx05cView::OnInitialUpdate()
{
    CScrollView::OnInitialUpdate();
    CSize sizeTotal(20000, 30000); // 20 by 30 cm
    CSize sizePage(sizeTotal.cx / 2, sizeTotal.cy / 2);
    CSize sizeLine(sizeTotal.cx / 50, sizeTotal.cy / 50);
    SetScrollSizes(MM_HIMETRIC, sizeTotal, sizePage, sizeLine);
}
```

4. **Use the Class View's Properties window to add a message handler for the *WM_KEYDOWN* message.** The code wizards available from the Properties window generate the member function *OnKeyDown* along with the necessary message map entries and prototypes. Edit the code as follows:

```
void CEx05cView::OnKeyDown(UINT nChar, UINT nRepCnt, UINT nFlags)
{
    switch (nChar) {
    case VK_HOME:
        OnVScroll(SB_TOP, 0, NULL);
```

(continued)

```
            OnHScroll(SB_LEFT, 0, NULL);
            break;
        case VK_END:
            OnVScroll(SB_BOTTOM, 0, NULL);
            OnHScroll(SB_RIGHT, 0, NULL);
            break;
        case VK_UP:
            OnVScroll(SB_LINEUP, 0, NULL);
            break;
        case VK_DOWN:
            OnVScroll(SB_LINEDOWN, 0, NULL);
            break;
        case VK_PRIOR:
            OnVScroll(SB_PAGEUP, 0, NULL);
            break;
        case VK_NEXT:
            OnVScroll(SB_PAGEDOWN, 0, NULL);
            break;
        case VK_LEFT:
            OnHScroll(SB_LINELEFT, 0, NULL);
            break;
        case VK_RIGHT:
            OnHScroll(SB_LINERIGHT, 0, NULL);
            break;
        default:
            break;
        }
}
```

5. **Edit the constructor and the *OnDraw* function.** Change the MFC Application Wizard–generated constructor and the *OnDraw* function in Ex05cView.cpp as follows:

```
CEx05cView::CEx05cView() : m_rectEllipse(0, 0, 4000, -4000)
{
    m_nColor = GRAY_BRUSH;
}
⋮
void CEx05cView::OnDraw(CDC* pDC)
{
    pDC->SelectStockObject(m_nColor);
    pDC->Ellipse(m_rectEllipse);
}
```

These functions are identical to those used in the Ex05a and Ex05b projects.

6. **Map the *WM_LBUTTONDOWN* message and edit the handler.** Make the following changes to the generated code:

```
void CEx05cView::OnLButtonDown(UINT nFlags, CPoint point)
{
    CClientDC dc(this);
    OnPrepareDC(&dc);
    CRect rectDevice = m_rectEllipse;
    dc.LPtoDP(rectDevice);
    if (rectDevice.PtInRect(point)) {
        if (m_nColor == GRAY_BRUSH) {
            m_nColor = WHITE_BRUSH;
        }
        else {
            m_nColor = GRAY_BRUSH;
        }
        InvalidateRect(rectDevice);
    }
}
```

This function is identical to the *OnLButtonDown* handler in the Ex05b project. It calls *OnPrepareDC* as before, but something is different. The *CEx05bView* class doesn't have an overridden *OnPrepareDC* function, so the call goes to *CScrollView::OnPrepareDC*. That function sets the mapping mode based on the first parameter to *SetScrollSizes*, and it sets the window origin based on the current scroll position. Even if your scroll view were to use the *MM_TEXT* mapping mode, you'd still need the coordinate conversion logic to adjust for the origin offset.

7. **Build and run the Ex05c program.** Check to be sure that the mouse hit logic is working even if the circle is scrolled partially out of the window. Also check the keyboard logic. The output should look like this:

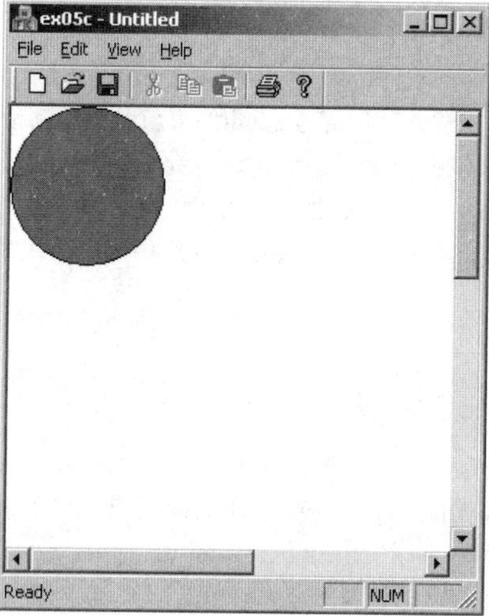

Using Other Windows Messages

The MFC library directly supports hundreds of Windows message-handling functions. In addition, you can define your own messages. You'll see plenty of message-handling examples in later chapters, including handlers for menu items, child window controls, and so forth. In the meantime, five special Windows messages deserve special attention: *WM_CREATE*, *WM_CLOSE*, *WM_QUERYENDSESSION*, *WM_DESTROY*, and *WM_NCDESTROY*.

The *WM_CREATE* Message

This is the first message that Windows sends to a view. It is sent when the window's *Create* function is called by the framework. At that time, the window creation is not finished, so the window is not visible. Therefore, your *OnCreate* handler cannot call Windows functions that depend on the window being completely alive. You can call such functions in an overridden *OnInitialUpdate* function, but you must be aware that in an SDI application *OnInitialUpdate* can be called more than once in a view's lifetime.

The *WM_CLOSE* Message

Windows sends the *WM_CLOSE* message when the user closes a window from the system menu and when a parent window is closed. If you implement the *OnClose* message map function in your derived view class, you can control the closing process. If, for example, you need to prompt the user to save changes to a file, you can do it in *OnClose*. Only after you've determined that it is safe to close the window should you call the base class *OnClose* function, which will continue the close process. The view object and the corresponding window will both still be active.

> **Note** When you're using the full application framework, you probably won't use the *WM_CLOSE* message handler. You can override the *CDocument::SaveModified* virtual function instead, as part of the application framework's highly structured program exit procedure.

The *WM_QUERYENDSESSION* Message

Windows sends the *WM_QUERYENDSESSION* message to all running applications when the user exits Windows. The *OnQueryEndSession* message map function handles it. If you write a handler for *WM_CLOSE*, you should write one for *WM_QUERYENDSESSION*, too.

The *WM_DESTROY* Message

Windows sends the *WM_DESTROY* message after the *WM_CLOSE* message, and the *OnDestroy* message map function handles it. When your program receives this message, it should assume that the view window is no longer visible on the screen but that it is still active and its child windows are still active. You use this message handler to do cleanup that depends on the existence of the underlying window. Be sure to call the base class *OnDestroy* function. You cannot "abort" the window destruction process in your view's *OnDestroy* function. *OnClose* is the place to do that.

The *WM_NCDESTROY* Message

This is the last message that Windows sends when the window is being destroyed. All child windows have already been destroyed. You can do final processing in *OnNcDestroy* that doesn't depend on a window being active. Be sure to call the base class *OnNcDestroy* function.

> **Note** Do not try to destroy a dynamically allocated window object in *OnNcDestroy*. That job is reserved for a special *CWnd* virtual function, *PostNcDestroy*, that the base class *OnNcDestroy* calls. MFC Technical Note #17 in the online documentation offers hints about when it's appropriate to destroy a window object.

6

Classic GDI Functions, Fonts, and Bitmaps

You've already seen some elements of the Graphics Device Interface (GDI). Anytime your program draws to the screen or the printer, it can use the GDI or GDI+ functions. We'll look at the classic GDI functions in this chapter and discuss GDI+ functions when we cover .NET in Chapter 33.

The GDI provides functions for drawing points, lines, rectangles, polygons, ellipses, bitmaps, and text. You can draw circles and squares intuitively once you study the available functions, but text programming is more difficult. This chapter gives you the information you need to start using the GDI effectively in the Microsoft Visual C++ .NET environment. You'll also learn how to use fonts and bitmaps on the display and the printer.

The Device Context Classes

In Chapter 3 and Chapter 5, we passed the view class's *OnDraw* member function a pointer to a device context object. *OnDraw* selected a brush and then drew an ellipse. The Microsoft Windows device context is the key GDI element that represents a physical device. Each C++ device context object has an associated Windows device context, which is identified by a 32-bit handle of type HDC.

The Microsoft Foundation Class (MFC) library provides a number of device context classes. The base class *CDC* has all the member functions (including some virtual functions) that you'll need for drawing. Except for the oddball *CMetaFileDC* class, derived classes are distinct only in their constructors and destructors. If you (or the application framework) construct an object of a derived device context class, you can pass a *CDC* pointer to a function such as *OnDraw*.

For the display, the usual derived classes are *CClientDC* and *CWindowDC*. For other devices, such as printers or memory buffers, you construct objects of the base class *CDC*.

The "virtualness" of the *CDC* class is an important feature of the application framework. In Chapter 17, you'll see how easy it is to write code that works with both the printer and the display. A statement in *OnDraw* such as

```
pDC->TextOut(0, 0, "Hello");
```

sends text to the display, the printer, or the Print Preview window, depending on the class of the object referenced by the *CView::OnDraw* function's *pDC* parameter.

For display and printer device context objects, the application framework attaches the handle to the object. For other device contexts, such as the memory device context that you'll see in later chapters, you must call a member function after construction in order to attach the handle.

The *CClientDC* and *CWindowDC* Display Context Classes

Recall that a window's client area excludes the border, the caption bar, and the menu bar. If you create a *CClientDC* object, you have a device context that is mapped only to this client area—you can't draw outside it. The point (0, 0) usually refers to the upper left corner of the client area. As you'll see later, an MFC *CView* object corresponds to a child window that is contained inside a separate frame window, often along with a toolbar, a status bar, and scroll bars. The client area of the view therefore does not include these other windows. If the window contains a docked toolbar along the top, for example, (0, 0) refers to the point immediately *under* the left edge of the toolbar.

If you construct an object of class *CWindowDC*, the point (0, 0) is at the upper left corner of the nonclient area of the window. With this whole-window device context, you can draw in the window's border, in the caption area, and so forth. Don't forget that the view window doesn't have a nonclient area, so *CWindowDC* is more applicable to frame windows than it is to view windows.

Constructing and Destroying *CDC* Objects

If you construct a *CDC* object, it is important to destroy it as soon as you're done with it. Windows limits the number of available device contexts, and if you fail to release a Windows device context object, a small amount of memory will be lost until your program exits. You'll usually construct a device context object inside a message handler function such as *OnLButtonDown*. The easiest way to ensure that the device context object is destroyed (and that the underlying Windows device context is released) is to construct the object on the stack in the following way:

```
void CMyView::OnLButtonDown(UINT nFlags, CPoint point)
{
    CRect rect;

    CClientDC dc(this);  // constructs dc on the stack
    dc.GetClipBox(rect); // retrieves the clipping rectangle
} // dc automatically released
```

Notice that the *CClientDC* constructor takes a window pointer as a parameter. The destructor for the *CClientDC* object is called when the function returns. You can also get a device context pointer by using the *CWnd::GetDC* member function, as shown in the following code. You must be careful here to call the *ReleaseDC* function to release the device context.

```
void CMyView::OnLButtonDown(UINT nFlags, CPoint point)
{
    CRect rect;

    CDC* pDC = GetDC();     // a pointer to an internal dc
    pDC->GetClipBox(rect); // retrieves the clipping rectangle
    ReleaseDC(pDC);        // Don't forget this
}
```

> **Warning** Do not destroy the *CDC* object passed by the pointer to *OnDraw*. The application framework will handle the destruction for you.

The State of the Device Context

You already know that a device context is required for drawing. When you use a CDC object to draw an ellipse, for example, what you see on the screen (or on hard copy) depends on the current "state" of the device context. The state includes the following:

- Attached GDI drawing objects such as pens, brushes, and fonts.
- The mapping mode that determines the scale of items when they are drawn. (You already experimented with the mapping mode in Chapter 5.)
- Various details such as text alignment parameters and polygon filling mode.

You've seen, for example, that selecting a gray brush before drawing an ellipse results in the ellipse having a gray interior. When you create a device context object, it has certain default characteristics, such as a black pen for shape boundaries. All other state characteristics are assigned through *CDC* class member functions. GDI objects are selected into the device context by means of the overloaded *SelectObject* functions. A device context can, for example, have one pen, one brush, or one font selected at any given time.

The *CPaintDC* Class

You'll need the *CPaintDC* class only if you override your view's *OnPaint* function. The default *OnPaint* calls *OnDraw* with a properly set up device context, but sometimes you'll need display-specific drawing code. The *CPaintDC* class is special because its constructor and destructor do housekeeping unique to drawing to the display. Once you have a *CDC* pointer, however, you can use it as you would any other device context pointer.

Here's a sample *OnPaint* function that creates a *CPaintDC* object:

```
void CMyView::OnPaint()
{
    CPaintDC dc(this);
    OnPrepareDC(&dc); // explained later
    dc.TextOut(0, 0, "for the display, not the printer");
    OnDraw(&dc);      // stuff that's common to display and printer
}
```

For Win32 Programmers

The *CPaintDC* constructor calls *BeginPaint* for you, and the destructor calls *EndPaint*. If you construct your device context on the stack, the *EndPaint* call is completely automatic.

GDI Objects

A Windows GDI object type is represented by an MFC library class. *CGdiObject* is the abstract base class for the GDI object classes. A Windows GDI object is represented by a C++ object of a class derived from *CGdiObject*.

Here's a list of the GDI derived classes:

- **CBitmap** A bitmap is an array of bits in which one or more bits correspond to each display pixel. You can use bitmaps to represent images or to create brushes.

- **CBrush** A brush defines a bitmapped pattern of pixels that is used to fill areas with color.
- **CFont** A font is a complete collection of characters of a particular typeface and a particular size. Fonts are generally stored on disk as resources, and some are device-specific.
- **CPalette** A palette is a color-mapping interface that allows an application to take full advantage of the color capability of an output device without interfering with other applications.
- **CPen** A pen is a tool for drawing lines and shape borders. You can specify a pen's color and thickness and whether it draws solid, dotted, or dashed lines.
- **CRgn** A region is an area whose shape is a polygon, an ellipse, or a combination of polygons and ellipses. You can use regions for filling, clipping, and mouse hit-testing.

Constructing and Destroying GDI Objects

You never construct an object of class *CGdiObject*; instead, you construct objects of the derived classes. Constructors for some GDI derived classes, such as *CPen* and *CBrush*, allow you to specify enough information to create the object in one step. Others, such as *CFont* and *CRgn*, require a second creation step. For these classes, you construct the C++ object with the default constructor and then you call a create function such as *CreateFont* or *CreatePolygonRgn*.

The *CGdiObject* class has a virtual destructor. The derived class destructors delete Windows GDI objects that are attached to the C++ objects. If you construct an object of a class derived from *CGdiObject*, you must delete it before exiting the program. To delete a GDI object, you must first separate it from the device context. You'll see an example of this in the next section.

For Win32 Programmers

With Win32, the GDI memory is owned by the process and is released when your program terminates. Still, an unreleased GDI bitmap object can waste a significant amount of memory.

Tracking GDI Objects

OK, so you know you have to delete your GDI objects and that they must first be disconnected from their device contexts. But how do you disconnect them? A member of the *CDC::SelectObject* family of functions does the work of selecting a GDI object into the device context, and in the process it returns a pointer to the previously selected object (which gets deselected in the process). Trouble is, you can't deselect the old object without selecting a new object. One easy way to track the objects is to "save" the original GDI object when you select your own GDI object and "restore" the original object when you're finished. Then you'll be ready to delete your own GDI object. Here's an example:

```
void CMyView::OnDraw(CDC* pDC)
{
    CPen newPen(PS_DASHDOTDOT, 2, (COLORREF) 0);  // black pen,
                                                  //  2 pixels wide
    CPen* pOldPen = pDC->SelectObject(&newPen);

    pDC->MoveTo(10, 10);
    pDC->Lineto(110, 10);
    pDC->SelectObject(pOldPen);                   // newPen is deselected
} // newPen automatically destroyed on exit
```

When a device context object is destroyed, all of its GDI objects are deselected. Thus, if you know that a device context will be destroyed before its selected GDI objects are destroyed, you don't have to deselect the objects. If, for example, you declare a pen as a view class data member (and you initialize it when you initialize the view), you don't have to deselect the pen inside *OnDraw* because the device context, which is controlled by the view base class's *OnPaint* handler, will be destroyed first.

Stock GDI Objects

Windows contains a number of stock GDI objects that you can use. These objects are part of Windows, so you don't have to worry about deleting them. (Windows ignores requests to delete stock objects anyway.) The MFC library function *CDC::SelectStockObject* selects a stock object into the device context and returns a pointer to the previously selected object, which it deselects. Stock objects are handy when you want to deselect your own nonstock GDI object before its destruction. You can use a stock object as an alternative to the "old" object you used in the previous example, as shown here:

```
void CMyView::OnDraw(CDC* pDC)
{
    CPen newPen(PS_DASHDOTDOT, 2, (COLORREF) 0);  // black pen,
                                                  //  2 pixels wide
```

```
    pDC->SelectObject(&newPen);
    pDC->MoveTo(10, 10);
    pDC->Lineto(110, 10);
    pDC->SelectStockObject(BLACK_PEN);          // newPen is deselected
} // newPen destroyed on exit
```

The *MFC Library Reference* lists, under *CDC::SelectStockObject*, the stock objects available for pens, brushes, fonts, and palettes.

The Lifetime of a GDI Selection

For the display device context, you get a "fresh" device context at the beginning of each message handler function. No GDI selections (or mapping modes or other device context settings) persist after your function exits. You must therefore set up your device context from scratch each time. The *CView* class virtual member function *OnPrepareDC* is useful for setting the mapping mode, but you must manage your own GDI objects.

For other device contexts, such as those for printers and memory buffers, your assignments can last longer. For these long-life device contexts, things get a little more complicated. The complexity results from the temporary nature of GDI C++ object pointers returned by the *SelectObject* function. (The temporary "object" is destroyed by the application framework during the idle loop processing of the application, sometime after the handler function returns the call. See MFC Technical Note #3 in the online documentation.) You can't simply store the pointer in a class data member; instead, you must convert it to a Windows handle (the only permanent GDI identifier) with the *GetSafeHandle* member function. Here's an example:

```
// m_pPrintFont points to a CFont object created in CMyView's constructor
// m_hOldFont is a CMyView data member of type HFONT, initialized to 0

void CMyView::SwitchToCourier(CDC* pDC)
{
    m_pPrintFont->CreateFont(30, 10, 0, 0, 400, FALSE, FALSE,
                             0, ANSI_CHARSET, OUT_DEFAULT_PRECIS,
                             CLIP_DEFAULT_PRECIS, DEFAULT_QUALITY,
                             DEFAULT_PITCH | FF_MODERN,
                             "Courier New"); // TrueType
    CFont* pOldFont = pDC->SelectObject(m_pPrintFont);

    // m_hOldFont is the CGdiObject public data member that stores
    //  the handle
    m_hOldFont = (HFONT) pOldFont->GetSafeHandle();
}

void CMyView:SwitchToOriginalFont(CDC* pDC)
```

(continued)

```
{
    // FromHandle is a static member function that returns an
    //  object pointer
     if (m_hOldFont) {
        pDC->SelectObject(CFont::FromHandle(m_hOldFont));
    }
}

// m_pPrintFont is deleted in the CMyView destructor
```

> **Caution** Be careful when you delete an object whose pointer is returned by *SelectObject*. If you've allocated the object yourself, you can delete it. If the pointer is temporary, as it will be for the object initially selected into the device context, you won't be able to delete the C++ object.

Fonts

Old-fashioned character-mode applications could display only the boring system font on the screen. Windows provides multiple device-independent fonts in variable sizes. By using these Windows fonts effectively, you can significantly energize an application with minimum programming effort. TrueType fonts, which were first introduced with Windows 3.1, are easier to program than the original device-dependent fonts first introduced with Windows. You'll see several example programs that use various fonts later in this chapter.

Fonts Are GDI Objects

Fonts are an integral part of the Windows GDI. This means that fonts behave in the same way other GDI objects do. They can be scaled and clipped, and they can be selected into a device context just as a pen or a brush can be selected. All GDI rules about deselection and deletion apply to fonts.

Selecting a Font

You can choose between two font types—device-independent TrueType fonts and device-dependent fonts such as the Windows display System font and the LaserJet LinePrinter font—or you can specify a font category and size and let Windows select the font for you. If you let Windows select the font, it will choose a TrueType font if possible. The MFC library provides a font selection dialog box tied to the currently selected printer, so there's little need for printer font guesswork. You let the user select the exact font and size for the printer, and then you approximate the display the best you can.

Printing with Fonts

For text-intensive applications, you'll probably want to specify printer font sizes in points (1 point = 1/72 inch). Why? Most, if not all, built-in printer fonts are defined in terms of points. The LaserJet LinePrinter font, for example, comes in one size, 8.5 point. You can specify TrueType fonts in any point size. If you work in points, you need a mapping mode that easily accommodates points. That's what *MM_TWIPS* is for. An 8.5-point font is 8.5 × 20, or 170, twips, and that's the character height you'll want to specify.

Displaying Fonts

If you're not worried about the display matching the printed output, you have a lot of flexibility. You can select any of the scalable Windows TrueType fonts, or you can select the fixed-size system fonts (stock objects). With the TrueType fonts, it doesn't much matter what mapping mode you use; simply choose a font height and go for it. No need to worry about points.

Matching printer fonts to make printed output match the screen presents some problems, but TrueType makes it easier than it used to be. Even if you're printing with TrueType fonts, however, you'll never quite get the display to match the printer output. Why? Characters are ultimately displayed in pixels (or dots), and the width of a string of characters is equal to the sum of the pixel widths of its characters, possibly adjusted for kerning. The pixel width of the characters depends on the font, the mapping mode, and the resolution of the output device. Only if both the printer and the display are set to *MM_TEXT* mode (1 pixel or dot = 1 logical unit) will you get an exact correspondence. If you're using the *CDC::GetTextExtent* function to calculate line breaks, the screen breakpoint will occasionally be different from the printer breakpoint.

> **Note** In the MFC Print Preview mode, which we'll examine closely in Chapter 15, line breaks occur exactly as they do on the printer, but the print quality in the preview window suffers in the process.

If you're matching a printer-specific font on the screen, TrueType again makes the job easier. Windows substitutes the closest matching TrueType font. For the 8.5-point LinePrinter font, Windows comes pretty close with its Courier New font.

Logical Inches and Physical Inches on the Display

The *CDC* member function *GetDeviceCaps* returns various display measurements that are important to your graphics programming. The six indexes described in Table 6-1 provide information about the display size. The values listed are for a typical display card configured for a resolution of 640-by-480 pixels with Windows 2000 and Windows XP.

Table 6-1 Logical Inches vs. Physical Inches

Index	Description	Value
HORZSIZE	Physical width in millimeters	320
VERTSIZE	Physical height in millimeters	240
HORZRES	Width in pixels	640
VERTRES	Height in raster lines	480
LOGPIXELSX	Horizontal pixels per logical inch	96
LOGPIXELSY	Vertical pixels per logical inch	96

The indexes *HORZSIZE* and *VERTSIZE* represent the physical dimensions of your display. (These indexes might not be true because Windows doesn't know what size display you have connected to your video adapter.) You can also calculate a display size by dividing *HORZRES* and *VERTRES* by *LOGPIXELSX* and *LOGPIXELSY*, respectively. The size calculated this way is known as the *logical size* of the display. Using the values above and the fact that there are 25.4 millimeters per inch, we can quickly calculate the two display sizes for a 640-by-480 pixel display under Windows 2000 and Windows XP. The physical display size is 12.60 by 9.45 inches, and the logical size is 6.67 by 5.00 inches. So the physical size and the logical size need not be the same.

For Windows 2000 and Windows XP, it turns out that *HORZSIZE* and *VERTSIZE* are independent of the display resolution, and *LOGPIXELSX* and *LOGPIXELSY* are always 96. So the logical size changes for different display resolutions, but the physical size does not.

Whenever you use a fixed mapping mode such as *MM_HIMETRIC* or *MM_TWIPS*, the display driver uses the physical display size to do the mapping. So, for Windows 2000 and Windows XP, text is smaller on a small monitor, but that's not what you want. Instead, you want your font sizes to correspond to the logical display size, not the physical size.

You can invent a special mapping mode, called *logical twips*, for which one logical unit is equal to 1/1440 logical inch. This mapping mode is independent of the operating system and display resolution and is used by programs such as Microsoft Word. Here's the code that sets the mapping mode to logical twips:

```
pDC->SetMapMode(MM_ANISOTROPIC);
pDC->SetWindowExt(1440, 1440);
pDC->SetViewportExt(pDC->GetDeviceCaps(LOGPIXELSX),
                    -pDC->GetDeviceCaps(LOGPIXELSY));
```

> **Note** From the Windows Control Panel, you can adjust both the display font size and the display resolution. If you change the display font size from the default 100 percent to 200 percent, *HORZSIZE* becomes 160, *VERTSIZE* becomes 120, and the dots-per-inch value becomes 192. In that case, the logical size is divided by 2, and all text drawn with the logical twips mapping mode is doubled in size.

Computing Character Height

Five font height measurement parameters are available through the *CDC* function *GetTextMetrics*, but only three are significant. Figure 6-1 shows the important font measurements. The *tmHeight* parameter represents the full height of the font, including descenders (for the characters g, j, p, q, and y) and any diacritics that appear over capital letters. The *tmExternalLeading* parameter is the distance between the top of the diacritic and the bottom of the descender from the line above. The sum of *tmHeight* and *tmExternalLeading* is the total character height. The value of *tmExternalLeading* can be 0.

You would think that *tmHeight* would represent the font size in points. Wrong! Another *GetTextMetrics* parameter, *tmInternalLeading*, comes into play. The point size corresponds to the difference between *tmHeight* and *tmInternalLeading*. With the *MM_TWIPS* mapping mode in effect, a selected 12-point font might have a *tmHeight* value of 295 logical units and a *tmInternalLeading* value of 55. The font's net height of 240 corresponds to the point size of 12.

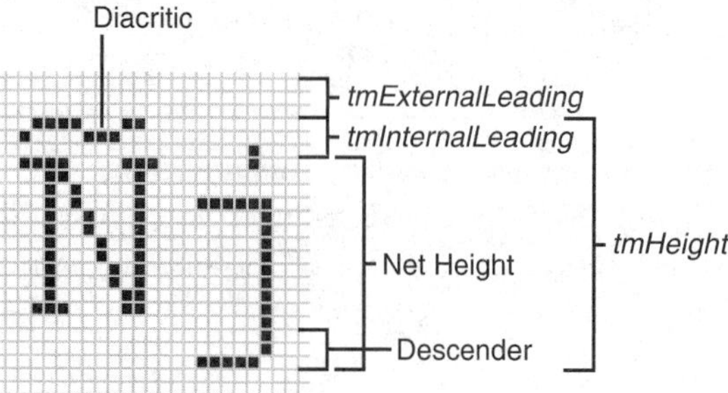

Figure 6-1 Font height measurements.

The Ex06a Example

This example sets up a view window with the logical twips mapping mode. A text string is displayed in 10-point sizes with the Arial TrueType font. Here are the steps for building the application:

1. **Use the MFC Application Wizard to generate the Ex06a project.** Start by choosing New from the File menu, and then select MFC Application. Select Single Document on the Application Type page, and deselect Printing And Print Preview on the Advanced Features page. Accept all the other default settings.

2. **Select the *CEx06aView* class in Class View, and then use the Properties window to override the *OnPrepareDC* function in the *CEx06aView* class.** Edit the code in Ex06aView.cpp as follows:

```
void CEx06aView::OnPrepareDC(CDC* pDC, CPrintInfo* pInfo)
{
    pDC->SetMapMode(MM_ANISOTROPIC);
    pDC->SetWindowExt(1440, 1440);
    pDC->SetViewportExt(pDC->GetDeviceCaps(LOGPIXELSX),
                        pDC->GetDeviceCaps(LOGPIXELSY));
}
```

3. **Add a private *ShowFont* helper function to the view class.** Add the following prototype in Ex06aView.h:

```
private:
    void ShowFont(CDC* pDC, int& nPos, int nPoints);
```

   Then add the function itself in Ex06aView.cpp:

```
void CEx06aView::ShowFont(CDC* pDC, int& nPos, int nPoints)
{
    TEXTMETRIC tm;
    CFont      fontText;
    CString    strText;
    CSize      sizeText;

    fontText.CreateFont(-nPoints * 20, 0, 0, 0, 400,
                        FALSE, FALSE, 0,
                        ANSI_CHARSET, OUT_DEFAULT_PRECIS,
                        CLIP_DEFAULT_PRECIS, DEFAULT_QUALITY,
                        DEFAULT_PITCH | FF_SWISS, "Arial");
    CFont* pOldFont = (CFont*) pDC->SelectObject(&fontText);
    pDC->GetTextMetrics(&tm);
    TRACE("points = %d, tmHeight = %d, tmInternalLeading = %d,"
          " tmExternalLeading = %d\n", nPoints, tm.tmHeight,
          tm.tmInternalLeading, tm.tmExternalLeading);
    strText.Format("This is %d-point Arial", nPoints);
    sizeText = pDC->GetTextExtent(strText);
    TRACE("string width = %d, string height = %d\n", sizeText.cx,
          sizeText.cy);
    pDC->TextOut(0, nPos, strText);
    pDC->SelectObject(pOldFont);
    nPos += tm.tmHeight + tm.tmExternalLeading;
}
```

4. **Edit the *OnDraw* function in Ex06aView.cpp.** The MFC Application Wizard always generates a skeleton *OnDraw* function for your view class. Find the function, and replace the code with the following:

```
void CEx06aView::OnDraw(CDC* pDC)
{
    int nPosition = 0;

    for (int i = 6; i <= 24; i += 2) {
        ShowFont(pDC, nPosition, i);
    }
    TRACE("LOGPIXELSX = %d, LOGPIXELSY = %d\n",
          pDC->GetDeviceCaps(LOGPIXELSX),
          pDC->GetDeviceCaps(LOGPIXELSY));
    TRACE("HORZSIZE = %d, VERTSIZE = %d\n",
          pDC->GetDeviceCaps(HORZSIZE),
          pDC->GetDeviceCaps(VERTSIZE));
    TRACE("HORZRES = %d, VERTRES = %d\n",
          pDC->GetDeviceCaps(HORZRES),
          pDC->GetDeviceCaps(VERTRES));
}
```

5. **Build and run the Ex06a program.** You must run the program from the debugger if you want to see the output from the *TRACE* statements. You can choose Start from the Debug menu in Visual C++ .NET, press the F5 key, or click the Continue button on the Debug toolbar (which will force the project to be built).

The resulting output (assuming the use of a standard VGA card) will look like the following:

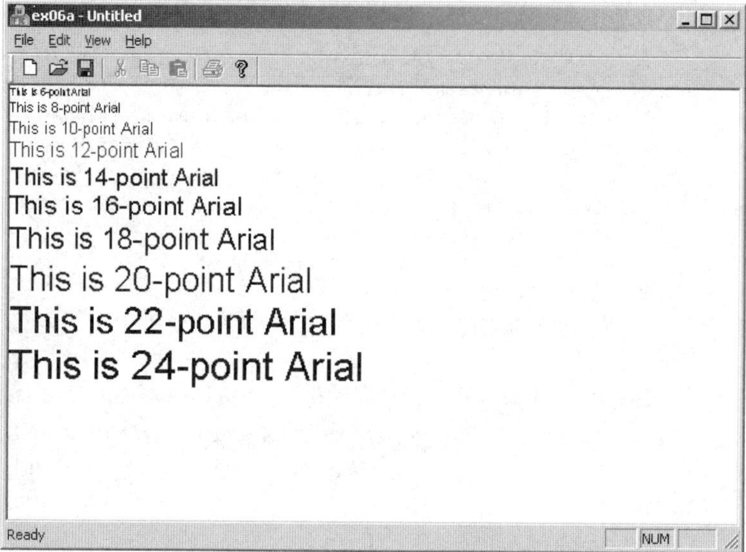

Notice that the output string sizes don't quite correspond to the point sizes. This discrepancy results from the font engine's conversion of logical units to pixels. The program's trace output, partially shown here, shows the printout of font metrics. (The numbers depend on your display driver and your video driver.)

```
points = 6, tmHeight = 150, tmInternalLeading = 30, tmExternalLeading = 4
string width = 990, string height = 150
points = 8, tmHeight = 210, tmInternalLeading = 45, tmExternalLeading = 5
string width = 1380, string height = 210
points = 10, tmHeight = 240, tmInternalLeading = 45, tmExternalLeading = 6
string width = 1770, string height = 240
points = 12, tmHeight = 270, tmInternalLeading = 30, tmExternalLeading = 8
string width = 2130, string height = 270
```

The Ex06a Program Elements

Following is a discussion of the important elements in the Ex06a example.

Setting the Mapping Mode in the *OnPrepareDC* Function

The application framework calls *OnPrepareDC* before calling *OnDraw*, so the *OnPrepareDC* function is the logical place to prepare the device context. If you had other message handlers that needed the correct mapping mode, those functions would have contained calls to *OnPrepareDC*.

The *ShowFont* Private Member Function

ShowFont contains code that is executed 10 times in a loop. With C, you would have made this a global function, but with C++ it's better to make it a private class member function, sometimes known as a *helper function*.

This function creates the font, selects it into the device context, prints a string to the window, and then deselects the font. If you choose to include debug information in the program, *ShowFont* also displays useful font metrics information, including the actual width of the string.

Calling *CFont::CreateFont*

This call includes lots of parameters, but the important ones are the first two—the font height and the width. A width value of 0 means that the aspect ratio of the selected font will be set to a value specified by the font designer. If you put a nonzero value here, as you'll see in the next example, you can change the font's aspect ratio.

> **Tip** If you want your font to be a specific point size, the *CreateFont* font height parameter (the first parameter) must be *negative*. If you're using the *MM_TWIPS* mapping mode for a printer, for example, a height parameter of –240 ensures a true 12-point font, with *tmHeight* – *tmInternalLeading* = 240. A +240 height parameter gives you a smaller font, with *tmHeight* = 240.

The last *CreateFont* parameter specifies the font name, in this case the Arial TrueType font. If you had used *NULL* for this parameter, the *FF_SWISS* specification (which indicates a proportional font without serifs) would have caused Windows to select the best matching font, which, depending on the specified size, might have been the System font or the Arial TrueType font. The font name takes precedence. If you had specified *FF_ROMAN* (which indicates a proportional font with serifs) with Arial, for example, you would have gotten Arial.

The Ex06b Example

This program is similar to Ex06a except that it shows multiple fonts. The mapping mode is *MM_ANISOTROPIC*, with the scale dependent on the window size. The characters change size along with the window. This program effectively shows off some TrueType fonts and contrasts them with the old-style fonts. Here are the steps for building the application:

1. **Run the MFC Application Wizard to generate the Ex06b project.** Make it an SDI application and deselect Printing And Print Preview on the Advanced Features page.

2. **Select the *CEx06bView* class in Class View, and then use the Properties window to override the *OnPrepareDC* function in the *CEx06bView* class.** Edit the code in Ex06bView.cpp as shown here:

```
void CEx06bView::OnPrepareDC(CDC* pDC, CPrintInfo* pInfo)
{
    CRect clientRect;

    GetClientRect(clientRect);
    pDC->SetMapMode(MM_ANISOTROPIC); // +y = down
    pDC->SetWindowExt(400, 450);
    pDC->SetViewportExt(clientRect.right, clientRect.bottom);
    pDC->SetViewportOrg(0, 0);
}
```

3. **Add a private *TraceMetrics* helper function to the view class.** Add the following prototype in Ex06bView.h:

```
private:
    void TraceMetrics(CDC* pDC);
```

Then add the function itself in Ex06bView.cpp:

```
void CEx06bView::TraceMetrics(CDC* pDC)
{
    TEXTMETRIC tm;
    char       szFaceName[100];

    pDC->GetTextMetrics(&tm);
    pDC->GetTextFace(99, szFaceName);
    TRACE("font = %s, tmHeight = %d, tmInternalLeading = %d,"
          " tmExternalLeading = %d\n", szFaceName, tm.tmHeight,
          tm.tmInternalLeading, tm.tmExternalLeading);
}
```

4. **Edit the *OnDraw* function in Ex06bView.cpp.** The MFC Application Wizard always generates a skeleton *OnDraw* function for your view class. Find the function, and edit the code as follows:

```
void CEx06bView::OnDraw(CDC* pDC)
{
    CFont fontTest1, fontTest2, fontTest3, fontTest4;

    fontTest1.CreateFont(50, 0, 0, 0, 400, FALSE, FALSE, 0,
                         ANSI_CHARSET, OUT_DEFAULT_PRECIS,
                         CLIP_DEFAULT_PRECIS, DEFAULT_QUALITY,
                         DEFAULT_PITCH | FF_SWISS, "Arial");
    CFont* pOldFont = pDC->SelectObject(&fontTest1);
    TraceMetrics(pDC);
    pDC->TextOut(0, 0, "This is Arial, default width");

    fontTest2.CreateFont(50, 0, 0, 0, 400, FALSE, FALSE, 0,
                         ANSI_CHARSET, OUT_DEFAULT_PRECIS,
                         CLIP_DEFAULT_PRECIS, DEFAULT_QUALITY,
                         DEFAULT_PITCH | FF_MODERN, "Courier");
                         // not TrueType
    pDC->SelectObject(&fontTest2);
    TraceMetrics(pDC);
    pDC->TextOut(0, 100, "This is Courier, default width");

    fontTest3.CreateFont(50, 10, 0, 0, 400, FALSE, FALSE, 0,
                         ANSI_CHARSET, OUT_DEFAULT_PRECIS,
                         CLIP_DEFAULT_PRECIS, DEFAULT_QUALITY,
                         DEFAULT_PITCH | FF_ROMAN, NULL);
    pDC->SelectObject(&fontTest3);
    TraceMetrics(pDC);
    pDC->TextOut(0, 200, "This is generic Roman, variable width");

    fontTest4.CreateFont(50, 0, 0, 0, 400, FALSE, FALSE, 0,
                         ANSI_CHARSET, OUT_DEFAULT_PRECIS,
                         CLIP_DEFAULT_PRECIS, DEFAULT_QUALITY,
                         DEFAULT_PITCH | FF_MODERN, "LinePrinter");
    pDC->SelectObject(&fontTest4);
    TraceMetrics(pDC);
    pDC->TextOut(0, 300, "This is LinePrinter, default width");
    pDC->SelectObject(pOldFont);
}
```

5. **Build and run the Ex06b program.** Run the program from the debugger to see the TRACE output. The program's window is shown here:

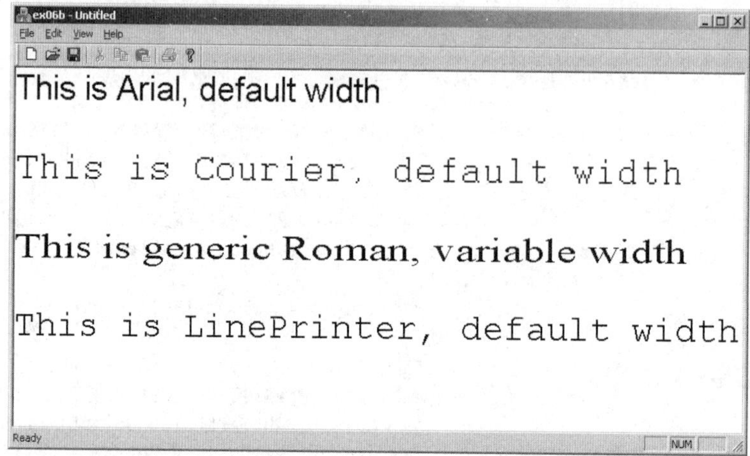

Resize the window to make it smaller, and watch the font sizes change. Compare the following window with the previous one:

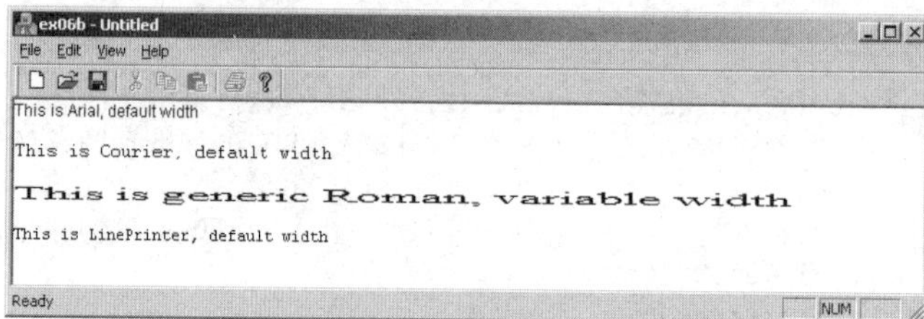

If you continue to downsize the window, notice how the Courier font stops shrinking after a certain size and how the Roman font width changes.

The Ex06b Program Elements

Following is a discussion of the important elements in the Ex06b example.

The *OnDraw* Member Function

The *OnDraw* function displays character strings in four fonts, as follows:

- **fontTest1** The TrueType font Arial with default width selection.
- **fontTest2** The old-style font Courier with default width selection. Notice how jagged the font appears in larger sizes.

- **fontTest3** The generic Roman font for which Windows supplies the TrueType font Times New Roman with programmed width selection. The width is tied to the horizontal window scale, so the font stretches to fit the window.
- **fontTest4** The LinePrinter font is specified, but because this is not a Windows font for the display, the font engine falls back on the *FF_MODERN* specification and selects the TrueType Courier New font.

The *TraceMetrics* Helper Function

The *TraceMetrics* helper function calls *CDC::GetTextMetrics* and *CDC::GetTextFace* to get the current font's parameters, which it prints in the Debug window.

The Ex06c Example: *CScrollView* Revisited

You saw the *CScrollView* class in Chapter 5 (in Ex05c). The Ex06c program allows the user to move an ellipse with a mouse by "capturing" the mouse, using a scrolling window with the *MM_LOENGLISH* mapping mode. Keyboard scrolling is left out, but you can add it by borrowing the *OnKeyDown* member function from Ex05c.

Instead of a stock brush, we'll use a pattern brush for the ellipse—a real GDI object. There's one complication with pattern brushes, however: You must reset the origin as the window scrolls; otherwise, strips of the pattern won't line up and the effect will be ugly.

As with the Ex05c program, this example involves a view class derived from *CScrollView*. Here are the steps to create the application:

1. **Run the MFC Application Wizard to generate the Ex06c project.** Make it an SDI application and deselect Printing And Print Preview on the Advanced Features page. Be sure to set the view base class to *CScrollView*.
2. **Edit the *CEx06cView* class header in the file Ex06cView.h.** Add the following lines in the class *CEx06cView* declaration:

```
private:
    const CSize m_sizeEllipse; // logical
    CPoint m_pointTopLeft; // logical, top left of ellipse rectangle
    CSize  m_sizeOffset; // device, from rect top left
                         //  to capture point
    BOOL   m_bCaptured;
```

3. **Select the *CEx06cView* class in Class View, and then use the Properties window to add three message handlers to the *CEx06cView* class.** Add the message handlers as follows:

Message	Member Function
WM_LBUTTONDOWN	OnLButtonDown
WM_LBUTTONUP	*OnLButtonUp*
WM_MOUSEMOVE	*OnMouseMove*

4. **Edit the *CEx06cView* message handler functions.** The code wizards available from the Properties window generated the skeletons for the functions listed in the preceding step. Find the functions in Ex06cView.cpp and code them as follows:

```
void CEx06cView::OnLButtonDown(UINT nFlags, CPoint point)
{
    // still logical
    CRect rectEllipse(m_pointTopLeft, m_sizeEllipse);
    CRgn  circle;

    CClientDC dc(this);
    OnPrepareDC(&dc);
    dc.LPtoDP(rectEllipse); // Now it's in device coordinates
    circle.CreateEllipticRgnIndirect(rectEllipse);
    if (circle.PtInRegion(point)) {
        // Capturing the mouse ensures subsequent LButtonUp message
        SetCapture();
        m_bCaptured = TRUE;
        CPoint pointTopLeft(m_pointTopLeft);
        dc.LPtoDP(&pointTopLeft);
        m_sizeOffset = point - pointTopLeft; // device coordinates
        // New mouse cursor is active while mouse is captured
        ::SetCursor(::LoadCursor(NULL, IDC_CROSS));
    }
}

void CEx06cView::OnLButtonUp(UINT nFlags, CPoint point)
{
    if (m_bCaptured) {
        ::ReleaseCapture();
        m_bCaptured = FALSE;
    }
}

void CEx06cView::OnMouseMove(UINT nFlags, CPoint point)
{
```

```
    if (m_bCaptured) {
         CClientDC dc(this);
        OnPrepareDC(&dc);
        CRect rectOld(m_pointTopLeft, m_sizeEllipse);
        dc.LPtoDP(rectOld);
        InvalidateRect(rectOld, TRUE);
        m_pointTopLeft = point - m_sizeOffset;
        dc.DPtoLP(&m_pointTopLeft);
        CRect rectNew(m_pointTopLeft, m_sizeEllipse);
        dc.LPtoDP(rectNew);
        InvalidateRect(rectNew, TRUE);
    }
}
```

5. **Edit the *CEx06cView* constructor, the *OnDraw* function, and the *OnInitialUpdate* function.** The MFC Application Wizard generated these skeleton functions. Find them in Ex06cView.cpp, and code them as follows:

```
CEx06cView::CEx06cView() : m_sizeEllipse(100, -100),
                           m_pointTopLeft(0, 0),
                           m_sizeOffset(0, 0)
{
    m_bCaptured = FALSE;
}

void CEx06cView::OnDraw(CDC* pDC)
{
    CBrush brushHatch(HS_DIAGCROSS, RGB(255, 0, 0));
    CPoint point(0, 0);                  // logical (0, 0)

    pDC->LPtoDP(&point);                 // In device coordinates,
    pDC->SetBrushOrg(point);             //  align the brush with
                                         //  the window origin
    pDC->SelectObject(&brushHatch);
    pDC->Ellipse(CRect(m_pointTopLeft, m_sizeEllipse));
    pDC->SelectStockObject(BLACK_BRUSH); // Deselect brushHatch
                                         // Test invalid rect
    pDC->Rectangle(CRect(100, -100, 200, -200));
}

void CEx06cView::OnInitialUpdate()
{
    CScrollView::OnInitialUpdate();

    CSize sizeTotal(800, 1050); // 8-by-10.5 inches
    CSize sizePage(sizeTotal.cx / 2, sizeTotal.cy / 2);
    CSize sizeLine(sizeTotal.cx / 50, sizeTotal.cy / 50);
    SetScrollSizes(MM_LOENGLISH, sizeTotal, sizePage, sizeLine);
}
```

6. **Build and run the Ex06c program.** The program allows an ellipse to be dragged with the mouse, and it allows the window to be scrolled through. The program's window should look like the one shown here. As you move the ellipse, observe the black rectangle. You should be able to see the effects of invalidating the rectangle.

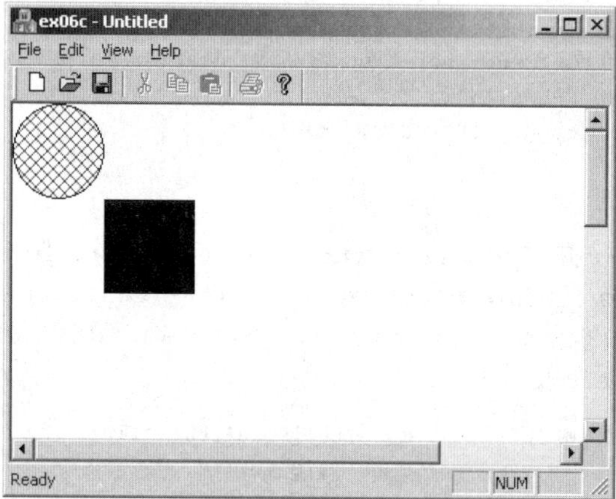

The Ex06c Program Elements

Following is a discussion of the important elements in the Ex06c example.

The *m_sizeEllipse* and *m_pointTopLeft* Data Members

Rather than store the ellipse's bounding rectangle as a single *CRect* object, the program separately stores its size (*m_sizeEllipse*) and the position of its top left corner (*m_pointTopLeft*). To move the ellipse, the program merely recalculates *m_pointTopLeft*, and any round-off errors in the calculation won't affect the size of the ellipse.

The *m_sizeOffset* Data Member

When *OnMouseMove* moves the ellipse, the relative position of the mouse within the ellipse must be the same as it was when the user first pressed the left mouse button. The *m_sizeOffset* object stores this original offset of the mouse from the top left corner of the ellipse rectangle.

The *m_bCaptured* Data Member

The *m_bCaptured* Boolean variable is set to *TRUE* when mouse tracking is in progress.

The *SetCapture* and *ReleaseCapture* Functions

SetCapture is the *CWnd* member function that "captures" the mouse, such that mouse movement messages are sent to this window even if the mouse cursor is outside the window. An unfortunate side effect of this function is that the ellipse can be moved outside the window and "lost." A desirable and necessary effect is that *all* subsequent mouse messages are sent to the window, including the *WM_LBUTTONUP* message, which would otherwise be lost. The Win32 *ReleaseCapture* function turns off mouse capture.

The *SetCursor* and *LoadCursor* Win32 Functions

The MFC library does not "wrap" some Win32 functions. By convention, we use the C++ scope resolution operator (::) when calling Win32 functions directly. In this case, there is no potential for conflict with a *CView* member function, but you can deliberately choose to call a Win32 function in place of a class member function with the same name. In that case, the :: operator ensures that you call the globally scoped Win32 function.

When the first parameter is *NULL*, the *LoadCursor* function creates a *cursor resource* from the specified predefined mouse cursor that Windows uses. The *SetCursor* function activates the specified cursor resource. This cursor remains active as long as the mouse is captured.

The *CScrollView::OnPrepareDC* Member Function

The *CView* class has a virtual *OnPrepareDC* function that does nothing. The *CScrollView* class implements the function for the purpose of setting the view's mapping mode and origin, based on the parameters that you passed to *SetScrollSizes* in *OnInitialUpdate*. The application framework calls *OnPrepareDC* for you prior to calling *OnDraw*, so you don't need to worry about it. You must call *OnPrepareDC* yourself in any other message handler function that uses the view's device context, such as *OnLButtonDown* and *OnMouseMove*.

The *OnMouseMove* Coordinate Transformation Code

As you can see, this function contains several translation statements. The logic can be summarized by the following steps:

1. Construct the previous ellipse rectangle and convert it from logical to device coordinates.
2. Invalidate the previous rectangle.
3. Update the top left coordinate of the ellipse rectangle.
4. Construct the new rectangle and convert it to device coordinates.
5. Invalidate the new rectangle.

The function calls *InvalidateRect* twice. Windows "saves up" the two invalid rectangles and computes a new invalid rectangle that is the union of the two, intersected with the client rectangle.

The *OnDraw* Function

The *SetBrushOrg* call is necessary to ensure that all of the ellipse's interior pattern lines up when the user scrolls through the view. The brush is aligned with a reference point, which is at the top left of the logical window, converted to device coordinates. This is a notable exception to the rule that *CDC* member functions require logical coordinates.

The *CScrollView SetScaleToFitSize* Mode

The *CScrollView* class has a stretch-to-fit mode that displays the entire scrollable area in the view window. The Windows *MM_ANISOTROPIC* mapping mode comes into play, with one restriction: positive *y* values always increase in the down direction, as in *MM_TEXT* mode.

To use the stretch-to-fit mode, make the following call in your view's function in place of the call to *SetScrollSizes*:

```
SetScaleToFitSize(sizeTotal);
```

You can make this call in response to a Shrink To Fit menu command. Thus, the display can toggle between scrolling mode and shrink-to-fit mode.

Using the Logical Twips Mapping Mode in a Scrolling View

The MFC *CScrollView* class allows you to specify only standard mapping modes. The Ex17a example in Chapter 17 shows a new class, *CLogScrollView*, that accommodates the logical twips mode.

Bitmaps

Without graphics images, Windows-based applications would be pretty dull. Some applications depend on images for their usefulness, but any application can be spruced up with the addition of decorative clip art from a variety of sources. Windows *bitmaps* are arrays of bits mapped to display pixels. That might sound simple, but you have to learn a lot about bitmaps before you can use them to create professional applications for Windows.

In the following sections, you'll learn how to create device-independent bitmaps (DIBs). By using DIBs, you'll have an easier time with colors and with the printer. In some cases, you'll get better performance. The Win32 function *CreateDIBSection* gives you the benefits of DIBs combined with all the features of GDI bitmaps.

You'll also learn how to use the MFC *CBitmapButton* class to put bitmaps on push buttons. (Using *CBitmapButton* to put bitmaps on pushbuttons has nothing to do with DIBs, but it's a useful technique that would be difficult to master without an example.)

GDI Bitmaps and Device-Independent Bitmaps

In this section, we'll spend more time looking at DIBs. The best place to check is the Platform SDK available through the MSDN help system. Windows has two kinds of bitmaps: GDI bitmaps and DIBs. GDI bitmaps have been around for quite a while, and you can find a great deal of information about them elsewhere.

GDI bitmap objects are represented by the MFC library *CBitmap* class. The GDI bitmap object has an associated Windows data structure, maintained inside the Windows GDI module, that is device-dependent. Your program can get a copy of the bitmap data, but the bit arrangement depends on the display hardware. GDI bitmaps can be freely transferred among programs on a single computer, but because of their device dependency, transferring bitmaps by disk or modem doesn't make sense.

A GDI bitmap is simply another GDI object, such as a pen or a font. You must somehow create a bitmap, and then you must select it into a device context. When you're finished with the object, you must deselect it and delete it. You know the drill.

There's a catch, though, because the "bitmap" of the display or printer device is effectively the display surface or the printed page itself. Therefore, you can't select a bitmap into a display device context or a printer device context. You have to create a special *memory device context* for your bitmaps, using the *CDC::CreateCompatibleDC* function. You must then use the *CDC* member function *StretchBlt* or *BitBlt* to copy the bits from the memory device context to the "real" device context. These "bit-blitting" functions are generally called in your view class's *OnDraw* function. Of course, you mustn't forget to clean up the memory device context when you're finished.

For Win32 Programmers

In Win32, you're allowed to put a GDI bitmap handle on the Clipboard for transfer to another process, but behind the scenes Windows converts the device-dependent bitmap to a DIB and copies the DIB to shared memory. That's a good reason to consider using DIBs from the start.

DIBs offer many programming advantages over GDI bitmaps. Because a DIB carries its own color information, color palette management is easier. DIBs also make it easy to control gray shades when you print. Any computer running Windows can process DIBs, which are usually stored in BMP disk files or as a resource in your program's EXE or DLL file. The wallpaper background on your monitor is read from a BMP file when you start Windows. The primary storage format for Microsoft Paint is the BMP file, and Visual C++ .NET uses BMP files for toolbar buttons and other images. Other graphic interchange formats are available, such as TIFF, GIF, and JPEG, but only the DIB format is directly supported by the Win32 API.

Color Bitmaps and Monochrome Bitmaps

Windows deals with color bitmaps a little differently from the way it deals with brush colors. Many color bitmaps are 16-color. A standard VGA board has four contiguous color planes, with one corresponding bit from each plane combining to represent a pixel. The 4-bit color values are set when the bitmap is created. With a standard VGA board, bitmap colors are limited to the standard 16 colors. Windows does not use dithered colors in bitmaps.

A monochrome bitmap has only one plane. Each pixel is represented by a single bit that is either off (0) or on (1). The *CDC::SetTextColor* function sets the "off" display color, and *SetBkColor* sets the "on" color. You can specify these pure colors individually with the Windows *RGB* macro.

DIBs and the *CDib* Class

MFC includes a class for plain GDI bitmaps (*CBitmap*). However, MFC does *not* include a class for managing DIBs, so this chapter includes a class for managing DIBs. It's a complete rewrite of the *CDib* class from the early editions of this book (before the fourth edition), and it takes advantage of Win32 features such as memory-mapped files, improved memory management, and DIB sections. It also includes palette support. Before you examine the *CDib* class, however, you need a little background on DIBs.

A Few Words About Palette Programming

Windows palette programming is quite complex, but you've got to deal with it if you expect your users to run their displays in the 8-bpp (bits per pixel) mode—and many users will if they have video cards with 1 MB or less of memory.

Suppose you're displaying a single DIB in a window. First, you must create a *logical palette*, a GDI object that contains the colors in the DIB. Then you must "realize" this logical palette into the hardware *system palette*, a table of the 256 colors that the video card can display at that instant. If your program is the foreground program, the realization process tries to copy all your colors into the system palette, but it doesn't touch the 20 standard Windows colors. For the most part, your DIB looks just like you want it to look.

But what if another program is the foreground program, and what if that program has a forest scene DIB with 236 shades of green? Your program will still realize its palette, but something different will happen. The system palette won't change, but Windows will set up a new mapping between your logical palette and the system palette. If your DIB contains a neon pink color, for example, Windows will map it to the standard red color. If your program forgets to realize its palette, your neon pink stuff will turn green when the other program becomes active.

The forest scene example is extreme because we assume that the other program grabs 236 colors. If the other program instead realizes a logical palette with only 200 colors, Windows will let your program load 36 of its own colors (including, one hopes, neon pink).

So when is a program supposed to realize its palette? The Windows message *WM_PALETTECHANGED* is sent to your program's main window whenever a program, including yours, realizes its palette. Another message, *WM_QUERYNEWPALETTE*, is sent whenever one of the windows in your program gets the input focus. Your program should realize its palette in response to both these messages (unless your program generated the message). These palette messages are not sent to your view window, however. You must map them in your application's main frame window and then notify the view. Chapter 14 will discuss the relationship between the frame window and the view.

You call the Win32 *RealizePalette* function to perform the realization, but first you must call *SelectPalette* to select your DIB's logical palette into the device context. *SelectPalette* has a flag parameter that you normally set to *FALSE* in your *WM_PALETTECHANGED* and *WM_QUERYNEWPALETTE* handlers. This flag ensures that your palette is realized as a foreground palette if your application is indeed running in the foreground. If you use a *TRUE* flag parameter here, you can force Windows to realize the palette as if the application were in the background.

You must also call *SelectPalette* for each DIB that you display in your *OnDraw* function. This time, you call it with a *TRUE* flag parameter. Things get complicated if you're displaying several DIBs, each with its own palette. Basically, you've got to select a palette for one of the DIBs and realize it (by selecting it with the *FALSE* parameter) in the palette message handlers. The selected DIB will end up looking better than the other DIBs. There are ways of merging palettes, but it might be easier to go out and buy more video memory.

DIBs, Pixels, and Color Tables

A DIB contains a two-dimensional array of elements called *pixels*. In many cases, each DIB pixel will be mapped to a display pixel, but the DIB pixel might be mapped to some logical area on the display, depending on the mapping mode and the display function stretch parameters.

A pixel consists of 1, 4, 8, 16, 24, or 32 contiguous bits, depending on the color resolution of the DIB. For 16-bpp, 24-bpp, and 32-bpp DIBs, each pixel represents an RGB color. A pixel in a 16-bpp DIB typically contains 5 bits each for red, green, and blue values; a pixel in a 24-bpp DIB has 8 bits for each color value. The 16-bpp and 24-bpp DIBs are optimized for video cards that can display 65,536 or 16.7 million simultaneous colors.

A 1-bpp DIB is a monochrome DIB, but these DIBs don't have to be black and white—they can contain any two colors selected from the color table that is built into each DIB. A monochrome bitmap has two 32-bit color table entries, each containing 8 bits for red, green, and blue values plus another 8 bits for flags. Zero (0) pixels use the first entry, and one (1) pixel uses the second. Whether you have a 65,536-color video card or a 16.7-million-color card, Windows can display the two colors directly. (Windows truncates 8-bits-per-color values to 5 bits for 65,536-color displays.) If your video card is running in 256-color palettized mode, your program can adjust the system palette to load the two specified colors.

Eight-bpp DIBs are quite common. Like a monochrome DIB, an 8-bpp DIB has a color table, but the color table has 256 (or fewer) 32-bit entries. Each pixel is an index into this color table. If you have a palettized video card, your program can create a logical palette from the 256 entries. If another program (running in the foreground) has control of the system palette, Windows will do its best to match your logical palette colors to the system palette.

What if you're trying to display a 24-bpp DIB with a 256-color palettized video card? If the DIB author was nice, he will have included a color table containing the most important colors in the DIB. Your program can build a logical palette from that table, and the DIB will look fine. If the DIB has no color table, use the palette returned by the Win32 *CreateHalftonePalette* function; it's better than the 20 standard colors you'd get with no palette at all. Another option is to analyze the DIB to identify the most important colors, but you can buy a utility to do that.

The Structure of a DIB Within a BMP File

You know that the DIB is the standard Windows bitmap format and that a BMP file contains a DIB. So let's look inside a BMP file to see what's there. Figure 6-2 shows a layout for a BMP file.

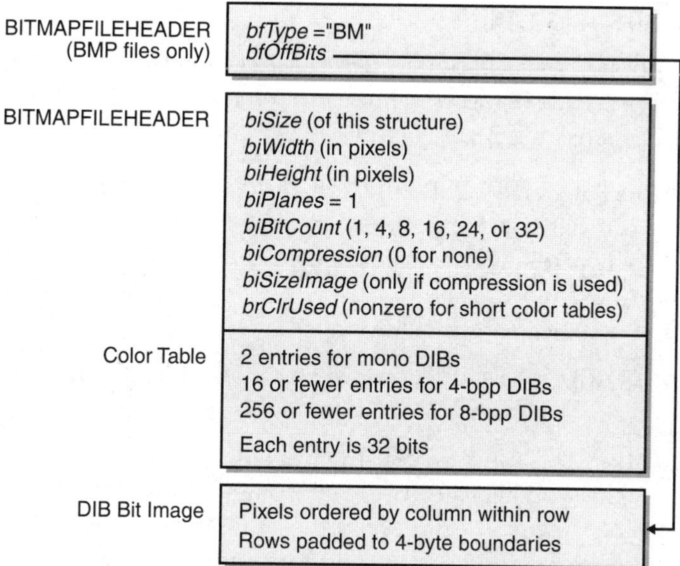

Figure 6-2 The layout for a BMP file.

The *BITMAPFILEHEADER* structure contains the offset to the image bits, which you can use to compute the combined size of the *BITMAPINFOHEADER* structure and the color table that follows. The *BITMAPFILEHEADER* structure contains a file size member, but you can't depend on it because you don't know whether the size is measured in bytes, words, or double words.

The *BITMAPINFOHEADER* structure contains the bitmap dimensions, the bits per pixel, compression information for both 4-bpp and 8-bpp bitmaps, and the number of color table entries. If the DIB is compressed, this header contains the size of the pixel array; otherwise, you can compute the size from the dimensions and the bits per pixel. Immediately following the header is the color table (if the DIB has a color table). The DIB image comes after that. The DIB image consists of pixels arranged by column within rows, starting with the bottom row. Each row is padded to a 4-byte boundary.

The only place you'll find a *BITMAPFILEHEADER* structure, however, is in a BMP file. If you get a DIB from the Clipboard, for example, there will be no file header. You can always count on the color table to follow the *BITMAPINFOHEADER* structure, but you can't count on the image to follow the color table. If you're using the *CreateDIBSection* function, for example, you must allocate the bitmap info header and color table and then let Windows allocate the image somewhere else.

DIB Access Functions

Windows supplies some important DIB access functions. None of these functions is wrapped by MFC, so you'll need to refer to the online Win32 documentation for details. Here's a summary:

- **SetDIBitsToDevice** This function displays a DIB directly on the display or printer. No scaling occurs; one bitmap bit corresponds to one display pixel or one printer dot. This scaling restriction limits the function's usefulness. The function doesn't work like *BitBlt* because *BitBlt* uses logical coordinates.
- **StretchDIBits** This function displays a DIB directly on the display or printer in a manner similar to that of *StretchBlt*.
- **GetDIBits** This function constructs a DIB from a GDI bitmap, using memory that you allocate. You have some control over the format of the DIB because you can specify the number of color bits per pixel and the compression. If you're using compression, you have to call *GetDIBits* twice—once to calculate the memory needed and once to generate the DIB data.
- **CreateDIBitmap** This function creates a GDI bitmap from a DIB. As for all these DIB functions, you must supply a device context pointer as a parameter. A display device context will do; you don't need a memory device context.
- **CreateDIBSection** This Win32 function creates a special kind of DIB known as a *DIB section*. It then returns a GDI bitmap handle. This function gives you the best features of DIBs and GDI bitmaps. You have direct access to the DIB's memory, and with the bitmap handle and a memory device context, you can call GDI functions to draw into the DIB.

The *CDib* Class

If DIBs look intimidating, don't worry. The *CDib* class makes DIB programming easy. The best way to get to know the *CDib* class is to look at the public member functions and data members. The *CDib* header file is shown below. Consult the Ex06d folder on the companion CD to see the implementation code.

CDib.h

```
#ifndef _INSIDE_VISUAL_CPP_CDIB
#define _INSIDE_VISUAL_CPP_CDIB
```

```
class CDib : public CObject
{
    enum Alloc {noAlloc, crtAlloc,
                heapAlloc}; // applies to BITMAPINFOHEADER
    DECLARE_SERIAL(CDib)
public:
    LPVOID  m_lpvColorTable;
    HBITMAP m_hBitmap;
    LPBYTE  m_lpImage;  // starting address of DIB bits
    LPBITMAPINFOHEADER m_lpBMIH; // buffer containing the
                                 //  BITMAPINFOHEADER
private:
    HGLOBAL m_hGlobal; // for external windows we need to free;
                       //  could be allocated by this class or
                       //  allocated externally
    Alloc m_nBmihAlloc;
    Alloc m_nImageAlloc;
    DWORD m_dwSizeImage; // of bits--not BITMAPINFOHEADER
                         // or BITMAPFILEHEADER
    int m_nColorTableEntries;

    HANDLE m_hFile;
    HANDLE m_hMap;
    LPVOID m_lpvFile;
    HPALETTE m_hPalette;
public:
    CDib();
    CDib(CSize size, int nBitCount);  // builds BITMAPINFOHEADER
    ~CDib();
    int GetSizeImage() {return m_dwSizeImage;}
    int GetSizeHeader()
        {return sizeof(BITMAPINFOHEADER) +
                sizeof(RGBQUAD) * m_nColorTableEntries;}
    CSize GetDimensions();
    BOOL AttachMapFile(const char* strPathname,
        BOOL bShare = FALSE);
    BOOL CopyToMapFile(const char* strPathname);
    BOOL AttachMemory(LPVOID lpvMem, BOOL bMustDelete = FALSE,
        HGLOBAL hGlobal = NULL);
    BOOL Draw(CDC* pDC, CPoint origin,
        CSize size); // until we implement CreateDibSection
    HBITMAP CreateSection(CDC* pDC = NULL);
    UINT UsePalette(CDC* pDC, BOOL bBackground = FALSE);
    BOOL MakePalette();
    BOOL SetSystemPalette(CDC* pDC);
    BOOL Compress(CDC* pDC,
        BOOL bCompress = TRUE); // FALSE means decompress
    HBITMAP CreateBitmap(CDC* pDC);
    BOOL Read(CFile* pFile);
```

(continued)

```
    BOOL ReadSection(CFile* pFile, CDC* pDC = NULL);
    BOOL Write(CFile* pFile);
    void Serialize(CArchive& ar);
    void Empty();
private:
    void DetachMapFile();
    void ComputePaletteSize(int nBitCount);
    void ComputeMetrics();
};
#endif // _INSIDE_VISUAL_CPP_CDIB
```

Here's a rundown of the *CDib* member functions, starting with the constructors and the destructor:

- **Default constructor** You'll use the default constructor in preparation for loading a DIB from a file or for attaching to a DIB in memory. The default constructor creates an empty DIB object.

- **DIB section constructor** If you need a DIB section that is created by the *CreateDIBSection* function, use this constructor. Its parameters determine DIB size and the number of colors. The constructor allocates info header memory but not image memory. You can also use this constructor if you need to allocate your own image memory.

Parameter	**Description**
size	*CSize* object that contains the width and height of the DIB
nBitCount	Bits per pixel; should be 1, 4, 8, 16, 24, or 32

- **Destructor** The *CDib* destructor frees all allocated DIB memory.

- ***AttachMapFile*** This function opens a memory-mapped file in read mode and attaches it to the *CDib* object. The return is immediate because the file isn't actually read into memory until it is used. When you access the DIB, however, a delay might occur as the file is paged in. The *AttachMapFile* function releases existing allocated memory and closes any previously attached memory-mapped file.

Parameter	**Description**
strPathname	Pathname of the file to be mapped
bShare	Flag that is *TRUE* if the file is to be opened in share mode; the default value is *FALSE*
Return value	*TRUE* if successful

- ***AttachMemory*** This function associates an existing *CDib* object with a DIB in memory. This memory can be in the program's resources, or it can be Clipboard or OLE data object memory. Memory might have been allocated from the CRT heap using the *new* operator, or it might have been allocated from the Windows heap using *GlobalAlloc*.

Parameter	Description
lpvMem	Address of the memory to be attached
bMustDelete	Flag that is *TRUE* if the *CDib* class is responsible for deleting this memory; the default value is *FALSE*
hGlobal	If memory was obtained with a call to the Win32 *GlobalAlloc* function, the *CDib* object needs to keep the handle in order to free it later, assuming that *bMustDelete* was set to *TRUE*
Return value	*TRUE* if successful

- ***Compress*** This function regenerates the DIB as a compressed or an uncompressed DIB. Internally, it converts the existing DIB to a GDI bitmap and then makes a new compressed or an uncompressed DIB. Compression is supported only for 4-bpp and 8-bpp DIBs. You can't compress a DIB section.

Parameter	Description
pDC	Pointer to the display device context
bCompress	*TRUE* (default) to compress the DIB; *FALSE* to uncompress it
Return value	*TRUE* if successful

- ***CopyToMapFile*** This function creates a new memory-mapped file and copies the existing *CDib* data to the file's memory, releasing any previously allocated memory and closing any existing memory-mapped file. The data isn't actually written to disk until the new file is closed, but that happens when the *CDib* object is reused or destroyed.

Parameter	Description
strPathname	Pathname of the file to be mapped
Return value	*TRUE* if successful

- ***CreateBitmap*** This function creates a GDI bitmap from an existing DIB and is called by the *Compress* function. Don't confuse this function with *CreateSection*, which generates a DIB and stores the handle.

Parameter	Description
pDC	Pointer to the display or printer device context
Return value	Handle to a GDI bitmap—*NULL* if unsuccessful. This handle is *not* stored as a public data member.

- ***CreateSection*** This function creates a DIB section by calling the Win32 *CreateDIBSection* function. The image memory will be uninitialized.

Parameter	Description
pDC	Pointer to the display or printer device context
Return value	Handle to a GDI bitmap—*NULL* if unsuccessful. This handle is stored as a public data member.

- ***Draw*** This function outputs the *CDib* object to the display (or to the printer) with a call to the Win32 *StretchDIBits* function. The bitmap will be stretched as necessary to fit the specified rectangle.

Parameter	Description
pDC	Pointer to the display or printer device context that will receive the DIB image
origin	*CPoint* object that holds the logical coordinates at which the DIB will be displayed
size	*CSize* object that represents the display rectangle's width and height in logical units
Return value	*TRUE* if successful

- ***Empty*** This function empties the DIB, freeing allocated memory and closing the map file if necessary.
- ***GetDimensions*** This function returns the width and height of a DIB in pixels.

Parameter	Description
Return value	*CSize* object

- ***GetSizeHeader*** This function returns the number of bytes in the info header and color table combined.

Parameter	**Description**
Return value	32-bit integer

- ***GetSizeImage*** This function returns the number of bytes in the DIB image (excluding the info header and the color table).

Parameter	**Description**
Return value	32-bit integer

- ***MakePalette*** If the color table exists, this function reads it and creates a Windows palette. The *HPALETTE* handle is stored in a data member.

Parameter	**Description**
Return value	*TRUE* if successful

- ***Read*** This function reads a DIB from a file into the *CDib* object. The file must have been successfully opened. If the file is a BMP file, reading starts from the beginning of the file. If the file is a document, reading starts from the current file pointer.

Parameter	**Description**
pFile	Pointer to a *CFile* object; the corresponding disk file contains the DIB
Return value	*TRUE* if successful

- ***ReadSection*** This function reads the info header from a BMP file, calls *CreateDIBSection* to allocate image memory, and then reads the image bits from the file into that memory. Use this function if you want to read a DIB from disk and then edit it by calling GDI functions. You can write the DIB back to disk using *Write* or *CopyToMapFile*.

Parameter	**Description**
pFile	Pointer to a *CFile* object; the corresponding disk file contains the DIB
pDC	Pointer to the display or printer device context
Return value	*TRUE* if successful

- ***Serialize*** Serialization is covered in Chapter 16. The *CDib::Serialize* function, which overrides the MFC *CObject::Serialize* function, calls the *Read* and *Write* member functions. See the MSDN Library for a description of the parameters.

- ***SetSystemPalette*** If you have a 16-bpp, 24-bpp, or 32-bpp DIB that doesn't have a color table, you can call this function to create for your *CDib* object a logical palette that matches the palette returned by the *CreateHalftonePalette* function. If your program is running on a 256-color palettized display and you don't call *SetSystemPalette*, you'll have no palette at all, and only the 20 standard Windows colors will appear in your DIB.

Parameter	Description
pDC	Pointer to the display context
Return value	*TRUE* if successful

- ***UsePalette*** This function selects the *CDib* object's logical palette into the device context and then realizes the palette. The *Draw* member function calls *UsePalette* before painting the DIB.

Parameter	Description
pDC	Pointer to the display device context for realization
bBackground	If this flag is *FALSE* (the default value) and the application is running in the foreground, Windows will realize the palette as the foreground palette. (It will copy as many colors as possible into the system palette.) If this flag is *TRUE*, Windows will realize the palette as a background palette. (It will map the logical palette to the system palette as best it can.)
Return value	Number of entries in the logical palette mapped to the system palette. If the function fails, the return value is *GDI_ERROR*.

- ***Write*** This function writes a DIB from the *CDib* object to a file. The file must have been successfully opened or created.

Parameter	Description
pFile	Pointer to a *CFile* object; the DIB will be written to the corresponding disk file
Return value	*TRUE* if successful

For your convenience, four public data members give you access to the DIB memory and to the DIB section handle. These members should give you a clue about the structure of a *CDib* object. A *CDib* is just a bunch of pointers to heap memory. That memory might be owned by the DIB or by someone else. Additional private data members determine whether the *CDib* class frees the memory.

DIB Display Performance

Optimized DIB processing is now a major feature of Windows. Modern video cards have frame buffers that conform to the standard DIB image format. If you have one of these cards, your programs can take advantage of the new Windows *DIB engine*, which speeds up the process of drawing directly from DIBs. If you're still running in VGA mode, however, you're out of luck; your programs will still work, but not as quickly.

If you're running Windows in 256-color mode, your 8-bpp bitmaps will be drawn quickly, either with *StretchBlt* or with *StretchDIBits*. If, however, you're displaying 16-bpp or 24-bpp bitmaps, those drawing functions will be too slow. Your bitmaps will appear more quickly in this situation if you create a separate 8-bbp GDI bitmap and then call *StretchBlt*. Of course, you must be careful to realize the correct palette before creating the bitmap and before drawing it.

Here's some code that you might insert just after loading your *CDib* object from a BMP file:

```
// m_hBitmap is a data member of type HBITMAP
// m_dcMem is a memory device context object of class CDC
m_pDib->UsePalette(&dc);
m_hBitmap = m_pDib->CreateBitmap(&dc); // could be slow
::SelectObject(m_dcMem.GetSafeHdc(), m_hBitmap);
```

Here's the code you use in place of *CDib::Draw* in your view's *OnDraw* member function:

```
  m_pDib->UsePalette(pDC); // could be in palette msg handler
CSize sizeDib = m_pDib->GetDimensions();
pDC->StretchBlt(0, 0, sizeDib.cx, sizeDib.cy, &m_dcMem,
                0, 0, sizeToDraw.cx, sizeToDraw.cy, SRCCOPY);
```

Don't forget to call *DeleteObject* for *m_hBitmap* when you're done with it.

The Ex06d Example

Now you'll put the *CDib* class to work in an application. The Ex06d program displays two DIBs, one from a resource and the other loaded from a BMP file that you select at run time. The program manages the system palette and displays the DIBs correctly on the printer.

Here are the steps to build Ex06d. It's a good idea to type in the view class code, but you'll want to use the cdib.h and cdib.cpp sample files.

1. **Run the MFC Application Wizard to generate the Ex06d project.** Accept all the defaults but two: Select Single Document and select the *CScrollView* view base class for *CEx06dView*.

2. **Import the Red Blocks bitmap.** Choose Add Resource from Visual C++ .NET's Project menu. In the Add Resource dialog box, click the Import button. Next, import Red Blocks.bmp from the \vcppnet\bitmaps directory on the companion CD. Visual C++ .NET will copy this bitmap file into your project's \res subdirectory. Assign *IDB_REDBLOCKS* as the ID, and save the changes.

3. **Integrate the *CDib* class with this project.** If you've created this project from scratch, copy the cdib.h and cdib.cpp files from \vcppnet\Ex06d on the companion CD. Simply copying the files to disk isn't enough; you must also add the *CDib* files to the project. Choose Add Existing Item from Visual C++ .NET's Project menu. Select cdib.h and cdib.cpp, and click the Open button. If you now switch to Class View or Solution Explorer, you'll see the class *CDib* and all of its member variables and functions.

4. **Add two private *CDib* data members to the class *CEx06dView*.** In Class View, right-click on the *CEx06dView* class. Choose Add Variable from the shortcut menu, and then add the *m_dibResource* member.

   Add *m_dibFile* in the same way. The result should be two data members at the bottom of the header file:

   ```
   CDib m_dibFile;
   CDib m_dibResource;
   ```

   Class View also adds this statement at the top of the Ex06dView.h file:

   ```
   #include "cdib.h"    // Added by Class View
   ```

5. **Edit the *OnInitialUpdate* member function in Ex06dView.cpp.** This function sets the mapping mode to *MM_HIMETRIC* and loads the *m_dibResource* object directly from the *IDB_REDBLOCKS* resource. The *CDib::AttachMemory* function connects the object to the resource in your EXE file. Add the following code shown in boldface:

   ```
   void CEx06dView::OnInitialUpdate()
   {
       CScrollView::OnInitialUpdate();
   ```

```
    CSize sizeTotal(30000, 40000); // 30-by-40 cm
    CSize sizeLine = CSize(sizeTotal.cx / 100, sizeTotal.cy / 100);
    SetScrollSizes(MM_HIMETRIC, sizeTotal, sizeTotal, sizeLine);

    LPVOID lpvResource = (LPVOID) ::LoadResource(NULL,
        ::FindResource(NULL, MAKEINTRESOURCE(IDB_REDBLOCKS),
        RT_BITMAP));
    m_dibResource.AttachMemory(lpvResource); // no need for
                                             //  ::LockResource
    CClientDC dc(this);
    TRACE("bits per pixel = %d\n", dc.GetDeviceCaps(BITSPIXEL));
}
```

6. **Edit the *OnDraw* member function in the file Ex06dView.cpp.** This code calls *CDib::Draw* for each of the DIBs. The *UsePalette* calls should really be made by message handlers for the *WM_QUERYNEWPALETTE* and *WM_PALETTECHANGED* messages. These messages are hard to deal with because they don't go to the view directly, so we'll take a shortcut. Add the following code shown in boldface:

```
void CEx06cView::OnDraw(CDC* pDC)
{
    BeginWaitCursor();
    m_dibResource.UsePalette(pDC); // should be in palette
    m_dibFile.UsePalette(pDC);     //  message handlers, not here
    pDC->TextOut(0, 0,
        "Press the left mouse button here to load a file.");
    CSize sizeResourceDib = m_dibResource.GetDimensions();
    sizeResourceDib.cx *= 30;
    sizeResourceDib.cy *= -30;
    m_dibResource.Draw(pDC, CPoint(0, -800), sizeResourceDib);
    CSize sizeFileDib = m_dibFile.GetDimensions();
    sizeFileDib.cx *= 30;
    sizeFileDib.cy *= -30;
    m_dibFile.Draw(pDC, CPoint(1800, -800), sizeFileDib);
    EndWaitCursor();
}
```

7. **Map the *WM_LBUTTONDOWN* message in the *CEx06dView* class.** Edit the file Ex06cView.cpp. *OnLButtonDown* contains code to read a DIB in two ways. If you leave the *MEMORY_MAPPED_FILES* definition intact, the *AttachMapFile* code will be activated to read a memory-mapped file. If you comment out the first line, the *Read* call will be activated. The *SetSystemPalette* call is there for DIBs that don't have a color table. Add the following code shown in boldface:

```
#define MEMORY_MAPPED_FILES
```

(continued)

```
void CEx06cView::OnLButtonDown(UINT nFlags, CPoint point)
{
    CFileDialog dlg(TRUE, "bmp", "*.bmp");
    if (dlg.DoModal() != IDOK) {
        return;
    }
#ifdef MEMORY_MAPPED_FILES
    if (m_dibFile.AttachMapFile(dlg.GetPathName(),
            TRUE) == TRUE) { // share
        Invalidate();
    }
 #else
    CFile file;
    file.Open(dlg.GetPathName(), CFile::modeRead);
    if (m_dibFile.Read(&file) == TRUE) {
        Invalidate();
    }
#endif // MEMORY_MAPPED_FILES
    CClientDC dc(this);
    m_dibFile.SetSystemPalette(&dc);
}
```

8. **Build and run the application.** The bitmaps directory on the companion CD contains several interesting bitmaps. The Chicago.bmp file is an 8-bpp DIB with 256-color table entries. The forest.bmp and clouds.bmp files are also 8-bpp, but they have smaller color tables. The balloons.bmp is a 24-bpp DIB with no color table. Try some other BMP files if you have them. Note that Red Blocks is a 16-color DIB that uses standard colors, which are always included in the system palette.

Going Further with DIBs

Each new version of Windows offers more DIB programming choices. Windows 2000 provides the *LoadImage* and *DrawDibDraw* functions, which are useful alternatives to the DIB functions already described. Experiment with these functions to see if they work well in your applications.

The *LoadImage* Function

The *LoadImage* function can read a bitmap directly from a disk file, returning a DIB section handle. Suppose you want to add an *ImageLoad* member function to *CDib* that works like *ReadSection*. You can add this code to cdib.cpp:

```
BOOL CDib::ImageLoad(const char* lpszPathName, CDC* pDC)
{
    Empty();
```

```
    m_hBitmap = (HBITMAP) ::LoadImage(NULL, lpszPathName,
        IMAGE_BITMAP, 0, 0,
        LR_LOADFROMFILE | LR_CREATEDIBSECTION | LR_DEFAULTSIZE);
    DIBSECTION ds;
    VERIFY(::GetObject(m_hBitmap, sizeof(ds), &ds) == sizeof(ds));
    // Allocate memory for BITMAPINFOHEADER
    //  and biggest possible color table
    m_lpBMIH = (LPBITMAPINFOHEADER) new
        char[sizeof(BITMAPINFOHEADER) + 256 * sizeof(RGBQUAD)];
    memcpy(m_lpBMIH, &ds.dsBmih, sizeof(BITMAPINFOHEADER));
    TRACE("CDib::LoadImage, biClrUsed = %d, biClrImportant = %d\n",
        m_lpBMIH->biClrUsed, m_lpBMIH->biClrImportant);
    ComputeMetrics(); // sets m_lpvColorTable
    m_nBmihAlloc = crtAlloc;
    m_lpImage = (LPBYTE) ds.dsBm.bmBits;
    m_nImageAlloc = noAlloc;
    // Retrieve the DIB section's color table
    //  and make a palette from it
    CDC memdc;
    memdc.CreateCompatibleDC(pDC);
    ::SelectObject(memdc.GetSafeHdc(), m_hBitmap);
    UINT nColors = ::GetDIBColorTable(memdc.GetSafeHdc(), 0, 256,
        (RGBQUAD*) m_lpvColorTable);
    if (nColors != 0) {
        ComputePaletteSize(m_lpBMIH->biBitCount);
        MakePalette();
    }
    // memdc deleted and bitmap deselected
    return TRUE;
}
```

Note that this function extracts and copies the *BITMAPINFOHEADER* structure and sets the values of the *CDib* pointer data members. You must do some work to extract the palette from the DIB section, but the Win32 *GetDIBColorTable* function gets you started. It's interesting that *GetDIBColorTable* can't tell you how many palette entries a particular DIB uses. If the DIB uses only 60 entries, for example, *GetDIBColorTable* generates a 256-entry color table with the last 196 entries set to 0.

The *DrawDibDraw* Function

Windows includes the Video for Windows (VFW) component, which is supported by Visual C++ .NET. The VFW *DrawDibDraw* function is an alternative to *StretchDIBits*. One advantage of *DrawDibDraw* is its ability to use dithered colors. Another is its increased speed in drawing a DIB with a bpp value that does not match the current video mode. The main disadvantage is the need to link the VFW code into your process at run time.

Here is a *DrawDib* member function for the *CDib* class that calls *DrawDib-Draw*:

```
BOOL CDib::DrawDib(CDC* pDC, CPoint origin, CSize size)
{
    if (m_lpBMIH == NULL) return FALSE;
    if (m_hPalette != NULL) {
        ::SelectPalette(pDC->GetSafeHdc(), m_hPalette, TRUE);
    }
    HDRAWDIB hdd = ::DrawDibOpen();
    CRect rect(origin, size);
    pDC->LPtoDP(rect); // Convert DIB's rectangle
                       //  to MM_TEXT coordinates
    rect -= pDC->GetViewportOrg();
    int nMapModeOld = pDC->SetMapMode(MM_TEXT);
    ::DrawDibDraw(hdd, pDC->GetSafeHdc(), rect.left, rect.top,
        rect.Width(), rect.Height(), m_lpBMIH, m_lpImage, 0, 0,
        m_lpBMIH->biWidth, m_lpBMIH->biHeight, 0);
    pDC->SetMapMode(nMapModeOld);
    VERIFY(::DrawDibClose(hdd));
    return TRUE;
}
```

Note that *DrawDibDraw* needs *MM_TEXT* coordinates and the *MM_TEXT* mapping mode. Thus, logical coordinates must be converted not to device coordinates but to pixels with the origin at the top left of the scrolling window.

To use *DrawDibDraw*, your program needs an *?include<vfw.h>* statement, and you must add vfw32.lib to the list of linker input files. *DrawDibDraw* might assume the bitmap it draws is in read/write memory—something to keep in mind if you map the memory to the BMP file.

Putting Bitmaps on Pushbuttons

The MFC library makes it easy to display a bitmap (instead of text) on a pushbutton. If you were to program this from scratch, you would set the Owner Draw property for your button and then write a message handler in your dialog class that would paint a bitmap on the button control's window. If you use the MFC *CBitmapButton* class instead, you end up doing a lot less work, but you have to follow a kind of "cookbook" procedure. Don't worry too much about how it all works (but be glad that you don't have to write much code!).

To make a long story short, you lay out your dialog resource as usual, with unique text captions for the buttons you designate for bitmaps. Next, you add some bitmap resources to your project, and you identify those resources by name rather than by numeric ID. Finally, you add some *CBitmapButton* data members to your dialog class, and you call the *AutoLoad* member function for each one, which matches a bitmap name to a button caption. If the button caption is *Copy*, you add two bitmaps: COPYU for the up state and COPYD for the down state. By the way, you must still set the button's Owner Draw property. (This will all make more sense when you write a program).

> **Note** If you look at the MFC source code for the *CBitmapButton* class, you'll see that the bitmap is an ordinary GDI bitmap painted with a *BitBlt* call. Thus, you can't expect any palette support. That's rarely a problem because bitmaps for buttons are usually 16-color bitmaps that depend on standard VGA colors.

The Ex06e Example

Ex06e shows how to show different bitmaps on a pushbutton. Here are the steps for building Ex06e:

1. **Run the MFC Application Wizard to produce the Ex06e project.** Accept all the defaults but two: Select Single Document and deselect Printing And Print Preview.

2. **Modify the project's *IDD_ABOUTBOX* dialog resource in Resource View.** We'll use the About dialog box that the MFC Application Wizard generates for hosting the bitmap button. Add three pushbuttons with captions, as shown below, accepting the default IDs *IDC_BUTTON1*, *IDC_BUTTON2*, and *IDC_BUTTON3*. The size of the buttons isn't important because the framework adjusts the button size at run time to match the bitmap size.

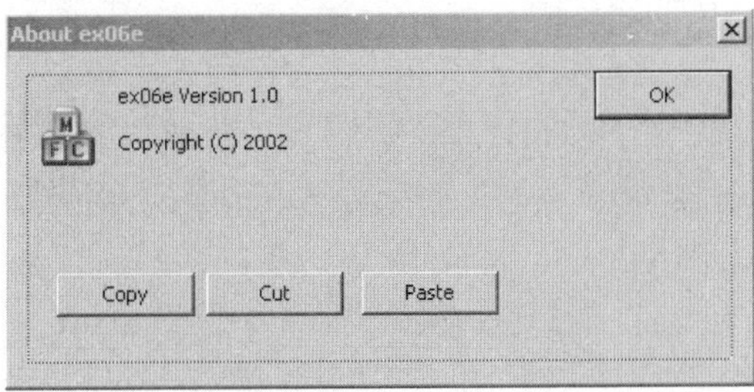

Set the Owner Draw property to *True* for all three buttons.

3. **Import EditCopy.bmp, EditPast.bmp, and EditCut.bmp from the \vcppnet\Ex06e directory on the companion CD.** Choose Add Resource from the Project menu, and then click the Import button to import the bitmaps into the project. Start with EditCopy.bmp. Assign the name *COPYU* to the button.

   Be sure to use quotes around the name in order to identify the resource by name rather than by ID. This is now the bitmap for the button's up state. Close the bitmap window and, from Resource View, use the Clipboard to make a copy of the bitmap. Rename the copy *COPYD* (down state), and then edit this bitmap. Choose Invert Colors from the Image menu. There are other ways of making a variation of the up image, but inversion is the quickest.

   Repeat the steps listed above for the EditCut and EditPast bitmaps. When you're finished, you should have the following bitmap resources in your project.

Resource Name	Original File	Invert Colors
"COPYU"	EditCopy.bmp	No
"COPYD"	EditCopy.bmp	Yes
"CUTU"	EditCut.bmp	No
"CUTD"	EditCut.bmp	Yes
"PASTEU"	EditPast.bmp	No
"PASTED"	EditPast.bmp	Yes

4. **Edit the code for the CAboutDlg class.** Both the declaration and the implementation for this class are contained in the Ex06e.cpp file. First add the three private data members shown here in the class declaration:

```
CBitmapButton m_editCopy;
CBitmapButton m_editCut;
CBitmapButton m_editPaste;
```

   Then use the code wizards available from the Properties window to override the *OnInitDialog* virtual function. This function is coded as follows:

```
BOOL CAboutDlg::OnInitDialog()
{
    CDialog::OnInitDialog();
    VERIFY(m_editCopy.AutoLoad(IDC_BUTTON1, this));
    VERIFY(m_editCut.AutoLoad(IDC_BUTTON2, this));
    VERIFY(m_editPaste.AutoLoad(IDC_BUTTON3, this));
```

```
    return TRUE;
 //return TRUE unless you set the focus to a control
 //EXCEPTION: OCX Property Pages should return FALSE
}
```

The *AutoLoad* function connects each button with the two matching resources. The *VERIFY* macro is an MFC diagnostic aid that displays a message box if you didn't code the bitmap names correctly.

5. **Edit the OnDraw function in Ex06eView.cpp.** Replace the code generated by the MFC Application Wizard with the following line:

```
pDC->TextOut(0, 0, "Choose About from the Help menu.");
```

6. **Build and test the application.** When the program starts, choose About from the Help menu and observe the button behavior. The following image shows the CUT button in the down state.

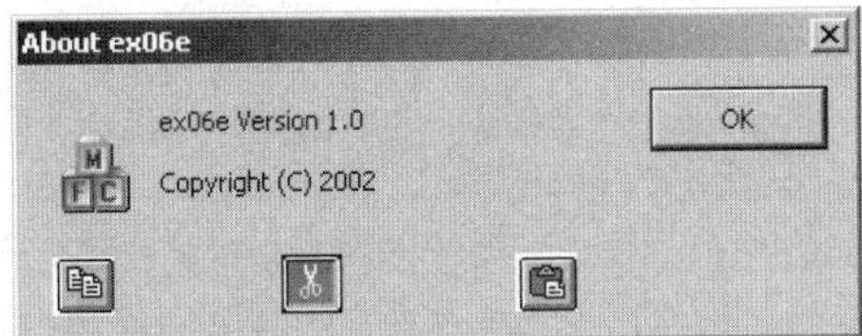

Note that bitmap buttons send *BN_CLICKED* notification messages just as ordinary buttons do. The code wizards available from the Properties window can, of course, map those messages in your dialog class.

Going Further with Bitmap Buttons

You've seen bitmaps for the buttons' up and down states. The *CBitmapButton* class also supports bitmaps for the focused and disabled states. For the Copy button, the focused bitmap name would be *COPYF*, and the disabled bitmap name would be *COPYX*. If you want to test the disabled option, make a COPYX bitmap, possibly with a red line through it, and then add the following line to your program:

```
m_editCopy.EnableWindow(FALSE);
```

7

Dialog Boxes

Almost every Microsoft Windows–based program uses dialog boxes to interact with the user. The dialog box might be a simple OK message box, or it might be a complex data entry form. Calling this powerful user interface element a dialog "box" does it an injustice—a dialog box is actually a window that receives messages, that can be moved and closed, and that can even accept drawing instructions in its client area.

The two kinds of dialog boxes are *modal* and *modeless*. This chapter explores both types. We'll also take a look at the special-purpose Windows common dialog boxes for opening files, selecting fonts, and so forth.

Modal vs. Modeless Dialog Boxes

The *CDialog* base class supports both modal and modeless dialog boxes. With a modal dialog box, such as the Open File dialog box, the user cannot work elsewhere in the same application (more correctly, in the same user interface thread) until the dialog box is closed. With a modeless dialog box, the user can work in another window in the application while the dialog box remains on the screen. Microsoft Word's Find and Replace dialog box is a good example of a modeless dialog box; you can edit your document while the dialog box is open.

Your choice of a modal or a modeless dialog box depends on the application. Modal dialog boxes are much easier to program, which might influence your decision.

Resources and Controls

If a dialog box is simply a window, what makes it different from the *CView* windows you've seen already? For one thing, a dialog box is almost always tied to a Windows resource that identifies the dialog box's elements and specifies their layout. Because you can use the dialog editor (one of the resource editors) to create and edit a dialog resource, you can quickly and efficiently produce dialog boxes in a visual manner.

A dialog box contains a number of elements called *controls*. Dialog controls include edit controls (text boxes), buttons, list boxes, combo boxes, static text (labels), tree views, progress indicators, and sliders. Windows manages these controls using special grouping and tabbing logic, and that relieves you of a major programming burden. The dialog controls can be referenced either by a *CWnd* pointer (because they are really windows) or by an index number (with an associated *#define* constant) assigned in the resource. A control sends a message to its parent dialog box in response to a user action such as typing text or clicking a button.

The Microsoft Foundation Class (MFC) library and Microsoft Visual Studio work together to enhance the dialog logic that Windows provides. Visual Studio can generate a class derived from *CDialog* and lets you associate dialog class data members with dialog controls. You can specify editing parameters such as maximum text length and numeric high and low limits. Visual Studio generates statements that call the MFC data exchange and data validation functions to move information back and forth between the screen and the data members.

Programming a Modal Dialog Box

Modal dialog boxes are the most frequently used dialog boxes. A user action (a menu choice, for example) brings up a dialog box on the screen, the user enters data in the dialog box, and then the user closes the dialog box. Here's a summary of the steps to add a modal dialog box to an existing project:

1. Use the dialog editor to create a dialog resource that contains various controls. The dialog editor updates the project's resource script (RC) file to include your new dialog resource, and it updates the project's resource.h file with corresponding *#define* constants.

2. Use the MFC Class Wizard to create a dialog class derived from *CDialog* and attached to the resource created in step 1. Visual Studio adds the associated code and header file to the Microsoft Visual C++ project.

Note When Visual Studio generates your derived dialog class, it generates a constructor that invokes a *CDialog* modal constructor, which takes a resource ID as a parameter. Your generated dialog header file contains the class enumerator constant *IDD*, which is set to the dialog resource ID. In the CPP file, the constructor implementation looks like this:

```
IMPLEMENT_DYNAMIC(CMyDialog, CDialog)
CMyDialog::CMyDialog(CWnd* pParent /*=NULL*/)
    : CDialog(CMyDialog::IDD, pParent)
{
    // initialization code here
}
```

The use of *enum IDD* decouples the CPP file from the resource IDs that are defined in the project's resource.h file.

3. Use Visual Studio to add data members, exchange functions, and validation functions to the dialog class.
4. Use Class View's Properties window to add message handlers for the dialog box's buttons and other event-generating controls.
5. Write the code for special control initialization (in *OnInitDialog*) and for the message handlers. Be sure the *CDialog* virtual member function *OnOK* is called when the user closes the dialog box (unless the user cancels the dialog box). (Note: *OnOK* is called by default.)
6. Write the code in your view class to activate the dialog box. This code consists of a call to your dialog class's constructor followed by a call to the *DoModal* dialog class member function. *DoModal* returns only when the user exits the dialog box.

Now we'll proceed with a real example, one step at a time.

The Ex07a Example: The Dialog Box That Ate Cincinnati

We'll dive in headfirst here and build a dialog box that contains almost every kind of control. The job will be easy because Visual Studio's dialog editor will help us. The finished product is shown in Figure 7-1.

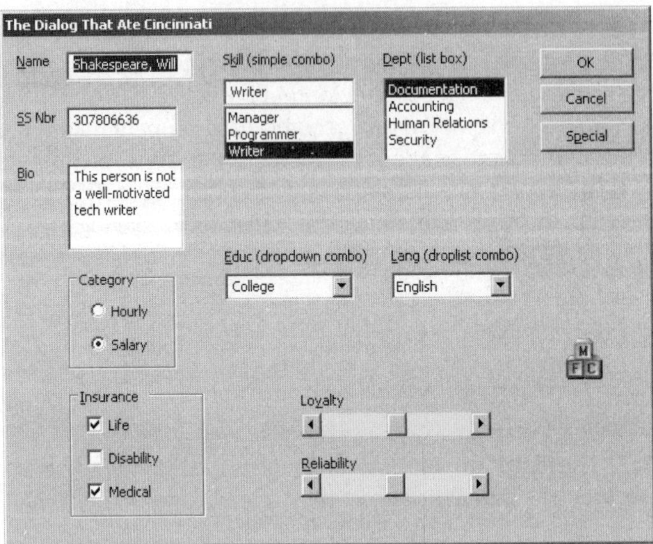

Figure 7-1 The finished dialog box in action.

As you can see, the dialog box supports a human resources application. The program is brightened a little by the use of Loyalty and Reliability scroll bar controls. Here is a classic example of direct action and visual representation of data! These are standard Windows controls we're looking at—we'll cover ActiveX controls in Chapter 9.

Building the Dialog Resource

Here are the steps for building the dialog resource:

1. **Run the MFC Application Wizard to generate a project named Ex07a.** Choose New Project from Visual Studio's File menu. In the New Project dialog box, select the MFC Application, type the name **Ex07a**, and click OK. In the MFC Application Wizard, accept all the defaults but two: On the Application Type page, select Single Document, and on the Advanced Features page, deselect Printing And Print Preview.

2. **Create a new dialog resource with ID *IDD_DIALOG1*.** Choose Add Resource from Visual Studio's Project menu. In the Add Resource dialog box, click Dialog and then click New. Visual Studio will create a new dialog resource and display it in the dialog editor, as shown here:

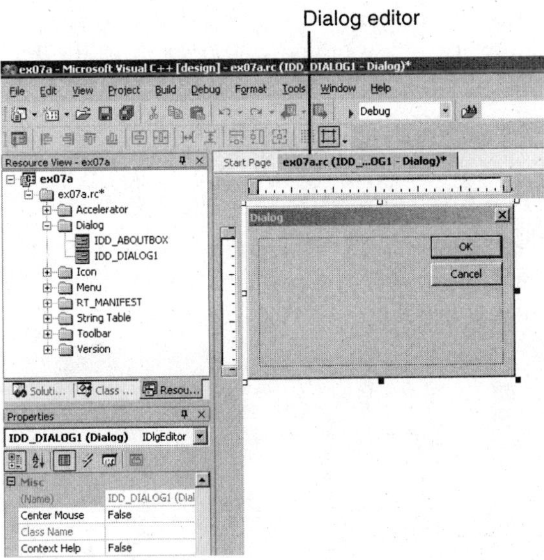

The dialog editor will assign the resource ID *IDD_DIALOG1* to the new dialog box. Notice that the dialog editor inserts OK and Cancel buttons for the new dialog box.

3. **Size the dialog box and set its properties.** Enlarge the dialog box so that it is about 6 inches wide and 5 inches tall.

   Right-click on the new dialog box and choose Properties from the shortcut menu. The Properties window will appear (usually on the right side of the screen, depending upon your profile settings):

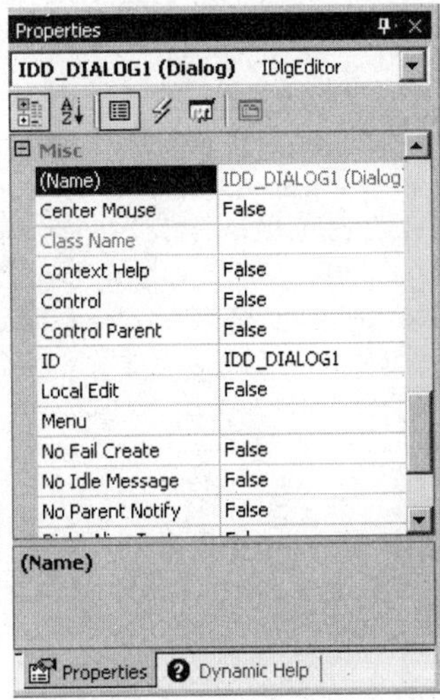

The state of the pushpin button in the title bar of the Properties window determines whether the Properties window stays visible.

(When the pushpin is "pushed in," the dialog box stays visible and does not slide out of view when not in use.) In the Properties window, change the *Caption* property for the new dialog box to *The Dialog Box That Ate Cincinnati.* Change the *System Menu* property to *False* to remove the close button from the dialog box title bar.

4. **Add the dialog box's controls.** Use the Toolbox to add each control. (If the Toolbox is not visible, choose Toolbox from the View menu.) Drag controls from the Toolbox to the new dialog box, and then position and size the controls, as shown in Figure 7-1. Here are the Toolbox controls:

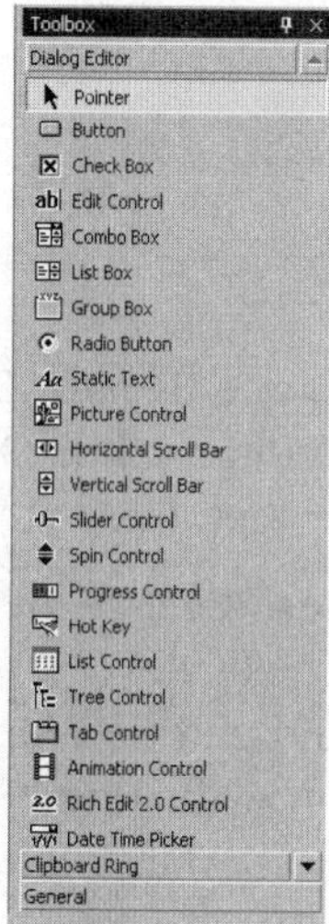

> **Note** The dialog editor displays the position and size of each control in the lower right corner of the status bar. The position units are special "dialog units," or DLUs, *not* device units. A horizontal DLU is the average width of the dialog font divided by 4. A vertical DLU is the average height of the font divided by 8. The dialog font is normally 8-point MS Sans Serif.

Here's a brief description of the dialog box's controls:

- **The static text control for the Name field.** A static text control simply paints characters on the screen. No user interaction occurs at run time. You can type the text after you position the bounding rectangle (which sets the *Caption* property in the Properties window), and you can resize the rectangle as needed.

Add a static text control for the *Name* field and set the *Caption* property to *&Name*. Follow the same procedure for the other static text controls in the dialog box. All static text controls have the same ID, but that's okay because the program doesn't need to access any of them.

> **Note** If you include an ampersand (&) in the *Caption* property for a static text control, at run time an underline will appear below the character that follows when the Alt key is pressed. This enables the user to jump to selected controls by holding down the Alt key and pressing the key corresponding to the underlined character. The related control must immediately follow the static text in the tabbing order. (I'll discuss tabbing order later in the chapter.) Thus, Alt+N jumps to the Name edit control and Alt+K jumps to the Skill combo box. (See Figure 7-1, shown earlier.) Needless to say, designated jump characters should be unique within the dialog box. The Skill control uses Alt+K because the SS Nbr control uses Alt+S.

- **The Name edit control.** An edit control is the primary means of entering text in a dialog box. Add a Name edit control and in the Properties window change this control's ID from *IDC_EDIT1* to *IDC_NAME*. Leave the defaults for the rest of the properties. Notice that the default sets *Auto HScroll* to *True*, which means that the text scrolls horizontally when the box is filled.
- **The SS Nbr (social security number) edit control.** The SS Nbr control is similar to the Name edit control. Simply change its ID to *IDC_SSN*. Later, you'll use the Add Member Variable Wizard to make this a numeric field.

> **Note** To align two or more controls, first select the controls by dragging or by clicking on the first control and then Shift+clicking on the other controls you want to align. Next, choose one of the alignment commands (Lefts, Centers, Rights, Tops, Middles, or Bottoms) from the Format menu's Align submenu.
>
> You can also align controls to a grid. To turn on the grid, click the Toggle Grid button (on the Dialog Editor toolbar) to reveal the grid and to help align controls.

- **The Bio (biography) edit control.** This is a multi-line edit control. To make an edit control multi-line, set the *Multiline* property to *True*. Set *Auto HScroll* to *False* and change its ID to *IDC_BIO*.
- **The Category group box.** This control serves only to group two radio buttons visually. Set the *Caption* property to *&Category*. The default ID is sufficient.
- **The Hourly and Salary radio buttons.** Position these radio buttons inside the Category group box. For the Hourly radio button, set *Caption* to *Hourly*, *Group* to *True*, *ID* to *IDC_CAT*, and *Tabstop* to *True*. For the Salary radio button, set *Caption* to *Salary* and *Tabstop* to *True*.

  Be sure that both buttons have the *Auto* property set to *True* (the default) and that only the Hourly button has the *Group* property set to *True*. Setting the *Group* property to *True* indicates that the Hourly radio button is the first control in the Category group. When these properties are set correctly, Windows will ensure that only one of the two buttons can be selected at a time. The Category group box has no effect on the buttons' operation.
- **The Insurance group box.** This control holds three check boxes. Set the *Caption* property to *&Insurance* and set the *Group* property to *True*.

> **Note** Later, when you set the dialog box's tab order, you can ensure that the Insurance group box follows the last radio button of the Category group. Setting the *Group* property to *True* will "terminate" the previous group. If you fail to do this, it isn't a serious problem, but you'll get several warning messages when you run the program through the debugger.

- **The Life, Disability, and Medical check boxes.** Place these controls inside the Insurance group box. Set the *Caption* properties to *Life*, *Disability*, and *Medical* and set the IDs to *IDC_LIFE*, *IDC_DIS*, and *IDC_MED*. Unlike radio buttons, check boxes are independent; the user can set any combination.
- **The Skill combo box.** This is the first of three types of combo boxes. Change the ID to *IDC_SKILL*, and then set the

Type property to *Simple*. Increase the height of the control to accommodate multiple lines. In the *Data* property, add the three skills *Manager*, *Programmer*, and *Writer* (separating each line with a semicolon).

This is a combo box of type Simple. The user can type anything in the top edit control, use the mouse to select an item from the attached list box, or use the Up or Down direction key to select an item from the attached list box.

- **The Educ (education) combo box.** Change the ID to *IDC_EDUC* and set the *Sort* property to *False*. In the *Data* property, add the three education levels *High School*, *College*, and *Graduate* (separating each line with a semicolon. In this drop-down combo box, the user can type anything in the edit box, click on the arrow, and then select an item from the drop-down list or use the Up or Down direction key to select an item from the attached list box.

> **Note** To set the size for the drop-down portion of a combo box, click on the box's arrow and drag down from the center of the bottom of the rectangle.

- **The Dept (department) list box.** Change the *ID* to *IDC_DEPT*; otherwise, leave the defaults. In this list box, the user can select only a single item by using the mouse, by using the Up or Down direction key, or by typing the first character of a selection. Note that the list box doesn't have a *Data* property, so you can't enter the initial choices. You'll see how to programmatically set these choices later in the chapter.
- **The Lang (language) combo box.** Change the *ID* to *IDC_LANG*, and then set the *Type* property to *Drop List*. In the *Data* property, add the languages *English*, *French*, and *Spanish* (separating each line with a semicolon). With this drop-down combo box, the user can select only from the attached list box. To select, the user can click on the arrow and then select an entry from the drop-down list, or the user can type in the first letter of the selection and then refine the selection using the Up or Down direction key.

- **The Loyalty and Reliability horizontal scroll bars.** Do not confuse scroll bar controls with a window's built-in scroll bars (as seen in scrolling views). A scroll bar control behaves in the same manner as other controls do and can be resized at design time. Position and size the horizontal scroll bar controls as shown earlier in Figure 7-1, and then assign the IDs *IDC_LOYAL* and *IDC_RELY*.

- **The OK, Cancel, and Special buttons.** Add a button control below the existing OK and Cancel buttons. Set the *Caption* property to *S&pecial* and then set the ID *IDC_SPECIAL*. Later, you'll learn about special meanings that are associated with the default IDs *IDOK* and *IDCANCEL*.

- **Any icon.** (The MFC icon is shown as an example.) You can use the Picture control to display any icon or bitmap in a dialog box, as long as the icon or bitmap is defined in the resource script. We'll use the program's MFC icon, identified as *IDR_MAINFRAME*. Set the Type option to Icon, and set the *Image* property to *IDR_MAINFRAME*. Leave the ID as *IDC_STATIC*.

5. **Check the dialog box's tabbing order.** Choose Tab Order from the Format menu. Use the mouse to set the tabbing order shown below. Click on each control in the order shown, and then press Enter.

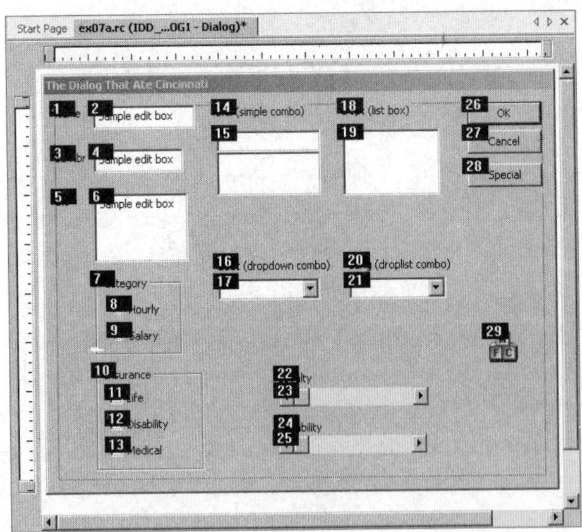

> **Tip** If you mess up the tab sequence partway through, you can recover with a Ctrl+left mouse click on the last correctly sequenced control. Subsequent mouse clicks will start with the next sequence number.

6. **Save the resource file on disk.** For safety, choose Save from the File menu or click the Save button on the toolbar to save Ex07a.rc. Keep the newly built dialog box open in the dialog editor.

Creating the Dialog Class

You've now built a dialog resource, but you can't use it without a corresponding dialog class. (The section titled "Understanding the Ex07a Application" later in this chapter explains the relationship between the dialog box and the underlying classes.) Class View works in conjunction with the dialog editor to create that class. Here are the steps to create a dialog class:

1. **Start the MFC Class Wizard.** In Class View, select the Ex07a project, as shown here.

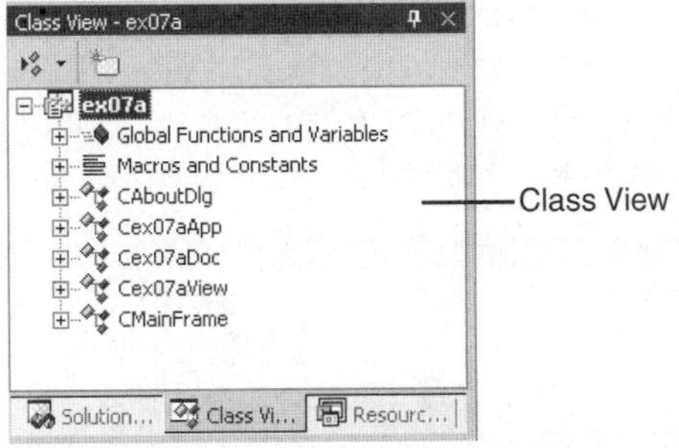

   On the Project menu, choose Add Class (or right-click on the project name in Class View and choose Add, Add Class). In the Add Class dialog box, select the MFC Class template. Click Open in the Add Class dialog box. The MFC Class Wizard will appear.

2. **Add the *CEx07aDialog* class.** Create a *CDialog*-based class by filling in the fields of the MFC Class Wizard, as shown below. Be sure the Dialog ID drop-down list is set to *IDD_DIALOG1* so the dialog resource you created earlier is used.

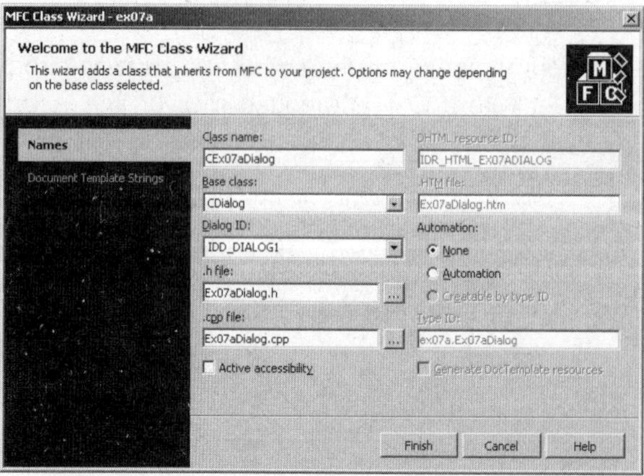

When you click Finish, the *CEx07aDialog* class will be added to Class View and its CPP file will be opened in the editor.

3. **Add the *CEx07aDialog* member variables.** After the *CEx07aDialog* class is added, you can add member variables using the Add Member Variable Wizard (shown below). To start the wizard, right-click on the *CEx07aDialog* class in Class View and choose Add, Add Variable.

   You must associate data members with each of the dialog box's controls. To do this, select the Control Variable check box, select a control from the Control ID drop-down list, and select Value from the Category drop-down list. Type a name in the Variable Name box and enter any other parameters. Here you can see the settings for adding the *CString* member variable named *m_strBio* for the Bio edit control:

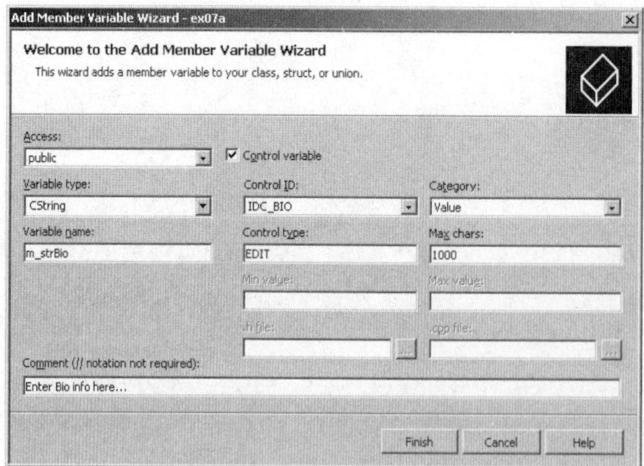

   When you're finished, click Finish and repeat this process for each of the controls listed in the table on the following page.

As you select controls in the Add Member Variables Wizard, you can set such things as the length of the string to enter or the range of numbers to enter. If you select a *CString* variable, you can set its maximum number of characters; if you select a numeric variable, you can set its minimum and maximum values. Set the minimum value for *IDC_SSN* to 0 and the maximum value to 999999999.

Most relationships between control types and variable types are obvious. The way in which radio buttons correspond to variables is not so intuitive, however. You should associate an integer variable with each radio button group, with the first radio button corresponding to value 0, the second to 1, and so forth.

Control ID	Data Member	Type	Parameters
IDC_BIO	*m_strBio*	*CString*	*Max chars = 1000*
IDC_CAT	*m_bCat*	*int*	
IDC_DEPT	*m_strDept*	*CString*	
IDC_DIS	*m_bInsDis*	*BOOL*	
IDC_EDUC	*m_strEduc*	*CString*	
IDC_LANG	*m_strLang*	*CString*	
IDC_LIFE	*m_bInsLife*	*BOOL*	
IDC_LOYAL	*m_nLoyal*	*int*	
IDC_MED	*m_bInsMed*	*BOOL*	
IDC_NAME	*m_strName*	*CString*	
IDC_RELY	*m_nRely*	*int*	
IDC_SKILL	*m_strSkill*	*CString*	
IDC_SSN	*m_nSsn*	*int*	*Min value = 0* *Max value = 999999999*

4. **Add the message-handling function for the Special button.** *CEx07aDialog* doesn't need many message-handling functions because the *CDialog* base class, with the help of Windows, does most of the dialog management. When you specify the ID *IDOK* for the OK button, for example, the virtual *CDialog* function *OnOK* gets called when the user clicks the button. For other buttons, however, you need message handlers.

   With the *CEx07aDialog* class selected in Class View, click the Events button at the top of the Properties window to add event handlers. The Properties window should contain an entry for

IDC_SPECIAL. Expand the *IDC_SPECIAL* tree and click the *BN_CLICKED* message. Click the down arrow for the *BN_CLICKED* message, as shown here:

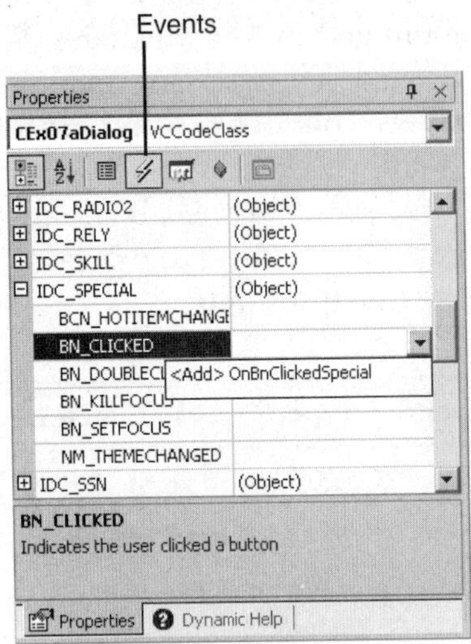

Visual Studio invents a message handler named *OnBnClicked-Special*. Click <Add> OnBnClickedSpecial to add the message handler. Visual Studio opens the file Ex07aDialog.cpp and moves to the *OnBnClickedSpecial* function. Insert a *TRACE* statement in the *OnBnclickedSpecial* function by typing in the following boldface code, which replaces the existing code:

```
void CEx07aDialog:: OnBnClickedSpecial ()
{
    TRACE("CEx07aDialog::OnBnClickedSpecial\n");
}
```

5. **Add an *OnInitDialog* message-handling function.** As you'll see in a moment, Visual Studio generates code that initializes a dialog box's controls. This DDX (Dialog Data Exchange) code won't initialize the list-box choices, however, so you must override the *CDialog::OnInit-Dialog* function. Although *OnInitDialog* is a virtual member function, Visual Studio generates the prototype and skeleton if you map the *WM_INITDIALOG* message in the derived dialog class. With the *CEx07aDialog* class selected in Class View, click the Overrides button at the top of the Properties window. In the list of overrides, select the *OnInitDialog* function and click the down arrow to select the method.

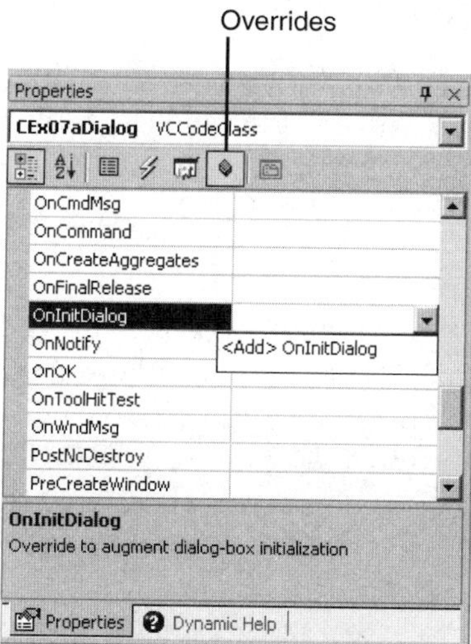

Click *<Add> OnInitDialog*. Visual Studio will place the *OnInitDialog* function in Ex07aDialog.cpp and open the source code file so you can edit the function. Type in the boldface code shown here to replace the existing code:

```
BOOL CEx07aDialog::OnInitDialog()
{
    // Be careful to call CDialog::OnInitDialog
    //  only once in this function
    CListBox* pLB = (CListBox*) GetDlgItem(IDC_DEPT);
    pLB->InsertString(-1, "Documentation");
    pLB->InsertString(-1, "Accounting");
    pLB->InsertString(-1, "Human Relations");
    pLB->InsertString(-1, "Security");

    // Call after initialization
    return CDialog::OnInitDialog();
}
```

This code initializes the Dept list box with four values. You can also use the same initialization technique for the combo boxes in place of setting the *Data* property in the resource.

Connecting the Dialog Box to the View

Now we've got the resource and the code for a dialog box, but it's not connected to the view. In most applications, you would probably use a menu command to display a dialog box, but we haven't studied menus yet. Here we'll use the familiar mouse-click message *WM_LBUTTONDOWN* to display the dialog box. The steps are as follows:

1. **Add the *OnLButtonDown* member function.** You've done this in the examples in earlier chapters. Simply select the *CEx07aView* class in Class View, and at the top of the Properties window, click the Messages button to display the list of messages for *CEx07aView*. Select the *WM_LBUTTONDOWN* entry, click the down arrow, and select *<Add> OnLButtonDown* to add the *OnLButtonDown* member function to Ex07aView.cpp.

2. **Write the code for *OnLButtonDown* in file Ex07aView.cpp.** Add the boldface code shown below. Most of the code consists of *TRACE* statements to print the dialog data members after the user exits the dialog box, but the *CEx07aDialog* constructor call and the *DoModal* call are the critical statements.

```
void CEx07aView::OnLButtonDown(UINT nFlags, CPoint point)
{
    CEx07aDialog dlg;
    dlg.m_strName  = "Shakespeare, Will";
    dlg.m_nSsn     = 307806636;
    dlg.m_nCat = 1;  // 0 = hourly, 1 = salary
    dlg.m_strBio = "This person is not a well-motivated tech writer";
    dlg.m_bInsLife = TRUE;
    dlg.m_bInsDis  = FALSE;
    dlg.m_bInsMed  = TRUE;
    dlg.m_strDept  = "Documentation";
    dlg.m_strSkill = "Writer";
    dlg.m_nLang    = 0;
    dlg.m_strEduc  = "College";
    dlg.m_nLoyal   = dlg.m_nRely = 50;
    int ret = dlg.DoModal();
    TRACE("DoModal return = %d\n", ret);
    TRACE("name = %s, ssn = %d, hourly = %d salary = %d\n",
        dlg.m_strName, dlg.m_nSsn, dlg.m_nCat);
    TRACE("dept = %s, skill = %s, lang = %d, educ = %s\n",
        dlg.m_strDept, dlg.m_strSkill, dlg.m_nLang, dlg.m_strEduc);
    TRACE("life = %d, dis = %d, med = %d, bio = %s\n",
        dlg.m_bInsLife, dlg.m_bInsDis, dlg.m_bInsMed, dlg.m_strBio);
```

```
    TRACE("loyalty = %d, reliability = %d\n",
          dlg.m_nLoyal, dlg.m_nRely);
}
```

3. **Add code to the virtual *OnDraw* function in the file Ex07aView.cpp.** To prompt the user to press the left mouse button, code the *CEx07aView::OnDraw* function. (The skeleton was generated by MFC Application Wizard.) The boldface code shown here (which you type in) replaces the existing code:

```
void CEx07aView::OnDraw(CDC* pDC)
{
    CEx07aDoc* pDoc = GetDocument();
    ASSERT_VALID(pDoc);

    pDC->TextOut(0, 0, "Press the left mouse button here.");
}
```

4. **Add the dialog class include statement to Ex07aView.cpp.** The *OnLButtonDown* function shown above depends on the declaration of class *CEx07aDialog*. You must insert the include statement

```
#include "Ex07aDialog.h"
```

at the top of the *CEx07aView* class source code file (Ex07aView.cpp), after the following statement:

```
#include "Ex07aView.h"
```

5. **Build and test the application.** If you've done everything correctly, you should be able to build and run the Ex07a application through Visual C++. Try entering data in each control, and then click OK and observe the *TRACE* results in the Output window. Notice that the scroll bar controls don't do much yet; we'll attend to them later. Notice what happens when you press Enter while typing in text data in a control: The dialog box closes immediately. Here's an example of the *TRACE* results in the Output window:

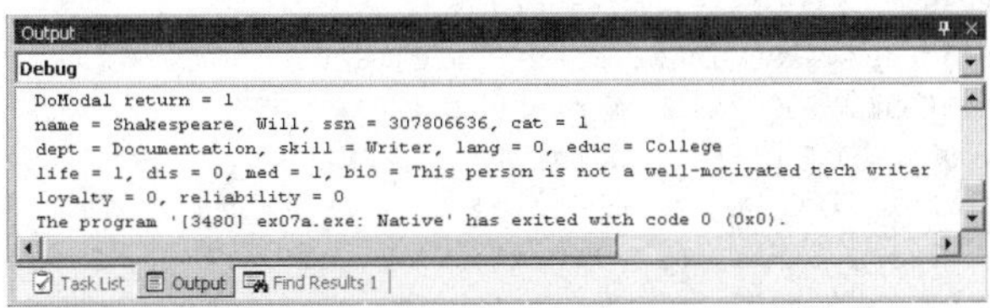

Understanding the Ex07a Application

When your program calls *DoModal*, control is returned to your program only when the user closes the dialog box. If you understand that, you understand modal dialog boxes. When you start creating modeless dialog boxes, you'll begin to appreciate the programming simplicity of modal dialog boxes. A lot happens "out of sight" as a result of that *DoModal* call, however. Here's a "what calls what" summary:

CDialog::DoModal
  CEx07aDialog::OnInitDialog
    ...additional initialization...
    CDialog::OnInitDialog
      CWnd::UpdateData(FALSE)
        CEx07aDialog::DoDataExchange
  user enters data...
  user clicks the OK button
  CEx07aDialog::OnOK
    ...additional validation...
    CDialog::OnOK
      CWnd::UpdateData(TRUE)
        CEx07aDialog::DoDataExchange
      CDialog::EndDialog(IDOK)

OnInitDialog and *DoDataExchange* are virtual functions overridden in the *CEx07aDialog* class. Windows calls *OnInitDialog* as part of the dialog box initialization process, and that results in a call to *DoDataExchange*, a *CWnd* virtual function that was overridden by Visual Studio. Here is a listing of that function:

```
void CEx07aDialog::DoDataExchange(CDataExchange* pDX)
{
    CDialog::DoDataExchange(pDX);
    DDX_Text(pDX, IDC_BIO, m_strBio);
    DDV_MaxChars(pDX, m_strBio, 1000);
    DDX_Radio(pDX, IDC_CAT, m_nCat);
    DDX_LBString(pDX, IDC_DEPT, m_strDept);
    DDX_Check(pDX, IDC_DIS, m_bInsDis);
    DDX_CBString(pDX, IDC_EDUC, m_strEduc);
    DDX_CBIndex(pDX, IDC_LANG, m_nLang);
    DDX_Check(pDX, IDC_LIFE, m_bInsLife);
    DDX_Scroll(pDX, IDC_LOYAL, m_nLoyal);
    DDX_Check(pDX, IDC_MED, m_bInsMed);
    DDX_Text(pDX, IDC_NAME, m_strName);
    DDX_Scroll(pDX, IDC_RELY, m_nRely);
    DDX_CBString(pDX, IDC_SKILL, m_strSkill);
    DDX_Text(pDX, IDC_SSN, m_nSsn);
    DDV_MinMaxInt(pDX, m_nSsn, 0, 999999999);
}
```

The *DoDataExchange* function and the *DDX_* (exchange) and *DDV_* (validation) functions are "bidirectional." If *UpdateData* is called with a *FALSE* parameter, the functions transfer data from the data members to the dialog box controls. If the parameter is *TRUE*, the functions transfer data from the dialog box controls to the data members. *DDX_Text* is overloaded to accommodate a variety of data types.

The *EndDialog* function is critical to the dialog box exit procedure. *DoModal* returns the parameter passed to *EndDialog*. *IDOK* accepts the dialog box's data, and *IDCANCEL* cancels the dialog box.

> **Tip** You can write your own "custom" DDX function and wire it into Visual C++. This feature is useful if you're using a unique data type throughout your application. For details, see the "TN026: DDX and DDV Routines" topic in the Visual Studio documentation.

Enhancing the Ex07a Application

The Ex07a application requires little coding for a lot of functionality. Now we'll make a new version of the program that uses some hand-coding to add extra features. We'll eliminate Ex07a's rude habit of dumping the user in response to a press of the Enter key, and we'll hook up the scroll bar controls.

Taking Control of the *OnOK* Exit

In the original Ex07a application, the *CDialog::OnOK* virtual function handles the OK button, which triggers data exchange and the exit from the dialog box. Pressing the Enter key happens to have the same effect, and that might or might not be what you want. If the user presses Enter while in the Name edit control, for example, the dialog box closes immediately.

What's going on here? When the user presses Enter, Windows looks to see which button has the input focus, as indicated on the screen by a dotted rectangle. If no button has the focus, Windows looks for the default button that the program or the resource specifies. (The default button has a thicker border.) If the dialog box has no default button, the virtual *OnOK* function is called, even if the dialog box does not contain an OK button.

You can disable the Enter key by writing a do-nothing *CEx07aDialog::OnOK* function and adding the exit code to a new function that responds to clicking the OK button. Here are the steps:

1. **"Map" the IDOK button to the virtual *OnOK* function.** In Class View, select the *CEx07aDialog* class. At the top of the Properties window, click the Overrides button to get the list of overridden functions. Click *OnOK* from the function list, click the down arrow, and click *<Add> OnOK*. This action generates the prototype and skeleton for *OnOK*. Leave the *OnOK* function as is for now.

2. **Use the dialog editor to change the OK button ID.** Display the *IDD_DIALOG1* resource and select the OK button. In the Properties window, change its ID from *IDOK* to *IDC_OK*, and then set the Default Button property to False.

3. **Create a member function named *OnClickedOk*.** In Class View, select the *CEx07aDialog* class. Click the Events button at the top of the Properties window. Expand the *IDC_OK* item, select the *BN_CLICKED* message, and then click *<Add> OnBnClickedOk* to add the *OnBnClicked* message handler for the newly renamed control *IDC_OK*.

4. **Edit the body of the *OnClickedOk* function in Ex07aDialog.cpp.** This function calls the base class *OnOK* function, as did the original *CEx07aDialog::OnOK* function. Here is the code:

```
void CEx07aDialog::OnClickedOk()
{
    TRACE("CEx07aDialog::OnClickedOk\n");
    CDialog::OnOK();
}
```

5. **Edit the original *OnOK* function in Ex07aDialog.cpp.** This function is a "leftover" handler for the old *IDOK* button. Edit the code as shown here:

```
void CEx07aDialog::OnOK()
{
    // dummy OnOK function -- do NOT call CDialog::OnOK()
    TRACE("CEx07aDialog::OnOK\n");
}
```

6. **Build and test the application.** Try pressing the Enter key now. Nothing should happen, but *TRACE* output should appear in the Output window. Clicking the OK button should exit the dialog box as before, however.

OnCancel Processing

Just as pressing the Enter key triggers a call to *OnOK*, pressing the Esc key triggers a call to *OnCancel*, which results in an exit from the dialog box with a *DoModal* return code of *IDCANCEL*. Ex07a does no special processing for

IDCANCEL; therefore, pressing the Esc key (or clicking the Close button) closes the dialog box. You can circumvent this process by substituting a dummy *OnCancel* function, following approximately the same procedure you used for the OK button.

Hooking Up the Scroll Bar Controls

The dialog editor allows you to include scroll bar controls in your dialog box, and the Add Member Variable Wizard lets you add integer data members. You must add code to make the Loyalty and Reliability scroll bars work.

Scroll bar controls have position and range values that can be read and written. If you set the range to (0, 100), for example, a corresponding data member with a value of 50 will position the scroll box at the center of the bar. (The function *CScrollBar::SetScrollPos* also sets the scroll box position.) The scroll bars send the *WM_HSCROLL* and *WM_VSCROLL* messages to the dialog box when the user drags the scroll box or clicks the arrows. The dialog box's message handlers must decode these messages and position the scroll box accordingly.

Each control you've seen so far has had its own individual message handler function. Scroll bar controls are different because all horizontal scroll bars in a dialog are tied to a single *WM_HSCROLL* message handler and all vertical scroll bars are tied to a single *WM_VSCROLL* handler. Because this monster dialog contains two horizontal scroll bars, the single *WM_HSCROLL* message handler must figure out which scroll bar sent the scroll message.

Here are the steps for adding the scroll bar logic to Ex07a:

1. **Add the class *enum* statements for the minimum and maximum scroll range.** In Ex07aDialog.h, add the following lines at the top of the class declaration:

```
enum { nMin = 0 };
enum { nMax = 100 };
```

2. **Edit the *OnInitDialog* function to initialize the scroll ranges.** In the *OnInitDialog* function, we'll set the minimum and the maximum scroll values such that the *CEx07aDialog* data members represent percentage values. A value of 100 means "Set the scroll box to the extreme right"; a value of 0 means "Set the scroll box to the extreme left."

   Add the following code to the *CEx07aDialog* member function *OnInitDialog* in the file Ex07aDialog.cpp:

```
CScrollBar* pSB = (CScrollBar*) GetDlgItem(IDC_LOYAL);
pSB->SetScrollRange(nMin, nMax);

pSB = (CScrollBar*) GetDlgItem(IDC_RELY);
pSB->SetScrollRange(nMin, nMax);
```

3. **Add a scroll bar message handler to *CEx07aDialog*.** Select *CEx07aDialog* in Class View and click the Messages button at the top of the Properties window. Select the *WM_HSCROLL* message, and then add the member function *OnHScroll*. Enter the following code shown in boldface:

```
void CEx07aDialog::OnHScroll(UINT nSBCode, UINT nPos,
                             CScrollBar* pScrollBar)
{
    int nTemp1, nTemp2;

    nTemp1 = pScrollBar->GetScrollPos();
    switch(nSBCode) {
    case SB_THUMBPOSITION:
        pScrollBar->SetScrollPos(nPos);
        break;
    case SB_LINELEFT: // left arrow button
        nTemp2 = (nMax - nMin) / 10;
        if ((nTemp1 - nTemp2) > nMin) {
            nTemp1 -= nTemp2;
        }
        else {
            nTemp1 = nMin;
        }
        pScrollBar->SetScrollPos(nTemp1);
        break;
    case SB_LINERIGHT: // right arrow button
        nTemp2 = (nMax - nMin) / 10;
        if ((nTemp1 + nTemp2) < nMax) {
            nTemp1 += nTemp2;
        }
        else {
            nTemp1 = nMax;
        }
        pScrollBar->SetScrollPos(nTemp1);
        break;
    }
}
```

4. **Build and test the application.** Build and run Ex07a again. Do the scroll bars work this time? The scroll boxes should "stick" after you drag them with the mouse, and they should move when you click the scroll bars' arrows. (Notice that we haven't added logic to cover the user's click on the scroll bar itself.)

Identifying Controls: *CWnd* Pointers and Control IDs

When you lay out a dialog resource in the dialog editor, you identify each control by an ID such as *IDC_SSN*. In your program code, however, you often need access to a control's underlying window object. The MFC library provides the *CWnd::GetDlgItem* function for converting an ID to a *CWnd* pointer. You've seen this already in the *OnInitDialog* member function of class *CEx07aDialog*. The application framework "manufactured" this returned *CWnd* pointer because there never was a constructor call for the control objects. This pointer is temporary and should not be stored for later use.

> **Tip** If you need to convert a *CWnd* pointer to a control ID, use the MFC library *GetDlgCtrlID* member function of class *CWnd*.

Setting the Dialog Box Background Color or a Control Color

You can change the background color of individual dialog boxes or specific controls in a dialog box, but you have to do some extra work. The parent dialog is sent a *WM_CTLCOLOR* message for each control immediately before the control is displayed. A *WM_CTLCOLOR* message is also sent on behalf of the dialog box itself. If you map this message in your derived dialog class, you can set the foreground and background text colors and select a brush for the control or dialog nontext area.

Following is a sample *OnCtlColor* function that sets all edit control backgrounds to yellow and the dialog box background to red. The *m_hYellowBrush* and *m_hRedBrush* variables are data members of type *HBRUSH*, which are initialized in the dialog box's *OnInitDialog* function. The *nCtlColor* parameter indicates the type of control, and the *pWnd* parameter identifies the specific control. If you wanted to set the color for an individual edit control, you can convert *pWnd* to a child window ID and test it.

```
HBRUSH CMyDialog::OnCtlColor(CDC* pDC, CWnd* pWnd, UINT nCtlColor)
{
    if (nCtlColor == CTLCOLOR_EDIT) {
        pDC->SetBkColor(RGB(255, 255, 0)); // yellow
        return m_hYellowBrush;
    }
    if (nCtlColor == CTLCOLOR_DLG) {
        pDC->SetBkColor(RGB(255, 0, 0));    // red
        return m_hRedBrush;
    }
    return CDialog::OnCtlColor(pDC, pWnd, nCtlColor);
}
```

> **Note** The dialog box does not post the *WM_CTLCOLOR* message in the message queue; instead, it calls the Win32 *SendMessage* function to send the message immediately. The message handler can then return a parameter, in this case a handle to a brush. This is not an MFC *CBrush* object but rather a Win32 *HBRUSH*. You can create the brush by calling the Win32 functions *CreateSolidBrush*, *CreateHatchBrush*, and so forth.

Adding Dialog Controls at Run Time

You've seen how to use the resource editor to create dialog controls at build time. If you need to add a dialog control at run time, here are the programming steps:

1. **Add an embedded control window data member to your dialog class.** The MFC control window classes include *CButton*, *CEdit*, *CListBox*, and *CComboBox*. An embedded control C++ object is constructed and destroyed along with the dialog object.
2. **Add an ID constant for the new control.** Right-click on the dialog class in Resource View and choose Resource Symbols to open the Resource Symbols dialog box. Add the new constant.
3. **Use Class View's Property Page to override *CDialog::OnInitDialog*.** This function should call the embedded control window's *Create* member function. This call displays the new control in the dialog box. Windows will destroy the control window when it destroys the dialog box.
4. **In your derived dialog class, manually add the necessary notification message handlers for your new control.**

In Chapter 12, you'll add a rich edit control to a view at run time.

Using Other Control Features

You've seen how to customize the control class *CScrollBar* by adding code in the dialog box's *OnInitDialog* member function. You can program other controls in a similar fashion. In the Visual Studio documentation, look at the control classes, particularly *CListBox* and *CComboBox*. Each has a number of features that the Properties window and the Visual Studio wizards do not directly support. Some combo boxes, for example, can support multiple selections by applying the LBS_MULTIPLESEL list box style to the combo box. If you want to use these features, don't try to use Class View to add data members. Instead, define your own data members and add your own exchange code in *OnInitDialog* and *OnBnClickedOk*.

Windows Common Dialog Boxes

Windows provides a group of standard user interface dialog boxes (in COMDLG32.DLL), and these are supported by the MFC library classes. You're probably familiar with all or most of these dialog boxes because so many Windows-based applications, including Visual C++ applications, already use them. All the common dialog classes are derived from a common base class, *CCommonDialog*. Table 7-1 shows lists the *CCommonDialog* classes.

Table 7-1 *CCommonDialog* Classes

Class	Purpose
CColorDialog	Allows the user to select or create a color
CFileDialog	Allows the user to open or save a file
CFindReplaceDialog	Allows the user to substitute one string for another
CFontDialog	Allows the user to select a font from a list of available fonts
COleDialog	Useful for inserting OLE objects
CPageSetupDialog	Allows the user to input page measurement parameters
CPrintDialog	Allows the user to set up the printer and print a document
CPrintDialogEx	Printing and Print Preview for Windows 2000

One characteristic that all common dialog boxes share is that they gather information from the user but don't do anything with it. The file dialog box can help the user select a file to open, but it really just provides your program with the pathname—your program must make the call that opens the file. Similarly, a font dialog box fills in a structure that describes a font, but it doesn't create the font.

Using the *CFileDialog* Class Directly

Using the *CFileDialog* class to open a file is easy. The following code opens a file that the user has selected using the dialog box:

```
CFileDialog dlg(TRUE, "bmp", "*.bmp");
if (dlg.DoModal() == IDOK) {
    CFile file;
    VERIFY(file.Open(dlg.GetPathName(), CFile::modeRead));
}
```

The first constructor parameter (*TRUE*) specifies that this object is a File Open dialog box instead of a File Save dialog box. The default file extension is BMP, and **.bmp* appears first in the filename edit box. The *CFileDialog::Get-Path-Name* function returns a *CString* object that contains the full pathname of the selected file.

Deriving from the Common Dialog Classes

You can usually use the common dialog classes directly. If you derive your own classes, you can add functionality without duplicating code. Each COMDLG32 dialog works a little differently, however. The next example is specific to the file dialog box, but it should give you some ideas for customizing the other common dialog boxes.

Nested Dialog Boxes

Win32 provides a way to "nest" one dialog box inside another so that multiple dialog boxes appear as one seamless whole. You must first create a dialog resource template with a "hole" in it—typically a group box control—with the specific child window ID *stc32 (=0x045f)*. Your program sets some parameters that tell COMDLG32 to use your template. In addition, your program must hook into the COMDLG32 message loop so that it gets first crack at selected notifications. When you're done with all of this, you'll notice that you've created a dialog box that is a child of the COMDLG32 dialog box, even though your template wraps COMDLG32's template. This sounds difficult, and it is, unless you use MFC. With MFC, you build the dialog resource template with a "hole" in it as described above, derive a class from one of the common dialog base classes, add the class-specific connection code in *OnInitDialog*, and then happily use the Properties window for a class to map the messages that originate from your template's new controls.

The Ex07b Example: *CFileDialog*

In this example, we'll derive a class *CEx07bDialog* that adds a working Delete All Matching Files button to the standard file dialog box. It will also change the dialog box's title and change the Open button's caption to Delete (to delete a single file). The example illustrates how you can use nested dialog boxes to add new controls to standard common dialog boxes. The new file dialog box is activated as in the previous examples—by pressing the left mouse button when the mouse cursor is in the view window. Because you should be gaining skill with Visual C++, the following steps won't be as detailed as those for the earlier examples. Figure 7-2 shows what the dialog box looks like.

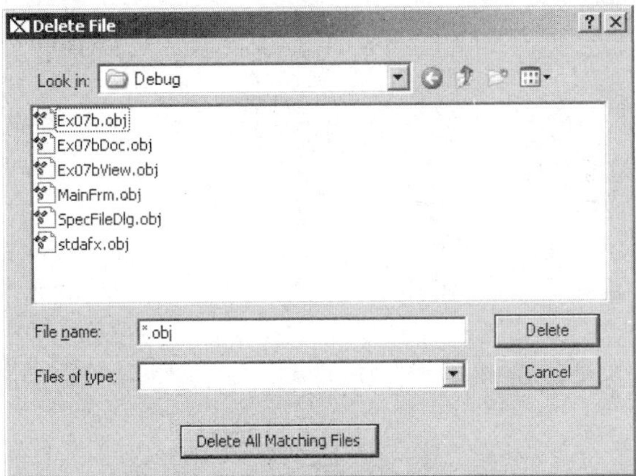

Figure 7-2 The Delete File dialog box in action.

Follow these steps to build the Ex07b application:

1. **Create a new MFC Application project named Ex07b.** In the MFC Application Wizard, accept all the defaults but two: On the Application Type page, select Single Document, and on the Advanced Features page, deselect Printing And Print Preview.

2. **Create a new dialog resource and set its properties.** On the Project menu, choose Add Resource and add a new dialog box. Make the dialog box about 3 by 5 inches. Using the Properties window for the dialog box, change the ID property to *IDD_FILESPECIAL*, set the Style property to Child, set the Border property to None, and set the Clip Siblings and Visible properties to True.

3. **Specify controls for the dialog box.** Delete the existing OK and Cancel buttons on the dialog box. Add a button at the bottom of the dialog box and set the ID to *IDC_DELETE* and set the Caption to Delete All Matching Files. Add a group box, set the ID to *stc32=0x045f*, and set the Visible property to False, as shown here.

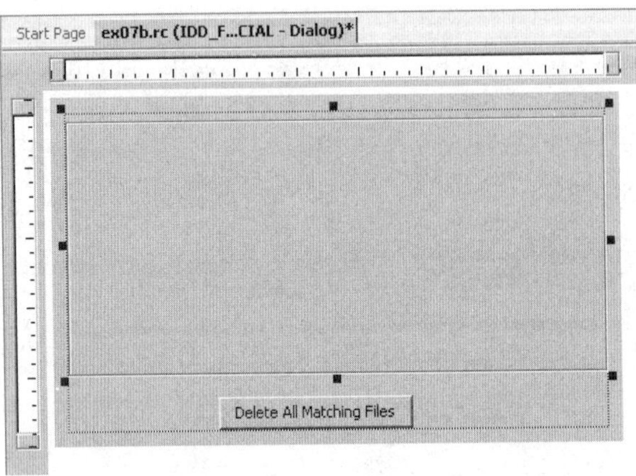

Check your work by right-clicking on the *IDD_FILESPECIAL* dialog resource in Resource View and choosing Resource Symbols. You should see a symbol list like the one shown here.

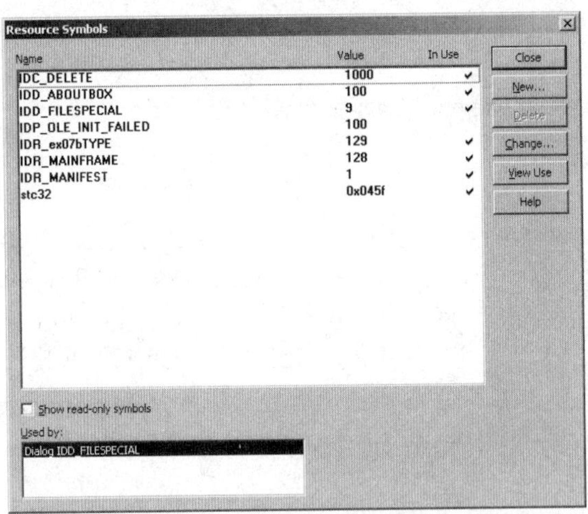

4. **Use the MFC Class Wizard to create the *CSpecialFileDialog* class.** In Class View, right-click on the Ex07b project, choose Add, Add Class, select the MFC Class template, and click Open to start the MFC Class Wizard. Fill in the wizard, as shown below. Be sure to change the filenames to SpecFileDlg.h and SpecFileDlg.cpp.

Unfortunately, we cannot use the Base Class drop-down list to change the base class to *CFileDialog*—that would decouple our class from the *IDD_FILESPECIAL* template. We have to change the base class by hand. When you're finished, click the Finish button.

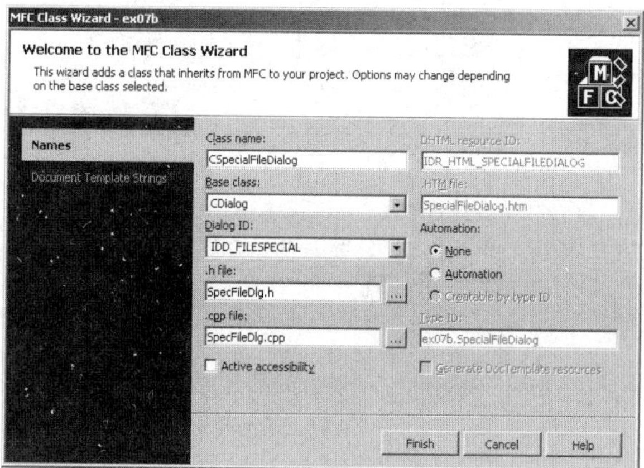

5. **Edit the file SpecFileDlg.h.** Change the line

```
class CSpecialFileDialog : public CDialog
```

to

```
class CSpecialFileDialog : public CFileDialog
```

Add the following two public data members:

```
CString m_strFilename;
BOOL m_bDeleteAll;
```

Finally, edit the constructor declaration:

```
CSpecialFileDialog(BOOL bOpenFileDialog,
    LPCTSTR lpszDefExt = NULL,
    LPCTSTR lpszFileName = NULL,
    DWORD dwFlags = OFN_HIDEREADONLY | OFN_OVERWRITEPROMPT,
    LPCTSTR lpszFilter = NULL,
    CWnd* pParentWnd = NULL);
```

6. **Replace *CDialog* with *CFileDialog* in SpecFileDlg.cpp.** Choose Find And Replace, Replace from the Edit menu, and replace this name globally.

7. **Edit the *CSpecialFileDialog* constructor in SpecFileDlg.cpp.** The derived class constructor must invoke the base class constructor and initialize the *m_bDeleteAll* data member. In addition, it must set some members of the *CFileDialog* base class data member *m_ofn*,

which is an instance of the Win32 *OPENFILENAME* structure. The *Flags* and *lpTemplateName* members control the coupling to your *IDD_FILESPECIAL* dialog template, and the *lpstrTitle* member changes the main dialog box title. Edit the constructor as follows:

```
CSpecialFileDialog::CSpecialFileDialog(BOOL bOpenFileDialog,
        LPCTSTR lpszDefExt, LPCTSTR lpszFileName, DWORD dwFlags,
        LPCTSTR lpszFilter, CWnd* pParentWnd)
    : CFileDialog(bOpenFileDialog, lpszDefExt, lpszFileName,
        dwFlags, lpszFilter, pParentWnd)
{
    m_ofn.Flags |= OFN_ENABLETEMPLATE;
    m_ofn.lpTemplateName = MAKEINTRESOURCE(IDD_FILESPECIAL);
    m_ofn.lpstrTitle = "Delete File";
    m_bDeleteAll = FALSE;
}
```

8. **Override the *OnInitDialog* function in the *CSpecialDialog* class.** Select the *CSpecialFileDialog* class in Class View, click the Overrides button in the Properties window, and add the *OnInit-Dialog* function. The *OnInitDialog* member function needs to change the common dialog box's Open button caption to Delete. The child window ID is *IDOK*. Edit the code as follows.

```
BOOL CSpecialFileDialog::OnInitDialog()
    BOOL bRet = CFileDialog::OnInitDialog();
    if (bRet == TRUE) {
        GetParent()->GetDlgItem(IDOK)->SetWindowText("Delete");
    }
    return bRet;
}
```

9. **Add a *BN_CLICKED* message handler for the new *IDC_DELETE* button (Delete All Matching Files) in the *CSpecialDialog* class.** Select the *CSpecialFileDialog* class in Class View, click the Events button in the Properties window, and add the *OnBnClickedDe-lete* message handler. The *OnBnClickedDelete* member function sets the *m_bDeleteAll* flag and then forces the main dialog box to exit as if the Cancel button had been clicked. The client program (in this case, the view) gets the *IDCANCEL* return from *DoModal* and reads the flag to see whether it should delete all files. Edit the code as follows:

```
void CSpecialFileDialog::OnBnClickedDelete()
{
    m_bDeleteAll = TRUE;
    // 0x480 is the child window ID of the File Name edit control
    //  (as determined by SPYXX)
```

```
        GetParent()->GetDlgItem(0x480)->GetWindowText(m_strFilename);
        GetParent()->SendMessage(WM_COMMAND, IDCANCEL);
    }
```

10. **Add code to the virtual *OnDraw* function in file Ex07bView.cpp.** The *CEx07bView OnDraw* function (whose skeleton was generated by MFC Application Wizard) should be coded as follows to prompt the user to press the mouse button:

```
void CEx07bView::OnDraw(CDC* pDC)
{
    CEx07bDoc* pDoc = GetDocument();
    ASSERT_VALID(pDoc);

    pDC->TextOut(0, 0, "Press the left mouse button here.");
}
```

11. **Add the *WM_LBUTTONDOWN* message handler to the *CEx07bView* class.** Select the *CEx07bView* class in Class View, click the Messages button in the Properties window, and add the *OnLButtonDown* message handler. Edit the code as follows:

```
void CEx07bView::OnLButtonDown(UINT nFlags, CPoint point)
{
    CSpecialFileDialog dlgFile(TRUE, NULL, "*.obj");
    CString strMessage;
    int nModal = dlgFile.DoModal();
    if ((nModal == IDCANCEL) && (dlgFile.m_bDeleteAll)) {
        strMessage.Format(
            "Are you sure you want to delete all %s files?",
            dlgFile.m_strFilename);
        if (AfxMessageBox(strMessage, MB_YESNO) == IDYES) {
            HANDLE h;
            WIN32_FIND_DATA fData;
            while((h = ::FindFirstFile(
            dlgFile.m_strFilename, &fData))
            != (HANDLE) 0xFFFFFFFF) { // no MFC equivalent
                if (::DeleteFile(fData.cFileName) == FALSE) {
                    strMessage.Format("Unable to delete file %s\n",
                        fData.cFileName);
                    AfxMessageBox(strMessage);
                    break;
                }
            }
        }
    }
```

(continued)

```
        else if (nModal == IDOK) {
            CString strSingleFilename = dlgFile.GetPathName();
            strMessage.Format(
                "Are you sure you want to delete %s?",
                strSingleFilename);
            if (AfxMessageBox(strMessage, MB_YESNO) == IDYES) {
                CFile::Remove(strSingleFilename);
            }
        }
    }
```

Remember that common dialog boxes only gather data. Because the view is the client of the dialog box, the view must call *DoModal* for the file dialog object and then figure out what to do with the information returned. In this case, the view has the return value from *DoModal* (either *IDOK* or *IDCANCEL*) and the value of the public *m_bDeleteAll* data member, and it can call various *CFileDialog* member functions such as *GetPathName*. If *DoModal* returns *IDCANCEL* and the flag is *TRUE*, the function makes the Win32 file system calls necessary to delete all the matching files. If *DoModal* returns *IDOK*, the function can use the MFC *CFile* functions to delete an individual file.

Using the global *AfxMessageBox* function is a convenient way to pop up a simple dialog that displays some text and then queries the user for a Yes/No answer. The Visual Studio documentation describes all of the message box variations and options.

12. **Include *SpecFileDlg.h* in Ex07bView.cpp.** Of course, you'll need to include the statement

    ```
    #include "SpecFileDlg.h"
    ```

    after the line

    ```
    #include "Ex07bView.h"
    ```

13. **Build and test the application.** Build and run Ex07b. Pressing the left mouse button should bring up the Delete File dialog box, and you should be able to use it to navigate through the disk directory and delete files. Be careful not to delete your important source files!

Other Customizations for *CFileDialog*

In the Ex07b example, you added a button to the dialog box. It's easy to add other controls, too. Just put them in the dialog resource template, and if they're standard Windows controls such as edit controls or list boxes, you can use the

Add Member Variable Wizard to add data members and DDX/DDV code to your derived class. The client program can set the data members before calling *DoModal*, and it can retrieve the updated values after *DoModal* returns.

> **Note** Even if you don't use nested dialog boxes, two windows are still associated with a *CFileDialog* object. Suppose you have overridden *OnInitDialog* in a derived class and you want to assign an icon to the file dialog box. You must call *CWnd::GetParent* to get the top-level window, just as you did in the Ex07b example. Here's the code:

```
HICON hIcon = AfxGetApp()->LoadIcon(IDI_MYICON);
GetParent()->SetIcon(hIcon, TRUE);          // Set big icon
GetParent()->SetIcon(hIcon, FALSE);         // Set small icon
```

Programming a Modeless Dialog Box

The dialog boxes we've worked with so far in this chapter have been ordinary modal dialog boxes. Now let's move on to the modeless dialog box and to the common dialog boxes for modern versions of the Windows base class *CDialog*. They both use a dialog resource that you can build with the dialog editor. If you're using a modeless dialog box with a view, you'll need to know some specialized programming techniques.

Creating Modeless Dialog Boxes

For modal dialog boxes, you've already learned that you construct a dialog object using a *CDialog* constructor that takes a dialog resource template ID as a parameter, and then you display the modal dialog box by calling the *DoModal* member function. The window ceases to exist as soon as *DoModal* returns. Thus, you can construct a modal dialog object on the stack, knowing that the dialog box has been destroyed by the time the dialog object goes out of scope.

Modeless dialog boxes are more complicated. You start by invoking the *CDialog* default constructor to construct the dialog object, but to create the dialog box you need to call the *CDialog::Create* member function instead of *DoModal*. *Create* takes the resource ID as a parameter and returns immediately with the dialog box still on the screen. You must worry about exactly when to construct the dialog object, when to create the dialog box, when to destroy the dialog box, and when to process user-entered data.

Table 7-2 summarizes the differences between creating a modal dialog box and a modeless dialog box.

Table 7-2 Modal vs. Modeless Dialog Boxes

	Modal Dialog Box	Modeless Dialog Box
Constructor Used	Constructor with resource ID param	Default constructor (no params)
Function Used to Create Window	*DoModal*	*Create* with resource ID param

User-Defined Messages

Suppose you want the modeless dialog box to be destroyed when the user clicks the dialog box's OK button. This presents a problem. How does the view know that the user has clicked the OK button? The dialog box could call a view class member function directly, but that would "marry" the dialog box to a particular view class. A better solution is for the dialog box to send the view a user-defined message as the result of a call to the OK button message-handling function. When the view gets the message, it can destroy the dialog box (but not the object so that it can maintain any user data specified in the dialog box). This sets the stage for the creation of a new dialog box.

You have two options for sending Windows messages: the *CWnd::SendMessage* function or the *PostMessage* function. The former causes an immediate call to the message-handling function, and the latter posts a message in the Windows message queue. Because there's a slight delay with the *PostMessage* option, it's reasonable to expect that the handler function has returned by the time the view gets the message.

Dialog Box Ownership

Now suppose you've accepted the dialog box default pop-up style, which means that the dialog box isn't confined to the view's client area. As far as Windows is concerned, the dialog box's "owner" is the application's main frame window (which you'll see in Chapter 12), not the view. You need to know the dialog box's view to send the view a message. Therefore, your dialog class must track its own view through a data member that the constructor sets. The *CDialog* constructor's *pParent* parameter doesn't have any effect here, so don't bother using it.

The Ex07c Example: A Modeless Dialog Box

We could convert the monster dialog box created earlier in the chapter to a modeless dialog box, but starting from scratch with a simpler dialog box is easier. Example Ex07c uses a dialog box with one edit control, an OK button, and a Cancel button. As in the Dialog Box That Ate Cincinnati example, pressing the left mouse button while the mouse cursor is inside the view window brings up the dialog box, but now we have the option of destroying it in response to another event—pressing the *right* mouse button when the mouse cursor is inside the view window. We'll allow only one open dialog box at a time, so we must be sure that a second left button press doesn't bring up a duplicate dialog box.

To summarize the upcoming steps, the Ex07c view class has a single associated dialog object that is constructed on the heap when the view is constructed. The dialog box is created and destroyed in response to user actions, but the dialog object is not destroyed until the application terminates.

Here are the steps to create the Ex07c example:

1. **Create a new MFC Application project named Ex07c.** In the MFC Application Wizard, accept all the defaults but two: On the Application Type page, select Single Document, and on the Advanced Features page, deselect Printing And Print Preview.

2. **Create a new dialog resource.** On the Project menu, select Add Resource and add a new dialog box. The dialog editor assigns the ID *IDD_DIALOG1* to the new dialog box. Using the Properties window for the dialog box, change the *Caption* property to *Modeless Dialog* and set the *Visible* property to *True*. Leave the default OK and Cancel buttons with IDs *IDOK* and *IDCANCEL*

3. **Add controls to the dialog box.** Add a static text control and an edit control with the default ID *IDC_EDIT1*. Change the Caption property of the static text control to Edit 1. Here is the completed dialog box:

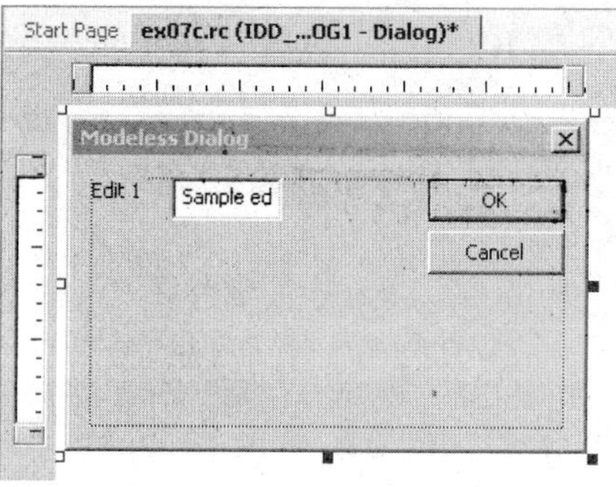

4. **Use the MFC Class Wizard to create the *CEx07cDialog* class.** In Class View, right-click on the Ex07c project, choose Add and then Add Class, select the MFC Class template, and click Open to start the MFC Class Wizard. Name the class *CEx07cDialog*, make sure it derives from *CDialog*, and set the Dialog ID to *IDD_DIALOG1*, as shown here. When you're finished, click the Finish button.

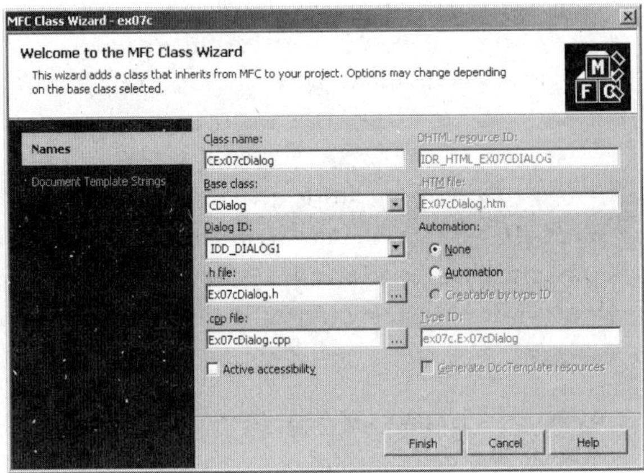

5. **Add message handlers for *IDCANCEL* and *IDOK*.** Select the *CEx07cDialog* class in Class View, click the Events button in the Properties window, and add the *OnBnClickedCancel* and *OnBnClickedOk* message handlers as shown in the following table.

Object ID	Message	Member Function
IDCANCEL	*BN_CLICKED*	*OnBnClickedCancel*
IDOK	*BN_CLICKED*	*OnBnClickedOk*

6. **Add a variable to the *CEx07cDialog* class.** Select the *CEx07cDialog* class in Class View. Choose Add Variable from the Project menu, and use the Add Member Variable Wizard to add member variables for the *IDC_EDIT1* control. Make the variable of type *CString* and name it *m_strEdit1*, as shown here:

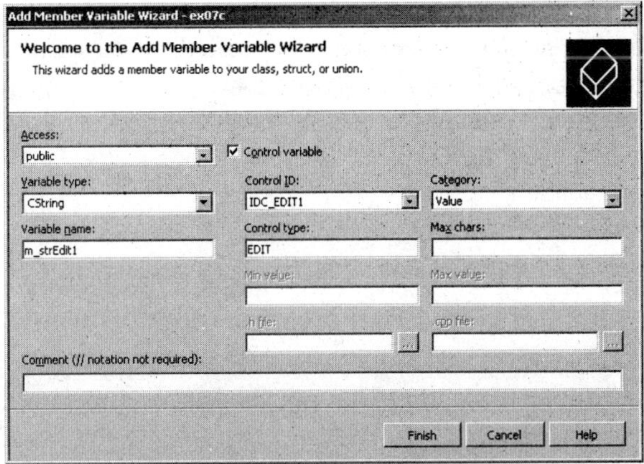

7. **Edit Ex07cDialog.h to add a view pointer and function prototypes.** Type the following boldface code in the *CEx07cDialog* class declaration:

```
private:
    CView* m_pView;
```

Also, add the function prototypes as follows:

```
public:
    CEx07cDialog(CView* pView);
    BOOL Create();
```

> **Note** Using the *CView* class rather than the *CEx07cView* class allows the dialog class to be used with any view class.

8. **Edit Ex07cDialog.h to define the *WM_GOODBYE* message ID.** Add the following line of code at the top of Ex07cDialog.h:

```
#define WM_GOODBYE      WM_USER + 5
```

The Windows constant *WM_USER* is the first message ID available for user-defined messages. The application framework uses a few of these messages, so we'll skip over the first five messages.

> **Note** Visual C++ maintains a list of symbol definitions in your project's resource.h file, but the resource editor does not understand constants based on other constants. Don't manually add *WM_GOODBYE* to resource.h because Visual C++ might delete it.

9. **Add the modeless constructor in the file Ex07cDialog.cpp.** You could modify the existing *CEx07cDialog* constructor, but if you add a separate one, the dialog class can serve for both modal and modeless dialog boxes. Add the following code to Ex07cDialog.cpp.

```
CEx07cDialog::CEx07cDialog(CView* pView)  // modeless constructor
: m_strEdit1(_T(""))
{
    m_pView = pView;
}
```

You should also add the following line to the modal constructor generated by the MFC Application Wizard:

```
IMPLEMENT_DYNAMIC(CEx07cDialog, CDialog)
CEx07cDialog::CEx07cDialog(CWnd* pParent /*=NULL*/)
    : CDialog(CEx07cDialog::IDD, pParent)
    , m_strEdit1(_T(""))
{
    m_pView = NULL;
}
```

The C++ compiler is clever enough to distinguish between the modeless constructor *CEx07cDialog(CView*)* and the modal constructor *CEx07cDialog(CWnd*)*. If the compiler sees an argument of class *CView* or a derived *CView* class, it generates a call to the modeless constructor. If it sees an argument of class *CWnd* or another derived *CWnd* class, it generates a call to the modal constructor.

10. **Add the *Create* function in Ex07cDialog.cpp.** This derived dialog class *Create* function calls the base class function with the dialog resource ID as a parameter. Add the following lines:

```
BOOL CEx07cDialog::Create()
{
    return CDialog::Create(CEx07cDialog::IDD);
}
```

> **Note** *Create* is not a virtual function. You can choose a different name if you want to.

11. **Edit the *OnBnClickedCancel* and *OnBnClickedOk* functions in Ex07cDialog.cpp.** These virtual functions generated in an earlier step are called in response to dialog button clicks. Add the following code shown in boldface:

```
void CEx07cDialog::OnBnClickedCancel()
{
    if (m_pView != NULL) {
        // modeless case -- do not call base class OnCancel
        m_pView->PostMessage(WM_GOODBYE, IDCANCEL);
    }
    else {
        CDialog::OnCancel(); // modal case
    }
}

void CEx07cDialog::OnBnClickedOk()
{
    if (m_pView != NULL) {
        // modeless case -- do not call base class OnOK
        UpdateData(TRUE);
         m_pView->PostMessage(WM_GOODBYE, IDOK);
    }
    else {
        CDialog::OnOK(); // modal case
    }
}
```

If the dialog box is being used as a modeless dialog box, it sends the user-defined message *WM_GOODBYE* to the view. We'll worry about handling the message later.

> **Important** For a modeless dialog box, be sure to *not* call the *CDialog::OnOK* or *CDialog::OnCancel* function. This means you must override these virtual functions in your derived class; otherwise, using the Esc key, the Enter key, or a button click will result in a call to the base class functions, which call the Windows *EndDialog* function. *EndDialog* is appropriate only for modal dialog boxes. In a modeless dialog box, you must call *DestroyWindow* instead and, if necessary, you must call *UpdateData* to transfer data from the dialog controls to the class data members.

12. **Edit the Ex07cView.h header file.** You need a data member to hold the dialog box pointer:

```
private:
    CEx07cDialog* m_pDlg;
```

You also need to add the forward declaration at the beginning of Ex07cView.h:

```
class CEx07cDialog;
```

You won't have to include Ex07cDialog.h in every module that includes Ex07cView.h.

13. **Modify the *CEx07cView* constructor and destructor in the file Ex07cView.cpp.** The *CEx07cView* class has a data member, *m_pDlg*, that points to the view's *CEx07cDialog* object. The view constructor constructs the dialog box object on the heap, and the view destructor deletes it. Add the following code shown in boldface:

```
CEx07cView::CEx07cView()
{
    m_pDlg = new CEx07cDialog(this);
}

CEx07cView::~CEx07cView()
{
    delete m_pDlg; // destroys window if not already destroyed
}
```

14. **Add code to the virtual *OnDraw* function in the Ex07cView.cpp file.** Edit the *CEx07cView OnDraw* function (whose skeleton was

generated by the MFC Application Wizard) as follows to prompt the user to press the mouse button:

```
void CEx07cView::OnDraw(CDC* pDC)
{
    CEx07cDoc* pDoc = GetDocument();
    ASSERT_VALID(pDoc);

    pDC->TextOut(0, 0, "Press the left mouse button here.");
}
```

15. **Add message handlers in *CEx07cView* for *WM_LBUTTONDOWN* and *WM_RBUTTONDOWN*.** Select the *CEx07cView* class in Class View, click the Messages button in the Properties window, and add the *OnLButtonDown* and *OnRButtonDown* functions. Then edit the code in file Ex07cView.cpp as follows:

```
void CEx07cView::OnLButtonDown(UINT nFlags, CPoint point)
{
    // creates the dialog if not created already
    if (m_pDlg->GetSafeHwnd() == 0) {
        m_pDlg->Create(); // displays the dialog window
    }
}

void CEx07cView::OnRButtonDown(UINT nFlags, CPoint point)
{
    m_pDlg->DestroyWindow();
    // no problem if window was already destroyed
}
```

For most window types except main frame windows, the *DestroyWindow* function does not destroy the C++ object. We want this behavior because we'll take care of the dialog object's destruction in the view destructor.

16. **Add the dialog box header include statement to the file Ex07cView.cpp.** While you're in Ex07cView.cpp, add the following dialog box header include statement after the view header include statement:

```
#include "Ex07cView.h"
#include "Ex07cDialog.h"
```

17. **Add your own message code for the *WM_GOODBYE* message.** Because Class View does not support user-defined messages, you must write the code yourself. This task makes you appreciate the work Visual Studio does for the other messages.

In Ex07cView.cpp, add the following line between the *BEGIN_MESSAGE_MAP* and *END_MESSAGE_MAP* statements:

```
ON_MESSAGE(WM_GOODBYE, OnGoodbye)
```

Also in Ex07cView.cpp, add the message handler function itself:

```
LRESULT CEx07cView::OnGoodbye(WPARAM wParam, LPARAM lParam)
{
    // message received in response to modeless dialog OK
    //  and Cancel buttons
    TRACE("CEx07cView::OnGoodbye %x, %lx\n", wParam, lParam);
    TRACE("Dialog edit1 contents = %s\n",
          (const char*) m_pDlg->m_strEdit1);
    m_pDlg->DestroyWindow();
    return 0L;
}
```

In Ex07cView.h, add the following function prototype after the *afx_msg* prototypes for *OnLButtonDown* and *OnRButtonDown*:

```
afx_msg LRESULT OnGoodbye(WPARAM wParam, LPARAM lParam);
```

With Win32, the *wParam* and *lParam* parameters are the usual means of passing message data. In a mouse button down message, for example, the mouse *x* and *y* coordinates are packed into the *lParam* value. With the MFC library, message data is passed in more meaningful parameters. The mouse position is passed as a *CPoint* object. User-defined messages must use *wParam* and *lParam*, so you can use these two variables however you want. In this example, we've put the button ID in *wParam*.

18. **Build and test the application.** Build and run Ex07c. Press the left mouse button and then the right mouse button. (Be sure the mouse cursor is outside the dialog box when you press the right mouse button.) Press the left mouse button again and enter some data in the Edit 1 cdit control, and then click the dialog box's OK button. Does the view's *TRACE* statement correctly list the edit control's contents?

> **Note** If you use the Ex07c view and dialog classes in an MDI application, each MDI child window can have one modeless dialog box. When the user closes an MDI child window, the child's modeless dialog box will be destroyed because the view's destructor calls the dialog box destructor, which in turn destroys the dialog box.

8

Common Controls

In Chapter 7, we looked at some of the standard controls that come with Microsoft Windows, including the button control, the check box, the radio button, the static text box, the list box, and the combo box. In this chapter, we'll look at a bunch of other controls—the common controls. These are included in a DLL named COMCTL32.DLL and the latest version of the DLL is 6.0. The common controls update all of the existing controls and add a variety of advanced new controls. Microsoft Visual C++ and Microsoft Foundation Class (MFC) library have added a great deal of support for these new controls.

> **Note** The version of COMCTL32.DLL installed on a system depends on the version of Windows and the version of Microsoft Internet Explorer. Windows 95 included a version of COMCTL32.DLL, but COMCTL32.DLL was not included in Windows NT 4.0. Subsequent versions of Windows (including Windows 2000 and Windows XP) include a recent version COMCTL32.DLL. Internet Explorer 3.0 and later included a version of COMCTL32.DLL.
>
> To be safe when targeting older systems, you should redistribute a recent version of COMCTL32.DLL as part of your installation. You can upgrade COMCTL32.DLL by installing the latest version of Internet Explorer. A component package that upgrades COMCTL32.DLL might also be available. Be sure to check the Microsoft Knowledge Base article "Redistribution of COMCTL32.DLL" (Q186176) and *http://msdn.microsoft.com* for the latest news on this subject.

Standard Common Controls

The standard common controls are the progress control, the slider control, the spin control, the list control, and the tree control. Figure 8-1 shows the Windows common controls dialog box example from this chapter.

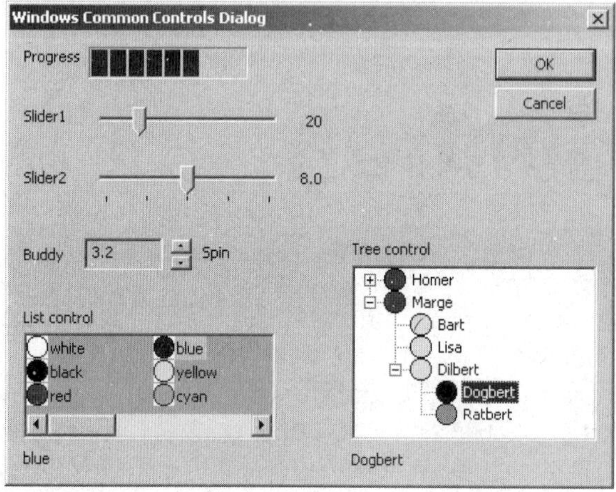

Figure 8-1 The Windows common controls dialog box.

The Progress Control

The progress control is the easiest common control to program and is represented by the MFC *CProgressCtrl* class. It is generally used only for output. To initialize the progress control, you call the *SetRange* and *SetPos* member functions in your *OnInitDialog* function, and then you call *SetPos* anytime in your message handlers. The progress control shown in Figure 8-1 has a range of 0 to 100, which is the default.

The Slider Control

The slider control (class *CSliderCtrl*), sometimes called a trackbar, allows the user to set an "analog" value. (In the Ex07a example in Chapter 7, slider controls would have been more effective than the horizontal Loyalty and Reliability scroll bars.) If you specify a large range for this control—0 to 100 or more, for example—the slider's motion will appear continuous. If you specify a small range, such as 0 to 5, the slider will move in discrete increments. You can program tick marks to match the increments. In this discrete mode, you can use a slider to set such items as the display screen resolution, lens f-stop values, and so forth. The slider does not have a default range.

The slider is easier to program than the scroll bar because you don't have to map the *WM_HSCROLL* or *WM_VSCROLL* messages in the dialog class hosting the controls. As long as you set the range, the slider will move when the user slides it or clicks in the body of the slider. You might choose to map the scroll messages anyway if you want to show the position value in another control. The *GetPos* member function returns the current position value. The top slider in Figure 8-1 operates continuously in the range 0 to 100. The bottom slider has a range of 0 to 4, and those indexes are mapped to a series of double-precision values (4.0, 5.6, 8.0, 11.0, and 16.0).

The Spin Control

The spin control (class *CSpinButtonCtrl*), sometimes called a spin button, is a tiny scroll bar that's most often used in conjunction with an edit control. The edit control, located just ahead of the spin control in the dialog box's tabbing order, is known as the spin control's *buddy*. The idea is that the user holds down the left mouse button on the spin control to raise or lower the value in the edit control. The spin speed accelerates as the user continues to hold down the mouse button.

If your program uses an integer in the buddy, you can avoid C++ programming almost entirely. Just use Visual Studio to attach an integer data member to the edit control and set the spin control's range in the *OnInitDialog* function. (You probably won't want the spin control's default range, which runs backward from a minimum of 100 to a maximum of 0.) Don't forget to set the *Auto Buddy* and *Set Buddy Integer* properties for the spin control. You can call the *SetRange* and *SetAccel* member functions in your *OnInitDialog* function to change the range and the acceleration profile.

If you want your edit control to display a noninteger, such as a time or a floating-point number, you must map the spin control's *WM_VSCROLL* (or *WM_HSCROLL*) messages and write handler code to convert the spin control's integer to the buddy's value.

The List Control

You use the list control (class *CListCtrl*) if you want a list that contains images as well as text. In Figure 8-1, shown earlier, you can see a list control with a "list view" style and small icons. The elements are arranged in a grid, and the control includes horizontal scrolling. When the user selects an item, the control sends a notification message, which you map in your dialog class. That message handler can determine which item the user selected. Items are identified by a zero-based integer index.

Both the list control and the tree control get their graphic images from a common control element called an *image list* (class *CImageList*). Your program must assemble the image list from icons or bitmaps and then pass an image list pointer to the list control. Your *OnInitDialog* function is a good place to create and attach the image list and to assign text strings. The *InsertItem* member function serves this purpose.

List control programming is straightforward if you stick with strings and icons. If you implement drag-and-drop or if you need custom owner-drawn graphics, you've got more work to do.

The Tree Control

You're already familiar with tree controls if you've used Windows Explorer or Visual Studio's Solution Explorer. The MFC *CTreeCtrl* class makes it easy to add this same functionality to your own programs. In Figure 8-1, you saw a tree control that shows a modern American combined family. The user can expand and collapse elements by clicking the + and – buttons or by double-clicking the elements. The icon next to each item is programmed to change when the user selects the item with a single click.

The list control and the tree control have some things in common: They can both use the same image list, and they share some of the same notification messages. Their methods of identifying items are different, however. The tree control uses an *HTREEITEM* handle instead of an integer index. To insert an item, you call the *InsertItem* member function, but first you must build up a *TV_INSERTSTRUCT* structure that identifies (among other things) the string, the image list index, and the handle of the parent item (which is null for top-level items).

As with list controls, infinite customization possibilities are available for the tree control. For example, you can allow the user to edit items and to insert and delete items.

The *WM_NOTIFY* Message

The original Windows controls sent their notifications in *WM_COMMAND* messages. But the standard 32-bit *wParam* and *lParam* message parameters are not sufficient for the information that a common control needs to send to its parent. Microsoft solved this "bandwidth" problem by defining a new message, *WM_NOTIFY*. With the *WM_NOTIFY* message, *wParam* is the control ID and *lParam* is a pointer to an *NMHDR* structure, which is managed by the control. This C structure is defined by the following code:

```
typedef struct tagNMHDR {
    HWND hwndFrom; // handle to control sending the message
    UINT idFrom;   // ID of control sending the message
    UINT code;     // control-specific notification code
} NMHDR;
```

However, many controls send *WM_NOTIFY* messages with pointers to structures larger than *NMHDR*. Those structures contain the three members above plus appended control-specific members. Many tree control notifications, for example, pass a pointer to an *NM_TREEVIEW*ture that contains *TV_ITEM* structures, a drag point, and so forth. When Visual Studio maps a *WM_NOTIFY* message, it generates a pointer to the appropriate structure.

The Ex08a Example: Standard Common Controls

To get an idea of how these common controls work, we'll put them in a modal dialog box. The steps are as follows.

1. **Run the MFC Application Wizard to generate a project named Ex08a.** Choose New Project from Visual Studio's File menu. In the New Project dialog box, select the MFC Application template, type the name **Ex08a**, and click OK. In the MFC Application Wizard, accept all the defaults but two: On the Application Type page, select Single Document, and on the Advanced Features page, deselect Printing And Print Preview. When you're finished, click Finish.

2. **Create a new dialog resource with ID IDD_DIALOG1.** Choose Add Resource from the Project menu and add a new dialog resource. Using the Toolbox, add controls to the dialog box. The following is a list of the control types, their IDs, and their tab order. After you set the *Caption* properties to the appropriate text, the dialog box should have the following controls and tab order:

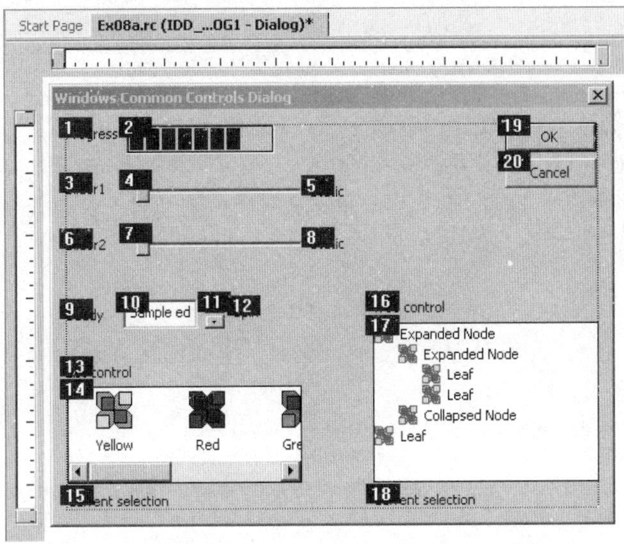

Don't worry about the other properties now—you'll set those in the following steps. (Some controls might look different than they do in Figure 8-1 until you set their properties.)

Control Type	ID	Tab Order
Static Text	*IDC_STATIC*	1
Progress	*IDC_PROGRESS1*	2
Static Text	*IDC_STATIC*	3
Slider	*IDC_SLIDER1*	4
Static Text	*IDC_STATIC_SLIDER1*	5
Static Text	*IDC_STATIC*	6
Slider	*IDC_SLIDER2*	7
Static Text	*IDC_STATIC_SLIDER2*	8
Static Text	*IDC_STATIC*	9
Edit	*IDC_BUDDY_SPIN1*	10
Spin	*IDC_SPIN1*	11
Static Text	*IDC_STATIC*	12
Static Text	*IDC_STATIC*	13
List control	*IDC_LISTVIEW1*	14
Static Text	*IDC_STATIC_LISTVIEW1*	15
Static Text	*IDC_STATIC*	16
Tree control	*IDC_TREEVIEW1*	17
Static Text	*IDC_STATIC_TREEVIEW1*	18
Button	*IDOK*	19
Button	*IDCANCEL*	20

3. **Use the MFC Class Wizard to create a new class, CEx08aDialog, derived from *CDialog*.** Choose Add Class from Project menu to display the MFC Class Wizard. Select *CDialog* as the base class and *IDD_DIALOG1* as the name of the Dialog ID, as shown here:

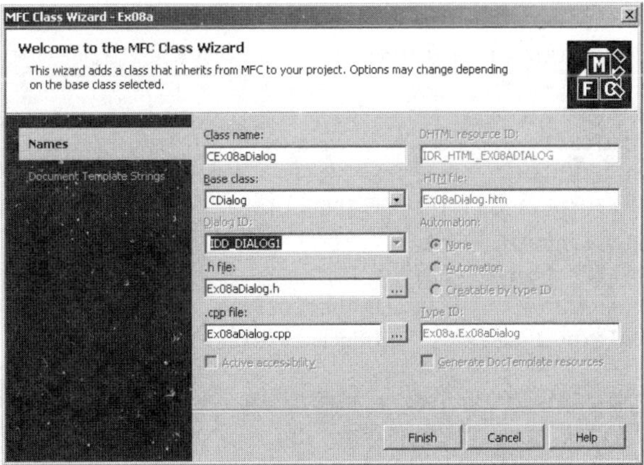

4. **Override the *OnInitDialog* function and handle the *WM_HSCROLL* and the *WM_VSCROLL* messages.** Select the CEx08aDialog class in Class View. Click the Overrides button at the top of the Properties window and add the *OnInitDialog* function. Click the Messages button at the top of the Properties window and add the *OnHScroll* and *OnVScroll* functions for the *WM_HSCROLL* and *WM_VSCROLL* messages.

5. **Program the progress control.** Visual Studio won't generate a data member for this control, so you must do it yourself. Add a public integer data member named *m_nProgress* in the *CEx08aDialog* class header, and set it to 0 in the constructor. Also, add the following code in the *OnInitDialog* member function:

```
// Progress control
CProgressCtrl* pProg =
    (CProgressCtrl*) GetDlgItem(IDC_PROGRESS1);
pProg->SetRange(0, 100);
pProg->SetPos(m_nProgress);
```

6. **Program the "continuous" slider control.** Add a public integer data member named *m_nSlider1* to the *CEx08aDialog* header, and set it to 0 in the constructor. Then add the following code in the *OnInitDialog* member function to set the slider's range, initialize its

position from the data member, and set the neighboring static control to the slider's current value:

```
// Slider control
CString strText1;
CSliderCtrl* pSlide1 =
    (CSliderCtrl*) GetDlgItem(IDC_SLIDER1);
pSlide1->SetRange(0, 100);
pSlide1->SetPos(m_nSlider1);
strText1.Format("%d", pSlide1->GetPos());
SetDlgItemText(IDC_STATIC_SLIDER1, strText1);
```

To keep the static control updated, you must map the *WM_HSCROLL* message that the slider sends to the dialog box. Add the following boldface code to the *OnHScroll* handler, replacing the existing code:

```
void CEx08aDialog::OnHScroll(UINT nSBCode, UINT nPos,
                             CScrollBar* pScrollBar)
{
    CSliderCtrl* pSlide = (CSliderCtrl*) pScrollBar;
    CString strText;
    strText.Format("%d", pSlide->GetPos());
    SetDlgItemText(IDC_STATIC_SLIDER1, strText);
}
```

Finally, you need to update the slider's *m_nSlider1* data member when the user clicks OK. Your natural instinct might be to put this code in the *OnOK* button handler. You would have a problem, however, if a data exchange validation error occurred that involved any other control in the dialog box. Your handler would set *m_nSlider1* even if the user chose to cancel the dialog box. To avoid this problem, add your code in the *DoDataExchange* function as shown below. If you do your own validation and detect a problem, call the *CDataExchange::Fail* function, which alerts the user with a message box.

```
void CEx08aDialog::DoDataExchange(CDataExchange* pDX)
{
    if (pDX->m_bSaveAndValidate) {
        TRACE("updating slider data members\n");
        CSliderCtrl* pSlide1 =
            (CSliderCtrl*) GetDlgItem(IDC_SLIDER1);
        m_nSlider1 = pSlide1->GetPos();
    }

    CDialog::DoDataExchange(pDX);
}
```

7. **Program the "discrete" slider control.** Add a public integer data member named *m_nSlider2* to the *CEx08aDialog* header, and set it to 0 in the constructor. This data member is a zero-based index into the *dValue*, the array of numbers (4.0, 5.6, 8.0, 11.0, and 16.0) that the slider can represent. Define *dValue* as a public static double array member variable in Ex08aDialog.h:

```
static double dValue[5];
```

Initialize *dValue* at the top of Ex08aDialog.cpp using the following line:

```
double CEx08aDialog::dValue[5] = {4.0, 5.6, 8.0, 11.0, 16.0};
```

Next, add code in the *OnInitDialog* member function to set the slider's range and initial position.

```
CString strText2;
CSliderCtrl* pSlide2 =
    (CSliderCtrl*) GetDlgItem(IDC_SLIDER2);
pSlide2->SetRange(0, 4);
pSlide2->SetPos(m_nSlider2);
strText2.Format("%3.1f", dValue[pSlide2->GetPos()]);
SetDlgItemText(IDC_STATIC_SLIDER2, strText2);
```

If you had only one slider, the *WM_HSCROLL* handler in step 5 would work. But because you have two sliders that send *WM_HSCROLL* messages, the handler must differentiate between them. Here's the new code:

```
void CEx08aDialog::OnHScroll(UINT nSBCode, UINT nPos,
                             CScrollBar* pScrollBar)
{
    CSliderCtrl* pSlide = (CSliderCtrl*) pScrollBar;
    CString strText;

    // Two sliders are sending
    //  HSCROLL messages (different processing)
    switch(pScrollBar->GetDlgCtrlID()) {
    case IDC_SLIDER1:
        strText.Format("%d", pSlide->GetPos());
        SetDlgItemText(IDC_STATIC_SLIDER1, strText);
        break;
    case IDC_SLIDER2:
        strText.Format("%3.1f", dValue[pSlide->GetPos()]);
        SetDlgItemText(IDC_STATIC_SLIDER2, strText);
        break;
    }
}
```

Slider2 needs tick marks, so display the dialog editor and set the control's *Tick Marks* and *Auto Ticks* properties to *True* in the Properties window. With *Auto Ticks* set to *True*, the slider will place a tick at every increment. If you don't see the tick marks after setting these properties, you might need to increase the height of the control.

The same data exchange considerations that applied to the previous slider apply to this slider. Add the following code in the dialog class *DoDataExchange* member function inside the block for the *if* statement you added in the previous step:

```
CSliderCtrl* pSlide2 =
    (CSliderCtrl*) GetDlgItem(IDC_SLIDER2);
m_nSlider2 = pSlide2->GetPos();
```

Display the dialog editor and set the *Point* property of both sliders to *Bottom/Right*. Select the *IDC_STATIC_SLIDER1* and *IDC_STATIC_SLIDER2* static controls and set the *Align Text* property to *Right*.

8. **Program the spin button control.** The spin control depends on its buddy edit control, which is located immediately before it in the tab order. Use the Add Member Variable Wizard to add a double-precision data member named *m_dSpin* for the *IDC_BUDDY_SPIN1* edit control. We're using a *double* instead of an *int* because the *int* would require almost no programming, and that would be too easy. We want the edit control range to be 0.0 to 10.0, but the spin control itself needs an integer range. You can start the Add Member Variable Wizard by selecting the *CEx08aDialog* class in Class View and then choosing Add Variable from the Project menu. The settings for the wizard are shown here:

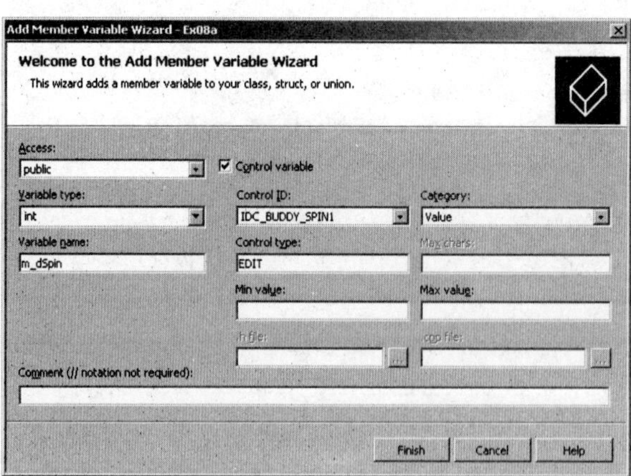

Add the following code to *OnInitDialog* to set the spin control range from 0 to 100 and set its initial value to *m_dSpin * 10.0*:

```
// Spin control
CSpinButtonCtrl* pSpin =
    (CSpinButtonCtrl*) GetDlgItem(IDC_SPIN1);
pSpin->SetRange(0, 100);
pSpin->SetPos((int) (m_dSpin * 10.0));
```

To display the current value in the buddy edit control, you need to handle the *WM_VSCROLL* message that the spin control sends to the dialog box. Add the following boldfaced code to *OnVScroll*:

```
void CEx08aDialog::OnVScroll(UINT nSBCode, UINT nPos,
                              CScrollBar* pScrollBar)
{
    if (nSBCode == SB_ENDSCROLL) {
        return; // Reject spurious messages
    }
    // Process scroll messages from IDC_SPIN1 only
    if (pScrollBar->GetDlgCtrlID() == IDC_SPIN1) {
        CString strValue;
        strValue.Format("%3.1f", (double) nPos / 10.0);
        ((CSpinButtonCtrl*) pScrollBar)->GetBuddy()
                                        ->SetWindowText(strValue);
    }

    CDialog::OnVScroll(nSBCode, nPos, pScrollBar);
}
```

There's no need to add code in *OnOK* or in *DoDataExchange* because the Dialog Data Exchange (DDX) code processes the contents of the edit control.

Display the dialog editor and set the *Auto Buddy* property for the spin control to *True*. Set the *Read Only* property for the buddy edit control to *True*.

9. **Set up an image list.** Both the list control and the tree control need an image list, and the image list needs icons. The companion CD contains icons in the Ex08a\res folder. These icons are circles with black outlines and different-colored interiors. Use fancier icons if you have them.

   To import these icons into the Ex08a project, first copy the .ico files to your Ex08a\res folder and then choose Add Resource from the Project menu. In the Add Resource dialog box, click Import. In the Import dialog box, navigate to the icon files. Set the Files Of

Type drop-down list to Icon Files. Select Icon0.ico to Icon7.ico and click Open. The icons will be opened in the image editor and added to the Icon folder in Resource View. Using the Properties window, set the *ID* property for each icon as shown here, and then close the icons in the icon editor.

Icon File	ID
Icon0.ico	*IDI_WHITE*
Icon1.ico	*IDI_BLACK*
Icon2.ico	*IDI_RED*
Icon3.ico	*IDI_BLUE*
Icon4.ico	*IDI_YELLOW*
Icon5.ico	*IDI_CYAN*
Icon6.ico	*IDI_PURPLE*
Icon7.ico	*IDI_GREEN*

When you're finished, the Icon folder in Resource View will look like the following:

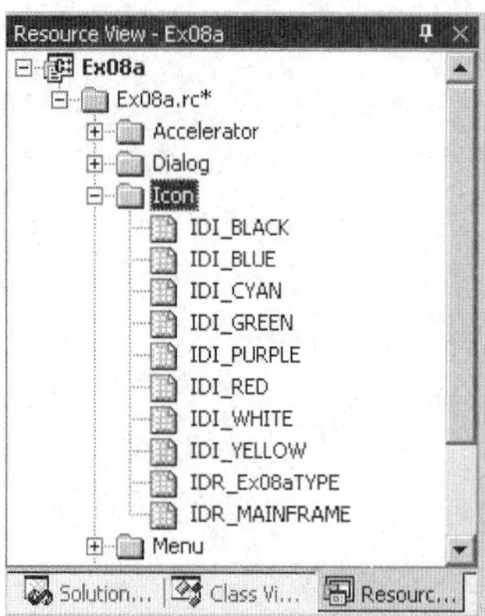

About Icons

You probably know that a bitmap is an array of bits that represent pixels on the display. (Bitmaps were discussed in Chapter 6.) In Windows, an icon is a "bundle" of bitmaps. First of all, an icon has different bitmaps for different sizes. Typically, small icons are 16 by 16 pixels and large icons are 32 by 32 pixels. Within each size are two separate bitmaps: one 4-bit-per-pixel bitmap for the color image and one monochrome (1-bit-per-pixel) bitmap for the "mask." If a mask bit is 0, the corresponding image pixel represents an opaque color. If the mask bit is 1, an image color of black (0) means that the pixel is transparent and an image color of white (0xF) means that the background color is inverted at the pixel location.

Small icons were new with Windows 95. They're used on the taskbar, in Windows Explorer, and in your list and tree controls, if you want them there. If an icon doesn't have a 16-by-16-pixel bitmap, Windows manufactures a small icon out of the 32-by-32-pixel bitmap, but it won't be as neat as one you draw yourself. The image editor in Visual Studio lets you create and edit icons. The following shows the image editor and the Colors palette.

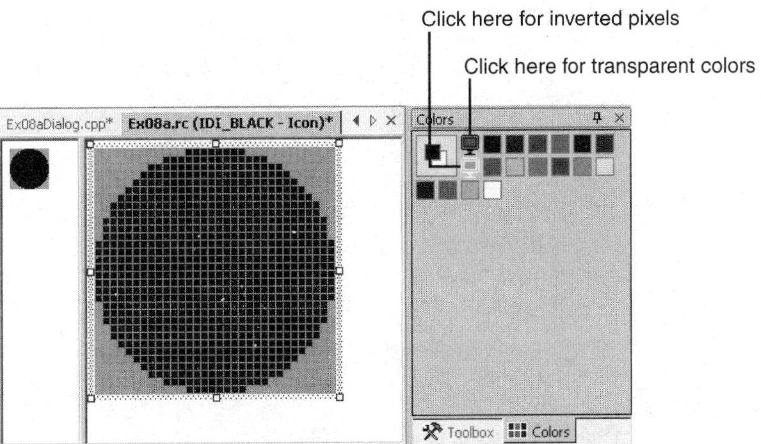

The top square in the upper left portion of the Colors palette shows you the main color for brushes, shape interiors, and so on, and the square underneath it shows the border color for shape outlines. You select a main color by left-clicking on a color, and you select a border color by right-clicking on a color. Now look at the two "monitors" to the right of the upper left square of the Colors palette. You click on the upper monitor to paint transparent pixels, which are drawn in dark cyan. You click on the lower monitor to paint inverted pixels, which are drawn in red.

Next, add a public *CImageList* data member named *m_imageList* in the *CEx08aDialog* class header, and then add the following code to *OnInitDialog*:

```
// Icons
HICON hIcon[8];
int n;
m_imageList.Create(16, 16, 0, 8, 8); // 32, 32 for large icons
hIcon[0] = AfxGetApp()->LoadIcon(IDI_WHITE);
hIcon[1] = AfxGetApp()->LoadIcon(IDI_BLACK);
hIcon[2] = AfxGetApp()->LoadIcon(IDI_RED);
hIcon[3] = AfxGetApp()->LoadIcon(IDI_BLUE);
hIcon[4] = AfxGetApp()->LoadIcon(IDI_YELLOW);
hIcon[5] = AfxGetApp()->LoadIcon(IDI_CYAN);
hIcon[6] = AfxGetApp()->LoadIcon(IDI_PURPLE);
hIcon[7] = AfxGetApp()->LoadIcon(IDI_GREEN);
for (n = 0; n < 8; n++) {
    m_imageList.Add(hIcon[n]);
}
```

10. **Program the list control.** In the dialog editor, set the following properties for the list control.

List Control Property	Value
Alignment	*Top*
Always Show Selection	*True*
Single Selection	*True*
View	*List*

Then add the following code to *OnInitDialog*:

```
// List control
static char* color[] = {"white", "black", "red",
                        "blue", "yellow", "cyan",
                        "purple", "green"};
CListCtrl* pList =
    (CListCtrl*) GetDlgItem(IDC_LISTVIEW1);
pList->SetImageList(&m_imageList, LVSIL_SMALL);
for (n = 0; n < 8; n++) {
    pList->InsertItem(n, color[n], n);
}
pList->SetBkColor(RGB(0, 255, 255)); // UGLY!
pList->SetTextBkColor(RGB(0, 255, 255));
```

As the last two lines illustrate, you don't use the *WM_CTLCOLOR* message with common controls; you just call a function to set the background color. As you'll see when you run the program, however, the icons' inverse-color pixels look shabby.

If you use the list control's *LVN_ITEMCHANGED* notification message, you'll be able to track the user's selection of items. In Class View, select the *CEx08aDialog* class. In the Properties window, click the Events button, expand the *IDC_LISTVIEW1* item, select the *LVN_ITEMCHANGED* event, and then add the *OnLvnItemchangedListview1* handler. Add the following code to the *OnLvnItemchangedListview1* handler to display the selected item's text in a static control:

```
void CEx08aDialog::OnLvnItemchangedListview1(NMHDR* pNMHDR,
                                             LRESULT* pResult)
{
    LPNMLISTVIEW pNMLV = reinterpret_cast<LPNMLISTVIEW>(pNMHDR);
    CListCtrl* pList =
        (CListCtrl*) GetDlgItem(IDC_LISTVIEW1);
    int nSelected = pNMLV->iItem;
    if (nSelected >= 0) {
        CString strItem = pList->GetItemText(nSelected, 0);
         SetDlgItemText(IDC_STATIC_LISTVIEW1, strItem);
    }
    *pResult = 0;
}
```

The *NM_LISTVIEW* structure has a data member called *iItem* that contains the index of the selected item.

11. **Program the tree control.** In the dialog editor, set the following properties for the tree control.

Tree Control Property	Value
Has Buttons	True
Has Lines	True
Lines At Root	True
Scroll	*True*

Next, add the following lines to *OnInitDialog*:

```
// Tree control
CTreeCtrl* pTree = (CTreeCtrl*) GetDlgItem(IDC_TREEVIEW1);
pTree->SetImageList(&m_imageList, TVSIL_NORMAL);
// tree structure common values
TV_INSERTSTRUCT tvinsert;
tvinsert.hParent = NULL;
tvinsert.hInsertAfter = TVI_LAST;
tvinsert.item.mask = TVIF_IMAGE | TVIF_SELECTEDIMAGE |
                     TVIF_TEXT;
tvinsert.item.hItem = NULL;
```

(continued)

```
tvinsert.item.state = 0;
tvinsert.item.stateMask = 0;
tvinsert.item.cchTextMax = 6;
tvinsert.item.iSelectedImage = 1;
tvinsert.item.cChildren = 0;
tvinsert.item.lParam = 0;
// top level
tvinsert.item.pszText = "Homer";
tvinsert.item.iImage = 2;
HTREEITEM hDad = pTree->InsertItem(&tvinsert);
tvinsert.item.pszText = "Marge";
HTREEITEM hMom = pTree->InsertItem(&tvinsert);
// second level
tvinsert.hParent = hDad;
tvinsert.item.pszText = "Bart";
tvinsert.item.iImage = 3;
pTree->InsertItem(&tvinsert);
tvinsert.item.pszText = "Lisa";
pTree->InsertItem(&tvinsert);
// second level
tvinsert.hParent = hMom;
tvinsert.item.pszText = "Bart";
tvinsert.item.iImage = 4;
pTree->InsertItem(&tvinsert);
tvinsert.item.pszText = "Lisa";
pTree->InsertItem(&tvinsert);
tvinsert.item.pszText = "Dilbert";
HTREEITEM hOther = pTree->InsertItem(&tvinsert);
// third level
tvinsert.hParent = hOther;
tvinsert.item.pszText = "Dogbert";
tvinsert.item.iImage = 7;
pTree->InsertItem(&tvinsert);
tvinsert.item.pszText = "Ratbert";
pTree->InsertItem(&tvinsert);
```

As you can see, this code sets *TV_INSERTSTRUCT* text and image indexes and calls *InsertItem* to add nodes to the tree.

Finally, add the *TVN_SELCHANGED* notification for the tree control. In Class View, select the *CEx08aDialog* class. In the Properties window, click the Events button, expand the *IDC_TREEVIEW1* item, select the *TVN_SELCHANGED* event, and then add the *OnTvnSelchangedTreeview1* handler. Add the following boldface code to display the selected text in a static control:

```
void CEx08aDialog::OnTvnSelchangedTreeview1 (NMHDR* pNMHDR,
                                             LRESULT* pResult)
{
```

```
    LPNMTREEVIEW pNMTreeView = reinterpret_cast<LPNMTREEVIEW>(pNMHDR;
    CTreeCtrl* pTree = (CTreeCtrl*) GetDlgItem(IDC_TREEVIEW1);
    HTREEITEM hSelected = pNMTreeView->itemNew.hItem;
    if (hSelected != NULL) {
        char text[31];
        TV_ITEM item;
        item.mask = TVIF_HANDLE | TVIF_TEXT;
        item.hItem = hSelected;
        item.pszText = text;
        item.cchTextMax = 30;
        VERIFY(pTree->GetItem(&item));
        SetDlgItemText(IDC_STATIC_TREEVIEW1, text);
    }
    *pResult = 0;
}
```

The *NM_TREEVIEW* structure has a data member called *itemNew* that contains information about the selected node; *itemNew.hItem* is the handle of that node. The *GetItem* function retrieves the node's data, storing the text using a pointer supplied in the *TV_ITEM* structure. The *mask* variable tells Windows that the *hItem* handle is valid going in and that text output is desired.

12. **Add code to the virtual *OnDraw* function in the file Ex08aView.cpp.**
Add the following boldface code:

```
void CEx08aView::OnDraw(CDC* pDC)
{
    CEx08aDoc* pDoc = GetDocument();
    ASSERT_VALID(pDoc);

    pDC->TextOut(0, 0, "Press the left mouse button here.");
}
```

13. **Add the *OnLButtonDown* member function.** Select the *CEx08aView* class in Class View. In the Properties window, click the Messages button, select the *WM_LBUTTONDOWN* message, and add the *OnLButtonDown* function. Add the following boldface code:

```
void CEx08aView::OnLButtonDown(UINT nFlags, CPoint point)
{
    CEx08aDialog dlg;

    dlg.m_nSlider1 = 20;
    dlg.m_nSlider2 = 2; // index for 8.0
    dlg.m_nProgress = 70; // write-only
    dlg.m_dSpin = 3.2;
```

(continued)

```
        dlg.DoModal();

        CView::OnLButtonDown(nFlags, point);
    }
```

In Ex08aView.cpp, add a statement to include Ex08aDialog.h:

```
#include "Ex08aDialog.h"
```

14. **Compile and run the program.** Experiment with the controls to see how they work. We haven't added code to make the progress indicator functional; we'll cover that in Chapter 13.

Advanced Common Controls

In addition to the standard common controls, Windows includes a set of advanced common controls, including the date and time picker, the month calendar, the internet protocol address control, and the extended combo box control. Example Ex08b uses each of these common controls. Figure 8-2 shows the dialog box from that example. You can refer back to that example as you read the descriptions that follow.

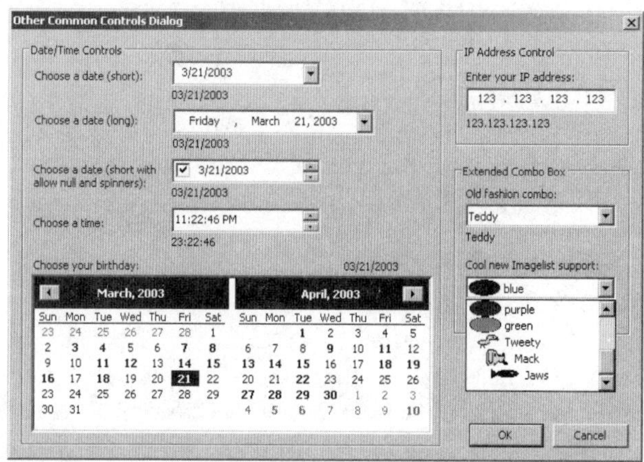

Figure 8-2 Advanced common controls in a dialog box.

The Date and Time Picker

A common field on a dialog box is a place for the user to enter a date and time. Before there was a date and time picker, developers had to either use a third-party control or subclass an MFC edit control to do significant data validation to ensure that the entered date was valid. The date and time picker control prompts the user for a date or time while offering the developer a wide variety of styles and options. For example, dates can be displayed in short formats (8/14/68) or long formats (August 14, 1968). A time mode lets the user enter a time using a familiar hours/minutes/seconds AM/PM format.

The control also lets you decide if you want the user to select the date using in-place editing, a pull-down calendar, or a spin button. Several selection options are available, including single and multiple select (for a range of dates) and the ability to turn on and off the "circling" in red ink of the current date. The control even has a mode that lets the user select "no date" via a check box. In Figure 8-2, the first four controls on the left illustrate the variety of configurations available with the date and time picker control.

The MFC class *CDateTimeCtrl* provides the MFC interface to the date and time picker common control. This class provides a variety of notifications that enhance the programmability of the control. *CDateTimeCtrl* provides member functions for dealing with either *CTime* or *COleDateTime* time structures.

You set the date and time in a *CDateTimeCtrl* using the *SetTime* member function. You can retrieve the date and time using the *GetTime* function. You can create custom formats using the *SetFormat* member function and change a variety of other configurations using the *CDateTimeCtrl* interface.

CTime vs. *COleDateTime*

Most "longtime" MFC developers are accustomed to using the *CTime* class. However, because *CTime's* valid dates are limited to dates between January 1, 1970, and January 18, 2038, many developers need an alternative. One popular alternative is *COleDateTime*, which is provided for OLE automation support and handles dates from 1 January 100 through 31 December 9999. Both classes have pros and cons. For example, *CTime* handles all the issues of daylight saving time, while *COleDateTime* does not.

Many developers choose *COleDateTime* because of its much larger range. Any application that uses *CTime* will need to be reworked in approximately 40 years because the maximum value is the year 2038. The class you decide to use must depend on your particular needs and the potential longevity of your application.

The Month Calendar

The large display at the bottom left of Figure 8-2 is a month calendar. Like the date and time picker control, the month calendar control lets the user select a date. However, the month calendar control can also be used to implement a small personal information manager in your applications. You can show as many months as you have room for—from one month to a year's worth of months, if you want. Ex08b uses the month calendar control to show only two months.

The month calendar control supports single or multiple selection and allows you to display a variety of options, such as numbered months and a circled "today's date." Notifications for the control let the developer specify which dates are in boldface. It is entirely up to the developer to decide what boldface dates might represent. For example, you could use the bold feature to indicate holidays, appointments, or unusable dates. The MFC class *CMonthCalCtrl* implements this control.

To initialize the *CMonthCalCtrl* class, you can call the *SetToday* member function. *CMonthCalCtrl* provides members that deal with both *CTime* and *COleDateTime*, including *SetToday*.

The Internet Protocol Address Control

If you write an application that uses any form of Internet or TCP/IP functionality, you might need to prompt the user for an Internet Protocol (IP) address. The common controls include an IP address edit control, as shown in the top right of Figure 8-2. In addition to letting the user enter a 4-byte IP address, this control performs an automatic validation of the entered IP address. *CIPAddressCtrl* provides MFC support for the IP address control.

An IP address consists of four "fields," as shown in Figure 8-3. The fields are numbered from left to right.

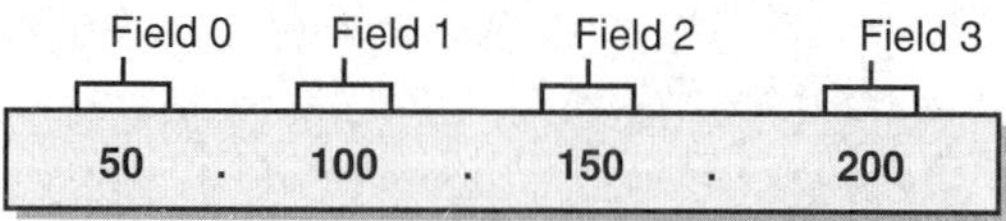

Figure 8-3 The fields of an IP address control.

To initialize an IP address control, you call the *SetAddress* member function in your *OnInitDialog* function. *SetAddress* takes a *DWORD*, with each byte in the *DWORD* representing one of the fields. In your message handlers, you can call the *GetAddress* member function to retrieve a *DWORD* or a series of *BYTES* to retrieve the various values of the four IP address fields.

The Extended Combo Box

The "old-fashioned" combo box was developed in the early days of Windows. Its inflexible design has been the source of much developer confusion. With the common controls, Microsoft has released a much more flexible version of the combo box called the extended combo box.

The extended combo box gives the developer much easier access to and better control over the edit control portion of the combo box. In addition, the extended combo box lets you attach an image list to the items in the combo box. You can display graphics in the extended combo box easily, especially compared with the old days of using owner-drawn combo boxes. Each item in the extended combo box can be associated with three images: a selected image, an unselected image, and an overlay image. You can use these images to provide a variety of graphical displays in the combo box, as we'll see shortly in the Ex08b sample. The two combo boxes on the right in Figure 8-2 are both extended combo boxes. The MFC *CComboBoxEx* class provides comprehensive extended combo box support.

Like the list control introduced earlier in this chapter, *CComboBoxEx* can be attached to a *CImageList* that will automatically display graphics next to the text in the extended combo box. If you're familiar with *CComboBox*, *CComboBoxEx* might cause some confusion: Instead of containing strings, the extended combo box contains items of type *COMBOBOXEXITEM*, a structure that consists of the following fields:

- *UINT mask* A set of bit flags that specify which operations are to be performed using the structure. For example, set the *CBEIF_IMAGE* flag if the image field is to be set or retrieved in an operation.
- *INT_PTR iItem* The extended combo box item number. Like the older style of combo box, the extended combo box uses zero-based indexing.
- *LPSTR pszText* The text of the item.
- *int cchTextMax* The length of the buffer available in *pszText*.
- *int iImage* A zero-based index into an associated image list.
- *int iSelectedImage* An index of the image in the image list to be used to represent the "selected" state.
- *int iOverlay* An index of the image in the image list to be used to overlay the current image.
- *int iIndent* The number of 10-pixel indentation spaces.
- *LPARAM lParam* A 32-bit parameter for the item.

You'll see how to use this structure in the upcoming Ex08b example.

The Ex08b Example: Advanced Common Controls

In this example, we'll build a dialog box that demonstrates how to create and program each type of advanced common control. The steps required to create the dialog box are as follows:

1. **Run the MFC Application Wizard to generate a project named Ex08b.** Choose New Project from the Visual Studio File menu. In the New Project dialog box, select the MFC Application template, type the name **Ex08b**, and click OK. In the MFC Application Wizard, accept all the defaults but one: On the Application Type page, select Single Document.

2. **Create a new dialog resource with ID *IDD_DIALOG1*.** Choose Add Resource from the Project menu and add a new dialog resource. Using the Toolbox, add controls to the dialog box. The following is a list of the control types, their *IDs*, and their tab order. After you set the *Caption* properties for the static text controls to the appropriate text, the dialog box should have the following controls and tab order:

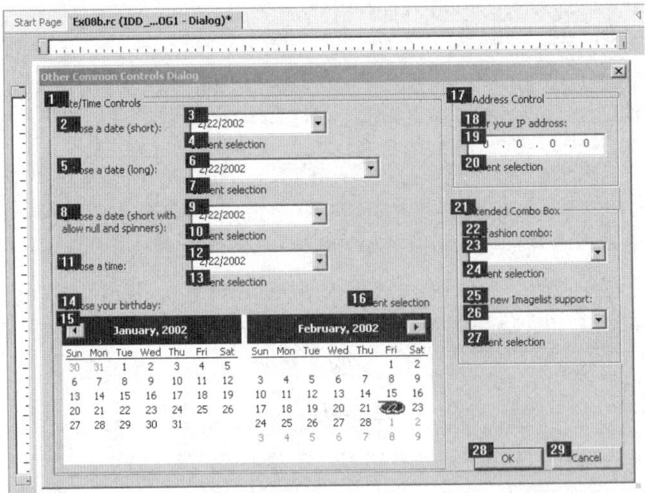

Until we set some properties, your dialog box will not look exactly like the one shown earlier in Figure 8-2.

Control Type	ID	Tab Order
Group Box	*IDC_STATIC*	1
Static	*IDC_STATIC*	2
Date Time Picker	*IDC_DATETIMEPICKER1*	3
Static	*IDC_STATIC1*	4
Static	*IDC_STATIC*	5
Date Time Picker	*IDC_DATETIMEPICKER2*	6
Static	*IDC_STATIC2*	7
Static	*IDC_STATIC*	8
Date Time Picker	*IDC_DATETIMEPICKER3*	9
Static	*IDC_STATIC3*	10
Static	*IDC_STATIC*	11
Date Time Picker	*IDC_DATETIMEPICKER4*	12
Static	*IDC_STATIC4*	13
Static	*IDC_STATIC*	14
Month Calendar	*IDC_MONTHCALENDAR1*	15
Static	*IDC_STATIC5*	16
Group Box	*IDC_STATIC*	17
Static	*IDC_STATIC*	18
IP Address	*IDC_IPADDRESS1*	19
Static	*IDC_STATIC6*	20
Group Box	*IDC_STATIC*	21
Static	*IDC_STATIC*	22
Extended Combo Box	*IDC_COMBOBOXEX1*	23
Static	*IDC_STATIC7*	24
Static	*IDC_STATIC*	25
Extended Combo Box	*IDC_COMBOBOXEX2*	26
Static	*IDC_STATIC8*	27
Button	*IDOK*	28
Button	*IDCANCEL*	29

3. **Use the MFC Class Wizard to create a new class, *CEx08bDialog*, that is derived from *CDialog*.** Choose Add Class from the Project menu to start the MFC Class Wizard. Select *CDialog* as the base class and *IDD_DIALOG1* as the name of the Dialog ID, as shown here:

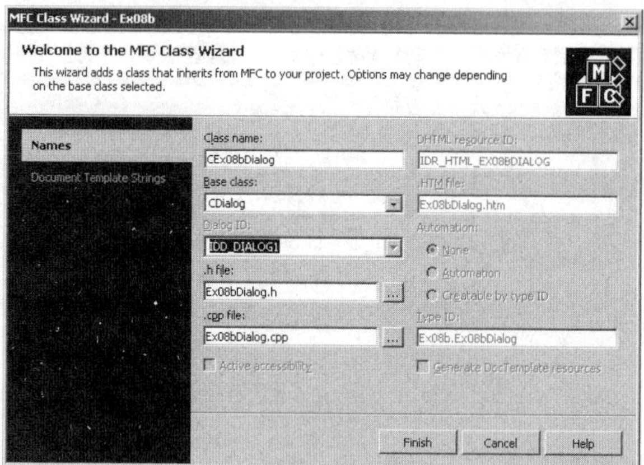

Override the *OnInitDialog* function. Select the *CEx08bDialog* class in Class View. Click the Overrides button at the top of the Properties window and add the *OnInitDialog* function.

4. **Set the properties for the dialog box's controls.** To demonstrate the full range of controls, we'll need to set a variety of properties for each of the common controls in this example. Here's a brief overview of each property you'll need to set:

   - **The Short Date and Time Picker** For the first date and time picker control (*IDC_DATETIMEPICKER1*), be sure the *Format* property is set to *Short Date* (the default).
   - **The Long Date and Time Picker** For the second date and time picker control (*IDC_DATETIMEPICKER2*), set the *Format* property to *Long Date.*
   - **The Short and NULL Date and Time Picker** For the third date and time picker control (*IDC_DATETIMEPICKER3*), be sure the *Format* property is set to *Short Date* and set the *Allow Edit*, *Show None*, and *Use Spin Control* properties to *True.*
   - **The Time Picker** The fourth date and time picker control (*IDC_DATETIMEPICKER4*) is configured to let the user select a time. Set the *Format* property to *Time*, and set the *Use Spin Control* property to *True.*

- **The Month Calendar** To configure the month calendar, you must set a few properties. First set the *Day States* property to *True*. With the default properties, the month calendar does not look like a control in the dialog box. No borders are drawn. To make the control fit in with the other controls in the dialog box, set the *Client Edge* and *Static Edge* properties to *True*.
- **The IP Address** This control (*IDC_IPADDRESS1*) does not require any special properties.
- **Extended Combo Boxes** These controls (*IDC_COMBOBOXEX1* and *IDC_COMBOBOXEX2*) do not require any special properties.

5. **Add the variables to *CEx08bDialog*.** Use the Add Member Variable Wizard to add member variables to *CEx08bDialog*. To start the wizard, select the *CEx08bDialog* class in Class View and then choose Add Variable from the Project menu. Enter the following member variables for each control listed.

Control ID	Category	Variable Type	Variable Name
IDC_DATETIMEPICKER1	Control	*CDateTimeCtrl*	*m_MonthCal1*
IDC_DATETIMEPICKER2	Control	*CDateTimeCtrl*	*m_MonthCal2*
IDC_DATETIMEPICKER3	Control	*CDateTimeCtrl*	*m_MonthCal3*
IDC_DATETIMEPICKER4	Control	*CDateTimeCtrl*	*m_MonthCal4*
IDC_IPADDRESS1	Control	*CIPAddressCtrl*	*m_ptrIPCtrl*
IDC_MONTHCALENDAR1	Control	*CMonthCalCtrl*	*m_MonthCal5*
IDC_STATIC1	Value	*CString*	*m_strDate1*
IDC_STATIC2	Value	*CString*	*m_strDate2*
IDC_STATIC3	Value	*CString*	*m_strDate3*
IDC_STATIC4	Value	*CString*	*m_strDate4*
IDC_STATIC5	Value	*CString*	*m_strDate5*
IDC_STATIC6	Value	*CString*	*m_strIPValue*
IDC_STATIC7	Value	*CString*	*m_strComboEx1*
IDC_STATIC8	Value	*CString*	*m_strComboEx2*

6. **Program the short date and time picker.** In this example, we don't mind if the first date and time picker starts with the current date, so we don't have any *OnInitDialog* handling for this control. (If we did want to change the date, we could make a call to *SetTime* for the control in *OnInitDialog*.) At run time, when the user selects a new date in the first date and time picker, the companion static control will be automatically updated. To achieve this, we need to add a handler for the

DTN_DATETIMECHANGE message. Select the *CEx08bDialog* class in Class View, click the Events button in the Properties window, expand the *IDC_DATETIMEPICKER1* item, select the *DTN_DATETIMECHANGE* message, and add the *OnDtnDatetimechangeDatetimepicker1* handler. Repeat this step for each of the other three *IDC_DATETIMEPICKER* IDs. Next, add the following boldface code to the handler for *Datetimepicker1* created by Visual Studio:

```
void CEx08bDialog::OnDtnDatetimechangeDatetimepicker1 (NMHDR* pNMHDR,
    LRESULT* pResult)
{
    LPNMDATETIMECHANGE pDTChange =
        reinterpret_cast<LPNMDATETIMECHANGE>(pNMHDR);
    CTime ct;
    m_MonthCal1.GetTime(ct);
    m_strDate1.Format(_T("%02d/%02d/%2d"),
                      ct.GetMonth(),ct.GetDay(),ct.GetYear());
    UpdateData(FALSE);
    *pResult = 0;
}
```

This code uses the *m_MonthCal1* data member that maps to the first date and time picker to retrieve the time into the *CTime* object variable *ct*. It then calls the *CString::Format* member function to set the companion static string. Finally, the call to *UpdateData(FALSE)* triggers MFC's *DDX* and causes the static to be automatically updated to *m_strDate1*.

7. **Program the long date and time picker.** Now we need to provide a similar handler for the second date and time picker:

```
void CEx08bDialog::OnDtnDatetimechangeDatetimepicker2(NMHDR* pNMHDR,
    LRESULT* pResult)
{
    LPNMDATETIMECHANGE pDTChange =
        reinterpret_cast<LPNMDATETIMECHANGE>(pNMHDR);
    CTime ct;
    m_MonthCal2.GetTime(ct);
    m_strDate2.Format(_T("%02d/%02d/%2d"),
                      ct.GetMonth(),ct.GetDay(),ct.GetYear());
    UpdateData(FALSE);
    *pResult = 0;
}
```

8. **Program the third date and time picker.** The third date and time picker needs a similar handler, but because we set the *Show None* style in the dialog box properties, it is possible for the user to specify a *NULL* date by selecting the inline check box. Instead of blindly calling *GetTime*, we have to check the return value. If the return value of the

GetTime call is nonzero, the user has selected a *NULL* date. If the return value is zero, a valid date has been selected. As in the previous two handlers, when a *CTime* object is returned, it is converted into a string and automatically displayed in the companion static control.

```
void CEx08bDialog::OnDtnDatetimechangeDatetimepicker3(NMHDR* pNMHDR,
    LRESULT* pResult)
{
    LPNMDATETIMECHANGE pDTChange =
        reinterpret_cast<LPNMDATETIMECHANGE>(pNMHDR);
    //NOTE: this one can be null!
    CTime ct;
    int nRetVal = m_MonthCal3.GetTime(ct);
    if (nRetVal) //If not zero, it's null; and if it is,
                 // do the right thing.
    {
        m_strDate3 = "NO DATE SPECIFIED!!";
    }
    else
    {
        m_strDate3.Format(_T("%02d/%02d/%2d"),ct.GetMonth(),
                          ct.GetDay(),ct.GetYear());
    }
    UpdateData(FALSE);
    *pResult = 0;
}
```

9. **Program the time picker.** The time picker needs a similar handler, but this time the format displays hours/minutes/seconds instead of months/days/years:

```
void CEx08bDialog::OnDtnDatetimechangeDatetimepicker4(NMHDR* pNMHDR,
    LRESULT* pResult)
{
    LPNMDATETIMECHANGE pDTChange =
        reinterpret_cast<LPNMDATETIMECHANGE>(pNMHDR);
    CTime ct;
    m_MonthCal4.GetTime(ct);
    m_strDate4.Format(_T("%02d:%02d:%2d"),
                      ct.GetHour(),ct.GetMinute(),ct.GetSecond());
    UpdateData(FALSE);
    *pResult = 0;
}
```

10. **Program the month selector.** You might think that the month selector handler is similar to the date and time picker's handler, but they're actually somewhat different. First of all, the message you need to handle for detecting when the user has selected a new date is the *MCN_SELCHANGE* message. Select the *CEx08bDialog* class in Class View, click the Events button in the Properties window, expand the

IDC_MONTHCALENDER1 item, select the *MCN_SELCHANGE* message, and add the *OnMcnSelchangeMonthcalender1* handler. In addition to the different message handler, this control uses *GetCurSel* as the date and time picker instead of *GetTime*. The following code shows the *MCN_SELCHANGE* handler for the month calendar control.

```
void CEx08bDialog::OnMcnSelchangeMonthcalendar1(NMHDR* pNMHDR,
    LRESULT* pResult)
{
    LPNSELCHANGE pSelChange =
        reinterpret_cast<LPNMSELCHANGE>(pNMHDR);
    CTime ct;
    m_MonthCal5.GetCurSel(ct);
    m_strDate5.Format(_T("%02d/%02d/%2d"),
                      ct.GetMonth(),ct.GetDay(),ct.GetYear());
    UpdateData(FALSE);
    *pResult = 0;
}
```

11. **Program the IP control.** First, we need to make sure the control is initialized. In this example, we initialize the control to 0 by giving it a 0 *DWORD* value. If you don't initialize the control, each segment will be blank. To initialize the control, add this call to the *CEx08bDialog::OnInitDialog* function:

```
// Initialize the IP control
m_ptrIPCtrl.SetAddress(0L);
```

Now we need to add a handler to update the companion static control whenever the IP address control changes. First, we need to add a handler for the *IPN_FIELDCHANGED* notification message. Select the *CEx08bDialog* class in Class View, click the Events button in the Properties window, expand the *IDC_IPADDRESS1* item, select the *IPN_FIELDCHANGED* message, and add the *OnIpnFieldchanged-Ipaddress1* handler.

Next, we need to implement the handler as follows:

```
void CEx08bDialog::OnIpnFieldchangedIpaddress1(NMHDR* pNMHDR,
    LRESULT* pResult)
{
    LPNMIPADDRESS pIPAddr =
        reinterpret_case<LPNMIADDRESS>(pNMHDR);
    DWORD dwIPAddress;
    m_ptrIPCtrl.GetAddress(dwIPAddress);

    m_strIPValue.Format("%d.%d.%d.%d   %x.%x.%x.%x",
        HIBYTE(HIWORD(dwIPAddress)),
        LOBYTE(HIWORD(dwIPAddress)),
        HIBYTE(LOWORD(dwIPAddress)),
        LOBYTE(LOWORD(dwIPAddress)),
```

```
        HIBYTE(HIWORD(dwIPAddress)),
        LOBYTE(HIWORD(dwIPAddress)),
        HIBYTE(LOWORD(dwIPAddress)),
        LOBYTE(LOWORD(dwIPAddress)));
    UpdateData(FALSE);
    *pResult = 0;
}
```

The first call to *CIPAddressCtrl::GetAddress* retrieves the current IP address into the local *dwIPAddress DWORD* variable. Next, we make a fairly complex call to *CString::Format* to deconstruct the *DWORD* into the various fields. This call uses the *LOWORD* macro to first get to the bottom word of the *DWORD* and then uses the *HIBYTE/LOBYTE* macros to further deconstruct the fields in order from field 0 to field 3.

12. **Add Items to the first extended combo box.** Add this code to *OnInitDialog* to programmatically add three items ("George", "Sandy", and "Teddy") to the first extended combo box. Can you spot how this differs from a "normal" combo box control?

```
// Initialize IDC_COMBOBOXEX1
CComboBoxEx* pCombo1 =
    (CComboBoxEx*) GetDlgItem(IDC_COMBOBOXEX1);
CString rgstrTemp1[3];
rgstrTemp1[0] = "George";
rgstrTemp1[1] = "Sandy";
rgstrTemp1[2] = "Teddy";

COMBOBOXEXITEM cbi1;
cbi1.mask = CBEIF_TEXT;
for (int nCount = 0; nCount < 3; nCount++)
{
    cbi1.iItem = nCount;
    cbi1.pszText = (LPTSTR)(LPCTSTR)rgstrTemp1[nCount];
    cbi1.cchTextMax = 256;
    pCombo1->InsertItem(&cbi1);
}
```

The first thing you probably noticed is the use of the *COMBOBOXEXITEM* structure for the extended combo box instead of the plain integers used for items in an older combo box.

13. **Add a handler for the first extended combo box.** We need to handle the *CBN_SELCHANGE* message for the first extended combo box. Select the *CEx08bDialog* class in Class View, click the Events button in the Properties window, expand the *IDC_COMBOBOX1* item, select the *CBN_SELCHANGE* message, and add the *OnCbnSelchangeComboboxex1* handler. The following code shows the extended combo box handler.

```
void CEx08bDialog::OnCbnSelchangeComboboxex1 ()
{
    COMBOBOXEXITEM cbi;
    CString str ("dummy_string");
    CComboBoxEx * pCombo = (CComboBoxEx *)GetDlgItem(IDC_COMBOBOXEX1);

    int nSel = pCombo->GetCurSel();
    cbi.iItem = nSel;
    cbi.pszText = (LPTSTR)(LPCTSTR)str;
    cbi.mask = CBEIF_TEXT;
    cbi.cchTextMax = str.GetLength();
    pCombo->GetItem(&cbi);
    SetDlgItemText(IDC_STATIC7,str);
    return;
}
```

Once the handler retrieves the item, it extracts the string and calls *SetDlgItemText* to update the companion static control.

14. **Add Images to the items in the second extended combo box.** The first extended combo box does not need any special programming. It simply demonstrates how to implement a simple extended combo box that is similar to the older, nonextended combo box. The second combo box requires a good bit of programming. First, we created six bitmaps and eight icons that we need to add to the resources for the project. Of course, you're free to grab these images from the companion CD instead of recreating them all by hand, or you can choose to use any bitmaps and icons. Add these bitmaps and icons to Resource View and set their *IDs* as shown here:

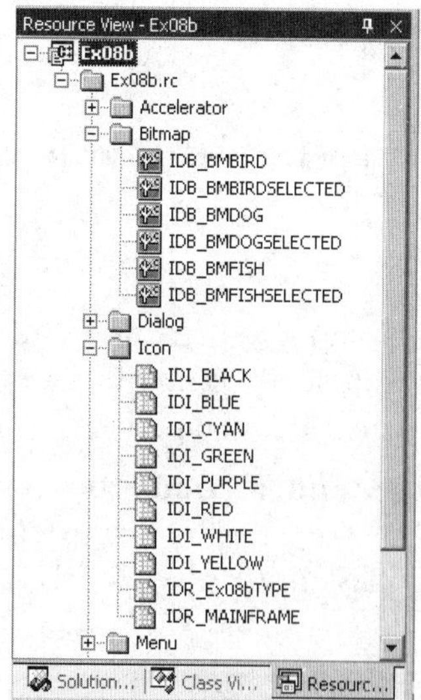

Before we start adding graphics to the extended combo box, let's create a public *CImageList* data member in the *CEx08bDialog* class named *m_imageList.* Add the following code toEx08bDialog.h:

```
CImageList m_imageList;
```

Now we can add some of the bitmap images to the image list and then "attach" the images to the three items already in the extended combo box. Add the following code to your *CEx08bDialog's OnInitDialog* method to achieve this:

```
// Initialize IDC_COMBOBOXEX2
CComboBoxEx* pCombo2 =
    (CComboBoxEx*) GetDlgItem(IDC_COMBOBOXEX2);
// First let's add images to the items there.
// We have six images in bitmaps to match to our strings:

m_imageList.Create(32,16,ILC_MASK,12,4);

CBitmap bitmap;

bitmap.LoadBitmap(IDB_BMBIRD);
m_imageList.Add(&bitmap, (COLORREF)0xFFFFFF);
bitmap.DeleteObject();

bitmap.LoadBitmap(IDB_BMBIRDSELECTED);
m_imageList.Add(&bitmap, (COLORREF)0xFFFFFF);
bitmap.DeleteObject();

bitmap.LoadBitmap(IDB_BMDOG);
m_imageList.Add(&bitmap, (COLORREF)0xFFFFFF);
bitmap.DeleteObject();

bitmap.LoadBitmap(IDB_BMDOGSELECTED);
m_imageList.Add(&bitmap, (COLORREF)0xFFFFFF);
bitmap.DeleteObject();

bitmap.LoadBitmap(IDB_BMFISH);
m_imageList.Add(&bitmap, (COLORREF)0xFFFFFF);
bitmap.DeleteObject();

bitmap.LoadBitmap(IDB_BMFISHSELECTED);
m_imageList.Add(&bitmap, (COLORREF)0xFFFFFF);
bitmap.DeleteObject();

// Set the imagelist
pCombo2->SetImageList(&m_imageList);
```

(continued)

```
CString rgstrTemp2[3];
rgstrTemp2[0] = "Tweety";
rgstrTemp2[1] = "Mack";
rgstrTemp2[2] = "Jaws";

COMBOBOXEXITEM cbi2;
cbi2.mask = CBEIF_TEXT|CBEIF_IMAGE|CBEIF_SELECTEDIMAGE|CBEIF_INDENT;
int nBitmapCount = 0;
for (int nCount = 0; nCount < 3; nCount++)
{
    cbi2.iItem = nCount;
    cbi2.pszText = (LPTSTR)(LPCTSTR)rgstrTemp2[nCount];
    cbi2.cchTextMax = 256;
    cbi2.iImage = nBitmapCount++;
    cbi2.iSelectedImage = nBitmapCount++;
    cbi2.iIndent = (nCount & 0x03);
    pCombo2->InsertItem(&cbi2);
}
```

The extended combo box initialization code first creates a pointer to the control using *GetDlgItem*. Then it calls *Create* to create memory for the images to be added and to initialize the image list. The next series of calls loads each bitmap, adds them to the image list, and then deletes the resource allocated in the load.

CComboBoxEx::SetImageList is called to associate the *m_imageList* with the extended combo box. Then a *COMBOBOXEXITEM* structure is initialized with a mask, and the *for* loop iterates from 0 through 2, setting the selected and unselected images with each pass through the loop. There's an array of strings named *rgstrTemp* that's associated with each picture. The *rgstrTemp* array includes the strings "Tweety", "Mack", and "Jaws". The variable *nBitmapCount* is used to set the string in the extended combo box. The variable *nBitmapCount* also increments through the image list to ensure that the correct image *ID* is put into the *COMBOBOXEXITEM* structure. Then the loop sets up the images for the list item and finally calls *CComboBoxEx::InsertItem* to put the *COMBOBOXEXITEM* structure back into the extended combo box and complete the association of images with the existing items in the list.

15. **Add items to the second extended combo box.** The other technique available for putting images into an extended combo box is to add them dynamically, as shown in the following code. Add this code to *OnInitDialog*:

```
HICON hIcon[8];
int n;
```

```
// Now let's insert some color icons
hIcon[0] = AfxGetApp()->LoadIcon(IDI_WHITE);
hIcon[1] = AfxGetApp()->LoadIcon(IDI_BLACK);
hIcon[2] = AfxGetApp()->LoadIcon(IDI_RED);
hIcon[3] = AfxGetApp()->LoadIcon(IDI_BLUE);
hIcon[4] = AfxGetApp()->LoadIcon(IDI_YELLOW);
hIcon[5] = AfxGetApp()->LoadIcon(IDI_CYAN);
hIcon[6] = AfxGetApp()->LoadIcon(IDI_PURPLE);
hIcon[7] = AfxGetApp()->LoadIcon(IDI_GREEN);
for (n = 0; n < 8; n++) {
    m_imageList.Add(hIcon[n]);
}

static char* color[] = {"white", "black", "red",
                        "blue", "yellow", "cyan",
                        "purple", "green"};

cbi2.mask = CBEIF_IMAGE|CBEIF_TEXT|CBEIF_OVERLAY|
            CBEIF_SELECTEDIMAGE;

for (n = 0; n < 8; n++) {
    cbi2.iItem = n;
    cbi2.pszText = color[n];
    cbi2.iImage = n+6; // 6 is the offset into the image list from
    cbi2.iSelectedImage = n+6; // the first six items we added...
    cbi2.iOverlay = n+6;
    int nItem = pCombo2->InsertItem(&cbi2);
    ASSERT(nItem == n);
}
```

The addition of the icons above is similar to the Ex08a list control example shown earlier in this chapter. The *for* loop fills out the *COMBOBOXEXITEM* structure and then calls *CComboBoxEx::InsertItem* with each item to add it to the list.

16. **Add a handler for the second extended combo box.** Select the *CEx08bDialog* class in Class View, click the Events button in the Properties window, expand the *IDC_COMBOBOX2* item, select the *CBN_SELCHANGE* message, and add the *OnCbnSelchangeComboboxex2* handler. Add the following boldface code to the second extended combo box handler. The handler is essentially the same as the first.

```
void CEx08bDialog::OnCbnSelchangeComboboxex2()
{
    COMBOBOXEXITEM cbi;
    CString str ("dummy_string");
    CComboBoxEx * pCombo = (CComboBoxEx *)GetDlgItem(IDC_COMBOBOXEX2);
```

(continued)

```
        int nSel = pCombo->GetCurSel();
        cbi.iItem = nSel;
        cbi.pszText = (LPTSTR)(LPCTSTR)str;
        cbi.mask = CBEIF_TEXT;
        cbi.cchTextMax = str.GetLength();
        pCombo->GetItem(&cbi);
        SetDlgItemText(IDC_STATIC8,str);
        return;
    }
```

17. **Connect the view and the dialog box.** Add code to the virtual *OnDraw* function in Ex08bView.cpp. Edit the code as follows:

```
void CEx08bView::OnDraw(CDC* pDC)
{
    CEx08vDoc* pDoc = GetDocument();
    ASSERT_VALID(pDoc);

    pDC->TextOut(0, 0, "Press the left mouse button here.");
}
```

18. **Add the *OnLButtonDown* member function to the *CEx08aView* class.** Select the *CEx08bView* class in Class View, click the Messages button in the Properties window, select the *WM_LBUTTONDOWN* message, and add the *OnLButtonDown* handler. Edit the code as follows:

```
void CEx08aView::OnLButtonDown(UINT nFlags, CPoint point)
{
    CEx08bDialog dlg;
    dlg.DoModal();

    CView::OnLButtonDown(nFlags, point);
}
```

Add a statement to include Ex08bDialog.h in file Ex08aView.cpp.

```
#include "Ex08bDialog.h"
```

19. **Compile and run the program.** Now you can experiment with the various common controls to see how they work.

9

Using ActiveX Controls

Developers have long searched for a way to "componentize" user interface elements. Even though Microsoft Windows has user interface elements such as buttons and edit boxes built into it, it's useful to have other controls—charts or grids, for example. The solution to this problem in classic Windows development is ActiveX controls (formerly known as OLE controls, or OCXs). Developers can use ActiveX controls in both Microsoft Visual Basic and Microsoft Visual C++.

Even with Microsoft .NET coming down the line, ActiveX controls are still useful, and you'll find a ton of them out there. This chapter is about using ActiveX controls in a Visual C++ .NET application. The premise here is that you can learn to use ActiveX controls without knowing much about the Component Object Model (COM) on which they're based. After all, Microsoft doesn't require that Visual Basic programmers be COM experts. In order to effectively write ActiveX controls, however, you need to know a bit more, starting with the fundamentals of COM. We'll take a close look at COM as well as using ATL to create ActiveX controls in Chapters 22 through 28. You might also pick up a copy of Adam Denning's *ActiveX Controls Inside Out* (Microsoft Press, 1997) if you're serious about creating ActiveX controls. Of course, knowing more ActiveX control theory won't hurt when you're using the controls in your programs. Chapter 24, Chapter 25, and Chapter 30 of this book are a good place to start. Even in the Microsoft .NET world, ActiveX will continue to play a part in building customizable, componentized application user interfaces.

ActiveX Controls vs. Ordinary Windows Controls

An ActiveX control is a software module that plugs into your C++ program in the same way that a Windows control does. At least that's the way it seems at first. It's worthwhile here to analyze the similarities and differences between ActiveX controls and the controls you already know.

Ordinary Controls: A Frame of Reference

In Chapter 8, you used ordinary Windows controls such as the edit control and the list box, and you saw the Windows common controls that work in much the same way. These controls are all child windows that you use most often in dialog boxes, and they are represented by MFC classes such as *CEdit* and *CTreeCtrl*. The client program is always responsible for the creation of the control's child window.

Ordinary controls send notification command messages (standard Windows messages), such as *BN_CLICKED*, to the dialog box. If you want to perform an action on the control, you call a C++ control class member function, which sends a Windows message to the control. The controls are all windows in their own right. All the MFC control classes are derived from *CWnd*, so if you want to get the text from an edit control, you call *CWnd::GetWindowText*. But even that function works by sending a message to the control.

Windows controls are an integral part of Windows, even though the Windows common controls are in a separate DLL. Another species of ordinary control, the so-called *custom control*, is a programmer-created control that acts as an ordinary control in that it sends *WM_COMMAND* notifications to its parent window and receives user-defined messages. You'll see one of these in Chapter 22.

How ActiveX Controls Are Similar to Ordinary Controls

You can consider an ActiveX control to be a child window, just as an ordinary control is. If you want to include an ActiveX control in a dialog box, you use the dialog editor to place it there, and the identifier for the control will turn up in the resource template. If you're creating an ActiveX control on the fly, you call a *Create* member function for a class that represents the control, usually in the *WM_CREATE* handler for the parent window. To manipulate an ActiveX control, you call a C++ member function, just as you do for a Windows control. The window that contains a control is called a *container*.

How ActiveX Controls Differ from Ordinary Controls: Properties and Methods

The most prominent ActiveX control features are properties and methods. Those C++ member functions that you call to manipulate a control instance all revolve around properties and methods. Properties have symbolic names that are matched to integer indexes. (These are actually DISPIDs, which we'll look at in Chapter 23.) For each property, the control designer assigns a property name, such as *BackColor* or *GridCellEffect*, and a property type, such as string, integer, or double. There's even a picture type for bitmaps and icons. The client program can set an individual ActiveX control property by specifying the property's integer index and its value. The client can get a property by specifying the index and accepting the appropriate return value. In certain cases, Visual Studio .NET lets you define data members in your client window class that are associated with the properties of the controls that the client class contains. The generated Dialog Data Exchange (DDX) code exchanges data between the control properties and the client class data members.

ActiveX control methods are like functions. A method has a symbolic name, a set of parameters, and a return value. You call a method by calling a C++ member function of the class that represents the control. A control designer can define any needed methods, such as *PreviousYear* or *LowerControlRods*.

An ActiveX control doesn't send *WM_* notification messages to its container the way an ordinary control does; instead, it "fires events." An event has a symbolic name and can have an arbitrary sequence of parameters—it's really a container function that the control calls. Like ordinary control notification messages, events don't return a value to the ActiveX control. Examples of events are *Click*, *KeyDown*, and *NewMonth*. Events are mapped in your client class just as control notification messages are.

In the MFC world, ActiveX controls act just like child windows, but there's a significant layer of code between the container window and the control window. In fact, the control might not even have a window. When you call *Create*, the control's window isn't created directly; instead, the control code is loaded and given the command for "in-place activation." The ActiveX control then creates its own window, which MFC lets you access through a *CWnd* pointer. It's not a good idea for the client to use the control's *hWnd* directly, however.

A DLL is used to store one or more ActiveX controls, but the DLL often has an OCX filename extension instead of a DLL extension. Your container program loads the DLLs when it needs them, using sophisticated COM techniques that rely on the Windows Registry. For the time being, simply accept the fact that once you specify an ActiveX control at design time, it will be loaded for you at run time. Obviously, when you ship a program that requires special ActiveX controls, you'll have to include the OCX files and an appropriate setup program.

Installing ActiveX Controls

Let's assume you've found a nifty ActiveX control that you want to use in your project. Your first step is to copy the control's DLL to your hard disk. You could put it anywhere, but it's easier to track your ActiveX controls if you put them in one place, such as in the system directory (typically \Windows\System for Windows 95/98 or \Winnt\System32 for Windows 2000 or Windows XP). Copy associated files such as help (HLP) or license (LIC) files to the same directory.

Your next step is to register the control in the Windows Registry. Actually, the ActiveX control registers itself when a client program calls a special exported function. The Windows utility Regsvr32 is a tool that accepts the control name on the command line. Regsvr32 is suitable for installation scripts, but another program, RegComp, in the project REGCOMP on the book's companion CD, lets you find your control by browsing the disk. Some controls have licensing requirements, which might involve extra entries to the Registry. (See Chapter 15, Chapter 17, Chapter 24, and Chapter 25 for information about how the Windows Registry works.) Licensed controls usually come with setup programs that take care of those details.

After you register your ActiveX control, you must install it in each project that uses it. That doesn't mean that the OCX file gets copied. It means that Visual Studio .NET generates a C++ wrapper class for the specific control, and that the control shows up in the dialog editor control palette for that project.

To install an ActiveX control in a project, choose Add Class from the Project menu and then choose MFC Class From ActiveX Control, as shown here:

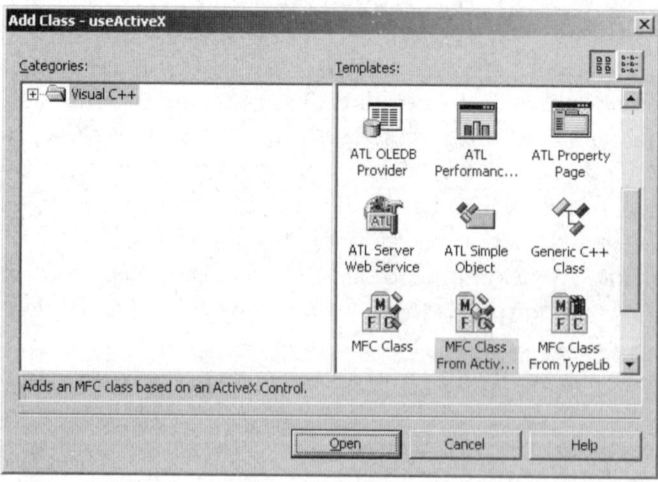

Select an ActiveX control in the Add Class From ActiveX Control Wizard. This gets you the list of all the ActiveX controls currently registered on your system. A typical list is shown here:

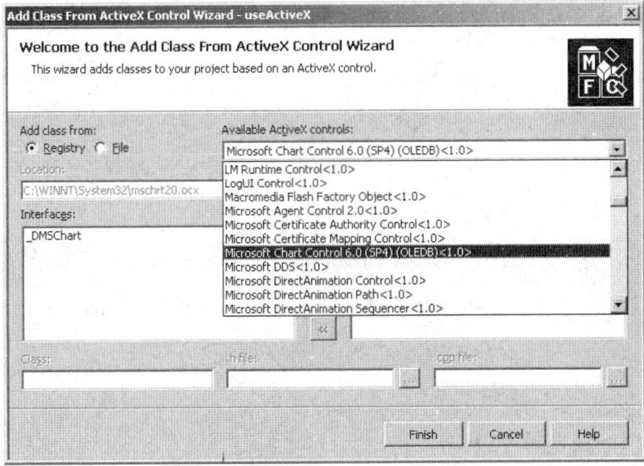

The Calendar Control

The MSCal.ocx control is a popular ActiveX calendar control that's probably already installed and registered on your computer. If it isn't there, don't worry. It's on the companion CD.

Figure 9-1 shows the calendar control inside a modal dialog box.

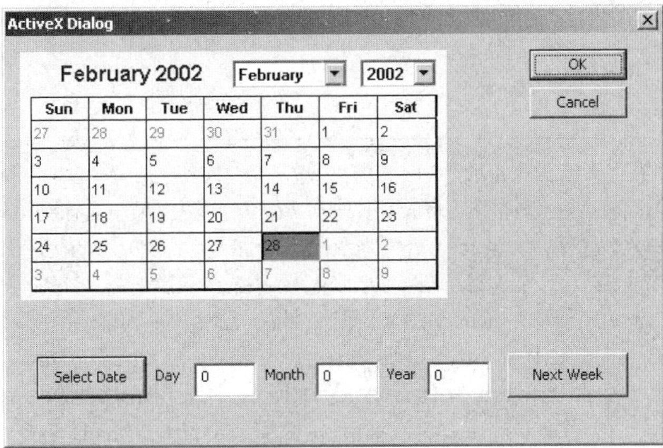

Figure 9-1 The calendar control in use.

The calendar control comes with a help file that lists the control's properties, methods, and events, as shown in Table 9-1.

Table 9-1 Properties, Methods, and Events of the Calendar Control

Properties	Methods	Events
BackColor	AboutBox	AfterUpdate
Day	*NextDay*	*BeforeUpdate*
DayFont	*NextMonth*	*Click*
DayFontColor	*NextWeek*	*DblClick*
DayLength	*NextYear*	*KeyDown*
FirstDay	*PreviousDay*	*KeyPress*
GridCellEffect	*PreviousMonth*	*KeyUp*
GridFont	*PreviousWeek*	*NewMonth*
GridFontColor	*PreviousYear*	*NewYear*
GridLinesColor	*Refresh*	
Month	*Today*	
MonthLength		
ShowDateSelectors		
ShowDays		
ShowHorizontalGridlines		
ShowTitle		
ShowVerticalGridlines		
TitleFont		
TitleFontColor		
Value		
ValueIsNull		
Year		

You'll be using the *BackColor*, *Day*, *Month*, *Year*, and *Value* properties in the Ex09a example later in this chapter. *BackColor* is an unsigned long, but it is used as an *OLE_COLOR*, which is almost the same as a *COLORREF*. *Day*, *Month*, and *Year* are short integers. *Value*'s type is the special type *VARIANT*, which is described in Chapter 25. It holds the entire date as a 64-bit value.

Each of the properties, methods, and events listed in the table has a corresponding integer identifier. Information about the names, types, parameter sequences, and integer IDs is stored inside the control and is accessible to Visual Studio .NET at container design time.

ActiveX Control Container Programming

MFC and Visual Studio .NET support ActiveX controls both in dialog boxes and as "child windows." To use ActiveX controls, you must understand how a control grants access to properties, and you must understand the interactions between your DDX code and those property values.

Property Access

The ActiveX control developer designates certain properties for access at design time. Those properties are specified in the property pages that the control displays in the dialog editor when you right-click on a control and choose Properties. The calendar control's main property page looks like this:

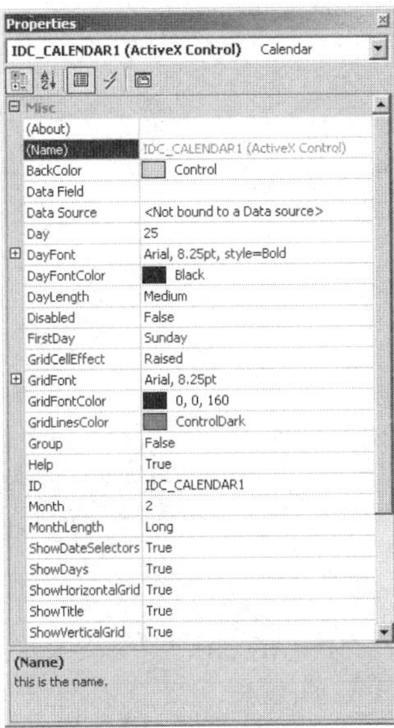

All the control's properties, including the design-time properties, are accessible at runtime. Some properties, however, might be designated as read-only.

Visual Studio .NET's C++ Wrapper Classes for ActiveX Controls

When you insert an ActiveX control into a project, Visual Studio .NET generates a C++ wrapper class, derived from *CWnd*, that is tailored to your control's methods and properties. The class has member functions for all properties and methods, and it has constructors that you can use to dynamically create an instance of the control. (Visual Studio .NET also generates wrapper classes for objects used by the control.) Here are a few typical member functions from the file CCalendar.h that Visual Studio .NET generates for the calendar control:

```
unsigned long get_BackColor()
{
    unsigned long result;
    InvokeHelper(DISPID_BACKCOLOR,
         DISPATCH_PROPERTYGET, VT_UI4, (void*)&result, NULL);
    return result;
}
void put_BackColor(unsigned long newValue)
{
    static BYTE parms[] = VTS_UI4 ;
    InvokeHelper(DISPID_BACKCOLOR, DISPATCH_PROPERTYPUT,
                 VT_EMPTY, NULL, parms, newValue);
}
short get_Day()
{
    short result;
    InvokeHelper(0x11, DISPATCH_PROPERTYGET,
                 VT_I2, (void*)&result, NULL);
    return result;
}
void put_Day(short newValue)
{
    static BYTE parms[] = VTS_I2 ;
    InvokeHelper(0x11, DISPATCH_PROPERTYPUT, VT_EMPTY,
                 NULL, parms, newValue);
}
LPDISPATCH get_DayFont()
{
    LPDISPATCH result;
    InvokeHelper(0x1, DISPATCH_PROPERTYGET,
                 VT_DISPATCH, (void*)&result, NULL);
    return result;
}
void put_DayFont(LPDISPATCH newValue)
{
    static BYTE parms[] = VTS_DISPATCH ;
    InvokeHelper(0x1, DISPATCH_PROPERTYPUT,
                 VT_EMPTY, NULL, parms, newValue);
}
unsigned long get_DayFontColor()
{
    unsigned long result;
    InvokeHelper(0x2, DISPATCH_PROPERTYGET, VT_UI4,
```

```
                (void*)&result, NULL);
    return result;
}
void put_DayFontColor(unsigned long newValue)
{
    static BYTE parms[] = VTS_UI4 ;
    InvokeHelper(0x2, DISPATCH_PROPERTYPUT,
                VT_EMPTY, NULL, parms, newValue);
}
short get_DayLength()
{
    short result;
    InvokeHelper(0x12, DISPATCH_PROPERTYGET, VT_I2,
                (void*)&result, NULL);
    return result;
}
void put_DayLength(short newValue)
{
    static BYTE parms[] = VTS_I2 ;
    InvokeHelper(0x12, DISPATCH_PROPERTYPUT,
                VT_EMPTY, NULL, parms, newValue);
}
short get_FirstDay()
{
    short result;
    InvokeHelper(0x13, DISPATCH_PROPERTYGET,
                VT_I2, (void*)&result, NULL);
    return result;
}
void put_FirstDay(short newValue)
{
    static BYTE parms[] = VTS_I2 ;
    InvokeHelper(0x13, DISPATCH_PROPERTYPUT,
                VT_EMPTY, NULL, parms, newValue);
}

void NextDay()
{
    InvokeHelper(0x16, DISPATCH_METHOD,
                VT_EMPTY, NULL, NULL);
}
void NextMonth()
{
    InvokeHelper(0x17, DISPATCH_METHOD,
                VT_EMPTY, NULL, NULL);
}
```

(continued)

```
void NextWeek()
{
    InvokeHelper(0x18, DISPATCH_METHOD,
                VT_EMPTY, NULL, NULL);
}
void NextYear()
{
    InvokeHelper(0x19, DISPATCH_METHOD,
                VT_EMPTY, NULL, NULL);
}
```

You don't have to concern yourself too much with the code inside these functions, but you can match up the first parameter of each *InvokeHelper* function with the dispatch ID for the corresponding property or method in the calendar control property list. As you can see, properties always have separate *put_* and *get_* functions. To call a method, you simply call the corresponding function. For example, to call the *NextDay* method from a dialog class function, you write code such as this:

```
m_calendar.NextDay();
```

In this case, *m_calendar* is an object of class *CCalendar*, the wrapper class for the calendar control.

MFC Application Wizard Support for ActiveX Controls

When the ActiveX Controls option (the default) is selected in the MFC Application Wizard, the wizard inserts the following line in your application class *InitInstance* member function:

```
AfxEnableControlContainer();
```

It also inserts the following line in the project's StdAfx.h file:

```
#include <afxdisp.h>
```

If you decide to add ActiveX controls to an existing project that doesn't include the two lines above, you can simply add the lines.

The Add Class Wizard and the Container Dialog Box

If you've used the dialog editor to generate a dialog template, you know that you can use the Add Class Wizard to generate a C++ class for the dialog window. If your template contains one or more ActiveX controls, you can use the Add Member Variable Wizard to add data members and the Class View's Properties window to add event handler functions.

Dialog Class Data Members vs. Wrapper Class Usage

What kind of data members can you add to the dialog box for an ActiveX control? If you want to set a control property before you call *DoModal* for the dialog box, you can add a dialog data member for that property. If you want to change properties inside the dialog member functions, you must take another approach: You add a data member that is an object of the wrapper class for the ActiveX control.

Now is a good time to review the MFC DDX logic. Look back at the Cincinnati dialog box in Chapter 8. The *CDialog::OnInitDialog* function calls *CWnd::UpdateData(FALSE)* to read the dialog class data members, and the *CDialog::OnOK* function calls *UpdateData(TRUE)* to write the members. Suppose you add a data member for each ActiveX control property and you need to get the *Value* property value in a button handler. If you call *UpdateData(FALSE)* in the button handler, it will read all the property values from all the dialog's controls—clearly a waste of time. It's more effective to avoid using a data member and to call the wrapper class *get_* function instead. To call that function, you must first tell Visual Studio .NET to add a wrapper class object data member.

Suppose you have a calendar wrapper class *CCalendar* and you have an *m_calendar* data member in your dialog class. If you want to get the *Value* property, you do it like this:

```
COleVariant var = m_calendar.get_Value();
```

> **Note** The *VARIANT* type and *COleVariant* class are described in Chapter 23.

Now consider another case: You want to set the day to the 5th of the month before the control is displayed. To do this by hand, you add a dialog class data member *m_sCalDay* that corresponds to the control's short integer *Day* property. Then you add the following line to the *DoDataExchange* function:

```
DDX_OCShort(pDX, IDC_CALENDAR1, 0x11, m_sCalDay);
```

The third parameter is the *Day* property's integer index (its *DispID*), which you can find in the *get_Day* and *put_Day* functions generated by Visual Studio .NET for the control. Here's how you construct and display the dialog box:

```
CMyDialog dlg;
dlg.m_sCalDay = 5;
dlg.DoModal();
```

The DDX code takes care of setting the property value from the data member before the control is displayed. No other programming is needed. As you'd expect, the DDX code sets the data member from the property value when the user clicks the OK button.

> **Note** Even when Visual Studio .NET correctly detects a control's properties, it can't always generate data members for all of them. In particular, no DDX functions exist for *VARIANT* properties such as the calendar's *Value* property. You have to use the wrapper class for these properties.

Mapping ActiveX Control Events

The Class View's Properties window lets you map ActiveX control events in the same way that you map Windows messages and command messages from controls. If a dialog class contains one or more ActiveX controls, the code wizards available from the Properties window add and maintain an *event sink map* that connects mapped events to their handler functions. You can see the code in ActiveXDialog.h and ActiveXDialog.cpp later in this chapter.

> **Note** ActiveX controls have the annoying habit of firing events before your program is ready for them. If your event handler uses windows or pointers to C++ objects, it should verify the validity of those entities before using them.

Locking ActiveX Controls in Memory

Normally, an ActiveX control remains mapped in your process as long as its parent dialog box is active. That means it must be reloaded each time the user opens a modal dialog box. The reloads are usually quicker than the initial load because of disk caching, but you can lock the control into memory for better performance. To do so, add the following line in the overridden *OnInitDialog* function after the base class call:

```
AfxOleLockControl(m_calendar.GetClsid());
```

The ActiveX control remains mapped until your program exits or until you call the *AfxOleUnlockControl* function.

The Ex09a Example: An ActiveX Control Dialog Container

Now it's time to build an application that uses a calendar control in a dialog box. Here are the steps to create the Ex09a example:

1. **Verify that the calendar control is registered.** If the control does not appear in your system directory, copy the files MSCal.ocx, MSCal.hlp, and MSCal.cnt to your system directory and register the control by running the REGCOMP program.

2. **Run the MFC Application Wizard to generate the Ex09a project.** Accept all of the default settings but two: Select Single Document and deselect Printing And Print Preview. On the Advanced Features page, be sure the ActiveX Controls option is selected, as shown here:

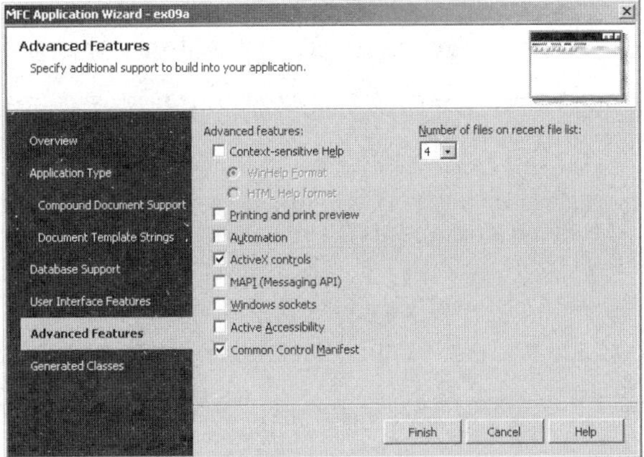

3. **Install the calendar control in the Ex09a project.** Choose Add Class from Visual C++ .NET's Project menu. Choose MFC Class From ActiveX Control and then click Open. Select Calendar Control 9.0 from the list of available controls in the Add Class From ActiveX Control Wizard. Visual Studio .NET will generate a class in the Ex09a directory. The Add Class From ActiveX Control Wizard is shown here:

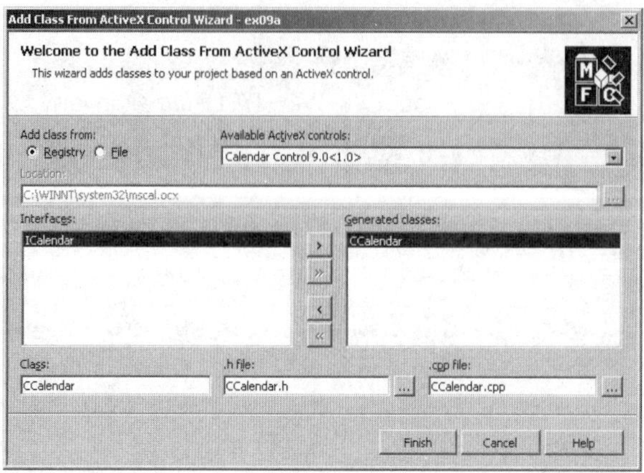

4. **Edit the calendar control class to handle help messages.** Add the following message map code to CCalendar.cpp:

```
BEGIN_MESSAGE_MAP(CCalendar, CWnd)
    ON_WM_HELPINFO()
END_MESSAGE_MAP()
```

In the same file, add the *OnHelpInfo* function:

```
BOOL CCalendar::OnHelpInfo(HELPINFO* pHelpInfo)
{
    // Edit the following string for your system
    ::WinHelp(GetSafeHwnd(), "c:\\winnt\\system32\\mscal.hlp",
              HELP_FINDER, 0);
    return FALSE;
}
```

In CCalendar.h, add the function prototype and declare the message map:

```
protected:
    afx_msg BOOL OnHelpInfo(HELPINFO* pHelpInfo);
    DECLARE_MESSAGE_MAP()
```

The *OnHelpInfo* function is called if the user presses the F1 key when the calendar control has the input focus. We have to add the message map code by hand because Visual Studio .NET doesn't modify generated ActiveX classes.

> **Note** The *ON_WM_HELPINFO* macro maps the *WM_HELP* message. You can use *ON_WM_HELPINFO* in any view or dialog class and then code the handler to activate any help system.

5. **Use the dialog editor to create a new dialog resource.** Choose Add Resource from Visual C++ .NET's Project menu, and then choose Dialog. The dialog editor will assign the ID *IDD_DIALOG1* to the new dialog box. Next, change the ID to *IDD_ACTIVEXDIALOG*, change the dialog caption to **ActiveX Dialog**, and set the dialog's Context Help property. Accept the default OK and Cancel buttons with the IDs *IDOK* and *IDCANCEL*, and then add the other controls as shown earlier in Figure 9-1. Make the Select Date button the default button. Right-click on the dialog box, select Insert ActiveX Control, and then select the calendar control from the list. Then set an appropriate tab order. While the dialog template is showing in the dialog editor, choose Tab Order from the Format menu. Click on the controls in the order you want them to tab. You'll see numbers next to the controls, indicating the tab order. Assign control IDs as shown in the following table.

Control	ID
Calendar control	*IDC_CALENDAR1*
Select Date button	*IDC_SELECTDATE*
Edit control	*IDC_DAY*
Edit control	*IDC_MONTH*
Edit control	*IDC_YEAR*
Next Week button	*IDC_NEXTWEEK*

6. **Use Visual Studio .NET to create the *CActiveXDialog* class.** Choose Add Class from Visual C++ .NET's Project menu. Choose MFC Class and click Open. In the MFC Class Wizard, create a *CDialog* derived class based on the *IDD_ACTIVEXDIALOG* template. Be sure to select *CDialog* as the base class. Name the class *CActiveXDialog*.

Right-click on the *CActiveXDialog* class in Class View and then choose Properties. Click the Overrides button on the Properties window toolbar to list virtual functions for *CActiveXDialog*. Add overriding functions for *OnInitDialog* and *OnOK*.

Click the Events button on the Properties window toolbar, and then add the message handler functions shown in the following table. To add a message handler function, click on an object ID, click on an event, click the drop-down combo box that appears next to the entry, and select *<Add>_*. The function will be written into the code and will appear inside the Code Editor.

Object ID	Event	Member Function
IDC_CALENDAR1	*NewMonth*	*NewMonthCalendar1*
IDC_SELECTDATE	*BN_CLICKED*	*OnBnClickedSelectdate*
IDC_NEXTWEEK	*BN_CLICKED*	*OnBnClickedNextweek*

7. **Use the Add Member Variable Wizard to add data members to the *CActiveXDialog* class.** Right-click on *CActiveDialog* in Class View and choose Add Variable from the shortcut menu, and then add the data members *m_calendar*, *m_sDay*, *m_sMonth*, and *m_sYear*, as shown here:

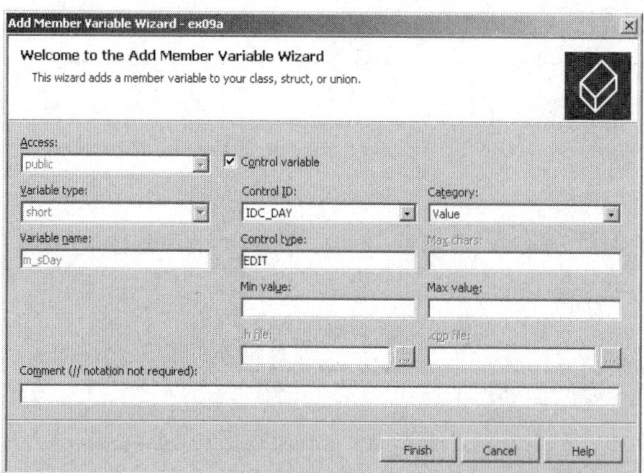

8. **Edit the *CActiveXDialog* class.** Add *m_varValue* and *m_BackColor* data members, and then edit the code for the two overriding functions and three handler functions (*OnInitDialog*, *NewMonthCalendar1*, *OnBnClickedSelectdate*, *OnBnClickedNextweek*, and *OnOK*). The following code shows all the code for the dialog class, with new code in boldface.

ActiveXDialog.h

```
#pragma once
#include "ccalendar.h"
//////////////////////////////////////////////////////////////////////
//
// CActiveXDialog dialog
class CActiveXDialog : public CDialog

 {
    DECLARE_DYNAMIC(CActiveXDialog)
public:
    CActiveXDialog(CWnd* pParent = NULL);   // standard constructor
    virtual ~ActiveXDialog();

// Dialog Data
    enum { IDD = IDD_ACTIVEXDIALOG };

    protected:
    virtual void DoDataExchange(CDataExchange* pDX); // DDX/DDV
                                                     //  support
    DECLARE_MESSAGE_MAP()
public:

    virtual BOOL OnInitDialog();
    void NewMonthCalendar1();
    afx_msg void OnBnClickedSelectdate();
    afx_msg void OnBnClickedNextweek();

    DECLARE_EVENTSINK_MAP()
public:
    CCalendar    m_calendar;
    short    m_sDay;
    short    m_sMonth;
    short    m_sYear;
    COleVariant m_varValue;
    unsigned long m_BackColor;

protected:
    virtual void OnOK();
};
```

ActiveXDialog.cpp

```
// ActiveXDialog.cpp : implementation file
//

#include "Stdafx.h"
#include "Ex09a.h"
#include "ActiveXDialog.h"
// CActiveXDialog dialog
IMPLEMENT_DYNAMIC(CActiveXDialog, CDialog)
CActiveXDialog::CActiveXDialog(CWnd* pParent /*=NULL*/)
    : CDialog(CActiveXDialog::IDD, pParent)
{
    m_sDay = 0;
    m_sMonth = 0;
    m_sYear = 0;
    m_BackColor = 0x8000000F;
}

ActiveXDialog::~ActiveXDialog()
{
}

void CActiveXDialog::DoDataExchange(CDataExchange* pDX)
{
    CDialog::DoDataExchange(pDX);

    DDX_Control(pDX, IDC_CALENDAR1, m_calendar);
    DDX_Text(pDX, IDC_DAY, m_sDay);
    DDX_Text(pDX, IDC_MONTH, m_sMonth);
    DDX_Text(pDX, IDC_YEAR, m_sYear);

    DDX_OCColor(pDX, IDC_CALENDAR1, DISPID_BACKCOLOR, m_BackColor);
}

BEGIN_MESSAGE_MAP(CActiveXDialog, CDialog)
    ON_BN_CLICKED(IDC_SELECTDATE, OnBnClickedSelectdate)
    ON_BN_CLICKED(IDC_NEXTWEEK, OnBnClickedNextweek)

END_MESSAGE_MAP()
```

```
//////////////////////////////////////////////////////////////////////
//
// CActiveXDialog message handlers

BEGIN_EVENTSINK_MAP(CActiveXDialog, CDialog)
    ON_EVENT(CActiveXDialog, IDC_CALENDAR1, 3,
             NewMonthCalendar1, VTS_NONE)
END_EVENTSINK_MAP()
BOOL CActiveXDialog::OnInitDialog()
{
    CDialog::OnInitDialog();
    m_calendar.put_Value(m_varValue); // no DDX for VARIANTs
    return TRUE;  //return TRUE unless you set
                  //the focus to a control
                  //EXCEPTION: OCX Property Pages
                  //should return FALSE

}
void CActiveXDialog::OnOK()
{
    CDialog::OnOK();
    m_varValue = m_calendar.get_Value(); // no DDX for VARIANTs
}

void CActiveXDialog::NewMonthCalendar1()
{
    AfxMessageBox("EVENT:  CActiveXDialog::NewMonthCalendar1");
}

void CActiveXDialog::OnBnClickedSelectdate()
{
    CDataExchange dx(this, TRUE);
    DDX_Text(&dx, IDC_DAY, m_sDay);
    DDX_Text(&dx, IDC_MONTH, m_sMonth);
    DDX_Text(&dx, IDC_YEAR, m_sYear);
    m_calendar.put_Day(m_sDay);
    m_calendar.put_Month(m_sMonth);
    m_calendar.put_Year(m_sYear);
}

void CActiveXDialog::OnBnClickedNextweek()
{
    m_calendar.NextWeek();
}
```

The *OnBnClickedSelectdate* function is called when the user clicks the Select Date button. The function gets the day, month, and year values from the three edit controls and transfers them to the control's properties. The Add Member Variable Wizard can't add DDX code for the *BackColor* property, so you must add it by hand. In addition, there's no DDX code for *VARIANT* types, so you must add code to the *OnInitDialog* and *OnOK* functions to set and retrieve the date with the control's *Value* property.

9. **Connect the dialog box to the view.** Use the Class View's Properties window to map the *WM_LBUTTONDOWN* message, and then edit the handler function as follows:

```
void CEx09aView::OnLButtonDown(UINT nFlags, CPoint point)
{
    CActiveXDialog dlg;
    dlg.m_BackColor = RGB(255, 251, 240); // light yellow
    COleDateTime today = COleDateTime::GetCurrentTime();
    dlg.m_varValue = COleDateTime(today.get_Year(),
                                  today.get_Month(),
                                  today.get_Day(), 0, 0, 0);
    if (dlg.DoModal() == IDOK) {
        COleDateTime date(dlg.m_varValue);
        AfxMessageBox(date.Format("%B %d, %Y"));
    }
}
```

The code sets the background color to light yellow and the date to today's date, displays the modal dialog box, and reports the date returned by the calendar control. You'll need to include ActiveXDialog.h in Ex09aView.cpp.

10. **Edit the virtual *OnDraw* function in the file Ex09aView.cpp.** To prompt the user to press the left mouse button, replace the code in the view class *OnDraw* function with this single line:

```
pDC->TextOut(0, 0, "Press the left mouse button here.");
```

11. **Build and test the Ex09a application.** Open the dialog box, enter a date in the three edit controls, and then click the Select Date button. Click the Next Week button. Try moving the selected date directly to a new month, and observe the message box that is triggered by the *NewMonth* event. Watch for the final date in another message box when you click OK.

For Win32 Programmers

If you use a text editor to look inside the Ex09a.rc file, you might be quite mystified. Here's the entry for the calendar control in the ActiveX dialog template:

```
CONTROL         "",IDC_CALENDAR1,
                "{8E27C92B-1264-101C-8A2F-040224009C02}",
                WS_TABSTOP,7,7,217,113
```

There's a 32-digit number sequence where the window class name should be. What's going on? Actually, the resource template isn't the one that Windows sees. The *CDialog::DoModal* function "preprocesses" the resource template before passing it on to the dialog box procedure within Windows. It strips out all the ActiveX controls and creates the dialog window without them. Then it loads the controls (based on their 32-digit identification numbers, called CLSIDs) and activates them in place, causing them to create their own windows in the correct places. The initial values for the properties you set in the dialog editor are stored in binary form inside the project's custom *DLGINIT* resource.

When the modal dialog box runs, the MFC code coordinates the messages sent to the dialog window both by the ordinary controls and by the ActiveX controls. This allows the user to tab between all the controls in the dialog box, even though the ActiveX controls are not part of the actual dialog template.

When you call the member functions for the control object, you might think you're calling functions for a child window. The control window is quite far removed, but MFC steps in to make it seem as if you're communicating with a real child window. In ActiveX terminology, the container owns a *site*, which is not a window. You call functions for the site, and ActiveX and MFC make the connection to the underlying window in the ActiveX control.

The container window is an object of a class derived from *CWnd*. The control site is also an object of a class derived from *CWnd*—the ActiveX control wrapper class. That means that the *CWnd* class has built-in support for both containers and sites.

ActiveX Controls in HTML Files

You've seen the ActiveX calendar control in an MFC modal dialog box. You can use the same control in a Web page. The following HTML code will work (if the person reading the page has the calendar control installed and registered on his or her machine):

```
<OBJECT
    CLASSID="clsid:8E27C92B-1264-101C-8A2F-040224009C02"
    WIDTH=300 HEIGHT=200 BORDER=1 HSPACE=5 ID=calendar>
    <PARAM NAME="Day" VALUE=7>
    <PARAM NAME="Month" VALUE=11>
    <PARAM NAME="Year" VALUE=1998>
</OBJECT>
```

The *CLASSID* attribute (the same number that was in the Ex09a dialog resource) identifies the calendar control in the Registry. A browser can download an ActiveX control.

Creating ActiveX Controls at Run Time

You've seen how to use the dialog editor to insert ActiveX controls at design time. If you need to create an ActiveX control at run time without a resource template entry, here are the programming steps:

1. Insert the component into your project. Visual Studio .NET will create the files for a wrapper class.
2. Add an embedded ActiveX control wrapper class data member to your dialog class or other C++ window class. An embedded C++ object will be constructed and destroyed along with the window object.
3. Choose Resource View from Visual C++ .NET's View menu. In Resource View, right-click on your RC file and choose Resource Symbols from the shortcut menu. Add an ID constant for the new control.
4. If the parent window is a dialog box, use Class View's Properties window to override *CDialog::OnInitDialog*. For other windows besides CDialog, use Class View's Properties window to map the *WM_CREATE* message. The new function should call the embedded control class's *Create* member function. This call indirectly displays the new control in the dialog box. The control will be properly destroyed when the parent window is destroyed.
5. In the parent window class, manually add the necessary event message handlers and prototypes for your new control. Don't forget to add the event sink map macros.

> **Tip** The code wizards available from Class View don't help you with event sink maps when you add a dynamic ActiveX control to a project. Consider inserting the target control in a dialog box in another temporary project. After you're finished mapping events, simply copy the event sink map code to the parent window class in your main project.

The Ex09b Example: The Web Browser ActiveX Control

Most of the functionality in Microsoft Internet Explorer is contained in one big ActiveX control, Shdocvw.dll. When you run Internet Explorer, you launch a small shell program that loads this Web browser control in its main window.

> **Note** You can find complete documentation for the Web browser control's properties, methods, and events in the online MSDN Library included with Visual Studio. NET.

Because of this modular architecture, you can write your own custom browser program with little effort. Ex09b creates a two-window browser that displays a search engine page side-by-side with the target page, as shown here:

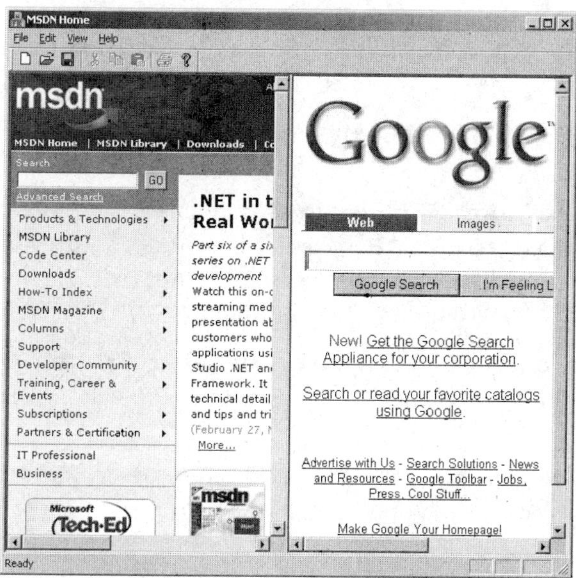

This view window contains two Web browser controls that are sized to occupy the entire client area. When the user clicks an item in the search (right-hand) control, the program intercepts the command and routes it to the target (left-hand) control.

Here are the steps for building the example:

1. **Be sure the Web browser control is registered.** You undoubtedly have the latest version of Internet Explorer installed, since Visual Studio .NET requires it, so the Web browser control should be registered. You can download Internet Explorer from *http://www.microsoft.com* if necessary.

2. **Run the MFC Application Wizard to generate the Ex09b project.** Accept all the default settings but two: Select Single Document and deselect Printing And Print Preview. Be sure the ActiveX Controls option is selected, as in Ex09a.

3. **Install the Web browser control in the Ex09b project.** Choose Add Class from the Project menu, and select the MFC Class From ActiveX Control template. Then select Microsoft Web Browser. Visual Studio .NET will present two interfaces for which to generate wrapper classes: *IWebBrowser* and *IWebBrowser2*. Select *IWebBrowser2*. Visual Studio .NET will generate the wrapper class *CWebBrowser2* and add the files to your project.

4. **Add two *CWebBrowser2* data members to the *CEx09bView* class.** It's easiest to add these member variables by hand in the header file:

```
private:
    CWebBrowser2 m_target;
    CWebBrowser2 m_search;
```

   Be sure to add an *#include* statement for the cwebbrowser2.h file.

5. **Add the child window ID constants for the two controls.** Right-click on the dialog class in Resource View and choose Resource Symbols from the shortcut menu. Add the symbols *ID_BROWSER_SEARCH* and *ID_BROWSER_TARGET*.

6. **Add a static character array data member for the Google URL.** Add the following static data member to the class declaration in Ex09bView.h:

```
private:
   static const char s_engineGoogle[];
```

Then add the following definition in Ex09bView.cpp, outside any function:

```
const char CEx09bView::s_engineGoogle[] = "http://www.google.com/";
```

7. **Use Class View's Properties window to map the view's *WM_CREATE* and *WM_SIZE* messages.** Edit the handler code in Ex09bView.cpp as follows:

```
int CEx09bView::OnCreate(LPCREATESTRUCT lpCreateStruct)
{
    if (CView::OnCreate(lpCreateStruct) == -1)
        return -1;

    DWORD dwStyle = WS_VISIBLE | WS_CHILD;
    if (m_search.Create(NULL, dwStyle, CRect(0, 0, 100, 100),
                        this, ID_BROWSER_SEARCH) == 0) {
        AfxMessageBox("Unable to create search control!\n");
        return -1;
    }
    m_search.Navigate(s_engineGoogle, NULL, NULL, NULL, NULL);

    if (m_target.Create(NULL, dwStyle, CRect(0, 0, 100, 100),
                        this, ID_BROWSER_TARGET) == 0) {
        AfxMessageBox("Unable to create target control!\n");
        return -1;
    }
    m_target.GoHome(); // as defined in Internet Explorer options

    return 0;
}

void CEx09bView::OnSize(UINT nType, int cx, int cy)
{
    CView::OnSize(nType, cx, cy);

    CRect rectClient;
    GetClientRect(rectClient);
    CRect rectBrowse(rectClient);
    rectBrowse.right = rectClient.right / 2;
    CRect rectSearch(rectClient);
    rectSearch.left = rectClient.right / 2;

    m_target.put_Width(rectBrowse.right - rectBrowse.left);
    m_target.put_Height(rectBrowse.bottom - rectBrowse.top);
    m_target.UpdateWindow();
```

(continued)

```
    m_search.put_Left(rectSearch.left);
    m_search.put_Width(rectSearch.right - rectSearch.left);
    m_search.put_Height(rectSearch.bottom - rectSearch.top);
    m_search.UpdateWindow();
}
```

The *OnCreate* function creates two browser windows inside the view window. The right-hand browser displays the top-level Google page, and the left-hand browser displays the "home" page as defined through the Internet Options icon in Control Panel. The *OnSize* function, which is called whenever the view window changes size, ensures that the browser windows completely cover the view window. The *CWebBrowser2* member functions *put_Width* and *put_Height* set the browser's *Width* and *Height* properties.

8. **Add the event sink macros in the CEx09bView files.** The code wizards available from Class View's Properties window can't map events from a dynamic ActiveX control, so you must do it manually. Add the following lines inside the class declaration in the file Ex09bView.h:

```
protected:
    afx_msg void OnBeforeNavigateExplorer1(LPCTSTR URL,
        long Flags, LPCTSTR TargetFrameName,
        VARIANT FAR* PostData, LPCTSTR Headers, BOOL FAR* Cancel);
    afx_msg void OnTitleChangeExplorer2(LPCTSTR Text);
    DECLARE_EVENTSINK_MAP()
```

Then add the following code in Ex09bView.cpp:

```
BEGIN_EVENTSINK_MAP(CEx09bView, CView)
    ON_EVENT(CEx09bView, ID_BROWSER_SEARCH, 100,
        OnBeforeNavigateExplorer1, VTS_BSTR VTS_I4 VTS_BSTR
        VTS_PVARIANT VTS_BSTR VTS_PBOOL)
    ON_EVENT(CEx09bView, ID_BROWSER_TARGET, 113,
        OnTitleChangeExplorer2, VTS_BSTR)
END_EVENTSINK_MAP()
```

9. **Add two event handler functions.** Add the following member functions in Ex09bView.cpp:

```
void CEx09bView::OnBeforeNavigateExplorer1(LPCTSTR URL,
    long Flags, LPCTSTR TargetFrameName,
    VARIANT FAR* PostData, LPCTSTR Headers, BOOL FAR* Cancel)
{
    TRACE("CEx09bView::OnBeforeNavigateExplorer1 -URL = %s\n", URL);
```

```
        if (!strnicmp(URL, s_engineGoogle, strlen(s_engineGoogle))) {
            return;
        }
        m_target.Navigate(URL, NULL, NULL, PostData, NULL);
        *Cancel = TRUE;
}

void CEx09bView::OnTitleChangeExplorer2(LPCTSTR Text)
{
    // Careful!  Event could fire before we're ready.
    CWnd* pWnd = AfxGetApp()->m_pMainWnd;
    if (pWnd != NULL) {
        if (::IsWindow(pWnd->m_hWnd)) {
            pWnd->SetWindowText(Text);
        }
    }
}
```

The *OnBeforeNavigateExplorer1* handler is called when the user clicks on a link in the search page. The function compares the clicked URL (in the *URL* string parameter) with the search engine URL. If they match, the navigation proceeds in the search window; otherwise, the navigation is cancelled and the *Navigate* method is called for the target window. The *OnTitleChangeExplorer2* handler updates the Ex09b window title to match the title on the target page.

10. **Build and test the Ex09b application.** Search for something on the Google page, and then watch the information appear in the target page.

Picture Properties

Some ActiveX controls support picture properties, which can accommodate bitmaps, metafiles, and icons. If an ActiveX control has at least one picture property, Visual Studio .NET will generate a *CPicture* class in your project during the control's installation. You don't need to use this *CPicture* class, but you must use the MFC class *CPictureHolder*. To access the *CPictureHolder* class declaration and code, you need the following line in StdAfx.h:

```
#include <afxctl.h>
```

Suppose you have an ActiveX control with a picture property named *Picture*. Here's how you set the *Picture* property to a bitmap in your program's resources:

```
CPictureHolder pict;
pict.CreateFromBitmap(IDB_MYBITMAP); // from project's resources
m_control.SetPicture(pict.GetPictureDispatch());
```

> **Note** If you include the AfxCtl.h file, you can't statically link your program with the MFC library. If you need a standalone program that supports picture properties, you'll have to borrow code from the *CPictureHolder* class, located in the \Program Files\Microsoft Visual Studio .NET\VC7\atlmfc\src\mfc\ctlpict.cpp file.

Bindable Properties: Change Notifications

If an ActiveX control has a property designated as *bindable*, the control will send an *OnChanged* notification to its container when the value of the property changes inside the control. In addition, the control can send an *OnRequestEdit* notification for a property whose value is about to change but has not yet changed. If the container returns *FALSE* from its *OnRequestEdit* handler, the control should not change the property value.

MFC fully supports property change notifications in ActiveX control containers, but as of Visual C++ .NET, no wizard support is available. That means you must manually add entries to your container class's event sink map.

Suppose you have an ActiveX control with a bindable property named *Note* with a dispatch ID of *4*. You add an *ON_PROPNOTIFY* macro to the *EVENTSINK* macros in this way:

```
BEGIN_EVENTSINK_MAP(CAboutDlg, CDialog)
    ON_PROPNOTIFY(CAboutDlg, IDC_MYCTRL1, 4, OnNoteRequestEdit,
                  OnNoteChanged)
END_EVENTSINK_MAP()
```

You must then code the *OnNoteRequestEdit* and *OnNoteChanged* functions with return types and parameter types exactly as shown here:

```
BOOL CMyDlg::OnNoteRequestEdit(BOOL* pb)
{
    TRACE("CMyDlg::OnNoteRequestEdit\n");
    *pb = TRUE; // TRUE means change request granted
    return TRUE;
}

BOOL CMyDlg::OnNoteChanged()
{
    TRACE("CMyDlg::OnNoteChanged\n");
    return TRUE;
}
```

You'll also need corresponding prototypes in the class header, as shown here:

```
afx_msg BOOL OnNoteRequestEdit(BOOL* pb);
afx_msg BOOL OnNoteChanged();
```

10

Win32 Core Memory Management

Microsoft Windows has been through a great number of changes over the years. In the late 1980s, system memory was at a huge premium, and it was all you could do to squeeze the bytes out of the RAM installed on your machine. With Windows running at 32 bits, the story has changed dramatically. In 16-bit Windows, you had to perform an immense amount of housekeeping by calling the Win16 memory management functions (such as *GlobalAlloc* and *GlobalLock*). These functions were carried forward into Win32, but only for reasons of backward compatibility. Underneath, the original functions work very differently, and many new ones have been added.

This chapter covers Win32 memory management theory, including the virtual memory and the fundamental heap management functions. The chapter also covers how the C++ *new* and *delete* operators connect with the underlying heap functions. Finally, the chapter covers how to use the memory-mapped file functions, finishing with some practical tips on managing dynamic memory. For more in-depth information about Windows memory management, you'll want to look at Jeffrey Richter's *Programming Applications for Microsoft Windows*, Fourth Edition (Microsoft Press, 1999), which covers Windows 2000.

Processes and Memory Space

Before you learn how Windows manages memory, you must first understand what a *process* is. If you already know what a program is, you're on your way. A program is an EXE file that you can launch in various ways in Windows. Once a program is running, it's called a process. A process owns its memory, file handles, and other system resources. If you launch the same program twice in a row, you'll have two separate processes running simultaneously. The Windows Task Manager (right-click on the taskbar) gives you a detailed list of processes that are currently running, and they allow you to kill processes that are not responding. The SPYXX.exe program (which is also included with Visual Studio) shows the relationships among processes, threads, and windows.

> **Note** The Windows Task Manager shows running programs and active processes. The Processes tab shows active processes. A single process (such as Windows Explorer) might have several main windows, each supported by its own thread, and some processes don't have windows at all. (See Chapter 11 for a discussion of threads.)

> **Note** The Microsoft .NET Framework provides a new level of isolation: the AppDomain. We'll look at AppDomains in Chapter 10.

The important thing to know about a process is that it has its own "private" 4 GB virtual address space (which I'll describe in detail shortly). For now, pretend that your computer has hundreds of gigabytes of RAM and that each process gets 4 GB. Your program can access any byte of this space with a single 32-bit linear address. Each process's memory space contains a variety of items, including the following:

- Your program's EXE image
- Any nonsystem DLLs that your program loads, including the MFC DLLs
- Your program's global data (read-only as well as read/write)
- Your program's stack

- Dynamically allocated memory, including Windows and C runtime library (CRT) heaps
- Memory-mapped files
- Interprocess shared memory blocks
- Memory local to specific executing threads
- All sorts of special system memory blocks, including virtual memory tables
- The Windows kernel and executive, plus DLLs that are part of Windows

The Windows 95/98 Process Address Space

In Windows 95/98, only the bottom 2 GB (0 to 0x7FFFFFFF) of address space is truly private, and the bottom 4 MB of that is off-limits. The stack, heaps, and read/write global memory are mapped in the bottom 2 GB, along with application EXE and DLL files.

The top 2 GB of space is the same for all processes and is shared by all processes. The Windows 95/98 kernel, executive, virtual device drivers (VxDs), and file system code, along with important tables such as page tables, are mapped to the top 1 GB (0xC0000000 to 0xFFFFFFFF) of address space. Windows DLLs and memory-mapped files are located in the range 0x80000000 to 0xBFFFFFFF.

Figure 10-1 shows a memory map of two processes using the same program.

How safe is all this? It's next to impossible for one process to overwrite another process's stack, global, or heap memory because this memory, located in the bottom 2 GB of virtual address space, is assigned only to that specific process. All EXE and DLL code is flagged as read-only, so there's no problem if the code is mapped in several processes.

However, because important Windows read/write data is mapped there, the top 1 GB of address space is vulnerable. An errant program could wipe out important system tables located in this region. In addition, one process could mess up another process's memory-mapped files in the range 0x80000000 through 0xBFFFFFFF because this region is shared by all processes.

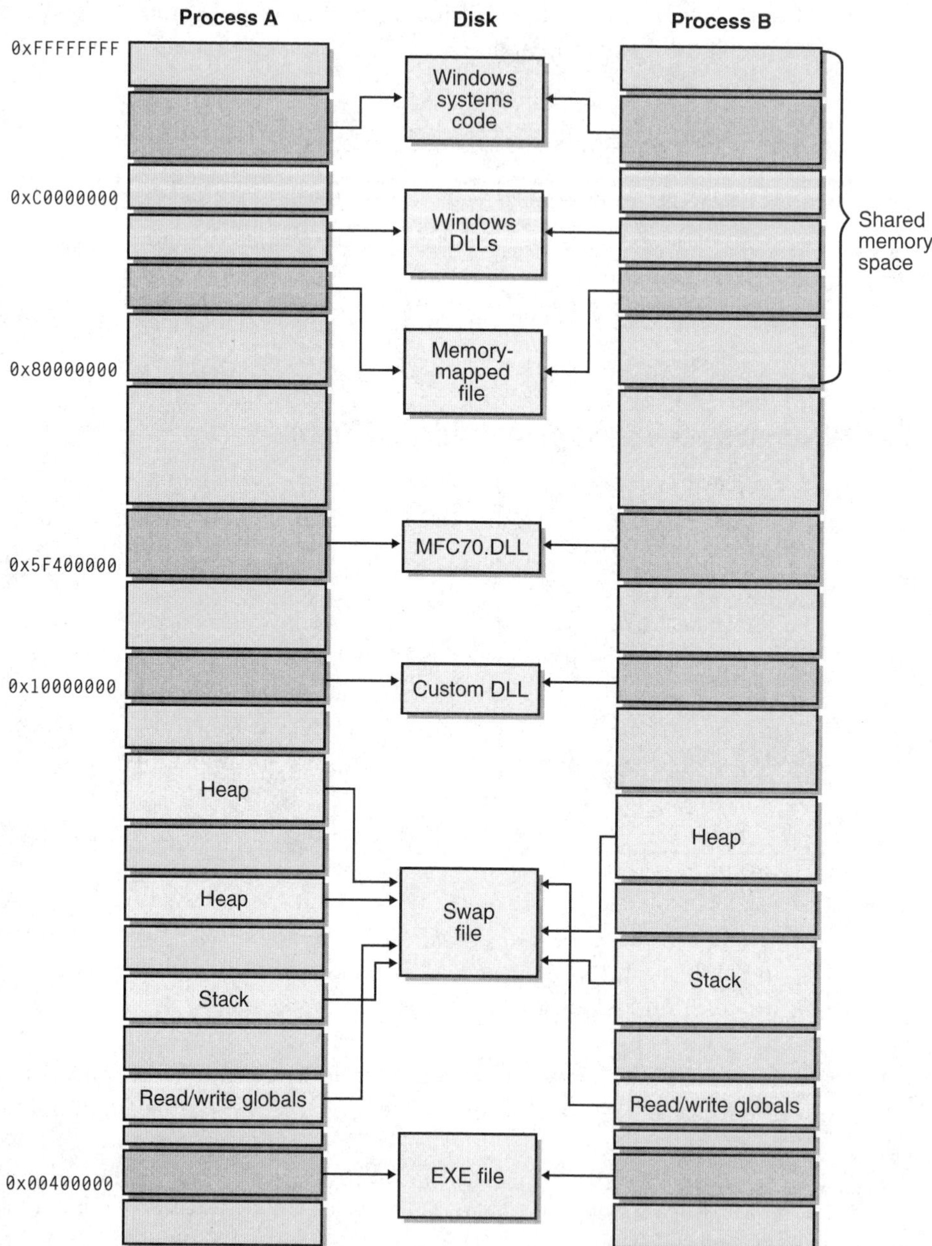

Figure 10-1 A typical Windows 95/98 virtual memory map for two processes linked to the same EXE file.

The Windows NT/2000/XP Process Address Space

A process in Windows NT/2000/XP can access only the bottom 2 GB of its address space, and the lowest and highest 64 KB of that is inaccessible. The EXE, the application's DLLs and Windows DLLs, and memory-mapped files all reside in this space between 0x00010000 and 0x7FFEFFFF. The Windows NT kernel, executive, and device drivers all reside in the upper 2 GB, where they're completely protected from any tampering by an errant program. Memory-mapped files are safer, too. One process cannot access another's memory-mapped file without knowing the file's name and explicitly mapping a view.

How Virtual Memory Works

You know that your computer doesn't really have hundreds of gigabytes of RAM. And it doesn't have hundreds of gigabytes of disk space either. Windows uses some smoke and mirrors here.

First of all, a process's 4 GB address space is used sparsely. Various programs and data elements will be scattered throughout the 4 GB address space in 4 KB units, starting on 4 KB boundaries. Each 4 KB unit, called a *page*, can hold either code or data. When a page is being used, it occupies physical memory, but you never see its physical memory address. The Intel microprocessor chip efficiently maps a 32-bit virtual address to both a physical page and an offset within the page, using two levels of 4 KB page tables, as shown in Figure 10-2. Note that individual pages can be flagged as either read-only or read/write. Also note that each process has its own set of page tables. The chip's CR3 register holds a pointer to the directory page, so when Windows switches from one process to another, it simply updates CR3.

So now our process is down from 4 GB to maybe 5 MB—a definite improvement. But if we're running several programs, along with Windows itself, we'll still run out of RAM. In Figure 10-2, you'll notice that the page table entry has a "present" bit that indicates whether the 4 KB page is currently in RAM. If we try to access a page that's not in RAM, an interrupt will fire and Windows will analyze the situation by checking its internal tables. If the memory reference was bogus, we'll get the dreaded "page fault" message and the program will exit. Otherwise, Windows will read the page from a disk file into RAM and update the page table by loading the physical address and setting the present bit. This is the essence of Win32 virtual memory.

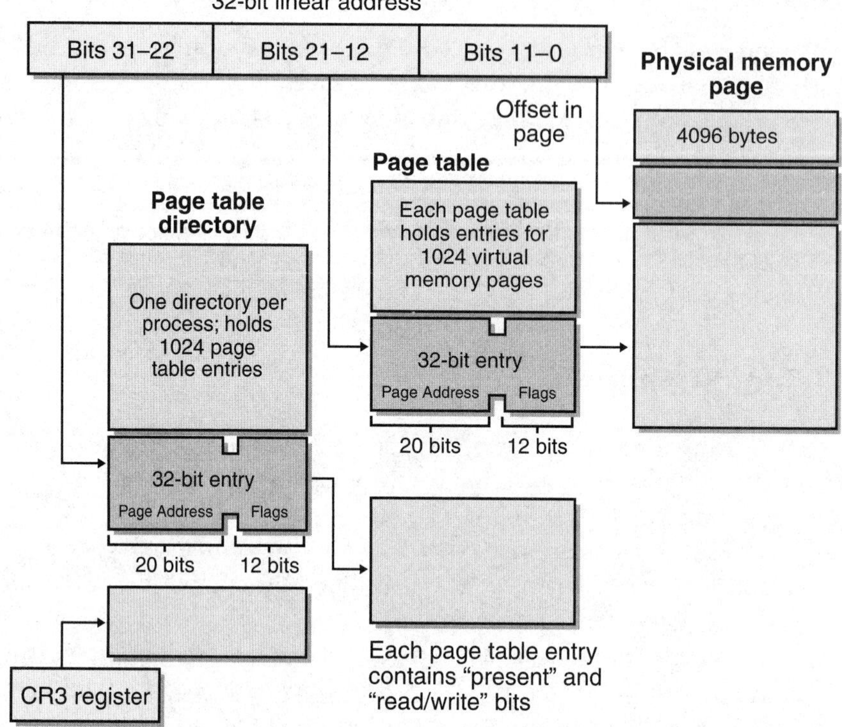

Figure 10-2 Win32 virtual memory management (Intel).

The Windows virtual memory manager figures out how to read and write 4 KB pages so that it optimizes performance. If one process hasn't used a page for a while and another process needs memory, the first page will be swapped out or discarded and the RAM will be used for the new process's page. Your program won't normally be aware that this is going on. The more disk I/O that happens, however, the worse your program's performance will be, so it stands to reason that more RAM is better.

I've mentioned the disk, but I haven't talked about files yet. All processes share a big system-wide swap file that's used for all read/write data and some read-only data. (Windows NT/2000/XP supports multiple swap files.) Windows determines the swap file size based on available RAM and free disk space, but there are ways to fine-tune the swap file's size and specify its physical location on disk.

The swap file isn't the only file used by the virtual memory manager, however. It wouldn't make sense to write code pages back to the swap file, so instead of using the swap file, Windows maps EXE and DLL files directly to their files on disk. Because the code pages are marked read-only, there's never a need to write them back to disk.

If two processes use the same EXE file, that file is mapped into each process's address space. The code and constants never change during program execution, so the same physical memory can be mapped for each process. The two processes cannot share global data, however, and Windows 95/98 and Windows NT/2000/XP handle this situation differently. Windows 95/98 maps separate copies of the global data to each process. In Windows NT/2000/XP, both processes use the same copy of each page of global data until one process attempts to write to that page. At that point, the page is copied; as a result, each process has its own private copy stored at the same virtual address.

> **Note** A DLL can be mapped directly to its DLL file only if the DLL can be loaded at its designated base address. If a DLL were statically linked to load at, say, 0x10000000 but that address range were already occupied by another DLL, Windows would have to "fix up" the addresses within the DLL code. Windows NT/2000/XP copies the altered pages to the swap file when the DLL is first loaded, but Windows 95/98 can do the fix-up "on the fly" when the pages are brought into RAM. Needless to say, it's important to build your DLLs with non-overlapping address ranges. If you're using the MFC DLLs, set the base address of your own DLLs outside the range 0x5F400000 through 0x5FFFFFFF. You'll see more on writing DLLs in Chapter 20.

Memory-mapped files are also mapped directly. These can be flagged as read/write and made available for sharing among processes.

For Win32 Programmers

If you've experimented with the Registers window in Visual Studio, you might have noticed the segment registers, particularly CS, DS, and SS. (To display the segment registers in Visual Studio .NET, you might need to right-click in the Registers window and select the CPU Segments group.) These 16-bit relics haven't gone away, but you can mostly ignore them. In 32-bit mode, the Intel microprocessor still uses segment registers, which are 16 bits long, to translate addresses before sending them through the virtual memory system. A table in RAM called the *descriptor table* has entries that contain the virtual memory base address and block size for code, data, and stack segments. In 32-bit mode, these segments can be up to 4 GB in size and can be flagged as read-only or read/write. For every memory reference, the chip uses the *selector*, the contents of a segment register, to look up the descriptor table entry for the purpose of translating the address.

Under Win32, each process has two segments—one for code and one for data and the stack. You can assume that both have a base value of 0 and a size of 4 GB, so they overlap. The net result is no translation at all, but Windows uses some tricks that exclude the bottom 16 KB from the data segment. If you try to access memory down there, you get a protection fault instead of a page fault, which is useful for debugging null pointers.

Some future operating system might someday use segments to get around that annoying 4 GB size limitation.

The *VirtualAlloc* Function: Committed and Reserved Memory

If your program needs dynamic memory, sooner or later the Win32 *VirtualAlloc* function will be called. Chances are that your program will never call *VirtualAlloc*; instead, you'll rely on the Windows heap or the CRT heap functions to call it directly. Knowing how *VirtualAlloc* works, however, will help you better understand the functions that call it.

First, you must understand what *reserved* and *committed* memory are. When memory is reserved, a contiguous virtual address range is set aside. If, for example, you know that your program is going to use a single memory block (known as a *region*) that is 5 MB in size but you don't need to use it all right away, you can call *VirtualAlloc* with a *MEM_RESERVE* allocation type parameter and a 5 MB size parameter. Windows will round the start address of the region to a 64 KB boundary and prevent your process from reserving other memory in the same range. You can specify a start address for your region, but more often you'll let Windows assign it for you. Nothing else will happen. No RAM will be allocated, and no swap file space will be set aside.

When you get more serious about needing memory, you can call *VirtualAlloc* again to commit the reserved memory, using a *MEM_COMMIT* allocation type parameter. Now the start and end addresses of the region will be rounded to 4 KB boundaries, and corresponding swap file pages will be set aside together with the required page table. The block will be designated as either read-only or read/write. Still, no RAM will be allocated, however; RAM allocation occurs only when you try to access the memory. If the memory was not previously reserved, no problem. If the memory was previously committed, still no problem. The rule is that memory must be committed before you can use it.

You can call the *VirtualFree* function to "decommit" committed memory, thereby returning the designated pages back to reserved status. *VirtualFree* can also free a reserved region of memory, but you have to specify the base address you got from a previous *VirtualAlloc* reservation call.

The Windows Heap and the *GlobalAlloc* Function Family

A *heap* is a memory pool for a specific process. When your program needs a block of memory, it calls a heap allocation function, and it calls a companion function to free the memory. There's no assumption about 4 KB page boundaries; the heap manager uses space in existing pages or calls *VirtualAlloc* to get more pages. We'll first look at Windows heaps, then we'll consider heaps managed by the CRT library for functions such as *malloc* and *new*.

Windows provides each process with a default heap, and the process can create any number of additional Windows heaps. The *HeapAlloc* function allocates memory in a Windows heap, and *HeapFree* releases it.

You might never need to call *HeapAlloc* yourself, but it will be called for you by the *GlobalAlloc* function that's left over from Win16. In the ideal 32-bit world, you wouldn't have to use *GlobalAlloc*, but in this world, you'll still run into some code ported from Win16 that uses "memory handle" (*HGLOBAL*) parameters instead of 32-bit memory addresses.

GlobalAlloc uses the default Windows heap. It does two different things, depending on its attribute parameter. If you specify *GMEM_FIXED*, *GlobalAlloc* will simply call *HeapAlloc* and return the address cast as a 32-bit *HGLOBAL* value. If you specify *GMEM_MOVEABLE*, the returned *HGLOBAL* value will be a pointer to a handle table entry in your process. That entry will contain a pointer to the actual memory, which is allocated with *HeapAlloc*.

Why bother with "movable" memory if it adds an extra level of indirection? You're looking at an artifact from Win16 in which, once upon a time, the operating system actually moved memory blocks around. In Win32, movable blocks exist only to support the *GlobalReAlloc* function, which allocates a new memory block, copies bytes from the old block to the new, frees the old block, and assigns the new block address to the existing handle table entry. If nobody ever called *GlobalReAlloc*, we could always use *HeapAlloc* instead of *GlobalAlloc*.

Unfortunately, many library functions use *HGLOBAL* return values and parameters instead of memory addresses. If such a function returns an *HGLOBAL* value, you should assume that memory was allocated with the *GMEM_MOVEABLE* attribute, and that means you must call the *GlobalLock* function to get the memory address. (If the memory block represented by the handle is fixed, the *GlobalLock* call just returns the handle as an address.) Call *GlobalUnlock* when you're finished accessing the memory. If you're required to supply an *HGLOBAL* parameter, to be absolutely safe you should generate it with a *GlobalAlloc(GMEM_MOVEABLE, ...)* call in case the called function decides to call *GlobalReAlloc* and expects the handle value to be unchanged.

The Small-Block Heap, the C++ *new* and *delete* Operators, and *_heapmin*

You can use the Windows *HeapAlloc* function in your programs, but you're more likely to use the *malloc* and *free* functions supplied by the CRT. If you write C++ code, you won't call these functions directly; instead, you'll use the *new* and *delete* operators, which map directly to *malloc* and *free*. If you use *new* to allocate a block larger than a certain threshold, the CRT will pass the call straight through to *HeapAlloc* to allocate memory from a Windows heap created for the CRT. For blocks smaller than the threshold, the CRT manages a small-block heap, calling *VirtualAlloc* and *VirtualFree* as necessary. Here is the algorithm:

1. Memory is reserved in 4 MB regions.
2. Memory is committed in 64 KB blocks (16 pages).

3. Memory is decommitted 64 KB at a time. As 128 KB becomes free, the last 64 KB is decommitted.

4. A 4 MB region is released when every page in that region has been decommitted.

As you can see, this small-block heap takes care of its own cleanup. The CRT's Windows heap doesn't automatically decommit and unreserve pages, however. To clean up the larger blocks, you must call the CRT *_heapmin* function, which calls the Windows *HeapCompact* function. (Unfortunately, the Windows 95/98 version of *HeapCompact* doesn't do anything—all the more reason to use Windows NT/2000/XP.) Once pages are decommitted, other programs can reuse the corresponding swap file space.

> **Note** In previous versions of the CRT, the free list pointers were stored inside the heap pages. This strategy required the *malloc* function to "touch" (read from the swap file) many pages to find free space, and this degraded performance. The current system, which stores the free list in a separate area of memory, is faster and minimizes the need for third-party heap management software.

If you want to change or access the block size threshold, use the CRT functions *_set_sbh_threshold* and *_get_sbh_threshold*.

A special debug version of *malloc*, *_malloc_dbg*, adds debugging information inside allocated memory blocks. The *new* operator calls *_malloc_dbg* when you build an MFC project with *_DEBUG* defined. Your program can then detect memory blocks that you forgot to free or that you inadvertently overwrote.

Memory-Mapped Files

In case you think you don't have enough memory management options already, I'll toss you another one. Suppose your program needs to read a device-independent bitmap (DIB) file. Your instinct might be to allocate a buffer of the correct size, open the file, and then call a read function to copy the whole disk file into the buffer. The Windows memory-mapped file is a more elegant tool for handling this problem, however. You simply map an address range directly to the file. When the process accesses a memory page, Windows allocates RAM and reads the data from disk.

Here's what the code looks like:

```
HANDLE hFile = ::CreateFile(strPathname, GENERIC_READ,
    FILE_SHARE_READ, NULL, OPEN_EXISTING, FILE_ATTRIBUTE_NORMAL, NULL);
ASSERT(hFile != NULL);
HANDLE hMap = ::CreateFileMapping(hFile, NULL, PAGE_READONLY,
    0, 0, NULL);
ASSERT(hMap != NULL);
LPVOID lpvFile = ::MapViewOfFile(hMap, FILE_MAP_READ,
    0, 0, 0); // Map whole file
DWORD dwFileSize = ::GetFileSize(hFile, NULL);  // useful info
// Use the file
::UnmapViewOfFile(lpvFile);
::CloseHandle(hMap);
::CloseHandle(hFile);
```

Here you're using virtual memory backed by the DIB file. Windows determines the file size, reserves a corresponding address range, and commits the file's storage as the physical storage for this range. In this case, *lpvFile* is the start address. The *hMap* variable contains the handle for the file-mapping object, which can be shared among processes if you want.

The DIB in the example above is a small file that you could read entirely into a buffer. Imagine a larger file for which you would normally issue seek commands. A memory-mapped file works for such a file as well because of the underlying virtual memory system. RAM is allocated and pages are read when you access them, and not before.

> **Note** By default, the entire file is committed when you map it, although it's possible to map only part of a file.

If two processes share a file mapping object (such as *hMap* in the sample code above), the file itself is, in effect, shared memory, but the virtual addresses returned by *MapViewOfFile* might be different. Indeed, this is the preferred Win32 method of sharing memory. (Calling the *GlobalAlloc* function with the *GMEM_SHARE* flag doesn't create shared memory as it did in Win16.) If memory sharing is all you want to do and you don't need a permanent disk file, you can omit the call to *CreateFile* and pass 0xFFFFFFFF as the *CreateFileMapping* *hFile* parameter. Now the shared memory will be backed by pages in the swap file. (See *Programming Applications for Microsoft Windows*, Fourth Edition by Jeffrey Richter for details on memory-mapped files.)

> **Note** If you intend to access only a few random pages of a file-mapping object that is backed by the swap file, you can use a technique that Jeffrey Richter describes in *Programming Applications for Microsoft Windows*. You call *CreateFileMapping* with a special flag, and then you commit specific address ranges later using the *VirtualAlloc* function.

> **Note** You might want to look carefully at the Windows message *WM_COPYDATA*. This message lets you transfer data between processes in shared memory without having to deal with the file mapping API. You must send this message rather than post it, which means that the sending process has to wait while the receiving process copies and processes the data.

Unfortunately, there's no direct support for memory-mapped files or shared memory in MFC. The *CSharedFile* class supports only clipboard memory transfers using *HGLOBAL* handles, so the class isn't as useful as its name implies.

Accessing Resources

Resources are contained inside EXEs and DLLs and thus occupy virtual address space that doesn't change during the life of the process. It is therefore easy to read a resource directly. If you need to access a bitmap, for example, you can get the DIB address with code like this:

```
LPVOID lpvResource = (LPVOID) ::LoadResource(NULL,
    ::FindResource(NULL, MAKEINTRESOURCE(IDB_REDBLOCKS),
    RT_BITMAP));
```

The *LoadResource* function returns an *HGLOBAL* value, but you can safely cast it to a pointer.

Tips for Managing Dynamic Memory

The more you use the heap, the more fragmented it will get and the more slowly your program will run. If your program is supposed to run for hours or days at a time, you have to be careful. It's better to allocate all the memory you need when your program starts and then free it when the program exits, but that's not always possible. The *CString* class is a nuisance because it's constantly allocating and freeing little bits of memory.

Don't forget to call *_heapmin* every once in a while if your program allocates blocks larger than the small-block heap threshold. And be sure to remember where heap memory comes from. You'd have a big problem, for instance, if you called *HeapFree* on a small-block pointer you got from *new*.

Be aware that your stack can be as big as it needs to be. Because you no longer have a 64 KB size limit, you can put large objects on the stack, thereby reducing the need for heap allocations.

Your program won't run at full speed and then suddenly throw an exception when Windows runs out of swap space. It will just slowly grind to a halt, making your customer unhappy. There's not much you can do except try to figure out which program is eating memory and why. Because the USER and GDI modules in Windows 95/98 still have 16-bit components, there is some possibility of exhausting the 64 KB heaps that hold GDI objects and window structures. This possibility is pretty remote, however, and if it happens, it probably indicates a bug in your program.

Optimizing Storage for Constant Data

Remember that the code in your program is backed not by the swap file but directly by its EXE and DLL files. If several instances of your program are running, the same EXE and DLL files will be mapped to each process's virtual address space. What about constant data? You would want that data to be part of the program rather than have it copied to another block of address space that's backed by the swap file.

You've got to work a little bit to ensure that constant data gets stored with the program. First, consider string constants, which often permeate your programs. You'd think that these would be read-only data, but guess again. Because you're allowed to write code like this (The compiler will compile this code, but you'll get a memory access error if you try to run it.)

```
char* pch = "test";
*pch = 'x';
```

The string "test" can't possibly be constant data, and it isn't. If you want "test" to be a constant, you must declare it as an initialized *const* static or a global variable. Here's the global definition:

```
const char g_pch[] = "test";
```

Now *g_pch* is stored with the code, but where, specifically? To answer that, you must understand the "data sections" that the Visual C++ linker generates. If you set the link options to generate a map file, you'll see a long list of the sections (memory blocks) in your program. Individual sections can be designated for code or data, and they can be read-only or read/write. Table 10-1 lists the important sections and describes their characteristics.

Table 10-1 Important Sections of a Program

Name	Type	Access	Contents
.text	Code	Read-only	Program code
.rdata	Data	Read-only	Constant initialized data
.data	Data	Read/write	Nonconstant initialized data
.bss	Data	Read/write	Nonconstant uninitialized data

The *.rdata* section is part of the EXE file, and that's where the linker puts the *g_pch* variable. The more stuff you put in the *.rdata* section, the better. The use of the *const* modifier does the trick.

You can put built-in types and even structures in the *.rdata* section, but you can't put C++ objects there if they have constructors. If you write a statement such as this one

```
const CRect g_rect(0, 0, 100, 100);
```

the linker puts the object into the *.bss* section, and it will be backed separately to the swap file for each process. If you think about it, this makes sense because the compiler must invoke the constructor function after the program is loaded.

Now suppose you wanted to do the worst possible thing: declare a *CString* global variable (or static class data member) like this:

```
const CString g_str("this is the worst thing I can do");
```

Now you've got the *CString* object (which is quite small) in the *.bss* section, and you've also got a character array in the *.data* section, neither of which can be backed by the EXE file. To make matters worse, when the program starts, the *CString* class must allocate heap memory for a copy of the characters. You'd be much better off using a *const* character array instead of a *CString* object.

11

Windows Message Processing and Multi-Threaded Programming

With its multi-tasking and multi-threading API, Win32 revolutionized programming for Microsoft Windows. If you've seen magazine articles and advanced programming books on these subjects, you might have been intimidated by the complexity of using multiple threads. You can stick with single-threaded programming for a long time and still write useful Win32 applications. But if you learn the fundamentals of threads, you'll be able to write more efficient and capable programs. You'll also be on your way to a better understanding of the Win32 programming model.

Windows Message Processing

In order to understand threads, you must first understand how 32-bit Windows processes messages. The best starting point is a single-threaded program that shows the importance of the message translation and dispatch process. You can improve that program by adding a second thread, which you'll control with a global variable and a simple message. Then you can experiment with events and critical sections. For heavy-duty multi-threading elements such as mutexes and semaphores, however, you'll need to refer to another book, such as Jeffrey Richter's *Programming Applications for Microsoft Windows*, Fourth Edition (Microsoft Press, 1999).

How a Single-Threaded Program Processes Messages

All the programs so far in this book have been single-threaded, which means that your code has only one path of execution. With Microsoft Visual Studio's help, you've written handler functions for various Windows messages and you've written *OnDraw* code that is called in response to the *WM_PAINT* message. It might seem as if Windows magically calls your handler when the message floats in, but it doesn't work that way. Deep inside the MFC code (which is linked to your program) are instructions that look something like this:

```
MSG message;
while (::GetMessage(&message, NULL, 0, 0)) {
    ::TranslateMessage(&message);
    ::DispatchMessage(&message);
}
```

Windows determines which messages belong to your program, and the *GetMessage* function returns when a message needs to be processed. If no messages are posted, your program is suspended and other programs can run. When a message eventually arrives, your program "wakes up." The *TranslateMessage* function translates key messages into character messages. For example, *WM_KEYDOWN* messages are translated into *WM_CHAR* messages containing ASCII characters. The *DispatchMessage* function passes control (via the window class) to the MFC message pump, which calls your function via the message map. When your handler is finished, it returns to the MFC code, which eventually causes *DispatchMessage* to return.

Yielding Control

What would happen if one of your handler functions were a pig and chewed up 10 seconds of CPU time? Back in the 16-bit days, that would have hung up the whole computer for the duration. Only cursor tracking and a few other interrupt-based tasks would have run. With Win32, multi-tasking got a whole lot better. Other applications can run because of preemptive multi-tasking—Windows simply interrupts your pig function when it needs to. However, even in Win32, your program will be locked out for 10 seconds. It won't be able to process any messages because *DispatchMessage* won't return until the pig returns.

There is a way around this problem, however, which works with both Win16 and Win32. You simply yield control once in a while by inserting the following instructions inside the main loop:

```
MSG message;
if (::PeekMessage(&message, NULL, 0, 0, PM_REMOVE)) {
    ::TranslateMessage(&message);
    ::DispatchMessage(&message);
}
```

The *PeekMessage* function works like *GetMessage*, except it returns immediately even if no message has arrived for your program. In that case, the messages keep flowing. If there is a message, however, the function pauses, the handler is called, and the message processing starts up again after the handler exits.

Timers

A Windows timer is a useful programming element that sometimes makes multithreaded programming unnecessary. If you need to read a communication buffer, for example, you can set up a timer to retrieve the accumulated characters every 100 milliseconds. You can also use a timer to control animation because the timer is independent of CPU clock speed.

Timers are easy to use. You simply call the *CWnd* member function *SetTimer* with an interval parameter, and then you provide a message handler function for the resulting *WM_TIMER* messages. Once you start the timer with a specified interval in milliseconds, *WM_TIMER* messages will be sent continuously to your window until you call *CWnd::KillTimer* or until the timer's window is destroyed. If you want to, you can use multiple timers, each identified by an integer. Because Windows isn't a real-time operating system, the interval between timer events becomes imprecise if you specify an interval much less than 100 milliseconds.

Like any other Windows messages, timer messages can be blocked by other handler functions in your program. Fortunately, timer messages don't stack up. Windows won't put a timer message in the queue if a message for that timer is already present.

The Ex11a Program

We're going to write a single-threaded program that contains a CPU-intensive computation loop. We want to let the program process messages after the user starts the computation; otherwise, the user won't be able to cancel the job. Also, we'd like to display the percent-complete status by using a progress indicator control, as shown in Figure 11-1. The Ex11a program allows message processing by yielding control in the compute loop. A timer handler updates the progress control based on compute parameters. The *WM_TIMER* messages could not be processed if the compute process didn't yield control.

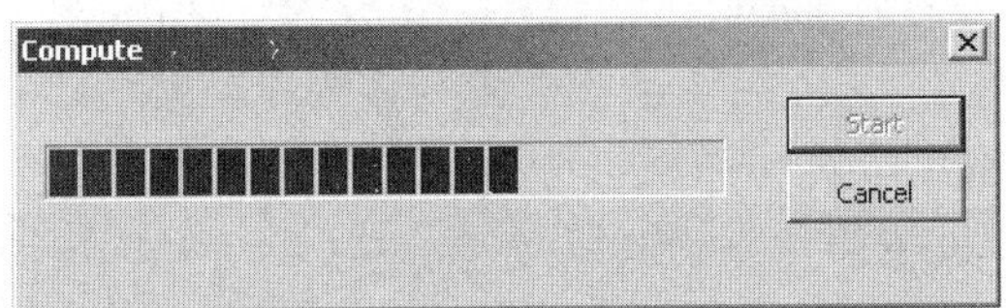

Figure 11-1 The Compute dialog box.

Here are the steps for building the Ex11a application:

1. **Run the MFC Application Wizard to generate a project named Ex11a.** Choose New Project from Visual Studio's File menu. In the New Project dialog box, select the MFC Application template, type the name **Ex11a**, and click OK. In the MFC Application Wizard, accept all the default settings but two: On the Application Type page, select Single Document, and on the Advanced Features page, deselect Printing And Print Preview.

2. **Create a new dialog resource named *IDD_COMPUTE*.** Choose Add Resource from the Project menu and add a new dialog resource. Change the *ID* property for the dialog box to *IDD_COMPUTE* and change the *Caption* property to *Compute*. For the OK button, change the *ID* property to *IDC_START* and change the *Caption* property to *Start*. For the Cancel button, change the *ID* property to *IDC_CANCEL*. Using the Toolbox, add a Progress control and leave the default *ID* property as *IDC_PROGRESS1*. When you're finished, your dialog box should look like the following:

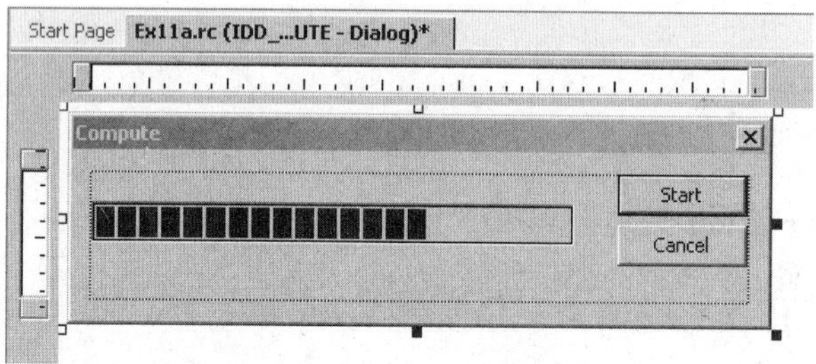

3. **Use the MFC Class Wizard to create the *CComputeDlg* class.** Choose Add Class from the Project menu to display the MFC Class Wizard. Type **CComputeDlg** as the class name, select *CDialog* as the base class, and set the dialog ID to *IDD_COMPUTE* to connect the new class to the dialog resource you just created.

4. **Add *WM_TIMER* and *BN_CLICKED* message handlers.** Select the *CComputeDlg* class in Class View. Click the Messages button at the top of the Properties window and add the *OnTimer* function for the *WM_TIMER* message. Click the Events button at the top of the Properties window and add the *OnBnClickedStart* and *OnBnClickedCancel* functions for *IDC_START* and *IDC_CANCEL*.

5. **Add three data members to the *CComputeDlg* class.** Edit the file ComputeDlg.h by adding the following protected data members:

```
int m_nTimer;
int m_nCount;
enum { nMaxCount = 50000 };
```

The *m_nCount* data member of class *CComputeDlg* is incremented during the compute process. It serves as a percent-complete measurement when divided by the "constant" *nMaxCount*.

6. **Add initialization code to the *CComputeDlg* constructor in the ComputeDlg.cpp file.** Add the following line to the constructor to ensure that the Cancel button will work if the compute process has not been started:

```
m_nCount = 0;
```

7. **Code the *OnBnClickedStart* function in ComputeDlg.cpp.** This code is executed when the user clicks the Start button. Add the following boldface code:

```
void CComputeDlg::OnBnClickedStart()
{
    MSG message;

    m_nTimer = SetTimer(1, 100, NULL); // 1/10 second
    ASSERT(m_nTimer != 0);
    GetDlgItem(IDC_START)->EnableWindow(FALSE);
    volatile int nTemp;
    for (m_nCount = 0; m_nCount < nMaxCount; m_nCount++) {
        for (nTemp = 0; nTemp < 10000; nTemp++) {
            // uses up CPU cycles
        }
        if (::PeekMessage(&message, NULL, 0, 0, PM_REMOVE)) {
            ::TranslateMessage(&message);
            ::DispatchMessage(&message);
        }
    }
    GetDlgItem(IDC_START)->EnableWindow(TRUE);
    CDialog::OnOK();
}
```

The main *for* loop is controlled by the value of *m_nCount*. At the end of each pass through the outer loop, *PeekMessage* allows other messages, including *WM_TIMER*, to be processed. The *EnableWindow(FALSE)* call disables the Start button during the computation. If we didn't take this precaution, the *OnBnClickedStart* function could be reentered. The second call to *EnableWindow(TRUE)* enables the Start button so the user can run the timer again.

8. **Code the *OnTimer* function in ComputeDlg.cpp.** When the timer fires, the progress indicator's position is set according to the value of *m_nCount*. Add the following boldface code:

```
void CComputeDlg::OnTimer(UINT nIDEvent)
{
    CProgressCtrl* pBar =
    (CProgressCtrl*) GetDlgItem(IDC_PROGRESS1);
    pBar->SetPos(m_nCount * 100 / nMaxCount);

    CDialog::OnTimer(nIDEvent);
}
```

9. **Update the *OnBnClickedCancel* function in ComputeDlg.cpp.** When the user clicks the Cancel button during computation, we don't destroy the dialog; instead, we set *m_nCount* to its maximum value, which causes *OnBnClickedStart* to exit the dialog box. If the computation hasn't started, it's okay to exit directly. Add the following boldface code:

```
void CComputeDlg::OnBnClickedCancel()
{
    TRACE("entering CComputeDlg::OnBnClickedCancel\n");
    if (m_nCount == 0) {         // prior to Start button
        CDialog::OnCancel();
    }
    else {                        // computation in progress
        m_nCount = nMaxCount;  // Force exit from OnBnClickedStart
    }
}
```

10. **Edit the *CEx11aView* class in Ex11aView.cpp.** First, edit the virtual *OnDraw* function to display a message, as shown here:

```
void CEx11aView::OnDraw(CDC* pDC)
{
    CEx11aDoc* pDoc = GetDocument();
    ASSERT_VALID(pDoc);

    pDC->TextOut(0, 0, "Press the left mouse button here.");
}
```

Then add the *OnLButtonDown* member function. Select the *CEx11aView* class in Class View. In the Properties window, click the Messages button, select the *WM_LBUTTONDOWN* message, and add the *OnLButtonDown* function. Add the following boldface code:

```
void Cex11aView::OnLButtonDown(UINT nFlags, CPoint point)
{
    CComputeDlg dlg;
```

```
        dlg.DoModal();

        CView::OnLButtonDown(nFlags, point);
    }
```

This code displays the modal dialog box whenever the user presses the left mouse button while the mouse cursor is in the view window.

While you're in Ex11aView.cpp, add the following *#include* statement:

```
#include "ComputeDlg.h"
```

11. **Build and run the application.** Press the left mouse button while the mouse cursor is inside the view window to display the dialog box. Click the Start button, and then click Cancel. The application should terminate the computation and fill the rest of the progress control.

On-Idle Processing

Before multi-threaded programming came along, Windows developers used on-idle processing for "background" tasks such as pagination. On-idle processing is no longer as important, but it's still useful. The application framework calls the virtual member function *OnIdle* of class *CWinApp*, and you can override this function to do background processing. *OnIdle* is called from the framework's message processing loop, which is actually a little more complicated than the simple *GetMessage/TranslateMessage/DispatchMessage* sequence you've seen.

Generally, once the *OnIdle* function completes its work, it is not called again until the next time the application's message queue has been emptied. If you override this function, your code will be called, but it won't be called continuously unless there is a constant stream of messages. The base class *OnIdle* updates the toolbar buttons and status indicators, and it cleans up various temporary object pointers. It makes sense for you to override *OnIdle* to update the user interface. The fact that your code won't be executed when no messages are coming is not important because the user interface shouldn't be changing.

Note If you do override *CWinApp::OnIdle*, don't forget to call the base class *OnIdle*. Otherwise, your toolbar buttons won't be updated and temporary objects won't be deleted.

OnIdle isn't called at all if the user is working in a modal dialog box or is using a menu. If you need to use background processing for modal dialog boxes and menus, you'll have to add a message handler function for the *WM_ENTERIDLE* message, but you must add it to the frame class rather than to the view class. That's because pop-up dialog boxes are always "owned" by the application's main frame window, not by the view window. Chapter 14 explores the relationship between the frame window and the view window.

Multi-Threaded Programming

As you'll recall from Chapter 10, a *process* is a running program that owns some memory, file handles, and other system resources. An individual process can contain separate execution paths, called *threads*. Don't look for separate code for separate threads, however, because a single function can be called from many threads. For the most part, all of a process's code and data space is available to all of the threads in the process. Two threads, for example, can access the same global variables. Threads are managed by the operating system, and each thread has its own stack.

Windows offers two kinds of threads, *worker threads* and *user interface threads*. The Microsoft Foundation Class (MFC) library supports both. A user interface thread has windows and therefore has its own message loop. A worker thread doesn't have windows, so it doesn't need to process messages. Worker threads are easier to program and are generally more useful. The remaining examples in this chapter illustrate worker threads. At the end of the chapter, however, you'll see an application for a user interface thread.

Don't forget that even a single-threaded application has one thread—the main thread. In the MFC hierarchy, *CWinApp* is derived from *CWinThread*. The samples in Chapter 2 refer to a method named *InitInstance* and a member variable named *m_pMainWnd* that appear to belong to *CWinApp*. The members are declared in *CWinThread*, but of course they're inherited by *CWinApp*. The important thing to remember here is that an application *is* a thread.

Writing the Worker Thread Function and Starting the Thread

If you haven't guessed already, using a worker thread for a long computation is more efficient than using a message handler that contains a *PeekMessage* call. Before you start a worker thread, however, you must write a global function for your thread's main program. This global function should return a *UINT*, and it should take a single 32-bit value (declared *LPVOID*) as a parameter. You can use the parameter to pass anything to your thread when you start it. The thread does its computation, and when the global function returns, the thread terminates. The thread will also be terminated if the process terminated, but it's preferable to ensure that the worker thread terminates first, which will guarantee that you'll have no memory leaks.

To start the thread (with function name *ComputeThreadProc*), your program makes the following call:

```
CWinThread* pThread =
    AfxBeginThread(ComputeThreadProc, GetSafeHwnd(),
                   THREAD_PRIORITY_NORMAL);
```

The compute thread code looks like this:

```
UINT ComputeThreadProc(LPVOID pParam)
{
    // Do thread processing
    return 0;
}
```

The *AfxBeginThread* function returns immediately; the return value is a pointer to the newly created thread object. You can use that pointer to suspend and resume the thread (*CWinThread::SuspendThread* and *ResumeThread*), but the thread object has no member function to terminate the thread. The second parameter is the 32-bit value that gets passed to the global function, and the third parameter is the thread's priority code. Once the worker thread starts, both threads run independently. Windows divides the time between the two threads (and among the threads that belong to other processes) according to their priority. If the main thread is waiting for a message, the compute thread can still run.

How the Main Thread Talks to a Worker Thread

The main thread (your application program) can communicate with the subsidiary worker thread in many different ways. One option that will *not* work, however, is a Windows message; the worker thread doesn't have a message loop. The simplest means of communication is a global variable because all the threads in the process have access to all the globals.

Suppose the worker thread increments and tests a global integer as it computes and then exits when the value reaches 100. The main thread could force the worker thread to terminate by setting the global variable to 100 or higher. The following code looks as if it should work, and when you test it, it probably will:

```
UINT ComputeThreadProc(LPVOID pParam)
{
    g_nCount = 0;
    while (g_nCount++ < 100) {
```

(continued)

```
        // Do some computation here
    }
    return 0;
}
```

There's a problem, however, that you can detect only by looking at the generated assembly code. The value of *g_nCount* gets loaded into a register, the register is incremented, and then the register value is stored back in *g_nCount*. Suppose *g_nCount* is 40 and Windows interrupts the worker thread just after the worker thread loads 40 into the register. Now the main thread gets control and sets *g_nCount* to 100. When the worker thread resumes, it increments the register value and stores 41 back into *g_nCount*, obliterating the previous value of 100. The thread loop doesn't terminate!

If you turn on the compiler's optimization switch, you'll have an additional problem. The compiler uses a register for *g_nCount*, and the register stays loaded for the duration of the loop. If the main thread changes the value of *g_nCount* in memory, it will have no effect on the worker thread's compute loop. (You can ensure that the counter isn't stored in a register, however, by declaring *g_nCount* as *volatile*.)

But suppose you rewrite the thread procedure as shown here:

```
UINT ComputeThreadProc(LPVOID pParam)
{
    g_nCount = 0;
    while (g_nCount < 100) {
        // Do some computation here
        ::InterlockedIncrement((long*) &g_nCount);
    }
    return 0;
}
```

The *InterlockedIncrement* function blocks other threads from accessing the variable while it is being incremented. The main thread can safely stop the worker thread.

Now you've seen some of the pitfalls of using global variables for communication. Using global variables is sometimes appropriate, as the next example illustrates, but there are alternative methods that are more flexible, as you'll see later in this chapter.

How the Worker Thread Talks to the Main Thread

It makes sense for the worker thread to check a global variable in a loop, but what if the main thread were to do that? Remember the earlier function that consumed CPU cycles? You definitely don't want your main thread to enter a loop because that would waste CPU cycles and stop your program's message processing. A Windows message is the preferred way for a worker thread to communicate with the main thread because the main thread always has a message loop. This implies, however, that the main thread has a window (visible or invisible) and that the worker thread has a handle to that window.

How does the worker thread get the handle? That's what the 32-bit thread function parameter is for. You pass the handle in the *AfxBeginThread* call. Why not pass the C++ window pointer instead? Doing so would be dangerous because you can't depend on the continued existence of the object and you're not allowed to share objects of MFC classes among threads. (This rule does not apply to objects derived directly from *CObject* or to simple classes such as *CRect* and *CString*.)

Do you send the message or post it? It's better to post it because sending it could cause reentry of the main thread's MFC message pump code, and that would create problems in modal dialog boxes. What kind of message do you post? Any user-defined message will do.

The Ex11b Program

The Ex11b program looks exactly like the Ex11a program when you run it. When you look at the code, however, you'll see some differences. The computation is done in a worker thread instead of in the main thread. The count value is stored in a global variable, *g_nCount*, which is set to the maximum value in the dialog box's Cancel button handler. When the thread exits, it posts a message to the dialog box, which causes *DoModal* to exit.

The document, view, frame, and application classes are the same except for their names, and the dialog resource is the same. The modal dialog class is still named *CComputeDlg*, but the code inside is quite different. The constructor, timer handler, and data exchange functions are pretty much the same.

The following code fragment shows the global variable definition and the global thread function as given in the \Ex11b\ComputeDlg.cpp file on the companion CD. Note that the function exits (and the thread terminates) when *g_nCount* is greater than a constant maximum value. Before it exits, however, the function posts a user-defined message to the dialog box.

```
int g_nCount = 0;

UINT ComputeThreadProc(LPVOID pParam)
{
    volatile int nTemp; // volatile else compiler optimizes too much

    for (g_nCount = 0; g_nCount < CComputeDlg::nMaxCount;
                       ::InterlockedIncrement((long*) &g_nCount)) {
```

(continued)

```
        for (nTemp = 0; nTemp < 50000; nTemp++) {
            // uses up CPU cycles
        }
    }
    // WM_THREADFINISHED is user-defined message
    ::PostMessage((HWND) pParam, WM_THREADFINISHED, 0, 0);
    g_nCount = 0;
    return 0; // ends the thread
}
```

The following *OnBnClickedStart* handler is mapped to the dialog box's Start button. Its job is to start the timer and the worker thread. You can change the worker thread's priority by changing the third parameter of *AfxBeginThread*—for example, the computation runs a little more slowly if you set the priority to *THREAD_PRIORITY_LOWEST*.

```
void CComputeDlg::OnBnClickedStart()
{
    m_nTimer = SetTimer(1, 100, NULL); // 1/10 second
    ASSERT(m_nTimer != 0);
    GetDlgItem(IDC_START)->EnableWindow(FALSE);
    AfxBeginThread(ComputeThreadProc, GetSafeHwnd(),
                   THREAD_PRIORITY_NORMAL);
}
```

The following *OnBnClickedCancel* handler is mapped to the dialog box's Cancel button. It sets the *g_nCount* variable to the maximum value, causing the thread to terminate.

```
void CComputeDlg::OnBnClickedCancel()
{
    if (g_nCount == 0) { // prior to Start button
        CDialog::OnCancel();
    }
    else { // computation in progress
        g_nCount = nMaxCount; // Force thread to exit
    }
}
```

The following *OnThreadFinished* handler is mapped to the dialog box's *WM_THREADFINISHED* user-defined message. It causes the dialog box's *DoModal* function to exit.

```
LRESULT CComputeDlg::OnThreadFinished(WPARAM wParam, LPARAM lParam)
{
    GetDlgItem(IDC_START)->EnableWindow(TRUE);

    CDialog::OnOK();
    return 0;
}
```

Using Events for Thread Synchronization

The global variable is a crude but effective means of interthread communication. Now let's try something more sophisticated. We want to think in terms of thread synchronization instead of simple communication. Our threads must carefully synchronize their interactions with one another.

An *event* is one type of kernel object that Windows provides for thread synchronization. (Processes and threads are also kernel objects.) An event is identified by a unique 32-bit handle within a process. It can be identified by name, or its handle can be duplicated for sharing among processes. An event can be either in the signaled (or true) state or in the unsignaled (or false) state. Events come in two types: manual reset and autoreset. We'll look at autoreset events here because they're ideal for the synchronization of two processes.

Let's go back to our worker thread example. We want the main (user interface) thread to "signal" the worker thread to make it start or stop, so we'll need a "start" event and a "kill" event. MFC provides a handy *CEvent* class that's derived from *CSyncObject*. By default, the constructor creates a Win32 autoreset event object in the unsignaled state. If you declare your events as global objects, any thread can easily access them. When the main thread wants to start or terminate the worker thread, it sets the appropriate event to the signaled state by calling *CEvent::SetEvent*.

Now the worker thread must monitor the two events and respond when one of them is signaled. MFC provides the *CSingleLock* class for this purpose, but it's easier to use the Win32 *WaitForSingleObject* function. This function suspends the thread until the specified object becomes signaled. When the thread is suspended, it's not using any CPU cycles, which is good. The first *WaitForSingleObject* parameter is the event handle. You can use a *CEvent* object for this parameter; the object will inherit from *CSyncObject* an operator *HANDLE* that returns the event handle it has stored as a public data member. The second parameter is the time-out interval. If you set this parameter to *INFINITE*, the function will wait forever until the event becomes signaled. If you set the time-out to 0, *WaitForSingleObject* will return immediately, with a return value of *WAIT_OBJECT_0* if the event was signaled.

The Ex11c Program

The Ex11c program uses two events to synchronize the worker thread with the main thread. Most of the Ex11c code is the same as Ex11b, but the *CComputeDlg* class is quite different. The StdAfx.h file contains the following line for the *CEvent* class:

```
#include <afxmt.h>
```

There are two global event objects, as shown here. Note that the constructors create the Windows events before the execution of the main program.

```
CEvent g_eventStart; // creates autoreset events
CEvent g_eventKill;
```

It's best to look at the worker thread global function first. The function increments *g_nCount*, just as it did in Ex11b. The worker thread is started by the *OnInitDialog* function instead of by the Start button handler. The first *WaitForSingleObject* call waits for the start event, which is signaled by the Start button handler. The *INFINITE* parameter means that the thread waits as long as necessary. The second *WaitForSingleObject* call is different—it has a 0 time-out value. It's located in the main compute loop and simply makes a quick test to see whether the kill event was signaled by the Cancel button handler. If the event was signaled, the thread terminates.

```
UINT ComputeThreadProc(LPVOID pParam)
{
    volatile int nTemp;

    ::WaitForSingleObject(g_eventStart, INFINITE);
    TRACE("starting computation\n");
    for (g_nCount = 0; g_nCount < CComputeDlg::nMaxCount;
                       g_nCount++) {
        for (nTemp = 0; nTemp < 10000; nTemp++) {
            // Simulate computation
        }
        if (::WaitForSingleObject(g_eventKill, 0) == WAIT_OBJECT_0) {
            break;
        }
    }
    // Tell owner window we're finished
    ::PostMessage((HWND) pParam, WM_THREADFINISHED, 0, 0);
    g_nCount = 0;
    return 0; // ends the thread
}
```

Here is the *OnInitDialog* function that's called when the dialog box is initialized. Note that it starts the worker thread, which doesn't do anything until the start event is signaled.

```
BOOL CComputeDlg::OnInitDialog()
{
    CDialog::OnInitDialog();
    AfxBeginThread(ComputeThreadProc, GetSafeHwnd());

    return TRUE;  // Return TRUE unless you set the focus to a control
                  // EXCEPTION: OCX Property Pages should return FALSE
}
```

The following Start button handler sets the start event to the signaled state, thereby starting the worker thread's compute loop:

```
void CComputeDlg::OnBnClickedStart()
{
    m_nTimer = SetTimer(1, 100, NULL); // 1/10 second
    ASSERT(m_nTimer != 0);
    GetDlgItem(IDC_START)->EnableWindow(FALSE);
    g_eventStart.SetEvent();
}
```

The following Cancel button handler sets the kill event to the signaled state, causing the worker thread's compute loop to terminate:

```
void CComputeDlg::OnBnClickedCancel()
{
    if (g_nCount == 0) { // prior to Start button
        // Must start it before we can kill it
        g_eventStart.SetEvent();
    }
    g_eventKill.SetEvent();
}
```

Note the awkward use of the start event when the user cancels without starting the compute process. It might be neater to define a new cancel event and then replace the first *WaitForSingleObject* call with a *WaitForMultipleObjects* call in the *ComputeThreadProc* function. If *WaitForMultipleObjects* were to detect a cancel event, it could cause an immediate thread termination.

Thread Blocking

The first *WaitForSingleObject* call in the *ComputeThreadProc* function above is an example of thread blocking. The thread simply stops executing until an event becomes signaled. A thread can be blocked in many other ways. You can call the Win32 *Sleep* function, for example, to put your thread to "sleep" for 500 milliseconds. Many functions block threads, particularly those functions that access hardware devices or Internet hosts. Back in the Win16 days, those functions took over the CPU until they were finished. In Win32, they allow other processes and threads to run.

You should avoid putting blocking calls in your main user interface thread. Remember that if your main thread is blocked, it can't process its messages, and that makes the program appear sluggish. If you have a task that requires heavy file I/O, put the code in a worker thread and synchronize it with your main thread.

Be careful of calls in your worker thread that could block indefinitely. Check the online documentation to determine whether you have the option of setting a time-out value for a particular I/O operation. If a call does block forever, the thread will be terminated when the main process exits, but then you'll have some memory leaks. You could call the Win32 *TerminateThread* function from your main thread, but you'd still have the memory-leak problem.

Critical Sections

Remember the problems with access to the *g_nCount* global variable? If you want to share global data among threads and you need more flexibility than simple instructions such as *InterlockedIncrement* can provide, the best synchronization tool for you might be *critical sections*—sections of code that require exclusive access to shared data. Events are good for signaling, but critical sections are good for controlling access to data.

MFC provides the *CCriticalSection* class, which wraps the Windows critical section handle. The constructor calls the Win32 *InitializeCriticalSection* function, the *Lock* and *Unlock* member functions call *EnterCriticalSection* and *LeaveCriticalSection*, and the destructor calls *DeleteCriticalSection*. Here's how you use the class to protect global data:

```
CCriticalSection g_cs;    // global variables accessible from all threads
int g_nCount;

void func()
{
    g_cs.Lock();
    g_nCount++;
    g_cs.Unlock();
}
```

Suppose your program tracks time values as hours, minutes, and seconds, each stored in a separate integer, and suppose two threads are sharing time values. Thread A is changing a time value but is interrupted by thread B after it has updated hours but before it has updated minutes and seconds. Thread B will have an invalid time value.

If you write a C++ class for your time format, it's easy to control data access by making the data members private and providing public member functions. The *CHMS* class, shown in the following code sample, does exactly that. Notice that the class has a data member of type *CCriticalSection*. Thus, a critical section object is associated with each *CHMS* object.

Notice that the other member functions call the *Lock* and *Unlock* member functions. If thread A is executing in the middle of *SetTime*, thread B will be blocked by the *Lock* call in *GetTotalSecs* until thread A calls *Unlock*. The *IncrementSecs* function calls *SetTime*, resulting in nested locks on the critical section. That's okay because Windows keeps track of the nesting level.

The *CHMS* class works well if you use it to construct global objects. If you share pointers to objects on the heap, you have another set of problems. Each thread must determine whether another thread has deleted the object, and that means you must synchronize access to the pointers.

HMS.h

```
#include "StdAfx.h"

class CHMS
{
private:
    int m_nHr, m_nMn, m_nSc;
    CCriticalSection m_cs;
public:
    CHMS() : m_nHr(0), m_nMn(0), m_nSc(0) {}

    ~CHMS() {}

    void SetTime(int nSecs)
    {
        m_cs.Lock();
        m_nSc = nSecs % 60;
        m_nMn = (nSecs / 60) % 60;
        m_nHr = nSecs / 3600;
        m_cs.Unlock();
    }

    int GetTotalSecs()
    {
        int nTotalSecs;
        m_cs.Lock();
        nTotalSecs = m_nHr * 3600 + m_nMn * 60 + m_nSc;
        m_cs.Unlock();
        return nTotalSecs;
    }

    void IncrementSecs()
    {
        m_cs.Lock();
        SetTime(GetTotalSecs() + 1);
        m_cs.Unlock();
    }
};
```

No sample program that uses the *CHMS* class is provided, but HMS.h is included on the book's companion CD. If you write a multi-threaded program, you can share global objects of the class. You don't need any other calls to the thread-related functions.

Mutexes and Semaphores

As I mentioned, I'm leaving these synchronization objects to Jeffrey Richter's *Programming Applications for Microsoft Windows*. You might need a mutex or a semaphore if you're controlling access to data across different processes because a critical section is accessible only within a single process. Mutexes and semaphores (along with events) are shareable by name.

User Interface Threads

The MFC library provides good support for user interface threads. You derive a class from *CWinThread*, and you use an overloaded version of *AfxBeginThread* to start the thread. Your derived *CWinThread* class has its own *InitInstance* function, and most important, it has its own message loop. You can construct windows and map messages as required.

Why might you want a user interface thread? If you want multiple top-level windows, you can create and manage them from your main thread. Suppose you allow the user to run multiple instances of your application but you want all instances to share memory. You can configure a single process to run multiple user interface threads such that users think they're running separate processes. That's exactly what Windows Explorer does. Check it out with SPY++.

Starting the second and subsequent threads is a little tricky because the user actually launches a new process for each copy of Windows Explorer. When the second process starts, it signals the first process to start a new thread, and then it exits. The second process can locate the first process by calling the Win32 *FindWindow* function or by declaring a shared data section. Shared data sections are explained in detail in Jeffrey Richter's book.

Part III

MFC's Document-View Architecture

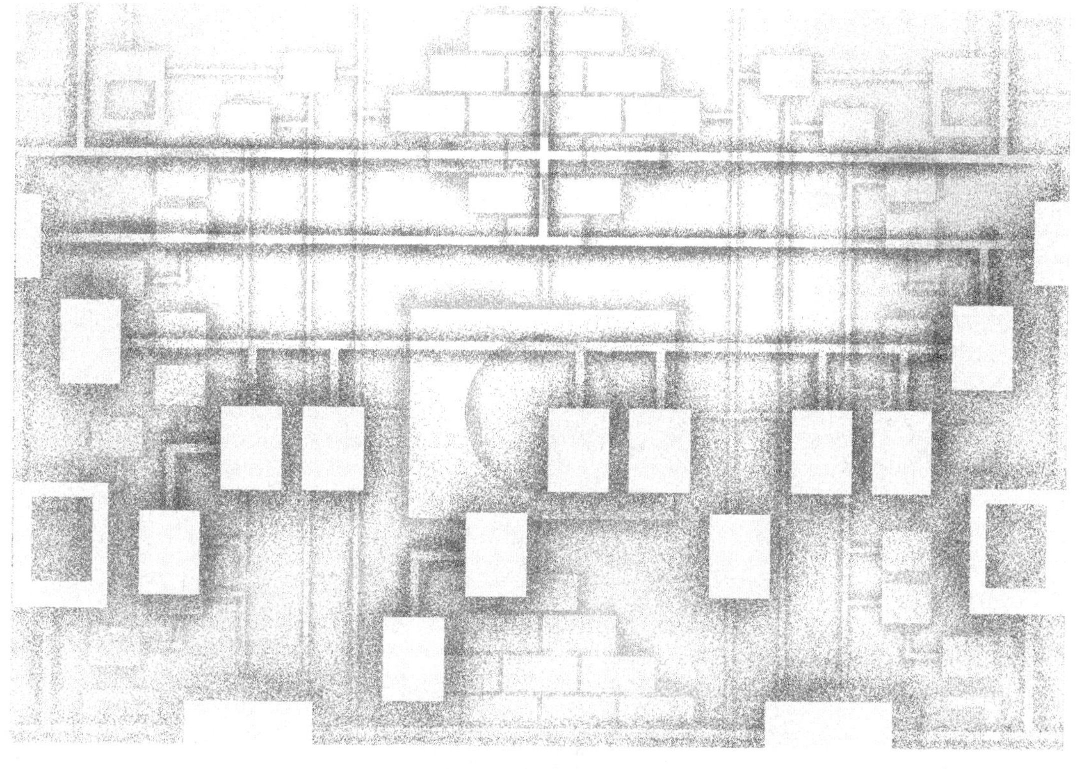

12

Menus, Keyboard Accelerators, the Rich Edit Control, and Property Sheets

In the book's examples so far, mouse clicks have triggered most program activity. Even though menu commands might have been more appropriate, we've used mouse clicks because mouse-click messages are handled simply and directly within the Microsoft Foundation Class (MFC) library view window. If you want program activity to be triggered when the user chooses a command from a menu, you must first become familiar with the other application framework elements.

This chapter concentrates on menus and the command routing architecture. Along the way, I'll introduce frames and documents and explain the relationships between these new application framework elements and the already familiar view element. You'll use the menu editor to lay out a menu visually, and you'll use the code wizards available from Class View to link document and view member functions to menu commands. You'll learn how to use special update command user interface member functions to enable and disable menu commands, and you'll learn how to use keyboard accelerators as menu shortcut keys.

Because you're probably tired of circles and dialog boxes, we'll first examine two new MFC building blocks: the rich edit common control, which can add powerful text editing features to your application, and property sheets, which are ideal for setting edit options.

The Main Frame Window and Document Classes

Up to now, we've been using a view window as if it were the application's only window. In a Single Document Interface (SDI) application, the view window sits inside another window—the application's main frame window. The main frame window has the title bar and the menu bar. Various child windows, including the toolbar window, the view window, and the status bar window, occupy the main frame window's client area, as shown in Figure 12-1. The application framework controls the interaction between the frame and the view by routing messages from the frame to the view.

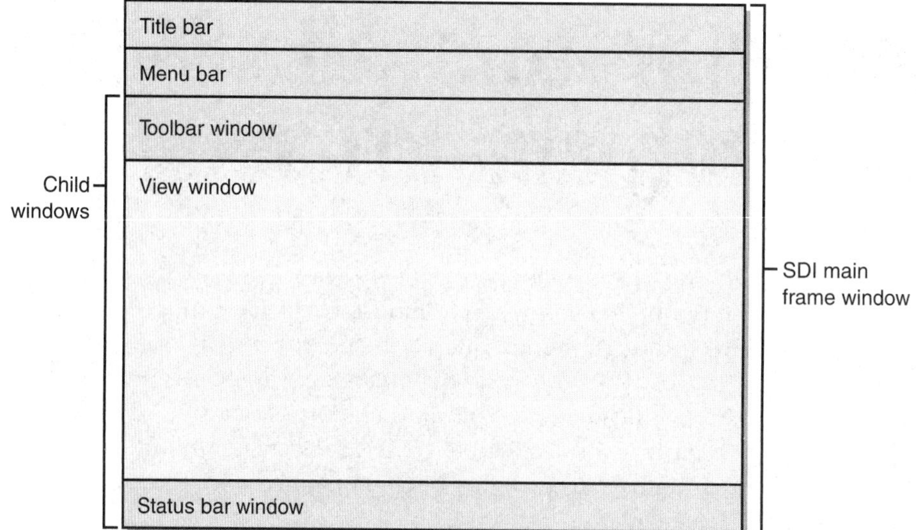

Figure 12-1 The child windows within an SDI main frame window.

Look again at any project files generated by the MFC Application Wizard. The MainFrm.h and MainFrm.cpp files contain the code for the application's main frame window class, which is derived from the class *CFrameWnd*. Other files, with names such as Ex12aDoc.h and Ex12aDoc.cpp, contain code for the application's document class, which is derived from *CDocument*. In this chapter, you'll begin working with the MFC document class. You'll start by learning that each view object has exactly one document object attached and that the view's inherited *GetDocument* member function returns a pointer to that object. You'll learn much more about the document-view interactions in Chapter 15.

Windows Menus

A Microsoft Windows menu is a familiar application element that consists of a top-level horizontal list of menus with submenus that appear when the user selects a top-level command. Most of the time, you define for a frame window a default menu resource that loads when the window is created. You can also define a menu resource independent of a frame window. In that case, your program must call the functions necessary to load and activate the menu.

A menu resource completely defines the initial appearance of a menu. Menu commands can be grayed out or have check marks, and bars can separate groups of menu commands. Multiple levels of associated menus are possible. If a first-level menu command is associated with a submenu, the menu command carries a right-pointing arrow symbol, as shown next to the Windows menu command in Figure 12-2.

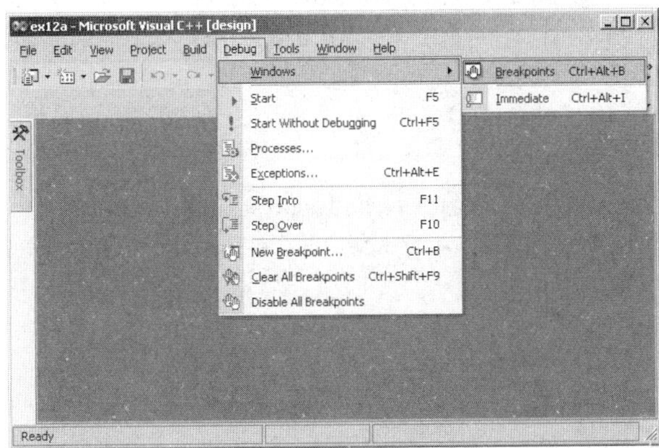

Figure 12-2 Submenus (shown in Microsoft Visual C++ .NET).

Visual C++ .NET includes an easy-to-use menu-resource editing tool. This tool lets you edit menus in a WYSIWYG environment. Each menu command has a properties dialog box that defines all the characteristics of that command. The resulting resource definition is stored in the application's resource script (RC) file. Each command is associated with an ID, such as *ID_FILE_OPEN*, that is defined in the Resource.h file.

The MFC library extends the functionality of the standard menus for Windows. Each menu command can have a prompt string that appears in the frame's status bar when the command is highlighted. These prompts are really Windows string resource elements linked to the menu command by a common ID. From the point of view of the menu editor and your program, the prompts appear to be part of the menu command definition.

Keyboard Accelerators

You've probably noticed that most menu commands contain an underlined letter. In Visual C++ .NET (and most other applications), pressing Alt+F,S activates the File Save menu command. This shortcut system is the standard Windows method of using the keyboard to choose commands from menus. If you look at an application's menu resource script (or the menu editor's properties dialog box), you'll see an ampersand (&) preceding the character that is underlined in each of the application's menu commands.

Windows offers an alternative way of linking keystrokes to menu commands. The keyboard accelerator resource consists of a table of key combinations with associated command IDs. The Edit Copy command (with the command ID *ID_EDIT_COPY*), for example, might be linked to the Ctrl+C key combination through a keyboard accelerator entry. A keyboard accelerator entry does not have to be associated with a menu command. If no Edit Copy command were present, the Ctrl+C key combination would nevertheless activate the *ID_EDIT_COPY* command.

> **Note** If a keyboard accelerator is associated with a menu command or toolbar button, the accelerator key will be disabled when the command or button is disabled.

Command Processing

As you saw in Chapter 2, the application framework provides a sophisticated routing system for command messages. These messages originate from menu commands, keyboard accelerators, and toolbar and dialog box button clicks. Command messages can also be sent by calls to the *CWnd::SendMessage* or *PostMessage* function. Each message is identified by a *#define* constant that is often assigned by a resource editor. The application framework has its own set of internal command message IDs, such as *ID_FILE_PRINT* and *ID_FILE_OPEN*. Your project's Resource.h file contains IDs that are unique to your application.

Most command messages originate in the application's frame window, and without the application framework in the picture, that's where you would put the message handlers. With command routing, however, you can handle a message almost anywhere. When the application framework sees a frame window command message, it starts looking for message handlers in one of the sequences listed here.

SDI Application	MDI Application
View	View
Document	Document
SDI main frame window	MDI child frame window
Application	MDI main frame window application

Most applications have a particular command handler in only one class, but suppose your one-view application has an identical handler in both the view class and the document class. Because the view is higher in the command route, only the view's command handler function will be called.

What is required to install a command handler function? The installation requirements are similar to those of the window message handlers you've already seen. You need the function itself, a corresponding message map entry, and the function prototype. Suppose you have a menu command named Zoom (with *IDM_ZOOM* as the associated ID) that you want your view class to handle. You first add the following code to your view implementation file:

```
BEGIN_MESSAGE_MAP(CMyView, CView)
    ON_COMMAND(IDM_ZOOM, OnZoom)
END_MESSAGE_MAP()

void CMyView::OnZoom()
{
    // command message processing code
}
```

Next, add the following function prototype to the *CMyView* class header file (before the *DECLARE_MESSAGE_MAP* macro):

```
afx_msg void OnZoom();
```

Of course, Visual Studio .NET automates the process of inserting command message handlers the same way it facilitates the insertion of window message handlers. You'll learn how this works in the next example, Ex12a.

Command Message Handling in Derived Classes

The command routing system is one dimension of command message handling. The class hierarchy is a second dimension. If you look at the source code for the MFC library classes, you'll see lots of *ON_COMMAND* message map entries. When you derive a class from one of these base classes—for example, *CView*—the derived class inherits all the *CView* message map functions, including the command message functions. To override one of the base class message map functions, you must add both a function and a message map entry to your derived class.

Update Command User Interface Handlers

You often need to change the appearance of a menu command to match the internal state of your application. If your application's Edit menu includes a Clear All command, for example, you might want to disable that command if there's nothing to clear. You've undoubtedly seen such grayed-out commands in Windows-based applications, and you've probably also seen check marks next to commands.

With Win32 programming, it's difficult to keep menu commands synchronized with the application's state. Every piece of code that changes the internal state must contain statements to update the menu. The MFC library takes a different approach by calling a special update command user interface handler function whenever a submenu is first displayed. The handler function's argument is a *CCmdUI* object, which contains a pointer to the corresponding command. The handler function can then use this pointer to modify the command's appearance. Update command user interface handlers apply only to commands on submenus, not to top-level menu commands that are permanently displayed. For example, you can't use an update command user interface handler to disable a File menu command.

The update command user interface coding requirements are similar to those for commands. You need the function itself, a special message map entry, and of course the prototype. The associated ID—in this case, *IDM_ZOOM*—is the same constant used for the command. Here is an example of the necessary additions to the view class code file:

```
BEGIN_MESSAGE_MAP(CMyView, CView)
    ON_UPDATE_COMMAND_UI(IDM_ZOOM, OnUpdateZoom)
END_MESSAGE_MAP()

void CMyView::OnUpdateZoom(CCmdUI* pCmdUI)
{
    pCmdUI->SetCheck(m_bZoomed); // m_bZoomed is a class data member
}
```

Here is the function prototype that you must add to the class header (before the *DECLARE_MESSAGE_MAP* macro):

```
afx_msg void OnUpdateZoom(CCmdUI* pCmdUI);
```

Needless to say, the code wizards available from Class View's Properties window automate the process of inserting update command user interface handlers.

Commands That Originate in Dialog Boxes

Suppose you have a pop-up dialog box with buttons, and you want a particular button to send a command message. Command IDs must be in the range

0x8000 to 0xDFFF, the same ID range that the resource editor uses for your menu commands. If you assign an ID in this range to a dialog box button, the button will generate a routable command. The application framework first routes this command to the main frame window because the frame window owns all pop-up dialog boxes. The command routing then proceeds normally; if your view has a handler for the button's command, that's where it will be handled. To ensure that the ID is in the range 0x8000 to 0xDFFF, you must use Visual C++ .NET's Resource Symbols dialog box to enter the ID before you assign the ID to a button.

The Application Framework's Built-in Menu Commands

You don't have to start each frame menu from scratch—the MFC library defines some useful menu commands for you, along with all the command handler functions, as shown in Figure 12-3.

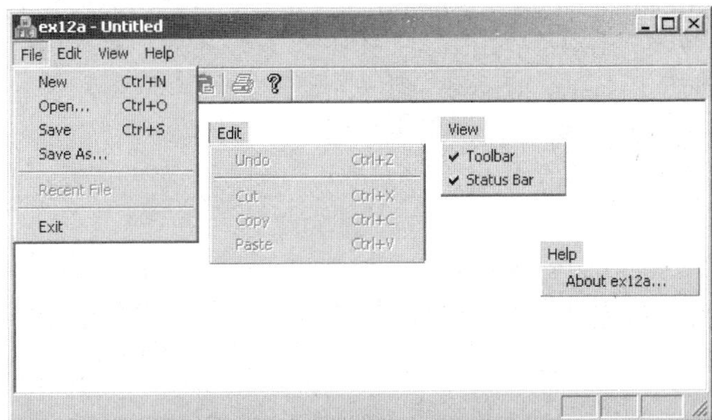

Figure 12-3 The standard SDI frame menus.

The menu commands and command message handlers that you get depend on the options you select in the MFC Application Wizard. If you deselect Printing And Print Preview, for example, the Print and Print Preview commands won't appear. Because printing is optional, the message map entries are not defined in the *CView* class but are generated in your derived view class. That's why entries such as the following are defined in the *CMyView* class instead of in the *CView* class:

```
ON_COMMAND(ID_FILE_PRINT, CView::OnFilePrint)
ON_COMMAND(ID_FILE_PRINT_PREVIEW, CView::OnFilePrintPreview)
```

Enabling and Disabling Menu Commands

The application framework can disable a menu command if it does not find a command message handler in the current command route. This feature saves you the trouble of having to write *ON_UPDATE_COMMAND_UI* handlers. You can disable the feature if you set the *CFrameWnd* data member *m_bAutoMenuEnable* to *FALSE*.

Suppose you have two views for one document but only the first view class has a message handler for the *IDM_ZOOM* command. The Zoom command on the frame menu will be enabled only when the first view is active. Or consider the Edit Cut, Copy, and Paste commands, which are supplied with the application framework. These will be disabled if you haven't provided message handlers in your derived view or document class.

MFC Text Editing Options

Windows itself supplies two text editing tools: the edit control and the rich edit common control. Both can be used as controls within dialog boxes, but both can also be made to look like view windows. The MFC library supports this versatility with the *CEditView* and *CRichEditView* classes.

The *CEditView* Class

This class is based on the Windows edit control. The MFC Application Wizard gives you the option of making *CEditView* the base class of your view class. When the framework gives you an edit view object, it has all the functionality of both *CView* and *CEdit*. There's no multiple inheritance here, just some magic that involves window subclassing. The *CEditView* class implements and maps the Clipboard cut, copy, and paste functions, so they appear active on the Edit menu. The default character limit for *CEditView* is 1,048,575. You can change the character limit by sending the *EM_LIMITTEXT* message to the underlying edit control. However, the limits are different depending on the operating system and the type of edit control (single or multi-line). See the MSDN Library for more information on these limits.

The *CRichEditView* Class

This class uses the rich edit control, so it supports mixed formats and large quantities of text. The *CRichEditView* class is designed to be used with the *CRichEditDoc* and *CRichEditCntrItem* classes to implement a complete ActiveX container application.

The *CRichEditCtrl* Class

This class wraps the rich edit control, and you can use it to make a fairly decent text editor. That's exactly what we'll do in the upcoming Ex12a example. We'll use an ordinary view class derived from *CView*, and we'll cover the view's client area with a big rich edit control that resizes itself when the view size changes. The *CRichEditCtrl* class has dozens of useful member functions, and it picks up other functions from its *CWnd* base class. The functions we'll use in this chapter are listed in Table 12-1.

Table 12-1 Commonly Used *CRichEditCtrl* Functions

Function	Description
Create	Creates the rich edit control window (which is called from the parent's *WM_CREATE* handler).
SetWindowPos	Sets the size and position of the edit window (sizes the control to cover the view's client area).
GetWindowText	Retrieves plain text from the control. (*CRichEditCtrl* includes other functions for retrieving the text using rich text formatting codes.)
SetWindowText	Stores plain text in the control.
GetModify	Gets a flag that is *TRUE* if the text has been modified (when the user types in the control or the program calls *SetModify(TRUE)*).
SetModify	Sets the modify flag to *TRUE* or *FALSE*.
GetSel	Gets a flag that indicates whether the user has selected text
SetDefaultCharFormat	Sets the control's default format characteristics.
SetSelectionCharFormat	Sets the format characteristics of the selected text.

> **Note** If you use the dialog editor to add a rich edit control to a dialog resource, your application class *InitInstance* member function must call the function *AfxInitRichEdit*.

The Ex12a Example

This example illustrates the routing of menu and keyboard accelerator commands to both documents and views. The application's view class is derived from *CView* and contains a rich edit control. View-directed menu commands, originating from a new submenu named Transfer, move data between the view object and the document object, and a Clear Document command erases the document's contents. On the Transfer menu, the Store Data In Document command is grayed out if the view hasn't been modified since the last time the data was transferred. The Clear Document command, located on the Edit menu, is grayed out when the document is empty. Figure 12-4 shows the first version of the Ex12a program in use.

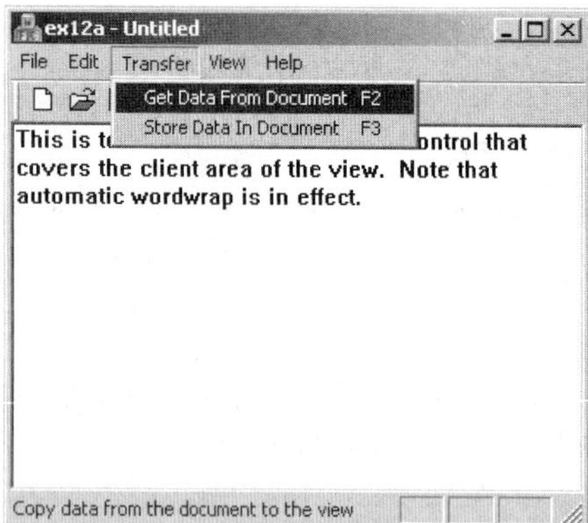

Figure 12-4 The Ex12a program in use.

If we were to exploit the document-view architecture fully, we would tell the rich edit control to keep its text inside the document, but that's rather difficult to do. Instead, we'll define a document *CString* data member named *m_strText*, the contents of which the user can transfer to and from the control. The initial value of *m_strText* is a Hello message; choosing Clear Document from the Edit menu sets it to empty. By running this example, you'll start to understand the separation of the document and the view.

The first part of the Ex12a example uses Visual C++ .NET's WYSIWYG menu editor and keyboard accelerator editor along with the code wizards available from Class View's Properties window. You'll need to do very little C++ coding. Simply follow these steps:

1. **Run the MFC Application Wizard to generate the Ex12a project.** Accept all the default settings but two: Select Single Document and deselect Printing And Print Preview.

2. **Use the resource editor to edit the application's main menu.** In Resource View, edit the *IDR_MAINFRAME* menu resource to add a separator and a Clear Document command to the Edit menu, as shown here:

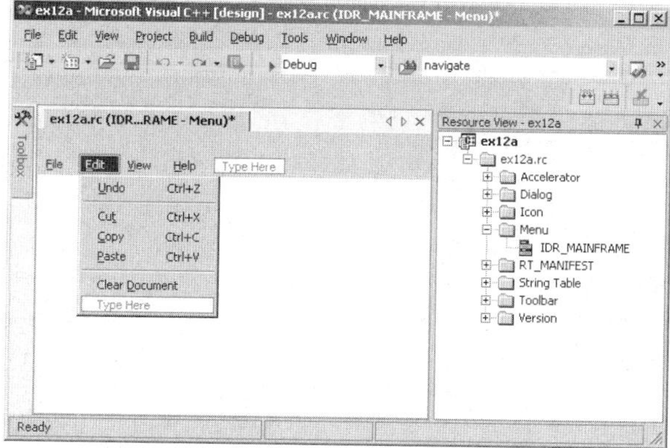

> **Tip** The resource editor's menu resource editor is intuitive, but you might need some help the first time you insert a command in the middle of a menu. Just right-click where you want to insert the command and choose Insert New from the shortcut menu. You'll automatically see where to add the command. To insert a separator, choose Insert Separator from the shortcut menu.

Now add a Transfer menu, and then define the underlying commands:

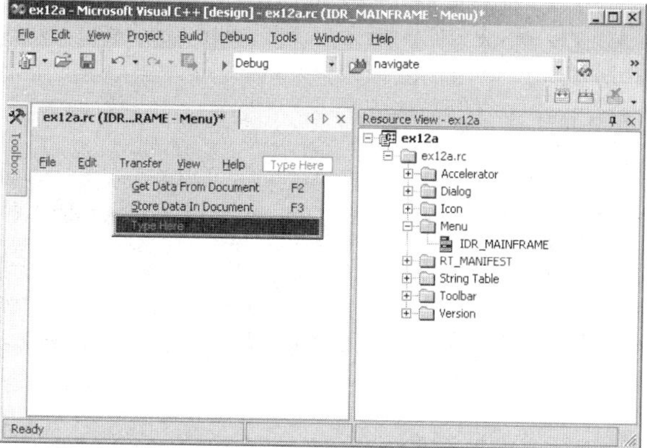

The MFC library has defined the following command IDs for your new menu commands in the Resource Symbols dialog box. (Note that \t is a tab character—but type **\t**; don't press the Tab key.)

Menu	Caption	Command ID
Edit	Clear &Document	*ID_EDIT_CLEARDOCUMENT*
Transfer	&Get Data From Document\tF2	*ID_TRANSFER_GETDATAFROM-DOCUMENT*
Transfer	&Store Data In Document\tF3	*ID_TRANSFER_STOREDATAIN-DOCUMENT*

After you add the commands, right-click on each of them and choose Properties from the shortcut menu. Type an appropriate prompt string in each command's Properties window. These prompts will appear in the application's status bar window when the command is highlighted.

3. **Use the resource editor to add keyboard accelerators.** Open the *IDR_MAINFRAME* accelerator table by double-clicking on its icon in Resource View, and then click on the empty row entry at the bottom of the table to add the following items.

Accelerator ID	Key
ID_TRANSFER_GETDATAFROMDOCUMENT	VK_F2
ID_TRANSFER_STOREDATAINDOCUMENT	VK_F3

Be sure to select None from the drop-down list in the Modifier box to turn off the Ctrl, Alt, and Shift modifiers.

4. **Use Class View's Properties window for the *CEx12aView* class to add the view class command and update command user interface message handlers.** Select the CEx12aView class, and then add the following member functions:

Object ID	Event	Member Function
ID_TRANSFER_GET-DATAFROMDOCUMENT	*COMMAND*	*OnTransferGetdata-fromdocument*
ID_TRANSFER_STORE-DATAINDOCUMENT	*COMMAND*	*OnTransferStoredatain-document*
ID_TRANSFER_STORE-DATAINDOCUMENT	*UPDATE_COMMAND_UI*	*OnUpdateTransferStore-dataindocument*

5. **Use Class View's Properties window for the *CEx12aDoc* class to add the document class command and update command user interface message handlers.** Select the *CEx12aDoc* class, and then add the following member functions:

Object ID	Event	Member Function
ID_EDIT_CLEAR-DOCUMENT	*COMMAND*	*OnEditCleardocument*
ID_EDIT_CLEAR-DOCUMENT	*UPDATE_COMMAND_UI*	*OnUpdateEditCleardocument*

6. Insert the following line in the Ex12aDoc.cpp file:

```
#include "Ex12aView.h"
```

7. **Add a *CString* data member to the *CEx12aDoc* class.** Edit the file Ex12aDoc.h or use Class View.

```
public:
    CString m_strText;
```

8. **Edit the document class member functions in Ex12aDoc.cpp.** The *OnNewDocument* function was generated by Visual Studio .NET. The framework calls this function after it first constructs the document and when the user chooses New from the File menu. Your version sets some text in the string data member. Add the following boldface code:

```
BOOL CEx12aDoc::OnNewDocument()
{
    if (!CDocument::OnNewDocument())
        return FALSE;
    m_strText = "Hello (from CEx12aDoc::OnNewDocument)";
    return TRUE;
}
```

The Edit Clear Document message handler sets *m_strText* to empty, and the update command user interface handler grays out the command if the string is already empty. Remember that the framework calls *OnUpdateEditCleardocument* when the Edit menu is displayed. Add the following boldface code:

```
void CEx12aDoc::OnEditCleardocument()
{
    m_strText.Empty();
    //reflect changes to the views
```

(continued)

```
    POSITION pos = GetFirstViewPosition();
    while (pos != NULL)
    {
        CEx12aView* pView = (CEx12aView*) GetNextView(pos);
        pView->m_rich.SetWindowText(m_strText);
    }
}

void CEx12aDoc::OnUpdateEditCleardocument(CCmdUI *pCmdUI)
{
    pCmdUI->Enable(!m_strText.IsEmpty());
}
```

9. **Add a *CRichEditCtrl* data member to the *CEx12aView* class.** Edit the file Ex12aView.h or use Class View.

```
public:
    CRichEditCtrl m_rich;
```

10. **Use Class View's Properties window to map the *WM_CREATE* and *WM_SIZE* messages in the *CEx12aView* class.** The *OnCreate* function creates the rich edit control. The control's size is 0 here because the view window doesn't have a size yet. Add the following boldface code:

```
int CEx12aView::OnCreate(LPCREATESTRUCT lpCreateStruct)
{
    CRect rect(0, 0, 0, 0);
    if (CView::OnCreate(lpCreateStruct) == -1)
        return -1;
    m_rich.Create(ES_AUTOVSCROLL | ES_MULTILINE | ES_WANTRETURN |
        WS_CHILD | WS_VISIBLE | WS_VSCROLL, rect, this, 1);
    return 0;
}
```

Windows sends the *WM_SIZE* message to the view as soon as the view's initial size is determined and again each time the user changes the frame size. This handler simply adjusts the rich edit control's size to fill the view client area. Add the following boldface code:

```
void CEx12aView::OnSize(UINT nType, int cx, int cy)
{
    CRect rect;
    CView::OnSize(nType, cx, cy);
    GetClientRect(rect);
    m_rich.SetWindowPos(&wndTop, 0, 0, rect.right - rect.left,
                        rect.bottom - rect.top, SWP_SHOWWINDOW);
}
```

11. **Edit the menu command handler functions in Ex12aView.cpp.** Visual Studio .NET generated these skeleton functions when you mapped the menu commands in step 4. The *OnTransferGetdatafromdocument* function gets the text from the document data member and puts it in the rich edit control. The function then clears the control's modified flag. There is no update command user interface handler. Add the following boldface code:

```
void CEx12aView::OnTransferGetdatafromdocument()
{
    CEx12aDoc* pDoc = GetDocument();
    m_rich.SetWindowText(pDoc->m_strText);
    m_rich.SetModify(FALSE);
}
```

The *OnTransferStoredataindocument* function copies the text from the view's rich edit control to the document string and resets the control's modified flag. The corresponding update command user interface handler grays out the command if the control has not been changed since it was last copied to or from the document. Add the following boldface code:

```
void CEx12aView::OnTransferStoredataindocument()
{
    CEx12aDoc* pDoc = GetDocument();
    m_rich.GetWindowText(pDoc->m_strText);
    m_rich.SetModify(FALSE);
}

void CEx12aView::OnUpdateTransferStoredataindocument(CCmdUI* pCmdUI)
{
    pCmdUI->Enable(m_rich.GetModify());
}
```

12. **Build and test the Ex12a application.** When the application starts, the Clear Document command on the Edit menu should be enabled. Choose Get Data From Document from the Transfer menu. Some text should appear. Edit the text, and then choose Store Data In Document. That command should now appear gray. Try choosing the Clear Document command, and then choose Get Data From Document again.

Property Sheets

You've already seen property sheets in Visual C++ .NET and in many other modern Windows-based programs. A property sheet is a nice user interface element that allows you to cram lots of categorized information into a small dialog box. The user selects pages by clicking on their tabs. Windows offers a tab control that you can insert in a dialog box, but it's more likely that you'll want to put dialog boxes inside the tab control. The MFC library supports this, and the result is called a *property sheet*. The individual dialog boxes are called *property pages*.

Building a Property Sheet

Follow these general steps to build a property sheet using the Visual C++ .NET tools:

1. Use the resource editor to create a series of dialog templates that are all approximately the same size. The captions are the strings that you want to display on the tabs.
2. Use the MFC Class Wizard to generate a class for each template. Select *CPropertyPage* as the base class. Add data members for the controls.
3. Use the MFC Class Wizard to generate a single class derived from *CPropertySheet*.
4. To the sheet class, add one data member for each page class.
5. In the sheet class constructor, call the *AddPage* member function for each page, specifying the address of the embedded page object.
6. In your application, construct an object of the derived *CPropertySheet* class, and then call *DoModal*. You must specify a caption in the constructor call, but you can change the caption later by calling *CPropertySheet::SetTitle*.
7. Take care of programming for the Apply button.

Property Sheet Data Exchange

The framework puts three buttons on a property sheet (as in Figure 12-5 in the next section.) Be aware that the framework calls the Dialog Data Exchange (DDX) code for a property page each time the user switches to and from that page. As you would expect, the framework calls the DDX code for a page when the user clicks OK, thus updating that page's data members. From these statements, you can conclude that all data members for all pages are updated when the user clicks OK to exit the sheet. All this with no C++ programming on your part!

> **Note** With a normal modal dialog box, if the user clicks the Cancel button, the changes will be discarded and the dialog class data members will remain unchanged. With a property sheet, however, the data members will be updated if the user changes one page and then moves to another, even if the user exits by clicking the Cancel button.

What does the Apply button do? Nothing at all if you don't write some code. It won't even be enabled. To enable it for a given page, you must set the page's modified flag by calling *SetModified(TRUE)* when you detect that the user has made changes on the page.

If you've enabled the Apply button, you can write a handler function for it in your page class by overriding the virtual *CPropertyPage::OnApply* function. Don't try to understand property page message processing in the context of normal modal dialog boxes; it's quite different. The framework gets a *WM_NOTIFY* message for all button clicks. It calls the DDX code for the page if the OK or Apply button was clicked. It then calls the virtual *OnApply* functions for *all* the pages, and it resets the modified flag, which disables the Apply button. Don't forget that the DDX code has already been called to update the data members in all pages, so you need to override *OnApply* in only one page class.

What you put in your *OnApply* function is your business, but one option is to send a user-defined message to the object that created the property sheet. The message handler can get the property page data members and process them. Meanwhile, the property sheet stays on the screen.

The Ex12a Example Revisited

Now we'll add a property sheet to Ex12a that allows the user to change the rich edit control's font characteristics. Of course, we could use the standard MFC *CFontDialog* function, but then you wouldn't learn how to create property sheets. Figure 12-5 shows the property sheet that you'll build as you continue with Ex12a.

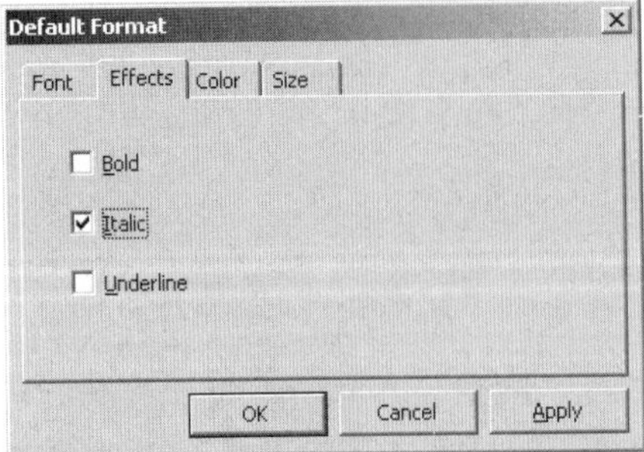

Figure 12-5 The property sheet from Ex12a.

If you haven't built Ex12a, follow the instructions that begin on page 285 to build it. If you already have Ex12a working with the Transfer menu commands, just continue on with these steps:

1. **Use the resource editor to edit the application's main menu.** In Resource View, edit the *IDR_MAINFRAME* menu resource to add a Format menu that looks like this.

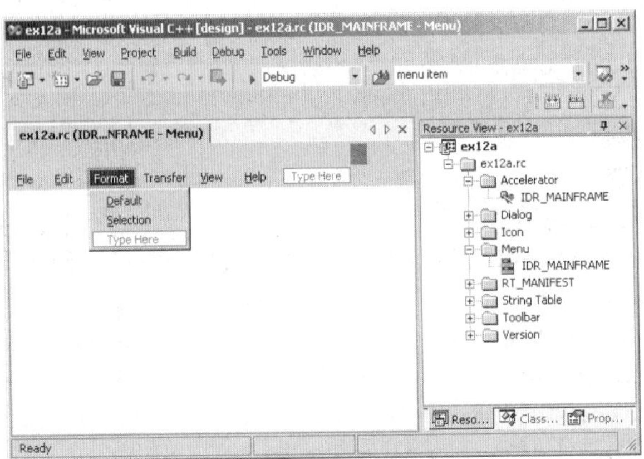

The MFC library has defined the following command IDs for the new Format menu commands.

Caption	Command ID
&Default	*ID_FORMAT_DEFAULT*
&Selection	*ID_FORMAT_SELECTION*

Add appropriate prompt strings for the two menu commands using the Properties window.

2. **Use Class View's Properties window to add the view class command and update command user interface message handlers.** Select the *CEx12aView* class in Class View, and then add the following member functions.

Object ID	Event	Member Function
ID_FORMAT_DEFAULT	*COMMAND*	*OnFormatDefault*
ID_FORMAT_SELECTION	*COMMAND*	*OnFormatSelection*
ID_FORMAT_SELECTION	*UPDATE_COMMAND_UI*	*OnUpdateFormatSelection*

3. **Use the resource editor to add four property page dialog templates.** Right-click on the RC file in Resource View and choose Add Resource from the shortcut menu. In the Add Resource dialog box, select the small property page template. The templates are shown here with their associated IDs:

IDD—PAGE 1 *IDD—PAGE 2*

IDD—PAGE 3 *IDD—PAGE 4*

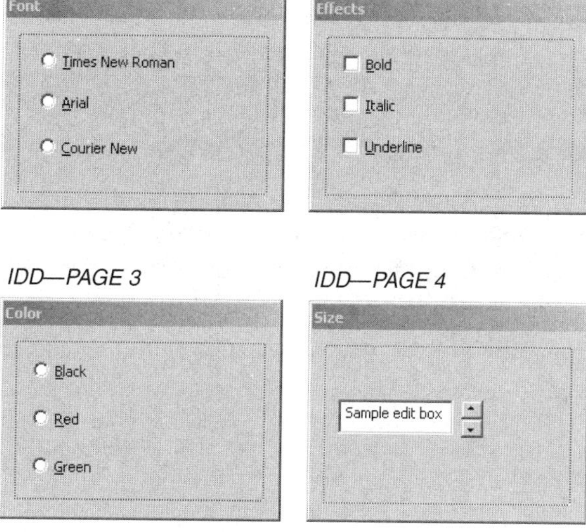

Use the IDs listed below for the controls in the dialog boxes. Set the *Auto Buddy* and the *Set Buddy Integer* properties for the Spin control, and set the *Group* property for the *IDC_FONT* and *IDC_COLOR* radio buttons. Set the minimum value of *IDC_FONTSIZE* to *8* and its maximum value to *24*.

Use the MFC Class Wizard to create the classes *CPage1*, *CPage2*, *CPage3*, and *CPage4*. In each case, select *CPropertyPage* as the base class. Have the MFC Class Wizard generate the code for all these classes in the files Property.h and Property.cpp by changing the filenames within the text boxes for the header file and the CPP file. When Visual Studio .NET asks you whether you want to merge the files, click Yes. Then add the data members shown here:

Dialog Box	Control	ID	Type	Data Member
IDD_PAGE1	First radio button	*IDC_FONT*	*int*	*m_nFont*
IDD_PAGE2	Bold check box	*IDC_BOLD*	*BOOL*	*m_bBold*
IDD_PAGE2	Italic check box	*IDC_ITALIC*	*BOOL*	*m_bItalic*
IDD_PAGE2	Underline check box	*IDC_UNDER-LINE*	*BOOL*	*m_bUnderline*
IDD_PAGE3	First radio button	*IDC_COLOR*	*int*	*m_nColor*
IDD_PAGE4	Edit control	*IDC_FONT SIZE*	*int*	*m_nFontSize*
IDD_PAGE4	Spin control	*IDC_SPIN1*		

Finally, use Class View's Properties window to override the *OnInitDialog* virtual function for *CPage4*.

4. **Use the MFC Class Wizard to create a class derived from *CPropertySheet*.** Select the name *CFontSheet*. Generate the code in the files Property.h and Property.cpp, the same files you used for the property page classes. The following code shows these files with the added code in boldface:

Property.h

```
#pragma once
// Property.h : header file
//

#define WM_USERAPPLY WM_USER + 5
extern CView* g_pView;

////////////////////////////////////////////////////////////////////////
// CPage1 dialog
```

```
class CPage1 : public CPropertyPage
{
    DECLARE_DYNCREATE(CPage1)

public:
    CPage1();
    virtual ~CPage1();

// Dialog Data
    enum { IDD = IDD_PAGE1 };
    int     m_nFont;


protected:
    virtual void DoDataExchange(CDataExchange* pDX); // DDX/DDV
    virtual BOOL OnApply();
    virtual BOOL OnCommand(WPARAM wParam, LPARAM lParam);

    DECLARE_MESSAGE_MAP()

};

///////////////////////////////////////////////////////////////////////////
// CPage2 dialog

class CPage2 : public CPropertyPage
{
    DECLARE_DYNCREATE(CPage2)

public:
    CPage2();
    virtual ~CPage2();

// Dialog Data
    enum { IDD = IDD_PAGE2 };
    BOOL    m_bBold;
    BOOL    m_bItalic;
    BOOL    m_bUnderline;

protected:
    virtual void DoDataExchange(CDataExchange* pDX); // DDX/DDV
    virtual BOOL OnCommand(WPARAM wParam, LPARAM lParam);

    DECLARE_MESSAGE_MAP()

};
```

(continued)

```
///////////////////////////////////////////////////////////////////////////
// CPage3 dialog

class CPage3 : public CPropertyPage
{
    DECLARE_DYNCREATE(CPage3)
public:
   CPage3();
    virtual ~CPage3();
// Dialog Data
    enum { IDD = IDD_PAGE3 };
    int      m_nColor;

protected:
    virtual void DoDataExchange(CDataExchange* pDX); // DDX/DDV
    virtual BOOL OnCommand(WPARAM wParam, LPARAM lParam);
    DECLARE_MESSAGE_MAP()
};

///////////////////////////////////////////////////////////////////////////
// CPage4 dialog

class CPage4 : public CPropertyPage
{
    DECLARE_DYNCREATE(CPage4)
public:
    CPage4();
    virtual ~CPage4();
// Dialog Data
    enum { IDD = IDD_PAGE4 };
    int      m_nFontSize;

protected:
    virtual void DoDataExchange(CDataExchange* pDX); // DDX/DDV
                                                     // support
    virtual BOOL OnCommand(WPARAM wParam, LPARAM lParam);
    DECLARE_MESSAGE_MAP()
public:
    virtual BOOL OnInitDialog();
};

///////////////////////////////////////////////////////////////////////////
// CFontSheet

class CFontSheet : public CPropertySheet
{
    DECLARE_DYNAMIC(CFontSheet)
```

```
public:
    CPage1 m_page1;
    CPage2 m_page2;
    CPage3 m_page3;
    CPage4 m_page4;

public:
    CFontSheet(UINT nIDCaption, CWnd* pParentWnd = NULL,
               UINT iSelectPage = 0);
    CFontSheet(LPCTSTR pszCaption, CWnd* pParentWnd = NULL,
               UINT iSelectPage = 0);
    virtual ~CFontSheet();

protected:
    DECLARE_MESSAGE_MAP()
};
```

Property.cpp

```
// Property.cpp : implementation file

#include "stdafx.h"
#include "Ex12a.h"
#include "Property.h"

CView* g_pView;

//////////////////////////////////////////////////////////////////////
// CPage1 dialog

IMPLEMENT_DYNCREATE(CPage1, CPropertyPage)

CPage1::CPage1() : CPropertyPage(CPage1::IDD)
{
    m_nFont = -1;
}

CPage1::~CPage1()
{
}

BOOL CPage1::OnApply()
{
    TRACE("CPage1::OnApply\n");
    g_pView->SendMessage(WM_USERAPPLY);
    return TRUE;
}
```

(continued)

```
BOOL CPage1::OnCommand(WPARAM wParam, LPARAM lParam)
{
    SetModified(TRUE);
    return CPropertyPage::OnCommand(wParam, lParam);
}

void CPage1::DoDataExchange(CDataExchange* pDX)
{
    TRACE("Entering CPage1::DoDataExchange -- %d\n",
          pDX->m_bSaveAndValidate);
    CPropertyPage::DoDataExchange(pDX);
    DDX_Radio(pDX, IDC_FONT, m_nFont);
}


BEGIN_MESSAGE_MAP(CPage1, CPropertyPage)
END_MESSAGE_MAP()

//////////////////////////////////////////////////////////////////////
// CPage1 message handlers

//////////////////////////////////////////////////////////////////////
// CPage2 dialog

IMPLEMENT_DYNCREATE(CPage2, CPropertyPage)

CPage2::CPage2() : CPropertyPage(CPage2::IDD)
{
    m_bBold = FALSE;
    m_bItalic = FALSE;
    m_bUnderline = FALSE;
}

CPage2::~CPage2()
{
}

BOOL CPage2::OnCommand(WPARAM wParam, LPARAM lParam)
{
    SetModified(TRUE);
    return CPropertyPage::OnCommand(wParam, lParam);
}

void CPage2::DoDataExchange(CDataExchange* pDX)
{
    TRACE("Entering CPage2::DoDataExchange -- %d\n",
          pDX->m_bSaveAndValidate);
    CPropertyPage::DoDataExchange(pDX);
    DDX_Check(pDX, IDC_BOLD, m_bBold);
```

```
    DDX_Check(pDX, IDC_ITALIC, m_bItalic);
    DDX_Check(pDX, IDC_UNDERLINE, m_bUnderline);
}

BEGIN_MESSAGE_MAP(CPage2, CPropertyPage)
END_MESSAGE_MAP()

//////////////////////////////////////////////////////////////////////
// CPage2 message handlers

//////////////////////////////////////////////////////////////////////
// CPage3 dialog

IMPLEMENT_DYNCREATE(CPage3, CPropertyPage)

CPage3::CPage3() : CPropertyPage(CPage3::IDD)
{
    m_nColor = -1;
}

CPage3::~CPage3()
{
}

BOOL CPage3::OnCommand(WPARAM wParam, LPARAM lParam)
{
    SetModified(TRUE);
    return CPropertyPage::OnCommand(wParam, lParam);
}

void CPage3::DoDataExchange(CDataExchange* pDX)
{
    TRACE("Entering CPage3::DoDataExchange -- %d\n",
          pDX->m_bSaveAndValidate);
    CPropertyPage::DoDataExchange(pDX);
    DDX_Radio(pDX, IDC_COLOR, m_nColor);
}

BEGIN_MESSAGE_MAP(CPage3, CPropertyPage)
END_MESSAGE_MAP()

//////////////////////////////////////////////////////////////////////
// CPage3 message handlers

//////////////////////////////////////////////////////////////////////
// CPage4 dialog

IMPLEMENT_DYNCREATE(CPage4, CPropertyPage)
```

(continued)

```
CPage4::CPage4() : CPropertyPage(CPage4::IDD)
{
    m_nFontSize = 0;
}

CPage4::~CPage4()
{
}

BOOL CPage4::OnCommand(WPARAM wParam, LPARAM lParam)
{
    SetModified(TRUE);
    return CPropertyPage::OnCommand(wParam, lParam);
}

void CPage4::DoDataExchange(CDataExchange* pDX)
{
    TRACE("Entering CPage4::DoDataExchange -- %d\n",
          pDX->m_bSaveAndValidate);
    CPropertyPage::DoDataExchange(pDX);
    DDX_Text(pDX, IDC_FONTSIZE, m_nFontSize);
    DDV_MinMaxInt(pDX, m_nFontSize, 8, 24);
}

BEGIN_MESSAGE_MAP(CPage4, CPropertyPage)
END_MESSAGE_MAP()

////////////////////////////////////////////////////////////////////
// CPage4 message handlers

BOOL CPage4::OnInitDialog()
{
    CPropertyPage::OnInitDialog();
    ((CSpinButtonCtrl*) GetDlgItem(IDC_SPIN1))->SetRange(8, 24);
    return TRUE;  //
 return TRUE unless you set the focus to a control
                  //
  EXCEPTION: OCX Property Pages should return FALSE
}

 ///////////////////////////////////////////////////////////////////
/
// CFontSheet

IMPLEMENT_DYNAMIC(CFontSheet, CPropertySheet)
CFontSheet::CFontSheet(UINT nIDCaption, CWnd* pParentWnd,
                       UINT iSelectPage)
    :CPropertySheet(nIDCaption, pParentWnd, iSelectPage)
{
}
```

```
CFontSheet::CFontSheet(LPCTSTR pszCaption, CWnd* pParentWnd,
                       UINT iSelectPage)
    :CPropertySheet(pszCaption, pParentWnd, iSelectPage)
{
    AddPage(&m_page1);
    AddPage(&m_page2);
    AddPage(&m_page3);
    AddPage(&m_page4);
}

CFontSheet::~CFontSheet()
{
}
BEGIN_MESSAGE_MAP(CFontSheet, CPropertySheet)
END_MESSAGE_MAP()

//////////////////////////////////////////////////////////////////////
// CFontSheet message handlers
```

5. **Insert the following line in the Ex12aView.h file:**

```
#include "Property.h"
```

6. **Add two data members and two prototypes to the *CEx12aView* class:**

```
private:
    CFontSheet m_sh;
    BOOL m_bDefault; // TRUE default format, FALSE selection
```

Now add the prototype for the private function *Format*:

```
void Format(CHARFORMAT &cf);
```

Insert the prototype for the protected function *OnUserApply* before the *DECLARE_MESSAGE_MAP* macro:

```
afx_msg LRESULT OnUserApply(WPARAM wParam, LPARAM lParam);
```

7. **Edit and add code in the file Ex12aView.cpp.** Map the user-defined *WM_USERAPPLY* message, as shown here:

```
ON_MESSAGE(WM_USERAPPLY, OnUserApply)
```

Add the following lines to the *OnCreate* function, just before the *return 0* statement:

```
CHARFORMAT cf;
Format(cf);
m_rich.SetDefaultCharFormat(cf);
```

Edit the view constructor to set default values for the property sheet data members, as follows:

```
CEx12aView::CEx12aView() : m_sh("")
{
    m_sh.m_page1.m_nFont = 0;
    m_sh.m_page2.m_bBold = FALSE;
    m_sh.m_page2.m_bItalic = FALSE;
    m_sh.m_page2.m_bUnderline = FALSE;
    m_sh.m_page3.m_nColor = 0;
    m_sh.m_page4.m_nFontSize = 12;
    g_pView = this;
    m_bDefault = TRUE;
}
```

Edit the format command handlers, as shown here:

```
void CEx12aView::OnFormatDefault()
{
    m_sh.SetTitle("Default Format");
    m_bDefault = TRUE;
    m_sh.DoModal();
}

void CEx12aView::OnFormatSelection()
{
    m_sh.SetTitle("Selection Format");
    m_bDefault = FALSE;
    m_sh.DoModal();
}

void CEx12aView::OnUpdateFormatSelection(CCmdUI* pCmdUI)
{
    long nStart, nEnd;
    m_rich.GetSel(nStart, nEnd);
    pCmdUI->Enable(nStart != nEnd);
}
```

Add the following handler for the user-defined *WM_USERAPPLY* message:

```
LRESULT CEx12aView::OnUserApply(WPARAM wParam, LPARAM lParam)
{
    TRACE("CEx12aView::OnUserApply -- wParam = %x\n", wParam);
    CHARFORMAT cf;
    Format(cf);
    if (m_bDefault) {
        m_rich.SetDefaultCharFormat(cf);
    }
    else {
```

```
        m_rich.SetSelectionCharFormat(cf);
    }
    return 0;
}
```

Add the *Format* helper function, as shown below, to set a *CHARFORMAT* structure based on the values of the property sheet data members:

```
void CEx12aView::Format(CHARFORMAT& cf)
{
    cf.cbSize = sizeof(CHARFORMAT);
    cf.dwMask = CFM_BOLD | CFM_COLOR | CFM_FACE |
                CFM_ITALIC | CFM_SIZE | CFM_UNDERLINE;
    cf.dwEffects = (m_sh.m_page2.m_bBold ? CFE_BOLD : 0) |
                   (m_sh.m_page2.m_bItalic ? CFE_ITALIC : 0) |
                   (m_sh.m_page2.m_bUnderline ? CFE_UNDERLINE : 0);
    cf.yHeight = m_sh.m_page4.m_nFontSize * 20;
    switch(m_sh.m_page3.m_nColor) {
    case -1:
    case 0:
        cf.crTextColor = RGB(0, 0, 0);
        break;
    case 1:
        cf.crTextColor = RGB(255, 0, 0);
        break;
    case 2:
        cf.crTextColor = RGB(0, 255, 0);
        break;
    }
    switch(m_sh.m_page1.m_nFont) {
    case -1:
    case 0:
        strncpy(cf.szFaceName, "Times New Roman" ,LF_FACESIZE);
        break;
    case 1:
        strncpy(cf.szFaceName, "Arial" ,LF_FACESIZE);
        break;
    case 2:
        strncpy(cf.szFaceName, "Courier New" ,LF_FACESIZE);
        break;
    }
    cf.bCharSet = 0;
    cf.bPitchAndFamily = 0;
}
```

8. **Build and test the enhanced Ex12a application.** Type some text, and then choose Default from the Format menu. Observe the *TRACE* messages in the Debug window as you click on property sheet tabs and click the Apply button. Try highlighting some text and then formatting the selection.

Apply Button Processing

You might be curious about the way the property sheet classes process the Apply button. In all the page classes, the overridden *OnCommand* functions enable the Apply button whenever a control sends a message to the page. This works fine for pages 1 through 3 in Ex12a, but for page 4, *OnCommand* is called during the initial conversation between the Spin control and its buddy.

The *OnApply* virtual override in the *CPage1* class sends a user-defined message to the view. The function finds the view in an expedient way—by using a global variable set by the view class. A better approach would be to pass the view pointer to the sheet constructor and then to the page constructor.

The view class calls the property sheet's *DoModal* function for both default formatting and selection formatting. It sets the *m_bDefault* flag to indicate the mode. We don't need to check the return from *DoModal* because the user-defined message is sent for both the OK button and the Apply button. If the user clicks Cancel, no message is sent.

The *CMenu* Class

Up to this point, the application framework and the menu editor have shielded you from the menu class, *CMenu*. A *CMenu* object can represent each Windows menu, including the top-level menu commands and submenus. Most of the time, the menu's resource is directly attached to a frame window when the window's *Create* or *LoadFrame* function is called, and a *CMenu* object is never explicitly constructed. The *CWnd* member function *GetMenu* returns a temporary *CMenu* pointer. Once you have this pointer, you can freely access and update the menu object.

Suppose you want to switch menus after the application starts. *IDR_MAINFRAME* always identifies the initial menu in the resource script. If you want a second menu, you use the menu editor to create a menu resource with your own ID. Then, in your program, you construct a *CMenu* object, use the *CMenu::LoadMenu* function to load the menu from the resource, and call the *CWnd::SetMenu* function to attach the new menu to the frame window. You then call the *Detach* member function to separate the object's *HMENU* handle so the menu is not destroyed when the *CMenu* object goes out of scope.

You can use a resource to define a menu, and then your program can modify the commands at run time. If necessary, however, you can build the whole menu at run time, without benefit of a resource. In either case, you can use *CMenu* member functions such as *ModifyMenu*, *InsertMenu*, and *DeleteMenu*. Each of these functions operates on an individual command identified by ID or by a relative position index.

A menu object is actually composed of a nested structure of submenus. You can use the *GetSubMenu* member function to get a *CMenu* pointer to a submenu contained in the main *CMenu* object. The *CMenu::GetMenuString* function returns the menu command string corresponding to either a zero-based index or a command ID. If you use the command ID option, the menu is searched, together with any submenus.

Creating Floating Shortcut Menus

Floating shortcut menus are one of the latest trends in user interface design. The user clicks the right mouse button and a floating menu offers commands that relate to the current selection. It's easy to create these menus using the resource editor and the MFC library *CMenu::TrackPopupMenu* function. Just follow these steps:

1. Use the menu editor to insert a new, empty menu in your project's resource file.
2. Type some characters in the left top-level command, and then add commands in the resulting shortcut menu.
3. Use Class View's Properties window to add a *WM_CONTEXTMENU* message handler in your view class or in some other window class that receives mouse-click messages. Code the handler as shown here:

```
void CMyView::OnContextMenu(CWnd *pWnd, CPoint point)
{
    CMenu menu;
    menu.LoadMenu(IDR_MYFLOATINGMENU);
    menu.GetSubMenu(0)
        ->TrackPopupMenu(TPM_LEFTALIGN | TPM_RIGHTBUTTON,
        point.x, point.y, this);
}
```

You can use Class View's Properties window to map the floating menu's command IDs in the same way you would map the frame menu's command IDs.

Extended Command Processing

In addition to the *ON_COMMAND* message map macro, the MFC library provides an extended variation, *ON_COMMAND_EX*. The extended command message map macro provides two features not supplied by the regular command message—a command ID function parameter and the ability to reject a command at run time, sending it to the next object in the command route. If the extended command handler returns *TRUE*, the command goes no further; if it returns *FALSE*, the application framework looks for another command handler.

The command ID parameter is useful when you want one function to handle several related command messages. You might invent some of your own uses for the rejection feature.

The code wizards available from Class View's Properties window can't help you with extended command handlers, so you have to do the coding yourself, outside the *AFX_MSG_MAP* brackets. Assume that *IDM_ZOOM_1* and *IDM_ZOOM_2* are related command IDs defined in Resource.h. Here's the class code you need to process both messages with one function, *OnZoom*:

```
BEGIN_MESSAGE_MAP(CMyView, CView)
    ON_COMMAND_EX(IDM_ZOOM_1, OnZoom)
    ON_COMMAND_EX(IDM_ZOOM_2, OnZoom)
END_MESSAGE_MAP()

BOOL CMyView::OnZoom(UINT nID)
{
    if (nID == IDM_ZOOM_1) {
        // code specific to first zoom command
    }
    else {
        // code specific to second zoom command
    }
    // code common to both commands
    return TRUE; // Command goes no further
}
```

Here's the function prototype:

```
afx_msg BOOL OnZoom(UINT nID);
```

Other MFC message map macros are helpful for processing ranges of commands, as you might see in dynamic menu applications. These macros include *ON_COMMAND_RANGE*, *ON_COMMAND_EX_RANGE*, and *ON_UPDATE_COMMAND_UI_RANGE*.

If the values of *IDM_ZOOM_1* and *IDM_ZOOM_2* were consecutive, you could rewrite the *CMyView* message map as follows:

```
BEGIN_MESSAGE_MAP(CMyView, CView)
    ON_COMMAND_EX_RANGE(IDM_ZOOM_1, IDM_ZOOM_2, OnZoom)
END_MESSAGE_MAP()
```

Now *OnZoom* is called for both menu commands, and the handler can determine the command from the integer parameter.

13

Toolbars and Status Bars

All of the book's Microsoft Visual C++ examples up to this point have included toolbars and status bars. The MFC Application Wizard generates the code that initializes these application framework elements if you accept the wizard's default Standard Docking Toolbar and Initial Status Bar user interface features. The default toolbar provides graphics equivalents for many of the standard application framework menu commands, and the default status bar displays menu prompts together with the keyboard state indicators CAP, NUM, and SCRL.

This chapter shows you how to customize the toolbar and the status bar for your application. You can add your own toolbar graphical buttons and control their appearance. You can also disable the status bar's normal display of menu prompts and keyboard indicators so that your application can take over the status bar for its own use.

Control Bars and the Application Framework

The toolbar is an object of class *CToolBar*, and the status bar is an object of class *CStatusBar*. Both of these classes are derived from class *CControlBar*, which is itself derived from *CWnd*. The *CControlBar* class supports control bar windows that are positioned inside frame windows. These control bar windows resize and reposition themselves as the parent frame moves and changes size. The application framework takes care of the construction and destruction of the control bar objects and window creation. The MFC Application Wizard generates control bar code for its derived frame class located in the files MainFrm.cpp and MainFrm.h.

In a typical Single Document Interface (SDI) application, a *CToolBar* object occupies the top portion of the *CMainFrame* client area and a *CStatusBar* object occupies the bottom portion. The view occupies the remaining (middle) part of the frame.

Beginning with version 4.0 of the Microsoft Foundation Class (MFC) library, the toolbar has been built around the toolbar common control that was first introduced with Microsoft Windows 95. Thus the toolbar is fully dockable. The programming interface is much the same as it was in earlier versions of the MFC library, however. The button images are easy to work with because a special resource type is supported by the resource editor.

Assuming that MFC Application Wizard has generated the control bar code for your application, the user can enable and disable the toolbar or the status bar individually by choosing commands from the application's View menu. When a control bar is disabled, it disappears and the view size is recalculated. Apart from the common behavior just described, toolbar and status bar objects operate independently of each other and have rather different characteristics.

Version 6.0 of the MFC library, introduced a new MFC toolbar called the *rebar*. The rebar is based on the controls that come with the common controls and provides a Microsoft Internet Explorer–style "sliding" toolbar. I'll cover the rebar later in this chapter.

Toolbars

A toolbar consists of a number of horizontally (or vertically) arranged graphical buttons that might be clustered in groups. The programming interface determines the grouping. The graphical images for the buttons are stored in a single bitmap that is attached to the application's resource file. When a button is clicked, it sends a command message, as menus and keyboard accelerators do. An update command user interface message handler is used to update the button's state, which in turn is used by the application framework to modify the button's graphical image.

The Toolbar Bitmap

Each button on a toolbar appears to have its own bitmap, but actually a single bitmap serves the entire toolbar. The toolbar bitmap has a tile, 15 pixels high and 16 pixels wide, for each button. The application framework supplies the button borders, and it modifies these borders, together with the button's bitmap tile color, to reflect the current button state. Figure 13-1 shows the relationship between the toolbar bitmap and the corresponding toolbar.

Figure 13-1 A toolbar bitmap and an actual toolbar.

The toolbar bitmap is stored in the file Toolbar.bmp in the application's \res subdirectory. The bitmap is identified in the resource script (RC) file as *IDR_MAINFRAME*. You don't edit the toolbar bitmap directly; instead, you use Microsoft Visual Studio's special toolbar editing facility.

Toolbar Button States

Each toolbar button can assume the states listed in Table 13-1. (There are additional states for later toolbar versions.)

Table 13-1 Toolbar States

State	Description
0	Normal, unpressed state.
TBSTATE_CHECKED	Checked (down) state.
TBSTATE_ENABLED	Available for use. Button is grayed-out and unavailable if this state is not set.
TBSTATE_HIDDEN	Not visible.
TBSTATE_INDETERMINATE	Grayed-out.
TBSTATE_PRESSED	Currently selected (pressed) using the mouse.
TBSTATE_WRAP	Line break follows the button.

A toolbar button can be a pushbutton, which is down only when currently clicked by the mouse, or it can be a check box button, which can be toggled up and down with mouse clicks. All toolbar buttons in the standard application framework toolbar are pushbuttons.

The Toolbar and Command Messages

When the user clicks a toolbar button with the mouse, a command message is generated. This message is routed like the menu command messages you saw in Chapter 12. Most of the time, a toolbar button matches a menu command. In the standard application framework toolbar, for example, the Disk button is equivalent to the File Save menu command—both generate the *ID_FILE_SAVE* command. The object receiving the command message doesn't need to know whether the message was produced by a button click or by the menu command.

A toolbar button doesn't have to mirror a menu command. If you don't provide an equivalent menu command, however, you should define a keyboard accelerator for the button so the user can activate the command with the keyboard or with a keyboard macro product for Windows. You can use Class View and the Properties window to define commands and update command user interface message handlers for toolbar buttons, whether or not they have corresponding menu commands.

A toolbar has an associated bitmap resource and, in the RC file, a companion toolbar resource that defines the menu commands associated with the buttons. Both the bitmap and the toolbar resource have the same ID, typically *IDR_MAINFRAME*. The text of the toolbar resource generated by the MFC Application Wizard is shown here:

```
IDR_MAINFRAME TOOLBAR   16, 15
BEGIN
    BUTTON      ID_FILE_NEW
    BUTTON      ID_FILE_OPEN
    BUTTON      ID_FILE_SAVE
        SEPARATOR
    BUTTON      ID_EDIT_CUT
    BUTTON      ID_EDIT_COPY
    BUTTON      ID_EDIT_PASTE
        SEPARATOR
    BUTTON      ID_FILE_PRINT
    BUTTON      ID_APP_ABOUT
END
```

The *SEPARATOR* constants serve to group the buttons by inserting corresponding spaces on the toolbar. If the number of toolbar bitmap panes exceeds the number of resource elements (excluding separators), the extra buttons are not displayed.

When you edit the toolbar using the resource editor, you're editing both the bitmap resource and the toolbar resource. You select a button image, and then you edit the properties, including the button's ID, in the Properties window.

Toolbar Update Command User Interface Message Handlers

You'll recall from Chapter 12 that update command user interface message handlers are used to disable or add check marks to menu commands. These same message handlers apply to toolbar buttons. If your update command user interface message handler calls the *CCmdUI::Enable* member function with a *FALSE* parameter, the corresponding button will be set to the disabled (grayed-out) state and no longer respond to mouse clicks.

Next to a menu command, the *CCmdUI::SetCheck* member function displays a check mark. For the toolbar, the *SetCheck* function implements check box buttons. If the update command user interface message handler calls *SetCheck* with a parameter value of 1, the button will be toggled to the down (checked) state; if the parameter is 0, the button will be toggled up (unchecked).

> **Note** If the *SetCheck* parameter value is 2, the button will be set to the indeterminate state. This state looks like the disabled state, but the button is still active and its color is a bit brighter.

The update command user interface message handlers for a shortcut menu are called only when the menu is painted. The toolbar is displayed all the time, so when are its update command user interface message handlers called? They're called during the application's idle processing so the buttons can be updated continuously. If the same handler covers a menu command and a toolbar button, it is called both during idle processing and when the shortcut menu is displayed.

ToolTips

You've seen ToolTips in various Windows applications, including Visual Studio. When the user positions the mouse on a toolbar button for a certain interval of time, text is displayed in a little ToolTip box next to the button. In Chapter 12, you learned that menu commands can have associated prompt strings, which are string resource elements with matching IDs. To create a ToolTip, you simply add the tip text to the end of the menu prompt, preceded by a newline (*n*) character. The resource editor lets you edit the prompt string while you're editing the toolbar images. Just select a toolbar image and edit the Prompt property in the Properties window.

Locating the Main Frame Window

The toolbar and status bar objects you'll be working with are attached to the application's main frame window, not to the view window. How does your view find its main frame window? In an SDI application, you can use the

CWnd::GetParentFrame function. Unfortunately, this function won't work in an MDI application because the view's parent frame is the MDI child frame, not the MDI frame window.

If you want your view class to work in both SDI and MDI applications, you must find the main frame window through the application object. The *AfxGetApp* global function returns a pointer to the application object. You can use that pointer to get the *CWinApp* data member *m_pMainWnd.* In an MDI application, the MFC Application Wizard generates code that sets *m_pMainWnd*, but in an SDI application, the framework sets *m_pMainWnd* during the view creation process. Once *m_pMainWnd* is set, you can use it in a view class to get the frame's toolbar with statements such as this:

```
CMainFrame* pFrame = (CMainFrame*) AfxGetApp()->m_pMainWnd;
CToolBar* pToolBar = &pFrame->m_wndToolBar;
```

> **Note** You'll need to cast *m_pMainWnd* from *CFrameWnd** to *CMainFrame** because *m_wndToolBar* is a member of that derived class. You'll also have to make *m_wndToolBar* public or make your class a friend of *CMainFrame*.

You can use similar logic to locate menu commands, status bar objects, and dialog objects.

> **Note** In an SDI application, the value of *m_pMainWnd* is not set when the view's *OnCreate* message handler is called. If you need to access the main frame window in your *OnCreate* function, you must use the *GetParentFrame* function.

The Ex13a Example: Using Toolbars

In this example, we'll add three special-purpose buttons that control drawing in the view window. We'll also construct a Draw menu with three commands, as follows:

Command	Function
Circle	Draws a circle in the view window
Square	Draws a square in the view window
Pattern	Toggles a diagonal line fill pattern for new squares and circles

The menu and toolbar choices force the user to alternate between drawing circles and squares. After the user draws a circle, the Circle command and toolbar button are disabled; after the user draws a square, the Square command and toolbar button are disabled.

On the application's Draw menu, the Pattern command gets a check mark when pattern fill is active. On the toolbar, the corresponding button is a check box button that is down when pattern fill is active and up when it is not active.

Figure 13-2 shows the application in action. The user has just drawn a square with pattern fill. Notice the states of the three drawing buttons.

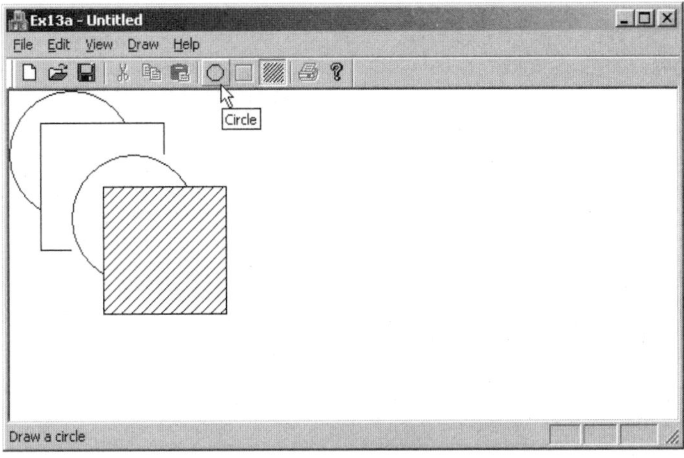

Figure 13-2 The Ex13a program in action.

The Ex13a example introduces the resource editor for toolbars. You'll need to do very little C++ coding. Simply follow these steps:

1. **Run the MFC Application Wizard to generate a project named Ex13a.** Choose New Project from Visual Studio's File menu. In the New Project dialog box, select the MFC Application template, type the name **Ex13a**, and click OK. In the MFC Application Wizard, accept all the defaults but two: On the Application Type page, select Single Document, and on the Advanced Features page, deselect Printing And Print Preview.

2. **Use the resource editor to edit the application's main menu.** In Resource View, double-click on *IDR_MAINFRAME* under Menu. Edit the *IDR_MAINFRAME* menu resource to create a new Draw menu that looks like the following. To reposition a menu, you can just drag the menu.

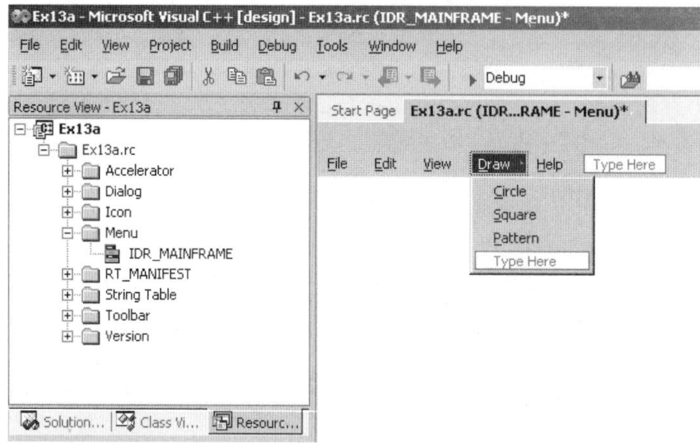

In the Properties window, verify that the following properties are set for your new Draw menu commands:

Caption	ID	Prompt
&Circle	*ID_DRAW_CIRCLE*	Draw a circle\nCircle
&Square	*ID_DRAW_SQUARE*	Draw a square\nSquare
&Pattern	*ID_DRAW_PATTERN*	Change the pattern\nPattern

3. **Use the resource editor to update the application's toolbar.** Edit the *IDR_MAINFRAME* toolbar resource to create a group of three new buttons that looks like this:

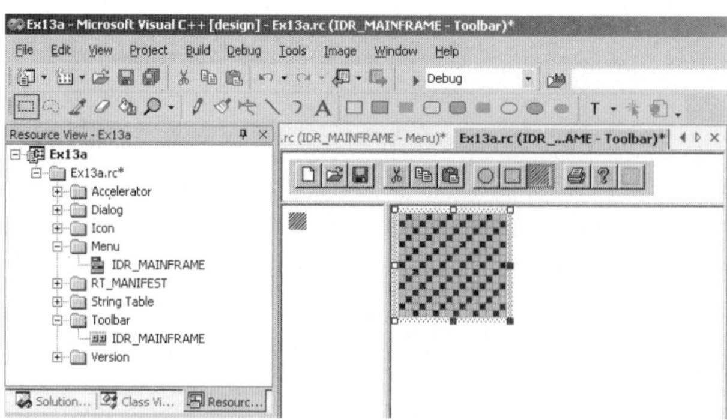

The toolbar editor is fairly intuitive. You add new buttons by editing the blank button at the far right of the toolbar. Use the Ellipsis, Rectangle, and Line tools on the Image Editor toolbar to draw on a button. You can move buttons around by dragging them with the mouse. To add a separator between buttons, drag the button where the separator should appear slightly to the right or left and the buttons will be nudged over. The Delete key erases a button's pixels. If you want to eliminate a button entirely, just drag it off the toolbar.

In the Properties window, set the ID property for the new buttons to *ID_DRAW_CIRCLE*, *ID_DRAW_SQUARE*, and *ID_DRAW_PATTERN*.

4. **Add the *CEx13aView* class message handlers.** Select the *CEx13aView* class in Class View, click the Events button in the Properties window, and add message handlers for the following command and update command user interface messages:

Object ID	Message	Member Function
ID_DRAW_CIRCLE	*COMMAND*	*OnDrawCircle*
ID_DRAW_CIRCLE	*UPDATE_COMMAND_UI*	*OnUpdate-DrawCircle*
ID_DRAW_PATTERN	*COMMAND*	*OnDrawPattern*
ID_DRAW_PATTERN	*UPDATE_COMMAND_UI*	*OnUpdateDraw-Pattern*
ID_DRAW_SQUARE	*COMMAND*	*OnDrawSquare*
ID_DRAW_SQUARE	*UPDATE_COMMAND_UI*	*OnUpdateDraw-Square*

5. **Add three data members to the *CEx13aView* class.** Add the following code to Ex13aView.h:

```
protected:
    CRect m_rect;
    BOOL  m_bCircle;
    BOOL  m_bPattern;
```

6. **Edit the Ex13aView.cpp file.** The *CEx13aView* constructor simply initializes the class data members. Add the following boldface code:

```
CEx13aView::CEx13aView() : m_rect(0, 0, 100, 100)
{
    m_bCircle = TRUE;
    m_bPattern = FALSE;
}
```

The *OnDraw* function draws an ellipse or a rectangle, depending on the value of the *m_bCircle* flag. The brush is plain white or a diagonal pattern, depending on the value of *m_bPattern*.

```
void CEx13aView::OnDraw(CDC* pDC)
{
    Cex13aDoc* pDoc = GetDocument();
    ASSERT_VALID(pDoc);

    CBrush brush(HS_BDIAGONAL, 0L); // brush with diagonal pattern

    if (m_bPattern) {
        pDC->SelectObject(&brush);
    }
    else {
        pDC->SelectStockObject(WHITE_BRUSH);
    }
    if (m_bCircle) {
        pDC->Ellipse(m_rect);
    }
    else {
        pDC->Rectangle(m_rect);
    }
    pDC->SelectStockObject(WHITE_BRUSH); // Deselects brush
                                          //  if selected
}
```

The *OnDrawCircle* function handles the *ID_DRAW_CIRCLE* command message, and the *OnDrawSquare* function handles the *ID_DRAW_SQUARE* command message. These two functions move the drawing rectangle down and to the right, and then they invalidate the rectangle, causing the *OnDraw* function to redraw it. The effect of this invalidation strategy is a diagonal cascading of alternating squares and circles. Also, the display is not buffered, so when the window is hidden or minimized, previously drawn items are not redisplayed.

```
void CEx13aView::OnDrawCircle()
{
    m_bCircle = TRUE;
    m_rect += CPoint(25, 25);
    InvalidateRect(m_rect);
}

void CEx13aView::OnDrawSquare()
{
    m_bCircle = FALSE;
```

```
    m_rect += CPoint(25, 25);
    InvalidateRect(m_rect);
}
```

The following two update command user interface functions alternately enable and disable the Circle and Square buttons and corresponding menu commands. Only one item can be enabled at a time.

```
void CEx13aView::OnUpdateDrawCircle(CCmdUI* pCmdUI)
{
    pCmdUI->Enable(!m_bCircle);
}

void CEx13aView::OnUpdateDrawSquare(CCmdUI* pCmdUI)
{
    pCmdUI->Enable(m_bCircle);
}
```

The *OnDrawPattern* function toggles the state of the *m_bPattern* flag.

```
void CEx13aView::OnDrawPattern()
{
    m_bPattern ^= 1;
}
```

The *OnUpdateDrawPattern* function updates the Pattern button and menu command according to the state of the *m_bPattern* flag. The toolbar button appears to move in and out, and the command check mark appears and disappears.

```
void CEx13aView::OnUpdateDrawPattern(CCmdUI* pCmdUI)
{
    pCmdUI->SetCheck(m_bPattern);
}
```

7. **Build and test the Ex13a application.** Notice the behavior of the toolbar buttons. Try the corresponding menu commands, and notice that they too are enabled, disabled, and checked as the application's state changes. Observe the ToolTip and the prompt in the status bar when you stop the mouse pointer on one of the new toolbar buttons.

Status Bars

The status bar window neither accepts user input nor generates command messages. Its job is simply to display text in panes under program control. The status bar supports two types of text panes—message line panes and status indicator panes. To use the status bar for application-specific data, you must first disable the standard status bar that displays the menu prompt and keyboard status.

The Status Bar Definition

The static *indicators* array that the MFC Application Wizard generates in the MainFrm.cpp file defines the panes for the application's status bar. The constant *ID_SEPARATOR* identifies a message line pane; the other constants are string resource IDs that identify indicator panes. Figure 13-3 shows the *indicators* array and its relationship to the standard framework status bar.

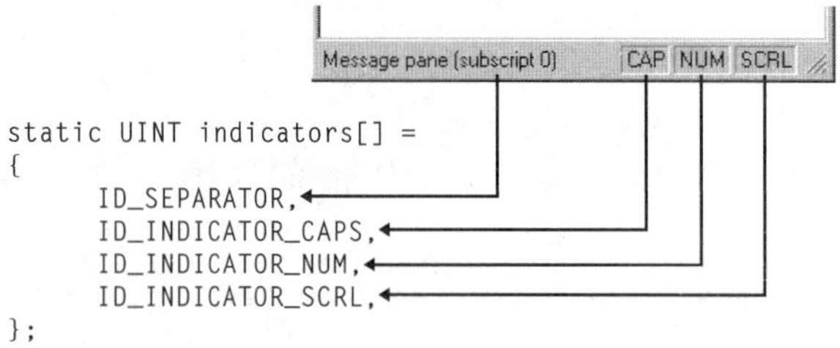

Message pane (subscript 0) CAP NUM SCRL

```
static UINT indicators[] =
{
    ID_SEPARATOR,
    ID_INDICATOR_CAPS,
    ID_INDICATOR_NUM,
    ID_INDICATOR_SCRL,
};
```

Figure 13-3 The status bar and the *indicators* array.

The *CStatusBar::SetIndicators* member function, called in the application's derived frame class, configures the status bar according to the contents of the *indicators* array.

The Message Line

A message line pane displays a string that the program supplies dynamically. To set the value of the message line, you must first get access to the status bar object and then you must call the *CStatusBar::SetPaneText* member function with a zero-based index parameter. Pane 0 is the leftmost pane, 1 is the next pane to the right, and so forth.

The following code fragment is part of a view class member function. Note that you must navigate up to the application object and then back down to the main frame window.

```
CMainFrame* pFrame = (CMainFrame*) AfxGetApp()->m_pMainWnd;
CStatusBar* pStatus = &pFrame->m_wndStatusBar;
pStatus->SetPaneText(0, "message line for first pane");
```

Normally, the length of a message line pane is exactly one-fourth the width of the display. If, however, the message line is the first (index 0) pane, it is a stretchy pane without a beveled border. Its minimum length is one-fourth the display width, and it expands if room is available in the status bar.

The Status Indicator

A status indicator pane is linked to a single resource-supplied string that is displayed or hidden by logic in an associated update command user interface message handler function. An indicator is identified by a string resource ID, and that same ID is used to route update command user interface messages. The Caps Lock indicator is handled in the frame class by a message map entry and a handler function equivalent to those shown below. The *Enable* function turns on the indicator if the Caps Lock mode is set.

```
ON_UPDATE_COMMAND_UI(ID_INDICATOR_CAPS, OnUpdateKeyCapsLock)

void CMainFrame::OnUpdateKeyCapsLock(CCmdUI* pCmdUI)
{
    pCmdUI->Enable(::GetKeyState(VK_CAPITAL) & 1);
}
```

The status bar update command user interface functions are called during idle processing so that the status bar is updated whenever your application receives messages.

The length of a status indicator pane is the exact length of the corresponding resource string.

Taking Control of the Status Bar

In the standard application framework implementation, the status bar has the child window ID *AFX_IDW_STATUS_BAR*. The application framework looks for this ID when it wants to display a menu prompt. The update command user interface handlers for the keyboard state indicators, embedded in the frame window base class, are linked to the following string IDs: *ID_INDICATOR_CAPS*, *ID_INDICATOR_NUM*, and *ID_INDICATOR_SCRL*. To take control of the status bar, you must use a different child window ID and different indicator ID constants.

> **Note** The only reason to change the status bar's child window ID is to prevent the framework from writing menu prompts in pane 0. If you like the menu prompts, you can disregard the following instructions.

The status bar window ID is assigned in the *CStatusBar::Create* function called by the derived frame class *OnCreate* member function. That function is contained in the MainFrm.cpp file that the MFC Application Wizard generates. The window ID is the third *Create* parameter, and it defaults to *AFX_IDW_STATUS_BAR*.

To assign your own ID, you must replace this call

```
m_wndStatusBar.Create(this);
```

with this call

```
m_wndStatusBar.Create(this, WS_CHILD | WS_VISIBLE | CBRS_BOTTOM,
                      ID_MY_STATUS_BAR);
```

You must also, of course, define the *ID_MY_STATUS_BAR* constant in the resource.h file (using Visual C++'s resource symbol editor).

We left out one thing. The standard application framework's View menu allows the user to turn the status bar on and off. That logic is pegged to the *AFX_IDW_STATUS_BAR* window ID, so you have to change the menu logic, too. In your derived frame class, you must write message map entries and handlers for the *ID_VIEW_STATUS_BAR* command and update command user interface messages. *ID_VIEW_STATUS_BAR* is the ID of the Status Bar menu command. The derived class handlers override the standard handlers in the *CFrameWnd* base class. See the upcoming Ex13b example for code details.

The Ex13b Example: Using Status Bars

The Ex13b example replaces the standard application framework status bar with a new status bar that has the following text panes:

Pane Index	String ID	Type	Description
0	*ID_SEPARATOR* (0)	Message line	*x* cursor coordinate
1	*ID_SEPARATOR* (0)	Message line	*y* cursor coordinate
2	*ID_INDICATOR_LEFT*	Status indicator	Left mouse button status
3	*ID_INDICATOR_RIGHT*	Status indicator	Right mouse button status

The resulting status bar is shown in Figure 13-4. Notice that the leftmost pane stretches past its normal screen length as the displayed frame window expands.

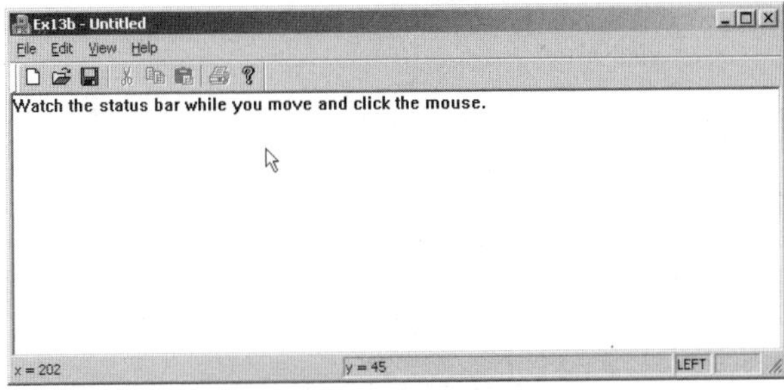

Figure 13-4 The status bar of the Ex13b example.

Follow these steps to produce the Ex13b example:

1. **Run the MFC Application Wizard to generate a project named Ex13b.** Choose New Project from Visual Studio's File menu. In the New Project dialog box, select the MFC Application template, type the name **Ex13b**, and click OK. In the MFC Application Wizard, accept all the defaults but two: On the Application Type page, select Single Document, and on the Advanced Features page, deselect Printing And Print Preview.

2. **Use the string editor to edit the application's string table resource.** The application has a single string table resource with artificial "segment" divisions left over from the 16-bit era. In Resource View, double-click on the String Table icon in the String Table folder to bring up the string editor. Then select the empty entry at the end of the list and add the following two strings:

String ID	String Caption
ID_INDICATOR_LEFT	LEFT
ID_INDICATOR_RIGHT	RIGHT

When you're finished, the string table should appear as follows:

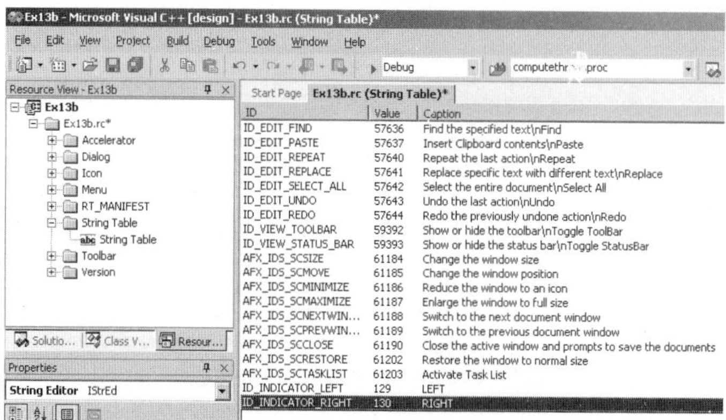

3. **Edit the application's symbols.** Choose Resource Symbols from the Edit menu. Click the New button and add the new status bar identifier, *ID_MY_STATUS_BAR*, and accept the default value as shown here:

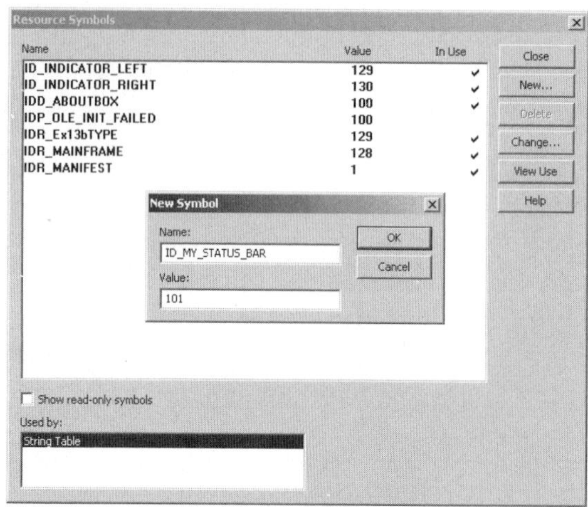

4. **Add View menu command handlers in the class *CmainFrame*.** Select the *CMainFrame* class in Class View, click the Events button in the Properties window, and add the following command message handlers:

Object ID	Message	Member Function
ID_VIEW_STATUS_BAR	*COMMAND*	*OnViewStatusBar*
ID_VIEW_STATUS_BAR	*UPDATE_COMMAND_UI*	*OnUpdateView-StatusBar*

5. **Add the following function prototypes to MainFrm.h.** You must add these *CMainFrame* message handler prototypes manually because Visual Studio doesn't recognize the associated command message IDs.

```
afx_msg void OnUpdateLeft(CCmdUI* pCmdUI);
afx_msg void OnUpdateRight(CCmdUI* pCmdUI);
```

While MainFrm.h is open, make *m_wndStatusBar* public rather than protected.

6. **Edit the MainFrm.cpp file.** Replace the original *indicators* array with the following boldface code:

```
static UINT indicators[] =
{
    ID_SEPARATOR,  // first message line pane
    ID_SEPARATOR,  // second message line pane
    ID_INDICATOR_LEFT,
    ID_INDICATOR_RIGHT,
};
```

Next, edit the *OnCreate* member function. Replace the following statement

```
if (!m_wndStatusBar.Create(this) ||
    !m_wndStatusBar.SetIndicators(indicators,
      sizeof(indicators)/sizeof(UINT)))
{
    TRACE0("Failed to create status bar\n");
    return -1;      // fail to create
}
```

with the statement shown here:

```
if (!m_wndStatusBar.Create(this,
        WS_CHILD | WS_VISIBLE | CBRS_BOTTOM, ID_MY_STATUS_BAR) ||
    !m_wndStatusBar.SetIndicators(indicators,
      sizeof(indicators)/sizeof(UINT)))
{
```

(continued)

```
    TRACE0("Failed to create status bar\n");
    return -1;      // fail to create
}
```

The modified call to *Create* uses our own status bar ID, *ID_MY_STATUS_BAR*, instead of *AFX_IDW_STATUS_BAR* (the application framework's status bar object).

Now add the following message map entries for the class *CMainFrame*. Visual Studio can't add these for you because it doesn't recognize the string table IDs as object IDs.

```
ON_UPDATE_COMMAND_UI(ID_INDICATOR_LEFT, OnUpdateLeft)
ON_UPDATE_COMMAND_UI(ID_INDICATOR_RIGHT, OnUpdateRight)
```

Add the following *CMainFrame* member functions that update the two status indicators:

```
void CMainFrame::OnUpdateLeft(CCmdUI* pCmdUI)
{
    pCmdUI->Enable(::GetKeyState(VK_LBUTTON) < 0);
}

void CMainFrame::OnUpdateRight(CCmdUI* pCmdUI)
{
    pCmdUI->Enable(::GetKeyState(VK_RBUTTON) < 0);
}
```

Note that the left and right mouse buttons have virtual key codes like keys on the keyboard have. You don't have to depend on mouse-click messages to determine the button status.

Finally, edit the following View menu functions in MainFrm.cpp:

```
void CMainFrame::OnViewStatusBar()
{
    m_wndStatusBar.ShowWindow((m_wndStatusBar.GetStyle() &
                              WS_VISIBLE) == 0);
    RecalcLayout();
}
void CMainFrame::OnUpdateViewStatusBar(CCmdUI* pCmdUI)
{
    pCmdUI->SetCheck((m_wndStatusBar.GetStyle() & WS_VISIBLE) != 0);
}
```

These functions ensure that the View menu's Status Bar command is properly linked to the new status bar.

7. **Edit the *OnDraw* function in Ex13bView.cpp.** The *OnDraw* function displays a message in the view window. Add the following boldface code:

```
void CEx13bView::OnDraw(CDC* pDC)
{
    CEx13bDoc* pDoc = GetDocument();
    ASSERT_VALID(pDoc);

    pDC->TextOut(0, 0,
        "Watch the status bar while you move and click the mouse.");
}
```

8. **Add a *WM_MOUSEMOVE* handler in the *CEx13bView* class.** Select the *CEx13bView* class in Class View, click the Messages button in the Properties window, and add the *OnMouseMove* function. Edit the function as shown below. This function gets a pointer to the status bar object and then calls the *SetPaneText* function to update the first and second message line panes.

```
void CEx13bView::OnMouseMove(UINT nFlags, CPoint point)
{
    CString str;
    CMainFrame* pFrame = (CMainFrame*) AfxGetApp()->m_pMainWnd;
    CStatusBar* pStatus = &pFrame->m_wndStatusBar;
    if (pStatus) {
        str.Format("x = %d", point.x);
        pStatus->SetPaneText(0, str);
        str.Format("y = %d", point.y);
        pStatus->SetPaneText(1, str);
    }
}
```

Finally, add the statement

```
#include "MainFrm.h"
```

near the top of the file Ex13bView.cpp.

9. **Build and test the Ex13b application.** Move the mouse and observe that the first two status bar panes accurately reflect the mouse cursor's position. Try the left and right mouse buttons. Can you toggle the status bar on and off from the View menu?

Note If you want the first (index 0) status bar pane to have a beveled border like the other panes and you want the status bar to grow and resize to fit the contents, include the following two lines in the *CMainFrame::OnCreate* function, following the call to the status bar *Create* function.

```
m_wndStatusBar.SetPaneInfo(0, 0, 0, 50);
m_wndStatusBar.SetPaneInfo(1, 0, SBPS_STRETCH, 50);
```

These statements change the width of the first two panes (from their default of one-fourth the display size) and make the second pane (index 1) the stretchy one.

Rebars

As you learned in Chapter 8, Visual C++ contains features originally found in Internet Explorer: the common controls. One of these is a new kind of toolbar called a rebar. You're probably familiar with the rebar if you've used Internet Explorer. The rebar differs from the default MFC toolbar in that it provides grippers and allows the user to "slide" its horizontal and vertical positions. In contrast, you change the MFC toolbar's position using drag-and-drop docking. Rebars also allow the developer to provide many more internal control types—such as drop-down menus—than are available in *CToolBar*.

Anatomy of a Rebar

Figure 13-5 shows the various terms used on a rebar. Each internal toolbar in a rebar is called a *band*. The raised edge where the user slides the band is called a *gripper*. Each band can also have a label.

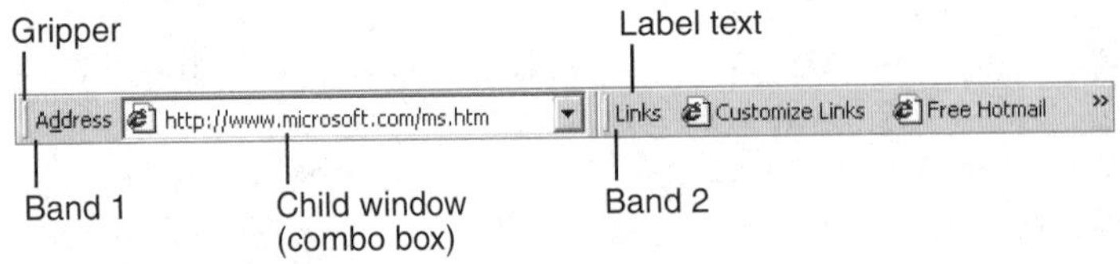

Figure 13-5 Rebar terminology.

MFC provides two classes that facilitate working with rebars:

- ***CReBar*** A high-level abstraction class that provides members for adding *CToolBar* and *CDialogBar* classes to rebars as bands. *CReBar* also handles communication (such as message notifications) between the underlying control and the MFC framework.
- ***CReBarCtrl*** A low-level wrapper class that wraps the ReBar control. This class provides numerous members for creating and manipulating rebars but does not provide the niceties that are found in *CReBar*.

Most MFC applications use *CReBar* and call the member function *GetReBarCtrl*, which returns a *CReBarCtrl* pointer to gain access to the lower-level control if needed.

The Ex13c Example: Using Rebars

Let's get familiar with the rebar by jumping into an example. This example creates an SDI application that has a rebar with two bands: a familiar toolbar band and a dialog bar band. Figure 13-6 shows the example in action.

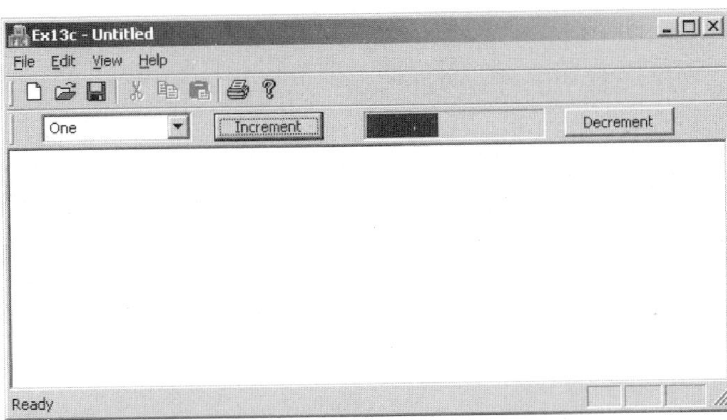

Figure 13-6 Ex13c rebar example.

Here are the steps required to create the Ex13c example:

1. **Run the MFC Application Wizard to generate a project named Ex13c.** Choose New Project from Visual Studio's File menu. In the New Project dialog box, select the MFC Application template, type the name **Ex13c**, and click OK. In the MFC Application Wizard, accept all the defaults but two: On the Application Type page, select Single Document, and on the User Interface Features page under Toolbars, select Standard Docking and Browser Style.

2. **Compile and run the application.** When you run the application, you'll see that the MFC Application Wizard has automatically created a rebar with two bands. One band contains a conventional toolbar and the other contains the text *TODO: layout dialog bar* in the band.

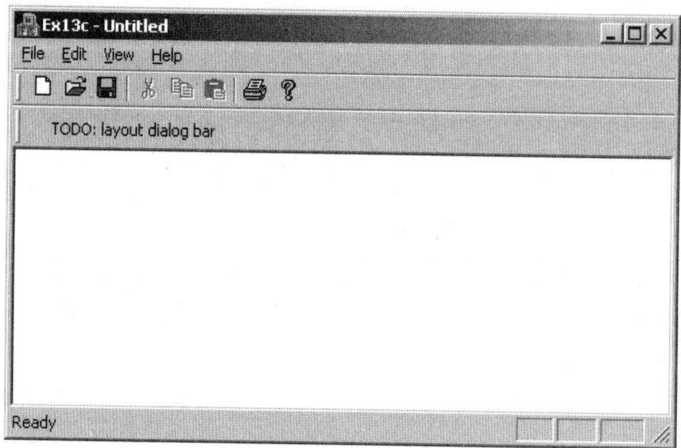

Open the MainFrm.h header file and see the code below, which declares the *CReBar* data member *m_ndReBar*.

```
protected:  // control bar embedded members
    CStatusBar  m_wndStatusBar;
    CToolBar    m_wndToolBar;
    CReBar      m_wndReBar;
    CDialogBar  m_wndDlgBar;
```

In the MainFrm.cpp file, you can see the code that adds the toolbar and the dialog bar to the *CReBar* object:

```
if (!m_wndReBar.Create(this) ||
    !m_wndReBar.AddBar(&m_wndToolBar) ||
    !m_wndReBar.AddBar(&m_wndDlgBar))
{
    TRACE0("Failed to create rebar\n");
    return -1;      // fail to create
}
```

3. **Lay out the dialog bar.** In Resource View, under the Dialog node, you'll find a dialog resource for the dialog bar with the ID *IDR_MAINFRAME*. Open *IDR_MAINFRAME*, and you'll see the dialog bar with the text *TODO: layout dialog bar*. Let's put some real controls onto the dialog bar. First, delete the static control with the *TODO* text in it. Then place a combo box on the dialog bar and use the Properties window to enter the following default data items in

the *Data* property: **One;Two;Buckle;My;Shoe!;**. Now place a button on the dialog bar and change the button's *Caption* property to *Increment*. Place a progress control on the dialog bar and set the *Smooth* property to *True*. Finally, place another button on the dialog bar and change the *Caption* property to *Decrement*. When you're done laying out out the dialog bar, it should look similar to this.

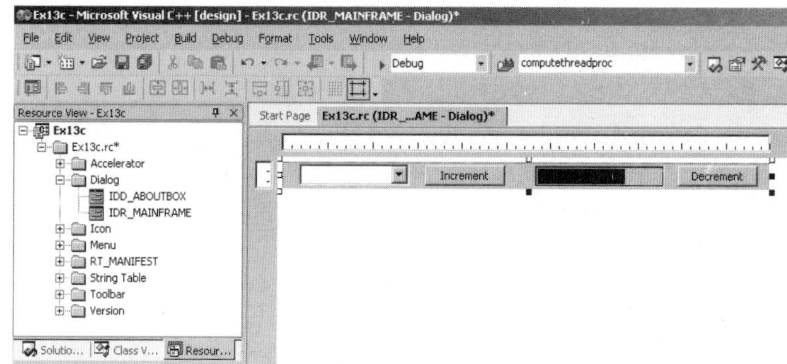

4. **Edit the MainFrm.h file.** Visual Studio doesn't understand how to connect the controls on the dialog bar with handlers in the *CMainFrame* class. We need to add them by hand. Open up MainFrm.h and add the following prototypes to *CMainFrame*.

```
afx_msg void OnButton1();
afx_msg void OnButton2();
```

5. **Edit the MainFrm.cpp file.** Open MainFrm.cpp and add the following message maps for Button1 and Button2:

```
BEGIN_MESSAGE_MAP(CMainFrame, CFrameWnd)
    ON_WM_CREATE()
    ON_BN_CLICKED(IDC_BUTTON1, OnButton1)
    ON_BN_CLICKED(IDC_BUTTON2, OnButton2)
END_MESSAGE_MAP()
```

Add the following *OnButton1* and *OnButton2* methods to CMainFrame.cpp:

```
void CMainFrame::OnButton1()
{
    CProgressCtrl * pProgress =
      (CProgressCtrl*)m_wndDlgBar.GetDlgItem(IDC_PROGRESS1);
    pProgress->StepIt();
}
```

```
void CMainFrame::OnButton2()
{
    CProgressCtrl * pProgress =
      (CProgressCtrl*)m_wndDlgBar.GetDlgItem(IDC_PROGRESS1);
    int nCurrentPos = pProgress->GetPos();
    pProgress->SetPos(nCurrentPos-10);
}
```

The *OnButton1* handler first gets a pointer to the progress control and then calls *StepIt* to increment the progress control. *OnButton2* decrements the current progress position by 10.

6. **Compile and test the Ex13c application.** Now you can compile and run Ex13c to see your custom rebar in action. The Increment button increases the progress bar and the Decrement button decreases it.

14

A Reusable Frame Window Base Class

C++ offers programmers the ability to produce "software building blocks" that can be taken off the shelf and fitted easily into an application. The Microsoft Foundation Class (MFC) library classes are a good example of this kind of reusable software. This chapter shows you how to build your own reusable base class by taking advantage of what the MFC library already provides.

In the process of building the reusable class, you'll learn a few more things about Microsoft Windows and the MFC library. In particular, you'll see how the application framework allows access to the Windows Registry, you'll learn more about the mechanics of the *CFrameWnd* class, and you'll get more exposure to static class variables and the *CString* class.

Why Reusable Base Classes Are Difficult to Write

In a normal application, you write code for software components that solve particular problems. It's usually a simple matter of meeting the project specification. With reusable base classes, however, you must anticipate future programming needs, both your own and those of others. You have to write a class that is general and complete yet efficient and easy to use.

This chapter's example shows the difficulty of building reusable software. The class was originally intended to be a frame class that would "remember" its window size and position. In addition to remembering their window sizes, many existing Windows-based programs also remember whether they've been minimized to the taskbar or whether they've been maximized to full screen. Then there is the oddball case of a window that is both minimized and maximized. In addition, the frame class needs to manage the toolbar and the status bar, and the class has to work in a dynamic-link library (DLL). In short, it's surprisingly difficult to write a frame class that would do everything that a programmer might expect.

In a production programming environment, reusable base classes might fall out of the normal software development cycle. A class written for one project might be extracted and further generalized for another project. There's always the temptation, though, to cut and paste existing classes without asking, "What can I factor out into a base class?" If you're in the software business for the long term, it's beneficial to start building your library of truly reusable components.

The *CPersistentFrame* Class

In this chapter, we'll use a class named *CPersistentFrame* that's derived from the *CFrameWnd* class. This *CPersistentFrame* class supports a persistent Single Document Interface (SDI) frame window that remembers the following characteristics:

- Window size
- Window position
- Maximized status
- Minimized status
- Toolbar and status bar enablement and position

When you terminate an application that's built with the *CPersistentFrame* class, the above information is saved on disk in the Windows Registry. When the application starts again, it reads the Registry and restores the frame to its state at the previous exit.

You can use the persistent view class in any SDI application, including the examples in this book. All you have to do is substitute *CPersistentFrame* for *CFrameWnd* in your application's derived frame class files.

The *CFrameWnd::ActivateFrame* Member Function

Why choose *CFrameWnd* as the base class for a persistent window? Why not have a persistent view class instead? In an MFC SDI application, the main frame window is always the parent of the view window. This frame window is created first, and then the control bars and the view are created as child windows. The application framework ensures that the child windows shrink and expand appropriately as the user changes the size of the frame window. It wouldn't make sense to change the view size after the frame was created.

The key to controlling the frame's size is the *CFrameWnd::ActivateFrame* member function. The application framework calls this virtual function (which is declared in *CFrameWnd*) during the SDI main frame window creation process (and in response to the File New and File Open commands). The framework's job is to call the *CWnd::ShowWindow* function with the parameter *nCmdShow*. *ShowWindow* makes the frame window visible along with its menu, view window, and control bars. The *nCmdShow* parameter determines whether the window is maximized or minimized.

If you override *ActivateFrame* in your derived frame class, you can change the value of *nCmdShow* before passing it to the *CFrameWnd::ActivateFrame* function. You can also call the *CWnd::SetWindowPlacement* function, which sets the size and position of the frame window, and you can set the visible status of the control bars. Because all changes are made before the frame window becomes visible, no annoying flash occurs on the screen.

You must be careful not to reset the frame window's position and size after every File New or File Open command. A first-time flag data member ensures that your *CPersistentFrame::ActivateFrame* function operates only when the application starts.

The *PreCreateWindow* Member Function

PreCreateWindow, which is declared at the *CWnd* level, is another virtual function that you can override to change the characteristics of your window before it is displayed. The framework calls this function before it calls *ActivateFrame*. The MFC Application Wizard *always* generates an overridden *PreCreateWindow* function in your project's view and frame window classes.

This function has a *CREATESTRUCT* structure as a parameter, and two of the data members in this structure are *style* and *dwExStyle*. You can change these data members before passing the structure on to the base class *PreCreateWindow* function. The *style* flag determines whether the window has a border, scroll bars, a minimize box, and so on. The *dwExStyle* flag controls other characteristics, such as always-on-top status. See the Window Styles and Extended Window Styles sections of the MFC Library Reference for details.

The *CREATESTRUCT* member *lpszClass* is also useful for changing the window's background brush, cursor, or icon. It makes no sense to change the brush or cursor in a frame window because the view window covers the client area. If you want an ugly red view window with a special cursor, for example, you can override your view's *PreCreateWindow* function like this:

```
BOOL CMyView::PreCreateWindow(CREATESTRUCT& cs)
{
    if (!CView::PreCreateWindow(cs)) {
        return FALSE;
    }
    cs.lpszClass =
        AfxRegisterWndClass(CS_DBLCLKS | CS_HREDRAW | CS_VREDRAW,
                            AfxGetApp()->LoadCursor(IDC_MYCURSOR),
                            ::CreateSolidBrush(RGB(255, 0, 0)));
    if (cs.lpszClass != NULL) {
        return TRUE;
    }
    else {
        return FALSE;
    }
}
```

If you override the *PreCreateWindow* function in your persistent frame class, windows of all derived classes will share the characteristics you programmed in the base class. Of course, derived classes can have their own overridden *PreCreateWindow* functions, but then you'll have to be careful about the interaction between the base class and derived class functions.

The Windows Registry

If you've used Win16-based applications, you've probably seen INI files. You can still use INI files in Win32-based applications, but Microsoft recommends that you use the Windows Registry instead. The Registry is a set of system files, managed by Windows, in which Windows and individual applications can store and access permanent information. The Registry is organized as a kind of hierarchical database in which string and integer data is accessed by a multipart key.

For example, a text processing application, TEXTPROC, might need to store the most recent font and point size in the Registry. Suppose that the program name forms the root of the key (a simplification) and that the application maintains two hierarchy levels below the name. The structure looks something like this:

TEXTPROC
  Text formatting
    Font = Times New Roman
    Points = 10

Unicode

European languages use characters that can be encoded in 8 bits—even characters with diacritics. Most Asian languages require 16 bits for their characters. Many programs use the double-byte character set (DBCS) standard; some characters use 8 bits and others 16 bits, depending on the value of the first 8 bits. DBCS is being replaced by Unicode, in which all characters are 16-bit "wide" characters. No specific Unicode character ranges are set aside for individual languages: If a character is used in both the Chinese and the Japanese languages, for example, that character appears only once in the Unicode character set.

When you look at MFC source code and the code that the MFC Application Wizard generates, you'll see the types *TCHAR*, *LPTSTR*, and *LPCTSTR* and you'll see literal strings such as *_T("string")*. You're looking at Unicode macros. If you build your project without defining *_UNICODE*, the compiler will generate code for ordinary 8-bit ANSI characters *(CHAR)* and pointers to 8-bit character arrays *(LPSTR, LPCSTR)*. If you do define *_UNICODE*, the compiler will generate code for 16-bit Unicode characters *(WCHAR)*, pointers *(LPWSTR, LPCWSTR)*, and literals *(L"wide string")*.

The *_UNICODE* preprocessor symbol also determines which Windows functions your program will call. Many Win32 functions have two versions. When your program calls *CreateWindowEx*, for example, the compiler will generate code to call either *CreateWindowExA* (with ANSI parameters) or *CreateWindowExW* (with Unicode parameters). In Windows NT, Windows 2000, and Windows XP, which use Unicode internally, *CreateWindowExW* passes all parameters straight through, but *CreateWindowExA* converts ANSI string and character parameters to Unicode. In Windows 95, Windows 98, and Windows Me, which use ANSI internally, *CreateWindowExW* is a stub that returns an error and *CreateWindowExA* passes the parameters straight through.

If you want to create a Unicode application, you should target it for Windows NT/2000/XP and use the macros throughout. You can write Unicode applications for Windows 95/98/Me, but you'll do extra work to call the "A" versions of the Win32 functions. As shown in Chapters 24 through 30, COM calls that support Automation always use wide characters. Although Win32 functions are available for converting between ANSI and Unicode, if you're using the *CString* class you can rely on a wide character constructor and the *AllocSysString* member function to do the conversions.

(continued)

Unicode *(continued)*

For simplicity, this book's example programs use ANSI only. The code generated by the MFC Application Wizard uses Unicode macros, but the code I wrote uses 8-bit literal strings and the *char*, *char**, and *const char** types.

The MFC library provides four *CWinApp* member functions, which are holdovers from the days of INI files, for accessing the Registry. The MFC Application Wizard generates a call to *CWinApp::SetRegistryKey* in your application's *InitInstance* function, as shown here:

```
SetRegistryKey(_T("Local AppWizard-Generated Applications"));
```

If you remove this call, your application will not use the Registry but will create and use an INI file in the Windows directory. The *SetRegistryKey* function's string parameter establishes the top of the hierarchy, and the following Registry functions define the bottom two levels, called the *heading name* and the *entry name*.

- *GetProfileInt*
- *WriteProfileInt*
- *GetProfileString*
- *WriteProfileString*

These functions treat Registry data as *CString* objects or unsigned integers. If you need floating-point values as entries, you must use the string functions and do the conversion yourself. All the functions take a heading name and an entry name as parameters. In the TEXTPROC example shown earlier, the heading name is Text Formatting and the entry names are Font and Points.

To use the Registry access functions, you need a pointer to the application object. The global function *AfxGetApp* does the job. In the previous sample Registry, the Font and Points entries were set with the following code:

```
AfxGetApp()->WriteProfileString("Text formatting", "Font",
                                "Times New Roman");
AfxGetApp()->WriteProfileInt("Text formatting", "Points", 10);
```

You'll see a real Registry example shortly, in Ex14a, and you'll learn to use the Windows Regedit program to examine and edit the Registry.

> **Note** The application framework stores a list of most recently used files in the Registry under the heading Recent File List.

Using the *CString* Class

The MFC *CString* class is a significant *de facto* extension of the C++ language. The *CString* class has many useful operators and member functions, but perhaps its most important feature is its dynamic memory allocation. You never have to worry about the size of a *CString* object. The following statements represent typical uses of *CString* objects:

```
CString strFirstName("Elvis");
CString strLastName("Presley");
CString strTruth = strFirstName + " " + strLastName; // concatenation
strTruth += " is alive";
ASSERT(strTruth == "Elvis Presley is alive");
ASSERT(strTruth.Left(5) == strFirstName);
ASSERT(strTruth[2] == 'v'); // subscript operator
```

In a perfect world, C++ programs would use all *CString* objects and never use ordinary zero-terminated character arrays. Unfortunately, many runtime library functions still use character arrays, so programs must always mix and match their string representations. Fortunately, the *CString* class provides a *const char*()* operator that converts a *CString* object to a character pointer. Many of the MFC library functions have *const char** parameters. Take the global *AfxMessageBox* function, for example. Here is one of the function's prototypes:

```
int AFXAPI AfxMessageBox(LPCTSTR lpszText, UINT nType = MB_OK,
                         UINT nIDHelp = 0);
```

Note that *LPCTSTR* is not a pointer to a *CString* object but is a Unicode-enabled replacement for *const char**.

You can call *AfxMessageBox* in this way

```
char szMessageText[] = "Unknown error";
AfxMessageBox(szMessageText);
```

or this way:

```
CString strMessageText("Unknown error");
AfxMessageBox(strMessageText);
```

Now suppose you want to generate a formatted string. *CString::Format* does the job, as shown here:

```
int nError = 23;
CString strMessageText;
strMessageText.Format("Error number %d", nError);
AfxMessageBox(strMessageText);
```

> **Note** Suppose you want direct write access to the characters in a *CString* object. If you write code like this:
>
> ```
> CString strTest("test");
> strncpy(strTest, "T", 1);
> ```
>
> you'll get a compile error because the first parameter of *strncpy* is declared *char**, not *const char**. The *CString::GetBuffer* function "locks down" the buffer with a specified size and returns a *char**. You must call the *ReleaseBuffer* member function later to make the string dynamic again. The correct way to capitalize the *T* is shown in the following example.
>
> ```
> CString strTest("test");
> strncpy(strTest.GetBuffer(5), "T", 1);
> strTest.ReleaseBuffer();
> ASSERT(strTest == "Test");
> ```

The *const char** operator takes care of converting a *CString* object to a constant character pointer, but what about conversion in the other direction? It so happens that the *CString* class has a constructor that converts a constant character pointer to a *CString* object, and it has a set of overloaded operators for these pointers. That's why statements such as the following work:

```
strTruth += " is alive";
```

The special constructor works with functions that take a *CString* reference parameter, such as *CDC::TextOut*. In the following statement, a temporary *CString* object is created on the calling program's stack and then the object's address is passed to *TextOut*:

```
pDC->TextOut(0, 0, "Hello, world!");
```

It's more efficient to use the other overloaded version of *CDC::TextOut* if you're willing to count the characters:

```
pDC->TextOut(0, 0, "Hello, world!", 13);
```

If you're writing a function that takes a string parameter, you've got some design choices. Here are some programming rules:

- If the function doesn't change the contents of the string and you're willing to use C runtime functions such as *strncpy*, use a *const char** parameter.
- If the function doesn't change the contents of the string but you want to use *CString* member functions inside the function, use a *const CString&* parameter.
- If the function changes the contents of the string, use a *CString&* parameter.

The Position of a Maximized Window

As a Windows user, you know that you can maximize a window from the system menu or by clicking a button at the top right corner of the window. You can return a maximized window to its original size in a similar fashion. It's obvious that a maximized window remembers its original size and position.

The *CWnd* function *GetWindowRect* retrieves the screen coordinates of a window. If a window is maximized, *GetWindowRect* returns the coordinates of the screen rather than the window's unmaximized coordinates. If a persistent frame class is to work for maximized windows, it has to know the window's unmaximized coordinates. *CWnd::GetWindowPlacement* retrieves the unmaximized coordinates together with some flags that indicate whether the window is currently minimized or maximized.

The companion *SetWindowPlacement* function lets you set the maximized and minimized status and the size and position of the window. To calculate the position of the top left corner of a maximized window, you need to account for the window's border size, which is obtainable from the Win32 *GetSystemMetrics* function. Later in the chapter, you'll see the Persist.cpp file, in which the *CPersistentFrame::ActivateFrame* code shows an example of how *SetWindowPlacement* is used.

Control Bar Status and the Registry

The MFC library provides two *CFrameWnd* member functions, *SaveBarState* and *LoadBarState*, for saving and loading control bar status to and from the Registry, respectively. These functions process the size and position of the status bar and docked toolbars. They don't process the position of floating toolbars, however.

Static Data Members

The *CPersistentFrame* class stores its Registry key names in *static const char* array data members. What would the other storage choices be? String resource entries won't work because the strings need to be defined with the class itself. (String resources make sense if *CPersistentFrame* is made into a DLL, however.) Global variables are generally not recommended because they defeat encapsulation. Static *CString* objects don't make sense because the characters must be copied to the heap when the program starts.

An obvious choice would be regular data members. But static data members are better because, as constants, they're segregated into the program's read-only data section and can be mapped to multiple instances of the same program. If the *CPersistentFrame* class is part of a DLL, all processes that are using the DLL can map the character arrays. Static data members are really global variables, but they're scoped to their class so there's no chance of name collisions.

The Default Window Rectangle

You're used to defining rectangles using device or logical coordinates. A *CRect* object constructed with the following statement has a special meaning:

```
CRect rect(CW_USEDEFAULT, CW_USEDEFAULT, 0, 0);
```

When Windows creates a new window with this special rectangle, it positions the window in a cascade pattern with the top left corner below and to the right of the window most recently created. The right and bottom edges of the window are always within the display's boundaries.

The *CFrameWnd* class's static *rectDefault* data member is constructed using *CW_USEDEFAULT* in this way, so it contains the special rectangle. The *CPersistentFrame* class declares its own *rectDefault* default window rectangle with a fixed size and position as a static data member, thus hiding the base class member.

The Ex14a Example: Using a Persistent Frame Window Class

The Ex14a program illustrates the use of a persistent frame window class, *CPersistentFrame*. The following code shows the contents of the files Persist.h and Persist.cpp, which are included in the Ex14a project on the companion CD. In this example, we'll insert the new frame class into an MFC Application Wizard–generated SDI application. Ex14a is a "do-nothing" application, but you can insert the persistent frame class into any of your own SDI "do-something" applications.

Persist.h

```
// Persist.h

#ifndef _INSIDE_VISUAL_CPP_PERSISTENT_FRAME
#define _INSIDE_VISUAL_CPP_PERSISTENT_FRAME

class CPersistentFrame : public CFrameWnd
{ // remembers where it was on the desktop
    DECLARE_DYNAMIC(CPersistentFrame)
private:
    static const CRect s_rectDefault;
    static const char s_profileHeading[];
    static const char s_profileRect[];
    static const char s_profileIcon[];
    static const char s_profileMax[];
    static const char s_profileTool[];
    static const char s_profileStatus[];
    BOOL m_bFirstTime;
protected: // Create from serialization only
    CPersistentFrame();
    ~CPersistentFrame();

    public:
    virtual void ActivateFrame(int nCmdShow = -1);
    protected:
    afx_msg void OnDestroy();
    DECLARE_MESSAGE_MAP()
};

#endif // _INSIDE_VISUAL_CPP_PERSISTENT_FRAME
```

Persist.cpp

```
// Persist.cpp Persistent frame class for SDI apps

#include "stdafx.h"
#include "persist.h"

#ifdef _DEBUG
#undef THIS_FILE
static char BASED_CODE THIS_FILE[] = __FILE__;
#endif
///////////////////////////////////////////////////////////////
// CPersistentFrame

const CRect CPersistentFrame::s_rectDefault(10, 10,
```

(continued)

```
                                                    500, 400);  // static
const char CPersistentFrame::s_profileHeading[] = "Window size";
const char CPersistentFrame::s_profileRect[] = "Rect";
const char CPersistentFrame::s_profileIcon[] = "icon";
const char CPersistentFrame::s_profileMax[] = "max";
const char CPersistentFrame::s_profileTool[] = "tool";
const char CPersistentFrame::s_profileStatus[] = "status";
IMPLEMENT_DYNAMIC(CPersistentFrame, CFrameWnd)

BEGIN_MESSAGE_MAP(CPersistentFrame, CFrameWnd)
    ON_WM_DESTROY()
END_MESSAGE_MAP()

///////////////////////////////////////////////////////////////////
CPersistentFrame::CPersistentFrame(){
    m_bFirstTime = TRUE;
}
///////////////////////////////////////////////////////////////////
CPersistentFrame::~CPersistentFrame()
{
}
///////////////////////////////////////////////////////////////////
void CPersistentFrame::OnDestroy()
{
    CString strText;
    BOOL bIconic, bMaximized;

    WINDOWPLACEMENT wndpl;
    wndpl.length = sizeof(WINDOWPLACEMENT);
    // gets current window position and
    //  iconized/maximized status
    BOOL bRet = GetWindowPlacement(&wndpl);
    if (wndpl.showCmd == SW_SHOWNORMAL) {
        bIconic = FALSE;
        bMaximized = FALSE;
    }
    else if (wndpl.showCmd == SW_SHOWMAXIMIZED) {
        bIconic = FALSE;
        bMaximized = TRUE;
    }
    else if (wndpl.showCmd == SW_SHOWMINIMIZED) {
        bIconic = TRUE;
        if (wndpl.flags) {
            bMaximized = TRUE;
        }
        else {
            bMaximized = FALSE;
        }
    }
```

```
    strText.Format("%04d %04d %04d %04d",
                   wndpl.rcNormalPosition.left,
                   wndpl.rcNormalPosition.top,
                   wndpl.rcNormalPosition.right,
                   wndpl.rcNormalPosition.bottom);
    AfxGetApp()->WriteProfileString(s_profileHeading,
                                    s_profileRect, strText);
    AfxGetApp()->WriteProfileInt(s_profileHeading,
                                 s_profileIcon, bIconic);
    AfxGetApp()->WriteProfileInt(s_profileHeading,
                                 s_profileMax, bMaximized);
    SaveBarState(AfxGetApp()->m_pszProfileName);
    CFrameWnd::OnDestroy();
}

///////////////////////////////////////////////////////////////////
void CPersistentFrame::ActivateFrame(int nCmdShow)
{
    CString strText;
    BOOL bIconic, bMaximized;
    UINT flags;
    WINDOWPLACEMENT wndpl;
    CRect rect;

    if (m_bFirstTime) {
        m_bFirstTime = FALSE;
        strText = AfxGetApp()->GetProfileString(s_profileHeading,
                                                s_profileRect);
        if (!strText.IsEmpty()) {
            rect.left = atoi((const char*) strText);
            rect.top = atoi((const char*) strText + 5);
            rect.right = atoi((const char*) strText + 10);
            rect.bottom = atoi((const char*) strText + 15);
        }
        else {
            rect = s_rectDefault;
        }
        bIconic = AfxGetApp()->GetProfileInt(s_profileHeading,
                                             s_profileIcon, 0);
        bMaximized = AfxGetApp()->GetProfileInt(s_profileHeading,
                                                s_profileMax, 0);
        if (bIconic) {
            nCmdShow = SW_SHOWMINNOACTIVE;
            if (bMaximized) {
                flags = WPF_RESTORETOMAXIMIZED;
            }
            else {
                flags = WPF_SETMINPOSITION;
            }
```

(continued)

```
        }
        else {
            if (bMaximized) {
                nCmdShow = SW_SHOWMAXIMIZED;
                flags = WPF_RESTORETOMAXIMIZED;
            }
            else {
                nCmdShow = SW_NORMAL;
                flags = WPF_SETMINPOSITION;
            }
        }
        wndpl.length = sizeof(WINDOWPLACEMENT);
        wndpl.showCmd = nCmdShow;
        wndpl.flags = flags;
        wndpl.ptMinPosition = CPoint(0, 0);
        wndpl.ptMaxPosition =
            CPoint(-::GetSystemMetrics(SM_CXBORDER),
                   -::GetSystemMetrics(SM_CYBORDER));
        wndpl.rcNormalPosition = rect;
        LoadBarState(AfxGetApp()->m_pszProfileName);
        // sets window's position and minimized/maximized status
        BOOL bRet = SetWindowPlacement(&wndpl);
    }
    CFrameWnd::ActivateFrame(nCmdShow);
}
```

Here are the steps for building the Ex14a application:

1. **Run the MFC Application Wizard to generate the Ex14a project.** Accept all default settings but two: Select Single Document and deselect Printing And Print Preview.

2. **Modify MainFrm.h.** You must change the base class of *CMainFrame.*

   To do this, simply change the line

   ```
   class CMainFrame : public CFrameWnd
   ```

   to

   ```
   class CMainFrame : public CPersistentFrame
   ```

   Also, add this line:

   ```
   #include "persist.h"
   ```

3. **Modify MainFrm.cpp.** Globally replace all occurrences of *CFrameWnd* with *CPersistentFrame.*

4. **Modify Ex14a.cpp.** Replace the line

   ```
   SetRegistryKey(_T("Local AppWizard-Generated Applications"));
   ```

with this line:

```
SetRegistryKey("Programming Visual C++ .NET");
```

5. **Add the Persist.cpp file to the project.** You can type in the Persist.h and Persist.cpp files from the previous code listing, or you can copy the files from the companion CD. Having the files in the \vcppnet\Ex14a directory is not sufficient. You must add the names of the files to the solution. Choose Add Existing Item from Visual C++ .NET's Project menu, and select Persist.h and Persist.cpp from the list.

6. **Build and test the Ex14a application.** Size and move the application's frame window, and then close the application. When you restart the application, does its window open at the same location at which it was closed? Experiment with maximizing and minimizing, and then change the status and position of the control bars. Does the persistent frame remember its settings?

7. **Examine the Windows Registry.** Run the Windows Regedit.exe program. Navigate to the HKEY_CURRENT_USER\Software\Programming Visual C++ .NET\Ex14a key. You should see data values similar to those shown here:

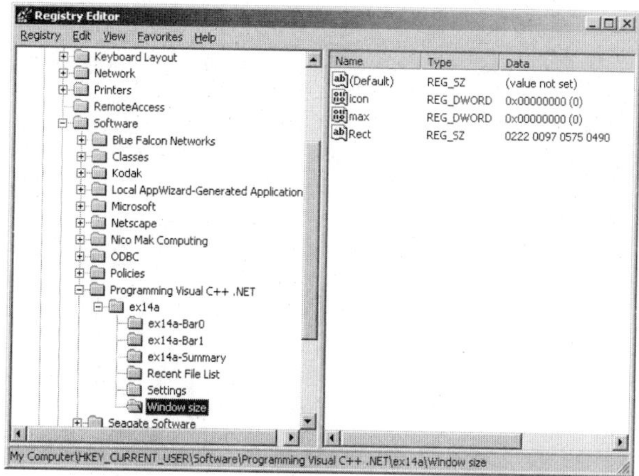

Notice the relationship between the Registry key and the *SetRegistryKey* function parameter, *"Programming Visual C++ .NET"*. If you supply an empty string as the *SetRegistryKey* parameter, the program name (Ex14a, in this case) will be positioned directly below the Software key.

Persistent Frames in MDI Applications

We won't get into Multiple Document Interface (MDI) applications until Chapter 16, but if you're using this book as a reference, you might want to apply the persistent frame technique to MDI applications.

The *CPersistentFrame* class, as presented in this chapter, won't work in an MDI application because the MDI main frame window's *ShowWindow* function is called, not by a virtual *ActivateFrame* function, but directly by the application class's *InitInstance* member function. If you need to control the characteristics of an MDI main frame window, add the necessary code to *InitInstance*.

The *ActivateFrame* function is called, however, for *CMDIChildWnd* objects. This means your MDI application could remember the sizes and positions of its child windows. You could store the information in the Registry, but you would have to accommodate multiple windows. You would have to modify the *CPersistentFrame* class for this purpose.

15

Separating the Document from Its View

Now you'll finally get to see the interaction between documents and views. Chapter 12 gave you a preview of this interaction when it showed the routing of command messages to both view objects and document objects. In this chapter, you'll see how the document maintains the application's data and how the view presents the data to the user. You'll also learn how the document and view objects talk to each other while the application executes.

The two examples in this chapter both use the *CFormView* class as the base class for their views. The first example is as simple as possible, with the document holding only one simple object of class *CStudent*, which represents a single student record. The view shows the student's name and grade and allows editing. With the *CStudent* class, you'll get some practice writing classes to represent real-world entities. You'll also get to use the Microsoft Foundation Class (MFC) library diagnostic dump functions.

The second example goes further by introducing pointer collection classes—the *CObList* and *CTypedPtrList* classes in particular. The document holds a collection of student records, and the view allows the sequencing, insertion, and deletion of individual records.

Document-View Interaction Functions

You already know that the document object holds the data and that the view object displays the data and allows editing. A Single Document Interface (SDI) application has a document class derived from *CDocument*, and it has one or more view classes, each ultimately derived from *CView*. A complex handshaking process takes place among the document, the view, and the rest of the application framework.

To understand this process, you need to know about five important member functions in the document and view classes. Two are nonvirtual base class functions that you call in your derived classes; three are virtual functions that you often override in your derived classes. Let's look at these functions one at a time.

The *CView::GetDocument* Function

A view object has one and only one associated document object. The *GetDocument* function allows an application to navigate from a view to its document. Suppose a view object gets a message that the user has entered new data into an edit control. The view must tell the document object to update its internal data accordingly. The *GetDocument* function provides the document pointer that can be used to access document class member functions or public data members.

> **Note** The *CDocument::GetNextView* function navigates from the document to the view, but because a document can have more than one view, you have to call this member function once for each view, inside a loop. You'll seldom call *GetNextView* because the application framework provides a better method of iterating through a document's views.

When the MFC Application Wizard generates a derived *CView* class, it creates two special type-safe versions of the *GetDocument* function (a debug version and a non-debug version) that return a pointer to an object of your derived document class. The non-debug version (which appears in the view header file) looks like this:

```
inline CMyDoc* CMyView::GetDocument() const
   { return reinterpret_cast<CMyDoc*>(m_pDocument); }
```

The debug version (which appears in the view source code file and is compiled when debugging is defined) looks like this:

```
CMyDoc* CMyView::GetDocument() const // non-debug version is inline
{
    ASSERT(m_pDocument->IsKindOf(RUNTIME_CLASS(CMyDoc)));
    return (CMyDoc*)m_pDocument;
}
```

When the compiler sees a call to *GetDocument* in your view class code, it uses *CMyView::GetDocument*, which returns *CMyDocument* *, instead of using *CView::GetDocument*, which returns *CDocument* *. Because *CMyDocument* * is returned, you do not have to cast the returned pointer to your derived document class. Without a helper function like this, the compiler would call the base class's *GetDocument* function and thus return a pointer to a *CDocument* object.

Notice that a statement such as the following always calls the base class's *GetDocument* function—whether or not you have the previous helper function in your program—because the *CView::GetDocument* function is not a virtual function:

```
pView->GetDocument(); // pView is declared CView*
```

The *CDocument::UpdateAllViews* Function

If the document data changes for any reason, all views must be notified so they can update their representations of that data. If *UpdateAllViews* is called from a member function of a derived document class, its first parameter, pSender, is NULL. If *UpdateAllViews* is called from a member function of a derived view class, set the *pSender* parameter to the current view, like this:

```
GetDocument()->UpdateAllViews(this);
```

The non-null parameter prevents the application framework from notifying the current view. The assumption here is that the current view has already updated itself.

The function has optional hint parameters that you can use to give view-specific and application-dependent information about which parts of the view to update. This is an advanced use of the function.

How exactly is a view notified when *UpdateAllViews* gets called? Take a look at the next function, *OnUpdate*.

The *CView::OnUpdate* Function

This virtual function is called by the application framework in response to your application's call to the *CDocument::UpdateAllViews* function. You can, of course, call it directly within your derived *CView* class. Typically, your derived view class's *OnUpdate* function accesses the document, gets the document's data, and then updates the view's data members or controls to reflect the changes. Alternatively, *OnUpdate* can invalidate a portion of the view, causing the view's *OnDraw* function to use document data to draw in the window. The *OnUpdate* function might look something like this:

```
void CMyView::OnUpdate(CView* pSender, LPARAM lHint, CObject* pHint)
{
    CMyDocument* pMyDoc = GetDocument();
    CString lastName = pMyDoc->GetLastName();
    m_pNameStatic->SetWindowText(lastName); // m_pNameStatic is
                                            //  a CMyView data member
}
```

The hint information is passed through directly from the call to *UpdateAllViews*. The default *OnUpdate* implementation invalidates the entire window rectangle. In your overridden version, you can choose to define a smaller invalid rectangle as specified by the hint information.

If the *CDocument* function *UpdateAllViews* is called with the *pSender* parameter pointing to a specific view object, *OnUpdate* is called for all the document's views *except* the specified view.

The *CView::OnInitialUpdate* Function

This virtual *CView* function is called when the application starts, when the user chooses New from the File menu, or when the user chooses Open from the File menu. The *CView* base class version of *OnInitialUpdate* does nothing but call *OnUpdate*. If you override *OnInitialUpdate* in your derived view class, be sure that the view class calls the base class's *OnInitialUpdate* function or the derived class's *OnUpdate* function.

You can use your derived class's *OnInitialUpdate* function to initialize your view object. When the application starts, the application framework calls *OnInitialUpdate* immediately after *OnCreate* (if you've mapped *OnCreate* in your view class). *OnCreate* is called once, but *OnInitialUpdate* can be called many times.

The *CDocument::OnNewDocument* Function

The framework calls this virtual function after a document object is first constructed or when the user chooses New from the File menu in an SDI application. This is a good place to set the initial values of your document's data members. The MFC Application Wizard generates an overridden *OnNewDocument* function in your derived document class. Be sure to retain the call to the base class function.

The Simplest Document-View Application

Suppose you don't need multiple views of your document, but you plan to take advantage of the application framework's file support. In this case, you can forget about the *UpdateAllViews* and *OnUpdate* functions. Simply follow these steps when you develop the application:

1. In your derived document class header file (generated by the MFC Application Wizard), declare your document's data members. These data members are the primary data storage for your application. You can make these data members public, or you can declare the derived view class a friend of the document class.

2. In your derived view class, override the *OnInitialUpdate* virtual member function. The application framework calls this function after the document data has been initialized or read from disk. (Chapter 16 discusses disk file I/O.) *OnInitialUpdate* should update the view to reflect the current document data.

3. In your derived view class, let your window message handlers, command message handlers, and your *OnDraw* function read and update the document data members directly, using *GetDocument* to access the document object.

The sequence of events for this simplified document-view environment is as follows:

Application starts	*CMyDocument* object is constructed
	CMyView object is constructed
	View window is created
	CMyView::OnCreate is called (if it is mapped)
	CMyDocument::OnNewDocument is called
	CMyView::OnInitialUpdate is called
	View object is initialized
	View window is invalidated
	CMyView::OnDraw is called
User edits data	*CMyView* functions update *CMyDocument* data members
User exits application	*CMyView* object is destroyed
	CMyDocument object is destroyed

The *CFormView* Class

The *CFormView* class is a useful view class that has many of the characteristics of a modeless dialog box. Like a class derived from *CDialog*, a derived *CFormView* class is associated with a dialog resource that defines the frame characteristics and enumerates the controls. The *CFormView* class supports the same dialog data exchange and validation (DDX and DDV) functions that you saw in the *CDialog* examples in Chapter 7.

A *CFormView* object receives notification messages directly from its controls, and it receives command messages from the application framework. This application framework command-processing ability clearly separates *CFormView* from *CDialog*, and it makes controlling the view from the frame's main menu or toolbar easy.

> **Warning** If the MFC Application Wizard generates a Form View dialog box, the properties are set correctly, but if you use the dialog editor to make a dialog box for a form view, you *must* specify the following items in the Dialog Properties window:
>
> *Style = Child*
> *Border = None*
> *Visible = unchecked*

The *CFormView* class is derived from *CView* (actually, from *CScrollView*) and not from *CDialog*. You can't, therefore, assume that *CDialog* member functions are supported. *CFormView* does *not* have virtual *OnInitDialog*, *OnOK*, and *OnCancel* functions. *CFormView* member functions do not call *UpdateData* and the DDX functions. You have to call *UpdateData* yourself at the appropriate times, usually in response to control notification messages or command messages.

Even though the *CFormView* class is not derived from the *CDialog* class, it is built around the Microsoft Windows dialog box. For this reason, you can use many of the *CDialog* class member functions such as *GotoDlgCtrl* and *NextDlgCtrl*. All you have to do is cast your *CFormView* pointer to a *CDialog* pointer. The following statement, extracted from a member function of a class derived from *CFormView*, sets the focus to a specified control. *GetDlgItem* is a *CWnd* function and is thus inherited by the derived *CFormView* class.

```
((CDialog*) this)->GotoDlgCtrl(GetDlgItem(IDC_NAME));
```

The MFC Application Wizard gives you the option of using *CFormView* as the base class for your view. When you select *CFormView*, the MFC Application Wizard generates an empty dialog box with the correct style properties set. The next step is to use the Class View's Properties window to add control notification message handlers, command message handlers, and update command user interface handlers. (The example steps show you what to do.) You can also define data members and validation criteria.

The *CObject* Class

If you study the MFC library hierarchy, you'll notice that the *CObject* class is at the top. Most other classes are derived from the *CObject* root class. When a class is derived from *CObject*, it inherits a number of important characteristics. The many benefits of *CObject* derivation will become clear as you read the chapters that follow.

In this chapter, you'll see how *CObject* derivation allows objects to participate in the diagnostic dumping scheme and allows objects to be elements in the collection classes.

Diagnostic Dumping

The MFC library gives you some useful tools for diagnostic dumping. You enable these tools when you select the Debug configuration. When you select the Release configuration, diagnostic dumping is disabled and the diagnostic code is not linked to your program. All diagnostic output goes to the Debug view in the debug Output window.

> **Tip** To clear diagnostic output from the debug Output window, position the cursor in the Output window and click the right mouse button. Then choose Clear All from the shortcut menu.

The *TRACE* Macro

We've been using the *TRACE* macro throughout the preceding examples in this book. *TRACE* statements are active whenever the constant *_DEBUG* is defined (when you select the Debug configuration and when the *afxTraceEnabled* variable is set to *TRUE*). *TRACE* statements work like C language *printf* statements, but they're completely disabled in the release version of the program. Here's a typical *TRACE* statement:

```
int nCount = 9;
CString strDesc("total");
TRACE("Count = %d, Description = %s\n", nCount, strDesc);
```

Even though the *TRACE* macro is deprecated (the documentation suggests using *ATLTRACE*), it is still available and works just fine.

The *afxDump* Object

An alternative to the *TRACE* statement is more compatible with the C++ language. The MFC *afxDump* object accepts program variables with a syntax similar to that of *cout*, the C++ output stream object. You don't need complex formatting strings; instead, overloaded operators control the output format. The *afxDump* output goes to the same destination as the *TRACE* output, but the *afxDump* object is defined only in the Debug version of the MFC library.

Here is a typical stream-oriented diagnostic statement that produces the same output as the *TRACE* statement above:

```
int nCount = 9;
CString strDesc("total");
#ifdef _DEBUG
    afxDump << "Count = " << nCount
            << ", Description = " << strDesc << "\n";
#endif // _DEBUG
```

Although both *afxDump* and *cout* use the same insertion operator (<<), they don't share any code. The *cout* object is part of the Microsoft Visual C++ iostream library, and *afxDump* is part of the MFC library. Don't assume that any of the *cout* formatting capability is available through *afxDump*.

Classes that aren't derived from *CObject*, such as *CString*, *CTime*, and *CRect*, contain their own overloaded insertion operators for *CDumpContext* objects. The *CDumpContext* class, of which *afxDump* is an instance, includes the overloaded insertion operators for the native C++ data types *(int, double, char**, and so on). The *CDumpContext* class also contains insertion operators for *CObject* references and pointers, and that's where things get interesting.

The Dump Context and the *CObject* Class

If the *CDumpContext* insertion operator accepts *CObject* pointers and references, it must also accept pointers and references to derived classes. Consider a trivial class, *CAction*, which is derived from *CObject*, as shown here:

```
class CAction : public CObject
{
public:
    int m_nTime;
};
```

What happens when the following statement executes?

```
#ifdef _DEBUG
    afxDump << action; // action is an object of class CAction
#endif // _DEBUG
```

The virtual *CObject::Dump* function gets called. If you haven't overridden *Dump* for *CAction*, you don't get much except for the address of the object. If you've overridden *Dump*, however, you can get the internal state of your object. Here's a *CAction::Dump* function:

```
#ifdef _DEBUG
void CAction::Dump(CDumpContext& dc) const
{
    CObject::Dump(dc); // Always call base class function
    dc << "time = " << m_nTime << "\n";
}
#endif // _DEBUG
```

The base class *(CObject) Dump* function prints a line such as this:

```
a CObject at $4115D4
```

If you have called the *DECLARE_DYNAMIC* macro in your *CAction* class definition and the *IMPLEMENT_DYNAMIC* macro in your *CAction* declaration, you'll see the name of the class in your dump, as shown here

```
a CAction at $4115D4
```

even if your dump statement looks like this:

```
#ifdef _DEBUG
    afxDump << (CObject&) action;
#endif // _DEBUG
```

The two macros work together to include the MFC library runtime class code in your derived *CObject* class. With this code in place, your program can determine an object's class name at run time (for the dump, for example) and it can obtain class hierarchy information.

> **Note** The *(DECLARE_SERIAL, IMPLEMENT_SERIAL)* and *(DECLARE_DYNCREATE, IMPLEMENT_DYNCREATE)* macro pairs provide the same runtime class features as those provided by the *(DECLARE_DYNAMIC, IMPLEMENT_DYNAMIC)* macro pair.

Automatic Dump of Undeleted Objects

When the Debug configuration is selected, the application framework dumps all objects that are undeleted when your program exits. This dump is a useful diagnostic aid, but if you want it to be really useful, you must be sure to delete *all* your objects, even the ones that would normally disappear after the exit. This object cleanup is good programming discipline.

The code that adds debug information to allocated memory blocks is now in the Debug version of the C runtime (CRT) library rather than in the MFC library. If you choose to dynamically link MFC, the MSVCRTD DLL will be loaded along with the necessary MFC DLLs. When you add the following line at the top of a CPP file, the CRT library will list the filename and line number at which the allocations were made:

```
#define new DEBUG_NEW
```

The MFC Application Wizard puts this line at the top of all the CPP files it generates.

Window Subclassing for Enhanced Data-Entry Control

What if you want an edit control (in a dialog box or a form view) that accepts only numeric characters? That's easy. You just set the *Number* style in the control's property sheet. If, however, you want to exclude numeric characters or change the case of alphabetic characters, you must do some programming.

The MFC library provides a convenient way to change the behavior of any standard control, including the edit control. Two other ways are available: You can derive your own classes from *CEdit*, *CListBox*, and so forth (with their own message handler functions) and then create control objects at run time. Or you can register a special window class, as a Win32 programmer would, and integrate it into the project's resource file with a text editor. Neither of these methods, however, allows you to use the dialog editor to position controls in the dialog resource.

The easy way to modify a control's behavior is to use the MFC library's window subclassing feature. You use the dialog editor to position a normal control in a dialog resource, and then you write a new C++ class that contains message handlers for the events that you want to handle yourself. Here are the steps for subclassing an edit control:

1. With the dialog editor, position an edit control in your dialog resource. Assume that it has the child window ID *IDC_EDIT1*.

2. Write a new class—for example, *CNonNumericEdit*—that is derived from *CEdit*. Map the *WM_CHAR* message and write a handler like this:

```
void CNonNumericEdit::OnChar(UINT nChar, UINT nRepCnt, UINT nFlags)
{
    if (!isdigit(nChar)) {
        CEdit::OnChar(nChar, nRepCnt, nFlags);
    }
}
```

3. In your derived dialog or form view class header, declare a data member of class *CNonNumericEdit* in this way:

```
private:
    CNonNumericEdit m_nonNumericEdit;
```

4. If you're working with a dialog class, add the following line to your *OnInitDialog* override function:

```
m_nonNumericEdit.SubclassDlgItem(IDC_EDIT1, this);
```

5. If you're working with a form view class, add the following code to your *OnInitialUpdate* override function:

```
if (m_nonNumericEdit.m_hWnd == NULL) {
    m_nonNumericEdit.SubclassDlgItem(IDC_EDIT1, this);
}
```

The *CWnd::SubclassDlgItem* member function ensures that all messages are routed through the application framework's message dispatch system before being sent to the control's built-in window procedure. This technique is called *dynamic subclassing* and is explained in more detail in Technical Note #14 in the *MFC Library Reference*.

The code in the preceding steps only accepts or rejects a character. If you want to change the value of a character, your handler must call *CWnd::DefWindowProc*, which bypasses some MFC logic that stores parameter values in thread object data members. Here's a sample handler that converts lowercase characters to uppercase:

```
void CUpperEdit::OnChar(UINT nChar, UINT nRepCnt, UINT nFlags)
{
    if (islower(nChar)) {
        nChar = toupper(nChar);
    }
    DefWindowProc(WM_CHAR, (WPARAM) nChar,
                  (LPARAM) (nRepCnt | (nFlags << 16)));
}
```

You can also use window subclassing to handle reflected messages, which were mentioned in Chapter 7. If an MFC window class doesn't map a message from one of its child controls, the framework will reflect the message back to the control. Technical Note #62 in the *MFC Library Reference* explains the details.

If you need an edit control with a yellow background, for example, you can derive a class *CYellowEdit* from *CEdit* and use Class View's Properties window to map the =*WM_CTLCOLOR* message in *CYellowEdit*. (The Properties window lists the message name with an equal sign in front to indicate that it is reflected.) The handler code, shown below, is substantially the same as the nonreflected *WM_CTLCOLOR* handler shown on page 157. (Member variable *m_hYellowBrush* is defined in the control class's constructor.)

```
HBRUSH CYellowEdit::CtlColor(CDC* pDC, UINT nCtlColor)
{
    pDC->SetBkColor(RGB(255, 255, 0)); // yellow
    return m_hYellowBrush;
}
```

The Ex15a Example: A Simple Document-View Interaction

The first of this chapter's two examples shows a very simple document-view interaction. The *CEx15aDoc* document class, which is derived from *CDocument*, allows for a single embedded *CStudent* object. The *CStudent* class represents a student record composed of a *CString* name and an integer grade. The *CEx15aView* view class is derived from *CFormView*. It is a visual representation of a student record that has edit controls for the name and grade. The default Enter pushbutton updates the document with data from the edit controls. Figure 15-1 shows the Ex15a program window.

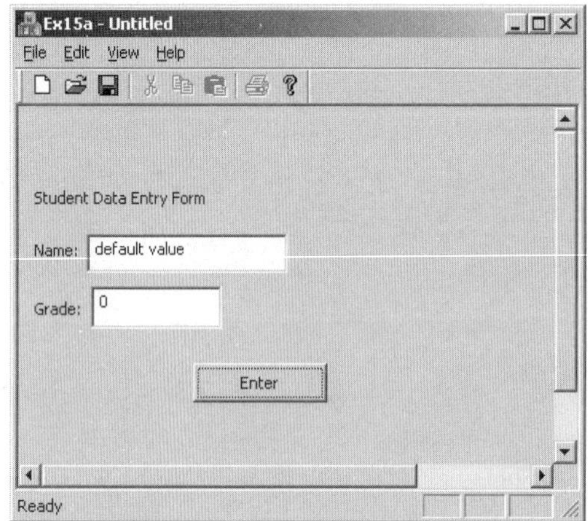

Figure 15-1 The Ex15a program in action.

The code for the *CStudent* class is shown below. Most of the class's features serve Ex15a, but a few items carry forward to Ex15b and the programs discussed in Chapter 16. For now, take note of the two data members, the default constructor, the operators, and the *Dump* function declaration. The *DECLARE_DYNAMIC* and *IMPLEMENT_DYNAMIC* macros ensure that the class name is available for the diagnostic dump.

Student.h

```
// student.h

#ifndef _INSIDE_VISUAL_CPP_STUDENT
#define _INSIDE_VISUAL_CPP_STUDENT
class CStudent : public CObject
{
    DECLARE_DYNAMIC(CStudent)
```

```
public:
    CString m_strName;
    int m_nGrade;

    CStudent()
    {
        m_nGrade = 0;
    }

    CStudent(const char* szName, int nGrade) : m_strName(szName)
    {
        m_nGrade = nGrade;
    }

    CStudent(const CStudent& s) : m_strName(s.m_strName)
    {
        // copy constructor
        m_nGrade = s.m_nGrade;
    }

    const CStudent& operator =(const CStudent& s)
    {
        m_strName = s.m_strName;
        m_nGrade = s.m_nGrade;
        return *this;
    }

    BOOL operator ==(const CStudent& s) const
    {
        if ((m_strName == s.m_strName) && (m_nGrade == s.m_nGrade)) {
            return TRUE;
        }
        else {
            return FALSE;
        }
    }

    BOOL operator !=(const CStudent& s) const
    {
        // Let's make use of the operator we just defined!
        return !(*this == s);
    }
#ifdef _DEBUG
    void Dump(CDumpContext& dc) const;
#endif // _DEBUG
};

#endif // _INSIDE_VISUAL_CPP_STUDENT
```

Student.cpp

```
#include "stdafx.h"
#include "student.h"

IMPLEMENT_DYNAMIC(CStudent, CObject)

#ifdef _DEBUG
void CStudent::Dump(CDumpContext& dc) const
{
    CObject::Dump(dc);
    dc << "m_strName = " << m_strName << "\nm_nGrade = " << m_nGrade;
}
#endif // _DEBUG
```

Follow these steps to build the Ex15a example:

1. **Run the MFC Application Wizard to generate the Ex15a project.** Make it an SDI application. On the Generated Classes page, change the view's base class to *CFormView*, as shown here.

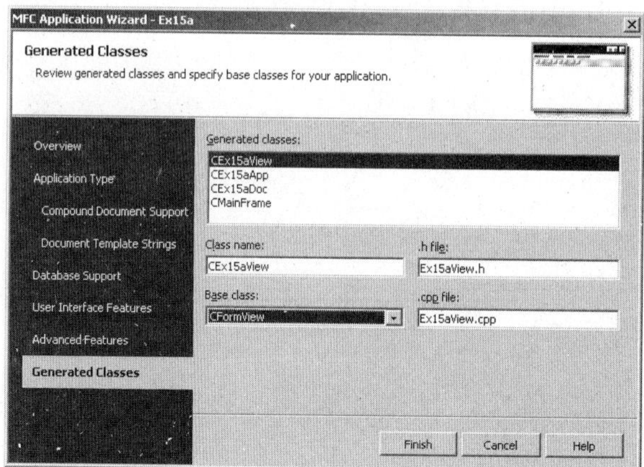

2. **Use the menu editor to replace the Edit menu commands.** Delete the current Edit menu commands and replace them with a Clear All command. Use the default constant ID_EDIT_CLEARALL, which is assigned by the application framework.

3. **Use the dialog editor to modify the *IDD_EX15A_FORM* dialog box. Open the MFC Application Wizard–generated dialog box *IDD_EX15A_FORM*,** and then add controls as shown here.

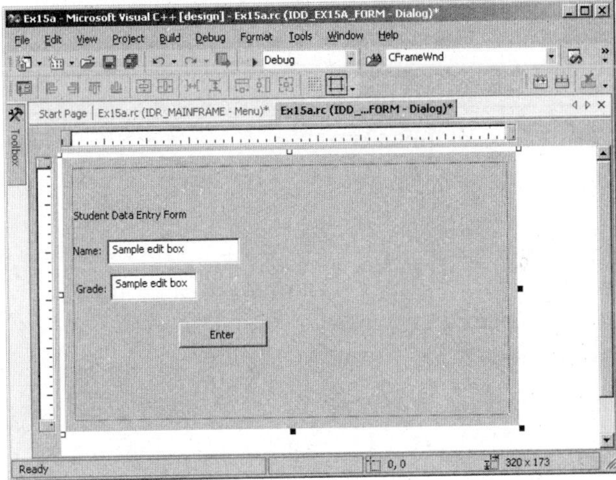

Be sure that you set the following properties in the dialog editor's Properties window: *Style* = *Child*, *Border* = *None*, *Visible* = *False*. Use the following IDs for the controls.

Control	ID
Name edit control	*IDC_NAME*
Grade edit control	*IDC_GRADE*
Enter button	*IDC_ENTER*

4. **Use Class View's Properties window to add message handlers for *CEx15aView*.** Select the CEx15aView class, and then add handlers for the following messages. Accept the default function names.

Object ID	Message	Member Function
IDC_ENTER	*BN_CLICKED*	*OnBnClickedEnter*
ID_EDIT_CLEARALL	*COMMAND*	*OnEditClearall*
ID_EDIT_CLEARALL	*UPDATE_COMMAND_UI*	*OnUpdateEditClearall*

5. **Use the Add Member Variable Wizard to add variables for *CEx15aView*.** In Class View, right-click on CEx15aView and choose Add Variable. Add the following variables:

Control ID	Member Variable	Category	Variable Type
IDC_GRADE	*m_nGrade*	Value	*int*
IDC_NAME	*m_strName*	Value	*CString*

   For *m_nGrade*, enter a minimum value of 0 and a maximum value of 100. Notice that the Add Member Variable Wizard generates the code necessary to validate data entered by the user.

6. **Add a prototype for the helper function *UpdateControlsFromDoc*.** In Class View, right-click on CEx15aView and choose Add Function. Fill out the dialog box to add the following function:

```
private:
    void UpdateControlsFromDoc(void);
```

7. **Edit the file Ex15aView.cpp.** The MFC Application Wizard generated the skeleton *OnInitialUpdate* function, and the Add Member Function Wizard available from Class View generated the skeleton *UpdateControlsFromDoc* function. *UpdateControlsFromDoc* is a private helper member function that transfers data from the document to the *CEx15aView* data members and then to the dialog edit controls. Edit the code as shown here:

```
void CEx15aView::OnInitialUpdate()
{   // called on startup
    CFormView::OnInitialUpdate();
    UpdateControlsFromDoc();
}
void CEx15aView::UpdateControlsFromDoc(void)
{   // called from OnInitialUpdate and OnEditClearall
    CEx15aDoc* pDoc = GetDocument();
    m_nGrade = pDoc->m_student.m_nGrade;
    m_strName = pDoc->m_student.m_strName;
    UpdateData(FALSE); // calls DDX
}
```

   The *OnBnClickedEnter* function replaces the *OnOK* function you'd expect to see in a dialog class. The function transfers data from the edit controls to the view's data members and then to the document. Add the boldface code shown here:

```
void CEx15aView::OnBnClickedEnter()
{
    CEx15aDoc* pDoc = GetDocument();
    UpdateData(TRUE);
    pDoc->m_student.m_nGrade = m_nGrade;
    pDoc->m_student.m_strName = m_strName;
}
```

In a complex multi-view application, the Edit Clear All command would be routed directly to the document. In this simple example, it's routed to the view. The update command user interface handler disables the menu command if the document's student object is already blank. Add the following boldface code:

```
void CEx15aView::OnEditClearall()
{
    GetDocument()->m_student = CStudent(); // "blank" student object
    UpdateControlsFromDoc();
}
void CEx15aView::OnUpdateEditClearall(CCmdUI* pCmdUI)
{
    pCmdUI->Enable(GetDocument()->m_student != CStudent()); //
 blank?
}
```

8. **Edit the Ex15a project to add the files for *CStudent*.** Be sure that Student.h and Student.cpp are in your project directory. Choose Add Existing Item from the Project menu and select the Student.h header and the Student.cpp source code files. Visual C++ .NET will add the files' names to the project's project file so that they will be compiled when you build the project.

9. **Add a *CStudent* data member to the *CEx15aDoc* class.** Edit the code in Ex15aDoc.h and remember to include Student.h in the CEx15aDoc.h file.

```
public:
    CStudent m_student;
```

The *CStudent* constructor is called when the document object is constructed, and the *CStudent* destructor is called when the document object is destroyed.

10. **Edit the Ex15aDoc.cpp file.** Use the *CEx15aDoc* constructor to initialize the student object, as shown here:

```
CEx15aDoc::CEx15aDoc() : m_student("default value", 0)
{
    TRACE("Document object constructed\n");
}
```

We can't tell whether the Ex15a program works properly unless we dump the document when the program exits. We'll use the destructor to call the document's *Dump* function, which calls the *CStudent::Dump* function shown here:

```
CEx15aDoc::~CEx15aDoc()
{
#ifdef _DEBUG
    Dump(afxDump);
#endif // _DEBUG
}

void CEx15aDoc::Dump(CDumpContext& dc) const
{
    CDocument::Dump(dc);
    dc << "\n" << m_student << "\n";
}
```

11. **Build and test the Ex15a application.** Type a name and a grade, and then click Enter. Now exit the application. Does the Debug window show messages similar to those shown here?

```
a CEx15aDoc at $411580
m_strTitle = Untitled
m_strPathName =
m_bModified = 0
m_pDocTemplate = $4113A0

a CStudent at $4115D4
m_strName = Sullivan, Walter
m_nGrade = 78
```

> **Note** To see these messages, you must compile the application with the *DEBUG* symbol defined or with the Debug configuration selected.

A More Advanced Document-View Interaction

If you're laying the groundwork for a multi-view application, the document-view interaction must be more complex than the simple interaction shown in example Ex15a. The fundamental problem is this: The user edits in view #1, so view #2 (and any other views) must be updated to reflect the changes. Now you need the *UpdateAllViews* and *OnUpdate* functions because the document will act as the clearinghouse for all view updates. The development steps are shown here:

1. In your derived document class header file (generated by the MFC Application Wizard), declare your document's data members. If you want to, you can make these data members private and you can define member functions to access them or declare the view class as a friend of the document class.
2. In your derived view class, use Class View's Properties window to override the *OnUpdate* virtual member function. The application framework calls this function whenever the document data has changed for any reason. *OnUpdate* should update the view with the current document data.
3. Evaluate all your command messages. Determine whether each one is document-specific or view-specific. (A good example of a document-specific command is the Clear All command on the Edit menu.) Now map the commands to the appropriate classes.
4. In your derived view class, allow the appropriate command message handlers to update the document data. Be sure that these message handlers call the *CDocument::UpdateAllViews* function before they exit. Use the type-safe version of the *CView::GetDocument* member function to access the view's document.
5. In your derived document class, allow the appropriate command message handlers to update the document data. Be sure that these message handlers call the *CDocument::UpdateAllViews* function before they exit.

The sequence of events for the complex document-view interaction is shown here:

Application starts	*CMyDocument* object is constructed *CMyView* object is constructed Other view objects are constructed View windows are created *CMyView::OnCreate* is called (if it is mapped) *CDocument::OnNewDocument* is called *CView::OnInitialUpdate* is called *CMyView::OnUpdate is called* The view is initialized
User executes view command	*CMyView* functions update *CMyDocument* data members *CDocument::UpdateAllViews* is called *OnUpdate* functions are called for other views
User executes document command	*CMyDocument* functions update data members *CDocument::UpdateAllViews* is called *CMyView::OnUpdate* is called Other views' *OnUpdate* functions are called
User exits application	View objects are destroyed *CMyDocument* object is destroyed

The *CDocument::DeleteContents* Function

At some point, you'll need a function to delete the contents of your document. You could write your own private member function, but it happens that the application framework declares a virtual *DeleteContents* function for the *CDocument* class. The application framework calls your overridden *DeleteContents* function when the document is closed and, as you'll see in the next chapter, at other times as well.

The *CObList* Collection Class

Once you get to know the collection classes, you'll wonder how you ever got along without them. The *CObList* class is a useful representative of the collection class family. If you're familiar with this class, it's easy to learn the other list classes, the array classes, and the map classes.

You might think that collections are something new, but the C programming language has always supported one kind of collection: the array. C arrays must be fixed in size, and they do not support insertion of elements. Many C programmers have written function libraries for other collections, including linked lists, dynamic arrays, and indexed dictionaries. For implementing collections, the C++ class is an obvious and good alternative to a C function library. A list object, for example, neatly encapsulates the list's internal data structures.

The *CObList* class supports ordered lists of pointers to objects of classes derived from *CObject*. Another MFC collection class, *CPtrList*, stores *void* pointers instead of *CObject* pointers. Why not use *CPtrList* instead? The *CObList* class offers advantages for diagnostic dumping, which you'll see in this chapter, and for serialization, which you'll see in the next chapter. One important feature of *CObList* is that it can contain mixed pointers. In other words, a *CObList* collection can hold pointers to both *CStudent* objects and *CTeacher* objects, assuming that both *CStudent* and *CTeacher* were derived from *CObject*.

Using the *CObList* Class for a First-In, First-Out List

One of the easiest ways to use a *CObList* object is to add new elements to the tail, or bottom, of the list and to remove elements from the head, or top, of the list. The first element added to the list will always be the first element removed from the head of the list. Suppose you're working with element objects of class *CAction*, which is your own custom class derived from *CObject*. A command-line program that puts five elements into a list and then retrieves them in the same sequence is shown here:

```
#include <afx.h>
#include <afxcoll.h>

class CAction : public CObject
{
private:
    int m_nTime;
public:
    CAction(int nTime) { m_nTime = nTime; } // Constructor stores
                                            //  integer time value
    void PrintTime() { TRACE("time = %d\n", m_nTime); }
};
```

(continued)

```
int main()
{
    CAction* pAction;
    CObList actionList; // action list constructed on stack
    int i;

    // inserts action objects in sequence {0, 1, 2, 3, 4}
    for (i = 0; i < 5; i++) {
        pAction = new CAction(i);
        actionList.AddTail(pAction); // no cast necessary for pAction
    }

    // retrieves and removes action objects in sequence {0, 1, 2, 3, 4}
    while (!actionList.IsEmpty()) {
        pAction =                                 // cast required for
            (CAction*) actionList.RemoveHead(); //  return value
         pAction->PrintTime();
        delete pAction;
    }

    return 0;
}
```

Here's what's going on in the program. First, a *CObList* object, *actionList*, is constructed. Then the *CObList::AddTail* member function inserts pointers to newly constructed *CAction* objects. No casting is necessary for *pAction* because *AddTail* takes a *CObject* pointer parameter and *pAction* is a pointer to a derived class.

Next, the *CAction* object pointers are removed from the list of the objects deleted. A cast is necessary for the returned value of *RemoveHead* because *RemoveHead* returns a *CObject* pointer that is higher in the class hierarchy than *CAction*.

When you remove an object pointer from a collection, the object is not automatically deleted. The *delete* statement is necessary for deleting the *CAction* objects.

CObList Iteration: The *POSITION* Variable

Suppose you want to iterate through the elements in a list. The *CObList* class provides a *GetNext* member function that returns a pointer to the "next" list element, but using it is a little tricky. *GetNext* takes a parameter of type *POSITION*, which is a 32-bit variable. The *POSITION* variable is an internal representation of the retrieved element's position in the list. Because the *POSITION* parameter is declared as a reference (&), the function can change its value.

GetNext does the following:

1. It returns a pointer to the "current" object in the list, which is identified by the incoming value of the *POSITION* parameter.
2. It increments the value of the *POSITION* parameter to the next list element.

Here's what a *GetNext* loop looks like, assuming you're using the list generated in the previous example:

```
CAction* pAction;
POSITION pos = actionList.GetHeadPosition();
while (pos != NULL) {
    pAction = (CAction*) actionList.GetNext(pos);
    pAction->PrintTime();
}
```

Now suppose you have an interactive Windows-based application that uses toolbar buttons to sequence forward and backward through the list one element at a time. You can't use *GetNext* to retrieve the entry because *GetNext* always increments the *POSITION* variable and you don't know in advance whether the user will want the next element or the previous element. Here's a sample view class command message handler function that gets the next list entry. In the *CMyView* class, *m_actionList* is an embedded *CObList* object and the *m_position* data member is a *POSITION* variable that holds the current list position.

```
CMyView::OnCommandNext()
{
    POSITION pos;
    CAction*  pAction;

    if ((pos = m_position) != NULL) {
        m_actionList.GetNext(pos);
        if (pos != NULL) { // pos is NULL at end of list
            pAction = (CAction*) m_actionList.GetAt(pos);
            pAction->PrintTime();
            m_position = pos;
        }
        else {
            AfxMessageBox("End of list reached");
        }
    }
}
```

GetNext is now called first to increment the list position, and the *CObList::GetAt* member function is called to retrieve the entry. The *m_position* variable is updated only when we're sure we're not at the tail of the list.

The *CTypedPtrList* Template Collection Class

The *CObList* class works fine if you want a collection to contain mixed pointers. If, on the other hand, you want a type-safe collection that contains only one type of object pointer, you should look at the MFC library template pointer collection classes. *CTypedPtrList* is a good example. Templates were introduced in Visual C++ version 2.0. *CTypedPtrList* is a template class that you can use to create a list of any pointers to objects of any specified class. To make a long story short, you use the template to create a custom derived list class, using either *CPtrList* or *CObList* as a base class.

To declare an object for *CAction* pointers, you write the following line of code:

```
CTypedPtrList<CObList, CAction*> m_actionList;
```

The first parameter is the base class for the collection, and the second parameter is the type for parameters and return values. Only *CPtrList* and *CObList* are permitted for the base class because those are the only two MFC library pointer list classes. If you're storing objects of classes derived from *CObject*, you should use *CObList* as your base class; otherwise, use *CPtrList*.

By using the template as shown above, the compiler ensures that all list member functions return a *CAction* pointer. Thus, you can write the following code:

```
pAction = m_actionList.GetAt(pos); // no cast required
```

If you want to clean up the notation a little, use a *typedef* statement to generate what looks like a class, as shown here:

```
typedef CTypedPtrList<CObList, CAction*> CActionList;
```

Now you can declare *m_actionList* as follows:

```
CActionList m_actionList;
```

The Dump Context and Collection Classes

The *Dump* function for *CObList* and the other collection classes has a useful property. If you call *Dump* for a collection object, you can get a display of each object in the collection. If the element objects use the *DECLARE_DYNAMIC* and *IMPLEMENT_DYNAMIC* macros, the dump will show the class name for each object.

The default behavior of the collection *Dump* functions is to display only class names and addresses of element objects. If you want the collection *Dump* functions to call the *Dump* function for each element object, you must, somewhere at the start of your program, make the following call:

```
#ifdef _DEBUG
    afxDump.SetDepth(1);
#endif
```

Now the following statement

```
#ifdef _DEBUG
    afxDump << actionList;
#endif
```

will produce output such as this:

```
a CObList at $411832
with 4 elements
    a CAction at $412CD6
time = 0
    a CAction at $412632
time = 1
    a CAction at $41268E
time = 2
    a CAction at $4126EA
time = 3
```

If the collection contains mixed pointers, the virtual *Dump* function will be called for the object's class and the appropriate class name will be printed.

The Ex15b Example: A Multi-View SDI Application

This second SDI example improves on Ex15a in the following ways:

- Instead of a single embedded *CStudent* object, the document contains a list of *CStudent* objects. (Now you see the reason for using the *CStudent* class instead of making *m_strName* and *m_nGrade* data members of the document.)
- Toolbar buttons allow the user to sequence through the list.
- The application is structured to allow the addition of extra views. The Edit Clear All command is now routed to the document object, so the document's *UpdateAllViews* function and the view's *OnUpdate* function are brought into play.
- The student-specific view code is isolated so that the *CEx15bView* class can later be transformed into a base class that contains only general-purpose code. Derived classes can override selected functions to accommodate lists of application-specific objects.

The Ex15b window, shown in Figure 15-2, looks a little different from the Ex15a window shown earlier in Figure 15-1. The toolbar buttons are enabled only when appropriate. The Next (down arrow) button, for example, is disabled when we're positioned at the bottom of the list.

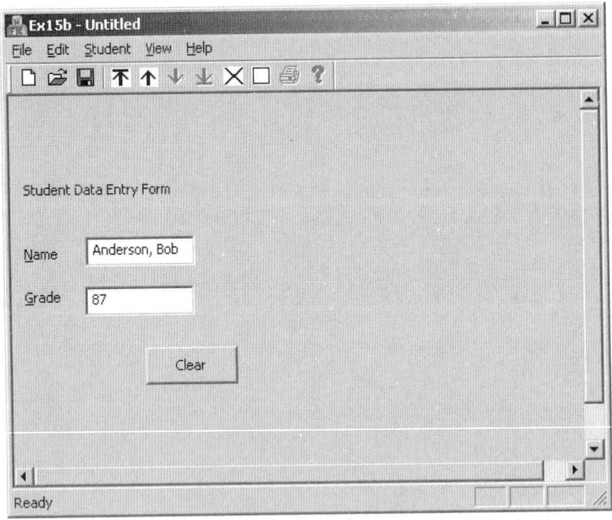

Figure 15-2 The Ex15b program in action.

The toolbar buttons function as follows.

Button	Function
⤒	Retrieves the first student record
⤓	Retrieves the last student record
↑	Retrieves the previous student record
↓	Retrieves the next student record
☐	Inserts a new student record
✕	Deletes the current student record

The Clear button in the view window clears the contents of the Name and Grade edit controls. The Clear All command on the Edit menu deletes all the student records in the list and clears the view's edit controls.

This example deviates from the step-by-step format in the previous examples. There's now more code, so we'll simply show selected code and the resource requirements. Boldface code indicates additional code or other changes that you enter in the output from the MFC Application Wizard and the code wizards available from Class View's Properties window. The frequent use of *TRACE* statements lets you follow the program's execution in the debugging window.

Resource Requirements

The file Ex15b.rc defines the application's resources as follows.

Toolbar

The toolbar (visible in Figure 15-2) was created by erasing the Edit Cut, Copy, and Paste tiles (fourth, fifth, and sixth from the left) and replacing them with six new patterns. The Flip Vertical command (on the Image menu) was used to duplicate some of the tiles. The Ex15b.rc file defines the linkage between the command IDs and the toolbar buttons.

Student Menu

It isn't absolutely necessary to have menu commands that correspond to the new toolbar buttons. (Class View's Properties window allows you to map toolbar button commands just as easily as menu commands.) However, most applications for Windows have corresponding menu commands, so users generally expect them.

Edit Menu

On the Edit menu, the clipboard commands are replaced by the Clear All command. See step 2 of the Ex15a example for an illustration of the Edit menu.

The *IDD_EX15B_FORM* Dialog Template

The *IDD_EX15B_FORM* dialog template is similar to the Ex15a dialog box shown in Figure 15-1 except that the Enter pushbutton has been replaced by the Clear pushbutton.

The following IDs identify the controls:

Control	ID
Name edit control	*IDC_NAME*
Grade edit control	*IDC_GRADE*
Clear pushbutton	*IDC_CLEAR*

The controls' styles are the same as for the Ex15a program.

Code Requirements

Here's a list of the files and classes in the Ex15b example.

Header File	Source Code File	Classes	Description
Ex15b.h	Ex15b.cpp	*CEx15bApp*	Application class (from the MFC Application Wizard)
		CAboutDlg	About dialog box
MainFrm.h	MainFrm.cpp	*CMainFrame*	SDI main frame
Ex15bDoc.h	Ex15bDoc.cpp	*Ex15bDoc*	Student document
Ex15b.h	Ex15b.cpp	*Ex15bView*	Student form view (derived from *CFormView*)
Student.h	Student.cpp	*Cstudent*	Student record (similar to Ex15a)
StdAfx.h	StdAfx.cpp		Includes the standard precompiled headers

CEx15bApp

The files Ex15b.cpp and Ex15b.h are the standard MFC Application Wizard output.

CMainFrame

The code for the *CMainFrame* class in MainFrm.cpp is the standard MFC Application Wizard output.

CStudent

This is the code from Ex15a, except for the following line added at the end of Student.h:

```
typedef CTypedPtrList<CObList, CStudent*> CStudentList;
```

> **Note** Use of the MFC template collection classes requires the following statement in StdAfx.h:
>
> ```
> #include <afxtempl.h>
> ```

CEx15bDoc

The MFC Application Wizard originally generated the *CEx15bDoc* class. The code used in the Ex15b example is shown here:

Ex15bDoc.h

```
// Ex15bDoc.h : interface of the CEx15bDoc class
//

#pragma once

#include "student.h"

class CEx15bDoc : public CDocument
{
protected: // create from serialization only
    CEx15bDoc();
    DECLARE_DYNCREATE(CEx15bDoc)

// Attributes
public:
    CStudentList* GetList() {
        return &m_studentList;
    }

// Operations
public:

// Overrides
    public:
    virtual BOOL OnNewDocument();
    virtual void Serialize(CArchive& ar);

// Implementation
public:
    virtual ~CEx15bDoc();
#ifdef _DEBUG
    virtual void AssertValid() const;
    virtual void Dump(CDumpContext& dc) const;
#endif

protected:

// Generated message map functions
protected:
    DECLARE_MESSAGE_MAP()

private:
    CStudentList m_studentList;

};
```

Ex15bDoc.cpp

```
// Ex15bDoc.cpp : implementation of the CEx15bDoc class
//

#include "stdafx.h"
#include "Ex15b.h"

#include "Ex15bDoc.h"

#ifdef _DEBUG
#define new DEBUG_NEW
#endif


// CEx15bDoc

IMPLEMENT_DYNCREATE(CEx15bDoc, CDocument)

BEGIN_MESSAGE_MAP(CEx15bDoc, CDocument)
    ON_COMMAND(ID_EDIT_CLEARALL, OnEditClearall)
    ON_UPDATE_COMMAND_UI(ID_EDIT_CLEARALL, OnUpdateEditClearall)
END_MESSAGE_MAP()


// CEx15bDoc construction/destruction

CEx15bDoc::CEx15bDoc()
{
    TRACE("Entering CEx15bDoc constructor\n");
#ifdef _DEBUG
    afxDump.SetDepth(1); // Ensure dump of list elements
#endif // _DEBUG
}

CEx15bDoc::~CEx15bDoc()
{
}

BOOL CEx15bDoc::OnNewDocument()
{
   TRACE("Entering CEx15bDoc::OnNewDocument\n");
    if (!CDocument::OnNewDocument())
        return FALSE;

    // TODO: add reinitialization code here
    // (SDI documents will reuse this document)

    return TRUE;
}

// CEx15bDoc serialization
```

```
void CEx15bDoc::Serialize(CArchive& ar)
{
    if (ar.IsStoring())
    {
        // TODO: add storing code here
    }
    else
    {
        // TODO: add loading code here
    }
}


// CEx15bDoc diagnostics

#ifdef _DEBUG
void CEx15bDoc::AssertValid() const
{
    CDocument::AssertValid();
}

void CEx15bDoc::Dump(CDumpContext& dc) const
{
    CDocument::Dump(dc);
    dc << "\n" << m_studentList << "\n";
}
#endif //_DEBUG


// CEx15bDoc commands

void CEx15bDoc::DeleteContents()
{
#ifdef _DEBUG
    Dump(afxDump);
#endif
    while (m_studentList.GetHeadPosition()) {
        delete m_studentList.RemoveHead();
    }
}

void CEx15bDoc::OnEditClearall()
{
    DeleteContents();
    UpdateAllViews(NULL);
}

void CEx15bDoc::OnUpdateEditClearall(CCmdUI *pCmdUI)
{
    pCmdUI->Enable(!m_studentList.IsEmpty());
}
```

Message Handlers for *CEx15bDoc*

The Edit Clear All command is handled in the document class. The following message handlers were added through Class View's Properties window.

Object ID	Message	Member Function
ID_EDIT_CLEARALL	*COMMAND*	*OnEditClearall*
ID_EDIT_CLEARALL	*ON_UPDATE_COMMAND_UI*	*OnUpdateEditClearall*

Data Members

The document class provides for an embedded *CStudentList* object, the *m_studentList* data member, which holds pointers to *CStudent* objects. The list object is constructed when the *CEx15bDoc* object is constructed, and it is destroyed at program exit. *CStudentList* is a *typedef* for a *CTypedPtrList* for *CStudent* pointers.

Constructor

The document constructor sets the depth of the dump context so that a dump of the list causes dumps of the individual list elements.

GetList

The inline *GetList* function helps isolate the view from the document. The document class must be specific to the type of object in the list—in this case, objects of the class *CStudent*. A generic list view base class, however, can use a member function to get a pointer to the list without knowing the name of the list object.

DeleteContents

The *DeleteContents* function is a virtual override function that is called by other document functions and by the application framework. Its job is to remove all student object pointers from the document's list and to delete those student objects. An important point to remember here is that SDI document objects are reused after they're closed. *DeleteContents* also dumps the student list.

Dump

The MFC Application Wizard generates the *Dump* function skeleton between the lines *#ifdef _DEBUG* and *#endif*. Because the *afxDump* depth was set to 1 in the document constructor, all the *CStudent* objects contained in the list are dumped.

CEx15bView

The code for the *CEx15bView* class is shown in the following code listing.

Ex15bView.h

```
// Ex15bView.h : interface of the CEx15bView class
//

#pragma once

class CEx15bView : public CFormView
{
protected:
    POSITION      m_position; // current position in document list
    CStudentList* m_pList;    // copied from document

protected: // create from serialization only
    CEx15bView();
    DECLARE_DYNCREATE(CEx15bView)

public:
    enum{ IDD = IDD_EX15B_FORM };

// Attributes
public:
    CEx15bDoc* GetDocument() const;

// Operations
public:

// Overrides
    public:
    virtual BOOL PreCreateWindow(CREATESTRUCT& cs);
    protected:
    virtual void DoDataExchange(CDataExchange* pDX);  // DDX/DDV support
    virtual void OnInitialUpdate(); // called first time after construct

// Implementation
public:
    virtual ~CEx15bView();
#ifdef _DEBUG
    virtual void AssertValid() const;
    virtual void Dump(CDumpContext& dc) const;
#endif

protected:
    virtual void ClearEntry();
    virtual void InsertEntry(POSITION position);
    virtual void GetEntry(POSITION position);
```

```
// Generated message map functions
protected:
    DECLARE_MESSAGE_MAP()
public:
    afx_msg void OnStudentHome();
    afx_msg void OnStudentDelete();
    afx_msg void OnStudentEnd();
    afx_msg void OnStudentInsert();
    afx_msg void OnStudentNext();
    afx_msg void OnStudentPrevious();
    afx_msg void OnUpdateStudentHome(CCmdUI *pCmdUI);
    afx_msg void OnUpdateStudentDelete(CCmdUI *pCmdUI);
    afx_msg void OnUpdateStudentEnd(CCmdUI *pCmdUI);
    afx_msg void OnUpdateStudentNext(CCmdUI *pCmdUI);
    afx_msg void OnUpdateStudentPrevious(CCmdUI *pCmdUI);
    int m_nGrade;
    CString m_strName;
protected:
    virtual void OnUpdate(Cview* /*pSender/,
                          LPARAM /*lHint*/, CObject* /*pHint*/)
public:
    afx_msg void OnBnClickedClear();
};

#ifndef _DEBUG  // debug version in Ex15bView.cpp
inline CEx15bDoc* CEx15bView::GetDocument() const
   { return reinterpret_cast<CEx15bDoc*>(m_pDocument); }
#endif
```

Ex15bView.cpp

```
// Ex15bView.cpp : implementation of the CEx15bView class
//

#include "stdafx.h"
#include "Ex15b.h"

#include "Ex15bDoc.h"
#include "Ex15bView.h"

#ifdef _DEBUG
#define new DEBUG_NEW
#endif


// CEx15bView

IMPLEMENT_DYNCREATE(CEx15bView, CFormView)
```

```
BEGIN_MESSAGE_MAP(CEx15bView, CFormView)
    ON_COMMAND(ID_STUDENT_HOME, OnStudentHome)
    ON_COMMAND(ID_STUDENT_DELETE, OnStudentDelete)
    ON_COMMAND(ID_STUDENT_END, OnStudentEnd)
    ON_COMMAND(ID_STUDENT_INSERT, OnStudentInsert)
    ON_COMMAND(ID_STUDENT_NEXT, OnStudentNext)
    ON_COMMAND(ID_STUDENT_PREVIOUS, OnStudentPrevious)
    ON_UPDATE_COMMAND_UI(ID_STUDENT_HOME, OnUpdateStudentHome)
    ON_UPDATE_COMMAND_UI(ID_STUDENT_DELETE, OnUpdateStudentDelete)
    ON_UPDATE_COMMAND_UI(ID_STUDENT_END, OnUpdateStudentEnd)
    ON_UPDATE_COMMAND_UI(ID_STUDENT_NEXT, OnUpdateStudentNext)
    ON_UPDATE_COMMAND_UI(ID_STUDENT_PREVIOUS, OnUpdateStudentPrevious)
    ON_BN_CLICKED(IDC_CLEAR, OnBnClickedClear)
END_MESSAGE_MAP()

// CEx15bView construction/destruction

CEx15bView::CEx15bView()
    : CFormView(CEx15bView::IDD)
    , m_nGrade(0)
    , m_strName(_T(""))
    , m_position(NULL)
{
    TRACE("Entering CEx15bView constructor\n");
}

CEx15bView::~CEx15bView()
{
}

void CEx15bView::DoDataExchange(CDataExchange* pDX)
{
    CFormView::DoDataExchange(pDX);
    DDX_Text(pDX, IDC_GRADE, m_nGrade);
    DDX_Text(pDX, IDC_NAME, m_strName);
}

BOOL CEx15bView::PreCreateWindow(CREATESTRUCT& cs)
{
    // TODO: Modify the Window class or styles here by modifying
    //  the CREATESTRUCT cs

    return CFormView::PreCreateWindow(cs);
}

void CEx15bView::OnInitialUpdate()
```

(continued)

```
{
    TRACE("Entering CEx15bView::OnInitialUpdate\n");
    m_pList = GetDocument()->GetList();
    CFormView::OnInitialUpdate();
}


// CEx15bView diagnostics

#ifdef _DEBUG
void CEx15bView::AssertValid() const
{
    CFormView::AssertValid();
}

void CEx15bView::Dump(CDumpContext& dc) const
{
    CFormView::Dump(dc);
}

CEx15bDoc* CEx15bView::GetDocument() const // non-debug version is inline
{
    ASSERT(m_pDocument->IsKindOf(RUNTIME_CLASS(CEx15bDoc)));
    return (CEx15bDoc*)m_pDocument;
}
#endif //_DEBUG


// CEx15bView message handlers

void CEx15bView::OnStudentHome()
{
    TRACE("Entering CEx15bView::OnStudentHome\n");
    // need to deal with list empty condition
    if (!m_pList->IsEmpty()) {
        m_position = m_pList->GetHeadPosition();
        GetEntry(m_position);
    }
}

void CEx15bView::OnUpdateStudentHome(CCmdUI *pCmdUI)
{
    // called during idle processing and when Student menu drops down
    POSITION pos;

    // enables button if list not empty and not at home already
    pos = m_pList->GetHeadPosition();
    pCmdUI->Enable((m_position != NULL) && (pos != m_position));
}
```

```
void CEx15bView::OnStudentDelete()
{
    // deletes current entry and positions to next one or head
    POSITION pos;
    TRACE("Entering CEx15bView::OnStudentDelete\n");
    if ((pos = m_position) != NULL) {
        m_pList->GetNext(pos);
        if (pos == NULL) {
            pos = m_pList->GetHeadPosition();
            TRACE("GetHeadPos = %ld\n", pos);
            if (pos == m_position) {
                pos = NULL;
            }
        }
        GetEntry(pos);
        CStudent* ps = m_pList->GetAt(m_position);
        m_pList->RemoveAt(m_position);
        delete ps;
        m_position = pos;
        GetDocument()->SetModifiedFlag();
        GetDocument()->UpdateAllViews(this);
    }
}

void CEx15bView::OnUpdateStudentDelete(CCmdUI *pCmdUI)
{
    // called during idle processing and when Student menu drops down
    pCmdUI->Enable(m_position != NULL);
}

void CEx15bView::OnStudentEnd()
{
    TRACE("Entering CEx15bView::OnStudentEnd\n");
    if (!m_pList->IsEmpty()) {
        m_position = m_pList->GetTailPosition();
        GetEntry(m_position);
    }
}

void CEx15bView::OnUpdateStudentEnd(CCmdUI *pCmdUI)
{
    // called during idle processing and when Student menu drops down
    POSITION pos;

    // enables button if list not empty and not at end already
    pos = m_pList->GetTailPosition();
    pCmdUI->Enable((m_position != NULL) && (pos != m_position));
}
```

(continued)

```
void CEx15bView::OnStudentInsert()
{
    TRACE("Entering CEx15bView::OnStudentInsert\n");
    InsertEntry(m_position);
    GetDocument()->SetModifiedFlag();
    GetDocument()->UpdateAllViews(this);
}

void CEx15bView::OnStudentNext()
{
    POSITION pos;
    TRACE("Entering CEx15bView::OnStudentNext\n");
    if ((pos = m_position) != NULL) {
        m_pList->GetNext(pos);
        if (pos) {
            GetEntry(pos);
            m_position = pos;
        }
    }
}

void CEx15bView::OnUpdateStudentNext(CCmdUI *pCmdUI)
{
    OnUpdateStudentEnd(pCmdUI);
}

void CEx15bView::OnStudentPrevious()
{
    POSITION pos;
    TRACE("Entering CEx15bView::OnStudentPrevious\n");
    if ((pos = m_position) != NULL) {
        m_pList->GetPrev(pos);
        if (pos) {
            GetEntry(pos);
            m_position = pos;
        }
    }
}

void CEx15bView::OnUpdateStudentPrevious(CCmdUI *pCmdUI)
{
    OnUpdateStudentHome(pCmdUI);
}

void CEx15bView::OnUpdate(CView* /*pSender*/,
    LPARAM /*lHint*/, CObject* /*pHint*/)
```

```
{
    // called by OnInitialUpdate and by UpdateAllViews
    TRACE("Entering CEx15bView::OnUpdate\n");
    m_position = m_pList->GetHeadPosition();
    GetEntry(m_position); // initial data for view
}

void CEx15bView::ClearEntry()
{
    m_strName = "";
    m_nGrade = 0;
    UpdateData(FALSE);
    ((CDialog*) this)->GotoDlgCtrl(GetDlgItem(IDC_NAME));
}

void CEx15bView::GetEntry(POSITION position)
{
    if (position) {
        CStudent* pStudent = m_pList->GetAt(position);
        m_strName = pStudent->m_strName;
        m_nGrade = pStudent->m_nGrade;
    }
    else {

        ClearEntry();
    }
    UpdateData(FALSE);
}

void CEx15bView::InsertEntry(POSITION position)
{
    if (UpdateData(TRUE)) {
        // UpdateData returns FALSE if it detects a user error
        CStudent* pStudent = new CStudent;
        pStudent->m_strName = m_strName;
        pStudent->m_nGrade = m_nGrade;
        m_position = m_pList->InsertAfter(m_position, pStudent);
    }
}


void CEx15bView::OnBnClickedClear()
{
    TRACE("Entering CEx15bView::OnBnClickedClear\n");
    ClearEntry();
}
```

Message Handlers for *CEx15bView*

Class View's Properties window was used to map the *CEx15bView* Clear push-button notification message as follows:

Object ID	Message	Member Function
IDC_CLEAR	*BN_CLICKED*	*OnBnClickedClear*

Because *CEx15bView* is derived from *CFormView*, Class View supports the definition of dialog data members. The variables shown here were added using the Add Member Variable Wizard:

Control ID	Member Variable	Category	Variable Type
IDC_GRADE	*m_nGrade*	Value	*int*
IDC_NAME	*m_strName*	Value	*CString*

You can use Class View's Properties window to map toolbar button commands to their handlers. Here are the commands and the handler functions to which they were mapped:

Object ID	Message	Member Function
ID_STUDENT_HOME	*COMMAND*	*OnStudentHome*
ID_STUDENT_END	*COMMAND*	*OnStudentEnd*
ID_STUDENT_PREVIOUS	*COMMAND*	*OnStudentPrevious*
ID_STUDENT_NEXT	*COMMAND*	*OnStudentNext*
ID_STUDENT_INSERT	*COMMAND*	*OnStudentInsert*
ID_STUDENT_DELETE	*COMMAND*	*OnStudentDelete*

Each command handler has built-in error checking.

The following update command user interface message handlers are called during idle processing to update the state of the toolbar buttons and, when the Student menu is painted, to update the menu commands.

Object ID	Message	Member Function
ID_STUDENT_HOME	*UPDATE_COMMAND_UI*	*OnUpdateStudentHome*
ID_STUDENT_END	*UPDATE_COMMAND_UI*	*OnUpdateStudentEnd*
ID_STUDENT_PREVIOUS	*UPDATE_COMMAND_UI*	*OnUpdateStudentPrevious*
ID_STUDENT_NEXT	*UPDATE_COMMAND_UI*	*OnUpdateStudentNext*
ID_STUDENT_DELETE	*UPDATE_COMMAND_UI*	*OnUpdateCommandDelete*

For example, the Following button, which retrieves the first student record, is disabled when the list is empty and when the *m_position* variable is already set to the head of the list.

The Previous button is disabled under the same circumstances, so it uses the same update command user interface handler. The End and the Next buttons share a handler for similar reasons. Because a delay sometimes occurs in calling the update command user interface functions, the command message handlers must look for error conditions.

Data Members

The *m_position* data member is a kind of cursor for the document's collection. It contains the position of the *CStudent* object that is currently displayed. The *m_pList* variable provides a quick way to get at the student list in the document.

OnInitialUpdate

The virtual *OnInitialUpdate* function is called when you start the application. It sets the view's *m_pList* data member for subsequent access to the document's list object.

OnUpdate

The virtual *OnUpdate* function is called both by the *OnInitialUpdate* function and by the *CDocument::UpdateAllViews* function. It resets the list position to the head of the list, and it displays the head entry. In this example, the *UpdateAllViews* function is called only in response to the Edit Clear All command. In a multi-view application, you might need a different strategy for setting the *CEx15bView m_position* variable in response to document updates from another view.

Protected Virtual Functions

The following three functions are protected virtual functions that deal specifically with *CStudent* objects: *GetEntry*, *InsertEntry*, and *ClearEntry*. You can transfer these functions to a derived class if you want to isolate the general-purpose list-handling features in a base class.

Testing the Ex15b Application

Fill in the student name and grade fields, and then click this button to insert the entry into the list:

Repeat this action several times, using the Clear pushbutton to erase the data from the previous entry. When you exit the application, the debug output should look similar to this:

```
 a CEx15bDoc at $4116D0
m_strTitle = Untitled
m_strPathName =
m_bModified = 1
m_pDocTemplate = $4113F1

a CObList at $411624
with 4 elements
    a CStudent at $412770
m_strName = Fisher, Lon
m_nGrade = 67
    a CStudent at $412E80
m_strName = Meyers, Lisa
m_nGrade = 80
    a CStudent at $412880
m_strName = Seghers, John
m_nGrade = 92
    a CStudent at $4128F0
m_strName = Anderson, Bob
m_nGrade = 87
```

Two Exercises for the Reader

You might have noticed the absence of a Modify button on the toolbar. Without such a button, you can't modify an existing student record. Can you add the necessary toolbar button and message handlers? The most difficult task might be designing a graphic for the button's tile.

Recall that the *CEx15bView* class is just about ready to be a general-purpose base class. Try separating the *CStudent*-specific virtual functions into a derived class. After that, make another derived class that uses a new element class other than *CStudent*.

16

Reading and Writing Documents

As you've probably noticed, every MFC Application Wizard–generated program has a File menu with the familiar New, Open, Save, and Save As commands. In this chapter, you'll learn how to make your application respond to these read and write document commands.

We'll look at both Single Document Interface (SDI) and Multiple Document Interface (MDI) applications. As you learn about reading and writing documents, you'll get a heavy but necessary dose of application framework theory; you'll learn a lot about the various helper classes that have been concealed up to this point. Knowing these details will help you to get the most out of the application framework.

This chapter includes three examples: an SDI application, an MDI application based on the Ex15b example from the previous chapter, and a Multiple Top-Level Interface (MTI) application. All these examples use the student list document with a *CFormView*-derived view class. The student list can be written to and read from disk through a process called *serialization*.

What Is Serialization?

In the world of object-oriented programming, objects can be persistent, which means they can be saved on disk when a program exits and then restored when the program is restarted. This process of saving and restoring objects is called *serialization*. In the Microsoft Foundation Class (MFC) library, designated classes have a member function named *Serialize*. When the application framework calls *Serialize* for a particular object—for example, an object of class *CStudent*—the data for the student is either saved on disk or read from disk.

In the MFC library, serialization is not a substitute for a database management system. All the objects associated with a document are sequentially read from or written to a single disk file. It's not possible to access individual objects at random disk file addresses. If you need database capability in your application, consider using the database support within MFC and the Active Template Library (ATL).

Disk Files and Archives

How do you know whether *Serialize* should read or write data? How is *Serialize* connected to a disk file? With the MFC library, objects of class *CFile* represent disk files. A *CFile* object encapsulates the binary file handle that you get through the Win32 function *CreateFile*. This is *not* the buffered *FILE* pointer that you'd get with a call to the C runtime *fopen* function; rather, it's a handle to a binary file. The application framework uses this file handle for Win32 *ReadFile*, *WriteFile*, and *SetFilePointer* calls.

If your application does no direct disk I/O but instead relies on the serialization process, you can avoid direct use of *CFile* objects. Between the *Serialize* function and the *CFile* object is an archive object (of class *CArchive*), as shown in Figure 16-1.

The *CArchive* object buffers data for the *CFile* object, and it maintains an internal flag that indicates whether the archive is storing (writing to disk) or loading (reading from disk). Only one active archive is associated with a file at any one time. The application framework takes care of constructing the *CFile* and *CArchive* objects, opening the disk file for the *CFile* object, and associating the archive object with the file. All you have to do (in your *Serialize* function) is load data from or store data in the archive object. The application framework calls the document's *Serialize* function during the File Open and File Save processes.

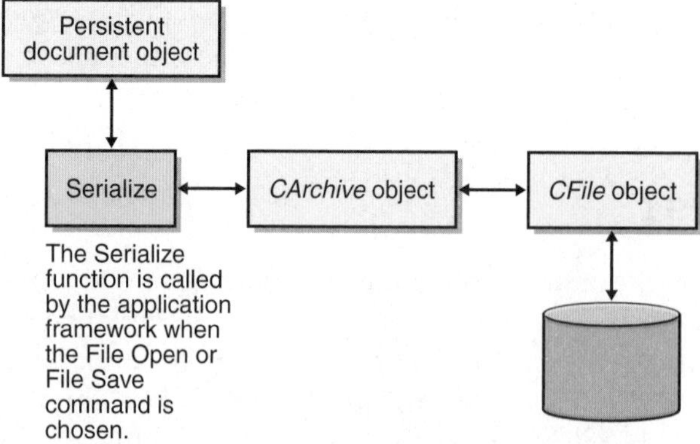

Figure 16-1 The serialization process.

Making a Class Serializable

A serializable class must be derived directly or indirectly from *CObject*. Also (with some exceptions), the class declaration must contain the *DECLARE_SERIAL* macro call, and the class implementation file must contain the *IMPLEMENT_SERIAL* macro call. (See the *MFC Library Reference* for a description of these macros.) This chapter's *CStudent* class example is modified from the class in Chapter 15 to include these macros.

Writing a *Serialize* Function

In Chapter 15, you saw a *CStudent* class, derived from *CObject*, with these data members:

```
public:
    CString m_strName;
    int     m_nGrade;
```

Now your job is to write a *Serialize* member function for *CStudent*. Because *Serialize* is a virtual member function of class *CObject*, you must be sure that the return value and parameter types match the *CObject* declaration. The *Serialize* function for the *CStudent* class is shown here:

```
void CStudent::Serialize(CArchive& ar)
{
    TRACE("Entering CStudent::Serialize\n");
    if (ar.IsStoring()) {
        ar << m_strName << m_nGrade;
    }
    else {
        ar >> m_strName >> m_nGrade;
    }
}
```

Most serialization functions call the *Serialize* functions of their base classes. If *CStudent* were derived from *CPerson*, for example, this would be the first line of the *Serialize* function:

```
CPerson::Serialize(ar);
```

The *Serialize* function for *CObject* (and for *CDocument*, which doesn't override it) doesn't do anything useful, so there's no need to call it.

Notice that *ar* is a *CArchive* reference parameter that identifies the application's archive object. The *CArchive::IsStoring* member function tells you whether the archive is currently being used for storing. The *CArchive* class has overloaded insertion operators (<<) and extraction operators (>>) for many of the C++ built-in types, as shown in Table 16-1.

Table 16-1 Types Supported by *CArchive*'s Insertion and Extraction Operators

Type	Description
BYTE	8 bits, unsigned
WORD	16 bits, unsigned
LONG	32 bits, signed
DWORD	32 bits, unsigned
float	32 bits
double	64 bits, IEEE standard
int	32 bits, signed
short	16 bits, signed
char	8 bits, unsigned
unsigned	32 bits, unsigned

The insertion operators are overloaded for values; the extraction operators are overloaded for references. Sometimes you must use a cast to satisfy the compiler. Suppose you have a data member *m_nType* that is an enumerated type. Here's the code you would use:

```
ar << (int) m_nType;
ar >> (int&) m_nType;
```

MFC classes that are not derived from *CObject*, such as *CString* and *CRect*, have their own overloaded insertion and extraction operators for *CArchive*.

Loading from an Archive: Embedded Objects vs. Pointers

Now suppose your *CStudent* object has other objects embedded in it, and that these objects are not instances of standard classes such as *CString*, *CSize*, and *CRect*. Let's add a new data member to the *CStudent* class:

```
public:
    CTranscript m_transcript;
```

Assume that *CTranscript* is a custom class, derived from *CObject*, with its own *Serialize* member function. There's no overloaded << or >> operator for *CObject*, so the *CStudent::Serialize* function now looks like this:

```
void CStudent::Serialize(CArchive& ar)
{
    if (ar.IsStoring()) {
        ar << m_strName << m_nGrade;
    }
```

```
    else {
        ar >> m_strName >> m_nGrade;
    }
    m_transcript.Serialize(ar);
}
```

Before the *CStudent::Serialize* function can be called to load a student record from the archive, a *CStudent* object must exist somewhere. The embedded *CTranscript* object *m_transcript* is constructed along with the *CStudent* object before the call to the *CTranscript::Serialize* function. When the virtual *CTranscript::Serialize* function does get called, it can load the archived transcript data into the embedded *m_transcript* object. If you're looking for a rule, here it is: Always make a direct call to *Serialize* for embedded objects of classes derived from *CObject*.

Suppose that, instead of an embedded object, your *CStudent* object contains a *CTranscript* pointer data member such as this:

```
public:
    CTranscript* m_pTranscript;
```

You could use the *Serialize* function, as shown here, but as you can see, you would have to construct a new *CTranscript* object yourself:

```
void CStudent::Serialize(CArchive& ar)
{
    if (ar.IsStoring())
        ar << m_strName << m_nGrade;
    else {
        m_pTranscript = new CTranscript;
        ar >> m_strName >> m_nGrade;
    }
    m_pTranscript->Serialize(ar);
}
```

Because the *CArchive* insertion and extraction operators are indeed overloaded for *CObject* pointers, you can write *Serialize* in this way instead:

```
void CStudent::Serialize(CArchive& ar)
{
    if (ar.IsStoring())
        ar << m_strName << m_nGrade << m_pTranscript;
    else
        ar >> m_strName >> m_nGrade >> m_pTranscript;
}
```

But how is the *CTranscript* object constructed when the data is loaded from the archive? That's where the *DECLARE_SERIAL* and *IMPLEMENT_SERIAL* macros in the *CTranscript* class come in.

When the *CTranscript* object is written to the archive, the macros ensure that the class name is written along with the data. When the archive is read, the class name is read in and an object of the correct class is dynamically constructed, under the control of code generated by the macros. Once the *CTranscript* object has been constructed, the overridden *Serialize* function for *CTranscript* can be called to do the work of reading the student data from the disk file. Finally, the *CTranscript* pointer is stored in the *m_pTranscript* data member. To avoid a memory leak, you must be sure that *m_pTranscript* does not already contain a pointer to a *CTranscript* object. If the *CStudent* object was just constructed and thus was not previously loaded from the archive, the transcript pointer will be null.

The insertion and extraction operators do not work with embedded objects of classes derived from *CObject*, as shown here:

```
ar >> m_strName >> m_nGrade >> &m_transcript; // Don't try this
```

Serializing Collections

Because all collection classes are derived from the *CObject* class and the collection class declarations contain the *DECLARE_SERIAL* macro call, you can conveniently serialize collections with a call to the collection class's *Serialize* member function. If you call *Serialize* for a *CObList* collection of *CStudent* objects, for example, the *Serialize* function for each *CStudent* object will be called in turn. You should, however, remember the following specifics about loading collections from an archive:

- If a collection contains pointers to objects of mixed classes (all derived from *CObject*), the individual class names will be stored in the archive so that the objects can be properly constructed with the appropriate class constructor.
- If a container object, such as a document, contains an embedded collection, loaded data is appended to the existing collection. You might need to empty the collection before loading from the archive. This is usually done in the document's virtual *DeleteContents* function, which is called by the application framework.
- When a collection of *CObject* pointers is loaded from an archive, the following processing steps take place for each object in the collection:
    - The object's class is identified.
    - Heap storage is allocated for the object.
    - The object's data is loaded into the newly allocated storage.
    - A pointer to the new object is stored in the collection.

The Ex16a example shows serialization of an embedded collection of *CStudent* records.

The *Serialize* Function and the Application Framework

OK, so you know how to write *Serialize* functions, and you know that these function calls can be nested. But do you know when the first *Serialize* function gets called to start the serialization process? With the application framework, everything is keyed to the document (the object of a class derived from *CDocument*). When you choose Save or Open from the File menu, the application framework creates a *CArchive* object (and an underlying *CFile* object) and then calls your document class's *Serialize* function, passing a reference to the *CArchive* object. Your derived document class *Serialize* function then serializes each of its nontemporary data members.

> **Note** If you take a close look at any MFC Application Wizard–generated document class, you'll notice that the class includes the *DECLARE_DYNCREATE* and *IMPLEMENT_DYNCREATE* macros rather than the *DECLARE_SERIAL* and *IMPLEMENT_SERIAL* macros. The *SERIAL* macros are not needed because document objects are never used in conjunction with the *CArchive* extraction operator or included in collections; the application framework calls the document's *Serialize* member function directly. You should include the *DECLARE_SERIAL* and *IMPLEMENT_SERIAL* macros in all other serializable classes.

The SDI Application

You've seen many SDI applications that have one document class and one view class. We'll stick to a single view class in this chapter, but we'll explore the interrelationships among the application object, the main frame window, the document, the view, the document template object, and the associated string and menu resources.

The Windows Application Object

For each of your applications, the MFC Application Wizard has been quietly generating a class derived from *CWinApp*. It has also been generating a statement such as this:

```
CMyApp theApp;
```

What you're seeing here is the mechanism that starts an MFC application. The class *CMyApp* is derived from the class *CWinApp*, and *theApp* is a globally declared instance of the class. This global object is called the Windows application object.

Here's a summary of the startup steps in a Microsoft Windows MFC library application:

1. Windows loads your program into memory.
2. The global object *theApp* is constructed. (All globally declared objects are constructed immediately when the program is loaded.)
3. Windows calls the global function *WinMain*, which is part of the MFC library. (*WinMain* is equivalent to the non-Windows *main* function—each is a main program entry point.)
4. *WinMain* searches for the one and only instance of a class derived from *CWinApp*.
5. *WinMain* calls the *InitInstance* member function for *theApp*, which is overridden in your derived application class.
6. Your overridden *InitInstance* function starts the process of loading a document and displaying the main frame and view windows.
7. *WinMain* calls the *Run* member function for *theApp*, which starts the processes of dispatching window messages and command messages.

You can override another important *CWinApp* member function. The *ExitInstance* function is called when the application terminates, after all its windows are closed.

> **Note** Windows allows multiple instances of programs to run. The *InitInstance* function is called each time a program instance starts up. In Win32, each instance runs as an independent process. It's only incidental that the same code is mapped to the virtual memory address space of each process. If you want to locate other running instances of your program, you must either call the Win32 *FindWindow* function or set up a shared data section or memory-mapped file for communication.

The Document Template Class

If you look at the *InitInstance* function that the MFC Application Wizard generates for your derived application class, you'll see that the following statements are featured:

```
CSingleDocTemplate* pDocTemplate;
pDocTemplate = new CSingleDocTemplate(
    IDR_MAINFRAME,
    RUNTIME_CLASS(CEx16aDoc),
    RUNTIME_CLASS(CMainFrame),       // main SDI frame window
    RUNTIME_CLASS(CEx16aView));
AddDocTemplate(pDocTemplate);
```

Unless you start doing fancy things with splitter windows and multiple views, this is the only time you'll actually see a document template object. In this case, it's an object of class *CSingleDocTemplate*, which is derived from *CDocTemplate*. The *CSingleDocTemplate* class applies only to SDI applications because SDI applications are limited to one document object. *AddDocTemplate* is a member function of class *CWinApp*.

The *AddDocTemplate* call, together with the document template constructor call, establishes the relationships among classes—the application class, the document class, the view window class, and the main frame window class. The application object exists, of course, before template construction, but the document, view, and frame objects are not constructed at this time. The application framework dynamically constructs these objects later, when they're needed.

This dynamic construction is a sophisticated use of the C++ language. The *DECLARE_DYNCREATE* and *IMPLEMENT_DYNCREATE* macros in a class declaration and implementation enable the MFC library to construct objects of the specified class dynamically. If this dynamic construction capability weren't present, more relationships among your application's classes would have to be hard-coded. Your derived application class, for example, would need code for constructing document, view, and frame objects of your specific derived classes. This would compromise the object-oriented nature of your program.

With the template system, all that's required in your application class is use of the *RUNTIME_CLASS* macro. Notice that the target class's declaration must be included for this macro to work.

Figure 16-2 illustrates the relationships among the various classes, and Figure 16-3 illustrates the object relationships. An SDI application can have only one template (and associated class groups), and when the SDI program is running, there can be only one document object and only one main frame window object.

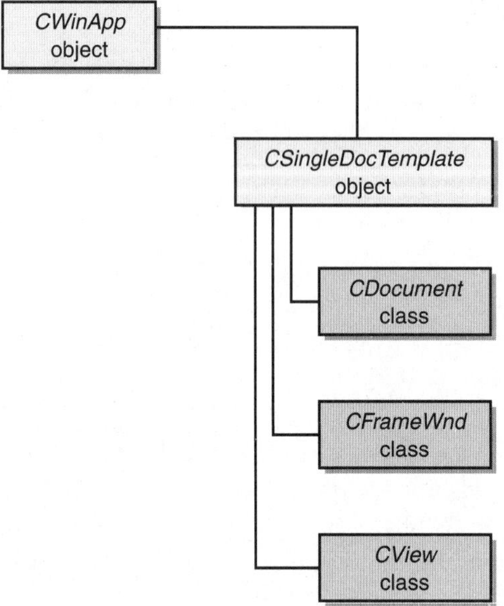

Figure 16-2 Class relationships.

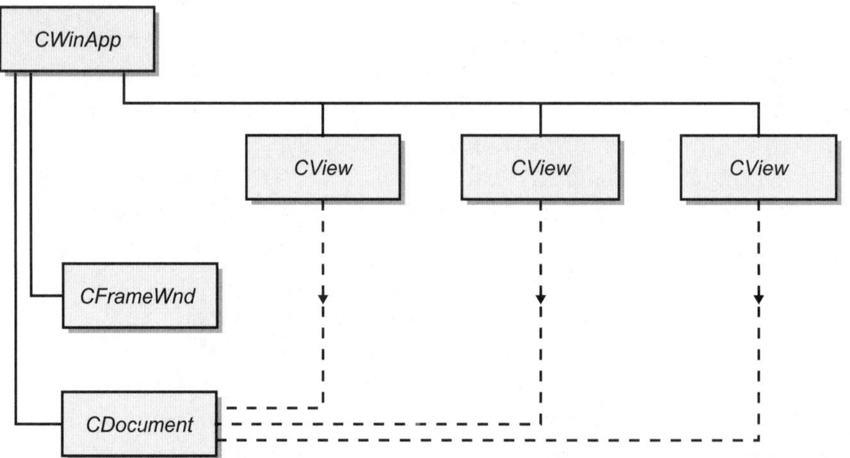

Figure 16-3 Object relationships.

> **Note** The MFC library dynamic construction capability was designed before the runtime type information (RTTI) feature was added to the C++ language. The original MFC implementation goes beyond RTTI, and the MFC library continues to use it for dynamic object construction.

The Document Template Resource

The first *AddDocTemplate* parameter is *IDR_MAINFRAME*, the identifier for a string table resource. Here is the corresponding string that the MFC Application Wizard generates for Ex16a in the application's RC file:

```
IDR_MAINFRAME
    "Ex16a\n"                  // application window caption
    "\n"                       // root for default document name
                               //  ("Untitled" used if none provided)
    "Ex16a\n"                  // document type name
    "Ex16a Files (*.16a)\n"    // document type description and filter
    ".16a\n"                   // extension for documents of this type
    "Ex16a.Document\n"         // Registry file type ID
    "Ex16a.Document"           // Registry file type description
```

> **Note** The resource compiler won't accept the string concatenations as shown in this example. If you examine the Ex16a.rc file, you'll see the substrings combined in one long string.

IDR_MAINFRAME specifies one string that is separated into substrings by newline characters (*\n*). The substrings show up in various places when the application executes. The string *16a* is the default document file extension specified to the MFC Application Wizard.

The *IDR_MAINFRAME* ID, in addition to specifying the application's strings, identifies the application's icon, toolbar resources, and menu. The MFC Application Wizard generates these resources, and you can maintain them using the resource editors.

So now you've seen how the *AddDocTemplate* call ties all the application elements together. Be aware, though, that no windows have been created yet and so nothing appears on the screen.

Multiple Views of an SDI Document

Providing multiple views of an SDI document is a little more complicated. You could provide a menu command that allows the user to choose a view, or you could allow multiple views in a splitter window. We'll look at both techniques in Chapter 18.

Creating an Empty Document: The *CWinApp::OnFileNew* Function

After your application class's *InitInstance* function calls the *AddDocTemplate* member function, it calls *OnFileNew* (indirectly through *CWinApp::ProcessShellCommand*), another important *CWinApp* member function. *OnFileNew* sorts through the web of interconnected class names and does the following:

1. Constructs the document object but does not attempt to read data from disk.
2. Constructs the main frame object (of class *CMainFrame*); it also creates the main frame window but does not show it. The main frame window includes the *IDR_MAINFRAME* menu, the toolbar, and the status bar.
3. Constructs the view object; it also creates the view window but doesn't show it.
4. Establishes connections among the document, main frame, and view objects. Do not confuse these object connections with the class connections established by the call to *AddDocTemplate*.
5. Calls the virtual *CDocument::OnNewDocument* member function for the document object, which calls the virtual *DeleteContents* function.
6. Calls the virtual *CView::OnInitialUpdate* member function for the view object.
7. Calls the virtual *CFrameWnd::ActivateFrame* for the frame object to show the main frame window together with the menus, view window, and control bars.

> **Note** Some of the functions listed here are not called directly by *OnFileNew* but are called indirectly through the application framework.

In an SDI application, the document, main frame, and view objects are created only once, and they last for the life of the program. The *CWinApp::OnFileNew* function is called by *InitInstance*. It's also called in response to the user choosing the File New command. In this case, *OnFileNew* must behave a little differently. It can't construct the document, frame, and view objects because they're already constructed. Instead, it reuses the existing document object and performs steps 5, 6, and 7 above. Notice that *OnFileNew* always calls *DeleteContents* (indirectly) to empty the document.

The Document Class's *OnNewDocument* Function

You've seen the view class *OnInitialUpdate* member function and the document class *OnNewDocument* member function in Chapter 15. If an SDI application didn't reuse the same document object, you wouldn't need *OnNewDocument* because you could perform all document initialization in your document class constructor. Now you must override *OnNewDocument* to initialize your document object each time the user chooses File New or File Open. The MFC Application Wizard helps you by providing a skeleton function in the derived document class it generates.

> **Note** It's a good idea to minimize the work you do in constructor functions. The fewer things you do, the less chance there is for the constructor to fail—and constructor failures are messy. Functions such as *CDocument::OnNewDocument* and *CView::OnInitialUpdate* are excellent places to do initial housekeeping. If anything fails at creation time, you can display a message box, and in the case of *OnNewDocument*, you can return *FALSE*. Be advised that both functions can be called more than once for the same object. If you need certain instructions executed only once, declare a "first time" flag data member and then test/set it appropriately.

Connecting File Open to Your Serialization Code: The *OnFileOpen* Function

When the MFC Application Wizard generates an application, it maps the File Open menu command to the *CWinApp::OnFileOpen* member function. When called, this function invokes a sequence of functions to accomplish these steps:

1. Prompts the user to select a file.
2. Calls the virtual function *CDocument::OnOpenDocument* for the already existing document object. This function opens the file, calls *CDocument::DeleteContents*, and constructs a *CArchive* object set for loading. It then calls the document's *Serialize* function, which loads data from the archive.
3. Calls the view's *OnInitialUpdate* function.

The Most Recently Used (MRU) file list is a handy alternative to the File Open command. The application framework tracks the four most recently used files and displays their names on the File menu. These filenames are stored in the Windows Registry between program executions.

> **Note** You can change the number of recent files tracked by supplying a parameter to the *LoadStdProfileSettings* function in the application class *InitInstance* function.

The Document Class's *DeleteContents* Function

When you load an existing SDI document object from a disk file, you must somehow erase the existing contents of the document object. The best way to do this is to override the *CDocument::DeleteContents* virtual function in your derived document class. The overridden function, as you've seen in Chapter 15, does whatever is necessary to clean up your document class's data members. In response to both the File New and File Open menu commands, the *CDocument* functions *OnNewDocument* and *OnOpenDocument* both call the *DeleteContents* function, which means *DeleteContents* is called immediately after the document object is first constructed. It's called again when you close a document.

If you want your document classes to work in SDI applications, plan on emptying the document's contents in the *DeleteContents* member function rather than in the destructor. Use the destructor only to clean up items that last for the life of the object.

Connecting the File Save and File Save As Commands to Your Serialization Code

When the MFC Application Wizard generates an application, it maps the File Save menu command to the *OnFileSave* member function of the *CDocument* class. *OnFileSave* calls the *CDocument* function *OnSaveDocument*, which in turn calls your document's *Serialize* function with an archive object set for storing. The File Save As menu command is handled in a similar manner: It is mapped to the *CDocument* function *OnFileSaveAs*, which calls *OnSaveDocument*. Here the application framework does all the file management necessary to save a document on disk.

> **Note** The File New and File Open menu commands are mapped to application class member functions, but File Save and File Save As are mapped to document class member functions. File New is mapped to *OnFileNew*. The SDI version of *InitInstance* also calls *OnFileNew* (indirectly). No document object exists when the application framework calls *InitInstance*, so *OnFileNew* can't possibly be a member function of *CDocument*. When a document is saved, however, a document object certainly exists.

The Document's "Dirty" Flag

Many document-oriented applications for Windows track the user's modifications of a document. If the user tries to close a document or exit the program, a message box asks whether the user wants to save the document. The MFC application framework directly supports this behavior with the *CDocument* data member *m_bModified*. This Boolean variable is *TRUE* if the document has been modified (has become "dirty"); otherwise, it is *FALSE*.

The protected *m_bModified* flag is accessed through the *CDocument* member functions *SetModifiedFlag* and *IsModified*. The framework sets the document object's flag to *FALSE* when the document is created or read from disk and when it is saved on disk. The programmer must use the *SetModifiedFlag* function to set the flag to *TRUE* when the document data changes. The virtual function *CDocument::SaveModified*, which the framework calls when the user closes the document, displays a message box if the *m_bModified* flag is set to *TRUE*. You can override this function if you need to do something else.

In the Ex16a example, you'll see how a one-line update command user interface function can use *IsModified* to control the state of the disk button and the corresponding menu command. When the user modifies the file, the disk button is enabled; when the user saves the file, the button is grayed out.

> **Note** In one respect, MFC SDI applications behave a little differently from other Windows-based SDI applications such as Notepad. Here's a typical sequence of events:
>
> 1. The user creates a document and saves it on disk (for example, under the name test.dat).
> 2. The user modifies the document.
> 3. The user chooses File Open and then specifies test.dat.
>
> When the user chooses File Open, Notepad asks whether the user wants to save the changes made to the document (in step 2 above). If the user answers no, the program will reread the document from disk. An MFC application, on the other hand, will assume that the changes are permanent and will not reread the file.

The Ex16a Example: SDI with Serialization

The Ex16a example is similar to example Ex15b. The dialog template and the toolbar are the same, and the view class is the same. Serialization has been added, together with an update command user interface function for File Save.

The header and implementation files for the view and document classes will be reused in example Ex16b.

All the new code (code that is different from Ex15b) is listed, with additions and changes to the wizard-generated code shown in boldface. The files and classes in the Ex16a example are listed in Table 16-2.

Table 16-2 Files and Classes in Ex16a

Header File	Source Code File	Class	Description
Ex16a.h	Ex16a.cpp	*CEx16aApp*	Application class (from the MFC Application Wizard)
		CAboutDlg	About dialog box
MainFrm.h	MainFrm.cpp	*CMainFrame*	SDI main frame
Ex16aDoc.h	Ex16aDoc.cpp	*CEx16aDoc*	Student document
Ex16aView.h	Ex16aView.cpp	*CEx16aView*	Student form view (borrowed from Ex15b)
Student.h	Student.cpp	*CStudent*	Student record
StdAfx.h	StdAfx.cpp		Precompiled headers (with afxtempl.h included)

CStudent

The Ex16a Student.h file is almost the same as the file in the Ex15b project. The header contains the macro

```
DECLARE_SERIAL(CStudent)
```

instead of

```
DECLARE_DYNAMIC(CStudent)
```

and the implementation file contains the macro

```
IMPLEMENT_SERIAL(CStudent, CObject, 0)
```

instead of

```
IMPLEMENT_DYNAMIC(CStudent, CObject)
```

The virtual *Serialize* function (as shown on page 394) has also been added.

CEx16aApp

The application class files shown in the following example contain only code generated by the MFC Application Wizard. The application was generated with a default file extension and with the Windows Explorer launch and drag-and-drop capabilities. These features are described later in this chapter.

To generate additional code, when you first run the MFC Application Wizard you must enter the filename extension in the File Extension box of the wizard's Document Template Strings Page, as shown here:

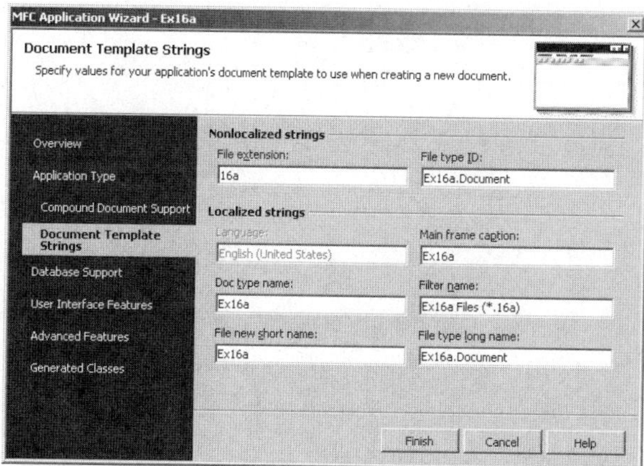

This ensures that the document template resource string contains the correct default extension and that the correct Windows Explorer–related code is inserted into your application class *InitInstance* member function. You can change some of the other resource substrings if you want.

Ex16a.h

```
// Ex16a.h : main header file for the Ex16a application
#pragma once

#ifndef __AFXWIN_H__
    #error include 'stdafx.h' before including this file for PCH
#endif

#include "resource.h"       // main symbols

// CEx16aApp:
// See Ex16a.cpp for the implementation of this class
class CEx16aApp : public CWinApp
{
public:
    CEx16aApp();
// Overrides
public:
    virtual BOOL InitInstance();

// Implementation
    afx_msg void OnAppAbout();
    DECLARE_MESSAGE_MAP()
};
extern CEx16aApp theApp;
```

Ex16a.cpp

```
// Ex16a.cpp : Defines the class behaviors for the application.

#include "stdafx.h"
#include "Ex16a.h"
#include "MainFrm.h"
#include "Ex16aDoc.h"
#include "Ex16aView.h"

#ifdef _DEBUG
#define new DEBUG_NEW
#endif

// CEx16aApp

BEGIN_MESSAGE_MAP(CEx16aApp, CWinApp)
    ON_COMMAND(ID_APP_ABOUT, OnAppAbout)
    // Standard file based document commands
    ON_COMMAND(ID_FILE_NEW, CWinApp::OnFileNew)
    ON_COMMAND(ID_FILE_OPEN, CWinApp::OnFileOpen)
END_MESSAGE_MAP()

// CEx16aApp construction

CEx16aApp::CEx16aApp()
{
    // TODO: add construction code here,
    // Place all significant initialization in InitInstance
}

// The one and only CEx16aApp object
CEx16aApp theApp;

// CEx16aApp initialization

BOOL CEx16aApp::InitInstance()
{
    // InitCommonControls() is required on Windows XP if an application
    // manifest specifies use of ComCtl32.dll version 6 or later to enable
    // visual styles.  Otherwise, any window creation will fail.
    InitCommonControls();
    CWinApp::InitInstance();

    // Initialize OLE libraries
    if (!AfxOleInit())
    {
        AfxMessageBox(IDP_OLE_INIT_FAILED);
        return FALSE;
    }
```

```
    AfxEnableControlContainer();
    // Standard initialization
    // If you are not using these features and wish to reduce the size
    // of your final executable, you should remove from the following
    // the specific initialization routines you do not need
    // Change the registry key under which our settings are stored
    // TODO: You should modify this string to be something appropriate
    // such as the name of your company or organization
    SetRegistryKey(_T("Local AppWizard-Generated Applications"));
    LoadStdProfileSettings(4); // Load standard INI file
                               // options (including MRU)
    // Register the application's document templates.  Document templates
    //  serve as the connection between documents, frame windows and views
    CSingleDocTemplate* pDocTemplate;
    pDocTemplate = new CSingleDocTemplate(
        IDR_MAINFRAME,
        RUNTIME_CLASS(CEx16aDoc),
        RUNTIME_CLASS(CMainFrame),       // main SDI frame window
        RUNTIME_CLASS(CEx16aView));
    AddDocTemplate(pDocTemplate);
    // Enable DDE Execute open
    EnableShellOpen();
    RegisterShellFileTypes(TRUE);
    // Parse command line for standard shell commands, DDE, file open
    CCommandLineInfo cmdInfo;
    ParseCommandLine(cmdInfo);
    // Dispatch commands specified on the command line.  Will return FALSE if
    // app was launched with /RegServer, /Register, /Unregserver
    // or /Unregister.
    if (!ProcessShellCommand(cmdInfo))
        return FALSE;
    // The one and only window has been initialized, so show and update it
    m_pMainWnd->ShowWindow(SW_SHOW);
    m_pMainWnd->UpdateWindow();
    // call DragAcceptFiles only if there's a suffix
    //  In an SDI app, this should occur after ProcessShellCommand
    // Enable drag/drop open
    m_pMainWnd->DragAcceptFiles();
    return TRUE;
}
// CAboutDlg dialog used for App About

class CAboutDlg : public CDialog
{
public:
    CAboutDlg();

// Dialog Data
    enum { IDD = IDD_ABOUTBOX };
```

(continued)

```
protected:
    virtual void DoDataExchange(CDataExchange* pDX);    // DDX/DDV support

// Implementation
protected:
    DECLARE_MESSAGE_MAP()
};

CAboutDlg::CAboutDlg() : CDialog(CAboutDlg::IDD)
{
}
void CAboutDlg::DoDataExchange(CDataExchange* pDX)
{
    CDialog::DoDataExchange(pDX);
}
BEGIN_MESSAGE_MAP(CAboutDlg, CDialog)
END_MESSAGE_MAP()

// App command to run the dialog
void CEx16aApp::OnAppAbout()
{
    CAboutDlg aboutDlg;
    aboutDlg.DoModal();
}
// CEx16aApp message handlers
```

CMainFrame

The main frame window class code, shown in the following example, is almost unchanged from the code that the MFC Application Wizard generated. The overridden *ActivateFrame* function and the *WM_DROPFILES* handler exist solely for trace purposes.

MainFrm.h

```
// MainFrm.h : interface of the CMainFrame class
#pragma once
class CMainFrame : public CFrameWnd
{
protected: // create from serialization only
    CMainFrame();
    DECLARE_DYNCREATE(CMainFrame)

// Attributes
public:
// Operations
public:
// Overrides
```

```
public:
    virtual BOOL PreCreateWindow(CREATESTRUCT& cs);

// Implementation
public:
    virtual ~CMainFrame();
#ifdef _DEBUG
    virtual void AssertValid() const;
    virtual void Dump(CDumpContext& dc) const;
#endif
protected:  // control bar embedded members
    CStatusBar  m_wndStatusBar;
    CToolBar    m_wndToolBar;

// Generated message map functions
protected:
    afx_msg int OnCreate(LPCREATESTRUCT lpCreateStruct);
    DECLARE_MESSAGE_MAP()
public:
    afx_msg void OnDropFiles(HDROP hDropInfo);
    virtual void ActivateFrame(int nCmdShow = -1);
};
```

MainFrm.cpp

```
// MainFrm.cpp : implementation of the CMainFrame class
#include "stdafx.h"
#include "Ex16a.h"
#include "MainFrm.h"

#ifdef _DEBUG
#define new DEBUG_NEW
#endif
// CMainFrame
IMPLEMENT_DYNCREATE(CMainFrame, CFrameWnd)
BEGIN_MESSAGE_MAP(CMainFrame, CFrameWnd)
    ON_WM_CREATE()
    ON_WM_DROPFILES()
END_MESSAGE_MAP()

static UINT indicators[] =
{
    ID_SEPARATOR,           // status line indicator
    ID_INDICATOR_CAPS,
    ID_INDICATOR_NUM,
    ID_INDICATOR_SCRL
};
```

(continued)

```
// CMainFrame construction/destruction
CMainFrame::CMainFrame()
{
    // TODO: add member initialization code here
}
CMainFrame::~CMainFrame()
{
}
int CMainFrame::OnCreate(LPCREATESTRUCT lpCreateStruct)
{
    if (CFrameWnd::OnCreate(lpCreateStruct) == -1)
        return -1;

    if (!m_wndToolBar.CreateEx(this, TBSTYLE_FLAT,
        WS_CHILD | WS_VISIBLE | CBRS_TOP
        | CBRS_GRIPPER | CBRS_TOOLTIPS | CBRS_FLYBY | CBRS_SIZE_DYNAMIC) ||
        !m_wndToolBar.LoadToolBar(IDR_MAINFRAME))
    {
        TRACE0("Failed to create toolbar\n");
        return -1;      // fail to create
    }
    if (!m_wndStatusBar.Create(this) ||
        !m_wndStatusBar.SetIndicators(indicators,
          sizeof(indicators)/sizeof(UINT)))
    {
        TRACE0("Failed to create status bar\n");
        return -1;      // fail to create
    }

    m_wndToolBar.EnableDocking(CBRS_ALIGN_ANY);
    EnableDocking(CBRS_ALIGN_ANY);
    DockControlBar(&m_wndToolBar);
    return 0;
}
BOOL CMainFrame::PreCreateWindow(CREATESTRUCT& cs)
{
    if( !CFrameWnd::PreCreateWindow(cs) )
        return FALSE;
    // TODO: Modify the Window class or styles here by modifying
    //  the CREATESTRUCT cs
    return TRUE;
}

// CMainFrame diagnostics
#ifdef _DEBUG
```

```
void CMainFrame::AssertValid() const
{
    CFrameWnd::AssertValid();
}
void CMainFrame::Dump(CDumpContext& dc) const
{
    CFrameWnd::Dump(dc);
}
#endif //_DEBUG
// CMainFrame message handlers
void CMainFrame::OnDropFiles(HDROP hDropInfo)
{
    TRACE("Entering CMainFrame::OnDropFiles\n");
    CFrameWnd::OnDropFiles(hDropInfo);
}
void CMainFrame::ActivateFrame(int nCmdShow)
{
    TRACE("Entering CMainFrame::ActivateFrame\n");
    CFrameWnd::ActivateFrame(nCmdShow);
}
```

The *CEx16aDoc* Class

The *CEx16aDoc* class is the same as the *CEx15bDoc* class from the previous chapter except for four functions: *Serialize*, *DeleteContents*, *OnOpenDocument*, and *OnUpdateFileSave*.

Serialize

One line has been added to the MFC Application Wizard–generated function to serialize the document's student list, as shown here:

```
//////////////////////////////////////////////////////////////////////////
// CEx16aDoc serialization

void CEx16aDoc::Serialize(CArchive& ar)
{
    TRACE("Entering CEx16aDoc::Serialize\n");
    if (ar.IsStoring())
    {
        // TODO: add storing code here
    }
    else
    {
        // TODO: add loading code here
    }
    m_studentList.Serialize(ar);
}
```

DeleteContents

The *Dump* statement is replaced by a simple *TRACE* statement. Here is the modified code:

```
void CEx16aDoc::DeleteContents()
{
    TRACE("Entering CEx16aDoc::DeleteContents\n");
    while (m_studentList.GetHeadPosition()) {
        delete m_studentList.RemoveHead();
    }
}
```

OnOpenDocument

This virtual function is overridden only for the purpose of displaying a *TRACE* message, as shown here:

```
BOOL CEx16aDoc::OnOpenDocument(LPCTSTR lpszPathName)
{
    TRACE("Entering CEx16aDoc::OnOpenDocument\n");
     if (!CDocument::OnOpenDocument(lpszPathName))
        return FALSE;

    // TODO: Add your specialized creation code here

    return TRUE;
}
```

OnUpdateFileSave

This message map function grays out the File Save toolbar button when the document is in the unmodified state. The view controls this state by calling the document's *SetModifiedFlag* function, as shown here:

```
void CEx16aDoc::OnUpdateFileSave(CCmdUI* pCmdUI)
{
    // Disable disk toolbar button if file is not modified
    pCmdUI->Enable(IsModified());
}
```

The *CEx16aView* Class

The code for the *CEx16aView* class borrows code from the *CEx15bView* class in Chapter 15.

Testing the Ex16a Application

Build the program and start it from the debugger, and then test it by typing some data and saving it on disk with the filename Test.16a. (You don't need to type the *.16a* part.)

Exit the program, and then restart it and open the file you saved. Did the data you typed come back? Take a look at the Debug window and observe the sequence of function calls. You should see the trace messages showing the student document being read and written as you load and save the document.

Windows Explorer Launch and Drag and Drop

In the past, PC users were accustomed to starting up a program and then selecting a disk file (sometimes called a document) that contained data the program understood. Many MS-DOS–based programs worked this way. The old Windows Program Manager improved things by allowing the user to double-click on a program icon instead of typing a program name. Meanwhile, Apple Macintosh users were double-clicking on a document icon; the Macintosh operating system figured out which program to run.

Windows Explorer still lets users double-click on a program, but it also lets users double-click on a document icon to run the document's program. But how does Windows Explorer know which program to run? Windows Explorer uses the Windows Registry to make the connection between document and program. The link starts with the filename extension that you typed into the MFC Application Wizard, but as you'll see, there's more to it than that. Once the association is made, users can launch your program by double-clicking on its document icon or by dragging the icon from Windows Explorer to a running instance of your program. In addition, users can drag the icon to a printer, and your program will print it.

Program Registration

In Chapter 14, you saw how MFC applications store data in the Windows Registry by calling *SetRegistryKey* from the *InitInstance* function. Independent of this *SetRegistryKey* call, your program can write file association information in a different part of the Registry on startup. To activate this feature, you must type in the filename extension when you create the application with the MFC Application Wizard. After you do that, the MFC Application Wizard adds the extension as a substring in your template string and adds the following line in your *InitInstance* function:

```
RegisterShellFileTypes(TRUE);
```

Now your program adds two items to the Registry. Under the *HKEY_CLASSES_ROOT* top-level key, it adds a subkey and a data string as shown here (for the Ex16a example):

```
.16a = Ex16a.Document
```

The data item is the file type ID that the MFC Application Wizard has chosen for you. Ex16a.Document, in turn, is the key for finding the program itself. The Registry entries for Ex16a.Document, also beneath *HKEY_CLASSES_ROOT*, are shown here.

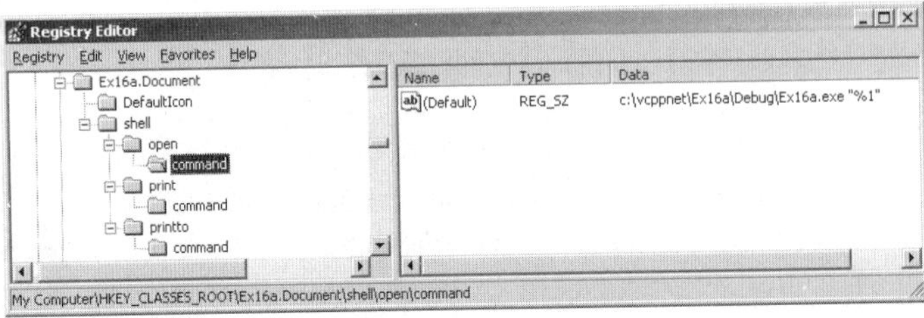

The Registry contains the full pathname of the Ex16a program. Now Windows Explorer can use the Registry to navigate from the extension to the file type ID to the actual program itself. After the extension is registered, Windows Explorer will find the document's icon and display it next to the filename.

Double-Clicking on a Document

When the user double-clicks on a document icon, Windows Explorer executes the associated SDI program, passing in the selected filename on the command line. You might notice that the MFC Application Wizard generates a call to *EnableShellOpen* in the application class *InitInstance* function. This supports execution via DDE message, the technique used by the File Manager in Windows NT 3.51. Windows Explorer can launch your SDI application without this call.

Enabling Drag and Drop

If you want your already-running program to open files dragged from Windows Explorer, you must call the *CWnd* function *DragAcceptFiles* for the application's main frame window. The application object's public data member *m_pMainWnd* points to the *CFrameWnd* (or *CMDIFrameWnd*) object. When the user drops a file anywhere inside the frame window, the window receives a *WM_DROPFILES* message, which triggers a call to *FrameWnd::OnDropFiles*. The following line in *InitInstance*, generated by the MFC Application Wizard, enables drag and drop:

```
m_pMainWnd->DragAcceptFiles();
```

Program Startup Parameters

When you choose Run from the Start menu or when you double-click the program directly in Windows Explorer, there is no command-line parameter. The *InitInstance* function processes the command line with calls to *ParseCommandLine* and *ProcessShellCommand*. If the command line contains something that looks like a filename, the program immediately loads that file. Thus, you create a Windows shortcut that can run your program with a specific document file.

Experimenting with Explorer Launch and Drag and Drop

Once you've built Ex16a, you can try running it from Windows Explorer. You must execute the program directly, however, in order to write the initial entries in the Registry. Be sure that you've saved at least one 16A file to disk, and then exit Ex16a. Start Windows Explorer and locate the directory in which you saved 16A files. Double-click on one of the 16A files in the panel on the right. Your program should start with the selected file loaded. Now, with both Ex16a and Windows Explorer open on the desktop, try dragging another file from Windows Explorer to the Ex16a window. The program should open the new file just as if you had chosen File Open from the Ex16a menu.

You might also want to look at the Ex16a entries in the Registry. Run the Regedit program (possibly named Regedt32 in Windows 2000 and Windows XP), and expand the *HKEY_CLASSES_ROOT* key. Look under .16a and Ex16a.Document. Also expand the *HKEY_CURRENT_USER* key, and look at Local AppWizard-Generated Applications under Software. You should see a Recent File List under the subkey Ex16a. The Ex16a program calls *SetRegistryKey* with the string *Local AppWizard-Generated Applications*, so the program name goes beneath the Ex16a subkey.

MDI Support

In addition to SDI applications, MFC supports MDI applications. In this section, we'll look at MDI applications and see how they read and write their document files. For a long time, MDI applications were the preferred MFC library program style. It's the MFC Application Wizard default, and most of the sample programs that come with Visual C++ are MDI applications.

In addition, you'll learn the similarities and differences between SDI and MDI applications, and you'll learn how to convert an SDI application to an MDI application. Be sure that you thoroughly understand the SDI application described earlier in this chapter before you attack the MDI application in this section.

Before you look at the MFC library code for MDI applications, you should be familiar with the operation of Windows MDI programs. Take a close look at Visual C++ .NET now. It's an MDI application whose "multiple documents" are program source code files. Visual C++ .NET is not the most typical MDI application, however, because it collects its documents into projects. It's better to examine Microsoft Word or, better yet, a real MFC library MDI application—the kind that the MFC Application Wizard generates.

A Typical MDI Application, MFC Style

Ex16b is an MDI version of Ex16a. Figure 16-4 shows the Ex16b program in use.

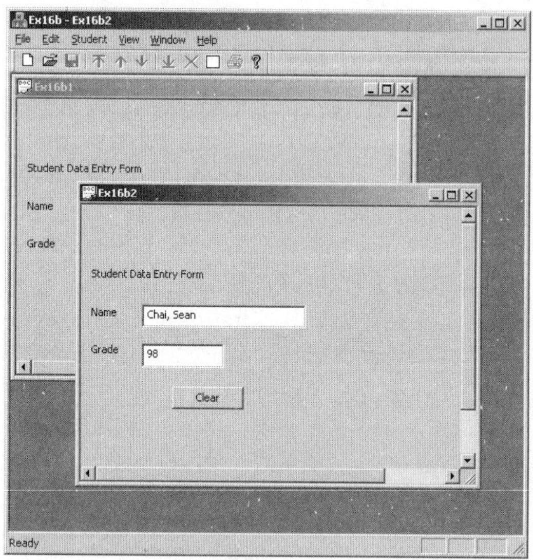

Figure 16-4 The Ex16b application with two files open.

The user has two separate document files open, each in a separate MDI child window. Only one child window is active at a time. The application has only one menu and one toolbar, and all commands are routed to the active child window. The main window's title bar reflects the name of the active child window's document file.

The child window's minimize box allows the user to reduce the child window to an icon in the main window. The application's Window menu (shown in Figure 16-4) lets the user control the presentation through the following commands.

Menu Command	Action
New Window	Opens as an additional child window for the selected document
Cascade	Arranges the existing windows in an overlapped pattern
Tile	Arranges the existing windows in a nonoverlapped, tiled pattern
Arrange Icons	Arranges minimized windows in the frame window
(document names)	Selects the corresponding child window and brings it to the top

The menus and toolbars in an MDI application are dynamic. When all the windows in an MDI application are closed, the File menu changes, most toolbar buttons are disabled, and the window caption does not show a filename. The only choice the user has is to start a new document or to open an existing document from disk.

As the user creates new files, the empty child window gets the default document name Ex16b1. This name is based on the Doc Type Name (Ex16b) selected in the Document Template Strings page of the MFC Application Wizard. The first new file is Ex16b1, the second is Ex16b2, and so forth. The user normally chooses a different name when saving the document.

An MFC library MDI application, like many commercial MDI applications, starts up with a new, empty document. (Visual C++ .NET is an exception.) If you want your application to start up with a blank frame, you can modify the argument to the *ProcessShellCommand* call in the application class file, as shown in example Ex16b.

The MDI Application Object

You're probably wondering how an MDI application works and what code makes it different from an SDI application. Actually, the startup sequences are pretty much the same. An application object of a class derived from class *CWinApp* has an overridden *InitInstance* member function. This *InitInstance* function is somewhat different from the SDI *InitInstance* function, starting with the call to *AddDocTemplate*.

The MDI Document Template Class

The MDI template construction call in *InitInstance* looks like this:

```
CMultiDocTemplate* pDocTemplate;
pDocTemplate = new CMultiDocTemplate(
    IDR_EX16BTYPE,
    RUNTIME_CLASS(CEx16bDoc),
    RUNTIME_CLASS(CChildFrame), // custom MDI child frame
    RUNTIME_CLASS(CEx16b));
AddDocTemplate(pDocTemplate);
```

Unlike Ex16a, an MDI application can use multiple document types and allows the simultaneous existence of more than one document object. This is the essence of the MDI application.

The single *AddDocTemplate* call shown in the previous example permits the MDI application to support multiple child windows, each connected to a document object and a view object. It's also possible to have several child windows (and corresponding view objects) connected to the same document object. In this chapter, we'll start with only one view class and one document class. You'll see multiple view classes and multiple document classes in Chapter 18.

> **Note** When your application is running, the document template object maintains a list of active document objects that were created from the template. The *CMultiDocTemplate* member functions *GetFirstDocPosition* and *GetNextDoc* allow you to iterate through the list. Use *CDocument::GetDocTemplate* to navigate from a document to its template.

The MDI Frame Window and the MDI Child Window

The SDI examples had only one frame window class and only one frame window object. For SDI applications, the MFC Application Wizard generated a class named *CMainFrame*, which was derived from the class *CFrameWnd*. An MDI application has two frame window classes and many frame objects, as shown in the following table. The MDI frame–view window relationship is shown in Figure 16-5.

Base Class	MFC Application Wizard–Generated Class	Number of Objects	Menu and Control Bars	Contains a View	Object Constructed
CMDIFrameWnd	*CMainFrame*	1 only	Yes	No	In application class's *InitInstance* function
CMDIChildWnd	*CChildFrame*	1 per child window	No	Yes	By application framework when a new child window is opened

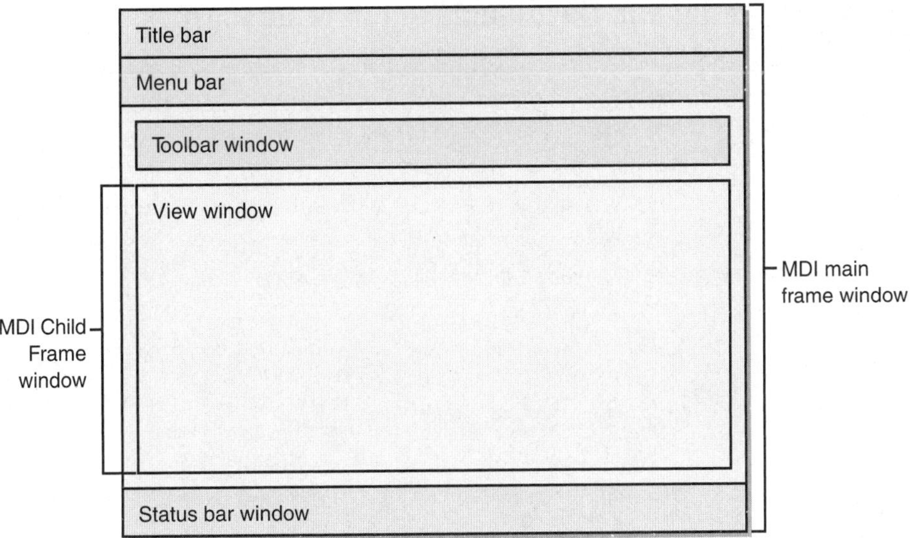

Figure 16-5 The MDI frame–view window relationship.

In an SDI application, the *CMainFrame* object frames the application and contains the view object. In an MDI application, the two roles are separated. Now the *CMainFrame* object is explicitly constructed in *InitInstance*, and the *CChildFrame* object contains the view. The MFC Application Wizard generates the following code:

```
CMainFrame* pMainFrame = new CMainFrame;
if (!pMainFrame->LoadFrame(IDR_MAINFRAME))
    return FALSE;
m_pMainWnd = pMainFrame;
⋮
pMainFrame->ShowWindow(m_nCmdShow);
pMainFrame->UpdateWindow();
```

The application framework can create the *CChildFrame* objects dynamically because the *CChildFrame* runtime class pointer is passed to the *CMultiDocTemplate* constructor.

> **Note** The MDI *InitInstance* function sets the *CWinApp* data member *m_pMainWnd* to point to the application's main frame window. This means you can access *m_pMainWnd* through the global *AfxGetApp* function anytime you need to get your application's main frame window.

The Main Frame and Document Template Resources

An MDI application (such as Ex16b, described later in this chapter) has two separate string and menu resources, identified by the *IDR_MAINFRAME* and *IDR_EX16BTYPE* constants. The first resource set goes with the empty main frame window; the second set goes with the occupied main frame window. Here are the two string resources with substrings broken out:

```
IDR_MAINFRAME
    "Ex16b"                     // application window caption

IDR_EX16BTYPE
    "\n"                        // (not used)
    "Ex16b\n"                   // root for default document name
    "Ex16b\n"                   // document type name
    "Ex16b Files (*.16b)\n"     // document type description and filter
    ".16b\n"                    // extension for documents of this type
    "Ex16b.Document\n"          // Registry file type ID
    "Ex16b.Document"            // Registry file type description
```

> **Note** The resource compiler won't accept the string concatenations as shown here. If you examine the Ex16b.rc file, you'll see the substrings combined in one long string.

The application window caption comes from the *IDR_MAINFRAME* string. When a document is open, the document filename is appended. The last two substrings in the *IDR_EX16BTYPE* string support embedded launch and drag and drop.

Creating an Empty Document

The *CWinApp::OnFileNew* function enables you to create an empty document. The MDI *InitInstance* function calls *OnFileNew* (through *ProcessShellCommand*), as did the SDI *InitInstance* function. This time, however, the main frame window has already been created. *OnFileNew*, through a call to the *CMultiDocTemplate* function *OpenDocumentFile*, now does the following:

1. Constructs a document object but does not attempt to read data from disk.

2. Constructs a child frame window object (of class *CChildFrame*). Also creates the child frame window but does not show it. In the main frame window, the *IDR_EX16BTYPE* menu replaces the *IDR_MAINFRAME* menu. *IDR_EX16BTYPE* also identifies an icon resource that is used when the child window is minimized within the frame.

3. Constructs a view object. Also creates the view window but does not show it.

4. Establishes connections among the document, the main frame, and view objects. Do not confuse these object connections with the class associations established by the call to *AddDocTemplate*.

5. Calls the virtual *OnNewDocument* member function for the document object.

6. Calls the virtual *OnInitialUpdate* member function for the view object.

7. Calls the virtual *ActivateFrame* member function for the child frame object to show the frame window and the view window.

The *OnFileNew* function is also called in response to the File New menu command. In an MDI application, *OnFileNew* performs exactly the same steps as it does when called from *InitInstance*.

> **Note** Some functions listed above are not called directly by *OpenDocumentFile* but are called indirectly through the application framework.

Creating an Additional View for an Existing Document

If you choose the New Window command from the Window menu, the application framework opens a new child window that is linked to the currently selected document. The associated *CMDIFrameWnd* function, *OnWindowNew*, does the following:

1. Constructs a child frame object (of class *CChildFrame*). Also creates the child frame window but does not show it.

2. Constructs a view object. Also creates the view window but does not show it.

3. Establishes connections between the new view object and the existing document and main frame objects.

4. Calls the virtual *OnInitialUpdate* member function for the view object.

5. Calls the virtual *ActivateFrame* member function for the child frame object to show the frame window and the view window.

Loading and Storing Documents

In MDI applications, documents are loaded and stored the same way as in SDI applications but with two important differences: A new document object is constructed each time a document file is loaded from disk, and the document object is destroyed when the child window is closed. Don't worry about clearing a document's contents before loading—but override the *CDocument::DeleteContents* function anyway to make the class portable to the SDI environment.

Multiple Document Templates

An MDI application can support multiple document templates through multiple calls to the *AddDocTemplate* function. Each template can specify a different combination of document, view, and MDI child frame classes. When the user chooses New from the File menu of an application with multiple templates, the application framework displays a list box that allows the user to select a template by name as specified in the string resource (document type substring). Multiple *AddDocTemplate* calls are not supported in SDI applications because the document, view, and frame objects are constructed once for the life of the application.

> **Note** When your application is running, the application object keeps a list of active document template objects. The *CWinApp* member functions *GetFirstDocTemplatePosition* and *GetNextDocTemplate* allow you to iterate through the list of templates. These functions, together with the *CDocTemplate* member functions *GetFirstDocPosition* and *GetNextDoc*, allow you to access all of the application's document objects.

If you don't want the template list box, you can edit the File menu to add a New menu command for each document type. Code the command message handlers as shown here, using the document type substring from each template:

```
void CMyApp::OnFileNewStudent()
{
    OpenNewDocument("Studnt");
}
void CMyApp::OnFileNewTeacher()
{
    OpenNewDocument("Teachr");
}
```

Then add the *OpenNewDocument* helper function as follows:

```
BOOL CMyApp::OpenNewDocument(const CString& strTarget)
{
    CString strDocName;
    CDocTemplate* pSelectedTemplate;
    POSITION pos = GetFirstDocTemplatePosition();
    while (pos != NULL) {
        pSelectedTemplate = (CDocTemplate*) GetNextDocTemplate(pos);
        ASSERT(pSelectedTemplate != NULL);
        ASSERT(pSelectedTemplate->IsKindOf(
            RUNTIME_CLASS(CDocTemplate)));
        pSelectedTemplate->GetDocString(strDocName,
            CDocTemplate::docName);
        if (strDocName == strTarget) { // from template's
                                       //  string resource
            pSelectedTemplate->OpenDocumentFile(NULL);
            return TRUE;
        }
    }
    return FALSE;
}
```

Explorer Launch and Drag and Drop

When you double-click on a document icon for an MDI application in Windows Explorer, the application launches only if it was not running already; otherwise, a new child window opens in the running application for the document you selected. The *EnableShellOpen* call in the application class *InitInstance* function is necessary for this to work. Drag and drop works much the same way in an MDI application as it does in an SDI application. If you drag a file from Windows Explorer to your MDI main frame window, the program opens a new child frame (with associated document and view) just as if you'd chosen the File Open command. As with SDI applications, you must use the Document Template Strings page of the MFC Application Wizard to specify the filename extension.

The Ex16b Example: An MDI Application

This example is the MDI version of the Ex16a example. It uses the same document and view class code and the same resources (except the program name). The application code and main frame class code are different, however. All the new code is listed here, including the code that the MFC Application Wizard generates. A list of the files and classes in the Ex16b example are shown in Table 16-3.

Table 16-3 Files and Classes in Ex16b

Header File	Source Code File	Class	Description
Ex16b.h	Ex16b.cpp	*CEx16bApp*	Application class (from the MFC Application Wizard)
		CAboutDlg	About dialog box
MainFrm.h	MainFrm.cpp	*CMainFrame*	MDI main frame
ChildFrm.h	ChildFrm.cpp	*CChildFrame*	MDI child frame
CEx16bDoc.h	CEx16bDoc.cpp	*CEx16bDoc*	Student document (borrowed from Ex16a)
CEx16bView.h	Ex16bView.cpp	*CEx16bView*	Student form view (borrowed from Ex16a)
Student.h	Student.cpp	*CStudent*	Student record (from Ex16a)
StdAfx.h	StdAfx.cpp		Precompiled headers (with afxtempl.h included)

CEx16bApp

In the *CEx16bApp* source code listing, the *OpenDocumentFile* member function is overridden only for the purpose of inserting a *TRACE* statement. Also, a few lines have been added before the *ProcessShellCommand* call in *InitInstance.* They check the argument to *ProcessShellCommand* and change it if necessary to prevent the creation of any empty document window on startup. The following shows the source code:

Ex16b.h

```
// Ex16b.h : main header file for the Ex16b application
//
#pragma once

#ifndef __AFXWIN_H__
    #error include 'stdafx.h' before including this file for PCH
#endif

#include "resource.h"       // main symbols

// CEx16bApp:
// See Ex16b.cpp for the implementation of this class
//

class CEx16bApp : public CWinApp
{
public:
    CEx16bApp();
```

```
// Overrides
public:
    virtual BOOL InitInstance();

// Implementation
    afx_msg void OnAppAbout();
    DECLARE_MESSAGE_MAP()
    virtual CDocument* OpenDocumentFile(LPCTSTR lpszFileName);
};
extern CEx16bApp theApp;
```

Ex16b.cpp

```
// Ex16b.cpp : Defines the class behaviors for the application.
//
#include "stdafx.h"
#include "Ex16b.h"
#include "MainFrm.h"
#include "ChildFrm.h"
#include "Ex16bDoc.h"
#include "Ex16bView.h"

#ifdef _DEBUG
#define new DEBUG_NEW
#endif

// CEx16bApp

BEGIN_MESSAGE_MAP(CEx16bApp, CWinApp)
    ON_COMMAND(ID_APP_ABOUT, OnAppAbout)
    // Standard file based document commands
    ON_COMMAND(ID_FILE_NEW, CWinApp::OnFileNew)
    ON_COMMAND(ID_FILE_OPEN, CWinApp::OnFileOpen)
END_MESSAGE_MAP()

// CEx16bApp construction

CEx16bApp::CEx16bApp()
{
    // TODO: add construction code here,
    // Place all significant initialization in InitInstance
}

// The one and only CEx16bApp object
CEx16bApp theApp;

// CEx16bApp initialization
BOOL CEx16bApp::InitInstance()
{
```

(continued)

```
// InitCommonControls() is required on Windows XP if an application
// manifest specifies use of ComCtl32.dll version 6 or later to enable
// visual styles.  Otherwise, any window creation will fail.
InitCommonControls();
CWinApp::InitInstance();

// Initialize OLE libraries
if (!AfxOleInit())
{
    AfxMessageBox(IDP_OLE_INIT_FAILED);
    return FALSE;
}
AfxEnableControlContainer();
// Standard initialization
// If you are not using these features and wish to reduce the size
// of your final executable, you should remove from the following
// the specific initialization routines you do not need
// Change the registry key under which our settings are stored
// TODO: You should modify this string to be something appropriate
// such as the name of your company or organization
SetRegistryKey(_T("Local AppWizard-Generated Applications"));
// Load standard INI file options (including MRU)
LoadStdProfileSettings(4);
// Register the application's document templates. Document templates
//  serve as the connection between documents, frame windows and views
CMultiDocTemplate* pDocTemplate;
pDocTemplate = new CMultiDocTemplate(
    IDR_Ex16bTYPE,
    RUNTIME_CLASS(CEx16bDoc),
    RUNTIME_CLASS(CChildFrame), // custom MDI child frame
    RUNTIME_CLASS(CEx16bView));
AddDocTemplate(pDocTemplate);
// create main MDI Frame window
CMainFrame* pMainFrame = new CMainFrame;
if (!pMainFrame->LoadFrame(IDR_MAINFRAME))
    return FALSE;
m_pMainWnd = pMainFrame;
// call DragAcceptFiles only if there's a suffix
//  In an MDI app, this should occur immediately after setting m_pMainWnd
// Enable drag/drop open
m_pMainWnd->DragAcceptFiles();
// Enable DDE Execute open
EnableShellOpen();
RegisterShellFileTypes(TRUE);
// Parse command line for standard shell commands, DDE, file open
CCommandLineInfo cmdInfo;
ParseCommandLine(cmdInfo);
```

```
    // no empty document window on startup
    if(cmdInfo.m_nShellCommand == CCommandLineInfo::FileNew) {
        cmdInfo.m_nShellCommand = CCommandLineInfo::FileNothing;
    }
    // Dispatch commands specified on the command line.  Will return FALSE
    // if app was launched with /RegServer, /Register, /Unregserver
    // or /Unregister.
    if (!ProcessShellCommand(cmdInfo))
        return FALSE;
    // The main window has been initialized, so show and update it
    pMainFrame->ShowWindow(m_nCmdShow);
    pMainFrame->UpdateWindow();
    return TRUE;
}

// CAboutDlg dialog used for App About
class CAboutDlg : public CDialog
{
public:
    CAboutDlg();
// Dialog Data
    enum { IDD = IDD_ABOUTBOX };

protected:
    virtual void DoDataExchange(CDataExchange* pDX);    // DDX/DDV support

// Implementation
protected:
    DECLARE_MESSAGE_MAP()
};
CAboutDlg::CAboutDlg() : CDialog(CAboutDlg::IDD)
{
}
void CAboutDlg::DoDataExchange(CDataExchange* pDX)
{
    CDialog::DoDataExchange(pDX);
}
BEGIN_MESSAGE_MAP(CAboutDlg, CDialog)
END_MESSAGE_MAP()

// App command to run the dialog
void CEx16bApp::OnAppAbout()
{
    CAboutDlg aboutDlg;
    aboutDlg.DoModal();
}

// CEx16bApp message handlers
CDocument* CEx16bApp::OpenDocumentFile(LPCTSTR lpszFileName)
{
    TRACE("CEx16bApp::OpenDocumentFile\n");
    return CWinApp::OpenDocumentFile(lpszFileName);
}
```

CMainFrame

This main frame class, as shown in the following code listings, is almost identical to the SDI version, except that it's derived from *CMDIFrameWnd* instead of *CFrameWnd*.

MainFrm.h

```
// MainFrm.h : interface of the CMainFrame class
//
#pragma once
class CMainFrame : public CMDIFrameWnd
{
    DECLARE_DYNAMIC(CMainFrame)
public:
    CMainFrame();
// Attributes
public:
// Operations
public:
// Overrides
public:
    virtual BOOL PreCreateWindow(CREATESTRUCT& cs);

// Implementation
public:
    virtual ~CMainFrame();
#ifdef _DEBUG
    virtual void AssertValid() const;
    virtual void Dump(CDumpContext& dc) const;
#endif

protected:  // control bar embedded members
    CStatusBar  m_wndStatusBar;
    CToolBar    m_wndToolBar;
// Generated message map functions
protected:
    afx_msg int OnCreate(LPCREATESTRUCT lpCreateStruct);
    DECLARE_MESSAGE_MAP()
};
```

MainFrm.cpp

```
// MainFrm.cpp : implementation of the CMainFrame class
//
#include "stdafx.h"
#include "Ex16b.h"
#include "MainFrm.h"
```

```
#ifdef _DEBUG
#define new DEBUG_NEW
#endif

// CMainFrame
IMPLEMENT_DYNAMIC(CMainFrame, CMDIFrameWnd)
BEGIN_MESSAGE_MAP(CMainFrame, CMDIFrameWnd)
    ON_WM_CREATE()
END_MESSAGE_MAP()

static UINT indicators[] =
{
    ID_SEPARATOR,           // status line indicator
    ID_INDICATOR_CAPS,
    ID_INDICATOR_NUM,
    ID_INDICATOR_SCRL
};

// CMainFrame construction/destruction
CMainFrame::CMainFrame()
{
    // TODO: add member initialization code here
}
CMainFrame::~CMainFrame()
{
}
int CMainFrame::OnCreate(LPCREATESTRUCT lpCreateStruct)
{
    if (CMDIFrameWnd::OnCreate(lpCreateStruct) == -1)
        return -1;

    if (!m_wndToolBar.CreateEx(this, TBSTYLE_FLAT,
        WS_CHILD | WS_VISIBLE | CBRS_TOP
        | CBRS_GRIPPER | CBRS_TOOLTIPS | CBRS_FLYBY
        | CBRS_SIZE_DYNAMIC) ||
        !m_wndToolBar.LoadToolBar(IDR_MAINFRAME))
    {
        TRACE0("Failed to create toolbar\n");
        return -1;      // fail to create
    }
    if (!m_wndStatusBar.Create(this) ||
        !m_wndStatusBar.SetIndicators(indicators,
          sizeof(indicators)/sizeof(UINT)))
    {
        TRACE0("Failed to create status bar\n");
        return -1;      // fail to create
    }
```

(continued)

```
    // TODO: Delete these three lines if you don't want the toolbar to
    // be dockable
    m_wndToolBar.EnableDocking(CBRS_ALIGN_ANY);
    EnableDocking(CBRS_ALIGN_ANY);
    DockControlBar(&m_wndToolBar);
    return 0;
}
BOOL CMainFrame::PreCreateWindow(CREATESTRUCT& cs)
{
    if( !CMDIFrameWnd::PreCreateWindow(cs) )
        return FALSE;
    // TODO: Modify the Window class or styles here by modifying
    //  the CREATESTRUCT cs

    return TRUE;
}
// CMainFrame diagnostics
#ifdef _DEBUG
void CMainFrame::AssertValid() const
{
    CMDIFrameWnd::AssertValid();
}
void CMainFrame::Dump(CDumpContext& dc) const
{
    CMDIFrameWnd::Dump(dc);
}
#endif //_DEBUG
// CMainFrame message handlers
```

CChildFrame

This child frame class, shown in the following code listings, lets you conveniently control the child frame window's characteristics by adding code in the *PreCreateWindow* function. You can also map messages and override other virtual functions.

ChildFrm.h

```
// ChildFrm.h : interface of the CChildFrame class
//
#pragma once

class CChildFrame : public CMDIChildWnd
{
    DECLARE_DYNCREATE(CChildFrame)
public:
    CChildFrame();
// Attributes
public:
```

```
// Operations
public:
// Overrides
    virtual BOOL PreCreateWindow(CREATESTRUCT& cs);

// Implementation
public:
    virtual ~CChildFrame();
#ifdef _DEBUG
    virtual void AssertValid() const;
    virtual void Dump(CDumpContext& dc) const;
#endif

// Generated message map functions
protected:
    DECLARE_MESSAGE_MAP()
public:
    virtual void ActivateFrame(int nCmdShow = -1);
};
```

ChildFrm.cpp

```
// ChildFrm.cpp : implementation of the CChildFrame class
//
#include "stdafx.h"
#include "Ex16b.h"
#include "ChildFrm.h"

#ifdef _DEBUG
#define new DEBUG_NEW
#endif

// CChildFrame
IMPLEMENT_DYNCREATE(CChildFrame, CMDIChildWnd)
BEGIN_MESSAGE_MAP(CChildFrame, CMDIChildWnd)
END_MESSAGE_MAP()

// CChildFrame construction/destruction
CChildFrame::CChildFrame()
{
    // TODO: add member initialization code here
}
CChildFrame::~CChildFrame()
{
}
BOOL CChildFrame::PreCreateWindow(CREATESTRUCT& cs)
{
    if( !CMDIChildWnd::PreCreateWindow(cs) )
        return FALSE;
    return TRUE;
}
```

(continued)

```
// CChildFrame diagnostics
#ifdef _DEBUG
void CChildFrame::AssertValid() const
{
    CMDIChildWnd::AssertValid();
}
void CChildFrame::Dump(CDumpContext& dc) const
{
    CMDIChildWnd::Dump(dc);
}
#endif //_DEBUG

// CChildFrame message handlers
void CChildFrame::ActivateFrame(int nCmdShow)
{
    TRACE("Entering CChildFrame::ActivateFrame\n");
    CMDIChildWnd::ActivateFrame(nCmdShow);
}
```

Testing the Ex16b Application

Do the build, run the program from Visual C++ .NET, and then make several documents. Try saving the documents on disk, closing them, and reloading them. Also, choose New Window from the Window menu. Notice that you now have two views (and child frames) attached to the same document. Now exit the program and start Windows Explorer. The files you created should show up with document icons. Double-click on a document icon and see whether the Ex16b program starts up. Now, with both Windows Explorer and Ex16b on the desktop, drag a document from Windows Explorer to Ex16b. Was the file opened?

MTI Support

Windows 2000 introduced a third type of application into its repertoire: the Multiple Top-Level Interface (MTI) application. This is the type of interface favored by Microsoft Office 2000 and Office XP applications. MTI applications are similar to SDI applications, but whereas SDI applications run as separate windows—one instance of the application for every window open—MTI applications have one instance serving all the open windows. When the user creates a new file, the application opens a new independent top-level window and a new document along with them—but they're tied to the same running instance of the application.

The Ex16c Example: An MTI Application

This example is an MTI version of the Ex16a we looked at in a previous section. To create this example, in the MFC Application Wizard select Multiple Top-Level Documents on the Application Type page and deselect Printing And Print Preview on the Advanced Features page. On the Generated Classes page, change the view's base class to *CFormView*.

Ex16c uses the same document and view class code and the same resources (except the resource name). The application code and main frame class code are different, however. You can examine all the new code in the Ex16c application on the companion CD. A list of files and classes in the Ex16c example are shown in Table 16-4.

Table 16-4 Files and Classes in Ex16c

Header File	Source Code File	Class	Description
Ex16c.h	Ex16c.cpp	*CEx16cApp*	Application class (from the MFC Application Wizard)
		CAboutDlg	About dialog box
MainFrm.h	MainFrm.cpp	*CMainFrame*	MTI main frame
CEx16cDoc.h	CEx16cDoc.cpp	*CEx16cDoc*	Student document (borrowed from Ex16a)
CEx16cView.h	Ex16cView.cpp	*CEx16cView*	Student form view (borrowed from Ex16a)
Student.h	Student.cpp	*CStudent*	Student record (from Ex16a)
StdAfx.h	StdAfx.cpp		Precompiled headers (with afxtempl.h included)

Unlike the MDI and SDI applications, the MTI application includes a New Frame command on the File menu. This command tells the application to open a new top-level window. The following listing illustrates handling the New Frame command:

```
void CEx16cApp::OnFileNewFrame()
{
    ASSERT(m_pDocTemplate != NULL);
    CDocument* pDoc = NULL;
    CFrameWnd* pFrame = NULL;

    // Create a new instance of the document referenced
    // by the m_pDocTemplate member.
    pDoc = m_pDocTemplate->CreateNewDocument();
```

(continued)

```
        if (pDoc != NULL)
        {
            // If creation worked, use create a new frame for
            // that document.
            pFrame = m_pDocTemplate->CreateNewFrame(pDoc, NULL);
            if (pFrame != NULL)
            {
                // Set the title, and initialize the document.
                // If document initialization fails, clean-up
                // the frame window and document.

                m_pDocTemplate->SetDefaultTitle(pDoc);
                if (!pDoc->OnNewDocument())
                {
                    pFrame->DestroyWindow();
                    pFrame = NULL;
                }
                else
                {
                    // Otherwise, update the frame
                    m_pDocTemplate->InitialUpdateFrame(pFrame, pDoc, TRUE);
                }
            }
        }

        // If we failed, clean up the document and show a
        // message to the user.
        if (pFrame == NULL || pDoc == NULL)
        {
            delete pDoc;
            AfxMessageBox(AFX_IDP_FAILED_TO_CREATE_DOC);
        }
    }
```

MTI applications use the *CMultiDocTemplate* class to manage the document, the frame, and the view. Notice that *OnFileNewFrame* creates a new document and then a new top-level frame window instead of depending on the framework to create the document, frame, and view classes. Otherwise, MTI applications manage their documents and views in the same way that SDI and MDI applications do.

Testing the Ex16c Application

To test the Ex16c application, run the application and choose New Frame from the File menu. Notice that a new frame opens up near the existing frame. The new top-level frame includes a new instance of the document, but the document is associated with the new frame (rather than with a new MDI child frame, as in Ex16b).

17

Printing and Print Preview

If you're depending on the Win32 API alone, printing will be one of the tougher programming jobs you'll face. The Microsoft Foundation Class (MFC) library application framework goes a long way toward making printing easier, and it adds a print preview capability that behaves like the print preview functions in commercial Microsoft Windows–based programs such as Microsoft Word and Microsoft Excel.

In this chapter, you'll learn how to use the MFC library print and print preview features. In the process, you'll get a feel for what's involved in Windows-based printing and how it's different from printing in MS-DOS. First, we'll do some WYSIWYG printing in which the printer output matches the screen display. This option requires careful use of mapping modes. Then we'll print a paginated data processing–style report that doesn't reflect the screen display at all. In that example, we'll use a template array to structure our document so the program can print any specified range of pages on demand.

Windows-Based Printing

In the old days, programmers had to worry about configuring their applications for dozens of printers. Windows makes life easier because it provides all of the printer drivers you'll ever need. It also supplies a consistent user interface for printing.

Standard Printer Dialog Boxes

When the user chooses Print from the File menu of a Windows-based application, the standard Print dialog box appears, as shown in Figure 17-1.

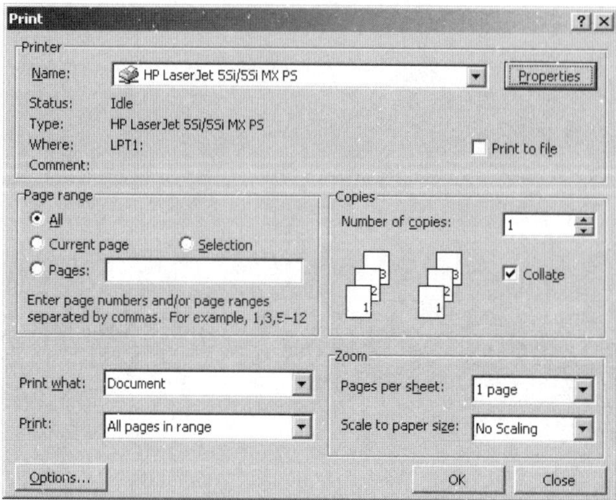

Figure 17-1 The standard Print dialog box.

If the user clicks the Properties button in the Print dialog box, the Document Properties dialog box appears, as shown in Figure 17-2.

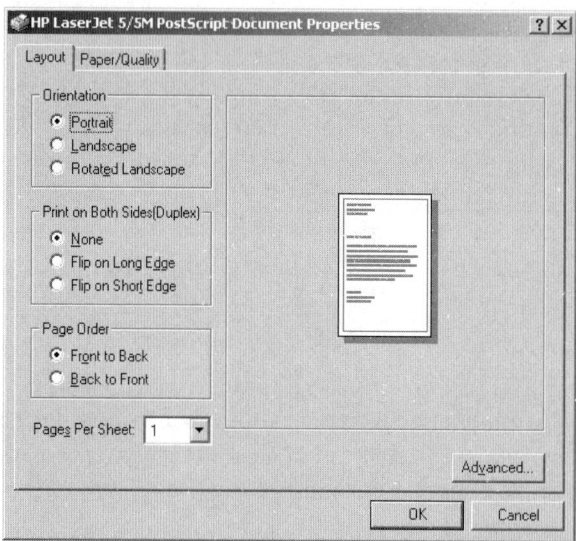

Figure 17-2 The Document Properties dialog box.

During the printing process, the application displays a standard printer status dialog box.

Interactive Print Page Selection

If you've worked in the data processing field, you might be used to batch-mode printing. A program reads a record and then formats and prints selected information as a line in a report. Let's say, for example, that every time 50 lines have been printed the program ejects the paper and prints a new page heading. The programmer assumes that the whole report will be printed at one time and therefore makes no allowance for interactively printing selected pages.

As Figure 17-1 shows, page numbers are important in Windows-based printing. A program must respond to a user's page selection by calculating which information to print and then printing the selected pages. If you're aware of this page selection requirement, you can design your application's data structures accordingly.

Remember the student list from Chapter 16? Let's say the list includes 1000 student names and the user wants to print page 5 of a student report. If each student record requires one print line and a page holds 50 lines, page 5 will include records 201 through 250. With an MFC list collection class, you're stuck iterating through the first 200 list elements before you can start printing. Maybe the list isn't the ideal data structure. How about an array collection instead? With the *CObArray* class (or one of the template array classes), you can directly access the 201st student record.

Not every application has elements that map to a fixed number of print lines. Suppose the student record contains a multi-line text biography field. You can't know how many biography lines each record includes, so you have to search through the entire file to determine the page breaks. If your program can remember those page breaks as it calculates them, its efficiency will increase.

Display Pages vs. Printed Pages

In many cases, you'll want a printed page to correspond to a display page. You cannot guarantee that objects will be printed exactly as they're displayed on screen, but with TrueType fonts, your printed page will be pretty close. If you're working with full-size paper and you want the corresponding display to be readable, you'll certainly want a display window that's larger than the screen. Thus, a scrolling view such as the one that the *CScrollView* class provides is ideal for your printable views.

At other times, you might not care about display pages. Perhaps your view holds its data in a list box, or maybe you don't need to display the data at all. In these cases, your program can contain stand-alone print logic that simply extracts data from the document and sends it to the printer. Of course, the program must properly respond to a user's page-range request. If you query the printer to determine the paper size and orientation (portrait or landscape), you can adjust the pagination accordingly.

Print Preview

The MFC library print preview feature shows you on screen the exact page and line breaks you'll get when you print your document on a selected printer. The fonts might look a little funny, especially in the smaller sizes, but that's not a problem. (Look at the Print Preview window that appears on page 455.)

Print preview is an MFC library feature, not a Windows feature. Don't underestimate how much effort went into programming print preview. (Just look at the source code.) The print preview program examines each character individually, determining its position based on the printer's device context. After selecting an approximating font, the program displays the character in the Print Preview window at the proper location.

Programming for the Printer

The application framework does most of the work for printing and print preview. To use the printer effectively, you must understand the sequence of function calls and know which functions to override.

The Printer Device Context and the *CView::OnDraw* Function

When your program prints on the printer, it uses a device context object of class *CDC*. Don't worry about where the object comes from; the application framework constructs it and passes it as a parameter to your view's *OnDraw* function. If your application uses the printer to duplicate the display, the *OnDraw* function can do double duty. If you're displaying, the *OnPaint* function calls *OnDraw* and the device context is the display context. If you're printing, *OnDraw* is called by another *CView* virtual function, *OnPrint*, with a printer device context as a parameter. The *OnPrint* function is called once to print an entire page.

In print preview mode, the *OnDraw* parameter is actually a pointer to a *CPreviewDC* object. Your *OnPrint* and *OnDraw* functions work the same regardless of whether you're printing or previewing.

The *CView::OnPrint* Function

You've seen that the base class *OnPrint* function calls *OnDraw* and that *OnDraw* can use both a display device context and a printer device context. The mapping mode should be set before *OnPrint* is called. You can override *OnPrint* to print items that you don't need on the display, such as a title page, headers, and footers. The *OnPrint* parameters are a pointer to the device context and a pointer to a print information object (*CPrintInfo*) that includes page dimensions, the current page number, and the maximum page number.

In your overridden *OnPrint* function, you can elect not to call *OnDraw* at all to support print logic that is totally independent of the display logic. The application framework calls the *OnPrint* function once for each page to be printed, with the current page number in the *CPrintInfo* structure. You'll find out shortly how the application framework determines the page number.

Preparing the Device Context: The *CView::OnPrepareDC* Function

If you need a display mapping mode other than *MM_TEXT* (and you often will), you'll usually set it in the view's *OnPrepareDC* function. You must override this function yourself if your view class is derived directly from *CView*, but it's already overridden if your view is derived from *CScrollView*. The *OnPrepareDC* function is called in *OnPaint* immediately before the call to *OnDraw*. If you're printing, the same *OnPrepareDC* function is called, this time immediately before the application framework calls *OnPrint*. Thus, the mapping mode is set before both the painting of the view and the printing of a page.

The second parameter of the *OnPrepareDC* function is a pointer to a *CPrintInfo* structure. This pointer is valid only if *OnPrepareDC* is being called before printing. You can test for this condition by calling the *CDC* member function *IsPrinting*. The *IsPrinting* function is particularly handy if you're using *OnPrepareDC* to set different mapping modes for the display and the printer.

If you do not know in advance how many pages your print job will require, your overridden *OnPrepareDC* function can detect the end of the document and reset the *m_bContinuePrinting* flag in the *CPrintInfo* structure. When this flag is *FALSE*, the *OnPrint* function won't be called again and control will pass to the end of the print loop.

The Start and End of a Print Job

When a print job starts, the application framework calls two *CView* functions, *OnPreparePrinting* and *OnBeginPrinting*. (The MFC Application Wizard generates the *OnPreparePrinting*, *OnBeginPrinting*, and *OnEndPrinting* functions for you if you select the Printing And Print Preview option.) The first function, *OnPreparePrinting*, is called before the display of the Print dialog box. If you know the first and last page numbers, call *CPrintInfo::SetMinPage* and *CPrintInfo::SetMaxPage* in *OnPreparePrinting*. The page numbers you pass to these functions will appear in the Print dialog box for the user to override.

The second function, *OnBeginPrinting*, is called after the Print dialog box closes. You override this function to create Graphics Device Interface (GDI) objects, such as fonts, that you need for the entire print job. A program runs faster if you create a font once instead of re-creating it for each page.

The *CView* function *OnEndPrinting* is called at the end of the print job, after the last page has been printed. You override this function to get rid of GDI objects created in *OnBeginPrinting*.

Table 17-1 lists the important overridable *CView* print loop functions.

Table 17-1 Overridable *CView* Print Loop Functions

Function	Common Override Behavior
OnPreparePrinting	Sets first and last page numbers
OnBeginPrinting	Creates GDI objects
OnPrepareDC (for each page)	Sets mapping mode and optionally detects end of print job
OnPrint (for each page)	Does print-specific output and then calls *OnDraw*
OnEndPrinting	Deletes GDI objects

The Ex17a Example: A WYSIWYG Print Program

This example displays and prints a single page of text stored in a document. The printed image should match the displayed image. The *MM_TWIPS* mapping mode is used for both printer and display. First, we'll use a fixed drawing rectangle, and then we'll base the drawing rectangle on the printable area rectangle supplied by the printer driver.

Here are the steps for building the example:

1. **Run the MFC Application Wizard to generate the Ex17a project.** Accept the default options. On the Generated Classes page, rename the document class *CPoemDoc* and the view class *CStringView*. Derive *CStringView* from *CScrollView*. Note that this is an MDI application.

2. **Add a *CStringArray* data member to the *CPoemDoc* class.** Edit the PoemDoc.h header file as follows:

```
public:
    CStringArray m_stringArray;
```

   The document data is stored in a string array. The MFC library *CStringArray* class holds an array of *CString* objects, which are accessible by a zero-based subscript. You need not set a maximum dimension in the declaration because the array is dynamic.

3. **Add a *CRect* data member to the *CStringView* class.** Edit the StringView.h header file as shown here:

```
private:
    CRect m_rectPrint;
```

4. **Edit three *CPoemDoc* member functions in the file PoemDoc.cpp.** The MFC Application Wizard generates skeleton *OnNewDocument* and *Serialize* functions, but we'll have to use Class View's Properties window to override the *DeleteContents* function. We'll initialize the poem document in the overridden *OnNewDocument* function. *DeleteContents* is called in *CDocument::OnNewDocument*, so by calling the base class function first we're sure the poem won't be deleted. (The text, by the way, is an excerpt from the 20th poem in Lawrence Ferlinghetti's book *A Coney Island of the Mind.*) Type 10 lines of your choice. You can substitute another poem or maybe your favorite Win32 function description. Add the following boldface code:

```
BOOL CPoemDoc::OnNewDocument()
{
    if (!CDocument::OnNewDocument())
        return FALSE;

    m_stringArray.SetSize(10);
    m_stringArray[0] = "The pennycandystore beyond the El";
    m_stringArray[1] = "is where I first";
    m_stringArray[2] = "                  fell in love";
    m_stringArray[3] = "                      with unreality";
    m_stringArray[4] = "Jellybeans glowed in the semi-gloom";
    m_stringArray[5] = "of that september afternoon";
    m_stringArray[6] = "A cat upon the counter moved among";
    m_stringArray[7] = "                     the licorice sticks";
    m_stringArray[8] = "                  and tootsie rolls";
    m_stringArray[9] = "          and Oh Boy Gum";

    return TRUE;
}
```

> **Note** The *CStringArray* class supports dynamic arrays, but here we're using the *m_stringArray* object as if it were a static array of 10 elements.

The application framework calls the document's virtual *DeleteContents* function when it closes the document; this action deletes the strings in the array. A *CStringArray* contains actual objects, and a *CObArray* contains pointers to objects. This distinction is important when it's time to delete the array elements. Here, the *RemoveAll* function actually deletes the string objects:

```
void CPoemDoc::DeleteContents()
{
    // called before OnNewDocument and when document is closed
    m_stringArray.RemoveAll();
}
```

Serialization isn't important in this example, but the following function shows how easy it is to serialize strings. The application framework calls the *DeleteContents* function before loading from the archive, so you don't have to worry about emptying the array. Add the following boldface code:

```
void CPoemDoc::Serialize(CArchive& ar)
{
    m_stringArray.Serialize(ar);
}
```

5. **Edit the *OnInitialUpdate* function in StringView.cpp.** You must override the function for all classes derived from *CScrollView*. This function's job is to set the logical window size and the mapping mode. Add the following boldface code:

```
void CStringView::OnInitialUpdate()
{
    CScrollView::OnInitialUpdate();
    CSize sizeTotal(m_rectPrint.Width(), -m_rectPrint.Height());
    CSize sizePage(sizeTotal.cx / 2,
                   sizeTotal.cy / 2);    // page scroll
    CSize sizeLine(sizeTotal.cx / 100,
                   sizeTotal.cy / 100); // line scroll
    SetScrollSizes(MM_TWIPS, sizeTotal, sizePage, sizeLine);
}
```

6. **Edit the *OnDraw* function in StringView.cpp.** The *OnDraw* function of class *CStringView* draws on both the display and the printer. In addition to displaying the poem text lines in 10-point Roman font, it draws a border around the printable area and a crude ruler along the top and left margins. *OnDraw* assumes the *MM_TWIPS* mapping mode, in which 1 inch = 1440 units. Add the boldface code shown here:

```
void CStringView::OnDraw(CDC* pDC)
{
    int        i, j, nHeight;
    CString    str;
    CFont      font;
    TEXTMETRIC tm;

    CPoemDoc* pDoc = GetDocument();
    // Draw a border -- slightly smaller to avoid truncation
    pDC->Rectangle(m_rectPrint + CRect(0, 0, -20, 20));
    // Draw horizontal and vertical rulers
    j = m_rectPrint.Width() / 1440;
    for (i = 0; i <= j; i++) {
        str.Format("%02d", i);
        pDC->TextOut(i * 1440, 0, str);
    }
    j = -(m_rectPrint.Height() / 1440);
    for (i = 0; i <= j; i++) {
        str.Format("%02d", i);
        pDC->TextOut(0, -i * 1440, str);
    }
    // Print the poem 0.5 inch down and over;
    //  use 10-point roman font
    font.CreateFont(-200, 0, 0, 0, 400, FALSE,
                    FALSE, 0, ANSI_CHARSET,
                    OUT_DEFAULT_PRECIS, CLIP_DEFAULT_PRECIS,
                    DEFAULT_QUALITY, DEFAULT_PITCH | FF_ROMAN,
                    "Times New Roman");
    CFont* pOldFont = (CFont*) pDC->SelectObject(&font);
    pDC->GetTextMetrics(&tm);
    nHeight = tm.tmHeight + tm.tmExternalLeading;
    TRACE("font height = %d, internal leading = %d\n",
          nHeight, tm.tmInternalLeading);
    j = pDoc->m_stringArray.GetSize();
    for (i = 0; i < j; i++) {
        pDC->TextOut(720, -i * nHeight - 720,
                     pDoc->m_stringArray[i]);
    }
    pDC->SelectObject(pOldFont);
    TRACE("LOGPIXELSX = %d, LOGPIXELSY = %d\n",
          pDC->GetDeviceCaps(LOGPIXELSX),
          pDC->GetDeviceCaps(LOGPIXELSY));
    TRACE("HORZSIZE = %d, VERTSIZE = %d\n",
          pDC->GetDeviceCaps(HORZSIZE),
          pDC->GetDeviceCaps(VERTSIZE));
}
```

7. **Edit the *OnPreparePrinting* function in StringView.cpp.** This function sets the maximum number of pages in the print job. This example has only one page. You must call the base class *DoPrepare-Printing* function in your overridden *OnPreparePrinting* function. Add the following boldface code:

```
BOOL CStringView::OnPreparePrinting(CPrintInfo* pInfo)
{
    pInfo->SetMaxPage(1);
    return DoPreparePrinting(pInfo);
}
```

8. **Edit the constructor in StringView.cpp.** The initial value of the print rectangle should be 8 by 15 inches, expressed in twips (1 inch = 1440 twips). Add the following boldface code:

```
CStringView::CStringView() : m_rectPrint(0, 0, 11520, -21600)
{
}
```

9. **Build and test the application.** If you run the Ex17a application under Windows NT, Window 2000, or Windows XP with the lowest screen resolution, your MDI child window will look like the one shown here. (The text will be larger with higher resolutions.)

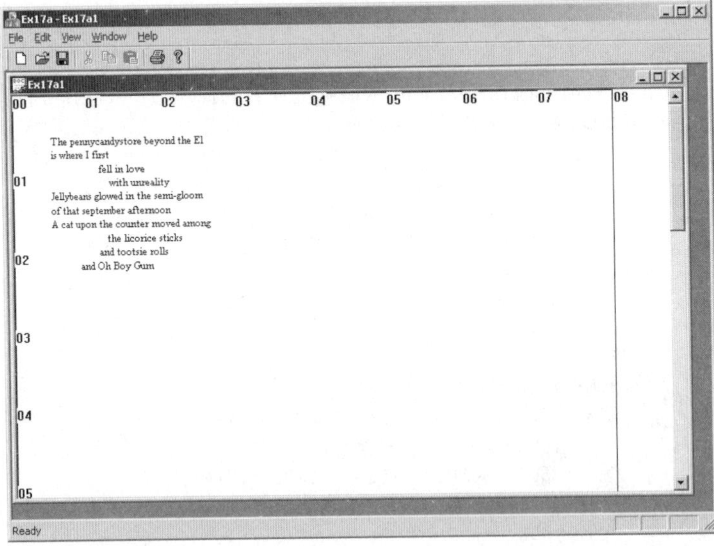

The window text is too small, isn't it? Go ahead and choose Print Preview from the File menu, and then click twice with the magnifying glass to enlarge the image. The Print Preview output is shown here:

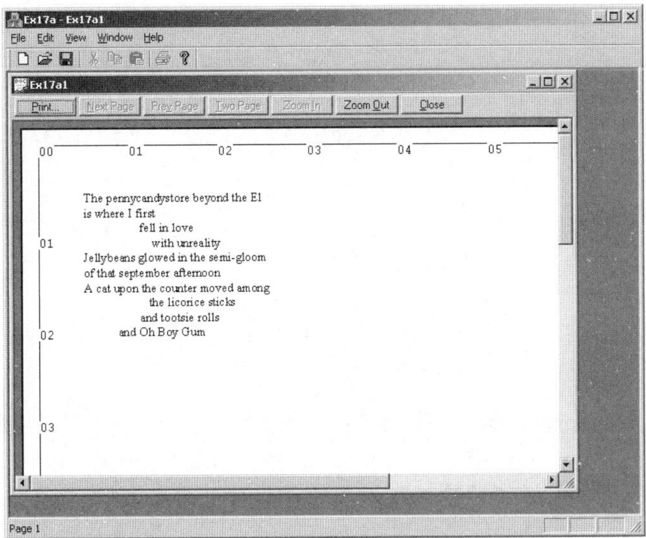

Remember logical twips from Chapter 6? We'll now use logical twips to enlarge type on the display while keeping the printed text the same size. This requires some extra work because the *CScrollView* class wasn't designed for nonstandard mapping modes. We'll change the view's base class from *CScrollView* to *CLogScrollView*, which is a class that borrows from the MFC code in ViewScrl.cpp. The files LogScrollView.h and LogScrollView.cpp are in the \vcppnet\Ex17a directory on the companion CD.

10. **Insert the *CLogScrollView* class into the project.** Copy the files LogScrollView.h and LogScrollView.cpp from the companion CD if you haven't done so already. Choose Add Existing Item from the Project menu. Select the two new files and click OK to insert them into the project.

11. **Edit the StringView.h header file.** Add the following line at the top of the file:

```
#include "LogScrollView.h"
```

Then change the line

```
class CStringView : public CScrollView
```

to

```
class CStringView : public CLogScrollView
```

12. **Edit the StringView.cpp file.** Globally replace all occurrences of *CScrollView* with *CLogScrollView*. Then edit the *OnInitialUpdate* function. Here's the edited code, which is much shorter:

```
void CStringView::OnInitialUpdate()
{
    CLogScrollView::OnInitialUpdate();
    CSize sizeTotal(m_rectPrint.Width(), -m_rectPrint.Height());
    SetLogScrollSizes(sizeTotal);
}
```

13. **Build and test the application again.** Now the screen should look like this:

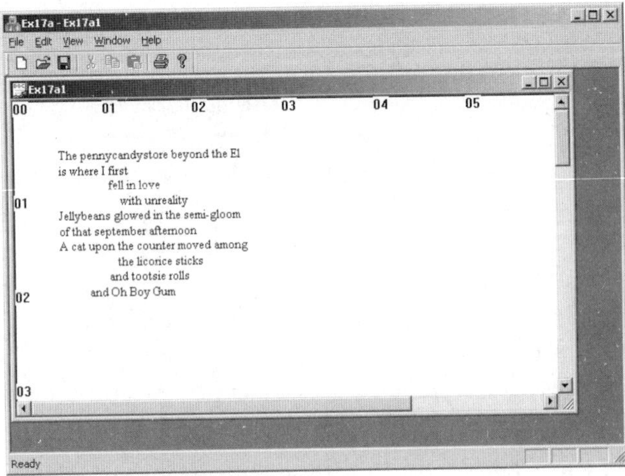

Reading the Printer Rectangle

The Ex17a program prints in a fixed-size rectangle that's appropriate for a laser printer set to portrait mode with 8.5-by-11-inch (letter-size) paper. But what if you load European-size paper or switch to landscape mode? The program should be able to adjust accordingly.

It's relatively easy to read the printer rectangle. Remember the *CPrintInfo* pointer that's passed to *OnPrint*? That structure has a data member *m_rectDraw* that contains the rectangle in logical coordinates. Your overridden *OnPrint* function simply stuffs the rectangle in a view data member, and *OnDraw* uses it. There's only one problem: You can't get the rectangle until you start printing, so the constructor still needs to set a default value for *OnDraw* to use before printing begins.

If you want the Ex17a program to read the printer rectangle and adjust the size of the scroll view, use Class View's Properties window to override *OnPrint* and then code the function as follows:

```
void CStringView::OnPrint(CDC* pDC, CPrintInfo* pInfo)
{
    m_rectPrint = pInfo->m_rectDraw;
    SetLogScrollSizes(CSize(m_rectPrint.Width(),
                      -m_rectPrint.Height()));
    CLogScrollView::OnPrint(pDC, pInfo);
}
```

Template Collection Classes Revisited: The *CArray* Class

In the Ex15b example in Chapter 15, you saw the MFC library *CTypedPtrList* template collection class, which was used to store a list of pointers to *CStudent* objects. Another collection class, *CArray*, is appropriate for our next example, Ex17b. This class is different from *CTypedPtrList* in two ways. First, it's an array, with elements accessible by index, just like *CStringArray* in Ex17a. Second, the array holds actual objects, not pointers to objects. In Ex17b, the elements are *CRect* objects. The elements' class does not have to be derived from *CObject*, and indeed, *CRect* is not.

As in Ex17b, a *typedef* makes the template collection easier to use. We'll use the following statement to define an array class that holds *CRect* objects and whose functions take *CRect* reference parameters. (It's cheaper to pass a 32-bit pointer than to copy a 128-bit object.)

```
typedef CArray<CRect, CRect&> CRectArray;
```

To use the template array, you declare an instance of *CRectArray* and then you call *CArray* member functions such as *SetSize*. You can also use the *CArray* subscript operator to get and set elements.

The template classes *CArray*, *CList*, and *CMap* are easy to use if the element class is sufficiently simple. The *CRect* class fits that description because it contains no pointer data members. Each template class uses a global function, *SerializeElements*, to serialize all the elements in the collection. The default *SerializeElements* function does a *bitwise* copy of each element to and from the archive.

If your element class contains pointers or is otherwise complex, you must write your own *SerializeElements* function. For example, if you write this function for the rectangle array (not required), your code will look like this:

```
void AFXAPI SerializeElements(CArchive& ar, CRect* pNewRects,
    int nCount)
{
    for (int i = 0; i < nCount; i++, pNewRects++) {
        if (ar.IsStoring()) {
            ar << *pNewRects;
        }
```

(continued)

```
            else {
                ar >> *pNewRects;
            }
        }
    }
```

When the compiler sees this function, it uses the function to replace the *SerializeElements* function inside the template. This only works, however, if the compiler sees the *SerializeElements* prototype before it sees the template class declaration.

> **Note** The template classes depend on two other global functions, *ConstructElements* and *DestructElements*. Starting with Microsoft Visual C++ version 4.0, these functions call the element class constructor and destructor for each object. Therefore, there's no real need to replace them.

The Ex17b Example: A Multi-Page Print Program

In this example, the document contains an array of 50 *CRect* objects that define circles. The circles are randomly positioned in a 6-by-6-inch area and have random diameters of as much as 0.5 inch. The circles, when drawn on the display, look like two-dimensional simulations of soap bubbles. Instead of drawing the circles on the printer, the application prints the corresponding *CRect* coordinates in numeric form, 12 to a page, with headers and footers. Here are the steps:

1. **Run the MFC Application Wizard to generate a project named Ex17b.** Select Single Document, and accept the defaults for all the other settings.

2. **Edit the StdAfx.h header file.** You'll need to bring in the declarations for the MFC template collection classes. Add the following statement:

   ```
   #include <afxtempl.h>
   ```

3. **Edit the Ex17bDoc.h header file.** In the Ex17a example, the document data consists of strings stored in a *CStringArray* collection. Because we're using a template collection for ellipse rectangles, we'll need a *typedef* statement outside the class declaration, as shown here:

   ```
   typedef CArray<CRect, CRect&> CRectArray;
   ```

Next, add the following public data members to the Ex17bDoc.h header file:

```
public:
    enum { nLinesPerPage = 12 };
    enum { nMaxEllipses = 50 };
    CRectArray m_ellipseArray;
```

The two enumerations are object-oriented replacements for *#defines*.

4. **Edit the Ex17bDoc.cpp implementation file.** The overridden *OnNewDocument* function initializes the ellipse array with some random values, and the *Serialize* function reads and writes the whole array. The MFC Application Wizard generated the skeletons for both functions. You don't need a *DeleteContents* function because the *CArray* subscript operator writes a new *CRect* object on top of any existing one. Add the following boldface code:

```
BOOL CEx17bDoc::OnNewDocument()
{
    if (!CDocument::OnNewDocument())
        return FALSE;

    int n1, n2, n3;
    // Make 50 random circles
    srand((unsigned) time(NULL));
    m_ellipseArray.SetSize(nMaxEllipses);

    for (int i = 0; i < nMaxEllipses; i++) {
        n1 = rand() * 600 / RAND_MAX;
        n2 = rand() * 600 / RAND_MAX;
        n3 = rand() * 50  / RAND_MAX;
        m_ellipseArray[i] = CRect(n1, -n2, n1 + n3, -(n2 + n3));
    }

    return TRUE;
}

void CEx17bDoc::Serialize(CArchive& ar)
{
    m_ellipseArray.Serialize(ar);
}
```

5. **Edit the Ex17bView.h header file.** Use the Add Member Variable Wizard and the Add Member Function Wizard, both available from Class View, to add the member variable and two function prototypes listed below. The Add Member Function Wizard will also generate skeletons for the functions in Ex17bView.cpp.

```
public:
    int m_nPage;
private:
    void PrintPageHeader(CDC *pDC);
    void PrintPageFooter(CDC *pDC);
```

The *m_nPage* data member holds the document's current page number for printing. The private functions are for the header and footer subroutines.

6. **Edit the *OnDraw* function in Ex17bView.cpp.** The overridden *OnDraw* function simply draws the bubbles in the view window. Add the boldface code shown here:

```
void CEx17bView::OnDraw(CDC* pDC)
{
    int i, j;

    CEx17bDoc* pDoc = GetDocument();
    j = pDoc->m_ellipseArray.GetUpperBound();
    for (i = 0; i < j; i++) {
        pDC->Ellipse(pDoc->m_ellipseArray[i]);
    }
}
```

7. **Insert the *OnPrepareDC* function in Ex17bView.cpp.** The view class is not a scrolling view, so the mapping mode must be set in this function. Use Class View's Properties window to override the *OnPrepareDC* function, and then add the following boldface code:

```
void CEx17bView::OnPrepareDC(CDC* pDC, CPrintInfo* pInfo)
{
    pDC->SetMapMode(MM_LOENGLISH);
}
```

8. **Insert the *OnPrint* function in Ex17bView.cpp.** The *CView* default *OnPrint* function calls *OnDraw*. In this example, we want the printed output to be entirely different from the displayed output, so the *OnPrint* function must take care of the print output without calling *OnDraw*. *OnPrint* first sets the mapping mode to *MM_TWIPS*, and then it creates a fixed-pitch font. After printing the numeric contents of 12 *m_ellipseArray* elements, *OnPrint* deselects the font. You could have created the font once in *OnBeginPrinting*, but you wouldn't have noticed the increased efficiency. Use Class View's Properties window to override the *OnPrint* function, and then add the following boldface code:

```
void CEx17bView::OnPrint(CDC* pDC, CPrintInfo* pInfo)
{
    int        i, nStart, nEnd, nHeight;
    CString    str;
    CPoint     point(720, -1440);
    CFont      font;
    TEXTMETRIC tm;

    pDC->SetMapMode(MM_TWIPS);
    CEx17bDoc* pDoc = GetDocument();
    m_nPage = pInfo->m_nCurPage; // for PrintPageFooter's benefit
    nStart = (m_nPage - 1) * CEx17bDoc::nLinesPerPage;
    nEnd = nStart + CEx17bDoc::nLinesPerPage;
     // 14-point fixed-pitch font
    font.CreateFont(-280, 0, 0, 0, 400, FALSE, FALSE,
                    0, ANSI_CHARSET, OUT_DEFAULT_PRECIS,
                    CLIP_DEFAULT_PRECIS, DEFAULT_QUALITY,
                    DEFAULT_PITCH | FF_MODERN, "Courier New");
                    // Courier New is a TrueType font
    CFont* pOldFont = (CFont*) (pDC->SelectObject(&font));
    PrintPageHeader(pDC);
    pDC->GetTextMetrics(&tm);
    nHeight = tm.tmHeight + tm.tmExternalLeading;
    for (i = nStart; i < nEnd; i++) {
        if (i > pDoc->m_ellipseArray.GetUpperBound()) {
            break;
        }
        str.Format("%6d %6d %6d %6d %6d", i + 1,
                   pDoc->m_ellipseArray[i].left,
                   pDoc->m_ellipseArray[i].top,
                   pDoc->m_ellipseArray[i].right,
                   pDoc->m_ellipseArray[i].bottom);
        point.y -= nHeight;
        pDC->TextOut(point.x, point.y, str);
    }
    PrintPageFooter(pDC);
    pDC->SelectObject(pOldFont);
}
```

9. **Edit the *OnPreparePrinting* function in Ex17bView.cpp.** The *OnPreparePrinting* function (whose skeleton is generated by the MFC Application Wizard) computes the number of pages in the document and then communicates that value to the application framework through the *SetMaxPage* function. Add the following boldface code:

```
BOOL CEx17bView::OnPreparePrinting(CPrintInfo* pInfo)
{
    CEx17bDoc* pDoc = GetDocument();
    pInfo->SetMaxPage(pDoc->m_ellipseArray.GetUpperBound() /
                      CEx17bDoc::nLinesPerPage + 1);
    return DoPreparePrinting(pInfo);
}
```

10. **Insert the page header and footer functions in Ex17bView.cpp.** These private functions, called from *OnPrint*, print the page headers and the page footers. The page footer includes the page number, stored by *OnPrint* in the view class data member *m_nPage*. The *CDC::GetTextExtent* function provides the width of the page number so that it can be right-justified. Add the boldface code shown here:

```
void CEx17bView::PrintPageHeader(CDC* pDC)
{
    CString str;

    CPoint point(0, 0);
    pDC->TextOut(point.x, point.y, "Bubble Report");
    point += CSize(720, -720);
    str.Format("%6.6s %6.6s %6.6s %6.6s %6.6s",
               "Index", "Left", "Top", "Right", "Bottom");
    pDC->TextOut(point.x, point.y, str);
}

void CEx17bView::PrintPageFooter(CDC* pDC)
{
    CString str;

    CPoint point(0, -14400); // Move 10 inches down
    CEx17bDoc* pDoc = GetDocument();
    str.Format("Document %s", (LPCSTR) pDoc->GetTitle());
    pDC->TextOut(point.x, point.y, str);
    str.Format("Page %d", m_nPage);
    CSize size = pDC->GetTextExtent(str);
    point.x += 11520 - size.cx;
    pDC->TextOut(point.x, point.y, str); // right-justified
}
```

11. **Build and test the application.** For one set of random numbers, the bubble view window looks like this:

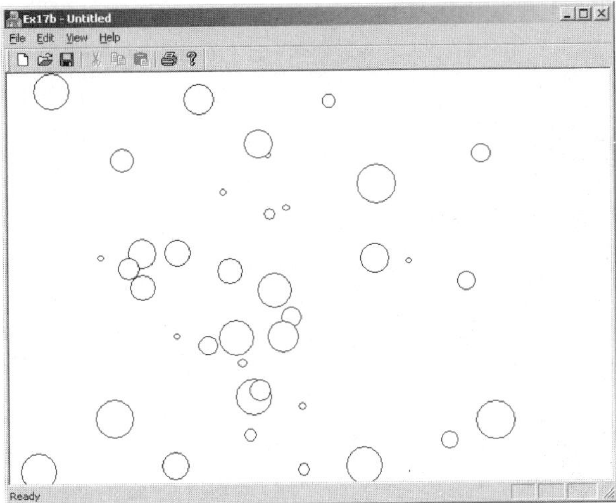

Each time you choose New from the File menu, you should see a different picture. In Print Preview, the first page of the output should look like this:

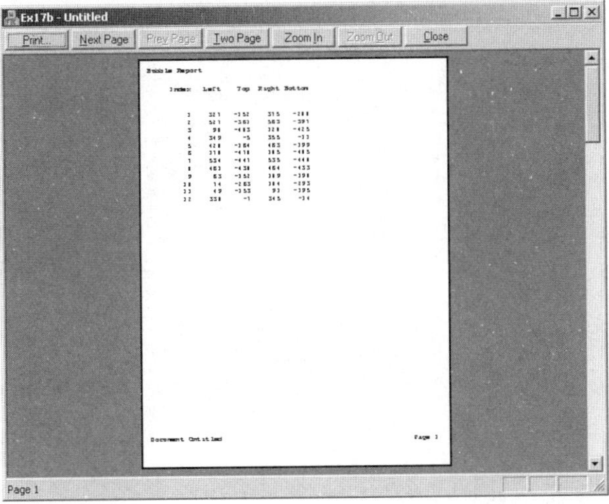

In the Print dialog box, you can specify any range of pages to print.

18

Splitter Windows and Multiple Views

Except for the Ex16b example, every program you've seen so far in this book has had only one view attached to a document. If you've used a Microsoft Windows–based word processor, you know that it's convenient to have two windows open simultaneously on different parts of a document. Both windows might show a normal view, or one window might show a print layout view and the other might show an outline view.

With the application framework, you can use a splitter window or multiple Multiple Document Interface (MDI) child windows to display multiple views. You'll learn about both presentation options in this chapter and learn how to make multiple view objects of the same view class (the normal view) in both cases. It's slightly more difficult, however, to use two or more view classes in the same application (say, the outline view and the print layout view).

This chapter emphasizes the selection and presentation of multiple views. The examples are based on a document with data initialized in the *OnNewDocument* function. You can refer back to Chapter 15 for a review of document-view communication.

The Splitter Window

A splitter window appears as a special type of frame window that holds several views in panes. The application can split the window on creation, or the user can split the window by choosing a menu command or by dragging a splitter box on the window's scroll bar. After the window has been split, the user can move the splitter bars with the mouse to adjust the relative sizes of the panes.

Splitter windows can be used in both Single Document Interface (SDI) and MDI applications. You can see examples of splitter windows on pages 461 and 463.

An object of class *CSplitterWnd* represents the splitter window. As far as Windows is concerned, a *CSplitterWnd* object is an actual window that fully occupies the frame window (*CFrameWnd* or *CMDIChildWnd*) client area. The view windows occupy the splitter window pane areas. The splitter window does not take part in the command dispatch mechanism. The active view window (in a splitter pane) is connected directly to its frame window.

View Options

When you combine multi-view presentation methods with application models, you get a number of permutations. Here are some of them:

- **SDI application with splitter window, single view class** This chapter's first example, Ex18a, illustrates this scenario. Each splitter window pane can be scrolled to a different part of the document. The programmer determines the maximum number of horizontal and vertical panes; the user makes the split at run time.
- **SDI application with splitter window, multiple view classes** The Ex18b example illustrates this scenario. The programmer determines the number of panes and the sequence of views; the user can change the pane size at run time.
- **SDI application with no splitter windows, multiple view classes** The Ex18c example illustrates this scenario. The user switches view classes by choosing a command from a menu.
- **MDI application with no splitter windows, single view class** This is the standard MDI application you saw in Chapter 16. The New Window menu command lets the user open a new child window for a document that's already open.
- **MDI application with no splitter windows, multiple view classes** A small change to the standard MDI application allows the use of multiple views. As example Ex18d shows, all you need to do is add a menu command and a handler function for each additional view class.
- **MDI application with splitter child windows** This scenario is covered thoroughly in the SCRIBBLE example in the *MFC Library Reference*.

Dynamic and Static Splitter Windows

A dynamic splitter window allows the user to split the window at any time by choosing a menu command or by dragging a splitter box on the scroll bar. The panes in a dynamic splitter window generally use the same view class. The top left pane is initialized to a particular view when the splitter window is created. In a dynamic splitter window, scroll bars are shared among the views. In a window with a single horizontal split, for example, the bottom scroll bar controls both views. A dynamic splitter application starts with a single view object. When the user splits the frame, other view objects are constructed. When the user unsplits the frame, view objects are destroyed.

The panes of a static splitter window are defined when the window is first created, and they cannot be changed. The user can move the bars but cannot unsplit or resplit the window. Static splitter windows can accommodate multiple view classes, with the configuration set at creation time. In a static splitter window, each pane has separate scroll bars. In a static splitter window application, all view objects are constructed when the frame is constructed, and they are all destroyed when the frame is destroyed.

The Ex18a Example: A Single View Class SDI Dynamic Splitter

In this example, the user can dynamically split the view into four panes with four separate view objects, all managed by a single view class. We'll use the document and the view code from the Ex17a example. The MFC Application Wizard lets you add a dynamic splitter window to a new application. You create an SDI project and select Split Window on the User Interface Features page, as shown here:

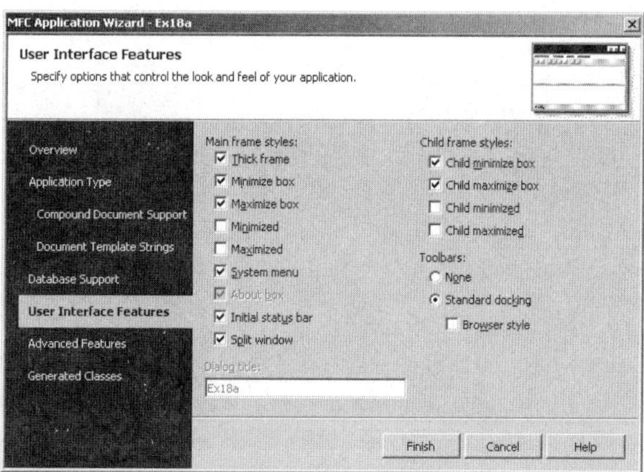

When you select the Split Window check box, the MFC Application Wizard adds code to your *CMainFrame* class. Of course, you can add the same code to the *CMainFrame* class of an existing application to add splitter capability.

Resources for Splitting

When the MFC Application Wizard generates an application with a splitter frame, it includes a Split menu command on the project's View menu. The *ID_WINDOW_SPLIT* command ID is mapped in the *CView* class within the MFC library.

CMainFrame

The application's main frame window class needs a splitter window data member and a prototype for an overridden *OnCreateClient* function. Here are the additions that the MFC Application Wizard makes to the MainFrm.h file:

```
protected:
    CSplitterWnd m_wndSplitter;
public:
    virtual BOOL OnCreateClient(LPCREATESTRUCT lpcs,
                                CCreateContext* pContext);
```

The application framework calls the *CFrameWnd::OnCreateClient* virtual member function when the frame object is created. The base class version creates a single view window as specified by the document template. The MFC Application Wizard–generated *OnCreateClient* override shown here (in MainFrm.cpp) creates a splitter window instead, and the splitter window creates the first view:

```
BOOL CMainFrame::OnCreateClient( LPCREATESTRUCT /*lpcs*/,
    CCreateContext* pContext)
{
    return m_wndSplitter.Create( this,
        2, 2,           // TODO: adjust the number of rows, columns
        CSize(10, 10),  // TODO: adjust the minimum pane size
        pContext);
}
```

The *CsplitterWnd::Create* member function creates a dynamic splitter window, and the *CSplitterWnd* object knows the view class because its name is embedded in the *CCreateContext* structure that's passed as a parameter to *Create*.

The second and third *Create* parameters (2, 2) specify that the window can be split into a maximum of two rows and two columns. If you change the parameters to (2, 1), you'll allow only a single horizontal split. The parameters (1, 2) allow only a single vertical split. The *CSize* parameter specifies the minimum pane size.

Testing the Ex18a Application

When the application starts, you can split the window by choosing Split from the View menu or by dragging the splitter boxes at the left and top of the scroll bars. Figure 18-1 shows a typical single view window with a four-way split. Multiple views share the scroll bars.

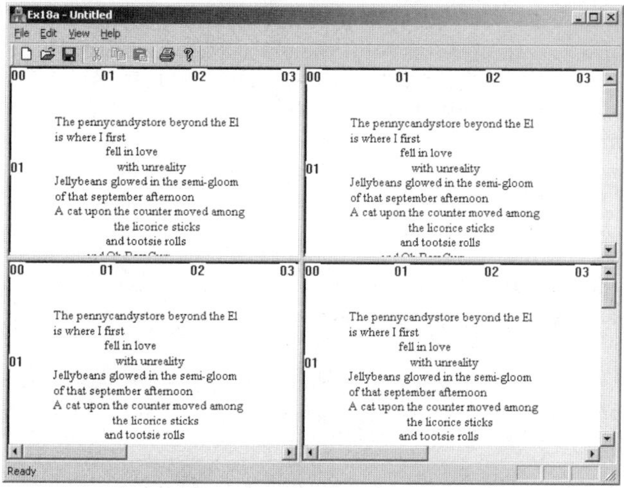

Figure 18-1 A single view window with a four-way split.

The Ex18b Example: A Double View Class SDI Static Splitter

In Ex18b, we'll extend Ex18a by defining a second view class and allowing a static splitter window to show the two views. (The H and CPP files are cloned from the original view class.) This time the splitter window works a little differently. Instead of starting off as a single pane, the splitter is initialized with two panes. The user can move the bar between the panes by dragging it with the mouse or by choosing the Window Split menu command.

The easiest way to generate a static splitter application is to let the MFC Application Wizard generate a dynamic splitter application and then edit the generated *CMainFrame::OnCreateClient* function.

CHexView

The *CHexView* class was written to allow programmers to appreciate poetry. It is essentially the same code used for *CStringView* except for the *OnDraw* member function:

```
void CHexView::OnDraw(CDC* pDC)
{
    // hex dump of document strings
    int        i, j, k, l, n, nHeight;
    CString    outputLine, str;
    CFont      font;
    TEXTMETRIC tm;

    CPoemDoc* pDoc = GetDocument();
    font.CreateFont(-160, 80, 0, 0, 400, FALSE, FALSE, 0,
        ANSI_CHARSET, OUT_DEFAULT_PRECIS, CLIP_DEFAULT_PRECIS,
        DEFAULT_QUALITY, DEFAULT_PITCH | FF_SWISS, "Arial");
    CFont* pOldFont = pDC->SelectObject(&font);
    pDC->GetTextMetrics(&tm);
    nHeight = tm.tmHeight + tm.tmExternalLeading;

    j = pDoc->m_stringArray.GetSize();
    for (i = 0; i < j; i++) {
        outputLine.Format("%02x   ", i);
        l = pDoc->m_stringArray[i].GetLength();
        for (k = 0; k < l; k++) {
            n = pDoc->m_stringArray[i][k] & 0x00ff;
            str.Format("%02x ", n);
            outputLine += str;
        }
        pDC->TextOut(720, -i * nHeight - 720, outputLine);
    }
    pDC->SelectObject(pOldFont);
}
```

This function displays a hexadecimal dump of all strings in the document's *m_stringArray* collection. Notice the use of the subscript operator to access individual characters in a *CString* object.

CMainFrame

As in Ex18a, the Ex18b application's main frame window class needs a splitter window data member and a prototype for an overridden *OnCreateClient* function. You can let the MFC Application Wizard generate the code by specifying Split Window, as in Ex18a. You don't have to modify the MainFrm.h file.

The implementation file, MainFrm.cpp, needs both view class headers (and the prerequisite document header), as shown here:

```
#include "PoemDoc.h"
#include "StringView.h"
#include "HexView.h"
```

The MFC Application Wizard generates dynamic splitter code in the *OnCreateClient* function, so you'll have to do some editing if you want a static splitter. Instead of calling *CSplitterWnd::Create*, you call the *CSplitterWnd::CreateStatic* function, which is tailored for multiple view classes. The following calls to *CSplitterWnd::CreateView* attach the two view classes. As the second and third *CreateStatic* parameters (2, 1) dictate, this splitter window contains only two panes. The horizontal split is initially 100 device units from the top of the window. The top pane is the string view; the bottom pane is the hex dump view. The user can change the splitter bar position, but not the view configuration.

```
BOOL CMainFrame::OnCreateClient( LPCREATESTRUCT /*lpcs*/,
    CCreateContext* pContext)
{
    VERIFY(m_wndSplitter.CreateStatic(this, 2, 1));
    VERIFY(m_wndSplitter.CreateView(0, 0, RUNTIME_CLASS(CStringView),
                                   CSize(100, 100), pContext));
    VERIFY(m_wndSplitter.CreateView(1, 0, RUNTIME_CLASS(CHexView),
                                   CSize(100, 100), pContext));
    return TRUE;
}
```

Testing the Ex18b Application

When you start the Ex18b application, the window should look like the one shown here. Notice the separate horizontal scroll bars for the two views.

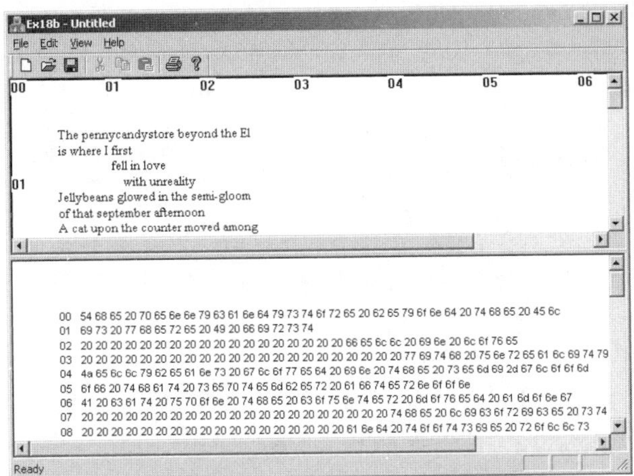

The Ex18c Example: Switching View Classes Without a Splitter

Sometimes you'll just want to switch view classes under program control and not be bothered with a splitter window. The Ex18c example is an SDI application that switches between *CStringView* and *CHexView* in response to commands on the View menu. Starting with what the MFC Application Wizard generates, all you need to do is add two new menu commands and then add some code to the *CMainFrame* class. You also need to change the *CStringView* and *CHexView* constructors from protected to public.

Resource Requirements

The following two commands have been added to the View menu in the *IDR_MAINFRAME* menu resource.

Caption	Command ID	*CMainFrame* Function
St&ring View	*ID_VIEW_STRINGVIEW*	*OnViewStringView*
&Hex View	*ID_VIEW_HEXVIEW*	*OnViewHexView*

The Class View's Properties window was used to add the command-handling functions and corresponding update command user interface handlers to the *CMainFrame* class.

CMainFrame

The *CMainFrame* class gets a new private helper function, *SwitchToView*, which is called from the two menu command handlers. The *enum* parameter tells the function which view to switch to. Here are the two added items in the MainFrm.h header file:

```
private:
    enum eView { STRING = 1, HEX = 2 };
    void SwitchToView(eView nView);
```

The *SwitchToView* function (in MainFrm.cpp) makes some low-level MFC calls to locate the requested view and activate it. Don't worry about how it works—just adapt it to your own applications when you want the view-switching feature. Add the following code:

```
void CMainFrame::SwitchToView(eView nView)
{
    CView* pOldActiveView = GetActiveView();
    CView* pNewActiveView = (CView*) GetDlgItem(nView);
    if (pNewActiveView == NULL) {
        switch (nView) {
```

```
        case STRING:
            pNewActiveView = (CView*) new CStringView;
            break;
        case HEX:
            pNewActiveView = (CView*) new CHexView;
            break;
        }
        CCreateContext context;
        context.m_pCurrentDoc = pOldActiveView->GetDocument();
        pNewActiveView->Create(NULL, NULL, WS_BORDER,
            CFrameWnd::rectDefault, this, nView, &context);
        pNewActiveView->OnInitialUpdate();
    }
    SetActiveView(pNewActiveView);
    pNewActiveView->ShowWindow(SW_SHOW);
    pOldActiveView->ShowWindow(SW_HIDE);
    pOldActiveView->SetDlgCtrlID(
        pOldActiveView->GetRuntimeClass() ==
        RUNTIME_CLASS(CStringView) ? STRING : HEX);
    pNewActiveView->SetDlgCtrlID(AFX_IDW_PANE_FIRST);
    RecalcLayout();
}
```

Finally, here are the menu command handlers and update command user interface handlers that the code wizard available from Class View's Properties window initially generated (along with message map entries and prototypes). The update command user interface handlers test the current view's class.

```
void CMainFrame::OnViewStringView()
{
    SwitchToView(STRING);
}

void CMainFrame::OnUpdateViewStringView(CCmdUI* pCmdUI)
{
    pCmdUI->Enable(
        !GetActiveView()->IsKindOf(RUNTIME_CLASS(CStringView)));
}

void CMainFrame::OnViewHexView()
{
    SwitchToView(HEX);
}

void CMainFrame::OnUpdateViewHexView(CCmdUI* pCmdUI)
{
    pCmdUI->Enable(
        !GetActiveView()->IsKindOf(RUNTIME_CLASS(CHexView)));
}
```

Testing the Ex18c Application

The Ex18c application initially displays the *CStringView* view of the document. You can toggle between the *CStringView* and *CHexView* views by choosing the appropriate command from the View menu. Both views of the document are shown side by side in Figure 18-2.

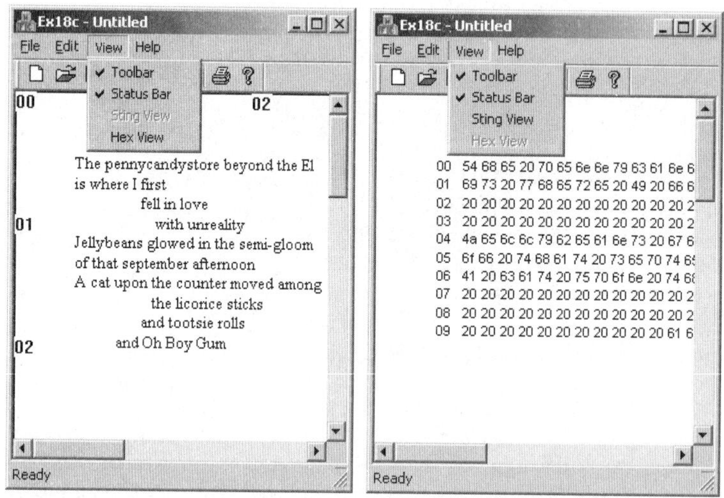

Figure 18-2 The CStringView view and the CHexView view of the document.

The Ex18d Example: A Multiple View Class MDI Application

The final example, Ex18d, uses the previous document and view classes to create a multiple view class MDI application without a splitter window. The logic is different from the logic in the other multiple view class applications. This time the action takes place in the application class in addition to the main frame class. As you study Ex18d, you'll gain more insight into the use of *CDocTemplate* objects.

This example was generated with the Context-Sensitive Help option on the Advanced Features page of the MFC Application Wizard. If you're starting from scratch, use the wizard to generate an ordinary MDI application with one of the view classes. Then add the second view class to the project and modify the application class files and main frame class files, as described in the following sections.

Resource Requirements

Two items have been added to the Window menu in the *IDR_Ex18dTYPE* menu resource:

Caption	Command ID	*CMainFrame* Function
New &String Window (replaces New Window item)	*ID_WINDOW_NEWSTRING-WINDOW*	*CMDIFrameWnd::OnWin-dowNew*
New &Hex Window	*ID_WINDOW_NEWHEX-WINDOW*	*OnWindowNewhexwindow*

Class View's Properties window was used to add the command-handling function *OnWindowNewhexwindow* to the *CMainFrame* class.

CEx18dApp

In the application class header file, Ex18d.h, the following data member and function prototype have been added:

```
public:
    CMultiDocTemplate* m_pTemplateHex;
```

The implementation file, Ex18d.cpp, contains the *#include* statements shown here:

```
#include "PoemDoc.h"
#include "StringView.h"
#include "HexView.h"
```

The *CEx18dApp InitInstance* member function has the code shown below inserted immediately after the *AddDocTemplate* function call:

```
m_pTemplateHex = new CMultiDocTemplate(
    IDR_Ex18dTYPE,
    RUNTIME_CLASS(CPoemDoc),
    RUNTIME_CLASS(CChildFrame),
    RUNTIME_CLASS(CHexView));
```

The *AddDocTemplate* call generated by the MFC Application Wizard established the primary document-frame-view combination for the application that is effective when the program starts. The template object above is a secondary template that can be activated in response to the New Hex Window menu command.

Now all you need is an *ExitInstance* member function, which overrides the *WinApp::ExitInstance* to clean up the secondary template:

```
int CEx18dApp::ExitInstance()
{
    delete m_pTemplateHex;
    return CWinApp::ExitInstance(); // saves profile settings
}
```

CMainFrame

The main frame class implementation file, MainFrm.cpp, has the *CHexView* class header (and the prerequisite document header) included:

```
#include "PoemDoc.h"
#include "HexView.h"
```

The base frame window class, *CMDIFrameWnd*, has an *OnWindowNew* function that is normally connected to the standard New Window command on the Window menu. The New String Window command is mapped to this function in Ex18d. The New Hex Window command is mapped to the command handler function below to create new hex child windows. The function is a clone of *OnWindowNew*, adapted for the hex view-specific template defined in *InitInstance*.

```
void CMainFrame::OnWindowNewhexwindow()
{
    CMDIChildWnd* pActiveChild = MDIGetActive();
    CDocument* pDocument;
    if (pActiveChild == NULL ||
            (pDocument = pActiveChild->GetActiveDocument()) == NULL) {
        TRACE("Warning:  No active document for WindowNew command\n");
        AfxMessageBox(AFX_IDP_COMMAND_FAILURE);
        return; // Command failed
    }

    // Otherwise, we have a new frame!
    CDocTemplate* pTemplate =
        ((CEx18dApp*) AfxGetApp())->m_pTemplateHex;
    ASSERT_VALID(pTemplate);
    CFrameWnd* pFrame =
        pTemplate->CreateNewFrame(pDocument, pActiveChild);
    if (pFrame == NULL) {
        TRACE("Warning:  failed to create new frame\n");
        AfxMessageBox(AFX_IDP_COMMAND_FAILURE);
        return; // Command failed
    }

    pTemplate->InitialUpdateFrame(pFrame, pDocument);
}
```

> **Note** The function cloning above is a useful MFC programming technique. You must first find a base class function that does almost what you want, and then copy it from the \Vc7\atlmfc\src\mfc subdirectory into your derived class, changing it as required. The only danger with cloning is that subsequent versions of the MFC library might implement the original function differently.

Testing the Ex18d Application

When you start the Ex18d application, a text view child window appears. Choose New Hex Window from the Window menu. The application should look like this:

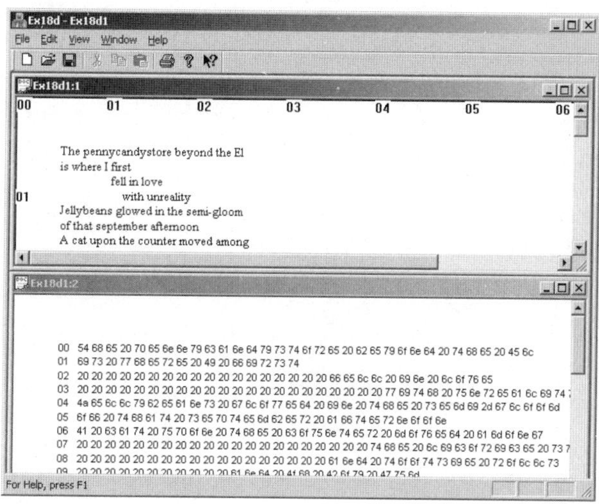

19

Context-Sensitive Help

Help technology comes in two flavors these days: HTML format and the classic WinHelp format. Microsoft Foundation Class (MFC) library application framework programs work with both WinHelp and HTML Help, but the trend is toward HTML Help. You can see an example of HTML Help in the Microsoft Visual C++ .NET online documentation.

This chapter shows you how to construct and process a simple standalone help file that has a table of contents and lets the user jump between topics. You'll also learn how your MFC library program activates the help system using help context IDs derived from window and command IDs keyed to an MFC Application Wizard–generated help file. Finally, you'll learn how to use the MFC library help message routing system to customize the help capability.

WinHelp vs. HTML Help

The choice between WinHelp and HTML Help is largely a personal one. The programmatic interface for accessing and managing each help system from MFC is the same. WinHelp uses Rich Text Format (RTF), whereas HTML Help uses HTML format. Over the last few years, several Microsoft Windows help tools such as RoboHELP from Blue Sky Software and ForeHelp from the Forefront Corporation have made writing standard WinHelp straightforward, but WinHelp implementations will probably eventually give way to HTML Help help systems.

The process of accessing topics in classic WinHelp is sequential—you get a list of topics via an index or table of contents, and when you select a topic

WinHelp takes you to another window. Here's an example of the default WinHelp produced by the MFC Application Wizard:

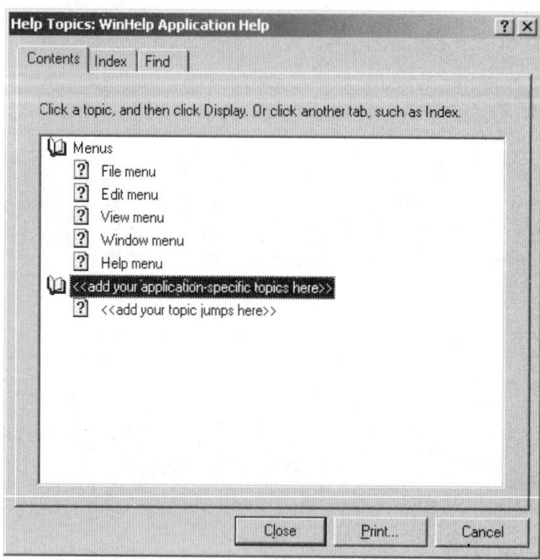

Here's the screen you see after selecting the "File menu commands" topic. You can get to the contents or the index or get back to the previous topic by clicking the appropriate button.

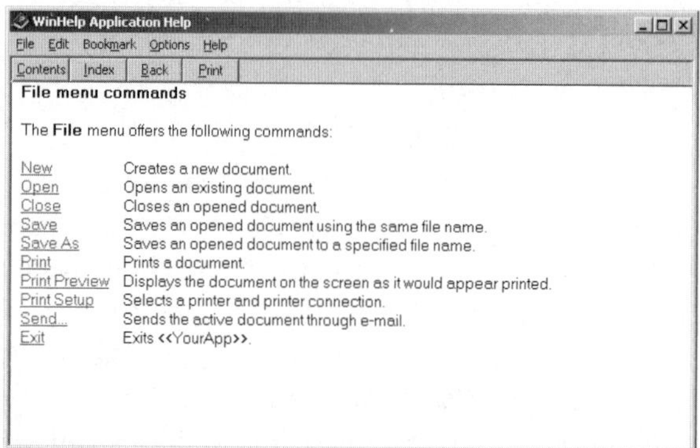

Here's an example of the default HTML Help produced by the MFC Application Wizard. Notice that the left pane of the window includes an Index tab, a Contents tab, and a Search tab, and that the topic content is shown in the right pane.

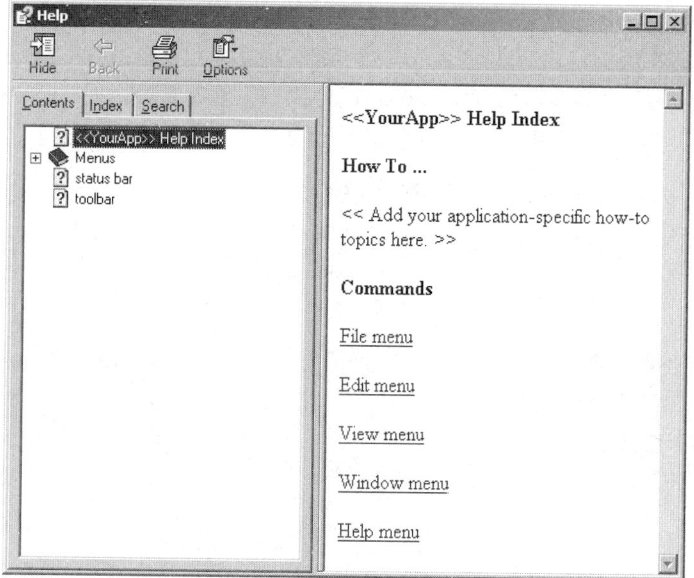

The HTML Help system is implemented as an ActiveX control named HHCtrl.ocx. HHCtrl.ocx provides navigation features and manages secondary windows and pop-up definitions. HHCtrl.ocx is flexible and will display topics from a precompiled help file as well as from HTML pages displayed in a Web browser.

Let's first look at using WinHelp in an MFC application.

The Windows WinHelp Program

If you've used commercial Windows-based applications, you're familiar with their sophisticated help screens, in which graphics, hyperlinks, and pop-ups abound. At some software firms, including Microsoft, help authoring has been elevated to a profession in its own right. This chapter won't turn you into a help expert, but you can get started by learning to prepare a simple no-frills help file.

Rich Text Format

The original Windows SDK documentation showed you how to format help files using the ASCII file format called Rich Text Format (RTF). We'll be using RTF too, but we'll be working in WYSIWYG mode to avoid the direct use of awkward escape sequences. You'll write with the same fonts, sizes, and styles that users will see on the help screens. You'll definitely need a word processor that handles RTF. Microsoft Word is just fine, but many other word processors also accommodate the RTF format.

Writing a Simple Help File

We're going to write a simple help file with a table of contents and three topics. This help file is designed to be run directly from WinHelp and started from Windows. No C++ programming is involved. Here are the steps:

1. **Create a \vcppnet\Ex19a subdirectory.**
2. **Write the main help text file.** Use Word (or another RTF-compatible word processor) to type text as shown here.

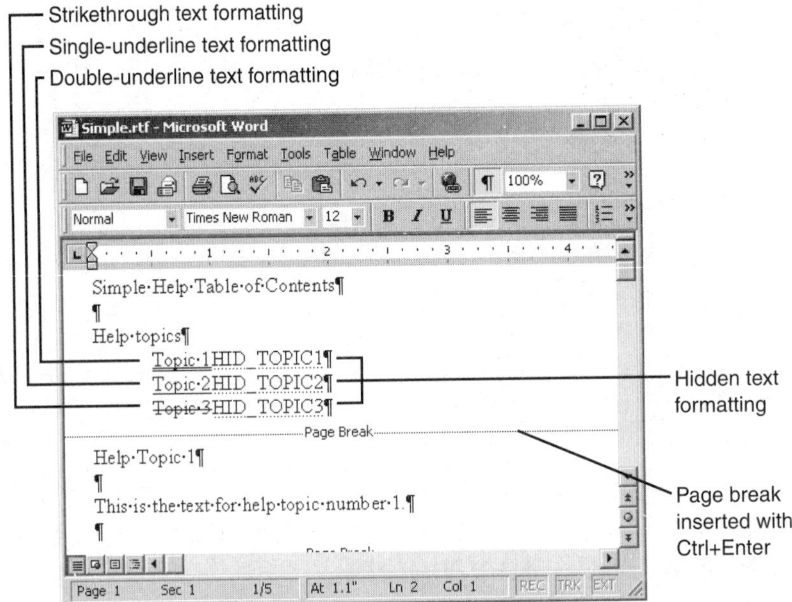

Be sure to apply the double-underline and hidden text formatting correctly and to insert the page break at the correct place.

> **Note** To see hidden text, you must turn on your word processor's hidden text viewing mode. In Word, choose Options from the Tools menu, click on the View tab, and then select All in the Formatting Marks section.

3. **Insert footnotes for the Table Of Contents screen.** The Table Of Contents screen is the first topic screen in this help system. Using the specified custom footnote marks, insert the following footnotes at the beginning of the topic title:

Footnote Mark	Text	Description
#	HID_CONTENTS	Help context ID
$	SIMPLE Help Contents	Topic title

When you're finished with this step, the document should look like this:

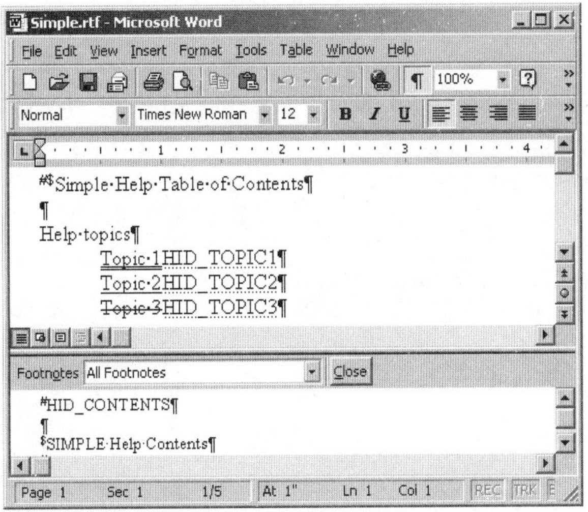

4. **Insert footnotes for the Help Topic 1 screen.** The Help Topic 1 screen is the second topic screen in the help system. Using the specified custom footnote marks, insert these footnotes:

Footnote Mark	Text	Description
#	HID_TOPIC1	Help context ID
$	SIMPLE Help Topic 1	Topic title
K	SIMPLE Topics	Keyword text

5. **Clone the Help Topic 1 screen.** Copy the entire Help Topic 1 section of the document—including the page break—to the Clipboard, and then paste two copies of the text into the document. The footnotes will be copied along with the text. In the first copy, change all occurrences of *1* to *2*. In the second copy, change all occurrences of *1* to *3*. Don't forget to change the footnotes. With Word, seeing which footnote goes with which topic can be a little difficult, so be

careful. When you're finished with this step, the document text (including footnotes) should look like this:

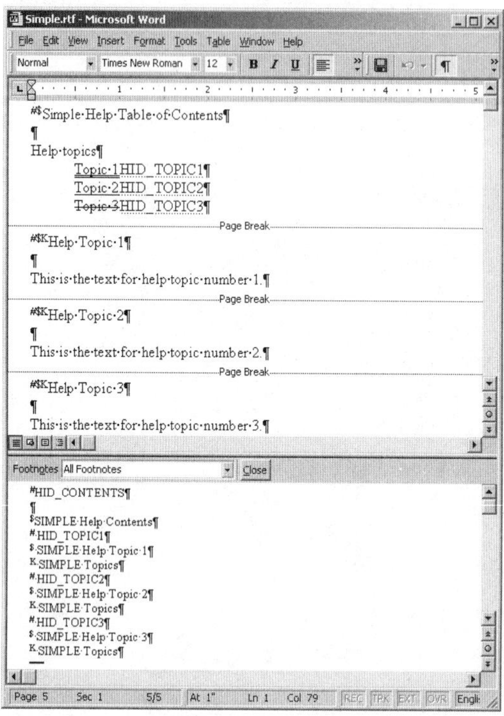

6. **Save the document.** Save the document as \vcppnet\Ex19a\Simple.rtf. Specify Rich Text Format as the file type.

7. **Write a help project file.** Using Visual C++ .NET or another text editor, create the file \vcppnet\Ex19a\Simple.hpj, as follows:

```
[OPTIONS]
CONTENTS=HID_CONTENTS
TITLE=SIMPLE Application Help
COMPRESS=true
WARNING=2

[FILES]
Simple.rtf
```

This file specifies the context ID of the Table Of Contents screen and the name of the RTF file that contains the help text. Be sure to save the file in text (ASCII) format.

8. **Build the help file.** From Windows, run the Microsoft Help Workshop (HCRTF) utility (located by default in Program Files\Microsoft Visual Studio .NET\Common7\Tools). Open the file \vcppnet\Ex19a\Simple.hpj, and then compile the help file by choosing Compile from the File menu.

   The Windows Help Compiler will run with the project file Simple.hpj. The output will be the help file Simple.hlp in the same directory.

9. **Run WinHelp with the new help file.** In Windows Explorer, double-click on the file \vcppnet\Ex19a\Simple.hlp. The Table Of Contents screen should look like this:

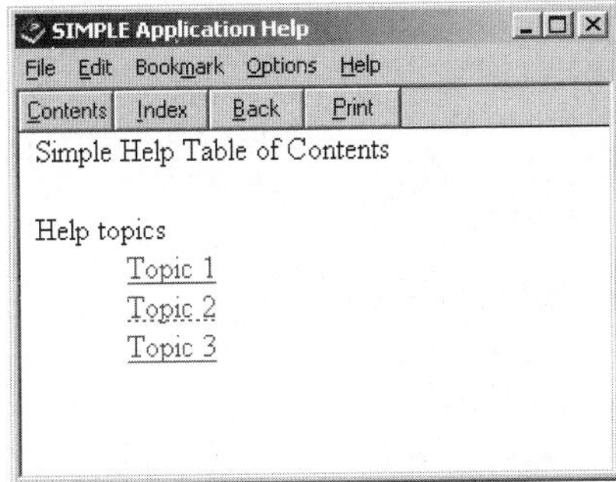

   Now move the cursor to Topic 1. Notice that the cursor changes from an arrow to a pointing hand. When you press the left mouse button, the Help Topic 1 screen should appear, as shown here:

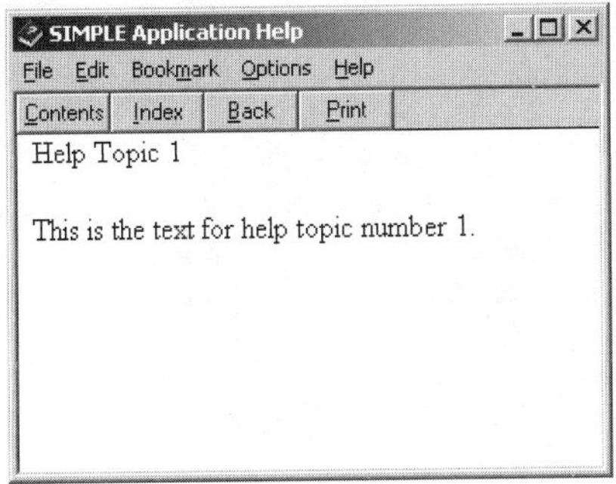

   The *HID_TOPIC1* text on the Table Of Contents screen links to the corresponding context ID (the # footnote) on the topic page. This link is known as a *jump*.

The link to Topic 2 is coded as a pop-up jump. When you click on Topic 2, here's what you'll see:

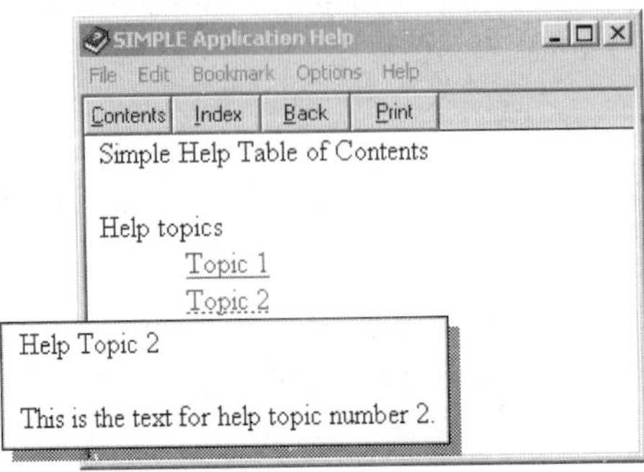

10. **Click the WinHelp Contents button.** Clicking this button should take you to the Table Of Contents screen, as shown at the beginning of step 9. WinHelp knows the ID of the Table Of Contents window because you specified it in the HPJ file.

11. **Click the WinHelp Index button.** When you click the Index button, WinHelp opens its Index dialog box, which displays the help file's list of keywords. In Simple.hlp, all topics (excluding the table of contents) have the same keyword (the K footnotes): SIMPLE Topics. When you double-click on this keyword, you'll see all associated topic titles (the $ footnotes), as shown here:

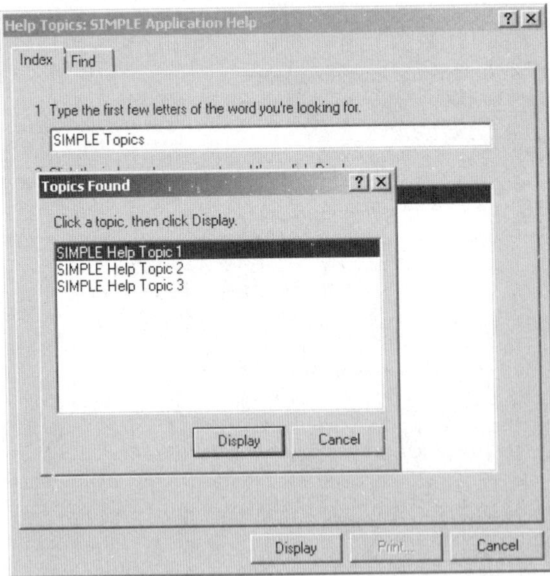

What we have here is a two-level help search hierarchy. The user can type the first few letters of the keyword and then select a topic from a list box. The more carefully you select your keywords and topic titles, the more effective your help system will be.

An Improved Table of Contents

You've been looking at an "old-style" help table of contents. The latest Win32 version of WinHelp can give you a modern, tree-view table of contents. All you need is a text file with a CNT extension. Add a new file, Simple.cnt, in the \vcppnet\Ex19a directory, containing this text:

```
:Base Simple.hlp
1 Help topics
2 Topic 1=HID_TOPIC1
2 Topic 2=HID_TOPIC2
2 Topic 3=HID_TOPIC3
```

Notice the context IDs that match the help file. The next time you run WinHelp with the Simple.hlp file, you'll see a new contents screen similar to the one shown here:

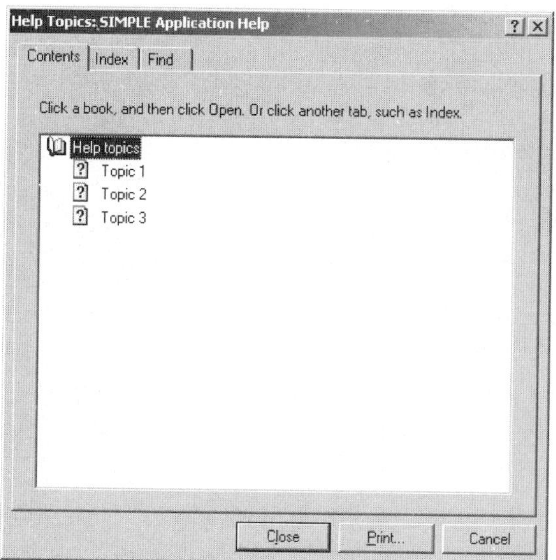

You can also use HCRTF to edit CNT files. The CNT file is independent of the HPJ file and the RTF files. If you update your RTF files, you must make corresponding changes in your CNT file.

The Application Framework and WinHelp

You've seen WinHelp running as a standalone program. The application framework and WinHelp cooperate to give you context-sensitive help. Here are some of the main elements:

1. You select the Context-Sensitive Help option when you run the MFC Application Wizard. Select WinHelp (rather than HTML Text) as the help system.
2. The MFC Application Wizard generates a Help Topics command on your application's Help menu, and it creates one or more generic RTF files together with an HPJ file and a batch file that runs the Help Compiler.
3. The MFC Application Wizard inserts a keyboard accelerator for the F1 key, and it maps the F1 key and the Help Topics command to member functions in the main frame window object.
4. When your program runs, it calls WinHelp when the user presses F1 or chooses the Help Topics command, passing a context ID that determines which help topic is displayed.

You now need to understand how WinHelp is called from another application and how your application generates context IDs for WinHelp.

Calling WinHelp

The *CWinApp* member function *WinHelp* activates WinHelp from within your application. If you look up *WinHelp* in the online documentation, you'll see a long list of actions that the optional second parameter controls. We'll ignore the second parameter and pretend that *WinHelp* has only one unsigned long integer parameter, *dwData*. This parameter corresponds to a help topic.

Suppose the SIMPLE help file is available and that your program contains the following statement:

```
AfxGetApp()->WinHelp(HID_TOPIC1);
```

When the statement is executed in response to the F1 key or some other event, the Help Topic 1 screen appears, as it would if the user had clicked on Topic 1 in the Help Table Of Contents screen.

"Wait a minute," you might say. "How does WinHelp know which help file to use?" The name of the help file matches the application name. If the executable program name is Simple.exe, the help file is named Simple.hlp.

> **Note** You can force *WinHelp* to use a different help file by setting the *CWinApp* data member *m_pszHelpFilePath*.

And how does WinHelp match the program constant *HID_TOPIC1* to the help file's context ID? The help project file must contain a MAP section that maps context IDs to numbers. If your application's resource.h file defines *HID_TOPIC1* as *101*, the Simple.hpj MAP section will look like this:

```
[MAP]
HID_TOPIC1        101
```

The program's *#define* constant name doesn't have to match the help context ID; only the numbers must match. Making the names correspond is good practice, however.

Using Search Strings

For a text-based application, you might need help based on a keyword rather than a numeric context ID. In this case, you can use the WinHelp *HELP_KEY* or *HELP_PARTIALKEY* option, as follows:

```
CString string("find this string");
AfxGetApp()->WinHelp((DWORD) (LPCSTR) string, HELP_KEY);
```

The double cast for *string* is necessary because the first *WinHelp* parameter is multi-purpose; its meaning depends on the value of the second parameter.

Calling WinHelp from the Application's Menu

The MFC Application Wizard generates a Help Topics command on the Help menu, and it maps that command to *CWnd::OnHelpFinder* in the main frame window, which calls WinHelp in this way:

```
AfxGetApp()->WinHelp(0L, HELP_FINDER);
```

With this call, WinHelp displays the Help Table Of Contents screen, and the user can navigate through the help file using jumps and searches.

If you want the old-style table of contents, you can call WinHelp in this way instead:

```
AfxGetApp()->WinHelp(0L, HELP_INDEX);
```

And if you want a "help on help" item, you can make this call:

```
AfxGetApp()->WinHelp(0L, HELP_HELPONHELP);
```

HELP_HELPONHELP is a standard identifier that asks the help system to display help on how to use Windows Help. This works only if the Winhlp32.hlp file is available.

Help Context Aliases

The ALIAS section of the HPJ file allows you to equate one context ID with another. Suppose your HPJ file contains the following statements:

```
[ALIAS]
HID_TOPIC1 = HID_GETTING_STARTED

[MAP]
HID_TOPIC1          101
```

Your RTF files can use *HID_TOPIC1* and *HID_GETTING_STARTED* interchangeably. Both will be mapped to the help context 101 as generated by your application.

Determining the Help Context

You now have enough information to add a simple context-sensitive help system to an MFC program. You define F1 (the standard MFC library Help key) as a keyboard accelerator, and then you write a command handler that maps the program's help context to a *WinHelp* parameter. You could invent your own method for mapping the program state to a context ID, but why not take advantage of the system that's already built into the application framework?

The application framework determines the help context based on the ID of the active program element. These identified program elements include menu commands, frame windows, dialog boxes, message boxes, and control bars. For example, a menu command might be identified as *ID_EDIT_CLEARALL*. The main frame window usually has the *IDR_MAINFRAME* identifier. You might expect these identifiers to map directly to help context IDs. *IDR_MAINFRAME*, for example, will map to a help context ID of the same name. But what if a frame ID and a command ID have the same numeric value? Obviously, you need a way to prevent such overlaps.

The application framework solves the overlap problem by defining a new set of help *#define* constants that are derived from program element IDs. These help constants are the sum of the element ID and a base value, as shown in the following table.

Program Element	Element ID Prefix	Help Context ID Prefix	Base (Hexadecimal)
Menu command or toolbar button	*ID_, IDM_*	*HID_, HIDM_*	10000
Frame or dialog box	*IDR_, IDD_*	*HIDR_, HIDD*	20000
Error message box	*IDP_*	*HIDP_*	30000
Nonclient area		*H...*	40000
Control bar	*IDW_*	*HIDW_*	50000
Dispatch error messages			60000

HID_EDIT_CLEARALL (0x1E121) corresponds to *ID_EDIT_CLEARALL* (0xE121), and *HIDR_MAINFRAME* (0x20080) corresponds to *IDR_MAINFRAME* (0x80).

F1 Help

Two separate context-sensitive help access methods are built into an MFC application and are available if you've selected the MFC Application Wizard's Context-Sensitive Help option. The first is standard F1 help. The user presses F1, the program makes its best guess about the help context, and then it calls WinHelp. In this mode, it is possible to determine the currently selected menu command or the currently selected window (frame, view, dialog box, or message box).

Shift+F1 Help

With Shift+F1 help, which is more powerful than the F1 mode, the program can identify the following help contexts:

- A menu command selected with the mouse cursor
- A toolbar button
- A frame window
- A view window
- A specific graphics element within a view window
- The status bar
- Various nonclient elements such as the system menu control

> **Note** Shift+F1 help doesn't work with modal dialog boxes or message boxes.

The user activates Shift+F1 help by pressing Shift+F1 or by clicking the Context Help toolbar button. In either case, the mouse cursor changes to include a question mark next to it. On the next mouse click, the help topic appears, with the position of the mouse cursor determining the context.

Message Box Help: The *AfxMessageBox* Function

The global function *AfxMessageBox* displays application framework error messages. This function is similar to the *CWnd::MessageBox* member function except that it has a help context ID as a parameter. The application framework maps this ID to a WinHelp context ID and then calls WinHelp when the user presses F1. If you can use the *AfxMessageBox* help context parameter, be sure to use prompt IDs that begin with *IDP_*. In your RTF file, use help context IDs that begin with *HIDP_*.

There are two versions of *AfxMessageBox*. In the first version, the prompt string is specified by a character-array pointer parameter. In the second version, the prompt ID parameter specifies a string resource. If you use the second version, your executable program will be more efficient. Both *AfxMessageBox* versions take a style parameter that makes the message box display an exclamation point, a question mark, or another graphics symbol.

Generic Help

When context-sensitive help is enabled, the MFC Application Wizard assembles a series of default help topics that are associated with standard MFC library program elements. Here are some of the standard topics:

- Menu and toolbar commands (File, Edit, and so forth)
- Nonclient window elements (maximize box, title bar, and so forth)
- Status bar
- Error message boxes

These topics are contained in the files AfxCore.rtf and AfxPrint.rtf, which are copied, along with the associated bitmap files, to the application's \hlp subdirectory. Your job is to customize the generic help files.

> **Note** The MFC Application Wizard generates AfxPrint.rtf only if you specify the Printing And Print Preview option.

A Help Example with No Programming Required

If you followed the instructions for the Ex18d example in Chapter 18, you selected the MFC Application Wizard's Context-Sensitive Help option. We'll now use that example to explore the application framework's built-in help capability. You'll see how easy it is to link help topics to menu command IDs and frame window resource IDs. We'll edit RTF files, not CPP files.

Here are the steps for customizing the help for Ex18d:

1. **Verify that the help file was built correctly.** If you've built the Ex18d project, the help file was probably created correctly as part of the build process. Check this by running the application and then pressing the F1 key. You should see the generic Application Help screen with the title "Modifying the Document," as shown here:

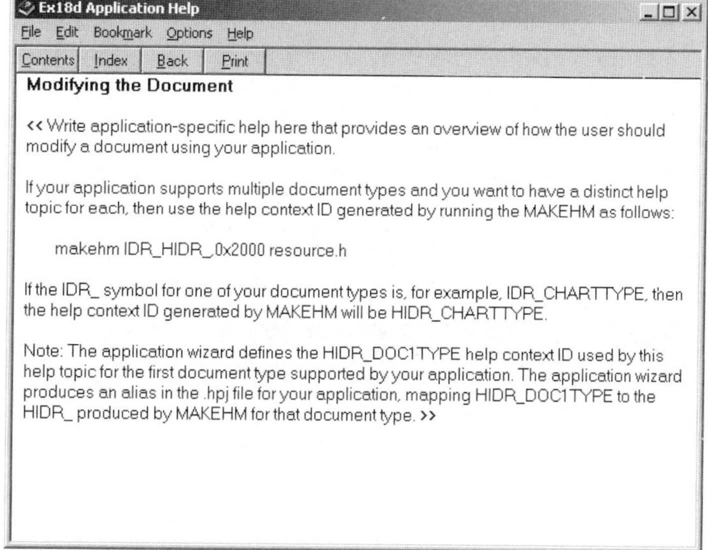

   If you do not see this screen, the help file was not built correctly. You can rebuild it by rebuilding the entire solution. Rerun the Ex18d program, and press F1 again.

2. **Test the generic help file.** Try the following experiments:

   - Close the Help dialog box, press Alt+F, and then press F1. This should open the help topic for the File New command. You can also press F1 while holding down the mouse button on the File New command to see the same help topic.

- ❑ Close the Help dialog box, click the Context Help toolbar button and then choose Save from the File menu. You should get the appropriate help topic.
- ❑ Click the Context Help toolbar button again, and then select the frame window's title bar. You should get an explanation of a Windows title bar.
- ❑ Close all child windows and then press F1. You should see a main index page that is also an old-style table of contents.

3. **Change the application title.** The file AfxCore.rtf, in the \vcppnet\Ex18d\hlp directory, contains the string <<*YourApp*>> throughout. Replace it globally with *Ex18d*.
4. **Change the Modifying The Document Help screen.** The file AfxCore.rtf in the \vcppnet\Ex18d\hlp directory contains text for the generic Application Help screen. Search on *Modifying the Document*, and then change the text to something appropriate for the application. This topic has the help context ID *HIDR_DOC1TYPE*. The generated Ex18d.hpj file provides the alias *HIDR_Ex18dTYPE*.
5. **Add a topic for the New String Window and New Hex Window commands on the Window menu.** The New String Window and New Hex Window commands were added to Ex18d, but without appropriate help text. Add a topic to AfxCore.rtf, as shown here.

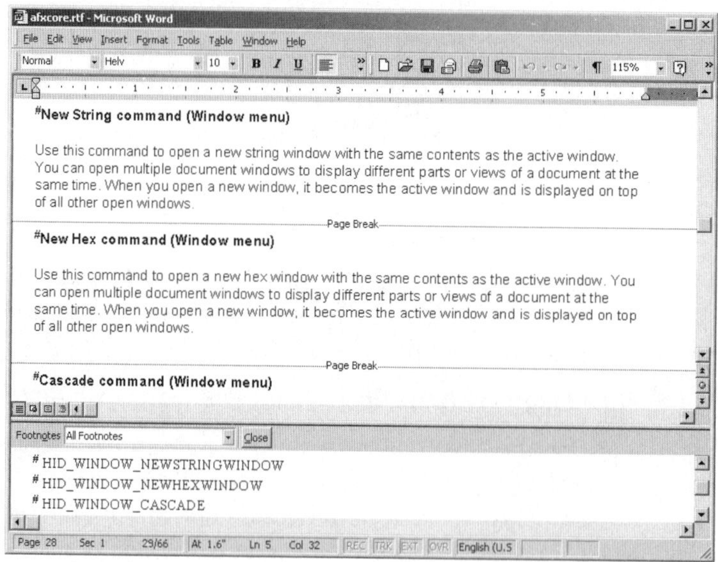

Be sure the # footnote that links the topic to the context ID uses *HID_WINDOW_NEWSTRINGWINDOW* and *HID_WINDOW_NEW-HEXWINDOW*, as defined in hlp\Ex18d.hm. The program's command ID for the New String Window command is *ID_WINDOW_NEW-STRINGWINDOW*. The command ID for a new hex window is *ID_WINDOW_NEWHEXWINDOW*.

6. **Rebuild and test the application.** Rebuild the entire application to synchronize the help files. Try the two new help links.

Help Command Processing

You've seen the components of a help file, and you've seen the effects of F1 and Shift+F1. You know how the application element IDs are linked to help context IDs. What you haven't seen is the application framework's internal processing of the help requests. Why should you be concerned? Suppose you want to provide help on a specific view window instead of a frame window. What if you need help topics linked to specific graphics items in a view window? You can address these and other needs by mapping the appropriate help messages in the view class.

Help command processing depends on whether the help request was an F1 request or a Shift+F1 request. Let's look at the processing of each help request separately.

F1 Processing

The F1 key is normally handled by a keyboard accelerator entry that the MFC Application Wizard inserts in the RC file. The accelerator associates the F1 key with an *ID_HELP* command that is sent to the *OnHelp* member function in the *CFrameWnd* class.

> **Note** In an active modal dialog box or a menu command in progress, the F1 key is processed by a Windows hook that causes the same *OnHelp* function to be called. The F1 accelerator key would otherwise be disabled.

The *CFrameWnd::OnHelp* function sends an MFC-defined *WM_COMMANDHELP* message to the innermost window, which is usually the view. If your view class does not map this message or if the handler returns

FALSE, the framework will route the message to the next outer window, which is either the MDI child frame or the main frame. If you have not mapped *WM_COMMANDHELP* in your derived frame window classes, the message will be processed in the MFC *CFrameWnd* class, which displays help for the symbol that the MFC Application Wizard generates for your application or document type.

If you map the *WM_COMMANDHELP* message in a derived class, your handler must call *CWinApp::WinHelp* with the proper context ID as a parameter.

For any application, the MFC Application Wizard adds the symbol *IDR_MAINFRAME* to your project and the HM file defines the help context ID *HIDR_MAINFRAME*, which is aliased to *main_index* in the HPJ file. The standard AfxCore.rtf file associates the main index with this context ID.

For an MDI application named SAMPLE, for example, the MFC Application Wizard will also add the symbol *IDR_SAMPLETYPE* to your project and the HM file will define the help context ID *HIDR_SAMPLETYPE*, which is aliased to *HIDR_DOC1TYPE* in the HPJ file. The standard AfxCore.rtf file will associate the topic "Modifying the Document" with this context ID.

Shift+F1 Processing

When the user presses Shift+F1 or clicks the Context Help toolbar button, a command message is sent to the *CFrameWnd* function *OnContextHelp*. When the user presses the mouse button again after positioning the mouse cursor, an MFC-defined *WM_HELPHITTEST* message is sent to the innermost window where the mouse click is detected. From that point on, the routing of this message is identical to that for the *WM_COMMANDHELP* message, described previously.

The *lParam* parameter of *OnHelpHitTest* contains the mouse coordinates in device units, relative to the upper left corner of the window's client area. The *y* value is in the high-order half; the *x* value is in the low-order half. You can use these coordinates to set the help context ID specifically for an item in the view. Your *OnHelpHitTest* handler should return the correct context ID; the framework will call *WinHelp*.

Example Ex19b: Help Command Processing

Ex19b is based on example Ex18d from Chapter 18. It's a two-view MDI application with view-specific help added. Each of the two view classes has an *OnCommandHelp* message handler to process F1 help requests and an *OnHelpHitTest* message handler to process Shift+F1 help requests.

Header Requirements

The compiler recognizes help-specific identifiers only if the following #include statement is present:

```
#include <afxpriv.h>
```

In Ex19b, the statement is in the StdAfx.h file.

CStringView

The modified string view in StringView.h needs message map function prototypes for both F1 help and Shift+F1 help, as shown here:

```
afx_msg LRESULT OnCommandHelp(WPARAM wParam, LPARAM lParam);
afx_msg LRESULT OnHelpHitTest(WPARAM wParam, LPARAM lParam);
```

Here are the message map entries in StringView.cpp:

```
ON_MESSAGE(WM_COMMANDHELP, OnCommandHelp)
ON_MESSAGE(WM_HELPHITTEST, OnHelpHitTest)
```

The *OnCommandHelp* message handler member function in StringView.cpp processes F1 help requests. It responds to the message sent from the MDI main frame and displays the help topic for the string view window, as shown here:

```
LRESULT CStringView::OnCommandHelp(WPARAM wParam, LPARAM lParam)
{
    if (lParam == 0) { // context not already determined
        lParam = HID_BASE_RESOURCE + IDR_STRINGVIEW;
    }
    AfxGetApp()->WinHelp(lParam);
    return TRUE;
}
```

Finally, the *OnHelpHitTest* member function handles Shift+F1 help, as shown here:

```
LRESULT CStringView::OnHelpHitTest(WPARAM wParam, LPARAM lParam)
{
    return HID_BASE_RESOURCE + IDR_STRINGVIEW;
}
```

In a more complex application, you might want *OnHelpHitTest* to set the help context ID based on the mouse cursor position.

CHexView

The *CHexView* class processes help requests the same way as the *CStringView* class does. Following is the necessary header code in HexView.h:

```
afx_msg LRESULT OnCommandHelp(WPARAM wParam, LPARAM lParam);
afx_msg LRESULT OnHelpHitTest(WPARAM wParam, LPARAM lParam);
```

Here are the message map entries in HexView.cpp:

```
ON_MESSAGE(WM_COMMANDHELP, OnCommandHelp)
ON_MESSAGE(WM_HELPHITTEST, OnHelpHitTest)
```

And here is the implementation code in HexView.cpp:

```
LRESULT CHexView::OnCommandHelp(WPARAM wParam, LPARAM lParam)
{
    if (lParam == 0) { // context not already determined
        lParam = HID_BASE_RESOURCE + IDR_HEXVIEW;
    }
    AfxGetApp()->WinHelp(lParam);
    return TRUE;
}

LRESULT CHexView::OnHelpHitTest(WPARAM wParam, LPARAM lParam)
{
    return HID_BASE_RESOURCE + IDR_HEXVIEW;
}
```

Resource Requirements

Two new symbols were added to the project's Resource.h file. Their values and corresponding help context IDs are shown here:

Symbol	Value	Help Context ID	Value
IDR_STRINGVIEW	101	*HIDR_STRINGVIEW*	0x20065
IDR_HEXVIEW	102	*HIDR_HEXVIEW*	0x20066

Help File Requirements

Two topics were added to the AfxCore.rtf file with the help context IDs *HIDR_STRINGVIEW* and *HIDR_HEXVIEW*, as shown here:

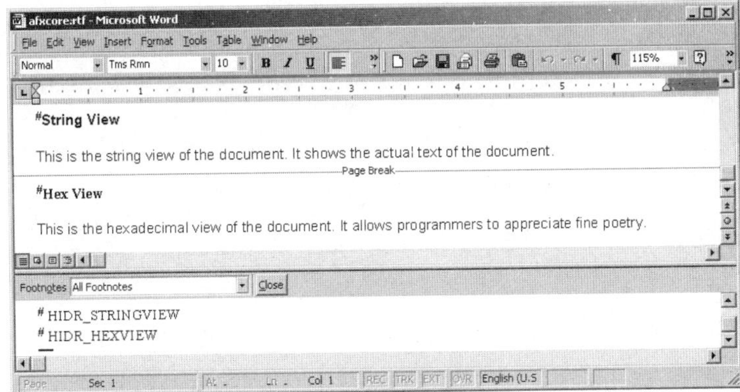

The generated Ex19b.hm file, which is in the project's \hlp subdirectory, should look like this:

```
// Commands (ID_* and IDM_*)
HID_WINDOW_NEWHEXWINDOW                         0x10082
HID_WINDOW_NEWSTRINGWINDOW                      0x10083

// Prompts (IDP_*)
HIDP_OLE_INIT_FAILED                    0x30064

// Resources (IDR_*)
HIDR_MANIFEST                           0x20001
HIDR_MAINFRAME                          0x20080
HIDR_Ex19bTYPE                          0x20081
HIDR_STRINGVIEW                         0x20065
HIDR_HEXVIEW                            0x20066

// Dialogs (IDD_*)
HIDD_ABOUTBOX                           0x20064

// Frame Controls (IDW_*)
```

Testing the Ex19b Application

To test the application, open a string child window and a hexadecimal child window. Test the action of F1 help and Shift+F1 help within those windows.

MFC and HTML Help

When you add help to your application, the second option is to use HTML Help. MFC applications access HTML Help in much the same way that they access WinHelp file. The application feeds context-sensitive help IDs into the help system, and the help system displays the appropriate help screen. However, HTML Help files are constructed differently than WinHelp files. HTML Help files are compiled from a number of HTML pages rather than from a single RTF file.

The following table shows the files generated by the MFC Application Wizard when you select HTML Help Format as the help system:

File	Description
HTMLDefines.h	Includes the context IDs for the entire project.
HTML help documents	HTML files that define the help text—generally one per help topic.
projectname.hhc	HTML Help Compiler file that contains instructions to the HTML Help compiler about how to compile the help contents.
projectname.hhp	HTML Help Compiler file that defines directives for compiling a help project.
Main_index.htm	Top-level HTM file. This is also where you add your own help topics.

Let's take a look at how to add HTML Help to an MFC application.

Example Ex19c: HTML Help

Ex19c is also based on example Ex18d. It is an MDI application that includes two views to a single document and uses HTML Help. The example was created using the MFC Application Wizard with HTML Help Format selected on the Advanced Features page.

If you look in the file hid_window_newhexwindow.htm, you'll see some updated help text reflecting the New String Window menu command. This is the text that appears whenever you select context-sensitive help for the New String Window command. Also notice a new file (one not generated by the MFC Application Wizard) named hid_window_newhex.htm, which is the help text that appears for the New Hex Window command.

If you're feeling gutsy, you can modify the help files with Notepad. The file includes tags that are used by the HTML help system, so tread lightly. However, a better option is to open the .HTM file in Visual Studio .NET. Visual Studio .NET understands HTML files and lets you edit them easily.

You might wonder how to create new help topics in the first place? The easiest way to create a new help topic is to take an existing HTM file, rename it appropriately, and then add new content to the file. Then you associate the new HTM file with the command ID as described below.

Visual Studio .NET adds help context IDs when you add new menu commands to the program and recompile it. Near the top of the HTMLDefines.h file, you'll see the following lines, which define help contexts for the New String Window menu command and the New Hex Window menu command:

```
#define HID_WINDOW_NEWSTRINGWINDOW                    0x10082
#define HID_WINDOW_NEWHEXWINDOW                       0x10083
```

In addition to the standard menu command help created by the MFC Application Wizard, Ex19c has a new help topic for the New Hex Window command. The help context ID was generously included by Visual Studio .NET when the command was added. Now it needs to be tied to the hid_window_newhexwindow.htm file. A line in the Ex19c.hhp file associates the help context ID with the help file:

```
hid_window_newhexwindow            = hid_window_newhexwindow.htm
```

Finally, the Ex19c.hhp file includes a reference to the new HTML file under the files tag:

```
[FILES]
afx_hidd_color.htm
afx_hidd_fileopen.htm
afx_hidd_filesave.htm
⋮
hid_window_newstringwindow.htm
hid_window_newhexwindow.htm
hid_window_split.htm
⋮
```

Once you relate the HTML files to the help command IDs, there's nothing else you need to do to get the help topics working. The rest of the built-in MFC help functionality will take care of the details for you. To see for yourself, run the Ex19c example, select various menu commands and push F1. You'll see the correct help screens appear after pressing F1.

20

Dynamic-Link Libraries

Dynamic-link libraries (DLLs) lie at the heart of the Microsoft Windows component model—even with the Microsoft .NET common language runtime right around the corner. Windows is itself composed of DLLs, which are binary modules. Binary modularity is different from source code modularity, which is what C++ employs. Instead of programming giant EXEs that you must rebuild and test each time you make a change, you can build smaller DLL modules and test them individually. You can, for example, put a C++ class in a DLL, which might be as small as 12 KB after compiling and linking. Client programs can load and link your DLL very quickly when they run.

DLLs have become quite easy to write. Win32 has greatly simplified the programming model, and more and better support is available from the Microsoft Foundation Class (MFC) DLL Wizard and the MFC library. This chapter shows you how to write DLLs in C++ and how to write client programs that use DLLs. We'll explore how Win32 maps DLLs into your processes, and you'll learn the differences between MFC library regular DLLs and MFC library extension DLLs. You'll see examples of simple DLLs of both types as well as a more complex DLL example that implements a custom control.

DLL Fundamentals

Before we look at the application framework's support for DLLs, you must understand how Win32 integrates DLLs into your process. You might want to review Chapter 10 to refresh your knowledge of processes and virtual memory. Remember that a process is a running instance of a program and that the program starts out as an EXE file on disk.

Basically, a DLL is a file on disk (usually with a DLL extension) consisting of global data, compiled functions, and resources that becomes part of your process. A DLL is compiled to load at a preferred base address, and if there's no conflict with other DLLs, the file is mapped to the same virtual address in your process. The DLL has various exported functions, and the client program (the program that loaded the DLL in the first place) imports those functions. Windows matches up the imports and exports when it loads the DLL.

> **Note** Win32 DLLs allow exported global variables as well as functions.

In Win32, each process gets its own copy of the DLL's read/write global variables. If you want to share memory among processes, you must use a memory-mapped file or declare a shared data section, as described in Jeffrey Richter's *Programming Applications for Microsoft Windows* (Microsoft Press, 1999). Whenever your DLL requests heap memory, that memory is allocated from the client process's heap.

How Imports Are Matched to Exports

A DLL contains a table of exported functions. These functions are identified to the outside world by their symbolic names and (optionally) by integers called *ordinal numbers*. The function table also contains the addresses of the functions within the DLL. When the client program first loads the DLL, it doesn't know the addresses of the functions it needs to call, but it does know the symbols or ordinals. The dynamic linking process then builds a table that connects the client's calls to the function addresses in the DLL. If you edit and rebuild the DLL, you don't need to rebuild your client program unless you've changed function names or parameter sequences.

> **Note** In a simple world, you'd have one EXE file that imports functions from one or more DLLs. In the real world, many DLLs call functions inside other DLLs. Thus, a particular DLL can have both exports and imports. This is not a problem because the dynamic linkage process can handle cross-dependencies.

In the DLL code, you must explicitly declare your exported functions as follows. (The alternative is to list your exported functions in a module-definition [DEF] file, but that's usually more troublesome.)

```
__declspec(dllexport) int MyFunction(int n);
```

On the client side, you must declare the corresponding imports like this:

```
__declspec(dllimport) int MyFunction(int n);
```

If you're using C++, the compiler generates a decorated name for *MyFunction* that other languages can't use. These decorated names are the long names that the compiler invents based on class name, function name, and parameter types. They are listed in the project's MAP file. If you want to use the plain name *MyFunction*, you have to write the declarations in this way:

```
extern "C" __declspec(dllexport) int MyFunction(int n);
extern "C" __declspec(dllimport) int MyFunction(int n);
```

> **Note** By default, the compiler uses the *__cdecl* argument-passing convention, which means that the calling program pops the parameters off the stack. Some client languages might require the *__stdcall* convention, which replaces the Pascal calling convention and results in the called function popping the stack. As a result, you might have to use the *__stdcall* modifier in your DLL export declaration.

Just having import declarations isn't enough to make a client link to a DLL. The client's project must specify the import library (LIB) to the linker, and the client program must actually contain a call to at least one of the DLL's imported functions. That call statement must be in an executable path in the program.

Implicit Linkage vs. Explicit Linkage

The preceding section primarily described *implicit linking*, which is what C++ programmers will probably use for their DLLs. When you build a DLL, the linker produces a companion import LIB file, which contains every DLL's exported symbols and (optionally) ordinals, but no code. The LIB file is a surrogate for the DLL that's added to the client program's project. When you build (statically link) the client, the imported symbols are matched to the exported symbols in the LIB file, and those symbols (or ordinals) are bound into the EXE file. The LIB file also contains the DLL filename (but not its full pathname), which gets stored in the EXE file. When the client is loaded, Windows finds and loads the DLL and then dynamically links it by symbol or by ordinal.

Explicit linking is more appropriate for interpreted languages such as Microsoft JScript, but you can use it from C++ if you need to. With explicit linking, you don't use an import file; instead, you call the Win32 *LoadLibrary* function, specifying the DLL's pathname as a parameter. *LoadLibrary* returns an

HINSTANCE parameter that you can use in a call to *GetProcAddress*, which converts a symbol (or an ordinal) to an address inside the DLL.

Suppose you have a DLL that exports a function such as this:

```
extern "C" __declspec(dllexport) double SquareRoot(double d);
```

Here's an example of a client's explicit linkage to the function:

```
typedef double (SQRTPROC)(double);
HINSTANCE hInstance;
SQRTPROC* pFunction;
VERIFY(hInstance = ::LoadLibrary("c:\\winnt\\system32\\mydll.dll"));
VERIFY(pFunction = (SQRTPROC*)::GetProcAddress(hInstance, "SquareRoot"));
double d = (*pFunction)(81.0); // Call the DLL function
```

With implicit linkage, all DLLs are loaded when the client is loaded, but with explicit linkage, you can determine when DLLs are loaded and unloaded. Explicit linkage allows you to determine at run time which DLLs to load. You can, for example, have one DLL with string resources in English and another with string resources in Spanish. Your application will load the appropriate DLL after the user chooses a language.

Symbolic Linkage vs. Ordinal Linkage

In Win16, the more efficient ordinal linkage was the preferred linkage option. In Win32, the efficiency of symbolic linkage has been improved. Microsoft now recommends symbolic over ordinal linkage. The DLL version of the MFC library, however, uses ordinal linkage.

A typical MFC program might link to hundreds of functions in the MFC DLL. Ordinal linkage permits that program's EXE file to be smaller because it does not have to contain the long symbolic names of its imports. If you build your own DLL with ordinal linkage, you must specify the ordinals in the project's DEF file, which doesn't have too many other uses in the Win32 environment. If your exports are C++ functions, you must use decorated names in the DEF file (or declare your functions with *extern "C")*.

Here's a short extract from one of the MFC library DEF files:

```
??0CRecentFileList@@QAE@IPBD0HH@Z @ 479 NONAME
??0CRecordset@@QAE@PAVCDatabase@@@Z @ 480 NONAME
??0CRecordView@@IAE@I@Z @ 481 NONAME
??0CRecordView@@IAE@PBD@Z @ 482 NONAME
??0CRectTracker@@QAE@PBUtagRECT@@I@Z @ 483 NONAME
??0CReObject@@QAE@PAVCRichEditCntrItem@@@Z @ 484 NONAME
??0CReObject@@QAE@XZ @ 485 NONAME
??0CResetPropExchange@@QAE@XZ @ 486 NONAME
??0CRichEditCntrItem@@QAE@PAU_reobject@@PAVCRichEditDoc@@@Z @ 487 NONAME
??0CRichEditDoc@@IAE@XZ @ 488 NONAME
```

```
??0CRichEditView@@QAE@XZ @ 489 NONAME
??0CScrollView@@IAE@XZ @ 490 NONAME
??0CSemaphore@@QAE@JJPBDPAU_SECURITY_ATTRIBUTES@@@Z @ 491 NONAME
??0CSharedFile@@QAE@II@Z @ 492 NONAME
```

The numbers after the @ symbols are the ordinals. (Kind of makes you want to use symbolic linkage instead, doesn't it?)

The DLL Entry Point: *DllMain*

By default, the linker assigns the main entry point *_DllMainCRTStartup* to your DLL. When Windows loads the DLL, it calls this function, which first calls the constructors for global objects and then calls the global function *DllMain*, which you're supposed to write. *DllMain* is called not only when the DLL is attached to the process but also when it is detached (and at other times as well).

Here's a skeleton *DllMain* function:

```
HINSTANCE g_hInstance;
extern "C" int APIENTRY
    DllMain(HINSTANCE hInstance, DWORD dwReason, LPVOID lpReserved)
{
    if (dwReason == DLL_PROCESS_ATTACH)
    {
        TRACE0("Ex20a.DLL Initializing!\n");
        // Do initialization here
    }
    else if (dwReason == DLL_PROCESS_DETACH)
    {
        TRACE0("Ex20a.DLL Terminating!\n");
        // Do cleanup here
    }
    return 1;   // ok
}
```

If you don't write a *DllMain* function for your DLL, a do-nothing version will be brought in from the runtime library.

The *DllMain* function is also called when individual threads are started and terminated, as indicated by the *dwReason* parameter. Richter's book tells you all you need to know about this complex subject.

Instance Handles: Loading Resources

Each DLL in a process is identified by a unique 32-bit *HINSTANCE* value. In addition, the process itself has an *HINSTANCE* value. All these instance handles are valid only within a particular process, and they represent the starting virtual address of the DLL or EXE. In Win32, the *HINSTANCE* and *HMODULE* values are the same and the types can be used interchangeably. The process (EXE) instance handle is almost always 0x400000, and the handle for a DLL loaded at the default base address is 0x10000000. If your program uses several DLLs, each will have a different *HINSTANCE* value, either because the DLLs had different base addresses specified at build time or because the loader copied and relocated the DLL code.

Instance handles are particularly important for loading resources. The Win32 *FindResource* function takes an *HINSTANCE* parameter. EXEs and DLLs can each have their own resources. If you want a resource from the DLL, you specify the DLL's instance handle. If you want a resource from the EXE file, you specify the EXE's instance handle.

How do you get an instance handle? If you want the EXE's handle, you call the Win32 *GetModuleHandle* function with a *NULL* parameter. If you want the DLL's handle, you call the Win32 *GetModuleHandle* function with the DLL name as a parameter. Later, you'll see that the MFC library has its own method of loading resources by searching various modules in sequence.

How the Client Program Finds a DLL

If you link explicitly using *LoadLibrary*, you can specify the DLL's full pathname. If you don't specify the pathname, or if you link implicitly, Windows will follows this search sequence to locate your DLL:

1. The directory containing the EXE file
2. The process's current directory
3. The Windows system directory
4. The Windows directory
5. The directories listed in the *Path* environment variable

Here's a trap you can easily fall into. You build a DLL as one project, copy the DLL file to the system directory, and then run the DLL from a client program. So far, so good. Next, you rebuild the DLL with some changes, but you forget to copy the DLL file to the system directory. The next time you run the client program, it loads the old version of the DLL. Be careful!

Debugging a DLL

Visual C++ makes debugging a DLL easy. You just run the debugger from the DLL project. The first time you do this, the debugger will ask for the pathname of the client EXE file. Every time you "run" the DLL from the debugger after this, the debugger will load the EXE, but the EXE will use the search sequence to find the DLL. This means that you must either set the *Path* environment variable to point to the DLL or copy the DLL to a directory in the search sequence.

MFC DLLs: Extension vs. Regular

We've been looking at Win32 DLLs that have a *DllMain* function and some exported functions. Now we'll move on to the MFC application framework, which adds its own support layer on top of the Win32 basics. The MFC Application Wizard lets you build two kinds of DLLs with MFC library support: extension DLLs and regular DLLs. You must understand the differences between these two types so you can decide which one is best for your needs.

> **Note** Of course, Visual C++ .NET lets you build a pure Win32 DLL without the MFC library, just as it lets you build a Windows-based program without the MFC library.

An extension DLL supports a C++ interface. In other words, the DLL can export whole classes and the client can construct objects of those classes or derive classes from them. An extension DLL dynamically links to the code in the DLL version of the MFC library. Therefore, an extension DLL requires that your client program be dynamically linked to the MFC library (the MFC Application Wizard default) and that both the client program and the extension DLL be synchronized to the same version of the MFC DLLs (mfc70.dll, mfc70d.dll, and so on). Extension DLLs are quite small; you can build a simple extension DLL with a size of 10 KB, which will load quickly.

If you need a DLL that can be loaded by any Win32 programming environment, you should use a regular DLL. A big restriction here is that the regular DLL can export only C-style functions. It can't export C++ classes, member functions, or overloaded functions because every C++ compiler has its own method of decorating names. You can, however, use C++ classes (and MFC library classes, in particular) inside your regular DLL. Implementing a COM interface for your DLL also solves the issue of integrating with Visual Basic.

When you build an MFC regular DLL, you can choose to statically link or dynamically link to the MFC library. If you choose static linking, your DLL will include a copy of all the MFC library code it needs and will thus be self-contained. A typical release-build statically linked regular DLL is about 144 KB. If you choose dynamic linking, the size will drop to about 17 KB but you'll have to ensure that the proper MFC DLLs are present on the target machine. That's no problem if the client program is already dynamically linked to the same version of the MFC library.

When you tell the MFC wizards what kind of DLL or EXE you want, compiler *#define* constants are set as shown in the following table.

	Dynamically Linked to Shared MFC Library	Statically Linked to MFC Library
Regular DLL	*_AFXDLL, _USRDLL*	_USRDLL
Extension DLL	*_AFXEXT, _AFXDLL*	Unsupported option
Client EXE	*_AFXDLL*	No constants defined

If you look inside the MFC source code and header files, you'll see a lot of *#ifdef* statements for these constants. This means that the library code is compiled quite differently depending on the kind of project you're producing.

MFC Extension DLLs: Exporting Classes

If your extension DLL contains only exported C++ classes, you'll have an easy time building and using it. The steps shown later for building the Ex20a example show you how to tell the MFC DLL Wizard that you're building an extension DLL skeleton. That skeleton has only the *DllMain* function. You simply add your own C++ classes to the project. There's only one special thing you must do: You must add the macro *AFX_EXT_CLASS* to the class declaration, as shown here:

```
class AFX_EXT_CLASS CStudent : public CObject
```

This modification goes into the H file that's part of the DLL project, and it also goes into the H file that client programs use. In other words, the H files are exactly the same for both client and DLL. The macro generates different code depending on the situation—it exports the class in the DLL and imports the class in the client.

The MFC Extension DLL Resource Search Sequence

If you build a dynamically linked MFC client application, many of the MFC library's standard resources (error message strings, print preview dialog templates, and so on) will be stored in the MFC DLLs, but your application will have its own resources, too. When you call an MFC function such as *CString::LoadString* or *CBitmap::LoadBitmap*, the framework will step in and search first the EXE file's resources and then the MFC DLL's resources.

If your program includes an extension DLL and your EXE needs a resource, the search sequence will be first the EXE file, then the extension DLL, and then the MFC DLLs. If you have a string resource ID, for example, that is unique among all resources, the MFC library will find it. If you have duplicate string IDs in your EXE file and your extension DLL file, the MFC library will load the string in the EXE file.

If the extension DLL loads a resource, the sequence will be first the extension DLL, then the MFC DLLs, and then the EXE.

You can change the search sequence if you need to. Suppose you want your EXE code to search the extension DLL's resources first. You can use code such as this:

```
HINSTANCE hInstResourceClient = AfxGetResourceHandle();
// Use DLL's instance handle
AfxSetResourceHandle(::GetModuleHandle("mydllname.dll"));
CString strRes;
strRes.LoadString(IDS_MYSTRING);
// Restore client's instance handle
AfxSetResourceHandle(hInstResourceClient);
```

You can't use *AfxGetInstanceHandle* instead of *::GetModuleHandle*. In an extension DLL, *AfxGetInstanceHandle* returns the EXE's instance handle, not the DLL's handle.

The Ex20a Example: An MFC Extension DLL

This example makes an extension DLL out of the *CPersistentFrame* class you saw in Chapter 14. First you'll build the Ex20a.dll file, and then you'll use it in a test client program, Ex20b.

Here are the steps for building the Ex20a example:

1. **Run the MFC DLL Wizard to produce the Ex20a project.** Choose New Project from the Visual Studio .NET File menu. Select Visual C++ Projects, and then select MFC DLL from the list of templates. On the Application Settings page, select the MFC Extension DLL, as shown here:

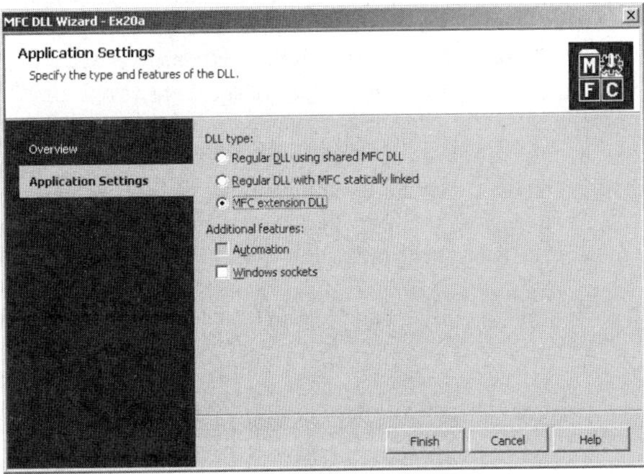

2. **Examine the Ex20a.cpp file.** The MFC DLL Wizard generates the following code, which includes the *DllMain* function:

```
// Ex20a.cpp : Defines the initialization routines for the DLL.
//
#include "stdafx.h"
#include <afxdllx.h>

#ifdef _DEBUG
#define new DEBUG_NEW
#endif

static AFX_EXTENSION_MODULE Ex20aDLL = { NULL, NULL };

extern "C" int APIENTRY
DllMain(HINSTANCE hInstance, DWORD dwReason, LPVOID lpReserved)
{
    // Remove this if you use lpReserved
    UNREFERENCED_PARAMETER(lpReserved);

    if (dwReason == DLL_PROCESS_ATTACH)
    {
        TRACE0("Ex20a.DLL Initializing!\n");

        // Extension DLL one-time initialization
        if (!AfxInitExtensionModule(Ex20aDLL, hInstance))
            return 0;

        // Insert this DLL into the resource chain
        // NOTE: If this Extension DLL is being implicitly
        // linked to by an MFC Regular DLL
        // (such as an ActiveX Control) instead of an
        // MFC application, then you will want to remove
        // this line from DllMain and put it in a separate
        // function exported from this Extension DLL.
        // The Regular DLL that uses this Extension DLL
        // should then explicitly call that function to
        // initialize this Extension DLL.
        // Otherwise, the CDynLinkLibrary object will not be
        // attached to the Regular DLL's resource chain,
        // and serious problems will result.

        new CDynLinkLibrary(Ex20aDLL);

    }
    else if (dwReason == DLL_PROCESS_DETACH)
    {
        TRACE0("Ex20a.DLL Terminating!\n");
```

```
            // Terminate the library before destructors are called
            AfxTermExtensionModule(Ex20aDLL);
        }
        return 1;   // ok
    }
```

3. **Insert the *CPersistentFrame* class into the project.** Choose Add Existing Item from the Project menu and locate the files Persist.h and Persist.cpp in the Ex14a folder on the companion CD. Add the class to the current project.

4. **Edit the Persist.h file.** Modify the line

```
class CPersistentFrame : public CFrameWnd
```

   to read

```
class AFX_EXT_CLASS CPersistentFrame : public CFrameWnd
```

5. **Build the project and copy the DLL file.** Copy the file Ex20a.dll from the \vcppnet\Ex20a\Debug directory to your system directory.

The Ex20b Example: A DLL Test Client Program

This example starts off as a client for Ex20a.dll. It imports the *CPersistentFrame* class from the DLL and uses it as a base class for the SDI frame window. Later, we'll add code to load and test the other sample DLLs in this chapter.

Here are the steps for building the Ex20b example:

1. **Run the MFC Application Wizard to produce the Ex20b project.** This is an ordinary MFC EXE program. Select Single Document. Otherwise, accept the default settings. Be absolutely sure that you accept the Use MFC In A Shared DLL option on the Application Type page.

2. **Copy the file persist.h from the \vcppnet\Ex20a directory.** Note that you're copying the header file, not the CPP file.

3. **Change the *CFrameWnd* base class to *CPersistentFrame*, as you did in Ex14a.** Replace all occurrences of *CFrameWnd* with *CPersistentFrame* in both MainFrm.h and MainFrm.cpp. Also insert the following line into MainFrm.h:

```
#include "persist.h"
```

4. **Add the Ex20a import library to the linker's input library list.** Choose Add Existing Item from the Visual Studio .NET Project menu.

5. **Locate the Ex20a.lib file in the \vcppnet\Ex20a\Debug directory on the companion CD.**
6. **Build and test the Ex20b program.** If you run the program from the debugger and Windows can't find the Ex20a DLL, Windows will display a message box when Ex20b starts. If all goes well, you should have a persistent frame application that works exactly like the one in Ex14a. The only difference is that the *CPersistentFrame* code will be in an extension DLL.

MFC Regular DLLs: The *AFX_EXTENSION_MODULE* Structure

When the MFC DLL Wizard generates a regular DLL, the *DllMain* function will be inside the framework and you'll end up with a structure of type *AFX_EXTENSION_MODULE* (and a global instance of the structure). *AFX_EXTENSION_MODULE* is used during initialization of MFC extension DLLs to hold the state of extension DLL module.

You usually don't need to do anything with this structure. You normally just write C functions and then export them using the *__declspec(dllexport)* modifier (or using entries in the project's DEF file).

Using the *AFX_MANAGE_STATE* Macro

When mfc70.dll is loaded as part of a process, it stores data in some truly global variables. If you call MFC functions from an MFC program or extension DLL, mfc70.dll will know how to set these global variables on behalf of the calling process. If you call into mfc70.dll from a regular MFC DLL, however, the global variables will not be synchronized and the effects will be unpredictable. To solve this problem, insert the following line at the start of all exported functions in your regular DLL:

```
AFX_MANAGE_STATE(AfxGetStaticModuleState());
```

If the MFC code is statically linked, the macro will have no effect.

The MFC Regular DLL Resource Search Sequence

When an EXE links to a regular DLL, resource loading functions inside the EXE will load the EXE's own resources. Resource loading functions inside the regular DLL will load the DLL's own resources.

If you want your EXE code to load resources from the DLL, you can use *AfxSetResourceHandle* to temporarily change the resource handle. If you're writing an application that needs to be localized, you can put language-specific strings, dialog boxes, menus, and so forth in an MFC regular DLL. You might, for example, include the modules English.dll, German.dll, and French.dll. Your client program will explicitly load the correct DLL and load the resources using regular resource-management function calls, which will have the same IDs in all the DLLs.

The Ex20c Example: An MFC Regular DLL

This example creates a regular DLL that exports a single square root function. First we'll build the Ex20c.dll file, and then we'll modify the test client program, Ex20b, to test the new DLL.

Here are the steps for building the Ex20c example:

1. **Run the MFC DLL Wizard to produce the project Ex20c.** Proceed as you did for Ex20a, but accept Regular DLL Using Shared MFC DLL (instead of selecting MFC Extension DLL) on the Application Settings page.

2. **Examine the Ex20c.cpp file.** The MFC DLL Wizard generates the following code:

```
// Ex20c.cpp : Defines the initialization routines for the DLL.
//
#include "stdafx.h"
#include "Ex20c.h"

#ifdef _DEBUG
#define new DEBUG_NEW
#endif

//
//    Note!
//        If this DLL is dynamically linked against the MFC
//        DLLs, any functions exported from this DLL which
//        call into MFC must have the AFX_MANAGE_STATE macro
//        added at the very beginning of the function.
//
//        For example:
//
//        extern "C" BOOL PASCAL EXPORT ExportedFunction()
//        {
//            AFX_MANAGE_STATE(AfxGetStaticModuleState());
//            // normal function body here
//        }
//
//        It is very important that this macro appear in each
//        function, prior to any calls into MFC.  This means that
//        it must appear as the first statement within the
//        function, even before any object variable declarations
//        as their constructors may generate calls into the MFC
//        DLL.
//
```

(continued)

```
//      Please see MFC Technical Notes 33 and 58 for additional
//      details.
//

// CEx20cApp
BEGIN_MESSAGE_MAP(CEx20cApp, CWinApp)
END_MESSAGE_MAP()

// CEx20cApp construction
CEx20cApp::CEx20cApp()
{
    // TODO: add construction code here,
    // Place all significant initialization in InitInstance
}

// The one and only CEx20cApp object
CEx20cApp theApp;


// CEx20cApp initialization
BOOL CEx20cApp::InitInstance()
{
    CWinApp::InitInstance();

    return TRUE;
}
```

3. **Add the code for the exported *Ex20cSquareRoot* function.** It's okay to add this code in the Ex20c.cpp file, although you can use a new file if you want to:

```
extern "C" __declspec(dllexport) double Ex20cSquareRoot(double d)
{
    AFX_MANAGE_STATE(AfxGetStaticModuleState());
    TRACE("Entering Ex20cSquareRoot\n");
    if (d >= 0.0) {
        return sqrt(d);
    }
    AfxMessageBox("Can't take square root of a negative number.");
    return 0.0;
}
```

You can see that there's no problem with the DLL displaying a message box or another modal dialog box. You'll need to include math.h in the file that contains this code.

Be sure to prototype the *Ex20cSquareRoot* function in the Ex20c.h file so external clients can see it.

4. **Build the project and copy the DLL file.** Copy the file Ex20c.dll from the \vcppnet\Ex20c\Debug directory to your system directory.

Updating the Ex20b Example: Adding Code to Test Ex20c.dll

When we built the Ex20b program, it linked dynamically to the Ex20a MFC extension DLL. Now we'll update the project to implicitly link to the Ex20c MFC regular DLL and to call the DLL's square root function.

Here are the steps for updating the Ex20b example:

1. **Add a new dialog resource and class to the Ex20b project.** Use the dialog editor to create the *IDD_EX20C* template, as shown here:

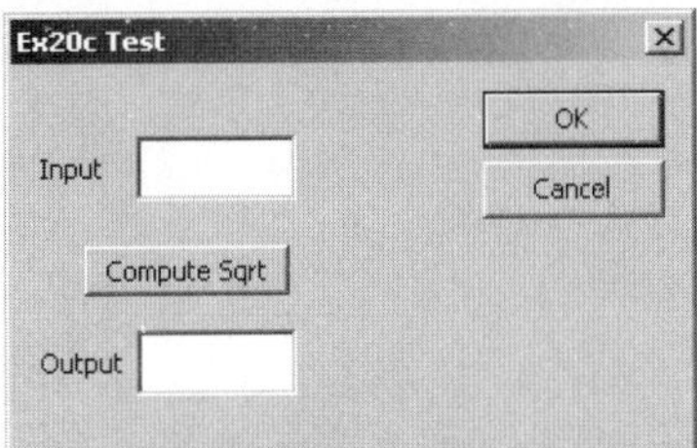

Use the Add Class Wizard to add a class *CTest20cDialog* that is derived from *CDialog*. The controls, data members, and message map function are shown in the following table.

Control ID	Type	Data Member	Message Map Function
IDC_INPUT	Edit control	*m_dInput* (double)	
IDC_OUTPUT	Edit control	*m_dOutput* (double)	
IDC_COMPUTE	Button		*OnBnClicked-Compute*

2. **Code the *OnBnClickedCompute* function to call the DLL's exported function.** Edit the generated function in Test20c-Dialog.cpp as shown here:

```
void CTest20cDialog::OnBnClickedCompute()
{
    UpdateData(TRUE);
    m_dOutput = Ex20cSquareRoot(m_dInput);
    UpdateData(FALSE);
}
```

You must declare the *Ex20cSquareRoot* function as an imported function. Add the following line to the Test20cDialog.h file:

```
extern "C" __declspec(dllimport) double Ex20cSquareRoot(double d);
```

3. **Integrate the *CTest20cDialog* class into the Ex20b application.** You must add a top-level menu, Test, and an Ex20c DLL option with the ID *ID_TEST_EX20CDLL*. Use Class View's Properties window to map this option to a member function in the *CEx20bView* class, and then code the handler in Ex20bView.cpp as follows:

```
void CEx20bView::OnTestEx20cdll()
{
    CTest20cDialog dlg;
    dlg.DoModal();
}
```

   Of course, you must add the following line to the Ex20bView.cpp file:

```
#include "Test20cDialog.h"
```

4. **Add the Ex20c import library to the linker's input library list.** Choose Add Existing Item from the Visual Studio .NET Project menu, and then add \vcppnet\Ex20c\Debug\Ex20c.lib to the project. Now the program should implicitly link to both the Ex20a DLL and the Ex20c DLL. As you can see, the client doesn't care whether the DLL is a regular DLL or an extension DLL. You just specify the LIB name to the linker.

5. **Build and test the updated Ex20b application.** Choose Ex20c DLL from the Test menu. Type a number in the Input edit control, and then click the Compute Sqrt button. The result should appear in the Output control.

A Custom Control DLL

Programmers have been using DLLs for custom controls since the early days of Windows because custom controls are neatly self-contained. The original custom controls were written in pure C and configured as standalone DLLs. Today, you can use the features of the MFC library in your custom controls, and the wizards help make coding easier. A regular DLL is the best choice for a custom control because the control doesn't need a C++ interface and it can be used by any development system that accepts custom controls (such as the Borland C++

compiler). You'll probably want to use the MFC dynamic linking option because the resulting DLL will be small and quick to load.

What Is a Custom Control?

You've seen ordinary controls in Chapter 7, Windows common controls in Chapter 8, and ActiveX controls in Chapter 9. The custom control acts like an ordinary control, such as the edit control, in that it sends *WM_COMMAND* notification messages to its parent window and receives user-defined messages. The dialog editor lets you position custom controls in dialog templates. That's what the custom control button on the control palette is for.

You have a lot of freedom in designing your custom control. You can paint anything you want in its window (which is managed by the client application), and you can define any notification and inbound messages you need. You can use Class View's Properties window to map normal Windows messages in the control (*WM_LBUTTONDOWN*, for example), but you must manually map the user-defined messages and manually map the notification messages in the parent window class.

A Custom Control's Window Class

A dialog resource template specifies its custom controls by their symbolic window class names. Don't confuse the Win32 window class with the C++ class; the only similarity is the name. A window class is defined by a structure that contains the following:

- The name of the class
- A pointer to the *WndProc* function that receives messages sent to windows of the class
- Miscellaneous attributes, such as the background brush

The Win32 *RegisterClass* function copies the structure into process memory so that any function in the process can use the class to create a window. When the dialog window is initialized, Windows creates the custom control child windows from the window class names stored in the template.

Suppose that the control's *WndProc* function is inside a DLL. When the DLL is initialized (by a call to *DllMain*), it can call *RegisterClass* for the control. Because the DLL is part of the process, the client program can create child windows of the custom control class. To summarize, the client knows the name string of a control window class and it uses that class name to construct the child window. All the code for the control, including the *WndProc* function, is inside the DLL. All that's necessary is that the client load the DLL before creating the child window.

The MFC Library and the *WndProc* Function

Okay, so Windows calls the control's *WndProc* function for each message sent to that window. But you really don't want to write an old-fashioned *switch-case* statement—you want to map those messages to C++ member functions, as you've been doing all along. Now, in the DLL, you must rig up a C++ class that corresponds to the control's window class. Once you've done that, you can use Class View's Properties window to map messages.

The obvious part is the writing of the C++ class for the control. You simply use the Add Class Wizard to create a new class that's derived from *CWnd*. The tricky part is wiring the C++ class to the *WndProc* function and to the application framework's message pump. You'll see a real *WndProc* in the Ex20d example, but here's the pseudocode for a typical control *WndProc* function:

```
LRESULT MyControlWndProc(HWND hWnd, UINT message
                         WPARAM wParam, LPARAM lParam)
{
    if (this is the first message for this window) {
        CWnd* pWnd = new CMyControlWindowClass();
        attach pWnd to hWnd
    }
    return AfxCallWndProc(pWnd, hWnd, message, WParam, lParam);
}
```

The MFC *AfxCallWndProc* function passes messages to the framework, which dispatches them to the member functions mapped in *CMyControlWindowClass*.

Custom Control Notification Messages

The control communicates with its parent window by sending it special *WM_COMMAND* notification messages with parameters, as shown here:

Parameter	Usage
(HIWORD) wParam	Notification code
(LOWORD) wParam	Child window ID
lParam	Child window handle

The meaning of the notification code is arbitrary and depends on the control. The parent window must interpret the code based on its knowledge of the control. For example, the code 77 might mean that the user typed a character while positioned on the control.

The control might send a notification message such as this:

```
GetParent()->SendMessage(WM_COMMAND,
    GetDlgCtrlID() | ID_NOTIFYCODE << 16, (LONG) GetSafeHwnd());
```

On the client side, you map the message with the MFC *ON_CONTROL* macro, like this:

```
ON_CONTROL(ID_NOTIFYCODE, IDC_MYCONTROL, OnClickedMyControl)
```

You then declare the handler function like this:

```
afx_msg void OnClickedMyControl();
```

User-Defined Messages Sent to the Control

User-defined messages (described in Chapter 7) are the means by which the client program communicates with the control. Because a standard message returns a 32-bit value if it is sent rather than posted, the client can obtain information from the control.

The Ex20d Example: A Custom Control

The Ex20d program is an MFC regular DLL that implements a traffic light control indicating off, red, yellow, and green states. When clicked with the left mouse button, the DLL sends a clicked notification message to its parent and responds to two user-defined messages, *RYG_SETSTATE* and *RYG_GETSTATE*. The state is an integer that represents the color. Credit for this example goes to Richard Wilton, who included the original C-language version of this control in his book *Windows 3 Developer's Workshop* (Microsoft Press, 1991).

The Ex20d project was originally generated using the MFC DLL Wizard, with linkage to the shared MFC DLL, just like Ex20c. The following is the code for the primary source file, with the added code in the *InitInstance* function in boldface. The dummy exported *Ex20dEntry* function exists solely to allow the DLL to be implicitly linked. The client program must include a call to this function. That call must be in an executable path in the program or the compiler will eliminate the call. Alternatively, the client program can call the Win32 *LoadLibrary* function in its *InitInstance* function to explicitly link the DLL.

Ex20d.cpp

```
// Ex20d.cpp : Defines the initialization routines for the DLL.
//
#include "stdafx.h"
#include "Ex20d.h"

#include "rygwnd.h"

#ifdef _DEBUG
#define new DEBUG_NEW
#endif

extern "C" __declspec(dllexport) void Ex20dEntry() {} // dummy function

// Application Wizard comments removed.
⋮
// CEx20dApp

BEGIN_MESSAGE_MAP(CEx20dApp, CWinApp)
END_MESSAGE_MAP()

// CEx20dApp construction
CEx20dApp::CEx20dApp()
{
    // TODO: add construction code here,
    // Place all significant initialization in InitInstance
}

// The one and only CEx20dApp object
CEx20dApp theApp;

// CEx20dApp initialization
BOOL CEx20dApp::InitInstance()
{
    CRygWnd::RegisterWndClass(AfxGetInstanceHandle());
    CWinApp::InitInstance();

    return TRUE;
}
```

The following is the code for the *CRygWnd* class, including the global *RygWndProc* function. You can use the Add Class Wizard to create this class by choosing Add Class from the Project menu. The code that paints the traffic light isn't very interesting, so we'll concentrate on the functions that are common to most custom controls. The static *RegisterWndClass* member function actually registers the *RYG* window class and must be called as soon as the DLL is loaded. The *OnLButtonDown* handler is called when the user presses the left mouse button inside the control window. It sends the clicked notification message to the parent window. The overridden *PostNcDestroy* function is important because it deletes the *CRygWnd* object when the client program destroys the control window. The *OnGetState* and *OnSetState* functions are called in response to user-defined messages sent by the client. Remember to copy the DLL to your system directory.

RygWnd.h

```
#pragma once

#define RYG_SETSTATE WM_USER + 0
#define RYG_GETSTATE WM_USER + 1

LRESULT CALLBACK AFX_EXPORT
    RygWndProc(HWND hWnd, UINT message, WPARAM wParam, LPARAM lParam);

// CRygWnd
class CRygWnd : public CWnd
{
private:
    int m_nState; // 0=off, 1=red, 2=yellow, 3=green

    static CRect  s_rect;
    static CPoint s_point;
    static CRect  s_rColor[3];
    static CBrush s_bColor[4];

public:
    static BOOL RegisterWndClass(HINSTANCE hInstance);
    DECLARE_DYNAMIC(CRygWnd)

public:
    CRygWnd();
    virtual ~CRygWnd();

private:
    void SetMapping(CDC* pDC);
    void UpdateColor(CDC* pDC, int n);

protected:
    afx_msg LRESULT OnSetState(WPARAM wParam, LPARAM lParam);
    afx_msg LRESULT OnGetState(WPARAM wParam, LPARAM lParam);
    DECLARE_MESSAGE_MAP()

};
```

RygWnd.cpp

```
// RygWnd.cpp : implementation file
//
#include "stdafx.h"
#include "Ex20d.h"
#include "RygWnd.h"

LRESULT CALLBACK AFX_EXPORT
    RygWndProc(HWND hWnd, UINT message, WPARAM wParam, LPARAM lParam)
{
    AFX_MANAGE_STATE(AfxGetStaticModuleState());

    CWnd* pWnd;

    pWnd = CWnd::FromHandlePermanent(hWnd);
    if (pWnd == NULL) {
        // Assume that client created a CRygWnd window
        pWnd = new CRygWnd();
        pWnd->Attach(hWnd);
    }
    ASSERT(pWnd->m_hWnd == hWnd);
    ASSERT(pWnd == CWnd::FromHandlePermanent(hWnd));
    LRESULT lResult = AfxCallWndProc(pWnd, hWnd, message,
                                     wParam, lParam);
    return lResult;
}


// static data members
CRect  CRygWnd::s_rect(-500, 1000, 500, -1000); // outer rectangle
CPoint CRygWnd::s_point(300, 300); // rounded corners
CRect  CRygWnd::s_rColor[] = {CRect(-250, 800, 250, 300),
                              CRect(-250, 250, 250, -250),
                              CRect(-250, -300, 250, -800)};
CBrush CRygWnd::s_bColor[] = {RGB(192, 192, 192),
                              RGB(0xFF, 0x00, 0x00),
                              RGB(0xFF, 0xFF, 0x00),
                              RGB(0x00, 0xFF, 0x00)};

BOOL CRygWnd::RegisterWndClass(HINSTANCE hInstance) // static member
                                                    //  function
{
    WNDCLASS wc;
    wc.lpszClassName = "RYG"; // matches class name in client
    wc.hInstance = hInstance;
    wc.lpfnWndProc = RygWndProc;
    wc.hCursor = ::LoadCursor(NULL, IDC_ARROW);
    wc.hIcon = 0;
```

```
    wc.lpszMenuName = NULL;
    wc.hbrBackground = (HBRUSH) ::GetStockObject(LTGRAY_BRUSH);
    wc.style = CS_GLOBALCLASS;
    wc.cbClsExtra = 0;
    wc.cbWndExtra = 0;
    return (::RegisterClass(&wc) != 0);
}

// CRygWnd
IMPLEMENT_DYNAMIC(CRygWnd, CWnd)
CRygWnd::CRygWnd()
{
    m_nState = 0;
    TRACE("CRygWnd constructor\n");
}

CRygWnd::~CRygWnd()
{
    TRACE("CRygWnd destructor\n");
}

BEGIN_MESSAGE_MAP(CRygWnd, CWnd)
    ON_MESSAGE(RYG_SETSTATE, OnSetState)
    ON_MESSAGE(RYG_GETSTATE, OnGetState)
    ON_WM_PAINT()
    ON_WM_LBUTTONDOWN()
END_MESSAGE_MAP()

void CRygWnd::SetMapping(CDC* pDC)
{
    CRect clientRect;
    GetClientRect(clientRect);
    pDC->SetMapMode(MM_ISOTROPIC);
    pDC->SetWindowExt(1000, 2000);
    pDC->SetViewportExt(clientRect.right, -clientRect.bottom);
    pDC->SetViewportOrg(clientRect.right / 2, clientRect.bottom / 2);
}

void CRygWnd::UpdateColor(CDC* pDC, int n)
{
    if (m_nState == n + 1) {
        pDC->SelectObject(&s_bColor[n+1]);
    }
    else {
        pDC->SelectObject(&s_bColor[0]);
    }
    pDC->Ellipse(s_rColor[n]);
}
```

(continued)

```
// CRygWnd message handlers
void CRygWnd::OnPaint()
{
    int i;
    CPaintDC dc(this); // device context for painting
    SetMapping(&dc);
    dc.SelectStockObject(DKGRAY_BRUSH);
    dc.RoundRect(s_rect, s_point);
    for (i = 0; i < 3; i++) {
        UpdateColor(&dc, i);
    }
}

void CRygWnd::OnLButtonDown(UINT nFlags, CPoint point)
{
    // Notification code is HIWORD of wParam, 0 in this case
    GetParent()->SendMessage(WM_COMMAND, GetDlgCtrlID(),
        (LONG) GetSafeHwnd()); // 0
}

void CRygWnd::PostNcDestroy()
{
    TRACE("CRygWnd::PostNcDestroy\n");
    delete this; // CWnd::PostNcDestroy does nothing
}

LRESULT CRygWnd::OnSetState(WPARAM wParam, LPARAM lParam)
{
    TRACE("CRygWnd::SetState, wParam = %d\n", wParam);
    m_nState = (int) wParam;
    Invalidate(FALSE);
    return 0L;
}

LRESULT CRygWnd::OnGetState(WPARAM wParam, LPARAM lParam)
{
    TRACE("CRygWnd::GetState\n");
    return m_nState;
}
```

Revising the Updated Ex20b Example: Adding Code to Test Ex20d.dll

The Ex20b program already links to the Ex20a and Ex20c DLLs. Now we'll revise the project to implicitly link to the Ex20d custom control.

Here are the steps for updating the Ex20b example:

1. **Add a new dialog resource and class to the Ex20b project.** Use the dialog editor to create the *IDD_EX20D* template with a custom control with the child window ID *IDC_RYG*, as shown here:

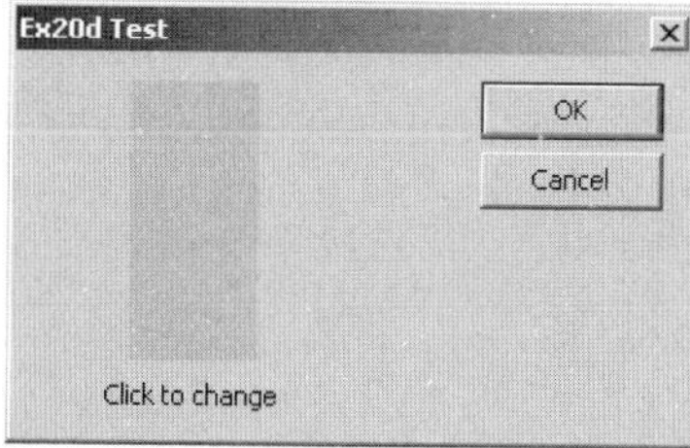

Specify *RYG* as the window class name of the custom control using the dialog editor's Properties window.

Then use the Add Class Wizard to generate a class *CTest20dDialog* that is derived from *CDialog*.

2. **Edit the Test20dDialog.h file.** Add the following private data member:

```
enum { OFF, RED, YELLOW, GREEN } m_nState;
```

Also add the following import and user-defined message IDs:

```
extern "C" __declspec(dllimport) void Ex20dEntry(); // dummy
                                                     // function
#define RYG_SETSTATE WM_USER + 0
#define RYG_GETSTATE WM_USER + 1
```

3. **Edit the constructor in Test20dDialog.cpp to initialize the state data member.** Add the following boldface code:

```
CTest20dDialog::CTest20dDialog(CWnd* pParent /*=NULL*/)
    : CDialog(CTest20dDialog::IDD, pParent)
{
    m_nState = OFF;
    Ex20dEntry(); // Make sure DLL gets loaded
}
```

4. **Map the control's clicked notification message.** You can't use Class View's Properties window here, so you must add the message map entry and handler function in the Test20dDialog.cpp file, as shown here:

```
void CTest20dDialog::OnClickedRyg()
{
    switch(m_nState) {
    case OFF:
        m_nState = RED;
        break;
    case RED:
        m_nState = YELLOW;
        break;
```

(continued)

```
        case YELLOW:
            m_nState = GREEN;
            break;
        case GREEN:
            m_nState = OFF;
            break;
        }
        GetDlgItem(IDC_RYG)->SendMessage(RYG_SETSTATE, m_nState);
        return;
}

BEGIN_MESSAGE_MAP(CTest20dDialog, CDialog)
    ON_CONTROL(0, IDC_RYG, OnClickedRyg) // Notification code is 0
END_MESSAGE_MAP()
```

When the dialog box gets the clicked notification message, it sends the *RYG_SETSTATE* message back to the control in order to change the color. Don't forget to add this prototype in the Test20dDialog.h file:

```
afx_msg void OnClickedRyg();
```

5. **Integrate the *CTest20dDialog* class into the Ex20b application.**

6. **You'll need to add a second command to the Test menu—an Ex20d DLL option with the ID *ID_TEST_EX20DDLL*.** Use Class View's Properties window to map this option to a member function in the *CEx20bView* class, and then code the handler in Ex20bView.cpp as follows:

```
void CEx20bView::OnTestEx20ddll()
{
    CTest20dDialog dlg;
    dlg.DoModal();
}
```

Of course, you have to add the following line to Ex20bView.cpp:

```
#include "Test20dDialog.h"
```

7. **Add the Ex20d import library to the linker's input library list.** Choose Add Existing Item from the Project menu. Add \vcppnet\Ex20d\Debug\Ex20.lib to the project. With this addition, the program should implicitly link to all three DLLs.

8. **Build and test the updated Ex20b application.** Choose Ex20d DLL from the Test menu. Try clicking the traffic light with the left mouse button. The traffic-light color should change.

21

MFC Programs Without Document or View Classes

The document-view architecture is useful for many applications, but sometimes a simpler program structure is sufficient. This chapter includes three sample applications: a dialog box–based program, a Single Document Interface (SDI) program, and a Multiple Document Interface (MDI) program. None of these programs uses document, view, or document-template classes, but they all use command routing and some other Microsoft Foundation Class (MFC) library features. In Microsoft Visual C++ .NET, you can create all three types of applications using the MFC Application Wizard.

In each example, we'll look at how the MFC Application Wizard generates code that doesn't rely on the document-view architecture and how you can add your own code.

The Ex21a Example: A Dialog Box–Based Application

For many applications, a dialog box is a sufficient user interface. The dialog box appears when the user starts the application. The user can minimize the dialog box, and as long as the dialog box is not system modal, the user can freely switch to other applications.

In this example, the dialog box functions as a simple calculator, as shown in Figure 21-1. The Add Member Variable Wizard takes care of defining the class data members and generating the DDX (Dialog Data Exchange) function calls—everything but the coding of the compute function. The application's resource script, Ex21a.rc, defines an icon as well as the dialog box.

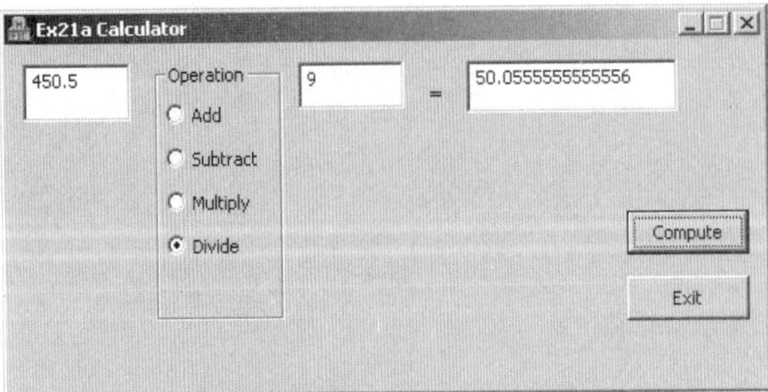

Figure 21-1 The Ex21a Calculator dialog box

The MFC Application Wizard gives you the option of generating a dialog box–based application. Here are the steps for building the Ex21a example:

1. **Run the MFC Application Wizard to produce the Ex21a project.** Select the Dialog Based option on the Application Type page, as shown here:

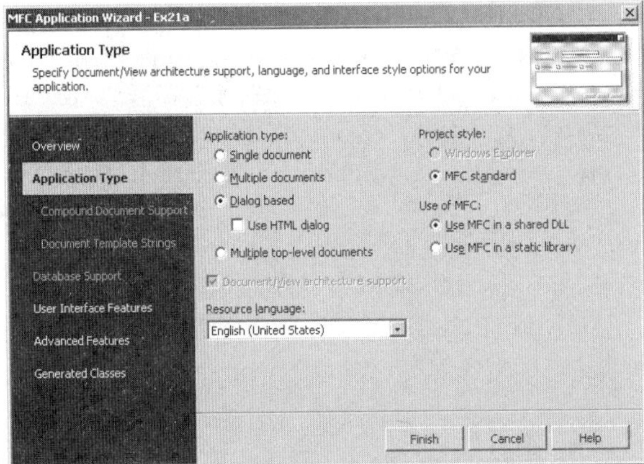

On the User Interface Features page, enter **Ex21a Calculator** as the dialog box title.

2. **Edit the *IDD_EX21A_DIALOG* resource.** Referring to Figure 21-1 as a guide, use the dialog editor to assign IDs to the controls shown in the following table. Then open the dialog box's Properties window. Set the *System Menu* and *Minimize Box* properties to *True*.

Control	ID
Left operand edit control	*IDC_LEFT*
Right operand edit control	*IDC_RIGHT*
Result edit control	*IDC_RESULT*
First radio button (group property set)	*IDC_OPERATION*
Compute button	*IDC_COMPUTE*

3. **Use the Add Member Variable Wizard to add member variables, and use Class View's Properties window to add a command handler.** The MFC Application Wizard has already generated a class *CEx21aDlg*. Add the following data members:

Control ID	Member Variable	Type
IDC_LEFT	*m_dLeft*	*Double*
IDC_RIGHT	*m_dRight*	*Double*
IDC_RESULT	*m_dResult*	*Double*
IDC_OPERATION	*m_nOperation*	*int*

Add the message handler *OnBnClickedCompute* for the *IDC_COMPUTE* button.

4. **Code the *OnBnClickedCompute* member function in the Ex21aDlg.cpp file.** Add the following boldface code:

```
void CEx21aDlg::OnBnClickedCompute()
{
    UpdateData(TRUE);
    if(m_nOperation == 0) {
        m_dResult = m_dLeft + m_dRight;
    } else if(m_nOperation == 1) {
        m_dResult = m_dLeft - m_dRight;
    } else if(m_nOperation == 2) {
        m_dResult = m_dLeft * m_dRight;
    } else if(m_nOperation == 3) {
        if(m_dRight == 0) {
            AfxMessageBox("Divide by zero");
        } else {
            m_dResult = m_dLeft / m_dRight;
        }
    }
    UpdateData(FALSE);
}
```

5. **Build and test the Ex21a application.** Notice that the program's icon appears on the Windows taskbar. Verify that you can minimize the dialog box.

The Application Class *InitInstance* Function

The critical element of the Ex21a application is the *CEx21aApp::InitInstance* function generated by the MFC Application Wizard. A normal *InitInstance* function creates a main frame window and returns *TRUE*, which allows the program's message loop to run. The Ex21a version constructs a modal dialog object, calls *DoModal*, and then returns *FALSE*. This means that the application exits after the user exits the dialog box. The *DoModal* function lets the Windows dialog procedure get and dispatch messages, as it always does. Note that the MFC Application Wizard does not generate a call to *CWinApp::SetRegistryKey*.

Here's the generated *InitInstance* code from Ex21a.cpp:

```
BOOL CEx21aApp::InitInstance()
{
    // InitCommonControls() is required on Windows XP if an application
    // manifest specifies use of ComCtl32.dll version 6 or later to enable
    // visual styles.  Otherwise, any window creation will fail.
    InitCommonControls();
    CWinApp::InitInstance();
    AfxEnableControlContainer();

    CEx21aDlg dlg;
    m_pMainWnd = &dlg;
    INT_PTR nResponse = dlg.DoModal();
    if (nResponse == IDOK)
    {
        // TODO: Place code here to handle when the dialog is
        //  dismissed with OK
    }
    else if (nResponse == IDCANCEL)
    {
        // TODO: Place code here to handle when the dialog is
        //  dismissed with Cancel
    }
    // Since the dialog has been closed, return FALSE so that we exit the
    //  application, rather than start the application's message pump.
    return FALSE;
}
```

The Dialog Class and the Program Icon

The generated *CEx21aDlg* class contains these two message map entries:

```
ON_WM_PAINT()
ON_WM_QUERYDRAGICON()
```

The associated handler functions take care of displaying the application's icon when the user minimizes the program. This code applies only to Microsoft Windows NT version 3.51, in which the icon is displayed on the desktop. You don't need these handlers for Windows 95/98/Me or Windows NT 4.0/2000/XP because those versions of Windows display the program's icon directly on the taskbar.

There is some icon code that you do need. It's in the dialog box's *OnInitDialog* handler, which is generated by the MFC Application Wizard. Notice the two *SetIcon* calls in the *OnInitDialog* function code shown below. If you selected the About box option, the MFC Application Wizard will generate code to add an About box to the System menu. The variable *m_hIcon* is a data member of the dialog class that is initialized in the constructor.

```
BOOL CEx21aDlg::OnInitDialog()
{
    CDialog::OnInitDialog();
    // Add "About..." menu item to system menu.
    // IDM_ABOUTBOX must be in the system command range.
    ASSERT((IDM_ABOUTBOX & 0xFFF0) == IDM_ABOUTBOX);
    ASSERT(IDM_ABOUTBOX < 0xF000);

    CMenu* pSysMenu = GetSystemMenu(FALSE);
    if (pSysMenu != NULL)
    {
        CString strAboutMenu;
        strAboutMenu.LoadString(IDS_ABOUTBOX);
        if (!strAboutMenu.IsEmpty())
        {
            pSysMenu->AppendMenu(MF_SEPARATOR);
            pSysMenu->AppendMenu(MF_STRING,
                                 IDM_ABOUTBOX, strAboutMenu);
        }
    }
    // Set the icon for this dialog.  The framework does this
    //  automatically when the application's main window
    //  is not a dialog.
    SetIcon(m_hIcon, TRUE);          // Set big icon
    SetIcon(m_hIcon, FALSE);         // Set small icon
    // TODO: Add extra initialization here
    return TRUE;  // return TRUE  unless you set the focus to a control
}
```

The Ex21b Example: An SDI Application

This SDI "Hello, world!" example builds on the code you saw way back in Chapter 2. The application has only one window—an object of a class derived from *CFrameWnd*. All drawing occurs inside the frame window, and all messages are handled there.

1. **Run the MFC Application Wizard to produce the Ex21b project.** Select the Single Document option on the Application Type page and deselect the Document/View Architecture Support option, as shown here:

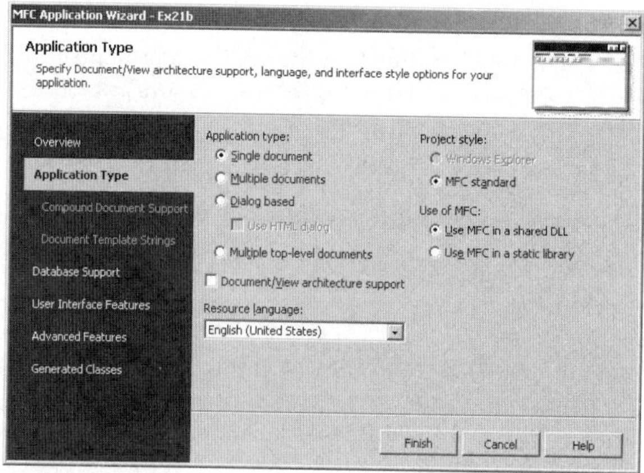

2. **Add code to paint in the view.** Add the following boldface code to the *CChildView::OnPaint* function in the ChildView.cpp source code file:

```
void CChildView::OnPaint()
{
    CPaintDC dc(this); // device context for painting

    dc.TextOut(0, 0, "Hello, world!");

    // Do not call CWnd::OnPaint() for painting messages
}
```

3. **Compile and run the application.** You now have a complete SDI application that has no dependencies on the document-view architecture.

The MFC Application Wizard automatically takes out dependencies on the document-view architecture and generates an application for you that has the following elements:

- **Main menu** You can have a Windows-based application without a menu—you don't even need a resource script. But Ex21b has both. The application framework routes menu commands to message handlers in the frame class.
- **Icon** An icon is useful if the program is to be activated from Windows Explorer. It's also useful when the application's main frame window is minimized. The icon is stored in the resource, along with the menu.
- **Window close message command handler** Many applications need to do special processing when the main window is closed. If you're using documents, you can override the *CDocument::SaveModified* function. But here, to take control of the close process, the MFC Application Wizard creates message handlers to process close messages sent as a result of user actions and by Windows itself when it shuts down.
- **Toolbar and status bar** The MFC Application Wizard automatically generates a default toolbar and status bar for you and sets up the routing even though there are no document-view classes.

Several interesting features in the SDI application have no document-view support, including:

- ***CChildView* class** Contrary to its name, this class is actually a *CWnd* derivative that is declared in ChildView.h and implemented in ChildView.cpp. *CChildView* implements only a virtual *OnPaint* member function, which contains any code that you want to draw in the frame window (as illustrated in step 2 of the Ex21b sample).
- ***CMainFrame* class** This class contains a data member, *m_wndView*, that is created and initialized in the *CMainFrame::OnCreate* member function.
- ***CMainFrame::OnSetFocus* function** This function makes sure the focus is translated to the *CChildView*:

```
void CMainFrame::OnSetFocus(CWnd* pOldWnd)
{
    // forward focus to the view window
    m_wndView.SetFocus();
}
```

- ***CMainFrame::OnCmdMsg* function** This function gives the view a chance to handle any command messages first:

```
BOOL CMainFrame::OnCmdMsg(UINT nID, int nCode, void* pExtra,
                          AFX_CMDHANDLERINFO* pHandlerInfo)
{
    // let the view have first crack at the command
    if (m_wndView.OnCmdMsg(nID, nCode, pExtra, pHandlerInfo))
        return TRUE;
    // otherwise, do default handling
    return CFrameWnd::OnCmdMsg(nID, nCode, pExtra, pHandlerInfo);
}
```

The Ex21c Example: An MDI Application

Now let's create an MDI application that doesn't use the document-view architecture.

1. **Run the MFC Application Wizard to produce the Ex21c project.** Select the Multiple Documents option on the Application Type page and deselect Document/View Architecture Support.

2. **Add code to paint in the dialog box.** Add the following boldface code to the *CChildView::OnPaint* function in the ChildView.cpp source code file:

```
void CChildView::OnPaint()
{
    CPaintDC dc(this); // device context for painting

    dc.TextOut(0, 0, "Hello, world!");

    // Do not call CWnd::OnPaint() for painting messages
}
```

3. **Compile and run the application.** You now have a complete MDI application without any dependencies on the document-view architecture.

   As in Ex21b, this example automatically creates a *CChildView* class. The main difference between Ex21b and Ex21c is that in Ex21c the *CChildView* class is created in the *CChildFrame::OnCreate* function instead of in the *CMainFrame* class.

Now that you've learned how to create three kinds of applications that do not depend on the document-view architecture, you can examine how they're generated to learn how MFC works. Try comparing the generated results to similar applications with document-view architecture support to get a complete picture of how the document-view classes work with the rest of MFC.

Part IV

COM, Automation, ActiveX, and OLE

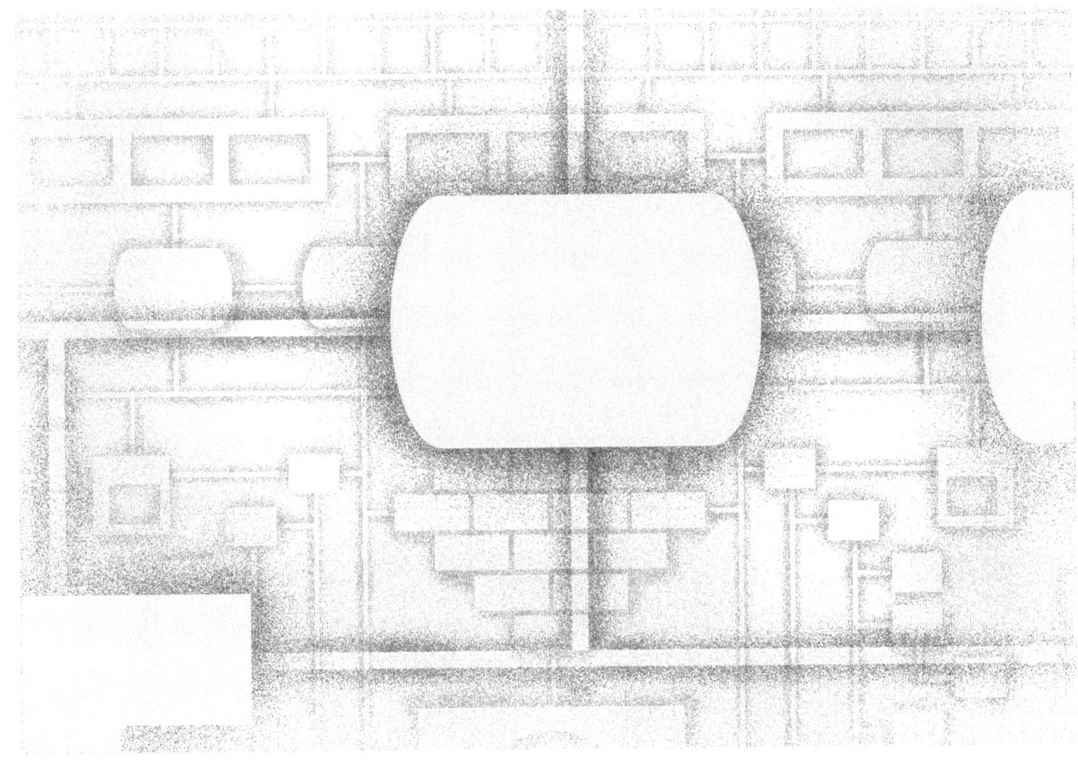

22

The Component Object Model

The Component Object Model (COM) is the foundation of Microsoft's ActiveX technology and has become an integral part of Microsoft Windows. A great deal of modern Windows programming involves COM, so it's important to understand the COM architecture. But where do you begin? You could start with the Microsoft Foundation Class classes for ActiveX Controls, Automation, and OLE, but as useful as those classes are, they obscure the real COM architecture. You've got to start with fundamental theory, and that includes COM and something called an *interface*.

This chapter covers the theory you need for the next six chapters. You'll learn about interfaces and how the MFC library implements interfaces through its macros and interface maps.

ActiveX Technology

It can be tricky to figure out how to use the terms *ActiveX* and *OLE*. You can think of ActiveX as something that was created when the "old" OLE was revamped to work with the Internet. ActiveX includes Windows features that are built on COM (which you'll study in this part of the book), the Microsoft Internet Information Services (IIS) family, and the WinInet programming interface.

Yes, OLE is still here, and once again it stands for Object Linking and Embedding, just as it did in the days of OLE 1.0. It's just another subset of ActiveX technology that includes odds and ends such as drag and drop. Unfortunately (or fortunately, if you have existing code), the MFC source code and the Windows API have not kept current with the naming conventions. As a result, you'll see lots of occurrences of *OLE* and *Ole* in class names and in function names even though some of those classes and functions go beyond linking and embedding. In this part of the book, you might also notice references to the "server" in the code generated by the MFC Application Wizard. Microsoft now reserves this term for database servers and Internet servers; *component* is the new term for OLE servers.

Bookstore computer sections are full of books on OLE, COM, and ActiveX. This book can't offer that level of detail, but you should come away with a pretty good understanding of COM theory. You'll find more on the connection to the MFC library classes than you might see in other books, with the exception of *MFC Internals* by George Shepherd and Scot Wingo (Addison-Wesley, 1996). The net result should be good preparation for the really heavy-duty ActiveX/COM books, including Kraig Brockschmidt's *Inside OLE*, 2nd edition (Microsoft Press, 1995) and Don Box's *Essential COM* (Addison-Wesley, 1998). A good mid-level book is Dale Rogerson's *Inside COM* (Microsoft Press, 1997).

As you'll see in the final section of this book, COM brings as many problems to the table as it solves. Most of this technology will be superseded by the .NET component model, which uses assemblies and the common language runtime. However, COM is still important for the time being. So let's get cracking.

What Is COM?

COM is a software architecture that facilitates the dynamic composition of software. The DLL model doesn't handle versioning well, and the raw remote procedure call (RPC) mechanism is difficult to manage. COM tries to solve these issues.

The "problem" is that there's no standard way for Windows program modules to communicate with one another. But what about the DLL, with its exported functions, Dynamic Data Exchange (DDE), the Windows Clipboard, and the Windows API itself, not to mention legacy standards such as Visual Basic custom controls (VBXs) and OLE 1? Aren't they good enough? Well, no. This potpourri of standards makes integrating software a nightmare.

The Essence of COM

What's wrong with the old standards? A lot. The Windows API has too large a programming "surface area"—more than 350 separate functions. VBXs don't work in the 32-bit world. DDE comes with a complicated system of applications, topics, and items. How you call a DLL is totally application-specific. COM, in contrast, provides a unified, expandable, object-oriented communications protocol for Windows that supports the following features:

- A standard, language-independent way for a Win32 client EXE to load and call a Win32 DLL
- A general-purpose way for one EXE to control another EXE on the same computer (the DDE replacement)
- A replacement for the VBX, called an ActiveX control
- A powerful new way for application programs to interact with the operating system
- Expansion to accommodate new protocols such as Microsoft's OLE DB database interface
- Distributed COM (DCOM), which allows one EXE to communicate with another EXE residing on a different computer, even if the computers use different microprocessor-chip families

So what is COM? That's an easier question to ask than to answer. At DevelopMentor, a training facility for software developers, the party line for years has been that "COM is love." That is, COM is a powerful integrating technology that allows you to mix all sorts of disparate software parts together at run time. COM allows developers to write software that runs together regardless of issues such as thread-awareness and language choice.

The COM protocol connects one software module with another and then drops out of the picture. After the connection is made, the two modules can communicate through a mechanism called an *interface*. Interfaces require no statically or dynamically linked entry points or hard-coded addresses other than the few general-purpose COM functions that start the communication process. *Interface* (more precisely, *COM interface*) is a term that you'll be seeing a lot of.

What Is a COM Interface?

Before digging into the topic of interfaces, let's reexamine the nature of inheritance and polymorphism in normal C++. We'll use a planetary-motion simulation to illustrate C++ inheritance and polymorphism. Imagine a spaceship that travels through our solar system under the influence of the sun's gravity. In ordinary C++, you can declare a *CSpaceship* class and write a constructor that sets the spaceship's initial position and acceleration. You can then write a nonvirtual member function named *Fly* that implements Kepler's laws to model the movement of the spaceship from one position to the next—say, over a period of 0.1 second. You can also write a *Display* function that paints an image of the spaceship in a window. The most interesting feature of the *CSpaceship* class is that the interface of the C++ class (the way the client talks to the class) and the implementation are tightly bound. One of the main goals of COM is to separate a class's interface from its implementation.

If we think of this example within the context of COM, the spaceship code can exist as a separate EXE or DLL (the component), which is a COM module. In COM, the simulation manager (the client program) can't call *Fly* or any *CSpaceship* constructor directly: COM provides only a standard global function to gain access to the spaceship object, and then the client and the object use interfaces to talk to one another.

Before we tackle real COM, let's build a COM simulation in which both the component and the client code are statically linked in the same EXE file. For our standard global function, we'll invent a function named *GetClassObject*. In this COM simulation, clients will use this global single abstract function for objects of a particular class. In real COM, clients get a class object first and then ask the class object to manufacture the real object in much the same way that MFC does dynamic creation.

GetClassObject has the following three parameters:

```
BOOL GetClassObject(int nClsid, int nIid, void** ppvObj);
```

The first parameter, *nClsid*, is a 32-bit integer that uniquely identifies the *CSpaceship* class. The second parameter, *nIid*, is the unique identifier of the interface that we want. The third parameter is a pointer to an interface to the object. Remember that we'll be dealing with interfaces, which are different from classes. As it turns out, a class can have several interfaces, so the last two parameters exist to manage interface selection. The function will return *TRUE* if the call is successful.

Now let's back up to the design of *CSpaceship*. We haven't really explained spaceship interfaces yet. A COM interface is a C++ base class (actually, a C++ *struct*) that declares a group of pure virtual functions. These functions completely control some aspect of derived class behavior. For *CSpaceship*, let's write an interface named *IMotion*, which controls the spaceship object's position. For simplicity's sake, we'll declare just two functions, *Fly* and *GetPosition*, and we'll keep things uncomplicated by making the position value an integer. The *Fly* function calculates the position of the spaceship, and the *GetPosition* function returns a reference to the current position. Here are the declarations:

```
struct IMotion
{
    virtual void Fly() = 0;
    virtual int& GetPosition() = 0;
};

class CSpaceship : public IMotion
{
protected:
    int m_nPosition;
```

```
public:
    CSpaceship() { m_nPosition = 0; }
    void Fly();
    int& GetPosition() { return m_nPosition; }
};
IMotion* pMot;
GetClassObject(CLSID_CSpaceship, IID_IMotion, (void**) &pMot);
```

Assume for the moment that COM can use the unique integer identifiers *CLSID_CSpaceship* and *IID_IMotion* to construct a spaceship object instead of some other kind of object. If the call is successful, *pMot* will point to a *CSpaceship* object that *GetClassObject* will somehow construct. As you can see, the *CSpaceship* class implements the *Fly* and *GetPosition* functions, and our main program can call them for the one particular spaceship object, as shown here:

```
int nPos = 50;
pMot->GetPosition() = nPos;
pMot->Fly();
nPos = pMot->GetPosition();
TRACE("new position = %d\n", nPos);
```

Now the spaceship is off and flying. We're controlling it entirely through the *pMot* pointer. Notice that *pMot* is technically not a pointer to a *CSpaceship* object. However, in this case, a *CSpaceship* pointer and an *IMotion* pointer are the same because *CSpaceship* is derived from *IMotion*. You can see how the virtual functions work here: It's classic C++ polymorphism.

Let's make things a little more complex by adding a second interface, *IVisual*, which handles the spaceship's visual representation. One function is enough—*Display*. Here's the whole base class:

```
struct IVisual
{
    virtual void Display() = 0;
};
```

Are you getting the idea that COM wants you to associate functions in groups? You're not imagining it. But why? Well, in our space simulation, we'll probably want to include other kinds of objects in addition to spaceships. Imagine that the *IMotion* and *IVisual* interfaces are being used for other classes. Perhaps a *CSun* class has an implementation of *IVisual* but does not have an implementation of *IMotion*, and perhaps a *CSpaceStation* class has other interfaces as well. If you "publish" your *IMotion* and *IVisual* interfaces, perhaps other space simulation software companies will adopt them.

You can think of an interface as a contract between two software modules. The idea is that interface declarations never change. If you want to upgrade your spaceship code, you don't change the *IMotion* or the *IVisual* interface;

rather, you add a new interface, such as *ICrew*. The existing spaceship clients can continue to run with the old interfaces, and new client programs can use the new *ICrew* interface as well. These client programs can find out at run time which interfaces a particular spaceship software version supports.

You can consider the *GetClassObject* function a more powerful alternative to the C++ *new* operator and class constructors. With the ordinary *new* operator and constructor mechanism, you obtain one object containing member functions. With the *GetClassObject* function, you obtain the object and a way to talk to the object (an interface). As you'll see later, you start with one interface and then use that interface to get other interfaces to the same object.

So how do you program two interfaces for *CSpaceship*? You could use C++ multiple inheritance, but that doesn't work if two interfaces have the same member function name. The MFC library uses nested classes instead, so that's what we'll use to illustrate multiple interfaces on the *CSpaceship* class. Here's a first cut at nesting interfaces within the *CSpaceship* class:

```
class CSpaceship
{
protected:
    int m_nPosition;
    int m_nAcceleration;
    int m_nColor;
public:
    CSpaceship()
        { m_nPosition = m_nAcceleration = m_nColor = 0; }
    class XMotion : public IMotion
    {
    public:
        XMotion() { }
        virtual void Fly();
        virtual int& GetPosition();
    } m_xMotion;

    class XVisual : public IVisual
    {
    public:
        XVisual() { }
        virtual void Display();
    } m_xVisual;

    friend class XVisual;
    friend class XMotion;
};
```

> **Note** It might make sense to make *m_nAcceleration* a data member of *XMotion* and make *m_nColor* a data member of *XVisual*. We'll make them data members of *CSpaceship* because that strategy is more compatible with the MFC macros, as you'll see later.

Notice that the implementations of *IMotion* and *IVisual* are contained within the "parent" *CSpaceship* class. In COM, this parent class is known as the class with *object identity*. Be aware that *m_xMotion* and *m_xVisual* are actually embedded data members of *CSpaceship*. Indeed, you could have implemented *CSpaceship* strictly with embedding. Nesting, however, offers two advantages: First, nested class member functions can access parent class data members without the need for *CSpaceship* pointer data members. Second, the nested classes are neatly packaged along with the parent while remaining invisible outside the parent. Look at the following code for the *GetPosition* member function:

```
int& CSpaceship::XMotion::GetPosition()
{
    METHOD_PROLOGUE(CSpaceship, Motion) // makes pThis
    return pThis->m_nPosition;
}
```

Notice the double-scope resolution operators, which are necessary for nested class member functions. *METHOD_PROLOGUE* is a one-line MFC macro that uses the C *offsetof* operator to retrieve the offset used in generating a *this* pointer to the parent class, *pThis*. The compiler always knows the offset from the beginning of parent class data to the beginning of nested class data. *GetPosition* can thus access the *CSpaceship* data member *m_nPosition*.

Now suppose you have two interface pointers, *pMot* and *pVis*, for a particular *CSpaceship* object. (Don't worry yet about how you got these pointers.) You can call interface member functions in the following manner:

```
pMot->Fly();
pVis->Display();
```

What's happening under the hood? In C++, each class (at least, each class that has virtual functions and is not an abstract base class) has a virtual function table, which is otherwise known as a *vtable*. In this example, that means there are vtables for *CSpaceship::XMotion* and *CSpaceship::XVisual*. For each object, there's a pointer to the object's data, the first element of which is a pointer to the class's vtable. The pointer relationships are shown on the following page.

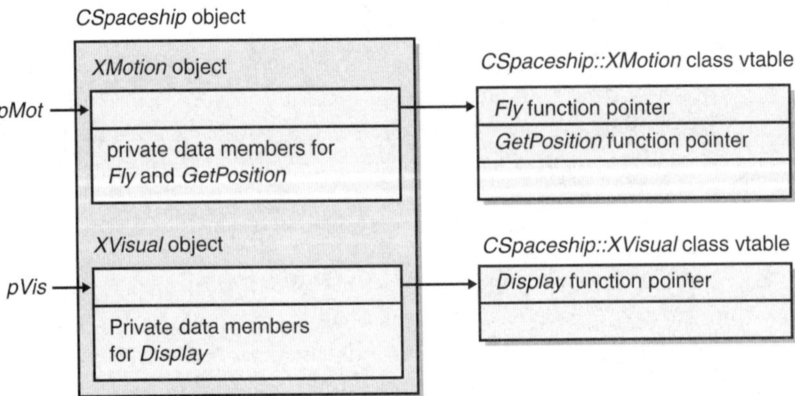

Theoretically, it's possible to program COM in C. If you look at the Windows header files, you'll see code such as this:

```
#ifdef __cplusplus
        // C++-specific headers
#else
        /* C-specific headers */
#endif
```

In C++, interfaces are declared as C++ structures, often with inheritance; in C, they're declared as C *typedef* structures with no inheritance. In C++, the compiler generates vtables for your derived classes; in C, you must "roll your own" vtables, and that gets tedious. It's important to realize, however, that in neither language do the interface declarations have data members, constructors, or destructors. Therefore, you can't rely on the interface having a virtual destructor—but that's not a problem because you never invoke a destructor for an interface.

The *IUnknown* Interface and the *QueryInterface* Member Function

Let's get back to the problem of how to obtain your interface pointers in the first place. COM declares a special interface named *IUnknown* for this purpose. As a matter of fact, all interfaces are derived from *IUnknown*, which has a pure virtual member function, *QueryInterface*, that returns an interface pointer based on the interface ID you feed it.

Once the interface mechanisms are hooked up, the client needs to get an *IUnknown* interface pointer (at the very least) or a pointer to one of the derived interfaces. Here's the new interface hierarchy, with *IUnknown* at the top:

```
struct IUnknown
{
    virtual BOOL QueryInterface(int nIid, void** ppvObj) = 0;
```

```
};
struct IMotion : public IUnknown
{
    virtual void Fly() = 0;
    virtual int& GetPosition() = 0;
};
struct IVisual : public IUnknown
{
    virtual void Display() = 0;
};
```

To satisfy the compiler, we must add *QueryInterface* implementations in both *CSpaceship::XMotion* and *CSpaceship::XVisual*. What do the vtables look like after this is done? For each derived class, the compiler builds a vtable with the base class function pointers on top, as shown here:

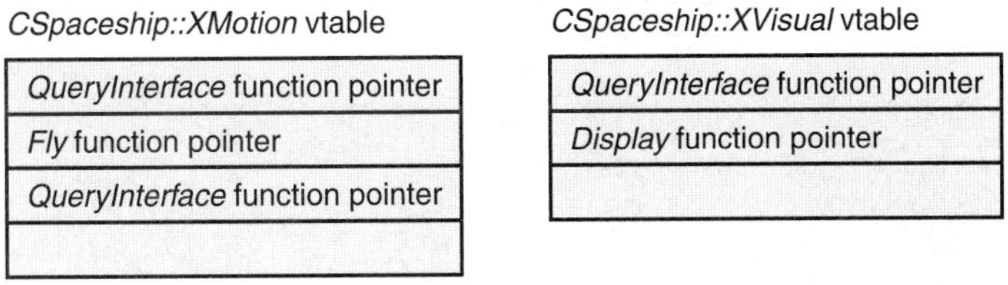

CSpaceship::XMotion vtable
QueryInterface function pointer
Fly function pointer
QueryInterface function pointer

CSpaceship::XVisual vtable
QueryInterface function pointer
Display function pointer

GetClassObject can get the interface pointer for a given *CSpaceship* object by getting the address of the corresponding embedded object. Here's the code for the *QueryInterface* function in *XMotion*:

```
BOOL CSpaceship::XMotion::QueryInterface(int nIid,
                                         void** ppvObj)
{
    METHOD_PROLOGUE(CSpaceship, Motion)
    switch (nIid) {
    case IID_IUnknown:
    case IID_IMotion:
        *ppvObj = &pThis->m_xMotion;
        break;
    case IID_IVisual:
        *ppvObj = &pThis->m_xVisual;
        break;
    default:
        *ppvObj = NULL;
        return FALSE;
    }
    return TRUE;
}
```

Because *IMotion* is derived from *IUnknown*, an *IMotion* pointer is a valid pointer if the caller asks for an *IUnknown* pointer.

Note The COM standard requires that *QueryInterface* return exactly the same *IUnknown* pointer value for *IID_IUnknown*, no matter which interface pointer you start with. Thus, if two *IUnknown* pointers match, you can assume that they refer to the same object. *IUnknown* is sometimes known as the "void*" of COM because it represents the object's identity.

The following is a *GetClassObject* function that uses the address of *m_xMotion* to obtain the first interface pointer for the newly constructed *CSpaceship* object:

```
BOOL GetClassObject(int& nClsid, int& nIid,
                    void** ppvObj)
{
    ASSERT(nClsid == CLSID_CSpaceship);
    CSpaceship* pObj = new CSpaceship();
    IUnknown* pUnk = &pObj->m_xMotion;
    return pUnk->QueryInterface(nIid, ppvObj);
}
```

Now your client program can call *QueryInterface* to obtain an *IVisual* pointer, as shown here:

```
IMotion* pMot;
IVisual* pVis;
GetClassObject(CLSID_CSpaceship, IID_IMotion, (void**) &pMot);
pMot->Fly();
pMot->QueryInterface(IID_IVisual, (void**) &pVis);
pVis->Display();
```

Notice that the client uses a *CSpaceship* object, but it never has an actual *CSpaceship* pointer. Thus, the client cannot directly access *CSpaceship* data members, even if they're public. Notice also that we haven't tried to delete the spaceship object yet—that will come shortly.

There's a special graphical representation for interfaces and COM classes. Interfaces are shown as small circles (or *jacks*) with lines attached to their class. The *IUnknown* interface, which every COM class supports, is at the top, and the others are on the left. The *CSpaceship* class can be represented like this:

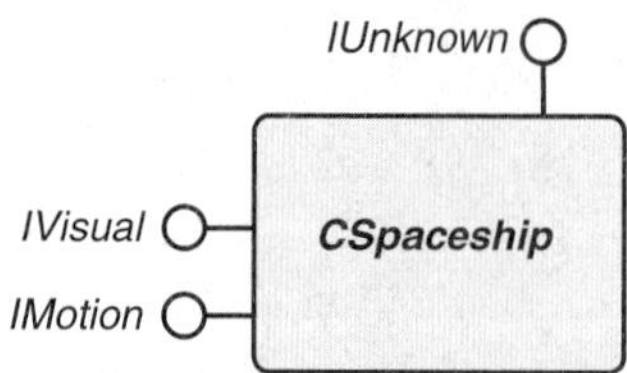

Reference Counting: The *AddRef* and *Release* Functions

COM interfaces don't have virtual destructors, so it isn't cool to write code like the following:

```
delete pMot;  // pMot is an IMotion pointer; don't do this
```

COM has a strict protocol for deleting objects. The two other *IUnknown* virtual functions, *AddRef* and *Release*, are the key. Each COM class has a data member—*m_dwRef* in the MFC library—that keeps track of how many "users" an object has. Each time the component program returns a new interface pointer (as in *QueryInterface*), the program calls *AddRef*, which increments *m_dwRef*. When the client program is finished with the pointer, it calls *Release*. When *m_dwRef* goes to 0, the object destroys itself. Here's an example of a *Release* function for the *CSpaceship::XMotion* class:

```
DWORD CSpaceship::XMotion::Release()
{
    METHOD_PROLOGUE(CSpaceship, Motion) // makes pThis
    if (pThis->m_dwRef == 0)
        return 0;
    if (--pThis->m_dwRef == 0) {
        delete pThis; // the spaceship object
        return 0;
    }
    return pThis->m_dwRef;
}
```

In MFC COM-based programs, the object's constructor sets *m_dwRef* to 1. This means that it isn't necessary to call *AddRef* after the object is first constructed. A client program should call *AddRef*, however, if it makes a copy of an interface pointer.

Class Factories

Object-oriented terminology can get a little fuzzy sometimes. Smalltalk programmers, for example, talk about objects the way C++ programmers talk about classes. The COM literature often uses the term *component object* to refer to the object plus the code associated with it. COM carries with it the notion of a *class object*, which is sometimes referred to as a *class factory*. To be more accurate, it should probably be called an *object factory*. A COM class object represents the global static area of a specific COM class. Its analog in MFC is the *CRuntimeClass*. A class object is sometimes called a *class factory* because it often implements a special COM interface named *IClassFactory*. This interface, like all interfaces, is derived from *IUnknown*. *IClassFactory*'s principal member function is *CreateInstance*, which in our COM simulation is declared like this:

```
virtual BOOL CreateInstance(int& nIid, void** ppvObj) = 0;
```

Why use a class factory? You've already seen that you can't call the target class constructor directly—you have to let the component module decide how to construct objects. The component provides the class factory for this purpose and thus encapsulates the creation step, as it should. Locating and launching component modules—and thus establishing the class factory—is expensive, but constructing objects with *CreateInstance* is cheap. We can therefore allow a single class factory to create multiple objects.

What does all this mean? It means we messed up when we let *GetClassObject* construct the *CSpaceship* object directly. We were supposed to construct a class factory object first and then call *CreateInstance* to cause the class factory (object factory) to construct the actual spaceship object.

Let's properly construct the spaceship simulation. First, we'll declare a new class, *CSpaceshipFactory*. To avoid complication, we'll derive the class from *IClassFactory* so we don't have to deal with nested classes. In addition, we'll add the code that tracks references:

```
struct IClassFactory : public IUnknown
{
    virtual BOOL CreateInstance(int& nIid, void** ppvObj) = 0;
};

class CSpaceshipFactory : public IClassFactory
{
private:
    DWORD m_dwRef;
public:
    CSpaceshipFactory() { m_dwRef = 1; }
    // IUnknown functions
    virtual BOOL QueryInterface(int& nIid,
                                void** ppvObj);
    virtual DWORD AddRef();
    virtual DWORD Release();
    // IClassFactory function
    virtual BOOL CreateInstance(int& nIid,
                                void** ppvObj);
};
```

Next, we'll write the *CreateInstance* member function:

```
BOOL CSpaceshipFactory::CreateInstance(int& nIid, void** ppvObj)
{
    CSpaceship* pObj = new CSpaceship();
    IUnknown* pUnk = &pObj->m_xMotion;
    return pUnk->QueryInterface(nIid, ppvObj);
}
```

Finally, the new *GetClassObject* function will construct a class factory object and return an *IClassFactory* interface pointer:

```
BOOL GetClassObject(int& nClsid, int& nIid,
                    void** ppvObj)
{
    ASSERT(nClsid == CLSID_CSpaceship);
    ASSERT((nIid == IID_IUnknown) || (nIid == IID_IClassFactory));
    CSpaceshipFactory* pObj = new CSpaceshipFactory();
    *ppvObj = pObj; // IUnknown* = IClassFactory* = CSpaceship*
}
```

The *CSpaceship* and *CSpaceshipFactory* classes work together and share the same class ID. Now the client code looks like this (without error-checking logic):

```
IMotion* pMot;
IVisual* pVis;
IClassFactory* pFac;
GetClassObject(CLSID_CSpaceship, IID_IClassFactory, (void**) &pFac);
pFac->CreateInstance(IID_IMotion, &pMot);
pMot->QueryInterface(IID_IVisual, (void**) &pVis);
pMot->Fly();
pVis->Display();
```

Notice that the *CSpaceshipFactory* class implements the *AddRef* and *Release* functions. It must do this because *AddRef* and *Release* are pure virtual functions in the *IUnknown* base class. We'll start using these functions in the next iteration of the program.

The *CCmdTarget* Class

We're still a long way from real MFC COM-based code, but we can take one more step in the COM simulation before we switch to the real thing. As you might guess, some code and data can be "factored out" of our spaceship COM classes into a base class. That's exactly what the MFC library does. The base class is *CCmdTarget*, the standard base class for document and window classes. *CCmdTarget*, in turn, is derived from *CObject*. We'll use *CSimulatedCmdTarget* instead, and we won't put too much in it—only the reference-counting logic and the *m_dwRef* data member. The *CSimulatedCmdTarget* functions *ExternalAddRef* and *ExternalRelease* can be called in derived COM classes. Because we're using *CSimulatedCmdTarget*, we'll bring *CSpaceshipFactory* in line with *CSpaceship* and we'll use a nested class for the *IClassFactory* interface.

We can also do some factoring out inside our *CSpaceship* class. The *QueryInterface* function can be "delegated" from the nested classes to the outer class helper function *ExternalQueryInterface*, which calls *ExternalAddRef*.

Thus, each *QueryInterface* function will increment the reference count, but *CreateInstance* will call *ExternalQueryInterface*, followed by a call to *ExternalRelease*. When the first interface pointer is returned by *CreateInstance*, the spaceship object will have a reference count of 1. A subsequent *QueryInterface* call will increment the count to 2, and in this case, the client will have to call *Release* twice to destroy the spaceship object.

One last thing: We'll make the class factory object a global object so we won't have to call its constructor. When the client calls *Release*, there won't be a problem because the class factory's reference count will be 2 by the time the client receives it. (The *CSpaceshipFactory* constructor sets the reference count to 1, and *ExternalQueryInterface*, called by *GetClassObject*, sets the count to 2.)

The Ex22a Example: Simulated COM

The following files show code for a working "simulated COM" program, Ex22a. This is a Win32 console application (without the MFC library) that uses a class factory to construct an object of class *CSpaceship*, calls its interface functions, and then releases the spaceship. The Interface.h header file contains the *CSimulatedCmdTarget* base class and the interface declarations that are used by both the client and component programs. The Spaceship.h header file contains the spaceship-specific class declarations that are used in the component program. Spaceship.cpp is the component that implements *GetClassObject*, and Client.cpp is the client that calls *GetClassObject*. What's phony here is that both client and component code are linked within the same Ex22a.exe program. Thus, our simulated COM is not required to make the connection at run time. (You'll see how that's done later in this chapter.)

Interface.h

```
// definitions that make our code look like MFC code
#define BOOL   int
#define DWORD  unsigned int
#define TRUE   1
#define FALSE  0
#define TRACE  printf
#define ASSERT assert
//----------definitions and macros-----------------------------
#define CLSID_CSpaceship    10
#define IID_IUnknown        0
#define IID_IClassFactory   1
#define IID_IMotion         2
#define IID_IVisual         3    // this macro for 16-bit Windows only
#define METHOD_PROLOGUE(theClass, localClass) \
    theClass* pThis = ((theClass*)((char*)(this) - \
    offsetof(theClass, m_x##localClass))); \
```

```
BOOL GetClassObject(int nClsid, int nIid, void** ppvObj);

//----------interface declarations-------------------------------
struct IUnknown
{
    IUnknown() { TRACE("Entering IUnknown ctor %p\n", this); }
    virtual BOOL QueryInterface(int nIid, void** ppvObj) = 0;
    virtual DWORD Release() = 0;
    virtual DWORD AddRef() = 0;
};
struct IClassFactory : public IUnknown
{
    IClassFactory()
        { TRACE("Entering IClassFactory ctor %p\n", this); }
    virtual BOOL CreateInstance(int nIid, void** ppvObj) = 0;
};
struct IMotion : public IUnknown
{
    IMotion() { TRACE("Entering IMotion ctor %p\n", this); }
    virtual void Fly() = 0; // pure
    virtual int& GetPosition() = 0;
};
struct IVisual : public IUnknown
{
    IVisual() { TRACE("Entering IVisual ctor %p\n", this); }
    virtual void Display() = 0;
};
class CSimulatedCmdTarget // 'simulated' CSimulatedCmdTarget
{
public:
    DWORD m_dwRef;
protected:
    CSimulatedCmdTarget() {
        TRACE("Entering CSimulatedCmdTarget ctor %p\n", this);
        m_dwRef = 1; // implied first AddRef
    }
    virtual ~CSimulatedCmdTarget()
        { TRACE("Entering CSimulatedCmdTarget dtor %p\n", this); }
    DWORD ExternalRelease() {
    TRACE("Entering CSimulatedCmdTarget::ExternalRelease--RefCount = %ld\n",
          m_dwRef);
        if (m_dwRef == 0)
            return 0;
        if(--m_dwRef == 0L) {
            TRACE("deleting\n");
            delete this;
            return 0;
        }
        return m_dwRef;
    }
    DWORD ExternalAddRef() { return ++m_dwRef; }
};
```

(continued)

Spaceship.h

```
class CSpaceship;
//----------class declarations-----------------------------------
class CSpaceshipFactory : public CSimulatedCmdTarget
{
public:
    CSpaceshipFactory()
        { TRACE("Entering CSpaceshipFactory ctor %p\n", this); }
    ~CSpaceshipFactory()
        { TRACE("Entering CSpaceshipFactory dtor %p\n", this); }
    BOOL ExternalQueryInterface(int lRid, void** ppvObj);
    class XClassFactory : public IClassFactory
    {
    public:
        XClassFactory()
            { TRACE("Entering XClassFactory ctor %p\n", this); }
        virtual BOOL QueryInterface(int lRid, void** ppvObj);
        virtual DWORD Release();
        virtual DWORD AddRef();
        virtual BOOL CreateInstance(int lRid, void** ppvObj);
    } m_xClassFactory;
    friend class XClassFactory;
};
class CSpaceship : public CSimulatedCmdTarget
{
private:
    int m_nPosition; // We can access these from
                     //  all the interfaces
    int m_nAcceleration;
    int m_nColor;
public:
    CSpaceship() {
        TRACE("Entering CSpaceship ctor %p\n", this);
        m_nPosition = 100;
        m_nAcceleration = 101;
        m_nColor = 102;
    }
    ~CSpaceship()
        { TRACE("Entering CSpaceship dtor %p\n", this); }
    BOOL ExternalQueryInterface(int lRid, void** ppvObj);
    class XMotion : public IMotion
    {
    public:
        XMotion()
            { TRACE("Entering XMotion ctor %p\n", this); }
        virtual BOOL QueryInterface(int lRid, void** ppvObj);
        virtual DWORD Release();
        virtual DWORD AddRef();
        virtual void Fly();
        virtual int& GetPosition();
    } m_xMotion;
```

```
    class XVisual : public IVisual
    {
    public:
        XVisual() { TRACE("Entering XVisual ctor\n"); }
        virtual BOOL QueryInterface(int lRid, void** ppvObj);
        virtual DWORD Release();
        virtual DWORD AddRef();
        virtual void Display();
    } m_xVisual;

    friend class XVisual;  // These must be at the bottom!
    friend class XMotion;
    friend class CSpaceshipFactory::XClassFactory;
};
```

Spaceship.cpp

```
#include <stdio.h>
#include <stddef.h> // for offsetof in METHOD_PROLOGUE
#include <ASSERT.h>
#include "Interface.h"
#include "Spaceship.h"

CSpaceshipFactory g_factory;
//----------member functions-------------------------------------
BOOL CSpaceshipFactory::ExternalQueryInterface(int nIid,
                                               void** ppvObj) {
    TRACE(
        "Entering CSpaceshipFactory::ExternalQueryInterface--nIid = %d\n",
        nIid);
    switch (nIid) {
    case IID_IUnknown:
    case IID_IClassFactory:
        *ppvObj = &m_xClassFactory;
        break;
    default:
        *ppvObj = NULL;
        return FALSE;
    }
    ExternalAddRef();
    return TRUE;
}
BOOL CSpaceshipFactory::XClassFactory::QueryInterface(int nIid,
                                               void** ppvObj) {
    TRACE("Entering CSpaceshipFactory::XClassFactory::\
          QueryInterface--nIid = %d\n", nIid);
    METHOD_PROLOGUE(CSpaceshipFactory, ClassFactory) // makes pThis
    return pThis->ExternalQueryInterface(nIid,
        ppvObj); // delegate to
                                           //  CSpaceshipFactory
}
```

(continued)

```
BOOL CSpaceshipFactory::XClassFactory::CreateInstance(int nIid,
                                                      void** ppvObj) {
    TRACE("Entering CSpaceshipFactory::XClassFactory::CreateInstance\n");
    METHOD_PROLOGUE(CSpaceshipFactory, ClassFactory) // makes pThis
    CSpaceship* pObj = new CSpaceship();
    if (pObj->ExternalQueryInterface(nIid, ppvObj)) {
        pObj->ExternalRelease(); // balance reference count
        return TRUE;
    }
    return FALSE;
}
DWORD CSpaceshipFactory::XClassFactory::Release() {
    TRACE("Entering CSpaceshipFactory::XClassFactory::Release\n");
    METHOD_PROLOGUE(CSpaceshipFactory, ClassFactory) // makes pThis
    return pThis->ExternalRelease(); // delegate to CSimulatedCmdTarget
}
DWORD CSpaceshipFactory::XClassFactory::AddRef() {
    TRACE("Entering CSpaceshipFactory::XClassFactory::AddRef\n");
    METHOD_PROLOGUE(CSpaceshipFactory, ClassFactory) // makes pThis
    return pThis->ExternalAddRef(); // delegate to CSimulatedCmdTarget
}
BOOL CSpaceship::ExternalQueryInterface(int nIid, void** ppvObj) {
    TRACE("Entering CSpaceship::ExternalQueryInterface--nIid = %d\n",
          nIid);
    switch (nIid) {
    case IID_IUnknown:
    case IID_IMotion:
        *ppvObj = &m_xMotion; // Both IMotion and IVisual are derived
        break;                // from IUnknown, so either pointer will do
    case IID_IVisual:
        *ppvObj = &m_xVisual;
        break;
    default:
        *ppvObj = NULL;
        return FALSE;
    }
    ExternalAddRef();
    return TRUE;
}
BOOL CSpaceship::XMotion::QueryInterface(int nIid, void** ppvObj) {
    TRACE("Entering CSpaceship::XMotion::QueryInterface--nIid = %d\n",
          nIid);
    METHOD_PROLOGUE(CSpaceship, Motion) // makes pThis
    return pThis->ExternalQueryInterface(nIid, ppvObj); // delegate to
                                                         //  CSpaceship
}
DWORD CSpaceship::XMotion::Release() {
    TRACE("Entering CSpaceship::XMotion::Release\n");
```

```
    METHOD_PROLOGUE(CSpaceship, Motion) // makes pThis
    return pThis->ExternalRelease(); // delegate to CSimulatedCmdTarget
}
DWORD CSpaceship::XMotion::AddRef() {
    TRACE("Entering CSpaceship::XMotion::AddRef\n");
    METHOD_PROLOGUE(CSpaceship, Motion) // makes pThis
    return pThis->ExternalAddRef(); // delegate to CSimulatedCmdTarget
}
void CSpaceship::XMotion::Fly() {
    TRACE("Entering CSpaceship::XMotion::Fly\n");
    METHOD_PROLOGUE(CSpaceship, Motion) // makes pThis
    TRACE("this = %p, pThis = %p\n", this, pThis);
    TRACE("m_nPosition = %d\n", pThis->m_nPosition);
    TRACE("m_nAcceleration = %d\n", pThis->m_nAcceleration);
}
int& CSpaceship::XMotion::GetPosition() {
    TRACE("Entering CSpaceship::XMotion::GetPosition\n");
    METHOD_PROLOGUE(CSpaceship, Motion) // makes pThis
    TRACE("this = %p, pThis = %p\n", this, pThis);
    TRACE("m_nPosition = %d\n", pThis->m_nPosition);
    TRACE("m_nAcceleration = %d\n", pThis->m_nAcceleration);
    return pThis->m_nPosition;
}
BOOL CSpaceship::XVisual::QueryInterface(int nIid, void** ppvObj) {
    TRACE("Entering CSpaceship::XVisual::QueryInterface--nIid = %d\n",
          nIid);
    METHOD_PROLOGUE(CSpaceship, Visual) // makes pThis
    return pThis->ExternalQueryInterface(nIid, ppvObj); // delegate to
                                                         //  CSpaceship
}
DWORD CSpaceship::XVisual::Release() {
    TRACE("Entering CSpaceship::XVisual::Release\n");
    METHOD_PROLOGUE(CSpaceship, Visual) // makes pThis
    return pThis->ExternalRelease(); // delegate to CSimulatedCmdTarget
}
DWORD CSpaceship::XVisual::AddRef() {
    TRACE("Entering CSpaceship::XVisual::AddRef\n");
    METHOD_PROLOGUE(CSpaceship, Visual) // makes pThis
    return pThis->ExternalAddRef(); // delegate to CSimulatedCmdTarget
}
void CSpaceship::XVisual::Display() {
    TRACE("Entering CSpaceship::XVisual::Display\n");
    METHOD_PROLOGUE(CSpaceship, Visual) // makes pThis
    TRACE("this = %p, pThis = %p\n", this, pThis);
    TRACE("m_nPosition = %d\n", pThis->m_nPosition);
    TRACE("m_nColor = %d\n", pThis->m_nColor);
}
//----------simulates COM component --------------------------------
// In real COM, this would be DllGetClassObject, which would be called
//  whenever a client called CoGetClassObject
```

(continued)

```
BOOL GetClassObject(int nClsid, int nIid, void** ppvObj)
{
    ASSERT(nClsid == CLSID_CSpaceship);
    ASSERT((nIid == IID_IUnknown) || (nIid == IID_IClassFactory));
    return g_factory.ExternalQueryInterface(nIid, ppvObj);
    // Refcount is 2, which prevents accidental deletion
}
```

Client.cpp

```
#include <stdio.h>
#include <stddef.h> // for offsetof in METHOD_PROLOGUE
#include <assert.h>
#include "interface.h"

//----------main program--------------------------------------------
int main() // simulates OLE client program
{
    TRACE("Entering client main\n");
    IUnknown* pUnk; // If you declare these void*, you lose type-safety
    IMotion* pMot;
    IVisual* pVis;
    IClassFactory* pClf;

    GetClassObject(CLSID_CSpaceship, IID_IClassFactory,
                   (void**) &pClf);

    pClf->CreateInstance(IID_IUnknown, (void**) &pUnk);
    pUnk->QueryInterface(IID_IMotion, (void**) &pMot); // All three
    pMot->QueryInterface(IID_IVisual, (void**) &pVis); //  pointers
                                                       //  should work
    TRACE("main: pUnk = %p, pMot = %p, pDis = %p\n", pUnk,
          pMot, pVis);

    // Test all the interface virtual functions
    pMot->Fly();
    int nPos = pMot->GetPosition();
    TRACE("nPos = %d\n", nPos);
    pVis->Display();

    pClf->Release();
    pUnk->Release();
    pMot->Release();
    pVis->Release();
    return 0;
}
```

Real COM with the MFC Library

So much for simulations. Now we'll get ready to convert the spaceship example to genuine COM. You need to acquire a little more knowledge before we start, though. First, you must learn about the *CoGetClassObject* function, then you must learn how COM uses the Windows Registry to load the component, and then you have to understand the difference between an *in-process component* (a DLL) and an *out-of-process component* (an EXE or a DLL running as a surrogate). Finally, you must become familiar with the MFC macros that support nested classes.

The net result will be an MFC regular DLL component that contains all the *CSpaceship* code with the *IMotion* and *IVisual* interfaces. A regular MFC library Windows application will act as the client. It will load and run the component when the user chooses a menu command.

The COM *CoGetClassObject* Function

In our simulation, we used a phony function named *GetClassObject*. In real COM, we'll use the global *CoGetClassObject* function. (Co stands for "component object.") Compare the following prototype to the *GetClassObject* function you saw earlier:

```
STDAPI CoGetClassObject(REFCLSID rclsid, DWORD dwClsContext,
    COSERVERINFO* pServerInfo, REFIID riid, LPVOID* ppvObj)
```

The interface pointer goes in the *ppvObj* parameter, and *pServerInfo* is a pointer to a machine on which the class object is instantiated (*NULL* if the machine is local). The types *REFCLSID* and *REFIID* are references to 128-bit globally unique identifiers (GUIDs) for COM classes and interfaces. *STDAPI* indicates that the function returns a 32-bit value of type *HRESULT*.

The standard GUIDs (for example, those that name interfaces that Microsoft has created) are defined in the Windows libraries that are dynamically linked to your program. You must define GUIDs for custom classes and interfaces, such as those for spaceship objects, in this way:

```
// {692D03A4-C689-11CE-B337-88EA36DE9E4E}
static const IID IID_IMotion =
    {0x692d03a4, 0xc689, 0x11ce, {0xb3, 0x37, 0x88, 0xea, 0x36,
     0xde, 0x9e, 0x4e}};
```

If the *dwClsContext* parameter is *CLSCTX_INPROC_SERVER*, the COM subsytem will look for a DLL. If the parameter is *CLSCTX_LOCAL_SERVER*, COM will look for an EXE. The two flags can be ORed together to indicate loading of a DLL if the DLL is available or an EXE if the DLL isn't available. For example, in-process servers are fastest because everybody shares the same address space. Communication EXE servers are considerably slower because the interprocess calls involve data copying as well as many thread context switches. The return value is an *HRESULT* value, which is 0 (*NOERROR*) if no error occurs.

> **Note** Another COM function, *CoCreateInstance*, combines the functionality of *CoGetClassObject* and *IClassFactory::CreateInstance*.

COM and the Windows Registry

In the Ex22a example, the component is statically linked to the client—a clearly bogus circumstance. In real COM, the component is either a DLL or a separate EXE. When the client calls the *CoGetClassObject* function, COM steps in and finds the correct component, which is located somewhere on disk. How does COM make the connection? It looks up the class's unique 128-bit class ID number in the Windows Registry. Thus, the class must be registered permanently on your computer.

If you run the Windows Regedit program, you'll see a screen similar to the one shown in Figure 22-1. This figure shows subfolders for four class IDs, three of which are class IDs associated with DLLs (InprocServer32) and one of which is a class ID associated with an EXE (LocalServer32). The *CoGetClassObject* function looks up the class ID in the Registry and then loads the DLL or EXE as required.

What if you don't want to track those ugly class ID numbers in your client program? No problem. COM supports another type of registration database entry that translates a human-readable program ID into the corresponding class ID. Figure 22-2 shows the Registry entries. The COM function *CLSIDFromProgID* reads the database and performs the translation.

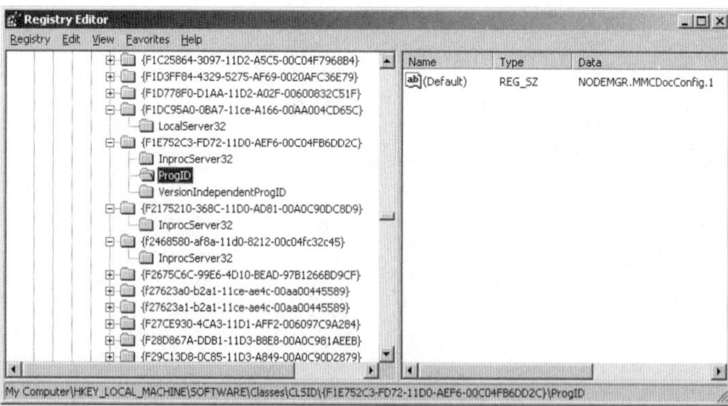

Figure 22-1 Subfolders of four class IDs in the Registry.

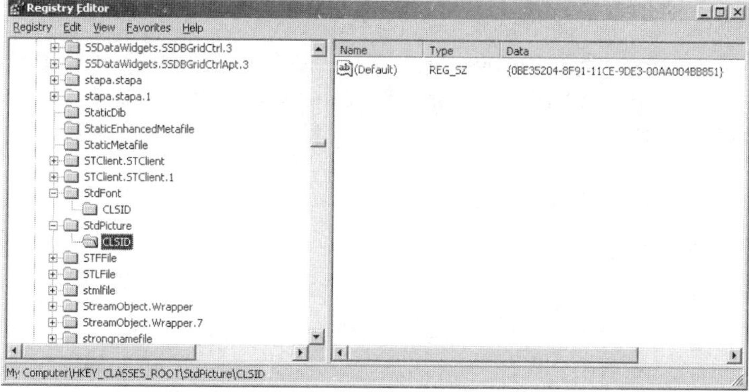

Figure 22-2 Human-readable program IDs in the Registry.

The first *CLSIDFromProgID* parameter is a string that holds the program ID, but it's not an ordinary string. This is your first exposure to double-byte characters in COM. All string parameters of COM functions (except Data Access Objects [DAO]) are Unicode character string pointers of type *OLECHAR**. The constant need to convert between double-byte strings and ordinary strings will make your life miserable. If you need a double-byte literal string, prefix the string with an *L* character, like this:

```
CLSIDFromProgID(L"Spaceship", &clsid);
```

You'll begin learning about the MFC library's Unicode string conversion capabilities in Chapter 23.

How does the registration information get into the Registry? You can program your component application to call Windows functions that directly update the Registry. The MFC library conveniently wraps these functions with the function *COleObjectFactory::UpdateRegistryAll*, which finds all your program's global class factory objects and registers their names and class IDs.

Runtime Object Registration

You've just seen how the Windows Registry registers COM classes on disk. Class factory objects also must be registered in memory for out-of-process servers. It's unfortunate that the word *register* is used in both contexts. Objects in out-of-process component modules are registered at run time with a call to the COM *CoRegisterClassObject* function, and the registration information is maintained in memory by the Windows DLLs. If the factory is registered in a mode that permits a single instance of the component module to create multiple COM objects, COM can use an existing process when a client calls *CoGetClassObject*.

How a COM Client Calls an In-Process Component

We're beginning with a DLL component instead of an EXE component because the program interactions are simpler. I'll show pseudocode here because you'll be using the MFC library classes, which hide much of the detail.

Client

```
CLSID clsid;
IClassFactory* pClf;
IUnknown* pUnk;
CoInitialize(NULL);  // Initialize COM
CLSIDFromProgID("componentname", &clsid);
```

COM

COM uses the Registry to look up the class ID from "componentname"

Client

```
CoGetClassObject(clsid, CLSCTX_INPROC_SERVER, NULL,
IID_IClassFactory, (void**) &pClf );
```

COM

```
COM uses the class ID to look for a component in memory
if (component DLL is not loaded already)
{
COM gets DLL filename from the Registry
COM loads the component DLL into process memory
}
```

DLL Component

```
if (component just loaded) {
Global factory objects are constructed
DLL's InitInstance called (MFC only)
}
```

COM

COM calls DLL's global exported DllGetClassObject with the CLSID value that was passed to CoGetClassObject

DLL Component

DllGetClassObject returns IClassFactory*

COM

COM returns IClassFactory* to client

Client	
	pClf->CreateInstance (NULL, IID_IUnknown, (void**) &pUnk);
DLL Component	
	Class factory's CreateInstance function called (called directly—through component's vtable) Constructs object of "componentname" class Returns requested interface pointer
Client	
	pClf->Release(); pUnk->Release();
DLL Component	

	"componentname" Release is called through vtable
	if (refcount == 0) {
	Object destroys itself
	}

Client	
	CoFreeUnusedLibraries();
COM	
	COM calls DLL's global exported DllCanUnloadNow
DLL Component	

	DllCanUnloadNow called if (all DLL's objects destroyed) {
	return TRUE
	}

Client	
	CoUninitialize(); // COM frees the DLL if DllCanUnloadNow returns TRUE just prior to exit
COM	
	COM releases resources
Client	
	Client exits
DLL Component	
	Windows unloads the DLL if it is still loaded and no other programs are using it

Some important points to note: First, the DLL's exported *DllGetClassObject* function is called in response to the client's *CoGetClassObject* call. Second, the class factory interface address returned is the actual physical address of the class factory vtable pointer in the DLL. Third, when the client calls *CreateInstance*—or any other interface function—the call is direct (through the component's vtable).

The COM linkage between a client EXE and a component DLL is quite efficient—as efficient as the linkage to any C++ virtual function in the same process, plus the full C++ parameter and return type-checking at compile time. The only penalty for using ordinary DLL linkage is the extra step of looking up the class ID in the Registry when the DLL is first loaded.

How a COM Client Calls an Out-of-Process Component

The COM linkage to a separate EXE component is more complicated than the linkage to a DLL component. The EXE component is in a different process, or possibly on a different computer. Don't worry, though. You should write your programs as if a direct connection existed. COM takes care of the details through its remoting architecture, which usually involves RPCs.

In an RPC, the client makes calls to a special DLL called a *proxy*. The proxy sends a stream of data to a *stub*, which is inside a DLL in the component's process. When the client calls a component function, the proxy alerts the stub by sending a message to the component program, which is processed by a hidden window. The mechanism of converting parameters to and from data streams is called *marshaling*.

If you use standard interfaces (those defined by Microsoft) such as IClassFactory and IPersist (an interface we'll look at later when we examine COM persistence), the proxy and the stub code, which implement marshaling, are provided by the Windows OLEAUT32 DLL. If you invent your own interfaces, such as IMotion and IVisual, you must write the proxies and stubs yourself. Fortunately, creating proxy and stub classes involves simply defining your interfaces in Interface Definition Language (IDL) and compiling the code produced by the Microsoft Interface Definition Language (MIDL) compiler.

Here's the pseudocode interaction between an EXE client and an EXE component. Compare it to the DLL version beginning on page 554. Notice that the client-side calls are exactly the same.

Client

```
CLSID clsid;
IClassFactory* pClf;
IUnknown* pUnk;
CoInitialize(NULL);  // Initialize COM
CLSIDFromProgID("componentname", &clsid);
```

COM	
	COM uses the Registry to look up the class ID from "componentname"
Client	
	CoGetClassObject(clsid, CLSCTX_LOCAL_SERVER, NULL, IID_IClassFactory, (void**) &pClf);
COM	

	COM uses the class ID to look for a component in memory if (component EXE is not loaded already, or if we need another instance) {
	COM gets EXE filename from the Registry
	COM loads the component EXE
	}

EXE Component	

	if (just loaded) {
	Global factory objects are constructed
	InitInstance called (MFC only)
	CoInitialize(NULL);
	for each factory object {
	CoRegisterClassObject(...);
	Returns IClassFactory* to COM
	}
	}

COM	
	COM returns the requested interface pointer to the client (client's pointer is not the same as the component's interface pointer)
Client	
	pClf->CreateInstance(NULL, IID_IUnknown, (void**) &pUnk);
EXE Component	
	Class factory's CreateInstance function called (called indirectly through marshaling) Constructs object of "componentname" class Returns requested interface pointer indirectly

(continued)

Client

pClf->Release();

pUnk->Release();

EXE Component

"componentname" Release is called indirectly

if (refcount == 0) {

Object destroys itself

}

if (all objects released) {

Component exits gracefully

}

Client

CoUninitialize(); // just prior to exit

COM

COM calls Release for any objects this client has failed to release

EXE Component

Component exits

COM

COM releases resources

Client

Client exits

As you can see, COM plays an important role in the communication between the client and the component. COM keeps an in-memory list of class factories that are in active EXE components, but it does not keep track of individual COM objects such as the *CSpaceship* object. Individual COM objects are responsible for updating the reference count and for destroying themselves through the *AddRef/Release* mechanism. COM does step in when a client exits. If that client is using an out-of-process component, COM will "listen in" on the communication and keep track of the reference count on each object. COM will disconnect from component objects when the client exits. Under certain circumstances, this will cause those objects to be released. Don't depend on this behavior, however. Be sure that your client program releases all its interface pointers before exiting.

The MFC Interface Macros

In Ex22a, you saw nested classes used for interface implementation. The MFC library has a set of macros that automate this process. For the *CSpaceship* class, which is derived from the real MFC *CCmdTarget* class, you use these macros inside the declaration:

```
BEGIN_INTERFACE_PART(Motion, IMotion)
    STDMETHOD_(void, Fly) ();
    STDMETHOD_(int&, GetPosition) ();
END_INTERFACE_PART(Motion)

BEGIN_INTERFACE_PART(Visual, IVisual)
    STDMETHOD_(void, Display) ();
END_INTERFACE_PART(Visual)

DECLARE_INTERFACE_MAP()
```

The *INTERFACE_PART* macros generate the nested classes, adding *X* to the first parameter to form the class name and adding *m_x* to form the embedded object name. The macros generate prototypes for the specified interface functions plus prototypes for *QueryInterface*, *AddRef*, and *Release*.

The *DECLARE_INTERFACE_MAP* macro generates the declarations for a table that holds the IDs of all the class's interfaces. The *CCmdTarget::ExternalQueryInterface* function uses the table to retrieve the interface pointers.

In the *CSpaceship* implementation file, use the following macros:

```
BEGIN_INTERFACE_MAP(CSpaceship, CCmdTarget)
    INTERFACE_PART(CSpaceship, IID_IMotion, Motion)
    INTERFACE_PART(CSpaceship, IID_IVisual, Visual)
END_INTERFACE_MAP()
```

These macros build the interface table used by *CCmdTarget::ExternalQueryInterface*. A typical interface member function looks like this:

```
STDMETHODIMP_(void) CSpaceship::XMotion::Fly()
{
    METHOD_PROLOGUE(CSpaceship, Motion)
    pThis->m_nPosition += 10;
    return;
}
```

Don't forget that you must implement all the functions for each interface, including *QueryInterface*, *AddRef*, and *Release*. Those three functions can delegate to functions in *CCmdTarget*.

> **Note** The *STDMETHOD_* and *STDMETHODIMP_* macros declare and implement functions using the *__stdcall* parameter passing convention, as required by COM. These macros allow you to specify the return value as the first parameter. Two other macros, *STDMETHOD* and *STDMETHODIMP*, assume an *HRESULT* return value.

The MFC *COleObjectFactory* Class

In the simulated COM example, you saw a *CSpaceshipFactory* class that was hard-coded to generate *CSpaceship* objects. The MFC library applies its dynamic creation technology to the problem. Thus, a single class, aptly named *COleObjectFactory*, can create objects of any class specified at run time. All you need to do is use macros like these in the class declaration:

```
DECLARE_DYNCREATE(CSpaceship)
DECLARE_OLECREATE(CSpaceship)
```

And use macros like these in the implementation file:

```
IMPLEMENT_DYNCREATE(CSpaceship, CCmdTarget)
// {692D03A3-C689-11CE-B337-88EA36DE9E4E}
IMPLEMENT_OLECREATE(CSpaceship, "Spaceship", 0x692d03a3, 0xc689, 0x11ce,
    0xb3, 0x37, 0x88, 0xea, 0x36, 0xde, 0x9e, 0x4e)
```

The *DYNCREATE* macros set up the standard dynamic creation mechanism. The *OLECREATE* macros declare and define a global object of class *COleObjectFactory* with the specified unique CLSID. In a DLL component, the exported *DllGetClassObject* function finds the specified class factory object and returns a pointer to it based on global variables set by the *OLECREATE* macros. In an EXE component, initialization code calls the static *COleObjectFactory::RegisterAll*, which finds all factory objects and registers each one by calling *CoRegisterClassObject*. The *RegisterAll* function is also called when a DLL is initialized. In that case, it merely sets a flag in the factory object(s).

We've really just scratched the surface of MFC's COM support. If you need more details, see Shepherd and Wingo's *MFC Internals*.

Wizard Support for COM In-Process Components

The MFC DLL Wizard isn't optimized for creating COM DLL components, but you can add COM support to your DLLs by requesting a regular DLL with Automation support. (Select Automation on the Application Settings page.) The following functions in the project's main source file are of interest:

```
BOOL CEx22bApp::InitInstance()
{
    CWinApp::InitInstance();
    // Register all OLE server (factories) as running.  This enables the
    //  OLE libraries to create objects from other applications.
    COleObjectFactory::RegisterAll();
    return TRUE;
}
// DllGetClassObject - Returns class factory
STDAPI DllGetClassObject(REFCLSID rclsid, REFIID riid, LPVOID* ppv)
{
    AFX_MANAGE_STATE(AfxGetStaticModuleState());
    return AfxDllGetClassObject(rclsid, riid, ppv);
}
// DllCanUnloadNow - Allows COM to unload DLL
STDAPI DllCanUnloadNow(void)
{
    AFX_MANAGE_STATE(AfxGetStaticModuleState());
    return AfxDllCanUnloadNow();
}
// DllRegisterServer - Adds entries to the system registry
STDAPI DllRegisterServer(void)
{
    AFX_MANAGE_STATE(AfxGetStaticModuleState());
    if (!AfxOleRegisterTypeLib(AfxGetInstanceHandle(), _tlid))
        return SELFREG_E_TYPELIB;

    if (!COleObjectFactory::UpdateRegistryAll())
        return SELFREG_E_CLASS;

    return S_OK;
}
// DllUnregisterServer - Removes entries from the system registry
STDAPI DllUnregisterServer(void)
{
    AFX_MANAGE_STATE(AfxGetStaticModuleState());
    if (!AfxOleUnregisterTypeLib(_tlid, _wVerMajor, _wVerMinor))
        return SELFREG_E_TYPELIB;

    if (!COleObjectFactory::UpdateRegistryAll(FALSE))
        return SELFREG_E_CLASS;

    return S_OK;
}
```

The four global functions are exported in the project's DEF file. By calling MFC functions, you ensure that the global functions do everything you need in a COM in-process component. The *DllRegisterServer* and *DllUnregisterServer* functions can be called by a utility program to update the system Registry.

Once you've created the skeleton project, your next step is to use MFC Class Wizard to add one or more COM-creatable classes to the project. Specify the class name, the base class, and filenames for the new class on the Names page, as shown here:

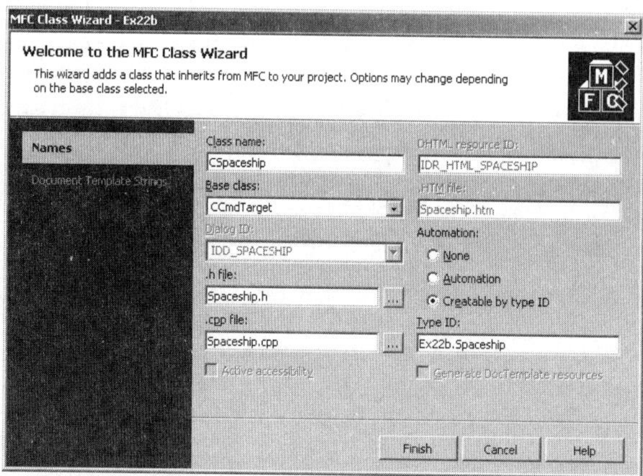

In your generated class, you end up with some Automation elements such as dispatch maps, but you can safely remove them. You can also remove the following two lines from StdAfx.h:

```
#include <afxodlgs.h>
#include <afxdisp.h>
```

MFC COM Client Programs

Writing an MFC COM client program is a no-brainer. You just use the MFC Application Wizard to generate a normal application, and then you add the following line in StdAfx.h:

```
#include <afxole.h>
```

Next, add the following line at the beginning of the application class InitInstance member function:

```
AfxOleInit();
```

You're now ready to add code that calls *CoGetClassObject*.

The Ex22b Example: An MFC COM In-Process Component

The Ex22b example is an MFC regular DLL that incorporates a true COM version of the *CSpaceship* class you saw in Ex22a. The MFC DLL Wizard generated the Ex22b.cpp and Ex22b.h files, as described previously. The Interface.h file, shown in the following listing, declares the *IMotion* and *IVisual* interfaces. The code for the *CSpaceship* class is shown after the Interface.h file. Compare that code to the code in Ex22a. Do you see how the use of the MFC macros reduces code size? Note that the MFC *CCmdTarget* class takes care of the reference counting and *QueryInterface* logic.

Interface.h

```
struct IMotion : public IUnknown
{
    STDMETHOD_(void, Fly) () = 0;
    STDMETHOD_(int&, GetPosition) () = 0;
};
struct IVisual : public IUnknown
{
    STDMETHOD_(void, Display) () = 0;
};
```

Spaceship.h

```
#pragma once
void ITrace(REFIID iid, const char* str);
// CSpaceship command target
class CSpaceship : public CCmdTarget
{
    DECLARE_DYNCREATE(CSpaceship)
private:
    int m_nPosition; // We can access this from all the interfaces
    int m_nAcceleration;
    int m_nColor;
public:
    CSpaceship();
    virtual ~CSpaceship();
    virtual void OnFinalRelease();
protected:
    DECLARE_MESSAGE_MAP()
    DECLARE_OLECREATE(CSpaceship)

    BEGIN_INTERFACE_PART(Motion, IMotion)
        STDMETHOD_(void, Fly) ();
        STDMETHOD_(int&, GetPosition) ();
    END_INTERFACE_PART(Motion)

    BEGIN_INTERFACE_PART(Visual, IVisual)
        STDMETHOD_(void, Display) ();
    END_INTERFACE_PART(Visual)
    DECLARE_INTERFACE_MAP()
};
```

Spaceship.cpp

```
// Spaceship.cpp : implementation file
//
#include "stdafx.h"
#include "Ex22b.h"
#include "Interface.h"
#include "Spaceship.h"

// CSpaceship
// {692D03A4-C689-11CE-B337-88EA36DE9E4E}
static const IID IID_IMotion =
    { 0x692d03a4, 0xc689, 0x11ce,
      { 0xb3, 0x37, 0x88, 0xea, 0x36, 0xde, 0x9e, 0x4e } };

// {692D03A5-C689-11CE-B337-88EA36DE9E4E}
static const IID IID_IVisual =
    { 0x692d03a5, 0xc689, 0x11ce,
      { 0xb3, 0x37, 0x88, 0xea, 0x36, 0xde, 0x9e, 0x4e } };

IMPLEMENT_DYNCREATE(CSpaceship, CCmdTarget)
CSpaceship::CSpaceship()
{
    TRACE("CSpaceship ctor\n");
    m_nPosition = 100;
    m_nAcceleration = 101;
    m_nColor = 102;
    // To keep the application running as long as an OLE automation
    //   object is active, the constructor calls AfxOleLockApp.
    AfxOleLockApp();
}
CSpaceship::~CSpaceship()
{
    TRACE("CSpaceship dtor\n");
    // To terminate the application when all objects created with
    //   OLE automation, the destructor calls AfxOleUnlockApp.
    AfxOleUnlockApp();
}
void CSpaceship::OnFinalRelease()
{
    // When the last reference for an automation object is released
    // OnFinalRelease is called.  The base class will automatically
    // delete the object.  Add additional cleanup required for your
    // object before calling the base class.
    delete this;
}
BEGIN_MESSAGE_MAP(CSpaceship, CCmdTarget)
END_MESSAGE_MAP()
// Note: we add support for IID_ISpaceship to support typesafe binding
//  from VBA.  This IID must match the GUID that is attached to the
//  dispinterface in the .IDL file.
```

```
// {E39B5EB0-A0DA-43F3-B9B0-206CF10890C1}
static const IID IID_ISpaceship =
    { 0xE39B5EB0, 0xA0DA, 0x43F3,
      { 0xB9, 0xB0, 0x20, 0x6C, 0xF1, 0x8, 0x90, 0xC1 } };

BEGIN_INTERFACE_MAP(CSpaceship, CCmdTarget)
    INTERFACE_PART(CSpaceship, IID_IMotion, Motion)
    INTERFACE_PART(CSpaceship, IID_IVisual, Visual)
END_INTERFACE_MAP()
// {13C4472C-84BB-4ED6-8164-83ED8EB136B5}
IMPLEMENT_OLECREATE_FLAGS(CSpaceship, "Ex22b.Spaceship",
    afxRegApartmentThreading, 0x13c4472c, 0x84bb, 0x4ed6, 0x81,
    0x64, 0x83, 0xed, 0x8e, 0xb1, 0x36, 0xb5)

STDMETHODIMP_(ULONG) CSpaceship::XMotion::AddRef()
{
    TRACE("CSpaceship::XMotion::AddRef\n");
    METHOD_PROLOGUE(CSpaceship, Motion)
    return pThis->ExternalAddRef();
}
STDMETHODIMP_(ULONG) CSpaceship::XMotion::Release()
{
    TRACE("CSpaceship::XMotion::Release\n");
    METHOD_PROLOGUE(CSpaceship, Motion)
    return pThis->ExternalRelease();
}
STDMETHODIMP CSpaceship::XMotion::QueryInterface(
    REFIID iid, LPVOID* ppvObj)
{
    ITrace(iid, "CSpaceship::XMotion::QueryInterface");
    METHOD_PROLOGUE(CSpaceship, Motion)
    return pThis->ExternalQueryInterface(&iid, ppvObj);
}
STDMETHODIMP_(void) CSpaceship::XMotion::Fly()
{
    TRACE("CSpaceship::XMotion::Fly\n");
    METHOD_PROLOGUE(CSpaceship, Motion)
    TRACE("m_nPosition = %d\n", pThis->m_nPosition);
    TRACE("m_nAcceleration = %d\n", pThis->m_nAcceleration);
    return;
}
STDMETHODIMP_(int&) CSpaceship::XMotion::GetPosition()
{
    TRACE("CSpaceship::XMotion::GetPosition\n");
    METHOD_PROLOGUE(CSpaceship, Motion)
    TRACE("m_nPosition = %d\n", pThis->m_nPosition);
    TRACE("m_nAcceleration = %d\n", pThis->m_nAcceleration);
    return pThis->m_nPosition;
}
```

(continued)

```
STDMETHODIMP_(ULONG) CSpaceship::XVisual::AddRef()
{
    TRACE("CSpaceship::XVisual::AddRef\n");
    METHOD_PROLOGUE(CSpaceship, Visual)
    return pThis->ExternalAddRef();
}
STDMETHODIMP_(ULONG) CSpaceship::XVisual::Release()
{
    TRACE("CSpaceship::XVisual::Release\n");
    METHOD_PROLOGUE(CSpaceship, Visual)
    return pThis->ExternalRelease();
}
STDMETHODIMP CSpaceship::XVisual::QueryInterface(
    REFIID iid, LPVOID* ppvObj)
{
    ITrace(iid, "CSpaceship::XVisual::QueryInterface");
    METHOD_PROLOGUE(CSpaceship, Visual)
    return pThis->ExternalQueryInterface(&iid, ppvObj);
}
STDMETHODIMP_(void) CSpaceship::XVisual::Display()
{
    TRACE("CSpaceship::XVisual::Display\n");
    METHOD_PROLOGUE(CSpaceship, Visual)
    TRACE("m_nPosition = %d\n", pThis->m_nPosition);
    TRACE("m_nColor = %d\n", pThis->m_nColor);
}
void ITrace(REFIID iid, const char* str)
{
    OLECHAR* lpszIID;
    ::StringFromIID(iid, &lpszIID);
    CString strTemp(lpszIID);
    TRACE("%s - %s\n", (const char*) strTemp, (const char*) str);
    AfxFreeTaskMem(lpszIID);
}
```

The Ex22c Example: An MFC COM Client

The Ex22c example is an MFC program that incorporates a true COM version of the client code you saw in Ex22a. This is a generic MFC Application Wizard–generated Single Document Interface (SDI) EXE program with an added *#include* statement for the MFC COM headers and a call to *AfxOleInit*, which initializes the DLL. A Spaceship command on an added Test menu is mapped to the view class handler function shown in the following code. The project also contains a copy of the Ex22b component's Interface.h file, shown in the previous section. You can see an *#include* statement for this file at the top of Ex22cView.cpp.

```
void CEx22cView::OnTestSpaceship()
{
    CLSID clsid;
    LPCLASSFACTORY pClf;
    LPUNKNOWN pUnk;
    IMotion* pMot;
    IVisual* pVis;

    HRESULT hr;
    if ((hr = ::CLSIDFromProgID(L"Ex22b.Spaceship", &clsid)) != NOERROR) {
        TRACE("unable to find Program ID -- error = %x\n", hr);
        return;
    }
    if ((hr = ::CoGetClassObject(clsid, CLSCTX_INPROC_SERVER,
        NULL, IID_IClassFactory, (void **) &pClf)) != NOERROR) {
        TRACE("unable to find CLSID -- error = %x\n", hr);
        return;
    }

    pClf->CreateInstance(NULL, IID_IUnknown, (void**) &pUnk);
    pUnk->QueryInterface(IID_IMotion, (void**) &pMot); // All three
    pMot->QueryInterface(IID_IVisual, (void**) &pVis); //  pointers
                                                        //  should work
    TRACE("main: pUnk = %p, pMot = %p, pDis = %p\n", pUnk, pMot, pVis);

    // Test all the interface virtual functions
    pMot->Fly();
    int nPos = pMot->GetPosition();
    TRACE("nPos = %d\n", nPos);
    pVis->Display();

    pClf->Release();
    pUnk->Release();
    pMot->Release();
    pVis->Release();
    AfxMessageBox("Test succeeded. See Debug window for output.");
}
```

To test the client and the component, you must first run the component to update the Registry. Several utilities will help you do this, but you might want to try the RegComp program in the \vcppnet\REGCOMP project on the companion CD. This program prompts you to select a DLL or an OCX file, and then it calls the exported *DllRegisterServer* function.

Both client and component show their progress through *TRACE* calls. To view the trace result, you need the debugger or some other utilities. You can run either the client or the component from the Visual Studio .NET debugger. If you try to run the component, you'll be prompted for the client pathname. In either case, you don't have to copy the DLL because Windows will find it through the Registry.

Containment vs. Aggregation vs. Inheritance

In normal C++ programming, you frequently use inheritance to factor out common behavior into a reusable base class. The *CPersistentFrame* class (discussed in Chapter 15) is an example of reusability through inheritance.

COM uses containment and aggregation instead of inheritance. Let's start with containment. Suppose you want to extend the spaceship simulation to include planets in addition to spaceships. Using C++ by itself, you would probably write a *COrbiter* base class that encapsulates the laws of planetary motion. With COM, you would have "outer" *CSpaceship* and *CPlanet* classes plus an "inner" *COrbiter* class. The outer classes would implement the *IVisual* interface directly, but they would delegate their *IMotion* interfaces to the inner class. The result would look something like this:

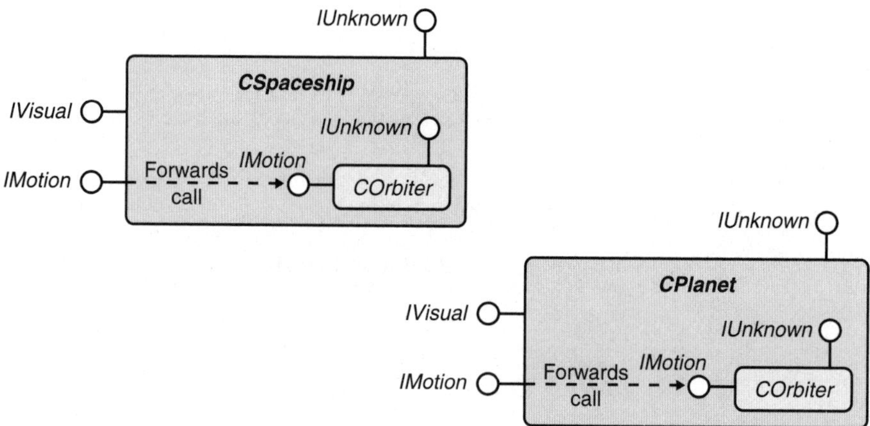

Note that the *COrbiter* object doesn't know that it's inside a *CSpaceship* or *CPlanet* object, but the outer object certainly knows that it has a *COrbiter* object embedded inside. The outer class needs to implement all its interface functions, but the *IMotion* functions, including *QueryInterface*, simply call the same *IMotion* functions of the inner class.

A more complex alternative to containment is aggregation. With aggregation, the client can have direct access to the inner object's interfaces. Here is the aggregation version of the space simulation:

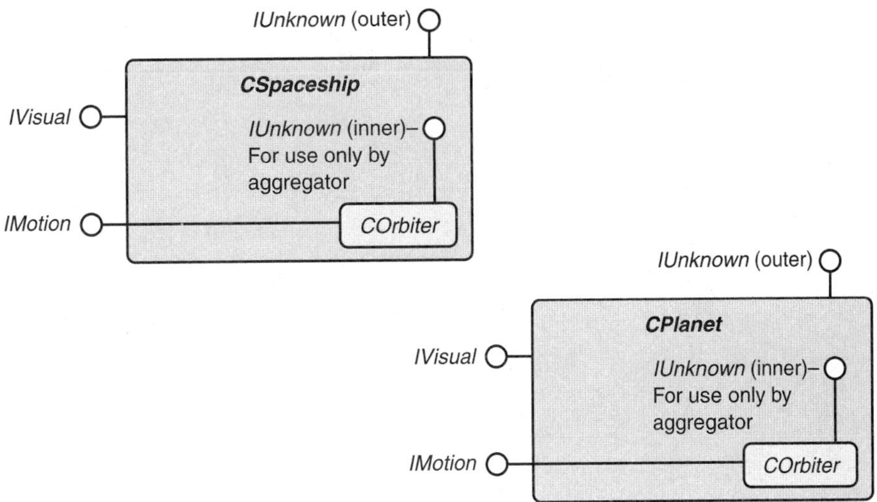

The orbiter is embedded in the spaceship and planet, just as it was in the containment case. Suppose the client obtains an *IVisual* pointer for a spaceship and then calls *QueryInterface* for an *IMotion* pointer. Using the outer *IUnknown* pointer will draw a blank because the *CSpaceship* class doesn't support *IMotion*. The *CSpaceship* class keeps track of the inner *IUnknown* pointer (of its embedded *COrbiter* object), so the class uses that pointer to obtain the *IMotion* pointer for the *COrbiter* object.

Now suppose the client obtains an *IMotion* pointer and then calls *QueryInterface* for *IVisual*. The inner object must be able to navigate to the outer object, but how? Take a close look at the *CreateInstance* call back on page 567. The first parameter is set to *NULL* in that case. If you're creating an aggregated (inner) object, you use that parameter to pass an *IUnknown* pointer for the outer object that you've already created. This pointer is called the *controlling unknown*. The *COrbiter* class saves this pointer in a data member and then uses it to call *QueryInterface* for interfaces that the class itself doesn't support.

The MFC library supports aggregation. The *CCmdTarget* class has a public data member, *m_pOuterUnknown*, that holds the outer object's *IUnknown* pointer (if the object is aggregated). The *CCmdTarget* member functions *ExternalQueryInterface*, *ExternalAddRef*, and *ExternalRelease* delegate to the outer *IUnknown* if it exists. The member functions *InternalQueryInterface*, *InternalAddRef*, and *InternalRelease* do not delegate. See Technical Note #38 in the *MFC Library Reference* for a description of the MFC macros that support aggregation.

Even though aggregation plays a major role in the underpinnings of COM (particularly with the proxy manager), you're unlikely to ever use it in standard COM applications.

23

Automation

After reading Chapter 22, you should know what an interface is. You've already seen two standard COM interfaces: *IUnknown* and *IClassFactory*. Now you're ready for "applied" COM, or at least one aspect of it—integrating with other applications via Automation (formerly known as OLE Automation). You'll learn about the COM *IDispatch* interface, which enables C++ programs to communicate with Microsoft Visual Basic for Applications (VBA) programs and with programs written in other scripting languages. In addition, *IDispatch* is the key to getting your COM object onto a Web page. You'll use the MFC library implementation of *IDispatch* to write C++ Automation component and client programs. We'll also explore both out-of-process components and in-process components.

But before we jump into C++ Automation programming, you need to know how the rest of the world writes programs. In this chapter, you'll get some exposure to VBA as it is implemented in Microsoft Excel. You'll run your C++ components from Excel, and you'll run Excel from a C++ client program.

Creating C++ Components for VBA

Not all programmers of Microsoft Windows–based applications will be C++ programmers, especially if they have to learn the intricacies of COM theory. If you've been paying attention, you've probably noticed a trend in which C++ programmers produce reusable modules. Programmers who use higher-level languages (Visual Basic, VBA, and Web scripting languages, for example) consume those modules by integrating them into applications. You can participate in this programming model by learning how to make your software script-friendly. Automation is one tool that the Microsoft Foundation Class library supports. ActiveX controls are another tool for C++/VBA integration and are very much a superset of Automation because both tools use the *IDispatch* interface. Using ActiveX controls, however, might be overkill in many situations. Many applications, including Excel, can support both Automation components and ActiveX controls. You'll be able to apply all that you learn about Automation when you write and use ActiveX controls.

Two factors are responsible for Automation's success. First, VBA is supported by most Microsoft applications, including Microsoft Word, Microsoft Access, and Excel, not to mention Microsoft Visual Basic itself. All these applications can be linked to other Automation-compatible components, including those written in C++ and VBA. For example, you can write a C++ program that uses the text-processing capability of Word, or you can write a C++ matrix inversion component that can be called from a VBA macro in an Excel worksheet.

The second factor underlying Automation's success is that dozens of software companies provide Automation programming interfaces for their applications, mostly for the benefit of VBA programmers. With a little effort, you can run these applications from C++. You can, for example, write an MFC program that controls the Microsoft Visio drawing program.

Automation isn't just for C++ and VBA programmers. Software tool companies are already announcing Automation-compatible, Basic-like languages that you can license for your own programmable applications. One version of Smalltalk even supports Automation.

Automation Clients and Components

A clearly defined "master-slave" relationship is always present in an Automation communication dialog. The master is the Automation client and the slave is the Automation component (server). The client initiates the interaction by constructing a component object (it might have to load the component program) or by attaching to an existing object in a component program that is already running. The client then calls interface functions in the component and releases those interfaces when it's finished.

Here are some interaction scenarios:

- A C++ Automation client uses a Microsoft or third-party application as a component. The interaction might trigger the execution of VBA code in the component application.

- A C++ Automation component is used from inside a Microsoft application (or a Visual Basic application), which acts as the Automation client. VBA code can thus construct and use C++ objects.
- A C++ Automation client uses a C++ Automation component.
- A Visual Basic program uses an Automation-aware application such as Excel. In this case, Visual Basic is the client and Excel is the component.

Excel: A Better Visual Basic Than Visual Basic

When the first three editions of this book were written, Visual Basic worked as an Automation client but you couldn't use it to create an Automation component. Since version 5.0, Visual Basic has let you write components, too—even ActiveX controls. The book originally used Excel instead of Visual Basic because Excel was the first Microsoft application to support VBA syntax and could serve as both a client and a component. Here, we'll stick with Excel because C++ programmers who look down their noses at Visual Basic might be inclined to buy Excel (if only to track their software royalties).

I strongly recommend that you get the latest version of Excel, which is a true 32-bit application and is a part of the Microsoft Office suite. With this version of Excel, you can write VBA code in a separate location that accesses worksheet cells in an object-oriented manner. Adding visual programming elements—such as buttons—is easy. Forget all you ever knew about the old spreadsheet programs that forced you to wedge macro code inside cells.

This chapter isn't meant to be an Excel tutorial, but it includes a simple Excel workbook. (A *workbook* is a file that can contain multiple worksheets plus separate VBA code.) This workbook demonstrates a VBA macro that executes from a button. You can use Excel to load Demo.xls from the \vcppnet\Ex23a subdirectory, or you can key in the example from scratch. Figure 23-1 shows the actual spreadsheet with the button and sample data.

In this spreadsheet, you highlight cells A4 through A9 and click the Process Col button. A VBA program iterates down the column and draws a hatched pattern on cells with numeric values greater than 10.

Figure 23-2 shows the macro code itself, which is "behind" the worksheet. In Excel, choose Macro from the Tools menu, and then choose Visual Basic Editor. (Alt+F11 is the shortcut.) As you can see, you're working in the standard VBA environment at this point.

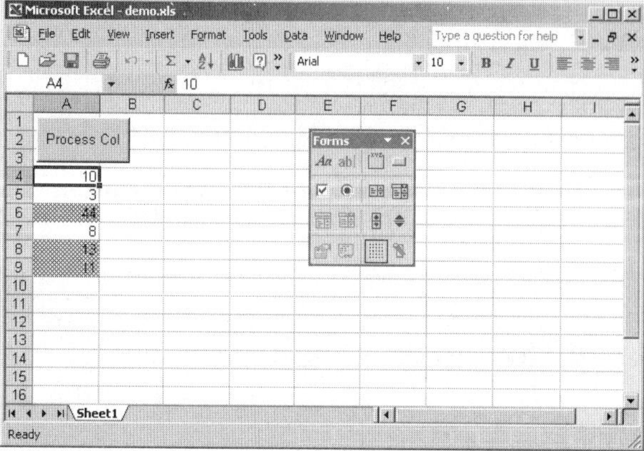

Figure 23-1 An Excel spreadsheet that uses VBA code.

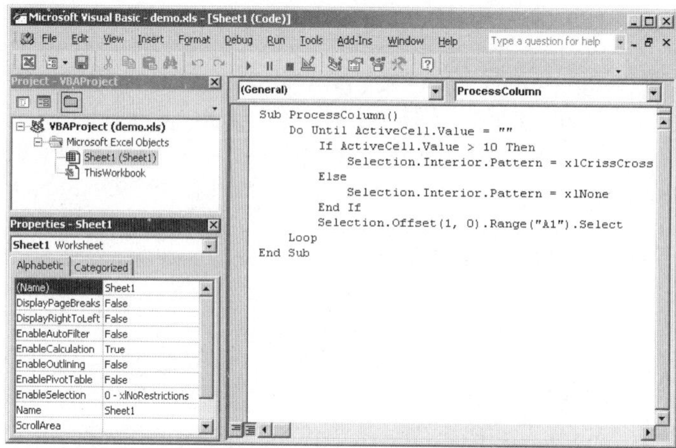

Figure 23-2 The VBA code for the Excel spreadsheet.

If you want to create the example yourself, follow these steps:

1. Start Excel with a new workbook, press Alt+F11, and then double-click Sheet1 in the top left window.
2. Type in the macro code shown in Figure 23-2.
3. Return to the Excel window by choosing Close And Return To Microsoft Excel from the File menu. Choose Toolbars from the View menu. Select Forms to display the Forms toolbar. (You can also access the list of toolbars by right-clicking on any existing toolbar.)

4. Click the Button control, and then create the button by dragging the mouse in the upper left corner of the worksheet. Assign the button to the *Sheet1.ProcessColumn* macro.
5. Size the button, and type the caption **Process Col** (as shown in Figure 23-1).
6. Type some numbers in the column starting at cell A4. Select the cells containing these numbers, and then click the button to test the program.

Pretty easy, isn't it?

Let's analyze an Excel VBA statement from the macro above:

```
Selection.Offset(1, 0).Range("A1").Select
```

The first element, *Selection*, is a property of an implied object, the Excel application. The *Selection* property in this case is assumed to be a *Range* object that represents a rectangular array of cells. The second element, *Offset*, is a property of the *Range* object that returns another *Range* object based on the two parameters. In this case, the returned *Range* object is the one-cell range that begins one row down from the original range. The third element, *Range*, is a property of the *Range* object that returns yet another range. This time it's the upper left cell in the second range. Finally, the *Select* method causes Excel to highlight the selected cell and makes it the new *Selection* property of the application.

As the program iterates through the loop, the preceding statement moves the selected cell down the worksheet one row at a time. This style of programming takes some getting used to, but it's fairly common—especially in Office environments that usually deal with lots of documents. The real value here is that you have all the capabilities of the Excel spreadsheet and graphics engine available to you in a seamless programming environment.

Properties, Methods, and Collections

The distinction between a property and a method is somewhat artificial. Basically, a property is a value that can be both set and retrieved. You can, for example, set and get the *Selection* property for an Excel application. Another example is Excel's *Width* property, which applies to many object types. Some Excel properties are read-only, but most are read/write.

Properties don't officially have parameters, but some properties are indexed. The property index acts a lot like a parameter. It doesn't have to be an integer, and it can have more than one element (a row and a column, for example). You'll find many indexed properties in Excel's object model, and Excel VBA can handle indexed properties in Automation components.

Methods are more flexible than properties. They can have zero or many parameters, and they can either set or retrieve object data. Most frequently, they perform some action, such as showing a window. Excel's *Select* method is an example of an action method.

The Excel object model supports collection objects. For example, if you use the *Worksheets* property of the *Application* object, you get back a *Sheets* collection object, which represents all the worksheets in the active workbook. You can use the *Item* property (with an integer index) to get a specific *Worksheet* object from a *Sheets* collection, or you can use an integer index directly on the collection.

Automation Interfaces

You've already learned that a COM interface is a useful way for Windows programs to communicate with one another, but you've also learned that designing your own COM interfaces is impractical in many cases. Automation's general-purpose interface, *IDispatch*, serves the needs of both C++ and VBA programmers. As you might guess from your glimpse of Excel VBA, this interface involves objects, methods, and properties.

You can write COM interfaces that include functions with any parameter types and return values you specify. *IMotion* and *IVisual*, which we created in Chapter 22, are examples. If you're going to let VBA programmers in, however, you can't play fast and loose anymore. You can solve the communication problem with one interface that has a member function smart enough to accommodate methods and properties as defined by VBA. Needless to say, *IDispatch* has such a function: Invoke. You use *IDispatch::Invoke* for COM objects that can be constructed and used in either C++ or VBA programs.

Now you're beginning to see what Automation does. It funnels all intermodule communication through the *IDispatch::Invoke* function. How does a client first connect to its component? *IDispatch* is merely another COM interface, so all the registration logic supported by COM comes into play. Automation components can be DLLs or EXEs, and they can be accessed over a network using Distributed COM (DCOM).

The *IDispatch* Interface

IDispatch is the heart of Automation. It's fully supported by COM marshaling (that is, Microsoft has already marshaled it for you), as are all the other standard

COM interfaces, and it's well supported by the MFC library. At the component end, you need a COM class with an *IDispatch* interface (plus the prerequisite class factory, of course). At the client end, you use standard COM techniques to obtain an *IDispatch* pointer. (As you'll see, the MFC library and the wizards take care of a lot of these details for you.)

Remember that *Invoke* is the principal member function of *IDispatch*. If you were to look up *IDispatch::Invoke* in the Visual C++ .NET online documentation, you'd see a really ugly set of parameters. Don't worry about those now. The MFC library steps in on both sides of the *Invoke* call, using a data-driven scheme to call component functions based on dispatch map parameters that you define with macros.

Invoke isn't the only *IDispatch* member function. Another function your controller might call is *GetIDsOfNames*. From the VBA programmer's point of view, properties and methods have symbolic names, but C++ programmers prefer more efficient integer indexes. *Invoke* uses integers to specify properties and methods, so *GetIDsOfNames* is useful at the start of a program for converting each name to a number if you don't know the index numbers at compile time. You've already seen that *IDispatch* supports symbolic names for methods. In addition, the interface supports symbolic names for a method's parameters. The *GetIDsOfNames* function returns those parameter names along with the method name. Unfortunately, the MFC *IDispatch* implementation doesn't support named parameters.

Automation Programming Choices

Suppose you're writing an Automation component in C++. You've got some choices to make. Do you want an in-process component or an out-of-process component? What kind of user interface do you want? Does the component need a user interface at all? Can users run your EXE component as a standalone application? If the component is an EXE, will it be Single Document Interface (SDI) or Multiple Document Interface (MDI)? Can the user shut down the component program directly?

If your component is a DLL, COM linkage will be more efficient than it would be with an EXE component because no marshaling is required. Most of the time, your in-process Automation components won't have their own user interfaces, except for modal dialog boxes. If you need a component that manages its own child window, you should use an ActiveX control, and if you want to use a main frame window, you should use an out-of-process component. As with any 32-bit DLL, an Automation DLL is mapped into the client's process memory. If two client programs happen to request the same DLL, Windows will load and link the DLL twice. Each client will be unaware that the other is using the same component.

With an EXE component, however, you must be careful to distinguish between a component program and a component object. When a client calls *IClassFactory::CreateInstance* to construct a component object, the component's class factory constructs the object, but COM might or might not need to start the component program.

Here are some scenarios:

- The component's COM-creatable class is programmed to require a new process for each object constructed. In this case, COM starts a new process in response to the second and subsequent *CreateInstance* calls, each of which returns an *IDispatch* pointer.
- Here's a special case of the above scenario that's specific to MFC applications. The component class is an MFC document class in an SDI application. Each time a client calls *CreateInstance*, a new component process starts, complete with a document object, a view object, and an SDI main frame window.
- The component class is programmed to allow multiple objects in a single process. Each time a client calls *CreateInstance*, a new component object is constructed. There is only one component process, however.
- Here's a special case of the above scenario that's specific to MFC applications. The component class is an MFC document class in an MDI application. There is a single component process with one MDI main frame window. Each time a client calls *CreateInstance*, a new document object is constructed, along with a view object and an MDI child frame window.

There's one more interesting case. Suppose a component EXE is running before the client needs it, and then the client decides to access a component object that already exists. You'll see this case with Excel. The user might have Excel running but minimized on the desktop, and the client might need access to Excel's one and only *Application* object. The client will call the COM function *GetActiveObject*, which provides an interface pointer for an existing component object. If the call fails, the client can create the object with *CoCreateInstance*.

For component object deletion, normal COM rules apply. Automation objects have reference counts, and they delete themselves when the client calls *Release* and the reference count goes to 0. In an MDI component, if the Automation object is an MFC document, its destruction will cause the corresponding MDI child window to close. In an SDI component, the destruction of the document object will cause the component process to exit. The client is responsible for calling *Release* for each *IDispatch* interface before the client exits. For EXE components, COM will intervene if the client exits without releasing an interface, thus allowing the component process to exit. You can't always depend on this intervention, however, so be sure that your client cleans up its interfaces!

With generic COM, a client application often obtains multiple interface pointers for a single component object. Look back at the spaceship example in Chapter 22, in which the simulated COM component class has both an *IMotion* pointer and an *IVisual* pointer. With Automation, however, there's usually only a single (*IDispatch*) pointer per object. As in all COM programming, you must be careful to release all your interface pointers. In Excel, for example, many properties return an *IDispatch* pointer to new or existing objects. If you fail to release a pointer to an in-process COM component, the Debug version of the MFC library will alert you with a memory-leak dump when the client program exits.

The MFC *IDispatch* Implementation

The component program can implement its *IDispatch* interface in several ways. The most common way passes off much of the work to the Windows COM DLLs by calling the COM function *CreateStdDispatch* or by delegating the *Invoke* call to the *ITypeInfo* interface, which involves the component's type library. A type library is a table, locatable through the Registry that allows a client to query the component for the symbolic names of objects, methods, and properties. A client can, for example, contain a browser that allows the user to explore the component's capabilities.

The MFC library supports type libraries, but it doesn't use them in its implementation of *IDispatch*, which is instead driven by a dispatch map. MFC programs don't call *CreateStdDispatch* at all, nor do they use a type library to implement *IDispatch::GetIDsOfNames*. This means you can't use the MFC library if you implement a multilingual Automation component—one that supports English and German property and method names, for example. (*CreateStdDispatch* doesn't support multilingual components either.)

Later in this chapter, you'll learn how a client can use a type library, and you'll see how MFC wizards create and maintain type libraries for you. Once your component has a type library, a client can use it for browsing, independent of the *IDispatch* implementation.

An MFC Automation Component

Let's look at what happens in an MFC Automation component—in this case, a simplified version of the Ex23c alarm clock program that's discussed later in this chapter. In the MFC library, the *IDispatch* implementation is part of the *CCmdTarget* base class, so you don't need *INTERFACE_MAP* macros. You write an Automation component class—*CClock*, for example—that's derived from *CCmdTarget*. This class's CPP file contains *DISPATCH_MAP* macros:

```
BEGIN_DISPATCH_MAP(CClock, CCmdTarget)
    DISP_PROPERTY(CClock, "Time", m_time, VT_DATE)
    DISP_PROPERTY_PARAM(CClock, "Figure", GetFigure,
                        SetFigure, VT_VARIANT, VTS_I2)
    DISP_FUNCTION(CClock, "RefreshWin", Refresh, VT_EMPTY, VTS_NONE)
    DISP_FUNCTION(CClock, "ShowWin", ShowWin, VT_BOOL, VTS_I2)
END_DISPATCH_MAP()
```

Looks a little like an MFC message map, doesn't it? The *CClock* class header file contains related code, shown here:

```
public:
    DATE m_time;
    afx_msg VARIANT GetFigure(short n);
    afx_msg void SetFigure(short n, const VARIANT& vaNew);
    afx_msg void Refresh();
    afx_msg BOOL ShowWin(short n);
    DECLARE_DISPATCH_MAP()
```

What does all this stuff mean? It means that the *CClock* class has the following properties and methods:

Name	**Type**	**Description**
Time	Property	Linked directly to class data member *m_time*.
Figure	Property	An indexed property that's accessed through member functions *GetFigure* and *SetFigure*. The first parameter is the index, and the second (for *SetFigure*) is the string value. (The figures are the *XII*, *III*, *VI*, and *IX* that appear on the clock face.)
RefreshWin	Method	Linked to the class member function *Refresh*. It has no parameters or return value.
ShowWin	Method	Linked to the class member function *ShowWin*. It is a short integer parameter with a Boolean return value.

How does the MFC dispatch map relate to *IDispatch* and the *Invoke* member function? The dispatch-map macros generate static data tables that the MFC library's *Invoke* implementation can read. A controller gets an *IDispatch* pointer for *CClock* (which is connected through the *CCmdTarget* base class), and it calls *Invoke* with an array of pointers as a parameter. The MFC library's implementation of *Invoke*, which is buried somewhere inside *CCmdTarget*, uses the *CClock* dispatch map to decode the supplied pointers and either calls one of your member functions or accesses *m_time* directly.

As you'll see in the examples, the Add Class Wizard can generate the Automation component class for you and help you code the dispatch map.

An MFC Automation Client Program

Let's move on to the client's end of the Automation conversation. How does an MFC Automation client program call *Invoke*? The MFC library provides a base class *COleDispatchDriver* for this purpose. This class has a data member, *m_lpDispatch*, that contains the corresponding component's *IDispatch* pointer. To shield you from the complexities of the *Invoke* parameter sequence, *COleDispatchDriver* has several member functions, including *InvokeHelper*, *GetProperty*, and *SetProperty*. These three functions call *Invoke* for an *IDispatch* pointer that links to the component. The *COleDispatchDriver* object incorporates the *IDispatch* pointer.

Suppose our client program has a class *CClockDriver* that's derived from *COleDispatchDriver* and that drives *CClock* objects in an Automation component. The functions that get and set the *Time* property are shown here:

```
DATE CClockDriver::GetTime()
{
    DATE result;
    GetProperty(1, VT_DATE, (void*)&result);
    return result;
}
void CClockDriver::SetTime(DATE propVal)
{
    SetProperty(1, VT_DATE, propVal);
}
```

Here are the functions for the indexed *Figure* property:

```
VARIANT CClockDriver::GetFigure(short i)
{
    VARIANT result;
    static BYTE parms[] = VTS_I2;
    InvokeHelper(2, DISPATCH_PROPERTYGET, VT_VARIANT,
                 (void*)&result, parms, i);
    return result;
}
void CClockDriver::SetFigure(short i, const VARIANT& propVal)
{
    static BYTE parms[] = VTS_I2 VTS_VARIANT;
    InvokeHelper(2, DISPATCH_PROPERTYPUT, VT_EMPTY, NULL,
                 parms, i, &propVal);
}
```

And here are the functions that access the component's methods:

```
void CClockDriver::RefreshWin()
{
    InvokeHelper(3, DISPATCH_METHOD, VT_EMPTY, NULL, NULL);
}
BOOL CClockDriver::ShowWin(short i)
{
    BOOL result;
    static BYTE parms[] = VTS_I2;
    InvokeHelper(4, DISPATCH_METHOD, VT_BOOL,
                 (void*)&result, parms, i);
    return result;
}
```

The function parameters identify the property or method, its return value, and its parameters. You'll learn about dispatch function parameters later, but for now take special note of the first parameter for the *InvokeHelper*, *GetProperty*, and *SetProperty* functions. This is the unique integer index, or dispatch ID (DISPID), for the property or method. Because you're using compiled C++, you can establish these IDs at compile time. If you're using an MFC Automation component with a dispatch map, the indexes will be determined by the map sequence, beginning with 1. If you don't know a component's dispatch indexes, you can call the *IDispatch* member function *GetIDsOfNames* to convert the symbolic property or method names to integers.

The following illustration shows the interactions between the client (or controller) and the component.

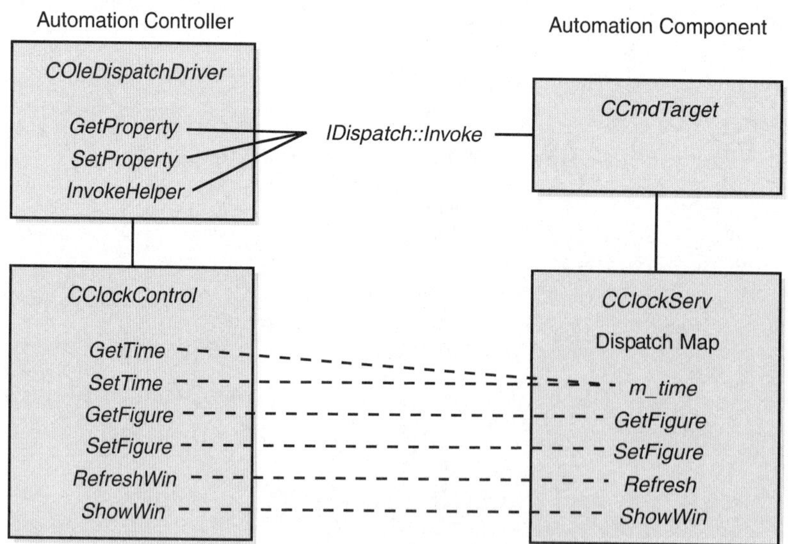

The solid lines show the actual connections through the MFC base classes and the *Invoke* function. The dotted lines represent the resulting logical connections between client class members and component class members.

Most Automation components have a binary type library file with a TLB extension. The Add Class Wizard can access this type library file to generate a class derived from *COleDispatchDriver*. (Choose Add Class from the Project menu and select MFC Class From TypeLib.) This generated controller class contains member functions for all the component's methods and properties with hard-coded DISPIDs. Sometimes you need to do some surgery on this generated code, but that's better than writing the functions from scratch.

After you have generated your driver class, you embed an object of this class in your client application's view class (or in another class), like this:

```
CClockDriver m_clock;
```

You then ask COM to create a clock component object using this statement:

```
m_clock.CreateDispatch("Ex23c.Document");
```

Now you're ready to call the dispatch driver functions:

```
m_clock.SetTime(COleDateTime::GetCurrentTime());
m_clock.RefreshWin();
```

When the *m_clock* object goes out of scope, its destructor releases the *IDispatch* pointer.

An Automation Client Program That Uses the Compiler's *#import* Directive

Now you can use an entirely new way of writing Automation client programs. Instead of using the Add Class Wizard to generate a class derived from *COleDispatchDriver*, you use the compiler to generate header and implementation files directly from a component's type library. For the clock component, your client program contains the following statement:

```
#import"..\Ex23c\debug\Ex23c.tlb" rename_namespace("ClockDriv") using namespace
 ClockDriv;
```

The compiler then generates (and processes) two files, Ex23c.tlh and Ex23c.tli, in the project's Debug or Release subdirectory. The TLH file contains the *IEx23c* clock driver class declaration plus this smart pointer declaration:

```
_COM_SMARTPTR_TYPEDEF(IEx23c, __uuidof(IDispatch));
```

The *_COM_SMARTPTR_TYPEDEF* macro generates the *IEx23cPtr* pointer type, which encapsulates the component's *IDispatch* pointer. The TLI file contains inline implementations of member functions, some of which are shown in the following code:

```
inline HRESULT IEx23c::RefreshWin ( ) {
    return _com_dispatch_method(this, 0x4, DISPATCH_METHOD,
                                VT_EMPTY, NULL, NULL);
}
inline DATE IEx23c::GetTime ( ) {
    DATE _result;
    _com_dispatch_propget(this, 0x1, VT_DATE, (void*)&_result);
    return _result;
}
inline void IEx23c::PutTime ( DATE _val ) {
    _com_dispatch_propput(this, 0x1, VT_DATE, _val);
}
```

Note the similarity between these functions and the *COleDispatchDriver* member functions you've already seen. The functions *_com_dispatch_method*, *_com_dispatch_propget*, and *_com_dispatch_propput* are in the runtime library.

In your Automation client program, you declare an embedded smart pointer member in your view class (or in another class), like this:

```
IEx23cPtr  m_clock;
```

You then create a clock component object using this statement:

```
m_clock.CreateInstance(__uuidof(Document));
```

Now you're ready to use the *IEx23cPtr* class's overloaded -> operator to call the member functions defined in the TLI file:

```
m_clock->PutTime(COleDateTime::GetCurrentTime());
m_clock->RefreshWin();
```

When the *m_clock* smart pointer object goes out of scope, its destructor calls the COM *Release* function.

The *#import* directive is the future of COM programming. With each new version of Visual C++, you'll see COM features moving into the compiler, along with the document-view architecture itself.

The *VARIANT* Type

No doubt you noticed the *VARIANT* type used in both Automation client and component functions in the previous example. *VARIANT* is an all-purpose data type that *IDispatch::Invoke* uses to transmit parameters and return values. The *VARIANT* type is the natural type to use when you exchange data with VBA. Here's a simplified version of the *VARIANT* definition in the Windows header files:

```
struct tagVARIANT {
    VARTYPE vt; // unsigned short integer type code
    WORD wReserved1, wReserved2, wReserved3;
    union {
        short      iVal;                 // VT_I2  short integer
        long       lVal;                 // VT_I4  long integer
        float      fltVal;               // VT_R4  4-byte float
        double     dblVal;               // VT_R8  8-byte IEEE float
        DATE       date;                 // VT_DATE stored as dbl
                                         //  date.time
        CY         vtCY                  // VT_CY 64-bit integer
        BSTR       bstrVal;              // VT_BSTR
        IUnknown*  punkVal;              // VT_UNKNOWN
        IDispatch* pdispVal;             // VT_DISPATCH
        short*     piVal;                // VT_BYREF | VT_I2
        long*      plVal;                // VT_BYREF | VT_I4
        float*     pfltVal;              // VT_BYREF | VT_R4
        double*    pdblVal;              // VT_BYREF | VT_R8
        DATE*      pdate;                // VT_BYREF | VT_DATE
        CY*        pvtCY;                // VT_BYREF | VT_CY
        BSTR*      pbstrVal;             // VT_BYREF | VT_BSTR
    }
};
typedef struct tagVARIANT VARIANT;
```

As you can see, the *VARIANT* type is a C structure that contains a type code *vt*, some reserved bytes, and a big union of types that you already know about. If *vt* is *VT_I2*, for example, you read the *VARIANT*'s value from *iVal*, which contains a 2-byte integer. If *vt* is *VT_R8*, you read this value from *dblVal*, which contains an 8-byte real value.

A *VARIANT* object can contain actual data or a pointer to data. If *vt* has the *VT_BYREF* bit set, you must access a pointer in *piVal*, *plVal*, and so on. Note that a *VARIANT* object can contain an *IUnknown* pointer or an *IDispatch* pointer. This means that you can pass a complete COM object using an Automation call, but if you want VBA to process that object, its class should have an *IDispatch* interface.

Strings are special. The *BSTR* type is yet another way to represent character strings. A *BSTR* variable is a pointer to a zero-terminated character array with a character count in front. A *BSTR* variable can therefore contain binary characters, including zeros. If you have a *VARIANT* object with *vt* = *VT_BSTR*, memory will look like this:

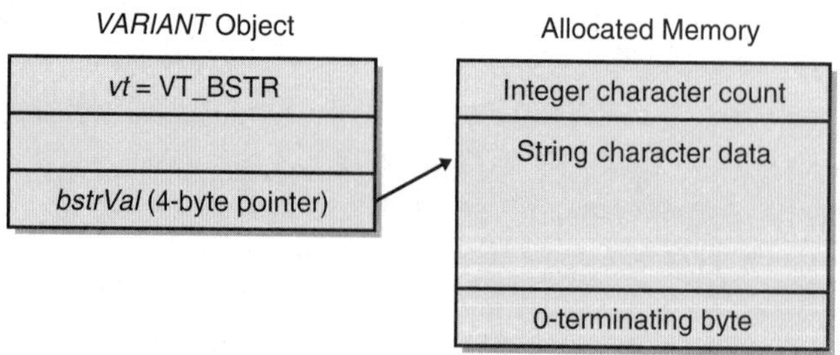

Because the string has a terminating 0, you can use *bstrVal* as if it were an ordinary *char* pointer, but you have to be very, very careful about memory cleanup. You can't simply delete the string pointer because the allocated memory begins with the character count. Windows provides the *SysAllocString* and *SysFreeString* functions for allocating and deleting *BSTR* objects.

> **Note** *SysAllocString* is another COM function that takes a wide string pointer as a parameter. This means that all *BSTR* variables contain wide characters, even if you haven't defined *_UNICODE*. Be careful!

Windows supplies some useful *VARIANT* manipulation functions, including those shown in the following table. If a *VARIANT* contains a *BSTR*, these functions ensure that memory is allocated and cleared properly. The *VariantInit* and *VariantClear* functions set *vt* to *VT_EMPTY*. All the variant functions are global functions and take a *VARIANT** parameter.

Function	Description
VariantInit	Initializes a *VARIANT*
VariantClear	Clears a *VARIANT*
VariantCopy	Frees memory associated with the destination *VARIANT* and copies the source *VARIANT*
VariantCopyInd	Frees the destination *VARIANT* and performs any indirection necessary to copy the source *VARIANT*
VariantChangeType	Changes the type of the *VARIANT*

The *COleVariant* Class

Writing a C++ class to wrap the *VARIANT* structure makes a lot of sense. Constructors can call *VariantInit*, and the destructor can call *VariantClear*. The class can have a constructor for each standard type, and it can have copy constructors and assignment operators that call *VariantCopy*. When a variant object goes out of scope, its destructor is called and memory is cleaned up automatically.

The MFC team created such a class that works well in Automation clients and components. A simplified declaration is shown here:

```
class COleVariant : public tagVARIANT
{
// Constructors
public:
    COleVariant();

    COleVariant(const VARIANT& varSrc);
    COleVariant(const COleVariant& varSrc);

    COleVariant(LPCTSTR lpszSrc);
    COleVariant(CString& strSrc);

    COleVariant(BYTE nSrc);
    COleVariant(short nSrc, VARTYPE vtSrc = VT_I2);
    COleVariant(long lSrc, VARTYPE vtSrc = VT_I4);

    COleVariant(float fltSrc);
    COleVariant(double dblSrc);
    COleVariant(const COleDateTime& dateSrc);
// Destructor
    ~COleVariant(); // deallocates BSTR
// Operations
public:
    void Clear(); // deallocates BSTR
    VARIANT Detach(); // more later
    void ChangeType(VARTYPE vartype, LPVARIANT pSrc = NULL);
};
```

In addition, the *CArchive* and *CDumpContext* classes have comparison operators, assignment operators, conversion operators, and friend insertion/extraction operators. See the *MFC Library Reference* for a complete description of this useful MFC *COleVariant* class.

Now let's see how the *COleVariant* class helps us write the component's *GetFigure* function that you saw referenced in the sample dispatch map. Assume that the component stores strings for four figures in a class data member:

```
private:
    CString m_strFigure[4];
```

Here's what we'd have to do if we used the *VARIANT* structure directly:

```
VARIANT CClock::GetFigure(short n)
{
    VARIANT vaResult;
    ::VariantInit(&vaResult);
    vaResult.vt = VT_BSTR;
    // CString::AllocSysString creates a BSTR
    vaResult.bstrVal = m_strFigure[n].AllocSysString();
    return vaResult; // Copies vaResult without copying BSTR
                     //  BSTR still must be freed later
}
```

Here's the equivalent, with a *COleVariant* return value:

```
VARIANT CClock::GetFigure(short n)
{
    return COleVariant(m_strFigure[n]).Detach();
}
```

Calling the *COleVariant::Detach* function is critical here. The *GetFigure* function constructs a temporary object that contains a pointer to a *BSTR*. That object gets bitwise-copied to the return value. If you didn't call *Detach*, the *COleVariant* destructor would free the *BSTR* memory and the calling program would get a *VARIANT* that contained a pointer to nothing.

A component's variant dispatch function parameters are declared as *const VARIANT&*. You can always cast a VARIANT pointer to a *COleVariant* pointer inside the function. Here's the *SetFigure* function:

```
void CClock::SetFigure(short n, const VARIANT& vaNew)
{
    COleVariant vaTemp;
    vaTemp.ChangeType(VT_BSTR, (COleVariant*) &vaNew);
    m_strFigure[n] = vaTemp.bstrVal;
}
```

Note Remember that all *BSTR* variables contain wide characters. The *CString* class has a constructor and an assignment operator for the *LPCWSTR* (wide-character pointer) type. Thus, the *m_strFigure* string will contain single-byte characters, even though *bstrVal* points to a wide-character array.

Client dispatch function variant parameters are also typed as *const VARIANT&*. You can call those functions with either a *VARIANT* or a *COleVariant* object. Here's an example of a call to the *CClockDriver::SetFigure* function:

```
pClockDriver->SetFigure(0, COleVariant("XII"));
```

> **Note** You can also use the standard classes *_bstr_t* and *_variant_t* to support *BSTR* and *VARIANT*. These classes are independent of the MFC library. The *_bstr_t* class encapsulates the *BSTR* data type; the *_variant_t* class encapsulates the *VARIANT* type. Both classes manage resource allocation and deallocation. For more information on these classes, see the Visual C++ .NET online documentation.

Parameter and Return Type Conversions for *Invoke*

All *IDispatch::Invoke* parameters and return values are processed internally as *VARIANT* types. Remember that! The MFC library implementation of Invoke is smart enough to convert between a *VARIANT* and whatever type you supply (where possible), so you have some flexibility in declaring parameter and return types. Suppose, for example, that your controller's *GetFigure* function specifies the return type *BSTR*. If a component returns an *int* or a *long*, all is well: COM and the MFC library will convert the number to a string. Suppose your component declares a *long* parameter and the controller supplies an *int*. Again, no problem.

> **Note** An MFC library Automation client specifies the expected return type as a *VT_* parameter to the *COleDispatchDriver* functions *GetProperty*, *SetProperty*, and *InvokeHelper*. An MFC library Automation component specifies the expected parameter types as *VTS_* parameters in the *DISP_PROPERTY* and *DISP_FUNCTION* macros.

Unlike C++, VBA is not a strongly typed language. VBA variables are often stored internally as *VARIANT* types. Take an Excel spreadsheet cell value, for example. A spreadsheet user can type a text string, an integer, a floating-point number, or a date/time in a cell. VBA treats the cell value as a *VARIANT* and returns a *VARIANT* object to an Automation client. If your client function declares a *VARIANT* return value, it can test *vt* and process the data accordingly.

VBA uses a date/time format that is distinct from the MFC library *CTime* class. Variables of type *DATE* hold both the date and the time in one double value. The fractional part represents time (.25 is 6:00 AM), and the whole part represents the date (the number of days since December 30, 1899). The MFC library provides a *COleDateTime* class that makes dates easy to deal with. You can construct a date in this way:

```
COleDateTime date(2001, 2, 11, 18, 0, 0);
```

The above declaration initializes the date to February 11, 2001, at 6:00 PM.

The *COleVariant* class has an assignment operator for *COleDateTime*, and the *COleDateTime* class has member functions for extracting date/time components. Here's how you print the time:

```
TRACE("time = %d:%d:%d\n",
      date.GetHour(),date.GetMinute(),date.GetSecond());
```

If you have a variant that contains a *DATE*, you use the *COleVariant::ChangeType* function to convert a date to a string, as shown here:

```
COleVariant vaTimeDate = date;
COleVariant vaTemp;
vaTemp.ChangeType(VT_BSTR, &vaTimeDate);
CString str = vaTemp.bstrVal;
TRACE("date = %s\n", str);
```

One last item concerning *Invoke* parameters: A dispatch function can have optional parameters. If the component declares trailing parameters as *VARIANT* types, the client doesn't have to supply them. If the client calls the function without supplying an optional parameter, the *VARIANT* object's *vt* value on the component end will be *VT_ERROR*.

Automation Examples

The remainder of this chapter presents five sample programs. The first three programs are Automation components—an EXE component with no user interface, a DLL component, and a multi-instance SDI EXE component. Each of these component programs comes with an Excel driver workbook file. The fourth sample program is an MFC Automation client program that drives the three components and also runs Excel using the *COleDispatchDriver* class. The last sample is a client program that uses the C++ *#import* directive instead of the MFC *COleDispatchDriver* class.

The Ex23a Example: An Automation Component EXE with No User Interface

The Ex23a example represents a typical use of Automation. It is similar to the Visual C++ .NET Autoclik example, which is an MDI framework application with the document object as the Automation component. (To find the Autoclik example, look in the MFC Library Reference and search for AutoClik.) However, unlike the Autoclik example, the Ex23a example has no user interface. There is one Automation-aware class, and in the first version of the program, a single process supports the construction of multiple Automation component objects. In the second version, a new process starts up each time an Automation client creates an object.

In the Ex23a example, a C++ component implements financial transactions. VBA programmers can write user-interface–intensive applications that rely on the audit rules imposed by the Automation component. A production component program would probably use a database, but Ex23a is simpler. It implements a bank account with two methods, *Deposit* and *Withdrawal*, and one read-only property, *Balance*. Obviously, *Withdrawal* can't permit withdrawals that make the balance negative. You can use Excel to control the component, as shown in Figure 23-3.

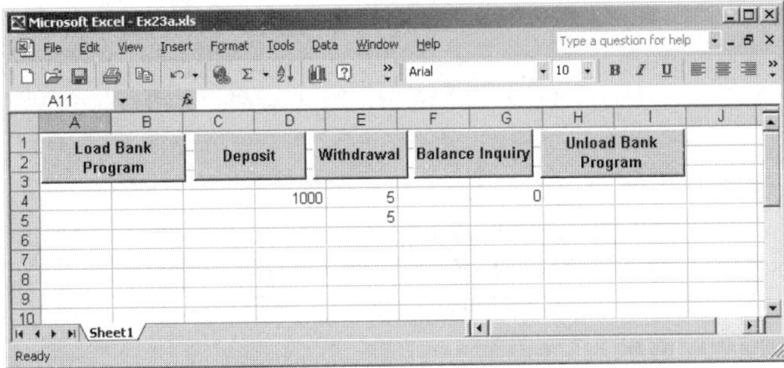

Figure 23-3 An Excel workbook controlling the Ex23a component.

Here are the steps for creating the program from scratch:

1. **Run the MFC Application Wizard to create the Ex23a project.** Select the Dialog Based option on the Application Type page. Deselect all options on the User Interface Features and the Advanced Features pages except the Automation check box on the Advanced Features page. This is the simplest application the MFC Application Wizard can generate.

2. **Eliminate the dialog class from the project.** Using Windows Explorer, delete the files Ex23aDlg.cpp, Ex23aDlg.h, DlgProxy.cpp, and DlgProxy.h. Remove Ex23aDlg.cpp, Ex23aDlg.h, DlgProxy.cpp, and DlgProxy.h from the project by deleting them from Solution Explorer. Edit Ex23a.cpp to remove the dialog *#include*, and remove all dialog-related code from the *InitInstance* function. In Resource View, delete the *IDD_EX23A_DIALOG* dialog resource template.

3. **Add code to enable Automation.** Selecting the Automation check box added this line in StdAfx.h:

```
#include <afxdisp.h>
```

   The *InitInstance* function (in Ex23a.cpp) now has COM initialization code in it. Be sure to add the *return TRUE* statement that's shown in boldface:

```
BOOL CEx23aApp::InitInstance()
{
    CWinApp::InitInstance();
    // Initialize OLE libraries
    if (!AfxOleInit())
    {
        AfxMessageBox(IDP_OLE_INIT_FAILED);
        return FALSE;
    }
    // Parse command line for automation or reg/unreg switches.
    CCommandLineInfo cmdInfo;
    ParseCommandLine(cmdInfo);

    // App was launched with /Embedding or /Automation switch.
    // Run app as automation server.
    if (cmdInfo.m_bRunEmbedded || cmdInfo.m_bRunAutomated)
    {
        // Register class factories via CoRegisterClassObject().
        COleTemplateServer::RegisterAll();
        return TRUE;
    }
    // App was launched with /Unregserver or /Unregister switch.
    // Remove entries from the registry.
    else if (cmdInfo.m_nShellCommand ==
    CCommandLineInfo::AppUnregister)
    {
        COleObjectFactory::UpdateRegistryAll(FALSE);
```

```
        AfxOleUnregisterTypeLib(_tlid, _wVerMajor, _wVerMinor);
        return FALSE;
    }
    // App was launched standalone or with other switches
    // (e.g. /Register or /Regserver).  Update registry entries,
    // including typelibrary.
    else
    {
        COleObjectFactory::UpdateRegistryAll();
        AfxOleRegisterTypeLib(AfxGetInstanceHandle(), _tlid);
        if (cmdInfo.m_nShellCommand ==
            CCommandLineInfo::AppRegister)
            return FALSE;
    }
    return FALSE;
}
```

4. **Use the Add Class Wizard to add a new class, *CBank*, as shown here:**

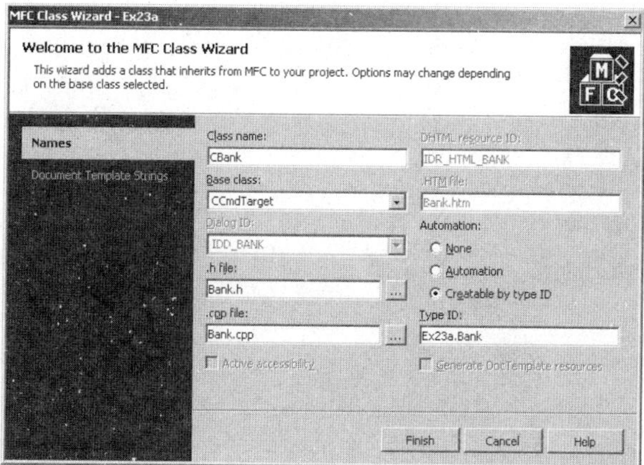

Be sure to select the Creatable By Type ID option.

5. **Use the Add Method Wizard and the Add Property Wizard to add two methods and a property.** To get to these wizards, open Class View, select the library node to expand the library information, and right-click on the IBank node. You'll see two commands: Add Method and Add Property. First, add a *Withdrawal* method, as shown here:

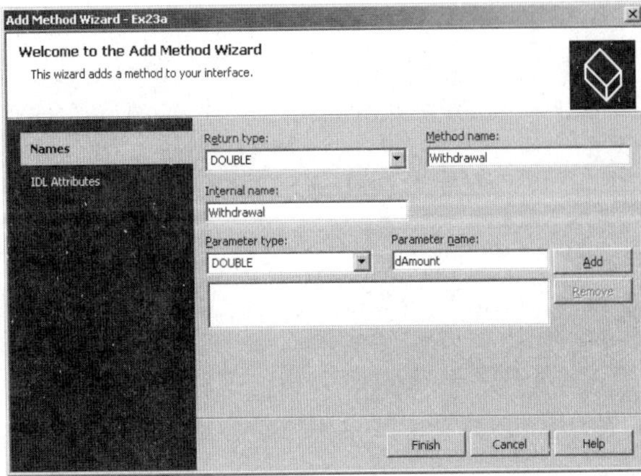

The *dAmount* parameter is the amount to be withdrawn, and the return value is the actual amount withdrawn. If you try to withdraw $100 from an account that contains $60, the amount withdrawn will be $60.

Add a similar *Deposit* method that returns *void*, and then add the *Balance* property, as shown here:

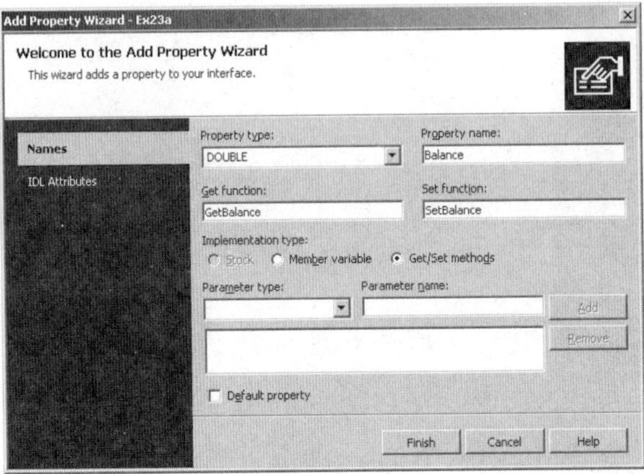

We could have selected direct access to a component data member, but then we wouldn't have read-only access. We selected Get/Set Methods so we can code the *SetBalance* function to do nothing.

6. **Add a public *m_dBalance* data member of type *double* to the *CBank* class.** Because we selected the Get/Set Methods option for the *Balance* property, the Add Property Wizard won't generate a data member. You should declare *m_dBalance* in the Bank.h file and initialize *m_dBalance* to 0.0 in the *CBank* constructor located in the Bank.cpp file.

7. **Edit the generated method and property functions.** Add the following boldface code:

```
DOUBLE CBank::Withdrawal(DOUBLE dAmount)
{
    AFX_MANAGE_STATE(AfxGetAppModuleState());
    if (dAmount < 0.0) {
        return 0.0;
    }
    if (dAmount <= m_dBalance) {
        m_dBalance -= dAmount;
         return dAmount;
    }
    double dTemp = m_dBalance;
    m_dBalance = 0.0;
    return dTemp;
}
void CBank::Deposit(DOUBLE dAmount)
{
    AFX_MANAGE_STATE(AfxGetAppModuleState());
    if (dAmount < 0.0) {
        return;
    }
    m_dBalance += dAmount;
}
DOUBLE CBank::GetBalance(void)
{
    AFX_MANAGE_STATE(AfxGetAppModuleState());
    return m_dBalance;
}
void CBank::SetBalance(DOUBLE newVal)
{
    AFX_MANAGE_STATE(AfxGetAppModuleState());
    TRACE("Sorry, Dave, I can't do that!\n");
}
```

8. **Build the Ex23a program, and run it once to register the component.**

9. **Set up five Excel macros in a new workbook file, Ex23a.xls.** Add the following code:

```
Dim Bank As Object
Sub LoadBank()
    Set Bank = CreateObject("Ex23a.Bank")
End Sub

Sub UnloadBank()
    Set Bank = Nothing
End Sub
```

(continued)

```
Sub DoDeposit()
    Range("D4").Select
    Bank.Deposit (ActiveCell.Value)
End Sub

Sub DoWithdrawal()
    Range("E4").Select
    Dim Amt
    Amt = Bank.Withdrawal(ActiveCell.Value)
    Range("E5").Select
    ActiveCell.Value = Amt
End Sub

Sub DoInquiry()
    Dim Amt
    Amt = Bank.Balance()
    Range("G4").Select
    ActiveCell.Value = Amt
End Sub
```

10. **Arrange an Excel worksheet as shown in Figure 23-3.** Attach the macros to the buttons (by right-clicking on the buttons).

11. **Test the Ex23a bank component.** Click the Load Bank Program button, enter a deposit value in cell D4, and click the Deposit button. Click the Balance Inquiry button, and watch the balance appear in cell G4. Enter a withdrawal value in cell E4, and click the Withdrawal button. To see the balance, click the Balance Inquiry button.

> **Note** Sometimes you have to click the buttons twice. The first click switches the focus to the worksheet, and the second click runs the macro. The hourglass pointer indicates that the macro is working.

What's happening in this program? Look closely at the *CEx23aApp::InitInstance* function. When you run the program directly from Windows, it displays a message box and then quits, but not before it updates the Registry. The *COleObjectFactory::UpdateRegistryAll* function hunts for global class factory objects, and the *CBank* class's *IMPLEMENT_OLECREATE* macro invocation defines such an object. (The *IMPLEMENT_OLECREATE_FLAGS* line was generated because we selected the Createable By Type ID check box when we added the *CBank* class.) The unique class ID and the program ID, *Ex23a.Bank*, are added to the Registry.

When Excel then calls *CreateObject*, COM loads the Ex23a program, which contains the global factory for *CBank* objects. COM then calls the factory object's *CreateInstance* function to construct the *CBank* object and return an *IDispatch* pointer. Here's the *CBank* class declaration that the Add Class Wizard generated in the Bank.h file, with unnecessary detail (and the method and property functions you've already seen) omitted:

```
#pragma once
// CBank command target
class CBank : public CCmdTarget
{
    DECLARE_DYNCREATE(CBank)
public:
    CBank();
    virtual ~CBank();
    virtual void OnFinalRelease();
    DOUBLE m_dBalance;
protected:
    DECLARE_MESSAGE_MAP()
    DECLARE_OLECREATE(CBank)
    DECLARE_DISPATCH_MAP()
    DECLARE_INTERFACE_MAP()
    DOUBLE Withdrawal(DOUBLE dAmount);
    enum
    {
        dispidBalance = 3, dispidDeposit = 2L, dispidWithdrawal = 1L
    };
    void Deposit(DOUBLE dAmount);
    DOUBLE GetBalance(void);
    void SetBalance(DOUBLE newVal);
};
```

Here's the code that was automatically generated by the Add Class Wizard in Bank.cpp:

```
// Bank.cpp : implementation file
//
#include "stdafx.h"
#include "Ex23a.h"
#include "Bank.h"

// CBank
IMPLEMENT_DYNCREATE(CBank, CCmdTarget)
CBank::CBank()
{
    EnableAutomation();
    // To keep the application running as long as an OLE automation
    //    object is active, the constructor calls AfxOleLockApp.
    AfxOleLockApp();
```

(continued)

```
    m_dBalance = 0.0;
}
CBank::~CBank()
{
    // To terminate the application when all objects created with
    //     with OLE automation, the destructor calls AfxOleUnlockApp.
    AfxOleUnlockApp();
}
void CBank::OnFinalRelease()
{
    // When the last reference for an automation object is released
    // OnFinalRelease is called.  The base class will automatically
    // delete the object.  Add additional cleanup required for your
    // object before calling the base class.
    CCmdTarget::OnFinalRelease();
}
BEGIN_MESSAGE_MAP(CBank, CCmdTarget)
END_MESSAGE_MAP()

BEGIN_DISPATCH_MAP(CBank, CCmdTarget)
 DISP_FUNCTION_ID(CBank, "Withdrawal", dispidWithdrawal,
                  Withdrawal, VT_R8, VTS_R8)
 DISP_FUNCTION_ID(CBank, "Deposit", dispidDeposit,
                  Deposit, VT_EMPTY, VTS_R8)
 DISP_PROPERTY_EX_ID(CBank, "Balance", dispidBalance,
                     GetBalance, SetBalance, VT_R8)
END_DISPATCH_MAP()

// Note: we add support for IID_IBank to support typesafe binding
//  from VBA.  This IID must match the GUID that is attached to the
//  dispinterface in the .IDL file.

// {8BAD2B0C-62CC-4952-811C-C736DA06858E}
static const IID IID_IBank =
    { 0x8BAD2B0C, 0x62CC, 0x4952,
     { 0x81, 0x1C, 0xC7, 0x36, 0xDA, 0x6, 0x85, 0x8E } };

BEGIN_INTERFACE_MAP(CBank, CCmdTarget)
    INTERFACE_PART(CBank, IID_IBank, Dispatch)
END_INTERFACE_MAP()

// {3EC6FA59-9F9F-4619-9F62-BA5FE37176F0}
IMPLEMENT_OLECREATE_FLAGS(CBank, "Ex23a.Bank",
    afxRegApartmentThreading, 0x3ec6fa59, 0x9f9f,
    0x4619, 0x9f, 0x62, 0xba, 0x5f, 0xe3, 0x71,
    0x76, 0xf0)
// CBank message handlers
:
```

This first version of the Ex23a program runs in single-process mode, as does the Autoclik program. If a second Automation client asks for a new *CBank* object, COM will call the class factory *CreateInstance* function again and the existing process will construct another *CBank* object on the heap. You can verify this by making a copy of the Ex23a.xls workbook (under a different name) and loading both the original and the copy. Click the Load Bank Program button in each workbook, and watch the Debug window. *InitInstance* should be called only once.

Debugging an EXE Component Program

When an Automation client launches an EXE component program, it sets the */Embedding* command-line parameter. If you want to debug your component, you must do the same. Right-click on the project in Solution Explorer. Choose Properties and then click Debugging in the Property Pages dialog box. Enter **/Automation** (or **/Embedding**) in the Command Arguments box, as shown here:

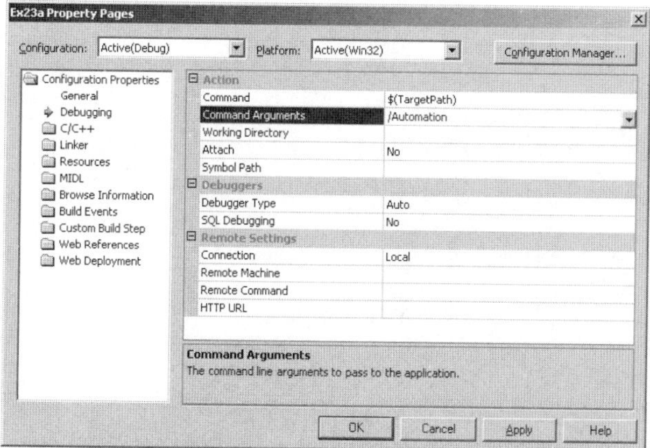

When you choose Start from the Debug menu or press F5, your program will start and then wait for a client to activate it. At this point, you should start the client program from Windows (if it is not already running) and then use it to create a component object. Your component program in the debugger should then construct its object. It might be a good idea to include a *TRACE* statement in the component object's constructor.

Remember that your component program must be registered before the client can find it. That means you have to run it once without the */Automation* (or the */Embedding*) flag. Many clients don't synchronize with Registry changes. If your client is running when you register the component, you might have to restart the client.

The Ex23b Example: An Automation Component DLL

You could easily convert Ex23a from an EXE to a DLL. The *CBank* class would be exactly the same, and the Excel driver would be similar. It's more interesting, though, to write a new application—this time with a minimal user interface. We'll use a modal dialog box because it's the most complex user interface we can conveniently use in an Automation DLL.

The Ex23b program is fairly simple. An Automation component class, identified by the registered name Ex23b.Auto, has the following properties and method:

Name	Description
LongData	Long integer property
TextData	*VARIANT* property
DisplayDialog	Method—no parameters, *BOOL* return

DisplayDialog displays the Ex23b data-gathering dialog box shown in Figure 23-4. An Excel macro passes two cell values to the DLL and then updates the same cells with the updated values.

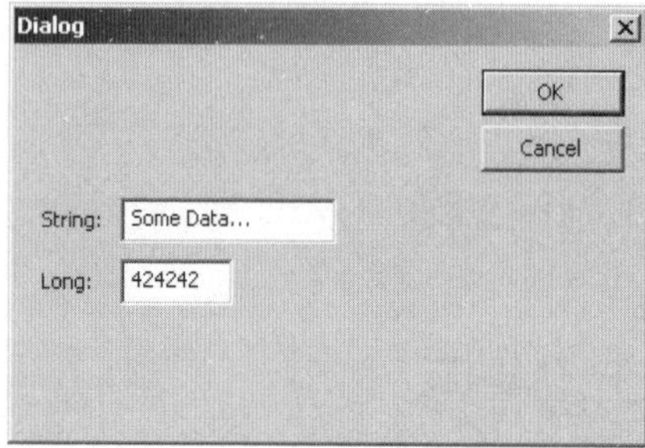

Figure 23-4 The Ex23b DLL dialog box in action.

Parameters Passed by Reference

So far, you've seen VBA parameters passed by value. VBA has pretty strange rules for calling methods. If the method has one parameter, you can use parentheses; if it has more than one, you can't (unless you're using the function's return value, in which case you must use parentheses). Here's some sample VBA code that passes the string parameter by value:

```
Object.Method1 parm1, "text"
Object.Method2("text")
Dim s as String
s = "text"
Object.Method2(s)
```

Sometimes, though, VBA passes the address of a parameter (a reference). In this example, the string is passed by reference:

```
Dim s as String
s = "text"
Object.Method1 parm1, s
```

You can override VBA's default behavior by prefixing a parameter with *ByVal* or *ByRef*. Your component can't predict if it's getting a value or a reference—it must prepare for both. The trick is to test *vt* to see whether its *VT_BYREF* bit is set. Here's a sample method implementation that accepts a string (in a *VARIANT*) passed either by reference or value:

```
void CMyComponent::Method(long nParm1, const VARIANT& vaParm2)
{
    CString str;
    if ((vaParm2.vt & 0x7f) == VT_BSTR) {
        if ((vaParm2.vt & VT_BYREF) != 0)
            str = *(vaParm2.pbstrVal); // byref
        else
            str = vaParm2.bstrVal; // byval
    }
    AfxMessageBox(str);
}
```

If you declare a *BSTR* parameter, the MFC library will do the conversion for you. Suppose your client program passes a *BSTR* reference to an out-of-process component and the component program changes the value. Because the component can't access the memory of the client process, COM must copy the string to the component and then copy it back to the client after the function returns. So, before you declare reference parameters, remember that passing references through *IDispatch* is not like passing references in C++.

The example was first generated as a normal MFC DLL using the MFC DLL Wizard with the Regular DLL Using Shared MFC DLL option and the Automation option selected. Here are the steps for building and testing the Ex23b component DLL from the code installed from the companion CD:

1. **In Visual Studio .NET, open the \vcppnet\Ex23b\Ex23b.sln solution.** Build the project.
2. **Register the DLL.** You can use the RegComp program in the \vcppnet\REGCOMP\Release directory on the companion CD; a file dialog box makes it easy to select the DLL file. Or you can use Regsvr32.exe.
3. **Start Excel, and then load the \vcppnet\Ex23b\Ex23b.xls workbook file.** Type an integer in cell C3, and then type some text in cell D3, as shown here:

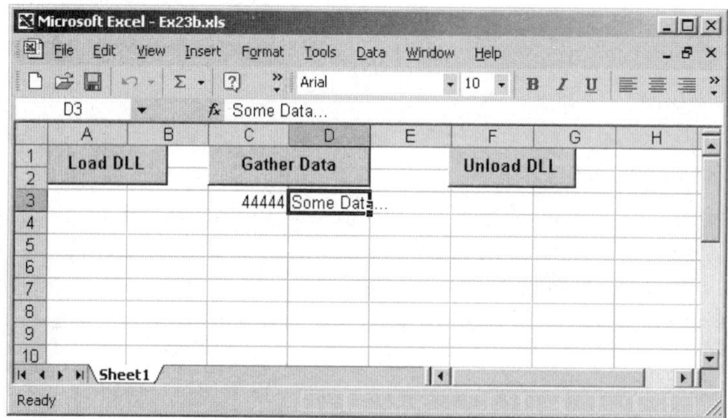

Click the Load DLL button, and then click the Gather Data button. Edit the data, click OK, and watch the new values appear in the spreadsheet.

4. **Click the Unload DLL button.** If you've started the DLL (and Excel) from the debugger, you can watch the Debug window to be sure the DLL's *ExitInstance* function is called.

Now let's look at the Ex23b code. Like an MFC EXE, an MFC regular DLL has an application class (derived from *CWinApp*) and a global application object. The overridden *InitInstance* member function in Ex23b.cpp looks like this:

```
BOOL CEx23bApp::InitInstance()
{
    TRACE("CEx23bApp::InitInstance\n");
    CWinApp::InitInstance();
```

```
    // Register all OLE server (factories) as running.  This enables the
    //  OLE libraries to create objects from other applications.
    COleObjectFactory::RegisterAll();

    return TRUE;
}
```

Debugging a DLL Component

To debug a DLL, you must tell the debugger which EXE file to load. Right-click on the project name in Solution Explorer and choose Properties. Click Debugging in the Property Pages dialog box and enter the controller's full pathname (including the EXE extension) in the Command box, as shown here:

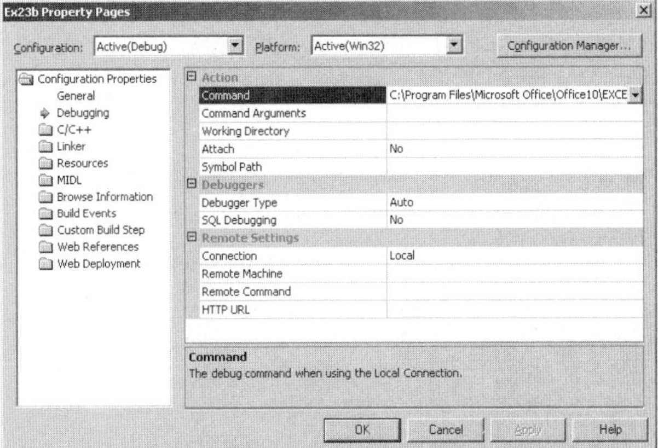

When you press F5, your controller will start. When you activate the component from the controller, the DLL will load.

It might be a good idea to include a *TRACE* statement in the component object's constructor. Don't forget that your DLL must be registered before the client can load it.

Here's another option: If you have the source code for the client program, you can start the client program in the debugger. When the client loads the component DLL, you can see the output from the component program's *TRACE* statements.

There's also the following code for the three standard COM DLL exported functions:

```
STDAPI DllGetClassObject(REFCLSID rclsid, REFIID riid, LPVOID* ppv)
{
    AFX_MANAGE_STATE(AfxGetStaticModuleState());
    return AfxDllGetClassObject(rclsid, riid, ppv);
}
// DllCanUnloadNow - Allows COM to unload DLL
STDAPI DllCanUnloadNow(void)
{
    AFX_MANAGE_STATE(AfxGetStaticModuleState());
    return AfxDllCanUnloadNow();
}
// DllRegisterServer - Adds entries to the system registry
STDAPI DllRegisterServer(void)
{
    AFX_MANAGE_STATE(AfxGetStaticModuleState());

    if (!AfxOleRegisterTypeLib(AfxGetInstanceHandle(), _tlid))
        return SELFREG_E_TYPELIB;

    if (!COleObjectFactory::UpdateRegistryAll())
        return SELFREG_E_CLASS;

    return S_OK;
}
// DllUnregisterServer - Removes entries from the system registry
STDAPI DllUnregisterServer(void)
{
    AFX_MANAGE_STATE(AfxGetStaticModuleState());

    if (!AfxOleUnregisterTypeLib(_tlid, _wVerMajor, _wVerMinor))
        return SELFREG_E_TYPELIB;

    if (!COleObjectFactory::UpdateRegistryAll(FALSE))
        return SELFREG_E_CLASS;

    return S_OK;
}
```

The PromptDlg.cpp file contains code for the *CPromptDlg* class, but that class is a standard class derived from *CDialog*. The file PromptDlg.h contains the *CPromptDlg* class header.

The *CEx23bAuto* class—the Automation component class initially generated by the Add Class Wizard (with the Createable By Type ID option)—is more interesting. This class is exposed to COM under the program ID Ex23b.Ex23bAuto. The following listing shows the header file Ex23bAuto.h:

Ex23bAuto.h

```
#pragma once
// CEx23bAuto command target
class CEx23bAuto : public CCmdTarget
{
    DECLARE_DYNCREATE(CEx23bAuto)
public:
    CEx23bAuto();
    virtual ~CEx23bAuto();
    virtual void OnFinalRelease();
protected:
    DECLARE_MESSAGE_MAP()
    DECLARE_OLECREATE(CEx23bAuto)
    DECLARE_DISPATCH_MAP()
    DECLARE_INTERFACE_MAP()
    void OnLongDataChanged(void);
    LONG m_lData;
    enum
    {
        dispidDisplayDialog = 3L,
        dispidTextData = 2,
        dispidLongData = 1
    };
    void OnTextDataChanged(void);
    VARIANT m_vaTextData;
    VARIANT_BOOL DisplayDialog(void);
};
```

The following listing shows the implementation file Ex23bAuto.cpp:

Ex23bAuto.cpp

```
// Ex23bAuto.cpp : implementation file
//
#include "stdafx.h"
#include "Ex23b.h"
#include "Ex23bAuto.h"
#include "Promptdlg.h"

// CEx23bAuto
IMPLEMENT_DYNCREATE(CEx23bAuto, CCmdTarget)
CEx23bAuto::CEx23bAuto()
{
    EnableAutomation();
    // To keep the application running as long as an OLE automation
    //    object is active, the constructor calls AfxOleLockApp.

    ::VariantInit(&m_vaTextData); // necessary initialization
    m_lData = 0;
```

(continued)

```
    AfxOleLockApp();
}
CEx23bAuto::~CEx23bAuto()
{
    // To terminate the application when all objects created with
    //     with OLE automation, the destructor calls AfxOleUnlockApp.
    AfxOleUnlockApp();
}
void CEx23bAuto::OnFinalRelease()
{
    // When the last reference for an automation object is released
    // OnFinalRelease is called.  The base class will automatically
    // delete the object.  Add additional cleanup required for your
    // object before calling the base class.
    CCmdTarget::OnFinalRelease();
}

BEGIN_MESSAGE_MAP(CEx23bAuto, CCmdTarget)
END_MESSAGE_MAP()

BEGIN_DISPATCH_MAP(CEx23bAuto, CCmdTarget)
    DISP_PROPERTY_NOTIFY_ID(CEx23bAuto, "LongData", dispidLongData, m_lData,
                            OnLongDataChanged, VT_I4)
    DISP_PROPERTY_NOTIFY_ID(CEx23bAuto, "TextData", dispidTextData,
                            m_vaTextData, OnTextDataChanged, VT_VARIANT)
    DISP_FUNCTION_ID(CEx23bAuto, "DisplayDialog", dispidDisplayDialog,
                     DisplayDialog, VT_BOOL, VTS_NONE)
END_DISPATCH_MAP()

// Note: we add support for IID_IEx23bAuto to support typesafe binding
//  from VBA.  This IID must match the GUID that is attached to the
//  dispinterface in the .IDL file.

// {125FECB2-734D-49FD-95C7-FE44B77FDE2C}
static const IID IID_IEx23bAuto =
    { 0x125FECB2, 0x734D, 0x49FD, { 0x95, 0xC7, 0xFE, 0x44, 0xB7,
      0x7F, 0xDE, 0x2C } };

BEGIN_INTERFACE_MAP(CEx23bAuto, CCmdTarget)
    INTERFACE_PART(CEx23bAuto, IID_IEx23bAuto, Dispatch)
END_INTERFACE_MAP()

// {BAF3D9ED-4518-43CA-B017-2EBA332CB618}
IMPLEMENT_OLECREATE_FLAGS(CEx23bAuto, "Ex23b.Ex23bAuto",
    afxRegApartmentThreading, 0xbaf3d9ed, 0x4518, 0x43ca,
    0xb0, 0x17, 0x2e, 0xba, 0x33, 0x2c, 0xb6, 0x18)

// CEx23bAuto message handlers
void CEx23bAuto::OnLongDataChanged(void)
```

```
{
    AFX_MANAGE_STATE(AfxGetStaticModuleState());
    TRACE("CEx23bAuto::OnLongDataChanged\n");
}
void CEx23bAuto::OnTextDataChanged(void)
{
    AFX_MANAGE_STATE(AfxGetStaticModuleState());
    TRACE("CEx23bAuto::OnTextDataChanged\n");
}
VARIANT_BOOL CEx23bAuto::DisplayDialog(void)
{
    AFX_MANAGE_STATE(AfxGetStaticModuleState());
    VARIANT_BOOL bRet;
    TRACE("Entering CEx23bAuto::DisplayDialog %p\n", this);
    bRet = TRUE;
    AfxLockTempMaps();  // See MFC Tech Note #3
    CWnd* pTopWnd = CWnd::FromHandle(::GetTopWindow(NULL));
    try {
        CPromptDlg dlg /*(pTopWnd)*/;
        if (m_vaTextData.vt == VT_BSTR){
            dlg.m_strData = m_vaTextData.bstrVal; // converts
                                                  //  double-byte
                                                  //  character to
                                                  //  single-byte
                                                  //  character
        }
        dlg.m_lData = m_lData;
        if (dlg.DoModal() == IDOK) {
            m_vaTextData = COleVariant(dlg.m_strData).Detach();
            m_lData = dlg.m_lData;
            bRet = TRUE;
        }
        else {
            bRet =  FALSE;
        }
    }
    catch (CException* pe) {
        TRACE("Exception: failure to display dialog\n");
        bRet =  FALSE;
        pe->Delete();
    }
    AfxUnlockTempMaps();
    return bRet;
}
```

The two properties, *LongData* and *TextData*, are represented by the class data members *m_lData* and *m_vaTextData*, which are both initialized in the constructor. When the *LongData* property was added in the Add Property Wizard, a notification function, *OnLongDataChanged*, was specified. This function is called whenever the controller changes the property value. Notification functions apply only to properties that are represented by data members. Don't confuse this notification with the notifications that ActiveX controls give their container when a bound property changes.

The *DisplayDialog* member function, which is the *DisplayDialog* method, is ordinary except that the *AfxLockTempMaps* and *AfxUnlockTempMaps* functions are necessary for cleaning up temporary object pointers that would normally be deleted in an EXE program's idle loop.

What about the Excel VBA code? Here are the three macros and the global declarations:

```
Dim Dllcomp As Object
Private Declare Sub CoFreeUnusedLibraries Lib "OLE32" ()

Sub LoadDllComp()
    Set Dllcomp = CreateObject("Ex23b.Ex23bAuto")
    Range("C3").Select
    Dllcomp.LongData = Selection.Value
    Range("D3").Select
    Dllcomp.TextData = Selection.Value
End Sub

Sub RefreshDllComp() 'Gather Data button
    Range("C3").Select
    Dllcomp.LongData = Selection.Value
    Range("D3").Select
    Dllcomp.TextData = Selection.Value
    Dllcomp.DisplayDialog
    Range("C3").Select
    Selection.Value = Dllcomp.LongData
    Range("D3").Select
    Selection.Value = Dllcomp.TextData
End Sub

Sub UnloadDllComp()
    Set Dllcomp = Nothing
    Call CoFreeUnusedLibraries
End Sub
```

The first line in *LoadDllComp* creates a component object as identified by the registered name *Ex23b.Ex23bAuto*. The *RefreshDllComp* macro accesses the component object's *LongData* and *TextData* properties. The first time you run *LoadDllComp*, it loads the DLL and constructs an *Ex23b.Auto* object. The second time you run it, something curious happens: A second object is constructed, and the original object is destroyed. If you run *LoadDllComp* from another copy of the workbook, you get two separate *Ex23b.Auto* objects. Of course, there's only one mapping of Ex23b.dll in memory at any time unless you're running more than one Excel process.

Look closely at the *UnloadDllComp* macro. When the *Set Dllcomp = Nothing* statement is executed, the DLL is disconnected, but it's not unmapped from Excel's address space, which means the component's *ExitInstance* function is not called. The *CoFreeUnusedLibraries* function calls the exported *DllCanUnloadNow* function for each component DLL and, if that function returns *TRUE*, *CoFreeUnusedLibraries* frees the DLL. MFC programs call *CoFreeUnusedLibraries* in the idle loop (after a one-minute delay), but Excel doesn't. That's why *UnloadDllComp* must call *CoFreeUnusedLibraries* after disconnecting the component.

The Ex23c Example: An SDI Automation Component EXE with User Interface

This Automation component example illustrates the use of a document component class in an SDI application in which a new process is started for each object. This component program demonstrates an indexed property plus a method that constructs a new COM object.

The first Automation component example, Ex23a, doesn't have a user interface. The global class factory constructs a *CBank* object that does the component's work. But what if you want your EXE component to have a window? If you've bought into the MFC document-view architecture, you'll want the document, view, and frame, with all the benefits they provide.

Suppose you create a regular MFC application and then add a COM-creatable class such as *CBank*. How do you attach the *CBank* object to the document and view? From a *CBank* class member function, you could navigate through the application object and main frame to the current document or view, but you'd have a tough time in an MDI application if you encountered several component objects and several documents. There's a better way: You make the document class the creatable class, and you have the full support of the MFC Application Wizard for this task. This is true for both MDI and SDI applications.

The MDI Autoclik example demonstrates how COM triggers the construction of new document, view, and child frame objects each time an Automation client creates a new component object. Because the Ex23c example is an SDI program, Windows starts a new process each time the client creates an object. Immediately after the program starts, COM, with the help of the MFC application framework, constructs not only the Automation-aware document but also the view and the main frame window.

Now is a good time to experiment with the Ex23c application, which was first generated by the MFC DLL Wizard with the Automation option selected. It's a Windows-based alarm clock program that's designed to be manipulated from an Automation client such as Excel. Ex23c has the following properties and methods:

Name	Description
Time	*DATE* property that holds a *COM DATE* (*m_vaTime*)
Figure	Indexed *VARIANT* property for the four figures on the clock face (*m_strFigure[]*)
RefreshWin	Method that invalidates the view window and brings the main frame window to the top (*Refresh*)
ShowWin	Method that displays the application's main window (*ShowWin*)
CreateAlarm	Method that creates a *CAlarm* object and returns its *IDispatch* pointer (*CreateAlarm*)

Here are the steps for building and running Ex23c from the companion CD:

1. **In Visual Studio .NET, open the solution \vcppnet\Ex23c\Ex23c.sln.** Build the project to produce the Ex23c.exe file in the project's Debug subdirectory.
2. **Run the program once to register it.** The program is designed to be executed either as a standalone application or as an Automation component. When you run it from Windows or from Visual Studio .NET, it updates the Registry and displays the face of a clock with the characters *XII*, *III*, *VI*, and *IX* at the 12, 3, 6, and 9 o'clock positions. Exit the program.
3. **Load the Excel workbook file \vcppnet\Ex23c\Ex23c.xls.** The worksheet should look like the one shown here:

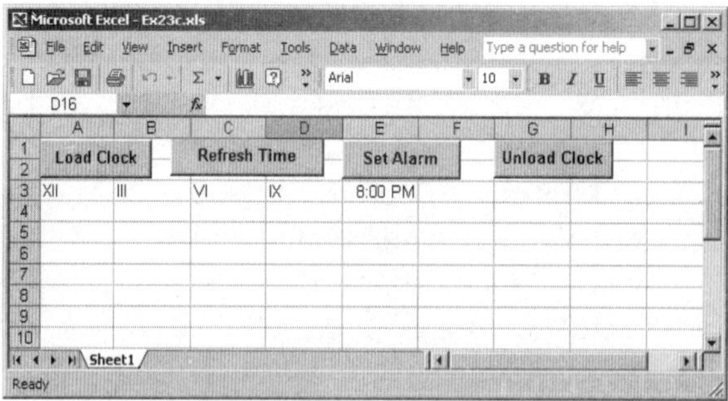

Click the Load Clock button, and then double-click the Set Alarm button. (There might be a long delay after you click the Load Clock button, depending on your system.) The clock should appear as shown here, with the letter *A* indicating the alarm setting:

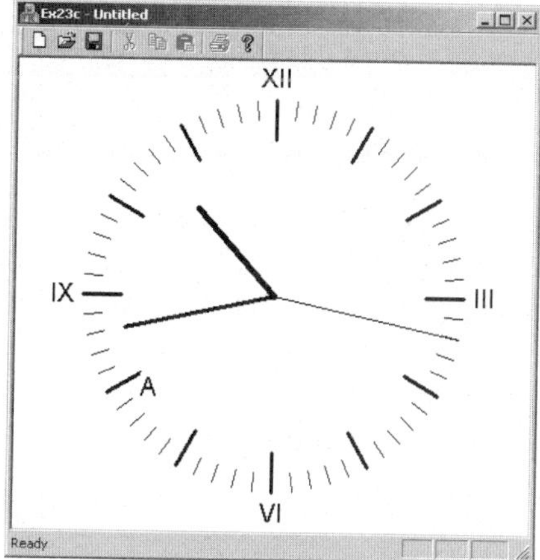

If you've started the component program from the debugger, you can watch the Debug window to see when *InitInstance* is called and when the document object is constructed.

If you're wondering why there's no menu, it's because of the following statement in the *CMainFrame::PreCreateWindow* function:

```
cs.hMenu = NULL;
```

4. **Close the Clock program and then click the Unload Clock button.** Or you can just click the Unload Clock button. The clock will go away.

The MFC Application Wizard did most of the work of setting up the document as an Automation component. In the derived application class *CEx23cApp*, it generated a data member for the component, as shown here:

```
public:
    COleTemplateServer m_server;
```

The MFC *COleTemplateServer* class is derived from *COleObjectFactory*. It is designed to create a COM document object when a client calls *IClassFactory::CreateInstance*. The class ID comes from the global *clsid* variable defined in Ex23c.cpp. The human-readable program ID (Ex23c.Document) comes from the *IDR_MAINFRAME* string resource.

In the *InitInstance* function (in Ex23c.cpp), the MFC Application Wizard generated the following code, which connects the component object (the document) to the application's document template:

```
CSingleDocTemplate* pDocTemplate;
pDocTemplate = new CSingleDocTemplate(
    IDR_MAINFRAME,
    RUNTIME_CLASS(CEx23cDoc),
```

(continued)

```
    RUNTIME_CLASS(CMainFrame),      // main SDI frame window
    RUNTIME_CLASS(CEx23cView));
AddDocTemplate(pDocTemplate);
:
m_server.ConnectTemplate(clsid, pDocTemplate, TRUE);
```

Now all the plumbing is in place for COM and the framework to construct the document, together with the view and frame. When the objects are constructed, however, the main window is not made visible. That's your job. You must write a method that shows the window.

The following *UpdateRegistry* call from the *InitInstance* function updates the Windows Registry with the contents of the project's *IDR_MAINFRAME* string resource:

```
m_server.UpdateRegistry(OAT_DISPATCH_OBJECT);
```

The following dispatch map in the Ex23cDoc.cpp file shows the properties and methods of the *CEx23cDoc* class. Note that the *Figure* property is an indexed property that the Add Property Wizard can generate if you specify a parameter. Later, you'll see the code you have to write for the *GetFigure* and *SetFigure* functions.

```
BEGIN_DISPATCH_MAP(CEx23cDoc, CDocument)
    DISP_PROPERTY_NOTIFY_ID(CEx23cDoc, "Time",
        dispidTime, m_time, OnTimeChanged, VT_DATE)
    DISP_FUNCTION_ID(CEx23cDoc, "ShowWin",
        dispidShowWin, ShowWin, VT_EMPTY, VTS_NONE)
    DISP_FUNCTION_ID(CEx23cDoc, "CreateAlarm",
        dispidCreateAlarm, CreateAlarm, VT_DISPATCH, VTS_DATE)
    DISP_FUNCTION_ID(CEx23cDoc, "RefreshWin",
        dispidRefreshWin, RefreshWin, VT_EMPTY, VTS_NONE)
    DISP_PROPERTY_PARAM_ID(CEx23cDoc, "Figure",
        dispidFigure, GetFigure, SetFigure, VT_VARIANT, VTS_I2)
END_DISPATCH_MAP()
```

The *ShowWin* and *RefreshWin* member functions aren't very interesting, but the *CreateAlarm* method is worth a close look. Here's the corresponding *CreateAlarm* member function:

```
IDispatch* CEx23cDoc::CreateAlarm(DATE time)
{
    AFX_MANAGE_STATE(AfxGetAppModuleState());
    TRACE("Entering CEx23cDoc::CreateAlarm, time = %f\n", time);
    // OLE deletes any prior CAlarm object
    m_pAlarm = new CAlarm(time);
    return m_pAlarm->GetIDispatch(FALSE);    // no AddRef here
}
```

We've chosen to have the component create an alarm object when a controller calls *CreateAlarm*. *CAlarm* is an Automation component class that we've generated with the Add Class Wizard. It is not COM-creatable, which means there's no *IMPLEMENT_OLECREATE* macro and no class factory. The *CreateAlarm* function constructs a *CAlarm* object and returns an *IDispatch* pointer. (The *FALSE* parameter for *CCmdTarget::GetIDispatch* means that the reference count is not incremented; the *CAlarm* object already has a reference count of 1 when it is constructed.)

The *CAlarm* class is declared in Alarm.h as follows:

```
#pragma once
// CAlarm command target
class CAlarm : public CCmdTarget
{
    DECLARE_DYNAMIC(CAlarm)
public:
    CAlarm(DATE time);
    virtual ~CAlarm();
    virtual void OnFinalRelease();
    DATE m_time;

protected:
    DECLARE_MESSAGE_MAP()
    DECLARE_DISPATCH_MAP()
    DECLARE_INTERFACE_MAP()
    void OnTimeChanged(void);

    enum
    {
        dispidTime = 1
    };
};
```

Notice the absence of the *DECLARE_DYNCREATE* macro.

Alarm.cpp contains a dispatch map, as follows:

```
BEGIN_DISPATCH_MAP(CAlarm, CCmdTarget)
    DISP_PROPERTY_NOTIFY_ID(CAlarm, "Time",
        dispidTime, m_time, OnTimeChanged, VT_DATE)
END_DISPATCH_MAP()
```

Why do we have a *CAlarm* class? We could have added an *AlarmTime* property in the *CEx23cDoc* class instead, but then we would have needed another property or method to turn the alarm on and off. By using the *CAlarm* class, what we're really doing is setting ourselves up to support multiple alarms—a collection of alarms.

To implement an Automation collection, we can write another class, *CAlarms*, that contains the methods *Add*, *Remove*, and *Item*. *Add* and *Remove* are self-explanatory; *Item* returns an *IDispatch* pointer for a collection element identified by an index, numeric, or some other key. We can also implement a read-only *Count* property that returns the number of elements. The document class (which owns the collection) will have an *Alarms* method with an optional *VARIANT* parameter. If the parameter is omitted, the method will return the *IDispatch* pointer for the collection. If the parameter specifies an index, the method will return an *IDispatch* pointer for the selected alarm.

> **Note** If we want our collection to support the VBA "For Each" syntax, we'll have some more work to do. We'll have to add an *IEnum VARIANT* interface to the *CAlarms* class to enumerate the collection of variants and implement the *Next* member function of this interface to step through the collection. Then we'll have to add a *CAlarms* method named *_NewEnum* that returns an *IEnumVARIANT* interface pointer. If we want the collection to be general, we must allow separate enumerator objects (with an *IEnum VARIANT* interface) and then implement the other *IEnumVARIANT* functions—*Skip*, *Reset*, and *Clone*.

The *Figure* property is an indexed property, which makes it interesting. The *Figure* property represents the four figures on the clock face—XII, III, VI, and IX. It's a *CString* array, so we can use Roman numerals. Here's the declaration in Ex23cDoc.h:

```
public:
    CString m_strFigure[4];
```

And here are the *GetFigure* and *SetFigure* functions in Ex23cDoc.cpp:

```
VARIANT CEx23cDoc::GetFigure(SHORT n)
{
    AFX_MANAGE_STATE(AfxGetAppModuleState());
    TRACE("Entering CEx23cDoc::GetFigure -- n = %d m_strFigure[n] = %s\n",
          n, m_strFigure[n]);
    return COleVariant(m_strFigure[n]).Detach();
}
void CEx23cDoc::SetFigure(SHORT n, VARIANT FAR& newVal)
{
    AFX_MANAGE_STATE(AfxGetAppModuleState());
    TRACE("Entering CEx23cDoc::SetFigure -- n = %d, vt = %d\n", n,
          newVal.vt);
```

```
    COleVariant vaTemp;
    vaTemp.ChangeType(VT_BSTR, (COleVariant*) &newVal);
    m_strFigure[n] = vaTemp.bstrVal; // converts double-to-single
    SetModifiedFlag();
}
```

These functions tie back to the *DISP_PROPERTY_PARAM* macro in the *CEx23cDoc* dispatch map. The first parameter is the index number, specified as a short integer by the last macro parameter. Property indexes don't have to be integers, and the index can have several components (row and column numbers, for example). The *ChangeType* call in *SetFigure* is necessary because the controller might otherwise pass numbers instead of strings.

You've just seen collection properties and indexed properties. What's the difference? A controller can't add or delete elements of an indexed property, but it can add elements to a collection and it can delete elements from a collection.

What draws the clock face? As you might expect, it's the *OnDraw* member function of the view class. This function uses *GetDocument* to get a pointer to the document object, and then it accesses the document's property data members and method member functions.

The Excel macro code is shown here:

```
Dim Clock As Object
Dim Alarm As Object

Sub LoadClock()
    Set Clock = CreateObject("Ex23c.Document")
    Range("A3").Select
    n = 0
    Do Until n = 4
        Clock.figure(n) = Selection.Value
        Selection.Offset(0, 1).Range("A1").Select
        n = n + 1
    Loop
    RefreshClock
    Clock.ShowWin
End Sub

Sub RefreshClock()
    Clock.Time = Now()
    Clock.RefreshWin
End Sub

Sub CreateAlarm()
    Range("E3").Select
    Set Alarm = Clock.CreateAlarm(Selection.Value)
    RefreshClock
End Sub
```

(continued)

```
Sub UnloadClock()
    Set Clock = Nothing
End Sub
```

Notice the *Set Alarm* statement in the *CreateAlarm* macro. It calls the *CreateAlarm* method to return an *IDispatch* pointer, which is stored in an object variable. If the macro is run a second time, a new alarm is created, but the original one is destroyed because its reference count goes to 0.

> **Warning** You've seen a modal dialog box in a DLL (Ex23b), and you've seen a main frame window in an EXE (Ex23c). Be careful with modal dialog boxes in EXEs. It's fine to have an About dialog box that's invoked directly by the component program, but it isn't a good idea to invoke a modal dialog box in an out-of-process component method function. The problem is that once the modal dialog box is on the screen, the user can switch back to the client program. MFC clients handle this situation with a special "Server Busy" message box, which appears right away. Excel does something similar, but it waits 30 seconds, and this can confuse the user.

The Ex23d Example: An Automation Client

So far, you've seen C++ Automation component programs. Now you'll see a C++ Automation client program that runs all the previous components and also controls Excel. The Ex23d program was originally generated by the MFC Application Wizard, but without any COM options. It was easier to add the COM code than it would have been to rip out the component-specific code. If you use the MFC Application Wizard to build such an Automation controller, add the following line at the end of StdAfx.h:

```
#include <afxdisp.h>
```

Then add this call at the beginning of the application's *InitInstance* function:

```
AfxOleInit();
```

To prepare Ex23d, open the \vcppnet\Ex23d\Ex23d.sln solution and do the build. Run the application, and you'll see a standard SDI application with a menu structure similar to that shown in Figure 23-5.

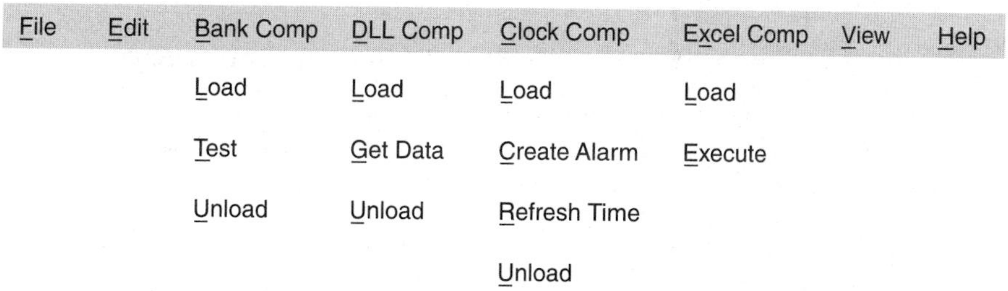

File	Edit	Bank Comp	DLL Comp	Clock Comp	Excel Comp	View	Help
		Load	Load	Load	Load		
		Test	Get Data	Create Alarm	Execute		
		Unload	Unload	Refresh Time			
				Unload			

Figure 23-5 A sample menu structure for a standard SDI application.

If you've built and registered all the components, you can test them from Ex23d. Notice that the DLL doesn't have to be copied to the \Winnt\System32 directory because Windows finds it through the Registry. For some components, you'll have to watch the Debug window to verify that the test results are correct. The program is reasonably modular. Menu commands and update command user interface events are mapped to the view class. Each component object has its own C++ controller class and an embedded data member in Ex23dView.h. We'll look at each part separately after we delve into type libraries.

Type Libraries and IDL Files

I've told you that type libraries aren't necessary for the MFC *IDispatch* implementation, but Visual C++ .NET has been quietly generating and updating type libraries for all your components. What good are these type libraries? VBA can use a type library to browse your component's methods and properties, and it can use the type library for improved access to properties and methods—a process called *early binding* (described later in this chapter). But we're building a C++ client program here, not a VBA program. It so happens that the Add Class Wizard can read a component's type library and use the information to generate C++ code for the client to use to "drive" an Automation component.

> **Note** The MFC Application Wizard initializes a project's Interface Definition Language (IDL) file when you first create it. The Add Property Wizard and the Add Method Wizard edit this file each time you generate a new Automation component class or add properties and methods to an existing class.

When you added properties and methods to your component classes, the Add Method Wizard and the Add Property Wizard updated the project's IDL file. This file is a text file that describes the component in IDL. (Your GUID will be different if you used the MFC Application Wizard to generate this project.) Here's the IDL file for the bank component:

```
// Ex23a.idl : type library source for Ex23a.exe
// This file will be processed by the MIDL compiler to produce the
// type library (Ex23a.tlb).
#include "olectl.h"
[ uuid(60BCA7D2-14D1-4832-A278-50670CD9975E), version(1.0) ]
library Ex23a
{
    importlib("stdole32.tlb");
    importlib("stdole2.tlb");

    //  Primary dispatch interface for CEx23aDoc
    [ uuid(1F013122-EA3D-414F-B58F-5A31A64EA5D5) ]
    dispinterface IEx23a
    {
        properties:
        methods:
    };
    //  Class information for CEx23aDoc
    [ uuid(5EE5C98C-5CCF-46F4-9E95-17BC06237D8B) ]
    coclass Ex23a
    {
        [default] dispinterface IEx23a;
    };
    //  Primary dispatch interface for Bank
    [ uuid(8BAD2B0C-62CC-4952-811C-C736DA06858E) ]
    dispinterface IBank
    {
        properties:
        [id(3), helpstring("property Balance")] DOUBLE Balance;
        methods:
        [id(1), helpstring("method Withdrawal")]
            DOUBLE Withdrawal(DOUBLE dAmount);
        [id(2), helpstring("method Deposit")]
            void Deposit(DOUBLE dAmount);
    };
    //  Class information for Bank
    [ uuid(3EC6FA59-9F9F-4619-9F62-BA5FE37176F0) ]
    coclass Bank
    {
        [default] dispinterface IBank;
    };
};
```

The IDL file has a unique GUID type library identifier, *60BCA7D2-14D1-4832-A278-50670CD9975E*, that completely describes the bank component's properties and methods under a dispinterface named *IBank*. In addition, it specifies the dispinterface GUID, *8BAD2B0C-62CC-4952-811C-C736DA06858E*, which is the same GUID that's in the interface map of the *CBank* class listed earlier. You'll see the significance of this GUID later in this chapter. The CLSID, *3EC6FA59-9F9F-4619-9F62-BA5FE37176F0*, is what a VBA browser can actually use to load your component.

Anyway, when you build your component project, Visual Studio .NET invokes the MIDL utility, which reads the IDL file and generates a binary TLB file in your project's debug or release subdirectory. By default, the type information is also included as part of the binary. When you develop a C++ client program, you can ask the Add Class Wizard to generate a driver class from the component project's TLB file.

To actually do this, you choose Add Class from the Project menu and select the MFC Class From TypeLib template. You navigate to the component project's TLB file, and then the Add Class Wizard shows you a dialog box similar to the one shown here:

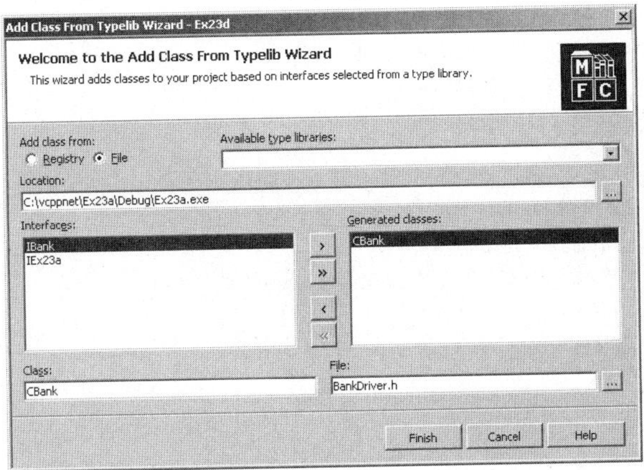

IBank is the dispinterface specified in the IDL file. You can keep this name for the class if you want, and you can specify the H filename. If a type library contains several interfaces, you can make multiple selections. You'll see the generated controller classes in the sections that follow.

The Controller Class for Ex23a.exe

The Add Class From Typelib Wizard generated the *IBank* class (derived from *COleDispatchDriver*) shown in the following listing. Look closely at the member function implementations. Note the first parameters of the *GetProperty*, *SetProperty*, and *InvokeHelper* function calls. These are hard-coded DISPIDs for the component's properties and methods, as determined by the component's dispatch map sequence.

BankDriver.h

```
class CBank : public COleDispatchDriver
{
public:
    CBank(){} // Calls COleDispatchDriver default constructor
    CBank(LPDISPATCH pDispatch) : COleDispatchDriver(pDispatch) {}
    CBank(const CBank& dispatchSrc) : COleDispatchDriver(dispatchSrc) {}
    // Attributes
public:
    // Operations
public:
    // IBank methods
public:
    double Withdrawal(double dAmount)
    {
        double result;
        static BYTE parms[] = VTS_R8 ;
        InvokeHelper(0x1, DISPATCH_METHOD, VT_R8, (void*)&result,
                     parms, dAmount);
        return result;
    }
    void Deposit(double dAmount)
    {
        static BYTE parms[] = VTS_R8 ;
        InvokeHelper(0x2, DISPATCH_METHOD, VT_EMPTY, NULL,
                     parms, dAmount);
    }
    // IBank properties
public:
    double GetBalance()
    {
        double result;
        GetProperty(0x3, VT_R8, (void*)&result);
        return result;
    }
    void SetBalance(double propVal)
    {
        SetProperty(0x3, VT_R8, propVal);
    }
};
```

The *CEx23dView* class has a data member *m_bank* of class *IBank*. The *CEx23dView* member functions for the Ex23a.Bank component are listed below. They are hooked up to options on the Ex23d main menu. Of particular interest is the *OnBankoleLoad* function. The *COleDispatchDriver::CreateDispatch* function loads the component program (by calling *CoGetClassObject* and *IClassFactory::CreateInstance*) and then calls *QueryInterface* to get an *IDispatch* pointer, which it stores in the object's *m_lpDispatch* data member. The *COleDispatchDriver::ReleaseDispatch* function, called in *OnBankoleUnload*, calls Release on the pointer.

```
void CEx23dView::OnBankoleLoad()
{
    if(!m_bank.CreateDispatch("Ex23a.Bank")) {
        AfxMessageBox("Ex23a.Bank component not found");
        return;
    }
}
void CEx23dView::OnUpdateBankoleLoad(CCmdUI *pCmdUI)
{
    pCmdUI->Enable(m_bank.m_lpDispatch == NULL);
}
void CEx23dView::OnBankoleTest()
{
    m_bank.Deposit(20.0);
    m_bank.Withdrawal(15.0);
    TRACE("new balance = %f\n", m_bank.GetBalance());
}
void CEx23dView::OnUpdateBankoleTest(CCmdUI *pCmdUI)
{
    pCmdUI->Enable(m_bank.m_lpDispatch != NULL);
}
void CEx23dView::OnBankoleUnload()
{
    m_bank.ReleaseDispatch();
}
void CEx23dView::OnUpdateBankoleUnload(CCmdUI *pCmdUI)
{
    pCmdUI->Enable(m_bank.m_lpDispatch != NULL);
}
```

The Controller Class for Ex23b.dll

The following listing shows the class header file generated by the Add Class From Typelib Wizard:

AutoDriver.h

```
// Machine generated IDispatch wrapper class(es) created with
// Add Class from Typelib Wizard

// CEx23bAuto wrapper class
class CEx23bAuto : public COleDispatchDriver
{
public:
    CEx23bAuto(){} // Calls COleDispatchDriver default constructor
    CEx23bAuto(LPDISPATCH pDispatch) : COleDispatchDriver(pDispatch) {}
    CEx23bAuto(const CEx23bAuto& dispatchSrc) :
        COleDispatchDriver(dispatchSrc) {}

    // Attributes
public:
    // Operations
public:
    // IEx23bAuto methods
public:
    BOOL DisplayDialog()
    {
        BOOL result;
        InvokeHelper(0x3, DISPATCH_METHOD, VT_BOOL,
                     (void*)&result, NULL);
        return result;
    }
    // IEx23bAuto properties
public:
    long GetLongData()
    {
        long result;
        GetProperty(0x1, VT_I4, (void*)&result);
        return result;
    }
    void SetLongData(long propVal)
    {
        SetProperty(0x1, VT_I4, propVal);
    }
    VARIANT GetTextData()
    {
        VARIANT result;
        GetProperty(0x2, VT_VARIANT, (void*)&result);
        return result;
    }
```

```
    void SetTextData(const VARIANT& propVal)
    {
        SetProperty(0x2, VT_VARIANT, &propVal);
    }
};
```

Notice that each property requires separate *Get* and *Set* functions in the client class, even though a data member in the component represents the property.

The view class header has a data member *m_auto* of class *CEx23bAuto*. Here are some DLL-related command handler member functions from Ex23dView.cpp:

```
void CEx23dView::OnDlloleGetdata()
{
    m_auto.DisplayDialog();
    COleVariant vaData = m_auto.GetTextData();
    ASSERT(vaData.vt == VT_BSTR);
    CString strTextData(vaData.bstrVal);
    long lData = m_auto.GetLongData();
    TRACE("CEx23dView::OnDlloleGetdata -- long = %ld, text = %s\n",
          lData, strTextData);
}
void CEx23dView::OnUpdateDlloleGetdata(CCmdUI *pCmdUI)
{
    pCmdUI->Enable(m_auto.m_lpDispatch != NULL);
}
void CEx23dView::OnDlloleLoad()
{
    if(!m_auto.CreateDispatch("Ex23b.Ex23bAuto")) {
        AfxMessageBox("Ex23b.Ex23bAuto component not found");
        return;
    }
    COleVariant va("test");
    m_auto.SetTextData(va);  // testing
    m_auto.SetLongData(79);  // testing
    // verify dispatch interface
    // {125FECB2-734D-49FD-95C7-FE44B77FDE2C}
    static const IID IID_IEx23bAuto =
        { 0x125FECB2, 0x734D, 0x49FD, { 0x95, 0xC7, 0xFE,
          0x44, 0xB7, 0x7F, 0xDE, 0x2C } };
    LPDISPATCH p;
    HRESULT hr = m_auto.m_lpDispatch->QueryInterface(IID_IEx23bAuto,
                                                     (void**) &p);
    TRACE("OnDlloleLoad -- QueryInterface result = %x\n", hr);
    p->Release();
}
void CEx23dView::OnUpdateDlloleLoad(CCmdUI *pCmdUI)
```

(continued)

```
{
   pCmdUI->Enable(m_auto.m_lpDispatch == NULL);
}
void CEx23dView::OnDlloleUnload()
{
   m_auto.ReleaseDispatch();
}
void CEx23dView::OnUpdateDlloleUnload(CCmdUI *pCmdUI)
{
   pCmdUI->Enable(m_auto.m_lpDispatch != NULL);
}
```

The Controller Class for Ex23c.exe

The following code shows the headers for the *CEx23c* and *CAlarm* classes, which drive the Ex23c Automation component:

ClockDriver.h

```
// Machine generated IDispatch wrapper class(es) created with
// Add Class from Typelib Wizard

// CEx23c wrapper class
class CEx23c : public COleDispatchDriver
{
public:
    CEx23c(){} // Calls COleDispatchDriver default constructor
    CEx23c(LPDISPATCH pDispatch) : COleDispatchDriver(pDispatch) {}
    CEx23c(const CEx23c& dispatchSrc) :
        COleDispatchDriver(dispatchSrc) {}

    // Attributes
public:
    // Operations
public:
    // IEx23c methods
public:
    void ShowWin()
    {
        InvokeHelper(0x2, DISPATCH_METHOD, VT_EMPTY, NULL, NULL);
    }
    LPDISPATCH CreateAlarm(DATE Time)
    {
        LPDISPATCH result;
        static BYTE parms[] = VTS_DATE ;
        InvokeHelper(0x3, DISPATCH_METHOD, VT_DISPATCH,
                    (void*)&result, parms, Time);
        return result;
    }
    void RefreshWin()
```

```
    {
        InvokeHelper(0x4, DISPATCH_METHOD, VT_EMPTY, NULL, NULL);
    }
    VARIANT get_Figure(short n)
    {
        VARIANT result;
        static BYTE parms[] = VTS_I2 ;
        InvokeHelper(0x5, DISPATCH_PROPERTYGET, VT_VARIANT,
                     (void*)&result, parms, n);
        return result;
    }
    void put_Figure(short n, VARIANT newValue)
    {
        static BYTE parms[] = VTS_I2 VTS_VARIANT ;
        InvokeHelper(0x5, DISPATCH_PROPERTYPUT, VT_EMPTY,
                     NULL, parms, n, &newValue);
    }
    // IEx23c properties
public:
    DATE GetTime()
    {
        DATE result;
        GetProperty(0x1, VT_DATE, (void*)&result);
        return result;
    }
    void SetTime(DATE propVal)
    {
        SetProperty(0x1, VT_DATE, propVal);
    }
};
```

CAlarm.h

```
class CAlarm : public COleDispatchDriver
{
public:
    CAlarm(){} // Calls COleDispatchDriver default constructor
    CAlarm(LPDISPATCH pDispatch) : COleDispatchDriver(pDispatch) {}
    CAlarm(const CAlarm& dispatchSrc) :
        COleDispatchDriver(dispatchSrc) {}

    // Attributes
public:
    // Operations
public:
    // IAlarm methods
public:
    // IAlarm properties
```

(continued)

```
public:
    DATE GetTime()
    {
        DATE result;
        GetProperty(0x1, VT_DATE, (void*)&result);
        return result;
    }
    void SetTime(DATE propVal)
    {
        SetProperty(0x1, VT_DATE, propVal);
    }
};
```

Of particular interest is the *CEx23c::CreateAlarm* member function in ClockDriver.h. This function can be called only after the clock object (document) has been constructed. It causes the Ex23c component to construct an alarm object and return an *IDispatch* pointer with a reference count of 1. The *COleDispatchDriver::AttachDispatch* function connects that pointer to the client's *m_alarm* object, but if that object already has a dispatch pointer, the old pointer is released. That's why, if you watch the Debug window, you'll see that the old Ex23c instance exits immediately after you ask for a new instance. You'll have to test this behavior with the Excel driver because Ex23d disables the Load menu command when the clock is running.

The view class has the data members *m_clock* and *m_alarm*. Here are the view class command handlers:

```
void CEx23dView::OnClockoleCreatealarm()
{
    CAlarmDialog dlg;
    if (dlg.DoModal() == IDOK) {
        COleDateTime dt(2002, 12, 23, dlg.m_nHours, dlg.m_nMinutes,
                        dlg.m_nSeconds);
        LPDISPATCH pAlarm = m_clock.CreateAlarm(dt);
        m_alarm.AttachDispatch(pAlarm);  // releases prior object!
        m_clock.RefreshWin();
    }
}
void CEx23dView::OnUpdateClockoleCreatealarm(CCmdUI *pCmdUI)
{
    pCmdUI->Enable(m_clock.m_lpDispatch != NULL);
}
void CEx23dView::OnClockoleLoad()
{
    if(!m_clock.CreateDispatch("Ex23c.Document")) {
        AfxMessageBox("Ex23c.Document component not found");
        return;
    }
```

```
    m_clock.put_Figure(0, COleVariant("XII"));
    m_clock.put_Figure(1, COleVariant("III"));
    m_clock.put_Figure(2, COleVariant("VI"));
    m_clock.put_Figure(3, COleVariant("IX"));
    OnClockoleRefreshtime();
    m_clock.ShowWin();
}
void CEx23dView::OnUpdateClockoleLoad(CCmdUI *pCmdUI)
{
    pCmdUI->Enable(m_clock.m_lpDispatch == NULL);
}
void CEx23dView::OnClockoleRefreshtime()
{
    COleDateTime now = COleDateTime::GetCurrentTime();
    m_clock.SetTime(now);
    m_clock.RefreshWin();
}
void CEx23dView::OnUpdateClockoleRefreshtime(CCmdUI *pCmdUI)
{
    pCmdUI->Enable(m_clock.m_lpDispatch != NULL);
}
void CEx23dView::OnClockoleUnload()
{
    m_clock.ReleaseDispatch();
}
void CEx23dView::OnUpdateClockoleUnload(CCmdUI *pCmdUI)
{
    pCmdUI->Enable(m_clock.m_lpDispatch != NULL);
}
```

Controlling Excel

The Ex23d program contains code that loads Excel, creates a workbook, and reads from and writes to cells from the active worksheet. Controlling Excel is exactly like controlling an MFC Automation component, but you need to know about a few Excel peculiarities.

If you study Excel VBA, you'll notice that you can use more than 100 "objects" in your programs. All of these objects are accessible through Automation, but if you write an MFC Automation client program, you'll need to know about the objects' properties and methods. Ideally, you want a C++ class for each object, with member functions coded to the proper dispatch IDs.

Excel has its own type library that is registered in the Registry. The Add Class From Typelib Wizard can read the type library after looking it up in the Registry. The wizard can create C++ driver classes for individual Excel objects. It makes sense to select the objects you need and then combine the classes into single files, as shown in Figure 23-6.

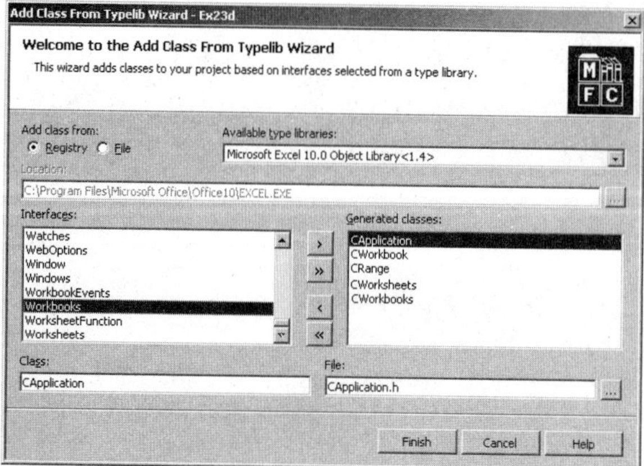

Figure 23-6 The Add Class From Typelib Wizard can create C++?? classes for the Excel objects listed in Excel's type library.

You might need to edit the generated code to suit your needs. Let's look at an example. If you use the Add Class From Typelib Wizard to generate a driver class for the *Worksheet* object, you get a *get_Range* member function, as shown here:

```
LPDISPATCH get_Range(VARIANT Cell1, VARIANT Cell2)
{
    LPDISPATCH result;
    static BYTE parms[] = VTS_VARIANT VTS_VARIANT ;
    InvokeHelper(0xc5, DISPATCH_PROPERTYGET, VT_DISPATCH,
                 (void*)&result, parms, &Cell1, &Cell2);
    return result;
}
```

You know (from the Excel VBA documentation) that you can call the method with either a single cell (one parameter) or a rectangular area specified by two cells (two parameters). Remember that you can omit optional parameters in a call to *InvokeHelper*. Now it makes sense to add a second overloaded *get_Range* function with a single cell parameter, like this:

```
LPDISPATCH get_Range( VARIANT Cell1) // added
{
    LPDISPATCH result;
    static BYTE parms[] = VTS_VARIANT;
    InvokeHelper(0xc5, DISPATCH_PROPERTYGET, VT_DISPATCH,
                 (void*)&result, parms, &Cell1);
    return result;
}
```

How do you know which functions to fix up? They're the functions you decide to use in your program. You'll have to read the Excel VBA reference manual to figure out the required parameters and return values. Perhaps someday soon someone will write a set of C++ Excel controller classes.

The Ex23d program uses the Excel objects and contains the corresponding classes shown in the following table. The code for these objects is contained in the files CApplication.h, CRange.h, CWorksheet.h, CWorksheets.h, and CWorkbooks.h.

Class	View Class Data Member
CApplication	*m_app*
CRange	*m_range[5]*
CWorksheet	*m_worksheet*
CWorkbooks	*m_workbooks*
CWorksheets	*m_worksheets*

The following view member function, *OnExceloleLoad*, handles the Excel Comp Load menu command. This function must work if the user already has Excel running on the desktop. The COM *GetActiveObject* function tries to return an *IUnknown* pointer for Excel. *GetActiveObject* requires a class ID, so we must first call *CLSIDFromProgID*. If *GetActiveObject* is successful, we call *QueryInterface* to get an *IDispatch* pointer and we attach it to the view's *m_app* controller object of class *CApplication*. If *GetActiveObject* is unsuccessful, we call *COleDispatchDriver::CreateDispatch*, as we did for the other components.

```
void CEx23dView::OnExceloleLoad()
{   // if Excel is already running, attach to it, otherwise start it
    LPDISPATCH pDisp;
    LPUNKNOWN pUnk;
    CLSID clsid;
    TRACE("Entering CEx23dView::OnExcelLoad\n");
    BeginWaitCursor();
    // Use Excel.Application.9 for Office 2000
    // Use Excel.Application.10 for Office XP
    ::CLSIDFromProgID(L"Excel.Application.10", &clsid); // from registry
    if(::GetActiveObject(clsid, NULL, &pUnk) == S_OK) {
        VERIFY(pUnk->QueryInterface(IID_IDispatch,
                (void**) &pDisp) == S_OK);
        m_app.AttachDispatch(pDisp);
        pUnk->Release();
        TRACE(" attach complete\n");
    }
    else {
        if(!m_app.CreateDispatch("Excel.Application.10")) {
            AfxMessageBox("Microsoft Excel program not found");
        }
```

(continued)

```
        TRACE(" create complete\n");
    }
    EndWaitCursor();
}
```

OnExceloleExecute is the command handler for the Execute command on the Excel Comp menu. Its first task is to find the Excel main window and bring it to the top. We must write some Windows code here because a method for this purpose couldn't be found. We must also create a workbook if no workbook is currently open.

We have to watch our method return values closely. The *Workbooks Add* method, for example, returns an *IDispatch* pointer for a *Workbook* object and, of course, increments the reference count. If we generated a class for *Workbook*, we could call *COleDispatchDriver::AttachDispatch* so that *Release* would be called when the *Workbook* object was destroyed. We don't need a *Workbook* class, so we'll simply release the pointer at the end of the function. If we don't properly clean up our pointers, we might get memory-leak messages from the Debug version of MFC.

The rest of the *OnExceloleExecute* function accesses the cells in the worksheet. It's easy to get and set numbers, dates, strings, and formulas. The C++ code is similar to the VBA code you would write to do the same job:

```
void CEx23dView::OnExceloleExecute()
{
    LPDISPATCH pRange, pWorkbooks;
    CWnd* pWnd = CWnd::FindWindow("XLMAIN", NULL);
    if (pWnd != NULL) {
        TRACE("Excel window found\n");
        pWnd->ShowWindow(SW_SHOWNORMAL);
        pWnd->UpdateWindow();
        pWnd->BringWindowToTop();
    }
    m_app.put_SheetsInNewWorkbook(1);

    VERIFY(pWorkbooks = m_app.get_Workbooks());
    m_workbooks.AttachDispatch(pWorkbooks);

    LPDISPATCH pWorkbook = NULL;
    if (m_workbooks.get_Count() == 0) {
        // Add returns a Workbook pointer, but we
        //  don't have a Workbook class
        pWorkbook = m_workbooks.Add(COleVariant((short) 0)); // Save the
                                          // pointer for later release
    }
    LPDISPATCH pWorksheets = m_app.get_Worksheets();
    ASSERT(pWorksheets != NULL);
    m_worksheets.AttachDispatch(pWorksheets);
```

```
LPDISPATCH pWorksheet = m_worksheets.get_Item(COleVariant((short) 1));

m_worksheet.AttachDispatch(pWorksheet);
m_worksheet.Select(COleVariant((short) 0));

VERIFY(pRange = m_worksheet.get_Range(COleVariant("A1"),
                                      COleVariant("A1")));
m_range[0].AttachDispatch(pRange);

VERIFY(pRange = m_worksheet.get_Range(COleVariant("A2"),
                                      COleVariant("A2")));
m_range[1].AttachDispatch(pRange);

VERIFY(pRange = m_worksheet.get_Range(COleVariant("A3"),
                                      COleVariant("A3")));
m_range[2].AttachDispatch(pRange);

VERIFY(pRange = m_worksheet.get_Range(COleVariant("A3"),
                                      COleVariant("C5")));
m_range[3].AttachDispatch(pRange);

VERIFY(pRange = m_worksheet.get_Range(COleVariant("A6"),
                                      COleVariant("A6")));
m_range[4].AttachDispatch(pRange);

m_range[4].put_Value(COleVariant(COleDateTime(2002, 4, 24,
                                              15, 47, 8)));
// retrieve the stored date and print it as a string
COleVariant vaTimeDate = m_range[4].get_Value();
TRACE("returned date type = %d\n", vaTimeDate.vt);
COleVariant vaTemp;
vaTemp.ChangeType(VT_BSTR, &vaTimeDate);
CString str(vaTemp.bstrVal);
TRACE("date = %s\n", (const char*) str);

m_range[0].put_Value(COleVariant("test string"));

COleVariant vaResult0 = m_range[0].get_Value();
if (vaResult0.vt == VT_BSTR) {
    CString str(vaResult0.bstrVal);
    TRACE("vaResult0 = %s\n", (const char*) str);
}
m_range[1].put_Value(COleVariant(3.14159));

COleVariant vaResult1 = m_range[1].get_Value();
if (vaResult1.vt == VT_R8) {
    TRACE("vaResult1 = %f\n", vaResult1.dblVal);
}
```

(continued)

```
        m_range[2].put_Formula(COleVariant("=$A2*2.0"));

        COleVariant vaResult2 = m_range[2].get_Value();
        if (vaResult2.vt == VT_R8) {
            TRACE("vaResult2 = %f\n", vaResult2.dblVal);
        }
        COleVariant vaResult2a = m_range[2].get_Formula();
        if (vaResult2a.vt == VT_BSTR) {
            CString str(vaResult2a.bstrVal);
            TRACE("vaResult2a = %s\n", (const char*) str);
        }
        m_range[3].FillRight();
        m_range[3].FillDown();
        // cleanup
        if (pWorkbook != NULL) {
            pWorkbook->Release();
        }
}
```

The Ex23e Example: An Automation Client

This program uses the *#import* directive to generate smart pointers. It behaves just like Ex23d except that it doesn't run Excel. The *#import* statements are in the StdAfx.h file to minimize the number of times the compiler has to generate the driver classes. Here is the added code:

```
#include <afxdisp.h>
#import "..\Ex23a\Debug\Ex23a.tlb" rename_namespace("BankDriv")
using namespace BankDriv;

#import "..\Ex23b\Debug\Ex23b.tlb" rename_namespace("Ex23bDriv")
using namespace Ex23bDriv;

#import "..\Ex23c\Debug\Ex23c.tlb" rename_namespace("ClockDriv")
using namespace ClockDriv;
```

If you have ActiveX controls turned on when you generate the code, the MFC Application Wizard will insert a call to *AfxOleInit* in your application class *InitInstance* member function. (Otherwise, you must add it by hand.)

The view class header contains embedded smart pointers, as shown here:

```
IEx23bAutoPtr m_auto;
IBankPtr m_bank;
IEx23cPtr m_clock;
IAlarmPtr m_alarm;
```

Here's the code for the view class menu command handlers:

```
void CEx23eView::OnBankoleLoad()
{
    if(m_bank.CreateInstance(__uuidof(Bank)) != S_OK) {
        AfxMessageBox("Bank component not found");
        return;
    }
}
void CEx23eView::OnUpdateBankoleLoad(CCmdUI *pCmdUI)
{
    pCmdUI->Enable(m_bank.GetInterfacePtr() == NULL);
}

void CEx23eView::OnBankoleTest()
{
    try {
        m_bank->Deposit(20.0);
        m_bank->Withdrawal(15.0);
        TRACE("new balance = %f\n", m_bank->GetBalance());
    } catch(_com_error& e) {
        AfxMessageBox(e.ErrorMessage());
    }
}
void CEx23eView::OnUpdateBankoleTest(CCmdUI *pCmdUI)
{
    pCmdUI->Enable(m_bank.GetInterfacePtr() != NULL);
}
void CEx23eView::OnBankoleUnload()
{
    m_bank.Release();
}
void CEx23eView::OnUpdateBankoleUnload(CCmdUI *pCmdUI)
{
    pCmdUI->Enable(m_bank.GetInterfacePtr() != NULL);
}
void CEx23eView::OnClockoleCreatealarm()
{
    CAlarmDlg dlg;
    try {
        if (dlg.DoModal() == IDOK) {
            COleDateTime dt(2001, 12, 23, dlg.m_nHours,
                            dlg.m_nMinutes, dlg.m_nSeconds);
            LPDISPATCH pAlarm = m_clock->CreateAlarm(dt);
            m_alarm.Attach((IAlarm*) pAlarm);  // releases prior object!
            m_clock->RefreshWin();
        }
```

(continued)

```
    } catch(_com_error& e) {
        AfxMessageBox(e.ErrorMessage());
    }
}
void CEx23eView::OnUpdateClockoleCreatealarm(CCmdUI *pCmdUI)
{
    pCmdUI->Enable(m_clock.GetInterfacePtr() != NULL);
}
void CEx23eView::OnClockoleLoad()
{
    if(m_clock.CreateInstance(__uuidof(CEx23cDoc)) != S_OK) {
        AfxMessageBox("Clock component not found");
        return;
    }
    try {
        m_clock->PutFigure(0, COleVariant("XII"));
        m_clock->PutFigure(1, COleVariant("III"));
        m_clock->PutFigure(2, COleVariant("VI"));
        m_clock->PutFigure(3, COleVariant("IX"));
        OnClockoleRefreshtime();
        m_clock->ShowWin();
    } catch(_com_error& e) {
        AfxMessageBox(e.ErrorMessage());
    }
}
void CEx23eView::OnUpdateClockoleLoad(CCmdUI *pCmdUI)
{
    pCmdUI->Enable(m_clock.GetInterfacePtr() == NULL);
}
void CEx23eView::OnClockoleRefreshtime()
{
    COleDateTime now = COleDateTime::GetCurrentTime();
    try {
        m_clock->PutTime(now);
        m_clock->RefreshWin();
    } catch(_com_error& e) {
        AfxMessageBox(e.ErrorMessage());
    }
}
void CEx23eView::OnUpdateClockoleRefreshtime(CCmdUI *pCmdUI)
{
    pCmdUI->Enable(m_clock.GetInterfacePtr() != NULL);
}
void CEx23eView::OnClockoleUnload()
{
    m_clock.Release();
}
```

```
void CEx23eView::OnUpdateClockoleUnload(CCmdUI *pCmdUI)
{
    pCmdUI->Enable(m_clock.GetInterfacePtr() != NULL);
}
void CEx23eView::OnDlloleGetdata()
{
    try {
        m_auto->DisplayDialog();
        COleVariant vaData = m_auto->GetTextData();
        ASSERT(vaData.vt == VT_BSTR);
        CString strTextData(vaData.bstrVal);
        long lData = m_auto->GetLongData();
        TRACE("CEx23dView::OnDlloleGetdata--long = %ld, text = %s\n",
              lData, strTextData);
    } catch(_com_error& e) {
        AfxMessageBox(e.ErrorMessage());
    }
}
void CEx23eView::OnUpdateDlloleGetdata(CCmdUI *pCmdUI)
{
    pCmdUI->Enable(m_auto.GetInterfacePtr() != NULL);
}
void CEx23eView::OnDlloleLoad()
{
    if(m_auto.CreateInstance(__uuidof(Ex23bAuto)) != S_OK) {
        AfxMessageBox("Ex23bAuto component not found");
        return;
    }
    IEx23bAuto* pEx23bAuto = 0;
    m_auto.QueryInterface(__uuidof(IEx23bAuto), (void**)&pEx23bAuto);
    if(pEx23bAuto) {
        pEx23bAuto->PutLongData(42);
        pEx23bAuto->Release();
    }
}
void CEx23eView::OnUpdateDlloleLoad(CCmdUI *pCmdUI)
{
    pCmdUI->Enable(m_auto.GetInterfacePtr() == NULL);
}
void CEx23eView::OnDlloleUnload()
{
    m_auto.Release();
}
void CEx23eView::OnUpdateDlloleUnload(CCmdUI *pCmdUI)
{
    pCmdUI->Enable(m_auto.GetInterfacePtr() != NULL);
}
```

Note the use of the *try/catch* blocks in the functions that manipulate the components. These blocks are particularly necessary for processing errors that occur when a component program stops running. In the previous example, Ex23d, the MFC *COleDispatchDriver* class took care of this detail.

VBA Early Binding

When you ran the Ex23a, Ex23b, and Ex23c components from Excel VBA, you used something called *late binding*. Normally, each time VBA accesses a property or a method, it calls *IDispatch::GetIDsOfNames* to look up the DISPID from the symbolic name. Not only is this inefficient, but VBA can't do type checking until it actually accesses a property or a method. Suppose, for example, that a VBA program tries to get a property value that it assumes is a number, but the component provides a string instead. VBA will give you a run-time error when it executes the *Property Get* statement.

With *early binding*, VBA can preprocess the Visual Basic code, converting property and method symbols to DISPIDs before it runs the component program. In so doing, it can check property types, method return types, and method parameters, giving you compile-time error messages. Where can VBA get the advance information it needs? From the component's type library, of course. It can use that same type library to allow the VBA programmer to browse the component's properties and methods. VBA reads the type library before it even loads the component program.

Registering a Type Library

You've already seen that Visual C++ .NET generates a TLB file for each component. In order for VBA to locate that type library, its location must be specified in the Windows Registry. Browsers use the TypeLib Registry entries, and the COM runtime uses the Interface Registry entries for run-time type-checking and, for an EXE component, marshaling the dispinterface.

How a Component Can Register Its Own Type Library

When an EXE component is run as a standalone, it can call the MFC *AfxRegisterTypeLib* function to make the necessary Registry entries, as shown here:

```
VERIFY(AfxOleRegisterTypeLib(AfxGetInstanceHandle(), theTypeLibGUID,
       "Ex23b.tlb"));
```

Here is *theTypeLibGUID*, which is a static variable of type *GUID*:

```
// {A9515ACA-5B85-11D0-848F-00400526305B}
static const GUID theTypeLibGUID =
```

```
{ 0xa9515aca, 0x5b85, 0x11d0, { 0x84, 0x8f, 0x00, 0x40, 0x05, 0x26,
  0x30, 0x5b } };
```

The *AfxRegisterTypeLib* function is declared in the Afxwin.h header and requires *_AFXDLL* to be defined. This means you can't use the function in a regular DLL unless you copy the code from the MFC source files.

The IDL File

Now is a good time to look at the IDL file for the same project:

```
// Ex23b.idl : type library source for Ex23b.dll
// This file will be processed by the MIDL compiler to produce the
// type library (Ex23b.tlb).

#include "olectl.h"
[ uuid(EE56DC40-B710-4543-8841-8D9C27ADA504), version(1.0) ]
library Ex23b
{
    importlib("stdole32.tlb");
    importlib("stdole2.tlb");
    //  Primary dispatch interface for Ex23bAuto

    [ uuid(125FECB2-734D-49FD-95C7-FE44B77FDE2C) ]
    dispinterface IEx23bAuto
    {
        properties:
        [id(1), helpstring("property LongData")] LONG LongData;
        [id(2), helpstring("property TextData")] VARIANT TextData;
        methods:
        [id(3), helpstring("method DisplayDialog")]
            VARIANT_BOOL DisplayDialog(void);
    };
    //  Class information for Ex23bAuto
    [ uuid(BAF3D9ED-4518-43CA-B017-2EBA332CB618) ]
    coclass Ex23bAuto
    {
        [default] dispinterface IEx23bAuto;
    };
};
```

As you can see, numerous connections exist among the Registry, the type library, the component, and the VBA client.

> **Note** The Visual C++ utility called OLEVIEW lets you examine registered components and their type libraries.

How Excel Uses a Type Library

Let's examine the sequence of steps that Excel takes to use your type library:

1. When Excel starts up, it reads the TypeLib section of the Registry to compile a list of all type libraries. It loads the type libraries for VBA and for the Excel object library.

2. After starting Excel, loading a workbook, and switching to the Visual Basic Editor, the user (or workbook author) chooses References from the Tools menu and checks the Ex23b LIB line, as shown below. When the workbook is saved, this reference information is saved with it.

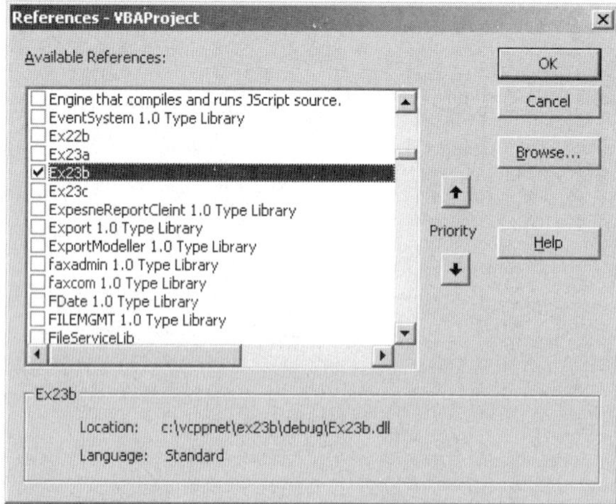

3. Now the Excel user can browse through the Ex23b properties and methods by choosing Object Browser from the Visual Basic Editor's View menu to view the Object Browser dialog box, as shown here:

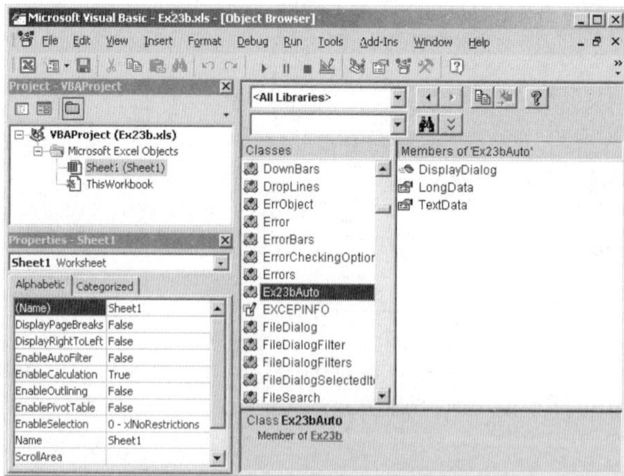

4. To make use of the type library in your VBA program, you simply replace the line

```
Dim DllComp as Object
```

with

```
Dim DllComp as IEx23bAuto
```

The VBA program will exit immediately if it can't find *IEx23bAuto* in its list of references.

5. Right after VBA executes the *CreateObject* statement and loads the component program, it calls *QueryInterface* for *IID_IEx23bAuto*, which is defined in the Registry, the type library, and the component class's interface map. (*IEx23bAuto* is really an *IDispatch* interface.) This is a sort of security check. If the component can't deliver this interface, the VBA program will exit. Theoretically, Excel can use the CLSID in the type library to load the component program, but it uses the CLSID from the Registry instead, just as it did in late binding mode.

Why Use Early Binding?

You might think that early binding will make your Automation component run faster. You probably won't notice any speed increase, though, because the *IDispatch::Invoke* calls are the limiting factor. A typical MFC *Invoke* call from a compiled C++ client to a compiled C++ component requires about 0.5 milliseconds.

The browse capability that the type library provides is probably more valuable than the compiled linkage. If you're writing a C++ controller, for example, you can load the type library through various COM functions, including *LoadTypeLib*, and then you can access it through the *ITypeLib* and *ITypeInfo* interfaces. Plan to spend some time on that project, however, because the type library interfaces are tricky.

Faster Client-Component Connections

Microsoft has recognized the limitations of the *IDispatch* interface. This interface is naturally slow because all data must be funneled through *VARIANT* arguments and possibly converted on both ends. There's a new variation, however, called a *dual interface*. In a dual interface, you define your own custom interface, which is derived from *IDispatch*. The *Invoke* and *GetIDsOfNames* functions are included, but so are other functions. If the client is smart enough, it can bypass the inefficient *Invoke* calls and use the specialized functions instead. Dual interfaces can either support only standard Automation types or support arbitrary types. (A detailed discussion of dual interfaces is beyond the scope of this book. See Kraig Brockschmidt's *Inside OLE*, 2d ed. [Microsoft Press, 1995], for more information.)

There is no direct MFC support for dual interfaces in Visual C++ .NET, but the ACDUAL Visual C++ sample should get you started.

24

Uniform Data Transfer: Clipboard Transfer and OLE Drag and Drop

COM includes a powerful mechanism for transferring data within and among Microsoft Windows–based applications: Uniform Data Transfer (UDT). As you'll see, UDT gives you all sorts of options for the formatting and storage of your transferred data, going well beyond standard Clipboard transfers. The COM *IDataObject* interface is the key element of UDT.

Microsoft Foundation Class (MFC) support is available for UDT, but that support is not so high-level that it obscures what's going on at the COM interface level. One useful application of UDT is OLE drag and drop. Many developers want to use drag-and-drop capabilities in their applications, and drag-and-drop support means that programs have a standard for information interchange. This chapter focuses on the MFC library support for drag-and-drop operations, together with Clipboard transfer.

The *IDataObject* Interface

The *IDataObject* interface is used for Clipboard transfers and drag-and-drop operations, but it's also used in compound documents, ActiveX controls, and custom OLE features. In his book *Inside OLE*, 2d ed. (Microsoft Press, 1995), Kraig Brockschmidt says, "Think of objects as little piles of stuff." The *IDataObject* interface helps you move those piles around, no matter what kind of stuff they contain.

If you were programming at the Win32 level, you'd write C++ code that supported the *IDataObject* interface. Your program would then construct data objects of this class, and you'd manipulate those objects using the *IDataObject* member functions. In this chapter, you'll see how to accomplish the same results using MFC's implementation of *IDataObject*. We'll start by taking a quick look at why the OLE Clipboard is an improvement over the regular Windows Clipboard.

How *IDataObject* Improves on Standard Clipboard Support

MFC has never provided much support for the Windows Clipboard. If you've written programs for the Clipboard, you've used Win32 Clipboard functions such as *OpenClipboard*, *CloseClipboard*, *GetClipboardData*, and *SetClipboardData*. One program copies a single data element of a specified format to the Clipboard, and another program selects the data by format code and pastes it. Standard Clipboard formats include global memory (specified by an *HGLOBAL* variable) and various Graphics Device Interface (GDI) objects such as bitmaps and metafiles (which are specified by their handles). Global memory can contain text as well as custom formats.

The *IDataObject* interface picks up where the Windows Clipboard leaves off. To make a long story short, you transfer a single *IDataObject* pointer to or from the Clipboard instead of transferring a series of discrete formats. The underlying data object can contain a whole array of formats. Those formats can carry information about target devices, such as printer characteristics, and they can specify the data's aspect, or view. The standard aspect is content. Other aspects include an icon for the data and a thumbnail picture.

Note that the *IDataObject* interface specifies the storage medium of a data object format. Conventional Clipboard transfer relies exclusively on global memory. The *IDataObject* interface permits the transmission of a disk filename or a structured storage pointer instead. Thus, if you want to transfer a very large block of data that's already in a disk file, you don't have to waste time copying it to and from a memory block.

In case you were wondering, *IDataObject* pointers are compatible with programs that use existing Clipboard transfer methods. The format codes are the same. Windows takes care of the conversion to and from the data object. Of course, if an OLE-aware program puts an *IStorage* pointer in a data object and puts the object on the Clipboard, older, non-OLE-aware programs will not be able to read that format.

The *FORMATETC* and *STGMEDIUM* Structures

Before you're ready for the *IDataObject* member functions, you need to examine two important COM structures that are used as parameter types: the *FORMATETC* structure and the *STGMEDIUM* structure.

FORMATETC

The *FORMATETC* structure is often used instead of a Clipboard format to represent data format information. However, unlike the Clipboard format, the *FORMATETC* structure includes information about a target device, the aspect or view of the data, and a storage medium indicator. Here are the members of the *FORMATETC* structure:

Type	Name	Description
CLIPFORMAT	*cfFormat*	A structure that contains Clipboard formats, such as standard interchange formats (for example, *CF_TEXT*, which is a text format, and *CF_DIB*, which is an image compression format), custom formats (such as rich text format), and OLE formats that are used to create linked or embedded objects.
*DVTARGETDEVICE**	*ptd*	A structure that contains information about the target device for the data, including the device driver name. (It can be *NULL*.)
DWORD	*dwAspect*	A *DVASPECT* enumeration constant (such as *DVASPECT_CONTENT*, or *DVASPECT _THUMBNAIL*)
LONG	*lindex*	Usually –1.
DWORD	*tymed*	Specifies the type of media used to transfer the object's data (such as *TYMED_HGLOBAL*, *TYMED_FILE*, or *TYMED_ISTORAGE*).

An individual data object accommodates a collection of *FORMATETC* elements, and the *IDataObject* interface provides a way to enumerate them. A useful macro for filling in a *FORMATETC* structure is shown here:

```
#define SETFORMATETC(fe, cf, asp, td, med, li)   \
    ((fe).cfFormat=cf, \
    (fe).dwAspect=asp, \
    (fe).ptd=td, \
    (fe).tymed=med, \
    (fe).lindex=li)
```

STGMEDIUM

The other important structure for *IDataObject* members is the *STGMEDIUM* structure. This structure is a global memory handle used for operations involving data transfer. Here are the members:

Type	Name	Description
DWORD	*tymed*	A storage medium value used in marshaling and unmarshaling routines
HBITMAP	*hBitmap*	Bitmap handle*
HMETAFILEPICT	*hMetaFilePict*	Metafile handle*
HENHMETAFILE	*hEnhMetaFile*	Enhanced metafile handle*
HGLOBAL	*hGlobal*	Global memory handle*
LPOLESTR	*lpszFileName*	Disk filename (double-byte)*
*ISTREAM**	*pstm*	*IStream* interface pointer*
*ISTORAGE**	*pstg*	*IStorage* interface pointer*
IUNKNOWN	*pUnkForRelease*	Used by clients to call *Release* for formats with interface pointers*

* This member is part of a union, including handles, strings, and interface pointers used by the receiving process to access the transferred data.

As you can see, the *STGMEDIUM* structure specifies where data is stored. The *tymed* variable determines which union member is valid.

IDataObject Interface Member Functions

The *IDataObject* interface has nine member functions. Both Brockschmidt and the *MFC Library Reference* do a good job describing all of them. We'll look in detail at the functions that are important for this chapter.

```
HRESULT EnumFormatEtc(DWORD dwDirection,
IEnumFORMATETC ppEnum);
```

If you have an *IDataObject* pointer for a data object, you can use *EnumFormatEtc* to enumerate all the formats that it supports. This is an ugly API that the MFC library insulates you from. You'll learn how this happens when you examine the *COleDataObject* class.

```
HRESULT GetData(FORMATETC* pFEIn, STGMEDIUM* pSTM);
```

GetData is the most important function in the interface. Somewhere, up in the sky, is a data object, and you have an *IDataObject* pointer to it. You specify, in a *FORMATETC* variable, the exact format you want to use when you retrieve the data, and you prepare an empty *STGMEDIUM* variable to accept the results. If the data object has the format you want, *GetData* will fill in the *STGMEDIUM* structure. Otherwise, you'll get an error return value.

```
HRESULT QueryGetData(FORMATETC* pFE);
```

You call *QueryGetData* if you're not sure whether the data object can deliver data in the format specified in the *FORMATETC* structure. The return value says, "Yes, I can" (*S_OK*) or "No, I can't" (an error code). Calling this function is definitely more efficient than allocating a *STGMEDIUM* variable and calling *GetData*.

```
HRESULT SetData(FORMATETC* pFEIn,
STGMEDIUM* pSTM, BOOL fRelease);
```

Data objects rarely support *SetData*. Data objects are normally loaded with formats in their own server module; clients retrieve data by calling *GetData*. With *SetData*, you'd be transferring data in the other direction—like pumping water from your house back to the water company.

Other *IDataObject* Member Functions: Advisory Connections

The interface contains other important functions that let you implement an advisory connection. When the program using a data object needs to be notified whether the object's data changes, the program can pass an *IAdviseSink* pointer to the object by calling the *IDataObject::DAdvise* function. The object will then call various *IAdviseSink* member functions, which the client program will implement. You don't need advisory connections for drag-and-drop operations.

MFC UDT Support

The MFC library does a lot to make data object programming easier. As you study the MFC data object classes, you'll start to see a pattern in MFC COM support. At the component end, the MFC library provides a base class that implements one or more OLE interfaces. The interface member functions call virtual functions that you override in your derived class. At the client end, the MFC library provides a class that wraps an interface pointer. You call simple member functions that use the interface pointer to make COM calls.

The terminology needs some clarification here. The *data object* I've described is the actual C++ object that you construct, and that's the way Brockschmidt uses the term. In the MFC documentation, a data object is what the client program sees through an *IDataObject* pointer. A *data source* is the object you construct in a component program.

The *COleDataSource* Class

When you want to use a data source, you construct an object of class *COleDataSource*, which implements the *IDataObject* interface (without advisory connection support). This class builds and manages a collection of data formats stored in a cache in memory. A data source is a regular COM object that keeps a reference count. Usually, you construct and fill a data source, and then you pass it to the Clipboard or drag and drop it in another location, never to worry about it again. If you decide to not pass off a data source, you can invoke the destructor, which cleans up all its formats.

Following are some of the more useful member functions of the *COleDataSource* class.

```
void CacheData(CLIPFORMAT cfFormat,
    STGMEDIUM* lpStgMedium,
    FORMATETC* lpFormatEtc = NULL);
```

This function inserts an element in the data object's cache for data transfer. The *lpStgMedium* parameter points to the data, and the *lpFormatEtc* parameter describes the data. If, for example, the *STGMEDIUM* structure specifies a disk filename, that filename gets stored inside the data object. If *lpFormatEtc* is set to NULL, the function fills in a *FORMATETC* structure with default values. It's safer, though, to create your *FORMATETC* variable with the *tymed* member set.

```
void CacheGlobalData(CLIPFORMAT cfFormat,
    HGLOBAL hGlobal, FORMATETC* lpFormatEtc = NULL);
```

You call this specialized version of *CacheData* to pass data in global memory (identified by an *HGLOBAL* variable). The data source object is considered the owner of that global memory block, so you should not free it after you cache it. You can usually omit the *lpFormatEtc* parameter. The *CacheGlobalData* function does not make a copy of the data.

```
DROPEFFECT DoDragDrop(DWORD dwEffects =
    DROPEFFECT_COPY|DROPEFFECT_MOVE|
    DROPEFFECT_LINK, LPCRECT lpRectStartDrag = NULL,
    COleDropSource* pDropSource = NULL);
```

You call this function for drag-and-drop operations on a data source. You'll see it used in the Ex24b example.

```
void SetClipboard(void);
```

The *SetClipboard* function, which you'll see in the Ex24a example, calls the *OleSetClipboard* function to put a data source on the Windows Clipboard. The Clipboard is responsible for deleting the data source and thus for freeing the global memory associated with the formats in the cache. When you construct a *COleDataSource* object and call *SetClipboard*, COM calls *AddRef* on the object.

The *COleDataObject* Class

This class is on the destination side of a data object transfer. Its base class is *CCmdTarget*, and it has a public member *m_lpDataObject* that holds an *IDataObject* pointer. That member must be set before you can effectively use the object. The class destructor calls *Release* only on the *IDataObject* pointer.

Following are a few of the more useful *COleDataObject* member functions.

```
BOOL AttachClipboard(void);
```

As Brockschmidt points out, OLE Clipboard processing is internally complex. From the developer's point of view, however, it's straightforward—as long as you use the *COleDataObject* member functions. You first construct an "empty" *COleDataObject* object, and then you call *AttachClipboard*, which calls the global *OleGetClipboard* function. Now the *m_lpDataObject* data member will point back to the source data object (or so it will appear), and you can access its formats.

If you call the *GetData* member function to get a format, you must remember that the Clipboard owns the format and you cannot alter its contents. If the format consists of an *HGLOBAL* pointer, you must not free that memory and you cannot hang onto the pointer. If you need to have long-term access to the data in global memory, consider calling *GetGlobalData* instead.

If a non-COM-aware program copies data to the Clipboard, the *AttachClipboard* function will still work because COM invents a data object that contains formats corresponding to the regular Windows data on the Clipboard.

```
void BeginEnumFormats(void);
BOOL GetNextFormat(FORMATETC* lpFormatEtc);
```

These two functions allow you to iterate through the formats that the data object contains. You call *BeginEnumFormats* first, and then you call *GetNextFormat* in a loop until it returns *FALSE*.

```
BOOL GetData(CLIPFORMAT cfFormat,
    STGMEDIUM* lpStgMedium
    FORMATETC* lpFormatEtc = NULL);
```

This function calls *IDataObject::GetData* and not much more. The function returns *TRUE* if the data source contains the format you asked for. You generally need to supply the *lpFormatEtc* parameter.

```
HGLOBAL GetGlobalData(CLIPFORMAT cfFormat,
    FORMATETC* lpFormatEtc = NULL);
```

Use the *GetGlobalData* function if you know that your requested format is compatible with global memory. This function makes a copy of the selected format's memory block, and it gives you an *HGLOBAL* handle that you must free later. You can often omit the *lpFormatEtc* parameter.

```
BOOL IsDataAvailable(CLIPFORMAT cfFormat,
    FORMATETC* lpFormatEtc = NULL);
```

The *IsDataAvailable* function tests whether the data object contains a given format.

MFC Data Object Clipboard Transfer

Now that you've seen the *COleDataObject* and *COleDataSource* classes, you'll have an easy time doing Clipboard data object transfers. But why not just do Clipboard transfers the old way using *GetClipboardData* and *SetClipboardData*? You can for most common formats, but if you write functions that process data objects, you can use those same functions for drag and drop.

Figure 24-1 shows the relationship between the Clipboard and the *COleDataSource* and *COleDataObject* classes. You construct a *COleDataSource* object on the copy side, and then you fill its cache with formats. When you call *SetClipboard*, the formats are copied to the Clipboard. On the paste side, you call *AttachClipboard* to attach an *IDataObject* pointer to a *COleDataObject* object, after which you can retrieve individual formats.

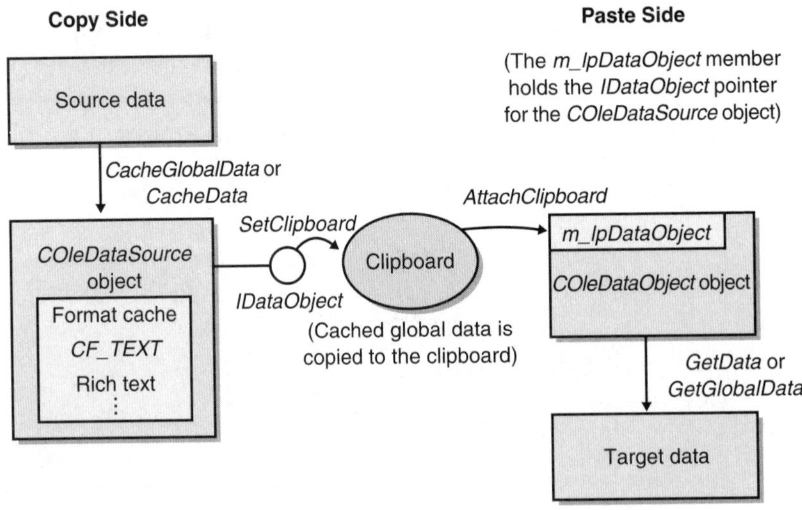

Figure 24-1 MFC OLE Clipboard processing.

Suppose you have a document-view application whose document has a *CString* data member called *m_strText*. You want to use view class command handler functions that copy to and paste from the Clipboard. Before you write those functions, you write two helper functions. The first, *SaveText*, creates a data source object from the contents of *m_strText*. The function constructs a *COleDataSource* object, and then it copies the string contents to global memory. Finally, it calls *CacheGlobalData* to store the *HGLOBAL* handle in the data source object. Here is the *SaveText* code:

```
COleDataSource* CMyView::SaveText()
{
    CEx24fDoc* pDoc = GetDocument();
    if (!pDoc->m_strtext.IsEmpty()) {
        COleDataSource* pSource = new COleDataSource();
        int nTextSize = GetDocument()->m_strText.GetLength() + 1;
        HGLOBAL hText = ::GlobalAlloc(GMEM_SHARE, nTextSize);
        LPSTR pText = (LPSTR) ::GlobalLock(hText);
        ASSERT(pText);
        strncpy(pText, GetDocument()->m_strText,
                    nTextSize - 1);
        ::GlobalUnlock(hText);
        pSource->CacheGlobalData(CF_TEXT, hText);
        return pSource;
    }
    return NULL;
}
```

The second helper function, *DoPasteText*, fills in *m_strText* from a data object specified as a parameter. We're using *COleDataObject::GetData* here instead of *GetGlobalData* because *GetGlobalData* makes a copy of the global memory block. That extra copy operation is unnecessary because we're copying the text to the *CString* object. We won't free the original memory block because the data object owns it. Here's the *DoPasteText* code:

```
// Memory is MOVEABLE, so we must use GlobalLock!
    SETFORMATETC(fmt, CF_TEXT, DVASPECT_CONTENT, NULL,
        TYMED_HGLOBAL, -1);
    VERIFY(pDataObject->GetData(CF_TEXT, &stg, &fmt));
    HGLOBAL hText = stg.hGlobal;
    GetDocument()->m_strText = (LPSTR) ::GlobalLock(hText);
    ::GlobalUnlock(hText);
    return TRUE;
}
```

Here are the two command handler functions:

```
void CMyView::OnEditCopy()
{
    COleDataSource* pSource = SaveText();
    if (pSource) {
        pSource->SetClipboard();
    }
}
void CMyView::OnEditPaste()
{
    COleDataObject dataObject;
    VERIFY(dataObject.AttachClipboard());
    DoPasteText(&dataObject);
    // dataObject released
}
```

The MFC *CRectTracker* Class

The *CRectTracker* class is useful in both OLE and non-OLE programs. It allows the user to move and resize a rectangular object in a view window. The class has two important data members: the *m_nStyle* member, which determines the border, resize handle, and other characteristics, and the *m_rect* member, which holds the device coordinates for the rectangle.

The important member functions follow.

```
void Draw(CDC* pDC) const;
```

The *Draw* function draws the tracker, including border and resize handles, but it does not draw anything inside the rectangle. That's your job.

```
BOOL Track(CWnd* pWnd, CPoint point,
    BOOL bAllowInvert = FALSE, CWnd* pWndClipTo = NULL);
```

You call this function in a *WM_LBUTTONDOWN* handler. If the cursor is on the rectangle border, the user can resize the tracker by holding down the mouse button. If the cursor is inside the rectangle, the user can move the tracker. If the cursor is outside the rectangle, *Track* will return *FALSE* immediately; otherwise, *Track* will return *TRUE* only when the user releases the mouse button. That means *Track* works a little like *CDialog::DoModal*. It contains its own message dispatch logic.

```
int HitTest(CPoint point) const;
```

Call *HitTest* if you need to distinguish between mouse button hits inside and on the tracker rectangle. The function returns immediately with the hit status in the return value.

```
BOOL SetCursor(CWnd* pWnd, UINT nHitTest) const;
```

Call this function in your view's *WM_SETCURSOR* handler to ensure that the cursor changes during tracking. If *SetCursor* returns *FALSE*, call the base class *OnSetCursor* function; if *SetCursor* returns *TRUE*, you return *TRUE*.

CRectTracker Rectangle Coordinate Conversion

You must deal with the fact that the *CRectTracker::m_rect* member stores device coordinates. If you're using a scrolling view or have otherwise changed the mapping mode or viewport origin, you must do coordinate conversion. Here's a strategy:

1. Define a *CRectTracker* data member in your view class. Use the name *m_tracker*.
2. Define a separate data member in your view class to hold the rectangle in logical coordinates. Use the name *m_rectTracker*.
3. In your view's *OnDraw* function, set *m_rect* to the updated device coordinates, and then draw the tracker. This adjusts for any scrolling since the last *OnDraw*. Some sample code is shown here:

```
m_tracker.m_rect = m_rectTracker;
pDC->LPtoDP(m_tracker.m_rect); // tracker requires device
                               //  coordinates
m_tracker.Draw(pDC);
```

4. In your mouse button down message handler, call *Track*, set *m_rectTracker* to the updated logical coordinates, and call *Invalidate*, as shown here:

```
if (m_tracker.Track(this, point, FALSE, NULL)) {
    CClientDC dc(this);
    OnPrepareDC(&dc);
    m_rectTracker = m_tracker.m_rect;
    dc.DPtoLP(m_rectTracker);
    Invalidate();
}
```

The Ex24a Example: A Data Object Clipboard

This example uses the *CDib* class from Ex06d. Here, you can move and resize the device-independent bitmap (DIB) image with a tracker rectangle, and you can copy and paste the DIB to and from the Clipboard using a COM data object. The example also includes functions for reading DIBs from and writing DIBs to BMP files.

If you create such an example from scratch, use the MFC Application Wizard without any ActiveX or Automation options and then add the following line in your StdAfx.h file:

```
#include <afxole.h>
```

Add the following call at the start of the application's *InitInstance* function:

```
AfxOleInit();
```

To prepare Ex24a, open the \vcppnet\Ex24a\Ex24a.sln solution and then build the project. Run the application, and paste a bitmap into the rectangle by choosing Paste From from the Edit menu. You'll see an MDI application similar to the one shown in Figure 24-2.

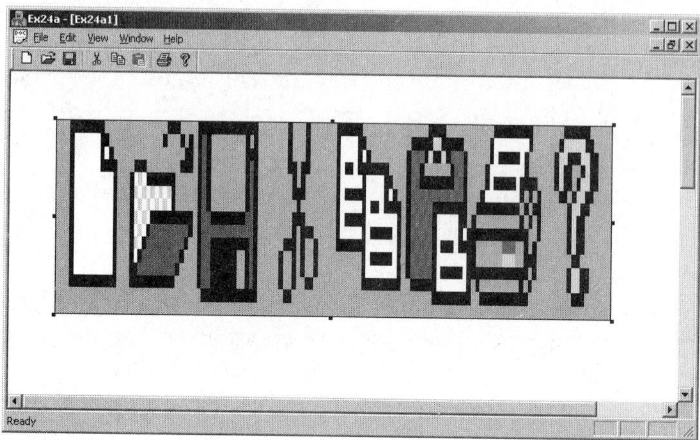

Figure 24-2 The Ex24a program in operation.

The *CMainFrame* Class

This class contains the handlers *OnQueryNewPalette* and *OnPaletteChanged* for the *WM_QUERYNEWPALETTE* and *WM_PALETTECHANGED* messages, respectively. These handlers send a user-defined *WM_VIEWPALETTECHANGED* message to all the views, and then the handler calls *CDib::UsePalette* to realize the palette. The value of *wParam* tells the view whether it should realize the palette in background mode or in foreground mode.

The *CEx24aDoc* Class

This class is pretty straightforward. It contains an embedded *CDib* object, *m_dib*, plus a Clear All command handler. The overridden *DeleteContents* member function calls the *CDib::Empty* function.

The *CEx24aView* Class

This class contains the Clipboard function command handlers, the tracking code, the DIB drawing code, and the palette message handler. The header and implementation files are shown below with manually entered code in boldface:

Ex24aView.h

```
// Ex24aView.h : interface of the CEx24aView class
//
#pragma once
#define WM_VIEWPALETTECHANGED  WM_USER + 5

class CEx24aView : public CScrollView
{
    // for tracking
    CRectTracker m_tracker;
    CRect m_rectTracker; // logical coordinates
    CSize m_sizeTotal;   // document size
protected: // create from serialization only
    CEx24aView();
    DECLARE_DYNCREATE(CEx24aView)
// Attributes
public:
    CEx24aDoc* GetDocument() const;
// Operations
public:
// Overrides
    public:
    virtual void OnDraw(CDC* pDC);  // overridden to draw this view
    virtual BOOL PreCreateWindow(CREATESTRUCT& cs);
protected:
    virtual BOOL OnPreparePrinting(CPrintInfo* pInfo);
    virtual void OnBeginPrinting(CDC* pDC, CPrintInfo* pInfo);
    virtual void OnEndPrinting(CDC* pDC, CPrintInfo* pInfo);
// Implementation
public:
```

(continued)

```
    virtual ~CEx24aView();
#ifdef _DEBUG
    virtual void AssertValid() const;
    virtual void Dump(CDumpContext& dc) const;
#endif
protected:
// Generated message map functions
protected:
    DECLARE_MESSAGE_MAP()
public:
    afx_msg void OnEditCopy();
    afx_msg void OnUpdateEditCopy(CCmdUI *pCmdUI);
    afx_msg void OnEditCut();
    afx_msg void OnEditPaste();
    afx_msg void OnUpdateEditPaste(CCmdUI *pCmdUI);
    afx_msg void OnEditCopyto();
    afx_msg void OnEditPastefrom();
    afx_msg void OnLButtonDown(UINT nFlags, CPoint point);
    afx_msg BOOL OnSetCursor(CWnd* pWnd, UINT nHitTest, UINT message);
    afx_msg void OnSetFocus(CWnd* pOldWnd);
    virtual void OnPrepareDC(CDC* pDC, CPrintInfo* pInfo = NULL);
    virtual void OnInitialUpdate();
    afx_msg LONG OnViewPaletteChanged(UINT wParam, LONG lParam);
    BOOL DoPasteDib(COleDataObject* pDataObject);
    COleDataSource* CEx24aView::SaveDib();
};
#ifndef _DEBUG  // debug version in Ex24aView.cpp
inline CEx24aDoc* CEx24aView::GetDocument() const
    { return reinterpret_cast<CEx24aDoc*>(m_pDocument); }
#endif
```

Ex24aView.cpp

```
// Ex24aView.cpp : implementation of the CEx24aView class
//
#include "stdafx.h"
#include "Ex24a.h"
#include "Ex24aDoc.h"
#include "Ex24aView.h"
#ifdef _DEBUG
#define new DEBUG_NEW
#endif
// CEx24aView
IMPLEMENT_DYNCREATE(CEx24aView, CScrollView)
BEGIN_MESSAGE_MAP(CEx24aView, CScrollView)
    // Standard printing commands
    ON_COMMAND(ID_FILE_PRINT, CScrollView::OnFilePrint)
    ON_COMMAND(ID_FILE_PRINT_DIRECT, CScrollView::OnFilePrint)
    ON_COMMAND(ID_FILE_PRINT_PREVIEW, CScrollView::OnFilePrintPreview)
```

```
    ON_COMMAND(ID_EDIT_COPY, OnEditCopy)
    ON_UPDATE_COMMAND_UI(ID_EDIT_COPY, OnUpdateEditCopy)
    ON_COMMAND(ID_EDIT_CUT, OnEditCut)
    ON_COMMAND(ID_EDIT_PASTE, OnEditPaste)
    ON_UPDATE_COMMAND_UI(ID_EDIT_PASTE, OnUpdateEditPaste)
    ON_COMMAND(ID_EDIT_COPYTO, OnEditCopyto)
    ON_COMMAND(ID_EDIT_PASTEFROM, OnEditPastefrom)
    ON_WM_LBUTTONDOWN()
    ON_WM_SETCURSOR()
    ON_WM_SETFOCUS()
    ON_WM_PALETTECHANGED()
END_MESSAGE_MAP()
// CEx24aView construction/destruction
CEx24aView::CEx24aView() : m_sizeTotal(800, 1050), // 8-by-10.5 inches
                                    //  when printed
m_rectTracker(50, 50, 250, 250)
{
}
CEx24aView::~CEx24aView()
{
}
BOOL CEx24aView::PreCreateWindow(CREATESTRUCT& cs)
{
    // TODO: Modify the Window class or styles here by modifying
    //  the CREATESTRUCT cs
    return CScrollView::PreCreateWindow(cs);
}
// CEx24aView drawing
void CEx24aView::OnDraw(CDC* pDC)
{
    CDib& dib = GetDocument()->m_dib;
    m_tracker.m_rect = m_rectTracker;
    pDC->LPtoDP(m_tracker.m_rect); // tracker wants device coordinates
    m_tracker.Draw(pDC);
    dib.Draw(pDC, m_rectTracker.TopLeft(), m_rectTracker.Size());
}
// CEx24aView printing
BOOL CEx24aView::OnPreparePrinting(CPrintInfo* pInfo)
{
    pInfo->SetMaxPage(1);
    return DoPreparePrinting(pInfo);
}
void CEx24aView::OnBeginPrinting(CDC* /*pDC*/, CPrintInfo* /*pInfo*/)
{
    // TODO: add extra initialization before printing
}
void CEx24aView::OnEndPrinting(CDC* /*pDC*/, CPrintInfo* /*pInfo*/)
{
```

(continued)

```
    // TODO: add cleanup after printing
}
// CEx24aView diagnostics
#ifdef _DEBUG
void CEx24aView::AssertValid() const
{
    CScrollView::AssertValid();
}
void CEx24aView::Dump(CDumpContext& dc) const
{
    CScrollView::Dump(dc);
}
CEx24aDoc* CEx24aView::GetDocument() const // non-debug version is inline
{
    ASSERT(m_pDocument->IsKindOf(RUNTIME_CLASS(CEx24aDoc)));
    return (CEx24aDoc*)m_pDocument;
}
#endif //_DEBUG

// helper functions used for clipboard and drag-drop
BOOL CEx24aView::DoPasteDib(COleDataObject* pDataObject)
{
    // update command user interface should keep us out of
    //  here if not CF_DIB
    if (!pDataObject->IsDataAvailable(CF_DIB)) {
        TRACE("CF_DIB format is unavailable\n");
        return FALSE;
    }
    CEx24aDoc* pDoc = GetDocument();
    // Seems to be MOVEABLE memory, so we must use GlobalLock!
    //  (hDib != lpDib) GetGlobalData copies the memory, so we can
    //  hang onto it until we delete the CDib.
    HGLOBAL hDib = pDataObject->GetGlobalData(CF_DIB);
    ASSERT(hDib != NULL);
    LPVOID lpDib = ::GlobalLock(hDib);
    ASSERT(lpDib != NULL);
     pDoc->m_dib.AttachMemory(lpDib, TRUE, hDib);
    pDoc->SetModifiedFlag();
    pDoc->UpdateAllViews(NULL);
    return TRUE;
}
COleDataSource* CEx24aView::SaveDib()
{
    CDib& dib = GetDocument()->m_dib;
    if (dib.GetSizeImage() > 0) {
        COleDataSource* pSource = new COleDataSource();
        int nHeaderSize = dib.GetSizeHeader();
        int nImageSize = dib.GetSizeImage();
        HGLOBAL hHeader = ::GlobalAlloc(GMEM_SHARE,
```

```
            nHeaderSize + nImageSize);
        LPVOID pHeader = ::GlobalLock(hHeader);
        ASSERT(pHeader != NULL);
        LPVOID pImage = (LPBYTE) pHeader + nHeaderSize;
        memcpy(pHeader, dib.m_lpBMIH, nHeaderSize);
        memcpy(pImage, dib.m_lpImage, nImageSize);
        // Receiver is supposed to free the global memory
        ::GlobalUnlock(hHeader);
        pSource->CacheGlobalData(CF_DIB, hHeader);
        return pSource;
    }
    return NULL;
}
// CEx24aView message handlers
void CEx24aView::OnEditCopy()
{
    COleDataSource* pSource = SaveDib();
    if (pSource) {
        pSource->SetClipboard(); // OLE deletes data source
    }
}
void CEx24aView::OnUpdateEditCopy(CCmdUI *pCmdUI)
{
    // serves Copy, Cut, and Copy To
    CDib& dib = GetDocument()->m_dib;
    pCmdUI->Enable(dib.GetSizeImage() > 0L);
}
void CEx24aView::OnEditCut()
{
    OnEditCopy();
    GetDocument()->OnEditClearall();
}
void CEx24aView::OnEditPaste()
{
    CEx24aDoc* pDoc = GetDocument();
    COleDataObject dataObject;
    VERIFY(dataObject.AttachClipboard());
    DoPasteDib(&dataObject);
    CClientDC dc(this);
    pDoc->m_dib.UsePalette(&dc);
    pDoc->SetModifiedFlag();
    pDoc->UpdateAllViews(NULL);
}
void CEx24aView::OnUpdateEditPaste(CCmdUI *pCmdUI)
{
    COleDataObject dataObject;
    BOOL bAvail = dataObject.AttachClipboard() &&
        dataObject.IsDataAvailable(CF_DIB);
```

(continued)

```
    pCmdUI->Enable(bAvail);
}
void CEx24aView::OnEditCopyto()
{
    CDib& dib = GetDocument()->m_dib;
    CFileDialog dlg(FALSE, "bmp", "*.bmp");
    if (dlg.DoModal() != IDOK) return;

    BeginWaitCursor();
    dib.CopyToMapFile(dlg.GetPathName());
    EndWaitCursor();
}
void CEx24aView::OnEditPastefrom()
{
    CEx24aDoc* pDoc = GetDocument();
    CFileDialog dlg(TRUE, "bmp", "*.bmp");
    if (dlg.DoModal() != IDOK) return;
    if (pDoc->m_dib.AttachMapFile(dlg.GetPathName(), TRUE)) { // share
        CClientDC dc(this);
        pDoc->m_dib.SetSystemPalette(&dc);
        pDoc->m_dib.UsePalette(&dc);
        pDoc->SetModifiedFlag();
         pDoc->UpdateAllViews(NULL);
    }
}
void CEx24aView::OnLButtonDown(UINT nFlags, CPoint point)
{
    if (m_tracker.Track(this, point, FALSE, NULL)) {
        CClientDC dc(this);
        OnPrepareDC(&dc);
        m_rectTracker = m_tracker.m_rect;
        dc.DPtoLP(m_rectTracker); // Update logical coordinates
        Invalidate();
    }
}
BOOL CEx24aView::OnSetCursor(CWnd* pWnd, UINT nHitTest, UINT message)
{
    if (m_tracker.SetCursor(pWnd, nHitTest)) {
        return TRUE;
    }
    else {
        return CScrollView::OnSetCursor(pWnd, nHitTest, message);
    }
}
void CEx24aView::OnSetFocus(CWnd* pOldWnd)
{
```

```
    CScrollView::OnSetFocus(pOldWnd);
    AfxGetApp()->m_pMainWnd->SendMessage(WM_PALETTECHANGED,
        (UINT) GetSafeHwnd());
}
void CEx24aView::OnPrepareDC(CDC* pDC, CPrintInfo* pInfo)
{
    // custom MM_LOENGLISH; positive y is down
    if (pDC->IsPrinting()) {
        int nHsize = pDC->GetDeviceCaps(HORZSIZE) * 1000 / 254;
        int nVsize = pDC->GetDeviceCaps(VERTSIZE) * 1000 / 254;
        pDC->SetMapMode(MM_ANISOTROPIC);
        pDC->SetWindowExt(nHsize, nVsize);
        pDC->SetViewportExt(pDC->GetDeviceCaps(HORZRES),
                            pDC->GetDeviceCaps(VERTRES));
    }
    else {
        CScrollView::OnPrepareDC(pDC, pInfo);
    }
}
void CEx24aView::OnInitialUpdate()
{
    SetScrollSizes(MM_TEXT, m_sizeTotal);
    m_tracker.m_nStyle = CRectTracker::solidLine |
        CRectTracker::resizeOutside;
    CScrollView::OnInitialUpdate();
}
LONG CEx24aView::OnViewPaletteChanged(UINT wParam, LONG lParam)
{
    TRACE("CEx24aView::OnViewPaletteChanged, HWND = %x, code = %d\n",
          GetSafeHwnd(), wParam);
    CClientDC dc(this);
    GetDocument()->m_dib.UsePalette(&dc, wParam);
    Invalidate();
    return 0;
}
```

Several interesting things happen in the view class. In the *DoPasteDib* helper, we can call *GetGlobalData* because we can attach the returned *HGLOBAL* variable to the document's *CDib* object. If we were to call *GetData*, we'd have to copy the memory block ourselves. The Paste From and Copy To command handlers rely on the memory-mapped file support in the *CDib* class. The *OnPrepareDC* function creates a special printer-mapping mode that is just like *MM_LOENGLISH* except that positive *y* is down. One pixel on the display corresponds to 0.01 inch on the printer.

MFC Drag and Drop

Drag and drop was the ultimate justification for the data object code you've been looking at. OLE supports this feature with its *IDropSource* and *IDropTarget* interfaces plus some library code that manages the drag-and-drop process. The MFC library offers good drag-and-drop support at the view level, so we'll use it. Be aware that drag-and-drop transfers are immediate and independent of the Clipboard. If the user cancels the operation, there's no "memory" of the object being dragged.

Drag-and-drop transfers should work consistently between applications, between windows of the same application, and within a window. When the user starts the operation, the cursor should change to an arrow-rectangle combination. If the user holds down the Ctrl key, the cursor turns into a plus sign (+), which indicates that the object is being copied rather than moved.

MFC also supports drag-and-drop operations for items in compound documents. This is the next level up in MFC OLE support, and it's not covered in this chapter. Look up the OCLIENT example in the MSDN Library under Visual C++ Samples.

The Source Side of the Transfer

When your source program starts a drag-and-drop operation for a data object, it calls *COleDataSource::DoDragDrop*. This function internally creates an object of MFC class *COleDropSource*, which implements the *IOleDropSource* interface. *DoDragDrop* is one of those functions that don't return for a while. It returns when the user drops the object or cancels the operation or when a specified number of milliseconds have elapsed.

If you're programming drag-and-drop operations to work with a *CRectTracker* object, you should call *DoDragDrop* only when the user clicks inside the tracking rectangle, not on its border. *CRectTracker::HitTest* gives you that information. When you call *DoDragDrop*, you must set a flag that tells you whether the user is dropping the object into the same view (or document) that it was dragged from.

The Destination Side of the Transfer

If you want to use the MFC library's view class drag-and-drop support, you must add a data member of class *COleDropTarget* to your derived view class. This class implements the *IDropTarget* interface, and it holds an *IDropSource* pointer that links back to the *COleDropSource* object. In your view's *OnInitialUpdate* function, you call the *Register* member function for the embedded *COleDropTarget* object.

After you've made your view a drop target, you must override four *CView* virtual functions, which the framework calls during the drag-and-drop operation. Here's a summary of what they should do, assuming that you're using a tracker:

Function	Description
OnDragEnter	Adjusts the focus rectangle and then calls *OnDragOver*
OnDragOver	Moves the dotted focus rectangle and sets the drop effect (determines cursor shape)
OnDragLeave	Cancels the transfer operation; returns the rectangle to its original position and size
OnDrop	Adjusts the focus rectangle and then calls the *DoPaste* helper function to get formats from the data object

The Drag-and-Drop Sequence

Figure 24-3 illustrates the MFC drag-and-drop process.

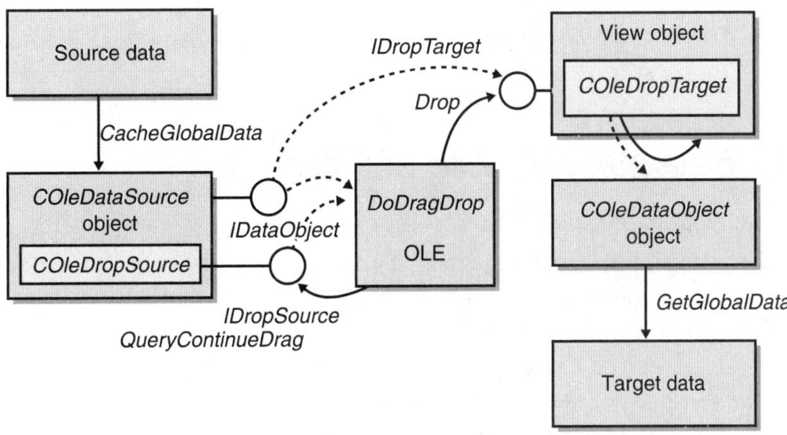

Figure 24-3 MFC OLE drag-and-drop processing.

Here's a summary of what's going on:

1. The user presses the left mouse button in the source view window.
2. The mouse button handler calls *CRectTracker::HitTest* and finds out that the cursor was inside the tracker rectangle.
3. The handler stores formats in a *COleDataSource* object.
4. The handler calls *COleDataSource::DoDragDrop* for the data source.

5. The user moves the cursor to the view window of the target application.

6. OLE calls *IDropTarget::OnDragEnter* and *OnDragOver* for the *COleDropTarget* object, which calls the corresponding virtual functions in the target's view. The *OnDragOver* function is passed a *COleDataObject* pointer for the source object, which the target tests for a format that it can understand.

7. *OnDragOver* returns a drop effect code, which OLE uses to set the cursor.

8. OLE calls *IDataSource::QueryContinueDrag* on the source side to find out whether the drag operation is still in progress. The MFC *COleDataSource* class responds appropriately.

9. The user releases the mouse button to drop the object in the target view window.

10. OLE calls *IDropTarget::OnDrop*, which calls *OnDrop* for the target's view. Because *OnDrop* is passed a *COleDataObject* pointer, it can retrieve the desired format from that object.

11. When *OnDrop* returns in the target program, *DoDragDrop* can return in the source program.

The Ex24b Example: OLE Drag and Drop

This example picks up where the Ex24a example left off. It adds drag-and-drop support, using the existing *SaveDib* and *DoPasteDib* helper functions. All of the Clipboard code is the same. You should be able to adapt Ex24b to other applications that require drag and drop for data objects.

To prepare Ex24b, open the \vcppnet\Ex24b\Ex24b.sln solution and build the project. Run the application, and test drag and drop between child windows and between instances of the program.

The *CEx24bDoc* Class

This class is just like the Ex24a version except for an added flag data member, *m_bDragHere*. This flag is *TRUE* when a drag-and-drop operation is in progress for this document. The flag is in the document and not in the view because it is possible to have multiple views attached to the same document. It doesn't make sense to drag a DIB from one view to another if both views reflect the document's *m_dib* member.

The *CEx24bView* Class

To start with, this class has three additional data members and a constructor that initializes all the data members, as shown here:

```
CRect m_rectTrackerEnter; // original logical coordinates
COleDropTarget m_dropTarget;
CSize m_dragOffset; // device coordinates

CEx24bView::CEx24bView() : m_sizeTotal(800, 1050), // 8-by-10.5 inches
                                                   //  when printed
    m_rectTracker(50, 50, 250, 250),
    m_dragOffset(0, 0),
    m_rectTrackerEnter(50, 50, 250, 250)
{
}
```

The *OnInitialUpdate* function needs one additional line to register the drop target:

```
m_dropTarget.Register(this);
```

Following are the drag-and-drop virtual override functions. Note that *OnDrop* replaces the DIB only if the document's *m_bDragHere* flag is *TRUE*, so if the user drops the DIB in the same window or in another window connected to the same document, nothing happens.

```
DROPEFFECT CEx24bView::OnDragEnter(COleDataObject* pDataObject,
                                   DWORD dwKeyState, CPoint point)
{
    TRACE("Entering CEx24bView::OnDragEnter, point = (%d, %d)\n",
          point.x, point.y);
    m_rectTrackerEnter = m_rectTracker; // Save original coordinates
                                        //  for cursor leaving
                                        //  rectangle
    CClientDC dc(this);
    OnPrepareDC(&dc);
    dc.DrawFocusRect(m_rectTracker); // will be erased in OnDragOver
    return OnDragOver(pDataObject, dwKeyState, point);
}
void CEx24bView::OnDragLeave()
{
    TRACE("Entering CEx24bView::OnDragLeave\n");
    CClientDC dc(this);
    OnPrepareDC(&dc);
    dc.DrawFocusRect(m_rectTracker);
    m_rectTracker = m_rectTrackerEnter; // Forget it ever happened
}
DROPEFFECT CEx24bView::OnDragOver(COleDataObject* pDataObject, DWORD
```

(continued)

```
                                      dwKeyState, CPoint point)
{
    if (!pDataObject->IsDataAvailable(CF_DIB)) {
        return DROPEFFECT_NONE;
    }
    MoveTrackRect(point);
    if((dwKeyState & MK_CONTROL) == MK_CONTROL) {
        return DROPEFFECT_COPY;
    }
    // Check for force move
    if ((dwKeyState & MK_ALT) == MK_ALT) {
        return DROPEFFECT_MOVE;
    }
    // default -- recommended action is move
    return DROPEFFECT_MOVE;
}
BOOL CEx24bView::OnDrop(COleDataObject* pDataObject,
                        DROPEFFECT dropEffect, CPoint point)
{
    TRACE("Entering CEx24bView::OnDrop -- dropEffect = %d\n", dropEffect);
    BOOL bRet;
    CEx24bDoc* pDoc = GetDocument();
    MoveTrackRect(point);
    if(pDoc->m_bDragHere) {
        pDoc->m_bDragHere = FALSE;
        bRet = TRUE;
    }
    else {
        bRet = DoPasteDib(pDataObject);
    }
    return bRet;
}
```

The handler for the *WM_LBUTTONDOWN* message needs a substantial overhaul. It must call *DoDragDrop* if the cursor is inside the rectangle and *Track* if it is on the rectangle border. The revised code is shown here:

```
void CEx24bView::OnLButtonDown(UINT nFlags, CPoint point)
{
    CEx24bDoc* pDoc = GetDocument();
    if(m_tracker.HitTest(point) == CRectTracker::hitMiddle) {
        COleDataSource* pSource = SaveDib();
        if(pSource) {
            // DoDragDrop returns only after drop is complete
            CClientDC dc(this);
            OnPrepareDC(&dc);
            CPoint topleft = m_rectTracker.TopLeft();
            dc.LPtoDP(&topleft);
```

```
                // 'point' here is not the same as the point parameter in
                //  OnDragEnter, so we use this one to compute the offset
                m_dragOffset = point - topleft;  // device coordinates
                pDoc->m_bDragHere = TRUE;
                DROPEFFECT dropEffect = pSource->DoDragDrop(
                    DROPEFFECT_MOVE|DROPEFFECT_COPY, CRect(0, 0, 0, 0));
                TRACE("after DoDragDrop -- dropEffect = %ld\n", dropEffect);
                if (dropEffect == DROPEFFECT_MOVE && pDoc->m_bDragHere) {
                    pDoc->OnEditClearall();
                }
                pDoc->m_bDragHere = FALSE;
                delete pSource;
            }
        }
        else {
            if(m_tracker.Track(this, point, FALSE, NULL)) {
                CClientDC dc(this);
                OnPrepareDC(&dc);
                // should have some way to prevent it going out of bounds
                m_rectTracker = m_tracker.m_rect;
                dc.DPtoLP(m_rectTracker); // Update logical coords
            }
        }
        Invalidate();
}
```

Finally, the new *MoveTrackRect* helper function, shown here, moves the tracker's focus rectangle each time the *OnDragOver* function is called. This job was done by *CRectTracker::Track* in the Ex24a example.

```
void CEx24bView::MoveTrackRect(CPoint point)
{
    CClientDC dc(this);
    OnPrepareDC(&dc);
    dc.DrawFocusRect(m_rectTracker);
    dc.LPtoDP(m_rectTracker);
    CSize sizeTrack = m_rectTracker.Size();
    CPoint newTopleft = point - m_dragOffset;  // still device
    m_rectTracker = CRect(newTopleft, sizeTrack);
    m_tracker.m_rect = m_rectTracker;
    dc.DPtoLP(m_rectTracker);
    dc.DrawFocusRect(m_rectTracker);
}
```

I tested Ex24b against the Microsoft Office XP suite using both drag-and-drop and Clipboard transfers. The *CF_DIB* format isn't supported. If you want pictures from Microsoft Excel, you must enhance Ex24b to process metafiles.

25

Introducing the Active Template Library

In this chapter, we'll look at the Active Template Library (ATL), the second framework included with Microsoft Visual C++ .NET. (MFC is the first.) We'll start by quickly revisiting the Component Object Model (COM) and looking at an alternative method of writing Chapter 22's *CSpaceship* object, which will illustrate that there's more than one way to write a COM class. (This will become important as you examine ATL's class composition methods.) Next, we'll investigate ATL, focusing first on C++ templates and raw C++ smart pointers and how they can be useful in COM development. We'll cover the client side of ATL programming and examine some of ATL's smart pointers. Finally, we'll check out the server side of ATL programming, reimplementing the Chapter 22 spaceship example using both classic ATL and attributed ATL to get a feel for ATL's architecture.

Revisiting COM

The most important concept to understand about COM programming is that it is interface-based. As you saw in Chapter 22, you don't need real COM or even Microsoft runtime support to use interface-based programming. All you need is some discipline.

Think back to the spaceship example in Chapter 22. We started out with a single class named *CSpaceship* that implemented several functions. Seasoned C++ developers usually sit down at the computer and start typing a class like this:

```
class CSpaceship {
    void Fly();
    int& GetPosition();
};
```

However, the procedure is a little different with interface-based development. Instead of writing the class directly, with interface-based programming you spell out an interface before implementing it. In Chapter 22, the *Fly* and *GetPosition* functions were moved into an abstract base class named *IMotion*:

```
struct IMotion {
    virtual void Fly() = 0;
    virtual int& GetPosition() = 0;
};
```

We then inherited the *CSpaceship* class from the *IMotion* interface, like this:

```
class CSpaceship : IMotion {
    void Fly();
    int& GetPosition();
};
```

Notice that at this point the motion interface has been separated from its implementation. When you practice interface development, the interface comes first. You can work on the interface as you develop it, making sure it's complete but not bloated. But once the interface has been published (that is, once a lot of other developers have started coding to it), it is frozen and can never change.

This subtle distinction between class-based programming and interface-based programming seems to introduce some programming overhead. But it turns out to be one of the key points for understanding COM. By collecting the *Fly* and the *GetPosition* functions in an interface, you develop a binary signature. That is, by defining the interface ahead of time and talking to the class through the interface, you give the client code a potentially language-neutral way of talking to the class.

Gathering functions together into interfaces is itself quite powerful. Say you want to describe something other than a spaceship—an airplane, for example. It's certainly conceivable that an airplane would also have *Fly* and *GetPosition* functions. Interface programming provides a more advanced form of polymorphism—polymorphism at the interface level, not only at the single-function level.

Separating interface from implementation is the basis of interface-based development. COM is centered on interface programming. It enforces the distinction between interface and implementation. In COM, the only way client code can talk to an object is through an interface. However, gathering functions together into interfaces isn't quite enough. One more ingredient is needed—a mechanism for discovering functionality at run time.

The Core Interface: *IUnknown*

The key element that makes COM different from ordinary interface programming is this rule: The first three functions of every COM interface are the same. The core interface in COM, *IUnknown*, looks like this:

```
struct IUnknown {
    virtual HRESULT QueryInterface(REFIID riid, void** ppv) = 0;
    virtual ULONG AddRef() = 0;
    virtual ULONG Release() = 0;
};
```

Every COM interface derives from this interface (which means that the first three functions of every COM interface you'll ever see will be *QueryInterface*, *AddRef*, and *Release*). To turn *IMotion* into a COM interface, you derive it from *IUnknown*, like this:

```
struct IMotion : IUnknown {
    void Fly();
    int& GetPosition();
};
```

> **Note** If you want these interfaces to work out-of-process, you have to make each function return an *HRESULT*. You'll see this when we cover attributed ATL later in the chapter.

AddRef and *Release* deserve some mention because they're part of *IUnknown*. *AddRef* and *Release* allow an object to control its own lifetime if it chooses to. As a rule, clients are supposed to treat interface pointers like resources: Clients acquire interfaces, use them, and then release them when they're done using them. Objects learn about new references to themselves via *AddRef*. Objects learn that they have been unreferenced through the *Release* function. Objects often use this information to control their lifetimes. For example, many objects self-destruct when their reference count reaches zero.

Here's how some client code might use the spaceship:

```
void UseSpaceship() {
    IMotion* pMotion = NULL;

    pMotion = GetASpaceship(); // This is a member of the
                               //  hypothetical Spaceship
                               //  API. It's presumably an
                               //  entry point into some DLL.
                               //  Returns an IMotion* and
                               //  causes an implicit AddRef.
    If(pMotion) {
        pMotion->Fly();
        int i = pMotion->GetPosition();
        pMotion->Release(); // done with this instance of CSpaceship
    }
}
```

The other (and more important) function within *IUnknown* is the first one: *QueryInterface*. *QueryInterface* is the COM mechanism for discovering functionality at run time. If someone gives you a COM interface pointer to an object and you don't want to use that pointer, you can use the pointer to ask the object for a different interface to the same object. This mechanism and the fact that interfaces remain constant once published are the key ingredients that allow COM-based software to evolve safely over time. The result is that you can add functionality to your COM software without breaking older versions of the clients running that software. In addition, clients will have a widely recognized means of acquiring that new functionality once they know about it.

For example, you add functionality to the implementation of *CSpaceship* by adding a new interface named *IVisual*. Adding this interface makes sense because you can have objects in three-dimensional space that move in and out of view. You might also have an invisible object in three-dimensional space (a black hole, for example). Here's the *IVisual* interface:

```
struct IVisual : IUnknown {
    virtual void Display() = 0;
};
```

A client might use the *IVisual* interface like this:

```
void UseSpaceship() {
    IMotion* pMotion = NULL;

    pMotion = GetASpaceship(); // Implicit AddRef
    if(pMotion) {
        pMotion->Fly();
        int i = pMotion->GetPosition();
```

```
        IVisual* pVisual = NULL;
        PMotion->QueryInterface(IID_IVisual, (void**) &pVisual);
        // Implicit AddRef within QueryInterface

        if(pVisible) {
            pVisual->Display(); // uncloaking now
            pVisual->Release(); // done with this interface
        }
    }
    pMotion->Release(); // done with this instance of IMotion
}
```

Notice that the preceding code uses interface pointers very carefully: It uses them only if the interface was acquired properly, and then it releases the interface pointers when it is done using them. This is raw COM programming at the lowest level—you acquire an interface pointer, you use the interface pointer, and you release it when you're done with it.

Writing COM Code

As you can see, writing COM client code isn't a whole lot different from writing regular C++ code. However, the C++ classes that the client talks to are abstract base classes. Instead of calling *operator new* as you would in C++, you create COM objects and acquire COM interfaces by explicitly calling some sort of API function. And instead of deleting the object outright, you simply follow the COM interface rule of balancing calls to *AddRef* with calls to *Release*.

What does it take to get the COM class up and running? You saw how to do it using MFC in Chapter 22. Here's another example of implementing *CSpaceship* as a COM class. This example uses the multiple inheritance approach to writing COM classes. That is, the C++ class inherits from several interfaces and then implements the union of all the functions (including *IUnknown*, of course).

```
struct CSpaceship : IMotion, IDisplay {
    ULONG m_cRef;
    int m_nPosition;

    CSpaceship() : m_cRef(0),
                   m_nPosition(0) {
    }

    HRESULT QueryInterface(REFIID riid,
                           void** ppv);
    ULONG AddRef() {
```

(continued)

```
            return InterlockedIncrement(&m_cRef);
        }
        ULONG Release() {
            ULONG cRef = InterlockedIncrement(&m_cRef);
            if(cRef == 0){
                delete this;
                return 0;
            } else
                return m_cRef;
        }
    // IMotion functions:
        void Fly() {
            // Do whatever it takes to fly here
        }
        int GetPosition() {
            return m_nPosition;
        }

        // IVisual functions:
        void Display() {
            // Uncloak
        }
    };
```

COM Classes That Use Multiple Inheritance

If you're used to seeing plain C++ code, the preceding code might look a little strange to you. It shows a less common form of multiple inheritance called *interface inheritance*. Most C++ developers are used to an implementation inheritance in which the derived class inherits everything from the base class—including the implementation. Interface inheritance simply means that the derived class inherits the interfaces of the base class. The preceding code effectively adds two data members to the *CSpaceship* class—a *vptr* for each implied vtable.

When you use the multiple inheritance approach to implementing interfaces, each interface shares *CSpaceship*'s implementation of *IUnknown*. This sharing illustrates a rather esoteric yet important concept known as *COM identity*. The basic idea of COM identity is that *IUnknown* is the *void** of COM. *IUknown* is the one interface guaranteed to be hanging off any object, and you can always get to it. COM identity also says (in the previous example) that the client can call *QueryInterface* through the *CSpaceship IMotion* interface to get the *IVisual* interface. Conversely, the client can call *QueryInterface* through the *CSpaceship IVisual* interface to get the *IMotion* interface. Finally, the client can call *QueryInterface* through *IUnknown* to acquire the *IMotion* or the *IVisual* interface, and the client can call *QueryInterface* through either *IMotion* or *IVisual* to get a pointer to *IUnknown*. To learn more about COM identity, see *Essential COM* by Don Box (Addison-Wesley, 1997) or *Inside COM* by Dale Rogerson (Microsoft Press, 1997).

Often you'll see COM classes illustrated with "lollipop" diagrams depicting the interfaces implemented by a COM class. You can see an example of a lollipop diagram on page 540 in Chapter 22.

The multiple inheritance method of implementing *CSpaceship* automatically fulfills the rules of COM identity. Note that all calls to *QueryInterface*, *AddRef*, and *Release* land in the same place in the C++ class, regardless of the interface through which they were called.

This is more or less the essence of COM. As a COM developer, your job is to create useful services and expose them through COM interfaces. At the most basic level, this means wiring up some function tables to follow COM's identity rules. You've seen two ways to accomplish this so far. (Chapter 22 showed you how to do it using nested classes and MFC. This chapter just showed you how to write a COM class that uses multiple inheritance in C++.) However, in addition to interface programming and writing classes to implement interfaces, there are several other pieces to the COM puzzle.

The COM Infrastructure

Once you get your mind around the concept of interface-based programming, you must implement quite a few details in order to get the class to mix in with the rest of the system. These details often overshadow the fundamental beauty of COM.

To start with, COM classes need a place to live, so you must package them in an EXE or a DLL. In addition, each COM class you write needs an accompanying class object (often referred to as a *class factory*). The way in which a COM server's class object is exposed will differ depending on how you package the COM class (in a DLL or an EXE). You must also consider the server lifetime. The server should stay in memory for as long as it's needed, and it should go away when it's not needed. To accomplish this, servers maintain global lock counts that indicate the number of objects with extant interface pointers. Finally, well-behaved servers insert the necessary values in the Windows Registry so client software can easily activate them.

We've spent a lot of time looking at MFC in this book. As you saw in Chapter 22, MFC takes care of most of the COM-based details for you. For example, *CCmdTarget* has an implementation of *IUnknown*. MFC has even created C++ classes and macros to implement class objects (such as *COleObjectFactory*, *COleTemplateServer*, *DECLARE_OLE_CREATE*, and *IMPLEMENT_OLE_CREATE*) that will put most of the correct entries into the Registry. MFC has the easiest-to-implement, zippiest version of *IDispatch* around—all you need is a *CCmdTarget* object and the Visual Studio .NET environment (specifically, the Add Property Wizard and the Add Method Wizard). And in case OLE drag and drop is your thing, MFC provides a standard implementation of the drag and drop protocol. Finally, MFC remains hands-down the easiest way to write fast, powerful ActiveX controls. (You can write ActiveX controls in Microsoft Visual Basic, but you don't have quite as much flexibility). These are all great features. However, using MFC has a downside.

To get these features, you must buy into MFC 100 percent. That's not necessarily a bad idea, but you should be aware of the cost of entry when you decide to use MFC. MFC is big. It has to be—it's a C++ framework with many capabilities.

As you can see from the examples we've looked at so far, implementing COM classes and making them available to clients involves writing a great deal of code—code that remains the same from one class implementation to another. *IUnknown* implementations are generally the same for every COM class you encounter—the main difference between them is the interfaces exposed by each class.

Let's take a quick peek at where COM and ATL fit into the big picture.

ActiveX, OLE, and COM

COM is simply the plumbing for a series of higher-level application integration technologies consisting of such items as ActiveX controls and OLE drag and drop. These technologies define protocols based on COM interfaces. You might choose to implement the higher-level features such as drag and drop or controls yourself. However, it makes more sense to let some sort of application framework do the grunt work. Of course, that's why there's MFC.

> **Note** For more information about how to implement higher-level features in raw C++, see Kraig Brockschmidt's *Inside OLE*, 2d. ed. (Microsoft Press, 1995).

ActiveX, MFC, and COM

While the pure plumbing of COM is quite interesting by itself (it's simply amazing to see how COM remoting works), the higher-level features are what sell applications. MFC is a huge framework geared toward creating entire Windows-based applications. Inside MFC, you'll find tons of utility classes and a data management/rendering mechanism (the document-view architecture), as well as support for drag and drop, Automation, and ActiveX controls. You probably don't want to develop an OLE drag and drop from scratch; you're much better off using MFC. However, if you need to create a small or medium-size COM-based service, you might want to turn away from MFC so you don't have to include all the baggage that MFC maintains for the higher-level features.

You can use raw C++ to create COM components, but you'll end up spending a good portion of your time hacking out the boilerplate code (*IUnknown* and class objects, for example). Using MFC to write COM-based applications turns out to be a less painful way of adding the big-ticket items to your application, but it's difficult to write lightweight COM classes in MFC. ATL sits between pure C++ and MFC as a way to implement COM-based software without requiring you to type in the boilerplate code or buy into all of MFC's architecture. ATL is basically a set of C++ templates and other kinds of support for writing COM classes.

An ATL Roadmap

If you look at the source code for ATL, you'll find that ATL consists of a collection of header files and C++ source code files. Most of it resides inside the ATLMFC\Include directory that comes with the installation of Microsoft Visual Studio .NET. Here's a rundown on some of the ATL files and what's inside each of them.

AtlBase.h

This file contains:

- ATL's function typedefs
- Structure and macro definitions
- Smart pointers for managing COM interface pointers
- Thread synchronization support classes
- Definitions for *CComBSTR*, *CComVariant*, threading, and apartment support

AtlCom.h

This file contains:

- Template classes for class object/class factory support
- *IUnknown* implementations
- Support for tear-off interfaces
- Type information management and support
- ATL's *IDispatch* implementation
- COM enumerator templates
- Connection point support

AtlConv.cpp and AtlConv.h

These two source code files include support for Unicode conversions.

AtlCtl.cpp and AtlCtl.h

These two files contain:

- The source code for ATL's *IDispatch* client support and event firing support
- *CComControlBase*
- The OLE embedding protocol support for controls
- Property page support

AtlIFace.idl and AtlIFace.h

AtlIFace.idl (which generates AtlIFace.h) includes an ATL-specific interface named *IRegistrar*.

AtlImpl.cpp

AtlImpl.cpp implements such classes as *CComBSTR*, which is declared in AtlBase.h.

AtlWin.cpp and AtlWin.h

These files provide windowing and user-interface support, including:

- A message-mapping mechanism
- A windowing class
- Dialog support

StatReg.cpp and StatReg.h

ATL features a COM component named the Registrar that handles putting appropriate entries into the Registry. The code for implementing this feature is in StatReg.h and StatReg.cpp.

Let's start our excursion into ATL by examining ATL's support for client-side COM development.

Client-side ATL Programming

There are basically two sides to ATL—client-side support and object-side support. By far the largest portion of support is on the object side because of all the code that's needed to implement ActiveX controls. However, the client-side support also turns out to be useful and interesting. We'll take a look at the client side of ATL next, with a little detour first to examine C++ templates, which are the cornerstone of ATL.

C++ Templates

The key to understanding ATL is understanding C++ templates. Despite the intimidating template syntax, the concept of templates is fairly straightforward. C++ templates are sometimes called *compiler-approved macros*, which is an appropriate description. Think about what macros do: When the preprocessor encounters a macro, it looks at the macro and expands it into regular C++ code. But the problem with macros is that they're sometimes error-prone and they're never type-safe. If you use a macro and pass an incorrect parameter, the compiler won't complain but your program might very well crash. Templates, however, are like type-safe macros. When the compiler encounters a template, it will expand the template just as it would a macro. But because templates are type-safe, the compiler will catch any type problems before the user encounters them.

Using templates to reuse code is different from what you're used to with conventional C++ development. Components written using templates reuse code by template substitution rather than by inheriting functionality from base classes. All the boilerplate code from templates is literally pasted into the project.

The archetypal example of using a template is a dynamic array. Imagine you need an array for holding integers. Rather than declaring the array with a fixed size, you want the array to grow as necessary. So you develop the array as a C++ class. Then someone you work with gets wind of your new class and says that she needs the exact same functionality. However, she wants to use floating point numbers in the array. Rather than pumping out the exact same code (except for using a different type of data), you can use a C++ template.

Here's an example of how you might use templates to solve the problem. The following is a dynamic array implemented as a template:

```
template <class T> class DynArray {
public:
    DynArray();
    ~DynArray(); // clean up and do memory management
    int Add(T Element); // adds an element and does
                        //  memory management
    void Remove(int nIndex) // remove element and
                            //  do memory management
    T GetAt(nIndex) const;
    int GetSize();
private:
    T* TArray;
    int m_nArraysize;
};

void UseDynArray() {
    DynArray<int> intArray;
    DynArray<float> floatArray;

    intArray.Add(4);
    floatArray.Add(5.0);

    intArray.Remove(0);
    floatArray.Remove(0);

    int x = intArray.GetAt(0);
    float f = floatArray.GetAt(0);
}
```

As you can imagine, creating templates is useful for implementing boilerplate COM code, and templates are the mechanism that ATL uses for providing COM support. The previous example is just one of the many uses for templates. Not only are templates useful for applying type information to a certain kind of data structure, but they're also useful for encapsulating algorithms. You'll see how when we take a closer look at ATL.

Smart Pointers

One of the most common uses of templates is for smart pointers. The traditional C++ literature calls C++'s built-in pointers "dumb" pointers. That's not a very nice name, but normal C++ pointers don't do much except point. It's often up to the client to perform details such as pointer initialization.

As an example, let's model two types of software developer who use C++ classes. We can start by creating the classes *CVBDeveloper* and *CCPPDeveloper*:

```
class CVBDeveloper {
public:
    CVBDeveloper() {
    }
    ~CVBDeveloper() {
        AfxMessageBox
            ("I used Visual Basic .NET, so I got home early.");
    }
    virtual void DoTheWork() {
        AfxMessageBox("Write them forms");
    }
};

class CCPPDeveloper {
public:
    CCPPDeveloper() {
    }
    ~CCPPDeveloper() {
        AfxMessageBox("Stay at work and fix those pointer problems");
    }
    virtual void DoTheWork() {
        AfxMessageBox("Hacking C++ code");
    }
};
```

The Visual Basic developer and the C++ developer both have functions for eliciting optimal performance. Now imagine some client code that looks like this:

```
//UseDevelopers.cpp

void UseDevelopers() {
    CVBDeveloper* pVBDeveloper;
    ⋮
    // The VBDeveloper pointer needs
    //  to be initialized
    //  sometime. But what if
    //  you forget to initialize and later
    //  on do something like this:
    if(pVBDeveloper) {
        // Get ready for fireworks
        //  because pVBDeveloper is
        //  NOT NULL, it points
        //  to some random data.
        c->DoTheWork();
    }
}
```

In this case, the client code forgot to initialize the *pVBDeveloper* pointer to *NULL*. (Of course, this never happens in real life!) Because *pVBDeveloper* contains a non-*NULL* value (the value is actually whatever happened to be on the stack at the time), the test to make sure the pointer is valid will succeed when in fact you expect it to fail. The client will gleefully proceed, believing all is well. The client will crash, of course, because the client is "calling into darkness." (Who knows where *pVBDeveloper* is pointing—probably to nothing that even resembles a Visual Basic developer.) Naturally, you'd like some mechanism for ensuring that the pointers are initialized. This is where smart pointers come in handy.

Now imagine a second scenario. You'd like to plug a little extra code into your developer-type classes that performs some sort of operation common to all developers. For example, you might like all the developers to do some design work before they begin coding. Consider the earlier Visual Basic developer and C++ developer examples. When the client calls *DoTheWork*, the developer will get right to coding without proper design, and he'll probably leave the poor clients in a lurch. What you'd like to do is add a generic hook to the developer classes so they make sure the design is done before coding begins.

The C++ solution to coping with these problems is the smart pointer.

Giving C++ Pointers Some Brains

Remember that a smart pointer is a C++ class for wrapping pointers. By wrapping a pointer in a class (and specifically, a template), you can make sure that certain operations are taken care of automatically rather than having mundane, boilerplate-type operations deferred to the client. One good example of such an operation is to make sure pointers are initialized correctly so that embarrassing crashes due to randomly assigned pointers don't occur. Another good example is to make certain that boilerplate code is executed before function calls are made through a pointer.

Let's invent a smart pointer for the developer model described earlier. Consider a template-based class named *SmartDeveloper*:

```
template<class T>
class SmartDeveloper {
    T* m_pDeveloper;

public:
    SmartDeveloper(T* pDeveloper) {
        ASSERT(pDeveloper != NULL);
        m_pDeveloper = pDeveloper;
    }
    ~SmartDeveloper() {
        AfxMessageBox("I'm smart so I'll get paid.");
    }
    SmartDeveloper &
      operator=(const SmartDeveloper& rDeveloper) {
        return *this;
    }
     T* operator->() const {
        AfxMessageBox("About to de-reference pointer. Make /
                       sure everything's okay. ");
        return m_pDeveloper;
    }
};
```

The *SmartDeveloper* template listed above wraps a pointer—any pointer. Because the *SmartDeveloper* class is based on a template, it can provide generic functionality regardless of the type associated with the class. You can think of templates as compiler-approved macros—declarations of classes (or functions) whose code can apply to any type of data.

We want the smart pointer to handle all developers, including those using Visual Basic, Visual C++, C#, and Delphi (among others). The *template <class T>* statement at the top accomplishes this. The *SmartDeveloper* template includes a pointer (*m_pDeveloper*) to the type of developer for which the class will be defined. The *SmartDeveloper* constructor takes a pointer to that type as a parameter and assigns it to *m_pDeveloper*. Notice that the constructor generates an assertion if the client passes a *NULL* parameter to construct *SmartDeveloper*.

In addition to wrapping a pointer, the *SmartDeveloper* implements several operators. The most important one is the -> operator (the member selection operator). This operator is the workhorse of any smart pointer class. Overloading the member selection operator is what turns a regular class into a smart pointer. Normally, using the member selection operator on a regular C++ dumb pointer tells the compiler to select a member belonging to the class or structure being pointed to. By overriding the member selection operator, you provide a way for the client to hook in and call some boilerplate code every time that client calls a method. In the *SmartDeveloper* example, the smart developer makes sure the work area is in order before working. (This example is somewhat contrived. In real life, you might want to put in a debugging hook, for example.)

Adding the -> operator to the class causes the class to behave like C++'s built-in pointer. In order to behave like native C++ pointers in other ways, smart pointer classes must implement the other standard operators, such as the dereferencing and assignment operators.

Using Smart Pointers

Using smart pointers is really no different from using the regular built-in C++ pointers. Let's start by looking at a client that uses plain vanilla developer classes:

```
void UseDevelopers() {
    CVBDeveloper VBDeveloper;
    CCPPDeveloper CPPDeveloper;
    VBDeveloper.DoTheWork();
    CPPDeveloper.DoTheWork();
}
```

No surprises here—executing this code causes the developers simply to come in and do the work. However, you want to use the smart developers—the ones that make sure the design is done before they actually start to hack. Here's the code that wraps the Visual Basic developer and C++ developer objects in the smart pointer class:

```
void UseSmartDevelopers {
    CVBDeveloper VBDeveloper;
    CCPPDeveloper CPPDeveloper;

    SmartDeveloper<CVBDeveloper> smartVBDeveloper(&VBDeveloper);
    SmartDeveloper<CCPPDeveloper> smartCPPDeveloper(&CPPDeveloper);
```

```
    smartVBDeveloper->DoTheWork();
    smartCPPDeveloper->DoTheWork();
}
```

Instead of bringing in any old developer to do the work (as in the previous example), the client asks the smart developers to do the work. The smart developers will automatically prepare the design before proceeding with coding.

Smart Pointers and COM

Although the last example was fabricated to make an interesting story, smart pointers do have useful applications in the real world. One of those applications is to make client-side COM programming easier.

Smart pointers are frequently used to implement reference counting. Because reference counting is a generic operation, hoisting client-side reference count management up into a smart pointer makes sense.

Because you're now familiar with COM, you understand that COM objects expose interfaces. To C++ clients, interfaces are simply pure abstract base classes, and C++ clients treat interfaces more or less like normal C++ objects. However, as you discovered in previous chapters, COM objects are a bit different from regular C++ objects. COM objects live at the binary level. As such, they are created and destroyed using language-independent means. COM objects are created via API functions calls. Most COM objects use a reference count to determine when to delete themselves from memory. Once a COM object is created, a client object can refer to it in a number of ways by referencing multiple interfaces belonging to the same COM object. In addition, several different clients can talk to a single COM object. In these situations, the COM object must stay alive for as long as it is referenced. Most COM objects destroy themselves when they're no longer referenced by any clients. COM objects use reference counting to accomplish this self-destruction.

To support this reference-counting scheme, COM defines a couple of rules for managing COM interfaces from the client side. The first rule is that creating a new copy of a COM interface should result in bumping the object's reference count up by one. The second rule is that clients should release interface pointers when they're finished with them. Reference counting is one of the more difficult aspects of COM to get right—especially from the client side. Keeping track of COM interface reference counting is a perfect use of smart pointers.

For example, the smart pointer's constructor might take the live interface pointer as an argument and set an internal pointer to the live interface pointer. Then the destructor might call the interface pointer's *Release* function to release the interface so the interface pointer will be released automatically when the smart pointer is deleted or falls out of scope. In addition, the smart pointer can help manage COM interfaces that are copied.

For example, imagine you've created a COM object and you're holding on to the interface pointer. You need to make a copy of the interface pointer, perhaps to pass it as an out parameter. At the native COM level, you must perform several steps. First, you must release the old interface pointer. Then you need to copy the old pointer to the new pointer. Finally, you must call *AddRef* on the new copy of the interface pointer. These steps must occur regardless of the interface being used, making this process ideal for boilerplate code. To implement this process in the smart pointer class, all you need to do is override the assignment operator. The client can then assign the old pointer to the new pointer. The smart pointer does all the work of managing the interface pointer, relieving the client of the burden.

ATL's Smart Pointers

Much of ATL's support for client-side COM development resides in a pair of ATL smart pointers: *CComPtr* and *CComQIPtr*. *CComPtr* is a basic smart pointer that wraps COM interface pointers. *CComQIPtr* adds a little more smarts by associating a GUID (for use as the interface ID) with a smart pointer. *CComPtr* has much of its functionality factored out in a class named *CComPtrBase*. Let's start by looking at *CComPtrBase*.

The *CComPtrBase* Class

CComPtrBase provides a basis for smart pointer classes that use COM-based memory functions. Here's *CComPtrBase*:

```
template <class T>
class CComPtrBase
{
protected:
    CComPtrBase() throw()
    {
        p = NULL;
    }
    CComPtrBase(int nNull) throw()
    {
        ATLASSERT(nNull == 0);
        (void)nNull;
        p = NULL;
    }
    CComPtrBase(T* lp) throw()
    {
```

```
        p = lp;
        if (p != NULL)
            p->AddRef();
    }
public:
    typedef T _PtrClass;
    ~CComPtrBase() throw()
    {
        if (p)
            p->Release();
    }
    operator T*() const throw()
    {
        return p;
    }
    T& operator*() const throw()
    {
        ATLASSERT(p!=NULL);
        return *p;
    }
    //The assert on operator& usually indicates a bug.  If this is really
    //what is needed, however, take the address of the p member explicitly.
    T** operator&() throw()
    {
        ATLASSERT(p==NULL);
        return &p;
    }
    _NoAddRefReleaseOnCComPtr<T>* operator->() const throw()
    {
        ATLASSERT(p!=NULL);
        return (_NoAddRefReleaseOnCComPtr<T>*)p;
    }
    bool operator!() const throw()
    {
        return (p == NULL);
    }
    bool operator<(T* pT) const throw()
    {
        return p < pT;
    }
    bool operator==(T* pT) const throw()
    {
        return p == pT;
    }
    // Release the interface and set to NULL
    void Release() throw()
```

(continued)

```
{
    T* pTemp = p;
    if (pTemp)
    {
        p = NULL;
        pTemp->Release();
    }
}
// Compare two objects for equivalence
bool IsEqualObject(IUnknown* pOther) throw()
{
    if (p == pOther)
        return true;

    if (p == NULL || pOther == NULL)
        return false; // One is NULL the other is not

    CComPtr<IUnknown> punk1;
    CComPtr<IUnknown> punk2;
    p->QueryInterface(__uuidof(IUnknown), (void**)&punk1);
    pOther->QueryInterface(__uuidof(IUnknown), (void**)&punk2);
    return punk1 == punk2;
}
// Attach to an existing interface (does not AddRef)
void Attach(T* p2) throw()
{
    if (p)
        p->Release();
    p = p2;
}
// Detach the interface (does not Release)
T* Detach() throw()
{
    T* pt = p;
    p = NULL;
    return pt;
}
HRESULT CopyTo(T** ppT) throw()
{
    ATLASSERT(ppT != NULL);
    if (ppT == NULL)
        return E_POINTER;
    *ppT = p;
    if (p)
        p->AddRef();
    return S_OK;
}
HRESULT SetSite(IUnknown* punkParent) throw()
{
```

```
        return AtlSetChildSite(p, punkParent);
    }
    HRESULT Advise(IUnknown* pUnk, const IID& iid, LPDWORD pdw) throw()
    {
        return AtlAdvise(p, pUnk, iid, pdw);
    }
    HRESULT CoCreateInstance(REFCLSID rclsid,
                             LPUNKNOWN pUnkOuter = NULL,
                             DWORD dwClsContext = CLSCTX_ALL) throw()
    {
        ATLASSERT(p == NULL);
        return ::CoCreateInstance(rclsid, pUnkOuter, dwClsContext,
                                  __uuidof(T), (void**)&p);
    }
    HRESULT CoCreateInstance(LPCOLESTR szProgID,
                             LPUNKNOWN pUnkOuter = NULL,
                             DWORD dwClsContext = CLSCTX_ALL) throw()
    {
        CLSID clsid;
        HRESULT hr = CLSIDFromProgID(szProgID, &clsid);
        ATLASSERT(p == NULL);
        if (SUCCEEDED(hr))
            hr = ::CoCreateInstance(clsid, pUnkOuter, dwClsContext,
                                    __uuidof(T), (void**)&p);
        return hr;
    }
    template <class Q>
    HRESULT QueryInterface(Q** pp) const throw()
    {
        ATLASSERT(pp != NULL);
        return p->QueryInterface(__uuidof(Q), (void**)pp);
    }
    T* p;
};
```

CComPtrBase is a fairly basic smart pointer. Notice the data member *p* of type T (the type introduced by the template parameter). *CComPtrBase*'s constructor performs an *AddRef* on the pointer while the destructor releases the pointer—no surprises here. *CComPtrBase* also has all the necessary operators for wrapping a COM interface. Only the assignment operator deserves special mention. The assignment does a raw pointer reassignment. The assignment operator calls a function named *AtlComPtrAssign*:

```
ATLINLINE ATLAPI_(IUnknown*) AtlComPtrAssign(IUnknown** pp,
                                             IUnknown* lp)
{
    if (lp != NULL)
        lp->AddRef();
    if (*pp)
```

(continued)

```
        (*pp)->Release();
    *pp = lp;
    return lp;
}
```

AtlComPtrAssign does a blind pointer assignment, *AddRef*-ing the assignee before calling *Release* on the assignor. You'll soon see a version of this function that calls *QueryInterface.*

CComPtrBase's main strength is that it helps you manage the reference count on a pointer to some degree. The next class down the hierarchy is *CComPtr*—the class you'd use in a real application.

The *CComPtr* Class

Because *CComPtr* derives from *CComPtrBase*, it includes all the interface pointer management functionality of *CComPtrBase*. *CComPtr* can help you manage *AddRef* and *Release* operations and code layout. A bit of code will help illustrate the usefulness of *CComPtr*. Imagine that your client code needs three interface pointers to get the work done, as shown here:

```
void GetLottaPointers(LPUNKNOWN pUnk){
    HRESULT hr;
    LPPERSIST pPersist;
    LPDISPATCH pDispatch;
    LPDATAOBJECT pDataObject;
    hr = pUnk->QueryInterface(IID_IPersist, (LPVOID *)&pPersist);
    if(SUCCEEDED(hr)) {
        hr = pUnk->QueryInterface(IID_IDispatch, (LPVOID *)
                                   &pDispatch);
        if(SUCCEEDED(hr)) {
            hr = pUnk->QueryInterface(IID_IDataObject,
                                   (LPVOID *) &pDataObject);
            if(SUCCEEDED(hr)) {
                DoIt(pPersist, pDispatch, pDataObject);
                pDataObject->Release();
            }
            pDispatch->Release();
        }
        pPersist->Release();
    }
}
```

You could use the controversial *goto* statement (and risk facing derisive comments from your coworkers) to try to make your code look cleaner, like this:

```
void GetLottaPointers(LPUNKNOWN pUnk){
    HRESULT hr;
```

```
    LPPERSIST pPersist;
    LPDISPATCH pDispatch;
    LPDATAOBJECT pDataObject;

    hr = pUnk->QueryInterface(IID_IPersist, (LPVOID *)&pPersist);
    if(FAILED(hr)) goto cleanup;

    hr = pUnk->QueryInterface(IID_IDispatch, (LPVOID *) &pDispatch);
    if(FAILED(hr)) goto cleanup;

    hr = pUnk->QueryInterface(IID_IDataObject,
                              (LPVOID *) &pDataObject);
    if(FAILED(hr)) goto cleanup;
    DoIt(pPersist, pDispatch, pDataObject);

cleanup:
    if (pDataObject) pDataObject->Release();
    if (pDispatch) pDispatch->Release();
    if (pPersist) pPersist->Release();
}
```

That might not be as elegant a solution as you'd like, however. Using *CComPtr* makes the same code a lot prettier and much easier to read, as shown here:

```
void GetLottaPointers(LPUNKNOWN pUnk){
    HRESULT hr;
    CComPtr<IUnknown> persist;
    CComPtr<IUnknown> dispatch;
    CComPtr<IUnknown> dataobject;

    hr = pUnk->QueryInterface(IID_IPersist, (LPVOID *)&persist);
    if(FAILED(hr)) return;

    hr = pUnk->QueryInterface(IID_IDispatch, (LPVOID *) &dispatch);
    if(FAILED(hr)) return;

    hr = pUnk->QueryInterface(IID_IDataObject,
                              (LPVOID *) &dataobject);
    if(FAILED(hr)) return;

    DoIt(pPersist, pDispatch, pDataObject);

    // Destructors call release...
}
```

At this point, you're probably wondering why *CComPtr* doesn't wrap *QueryInterface*. After all, *QueryInterface* is a hot spot for reference counting. Adding *QueryInterface* support for the smart pointer requires some way of associating a GUID with the smart pointer. *CComPtr* was introduced in the first version of ATL. Rather than disrupt any existing code base, Microsoft introduced a beefed-up version of *CComPtr* named *CComQIPtr*.

The *CComQIPtr* Class

Here's *CComQIPtr*'s definition:

```
template <class T, const IID* piid = &__uuidof(T)>
class CComQIPtr : public CComPtr<T>
{
public:
    CComQIPtr() throw()
    {
    }
    CComQIPtr(T* lp) throw() :
        CComPtr<T>(lp)
    {
    }
    CComQIPtr(const CComQIPtr<T,piid>& lp) throw() :
        CComPtr<T>(lp.p)
    {
    }
    CComQIPtr(IUnknown* lp) throw()
    {
        if (lp != NULL)
            lp->QueryInterface(*piid, (void **)&p);
    }
    T* operator=(T* lp) throw()
    {
        return static_cast<T*>(AtlComPtrAssign((IUnknown**)&p, lp));
    }
    T* operator=(const CComQIPtr<T,piid>& lp) throw()
    {
        return static_cast<T*>(AtlComPtrAssign((IUnknown**)&p, lp.p));
    }
    T* operator=(IUnknown* lp) throw()
    {
        return static_cast<T*>(AtlComQIPtrAssign((IUnknown**)&p,
                                        lp, *piid));
    }
};

//Specialization to make it work
template<>
class CComQIPtr<IUnknown, &IID_IUnknown> : public CComPtr<IUnknown>
{
```

```
public:
    CComQIPtr() throw()
    {
    }
    CComQIPtr(IUnknown* lp) throw()
    {
        //Actually do a QI to get identity
        if (lp != NULL)
            lp->QueryInterface(__uuidof(IUnknown), (void **)&p);
    }
    CComQIPtr(const CComQIPtr<IUnknown,&IID_IUnknown>& lp) throw() :
        CComPtr<IUnknown>(lp.p)
    {
    }
    IUnknown* operator=(IUnknown* lp) throw()
    {
        //Actually do a QI to get identity
        return AtlComQIPtrAssign((IUnknown**)&p, lp,
                                 __uuidof(IUnknown));
    }
    IUnknown* operator=(const CComQIPtr<IUnknown,&IID_IUnknown>& lp)
        throw()
    {
        return AtlComPtrAssign((IUnknown**)&p, lp.p);
    }
};
```

What makes *CComQIPtr* different from *CComPtr* is the second template parameter, *piid*—the interfaces's GUID. This smart pointer has several constructors: a default constructor, a copy constructor, a constructor that takes a raw interface pointer of unspecified type, and a constructor that accepts an *IUnknown* interface as a parameter. Notice in this last constructor that if the developer creates an object of this type and initializes it with a plain old *IUnknown* pointer, *CComQIPtr* will call *QueryInterface* using the GUID template parameter. Also notice that the assignment to an *IUnknown* pointer calls *AtlComQIPtrAssign* to make the assignment. As you can imagine, *AtlComQIPtrAssign* performs a *QueryInterface* under the hood using the GUID template parameter.

Using *CComQIPtr*

Here's how you might use *CComQIPtr* in some COM client code:

```
void GetLottaPointers(ISomeInterface* pSomeInterface){
    HRESULT hr;
    CComQIPtr<IPersist, &IID_IPersist> persist;
    CComQIPtr<IDispatch, &IID_IDispatch> dispatch;
    CComPtr<IDataObject, &IID_IDataObject> dataobject;
```

(continued)

```
    dispatch = pSomeInterface;   // implicit QI
    persist = pSomeInterface;    // implicit QI
    dataobject = pSomeInterface; // implicit QI

    DoIt(persist, dispatch, dataobject); // send to a function
                                         //  that needs IPersist*,
                                         //  IDispatch*, and
                                         //  IDataObject*

    // Destructors call release...
}
```

CComQIPtr is useful when you want the Java-style or Visual Basic–style type conversions. Notice that the code listed above doesn't require any calls to *QueryInterface* or *Release*. Those calls happen automatically.

ATL Smart Pointer Problems

Smart pointers can be convenient in some places (as in the *CComPtr* example, in which we eliminated the *goto* statement). Unfortunately, C++ smart pointers aren't the panacea that programmers pray for to solve their reference-counting and pointer-management problems. Smart pointers simply move these problems to a different level.

One situation in which you must be very careful with smart pointers is when you convert from code that is not smart-pointer-based to code that uses the ATL smart pointers. The problem is that the ATL smart pointers don't hide the *AddRef* and *Release* calls. This just means that you must take care to understand how the smart pointer works rather than be careful about how you call *AddRef* and *Release*.

For example, imagine taking this code:

```
void UseAnInterface(){
    IDispatch* pDispatch = NULL;

    HRESULT hr = GetTheObject(&pDispatch);
    if(SUCCEEDED(hr)) {
        DWORD dwTICount;
        pDispatch->GetTypeInfoCount(&dwTICount);
         pDispatch->Release();
    }
}
```

and capriciously converting it to use a smart pointer, like this:

```
void UseAnInterface() {
    CComPtr<IDispatch> dispatch = NULL;

    HRESULT hr = GetTheObject(&dispatch);
```

```
    if(SUCCEEDED(hr)) {
        DWORD dwTICount;
        dispatch->GetTypeInfoCount(&dwTICount);
        dispatch->Release();
    }
}
```

Because *CComPtr* and *CComQIPtr* do not hide calls to *AddRef* and *Release*, this blind conversion causes a problem when the release is called through the dispatch smart pointer. The *IDispatch* interface performs its own release, so the code above calls *Release* twice—the first time explicitly through the call *dispatch->Release()* and the second time implicitly at the function's closing curly bracket.

In addition, ATL's smart pointers include the implicit cast operator that allows smart pointers to be assigned to raw pointers. In this case, what's actually happening with the reference count starts to get confusing.

The bottom line is that even though smart pointers make some aspects of client-side COM development more convenient, they're not foolproof. You still have to have some knowledge about how smart pointers work if you want to use them safely.

Server-Side ATL Programming

Even though a fair amount of ATL is devoted to client-side development aids (such as smart pointers and BSTR wrappers), the bulk of ATL exists to support COM-based servers. Next, you'll get an overview of ATL so you can understand how the pieces fit together, then we'll reimplement the spaceship example in ATL to investigate the ATL Object Wizard and get a feel for what it takes to write COM classes using ATL.

ATL and COM Classes

Your job as a COM class developer is to wire up the function tables to their implementations and to make sure that *QueryInterface*, *AddRef*, and *Release* work as advertised. How you get that to happen is your own business. As far as users are concerned, they couldn't care less what methods you use. You've seen two basic approaches so far—the raw C++ method using multiple inheritance of interfaces and the MFC approach using macros and nested classes. The ATL approach to implementing COM classes is somewhat different from either of these approaches.

Compare the raw C++ approach to MFC's approach. Remember that one way of developing COM classes using raw C++ involves multiply inheriting a single C++ class from at least one COM interface and then writing all the code for the C++ class. At that point, you've got to add any extra features (such as supporting *IDispatch* or COM aggregation) by hand. The MFC approach to COM classes involves using macros that define nested classes (with one nested class implementing each interface). MFC supports *IDispatch* and COM aggregation—you don't have to do a lot to get those features up and running. However, it's difficult to paste any new interfaces onto a COM class without a lot of typing. (As you saw in Chapter 22, MFC's COM support uses some lengthy macros.)

The ATL approach to composing COM classes requires inheriting a C++ class from several template-based classes. However, Microsoft has already done the work of implementing *IUnknown* for you through the class templates within ATL.

Let's dive right in and create the spaceship example as a COM class. As always, start by choosing New Project from the File menu in Visual C++ .NET. In the New Project dialog box (shown in Figure 25-1), select ATL Project from the Visual C++ Projects folder. Give your project a useful name such as ATLSpaceShipSvr, and click OK. The ATL Project Wizard will launch.

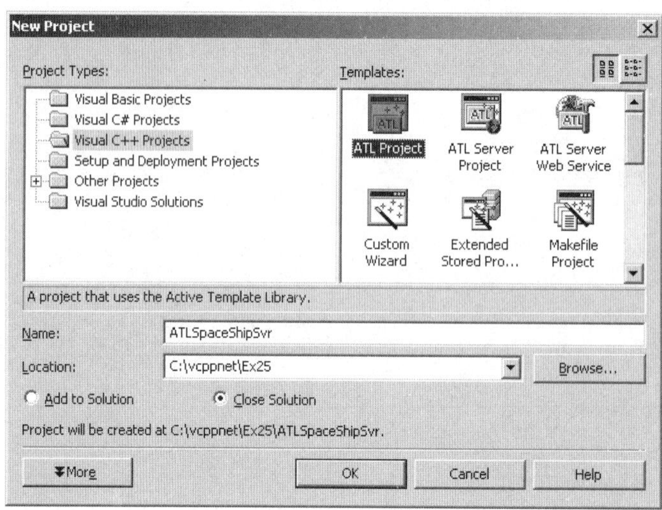

Figure 25-1 Selecting the ATL Project Wizard in the New Project dialog box.

ATL Project Options

On the Application Settings page of the ATL Project Wizard, shown in Figure 25-2, you can select the server type for your project. The wizard gives you the choice of creating a Dynamic Link Library (DLL), an executable (EXE), or a service (EXE). If you select the DLL option and deselect the Attributed option, the options for attaching the proxy/stub code to the DLL and for including MFC in your ATL project will be activated. There's also an option for supporting COM+ 1.0.

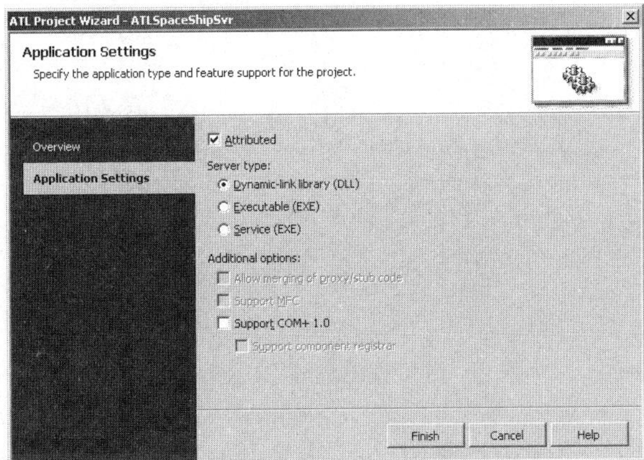

Figure 25-2 The Application Settings page of the ATL Project Wizard.

Selecting DLL as the server type will produce all the necessary pieces to make your server DLL fit into the COM milieu. Among these pieces are the following well-known COM functions: *DllGetClassObject*, *DllCanUnloadNow*, *DllRegisterServer*, and *DllUnregisterServer*. Also included are the correct server lifetime mechanisms for a DLL.

If you decide you might want to run your DLL out of process as a surrogate, select the Allow Merging Of Proxy/Stub Code option so you can package all your components into a single binary file. (Proxy/stub code has traditionally shipped as a separate DLL.) That way, you'll have to distribute only a single DLL. If you decide you absolutely must include MFC in your DLL, go ahead and select the Support MFC option. MFC support includes AfxWin.h and AfxDisp.h in your StdAfx.h file and links your project to the current version of MFC's import library. Using MFC can be very convenient and almost addictive at times, but beware of dependencies you'll inherit when you include MFC. You can also select Support COM+ 1.0 to add support for COM+ 1.0 run-time services.

If you elect to produce an executable EXE server, the ATL Project Wizard will produce code that compiles to an EXE file. The EXE will correctly register the class objects with the operating system by using *CoRegisterClassObject* and *CoRevokeClassObject*. The project will also insert the correct code for managing the lifetime of the executable server. Finally, if you select the Service (EXE) option, the wizard will add the necessary service-oriented code.

Attributed ATL vs. Classic ATL

I've mentioned the Attributed option on the Application Settings page of the ATL Project Wizard. Attributes are a new feature in Visual C++ .NET, and they're designed to simplify COM programming and .NET common language runtime development. Using attributes is like adding footnotes to your source code. By including attributes in your source files, you give the compiler instructions to work with provider DLLs to insert code or modify the code in the generated object files. These attributes help Visual C++ .NET create IDL files, interfaces, type libraries, and other COM elements. Attributes are supported by the Visual C++ .NET wizards and the Properties windows.

If you're familiar with Interface Definition Language (IDL), you'll understand attributes. Many of the separate declarations found in IDL become attributes that go directly in the source code rather than in the IDL code.

C++ was invented a long time ago—even back before Windows was a popular programming platform. As you've seen by looking at COM, C++ isn't the best solution for building DLLs and components—particularly because of all the intricacies built into the language. That's why COM exists. In many ways, COM takes the best parts of C++'s use of tables of virtual functions mapped to implementations and makes C++ DLLs distributable. Attributes go one step further.

Attributes extend C++ without breaking the classic structure of the language. Attributes let you add language functionality through provider DLLs. The primary goal of attributes is to simplify the authoring of COM components. You can apply attributes to most C++ constructs, including classes, data members, and member functions.

We'll look at classic ATL programming and at attributed ATL programming later in this chapter.

Using the ATL Project Wizard to write a lightweight COM server yields a project file for compiling your project. The project file ties together all the source code for the project and maintains the proper build instructions for each of the files.

Creating a Classic ATL COM Class

Once you've created a COM server, you're ready to start adding COM classes to the server. Fortunately, there's an easy way to do that with the ATL Simple Object Wizard, shown in Figure 25-3. To access this wizard, choose Add Class from the Project menu. Then select ATL Simple Object from among the templates.

> **Note** To create a classic COM DLL, be sure the Attributed check box is deselected on the Application Settings page of the ATL Project Wizard.

Using the ATL Simple Object Wizard to generate a new object will add a C++ source file and a header file containing the new class definition and implementation to your project. The wizard will also add an interface to the IDL code. Although the wizard takes care of pumping out a skeleton IDL file, you still need to understand IDL to some extent if you want to write effective COM interfaces (as you'll soon see).

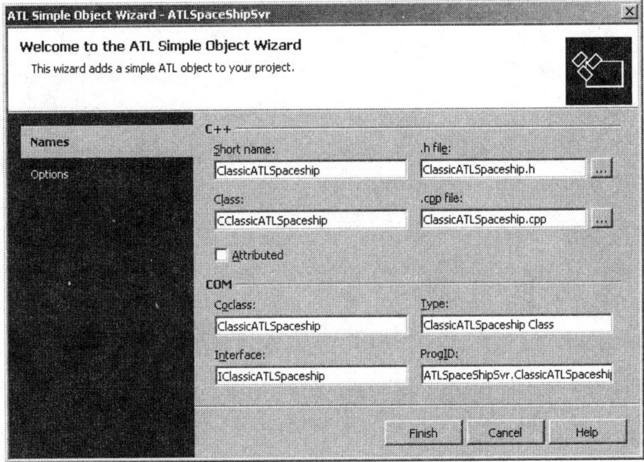

Figure 25-3 Using the ATL Simple Object Wizard to insert a new ATL-based COM class into the project.

The Options page of the ATL Simple Object Wizard allows you to select the threading model for your COM class and specify whether you want a dual (*IDispatch*-based) or a custom interface. It also allows you to choose how your class will support aggregation. The wizard also lets you easily include the *ISupportErrorInfo* interface and connection points in your class, and you can add Internet Explorer hosting support. Finally, you can aggregate to the free-threaded marshaler for objects that specify Both or Neutral as the threading model.

Apartments and Threading

To figure out COM, you have to understand that COM is centered on the notion of *abstraction*—hiding as much information as possible from the client. One piece of information that COM hides from the client is whether the COM class is thread-safe. The client should be able to use an object as it sees fit without worrying about whether an object properly serializes access to itself—that is, whether it properly protects access to its internal data. COM defines the notion of an *apartment* to provide this abstraction.

An apartment defines an execution context, or thread, that houses interface pointers. A thread enters an apartment by calling a function from the *CoInitialize* family: *CoInitialize*, *CoInitializeEx*, or *OleInitialize*. Then COM requires that all method calls to an interface pointer be executed within the apartment that initialized the pointer (in other words, from the same thread that called *CoCreateInstance*). COM defines two kinds of apartments—single-threaded apartments and multi-threaded apartments. Single-threaded apartments can house only one thread, and multi-threaded apartments can house several threads. A process can have only one multi-threaded apartment, but it can have many single-threaded apartments. An apartment can house any number of COM objects.

A single-threaded apartment guarantees that COM objects created within it will have method calls serialized through the remoting layer; a COM object created within a multi-threaded apartment will not. A helpful way to remember the difference between apartments is to think of it this way: Instantiating a COM object within the multi-threaded apartment is like putting a piece of data into the global scope where multiple threads can get to it. Instantiating a COM object within a single-threaded apartment is like putting data within the scope of only one thread. The bottom line is that COM classes that want to live in the multi-threaded apartment had better be thread-safe, and COM classes that are satisfied living in their own apartments need not worry about concurrent access to their data.

A COM object that lives within a different process space from its client has its method calls serialized automatically via the remoting layer. However, a

COM object that lives in a DLL might want to provide its own internal protection (using critical sections, for example) rather than having the remoting layer protect it. A COM class advertises its thread safety to the world via a Registry setting. This named value lives in the Registry under the CLSID under *HKEY_CLASSES_ROOT*, like this:

```
[HKCR\CLSID\{some GUID ...}\InprocServer32]
@="C:\SomeServer.DLL"
ThreadingModel=<thread model>
```

The *ThreadingModel* can be one of five values—*Single*, *Both*, *Free*, *Apartment*, or *Neutral*—or it can be blank. ATL provides support for all current threading models. Here's a rundown of what each value indicates:

- *Single* or blank indicates that the class executes in the main thread only (the first single thread created by the client).
- *Both* indicates that the class is thread-safe and can execute in both the single-threaded and multi-threaded apartments. This value tells COM to use the same kind of apartment as the client.
- *Free* indicates that the class is thread-safe. This value tells COM to force the object inside the multi-threaded apartment.
- *Apartment* indicates that the class isn't thread-safe and must live in its own single-threaded apartment.
- *Neutral* indicates that the class can live in the thread-neutral apartment. It follows the same rules as a multi-threaded class, but it can run on any thread.

When you select a threading model in the ATL Simple Object Wizard, the wizard will insert different code into your class depending on your selection. For example, if you select the Apartment model, the Object Wizard will derive your class from *CComObjectRootEx* and include *CComSingleThreadModel* as the template parameter, like this:

```
class ATL_NO_VTABLE CClassicATLSpaceship :
    public CComObjectRootEx<CComSingleThreadModel>,
    public CComCoClass<CClassicATLSpaceship,
                       &CLSID_ClassicATLSpaceship>,
    public IDispatchImpl<IClassicATLSpaceship,
                        &IID_IClassicATLSpaceship,
                        &LIBID_SPACESHIPSVRLib>
{
:
};
```

The *CComSingleThreadModel* template parameter mixes in the more efficient standard increment and decrement operations for *IUnknown* (because access to the class is automatically serialized). In addition, the ATL Simple Object Wizard will cause the class to insert the correct threading model value in the Registry. If you select the Single option in the wizard, the class will use the *CComSingleThreadModel* but leave the *ThreadingModel* value blank in the Registry.

Selecting the Both option or the Free option will cause the class to use the *CComMultiThreadModel* template parameter, which employs the thread-safe Win32 increment and decrement operations *InterlockedIncrement* and *InterlockedDecrement*. For example, a free-threaded class definition looks like this:

```
class ATL_NO_VTABLE CClassicATLSpaceship :
    public CComObjectRootEx<CComMultiThreadModel>,
    public CComCoClass<CClassicATLSpaceship,
                       &CLSID_ClassicATLSpaceship>,
    public IDispatchImpl<IClassicATLSpaceship,
                         &IID_IClassicATLSpaceship,
                         &LIBID_SPACESHIPSVRLib>
{
⋮
};
```

Selecting the Both threading model will insert *Both* as the data for the *ThreadingModel* value; selecting Free will insert the data value *Free* for the *ThreadingModel* value.

Connection Points and *ISupportErrorInfo*

Adding connection to your COM class is easy. Selecting the Connection Points check box causes the class to derive from *IConnectionPointImpl*. This option also adds a blank connection map to your class. Adding connection points (for example, an event set) to your class is simply a matter of performing the following four steps:

1. Define the callback interface in the IDL file.
2. Use the ATL proxy generator to create a proxy.
3. Add the proxy class to the COM class.
4. Add the connection points to the connection point map.

ATL also includes support for *ISupportErrorInfo*. The *ISupportErrorInfo* interface ensures that error information is propagated up the call chain correctly.

OLE Automation objects that use the error-handling interfaces must implement *ISupportErrorInfo*. Selecting Support ISupportErrorInfo in the ATL Simple Object Wizard will cause the ATL-based class to derive from *ISupportErrorInfoImpl*.

The Free-Threaded Marshaler

You can select the Free Threaded Marshaler option to aggregate the COM free-threaded marshaler to your class. As mentioned, this option is available only for objects that specify Both or Neutral as the threading model. The generated class does this by calling *CoCreateFreeThreadedMarshaler* in its *FinalConstruct* function. The free-threaded marshaler allows thread-safe objects to bypass the standard marshaling that occurs whenever cross-apartment interface methods are invoked, allowing threads living in one apartment to access interface methods in another apartment as if they were in the same apartment.

This process speeds up cross-apartment calls tremendously. The free-threaded marshaler does this by implementing the *IMarshal* interface. When the client asks the object for an interface, the remoting layer calls *QueryInterface*, asking for *IMarshal*. If the object implements *IMarshal* (in this case, the object implements *IMarshal* because the ATL Simple Object Wizard also adds an entry into the class's interface to handle *QueryInterface* requests for *IMarshal*) and the marshaling request is in process, the free-threaded marshaler will actually copy the pointer into the marshaling packet. That way, the client will receive an actual pointer to the object. The client can talk to the object directly without having to go through proxies and stubs. Of course, if you select the Free Threaded Marshaler option, all data in your object had better be thread-safe. Just be very cautious if you check this box.

Implementing the Spaceship Class Using Classic ATL

We'll create the spaceship class using the defaults provided by the ATL Simple Object Wizard. For example, the spaceship class will have a dual interface, so it will be accessible from environments such as JScript on a Web page. In addition, the spaceship class will be an apartment model object, which means that COM will manage most of the concurrency issues. The only information you need to supply to the ATL Simple Object Wizard is a clever name. Enter a value such as **ClassicATLSpaceship** in the Short Name text box on the Names page.

You don't need to set any of the other options right now. For instance, you don't need to set the Connection Points option because we'll cover connections in the next chapter. You can always add connection points later by typing them in by hand.

Here's the class definition generated by the wizard:

```
// CClassicATLSpaceship

class ATL_NO_VTABLE CClassicATLSpaceship :
    public CComObjectRootEx<CComSingleThreadModel>,
    public CComCoClass<CClassicATLSpaceship,
                      &CLSID_ClassicATLSpaceship>,
    public IDispatchImpl<IClassicATLSpaceship,
        &IID_IClassicATLSpaceship,
        &LIBID_ATLSpaceShipSvrLib, /*wMajor =*/ 1, /*wMinor =*/ 0>
{
public:
:
};
```

ATL includes quite a few COM-oriented C++ classes, but those listed in the spaceship class's inheritance list above are enough to give you a sense of how ATL works.

The most generic ATL-based COM objects derive from three base classes: *CComObjectRoot*, *CComCoClass*, and *IDispatch*. *CComObjectRoot* implements *IUnknown* and manages the identity of the class. This means that *CComObjectRoot* implements *AddRef* and *Release* and hooks into ATL's *QueryInterface* mechanism. *CComCoClass* manages the COM class's class object and some general error reporting. In the class definition above, *CComCoClass* adds the class object that knows how to create *CClassicATLSpaceship* objects. Finally, the code produced by the ATL Simple Object Wizard includes an implementation of *IDispatch* based on the type library produced by compiling the IDL. The default *IDispatch* is based on a dual interface (which is an *IDispatch* interface followed by the functions defined in the IDL).

As you can see, using ATL to implement COM classes is different from using pure C++. The Tao of ATL differs from what you might be used to when you develop normal C++ classes. With classic ATL, the most important part of the project is the interfaces, which are described in IDL. By adding functions to the interfaces in the IDL code, you automatically add functions to the concrete classes implementing the interfaces. The functions are added automatically because the projects are set up such that compiling the IDL file yields a C++ header file with those functions. All that's left for you to do after adding the functions in the interface is to implement those functions in the C++ class. The IDL file also provides a type library so the COM class can implement *IDispatch*. However, while ATL is useful for implementing lightweight COM services and objects, it is also a new means by which you can create ActiveX controls, as you'll see in the next chapter.

Basic ATL Architecture

If you've experimented at all with ATL, you've seen how it simplifies the process of implementing COM classes. The tool support is quite good—it's almost as easy to develop COM classes using Visual C++ .NET as it is to create MFC-based programs. You just use the ATL Project Wizard to create a server and the ATL Simple Object Wizard to create a new ATL-based class. As with MFC, you use Class View to add new function definitions to an interface. Then you simply fill in the functions within the C++ code generated by Class View. The code generated by the ATL Project Wizard includes all the necessary code for implementing your class, including an implementation of *IUnknown*, a server module to house your COM class, and a class object that implements *IClassFactory*.

Writing COM objects as just described is certainly more convenient than most other methods. But exactly what happens when you use the ATL Project Wizard to generate the code for you? Understanding how classic ATL works is important if you want to extend your ATL-based COM classes and servers much beyond what the ATL Project Wizard and Class View provide. For example, ATL provides support for advanced interface techniques such as tear-off interfaces. Unfortunately, there's no wizard option for implementing a tear-off interface. Even though ATL supports it, you've got to do a little work by hand to accomplish the tear-off interface. Understanding how ATL implements *IUnknown* is helpful in this situation.

Let's examine the *CClassicATLSpaceship* class in a bit more detail. Here's the entire definition:

```
// CClassicATLSpaceship
class ATL_NO_VTABLE CClassicATLSpaceship :
    public CComObjectRootEx<CComSingleThreadModel>,
    public CComCoClass<CClassicATLSpaceship,
                       &CLSID_ClassicATLSpaceship>,
    public IDispatchImpl<IClassicATLSpaceship,
        &IID_IClassicATLSpaceship,
        &LIBID_ATLSpaceShipSvrLib, /*wMajor =*/ 1, /*wMinor =*/ 0>
{
public:
    CClassicATLSpaceship()
    {
    }

DECLARE_REGISTRY_RESOURCEID(IDR_CLASSICATLSPACESHIP)

BEGIN_COM_MAP(CClassicATLSpaceship)
    COM_INTERFACE_ENTRY(IClassicATLSpaceship)
```

(continued)

```
    COM_INTERFACE_ENTRY(IDispatch)
END_COM_MAP()

    DECLARE_PROTECT_FINAL_CONSTRUCT()

    HRESULT FinalConstruct()
    {
        return S_OK;
    }
    void FinalRelease()
    {
    }
public:
};

OBJECT_ENTRY_AUTO(__uuidof(ClassicATLSpaceship), CClassicATLSpaceship)
```

While this is ordinary vanilla C++ source code, it differs from normal, everyday C++ source code for implementing a COM object in several ways. For example, while many COM class implementations derive strictly from COM interfaces, this COM class derives from several templates. In addition, this C++ class uses several odd-looking macros. As you examine the code, you'll see ATL's implementation of *IUnknown* as well as a few other interesting items, such as a technique for managing vtable bloat and an uncommon use for templates. Let's start by taking a look at the first symbol in the wizard-generated macro code: *ATL_NO_VTABLE*.

Managing Vtable Bloat

COM interfaces are easily expressed in C++ as pure abstract base classes. Writing COM classes that use multiple inheritance (there are other ways to write COM classes) is merely a matter of adding the COM interface base classes to your inheritance list and implementing the union of all the functions. Of course, this means that the memory footprint of your COM server will include a significant amount of vtable overhead for each interface implemented by your class. That's not a big deal if you have only a few interfaces and your C++ class hierarchy isn't very deep. However, implementing interfaces this way does add overhead that tends to accumulate as interfaces are added and hierarchies deepen. ATL provides a way to cut down on some of the overhead introduced by a lot of virtual functions. ATL defines the following symbol:

```
#define ATL_NO_VTABLE  __declspec(novtable)
```

Using *ATL_NO_VTABLE* prevents an object's vtable (*vtable*) from being initialized in the constructor, thereby eliminating from the linker the vtable and all the functions pointed to by the vtable for that class. This elimination can lower the size of your COM server somewhat, as long as the most-derived class does not use the *novtable declspec* shown above. You'll notice the size difference in classes with deep derivation lists. One caveat, however: Calling virtual functions from the constructor of any object that uses this *declspec* is unsafe because *vptr* is uninitialized.

The second line in the class declaration previously shown demonstrates that *CClassicATLSpaceship* derives from *CComObjectRootEx*. This is where you get to ATL's version of *IUnknown*.

ATL's *IUnknown*: *CComObjectRootEx*

CComObjectRootEx isn't at the top of the ATL hierarchy, but it's pretty close. The actual base class for a COM object in ATL is a class named *CComObjectRootBase*. (Both class definitions are located in AtlCom.h.) Looking at *CComObjectRootBase* reveals the code you might expect for a C++-based COM class. *CComObjectRootBase* includes a DWORD member named *m_dwRef* for reference counting. You'll also see *OuterAddRef*, *OuterRelease*, and *OuterQueryInterface* for supporting COM aggregation and tear-off interfaces. Looking at *CComObjectRootEx* reveals *InternalAddRef*, *InternalRelease*, and *InternalQueryInterface* for performing the regular native reference counting, and *QueryInterface* mechanisms for class instances with object identity.

Notice that *CClassicATLSpaceship*'s definition shows that the class is derived from *CComObjectRootEx* and that *CComObjectRootEx* is a parameterized template class. The following listing shows the definition of *CComObjectRootEx*:

```
template <class ThreadModel>
class CComObjectRootEx : public CComObjectRootBase
{
public:
    typedef ThreadModel _ThreadModel;
    typedef _ThreadModel::AutoCriticalSection _CritSec;
    typedef CComObjectLockT<_ThreadModel> ObjectLock;

    ULONG InternalAddRef()
    {
        ATLASSERT(m_dwRef != -1L);
        return _ThreadModel::Increment(&m_dwRef);
    }
    ULONG InternalRelease()
    {
#ifdef _DEBUG
        LONG nRef = _ThreadModel::Decrement(&m_dwRef);
```

(continued)

```
        if (nRef < -(LONG_MAX / 2))
        {
            ATLASSERT(0 && _T("Release called on a pointer "
                                "that has already been released"));
        }
        return nRef;
#else
        return _ThreadModel::Decrement(&m_dwRef);
#endif
    }

    void Lock() {m_critsec.Lock();}
    void Unlock() {m_critsec.Unlock();}
private:
    _CritSec m_critsec;
};
```

CComObjectRootEx is a template class that varies in type based on the kind of threading model class passed in as the template parameter. In fact, ATL supports several threading models: single-threaded apartments, multi-threaded apartments, and free threading. ATL includes three preprocessor symbols for selecting the various default threading models for your project: *_ATL_SINGLE_THREADED*, *_ATL_APARTMENT_THREADED*, and *_ATL_FREE_THREADED*.

Defining the preprocessor symbol *_ATL_SINGLE_THREADED* in Stdafx.h changes the default threading model to support only one STA-based thread. This option is useful for out-of-process servers that don't create any extra threads. Because the server supports only one thread, ATL's global state can remain unprotected by critical sections and the server will therefore be more efficient. The downside is that your server can support only one thread. Defining *_ATL_APARTMENT_THREADED* for the preprocessor will cause the default threading model to support multiple STA-based threads. This is useful for apartment model in-process servers (servers that support the *ThreadingModel=Apartment* Registry value). Because a server that employs this threading model can support multiple threads, ATL protects its global state using critical sections. Finally, defining the *_ATL_FREE_THREADED* preprocessor symbol creates servers compatible with any threading environment. That is, ATL protects its global state using critical sections, and each object in the server will have its own critical sections to maintain data safety.

These preprocessor symbols merely determine which threading class to plug into *CComObjectRootEx* as a template parameter. ATL provides three threading model classes. The classes provide support for the most efficient yet thread-safe behavior for COM classes within each of the three contexts listed above. The three classes are *CComMultiThreadModelNoCS*, *CComMultiThread-*

Model, and *CComSingleThreadModel*. The following listing shows the three threading model classes within ATL:

```
class CComMultiThreadModelNoCS
{
public:
    static ULONG WINAPI Increment(LPLONG p) throw()
        {return InterlockedIncrement(p);}
    static ULONG WINAPI Decrement(LPLONG p) throw()
        {return InterlockedDecrement(p);}
    typedef CComFakeCriticalSection AutoCriticalSection;
    typedef CComFakeCriticalSection CriticalSection;
    typedef CComMultiThreadModelNoCS ThreadModelNoCS;
};

class CComMultiThreadModel
{
public:
    static ULONG WINAPI Increment(LPLONG p) throw()
        {return InterlockedIncrement(p);}
    static ULONG WINAPI Decrement(LPLONG p) throw()
        {return InterlockedDecrement(p);}
    typedef CComAutoCriticalSection AutoCriticalSection;
    typedef CComCriticalSection CriticalSection;
    typedef CComMultiThreadModelNoCS ThreadModelNoCS;
};

class CComSingleThreadModel
{
public:
    static ULONG WINAPI Increment(LPLONG p) throw() {return ++(*p);}
    static ULONG WINAPI Decrement(LPLONG p) throw() {return --(*p);}
    typedef CComFakeCriticalSection AutoCriticalSection;
    typedef CComFakeCriticalSection CriticalSection;
    typedef CComSingleThreadModel ThreadModelNoCS;
};
```

Notice that each of these classes exports two static functions—*Increment* and *Decrement*—and various aliases for critical sections.

CComMultiThreadModel and *CComMultiThreadModelNoCS* both implement *Increment* and *Decrement* using the thread-safe Win32 *InterlockedIncrement* and *InterlockedDecrement* functions. *CComSingleThreadModel* implements Increment and Decrement using the more conventional ++ and -- operators.

In addition to implementing incrementing and decrementing differently, the three threading models also manage critical sections differently. ATL provides wrappers for two critical sections—a *CComCriticalSection* (which is a plain wrapper around the Win32 critical section API) and *CComAutoCriticalSection* (which is the same as *CComCriticalSection* with the addition of automatic initialization and cleanup of critical sections). ATL also defines a "fake" critical section class that has the same binary signature as the other critical section classes but doesn't do anything. As you can see from the class definitions, *CComMultiThreadModel* uses real critical sections while *CComMultiThreadModelNoCS* and *CComSingleThreadModel* use the fake no-op critical sections.

So now the minimal ATL class definition makes a bit more sense. *CComObjectRootEx* takes a thread model class whenever you define it. *CClassicATLSpaceship* is defined using the *CComSingleThreadModel* class, so it uses the *CComSingleThreadModel* methods for incrementing and decrementing as well as the fake no-op critical sections. Thus *CClassicATLSpaceship* uses the most efficient behavior because it doesn't need to worry about protecting data. However, you're not stuck with that model. If you want to make *CClassicATLSpaceship* safe for any threading environment, for example, you simply redefine *CClassicATLSpaceship* to derive from *CComObjectRootEx* using *CComMultiThreadModel* as the template parameter. *AddRef* and *Release* calls are automatically mapped to the correct *Increment* and *Decrement* functions.

ATL and *QueryInterface*

It looks as though ATL took a cue from MFC for implementing *QueryInterface*—ATL uses a lookup table just like MFC's version. Take a look at the middle of *CClassicATLSpaceship*'s definition—you'll see a construct based on macros called the *interface map*. ATL's interface maps constitute its *QueryInterface* mechanism.

Clients use *QueryInterface* to arbitrarily widen the connection to an object. That is, when a client needs a new interface, it will call *QueryInterface* through an existing interface. The object will then look at the name of the requested interface and compare it to all the interfaces implemented by the object. If the object implements the interface, it will hand the interface back to the client. Otherwise, *QueryInterface* will return an error indicating that no interface was found.

Traditional *QueryInterface* implementations usually consist of long if-then statements. For example, a standard implementation of *QueryInterface* for a multiple-inheritance COM class might look like this:

```
class CClassicATLSpaceship: public IDispatch,
                                   IClassicATLSpaceship {
    HRESULT QueryInterface(RIID riid,
                           void** ppv) {
        if(riid == IID_IDispatch)
```

```
            *ppv = (IDispatch*) this;
        else if(riid == IID_IClassicATLSpaceship ||
                riid == IID_IUnknown)
            *ppv = (IClassicATLSpaceship *) this;
        else {
            *ppv = 0;
            return E_NOINTERFACE;
        }

        ((IUnknown*)(*ppv))->AddRef();
        return NOERROR;
    }
    // AddRef, Release, and other functions
};
```

As you'll see in a moment, ATL uses a lookup table instead of this conventional if-then statement.

ATL's lookup table begins with a macro named *BEGIN_COM_MAP*. The following listing shows the full definition of *BEGIN_COM_MAP*:

```
#define BEGIN_COM_MAP(x) public: \
    typedef x _ComMapClass; \
    static HRESULT WINAPI _Cache(void* pv, \
        REFIID iid, void** ppvObject, \
        DWORD_PTR dw) throw() \
    { \
        _ComMapClass* p = (_ComMapClass*)pv; \
        p->Lock(); \
        HRESULT hRes = \
            ATL::CComObjectRootBase::_Cache(pv, iid, ppvObject, dw); \
        p->Unlock(); \
        return hRes; \
    } \
    IUnknown* _GetRawUnknown() throw() \
    { ATLASSERT(_GetEntries()[0].pFunc == _ATL_SIMPLEMAPENTRY); \
        return (IUnknown*)((INT_PTR)this+_GetEntries()->dw); } \
    _ATL_DECLARE_GET_UNKNOWN(x) \
    HRESULT _InternalQueryInterface(REFIID iid, \
        void** ppvObject) throw() \
    { return InternalQueryInterface(this, \
        _GetEntries(), iid, ppvObject); } \
    const static ATL::_ATL_INTMAP_ENTRY* WINAPI _GetEntries() \
        throw() { \
    static const ATL::_ATL_INTMAP_ENTRY _entries[] = \
        { DEBUG_QI_ENTRY(x)
```

Each class that uses ATL for implementing *IUnknown* specifies an interface map to provide to *InternalQueryInterface*. ATL's interface maps consist of structures containing interface ID (GUID)/DWORD/function pointer tuples. The following listing shows the type named *_ATL_INTMAP_ENTRY* that contains these tuples:

```
struct _ATL_INTMAP_ENTRY
{
    const IID* piid;       // the interface id (IID)
    DWORD_PTR dw;
    _ATL_CREATORARGFUNC* pFunc; //NULL:end, 1:offset, n:ptr
};
```

The first member is the interface ID (a GUID), and the second member indicates what action to take when the interface is queried. There are three ways to interpret the third member. If *pFunc* is equal to the constant *_ATL_SIMPLEMAPENTRY* (the value 1), *dw* is an offset into the object. If *pFunc* is non-null but not equal to 1, *pFunc* indicates a function to be called when the interface is queried. If *pFunc* is *NULL*, *dw* indicates the end of the *QueryInterface* lookup table.

Notice that *CClassicATLSpaceship* uses *COM_INTERFACE_ENTRY*. This is the interface map entry for regular interfaces. Here's the raw macro:

```
#define offsetofclass(base, derived) \
    ((DWORD_PTR) \
    (static_cast<base*>((derived*)_ATL_PACKING))-_ATL_PACKING)

#define COM_INTERFACE_ENTRY(x) \
    {&_ATL_IIDOF(x), \
    offsetofclass(x, _ComMapClass), \
    _ATL_SIMPLEMAPENTRY}
```

COM_INTERFACE_ENTRY fills the *_ATL_INTMAP_ENTRY* structure with the interface's GUID. In addition, notice how *offsetofclass* casts the *this* pointer to the right kind of interface and fills the *dw* member with that value. Finally, *COM_INTERFACE_ENTRY* fills the last field with *_ATL_SIMPLEMAPENTRY* to indicate that *dw* points to an offset into the class.

For example, the interface map for *CClassicATLSpaceship* looks like this after the preprocessor is done with it:

```
const static _ATL_INTMAP_ENTRY* __stdcall _GetEntries() {
    static const _ATL_INTMAP_ENTRY _entries[] = {
        {&IID_IClassicATLSpaceship,
         ((DWORD)(static_cast<IClassicATLSpaceship*>
             ((_ComMapClass*)8))-8),
        ((_ATL_CREATORARGFUNC*)1)},
        {&IID_IDispatch,
```

```
        ((DWORD)(static_cast<IDispatch*>((_ComMapClass*)8))-8),
        ((_ATL_CREATORARGFUNC*)1)},
        {0, 0, 0}
    };
    return _entries;
}
```

Right now, the *CClassicATLSpaceship* class supports two interfaces—*IClassicATLSpaceship* and *IDispatch*—so there are only two entries in the map.

CComObjectRootEx's implementation of *InternalQueryInterface* uses the *_GetEntries* function as the second parameter. *CComObjectRootEx::InternalQueryInterface* uses a global ATL function named *AtlInternalQueryInterface* to look up the interface in the map. *AtlInternalQueryInterface* simply walks through the map, trying to find the interface.

In addition to *COM_INTERFACE_ENTRY*, ATL includes 16 other macros for implementing composition techniques ranging from tear-off interfaces to COM aggregation. Now you'll see what it takes to beef up the *IClassicATLSpaceship* interface and add those two other interfaces, *IMotion* and *IVisual*. You'll also learn about the strange COM beast known as a dual interface.

Making the Spaceship Go

Now that you've got some ATL code staring you in the face, what can you do with it? This is COM, so the place to start is in the IDL file. Again, if you're a seasoned C++ developer, this is a new aspect of software development you're probably not used to. Remember that these days, software distribution and integration are becoming very important. You've been able to get away with hacking out C++ classes and throwing them together into a project because you (as a developer) know the entire picture. However, component technologies (such as COM) change that. The developer no longer knows the entire picture. Often you have only a component—you don't have the source code for the component. The only way to know how to talk to a component is through the interfaces it exposes.

Keep in mind that modern software developers use many different tools—not just C++. You've got Visual Basic developers, Delphi developers, and C developers. COM is all about making the edges line up so that software pieces created by these various components can all integrate smoothly when they come together. In addition, distributing software remotely (either out-of-process on the same machine or even to a different machine) requires some sort of interprocess communication. That's why there's IDL. Here's the default IDL file created by the ATL wizards with the new spaceship class:

```
import "oaidl.idl";
import "ocidl.idl";

[
    object,
    uuid(45896187-46FF-4A07-A9DC-557377380535),
    dual,
    nonextensible,
    helpstring("IClassicATLSpaceship Interface"),
    pointer_default(unique)
]
interface IClassicATLSpaceship : IDispatch{
};
[
    uuid(F5FD4043-22AE-470D-8C43-1AC904D2E8E0),
    version(1.0),
    helpstring("ATLSpaceShipSvr 1.0 Type Library")
]
library ATLSpaceShipSvrLib
{
    importlib("stdole2.tlb");
    [
        uuid(E485E21E-A23C-413F-A93B-909318565113),
        helpstring("ClassicATLSpaceship Class")
    ]
    coclass ClassicATLSpaceship
    {
        [default] interface IClassicATLSpaceship;
    };
};
```

The key concept involved here is that IDL is a purely declarative language. This language defines how other clients will talk to an object. Remember that you'll eventually run this code through the MIDL compiler to get a pure abstract base class (which is useful for C++ clients) and a type library (which is useful for Visual Basic and Java clients as well as others). If you understand plain C code, you're well on your way to understanding IDL. You might think of IDL as C with footnotes. The syntax of IDL dictates that attributes always precede what they describe. For example, attributes precede items such as interface declarations, library declarations, and method parameters.

If you look at the IDL file, you'll notice that it begins by importing Oaidl.idl and Ocidl.idl. Importing these files is somewhat akin to including Windows.h inside one of your C or C++ files. These IDL files include definitions for all of the basic COM infrastructures (including definitions for *IUnknown* and *IDispatch*).

An open square bracket ([) follows the *import* statement. In IDL, square brackets always enclose attributes. The first element described in this IDL file is the *IClassicATLSpaceship* interface. However, before you can describe the interface, you must apply some attributes to it. For example, it needs a name (a GUID), and you need to tell the MIDL compiler that this interface is COM-oriented rather than being used for standard remote procedure call (RPC) and that this is a dual interface. (More on dual interfaces shortly.) Next comes the actual interface itself. Notice how it appears very much like a normal C structure.

Once the interfaces are described in IDL, it can be useful to collect this information into a type library, which is what the next section of the IDL file does. Notice that the type library section also begins with an open square bracket, which designates that attributes are to follow. As always, the type library is a discrete "thing" in COM and as such requires a name (GUID). The library statement tells the MIDL compiler that this library includes a COM class named *ClassicATLSpaceship* and that clients of this class can acquire the *IClassicATLSpaceship* interface.

Adding Methods to an Interface

Right now, the *IClassicATLSpaceship* interface is pretty sparse. It looks as if it could use a method or two. Let's add one. When we added automation properties to the MFC-based COM classes, we used Class View. We'll do the same with ATL. Notice also that *CClassicATLSpaceship* derives from something named *IClassicATLSpaceship*. *IClassicATLSpaceship* is, of course, a COM interface. Double-clicking on *IClassicATLSpaceship* in Class View brings that specific section of the IDL into the editor window.

At this point, you could begin typing the COM interface into the IDL file. If you were to add functions and methods in this way (straight into the IDL file), you'd have to touch the ClassicATLSpaceship.h and ClassicATLSpaceship.cpp files and insert the methods by hand. A more effective way to add functions to the interface is through Class View, using the Add Method Wizard (shown in Figure 25-4). To edit the IDL using Class View, right-click on the interface in Class View. You'll see the Add Method and Add Property commands on the shortcut menu. Let's add a method named *CallStarFleet*.

To add a method, you simply type the name of the method in the Method Name text box. Then you type the method parameters into the Parameter Name and Parameter Type text boxes. Here's where it helps to understand a little bit about IDL.

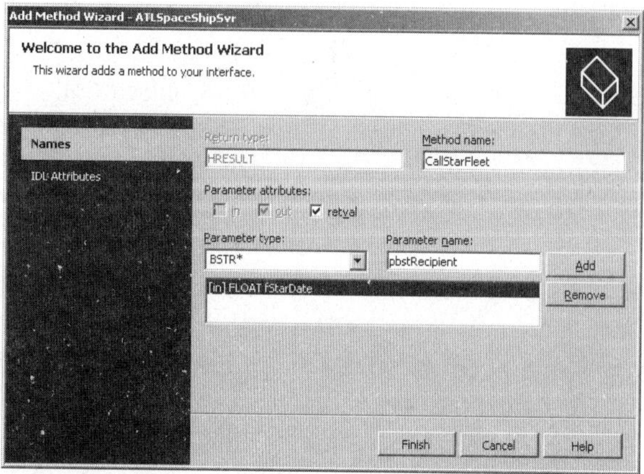

Figure 25-4 Adding a method to an interface.

Remember that IDL's purpose is to provide completely unambiguous information about how methods can be invoked. In the standard C++ world, you could often get away with ambiguities such as open-ended arrays because the caller and the callee shared the same stack frame—there was always a lot of wiggle room available. Now that method calls might eventually go over the wire, it's important to tell the remoting layer exactly what to expect when it encounters a COM interface. You do this by applying attributes to the method parameters (more square brackets).

The method call shown in Figure 25-4 (*CallStarFleet*) has two parameters in its list—a floating point number that indicates the star date and a BSTR that indicates who received the communication. Notice that the method definition spells out the parameter direction. The star date is passed into the method call, which is designated by the *[in]* attribute. A BSTR that identifies the recipient is passed back as a pointer to a BSTR. The *[out]* attribute indicates that the direction of the parameter is from the object back to the client. The *[retval]* attribute indicates that you can assign the result of this method to a variable in higher languages that support this feature.

Dual Interfaces

In Chapter 23, you had a chance to see the *IDispatch* interface. *IDispatch* makes it possible to expose functionality (at the binary level) to environments such as JScript that don't have a clue about vtables. In order for *IDispatch* to work, the client has to go through a lot of machinations before it can call *Invoke*. The client first has to acquire the invocation tokens. Then it has to set up the *VARIANT* arguments. On the object side, the object has to decode all those *VARIANT* parameters, make sure they're correct, put them on some sort of stack frame, and then make the function call. As you can imagine, all this work is complex and time-consuming.

If you're writing a COM object and you expect some of your clients to use scripting languages and other clients to use languages such as C++, you've got a dilemma. You've got to include *IDispatch* or you'll lock out your scripting language clients. If you provide only *IDispatch*, you'll make accessing your object from C++ very inconvenient. Of course, you can provide access through both *IDispatch* and a custom interface, but that involves a lot of bookkeeping work. Dual interfaces evolved to handle this problem.

A dual interface is simply *IDispatch* with functions pasted onto the end. For example, the *IMotion* interface described below is a valid dual interface:

```
interface IMotion : public IDispatch {
    virtual HRESULT Fly() = 0;
    virtual HRESULT GetPosition() = 0;
};
```

Because *IMotion* derives from *IDispatch*, the first seven functions of *IMotion* are those of *IDispatch*. Clients that understand only *IDispatch* (JScript, for instance) look at the interface as just another version of *IDispatch* and feed DISPIDs to the *Invoke* function in the hopes of invoking a function. Clients that understand vtable-style custom interfaces look at the entire interface, ignore the middle four functions (the *IDispatch* functions), and concentrate on the first three functions (*IUnknown*) and the last three functions (the ones that represent the interface's core functions). Figure 25-5 shows the vtable layout of *IMotion*.

Most raw C++ implementations load the type library right away and delegate to *ITypeInfo* to perform the nasty task of implementing *Invoke* and *GetIDsOfNames*. To get an idea of how this works, see Kraig Brockschmidt's *Inside OLE*, 2d. ed. (Microsoft Press, 1995) or Dale Rogerson's *Inside COM* (Microsoft Press, 1997).

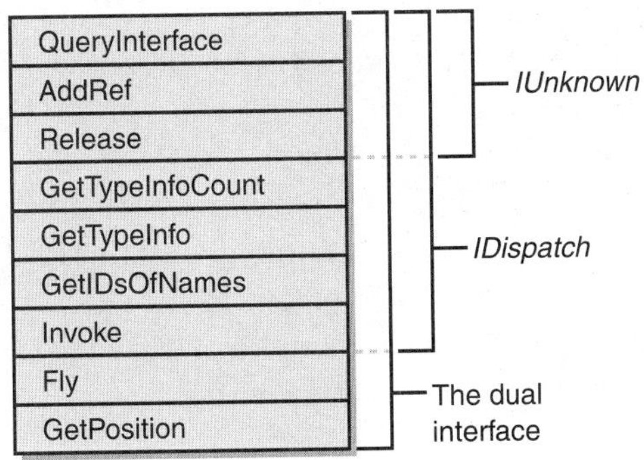

Figure 25-5 The layout of a dual interface.

ATL and *IDispatch*

ATL's implementation of *IDispatch* delegates to the type library. ATL's implementation of *IDispatch* lives in the class *IDispatchImpl*. Objects that want to implement a dual interface include the *IDispatchImpl* template in the inheritance list, like this:

```
class ATL_NO_VTABLE CClassicATLSpaceship :
    public CComObjectRootEx<CComSingleThreadModel>,
    public CComCoClass<CClassicATLSpaceship, &CLSID_ClassicATLSpaceship>,
    public IDispatchImpl<IClassicATLSpaceship, &IID_IClassicATLSpaceship,
                         &LIBID_SPACESHIPSVRLib>,
    public IDispatchImpl<IVisual, &IID_IVisual,
                         &LIBID_SPACESHIPSVRLib>,
    public IDispatchImpl<IMotion, &IID_IMotion,
                         &LIBID_SPACESHIPSVRLib>
{
:
};
```

In addition to including the *IDispatchImpl* template class in the inheritance list, the object includes entries for the dual interface and for *IDispatch* in the interface map so that *QueryInterface* works properly:

```
BEGIN_COM_MAP(CClassicATLSpaceship)
    COM_INTERFACE_ENTRY(IClassicATLSpaceship)
    COM_INTERFACE_ENTRY(IDispatch)
END_COM_MAP()
```

As you can see, the *IDispatchImpl* template class arguments include the dual interface itself, the GUID for the interface, and the GUID representing the type library that holds all the information about the interface. In addition to these template arguments, the *IDispatchImpl* class has some optional parameters not illustrated in Figure 25-5. The template parameter list also includes room for a major and minor version of the type library. Finally, the last template parameter is a class for managing the type information. ATL provides a default class named *CComTypeInfoHolder*.

In most raw C++ implementations of *IDispatch*, the class calls *LoadTypeLib* and *ITypeLib::GetTypeInfoOfGuid* in the constructor and holds on to the *ITypeInfo* pointer for the life of the class. ATL's implementation does things a little differently by using the *CComTypeInfoHolder* class to help manage the *ITypeInfo* pointer. *CComTypeInfoHolder* maintains an *ITypeInfo* pointer as a data member and wraps the critical *IDispatch*-related functions *GetIDsOfNames* and *Invoke*.

Clients acquire the dual interface by calling *QueryInterface* for *IID_IClassicATLSpaceship*. (The client can also get this interface by calling *QueryInterface* for *IDispatch*.) If the client calls *CallStarFleet* on the interface, the client will access those functions directly (as it would for any other COM interface).

When a client calls *IDispatch::Invoke*, the call lands inside *IDispatchImpl*'s *Invoke* function, as you'd expect. From there, *IDispatchImpl::Invoke* delegates to the *CComTypeInfoHolder* class to perform the invocation, the *CComTypeInfoHolder* class's *Invoke* function. The *CComTypeInfoHolder* class doesn't call *LoadTypeLib* until an actual call to *Invoke* or *GetIDsOfNames*. *CComTypeInfoHolder* has a member function named *GetTI* that consults the Registry for the type information (using the GUID and any major/minor version numbers passed in as a template parameter). Then *CComTypeInfoHolder* calls *ITypeLib::GetTypeInfo* to get the information about the interface. At that point, the type information holder delegates to the type information pointer. *IDispatchImpl* implements *IDispatch::GetIDsOfNames* in the same manner.

The *IMotion* and *IVisual* Interfaces

To get this COM class up to snuff with the other versions (the raw C++ version and the MFC version described in Chapter 22), you must add the *IMotion* and *IVisual* interfaces to the project and to the class. Unfortunately, Visual Studio .NET doesn't provide a wizard for adding an interface to a project. To get this to happen, you can use the ATL Simple Object Wizard to add a simple object. Alternatively, you can type the interfaces in by hand. Open the IDL file and position the cursor near the top (somewhere after the *#import* statements but before the *library* statement), and start typing interface definitions as described in the following paragraph.

Once you get the hang of IDL, your first instinct when you describe an interface should be to insert an open square bracket. Remember that in IDL, distinct items get attributes. One of the most important attributes for an interface is the name, or the GUID. In addition, at the very least the interface must have the *object* attribute to tell the MIDL compiler you're dealing with COM at this point (as opposed to regular RPC). You also want these interfaces to be dual interfaces. The keyword *dual* in the interface attributes indicates this and inserts certain Registry entries to get the universal marshaling working correctly. After the attributes are closed off with a closing square bracket, the interface keyword kicks in to describe the interface.

We'll make *IMotion* a dual interface and *IVisual* a plain custom interface to illustrate how the two different types of interfaces are attached to the *CSpaceship* class. Here are the *IMotion* and *IVisual* interfaces described in IDL:

```
[
    object,
    uuid(692D03A4-C689-11CE-B337-88EA36DE9E4E),
    dual,
    helpstring("IMotion interface")
]
interface IMotion : IDispatch
{
    HRESULT Fly();
    HRESULT GetPosition([out,retval]long* nPosition);
};

[
    object,
    uuid(692D03A5-C689-11CE-B337-88EA36DE9E4E),
    helpstring("IVisual interface")
]
interface IVisual : IUnknown
{
    HRESULT Display();
};
```

Once the interfaces are described in IDL, you run the IDL through the MIDL compiler again. The MIDL compiler will spit out a new copy of Spaceshipsvr.h with the pure abstract base classes for *IMotion* and *IVisual.*

Now you need to add these interfaces to the *CSpaceship* class. There are two steps here. The first step is to create the interface part of the COM class's identity. Let's do the *IMotion* interface first. Adding the *IMotion* interface to *CSpaceship* is easy. You just use the *IDispatchImpl* template to provide an implementation of a dual interface, like this:

```
class ATL_NO_VTABLE CClassicATLSpaceship :
    public CComObjectRootEx<CComSingleThreadModel>,
    public CComCoClass<CClassicATLSpaceship,
                       &CLSID_ClassicATLSpaceship>,
    public IDispatchImpl<IClassicATLSpaceship,
                         &IID_IClassicATLSpaceship,
                         &LIBID_SPACESHIPSVRLib>,
    public IDispatchImpl<IMotion, &IID_IMotion,
                         &LIBID_SPACESHIPSVRLib>
{
:
};
```

The second step involves beefing up the interface map so the client can acquire the *IMotion* interface. However, having two dual interfaces in a single COM class brings up an interesting issue. When a client calls *QueryInterface* for *IMotion*, the client should definitely get *IMotion*. However, when the client calls *QueryInterface* for *IDispatch*, which version of *IDispatch* should the client get—*IClassicATLSpaceship*'s dispatch interface or *IMotion*'s dispatch interface?

Multiple Dual Interfaces

Remember that all dual interfaces begin with the seven functions of *IDispatch*. A problem occurs whenever the client calls *QueryInterface* for *IID_IDispatch*. As a developer, you need to choose which version of *IDispatch* to pass out.

The interface map is where the *QueryInterface* for *IID_IDispatch* is specified. ATL has a specific macro for handling the dual interface situation. First, consider the interface map for *CClassicATLSpaceship* so far:

```
BEGIN_COM_MAP(CClassicATLSpaceship)
    COM_INTERFACE_ENTRY(IClassicATLSpaceship)
    COM_INTERFACE_ENTRY(IDispatch)
END_COM_MAP()
```

When the client calls *QueryInterface*, ATL rips through the table trying to match the requested IID to one in the table. The interface map above handles two interfaces: *IClassicATLSpaceship* and *IDispatch*. If you want to add another dual interface to the *CClassicATLSpaceship* class, you need a different macro.

The macro that handles multiple dispatch interfaces in an ATL-based COM class is named *COM_INTERFACE_ENTRY2*. To get *QueryInterface* working correctly, all you need to do is decide which version of *IDispatch* the client should get when it asks for *IDispatch*, like this:

```
BEGIN_COM_MAP(CClassicATLSpaceship)
    COM_INTERFACE_ENTRY(IClassicATLSpaceship)
    COM_INTERFACE_ENTRY(IMotion)
    COM_INTERFACE_ENTRY2(IDispatch, IClassicATLSpaceship)
END_COM_MAP()
```

In this case, a client that asks for *IDispatch* will get a pointer to *IClassicATLSpaceship* (whose first seven functions include the *IDispatch* functions).

Adding a nondual interface to an ATL-based COM class is even easier. You just add the interface to the inheritance list, like this:

```
class ATL_NO_VTABLE CClassicATLSpaceship :
    public CComObjectRootEx<CComSingleThreadModel>,
    public CComCoClass<CClassicATLSpaceship,
                       &CLSID_ClassicATLSpaceship>,
```

(continued)

```
    public IDispatchImpl<IClassicATLSpaceship,
                         &IID_IClassicATLSpaceship,
                         &LIBID_SPACESHIPSVRLib>,
    public IDispatchImpl<IMotion, &IID_IMotion,
                         &LIBID_SPACESHIPSVRLib>,
    public IDispatchImpl(IVisual, &IID_IVisual,
                         &LIBID_SPACESHIPSVRLib>
{
:
};
```

Then you add an interface map entry, like this:

```
BEGIN_COM_MAP(CClassicATLSpaceship)
    COM_INTERFACE_ENTRY(IClassicATLSpaceship)
    COM_INTERFACE_ENTRY(IMotion)
    COM_INTERFACE_ENTRY2(IDispatch, IClassicATLSpaceship)
    COM_INTERFACE_ENTRY(IVisual)
END_COM_MAP()
```

At this point, you have a viable, working COM server that will register itself and be able to play in the COM game of component software. But it turns out there's another way to implement COM servers using Visual C++ .NET: by using attributed programming.

Attributed Programming

Instead of adding COM support programmatically through C++ templates, you can employ a more declarative approach using attributed programming. Whereas classic ATL programming involves acquiring *IUnknown* support through template classes and interface map macros, attributed programming simply involves declaring a class as a COM class directly in the source code.

Let's create the same spaceship server using attributed programming. First, create a new ATL project, and this time select the Attributed check box on the Application Settings page of the ATL Project Wizard. Then use the ATL Simple Object Wizard to add an attributed class. Call the class *AttributedATLSpaceship*. When you page through the class options, you'll notice that the options are the same. That is, your class might be *Apartment Threaded*, *Free Threaded*, *Both*, or *Neutral*. You can also create support for *ISupportErrorInfo* and enable connection points.

However, when you look at the code emitted from the wizard, it will look quite a bit different from classic ATL-based code. Here's what you'll get:

```
// IAttributedATLSpaceShip
[
    object,
    uuid("4B8685BD-00F1-4D38-AFC1-3012C786480D"),
    dual,    helpstring("IAttributedATLSpaceShip Interface"),
    pointer_default(unique)
]
__interface IAttributedATLSpaceShip : IDispatch
{
};
// CAttributedATLSpaceShip
[
    coclass,
    threading("apartment"),
    vi_progid("AttributedATLSpaceShipSvr.AttributedATL"),
    progid("AttributedATLSpaceShipSvr.AttributedA.1"),
    version(1.0),
    uuid("CE07EBA4-0858-4A81-AD1C-C12710B4A1A2"),
    helpstring("AttributedATLSpaceShip Class")
]
class ATL_NO_VTABLE CAttributedATLSpaceShip :
    public IAttributedATLSpaceShip
{
public:
    CAttributedATLSpaceShip()
    {
    }
    DECLARE_PROTECT_FINAL_CONSTRUCT()
    HRESULT FinalConstruct()
    {
        return S_OK;
    }
    void FinalRelease()
    {
    }
public:
};
```

All the COM support brought in as C++ templates in classic ATL is brought into the ATL server through provider DLLs. The square-braced attributes at the top of the file instruct the compiler to add the COM infrastructure to the *CAttributedATLSpaceShip* class. That's a whole lot easier than keeping track of classes such as *CComObjectRootEx* and *CComCoClass* and macros such as *BEGIN_COM_MAP*.

Developing the COM class further is almost easy. For example, say you want to add the *IMotion* and *IVisible* interfaces to the class. In attributed ATL, you just put the interfaces directly into the ATL source code, like this:

```
[
    object,
    uuid("692D03A4-C689-11CE-B337-88EA36DE9E4E"),
    dual,
    helpstring("IMotion interface")
]
__interface IMotion : IDispatch
{
    HRESULT Fly();
    HRESULT GetPosition([out,retval]long* nPosition);
};
[
    object,
    uuid("692D03A5-C689-11CE-B337-88EA36DE9E4E"),
    helpstring("IVisual interface")
]
__interface IVisual : IUnknown
{
    HRESULT Display();
};
// More code
```

The attributes in front of the *__interface* keyword describe the interfaces as COM interfaces—dual interfaces, to be exact. Once these interfaces are described in the source code, you can implement the interfaces on the class by right-clicking on the class name in Class View, choosing Add, and then selecting Implement Interface. You can select the interfaces from registered type libraries or from the interfaces listed in the source code (*IMotion* and *IVisual*). Visual Studio .NET stubs out the functions for you; you need to fill them in.

The resulting DLL is a full-fledged COM DLL complete with the expected entry points: *DllMain*, *DllGetClassObject*, *DllCanUnloadnow*, *DllRegisterServer*, and *DllUnregisterServer*.

26

ATL and ActiveX Controls

If, after reading about COM and ATL, you're still wondering how COM will fit into your day-to-day programming activities, you're not alone. How to use COM in real life isn't always obvious at first glance. After all, you have to type in a whole lot of extra code just to get a COM object up and running. However, one very real application of COM is right under your nose—ActiveX controls. ActiveX controls are small gadgets (usually user-interface-oriented) that are written around COM.

Chapter 9 showed you how to use ActiveX controls within an MFC application. In Chapter 25, we examined COM classes that were created using ATL. In this chapter, you'll learn how to write a kind of COM class called an ActiveX control. You had a chance to work with ActiveX controls from the client side in Chapter 9. Now it's time to write your own.

Several steps are involved in creating an ActiveX control using ATL:

- Deciding what to draw
- Developing incoming interfaces for the control
- Developing outgoing interfaces (events) for the control
- Implementing a persistence mechanism for the control
- Providing a user interface for manipulating the control's properties

This chapter covers all these steps. Soon you'll be able to use ATL to create ActiveX controls that you (and other developers) can use in other programs.

What Are ActiveX Controls?

There's still some confusion about what really constitutes an ActiveX control. In 1994, Microsoft tacked some new interfaces onto its Object Linking and Embedding (OLE) protocol, packaged them in DLLs, and called them *OLE controls*. Originally, OLE controls implemented nearly the entire OLE document-embedding protocol. In addition, OLE controls supported the following:

- Dynamic invocation (Automation)
- Property pages (so the user could modify the control's properties)
- Outbound callback interfaces (event sets)
- Connections (a standard way for clients and controls to hook up the event callbacks)

When the Internet became a dominant factor in Microsoft's marketing plans, the company announced its intention to plant ActiveX controls on Web pages. At that point, the size of these components became an issue. Microsoft took its OLE control specification, changed the name from OLE controls to ActiveX controls, and stated that all the features listed above were optional. That means that under the new ActiveX control definition, a control's only requirement is that it be based on COM and that it implement *IUnknown*. Of course, in order for a control to be useful it really needs to implement most of the features listed above. So, in the end, ActiveX controls and OLE controls are more or less the same animal.

These days, Microsoft .NET (and especially ASP.NET) emphasizes pure HTML running in the browser as the dominant Web interface. The idea is to reduce the dependencies between your Web site and specific kinds of browsers. However, ActiveX controls work the same way they've always worked, and if you know that the browser on the other end of your Web site is Microsoft Internet Explorer, ActiveX controls will still offer a means of providing a rich user interface for the client.

Developers have been able to use MFC to create ActiveX controls since mid-1994. However, one downside to using MFC to create ActiveX controls is that the controls become bound to MFC. Sometimes you want your controls to be smaller or to work even if the end user doesn't have the MFC DLLs on her system. In addition, using MFC to create ActiveX controls forces you make certain design decisions. For example, if you decide to use MFC to write an ActiveX control, you more or less lock yourself out of using dual interfaces (unless you feel like writing a lot of extra code). Using MFC to create ActiveX controls also means that the control and its property pages must use *IDispatch* to communicate with each other.

To avoid the problems described so far, you can use ATL to create ActiveX controls. ATL now includes the facilities to create full-fledged ActiveX controls, complete with every feature an ActiveX control should have—including incoming interfaces, persistent properties, property pages, and connection points. If you've ever written an ActiveX control using MFC, you'll see how much more flexible using ATL can be.

Using ATL to Write an ActiveX Control

Although creating an ActiveX control using ATL is a pretty straightforward process, using ATL ends up being a bit more burdensome than using MFC. That's because ATL doesn't include all of MFC's amenities. For example, ATL doesn't include device context wrappers. When you draw on a device context, you have to use the raw device context handle.

Despite these issues, creating an ActiveX control using ATL is a whole lot easier than creating one from scratch. Also, using ATL gives you a certain amount of flexibility that you don't get when you use MFC. For example, adding dual interfaces to your control is a tedious process with MFC, but you get them for free when you use ATL. The ATL Control Wizard also makes it easy to add more COM classes (even noncontrol classes) to your project; adding new controls to an MFC-based DLL is a bit more difficult.

In this chapter's example, we'll represent a small pair of dice as an ATL-based ActiveX control. The dice control will illustrate the most important facets of ActiveX controls, including control rendering, incoming interfaces, properties, property pages, and events. We'll take a look at both classic ATL and attributed versions of this control.

Creating a Control

As always, the easiest way to create a COM server in ATL is to simply add an ATL class to your project using the ATL Control Wizard. You create a new ATL project by choosing New Project from the File menu and selecting ATL Project from the project templates. Name the project something clever, like *ClassicATLDiceSvr*. As you step through the ATL Project Wizard, leave the default options as they are except for the Attributed option—deselect that one.

After you create the DLL server, perform the following steps:

1. Choose Add Class from the Project menu. Select ATL Control from the class templates.

2. The Names page of the ATL Control Wizard (shown in Figure 26-1) lets you name the control. In the Short Name text box, give the control a name (such as ClassicATLDiceControl).

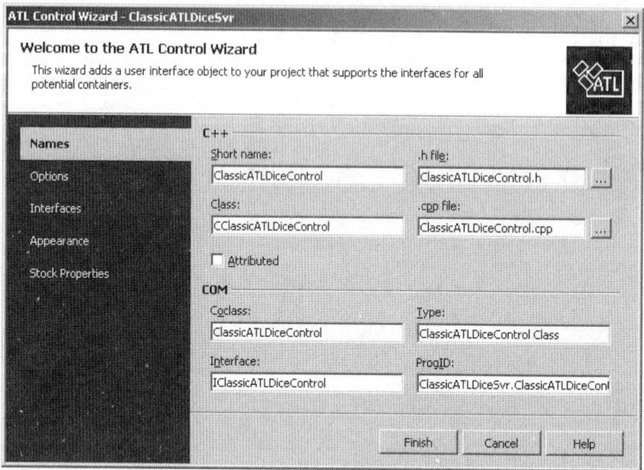

Figure 26-1 The Names page of the ATL Control Wizard.

3. On the Options page, you configure the control. For example, you can:

   - Select a standard control, a composite control, or a DHTML control (and minimal versions of each of these controls)
   - Designate the threading model for the control
   - Specify whether the main interface will be a dual or custom interface
   - Specify whether your control will support aggregation
   - Choose whether to use ActiveX control licensing and connection points in your control

4. To make your life easier later, select Connection Points as the support option. (This will save you some typing later on.) Leave everything else as the default value. Figure 26-2 shows what the Options page will look like.

5. On the Interfaces page, you specify what COM interfaces your control will support. Add IPropertyNotifySink to the supported list.

6. On the Appearance page (shown in Figure 26-3), you can apply various traits to your control. For example, you can give the control

behaviors based on regular Microsoft Windows controls such as buttons and edit controls. Other options include having your control appear invisible at run time or giving your control an opaque background.

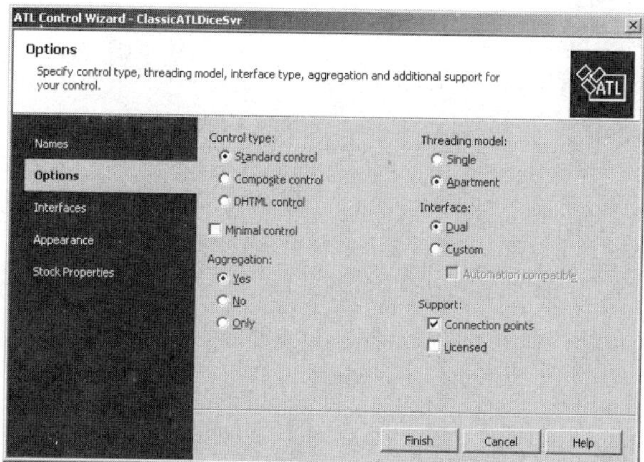

Figure 26-2 The Options page of the ATL Control Wizard.

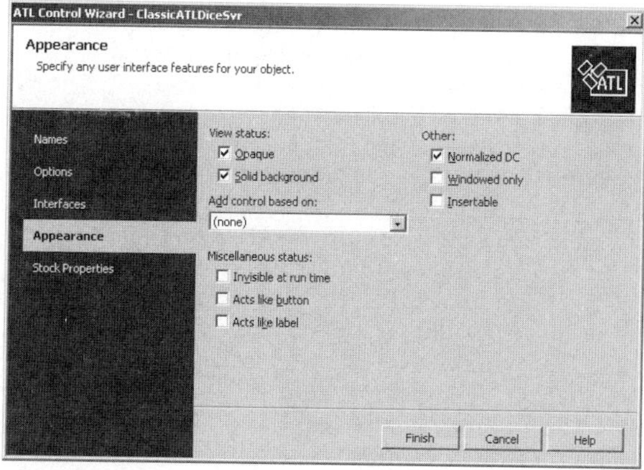

Figure 26-3 The Appearance page of the ATL Control Wizard.

7. Finally, select the Stock Properties page (shown in Figure 26-4) if you want to give your control some stock properties. Stock properties are properties that you might expect any control to have, including background colors, border colors, foreground colors, and a caption.

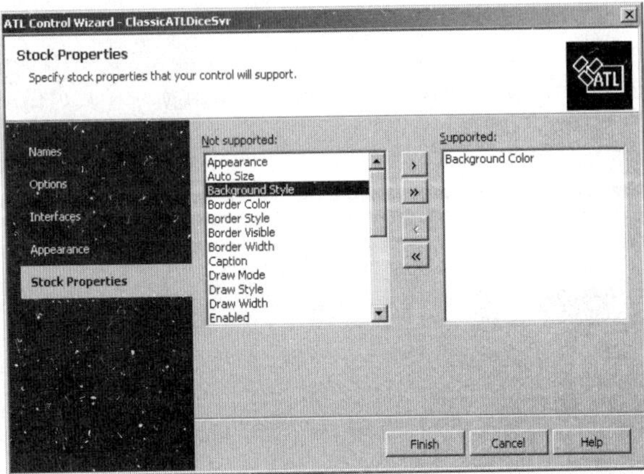

Figure 26-4 The Stock Properties page of the ATL Control Wizard.

8. When you've finished selecting the attributes for the control, click Finish.

The ATL Control Wizard will add a header file and a source file that define the new control. In addition, it will set aside space in the IDL file to hold the control's main interface and assign a GUID to the interface. Here's the C++ definition of the control produced by the wizard:

```
class ATL_NO_VTABLE CClassicATLDiceControl :
    public CComObjectRootEx<CComSingleThreadModel>,
    public CStockPropImpl<CClassicATLDiceControl,
        IClassicATLDiceControl>,
    public IPersistStreamInitImpl<CClassicATLDiceControl>,
    public IOleControlImpl<CClassicATLDiceControl>,
    public IOleObjectImpl<CClassicATLDiceControl>,
    public IOleInPlaceActiveObjectImpl<CClassicATLDiceControl>,
    public IViewObjectExImpl<CClassicATLDiceControl>,
    public IOleInPlaceObjectWindowlessImpl<CClassicATLDiceControl>,
    public ISupportErrorInfo,
    public IConnectionPointContainerImpl<CClassicATLDiceControl>,
    public CProxy_IClassicATLDiceControlEvents<CClassicATLDiceControl>,
    public IPersistStorageImpl<CClassicATLDiceControl>,
    public ISpecifyPropertyPagesImpl<CClassicATLDiceControl>,
    public IQuickActivateImpl<CClassicATLDiceControl>,
    public IDataObjectImpl<CClassicATLDiceControl>,
    public IProvideClassInfo2Impl<&CLSID_ClassicATLDiceControl,
        &__uuidof(_IClassicATLDiceControlEvents),
        &LIBID_ClassicATLDiceSvrLib>,
    public IPropertyNotifySinkCP<CClassicATLDiceControl>,
    public CComCoClass<CClassicATLDiceControl,
        &CLSID_ClassicATLDiceControl>,
    public CComControl<CClassicATLDiceControl>
{
  :
}
```

That's a pretty long inheritance list. You've already seen the template implementations of *IUnknown* and support for class objects. They exist in *CComObjectRootEx* and *CComCoClass*. You've also seen how ATL implements *IDispatch* within the *IDispatchImpl* template. However, for a basic control about 11 more interfaces are required to make everything work. These interfaces fall into several functional categories, as shown in the following table.

Function/Category	Interface
Handling self-description	*IProvideClassInfo2*
Handling persistence	*IPersistStreamInit* *IPersistStorage*
Handling activation	*IQuickActivate* (and some of *IOleObject*)
Interface from the original OLE control specification	*IOleControl*
Interface from the OLE Document specification	*IOleObject*
Rendering	*IOleInPlaceActiveObject* *IViewObjectEx* *IOleInPlaceObjectWindowless* *IDataObject*
Helping the container manage property pages	*ISpecifyPropertyPages*
Handling connections	*IPropertyNotifySinkCP* *IConnectionPointContainer*

Note The interfaces listed in the table are by and large boilerplate interfaces—ones that a COM class must implement in order to qualify as an ActiveX control. Most of the implementations are standard and vary only slightly (if at all) from one control to the next. The beauty of ATL is that it implements this standard behavior and gives you programmatic hooks into which you can plug in your custom code, so you don't have to burn your eyes out by looking directly at the COM code. You can live a full and rich life without understanding exactly how these interfaces work. However, if you want to know more about the internal workings of ActiveX controls, be sure to check out *Inside OLE* by Kraig Brockschmidt (Microsoft Press, 1995) and *ActiveX Controls Inside Out* by Adam Denning (Microsoft Press, 1997).

ATL's Control Architecture

At the highest level, an ActiveX control has two aspects: its external state (what it renders on the screen) and its internal state (its properties). Once an ActiveX control is hosted by some sort of container (such as a Microsoft Visual Basic .NET form or an MFC dialog box), it maintains a symbiotic relationship with that container. The client code talks to the control through incoming COM interfaces such as *IDispatch* and OLE document interfaces such as *IOleObject* and *IDataObject*.

The control also has the opportunity to talk back to the client. One method of implementing this two-way communication is for the client to implement an *IDispatch* interface to represent the control's event set. The container maintains a set of properties called *ambient properties* that the control can use to find out about its host. For instance, a control can camouflage itself within the container because the container makes the information stored in these properties available through a specifically named *IDispatch* interface. The container can implement an interface named *IPropertyNotifySink* to find out when the properties within a control might change. Finally, the container will implement *IOleClientSite* and *IOleControlSite* as part of the control-embedding protocol.

The interfaces listed earlier allow the client and the object to exhibit the behaviors expected of an ActiveX control. We'll tackle some of these interfaces as we go along. The best place to begin looking at ATL-based controls is the *CComControl* class and its base classes.

The *CComControl* Class

You can find the definition of *CComControl* in Microsoft's AtlCtl.h file under Atlmfc's Include directory. *CComControl* is a template class that takes two class parameters: the *CComControlBase* class and the base window class *WinBase*.

```
template <class T, class WinBase =  CWindowImpl< T > >
class ATL_NO_VTABLE CComControl : public CComControlBase,
                                  public WinBase
{
⋮
};
```

CComControl is a rather lightweight class that does little by itself—it derives functionality from *CComControlBase* and *WinBase*. *WinBase* is the base class that implements windowing functions, and it defaults to *CWindowImpl*. *CComControl* expects the template parameter to be an ATL-based COM object that's derived from *CComObjectRootEx*. *CComControl* requires the template parameter for various reasons, the primary one being that from time to time the control class will use the template parameter to call back to the control's *InternalQueryInterface*.

CComControl implements several functions that make it easy for the control to call back to the client. For example, it implements a function named *FireOnRequestEdit* to allow controls to tell the client that a specified property is about to change. This function calls back to the client through the client-implemented interface *IPropertyNotifySink*. *FireOnRequestEdit* notifies all connected *IPropertyNotifySink* interfaces that the property specified by a certain DISPID is about to change.

CComControl also implements the *FireOnChanged* function. *FireOnChanged* is very much like *FireOnRequestEdit* in that it calls back to the client through the *IPropertyNotifySink* interface. This function tells the clients of the control (all clients connected to the control through *IPropertyNotifySink*) that a property specified by a certain DISPID has already changed.

In addition to mapping the *IPropertyNotifySink* interface to some more easily understood functions, *CComControl* implements a function named *ControlQueryInterface*, which simply forwards the call to the control's *IUnknown* interface. (This is how you can get a control's *IUnknown* interface from inside the control.) You can also find an implementation of *MessageBox* in *CComControl* now. Finally, *CComControl* implements a function named *CreateControlWindow*. The default behavior for this function is to call *CWindowImpl::Create*. If you want, you can override this function to do something other than create a single window. For example, you might want to create multiple windows for your control.

Most of the real functionality for *CComControl* exists within those two other classes—*CComControlBase* and *CWindowImpl*. Let's take a look at those classes now.

The *CComControlBase* Class

CComControlBase is a much more substantial class than *CComControl*. To begin with, *CComControlBase* maintains all the pointers used by the control to talk back to the client. It uses ATL's *CComPtr* smart pointer to include member variables that wrap the following interfaces implemented for calling back to the client:

- A wrapper for *IOleInPlaceSite* (*m_spInPlaceSite*)
- An advise holder for the client's data advise sink (*m_spDataAdviseHolder*)
- An OLE advise holder for the client's OLE advise sink (*m_spOleAdviseHolder*)

- A wrapper for *IOleClientSite* (*m_spClientSite*)
- A wrapper for *IAdviseSink* (*m_spAdviseSink*)

CComControlBase also uses ATL's *CComDispatchDriver* to wrap the client's dispatch interface for exposing its ambient properties.

CComControlBase is also where you'll find the member variables that contain the control's sizing and positioning information: *m_sizeNatural*, *m_sizeExtent*, and *m_rcPos*. The other important data member within *CComControlBase* is the control's window handle. Most ActiveX controls are user interface gadgets, and as such they maintain a window. *CWindowImpl* and *CWindowImplBaseT* handle the windowing aspects of an ATL-based ActiveX control.

The *CWindowImpl* and *CWindowImplBaseT* Classes

CWindowImpl derives from *CWindowImplBaseT*, which derives from *CWindowImplRoot*, which in turn derives from *TBase* and *CMessageMap*. As a template class, *CWindowImpl* takes three parameters upon instantiation. The first template parameter is the control being created. *CWindowImpl* needs the control type because *CWindowImpl* calls back to the control during window creation. The second template parameter is the *Windowing* base class. The default is *CWindow*. The third parameter represents a set of windowing traits for the control, which applies the following traits to the control: *WS_CHILD*, *WS_VISIBLE*, *WS_CLIPCHILDREN*, and *WS_CLIPSIBLINGS*. Let's take a closer look at how ATL handles windowing.

ATL Windowing

Just as *CComControl* is relatively lightweight (most work happens in *CComControlBase*), so is *CWindowImpl*. *CWindowImpl* more or less handles only window creation. In fact, that's the only function it explicitly defines. *CWindowImpl::Create* creates a new window based on the window class information managed by a class named *_ATL_WNDCLASSINFO*. There's an ASCII character version and a wide-character version.

```
struct _ATL_WNDCLASSINFOA
{
    WNDCLASSEXA m_wc;
    LPCSTR m_lpszOrigName;
    WNDPROC pWndProc;
    LPCSTR m_lpszCursorID;
    BOOL m_bSystemCursor;
    ATOM m_atom;
    CHAR m_szAutoName[5+sizeof(void*)*CHAR_BIT];
    ATOM Register(WNDPROC* p)
    {
```

```
        return AtlWinModuleRegisterWndClassInfoA(&_AtlWinModule,
            &_AtlBaseModule, this, p);
    }
};

struct _ATL_WNDCLASSINFOW
{
    WNDCLASSEXW m_wc;
    LPCWSTR m_lpszOrigName;
    WNDPROC pWndProc;
    LPCWSTR m_lpszCursorID;
    BOOL m_bSystemCursor;
    ATOM m_atom;
    WCHAR m_szAutoName[5+sizeof(void*)*CHAR_BIT];
    ATOM Register(WNDPROC* p)
    {
        return AtlWinModuleRegisterWndClassInfoW(&_AtlWinModule,
            &_AtlBaseModule, this, p);
    }
};
```

ATL then uses typedefs to alias this structure to a single class named *CWndClassInfo*:

```
typedef _ATL_WNDCLASSINFOA CWndClassInfoA;
typedef _ATL_WNDCLASSINFOW CWndClassInfoW;
#ifdef UNICODE
#define CWndClassInfo CWndClassInfoW
#else
#define CWndClassInfo CWndClassInfoA
#endif
```

CWindowImpl uses a macro named *DECLARE_WND_CLASS* to add window class information to a *CWindowImpl*-derived class. *DECLARE_WND_CLASS* also adds a function named *GetWndClassInfo*. Here's the *DECLARE_WND_CLASS* macro:

```
#define DECLARE_WND_CLASS(WndClassName) \
static ATL::CWndClassInfo& GetWndClassInfo() \
{ \
    static ATL::CWndClassInfo wc = \
    { \
        { sizeof(WNDCLASSEX), \
            CS_HREDRAW | CS_VREDRAW | CS_DBLCLKS, StartWindowProc, \
            0, 0, NULL, NULL, NULL, (HBRUSH)(COLOR_WINDOW + 1), \
            NULL, WndClassName, NULL }, \
        NULL, NULL, IDC_ARROW, TRUE, 0, _T("") \
    }; \
    return wc; \
}
```

This macro expands to provide a *CWndClassInfo* structure for the control class. Because *CWndClassInfo* manages the information for a single window class, each window created through a specific instance of *CWindowImpl* will be based on the same window class.

CWindowImpl derives from *CWindowImplBaseT*. *CWindowImplBaseT* derives from *CWindowImplRoot*, which is specialized around the *CWindow* class and the *CControlWinTraits* classes, as follows:

```
template <class TBase = CWindow, class TWinTraits = CControlWinTraits>
class ATL_NO_VTABLE CWindowImplBaseT : public CWindowImplRoot< TBase >
{
⋮
};
```

CWindowImplRoot derives from *CWindow* by default and *CMessageMap*. *CWindowImplBaseT* manages the window procedure of a *CWindowImpl*-derived class. *CWindow* is a lightweight class that wraps window handles in the same way (but not as extensively) as MFC's *CWnd* class. *CMessageMap* is a tiny class that defines a single pure virtual function named *ProcessWindowMessage*. ATL-based message-mapping machinery assumes that this function is available, so ATL-based classes that want to use message maps must derive from *CMessageMap*. Let's take a quick look at ATL message maps.

ATL Message Maps

The root of ATL's message mapping machinery lies within the *CMessageMap* class. ATL-based controls expose message maps by virtue of indirectly deriving from *CWindowImplBase*. In MFC, by contrast, deriving from *CCmdTarget* enables message mapping. However, as in MFC, it's not enough to derive from a class that supports message maps. The message maps actually have to be there—and they are implemented via macros.

To implement a message map in an ATL-based control, you use message map macros. First, ATL's *BEGIN_MSG_MAP* macro goes into the control class's header file. *BEGIN_MSG_MAP* marks the beginning of the default message map. *CWindowImpl::WindowProc* uses this default message map to process messages sent to the window. The message map directs messages to the appropriate handler function or to another message map. ATL defines another macro named *END_MSG_MAP* to mark the end of a message map. Between *BEGIN_MSG_MAP* and *END_MSG_MAP* lie some other macros for mapping window messages to member functions in the control.

Here's a typical message map you might find in an ATL-based control:

```
BEGIN_MSG_MAP(CAFullControl)
    CHAIN_MSG_MAP(CComControl<CAFullControl>)
    DEFAULT_REFLECTION_HANDLER()
```

```
    MESSAGE_HANDLER(WM_TIMER, OnTimer);
    MESSAGE_HANDLER(WM_LBUTTONDOWN, OnLButton);
END_MSG_MAP()
```

This message map delegates most of the message processing to the control through the *CHAIN_MSG_MAP* macro and handles message reflection through the *DEFAULT_REFLECTION_HANDLER* macro. The message map also handles two window messages explicitly: *WM_TIMER* and *WM_LBUTTONDOWN*. These are standard window messages that are mapped using the *MESSAGE_HANDLER* macro. The macros simply produce a table that relates window messages to member functions in the class. In addition to handling regular messages, message maps are capable of handling other sorts of events. Here's a rundown of the kinds of macros that can go in a message map:

Macro	Description
MESSAGE_HANDLER	Maps a Windows message to a handler function
MESSAGE_RANGE_HANDLER	Maps a contiguous range of Windows-based messages to a handler function
COMMAND_HANDLER	Maps a *WM_COMMAND* message to a handler function based on the identifier and the notification code of the menu item, control, or accelerator
COMMAND_ID_HANDLER	Maps a *WM_COMMAND* message to a handler function based on the identifier of the menu item, control, or accelerator
COMMAND_CODE_HANDLER	Maps a *WM_COMMAND* message to a handler function based on the notification code
COMMAND_RANGE_HANDLER	Maps a contiguous range of *WM_COMMAND* messages to a handler function based on the identifier of the menu item, control, or accelerator
NOTIFY_HANDLER	Maps a *WM_NOTIFY* message to a handler function based on the notification code and the control identifier
NOTIFY_ID_HANDLER	Maps a *WM_NOTIFY* message to a handler function based on the control identifier
NOTIFY_CODE_HANDLER	Maps a *WM_NOTIFY* message to a handler function based on the notification code
NOTIFY_RANGE_HANDLER	Maps a contiguous range of *WM_NOTIFY* messages to a handler function based on the control identifier
NOTIFY_RANGE_CODE_HANDLER	Maps a *WM_NOTIFY* message to a handler function based on the notification code and a contiguous range of control identifiers

Handling messages within ATL works much the same as in MFC. ATL includes a single window procedure through which messages are routed. Technically, you can build your controls effectively without understanding everything about ATL's control architecture. However, such knowledge can be helpful as you develop a control, and it can be even more useful when you debug a control.

Developing a Control

Once the control is inserted into the server, you must add some code to make the control do something. If you were to compile and load ATL's default control into a container, the results wouldn't be particularly interesting. You'd simply see a blank rectangle with the string *ATL 7.0 : ClassicATLDiceControl*. You'd want to add code to render the control, to represent the internal state of the control, to respond to events, and to generate events to send back to the container.

Deciding What to Draw

A good place to start working on a control is its drawing code—you get instant gratification that way. Our control is visually represented by a couple of dice. The easiest way to render the dice control is to draw bitmaps representing each of the six possible dice faces and then show the bitmaps on the screen. This implies that the dice control will maintain some variables to represent its state. For example, the control needs to manage the bitmaps representing the dice as well as two numbers that represent the first value shown by each die. Here's the code from ClassicATLDiceControl.h that represents the state of the dice:

```
#define MAX_DIEFACES 6

HBITMAP m_dieBitmaps[MAX_DIEFACES];
unsigned short m_nFirstDieValue;
unsigned short m_nSecondDieValue;
```

Before diving headfirst into the control's drawing code, you need to do a bit of preliminary work—the bitmaps need to be loaded. Presumably, each die rendered by the dice control will show any one of six dice faces, so the control needs one bitmap for each face. Figure 26-5 shows what one of the dice bitmaps looks like.

Figure 26-5 A bitmap for the dice control.

If you draw the bitmaps one at a time, they'll have sequential identifiers in the resource.h file. Giving the bitmaps sequential identifiers will make them easier to load. Otherwise, you might need to modify the Resource.h file, which contains the following identifiers:

```
#define IDB_DICE1                        220
#define IDB_DICE2                        221
#define IDB_DICE3                        222
#define IDB_DICE4                        223
#define IDB_DICE5                        224
#define IDB_DICE6                        225
```

Loading bitmaps is fairly straightforward. You cycle through the bitmap array and load the bitmap resources. When they're stored in an array like this, grabbing the bitmap out of the array and showing it is much easier than if you don't use an array. Here's the function that loads the bitmaps into the array:

```
BOOL CClassicATLDiceControl::LoadBitmaps() {
    int i;
    BOOL bSuccess = TRUE;
    for(i=0; i<MAX_DIEFACES; i++) {
        DeleteObject(m_dieBitmaps[i]);
        m_dieBitmaps[i] = LoadBitmap(_AtlBaseModule.m_hInst,
                                     MAKEINTRESOURCE(nID+i));
        if(!m_dieBitmaps[i]) {
            ::MessageBox(NULL,
                         "Failed to load bitmaps",
                         NULL,
                         MB_OK);
            bSuccess = FALSE;
        }
    }
    return bSuccess;
}
```

The best place to call *LoadBitmaps* is from within the control's constructor, as shown in the following code. To simulate a random roll of the dice, you set the control's state so the first and second die values are random numbers between 0 and 5. (These numbers will be used when the dice control is drawn.)

```
class ATL_NO_VTABLE CClassicATLDiceControl : // big inheritance list {
    CClassicATLDiceControl () {
        LoadBitmaps();
        srand((unsigned)time(NULL));
        m_nFirstDieValue = (rand() % (MAX_DIEFACES)) + 1;
        m_nSecondDieValue = (rand() % (MAX_DIEFACES)) + 1;
        ⋮
    }
    ⋮
}
```

Once the bitmaps are loaded, you'll want to render them. The dice control should include a function for showing each die face based on the current internal state of the dice. Here's where you'll first encounter ATL's drawing machinery.

One of the most convenient things about ATL-based controls (and MFC-based controls) is that all the drawing code happens in one place: within the control's *OnDraw* function. *OnDraw* is a virtual function of *COleControlBase*. Here's *OnDraw*'s signature:

```
virtual HRESULT OnDraw(ATL_DRAWINFO& di);
```

OnDraw takes a single parameter: a pointer to an *ATL_DRAWINFO* structure. Among other things, the *ATL_DRAWINFO* structure contains a device context on which to render your control. Here's the *ATL_DRAWINFO* structure:

```
struct ATL_DRAWINFO {
    UINT cbSize;
    DWORD dwDrawAspect;
    LONG lindex;
    DVTARGETDEVICE* ptd;
    HDC hicTargetDev;
    HDC hdcDraw;
    LPCRECTL prcBounds; //Rectangle in which to draw
    LPCRECTL prcWBounds; //WindowOrg and Ext if metafile
    BOOL bOptimize;
    BOOL bZoomed;
    BOOL bRectInHimetric;
    SIZEL ZoomNum;      //ZoomX = ZoomNum.cx/ZoomNum.cy
    SIZEL ZoomDen;
};
```

As you can see, there's a lot more information here than a simple device context. Although you can count on the framework filling it out correctly for you, it's good to know where the information in the structure comes from and how it fits into the picture.

ActiveX controls are interesting because they're drawn in two contexts. The first and most obvious context is when the control is active and it draws within the actual drawing space of the client. The other, less obvious context is during design time (such as when an ActiveX control resides in a Visual Basic form in design mode). In the first context, ActiveX controls render themselves to a live screen device context. In the second context, ActiveX controls render themselves to a metafile device context.

Many ATL-based controls are composed of at least one window. So ATL controls need to render themselves during the *WM_PAINT* message. Once the control receives the *WM_PAINT* message, the message routing architecture passes control to *CComControlBase::OnPaint*. (Remember that *CComControl-*

Base is one of the control's base classes.) *CComControlBase::OnPaint* performs several steps. The function begins by creating a painting device context (using *BeginPaint*). Then it creates an *ATL_DRAWINFO* structure on the stack and initializes the fields within the structure. *OnPaint* sets up *ATL_DRAWINFO* to show the entire content. (The *dwDrawAspect* field is set to *DVASPECT_CONTENT*.) *OnPaint* also sets the *lindex* field to –1, sets the drawing device context to the newly created painting device context, and sets up the bounding rectangle to be the client area of the control's window. Then it goes on to call *OnDrawAdvanced*.

The default *OnDrawAdvanced* function prepares a normalized device context for drawing. You can override this method if you want to use the device context passed by the container without normalizing it. ATL then calls your control class's *OnDraw* method.

The second context in which the *OnDraw* function is called is when the control draws to a metafile. The control draws itself to a metafile whenever someone calls *IViewObjectEx::Draw*. (*IViewObjectEx* is one of the interfaces implemented by the ActiveX control.) ATL implements the *IViewObjectEx* interface through the template class *IViewObjectExImpl*. *IViewObjectExImpl::Draw* is called whenever the control needs to take a snapshot of its presentation space for the container to store. In this case, the container creates a metafile device context and hands it to the control. *IViewObjectExImpl* initializes an *ATL_DRAWINFO* structure and puts it on the stack. The bounding rectangle, the index, the drawing aspect, and the device contexts are all passed in as parameters by the client. The rest of the drawing is the same in this case—the control calls *OnDrawAdvanced*, which in turn calls your version of *OnDraw*.

Once you're armed with this knowledge, writing functions to render the bitmaps becomes fairly straightforward. To show the first die face, you create a memory-based device context, select the object into the device context, and *BitBlt* the memory device context into the real device context. Here's the code:

```
void CClassicATLDiceControl::ShowFirstDieFace(ATL_DRAWINFO& di) {

    BITMAP bmInfo;
    GetObject(m_dieBitmaps[m_nFirstDieValue-1],
              sizeof(bmInfo), &bmInfo);

    SIZE size;

    size.cx = bmInfo.bmWidth;
    size.cy = bmInfo.bmHeight;

    HDC hMemDC;
    hMemDC = CreateCompatibleDC(di.hdcDraw);

    HBITMAP hOldBitmap;
```

(continued)

```
    HBITMAP hbm = m_dieBitmaps[m_nFirstDieValue-1];
    hOldBitmap = (HBITMAP)SelectObject(hMemDC, hbm);

    if (hOldBitmap == NULL)
        return;     // destructors will clean up

    BitBlt(di.hdcDraw,
           di.prcBounds->left+1,
           di.prcBounds->top+1,
           size.cx,
           size.cy,
           hMemDC, 0,
           0,
           SRCCOPY);

    SelectObject(di.hdcDraw, hOldBitmap);
    DeleteDC(hMemDC);
}
```

Showing the second die face follows more or less the same process—just be sure that the dice are represented separately. For example, you probably want to change the call to *BitBlt* so the two dice bitmaps are shown side by side.

```
void CClassicATLDiceControl::ShowSecondDieFace(ATL_DRAWINFO& di) {
    //
    // This code is exactly the same as ShowFirstDieFace
    //  except the second die is positioned next to the first die.
    //
    BitBlt(di.hdcDraw,
           di.prcBounds->left+size.cx + 2,
           di.prcBounds->top+1,
           size.cx,
           size.cy,
           hMemDC, 0,
           0, SRCCOPY);
    // The rest is the same as in ShowFirstDieFace
}
```

The last step is to call these two functions whenever the control is asked to render itself—in the control's *OnDraw* function. *ShowFirstDieFace* and *ShowSecondDieFace* will show the correct bitmap based on the state of *m_nFirstDieValue* and *m_nSecondDieValue*:

```
HRESULT OnDraw(ATL_DRAWINFO& di)
    {
        RECT& rc = *(RECT*)di.prcBounds;

        HBRUSH hBrush = CreateSolidBrush(m_clrBackColor);
        HBRUSH hOldBrush = (HBRUSH)SelectObject(di.hdcDraw, hBrush);
```

```
        Rectangle(di.hdcDraw, rc.left, rc.top, rc.right, rc.bottom);

        SelectObject(di.hdcDraw, hOldBrush);
        DeleteObject(hBrush);

        ShowFirstDieFace(di);
        ShowSecondDieFace(di);

        return S_OK;
    }
```

Notice that the drawing code takes the background color into account. We'll be able to change the background color a little later.

At this point, if you compile and load this control into some ActiveX control container (such as a Visual Basic form or an MFC-based dialog box), you'll see two die faces staring back at you. Now it's time to add some code to enliven the control and roll the dice.

Responding to Window Messages

Just looking at two dice faces isn't that much fun. You want to make the dice work. A good way to get the dice to appear to jiggle is to use a timer to generate events and then respond to the timer by showing a new pair of dice faces. Setting up a Windows-based timer in the control means adding a function to handle the timer message and adding a macro to the control's message map. Let's start by using Class View's Properties window to add a handler for *WM_TIMER*. This will add a prototype for the *OnTimer* function and an entry into the message map to handle the *WM_TIMER* message. We'll then add some code to the *OnTimer* function to handle the *WM_TIMER* message. The following code shows the *OnTimer* function:

```
LRESULT CClassicATLDiceControl::OnTimer(UINT uMsg, WPARAM wParam,
    LPARAM lParam, BOOL& bHandled) {

    if(m_nTimesRolled > 15) {
        m_nTimesRolled = 0;
        KillTimer(1);         } else {
        m_nFirstDieValue = (rand() % (MAX_DIEFACES)) + 1;
        m_nSecondDieValue = (rand() % (MAX_DIEFACES)) + 1;
        FireViewChange();
        m_nTimesRolled++;
    }
    bHandled = TRUE;
    return 0;
}
```

This function responds to the timer message by generating two random numbers, setting up the control's state to reflect these two new numbers, and then asking the control to refresh itself by calling *FireViewChange*. Notice that the function kills the timer as soon as the dice have rolled a certain number of times. Also notice that the message handler tells the framework that it successfully handled the function by setting the *bHandled* variable to *TRUE*.

Notice there's an entry for *WM_TIMER* in the control's message map. Because *WM_TIMER* is just a plain vanilla window message, it's represented with a standard *MESSAGE_HANDLER* macro as follows:

```
BEGIN_MSG_MAP(CClassicATLDiceControl)
    MESSAGE_HANDLER(WM_TIMER, OnTimer)
    CHAIN_MSG_MAP(CComControl<CClassicATLDiceControl>)
    DEFAULT_REFLECTION_HANDLER()
END_MSG_MAP()
```

As you can tell from this message map, the dice control already handles the gamut of Windows-based messages through the *CHAIN_MSG_MAP* macro. However, now the pair of dice can simulate rolling by responding to the timer message. Setting a timer causes the control to repaint itself with a new pair of dice numbers every quarter of a second or so. Of course, you need some way to start the dice rolling. Because this is an ActiveX control, it's reasonable to allow client code to start rolling the dice via a call to a function in one of its incoming interfaces. We'll use Class View's Properties window to add a *RollDice* function to the main interface. Right-click on the *IClassicATLDiceControl* interface that appears in Class View and choose Add Method from the shortcut menu. Then add a *RollDice* function. Visual C++ .NET will add a function named *RollDice* to your control. You implement *RollDice* by setting the timer for a reasonably short interval and then returning *S_OK*. Add the following boldface code:

```
STDMETHODIMP CClassicATLDiceControl::RollDice()
{
    if(::IsWindow(m_hWnd)) {
    SetTimer(1, 250);
    }
    return S_OK;
}
```

If you load the dice into an ActiveX control container, you'll be able to browse and call the control's methods and roll the dice.

In addition to using the incoming interface to roll the dice, the user might reasonably expect to roll the dice by double-clicking on the control. To enable this behavior, you just add a message handler to trap the mouse-button-down message by adding a function to handle a left mouse double-click:

```
LRESULT CClassicATLDiceControl::OnLButtonDblClick(UINT uMsg,
                                                  WPARAM wParam,
```

```
                                          LPARAM lParam,
                                          BOOL& bHandled) {
    RollDice();
    bHandled = TRUE;
    return 0;
}
```

Then be sure to add an entry to the message map to handle the *WM_LBUTTONDOWN* message:

```
BEGIN_MSG_MAP(CClassicATLDiceControl)
    // Other message handlers
    MESSAGE_HANDLER(WM_LBUTTONDBLCLK, OnLButtonDblClick)
END_MSG_MAP()
```

When you load the dice control into a container and double-click on it, you should see the dice roll. Now that you've added rendering code and given the control the ability to roll, it's time to add some properties.

Adding Properties and Property Pages

You've just seen that ActiveX controls have an external presentation state. (The presentation state is the state reflected when the control draws itself.) Most ActiveX controls also have an internal state. This internal state is a set of variables exposed to the outside world via interface functions. These internal variables are also known as *properties*.

For example, imagine a simple grid implemented as an ActiveX control. The grid has an external presentation state and a set of internal variables for describing the state of the grid. The properties of a grid control would probably include the number of rows in the grid, the number of columns in the grid, the color of the lines composing the grid, the type of font used, and so forth.

As you saw in Chapter 25, adding properties to an ATL-based class means adding member variables to the class and then creating *get* and *put* functions to access these properties. For example, two member variables that you might add to the dice control include the dice color and the number of times the dice should roll before stopping. These two properties can easily be represented as a pair of short integers, as shown here:

```
class ATL_NO_VTABLE CClassicATLDiceControl :
⋮
{
    ⋮
    short m_nDiceColor;
    short m_nTimesToRoll;
    ⋮
};
```

To make these properties accessible to the client, you need to add *get* and *put* functions to the control. You do this by right-clicking on the interface symbol in Class View and choosing Add Property from the shortcut menu. Using Class View to add *DiceColor* and *TimesToRoll* properties to the control will add four new functions to the control: *get_DiceColor*, *put_DiceColor*, *get_TimesToRoll*, and *put_TimesToRoll*.

The *get_DiceColor* function should retrieve the state of *m_nDiceColor*:

```
STDMETHODIMP CClassicATLDiceControl::get_DiceColor(short * pVal)
{
    *pVal = m_nDiceColor;
    return S_OK;
}
```

To make the control interesting, *put_DiceColor* should change the colors of the dice bitmaps and redraw the control immediately. Our example will use red and blue dice as well as the original black and white dice. To make the control show the new color bitmaps immediately after the client sets the dice color, the *put_DiceColor* function should load the new bitmaps according to new color and redraw the control:

```
STDMETHODIMP ClassicATLDiceControl::put_DiceColor(short newVal)
{
    if(newVal < 3 && newVal >= 0)
        m_nDiceColor = newVal;
    LoadBitmaps();
    FireViewChange();
    return S_OK;
}
```

Of course, this means that *LoadBitmaps* needs to load the bitmaps based on the state of *m_nDiceColor*, so we need to add the following boldface code to our existing *LoadBitmaps* function:

```
BOOL CClassicATLDiceControl::LoadBitmaps() {
   int i;
   BOOL bSuccess = TRUE;
   int nID = IDB_WHITE1;

   switch(m_nDiceColor) {
      case 0:
         nID = IDB_WHITE1;
         break;

      case 1:
         nID = IDB_BLUE1;
         break;
```

```
        case 2:
            nID = IDB_RED1;
            break;

    }

    for(i=0; i<MAX_DIEFACES; i++) {
        DeleteObject(m_dieBitmaps[i]);
        m_dieBitmaps[i] = LoadBitmap(_AtlBaseModule.m_hInst,
                                     MAKEINTRESOURCE(nID+i));
        if(!m_dieBitmaps[i]) {
            ::MessageBox(NULL,
                         "Failed to load bitmaps",
                         NULL,
                         MB_OK);
            bSuccess = FALSE;
        }
    }
    return bSuccess;
}
```

Just as the dice color property reflects the color of the dice, the number of times the dice rolls should be reflected by the state of the *TimesToRoll* property. The *get_TimesToRoll* function needs to read the *m_nTimesToRoll* member, and the *put_TimesToRoll* function needs to modify *m_nTimesToRoll*. Add the boldface code shown here:

```
STDMETHODIMP CClassicATLDiceControl::get_TimesToRoll(short * pVal)
{
    *pVal = m_nTimesToRoll;
    return S_OK;
}

STDMETHODIMP CClassicATLDiceControl::put_TimesToRoll(short newVal)
{
    m_nTimesToRoll = newVal;
    return S_OK;
}
```

Finally, instead of hard-coding the number of times the dice rolls, use the *m_nTimesToRoll* variable to determine when to kill the timer:

```
LRESULT CClassicATLDiceControl::OnTimer(UINT uMsg, WPARAM wParam,
                                        LPARAM lParam, BOOL& bHandled)
{
    if(m_nTimesRolled > m_nTimesToRoll) {
        m_nTimesRolled = 0;
        KillTimer(1);
    } else {
```

(continued)

```
            m_nFirstDieValue = (rand() % (MAX_DIEFACES)) + 1;
            m_nSecondDieValue = (rand() % (MAX_DIEFACES)) + 1;
            FireViewChange();
            m_nTimesRolled++;
        }
        bHandled = TRUE;
        return 0;
    }
```

Now these two properties are exposed to the outside world. When the client code changes the color of the dice, the control will load a new set of bitmaps and redraw the control with the new dice faces. When the client code changes the number of times to roll, the dice control will use that information to determine the number of times the dice control should respond to the *WM_TIMER* message. So the next question is, "How are these properties accessed by the client code?" One way is through a control's property pages.

Property Pages

Because ActiveX controls are usually user interface gadgets that are meant to be mixed into much larger applications, they often find a home within such places as Visual Basic forms and MFC form views and dialog boxes. When a control is instantiated, the client code can usually reach into the control and manipulate its properties by calling certain functions on the control's incoming interface functions. However, when an ActiveX control is in design mode, accessing the properties through the interface functions isn't always practical. It would be unkind to tool developers to force them to go through the interface functions all the time just to tweak some properties in the control. Why should the tool vendor who's creating the client have to provide a user interface for managing control properties? That's what property pages are for. Property pages are sets of dialog boxes that are implemented by the control for manipulating properties. That way, the tool vendors don't have to keep re-creating dialog boxes for tweaking the properties of an ActiveX control.

How property pages are used Property pages are usually used in one of two ways. The first way is through the control's *IOleObject* interface. The client can call *IOleObject*'s *DoVerb* function, passing in the properties verb identifier (named OLEIVERB_PROPERTIES and defined as the number –7) to ask the control to show its property pages. The control then displays a dialog box, or property frame, that contains all of the control's property pages. For example, Figure 26-6 shows the Properties dialog box containing the property pages for the Microsoft Calendar 9.0 control.

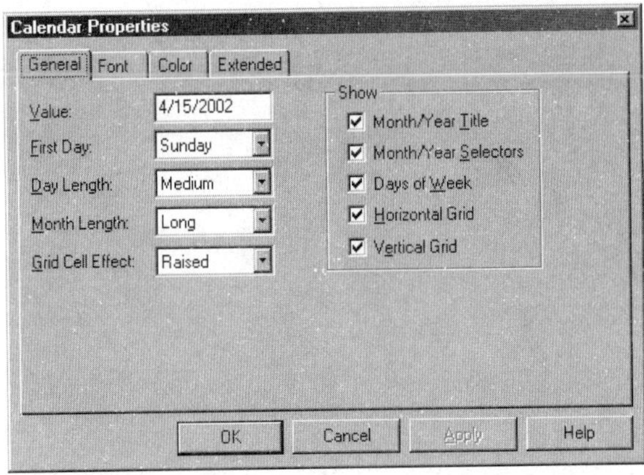

Figure 26-6 The Microsoft Calendar 9.0 control executing the properties verb.

Property pages are a testament to the power of COM. As it turns out, each single property page is a separate COM object (which is named using a GUID and registered like all the other COM classes on your system). When a client asks an ActiveX control to show its property pages via the properties verb, the control passes its own list of property page GUIDs into a system API function named *OleCreatePropertyFrame*. *OleCreatePropertyFrame* enumerates the property page GUIDs, calling *CoCreateInstance* for each property page. The property frame gets a copy of an interface so that the frame can change the properties within the control. *OleCreatePropertyFrame* calls back to the control when the user clicks OK or Apply.

The second way clients use property pages is when the client asks the control for a list of property page GUIDs. The then client calls *CoCreateInstance* on each property page and installs each property page in its own frame. Figure 26-7 shows an example of how Visual C++ .NET uses the Microsoft Calendar property pages in its own property dialog frame. To see a control's property pages, highlight the control in the dialog box and select Property Pages from the View menu.

This second method is by far the most common way for a control's property pages to be used. Notice that the property sheet in Figure 26-7 contains the same General tab shown in Figure 26-6. (The term *property sheet* generally refers to a collection of property pages.) The General property page in Figure 26-7 belongs to Visual C++. The Font and Color property pages are coming from the MFC libraries to which the control is linking (even though they're shown within the context of Visual C++).

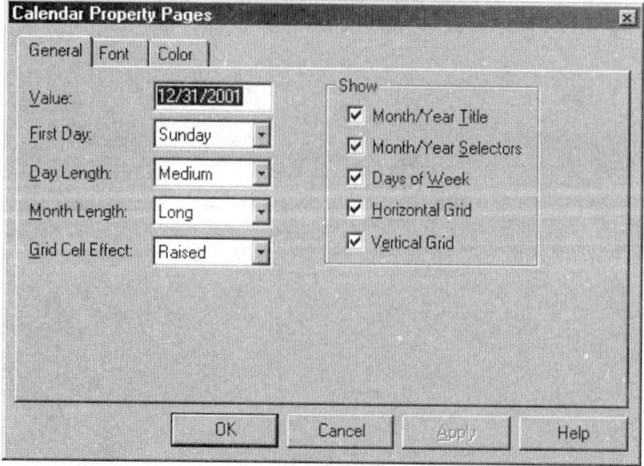

Figure 26-7 Visual C++ .NET inserting the Calendar 9.0 property pages into its own dialog box for editing resource properties.

In order for a property page to work correctly, the control that the property page is associated with must implement *ISpecifyPropertyPages* and the property page object must implement an interface named *IPropertyPage*. With this in mind, let's examine exactly how ATL implements property pages.

Adding a property page to your control You can use the Visual Studio .NET ATL Property Page Wizard to create property pages in your ATL project. To create a property page, perform the following steps:

1. Choose Add Class from the Project menu.
2. Select ATL Property Page from the template list. Fill in the required information on the ATL Property Page Wizard pages, and then click Finish.

The wizard will generate a dialog template and include it as part of a control's resources. In the dice control example, the two properties we're concerned with are the color of the dice and the number of times to roll the dice. The dialog template created by the ATL Property Page Wizard is blank, so you'll want to add a couple of controls to represent these properties. In this example, the user will be able to select the dice color from a combo box and enter the number of times the dice should roll in an edit control, as shown in Figure 26-8.

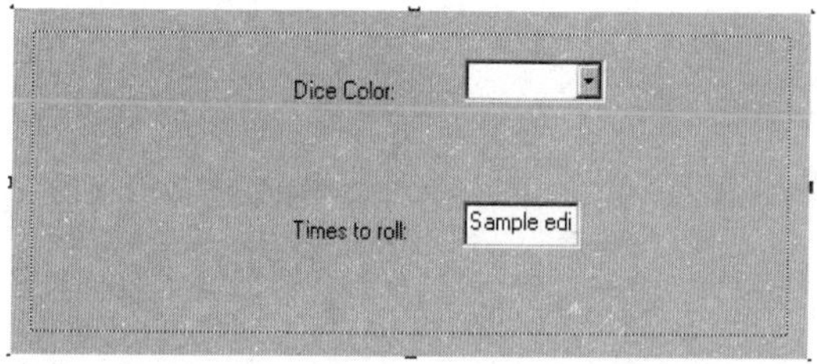

Figure 26-8 The property page dialog template.

The ATL Property Page Wizard also creates a C++ class for you that implements the interface necessary for the class to behave as a property page. In addition to generating this C++ class, the wizard makes the class part of the project. It adds the new property page class to the IDL file within the coclass section. In addition, the wizard appends the property page to the object map so *DllGetClassObject* can find the property page class. Finally, the wizard adds a new Registry script (so the DLL will make the correct Registry entries when the control is registered).

Here's the header file created by the ATL Property Page Wizard for a property page named *DiceMainPropPage*:

```
#pragma once

#include "resource.h"       // main symbols
#include "ClassicATLDiceSvr.h"

// CDiceMainPropPage
class ATL_NO_VTABLE CDiceMainPropPage :
    public CComObjectRootEx<CComSingleThreadModel>,
    public CComCoClass<CDiceMainPropPage, &CLSID_DiceMainPropPage>,
    public IPropertyPageImpl<CDiceMainPropPage>,
    public CDialogImpl<CDiceMainPropPage>
{
public:
    CDiceMainPropPage()
    {
        m_dwTitleID = IDS_TITLEDiceMainPropPage;
        m_dwHelpFileID = IDS_HELPFILEDiceMainPropPage;
        m_dwDocStringID = IDS_DOCSTRINGDiceMainPropPage;
    }

    DECLARE_PROTECT_FINAL_CONSTRUCT()

    HRESULT FinalConstruct()
    {
```

(continued)

```
        return S_OK;
    }

    void FinalRelease()
    {
    }

    enum {IDD = IDD_DICEMAINPROPPAGE};

DECLARE_REGISTRY_RESOURCEID(IDR_DICEMAINPROPPAGE)

BEGIN_COM_MAP(CDiceMainPropPage)
    COM_INTERFACE_ENTRY(IPropertyPage)
END_COM_MAP()

BEGIN_MSG_MAP(CDiceMainPropPage)
    CHAIN_MSG_MAP(IPropertyPageImpl<CDiceMainPropPage>)
END_MSG_MAP()

// Handler prototypes:
//  LRESULT MessageHandler(UINT uMsg, WPARAM wParam, LPARAM lParam,
//                         BOOL& bHandled);
//  LRESULT CommandHandler(WORD wNotifyCode, WORD wID, HWND hWndCtl,
//                         BOOL& bHandled);
//  LRESULT NotifyHandler(int idCtrl, LPNMHDR pnmh, BOOL& bHandled);
    STDMETHOD(Apply)(void)
    {
        ATLTRACE(_T("CDiceMainPropPage::Apply\n"));
        for (UINT i = 0; i < m_nObjects; i++)
        {
            // Do something interesting here
            // ICircCtl* pCirc;
            // m_ppUnk[i]->QueryInterface(IID_ICircCtl, (void**)&pCirc);
            // pCirc->put_Caption(CComBSTR("something special"));
            // pCirc->Release();
        }
        m_bDirty = FALSE;
        return S_OK;
    }
};

OBJECT_ENTRY_AUTO(__uuidof(DiceMainPropPage), CDiceMainPropPage)
```

Examining this property page listing reveals that ATL's property page classes are composed of several ATL templates: *CComObjectRootEx* (to implement *IUnknown*), *CComCoClass* (the class object for the property page), *IPropertyPageImpl* (for implementing *IPropertyPage*), and *CDialogImpl* (for implementing the dialog-specific behavior).

As with most other COM classes created by ATL's wizards, most of the code involved in getting a property page to work is boilerplate code. Notice that besides the constructor and some various maps, the only other function is one named *Apply*.

Before we get into the mechanics of implementing a property page, it'll be helpful for you to understand how the property page architecture works. The code you need to type in to get the property pages working will then make more sense.

When the client decides it's time to show some property pages, a modal dialog frame must be constructed. The frame is constructed by the client or by the control itself. If the property pages are being shown via the *DoVerb* function, the control will construct the frame. If the property pages are being shown within the context of another application—such as when Visual C++ .NET shows the control's property pages within the IDE—the client will construct the dialog frame. The key to the dialog frame is that it holds property page sites (small objects that implement *IPropertyPageSite*) for each property page.

The client code (the modal dialog frame, in this case) then enumerates through a list of GUIDs, calling *CoCreateInstance* on each one of them and asking for the *IPropertyPage* interface. If the COM object produced by *CoCreateInstance* is a property page, it implements the *IPropertyPage* interface. The dialog frame uses the *IPropertyPage* interface to talk to the property page. Here's the declaration of the *IPropertyPage* interface:

```
interface IPropertyPage : public IUnknown {
    HRESULT SetPageSite(IPropertyPageSite *pPageSite) = 0;
    HRESULT Activate(HWND hWndParent,
                     LPCRECT pRect,
                     BOOL bModal) = 0;
    HRESULT Deactivate( void) = 0;
    HRESULT GetPageInfo(PROPPAGEINFO *pPageInfo) = 0;
    HRESULT SetObjects(ULONG cObjects,
                       IUnknown **ppUnk) = 0;
    HRESULT Show(UINT nCmdShow) = 0;
    HRESULT Move(LPCRECT pRect) = 0;
    HRESULT IsPageDirty( void) = 0;
    HRESULT Apply( void) = 0;
    HRESULT Help(LPCOLESTR pszHelpDir) = 0;
    HRESULT TranslateAccelerator(MSG *pMsg) = 0;
};
```

Once a property page has been created, the property page and the client code need some channels to communicate back and forth with the control. After the property dialog frame successfully calls *QueryInterface* for *IPropertyPage* on the property page objects, the frame calls *IPropertyPage::SetPageSite* on each *IPropertyPage* interface pointer that it holds, passing in an *IPropertyPageSite* interface pointer. The property page sites within the property frame provide a way for each property page to call back to the frame. The property page site provides information to the property page and receives notifications from the page when changes occur. Here's the *IPropertyPageSite* interface:

```
interface IPropertyPageSite : public IUnknown {
    public:
        virtual HRESULT OnStatusChange(DWORD dwFlags) = 0;
        virtual HRESULT GetLocaleID(LCID *pLocaleID) = 0;
        virtual HRESULT GetPageContainer(IUnknown *ppUnk) = 0;
        virtual HRESULT TranslateAccelerator(MSG *pMsg) = 0;
};
```

In addition to the frame and control connecting to each other through *IPropertyPage* and *IPropertyPageSite*, each property page needs a way to talk back to the control. This is usually done when the dialog frame calls *IPropertyPage::SetObjects*, passing in the control's *IUnknown*. Figure 26-9 depicts the property page architecture.

Now that you understand how ActiveX control property pages work in general, understanding how they work within ATL will be a lot easier. You'll see how ATL's property pages work when the client code exercises the control's properties verb as well as when environments such as Visual C++ .NET integrate a control's property pages into the IDE.

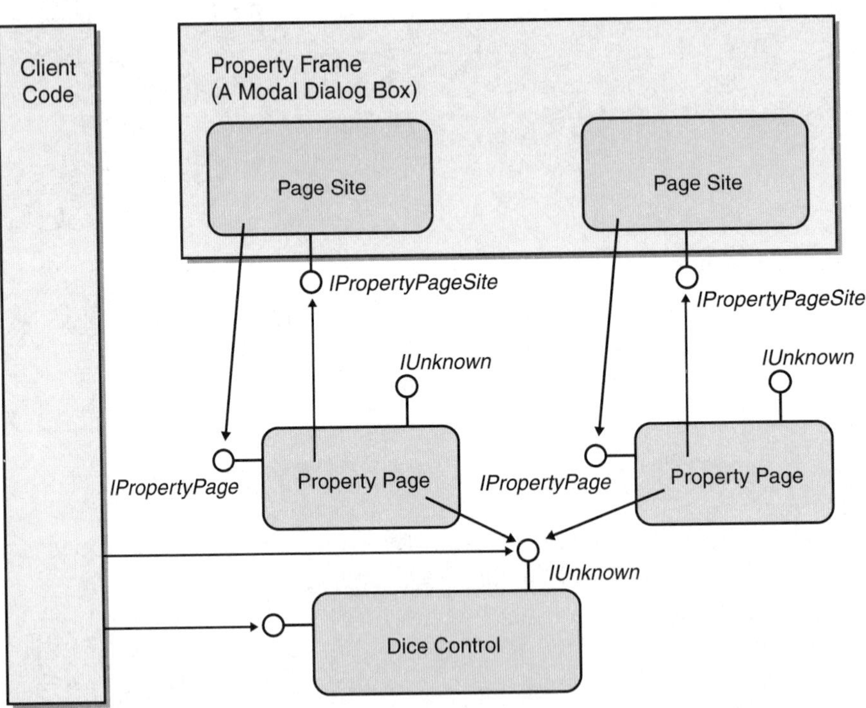

Figure 26-9 How the property pages, property frame, and property page sites communicate.

ATL and the properties verb The first way in which an ActiveX control shows its property pages is when the client invokes the properties verb by calling *IOleObject::DoVerb* using the constant *OLEIVERB_PROPERTIES*. When the client calls *DoVerb* in an ATL-based control, the call ends up in the function *CComControlBase::DoVerbProperties*, which simply calls *OleCreatePropertyFrame*, passing in its own *IUnknown* pointer and the list of property page GUIDs. *OleCreatePropertyFrame* takes the list of GUIDs, calling *CoCreateInstance* on each one to create the property pages, and arranges them within the dialog frame. *OleCreatePropertyFrame* uses each property page's *IPropertyPage* interface to manage the property page.

ATL property maps Of course, understanding how *OleCreatePropertyFrame* works from within the ATL-based control begs the next question: Where does the list of property pages actually come from? ATL uses macros to generate lists of property pages called *property maps*. When you add a new property page to an ATL-based control, you must set up the list of property pages using these macros. ATL includes several macros for implementing property maps: *BEGIN_PROPERTY_MAP*, *PROP_ENTRY*, *PROP_ENTRY_EX*, *PROP_PAGE*, *PROP_DATA_ENTRY*, and *END_PROPERTY_MAP*. Here are those macros in the raw:

```
struct ATL_PROPMAP_ENTRY
{
    LPCOLESTR szDesc;
    DISPID dispid;
    const CLSID* pclsidPropPage;
    const IID* piidDispatch;
    DWORD dwOffsetData;
    DWORD dwSizeData;
    VARTYPE vt;
};

#define BEGIN_PROPERTY_MAP(theClass) \
    __if_not_exists(__ATL_PROP_NOTIFY_EVENT_CLASS) \
    { \
        typedef ATL::_ATL_PROP_NOTIFY_EVENT_CLASS \
            __ATL_PROP_NOTIFY_EVENT_CLASS; \
    } \
    typedef theClass _PropMapClass; \
    static ATL::ATL_PROPMAP_ENTRY* GetPropertyMap()\
    {\
        static ATL::ATL_PROPMAP_ENTRY pPropMap[] = \
        { \
            {OLESTR("_cx"), 0, &CLSID_NULL, NULL, offsetof(_PropMapClass,
                m_sizeExtent.cx), sizeof(long), VT_UI4}, \
            {OLESTR("_cy"), 0, &CLSID_NULL, NULL, offsetof(_PropMapClass,
```

(continued)

```
                m_sizeExtent.cy), sizeof(long), VT_UI4},

// This one can be used on any type of object, but does not
// include the implicit m_sizeExtent
#define BEGIN_PROP_MAP(theClass) \
    __if_not_exists(__ATL_PROP_NOTIFY_EVENT_CLASS) \
    { \
        typedef ATL::_ATL_PROP_NOTIFY_EVENT_CLASS \
            __ATL_PROP_NOTIFY_EVENT_CLASS; \
    } \
    typedef theClass _PropMapClass; \
    static ATL::ATL_PROPMAP_ENTRY* GetPropertyMap()\
    {\
        static ATL::ATL_PROPMAP_ENTRY pPropMap[] = \
        {

#define PROP_ENTRY(szDesc, dispid, clsid) \
        {OLESTR(szDesc), dispid, &clsid, &__uuidof(IDispatch), 0, 0, 0},

#define PROP_ENTRY_EX(szDesc, dispid, clsid, iidDispatch) \
        {OLESTR(szDesc), dispid, &clsid, &iidDispatch, 0, 0, 0},

#define PROP_PAGE(clsid) \
        {NULL, NULL, &clsid, &IID_NULL, 0, 0, 0},

#define PROP_DATA_ENTRY(szDesc, member, vt) \
        {OLESTR(szDesc), 0, &CLSID_NULL, NULL, offsetof(_PropMapClass,
            member), sizeof(((_PropMapClass*)0)->member), vt},

#define END_PROPERTY_MAP() \
            {NULL, 0, NULL, &IID_NULL, 0, 0, 0} \
        }; \
        return pPropMap; \
    }

#define END_PROP_MAP() \
            {NULL, 0, NULL, &IID_NULL, 0, 0, 0} \
        }; \
        return pPropMap; \
    }
```

When you decide to add property pages to a COM class using ATL's property page macros, according to the ATL documentation you should put these macros into your class's header file. For example, if you want to add property pages to the dice control, you add the following code to the C++ class:

```
class ATL_NO_VTABLE CClassicATLDiceControl :
    ⋮
{
    ⋮

    BEGIN_PROP_MAP(CClassicATLDiceControl)

    PROP_DATA_ENTRY("_cx", m_sizeExtent.cx, VT_UI4)
    PROP_DATA_ENTRY("_cy", m_sizeExtent.cy, VT_UI4)
        PROP_ENTRY("Caption goes here...", 2,
                   CLSID_MainPropPage)
        PROP_ENTRY_EX("Caption goes here...", 3,
                      CLSID_SecondPropPage,
                      DIID_SecondDualInterface)
        PROP_PAGE(CLSID_StockColorPage)
    END_PROPERTY_MAP()

};
```

ATL's property map macros set up the list of GUIDs that represent property pages. ATL's property maps are composed of an array of *ATL_PROPMAP_ENTRY* structures. The *BEGIN_PROPERTY_MAP* macro declares a static variable of this structure. The *PROP_DATA_ENTRY* macros associate property dispatch names with internal class member variables (in this case the *x* and *y* extents). The *PROP_PAGE* macro inserts a GUID into the list of property pages. *PROP_ENTRY* inserts a property page GUID into the list and also associates a specific control property with the property page. The final macro, *PROP_ENTRY_EX*, lets you associate a certain dual interface to a property page. When client code invokes the control's properties verb, the control just rips through this list of GUIDs and hands the list over to the *OleCreatePropertyFrame* so the property can create the property pages.

Property pages and development tools Executing the properties verb isn't the only way for an ActiveX control to show its property pages. As mentioned before, folks who write tools such as Visual Basic .NET and Visual C++ .NET might want programmatic access to a control's property pages. For example, when you use MFC to work on a dialog box containing an ActiveX control, right-clicking on the control to view the properties will give you a dialog frame produced by Visual C++ .NET (as opposed to the dialog frame produced by *OleCreatePropertyFrame*).

Visual C++ .NET uses the control's *ISpecifyPropertyPages* interface to get the list of GUIDs (the list generated by the property page macros). Here's the *ISpecifyPropertyPages* interface definition:

```
interface ISpecifyPropertyPages : public IUnknown {
    HRESULT GetPages(CAUUID *pPages);
};

typedef struct tagCAUUID
{
    ULONG      cElems;
    GUID FAR*  pElems;
} CAUUID;
```

ATL implements the *ISpecifyPropertyPages::GetPages* function by cycling through the list of GUIDs (produced by the property map macros) and returning them within the *CAUUID* structure. Environments such as Visual C++ .NET use each GUID in a call to *CoCreateInstance* to create a new property page. The property page site and the property page exchange interfaces. The property page site holds onto the property page's *IPropertyPage* interface, and the property page holds onto the property site's *IPropertyPageSite* interface. After the dialog frame constructs the property pages, it must reflect the current state of the ActiveX control through the dialog controls. For that, you must override the property page's *Activate* method.

Showing the property page The property page's *Activate* method is called whenever the property page is about to be shown. A good thing for a property page to do at this time is to fetch the values from the ActiveX control and populate the property page's controls. Remember that the property page holds onto an array of unknown pointers. (They're held in the *IPropertyPageImpl*'s *m_ppUnk* array.) To access the ActiveX control's properties, you must call *QueryInterface* on the unknown pointers and ask for the interface that exposes the properties. In this case, the interface is *IClassicATLDiceCopntrol.* Once the property page has the interface, it can use the interface to fetch the properties and plug the values into the dialog box controls. Here's the overridden Activate method:

```
#include "ClassicATLDiceSvr.h"

class ATL_NO_VTABLE CDiceMainPropPage :
    public CComObjectRootEx<CComSingleThreadModel>,
    public CComCoClass<CDiceMainPropPage, &CLSID_DiceMainPropPage>,
    public IPropertyPageImpl<CDiceMainPropPage>,
    public CDialogImpl<CDiceMainPropPage>
{
    ⋮
```

```
STDMETHOD(Activate)(HWND hWndParent, LPCRECT prc, BOOL bModal)
{
    // If we don't have any objects, this method should not be called
    // Note that OleCreatePropertyFrame will call Activate even if a call
    // to SetObjects fails, so this check is required
    if (!m_ppUnk)
        return E_UNEXPECTED;

    // Use Activate to update the property page's UI with information
    // obtained from the objects in the m_ppUnk array

    // We update the page to display the Name and ReadOnly properties of
    // the document

    // Call the base class
    HRESULT hr;
    hr = IPropertyPageImpl<CDiceMainPropPage>::Activate(hWndParent,
                                                        prc, bModal);
    if (FAILED(hr))
        return hr;

    for (UINT i = 0; i < m_nObjects; i++)
    {
        CComQIPtr<IClassicATLDiceControl, &IID_IClassicATLDiceControl>
            pClassicATLDiceControl(m_ppUnk[i]);
        short nColor = 0;

        if FAILED(pClassicATLDiceControl->get_DiceColor(&nColor))
        {
            return E_FAIL;
        }
        HWND hWndComboBox = GetDlgItem(IDC_COLOR);
        ::SendMessage(hWndComboBox,
                      CB_SETCURSEL,
                      nColor, 0);

        short nTimesToRoll = 0;
        if FAILED(pClassicATLDiceControl->get_TimesToRoll
            (&nTimesToRoll))
        {
            return E_FAIL;
        }
        SetDlgItemInt(IDC_TIMESTOROLL, nTimesToRoll, FALSE);
    }
    return S_OK;
}
```

In addition to adding code to prepare to show the dialog box, you must add code to allow users to set the control's properties. Whenever the user changes a property, the property dialog box will activate the Apply button, indicating that the user can apply the newly set properties. When the user clicks the Apply button, control will jump to the property page's *Apply* function, so you must insert some code in here to make the Apply button work.

Handling the Apply button After the user finishes manipulating the properties, he'll click the Apply button or the OK button to save the changes. In response, the client code will ask the property page to apply the new properties to the control. Remember that the ActiveX control and the property page are separate COM objects, so they need to communicate via interfaces. Here's how the process works.

When you create a property page using the ATL Property Page Wizard, ATL overrides the *Apply* function from *IPropertyPage* for you. The property page site uses this function for notifying the property page of changes that need to be made to the control. When the property page's *Apply* function is called, it's time to synch up the state of the property page with the state of the control. Remember that the control's *IUnknown* interface was passed into the property page early in the game via a call to *IPropertyPage::SetObjects*. (The interface pointers are stored in the property page's *m_ppUnk* array.) Most property pages respond to the *Apply* function by setting the state of the ActiveX control properties through the interface provided. In the case of our ATL-based property page, this means examining the value in the combo box and the edit box and setting the new values inside the control itself, like this:

```
#include "ClassicATLDiceSvr.h"

class ATL_NO_VTABLE CDiceMainPropPage :
    public CComObjectRootEx<CComSingleThreadModel>,
    public CComCoClass<CDiceMainPropPage, &CLSID_DiceMainPropPage>,
    public IPropertyPageImpl<CDiceMainPropPage>,
    public CDialogImpl<CDiceMainPropPage>
{
   ⋮
    STDMETHOD(Apply)(void)
    {
        USES_CONVERSION;
            ATLTRACE(_T("CDiceMainPropPage::Apply\n"));
        for (UINT i = 0; i < m_nObjects; i++)
            {
                CComQIPtr<IClassicATLDiceControl,
                    &IID_IClassicATLDiceControl>
                    pClassicATLDiceControl(m_ppUnk[i]);
                HWND hWndComboBox = GetDlgItem(IDC_COLOR);
                short nColor   = (short)::SendMessage(hWndComboBox,
                                                       CB_GETCURSEL,
```

```
                                                    0, 0);
                if(nColor >= 0 && nColor <= 2) {
                if FAILED(pClassicATLDiceControl->put_DiceColor(nColor))
                {
                    CComPtr<IErrorInfo> pError;
                    CComBSTR            strError;
                    GetErrorInfo(0, &pError);
                    pError->GetDescription(&strError);
                    MessageBox(OLE2T(strError),
                               _T("Error"),
                               MB_ICONEXCLAMATION);
                    return E_FAIL;
                }
            }
            short nTimesToRoll = (short)GetDlgItemInt(IDC_TIMESTOROLL);
            if FAILED(pClassicATLDiceControl->put_TimesToRoll(nTimesToRoll))
            {
                CComPtr<IErrorInfo> pError;
                CComBSTR            strError;
                GetErrorInfo(0, &pError);
                pError->GetDescription(&strError);
                MessageBox(OLE2T(strError), _T("Error"), MB_ICONEXCLAMATION);
                return E_FAIL;
            }
        }
        m_bDirty = FALSE;
        return S_OK;
    }
```

Property Persistence

Once you've added properties to the control, you might want to have those properties persist with their container. For example, imagine that a gaming company buys your dice control to include in its Windows version of a new game. The game vendor uses your dice control within one of their dialog boxes and configures the control so that the dice are blue and they roll 23 times before stopping. If the dice control has a sound property, the game authors can configure the dice to emit a beep every time they roll. When someone plays the game and rolls the dice, that person will see a pair of blue dice that roll 23 times before stopping and they'll hear the dice make a sound while rolling. Remember that these properties are all properties of the control. If you're using the control in an application, chances are good that you'll want these properties to be saved with the application.

Fortunately, adding persistence support to your control is almost free when you use the ATL property macros. You've already seen how to add the property pages to the control DLL using the property map macros. As it turns out, these macros also make the properties persistent.

You can find ATL's code for handling the persistence of a control's properties within the *CComControlBase* class. *CComControlBase* has a member function named *IPersistStreamInit_Save* that handles saving a control's properties to a stream provided by the client. Whenever the container calls *IPersistStreamInit::Save*, ATL ends up calling *IPersistStreamInit_Save* to do the actual work. *IPersistStreamInit_Save* works by retrieving the control's property map—the list of properties maintained by the control. (Remember that the *BEGIN_PROPERTY_MAP* macro adds a function named *GetPropertyMap* to the control.) The first item written out by *IPersistStreamInit_Save* is the control's extents (its size on the screen). *IPersistStreamInit_Save* then cycles through the property map to write the contents of the property map out to the stream. For each property, the control calls *QueryInterface* on itself to get its own dispatch interface. As *IPersistStreamInit_Save* goes through the list of properties, the control calls *IDispatch::Invoke* on itself to get the property based on the DISPID associated with the property. (The property's DISPID is included as part of the property map structure.) The property comes back from *IDispatch::Invoke* as a variant, and *IPersistStreamInit_Save* writes the property to the stream provided by the client.

Bidirectional Communication (Events)

Now that the dice control has properties and property pages and renders itself to a device context, the last thing to do is to add some events to the control. Events provide a way for the control to call back to the client code and inform the client code of certain events as they occur.

For example, the user can roll the dice. Then, when the dice stop rolling, the client application can fish the dice values out of the control. Another way to implement the control is to set it up so that the control uses an event to notify the client application when the dice have rolled. We'll add some events to the dice control shortly. But first, we'll look at how ActiveX control events work.

How events work When a control is embedded in a container (such as a Visual Basic .NET form or an MFC-based dialog box), one of the steps the client code takes is to establish a connection to the control's event set. That is, the client implements an interface that has been described by the control and makes that interface available to the control. That way, the control can talk back to the container.

Part of developing a control involves defining an interface that the control can use to call back to the client. For example, if you're developing the control using MFC, the wizards will define the interface and produce some functions you can call from within the control to fire events back to the client. If you're developing the control in ATL, you can accomplish the same result by defining the event callback interface in the control's IDL and using Class View to create a set of callback proxy functions for firing the events to the container. When the callback interface is defined by the control, the container must implement that interface and hand it over to the control. The client and the control do this through the *IConnectionPointContainer* and *IConnectionPoint* interfaces.

IConnectionPointContainer is the interface that a COM object implements to indicate that it supports connections. *IConnectionPointContainer* represents a collection of connections available to the client. Within the context of ActiveX controls, one of these connections is usually the control's main event set. Here's the *IConnectionPointContainer* interface:

```
interface IConnectionPointContainer : IUnknown {
    HRESULT FindConnectionPoint(REFIID riid,
                                IConnectionPoint **ppcp) = 0;
    HRESULT EnumConnectionPoints(IEnumConnectionsPoint **ppec) = 0;
};
```

IConnectionPointContainer represents a collection of *IConnectionPoint* interfaces. Here's the *IConnectionPoint* interface:

```
interface IConnectionPoint : IUnknown {
    HRESULT GetConnectionInterface(IID *pid) = 0;
    HRESULT GetConnectionPointContainer(
        IConnectionPointContainer **ppcpc) = 0;
    HRESULT Advise(IUnknown *pUnk, DWORD *pdwCookie) = 0;
    HRESULT Unadvise(dwCookie) = 0;
    HRESULT EnumConnections(IEnumConnections **ppec) = 0;
}
```

The container creates the control by calling *CoCreateInstance* on the control. As the control and the container are establishing the interface connections between themselves, one of the interfaces the container will ask for is *IConnectionPointContainer*. (The container calls *QueryInterface* asking for *IID_IConnectionPointContainer*.) If the control supports connection points (if the control answers *Yes* when queried for *IConnectionPointContainer*), the control will use *IConnectionPointContainer::FindConnectionPoint* to get the *IConnectionPoint* interface that represents the main event set. The container will know the GUID that represents the main event set by looking at the control's type information as the control is inserted into the container.

If the container can establish a connection point to the control's main event set (if *IConnectionPointContainer::FindConnectionPoint* returns an *IConnectionPoint* interface pointer), the container will use *IConnection-Point::Advise* to subscribe to the callbacks. Of course, in order to do this the container must implement the callback interface defined by the control (which the container can learn about by using the control's type library). Once the connection is established, the control can call back to the container whenever the control fires off an event. Next, we'll look at what it takes to make events work within an ATL-based ActiveX control.

Adding events to the dice control There are several steps to adding event sets to your control. Some are hidden by clever wizardry. First, you use IDL to describe the events. Second, you add a proxy that encapsulates the connection points and event functions. Finally, you fill out the control's connection map so the client and the object have a way to connect to each other. Let's examine each step in detail.

When you use ATL to write an ActiveX control, IDL is the place to start adding events to your control. The event callback interface is described within the IDL so the client will know how to implement the callback interface correctly. The IDL is compiled into a type library that the client will use to figure out how to implement the callback interface. The easiest way to add events to the IDL is to select the event callback interface from within Class View and add the event methods. For example, if you want to add events to indicate that the dice were rolled, doubles were rolled, and snake eyes were rolled, you describe the callback interface with a *DiceRolled*, a *Doubles*, and a *SnakeEyes* method. It's just like defining methods within the main interface. Here's the control's IDL file after adding the methods:

```
[
    uuid(D66265FF-D959-47FB-BC36-585AFC4FFB49),
    version(1.0),
    helpstring("ClassicATLDiceSvr 1.0 Type Library")
]
library ClassicATLDiceSvrLib
{
    importlib("stdole2.tlb");
    [
        uuid(2FECDCBE-D2C8-46EF-A4A1-E86CDC63B321),
        helpstring("_IClassicATLDiceControlEvents Interface")
    ]
    dispinterface _IClassicATLDiceControlEvents
    {
        properties:
        methods:
            [id(1)]void Doubles(short n);
            [id(2)]void SnakeEyes();
            [id(3)]void DiceRolled(short x, short y);
```

```
    };
    [
        uuid(75E15528-7E89-431F-B170-D6991C26F944),
        helpstring("ClassicATLDiceControl Class")
    ]
    coclass ClassicATLDiceControl
    {
        [default] interface IClassicATLDiceControl;
        [default, source] dispinterface _IClassicATLDiceControlEvents;
    };
    [
        uuid(7A91E3F2-21BB-4286-B02E-4F067FD48DB3),
        helpstring("CDiceMainPropPage Class")
    ]
};
```

The control's callback interface is defined as a dispatch interface (note the *dispinterface* keyword) because that's the most generic kind of interface available. When it comes to callback interfaces, most environments understand only *IDispatch*. The code describes a callback interface to be implemented by the client (if the client decides it wants to receive these callbacks).

Implementing the connection point After you've described the callback interface within the IDL and compiled the control, the control's type information will contain the callback interface description so the client will know how to implement the callback interface. However, you don't yet have a convenient way to fire these events from the control. You could, of course, call back to the client by setting up calls to *IDispatch::Invoke* by hand. However, a better way is to set up a proxy (a set of functions that wrap calls to *IDispatch*) to handle the hard work for you. To generate a set of functions that you can call to fire events in the container, you can use the Implement Connection Point Wizard available from Class View.

In Class View, click the right mouse button while the cursor is hovering over the CClassicATLDiceControl symbol. This will bring up the shortcut menu for the CClassicATLDiceControl item. Choose Add, and then choose Add Connection Point to launch the Implement Connection Point Wizard. This wizard will ask you to locate the type information that describes the interface you expect to use when you call back to the container (the *_IClassicATLDiceControlEvents* interface, in this case). By default, the wizard will look at your control's type library and show the interfaces found within it. Select *_IClassicATLDiceControlEvents* and then click Finish to create a C++ class that wraps the dice events interface.

Given the above interface definition, here's the code generated by the Implement Connection Point Wizard:

```
#pragma once
template<class T>
class CProxy_IClassicATLDiceControlEvents :
    public IConnectionPointImpl<T,
        &__uuidof(_IClassicATLDiceControlEvents)>
{
public:
    HRESULT Fire_Doubles(short  n)
    {
        HRESULT hr = S_OK;
        T * pThis = static_cast<T *>(this);
        int cConnections = m_vec.GetSize();

        for (int iConnection = 0; iConnection < cConnections;
            iConnection++)
        {
            pThis->Lock();
            CComPtr<IUnknown> punkConnection = m_vec.GetAt(iConnection);
            pThis->Unlock();

            IDispatch * pConnection =
                static_cast<IDispatch *>(punkConnection.p);

            if (pConnection)
            {
                CComVariant avarParams[1];
                avarParams[0] = n;
                DISPPARAMS params = { avarParams, NULL, 1, 0 };
                hr = pConnection->Invoke(1, IID_NULL, LOCALE_USER_DEFAULT,
                    DISPATCH_METHOD, &params, NULL, NULL, NULL);
            }
        }
        return hr;
    }
    HRESULT Fire_SnakeEyes()
    {
        HRESULT hr = S_OK;
        T * pThis = static_cast<T *>(this);
        int cConnections = m_vec.GetSize();

        for (int iConnection = 0; iConnection < cConnections; iConnection++)
        {
            pThis->Lock();
            CComPtr<IUnknown> punkConnection = m_vec.GetAt(iConnection);
            pThis->Unlock();
```

```
            IDispatch * pConnection =
                static_cast<IDispatch *>(punkConnection.p);

            if (pConnection)
            {
                DISPPARAMS params = { NULL, NULL, 0, 0 };
                hr = pConnection->Invoke(2, IID_NULL, LOCALE_USER_DEFAULT,
                    DISPATCH_METHOD, &params, NULL, NULL, NULL);
            }
        }
        return hr;
    }
    HRESULT Fire_DiceRolled(short  x, short  y)
    {
        HRESULT hr = S_OK;
        T * pThis = static_cast<T *>(this);
        int cConnections = m_vec.GetSize();

        for (int iConnection = 0; iConnection < cConnections; iConnection++)
        {
            pThis->Lock();
            CComPtr<IUnknown> punkConnection = m_vec.GetAt(iConnection);
            pThis->Unlock();

            IDispatch * pConnection =
                static_cast<IDispatch *>(punkConnection.p);

            if (pConnection)
            {
                CComVariant avarParams[2];
                avarParams[1] = x;
                avarParams[0] = y;
                DISPPARAMS params = { avarParams, NULL, 2, 0 };
                hr = pConnection->Invoke(3, IID_NULL, LOCALE_USER_DEFAULT,
                    DISPATCH_METHOD, &params, NULL, NULL, NULL);
            }
        }
        return hr;
    }
};
```

The C++ class generated by the connection point generator serves a dual purpose. First, it acts as the specific connection point. (Notice that it derives from *IConnectionPointImpl*.) Second, it serves as a proxy to the interface implemented by the container. For example, if you want to call over to the client and tell the client that doubles were rolled, you can simply call the proxy's *Fire_Doubles* function. Notice how the proxy wraps the *IDispatch* call so you don't have to get your hands messy dealing with variants by yourself.

Establishing the connection and firing the events The final step in setting up the event set is to add the connection point to the dice control and turn on the *IConnectionPointContainer* interface. The Implement Connection Point Wizard added the *CProxy_IClassicATLDiceControlEvents* class to the dice control's inheritance list, which provides the *IConnectionPoint* implementation inside the control. An ATL class named *IConnectionPointContainerImpl* provides the implementation of *IConnectionPointContainer*. These two interfaces should be in the dice control's inheritance list, like this:

```
class ATL_NO_VTABLE CClassicATLDiceControl :
    public CComObjectRootEx<CComSingleThreadModel>,
    public CStockPropImpl<CClassicATLDiceControl, IClassicATLDiceControl>,
    public IPersistStreamInitImpl<CClassicATLDiceControl>,
    public IOleControlImpl<CClassicATLDiceControl>,
    public IOleObjectImpl<CClassicATLDiceControl>,
    public IOleInPlaceActiveObjectImpl<CClassicATLDiceControl>,
    public IViewObjectExImpl<CClassicATLDiceControl>,
    public IOleInPlaceObjectWindowlessImpl<CClassicATLDiceControl>,
    public ISupportErrorInfo,
    public IConnectionPointContainerImpl<CClassicATLDiceControl>,
    public CProxy_IClassicATLDiceControlEvents<CClassicATLDiceControl>,
    public IPersistStorageImpl<CClassicATLDiceControl>,
    public ISpecifyPropertyPagesImpl<CClassicATLDiceControl>,
    public IQuickActivateImpl<CClassicATLDiceControl>,
    public IDataObjectImpl<CClassicATLDiceControl>,
    public IProvideClassInfo2Impl<&CLSID_ClassicATLDiceControl,
        &__uuidof(_IClassicATLDiceControlEvents),
        &LIBID_ClassicATLDiceSvrLib>,
    public IPropertyNotifySinkCP<CClassicATLDiceControl>,
    public CComCoClass<CClassicATLDiceControl, &CLSID_ClassicATLDiceControl>,
    public CComControl<CClassicATLDiceControl>
{
⋮
}
```

Having these classes in the inheritance list will insert the machinery in your control that makes connection points work. When you want to fire an event to the container, all you need to do is call one of the functions in the proxy. For example, a good time to fire these events is from within the control's *OnTimer* method—firing a *DiceRolled* event whenever the timer stops, firing a *SnakeEyes* event whenever both die faces have the value 1, and firing a *Doubles* event when both die faces are equal:

```
LRESULT CClassicATLDiceControl::OnTimer(UINT uMsg, WPARAM wParam,
                                        LPARAM lParam, BOOL& bHandled)
{
    if(m_nTimesRolled > m_nTimesToRoll) {
```

```
        m_nTimesRolled = 0;
        KillTimer(1);

        Fire_DiceRolled(m_nFirstDieValue, m_nSecondDieValue);

        if(m_nFirstDieValue == m_nSecondDieValue) {
            Fire_Doubles(m_nFirstDieValue);
        }

        if(m_nFirstDieValue == 1 &&
           m_nSecondDieValue == 1) {
            Fire_SnakeEyes();
        }

    } else {
        m_nFirstDieValue = (rand() % (MAX_DIEFACES)) + 1;
        m_nSecondDieValue = (rand() % (MAX_DIEFACES)) + 1;
        FireViewChange();
        m_nTimesRolled++;
    }
    bHandled = TRUE;
    return 0;
}
```

Finally, notice the connection map contains entries for the control's connection points:

```
BEGIN_CONNECTION_POINT_MAP(CClassicATLDiceControl)
    CONNECTION_POINT_ENTRY(__uuidof(_IClassicATLDiceControlEvents))
END_CONNECTION_POINT_MAP()
```

The control uses this map to hand back connection points as the client requests them.

Using the Control

So, how do you use the control once you've written it? The beauty of COM is that as long as the client and the object agree on their shared interfaces, they don't need to know anything else about each other. All the interfaces implemented within the dice control are well understood by a number of programming environments. You've already seen how to use ActiveX controls within an MFC-based dialog box. The control you just wrote will work fine within an MFC-based dialog box—you just use the Customize Toolbox dialog box to add controls to the Toolbox.

To insert the *ClassicATLDiceControl* component into your project, choose Customize Toolbox from the Tools menu to open the Customize Toolbox dialog box. On the COM Components tab, select the ClassicATLDiceControl Class check box. Visual C++ .NET will read the dice control's type information and insert all the necessary COM glue to make the dialog box and the control talk with each other. (This includes all the OLE embedding interfaces as well as the connection and event interfaces.) You can also just as easily use this control from within a Visual Basic .NET form. When you're working on a Visual Basic .NET project, choose Add Reference from the Project menu, click on the COM tab, and select ClassicATLDiceSvr 1.0 Type Library to add the dice control to the Visual Basic .NET project.

Creating an Attributed Control

In addition to classic ATL-style programming for creating ActiveX controls, Visual Studio .NET also offers attributed ATL for programming controls. Recall from Chapter 22 and Chapter 25 that COM development requires a fair amount of boilerplate code—code that remains the same from one COM implementation to another. Attributed programming pushes the boilerplate COM code (*IUnknown* implementations, DLL entry points, and so forth) out of C++ templates and moves the boilerplate into injected code. That is, by declaring a few attributes before some C++ code, you can have the compiler and linker provide the boilerplate code.

If you go back and take a look at the listing for *ClassicATLDiceControl*, you'll see *CComObjectRootEx* and *CComCoClass* templates in the declaration. The following listing shows the attributed version of the same control (the dice control).

```
// IAttributedATLDiceControl
[
    object,
    uuid(5321A066-9E3A-4412-A11A-32D5ED060146),
    dual,
    helpstring("IAttributedATLDiceControl Interface"),
    pointer_default(unique)
]
__interface IAttributedATLDiceControl : public IDispatch
{
    [propput, bindable, requestedit, id(DISPID_BACKCOLOR)]
    HRESULT BackColor([in]OLE_COLOR clr);
    [propget, bindable, requestedit, id(DISPID_BACKCOLOR)]
    HRESULT BackColor([out,retval]OLE_COLOR* pclr);
    [propget, id(1), helpstring("property DiceColor")]
    HRESULT DiceColor([out, retval] SHORT* pVal);
    [propput, id(1), helpstring("property DiceColor")]
    HRESULT DiceColor([in] SHORT newVal);
    [propget, id(2), helpstring("property TimesToRoll")]
    HRESULT TimesToRoll([out, retval] SHORT* pVal);
    [propput, id(2), helpstring("property TimesToRoll")]
```

```
    HRESULT TimesToRoll([in] SHORT newVal);
    [id(3), helpstring("method RollDice")] HRESULT RollDice(void);
};

// _IAttributedATLDiceControlEvents
[
    uuid("4AB0D205-044E-4641-A0A5-B606D8685FE5"),
    dispinterface,
    helpstring("_IAttributedATLDiceControlEvents Interface")
]
__interface _IAttributedATLDiceControlEvents
{
    [id(1), helpstring("method Doubles")] HRESULT Doubles(SHORT n);
    [id(2), helpstring("method SnakeEyes")] HRESULT SnakeEyes(void);
    [id(3), helpstring("method DiceRolled")] HRESULT DiceRolled
        (SHORT x, SHORT y);
};

// CAttributedATLDiceControl
[
    coclass,
    threading("apartment"),
    vi_progid("AttributedATLDiceSvr.AttributedATLDiceC"),
    progid("AttributedATLDiceSvr.AttributedATLDic.1"),
    version(1.0),
    uuid("48350572-BE82-4FBB-AA6F-B4691E30173A"),
    helpstring("AttributedATLDiceControl Class"),
    event_source("com"),
    support_error_info(IAttributedATLDiceControl),
    registration_script("control.rgs")
]
class ATL_NO_VTABLE CAttributedATLDiceControl :
    public CStockPropImpl<CAttributedATLDiceControl,
        IAttributedATLDiceControl>,
    public IPersistStreamInitImpl<CAttributedATLDiceControl>,
    public IOleControlImpl<CAttributedATLDiceControl>,
    public IOleObjectImpl<CAttributedATLDiceControl>,
    public IOleInPlaceActiveObjectImpl<CAttributedATLDiceControl>,
    public IViewObjectExImpl<CAttributedATLDiceControl>,
    public IOleInPlaceObjectWindowlessImpl<CAttributedATLDiceControl>,
    public IPersistStorageImpl<CAttributedATLDiceControl>,
    public ISpecifyPropertyPagesImpl<CAttributedATLDiceControl>,
    public IQuickActivateImpl<CAttributedATLDiceControl>,
    public IDataObjectImpl<CAttributedATLDiceControl>,
    public CComControl<CAttributedATLDiceControl>
{
public:
    ⋮
```

(continued)

```
    __event __interface _IAttributedATLDiceControlEvents;
//Fire events:
    HRESULT Fire_Doubles(short x)
    {
      __raise Doubles(x);
      return S_OK;
    }

    HRESULT Fire_DiceRolled(short x, short y)
    {
      __raise DiceRolled(x, y);
      return S_OK;
    }

    HRESULT Fire_SnakeEyes()
    {
      __raise SnakeEyes();
      return S_OK;
    }
⋮
}
```

The *CComCoClass* and the *CComObjectRootEx* template classes are missing from the attributed version of the control. Other COM boilerplate code pulled in through the attributes declared includes an implementation of *ISupportErrorInfo*, connection point support, and an implementation of *IProvideClassInfo2*. Otherwise, the rest of the control is pretty much the same with the exception of managing events.

Control Events in Attributed ATL

Take a look at the previous listing for the attributed ATL control. In addition to declaring the main dice interface, the listing declares an event interface (the one with methods for telling the client code about the dice being rolled, snake eyes, and doubles). To declare the *_IAttributedATLDiceControlEvents* interface as the control's event interface, attributed ATL uses the keywords *__event __interface* together.

Unfortunately, the code wizards available from Class View's properties window won't write the event proxies for you—that you must do by hand. Notice the hand-coded methods *Fire_DiceRolled*, *Fire_Doubles*, and *Fire_SnakeEyes* in the previous code listing. To fire the event off to the client code, you simply raise the event using the *__raise* keyword before calling the event method.

27

The OLE DB Templates

The modern way to approach database access is through OLE DB. This chapter covers the OLE DB templates—the mechanism that Microsoft Visual C++ .NET provides for accessing data through OLE DB directly. OLE DB is designed to provide access to all types of data within a system, and it uses the Component Object Model (COM) to accomplish this. OLE DB is fairly flexible—it covers all the main SQL functionality, and it defines interfaces that are suitable for gaining access to non-SQL types of data.

OLE DB data access has two major parts: consumers and providers. We'll take a look at the basic OLE DB architecture and then examine how the consumer templates work, and then we'll look at how the provider-side templates work.

Why OLE DB?

OLE DB exists to provide a uniform way to access all sorts of disparate data sources. For example, imagine all the types of data sources you might find in a typical organization. These might include sources as varied as production systems, file systems, spreadsheets, personal databases (such as Xbase and Btrieve), and e-mail. The problem is that each of these sources requires its own protocol. If you want to access data from a specific source, you have to learn the protocol for managing the data source. (Ugh!) OLE DB is the middle layer that provides uniform access to various data sources. With OLE DB, client-side developers have to concentrate on only a few details to get access to data (instead of needing to know many different database access protocols).

The most important thing to realize about OLE DB is that it is built on COM. In other words, OLE DB is a set of interfaces for accessing data through

COM. The OLE DB interfaces are general enough to provide a uniform means of accessing data, regardless of the method that is used to store the data. For example, developers use the same OLE DB interfaces to get to data without having to be concerned about whether data is stored in a database management system (DBMS) or a non-DBMS information source. At the same time, OLE DB lets developers continue to take advantage of the benefits of the underlying database technology (such as speed and flexibility) without having to move data around just to access those benefits.

As mentioned earlier, at the highest level the OLE DB architecture consists of consumers and providers. A consumer is any bit of system or application code that uses an OLE DB interface. This includes OLE DB components themselves. A provider is any software component that exposes an OLE DB interface.

There are two types of OLE DB providers: data providers and service providers. The names are pretty self-explanatory. Data providers own data and expose that data in a tabular form as a *rowset*. (A rowset is just an abstraction for exposing data in a tabular form.) Examples of data providers include relational DBMSs, storage managers, spreadsheets, and indexed sequential access method (ISAM) databases.

A service provider is any OLE DB component that does not own data but encapsulates some service by massaging data through OLE DB interfaces. In one sense, a service component is both a consumer and a provider. For example, a heterogeneous query processor is a service component. If a consumer tries to join data from tables in two different data sources, as a consumer the query processor will retrieve rows from rowsets created over each of the base tables, and as a provider the query processor will create a rowset from these rows and return it to the consumer.

To sum up, there are many kinds of data and numerous ways of accessing that data in the real world, and many developers understand how to manipulate data using standard database management techniques. OLE DB defines an architecture that "componentizes" data access. As a component DBMS, OLE DB offers greater efficiency than traditional DBMSs by separating database functionality into the roles of consumers and producers. Because data consumers generally require only a portion of the database management functionality, OLE DB separates that functionality, thereby reducing client-side resource overhead.

OLE DB also reduces the burden on the provider side—providers need to worry only about providing data (not about any client-side junk). For example, OLE DB allows a simple tabular data provider to implement functionality that's native to its data store and provide a singular access protocol to get to the data. That way, a minimal implementation of a provider can choose to use only the interfaces that expose data as tables. This allows for the development of completely different query processor components that can consume tabular information from any provider that exposes its data through OLE DB. In addition, SQL DBMSs can expose their functionality in a more layered manner by using the OLE DB interfaces.

The Basic OLE DB Architecture

In addition to defining a basic relationship between consumers and providers, OLE DB defines the following components that make up the OLE DB architecture. (Each component is a COM object.)

- **Enumerators** Enumerators search for available data sources. Consumers that are not hardwired for a particular data source employ enumerators to search for a data source to use.
- **Data source objects** These contain the machinery to connect to a data source (such as a file or a DBMS). A data source object generates sessions.
- **Sessions** Sessions represent connections to a database. For example, sessions provide a context for database transactions. A single data source object can create multiple sessions. Sessions generate transactions, commands, and rowsets.
- **Transaction objects** These are used for managing database transactions in order to maintain database security.
- **Commands** Commands execute text commands, such as SQL statements. If the text command specifies a rowset, such as a SQL SELECT statement, the command will generate rowsets. A single session can create multiple commands.
- **Rowsets** Rowsets expose data in a tabular format. A special case of a rowset is an index. Rowsets can be created from the session or the command.
- **Errors** Errors can be created by any interface on any OLE DB object. They contain additional information about an error, including an optional custom error object.

Here's an example of how you might apply these components to create an OLE DB consumer. If you aren't sure where the data source is, you might first use an enumerator to find it. Once you've located a data source, you can create a session with it. The session will let you access the data as rowsets as well as create commands that generate rowsets.

The upside of using the OLE DB architecture is that you get a homogenous way to access heterogeneous data sources. The downside is that you have to implement a bunch of COM interfaces to make that happen. That's why the OLE DB templates exist.

The Basic OLE DB Template Architecture

Now that you understand the basic architecture behind OLE DB, let's look at a specific implementation of the OLE DB interfaces (provided by the new OLE DB consumer and provider templates). Like most other COM-based technologies, OLE DB involves implementing a bunch of interfaces. Of course, just as with ActiveX controls, you can choose to implement them by hand (which is often an inefficient approach—unless you're just trying to understand the technology inside-out) or you can find someone else to do most of the dirty work. While OLE DB is a rich and powerful data access technology, getting it up and running by hand is a somewhat tedious task.

Just as Visual C++ .NET provides a template library (the Active Template Library) for implementing ActiveX controls, Visual C++ .NET provides a template library that helps you manage OLE DB. The OLE DB template library provides classes that implement many of the commonly used OLE DB interfaces. In addition, Visual C++ .NET provides great wizard support for generating code to apply to common scenarios.

At a high level, you can divide the classes in this template library into the two groups defined by OLE DB itself: the consumer classes and the provider classes. The consumer classes help you implement database client (consumer) applications, and the provider classes help you implement database server (provider) applications. Remember that OLE DB consumers are applications that call the COM interfaces exposed by OLE DB service providers (regular providers) to access data. OLE DB providers are COM servers that provide data and services in a form that a consumer can understand.

The OLE DB Consumer Template Architecture

Microsoft has kept the top-layer classes in the OLE DB consumer templates as close to the OLE DB specification as possible. That is, OLE DB templates don't define another object model. They simply wrap the existing OLE DB object model. For each of the consumer-related components discussed in the previous section, you'll find a corresponding C++ template class. This design philosophy leverages the flexibility of OLE DB and allows more advanced features—such as multiple accessors on rowsets—to be available through the OLE DB templates.

The OLE DB templates are small and flexible. They're implemented using C++ templates and multiple inheritance. Because OLE DB templates are close to the metal (they wrap only the existing OLE DB architecture), each class mirrors an existing OLE DB component. For example, *CDataSource* corresponds to the data source object in OLE DB.

The OLE DB consumer template architecture can be divided into three parts: the general data source support classes, classes for supporting data access and rowset operations, and classes for handling tables and commands. A quick summary of these classes follows.

General Data Source Support

The data source (where the data comes from) is the most fundamental concept underlying data access using OLE DB. Of course, the OLE DB templates have support for data sources. General data source support comprises three classes, as described in the following table.

Class	Description
CDataSource	This class represents the data source component and manages the connection to a data source.
CEnumerator	This class provides a way to select a provider by cycling through a list of providers. Its functionality is equivalent to the *SQLBrowseConnect* and *SQLDriverConnect* functions.
CSession	This class handles transactions. You can use it to create rowsets, commands, and many other objects. A *CDataSource* object creates a *CSession* object using the *CSession::Open* method.

Data Access and Rowset Support

The OLE DB templates provide binding and rowset support through several classes. The accessor classes talk to the data source, and the rowset manages the data in tabular form. The data access and rowset components are implemented through the *CAccessorRowset* class. *CAccessorRowset* is a template class that's specialized on an accessor and a rowset. This class can handle multiple accessors of different types.

The OLE DB template library defines the accessors listed in the following table.

Class	Description
CAccessor	This class is used when a record is statically bound to a data source—it contains the preexisting data buffer and understands the data format up front. You use *CAccessor* when you know the structure and the type of the database ahead of time.
CDynamicAccessor	This class is used for retrieving data from a source whose structure is not known at design time. This class uses *IColumnsInfo::GetColumnInfo* to get the database column information. *CDynamicAccessor* creates and manages the data buffer.
CDynamicParameterAccessor	This class is similar to *CDynamicAccessor* except that it's used with commands. When used to prepare commands, *CDynamicParameterAccessor* can get parameter information from the *ICommandWithParameters* interface. This is especially useful for handling unknown command types.
CManualAccessor	This class lets you access any data types you want as long as the provider can convert the type. *CManualAccessor* handles both result columns and command parameters.

Along with the accessors, the OLE DB templates define three types of rowsets: single-fetching, bulk, and array. These are fairly self-explanatory. Clients use a function named *MoveNext* to navigate through the data. The difference between the single-fetching, bulk, and array rowsets lies in the number of row handles retrieved when *MoveNext* is called. Single-fetching rowsets retrieve a single rowset for each call to *MoveNext*, and bulk rowsets fetch multiple rows. Array rowsets provide a convenient array syntax for fetching data. The OLE DB templates provide the single row-fetching capability by default.

Table and Command Support

The final layer in the OLE DB consumer template architecture consists of two more classes: table and command classes (*CTable* and *CCommand*). These classes are used to open the rowset, execute commands, and initiate bindings. Both classes derive from *CAccessorRowset*.

The *CTable* class is a minimal class implementation that opens a table on a data source (which you can specify programmatically). You should use this class when you need bare-bones access to a source; *CTable* is designed for simple providers that do not support commands.

Other data sources do support commands. For those sources, you should use the OLE DB templates' *CCommand* class. As its name implies, *CCommand* is used mostly for executing commands. This class has a function named *Open* that executes singular commands. This class also has a function named *Prepare* for setting up a command to execute multiple times.

When you use the *CCommand* class, you specialize it using three template arguments: an accessor, a rowset, and a third template argument (which defaults to *CNoMultipleResults*). If you specify *CMultipleResults* for the third argument, the *CCommand* class will support the *IMultipleResults* interface for a command that returns multiple rowsets.

The OLE DB Provider Template Architecture

Remember that OLE DB is really just a set of interfaces that specify a protocol for managing data. OLE DB defines several interfaces (some mandatory and others optional) for the following types of objects: data source, session, rowset, and command. Let's discuss each type in turn and look at code snippets that show how the templates bring in the correct functionality for each component.

The Data Source Object

A data source object wraps most aspects of data access. For example, a data source consists of actual data and its associated DBMS, the platform on which the DBMS exists, and the network used to access that platform. A data source is just a COM object that implements a bunch of interfaces, as shown in Table 27-1.

> **Note** The upcoming tables describing interface requirements were compiled from the Visual Studio .NET MSDN Online Help.

Table 27-1 Data Source Object Interface Requirements

Interface	Required?	Implemented?
IDBInitialize	√	√
IDBCreateSession	√	√
IDBProperties	√	√
IPersist	√	√
IDBDataSourceAdmin		
IDBInfo		
IPersistFile		
ISupportErrorInfo		

Here's a code snippet showing the code inserted by the ATL OLE DB Provider Wizard when you create a data source for an OLE DB provider:

```
class ATL_NO_VTABLE CAProviderSource :
    public CComObjectRootEx<CComSingleThreadModel>,
    public CComCoClass<CAProviderSource, &CLSID_AProvider>,
    public IDBCreateSessionImpl<CAProviderSource, CAProviderSession>,
    public IDBInitializeImpl<CAProviderSource>,
    public IDBPropertiesImpl<CAProviderSource>,
    public IPersistImpl<CAProviderSource>,
    public IInternalConnectionImpl<CAProviderSource>
{
    ⋮
};
```

Notice that this is a normal COM class (with ATL's *IUnknown* implementation). The OLE DB data source object brings in implementations of the *IDBCreateSession*, *IDBInitialize*, *IDBProperties*, and *IPersist* interfaces through inheritance. Notice how the templates are specialized on the *CAProviderSource* and *CAProviderSession* classes. If you decide to add more functionality to your class, you can do so by inheriting from one of the OLE DB interface implementation classes.

The Command Object

Providers that support building and executing queries expose a command object. Command objects specify, prepare, and execute a database manipulation language (DML) query or data definition language (DDL) definition and its associated properties. For example, the command object translates a SQL-type command into an operation specific to the data source. A single session can be associated with multiple commands. Table 27-2 lists the interfaces used in a command object.

Here's a code snippet showing the code that the ATL OLE DB Provider Wizard inserts to implement a command object when you create an OLE DB provider:

```
class ATL_NO_VTABLE CAProviderCommand :
    public CComObjectRootEx<CComSingleThreadModel>,
    public IAccessorImpl<CAProviderCommand>,
    public ICommandTextImpl<CAProviderCommand>,
    public ICommandPropertiesImpl<CAProviderCommand>,
    public IObjectWithSiteImpl<CAProviderCommand>,
    public IConvertTypeImpl<CAProviderCommand>,
    public IColumnsInfoImpl<CAProviderCommand>,
    public IInternalCommandConnectionImpl<CAProviderCommand>

{
⋮
};
```

As with the data source, notice that this is just a regular COM class. This class brings in the required interfaces through inheritance. (For example, *IAccessor* comes in through the *IAccessorImpl* template.) A command object uses *IAccessor* to specify parameter bindings. Consumers call *IAccessor::CreateAccessor*, passing an array of *DBBINDING* structures. *DBBINDING* contains information on the column bindings (type, length, and so on). The provider receives the structures and determines how the data should be transferred and whether conversions are necessary.

The *ICommandText* interface provides a way to specify a text command. The *ICommandProperties* interface handles all of the command properties.

The command class is the heart of the data provider. Most of the action happens within this class.

Table 27-2 Command Object Interface Requirements

Interface	Required?	Implemented?
IAccessor	√	√
IColumnsInfo	√	√
ICommand	√	√
ICommandProperties	√	√
ICommandText	√	√
IConvertType	√	√
IColumnsRowset		
ICommandPrepare		
ICommandWithParameters		
ISupportErrorInfo		

The Session Object

Session objects define the scope of a transaction and generate rowsets from the data source. Session objects also generate command objects. The command object executes commands on the rowset. For providers that support commands, the session acts as a command factory. Calling *IDBCreateSession::CreateSession* creates a session from the data source object. A single data source object can be associated with many sessions. Table 27-3 lists the interfaces found on a session object.

Table 27-3 Session Object Interface Requirements

Interface	Required?	Implemented?
IGetDataSource	√	√
IOpenRowset	√	√
ISessionProperties	√	√
IDBCreateCommand		√
IDBSchemaRowset		√
IIndexDefinition		
ISupportErrorInfo		
ITableDefinition		
ITransactionJoin		
ITransactionLocal		
ITransactionObject		

Here's a code snippet showing the code that the ATL OLE DB Provider Wizard inserts to implement a session object when you create an OLE DB provider:

```
class ATL_NO_VTABLE CAProviderSession :
    public CComObjectRootEx<CComSingleThreadModel>,
    public IGetDataSourceImpl<CAProviderSession>,
    public IOpenRowsetImpl<CAProviderSession>,
    public ISessionPropertiesImpl<CAProviderSession>,
    public IObjectWithSiteSessionImpl<CAProviderSession>,
    public IDBSchemaRowsetImpl<CAProviderSession>,
    public IDBCreateCommandImpl<CAProviderSession, CAProviderCommand>
{
⋮
};
```

The Rowset Object

A rowset object represents tabular data. At the raw OLE DB level, rowsets are generated by calling *IOpenRowset::OpenRowset* on the session. For providers that support commands, rowsets are used to represent the results of row-returning queries. In addition to *IOpenRowset::OpenRowset*, OLE DB has a number of other methods that return rowsets. For example, the schema functions return rowsets. Single sessions can be associated with multiple rowsets. In addition, single command objects can be associated with multiple rowsets. Table 27-4 lists the interfaces associated with the rowset object.

Table 27-4 Rowset Object Interface Requirements

Interface	Required?	Implemented?
IAccessor	√	√
IColumnsInfo	√	√
IConvertType	√	√
IRowset	√	√
IRowsetInfo	√	√
IColumnsRowset		
IConnectionPointContainer		√ (through ATL)
IRowsetChange		
IRowsetIdentity	√ (for Level 0)	√
IRowsetLocate		
IRowsetResynch		
IRowsetScroll		
IRowsetUpdate		
ISupportErrorInfo		

Here's a code snippet showing the code that the ATL OLE DB Provider Wizard inserts to implement a rowset object when you create an OLE DB provider:

```
class CAProviderWindowsFile:
    public WIN32_FIND_DATA
{
public:
```

(continued)

```
BEGIN_PROVIDER_COLUMN_MAP(CAProviderWindowsFile)
    PROVIDER_COLUMN_ENTRY("FileAttributes", 1, dwFileAttributes)
    PROVIDER_COLUMN_ENTRY("FileSizeHigh", 2, nFileSizeHigh)
    PROVIDER_COLUMN_ENTRY("FileSizeLow", 3, nFileSizeLow)
    PROVIDER_COLUMN_ENTRY_STR("FileName", 4, cFileName)
    PROVIDER_COLUMN_ENTRY_STR("AltFileName", 5, cAlternateFileName)
END_PROVIDER_COLUMN_MAP()

};

class CAProviderRowset :
    public CRowsetImpl< CAProviderRowset,
                        CAProviderWindowsFile,
                        CAProviderCommand>
{
⋮
};
```

The wizard-generated rowset object implements the *IAccessor*, *IRowset*, and *IRowsetInfo* interfaces, among others. *IAccessorImpl* binds both output columns. The *IRowset* interface fetches rows and data. The *IRowsetInfo* interface handles the rowset properties. The *CWindowsFile* class represents the user record class. The class generated by the wizard is really just a placeholder—it doesn't do much. When you decide on the column format of your data provider, this is the class you'll modify.

How the Provider Parts Work Together

The purpose of the first part of the architecture—the data source—should be obvious. Every provider must include a data source object. When a consumer application needs data, the consumer calls *CoCreateInstance* to create the data source object and start the provider. Within the provider, the data source object creates a session object using the *IDBCreateSession* interface. The consumer uses this interface to connect to the data source object.

The command object does most of the work. To make the data provider actually do something, you modify the command class's *Execute* function.

Like most COM-based protocols, the OLE DB protocol makes sense once you've examined it for a while. Also, like most COM-based protocols, the OLE DB protocol involves a good amount of code to get going—code that could be easily implemented by some sort of framework. That's what the data consumer and data provider templates are all about. The rest of the chapter shows you what you need to do to create data consumers and data providers.

Creating an OLE DB Consumer

Creating an OLE DB consumer is pretty straightforward—most of the support comes through the ATL OLE DB Consumer Wizard. You can see an example of a consumer in the Ex27 folder on the companion CD. Here are the steps for creating a consumer using the ATL OLE DB Consumer Wizard:

1. Create an application or a control to drive the data consumption. For example, you might want to create an ActiveX control.
2. While you're in Visual Studio .NET, use the ATL OLE DB Consumer Wizard (shown in Figure 27-1) to insert a data consumer. (Choose Add Class from the Project menu and then select ATL OLE DB Consumer from the class templates.)
3. On the wizard's only page, name the class, select the data source, and specify a table or command object and the kinds of updates (change, insert, delete) to be supported in the consumer.

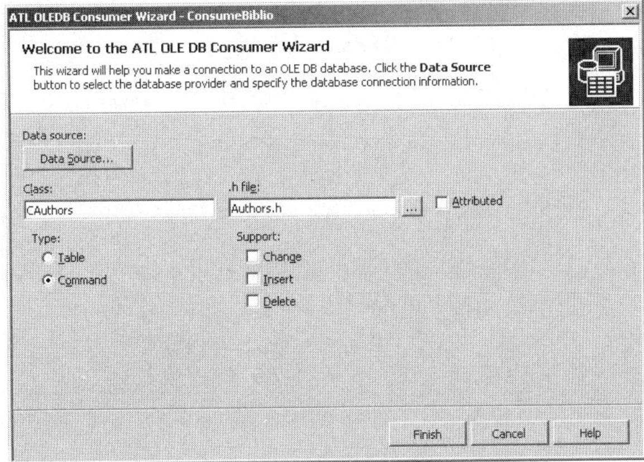

Figure 27-1 The ATL OLE DB Consumer Wizard.

4. Click the Data Source button to configure the data consumer. Once you've selected a data source, click OK. The wizard will create an OLE DB consumer template for you.

As an example, we took a Microsoft Access database named Biblio.mdb and made a data consumer out of it. The Biblio database includes the titles and the authors of various programming texts. Using the ATL OLE DB Consumer

Wizard to create the OLE DB consumer template for the authors in the database yielded these classes:

```
// Authors.h : Declaration of the CAuthors
#pragma once

// code generated on Wednesday, April 17, 2002, 10:25 AM
class CAuthorsAccessor
{
public:
    LONG m_Au_ID;
    TCHAR m_Author[51];
    SHORT m_YearBorn;

    // The following wizard-generated data members contain status
    // values for the corresponding fields in the column map. You
    // can use these values to hold NULL values that the database
    // returns or to hold error information when the compiler returns
    // errors. See Field Status Data Members in Wizard-Generated
    // Accessors in the Visual C++ documentation for more information
    // on using these fields.
    // NOTE: You must initialize these fields
    //       before setting/inserting data!

    DBSTATUS m_dwAu_IDStatus;
    DBSTATUS m_dwAuthorStatus;
    DBSTATUS m_dwYearBornStatus;

    // The following wizard-generated data members contain length
    // values for the corresponding fields in the column map.
    // NOTE: For variable-length columns, you must initialize these
    //       fields before setting/inserting data!

    DBLENGTH m_dwAu_IDLength;
    DBLENGTH m_dwAuthorLength;
    DBLENGTH m_dwYearBornLength;

    void GetRowsetProperties(CDBPropSet* pPropSet)
    {
        pPropSet->AddProperty(DBPROP_CANFETCHBACKWARDS,
            true, DBPROPOPTIONS_OPTIONAL);
        pPropSet->AddProperty(DBPROP_CANSCROLLBACKWARDS,
            true, DBPROPOPTIONS_OPTIONAL);
        pPropSet->AddProperty(DBPROP_IRowsetChange,
            true, DBPROPOPTIONS_OPTIONAL);
        pPropSet->AddProperty(DBPROP_UPDATABILITY,
            DBPROPVAL_UP_CHANGE | DBPROPVAL_UP_INSERT
            | DBPROPVAL_UP_DELETE);
    }
```

```
    HRESULT OpenDataSource()
    {
        CDataSource _db;
        HRESULT hr;
        // Here goes the _db.OpenFromInitializationString
        :
        if (FAILED(hr))
        {
#ifdef _DEBUG
            AtlTraceErrorRecords(hr);
#endif
            return hr;
        }
        return m_session.Open(_db);
    }

    void CloseDataSource()
    {
        m_session.Close();
    }

    operator const CSession&()
    {
        return m_session;
    }

    CSession m_session;
    DEFINE_COMMAND_EX(CAuthorsAccessor, L" \
     SELECT \
        Au_ID, \
        Author, \
        'Year Born' \
        FROM Authors")

    BEGIN_COLUMN_MAP(CAuthorsAccessor)
        COLUMN_ENTRY_LENGTH_STATUS(1, m_Au_ID,
           m_dwAu_IDLength, m_dwAu_IDStatus)
        COLUMN_ENTRY_LENGTH_STATUS(2,
           m_Author, m_dwAuthorLength, m_dwAuthorStatus)
        COLUMN_ENTRY_LENGTH_STATUS(3,
            m_YearBorn, m_dwYearBornLength, m_dwYearBornStatus)
    END_COLUMN_MAP()
};

class CAuthors : public CCommand<CAccessor<CAuthorsAccessor> >
{
public:
```

(continued)

```
    HRESULT OpenAll()
    {
        HRESULT hr;
        hr = OpenDataSource();
        if (FAILED(hr))
            return hr;
        __if_exists(GetRowsetProperties)
        {
            CDBPropSet propset(DBPROPSET_ROWSET);
            __if_exists(HasBookmark)
            {
                propset.AddProperty(DBPROP_IRowsetLocate, true);
            }
            GetRowsetProperties(&propset);
            return OpenRowset(&propset);
        }
        __if_not_exists(GetRowsetProperties)
        {
            __if_exists(HasBookmark)
            {
                CDBPropSet propset(DBPROPSET_ROWSET);
                propset.AddProperty(DBPROP_IRowsetLocate, true);
                return OpenRowset(&propset);
            }
        }
        return OpenRowset();
    }

    HRESULT OpenRowset(DBPROPSET *pPropSet = NULL)
    {
        HRESULT hr = Open(m_session, L"Authors", pPropSet);
#ifdef _DEBUG
        if(FAILED(hr))
            AtlTraceErrorRecords(hr);
#endif
        return hr;
    }

    void CloseAll()
    {
        Close();
        ReleaseCommand();
        CloseDataSource();
    }
};
```

The *CAuthorsAccessor* class defines the structure of the author record. Notice that the class includes an author ID field, a name field, and a field indicating when the author was born.

The *CAuthors* class represents the actual data consumer class that connects to the database. Notice that it's derived from *CCommand*. Remember that command objects represent a command (such as a SQL statement) and generate rowsets. The *COLUMN_MAP* represents data returned in the rowset. The *PARAM_MAP* represents parameter data for a command.

The column maps and the parameter maps represent the user's view of the accessor. As with many data structures in ATL and MFC, these maps are built up with macros. Here's how the maps work: Data returned by a database is contained in a contiguous block of memory. OLE DB templates work with this block of memory to extract the data. The data members in the entries represent offsets into that block of memory. The entries in the maps filter out the data from the database. That way, the developer doesn't have to worry about doing anything funky like performing pointer arithmetic on the block to get information.

Using the OLE DB Consumer Code

Using the database consumer class is just about as easy as creating it. Here's how to take advantage of the database consumer class:

1. Declare an instance of *CAuthors* wherever you need to use it:

```
class CUseAuthors : public CDialog {
    CAuthors m_authors;
    ⋮
};
```

2. Open the Authors table by calling *Open* on the database consumer object:

```
CUseAuthors::OnInitDialog() {
    m_authors.Open();
}
```

3. Use member functions to navigate through and manipulate the database. Here's a short sampling of some of the things you can do:

```
CUseAuthors::OnNext() {
    m_authors.MoveNext();
}
CUseAuthors::OnFirst() {
    m_authors.MoveFirst();
}
CUseAuthors::OnLast() {
    m_authors.MoveLast();
}
CUseAuthors::OnInsert() {
    m_authors.Insert();
}
```

4. As you navigate through the database, the data will end up in the member variables. For example, to find out the name of the next author in the database, you use code that looks like this:

```
m_authors.MoveNext();
m_strAuthorName = m_authors.m_Author;
```

As you can see, using the templates greatly simplifies getting the data out of the database. All you need to do is find the database, point the ATL OLE DB Consumer Wizard to it, and get the wizard to generate your code. You can then use accessor class functions to move around the database and fetch the data. The other half of the OLE DB template equation is the data provider, which we'll discuss next.

Creating an OLE DB Provider

It's pretty obvious how OLE DB consumers are useful. You just ask a wizard to create a wrapper for you, and you get a fairly easy way to access the data in a database. However, it might be a bit less obvious why you'd want to create an OLE DB provider.

Writing an OLE DB provider allows you to insert a layer between a client of some data and the data itself. Here are just a few reasons you might want to write a provider:

- Writing an OLE DB provider means that clients don't necessarily touch the data directly. Therefore, you can add additional capabilities to your data, such as query processing.
- In some cases, writing an OLE DB provider allows you to increase data access performance by controlling how the data is manipulated.
- Adding an OLE DB provider layer increases the potential audience of your data. For example, if you have a proprietary data format that can be accessed by only one programming language, you have a single point of failure. OLE DB providers give you a way to open that proprietary format to a wider variety of programmers, regardless of the programming language they use.

Working with the OLE DB providers is similar to working with the OLE DB consumers. The wizards do a lot of the work for you. You just need to know how to work with the generated classes. The steps for creating an OLE DB provider are as follows:

1. Decide what you want the provider to do. Remember the philosophy behind OLE DB: It's all about providing a singular way to access multiple data sources. For example, you might want to write a provider that recursively enumerates the contents of a structured storage file. Or you might want a provider that sifts through e-mail folders and allows clients database-style access to your e-mail system. The possibilities are nearly endless.

2. Use the ATL OLE DB Provider Wizard to create a provider. (Choose Add Class from the Project menu, and then select ATL OLE DB Provider from the class templates.) The wizard will ask you to provide a name for your object and will allow you to modify the default names for the files it will create.

3. After you click Finish, the ATL OLE DB Provider Wizard will create the code for a provider, including a data source, a rowset, and a session. A provider also supports one or more properties, which are defined in property maps within the files created by the wizard. When the wizard creates the files, it inserts maps for the properties belonging to the OLE DB property group that was defined for the object or objects included in those files. For example, the header file containing the data source object also contains the property map for the data source properties. The session header file contains the property map for the session properties. Finally, the rowset and command objects reside in a single header file, which includes properties for the command object.

For example, let's look at what the ATL OLE DB Provider Wizard produces for an OLE DB provider named AProvider. First, the wizard creates a data source object, which lives in a file named AProviderDS.h:

```
class ATL_NO_VTABLE CAProviderSource :
    public CComObjectRootEx<CComSingleThreadModel>,
    public CComCoClass<CAProviderSource, &CLSID_AProvider>,
    public IDBCreateSessionImpl<CAProviderSource, CAProviderSession>,
    public IDBInitializeImpl<CAProviderSource>,
    public IDBPropertiesImpl<CAProviderSource>,
    public IPersistImpl<CAProviderSource>,
    public IInternalConnectionImpl<CAProviderSource>
{
public:
    DECLARE_PROTECT_FINAL_CONSTRUCT()
```

(continued)

```
    HRESULT FinalConstruct()
    {
        return FInit();
    }

    void FinalRelease()
    {
    }

DECLARE_REGISTRY_RESOURCEID(IDR_APROVIDER)
BEGIN_COM_MAP(CAProviderSource)
    COM_INTERFACE_ENTRY(IDBCreateSession)
    COM_INTERFACE_ENTRY(IDBInitialize)
    COM_INTERFACE_ENTRY(IDBProperties)
    COM_INTERFACE_ENTRY(IPersist)
    COM_INTERFACE_ENTRY(IInternalConnection)
END_COM_MAP()

BEGIN_PROPSET_MAP(CAProviderSource)
    BEGIN_PROPERTY_SET(DBPROPSET_DATASOURCEINFO)
        PROPERTY_INFO_ENTRY(ACTIVESESSIONS)
        PROPERTY_INFO_ENTRY(DATASOURCEREADONLY)
        PROPERTY_INFO_ENTRY(BYREFACCESSORS)
        PROPERTY_INFO_ENTRY(OUTPUTPARAMETERAVAILABILITY)
        PROPERTY_INFO_ENTRY(PROVIDEROLEDBVER)
        PROPERTY_INFO_ENTRY(DSOTHREADMODEL)
        PROPERTY_INFO_ENTRY(SUPPORTEDTXNISOLEVELS)
        PROPERTY_INFO_ENTRY(USERNAME)
    END_PROPERTY_SET(DBPROPSET_DATASOURCEINFO)
    BEGIN_PROPERTY_SET(DBPROPSET_DBINIT)
        PROPERTY_INFO_ENTRY(AUTH_PASSWORD)
        PROPERTY_INFO_ENTRY(AUTH_PERSIST_SENSITIVE_AUTHINFO)
        PROPERTY_INFO_ENTRY(AUTH_USERID)
        PROPERTY_INFO_ENTRY(INIT_DATASOURCE)
        PROPERTY_INFO_ENTRY(INIT_HWND)
        PROPERTY_INFO_ENTRY(INIT_LCID)
        PROPERTY_INFO_ENTRY(INIT_LOCATION)
        PROPERTY_INFO_ENTRY(INIT_MODE)
        PROPERTY_INFO_ENTRY(INIT_PROMPT)
        PROPERTY_INFO_ENTRY(INIT_PROVIDERSTRING)
        PROPERTY_INFO_ENTRY(INIT_TIMEOUT)
    END_PROPERTY_SET(DBPROPSET_DBINIT)
    CHAIN_PROPERTY_SET(CAProviderSession)
    CHAIN_PROPERTY_SET(CAProviderCommand)
END_PROPSET_MAP()

public:
};
```

In addition to the data object, the ATL OLE DB Provider Wizard produces a command object and a rowset that both live in AProviderRS.h:

```
class ATL_NO_VTABLE CAProviderCommand :
    public CComObjectRootEx<CComSingleThreadModel>,
    public IAccessorImpl<CAProviderCommand>,
    public ICommandTextImpl<CAProviderCommand>,
    public ICommandPropertiesImpl<CAProviderCommand>,
    public IObjectWithSiteImpl<CAProviderCommand>,
    public IConvertTypeImpl<CAProviderCommand>,
    public IColumnsInfoImpl<CAProviderCommand>,
    public IInternalCommandConnectionImpl<CAProviderCommand>

{
public:

BEGIN_COM_MAP(CAProviderCommand)
    COM_INTERFACE_ENTRY(ICommand)
    COM_INTERFACE_ENTRY(IObjectWithSite)
    COM_INTERFACE_ENTRY(IAccessor)
    COM_INTERFACE_ENTRY(ICommandProperties)
    COM_INTERFACE_ENTRY2(ICommandText, ICommand)
    COM_INTERFACE_ENTRY(IColumnsInfo)
    COM_INTERFACE_ENTRY(IConvertType)
    COM_INTERFACE_ENTRY(IInternalConnection)
END_COM_MAP()

// ICommand
public:

    HRESULT FinalConstruct()
    {
        HRESULT hr = CConvertHelper::FinalConstruct();
        if (FAILED (hr))
            return hr;
        hr = IAccessorImpl<CAProviderCommand>::FinalConstruct();
        if (FAILED(hr))
            return hr;
        return CUtlProps<CAProviderCommand>::FInit();
    }
    void FinalRelease()
    {
        IAccessorImpl<CAProviderCommand>::FinalRelease();
    }

    HRESULT WINAPI Execute(IUnknown * pUnkOuter,
     REFIID riid, DBPARAMS * pParams,
      LONG * pcRowsAffected, IUnknown ** ppRowset);
```

(continued)

```
    static ATLCOLUMNINFO* GetColumnInfo(CAProviderCommand* pv,
                                        ULONG* pcInfo)
    {
        return CAProviderWindowsFile::GetColumnInfo(pv, pcInfo);
    }

BEGIN_PROPSET_MAP(CAProviderCommand)
    BEGIN_PROPERTY_SET(DBPROPSET_ROWSET)
        PROPERTY_INFO_ENTRY(IAccessor)
        PROPERTY_INFO_ENTRY(IColumnsInfo)
        PROPERTY_INFO_ENTRY(IConvertType)
        PROPERTY_INFO_ENTRY(IRowset)
        PROPERTY_INFO_ENTRY(IRowsetIdentity)
        PROPERTY_INFO_ENTRY(IRowsetInfo)
        PROPERTY_INFO_ENTRY(IRowsetLocate)
        PROPERTY_INFO_ENTRY(BOOKMARKS)
        PROPERTY_INFO_ENTRY(BOOKMARKSKIPPED)
        PROPERTY_INFO_ENTRY(BOOKMARKTYPE)
        PROPERTY_INFO_ENTRY(CANFETCHBACKWARDS)
        PROPERTY_INFO_ENTRY(CANHOLDROWS)
        PROPERTY_INFO_ENTRY(CANSCROLLBACKWARDS)
        PROPERTY_INFO_ENTRY(LITERALBOOKMARKS)
        PROPERTY_INFO_ENTRY(ORDEREDBOOKMARKS)
    END_PROPERTY_SET(DBPROPSET_ROWSET)
END_PROPSET_MAP()

};

class CAProviderRowset :
    public CRowsetImpl< CAProviderRowset,
                        CAProviderWindowsFile, CAProviderCommand>
{
public:

    HRESULT Execute(DBPARAMS * pParams, LONG* pcRowsAffected)
    {
        USES_CONVERSION;
        BOOL bFound = FALSE;
        HANDLE hFile;

        LPTSTR  szDir =
            (m_strCommandText == _T("")) ? _T("*.*") :
                OLE2T(m_strCommandText);

        CAProviderWindowsFile wf;
        hFile = FindFirstFile(szDir, &wf);
        if (hFile == INVALID_HANDLE_VALUE)
            return DB_E_ERRORSINCOMMAND;
        LONG cFiles = 1;
```

```
        BOOL bMoreFiles = TRUE;
        while (bMoreFiles)
        {
            _ATLTRY
            {
                m_rgRowData.Add(wf);
            }
            _ATLCATCH( e )
            {
                _ATLDELETEEXCEPTION( e )
                return E_OUTOFMEMORY;
            }
            bMoreFiles = FindNextFile(hFile, &wf);
            cFiles++;
        }
        FindClose(hFile);
        if (pcRowsAffected != NULL)
            *pcRowsAffected = cFiles;
        return S_OK;
    }
};
```

The wizard produces a session object in a file named AProviderSess.h, as shown in this code:

```
class ATL_NO_VTABLE CAProviderSession :
    public CComObjectRootEx<CComSingleThreadModel>,
    public IGetDataSourceImpl<CAProviderSession>,
    public IOpenRowsetImpl<CAProviderSession>,
    public ISessionPropertiesImpl<CAProviderSession>,
    public IObjectWithSiteSessionImpl<CAProviderSession>,
    public IDBSchemaRowsetImpl<CAProviderSession>,
    public IDBCreateCommandImpl<CAProviderSession, CAProviderCommand>
{
public:
    CAProviderSession()
    {
    }

    DECLARE_PROTECT_FINAL_CONSTRUCT()

    HRESULT FinalConstruct()
    {
        return FInit();
    }
    void FinalRelease()
    {
    }
```

(continued)

```
    STDMETHOD(OpenRowset)(IUnknown *pUnk, DBID *pTID,
                          DBID *pInID, REFIID riid,
                          ULONG cSets, DBPROPSET rgSets[],
                          IUnknown **ppRowset)
    {
        CAProviderRowset* pRowset;
        return CreateRowset(pUnk, pTID, pInID, riid, cSets,
                            rgSets, ppRowset, pRowset);
    }

    void SetRestrictions(ULONG cRestrictions,
        GUID* rguidSchema, ULONG* rgRestrictions)
    {
        for (ULONG l=0; l<cRestrictions; l++)
        {
            // We support restrictions on the table name but nothing else
            if (InlineIsEqualGUID(rguidSchema[l], DBSCHEMA_TABLES))
                rgRestrictions[l] = 0x04;
            else if (InlineIsEqualGUID(rguidSchema[l], DBSCHEMA_COLUMNS))
                rgRestrictions[l] = 0x04;
            else if (InlineIsEqualGUID(rguidSchema[l],
                    DBSCHEMA_PROVIDER_TYPES))
                rgRestrictions[l] = 0x00;
        }
    }

BEGIN_PROPSET_MAP(CAProviderSession)
    BEGIN_PROPERTY_SET(DBPROPSET_SESSION)
        PROPERTY_INFO_ENTRY(SESS_AUTOCOMMITISOLEVELS)
    END_PROPERTY_SET(DBPROPSET_SESSION)
END_PROPSET_MAP()

BEGIN_COM_MAP(CAProviderSession)
    COM_INTERFACE_ENTRY(IGetDataSource)
    COM_INTERFACE_ENTRY(IOpenRowset)
    COM_INTERFACE_ENTRY(ISessionProperties)
    COM_INTERFACE_ENTRY(IObjectWithSite)
    COM_INTERFACE_ENTRY(IDBCreateCommand)
    COM_INTERFACE_ENTRY(IDBSchemaRowset)
END_COM_MAP()

BEGIN_SCHEMA_MAP(CAProviderSession)
    SCHEMA_ENTRY(DBSCHEMA_TABLES, CAProviderSessionTRSchemaRowset)
    SCHEMA_ENTRY(DBSCHEMA_COLUMNS, CAProviderSessionColSchemaRowset)
    SCHEMA_ENTRY(DBSCHEMA_PROVIDER_TYPES,
                CAProviderSessionPTSchemaRowset)
END_SCHEMA_MAP()

};
⋮
```

Modifying the Provider Code

As with most wizard-generated code, the OLE DB provider code generated by the ATL OLE DB Provider Wizard is just boilerplate code—it doesn't do very much. You must take several steps to turn this boilerplate code into a real OLE DB provider. The two critical things you must do are to add the user record and code to manage a dataset and to set up the data as rows and columns.

The ATL OLE DB Provider Wizard provides a default user record named *CAProviderWindowsFile*. You'll probably want to scrap this user record and replace it with something useful in your domain. As a simple example, imagine that you want to write an OLE DB provider that enumerates a compound file. Your user record might look like this:

```
struct CStgInfo {
BEGIN_PROVIDER_COLUMN_MAP(CStgInfo)
    PROVIDER_COLUMN_ENTRY("StgName", 1, szName)
    PROVIDER_COLUMN_ENTRY("Size", 2, cbSizeLow)
    PROVIDER_COLUMN_ENTRY("Size", 2, cbSizeHigh)

END_PROVIDER_COLUMN_MAP()

    OLECHAR szName[256];
    long cbSizeLow;
    long cbSizeHigh;
};
```

This structure contains the data fields for the name and size of the substorage. The provider column map macros map the data into columns. You can actually derive the structure from a *STATSTG* structure (which is used to enumerate structured storages)—you just add entries to the provider column map to handle the members.

The other important addition to the provider is the code for opening the data set. This happens in the rowset's *Execute* function. Many kinds of functionality can go in here. For example, if you want to enumerate the top-level substorages in a compound file, you can open the storage and then enumerate the contents as shown in the following code snippet:

```
class RStgInfoProviderRowset :
    public CRowsetImpl<RStgInfoProviderRowset,
                       CStgInfo,
                       CStgInfoProviderCommand>
{
public:
    HRESULT Execute(DBPARAMS * pParams, LONG* pcRowsAffected)
    {
        USES_CONVERSION;
```

(continued)

```
LPTSTR  szFile =
       m_strCommandText == _T("")) ? _T("") :
           OLE2T(m_strCommandText);

IStorage* pStg = NULL;

HRESULT hr = StgOpenStorage(szFile, NULL,
                            STGM_READ|STGM_SHARE_EXCLUSIVE,
                            NULL, NULL, &pStg);

if(FAILED(hr))
    return DB_E_ERRORSINCOMMAND;

LONG cStgs = 0;

IEnumSTATSTG* pEnumSTATSTG;

hr = pStg->EnumElements(0, 0, 0, &pEnumSTATSTG);

if(pEnumSTATSTG) {

    STATSTG rgSTATSTG[100];
    ULONG nFetched;

    hr = pEnumSTATSTG->Next(100, rgSTATSTG, &nFetched);

    for(ULONG i = 0; i < nFetched; i++) {
        CStgInfo stgInfo;
        stgInfo.cbSizeLow = rgSTATSTG[i].cbSize.LowPart;
        stgInfo.cbSizeHigh = rgSTATSTG[i].cbSize.HighPart;

        wcsncpy(stgInfo.szName,
                rgSTATSTG[i].pwcsName,
                255);

        CoTaskMemFree(rgSTATSTG[i].pwcsName);

        if (!m_rgRowData.Add(stgInfo))
            return E_OUTOFMEMORY;
        cStgs++;
    }
    pEnumSTATSTG->Release();
}

if(pStg)
    pStg->Release();

if (pcRowsAffected != NULL)
```

```
            *pcRowsAffected = cStgs;
        return S_OK;
    }
}
```

When some client code tries to open the OLE DB data provider, the call will end up inside this function. This function simply opens the structured storage file that was passed in as the command text and uses the standard structured storage enumerator to find the top-level substorages. The *Execute* function then stores the name of the substorage and the size of the substorage in an array. The OLE DB provider uses this array to fulfill requests for the column data.

Enhancing the Provider

Of course, you can do a lot to beef up this OLE DB provider. We've barely scratched the surface of what you can do with a provider. When the ATL OLE DB Provider Wizard pumps out the default provider, it's a read-only provider—that is, users cannot change the contents of the data. The OLE DB templates provide support for locating rowsets and setting bookmarks. In most cases, enhancing the provider is a matter of tacking on implementations of COM interfaces provided by the OLE DB templates.

Attributed OLE DB Programming

Just as you can write ActiveX controls using attributed ATL, you can also write OLE DB templates using attributes. Six attributes apply to OLE DB consumer template programming. These are described in Table 27-5.

Table 27-5 OLE DB Consumer Attributes

Attribute	Description
db_accessor	Binds columns in a rowset and binds them to the corresponding accessor maps
db_column	Binds a specified column to the rowset
db_command	Executes an OLE DB command
db_param	Associates the specified member variable with an input or output parameter
db_source	Creates and encapsulates a connection, through a provider, to a data source
db_table	Opens an OLE DB table

Database development is another type of programming that involves a great deal of boilerplate code, so it's another great candidate for attributed programming. Remember that with attributed programming, you declare program features using attributes, and the compiler and linker inject code into your project. For example, here's an OLE DB consumer template for using the Titles table in the Biblio.mdb database:

```
// Titles.h : Declaration of the CTitles
#pragma once

[
    db_source(
        ⋮
        ),
    db_table(L"Titles")
]
class CTitles
{
public:
// This table/command contains column(s) that can be accessed
// via an ISequentialStream interface.  Not all providers, however,
// support this feature, and even those that do support it, are
// often limited to just one ISequentialStream per rowset.
// If you want to use streams in this accessor, use the sample
// line(s) of code below, and set the DBPROP_ISequentialStream
// rowset property to true.  You can than use the Read() method
// to read the data.  For more information on
// ISequentialStream binding see the documentation
// [ db_column(8, status=m_dwCommentsStatus,
//   length=m_dwCommentsLength) ] ISequentialStream* m_Comments;

  [ db_column(8, status=m_dwCommentsStatus,
            length=m_dwCommentsLength) ] TCHAR m_Comments[8000];

  [ db_column(5, status=m_dwDescriptionStatus,
            length=m_dwDescriptionLength) ] TCHAR m_Description[51];

  [ db_column(3, status=m_dwISBNStatus,
            length=m_dwISBNLength) ] TCHAR m_ISBN[21];

  [ db_column(6, status=m_dwNotesStatus,
            length=m_dwNotesLength) ] TCHAR m_Notes[51];

  [ db_column(4, status=m_dwPubIDStatus,
            length=m_dwPubIDLength) ] LONG m_PubID;

  [ db_column(7, status=m_dwSubjectStatus,
            length=m_dwSubjectLength) ] TCHAR m_Subject[51];
```

```
[ db_column(1, status=m_dwTitleStatus,
          length=m_dwTitleLength) ] TCHAR m_Title[256];

[ db_column(2, status=m_dwYearPublishedStatus,
          length=m_dwYearPublishedLength) ] SHORT m_YearPublished;

  // The following wizard-generated data members contain status
  // values for the corresponding fields. You
  // can use these values to hold NULL values that the database
  // returns or to hold error information when the compiler returns
  // errors. See Field Status Data Members in Wizard-Generated
  // Accessors in the Visual C++ documentation for more information
  // on using these fields.
  // NOTE: You must initialize these fields before
  //       setting/inserting data!

  DBSTATUS m_dwCommentsStatus;
  DBSTATUS m_dwDescriptionStatus;
  DBSTATUS m_dwISBNStatus;
  DBSTATUS m_dwNotesStatus;
  DBSTATUS m_dwPubIDStatus;
  DBSTATUS m_dwSubjectStatus;
  DBSTATUS m_dwTitleStatus;
  DBSTATUS m_dwYearPublishedStatus;

  // The following wizard-generated data members contain length
  // values for the corresponding fields.
  // NOTE: For variable-length columns, you must initialize these
  //       fields before setting/inserting data!

  DBLENGTH m_dwCommentsLength;
  DBLENGTH m_dwDescriptionLength;
  DBLENGTH m_dwISBNLength;
  DBLENGTH m_dwNotesLength;
  DBLENGTH m_dwPubIDLength;
  DBLENGTH m_dwSubjectLength;
  DBLENGTH m_dwTitleLength;
  DBLENGTH m_dwYearPublishedLength;

  void GetRowsetProperties(CDBPropSet* pPropSet)
  {
      pPropSet->AddProperty(DBPROP_CANFETCHBACKWARDS,
          true, DBPROPOPTIONS_OPTIONAL);
      pPropSet->AddProperty(DBPROP_CANSCROLLBACKWARDS,
          true, DBPROPOPTIONS_OPTIONAL);
      // pPropSet->AddProperty(DBPROP_ISequentialStream, true);
      pPropSet->AddProperty(DBPROP_IRowsetChange,
          true, DBPROPOPTIONS_OPTIONAL);
```

(continued)

```
            pPropSet->AddProperty(DBPROP_UPDATABILITY,
                DBPROPVAL_UP_CHANGE | DBPROPVAL_UP_INSERT
                | DBPROPVAL_UP_DELETE);
        }
};
```

The code is a C++ class representing the Titles table in the Biblio database. Using attributes shortens the code somewhat. Notice that the *COLUMN_MAP* that is present in the classic ATL OLE DB consumer template is missing; it's replaced by member variables of the *CTitles* class, preceded by the *db_column* attribute. Also notice the absence of a *CTitlesAccessor* class. (In the classic OLE DB consumer template, the *CAuthorsAccessor* class and the *CAuthors* class were separate entities.) The accessor information and the *CAuthors* class are wrapped up into one class: the *CTitles* class. Also notice that the database connection information is included as a set of attributes preceding the entire *CTitles* class. (In the classic OLE DB consumer example with the Authors table shown earlier, the database connection information was hard-coded into the *OpenDataSource* method.)

Using the attributed *CTitles* class is similar to using the *CAuthors* class. Here's how to use the attributed database consumer class:

1. Declare an instance of *CTitles* wherever you need to use it:

```
class CUseTitles : public CDialog {
    CTitles m_titles;
    ⋮
};
```

2. Open the database by calling *Open* on the database consumer object:

```
CUseTitles::OnInitDialog() {
    m_titles.Open();
}
```

3. Use member functions to navigate through and manipulate the database. Here's a sampling of some of the things you can do:

```
CUseTitles::OnNext() {
    m_titles.MoveNext();
}
CUseTitles::OnFirst() {
    m_titles.MoveFirst();
}
CUseTitles::OnLast() {
    m_titles.MoveLast();
}
```

```
CUseTitles::OnInsert() {
    m_titles.Insert();
}
```

4. As you navigate through the database, the data will end up in the member variables. For example, if you want to find out the name of the next title in the table, the code will look like this:

```
m_titles.MoveNext();
m_strTitle = m_titles.m_Title;
```

Using attributed OLE DB consumer templates greatly reduces the programming area you work with when you access OLE DB data sources.

Part V

Programming for the Internet

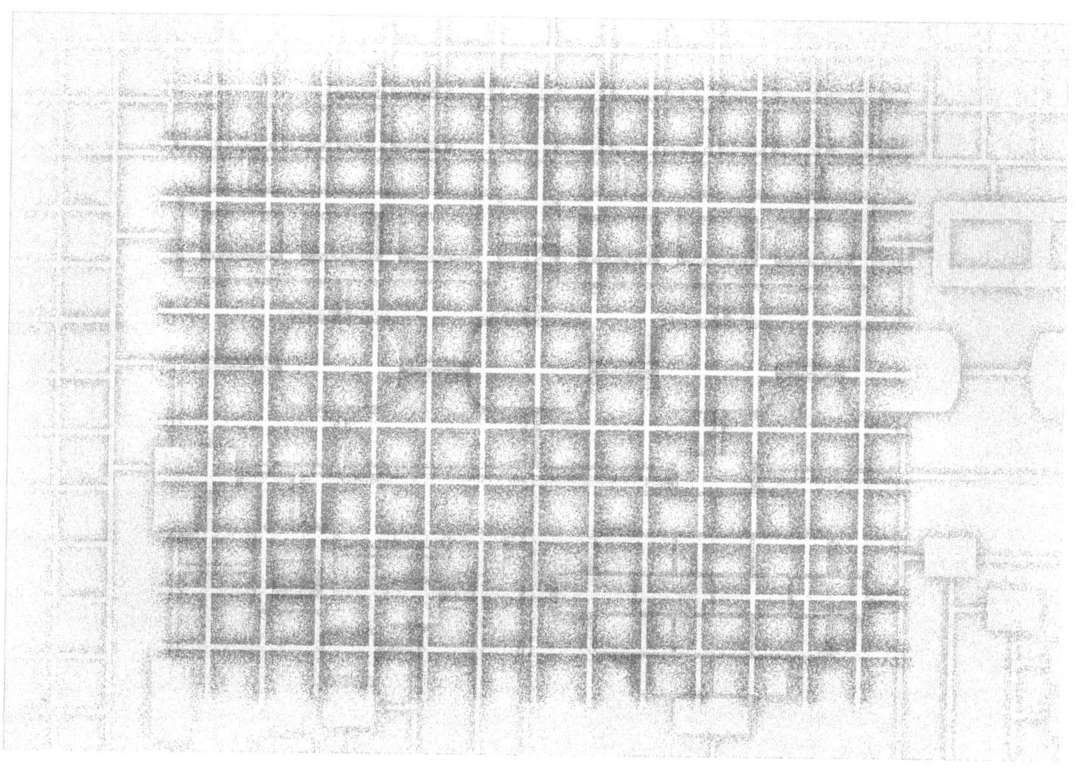

28

Internet Essentials

There was a time when you could get along as a developer and not worry about how Internet development differed from desktop development. These days, however, the Internet itself is becoming a development platform (especially with Microsoft .NET, which we'll look at in Part VI of this book). To be successful as a modern developer, you have to understand how the Internet works and how to write programs that can access other computers on the Internet. Somewhere, sometime in the near future, your software will probably have to touch the Internet. Of course, desktop-style programming will not be going away, but the Internet provides such compelling connectivity that you'll probably want to use it.

In this chapter, we'll start with a primer on Transmission Control Protocol/Internet Protocol (TCP/IP), which is used throughout the Internet, and then we'll move up one level to examine the workings of Hypertext Transfer Protocol (HTTP). Then it'll be time to get something running. We'll assemble our own intranet (a local version of the Internet) and study an HTTP client/server program based on Winsock, the fundamental API for TCP/IP. Finally, we'll move on to WinInet, which is a higher-level API than Winsock.

Classic Internet Development vs. .NET Development

Internet development can be divided roughly into two types: classic Internet development and Internet development using .NET. This part of the book, Part V, looks at classic Internet development. This chapter will examine how the Internet works at the wire level. In Chapter 29, we'll look at Dynamic HTML (DHTML), which lets you apply a much more responsive feel to your Web applications. Chapter 30 will cover ATL Server—a set of templates that provide low-level C++-style access to the Internet protocols.

The last part of this book, Part VI, covers .NET technology—which is the culmination of years of research and improvements with Internet development as its primary focus. The underpinnings of Internet development remain the same all over (even if you're using UNIX and Apache servers), but the amount of raw code necessary to get a Web site up and running is pretty phenomenal (as is the amount of code necessary to get a simple SDK-style window up and running). .NET offers a host of useful abstractions that hide the nitty-gritty of Web development—just as MFC and Microsoft Visual Basic .NET hide much of the complexity of the Windows API.

An Internet Primer

You can't write a good Winsock program without understanding the concept of a *socket*, which is used to send and receive packets of data across the network. To fully understand sockets, you need a thorough knowledge of the underlying Internet protocols. This section contains a concentrated dose of Internet theory. It should be enough to get you going, but you might want to refer to one of the TCP/IP textbooks if you want more theory.

Network Protocols and Layering

All networks use layering for their transmission protocols, and the collection of layers is often called a *stack*. The application program talks to the top layer, and the bottom layer talks to the network. Figure 28-1 shows the stack for a local area network (LAN) that's running TCP/IP. Each layer is logically connected to the corresponding layer at the other end of the communications channel. The server program, which is shown at the right side of the figure, continuously listens on one end of the channel, while the client program, shown on the left, periodically connects with the server to exchange data. You can think of the server as an HTTP-based World Wide Web (WWW) server, and you can think of the client as a browser program running on your computer.

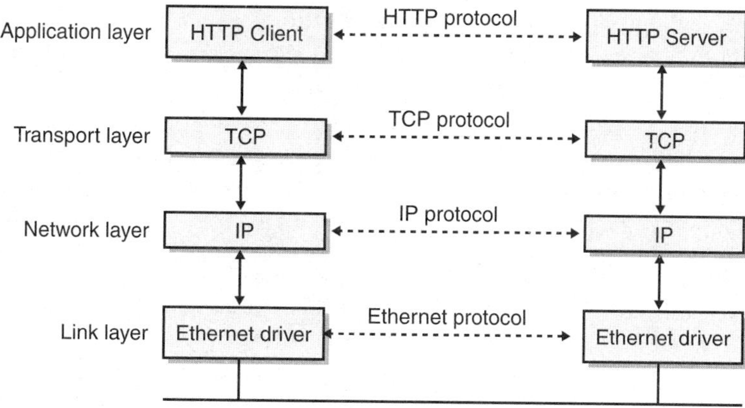

Figure 28-1 The stack for a LAN running TCP/IP.

IP

The IP layer is the best place to start in your quest to understand TCP/IP. The IP protocol defines packets called *datagrams* that are fundamental units of Internet communication. These packets, which are typically less than 1000 bytes in length, go bouncing all over the world when you open a Web page, download a file, or send e-mail. Figure 28-2 shows a simplified layout of an IP datagram.

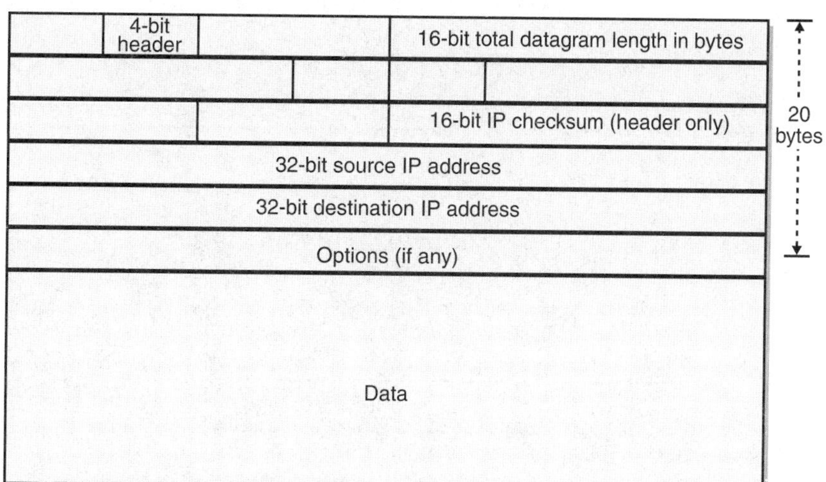

Figure 28-2 A simple IP datagram layout.

Notice that the IP datagram contains 32-bit addresses for both the source and destination computers. These IP addresses uniquely identify computers on the Internet and are used by *routers* (specialized computers that act like telephone switches) to direct the individual datagrams to their destinations. The routers don't care about what's inside a datagram—they're interested only in the datagram's destination address and total length. The routers' job is to resend the datagram as quickly as possible.

The IP layer doesn't tell the sending program whether a datagram has successfully reached its destination. That's a job for the next layer up the stack. The receiving program can look only at the checksum to determine whether the IP datagram header was corrupted.

UDP

The TCP/IP protocol should really be called TCP/UDP/IP because it includes User Datagram Protocol (UDP), which is a peer of TCP. All IP-based transport protocols store their own headers and data inside the IP data block. Figure 28-3 shows the UDP layout.

16-bit source port number	16-bit destination port number
16-bit length (UDP header + data)	16-bit checksum (UDP header + data)
Data (if any)	

Figure 28-3 A simple UDP layout

A complete UDP/IP datagram is shown in Figure 28-4.

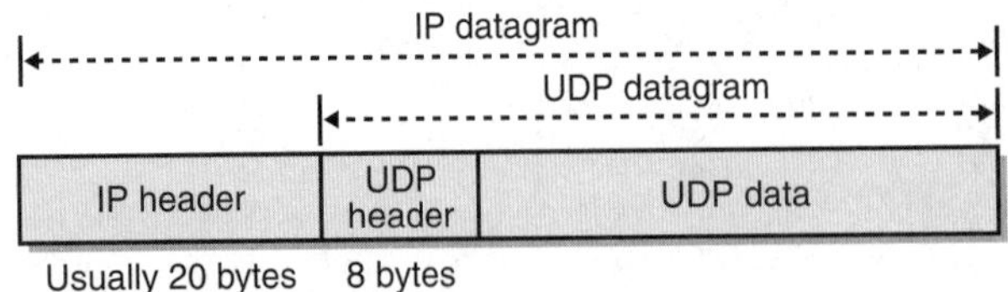

Figure 28-4 The relationship between the IP datagram and the UDP datagram.

UDP is only a small step up from IP, but applications never use IP directly. Like IP, UDP doesn't tell the sender when the datagram has arrived. That's up to the application. The sender can, for example, require that the receiver send a response, and the sender can retransmit the datagram if a response doesn't arrive within, say, 20 seconds. UDP is good for simple, one-shot messages and is used by the Internet Domain Name System (DNS), which we'll look at later in this chapter. (UDP is used for transmitting live audio and video, for which some lost or out-of-sequence data is not a big problem.)

Figure 28-3 shows that the UDP header *does* convey some additional information—namely, the source and destination port numbers. The application programs on each end use these 16-bit numbers. For example, a datagram that a client program sends to a server could have a source port number of 1701 and a destination port number of 1700. The server program will listen for any datagram that includes 1700 in its destination port number, and when it finds one, it can respond by sending another datagram back to the client, which will listen for a datagram that includes 1701 in its destination port number.

IP Address Format: Network Byte Order

You know that IP addresses are 32-bits long. You might think that 2^{32} (more than 4 billion) uniquely addressed computers could exist on the Internet, but that's not true. Part of the address identifies the LAN on which the host computer is located, and part of it identifies the host computer within the network. Most IP addresses are Class C addresses, which are formatted as shown in Figure 28-5.

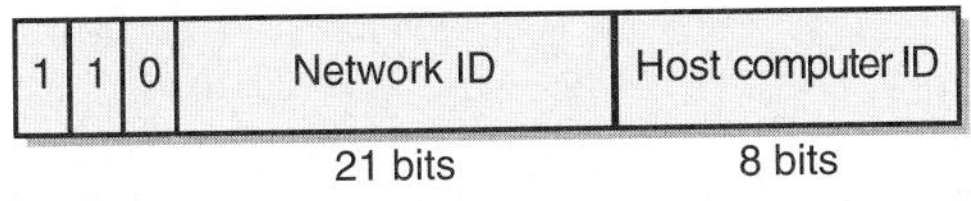

Figure 28-5 The layout of a Class C IP address.

This means that slightly more than 2 million networks can exist, and each of those networks can have 2^8 (256) addressable host computers. The Class A and Class B IP addresses, which allow more host computers on a network, are all used up.

> **Note** The Internet powers that be have recognized the shortage of IP addresses, so they have proposed a new standard, the IPv6 protocol (sometimes referred to as IP Next Generation, or IPng for short). IPv6 defines a new IP datagram format that uses 128-bit addresses instead of 32-bit addresses. With IPv6, you'll be able, for example, to assign a unique Internet address to each light switch in your house so you can switch off your bedroom light from your portable computer from anywhere in the world.

By convention, IP addresses are written in dotted-decimal format. The four parts of the address refer to the individual byte values. An example of a Class C IP address is 192.168.198.201. In a computer with an Intel CPU, the address bytes are stored low-order-to-the-left, in so-called *little endian* order. In most other computers, including the UNIX machines that first supported the Internet, bytes are stored high-order-to-the-left, in *big endian* order. Because the Internet imposes a machine-independent standard for data interchange, all multibyte numbers must be transmitted in big endian order. This means that programs running on Intel-based machines must convert between network byte order (big endian) and host byte order (little endian). This rule applies to 2-byte port numbers as well as to 4-byte IP addresses.

TCP

You've learned about the limitations of UDP. What you really need is a protocol that supports error-free transmission of large blocks of data. Obviously, you want the receiving program to be able to reassemble the bytes in the exact sequence in which they were transmitted, even though the individual datagrams might arrive in the wrong sequence. TCP is that protocol, and it's the principal transport protocol for all Internet applications, including HTTP and File Transfer Protocol (FTP). Figure 28-6 shows the layout of a TCP segment. (It's not called a datagram.) The TCP segment fits inside an IP datagram, as shown in Figure 28-7.

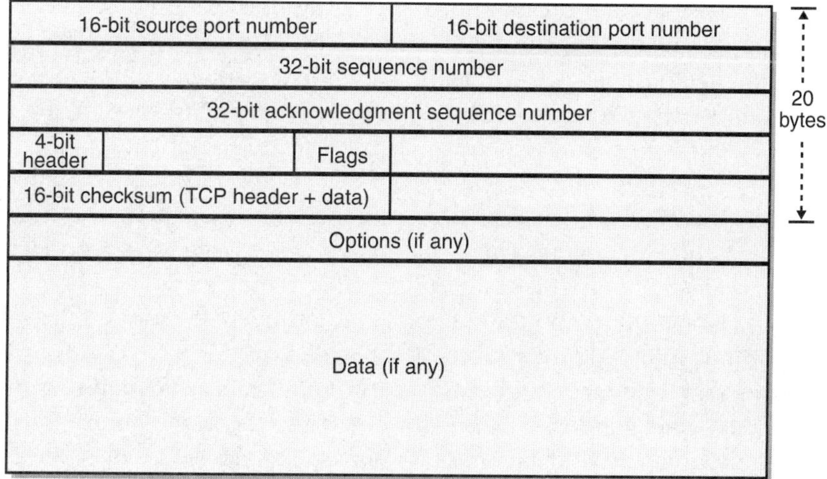

Figure 28-6 A simple layout of a TCP segment.

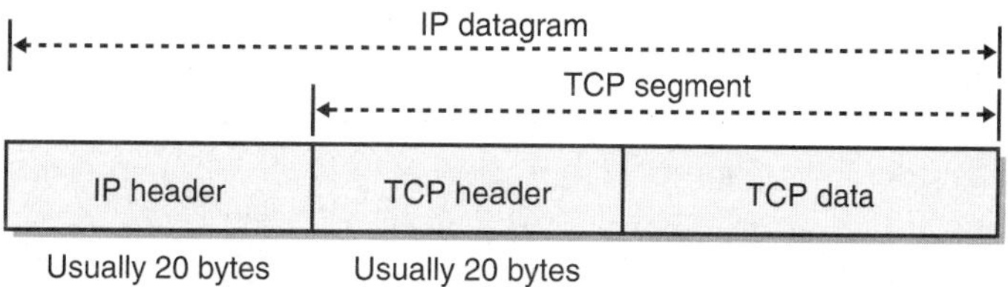

Figure 28-7 The relationship between an IP datagram and a TCP segment.

The TCP protocol establishes a full-duplex, point-to-point connection between two computers, and a program at each end of this connection uses its own port. The combination of an IP address and a port number is called a *socket*. The connection is first established with a three-way handshake. The initiating program sends a segment with the *SYN* flag set, the responding program sends a segment with both the *SYN* and *ACK* flags set, and then the initiating program sends a segment with the *ACK* flag set.

After the connection is established, each program can send a stream of bytes to the other program. TCP uses the sequence number fields together with *ACK* flags to control this flow of bytes. The sending program doesn't wait for each segment to be acknowledged but instead sends a number of segments together and then waits for the first acknowledgment. If the receiving program has data to send back to the sending program, it can piggyback its acknowledgment and outbound data together in the same segments.

The sending program's sequence numbers are not segment indexes but rather indexes into the byte stream. The receiving program sends back the sequence numbers (in the acknowledgment number field) to the sending program, thereby ensuring that all bytes are received and assembled in sequence. The sending program resends unacknowledged segments.

Each program closes its end of the TCP connection by sending a segment with the *FIN* flag set, which must be acknowledged by the program on the other end. A program can no longer receive bytes on a connection that has been closed by the program on the other end.

Don't worry about the complexity of the TCP protocol. The Winsock and WinInet APIs hide most of the details, so you don't have to worry about *ACK* flags and sequence numbers. Your program calls a function to transmit a block of data, and Windows takes care of splitting the block into segments and stuffing them inside IP datagrams. Windows also takes care of delivering the bytes on the receiving end, but that gets tricky, as you'll see later in this chapter.

DNS

When we surf the Web, we don't use IP addresses. Instead, we use human-friendly names such as *microsoft.com* or *www.cnn.com*. A significant portion of Internet resources is consumed when host names (such as *microsoft.com*) are translated into IP addresses that TCP/IP can use. A distributed network of name server (domain server) computers performs this translation by processing DNS queries. The entire Internet namespace is organized into domains, starting with an unnamed root domain. Under the root is a series of top-level domains such as *com*, *edu*, *gov*, and *org*.

> **Note** Don't confuse Internet domains with Windows NT/2000/XP domains. The latter are logical groups of networked computers that share a common security database.

Servers and Domain Names

Let's look at the server end first. Suppose a company named Consolidated Messenger has two host computers connected to the Internet, one for WWW service and the other for FTP service. Following convention, these host computers are named *www.consolidatedmessenger.com* and *ftp.consolidatedmessenger.com*, respectively, and both are members of the second-level domain *consolidated-messenger*, which Consolidated Messenger has registered with an organization called InterNIC. (See *http://www.internic.net*.)

Now Consolidated Messenger must designate two (or more) host computers as its name servers. Each name server for the *com* domain has a database entry for the *consolidatedmessenger* domain, and that entry contains the names and IP addresses of Consolidated Messenger's two name servers. Each of the two *consolidatedmessenger* name servers has database entries for both of Consolidated Messenger's host computers. These servers might also have database entries for hosts in other domains, and they might have entries for name servers in third-level domains. Thus, if a name server can't provide a host's IP address directly, it can redirect the query to a lower-level name server. Figure 28-8 illustrates Consolidated Messenger's domain configuration.

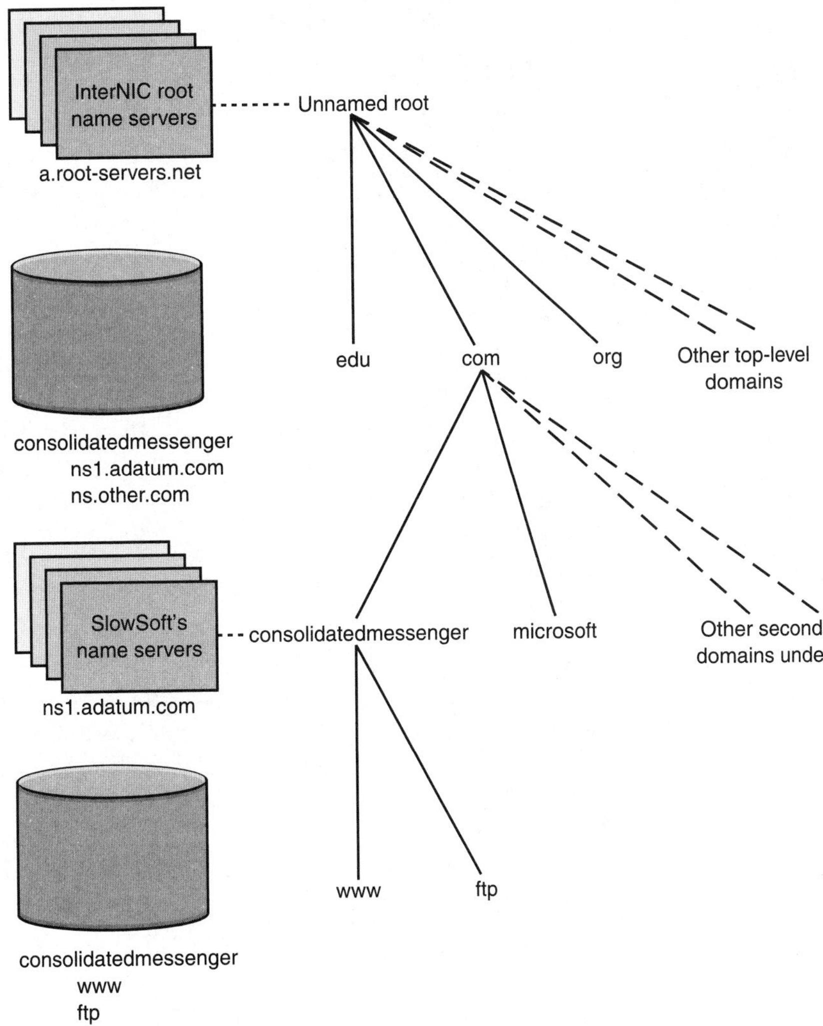

Figure 28-8 Consolidated Messenger's domain configuration.

> **Note** A top-level name server runs on its own host computer. InterNIC manages (at last count) 13 computers that serve the root domain and top-level domains. Lower-level name servers can be programs running on host computers anywhere on the Internet. Consolidated Messenger's Internet service provider (ISP), A.Datum Corporation, can furnish one of Consolidated Messenger's name servers. If the ISP is running Windows NT/2000 Server, the name server is usually the DNS program that comes bundled with the operating system. That name server might be designated *ns1.adatum.com*.

Clients and Domain Names

Now for the client side. A user types *http://www.consolidatedmessenger.com* in the browser. (The *http://* prefix tells the browser to use the HTTP protocol when it eventually finds the host computer.) The browser must then resolve *www.consolidatedmessenger.com* into an IP address, so it uses TCP/IP to send a DNS query to the default gateway IP address for which TCP/IP is configured. This default gateway address identifies a local name server, which might have the needed host IP address in its cache. If not, the local name server relays the DNS query up to one of the root name servers. The root server looks up *consolidatedmessenger* in its database and sends the query back down to one of Consolidated Messenger's designated name servers. In the process, the IP address for *www.consolidatedmessenger.com* is cached for later use if it was not cached already. If you want to go the other way, name servers are also capable of converting an IP address to a name.

HTTP

We'll do some Winsock programming soon, but just sending raw byte streams back and forth isn't very interesting. You need to use a higher-level protocol in order to be compatible with existing Internet servers and browsers. HTTP is a good place to start because it's the protocol of the Web and it's relatively simple.

HTTP is built on TCP, and this is the way it works: First, a server program listens on port 80. Then a client program (typically a browser) connects to the server (*www.consolidatedmessenger.com* in this case) after receiving the server's IP address from a name server. Using its own port number, the client sets up a two-way TCP connection to the server. When the connection is established, the client sends a request to the server, which might look like this:

```
GET /customers/newproducts.html HTTP/1.0
```

The server identifies the request as a *GET*, the most common type, and it concludes that the client wants a file named newproducts.html that's located in a server directory known as /customers (which might or might not be \customers on the server's hard disk). Immediately following are request headers, which mostly describe the client's capabilities.

```
Accept: image/gif, image/x-xbitmap, image/jpeg, image/pjpeg,
        image/x-jg, */*
Accept-Language: en
UA-pixels: 1024x768
UA-color: color8
UA-OS: Windows NT 5.0
UA-CPU: x86
User-Agent: Mozilla/4.0 (compatible; MSIE 6.0; AK; Windows NT 5.0)
Host: www.consolidatedmessenger.com
Connection: Keep-Alive
If-Modified-Since: Wed, 24 Apr 2002 20:23:04 GMT
(blank line)
```

The *If-Modified-Since* header tells the server not to bother to transmit newproducts.html unless the file has been modified since April 24, 2002. This implies that the browser already has a dated copy of this file stored in its cache. The blank line at the end of the request is crucial; it provides the only way for the server to tell that it is time to stop receiving and start transmitting, and that's because the TCP connection stays open.

Now the server springs into action. It sends newproducts.html, but first it sends an OK response:

```
HTTP/1.0 200 OK
```

This is immediately followed by some response header lines:

```
Server: Microsoft-IIS/6.0
Date: Thu, 25 Apr 2002 17:33:12 GMT
Content-Type: text/html
Accept-Ranges: bytes
Last-Modified: Wed, Apr 24 2002 20:23:04 GMT
Content-Length: 407
(blank line)
```

The contents of newproducts.html immediately follow the blank line:

```
<html>
<head><title>Consolidated Messenger's New Products</title></head>
<body><body background="/images/clouds.jpg">
<h1><center>Welcome to Consolidated Messenger's New Products List
</center></h1><p>
```

(continued)

```
Unfortunately, budget constraints have prevented Consolidated Messenger
 from introducing any new products this year. We suggest you keep
 enjoying the old products.<p>
<a href="default.htm">Consolidated Messenger's Home Page</a><p>
</body>
</html>
```

You're looking at elementary HTML code here, and the resulting Web page won't win any prizes. We won't go into the details because dozens of HTML books are already available. From these books, you'll learn that HTML tags are contained in angle brackets and that there's often an end tag (with a / character) for every start tag. Some tags, such as *<a>* (hypertext anchor), have attributes. In the example above, the following line creates a link to another HTML file:

```
<a href="default.htm">Consolidated Messenger's Home Page</a><p>
```

The user clicks on *Consolidated Messenger's Home Page*, and the browser requests default.htm from the original server.

Actually, newproducts.html references two server files, default.htm and /images/clouds.jpg. The clouds.jpg file is a JPEG file that contains a background picture for the page. The browser downloads each of these files as a separate transaction, establishing and closing a separate TCP connection each time. The server just dishes out files to any client that asks for them. In this case, the server doesn't know or care whether the same client requested newproducts.html and clouds.jpg. To the server, clients are simply IP addresses and port numbers. In fact, the port number is different for each request from a client. For example, if 10 of your company's programmers are surfing the Web via your company's proxy server (more on proxy servers later), the server will see the same IP address for each client.

Note Web pages typically use two graphics formats, GIF and JPEG. GIF files are compressed images that retain all the detail of the original uncompressed image but are usually limited to 256 colors. They support transparent regions and animation. JPEG files are smaller, but they don't carry all the detail of the original file. GIF files are often used for small images such as buttons, and JPEG files are often used for photographic images, for which detail is not critical. Visual C++ .NET can read, write, and convert both GIF and JPEG files, but the Win32 API cannot handle these formats unless you supply a special compression/decompression module.

The HTTP standard includes a *PUT* request type that enables a client program to upload a file to the server. Client programs and server programs seldom implement *PUT*.

FTP

FTP handles the uploading and downloading of server files plus directory navigation and browsing. A Windows command-line program called ftp (it doesn't work through a Web proxy server) lets you connect to an FTP server using UNIX-like keyboard commands. Browser programs usually support the FTP protocol (for downloading files only) in a more user-friendly manner. You can protect an FTP server's directories with a username/password combination, but both strings will be passed over the Internet as clear text. FTP is based on TCP. Two separate connections are established between the client and server, one for control and one for data.

Internet vs. Intranet

Up to now, we've assumed that client and server computers were connected to the Internet. The fact is, you can run exactly the same client and server software on a local intranet. An intranet is often implemented on a company's LAN and is used for distributed applications. Users see the familiar browser interface at their client computers, and server computers supply simple Web-like pages or do complex data processing in response to user input.

An intranet offers a lot of flexibility. If, for example, you know that all your computers are Intel-based, you can use ActiveX controls and ActiveX document servers that provide ActiveX document support. If necessary, your server and client computers can run custom TCP/IP software that allows communication beyond HTTP and FTP. To secure your company's data, you can separate your intranet completely from the Internet or you can connect it through a *firewall*, which is a security system that protects your company's network from external threats.

Building an Intranet

Building a Windows-based intranet is easy and cheap. Windows 95/98/Me and Windows NT/2000/XP all contain the necessary networking capabilities. If you don't want to spend the money, you can build a free intranet within a single computer. All the code in this chapter will run on this one-computer configuration.

NTFS vs. FAT File Systems

With Windows 95/98/Me, you're restricted to one file system, File Allocation Table (FAT)—or Virtual File Allocation Table (VFAT) for long filenames. With Windows NT/2000/XP, you get the NT file system (NTFS). Your intranet will be much more secure using NTFS because NTFS allows you to set user permissions for individual directories and files. Users log on to a Windows server (or to an attached workstation) and supply a username and password.

Intranet and Internet clients participate in this operating system security scheme because the server can log them on as if they were local users. Thus, you can restrict access to any server directory or file to specific users who must supply passwords. If those user workstations are Windows network clients (as would be the case with a LAN-based intranet), the username and password are passed through from the user's logon.

Network Hardware

You obviously need more than one computer to make a network. Your main development computer will probably be a Pentium-based computer, but chances are you'll have at least one old computer hanging around. It makes sense to connect it to your main computer for intranet testing and file backups.

You'll need a network board for each computer, but 10-megabit-per-second Ethernet boards are now extremely inexpensive. Choose a brand that comes with its own drivers for Windows 95/98/Me and Windows NT/2000/XP or is already supported by those operating systems. To see a list of supported boards in Windows NT and Windows 95/98/Me, click on the Network icon in Control Panel and then click the Add button to add an adapter. To see the list of supported boards in Windows 2000 and Windows XP, click on the Network And Dial-up Connections icon in Control Panel, right-click on any local area connection, click Properties, and then select Install to add an adapter.

Most network boards have connectors for both thin coaxial (coax) and 10BaseT twisted pair cable. With 10BaseT, you must buy a hub. Thin coax requires only coaxial cable (which is available in precut lengths with connectors) plus terminator plugs. With coax, you daisy-chain your computers together and put terminators on each end of the chain.

Follow the instructions that come with the network board. In most cases, you'll have to run an MS-DOS program that writes to the electrically erasable programmable read-only memory (EEPROM) on the board. Write down the values you select—you'll need them later.

Configuring Windows for Networking

Control Panel's Network applet lets you configure network settings. During configuration, you must select TCP/IP as one of your protocols if you want to run an intranet. You must also install the Windows driver for your network board, ensuring that the IRQ and I/O address values match what you put into the board's EEPROM. You must also assign an IP address to each of your network boards. If you're not connected directly to the Internet, you can choose any unique address you want.

That's actually enough configuring for an intranet, but you'll probably want to use your network for sharing files and printers, too. For Windows NT, install Client And Server Services and bind them to TCP/IP. For Windows 95/98/Me, install Client For Microsoft Networks and File And Printer Sharing For Microsoft Networks. For Windows 2000/XP, the File And Printer Sharing For Microsoft Networks component is installed and enabled by default. If you have an existing network with another protocol installed (Novell IPX/SPX or Microsoft NetBEUI, for example), you can continue to use that protocol on the network along with TCP/IP. In that case, Windows file and print sharing will use the existing protocol and your intranet will use TCP/IP. If you want one computer to share another computer's resources, you must enable sharing from Windows Explorer (for disk directories) or from the Printers folder (for printers).

Intranet Host Names and the HOSTS File

Both Internet and intranet users expect their browsers to use host names, not IP addresses. There are various methods of resolving names to addresses, including using your own DNS server, which is an installable component of Windows NT/2000 Server. The easiest way to map Internet host names to IP addresses, however, is to use the HOSTS file. In Windows NT/2000/XP, this is a text file in the \Winnt\System32\DRIVERS\ETC directory. In Windows 95/98/Me, it's in the \WINDOWS directory, in a prototype HOSTS.SAM file. Just copy that file to HOSTS and make the entries with Notepad. Be sure to copy the edited HOSTS file to all computers in the network.

Testing Your Intranet: The Ping Program

You can use the Windows Ping program to test your intranet. From the command line, type **ping**, followed by the IP address (in dotted-decimal format) or the host name of another computer on the network. If you get a positive response, you'll know that TCP/IP is configured correctly. If you get no response or an error message, proceed no further. Go back and troubleshoot your network connections and configuration.

An Intranet for One Computer: The TCP/IP Loopback Address

The first line in the HOSTS file should be the following:

```
127.0.0.1        localhost
```

This is the standard loopback IP address. If you start a server program to listen on this address, client programs running on the same machine can connect to localhost to get a TCP/IP connection to the server program. This works whether or not you have network boards installed.

Winsock Programming

Winsock is the lowest-level Windows API for TCP/IP programming. Part of the code (the exported functions that your program calls) is located in Wsock32.dll, and part is inside the Windows kernel. You can write both Internet server programs and Internet client programs using the Winsock API. This API is based on the original Berkeley Sockets API for UNIX. A new and much more complex version, Winsock 2, was included for the first time with Windows NT 4.0, but we'll stick with the old version because it's available in all versions of Windows.

Synchronous vs. Asynchronous Winsock Programming

Winsock was introduced first for Win16, which did not support multithreading. Consequently, most developers used Winsock in the asynchronous mode. In that mode, all sorts of hidden windows and *PeekMessage* calls enabled single-threaded programs to make Winsock send and receive calls without blocking, thus keeping the user interface alive. Asynchronous Winsock programs were complex. They often implemented "state machines" that processed callback functions to try to figure out what to do next based on what had just happened. Well, we're not in 16-bit land anymore, so we can do modern multithreaded programming. If this scares you, go back and review Chapter 11. Once you get used to multithreaded programming, you'll love it.

In this chapter, we'll make the most of our Winsock calls from worker threads so the program's main thread can carry on with the user interface. The worker threads contain nice, sequential logic consisting of blocking Winsock calls.

The MFC Winsock Classes

We've tried to use MFC classes where it makes sense to use them, but the MFC developers have informed us that the *CAsyncSocket* and *CSocket* classes are not appropriate for 32-bit synchronous programming. The Visual C++ .NET online help says you can use *CSocket* for synchronous programming, but if you look at the source code you'll see some ugly message-based code left over from Win16.

The Blocking Socket Classes

Since we couldn't use MFC, we had to write our own Winsock classes. *CBlockingSocket* is a thin wrapping of the Winsock API, designed only for synchronous use in a worker thread. The only fancy features are exception-throwing on errors and timeouts for sending and receiving data. The exceptions help you write cleaner code because you don't need to have error tests after every Winsock call. The timeouts (which are implemented with the Winsock *select* function) prevent a communication fault from blocking a thread indefinitely.

CHttpBlockingSocket is derived from *CBlockingSocket* and provides functions for reading HTTP data. *CSockAddr* and *CBlockingSocketException* are helper classes.

The *CSockAddr* Helper Class

Many Winsock functions take socket address parameters. As you might remember, a socket address consists of a 32-bit IP address plus a 16-bit port number. The actual Winsock type is a 16-byte *sockaddr_in* structure, which looks like this:

```
struct sockaddr_in {
    short   sin_family;
    u_short sin_port;
    struct  in_addr sin_addr;
    char    sin_zero[8];
};
```

The IP address is stored as type *in_addr*, which looks like this:

```
struct in_addr {
    union {
        struct { u_char s_b1,s_b2,s_b3,s_b4; } S_un_b;
        struct { u_short s_w1,s_w2; } S_un_w;
        u_long S_addr;
    } S_un;
}
```

These are ugly structures, so we'll derive a programmer-friendly C++ class from *sockaddr_in*. The file \vcppnet\Ex28a\Blocksock.h on the companion CD contains the following code for doing this, with inline functions included:

```
class CSockAddr : public sockaddr_in {
public:
    // constructors
```

(continued)

```
        CSockAddr()
        {
            sin_family = AF_INET;
            sin_port = 0;
            sin_addr.s_addr = 0;
        } // Default
        CSockAddr(const SOCKADDR& sa) { memcpy(this, &sa,
            sizeof(SOCKADDR)); }
        CSockAddr(const SOCKADDR_IN& sin) { memcpy(this, &sin,
            sizeof(SOCKADDR_IN)); }
        CSockAddr(const ULONG ulAddr, const USHORT ushPort = 0)
        // parms are host byte ordered
        {
            sin_family = AF_INET;
            sin_port = htons(ushPort);
            sin_addr.s_addr = htonl(ulAddr);
        }
        CSockAddr(const char* pchIP, const USHORT ushPort = 0)
        // dotted IP addr string
        {
            sin_family = AF_INET;
            sin_port = htons(ushPort);
            sin_addr.s_addr = inet_addr(pchIP);
        } // already network byte ordered
        // Return the address in dotted-decimal format
        CString DottedDecimal()
            { return inet_ntoa(sin_addr); }
        // constructs a new CString object
        // Get port and address (even though they're public)
        USHORT Port() const
            { return ntohs(sin_port); }
        ULONG IPAddr() const
            { return ntohl(sin_addr.s_addr); }
        // operators added for efficiency
        const CSockAddr& operator=(const SOCKADDR& sa)
        {
            memcpy(this, &sa, sizeof(SOCKADDR));
            return *this;
        }
        const CSockAddr& operator=(const SOCKADDR_IN& sin)
        {
            memcpy(this, &sin, sizeof(SOCKADDR_IN));
            return *this;
        }
        operator SOCKADDR()
            { return *((LPSOCKADDR) this); }
        operator LPSOCKADDR()
            { return (LPSOCKADDR) this; }
        operator LPSOCKADDR_IN()
            { return (LPSOCKADDR_IN) this; }
};
```

As you can see, this class has some useful constructors and conversion operators, which make the *CSockAddr* object interchangeable with the type *sockaddr_in* and the equivalent types *SOCKADDR_IN*, *sockaddr*, and *SOCKADDR*. There's a constructor and a member function for IP addresses in dotted-decimal format. The internal socket address is in network byte order, but the member functions all use host byte order parameters and return values. The Winsock functions *htonl*, *htons*, *ntohs*, and *ntohl* take care of the conversions between network and host byte order.

The *CBlockingSocketException* Class

All the *CBlockingSocket* functions throw a *CBlockingSocketException* object when Winsock returns an error. This class is derived from the MFC *CException* class and thus overrides the *GetErrorMessage* function. This function gives the Winsock error number and a character string that *CBlockingSocket* provided when it threw the exception.

The *CBlockingSocket* Class

The following code shows an excerpt from the header file for the *CBlockingSocket* class:

Blocksock.h

```
class CBlockingSocket : public CObject
{
    DECLARE_DYNAMIC(CBlockingSocket)
public:
    SOCKET m_hSocket;
    CBlockingSocket();  { m_hSocket = NULL; }
    void Cleanup();
    void Create(int nType = SOCK_STREAM);
    void Close();
    void Bind(LPCSOCKADDR psa);
    void Listen();
    void Connect(LPCSOCKADDR psa);
    BOOL Accept(CBlockingSocket& s, LPCSOCKADDR psa);
    int Send(const char* pch, const int nSize, const int nSecs);
    int Write(const char* pch, const int nSize, const int nSecs);
    int Receive(char* pch, const int nSize, const int nSecs);
    int SendDatagram(const char* pch, const int nSize, LPCSOCKADDR psa,
        const int nSecs);
    int ReceiveDatagram(char* pch, const int nSize, LPCSOCKADDR psa,
```

(continued)

```
        const int nSecs);
    void GetPeerAddr(LPCSOCKADDR psa);
    void GetSockAddr(LPCSOCKADDR psa);
    static CSockAddr GetHostByName(const char* pchName,
        const USHORT ushPort = 0);
    static const char* GetHostByAddr(LPCSOCKADDR psa);
    operator SOCKET();
        { return m_hSocket; }
};
```

Here are the *CBlockingSocket* member functions, starting with the constructor:

- **Constructor** The *CBlockingSocket* constructor makes an uninitialized object. You must call the *Create* member function to create a Windows socket and connect it to the C++ object.
- **Create** This function calls the Winsock *socket* function and then sets the *m_hSocket* data member to the returned 32-bit *SOCKET* handle.

Parameter	Description
nType	A type of socket; should be *SOCK_STREAM* (the default value) or *SOCK_DGRAM*

- **Close** This function closes an open socket by calling the Winsock *closesocket* function. The *Create* function must have been called previously. The destructor does not call this function because it would be impossible to catch an exception for a global object. Your server program can call *Close* anytime for a socket that is listening.
- **Bind** This function calls the Winsock *bind* function to bind a previously created socket to a specified socket address. Before calling *Listen*, your server program calls *Bind* with a socket address containing the listening port number and server's IP address. If you supply *INADDR_ANY* as the IP address, Winsock will decipher your computer's IP address.

Parameter	Description
psa	A *CSockAddr* object or a pointer to a variable of type *sockaddr*

- **Listen** This TCP function calls the Winsock *listen* function. Your server program calls *Listen* to begin listening on the port specified by the previous *Bind* call. The function returns immediately.

- **Accept** This TCP function calls the Winsock *accept* function. Your server program calls *Accept* immediately after calling *Listen*. *Accept* returns when a client connects to the socket, sending back a new socket (in a *CBlockingSocket* object that you provide) that corresponds to the new connection.

Parameter	Description
s	A reference to an existing *CBlockingSocket* object for which *Create* has not been called
psa	A *CSockAddr* object or a pointer to a variable of type *sockaddr* for the connecting socket's address
Return value	*TRUE* if successful

- **Connect** This TCP function calls the Winsock *connect* function. Your client program calls *Connect* after calling *Create*. *Connect* returns when the connection has been made.

Parameter	Description
psa	A *CSockAddr* object or a pointer to a variable of type *sockaddr*

- **Send** This TCP function calls the Winsock *send* function after calling *select* to activate the timeout. The number of bytes actually transmitted by each *Send* call depends on how quickly the program at the other end of the connection can receive the bytes. *Send* will throw an exception if the program at the other end closes the socket before it reads all the bytes.

Parameter	Description
pch	A pointer to a buffer that contains the bytes to send
nSize	The size (in bytes) of the block to send
nSecs	Timeout value in seconds
Return value	The actual number of bytes sent

- **Write** This TCP function calls *Send* repeatedly until all the bytes are sent or until the receiver closes the socket.

Parameter	Description
pch	A pointer to a buffer that contains the bytes to send
nSize	The size (in bytes) of the block to send
nSecs	Timeout value in seconds
Return value	The actual number of bytes sent

- **Receive** This TCP function calls the Winsock *recv* function after calling *select* to activate the timeout. This function returns only the bytes that have been received. For more information, see the description of the *CHttpBlockingSocket* class in the next section.

Parameter	Description
pch	A pointer to an existing buffer that will receive the incoming bytes
nSize	The maximum number of bytes to receive
nSecs	Timeout value in seconds
Return value	The actual number of bytes received

- **Send Datagram** This UDP function calls the Winsock *sendto* function. The program on the other end needs to call *ReceiveDatagram*. There is no need to call *Listen*, *Accept*, or *Connect* for datagrams. You must have previously called *Create* with the parameter set to *SOCK_DGRAM*.

Parameter	Description
pch	A pointer to a buffer that contains the bytes to send
nSize	The size (in bytes) of the block to send
psa	The datagram's destination address (a *CSockAddr* object or a pointer to a variable of type *sockaddr*)
nSecs	Timeout value in seconds
Return value	The actual number of bytes sent

- **Receive Datagram** This UDP function calls the Winsock *recvfrom* function. The function returns when the program at the other end of the connection calls *SendDatagram*. You must have previously called *Create* with the parameter set to *SOCK_DGRAM*.

Parameter	Description
pch	A pointer to an existing buffer that will receive the incoming bytes
nSize	The size (in bytes) of the block to send
psa	The datagram's destination address (a *CSockAddr* object or a pointer to a variable of type *sockaddr*)
nSecs	Timeout value in seconds
Return value	The actual number of bytes received

- **GetPeerAddr** This function calls the Winsock *getpeername* function. It returns the port and IP address of the socket on the other end of the connection. If you're connected to the Internet through a Web proxy server, the IP address will be the proxy server's IP address.

Parameter	Description
psa	A *CSockAddr* object or a pointer to a variable of type *sockaddr*

- **GetSockAddr** This function calls the Winsock *getsockname* function. It returns the socket address that Winsock assigns to this end of the connection. If the other program is a server on a LAN, the IP address will be the address assigned to this computer's network board. If the other program is a server on the Internet, your service provider will assign the IP address when you dial in. In both cases, Winsock will assign the port number, which is different for each connection.

Parameter	Description
psa	A *CSockAddr* object or a pointer to a variable of type *sockaddr*

- **GetHostByName** This static function calls the Winsock function *gethostbyname*. It queries a name server and then returns the socket address corresponding to the host name. The function times out by itself.

Parameter	Description
pchName	A pointer to a character array containing the host name to resolve
ushPort	The port number (default value 0) that will become part of the returned socket address
Return value	The socket address containing the IP address from the DNS plus the port number *ushPort*

- **GetHostByAddr** This static function calls the Winsock *gethostbyaddr* function. It queries a name server and then returns the host name that corresponds to the socket address. The function times out by itself.

Parameter	Description
psa	A *CSockAddr* object or a pointer to a variable of type *sockaddr*
Return value	A pointer to a character array containing the host name; the caller should not delete this memory

- **Cleanup** This function closes the socket if it is open. It doesn't throw an exception, so you can call it inside an exception catch block.
- **operator SOCKET** This overloaded operator lets you use a *CBlockingSocket* object in place of a *SOCKET* parameter.

The *CHttpBlockingSocket* Class

If you call *CBlockingSocket::Receive*, you'll have a difficult time knowing when to stop receiving bytes. Each call will return the bytes that are stacked up at your end of the connection at that instant. If there are no bytes, the call will block, but if the sender closed the socket, the call will return zero bytes.

In the earlier section on HTTP, you learned that the client sends a request terminated by a blank line. The server is supposed to send the response headers and data as soon as it detects the blank line, but the client must analyze the response headers before it reads the data. This means that as long as a TCP connection remains open, the receiving program must process the received data as it comes in. A simple but inefficient technique would be to call *Receive* for 1 byte at a time. A better way is to use a buffer.

The *CHttpBlockingSocket* class adds buffering to *CBlockingSocket*, and it provides two new member functions. Here's part of the \vcppnet\Ex28a\Blocksock.h file:

```
class CHttpBlockingSocket : public CBlockingSocket
{
public:
    DECLARE_DYNAMIC(CHttpBlockingSocket)
    enum {nSizeRecv = 1000}; // max receive buffer size (> hdr line
                             //  length)
    CHttpBlockingSocket();
    ~CHttpBlockingSocket();
    int ReadHttpHeaderLine(char* pch, const int nSize, const int nSecs);
    int ReadHttpResponse(char* pch, const int nSize, const int nSecs);
private:
    char* m_pReadBuf; // read buffer
    int m_nReadBuf; // number of bytes in the read buffer
};
```

The constructor and destructor take care of allocating and freeing a 1000-character buffer. The two new member functions are as follows:

- **ReadHttpHeaderLine** This function returns a single header line, terminated with a *<cr><lf>* pair. *ReadHttpHeaderLine* inserts a terminating zero at the end of the line. If the line buffer is full, the terminating zero is stored in the last position.

Parameter	Description
pch	A pointer to an existing buffer that will receive the incoming line (zero-terminated)
nSize	The size of the *pch* buffer
nSecs	Timeout value in seconds
Return value	The actual number of bytes received, excluding the terminating zero

- **ReadHttpResponse** This function returns the remainder of the server's response that's received when the socket is closed or when the buffer is full. Don't assume that the buffer will contain a terminating zero.

Parameter	Description
pch	A pointer to an existing buffer that will receive the incoming data
nSize	The maximum number of bytes to receive
nSecs	Time out value in seconds
Return value	The actual number of bytes received

A Simplified HTTP Server Program

Now it's time to use the blocking socket classes to write an HTTP server program. All the frills have been eliminated, but the code actually works with a browser. This server doesn't do much except return some hard-coded headers and HTML statements in response to any *GET* request. (See the Ex28a program later in this chapter for a more complete HTTP server.)

Initializing Winsock

Before making any Winsock calls, the program must initialize the Winsock library. The following statements in the application's *InitInstance* member function do the job:

```
WSADATA wsd;
WSAStartup(0x0101, &wsd);
```

Starting the Server

The server starts in response to some user action, such as a menu choice. Here's the command handler:

```
CBlockingSocket g_sListen; // one-and-only global socket for listening
void CSocketView::OnInternetStartServer()
{
    try {
        CSockAddr saServer(INADDR_ANY, 80);
        g_sListen.Create();
        g_sListen.Bind(saServer);
        g_sListen.Listen();
        AfxBeginThread(ServerThreadProc, GetSafeHwnd());
    }
    catch(CBlockingSocketException* e) {
        g_sListen.Cleanup();
        // Do something about the exception
        e->Delete();
    }
}
```

Pretty simple, really. The handler creates a socket, starts listening on it, and then starts a worker thread that waits for some client to connect to port 80. If something goes wrong, an exception will be thrown. The global *g_sListen* object lasts for the life of the program and is capable of accepting multiple simultaneous connections, each managed by a separate thread.

The Server Thread

Now let's look at the *ServerThreadProc* function:

```
UINT ServerThreadProc(LPVOID pParam)
{
    CSockAddr saClient;
    CHttpBlockingSocket sConnect;
    char request[100];
    char headers[] = "HTTP/1.0 200 OK\r\n"
        "Server: Inside Visual C++ .NET SOCK01\r\n"
        "Date: %s\r\n"
        "Content-Type: text/html\r\n"
        "Accept-Ranges: bytes\r\n"
        "Content-Length: 187\r\n"
        "\r\n"; // the important blank line
    char html[] =
        "<html><head><title>Inside Visual C++ Server</title></head>\r\n"
        "<body><body background=\"/samples/images/usa1.jpg\">\r\n"
        "<h1><center>This is a custom home page</center></h1><p>\r\n"
        "</body></html>\r\n\r\n";
     try {
        if(!g_sListen.Accept(sConnect, saClient)) {
            // Handler in view class closed the listening socket
            return 0;
        }
        AfxBeginThread(ServerThreadProc, pParam);
        // read request from client
        sConnect.ReadHttpHeaderLine(request, 100, 10);
        TRACE("SERVER: %s", request); // Print the first header
        if(strnicmp(request, "GET", 3) == 0) {
            do { // Process the remaining request headers
                sConnect.ReadHttpHeaderLine(request, 100, 10);
                TRACE("SERVER: %s", request); // Print the other headers
            } while(strcmp(request, "\r\n"));
            sConnect.Write(headers, strlen(headers), 10); // response hdrs
            sConnect.Write(html, strlen(html), 10); // HTML code
        }
        else {
            TRACE("SERVER: not a GET\n");
            // don't know what to do
        }
```

(continued)

```
        sConnect.Close(); // Destructor doesn't close it
    }
    catch(CBlockingSocketException* e) {
        // Do something about the exception
        e->Delete();
    }
    return 0;
}
```

The most important function call is the *Accept* call. The thread will block until a client connects to the server's port 80, and then *Accept* will return with a new socket, *sConnect*. The current thread will immediately start another thread.

In the meantime, the current thread must process the client's request, which just came in on *sConnect*. It first reads all the request headers by calling *ReadHttpHeaderLine* until it detects a blank line. Then it calls *Write* to send the response headers and the HTML statements. Finally, the current thread calls *Close* to close the connection socket. End of story for this connection. The next thread will be sitting, blocked at the *Accept* call, waiting for the next connection.

Cleaning Up

To avoid a memory leak on exit, the program must ensure that all worker threads have been terminated. The simplest way to do this is to close the listening socket. This forces any thread's pending *Accept* to return *FALSE*, causing the thread to exit.

```
try {
    g_sListen.Close();
    Sleep(340); // Wait for thread to exit
    WSACleanup(); // Terminate Winsock
}
catch(CUserException* e) {
    e->Delete();
}
```

A problem might arise if a thread is in the process of fulfilling a client request. In this case, the main thread should positively ensure that all threads have terminated before exiting.

A Simplified HTTP Client Program

Now for the client side of the story—a simple working program that does a blind *GET* request. When a server receives a *GET* request with a slash, as shown below, it's supposed to deliver its default HTML file:

```
GET / HTTP/1.0
```

If you were to type **http://www.consolidatedmessenger.com** in a browser, the browser would send the blind *GET* request.

This client program can use the same *CHttpBlockingSocket* class you've already seen, and it must initialize Winsock the same way the server did. A command handler simply starts a client thread with a call like this:

```
AfxBeginThread(ClientSocketThreadProc, GetSafeHwnd());
```

Here's the client thread code:

```
CString g_strServerName = "localhost"; // or some other host name
UINT ClientSocketThreadProc(LPVOID pParam)
{
    CHttpBlockingSocket sClient;
    char* buffer = new char[MAXBUF];
    int nBytesReceived = 0;
    char request[] = "GET / HTTP/1.0\r\n";
    char headers[] = // Request headers
        "User-Agent: Mozilla/1.22 (Windows; U; 32bit)\r\n"
        "Accept: */*\r\n"
        "Accept: image/gif\r\n"
        "Accept: image/x-xbitmap\r\n"
        "Accept: image/jpeg\r\n"
        "\r\n"; // need this
    CSockAddr saServer, saClient;
    try {
        sClient.Create();
        saServer = CBlockingSocket::GetHostByName(g_strServerName, 80);
        sClient.Connect(saServer);
        sClient.Write(request, strlen(request), 10);
        sClient.Write(headers, strlen(headers), 10);
        do { // Read all the server's response headers
            nBytesReceived = sClient.ReadHttpHeaderLine(buffer, 100, 10);
        } while(strcmp(buffer, "\r\n")); // through the first blank line
        nBytesReceived = sClient.ReadHttpResponse(buffer, 100, 10);
        if(nBytesReceived == 0) {
            AfxMessageBox("No response received");
        }
        else {
            buffer[nBytesReceived] = '\0';
            AfxMessageBox(buffer);
        }
    }
    catch(CBlockingSocketException* e) {
        // Log the exception
        e->Delete();
    }
    sClient.Close();
    delete [] buffer;
    return 0; // The thread exits
}
```

This thread first calls *CBlockingSocket::GetHostByName* to get the server computer's IP address. Then it creates a socket and calls *Connect* on that socket. Now there's a two-way communication channel to the server. The thread sends its *GET* request followed by some request headers, reads the server's response headers, and then reads the response file itself, which it assumes is a text file. After the thread displays the text in a message box, it exits.

Building a Web Server Using *CHttpBlockingSocket*

If you need a Web server, your best bet is to buy one or to use Microsoft Internet Information Services (IIS), which comes bundled with Windows NT/2000 Server. You can install it on Windows 2000 Professional and on Windows XP as well. Of course, you'll learn more if you build your own server and you'll also have a useful diagnostic tool. And what if you need features that IIS can't deliver? Suppose you want to add Web server capability to an existing Windows application, or suppose you have a custom ActiveX control that sets up its own non-HTTP TCP connection with the server. Take a good look at the server code in Ex28a. It might work as a foundation for your next custom server application.

Ex28a Server Limitations

The server part of the Ex28a program honors *GET* requests for files, and it has logic for processing *POST* requests. These are the two most common HTTP request types. Ex28a will not, however, launch Common Gateway Interface (CGI) scripts or load Internet Server Application Programming Interface (ISAPI) DLLs. Ex28a makes no provision for security, and it doesn't have FTP capabilities. Other than that, it's a great server! If you want the missing features, just write the code for them yourself.

Ex28a Server Architecture

You'll soon see that Ex28a combines an HTTP server, a Winsock HTTP client, and two WinInet HTTP clients. All three clients can talk to the built-in server or to any other server on the Internet. Any client program, including the Telnet utility and standard browsers such as Microsoft Internet Explorer, can communicate with the Ex28a server. You'll examine the client sections a little later in this chapter.

Ex28a is a standard MFC SDI document–view application with a view class derived from *CEditView*. The main menu includes Start Server and Stop Server menu choices as well as a Configuration command that brings up a tabbed dialog box for setting the home directory, the default file for blind *GET*s, and the listening port number (usually 80).

The Start Server command handler starts a global socket listening and then launches a thread, as in the simplified HTTP server described previously. Look at the *ServerThreadProc* function included in the ServerThread.cpp file of the Ex28a project on the companion CD. Each time a server thread processes a request, it logs the request by sending a message to the *CEditView* window. It also sends messages for exceptions, such as bind errors.

The primary job of the server is to deliver files. It first opens a file, storing a *CFile* pointer in *pFile*, and then it reads 5 KB (*SERVERMAXBUF*) blocks and writes them to the socket *sConnect*, as shown in the code below:

```
char* buffer = new char[SERVERMAXBUF];
DWORD dwLength = pFile->GetLength();
nBytesSent = 0;
DWORD dwBytesRead = 0;
UINT uBytesToRead;
while(dwBytesRead < dwLength) {
    uBytesToRead = min(SERVERMAXBUF, dwLength - dwBytesRead);
    VERIFY(pFile->Read(buffer, uBytesToRead) == uBytesToRead);
    nBytesSent += sConnect.Write(buffer, uBytesToRead, 10);
    dwBytesRead += uBytesToRead;
}
```

The server is programmed to respond to a *GET* request for a phony file named Custom. It generates some HTML code that displays the client's IP address, port number, and a sequential connection number. This is one possibility for server customization.

The server normally listens on a socket bound to address *INADDR_ANY*. This is the server's default IP address determined by the Ethernet board or assigned during your connection to your ISP. If your server computer has several IP addresses, you can force the server to listen to one of them by filling in the Server IP Address box on the Advanced tab of the Configuration dialog box. You can also change the server's listening port number on the Server tab. If you choose port 90, for example, browser users would connect to *http://localhost:90*.

The leftmost status bar indicator pane displays "Listening" when the server is running.

Using the Win32 *TransmitFile* Function

With Windows NT/2000/XP, you can make your server more efficient by using the Win32 *TransmitFile* function in place of the *CFile::Read* loop in the code excerpt shown above. *TransmitFile* sends bytes from an open file directly to a socket and is highly optimized. The Ex28a *ServerThreadProc* function contains the following line:

```
if (::TransmitFile(sConnect, (HANDLE) pFile >m_hFile, dwLength, 0,
    NULL, NULL, TF_DISCONNECT))
```

If you have Windows NT/2000/XP, uncomment the line

```
#define USE_TRANSMITFILE
```

at the top of ServerThread.cpp to activate the *TransmitFile* logic.

Building and Testing Ex28a

Open the Ex28a project in Visual C++ .NET, and then build the project. A directory under Ex28a, called Website, contains some HTML files and is set up as the Ex28a server's home directory, which appears to clients as the server's root directory.

> **Note** If you have another HTTP server running on your computer, stop it now. If you have installed IIS along with Windows NT/2000 Server, it is probably running now, so you must stop it. Ex28a reports a bind error (10048) if another server is already listening on port 80.

Run the program from the debugger, and then choose Start Server from the Internet menu. Now go to your Web browser and type *localhost*. You should see the Welcome To The Inside Visual C++ .NET Home Page complete with all graphics. The Ex28a window should look like this.

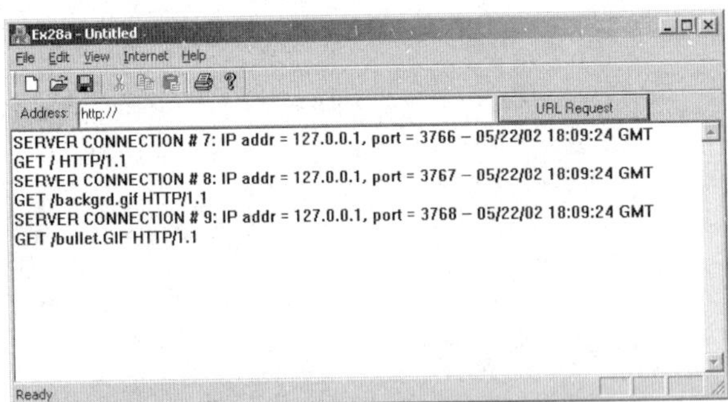

Look at the Visual C++ .NET debug window for a listing of the client's request headers.

If you click the browser's Refresh button, you might notice Ex28a error messages like this:

```
WINSOCK ERROR--SERVER: Send error #10054 -- 10/05/99 04:34:10 GMT
```

This tells you that the browser read the file's modified date from the server's response header and figured out that it didn't need the data because it already had the file in its cache. The browser then closed the socket, and the server detected an error. If the Ex28a server were smarter, it would have checked the client's If-Modified-Since request header before sending the file.

Of course, you can test the server on your intranet. Start the server on one computer, and then run the browser from another, typing in the server's host name as it appears in the HOSTS file.

Building a Web Client Using *CHttpBlockingSocket*

If you had written your own Internet browser program a few years ago, you could have made a billion dollars by now. But these days, you can download browsers for free, so it doesn't make sense to write one. It does make sense, however, to add Internet access features to your Windows applications. Winsock is not the best tool if you need HTTP or FTP access only, but it's a good learning tool.

The Ex28a Winsock Client

The Ex28a program implements a Winsock client in the file \vcppnet\Ex28a\ClientSockThread.cpp on the companion CD. The code is similar to the code for the simplified HTTP client shown earlier. The client thread uses global variables set by the Configuration dialog box, including server filename, server host name, server IP address and port, and client IP address. The client IP address is necessary only if your computer supports multiple IP addresses. When you run the client, it connects to the specified server and issues a *GET* request for the file that you specified. The Winsock client logs error messages in the Ex28a main window.

Ex28a Support for Proxy Servers

If your computer is connected to a LAN at work, chances are it's not exposed directly to the Internet but rather is connected through a *proxy server*. There are two kinds of proxy servers: Web and Winsock. Web proxy servers, sometimes called CERN proxies, support only the HTTP, FTP, and gopher protocols. (The gopher protocol, which predates HTTP, allows character-mode terminals to access Internet files.) A Winsock client program must be specially adapted to use a Web proxy server. A Winsock proxy server is more flexible and thus can support protocols such as RealAudio. Instead of modifying your client program source code, you link to a special remote Winsock DLL that can communicate with a Winsock proxy server.

The Ex28a client code can communicate through a Web proxy if you select the Use Web Proxy check box on the Client tab of the Configuration dialog box. In that case, you must know and enter the name of your proxy server. From that point on, the client code will connect to the proxy server instead of the real server. All *GET* and *POST* requests must then specify the full URL for the file.

If you were connected directly to Consolidated Messenger's server, for example, your *GET* request might look like this:

```
GET /customers/newproducts.html HTTP/1.0
```

But if you were connected through a Web proxy server, the *GET* would look like this:

```
GET http://consolidatedmessenger.com/customers/newproducts.html HTTP/1.0
```

Testing the Ex28a Winsock Client

The easiest way to test the Winsock client is by using the built-in Winsock server. Just start the server as before, and then choose Request (Winsock) from the Internet menu. You should see some HTML code in a message box. You can also test the client against IIS, the server running in another Ex28a process on the same computer, the Ex28a server running on another computer on the Net, and an Internet server. Ignore the Address URL in the dialog box bar for the time being; it's for one of the WinInet clients. You must enter the server name and filename on the Client tab of the Configuration dialog box.

WinInet

WinInet is a higher-level API than Winsock, but it works only for HTTP, FTP, and gopher client programs in either asynchronous or synchronous mode. You can't use it to build servers. The WININET DLL is independent of the WINSOCK32 DLL. Internet Explorer uses WinInet, and so do ActiveX controls.

WinInet's Advantages over Winsock

WinInet far surpasses Winsock in the support it gives to a professional-level client program. Here are just some of the WinInet benefits:

- **Caching** Just like Internet Explorer, your WinInet client program will cach HTML files and other Internet files. You don't have to do a thing. The second time your client requests a particular file, it will be loaded from a local disk instead of from the Internet.
- **Security** WinInet supports basic authentication, Windows NT/2000/XP challenge/response authentication, and Secure Sockets Layer (SSL).
- **Web proxy access** You enter proxy server information through Control Panel, and it will be stored in the Registry. WinInet reads the Registry and uses the proxy server when required.
- **Buffered I/O** WinInet's read function doesn't return until it can deliver the number of bytes you asked for. (It will return immediately, of course, if the server closes the socket.) Also, you can read individual text lines if you need to.
- **Easy API** Status callback functions are available for user interface update and cancellation. One function, *CInternetSession::OpenURL*, finds the server's IP address, opens a connection, and makes the file ready for reading, all in one call. Some functions even copy Internet files directly to and from disk.
- **User-friendliness** WinInet parses and formats headers for you. If a server has moved a file to a new location, it will send back the new URL in an HTTP Location header. WinInet will seamlessly access the new server for you. In addition, it will put a file's modified date in the request header for you.

The MFC WinInet Classes

WinInet is a modern API available only for Win32. The MFC wrapping is quite good, which means we didn't have to write our own WinInet class library. Yes, MFC WinInet supports blocking calls in multithreaded programs, and by now you know that makes us happy.

The MFC classes closely mirror the underlying WinInet architecture, and they add exception processing. These classes are summarized in the following sections.

CInternetSession

You need only one *CInternetSession* object for each thread that accesses the Internet. After you have your *CInternetSession* object, you can establish HTTP, FTP, or gopher connections or you can open remote files directly by calling the

OpenURL member function. You can use the *CInternetSession* class directly, or you can derive a class from it in order to support status callback functions.

The *CInternetSession* constructor calls the WinInet *InternetOpen* function, which returns an *HINTERNET* session handle that is stored inside the *CInternetSession* object. This function initializes your application's use of the WinInet library, and the session handle is used internally as a parameter for other WinInet calls.

CHttpConnection

An object of class *CHttpConnection* represents a "permanent" HTTP connection to a particular host. You know already that HTTP doesn't support permanent connections and that FTP doesn't either. (The connections last only for the duration of a file transfer.) WinInet gives the appearance of a permanent connection because it remembers the host name.

After you have your *CInternetSession* object, you call the *GetHttpConnection* member function, which returns a pointer to a *CHttpConnection* object. (Don't forget to delete this object when you're finished with it.)

The *GetHttpConnection* member function calls the WinInet *InternetConnect* function, which returns an *HINTERNET* connection handle that's stored inside the *CHttpConnection* object and used for subsequent WinInet calls.

CFtpConnection and *CGopherConnection*

These classes are similar to *CHttpConnection*, but they use the FTP and gopher protocols. The *CFtpConnection* member functions *GetFile* and *PutFile* allow you to transfer files directly to and from your disk.

CInternetFile

With HTTP, FTP, or gopher, your client program reads and writes byte streams. The MFC WinInet classes make these byte streams look like ordinary files. If you look at the class hierarchy, you'll see that *CInternetFile* is derived from *CStdioFile*, which is derived from *CFile*. Therefore, *CInternetFile* and its derived classes override familiar *CFile* functions such as *Read* and *Write*. For FTP files, you use *CInternetFile* objects directly, but for HTTP and gopher files, you use objects of the derived classes *CHttpFile* and *CGopherFile*. You don't construct a *CInternetFile* object directly—you call *CFtpConnection::OpenFile* to get a *CInternetFile* pointer.

If you have an ordinary *CFile* object, it has a 32-bit *HANDLE* data member that represents the underlying disk file. A *CInternetFile* object uses the same *m_hFile* data member, but that data member holds a 32-bit Internet file handle of type *HINTERNET*, which is not interchangeable with a *HANDLE*. The *CInternetFile* overridden member functions use this handle to call WinInet functions such as *InternetReadFile* and *InternetWriteFile*.

CHttpFile

This Internet file class has member functions that are unique to HTTP files, such as *AddRequestHeaders*, *SendRequest*, and *GetFileURL*. You don't construct a *CHttpFile* object directly, but you call the *CHttpConnection::OpenRequest* function, which calls the WinInet function *HttpOpenRequest* and returns a *CHttpFile* pointer. You can specify a *GET* or *POST* request for this call.

Once you have your *CHttpFile* pointer, you call the *CHttpFile::SendRequest* member function, which actually sends the request to the server. Then you call *Read*.

CFtpFileFind and *CGopherFileFind*

These classes let your client program explore FTP and gopher directories.

CInternetException

The MFC WinInet classes throw *CInternetException* objects that your program can process with *try/catch* logic.

Internet Session Status Callbacks

WinInet and MFC provide callback notifications as a WinInet operation progresses, and these status callbacks are available in both synchronous (blocking) and asynchronous modes. In synchronous mode (which we're using exclusively here), your WinInet calls will block even if you have status callbacks enabled.

Callbacks are easy in C++. You simply derive a class and override selected virtual functions. The base class for WinInet is *CInternetSession*. Now let's derive a class named *CCallbackInternetSession*:

```
class CCallbackInternetSession : public CInternetSession
{
public:
    CCallbackInternetSession( LPCTSTR pstrAgent = NULL,
        DWORD dwContext = 1,
        DWORD dwAccessType = PRE_CONFIG_INTERNET_ACCESS,
        LPCTSTR pstrProxyName = NULL, LPCTSTR pstrProxyBypass = NULL,
        DWORD dwFlags = 0 ) { EnableStatusCallback() }
protected:
    virtual void OnStatusCallback(DWORD dwContext,
        DWORD dwInternalStatus,
        LPVOID lpvStatusInformation,
        DWORD dwStatusInformationLength);
};
```

The only coding that's necessary is a constructor and a single overridden function, *OnStatusCallback*. The constructor calls *CInternetSession::EnableStatusCallback* to enable the status callback feature. Your WinInet client program makes its various Internet blocking calls, and when the status changes, *OnStatusCallback* is called. Your overridden function quickly updates the user interface and returns, and then the Internet operation continues. For HTTP, most of the callbacks originate in the *CHttpFile::SendRequest* function.

What kinds of events trigger callbacks? Here's a list of the codes passed in the *dwInternalStatus* parameter:

Code Passed	Action Taken
INTERNET_STATUS_RESOLVING_NAME	Looking up the IP address of the supplied name. The name is now in *lpvStatusInformation*.
INTERNET_STATUS_NAME_RESOLVED	Successfully found the IP address. The IP address is now in *lpvStatusInformation*.
INTERNET_STATUS_CONNECTING_TO_SERVER	Connecting to the socket.
INTERNET_STATUS_CONNECTED_TO_SERVER	Successfully connected to the socket.
INTERNET_STATUS_SENDING_REQUEST	Send the information request to the server.
INTERNET_STATUS_REQUEST_SENT	Successfully sent the information request to the server.
INTERNET_STATUS_RECEIVING_RESPONSE	Waiting for the server to respond to a request.
INTERNET_STATUS_RESPONSE_RECEIVED	Successfully received a response from the server.
INTERNET_STATUS_CLOSING_CONNECTION	Closing the connection to the server.
INTERNET_STATUS_CONNECTION_CLOSED	Successfully closed the connection to the server.
INTERNET_STATUS_HANDLE_CREATED	Program can now close the handle.
INTERNET_STATUS_HANDLE_CLOSING	Successfully terminated this handle value.
INTERNET_STATUS_REQUEST_COMPLETE	Successfully completed the asynchronous operation.

You can use your status callback function to interrupt a WinInet operation. You can, for example, test for an event set by the main thread when the user cancels the operation.

A Simplified WinInet Client Program

And now for the WinInet equivalent of our Winsock client program that implements a blind *GET* request. Because you're using WinInet in blocking mode, you must put the code in a worker thread. That thread is started from a command handler in the main thread:

```
AfxBeginThread(ClientWinInetThreadProc, GetSafeHwnd());
```

Here's the client thread code:

```
CString g_strServerName = "localhost"; // or some other host name
UINT ClientWinInetThreadProc(LPVOID pParam)
{
    CInternetSession session;
    CHttpConnection* pConnection = NULL;
    CHttpFile* pFile1 = NULL;
    char* buffer = new char[MAXBUF];
    UINT nBytesRead = 0;
    try {
        pConnection = session.GetHttpConnection(g_strServerName, 80);
        pFile1 = pConnection->OpenRequest(1, "/"); // blind GET
        pFile1->SendRequest();
        nBytesRead = pFile1->Read(buffer, MAXBUF - 1);
        buffer[nBytesRead] = '\0'; // necessary for message box
        char temp[10];
        if(pFile1->Read(temp, 10) != 0) {
            // makes caching work if read complete
            AfxMessageBox("File overran buffer -- not cached");
        }
        AfxMessageBox(buffer);
    }
    catch(CInternetException* e) {
        // Log the exception
        e->Delete();
    }
    if(pFile1) delete pFile1;
    if(pConnection) delete pConnection;
    delete [] buffer;
    return 0;
}
```

The second *Read* call needs some explanation. It has two purposes. If the first *Read* doesn't read the whole file, that means that it was longer than *MAXBUF –1*. The second *Read* will get some bytes, and that lets you detect the overflow problem. If the first *Read* reads the whole file, you still need the second *Read* to force WinInet to cache the file on your hard disk. Remember that WinInet tries to read all the bytes you ask it to—through the end of the file. Even so, you need to read 0 bytes after that.

Building a Web Client Using the MFC WinInet Classes

There are two ways to build a Web client with WinInet. The first method, using the *CHttpConnection* class, is similar to the simplified WinInet client discussed in the previous section. The second method, using *CInternetSession::OpenURL*, is even easier. We'll start with the *CHttpConnection* version.

The Ex28a WinInet Client #1: Using *CHttpConnection*

The Ex28a program implements a WinInet client in the file \vcppnet\Ex28a\ClientInetThread.cpp on the companion CD. Besides allowing the use of an IP address as well as a host name, the program uses a status callback function. That function, *CCallbackInternetSession::OnStatusCallback* in the file \vcppnet\Ex28a\Utility.cpp, puts a text string in a global variable *g_pchStatus*, using a critical section for synchronization. The function then posts a user-defined message to the application's main window. The message triggers an Update Command UI handler (called by *CWinApp::OnIdle*), which displays the text in the second status bar text pane.

Testing the WinInet Client #1

To test the WinInet client #1, you can follow the same procedure we used to test the Winsock client. Note the status bar messages as the connection is made. Note that the file appears more quickly the second time you request it.

The Ex28a WinInet Client #2: Using *OpenURL*

The Ex28a program implements a different WinInet client in the file ClientUrlThread.cpp on the companion CD. This client uses the Address URL (that you type to access the Internet site). Here's the actual code:

```
CString g_strURL = "http:// ";

UINT ClientUrlThreadProc(LPVOID pParam)
{
```

```
    char* buffer = new char[MAXBUF];
    UINT nBytesRead = 0;

    CInternetSession session; // can't get status callbacks for OpenURL
    CStdioFile* pFile1 = NULL; // could call ReadString to get 1 line
    try {
        pFile1 = session.OpenURL(g_strURL, 0,
            INTERNET_FLAG_TRANSFER_BINARY
            |INTERNET_FLAG_KEEP_CONNECTION);
         // If OpenURL fails, we won't get past here
        nBytesRead = pFile1->Read(buffer, MAXBUF - 1);
        buffer[nBytesRead] = '\0'; // necessary for message box
        char temp[100];
        if(pFile1->Read(temp, 100) != 0) {
            // makes caching work if read complete
            AfxMessageBox("File overran buffer -- not cached");
        }
        ::MessageBox(::GetTopWindow(::GetDesktopWindow()), buffer,
            "URL CLIENT", MB_OK);
    }
    catch(CInternetException* e) {
        LogInternetException(pParam, e);
        e->Delete();
    }
    if(pFile1) delete pFile1;
    delete [] buffer;
    return 0;
}
```

Note that *OpenURL* returns a pointer to a *CStdioFile* object. You can use that pointer to call *Read* as shown, or you can call *ReadString* to get a single line. The file class does all the buffering. As in the previous WinInet client, it's necessary to call *Read* a second time to cache the file. The *OpenURL* *INTERNET_FLAG_KEEP_CONNECTION* parameter is necessary for Windows NT/2000/XP challenge/response authentication. If you add the flag *INTERNET_FLAG_RELOAD*, the program will bypass the cache just as the browser does when you click the Refresh button.

Testing the WinInet Client #2

You can test the WinInet client #2 against any HTTP server. You run this client by typing in the URL address, not by using the menu. You must include the protocol (*http://* or *ftp://*) in the URL address. Type **http://localhost**. You should see the same HTML code in a message box. No status messages will appear here because the status callback doesn't work with *OpenURL*.

Asynchronous Moniker Files

Just when you thought you knew all the ways to download a file from the Internet, you're going to learn about another one. With asynchronous moniker files, you'll be doing all your programming in your application's main thread without blocking the user interface. Sounds like magic, doesn't it? The magic is inside the Windows URLMON DLL, which depends on WinInet and is used by Internet Explorer. The MFC *CAsyncMonikerFile* class makes the programming easy, but you should know a little theory first.

Monikers

A moniker is a "surrogate" COM object that holds the name (URL) of the "real" object, which can be an embedded component but more often is just an Internet file (HTML, JPEG, GIF, and so on). Monikers implement the *IMoniker* interface, which has two important member functions: *BindToObject* and *BindToStorage*. The *BindToObject* function puts an object into the running state, and the *BindToStorage* function provides an *IStream* or an *IStorage* pointer from which the object's data can be read. A moniker has an associated *IBindStatusCallback* interface with member functions such as *OnStartBinding* and *OnDataAvailable*, which are called during the process of reading data from a URL.

The callback functions are called in the thread that created the moniker. This means that the URLMON DLL must set up an invisible window in the calling thread and send the calling thread messages from another thread, which uses WinInet functions to read the URL. The window's message handlers call the callback functions.

The MFC *CAsyncMonikerFile* Class

Fortunately, MFC can shield you from the COM interfaces described above. The *CAsyncMonikerFile* class is derived from *CFile*, so it acts like a regular file. Instead of opening a disk file, the class's *Open* member function gets an *IMoniker* pointer and encapsulates the *IStream* interface that's returned from a call to *BindToStorage*. Furthermore, the class has virtual functions that are tied to the member functions of *IBindStatusCallback*. Using this class is a breeze—you construct an object or a derived class and call the *Open* member function, which returns immediately. Then you wait for calls to overridden virtual functions such as *OnProgress* and *OnDataAvailable* (which are named, not coincidentally, after their *IBindStatusCallback* equivalents).

Using the *CAsyncMonikerFile* Class in a Program

Suppose your application downloads data from a dozen URLs but has only one class derived from *CAsyncMonikerFile*. The overridden callback functions must figure out where to put the data. That means you must associate each derived class object with some user interface element in your program. The following steps illustrate one of many ways to do this. Suppose you want to list the text of an HTML file in an edit control that's part of a form view. This is what you can do:

1. Derive a class from *CAsyncMonikerFile*.
2. Add a character pointer data member *m_buffer*. Invoke *new* for this pointer in the constructor, and invoke *delete* in the destructor.
3. Add a public data member *m_edit* of class *CEdit*.
4. Override the *OnDataAvailable* function thus:

```
void CMyMonikerFile::OnDataAvailable(DWORD dwSize, DWORD bscfFlag)
{
    try {
        while (dwSize > 0){
            UINT nBytesRead = Read(m_buffer, MAXBUF - 1);
            dwSize -= nBytesRead;
        }
    }
    catch(CFileException* pe) {
        TRACE(_T("File exception %d\n"), pe->m_cause);
        pe->Delete();
    }
}
```

5. Embed an object of your new moniker file class in your view class.
6. In your view's *OnInitialUpdate* function, attach the *CEdit* member to the edit control like this:

```
m_myEmbeddedMonikerFile.m_edit.SubClassDlgItem(ID_MYEDIT, this);
```

7. In your view class, open the moniker file like this:

```
m_myEmbeddedMonikerFile.Open("http://host/filename");
```

For a large file, *OnDataAvailable* will be called several times, each time adding text to the edit control. If you override *OnProgress* or *OnStopBinding* in your derived moniker file class, your program can be alerted when the transfer is finished. You can also check the value of *bscfFlag* in *OnDataAvailable* to determine whether the transfer completed. Note that everything here is in your main thread and—most important—the moniker file object must exist for as long as the transfer is in progress. That's why it's a data member of the view class.

Asynchronous Moniker Files vs. WinInet Programming

In the WinInet examples earlier in this chapter, you started a worker thread that made blocking calls and sent a message to the main thread when it was finished. With asynchronous moniker files, the same thing happens—the transfer takes place in another thread, which sends messages to the main thread. You just don't see the other thread. There is one very important difference, however, between asynchronous moniker files and WinInet programming: with blocking WinInet calls, you need a separate thread for each transfer; with asynchronous moniker files, only one extra thread handles all transfers together. For example, if you're writing a browser that must download 50 bitmaps simultaneously, using asynchronous moniker files saves 49 threads, which makes the program much more efficient.

Of course, you have some extra control with WinInet, and it's easier to get information from the response headers, such as total file length. Therefore, your choice of programming tools will depend on your application. The more you know about your options, the better the choices you can make.

29

Introducing Dynamic HTML

Dynamic HTML (DHTML), which was introduced as part of Microsoft Internet Explorer 4.0, is a technology that provides significant benefits to Webmasters and developers. Why the buzz about DHTML? For clients who use Internet Explorer as their browser of choice, DHTML represents a dramatic change in how they experience the Web.

It began with the Internet Explorer 4.0 "HTML display engine"—sometimes called Trident in Microsoft literature. As part of the design of Internet Explorer 4.0, Microsoft made Trident a COM component that exposes many of its internal objects that are used for displaying HTML pages in Internet Explorer 4.0. This feature allows you to traverse the portions of an HTML page in script or code as if the HTML page were a data structure. Gone are the days of having to parse HTML or write grotesque Common Gateway Interface (CGI) scripts to get to data in a form. The real power of using DHTML, however, lies not in this ability to access the HTML objects but in the ability to actually change and manipulate the HTML page on the fly—thus the name Dynamic HTML.

Once you grasp the concept of DHTML, a million possible applications will come to mind. For Webmasters, DHTML means that much of the logic that manipulates a Web page can live in scripts that are downloaded to the client. C++ developers can embed DHTML in their applications and use it as an embedded Web client or as a super-flexible, dynamic "form" that their application can change on the fly.

Unfortunately, DHTML is so powerful and extensive that it requires a separate book to fill you in on all of the copious details. For example, to really leverage DHTML you need to understand all of the possible elements of an

HTML page: forms, lists, style sheets, and so on. *Inside Dynamic HTML* by Scott Isaacs (Microsoft Press, 1997) is a great resource for learning the details of DHTML.

Instead of covering all aspects of DHTML, I'll briefly introduce you to the DHTML object model, show you how to work with the model from the scripting angle (as a reference), and then show you how to work with the model from both the Microsoft Foundation Class (MFC) Library and the Active Template Library (ATL). These features are all made possible by the excellent DHTML support introduced in Microsoft Visual C++ .NET.

The DHTML Object Model

If you've been buried in a Visual C++ .NET project and haven't yet had time to take a peek at HTML, the first thing you should know is that HTML is an ASCII markup language format. Here is the code for a very basic HTML page:

```
<html>
<head>
<title>
This is an example of a very basic HTML page!
</title>
</head>
<body>
<h1>This is some text with H1!
</h1>
<h3>
This is some text with H3!
</h3>
</body>
</html>
```

This basic HTML "document" is composed of the following elements:

- **A head (or header)** In this example, the header contains a title: "This is an example of a very basic HTML page!"
- **The body of the document** The body in this example contains two text elements. The first has the heading 1 (h1) style and reads, "This is some text with H1!" The second text element has the heading 3 (h3) style and reads, "This is some text with H3!"

The end result is an HTML page that, when displayed in Internet Explorer, looks like Figure 29-1.

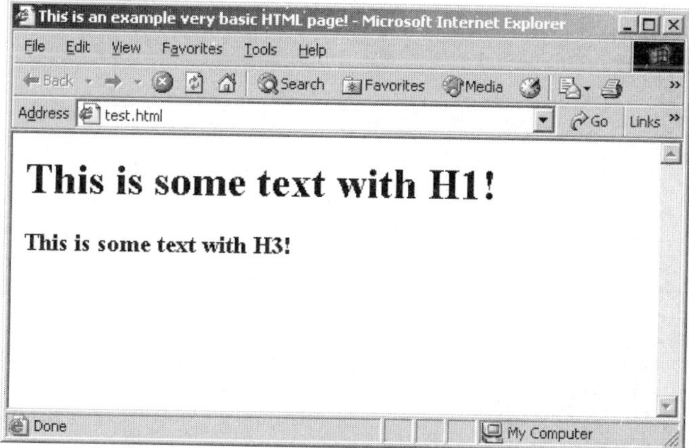

Figure 29-1 A very basic HTML page, as seen in Internet Explorer.

When Internet Explorer loads this sample HTML page, it creates an internal representation that you can traverse, read, and manipulate through the DHTML object model. Figure 29-2, on the following page, shows the basic hierarchy of the DHTML object model.

At the root of the object model is the *window* object. This object can be used from a script to perform some action, such as popping up a dialog box. Here's an example of some JScript that accesses the window object:

```
<SCRIPT LANGUAGE="JScript">
function about()
{
    window.showModalDialog("about.htm","",
        "dialogWidth:25em;dialogHeight13em")
}
</SCRIPT>
```

When the *about* script function is called, it calls the *showModalDialog* function in the *window* DHTML object to display a dialog box. This example also illustrates how scripts access the object model—through globally accessible objects that map directly to the corresponding object in the DTHML object model.

The window object has several "subobjects" that allow you to further manipulate portions of Internet Explorer. The *document* object is what we'll spend most of our time on in this chapter because it gives us programmatic access to the various elements of the currently loaded HTML document. On page 853, you'll see some JScript that shows how to create basic dynamic content that changes the document object.

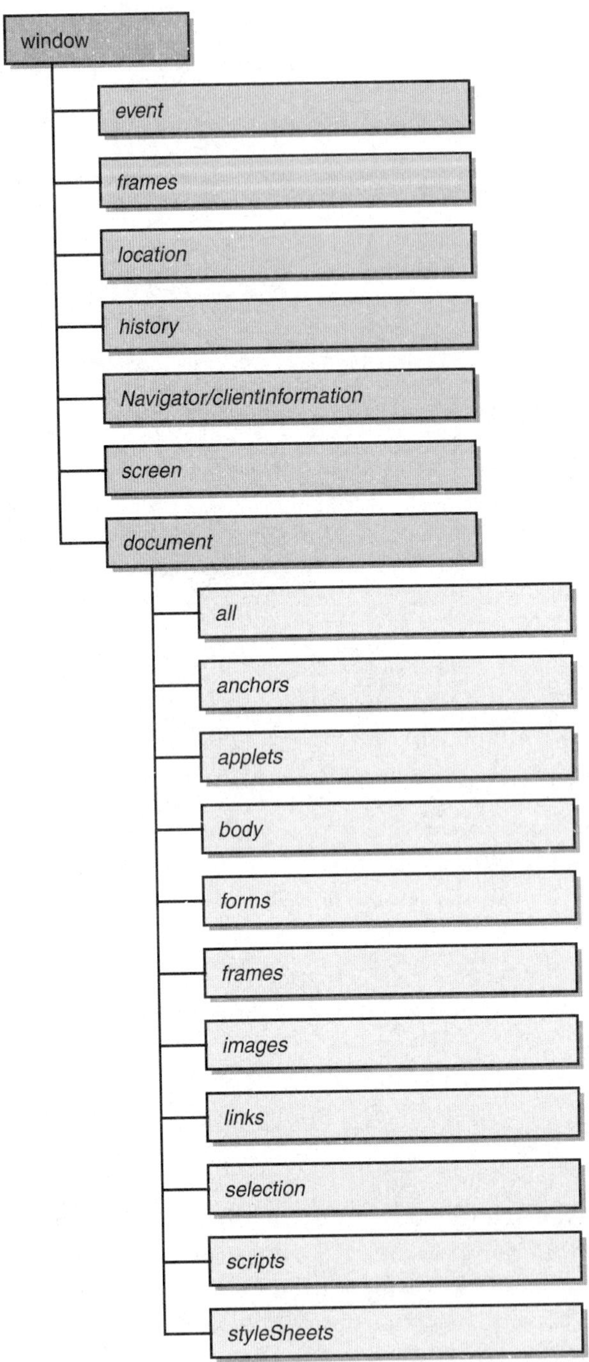

Figure 29-2 The basic hierarchy of the DHTML object model.

```
<HTML>
<HEAD>
<TITLE>Welcome!</TITLE>
<SCRIPT LANGUAGE="JScript">
function changeMe() {
    document.all.MyHeading.outerHTML =
        "<H1 ID=MyHeading>Dynamic HTML is magic!</H1>";
    document.all.MyHeading.style.color = "green";
    document.all.MyText.innerText = "Presto Change-o! ";
    document.all.MyText.align = "center";
    document.body.insertAdjacentHTML("BeforeEnd",
        "<P ALIGN=\"center\">Open Sesame!</P>");
}
</SCRIPT>
<BODY onclick="changeMe()">
<H3 ID=MyHeading> Dynamic HTML demo!</H3>
<P ID=MyText>Click anywhere to see the power of DHTML!</P>
</BODY>
</HTML>
```

This script changes the *MyHeading* and *MyText* objects in the HTML documents on the fly. Not only does it change the text, but it also changes attributes of the elements such as color and alignment. If you want to see this script in action, you can find it in the Ex29_1.html file on the companion CD.

Before we further deconstruct the DHTML object model, let's examine the DHTML concept of a collection. Collections in DHTML are logically equivalent to C++ data structures such as linked lists. In fact, access to the DHTML object model is performed largely by iterating through collections to search for a particular HTML element and then potentially iterating through another subcollection to get to yet another element. Elements contain several methods, such as *contains* and *length*, that you use to traverse the elements.

For example, one subelement of the *document* object is a collection named *all* that contains all of the document's elements. In fact, most of the subobjects of the *document* object are collections. The following script (Ex29_2.html) shows how to iterate through the *all* collection and list the various items of a document:

```
<HTML>
<HEAD>
<TITLE>Iterating through the all collection.</TITLE>
<SCRIPT LANGUAGE="JScript">
function listAllElements() {
    var tag_names = "";
```

(continued)

```
    for (i=0; i<document.all.length; i++)
        tag_names = tag_names + document.all(i).tagName + " ";
    alert("This document contains: " + tag_names);
}
</SCRIPT>
</HEAD>

<BODY onload="listAllElements()">
<H1>DHTML Rocks!</H1>
<P ID=MyText>This document is <B> very </B> short.</P>
</BODY>
</HTML>
```

Notice how easy it is to retrieve items with script. (The syntax calls for parentheses, much like when you access an array in C++.) Also notice that each element in an HTML document has properties such as *tagName* that allow you to programmatically "search" for various elements. For example, if you want to write a script that filters out all bold items, you can scan the *all* collection for an element with *tagName* equal to *B*.

Now you know the basics of the DHTML object model and you understand how to access them through scripts from the Webmaster's perspective. Let's look at how Visual C++ .NET lets us work with DHTML from an application developer's perspective.

Visual C++ .NET and DHTML

Visual C++ .NET supports DHTML through both MFC and ATL. Both MFC and ATL give you complete access to the DHTML object model. Unfortunately, access to the object model from languages such as C++ is obtained through OLE Automation (*IDispatch*) and in many cases isn't as cut-and-dried as some of the scripts we looked at earlier.

The DHTML object model is exposed to C++ developers through a set of COM objects with the prefix *IHTML* (*IHTMLDocument*, *IHTMLWindow*, *IHTMLElement*, *IHTMLBodyElement*, and so on). In C++, once you obtain the document interface, you can use any of the *IHTMLDocument2* interface methods to obtain or to modify the document's properties.

You can access the *all* collection by calling the *IHTMLDocument2::get_all* method. This method returns an *IHTMLElementCollection* collection interface that contains all the elements in the document. You can then iterate through the collection using the *IHTMLElementCollection::item* method (similar to the parentheses in the script above). The *IHTMLElementCollection::item* method supplies you with an *IDispatch* pointer that you can call *QueryInterface* on, requesting the *IID_IHTMLElement* interface. This call to *QueryInterface* will give you an *IHTMLElement* interface pointer that you can use to get or set information for the HTML element.

Most elements also provide a specific interface for working with that particular element type. These element-specific interface names take the form *IHTMLXXXXElement*, where *XXXX* is the name of the element (*IHTMLBodyElement*, for example). You must call *QueryInterface* on the *IHTMLElement* object to request the element-specific interface you need. This might sound confusing (and it can be!). But don't worry—you'll see plenty of samples in this chapter that demonstrate how it all ties together. You'll be writing DHTML code in no time.

The Ex29a Example: MFC and DHTML

MFC's support for DHTML starts with a new *CView* derivative, *CHtmlView*. *CHtmlView* allows you to embed an HTML view inside frame windows or splitter windows, and with some DHTML work it can act as a dynamic form. Example Ex29a demonstrates how to use the new *CHtmlView* class in a vanilla MDI application.

Follow these steps to create the Ex29a example:

1. **Run the MFC Application Wizard and create the Ex29a project.** Make the project an SDI application. Accept all the other defaults, except select *CHtmlView* as the base class on the Generated Classes page.

2. **Edit the URL to be loaded.** In the *CEx29aView::OnInitialUpdate* function, you'll see this line:

   ```
   Navigate2(_T("http://www.msdn.microsoft.com/visualc/"),NULL,NULL);
   ```

   You can edit this line to have the application load a local page or a URL other than the Visual C++ .NET page.

3. **Compile and run the application.** Figure 29-3 shows the application running with the default Web page.

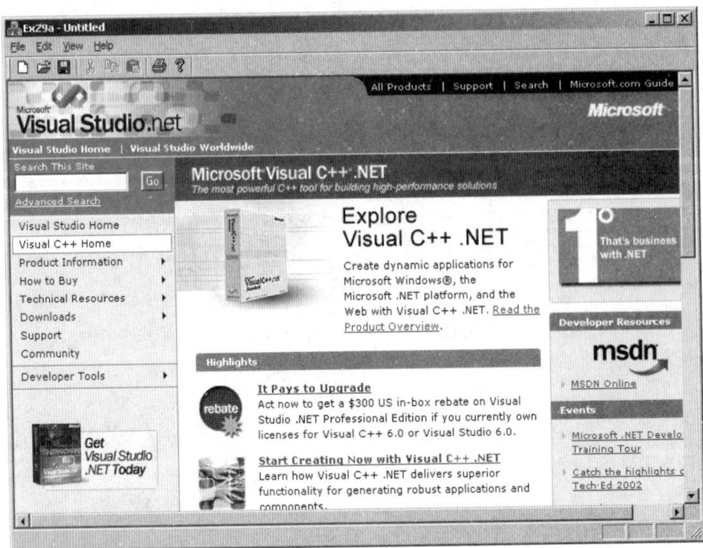

Figure 29-3 The Ex29a example.

The Ex29b Example: DHTML and MFC

Now let's create a sample that really shows how to use DHTML with MFC. Ex29b creates a *CHtmlView* object and a *CListView* object separated by a splitter. It then uses DHTML to enumerate the HTML elements in the *CHtmlView* object and displays the results in the *CListView* object. The end result is a DHTML explorer that you can use to view the DHTML object model of any HTML file.

Here are the steps to create Ex29b:

1. **Run the MFC Application Wizard and create the Ex29b project.** Accept all the defaults but three: Select Single Document and Windows Explorer on the Application Type page, and select *CHtmlView* as the base class on the Generated Classes page.

2. **Change the *CLeftView* to a *CListView* derivative.** By default, the MFC Application Wizard makes the *CLeftView* of the splitter window a *CTreeView* derivative. Open the LeftView.h file, and do a global search for *CTreeView* and replace it with *CListView*. Open LeftView.cpp, and do the same find and replace.

3. **Edit the URL to be loaded.** In the *CEx29bView::OnInitialUpdate* function, change the URL to *http://msdn.microsoft.com.*

4. **Add a *DoDHTMLExplore* function to *CMainFrame*.** First add the following declaration to the MainFrm.h file:

```
virtual void DoDHTMLExplore(void);
```

Then add the implementation for *DoHTMLExplore* to MainFrm.cpp:

```
void CMainFrame::DoDHTMLExplore(void)
{

    CLeftView *pListView =
        (CLeftView *)m_wndSplitter.GetPane(0,0);

    CEx29bView * pDHTMLView =
        (CEx29bView *)m_wndSplitter.GetPane(0,1);

    //Clear the listview
    pListView->GetListCtrl().DeleteAllItems();
    IDispatch* pDisp = pDHTMLView->GetHtmlDocument();

    if (pDisp != NULL )
    {
        IHTMLDocument2* pHTMLDocument2;
        HRESULT hr;

        hr = pDisp->QueryInterface( IID_IHTMLDocument2,
                    (void**)&pHTMLDocument2 );
        if (hr == S_OK)
        {
            IHTMLElementCollection* pColl = NULL;

            hr = pHTMLDocument2->get_all( &pColl );
            if (hr == S_OK && pColl != NULL)
            {
                LONG celem;
                hr = pColl->get_length( &celem );

                if ( hr == S_OK )
                {
                    for ( int i=0; i<celem; i++ )
                    {
```

(continued)

```
VARIANT varIndex;
varIndex.vt = VT_UINT;
varIndex.lVal = i;
VARIANT var2;
VariantInit( &var2 );
IDispatch* pDisp;

hr = pColl->item( varIndex, var2, &pDisp );
if ( hr == S_OK )
{
    IHTMLElement* pElem;

    hr = pDisp->QueryInterface(
        IID_IHTMLElement,
        (void **)&pElem);
    if ( hr == S_OK )
    {
        BSTR bstr;
        hr = pElem->get_tagName(&bstr);
        CString strTag (bstr);
        IHTMLImgElement* pImgElem;

         //Is it an image element?
        hr = pDisp->QueryInterface(
            IID_IHTMLImgElement,
            (void **)&pImgElem );
        if ( hr == S_OK )
        {
            pImgElem->get_href(&bstr);
            strTag += " - ";
            strTag += bstr;
            pImgElem->Release();
        }
        else
        {
            IHTMLAnchorElement* pAnchElem;

            //Is it an anchor?
            hr = pDisp->QueryInterface(
                IID_IHTMLAnchorElement,
                (void **)&pAnchElem );
            if ( hr == S_OK )
            {
                pAnchElem->get_href(&bstr);
                strTag += " - ";
                strTag += bstr;
                pAnchElem->Release();
            }
        }//end of else
```

```
                            pListView->GetListCtrl().InsertItem(
                                pListView->GetListCtrl()
                                .GetItemCount(), strTag);
                            pElem->Release();
                        }
                        pDisp->Release();
                    }
                }
            }
            pColl->Release();
        }
        pHTMLDocument2->Release();
    }
    pDisp->Release();
    }
}
```

To "explore" the HTML document using DHTML, the *DoHTMLExplore* function first gets pointers to the *CListView* and *CHtmlView* views in the splitter window. Then it makes a call to *GetHtmlDocument* to get an *IDispatch* pointer to the DHTML *document* object. Next, it gets the *IHTMLDocument2* interface, retrieves the *all* collection, and iterates through it. In each iteration, *DoHTMLExplore* checks the element type. If the element is an image or an anchor, *DoHTMLExplore* retrieves additional information such as the link for the image. The *all* collection loop then places the textual description of the HTML element in the *CListView* object.

5. **Be sure that Mainfrm.cpp includes mshtml.h.** Add the following line to the top of Mainfrm.cpp so the *DoHTMLExplore* code will compile:

```
#include <mshtml.h>
```

6. **Add a call to *DoHTMLExplore*.** For this example, we'll change the *CEx29bApp::OnAppAbout* function to call the *DoDHTMLExplore* function in the Ex29b.cpp file. Replace the existing code with the following boldface code:

```
void CEx29bApp::OnAppAbout()
{
    CMainFrame * pFrame = (CMainFrame*)AfxGetMainWnd();
    pFrame->DoDHTMLExplore();

}
```

7. **Customize the list view.** In the *CLeftView::PreCreateWindow* function (LeftView.cpp), add this line:

```
cs.style |= LVS_LIST;
```

8. **Compile and run the application.** Press the ? toolbar item or choose Help/About to invoke the explore function.

Figure 29-4 shows the Ex29b example in action.

Figure 29-4 The Ex29b example in action.

Now that you've seen how to use DHTML and MFC, let's look at how ATL implements DHMTL support.

The Ex29c Example: ATL and DHTML

ATL's support for DHTML comes in the form of an HTML object that can be embedded in any ATL ActiveX control. Ex29c creates an ATL control that illustrates DHTML support.

To create the example, follow these steps:

1. **Run the ATL Project Wizard and create the Ex29c project.** Select Executable as the server type on the Application Settings page.

2. **Insert an HTML control.** From the Project menu, choose Add Class. Select ATL Control from the list of templates, as shown here:

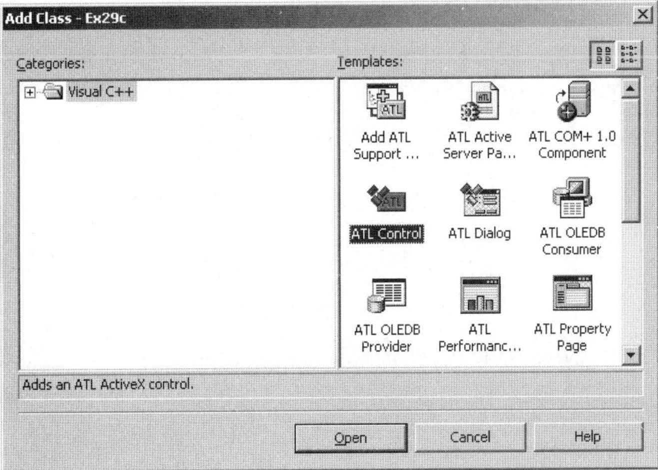

3. **Fill in the C++ Short Name on the Names page and select DHTML Control on the Options page, as shown here:**

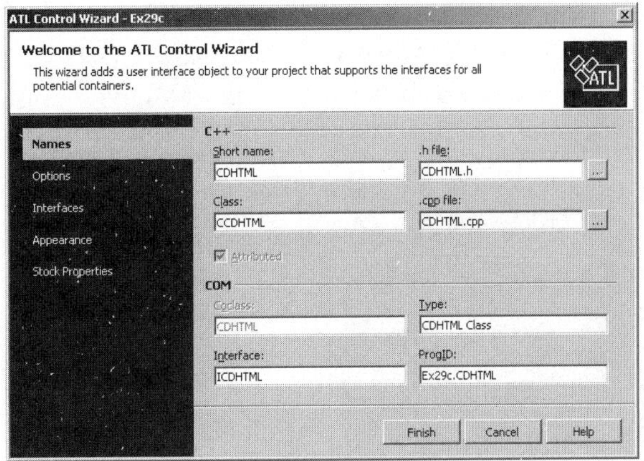

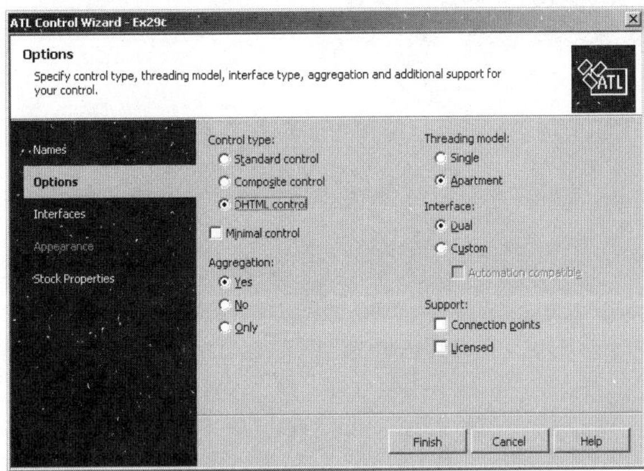

Note If you look at the *IDHTMLUI* object, you'll see this stock implementation of the *OnClick* handler:

```
STDMETHOD(OnClick)(IDispatch* pdispBody, VARIANT varColor)
    {
        CComQIPtr<IHTMLBodyElement> spBody(pdispBody);
        if (spBody != NULL)
            spBody->put_bgColor(varColor);
        return S_OK;
    }
```

The default *OnClick* handler uses *QueryInterface* on the *IDispatch* pointer to get the *IHTMLBodyElement* object. The handler then calls the *put_bgColor* method to change the background color.

4. **Compile, load, and run the control to see the ATL DHTML code in action.** After you build the project, run the ActiveX Control Test Container from the Tools menu. In the test container, choose Insert New Control from the Edit menu and select CDHTML Object from the list box. Figure 29-5 shows the resulting ActiveX control that uses DHTML to change the background when the user clicks the button.

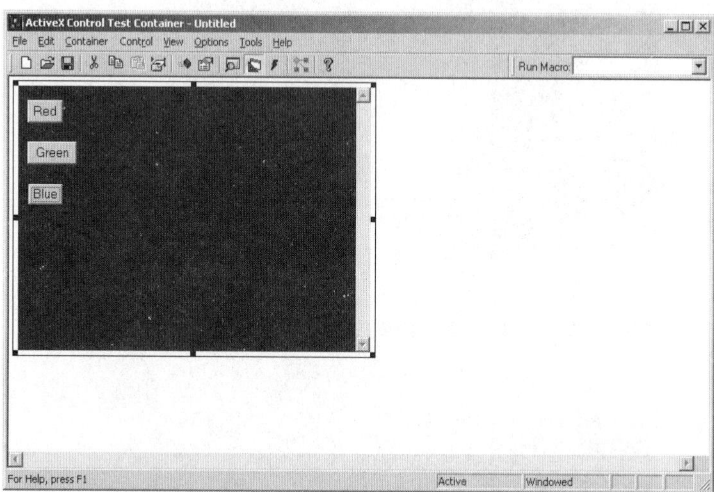

Figure 29-5 The Ex29c ActiveX control.

For More Information

The possibilities for using DHTML in your Visual C++ .NET applications are endless: You can create completely dynamic applications, applications that update from the Internet, client/server ActiveX controls, and so on. If you'd like to learn more about DHTML, here are some good resources:

- *Inside Dynamic HTML* by Scott Isaacs (Microsoft Press, 1997)
- *Dynamic HTML in Action* by William J. Pardi and Eric M. Schurman (Microsoft Press, 1998)
- The Platform SDK (an excellent resource on DHTML and other Microsoft technologies)
- *msdn.microsoft.com* (which discusses DHTML in several areas)

30

ATL Server

In Chapter 28, we used a "homemade" intranet based on the Winsock APIs. In this chapter, you'll learn how to use and extend Microsoft Internet Information Services (IIS), which is bundled with Microsoft Windows 2000 and Windows XP. IIS is actually three separate services—one for HTTP (for the World Wide Web), one for FTP, and one for SMTP/NNTP.

This chapter tells you how to write HTTP server extensions using ATL Server. ATL Server is a set of C++ classes that take the grunge work out of writing ISAPI DLLs. It uses a combination of ISAPI DLLs and extension DLLs written using C++ templates and substitutable tags to customize the content of your page. You'll see how ATL Server simplifies handling HTTP requests so you can write an interactive Web site more quickly than if you program by hand.

This chapter assumes that you have Windows NT 2000/XP (with IIS installed). Let's start by taking a look at IIS.

IIS

IIS is a high-performance Internet/intranet server that takes advantage of underlying Windows NT features such as I/O completion ports, the Win32 function *TransmitFile*, file-handle caching, and CPU scaling for threads.

When you install Windows NT 2000/XP, you're given the option of installing IIS. If you selected IIS at setup, the server will be running whenever Windows NT is running. IIS is a special kind of Win32 program called a *service* (actually three services—HTTP, FTP, and SMTP/NNTP—in one program called inetinfo.exe), which doesn't appear on the taskbar. You can control IIS from the Services icon in Control Panel, but you'll probably want to use the Internet Service Manager program instead.

Internet Service Manager

You can run Internet Service Manager from Control Panel using Administrative Tools. From the Start menu, choose Settings, Control Panel. In Control Panel, select Administration. Then select Internet Information Services. On Advanced Server, you can also get to the IIS manager by choosing All Programs, Administrative Tools from the Start menu and then selecting Internet Information Services.

> **Note** You can also run an HTML-based version of Internet Service Manager remotely from a browser. That version allows you to change service parameters, but it won't let you turn services on and off.

Figure 30-1 shows the Internet Service Manager screen with the World Wide Web (WWW) default site running and FTP services stopped.

You can select a service by clicking on its icon at the left. The Start Item and Stop Item toolbar buttons (triangle and square, respectively) allow you to turn the selected service on or off.

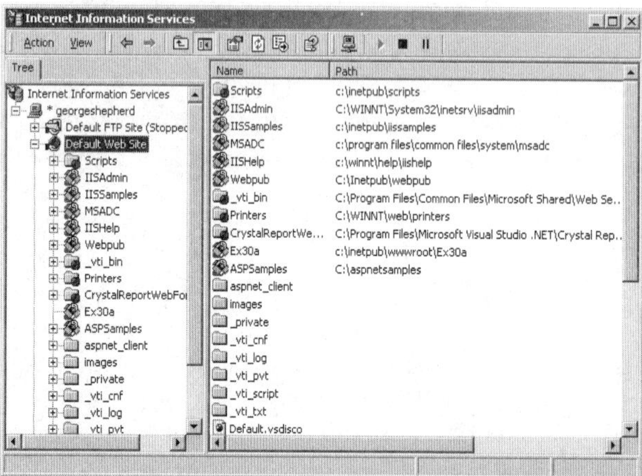

Figure 30-1 The Internet Service Manager screen.

IIS Security

Now that a throng of users can potentially get to your Web site through the Internet, security becomes a big deal. To configure IIS security, right-click on the Web site you want to control and then choose Properties from the shortcut menu to display the Web site's property sheet. Then select the Directory Security property page, as shown in Figure 30-2. Click the Edit button in the Anonymous Access And Authentication Control panel, and you'll see the Authentication Methods property sheet (shown in Figure 30-3). When a client browser requests a file, the server will impersonate a local user for the duration of the request, and that username will determine which files the client can access. Which local user will the server impersonate? Usually the one you see in the Username field, as shown in Figure 30-4. (Click the Edit button in the Authentication Methods dialog box to display the Anonymous User Account dialog box.)

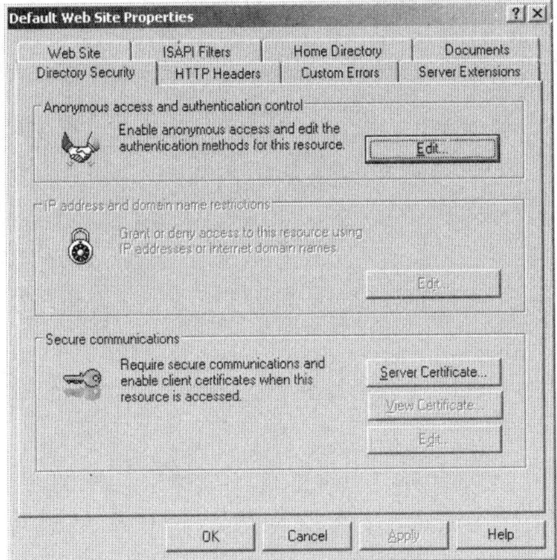

Figure 30-2 The IIS Directory Security property page.

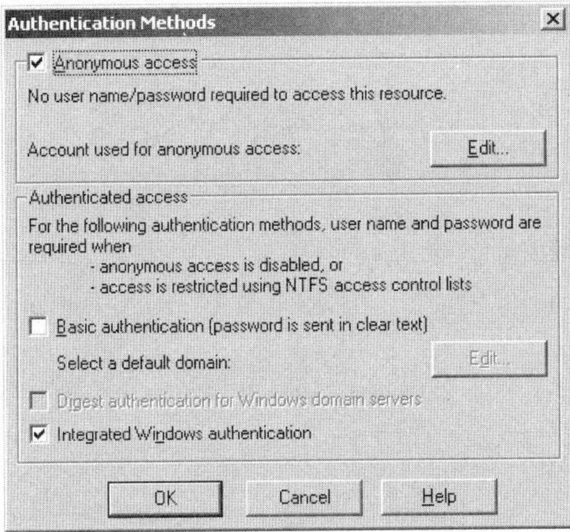

Figure 30-3 The IIS Authentication Methods property sheet.

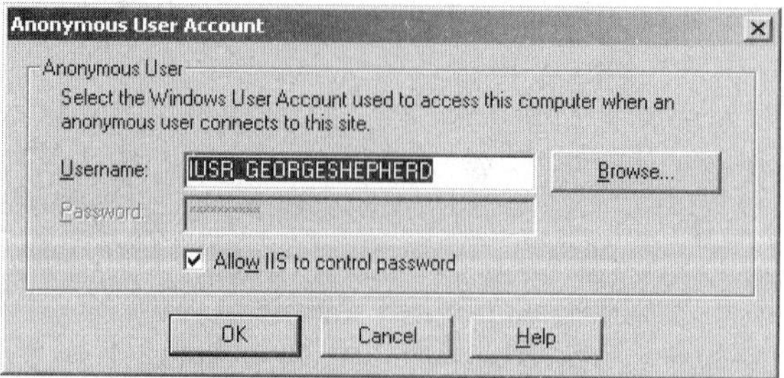

Figure 30-4 The Anonymous User Account dialog box.

Most Web page visitors don't supply a username and password, so they're considered anonymous users. They have the same rights they'd have if they had logged on to your server locally as IUSR_<MYMACHINENAME>. That means IUSR_<MYMACHINENAME> must appear in the list of users that's displayed when you run User Manager or User Manager For Domains (from the Administrative Tools menu), and the passwords must match. (Note that the MMC snap-in is named Computer Management.) The IIS Setup program normally defines this anonymous user for you. You can define your own WWW anonymous username, but you must be sure that the entry in the Anonymous User Account dialog box matches the entry in the computer's (or Windows NT domain's) user list.

Note also the Authenticated Access options in the Authentication Methods property sheet. IIS uses this username to get a security token when it runs a Web site that offers anonymous access. For the time being, stick to the Anonymous Access option only, which means that all Web users will be logged on as IUSR_<MYMACHINENAME.>

IIS Directories

Remember Consolidated Messenger's Web site from Chapter 28? If you requested the URL *http://consolidatedmessenger.com/newproducts.html*, the newproducts.html file would be displayed from the *consolidatedmessenger.com* home directory. Each server needs a home directory, even if that directory contains only subdirectories. The home directory does not need to be the server computer's root directory, however. As shown in Figure 30-5, the WWW home directory is really C:\WebHome, so clients read the disk file C:\WebHome\newproducts.html.

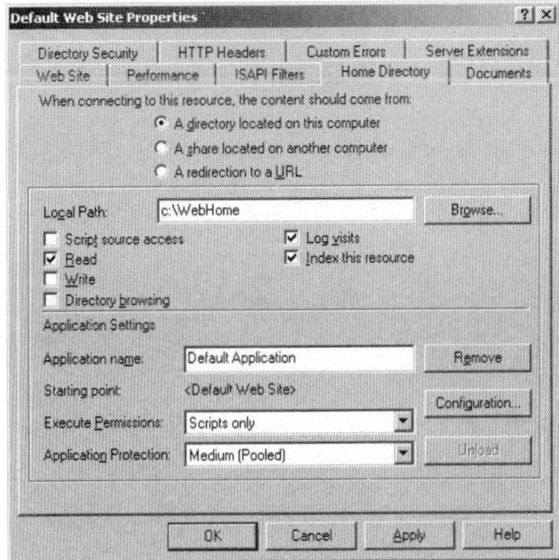

Figure 30-5 The \WebHome WWW home directory property page.

Your server could get by with a home directory only, but the IIS virtual directory feature might be useful. Suppose Consolidated Messenger wants to allow Web access to the directory \BF on the D drive. IIS lets you create a virtual directory, such as /BugsFixed, and map it to a real directory, such as D:\BF. Clients can then access files in the D:\BF directory with a URL similar to this: *http://consolidatedmessenger.com/BugsFixed/file1.html.*

> **Note** If your computer is configured for multiple IP addresses (see the Control Panel Network icon), IIS will allow you to define virtual Web servers. Each virtual server will have its own home directory (and virtual directories) attached to a specified IP address, making it appear as if you have several server computers. Unfortunately, the IIS Web server listens on all the computer's IP addresses, so you can't run IIS simultaneously with the Ex28a server with both listening on port 80.

As described in Chapter 28, browsers can issue a blind request. The Documents tab of the property sheet shown in Figure 30-5 lets you specify the file that a blind request selects, usually Default.htm. If you select the Directory Browsing option on the Home Directory page of the Web site's property sheet, browser clients can see a hypertext list of files in the server's directory instead.

IIS Logging

IIS is capable of making log entries for all connections. You control logging from the Web Site property page of the Web site's property sheet. You can specify text log files, or you can specify logging to an SQL/ODBC database. Log entries consist of date, time, client IP address, file requested, query string, and so forth.

Testing IIS

It's easy to test IIS with a browser or with any of the Ex30a clients. Just make sure that IIS is running and that the Ex30a server is not running. The default IIS home directory is \Winnt\System32\inetsrv\wwwroot (\inetpub\wwwroot on Windows XP), and some HTML files are installed there. If you're running a single machine, you can use the localhost host name. For a network, use a name from the Hosts file. If you can't access the server from a remote machine, run ping to make sure the network is configured correctly. Don't try to build and run ISAPI DLLs until you have successfully tested IIS on your computer.

ISAPI Server Extensions

An ISAPI server extension is a program (implemented as a DLL loaded by IIS) that runs in response to a *GET* or *POST* request from a client program (browser). The browser can pass parameters, which are often values that the browser user types into edit controls, selects from list boxes, and so forth, to the program. The ISAPI server extension typically sends back HTML code based on those parameter values. You'll understand this process better when you see an example.

CGI and ISAPI

Internet server programs were first developed for UNIX computers, so the standards were in place long before Microsoft introduced IIS. The Common Gateway Interface (CGI) standard, which is actually part of HTTP, evolved as a way for browser programs to interact with scripts or separate executable programs running on the server. Without altering the HTTP/CGI specifications, Microsoft designed IIS to allow any browser to load and run a server DLL. DLLs are part of the IIS process and thus are faster than scripts that might need to load separate executable programs. In this chapter, we'll write an ISAPI DLL in C++ using ATL Server. There are other ways to create Web pages, including writing PERL scripts, Active Server Pages (ASP), and ASP.NET.

CGI shifts the programming burden to the server. Using CGI parameters, the browser sends small amounts of information to the server computer, and the server can do absolutely anything with this information, including access a database, generate images, and control peripheral devices. The server sends a file (HTML or otherwise) back to the browser. The file can be read from the server's disk, or it can be generated by the program. No ActiveX controls are necessary, and the browser can be running on any type of computer.

A Simple ISAPI Server Extension *GET* Request

Suppose an HTML file contains the following tag:

```
<a href="scripts/maps.dll?State=Idaho">Idaho Weather Map</a><p>
```

When the user clicks on Idaho Weather Map, the browser will send the server a CGI *GET* request like this:

```
GET scripts/maps.dll?State=Idaho HTTP/1.0
```

IIS will then load maps.dll from its scripts (virtual) directory, call a default function (often named *Default*), and pass it the *State* parameter *Idaho*. The DLL will then go to work generating a JPG file containing the up-to-the-minute satellite weather map for Idaho and send it to the client.

If maps.dll has more than one function, the tag can specify the function name like this:

```
<a href="scripts/maps.dll?GetMap?State=Idaho&Res=5">Idaho Weather Map</a><p>
```

In this case, the function *GetMap* will be called with two parameters, *State* and *Res*.

You'll soon learn how to write an ISAPI server similar to maps.dll, but first you'll need to understand HTML forms because you don't often see CGI *GET* requests by themselves.

HTML Forms: *GET* vs. *POST*

In the HTML code for the simple CGI *GET* request above, the state name is hard-coded in the tag. Why not let the user select the state from a drop-down list? For that, you need a form, and here's a simple one that can do the job:

```
<html>
<head><title>Weathermap HTML Form</title>
</head>
<body>
<h1><center>Welcome to the Satellite Weathermap Service</center></h1>
<form action="scripts/maps.dll?GetMap" method=GET>
```

(continued)

```
    <p>Select your state:
    <select name="State">
        <option> Alabama
        <option> Alaska
        <option> Idaho
        <option> Washington
    </select>
<p><input type="submit"><input type="reset">
</form>
</body></html>
```

If you look at this HTML file with a browser, you'll see the form shown in Figure 30-6.

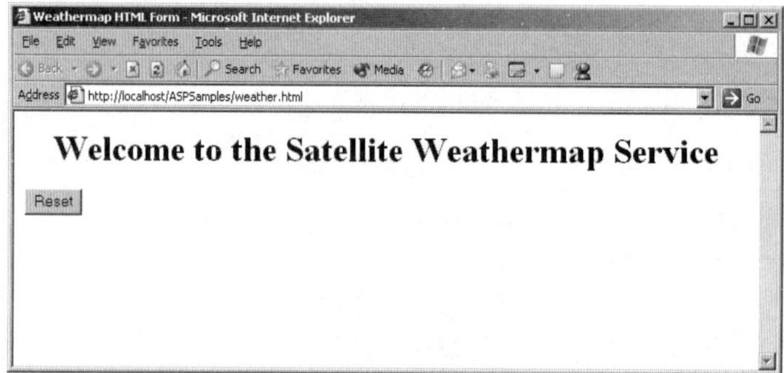

Figure 30-6 The Weathermap HTML Form window.

The select tag provides the state name from a list of four states, and the all-important *submit* input tag displays the pushbutton that sends the form data to the server in the form of a CGI *GET* request that looks like this:

```
GET scripts/maps.dll?GetMap?State=Idaho HTTP/1.0
(various request headers)
(blank line)
```

Unfortunately, some early versions of the Netscape browser omit the function name in form-originated *GET* requests, giving you two choices: provide only a default function in your ISAPI DLL or use the *POST* method inside a form instead of the *GET* method.

If you want to use the *POST* option, you can change one HTML line in the form to the following:

```
<form action="scripts/maps.dll?GetMap" method=POST>
```

Now here's what the browser will send to the server:

```
POST scripts/maps.dll?GetMap
(various request headers)
(blank line)
State=Idaho
```

Note that the parameter value is in the last line instead of in the request line.

> **Note** ISAPI DLLs are usually stored in a separate virtual directory on the server because these DLLs must have execute permission but do not need read permission. Clicking the Edit button shown in Figure 30-3 will allow you to access these permissions from Internet Service Manager, or you can double-click on a directory to change its properties.

You can use the Internet Services API to build high-performance Web applications with low-level control under IIS. You write a DLL using C/C++, and IIS uses a DLL to filter incoming requests or respond to them. These two kinds of ISAPI DLLs are called *filters* and *extensions*, respectively.

An ISAPI filter is a DLL that can receive event notifications from IIS as client requests are being processed. The filter can then modify the standard behavior of IIS. Filters can be used to provide compression, encryption, logging, and custom authentication schemes, among other things.

An ISAPI extension is a DLL that can receive client requests and send responses. C++ code can often generate the HTML that is sent to the client. The extension DLL must export the *GetExtensionVersion* and *HttpExtensionProc* entry points (and optionally *TerminateExtension*). For every client request, an *EXTENSION_CONTROL_BLOCK* structure is passed from IIS to the ISAPI extension DLL through *HttpExtensionProc*. This structure is used to get HTTP header information, call IIS helper functions, and read and write to the client stream.

In a moment, you'll see how ATL Server pushes the Extension Control Block (ECB, or *EXTENSION_CONTROL_BLOCK* as defined in the last paragraph) processing into a set of classes more akin to what C++ developers are used to seeing. As with most C++ code within Microsoft libraries, the ECB is still directly available from within ATL Server.

With low-level ISAPI control comes responsibility. For example, useful ASP intrinsic objects such as *Session* and *Response* are not available in ISAPI, although similar functions can ultimately be accessed. Programming the ECB in a normal C or C++-based ISAPI DLL involves manipulating buffers and other low-level elements. Furthermore, when you write an ISAPI extension, you typically create a thread pool to respond to incoming client requests. For more information on ISAPI, see the MSDN Online article "Developing ISAPI Extensions and Filters."

Enter ATL Server

MFC includes several classes to help you write ISAPI DLLs. These include *CHttpServer*, *CHttpServerContext*, and *CHtmlStream*. In addition, you can see that the creators of some real-world sites actually use MFC to write ISAPI DLLs for their sites.

There's a good amount of documentation on writing ISAPI DLLs using MFC, including earlier editions of this book. Suffice it to say that writing ISAPI DLLs by hand is a C++ process; as a result, it's prone to C++ foibles such as memory leaks and null pointers. The MFC classes make the process somewhat easier, and ATL Server makes the process easier still.

The modern way to write ISAPI DLLs is to use ATL Server. ATL Server is not solely for Web-based user interface development—it's also useful for developing Web services (programmable Web sites). Let's start by taking a look at the ATL Server architecture.

ATL vs. ATL Server

In Chapter 25, we looked at ATL as a COM development tool—a set of class libraries that hide the complexities of COM from the developer. In this chapter, we're looking at ATL Server, which actually has very little to do with COM. The ATL-based COM support is generally independent of ATL Server's support for ISAPI.

Where Does ATL Server Fit In?

There are many ways to handle an HTTP request on the Windows platform. They run the gamut from writing ISAPI DLLs by hand to writing ASP code, writing PERL scripts, and writing ASP.NET code. Each method has its advantages and disadvantages. For example, when you write ISAPI DLLs by hand, you have complete control over how to handle each request. However, you have little leverage over the response to the client. (That is, you have to generate every little part of the response programmatically.) In addition, writing ISAPI DLLs by hand means writing boilerplate code. On the other end of the spectrum is ASP, in which each page is usually a mixture of HTML, some script code, and perhaps some COM objects.

ATL Server tries to sit between the two. Developing Web-based content and user interfaces usually involves managing HTML tags (or perhaps some XML in the case of Web services) and developing logic to drive dynamic content. The executable part of an ATL Server application lives within some C++ classes. In this way, ATL Server provides performance similar to when you code C++ ISAPI DLLs from scratch, and it also includes some of the HTML management features of higher-level development tools such as ASP.NET. The ATL Server classes encapsulate the request, the response, cookies, forms, and the execution context. As a result, handling requests using ATL Server is much easier than when you use the raw ECB.

In addition to a fundamental architecture for managing ISAPI executable code and HTML, ATL Server includes other useful features such as a performance cache and a thread pool.

The ATL Server Architecture

At the end of the day, your job as a Web developer (and who isn't one these days, at least in some capacity?) is to respond to HTTP requests and shove some content out to the client that's connected to your server. You've already seen how to write a server using sockets and the MFC socket classes. Microsoft has already done the dirty work of managing port 80 by providing a service that will watch the port for you: IIS. As an application developer, you need to make IIS do something meaningful—generate well-formed HTML for the client. That's ATL Server's job.

At a high level, ATL Server applications are divided into roughly two parts: a collection of DLLs (both ISAPI extensions and application extension DLLs) and HTML generation templates called Server Response Files (SRF files for short). ATL Server's architecture clearly separates the application presentation from the application logic. The basic content of your page (the presentation) is laid out in SRF files, and then ATL Server uses the application DLLs to replace well-marked HTML code (HTML with embedded code that ATL Server understands) in the HTML text within the SRF files. An SRF file includes HTML content interspersed with well-defined substitution tags. The SRF file is fed to the ISAPI extensions and ATL Server DLLs (the application logic), which make substitutions for the tags.

From the C++ point of view, an ATL Server project comprises several DLLs: a single ISAPI extension DLL and one or more ATL Server application DLLs. The ISAPI extension DLL caches the loaded ATL Server DLLs and parsed SRF files. The ISAPI DLL also contains a thread pool for responding to client requests. The ATL Server application DLL has the smarts to parse the SRF files and replace SRF substitution tags with HTML.

The ISAPI DLL is responsible for hooking up to IIS, and the application DLLs contain code to handle requests. In ATL Server, classes for handling requests derive from *CRequestHandlerT* and contain whatever methods you write for replacing SRF substitution tags with HTML. In many ways, ATL Server is much like the application wizards we looked at in Chapter 4.

ATL Server handler classes contain a pair of dictionaries to associate request handler classes with request handler DLLs and to associate replacement methods with SRF tags. In addition to the replacement dictionaries, *CRequest-HandlerT* contains methods and member variables for accessing standard Web application elements such as form variables, cookies, request streams, and response streams. Figure 30-7 shows how ATL Server processes a client. It shows several application DLLs and a single ISAPI extension DLL.

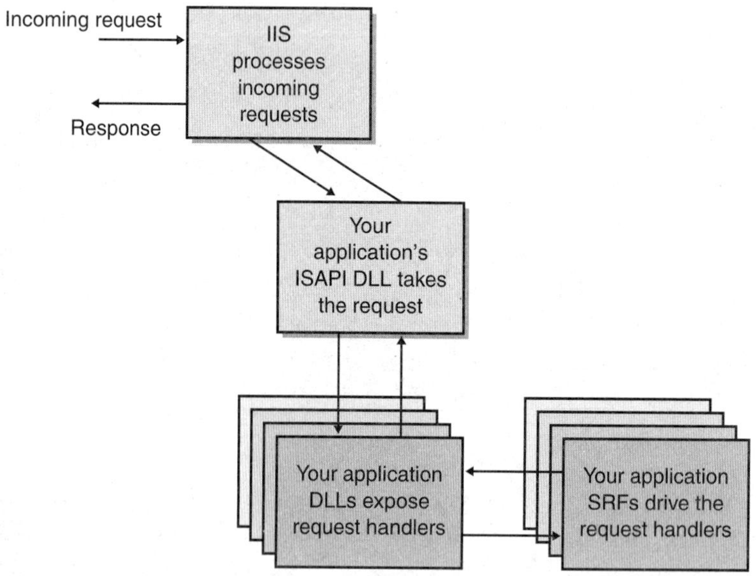

Figure 30-7 The ATL Server architecture.

Here's the path that a request follows through an ATL Server application:

1. The client requests an SRF file via HTTP (for example, *http://www.consolidatedmessenger.com/default.srf*).
2. IIS picks up the request and maps the extension to an ISAPI DLL. In the case of an ATL Server application, this is the ISAPI DLL for the application (which implements *HttpExtensionProc*).
3. The ISAPI DLL contains a thread pool and two caches: a DLL cache and a stencil cache. The DLL cache contains loaded ATL Server request handler DLLs, and the stencil cache contains loaded and token-parsed SRF files. The ISAPI DLL passes the request to a thread pool. (The caches will be used shortly.)
4. One of the worker threads from the pool handles the queued request by opening the SRF file to determine which application DLL should receive the request. (We'll look at the format of an SFR file in a moment.)

5. The worker thread expects to find a line in the SRF file indicating the application DLL to load. If the DLL isn't already loaded, the worker thread will load the DLL. The application will then pass the request to the default request handler class.

6. The SRF file is parsed into tokens (if necessary) and rendered into HTML. Each time the application encounters a token representing a substitution tag, it calls the corresponding replacement method in a handler class that resides in one of the application DLLs. The replacement method generates the output to the browser dynamically.

7. IIS sends the entire response to the client.

Now let's take a look at what those SRF files look like.

SRF Files

For the most part, SRF files are composed of HTML. The bulk of a response is usually the HTML contained in an SRF file. The SRF file also includes simple flow control tags such as *if* and *while*. SRF syntax also supports making method calls into C++ classes, and DLL function mappings.

The SRF tags we're about to look at actually make method calls into your C++ classes. Naturally, the SRF file contains a list of the application DLLs it uses. These appear as handler tags within the SRF file.

As an example, here's a simple SRF file that prints a greeting:

```
{{handler MyFirstApplication.dll/Default}}
<html>
<head>
</head>
<body>
{{HelloHandler}}<br>
</body>
</html>
```

Notice that the first line of the file names the application DLL (MyFirstApplication.dll) in which the handler map lives. (The handler map relates tags to specific C++ code that handle the tags.) The application DLL is used by the ISAPI extension to process the request. This line specifies the handler class and the DLL it lives in.

The next line includes double curly braces, which identify server-side tags to interpret or replace. The tag, *HelloHandler*, names the request handler method to invoke. The output from the request handler named within the tag is injected into the HTML buffer. Here's where the separation between the user interface and the code happens. Web designers can modify the HTML surrounding the handler tag without touching the C++ code.

Multiple Application DLLs

If you think about it, having a one-to-one mapping between application DLLs and SRF files would not work very well in a dynamic environment. A single SRF file can be processed in any number of ways, depending on the capabilities of the server. To support this, ATL Server allows an SRF file to be served by more than one application DLL and by more than one handler. The SRF file will include one default DLL, and the other DLLs will be named. Named DLLs are given IDs within the request comment block. The SRF file uses the IDs within the replacement tags to specify which hander and which method to call.

For example, the following code snippet shows an SRF file with two handlers:

```
{{handler HandlerOne.dll/Default}}
{{id=AlternateHandler handler=HandlerTwo.dll/OtherHandler}}
<html>
<body>
{{MainHandlerMethod}}<br>
{{AlternateHandler.AlternateMethod}}
</body>
</html>
```

This code specifies the default request handler class living in the HandlerOne.dll file and an alternate handler class named *OtherHandler* living within a second DLL named HandlerTwo.dll.

A tag can include SRF keywords (for example, flow control keywords such as *if* and *endif*), which we'll look at in a bit. If the string within the tag is *not* an SRF keyword, it is passed to a handler DLL for replacement. Look carefully at the example. Replacement tags devoid of IDs are managed by the default handler. Tags with identifiers are handled by the specified DLL. HandlerOne.dll interprets the *MainHandlerMethod* tag by mapping it to the default request handler class, and it calls the replacement method associated with the *MainHandlerMethod* tag. HandlerTwo.dll interprets the *AlternateHandler.AlternateMethod* tag by mapping it to the request handler class named *AlternateHandler*, and it calls the replacement method associated with the *AlternateMethod* tag.

Tag Handlers

Tag handlers are member functions of a handler class that lives within an application DLL. The handler classes derive from *CRequestHandlerT*, as shown in the next code snippet. The class includes a replacement method map. Notice that the snippet also includes a handler map (at the DLL-level scope) that maps the class to a replacement string.

```
class CMainHandler : public CRequestHandlerT<CMainHandler>
{
    public:
        DWORD ValidateAndExchange();
        DWORD OnMainHandlerMethod();
        BEGIN_REPLACEMENT_METHOD_MAP(CMainHandler)
            REPLACEMENT_METHOD_ENTRY("MainHandlerMethod",
                OnMainHandlerMethod)
        END_REPLACEMENT_METHOD_MAP()
};

BEGIN_HANDLER_MAP()
    HANDLER_ENTRY("Default", CMainHandler)
    // Other handlers within this DLL are mapped here.
END_HANDLER_MAP()
```

Each tag replacement method looks something like this:

```
HTTP_CODE OnMainHandlerMethod()
{
    CWriteStreamHelper os(m_pStream);
    os << "This text was generated by the application DLL." << endl;
    return HTTP_SUCCESS;
}
```

The *CWriteStreamHelper* class encapsulates the output buffer that will eventually be sent to the browser. If you're an MFC developer, you're probably familiar with the << streaming syntax. The code simply inserts "This text was generated by the application DLL" into the stream of text going back to the browser.

Control Flow

SRF files include replacement tags like those we've just seen. They also include keywords for managing control flow.

The *if*, *else*, and *endif* keywords support branching. For example, here's how to use branching within an SRF file:

```
{{handler MyFirstApplication.dll/Default}}
<html>
<head>
</head>
<body>
{{if IsUserRegistered}}
{{HelloHandler}}<br>
</body>
</html>
```

When the tag including *if IsUserRegistered* is encountered, execution flow ends up within a replacement method in MyFirstApplication.dll (presumably called *OnIsUserRegistered*). This method returns either *HTTP_SUCCESS* or *HTTP_S_FALSE*. For example, the replacement method for *IsUserRegistered* might look something like this:

```
// Member of the default handler class
HTTP_CODE OnIsUserRegistered()
{
    if (LookupUserInDatabase())
        return HTTP_SUCCESS;
    else
        return HTTP_S_FALSE;
}
```

This method simply controls the execution flow based on the state of the database.

The *while* and *endwhile* keywords control looping. The *while* keyword uses a replacement method's return value as the conditional. For example:

```
{{handler MyFirstApplication.dll/Default}}
<html>
<head>
</head>
<body>
{{while CustomersInDatabase}}
{{ShowNextCustomerHandler}}<br>
{{endwhile}}
</body>
</html>
```

Include Files

Finally, SRF files can include other files (SRF and HTML files)—as sort of a form of reuse. The *include* keyword brings in another file. The include mechanism uses a URL to specify the path to the file. A great use for include files is for managing standard user interface elements such as headers and footers. For example, here's how you might use the *include* statement in an SRF file:

```
{{handler MyFirstApplication.dll/Default}}
{{include menu.srf}}
<html>
<head>
</head>
<body>
{{while CustomersInDatabase}}
{{ShowNextCustomerHandler}}<br>
{{endwhile}}
</body>
</html>
```

Notice that ATL Server is mostly declarative. There's only HTML and replacement tags. There are no script blocks, no calls to *CreateObject*, and generally no executable code in the page. It's all in the code behind the page.

The Ex30a Example: An ATL Server Web Site

To see how ATL Server works, let's run through an example. Ex30a is a simple example with a couple of form elements on the page. Here are the steps for creating the example:

1. Create a new ATL Server project. Choose New from the File menu. Select ATL Server Project. Type **Ex30a** as the project name. Select the Memory-Backed Session-State Services option from the Session Services section of the Server Options page. Leave all the other options as the defaults.

2. Examine the code. Notice that there are two subprojects for your ATL Server project: Ex30a and Ex30Isapi. The former project is the application DLL. The latter is the ISAPI DLL that IIS will use. Inside the Ex30a project is a file named Ex30a.srf. This is the SRF file that will be used to process the Web page. Here's the code from the SRF file:

```
{{// use MSDN's "ATL Server Response File Reference"
     to learn about SRF  files.}}
{{handler Ex30a.dll/Default}}
This is a test: {{Hello}}
```

   The handler code lives inside Ex30a.dll. The source code for the handler is a class named *CEx30aHandler* that lives within the file Ex30a.h. Here's the default source code for the handler:

```
[ request_handler("Default") ]
class CEx30aHandler
{
// additional support goes here...
protected:
    // Here is an example of how to use a
    // replacement tag with the stencil processor
    [ tag_name(name="Hello") ]
    HTTP_CODE OnHello(void)
    {
        m_HttpResponse << "Hello World!";
        return HTTP_SUCCESS;
    }
}; // class CEx30aHandler
```

There are no templates appearing in this code because the ATL Server Project Wizard supports attributed programming by default. One of the default options within the wizard is to add deployment support. When this option is selected, Microsoft Visual Studio adds a virtual directory named Ex30a. You can see it by opening up IIS and expanding the Default Web Site node. The list of virtual directories is on the left side—select Ex30a to display the list of application files on the right side. Right-click on the file Ex30a.srf and choose Browse from the shortcut menu. Microsoft Internet Explorer will come up, and you should see a greeting within the browser that says, "This is a test: Hello World!"

3. Add some form elements to the SRF file. Open Ex30a.srf in Visual Studio and view the code in HTML mode. (There are Design and HTML tabs near the bottom of the editor window.) Add the following boldface code to the file:

```
<html>
{{// use MSDN's "ATL Server Response File Reference" to learn about
  SRF files.}}
<head>
</head>
<body>
<p>{{handler Ex30a.dll/Default}}
</p>
<p>{{Hello}}
</p>
<form action="Ex30a.srf" method="post" id="Form1">
<div id="DIV1" ms_positioning="FlowLayout">
<table height="15" cellSpacing="0" cellPadding="0" width="70"
       border="0" ms_1d_layout="TRUE" id="Table1">
<tr>
<td>Name:</td>
</tr>
</table>
</div>
<input id="Name" type="text" name="Name">
<p><input id="Submit" type="submit" value="Button" name="Submit"></p>
</form>
</body>
</html>
```

This code adds a text box and a submit button to the form. If you switch back to HTML view, you should see them.

Rebuild the application (or copy the new SRF file to the new virtual directory) and browse the page again. You should see the elements on the page.

4. Add a handler to personalize the greeting. Add the following handler to the tag handler class:

```
[ tag_name(name="PersonalGreeting") ]
HTTP_CODE OnPersonalGreeting(void)
{
    const CHttpRequestParams& FormFields =
        m_HttpRequest.GetFormVars();
    CString szName = FormFields.Lookup("Name");
    if (szName.Compare("") != 0) {
        m_HttpResponse <<  "You are " << szName;
    } else {
        m_HttpResponse <<  "I don't know you.";
    }
    return HTTP_SUCCESS;
}
```

This handler checks to see whether the Name text box has been filled in. If so, you'll see a personalized greeting. Otherwise, the browser will display "I don't know you."

Add a call to *OnPersonalGreeting* by adding a *PersonalGreeting* tag to the SRF file. You can do this in Design mode. Rebuild the application and browse the file. After you type a name in the text box and click the submit button, you should see a personalized greeting, as shown in Figure 30-8.

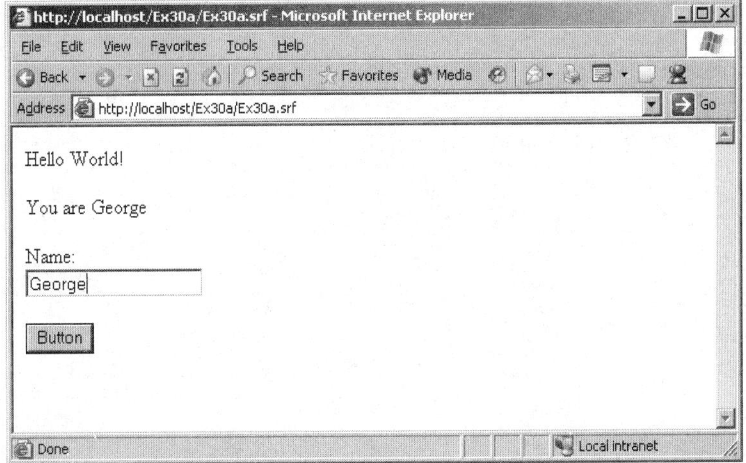

Figure 30-8 The ATL Server application in action.

Part VI

.NET and Beyond

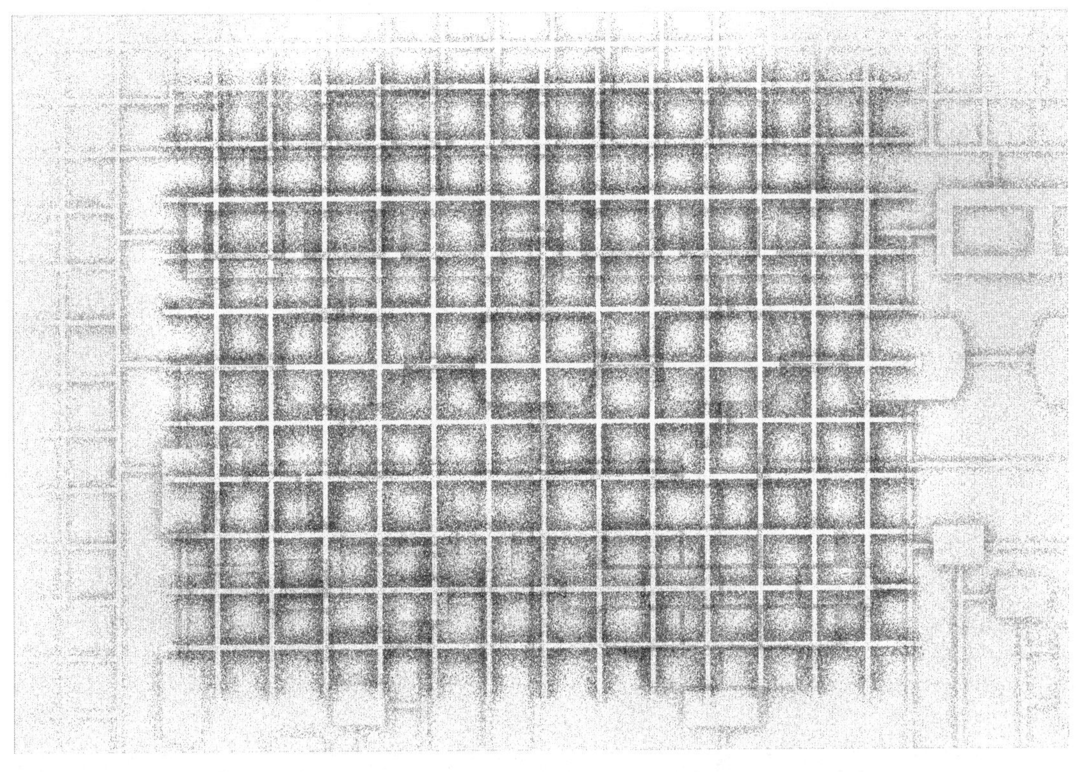

31

Microsoft .NET

You've no doubt heard a lot of buzz about Microsoft .NET. If you're in the Microsoft camp, there's no way to ignore it. .NET is a framework of technologies whose major goals include making software development for the PC much easier and connecting as much of the world as possible through the Internet.

At the heart of .NET is the common language runtime. This chapter mainly focuses on how the common language runtime works and the problems it solves. We'll start with a reevaluation of COM and DLL technology (Microsoft Windows component technology) and identify some of the problems that still exist within COM. Chapter 22 covered the technical details of COM but didn't provide a full historical perspective. A full understanding of component software evolution will help you understand the .NET common language runtime. We'll examine how the .NET common language runtime solves issues with COM, and in the process we'll look at such .NET features as cross-language integration, component versioning, deployment, and the system library provided by the runtime.

Windows Component Technology

As you saw in Chapter 10 when we examined DLLs, one of the most important evolutionary steps within software development has been that of component architectures. Component-based development makes software production more manageable. By dividing an application into components, you can isolate issues and find problems much more quickly. Let's take a look at component technology from a historical perspective.

Some Component History

In the world of classic Windows software development, DLLs are nearly synonymous with the notion of components and code sharing. Before dynamic linking, the only way to share code modules was by using static linking. The earliest PC applications were deployed as single executables. Shipping an application usually involved shipping the executable and perhaps some drivers along with it. Any code brought in from other sources came via raw source code or a precompiled binary code that was glued to the end of the application. Static linking enables you to partition your application into multiple segments, but it has one major drawback: you have to manage buggy code. Attaching the library to the client application forces you to rebuild and redeploy the entire application to fix the bug. The way around this issue is through dynamic linking.

As you saw in Chapter 20, dynamic linking uses a single copy of a library available on disk. The library is loaded on demand at run time by the client applications. If a copy of the library is already loaded, Windows simply maps the code pages into the client's memory space. At any rate, only one copy of the DLL remains loaded at run time.

DLLs contain loadable, executable code and Windows resources. Remember from Chapter 20 that Windows supports two forms of dynamic linking: implicit linking and explicit linking. Implicit linking involves linking your client application to the DLL's import library. When the linker links to an import library, it inserts a little bit of fix-up code for each function exported by the DLL. When the client application finally runs, the first code that is executed by the application is the set of address fix-ups stipulated by the import DLL. By contrast, explicit linking involves a good deal more work for the client developer. Clients link to DLL entry points by explicitly calling *LoadLibrary*, *FreeLibrary*, and *GetProcAddress*.

While DLLs provide the promise of real components—separate binaries that can be linked at run time—they don't quite make good on the promise.

What's Wrong with DLLs

One of the main challenges with plain-vanilla DLLs is keeping all the clients and DLLs synchronized as far as the exported functions are concerned. For applications that are developed and deployed atomically, this is not a problem. A great example is Windows itself, which is a set of atomically developed and deployed DLLs—user32.DLL, gdi32.dll, kernel32.dll, and so on. However, dynamic linking does pose problems for software whose modules are developed and deployed independently.

The promise of DLLs as a component technology lies in the ability it gives you to dynamically compose software—to change components at run time. As long as all the function signatures within the DLL remain the same as the ones expected by the client, there's no problem. However, if any of the method signatures change (perhaps with the addition of a parameter or the subtraction of a function) and the client application is not recompiled, the client application might not load (at the very least) or might crash (in the worst case). In another scenario, an older version of a popular library might be copied over a newer one, resulting in some sort of function mismatch between the client and the DLL.

The basic problem is that the notion of typing is missing from the normal DLL loading process. Type signatures are contained in the header files shared between the client and the DLL, but they're found nowhere else. If DLLs and clients are compiled with the different header files, the application won't work. This is one of the advantages COM provides: adding formal type checking to the loading process.

The COM Technology

We looked at COM in detail in Chapter 22. By applying the discipline of interface-based programming, COM introduces a layer of indirection between the client and the actual component code. COM interfaces are collections of functions named by a GUID. The interfaces are predictable and don't vary in the same way that raw DLL entry points can. In fact, COM programming stipulates a rule that interfaces not change once they've been published. A normal Windows DLL might have a multitude of entry points, but a COM DLL has only four standard DLL entry points: *DllGetClassObject*, *DllCanUnloadNow*, *DllRegisterServer*, and *DllUnregisterServer*. The functionality of the DLL is described by one or more COM interfaces. COM turns DLL loading into a typed operation. Code is loaded based on type, and that type is an interface.

For a more in-depth discussion of COM, see Chapter 22. For now, just recall these points:

- COM interfaces are collections of function signatures, usually described in Microsoft Visual C++ as a *struct*. All COM interfaces include the same three function signatures at the top: *QueryInterface*, *AddRef*, and *Release*. These three functions comprise the *IUnknown* interface. Interfaces have unique names called GUIDs. Once an interface is published and used widely, it should never change.
- COM implementations give life and behavior to these interfaces.

- COM class objects, or class factories, expose COM implementations to the system. COM class objects are named using GUIDs and appear in the registry.
- COM DLLs often include type information as a resource. This provides a level of reflection so clients of the DLL can understand what's inside the DLL.
- COM clients use API functions to instantiate the COM object (*CoCreateInstance*, *CoGetClassObject/IClassFactory::CreateObject*, or *CoCreateInstanceEx*). Visual Basic clients simply need to use the *New* keyword. However, Visual Basic uses the API functions underneath the hood.
- COM clients are responsible for managing the interface pointers they acquire. That is, they must call *AddRef* through an interface pointer when they duplicate the pointer, and they must call *Release* through an interface pointer when they discard the interface. Visual Basic developers don't need to pay attention to this rule because the runtime manages the interface pointers.

The Benefits of COM

COM is vastly superior to plain DLLs for composing software from components. In fact, many enterprises have built their core systems using COM. For example, the back end to Nasdaq.com is written using COM. COM works so well in so many cases for a number of reasons.

One key to COM's success is its emphasis on interfaces. Decoupling clients from the implementations encourages component-based architectures. When your program accesses services through interfaces instead of classes, it's possible to change implementations easily without breaking the client. This allows separate parties to develop software independently of each other.

COM loads services using named types. The name is the GUID, and the type is the interface definition. As you saw in Chapter 22, COM applications call *CoCreateInstance*, pass in the GUID representing the types—the interface ID and the class ID—and you get an instance of the class as well as a pointer to the interface. In addition, you can widen your connection at run time and get even more types by using QueryInterface. COM replaces the plain-vanilla *LoadLibrary*/*GetProcAddress* API calls with the single function *CoCreateInstance* and well-defined extensible interfaces to the code in the DLL. In a nutshell, COM introduced the notion of type into the DLL loading mechanism.

In addition to enforcing interface-based programming, COM adds the notion of reflection—the DLL's ability to describe itself. Think about how standard DLL functionality is exposed: The only way you can learn about the contents of a plain-vanilla DLL is by reading some documentation or a header file. COM DLLs include binary type information embedded within the DLL. This type information advertises the types (data types and interface types) and implementations (class IDs) contained within. Visual Basic and Visual C++ use this type information to implement IntelliSense, and the COM runtime uses type information to set up the proxy-stub pairs at run time.

The Drawbacks of COM

Although COM provides many benefits, it does come with its own issues. Some of COM's deficiencies are minor. For example, the names of the COM DLLs and accompanying configuration information all go into the registry, which leads to an overburdened registry. This is not the biggest problem in itself. However, because COM uses the registry (which is visible to every application), there's no way to isolate private components. If a new version of a component is installed on the system, the new changes will ripple—perhaps to a client that's not interested in the change. The second issue with the registry is that it adds complexity to an application's install and uninstall procedures.

Another minor problem with COM is that for COM to work, both clients and DLLs have to follow stringent rules. Some rules, such as calling AddRef and Release at appropriate times, are there to prevent resource leaks. If a client developer fails to call these methods properly, the client might suffer resource constraints. A more important rule is that interfaces must never change once published. Changing an interface after it's published undermines the reliability and predictability that using typed interfaces is supposed to provide. During COM's lifetime, most developers have followed these rules. However, it's easy to forget to release an interface pointer. And, indeed, in a few cases the interface consistency rule has been broken, resulting in broken applications. These issues aren't huge in themselves, but they can cause a certain amount of angst for developers and system administrators.

COM also has the major problem of inconsistencies within COM data types. As an MFC/C++ developer, you're used to developing code using pointers and perhaps object graphs such as linked lists. COM Interface Definition Language (IDL) fully supports such complex programming constructs. However, if your target audience includes users of Visual Basic programs, you cannot use such constructs. In Chapter 23, we looked at IDispatch and scriptable components, which allow you to target the Web with your software. Using IDispatch limits your data type selection to include only those types that fit in a *VARIANT*. So if you target your component for scripting, your available data types will decrease dramatically. Finally, the contents of a DLL's type library do not completely reflect the contents of the DLL in some cases.

Ultimately, COM-based applications are still built out of DLLs (often written using different development environments), and there will always be a boundary between the client and the object. That boundary is bridged using function signatures. COM adds the notion of type to the loader, adding some consistency and reliability to the loading process. However, COM supports disparate type systems and imposes some complex rules. These issues are spelling the end to COM's reign as the premier component technology for Windows. The goal of the common language runtime is to fix these issues.

The Common Language Runtime

COM led to a lot of great software and some very useful systems over the years. However, during its lifespan, the problems we just discussed emerged time and again (and we haven't even mentioned the problems with DCOM). The initial impetus behind COM was the question "How can we compose already-compiled binary software that was developed using different languages and tools?" The answer was "Build reliable, predictable bridges between separate components." COM concentrated on a well-established boundary—the one between the client and the object. COM makes sure the boundary is well-defined and named so there's no ambiguity between the client and the object.

It eventually became evident that the boundary between the client and the object didn't necessarily have to exist at all. What if a runtime environment were available that dissolved the boundary between the client and the object? That's what the common language runtime is all about—erasing the boundaries between components. The common language runtime basically reframes the entire component development problem.

No Boundaries

Recall that one of the biggest problems with COM is that different development environments work with different data types. The disparity in data types solidifies the boundary between the client and the DLL.

As mentioned, the main idea behind the common language runtime is to erase the boundaries between components. It does this in two ways: by providing a common runtime environment for components to live in, and by establishing a common type system (CTS). Any components targeted to live within the common language runtime must base themselves on the CTS. (We'll discuss CTS in detail later in this chapter.)

Figure 31-1 shows how COM components bridge DLL boundaries. Figure 31-2 shows how all common language runtime objects live within the same runtime and don't have to make boundary crossings.

Process Boundary

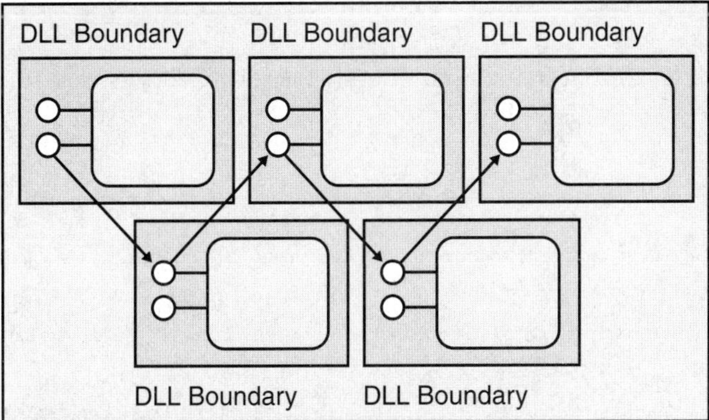

Figure 31-1 COM boundary crossings.

Process Boundary

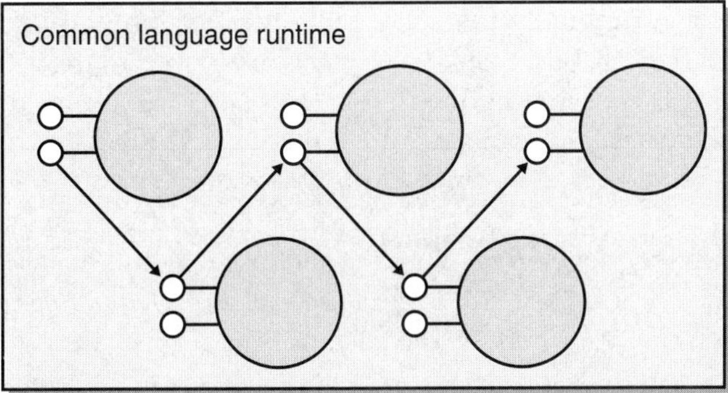

Figure 31-2 Common language runtime components don't have to worry about boundary crossings.

COM provided a modest amount of type information with its components, but the type information was sometimes incomplete due to the disparities between programming environments. The common language runtime and .NET development tools fix this. With the common language runtime and its pervasive type system, components reflect themselves accurately. You can know anything you want to about the code at run time and development time.

As you'll see later, the common language runtime provides garbage collection, memory layout management, and security control. To perform these services effectively, it has to know *everything* about the code that it's hosting. In fact, types living within the runtime are called managed types because all aspects of their creation and execution are managed by the runtime.

Mscoree.dll includes the basic functionality for the common language runtime. Another DLL, Mscorlib.dll, comprises the runtime library. Mscoree.dll is an unmanaged DLL that provides loading functionality and runtime services. Mscorlib.dll is a managed DLL that contains the core types used throughout the system. Your own managed executables use both Mscoree.dll and Mscorlib.dll.

It's All About Type

In normal C development, type consciousness was optional—everything was basically some form of an integer that you could cast any way you wanted to. C++ raised the bar of type-consciousness. However, you could easily defeat the C++ type system using a cast.

In .NET, types are king. Everything is a well-defined type—from the lowliest integer to the most complex class. All types within the common language runtime derive from a fundamental system type named *System.Object*. This is a bit different than in classical programming environments such as C++, whose types (primitives such as *int*, *long*, and *char*) mostly denote memory usage. Common language runtime types have built-in reflection and the facilities of *System.Object* at their disposal. *System.Object* is analogous to the *VARIANT* commonly found in COM's scripting interfaces, because a variant includes the data type (not just the data). You can always interrogate a VARIANT to find out what kind of data it represents. *System.Object* is also similar to MFC's *CObject* class because *System.Object* provides some fundamental services that are useful to both the runtime and developers. Some of the more useful *System.Object* functions include *Equals*, *GetType*, *ToString*, *Finalize*, and *MemberwiseClone*.

Equals determines whether two instances of a type are equal. *GetType* returns the type of an instance at run time, in much the same way that the CObject::IsKindOf method works in MFC. *ToString* returns a string representing the type of the instance. *Finalize* tells the object to free up resources and carry out other cleanup operations before being swept away by the garbage collector. *MemberwiseClone* is like the copy constructor in C++; it performs a deep copy of an instance of a common language runtime type.

Classic C++ supports composing your own types using the *typedef* statement or by defining structures and classes. When you define a type within the context of C++, you're telling the compiler about the structure of the type.

The common language runtime also supports composing your own types. But because custom types also derive from *System.Object*, these custom types automatically include type information and the other services provided by *System.Object*.

In summary, one of the most important goals of the common language runtime is to support cross-language programming. To accomplish this, it extends the notion of type much further than C++ or COM do. For example, types within a

C++ program are restricted to that language, and types within a Visual Basic program are restricted to the Visual Basic runtime. Types within the common language runtime must adhere to the rules of the common type system.

Common Language Runtime Types

As a C++ developer, you're probably accustomed to using C++ types denoted by such keywords as *long*, *float*, and *class*. However, if you met a Visual Basic 6.0 developer on the street and began talking about C++ types, he would have a very different notion of what you were talking about. Different development environments define their data types differently. The .NET approach is to define types within the context of a common runtime environment.

In the mid-1990s, each software development environment had its own runtime support. For example, Visual Basic 6.0 has its own runtime engine, Vbrun.dll. The data types within Visual Basic 6.0 are managed by Vbrun.dll. MFC has its own runtime support DLL as well: MFC*xxx*.dll (with *xxx* denoting whatever the current version is). The same goes for ATL, which has its own support DLL. Rather than depend on a specific language or on runtime support from a specialized library, .NET code relies on a single type system, a common runtime engine, and a common class library. Component integration is much easier because all the components of an application work with the same data types. Interop issues between .NET components are virtually nonexistent.

The basis for the common language runtime is the fact that data types are the same for every component running under the runtime. To enforce type compatibility between components, types targeted for the common language runtime must adhere to the CTS at run time. The CTS defines rules for various language implementations to follow.

The CTS defines several types, including value types, reference types, enumerations, arrays, delegates, interfaces, and classes. It also defines a pointer type for interoperating with unmanaged code (code not running within the common language runtime). Following is a rundown of each of these types.

Value Types

Value types represent flat values—data that takes up some flat memory as opposed to reference types that "point" to other types. When value types are copied across function calls as parameters, they are literally copied from the caller's context to the callee's context. The .NET common language runtime supports two kinds of value types: built-in value types and user-defined value types. Built-in value types include types such as *System.Int32* and *System.Boolean*. User-defined types are composed from primitive types and include structures. A good example of a user-defined type is a collection of coordinates that define a shape. Because value types simply define memory layout, they do not have the overhead associated with class. Value types are handled very efficiently by the runtime.

Reference Types

Whereas a variable of value type contains a value of that type, a variable of reference type is more akin to C++ pointers and contains a reference of that type. Reference types are managed by the runtime and live on the garbage-collected heap.

Boxing and Unboxing

Because of how value types and reference types differ, you sometimes need to convert value types to reference types. This process is known as *boxing*. Let's say you run across a function call that takes a reference type in the parameter list, and as the caller you hold only a value. If you try to pass a value type where a reference type is required, you'll encounter a runtime error. You can box the object, which will clone the object and create a reference to it. When boxed objects are copied back into the instance, this is known as *unboxing*. The managed C++ includes keywords for boxing and unboxing types, as you'll see in Chapter 32.

Enumerations

As a seasoned C++ developer, you're probably familiar with the C++ *enum* keyword, which defines a sequence as a type in the C++ type system. Enumerations as defined by the CTS are a special form of value type; they inherit from *System.Enum*. Enumerations are useful for describing collections such as the days of the week (Monday, Tuesday, Wednesday, and so forth) and months of the year (January, February, March, and so on). In classic C-style programming, you'd probably assign the values 1 through 12 to represent the months of the year, like so:

```
enum Months {
   January = 1,
   February,
   March,
   April,
   May,
   June,
   July,
   August,
   September,
   October,
   November,
   December
};
```

You can create variables of type *Months*, but the data type underlying the variable is an integer so you can just as easily use the number *2* whenever the month February is required. Using enumerations provides a higher level of type safety and code readability than when you use primitive types. One problem in C++ is that there's no way to relate the numbers of the month to their names except by writing some extra code. The strongly typed enumerations available in .NET get rid of this problem. When you declare an instance of a .NET enumeration, you can assign it a value from the enumerators defined in enumerations. We'll see an example of enumerations in Chapter 32.

The methods available through .NET enumerations include all the members from *System.Object* and the methods available from *System.Enum*. The *System.Enum* functions include *Format*, *GetNames*, *GetUnderlyingType*, *GetValues*, *IsDefined*, *Parse*, and *ToObject*.

Arrays

Arrays are homogenous and can hold only elements of a single type. In the unmanaged world we used to live in, arrays were just blocks of memory. Languages such as C and C++ provided syntax for indexing into arrays. Class libraries such as MFC and the standard template library (STL) provide useful classes for managing arrays without the headaches associated with managing raw pointers. For example, MFC includes a *CObArray* class that includes methods for adding and deleting objects from the array. Visual Basic 6.0 developers are used to working with arrays, too. However, a Visual Basic array ends up as a *SafeArray* when it's described with type information. As a C++ developer, catering to the Visual Basic 6.0 crowd means defining arrays using the COM *SAFEARRAY* structure (which is a self-describing multidimensional array of type *VARIANT*).

The CTS defines an array type that works the same no matter what environment you're working in. .NET arrays derive from *System.Array* and work similarly to STL-based arrays and MFC-based CObArrays. They grow as necessary and include functionality for adding and deleting elements, counting elements, and getting elements from specific positions within the array. You'll see an example of a managed array in Chapter 32.

Delegates

Any C++ developer who has worked with Windows for a while has dealt with function pointers. When you define function pointer types in C++, you describe a call stack that the compiler understands. In this way, you can have various sections of your code calling back and forth.

Delegates inherit from *System.Delegate*. Within the context of the CTS, delegates serve a similar purpose. Delegates point to .NET methods so you can execute them indirectly. They're managed types, so they're fully type-safe. Delegates are different from C++ function pointers. Many function pointers in C++ require special treatment. For example, normal C++ member functions include a hidden first parameter called the *this* parameter, which is a pointer to the instance of the class for which it is declared. Static and global functions do not have this hidden pointer. .NET delegates can reference all kinds of methods of classes and objects: static, virtual, and instance methods. You'll find delegates used mostly within the context of event handling and callbacks within .NET applications. Each instance of a delegate can forward a call to one or more methods with matching signatures. That is, delegates can be used to broadcast. You'll see an example of a managed C++ delegate in Chapter 32.

Interfaces

Until the mid-1990s, nobody paid any attention to the discipline of interface-based programming. As you saw when we looked at COM, one of most important contributions by COM was that of the interface. Using interface-based programming, you can describe type compatibility between different implementations. For example, you might define a *shape* interface that includes several methods for describing shapes. You might then implement several different shapes using the *shape* interface—for example, a square, a circle, and a line. Each of these shapes behaves very differently. However, by abstracting the shape behavior behind an interface, client code that deals only with the interface can work with all the shapes. The *shape* interface denotes type compatibility. .NET fully supports interfaces. .NET interfaces primarily serve to provide type compatibility for objects.

You'll see an example of using a managed interface in Chapter 32.

Classes

Classes within .NET are similar to classes you've worked with using C++. They have data members and methods. In .NET, data members are called the *fields* within a class. .NET classes can have both virtual and nonvirtual methods. Virtual methods work the way you'd expect them to—to ensure that the correct version of a function is called within a class hierarchy. .NET classes can also implement interfaces, just like C++ classes can. All code running within the common language runtime must somehow be scoped by a class.

.NET offers a bit more flexibility than C++ does as far as classes are concerned. .NET classes can be sealed at some point, and new classes can no longer be derived from them. Also, whole classes can be labeled as abstract, which means that new classes must be derived from them before they're used. .NET enforces visibility constraints for both the members within a class and the class itself. .NET class members can be public, private, or protected. These visibility modifiers have exactly the same meaning in .NET as they do in C++. .NET class members can also be marked as being visible either within the assembly in which they live or outside that assembly.

You'll see examples of .NET classes in the next three chapters.

Pointers

The final type available within .NET is the pointer type. The .NET runtime hides most of the details related to pointers, and you never have to see a regular address when you work in .NET. However, within the realm of managed C++, pointer types are available to you when you need them.

The three kinds of .NET pointers are managed pointers, unmanaged pointers, and unmanaged function pointers. When you work with managed code in the normal way (using C#, Visual Basic .NET, or managed C++), the common language runtime is working with managed pointers. For example, when reference types are passed as parameters or returned from methods, the common language runtime uses managed pointers. Only managed pointers are compliant with the Common Language Specification (CLS).

The common language runtime supports unmanaged pointers specifically to offer backward compatibility (with unmanaged C++). As a C++ developer, you're used to unmanaged pointers—they're just addresses in memory.

The most common use for pointers is for reading and writing raw data. When you're using managed references and pointers, you don't see the actual memory you're working with. If you're in a situation where you want to see raw memory, unmanaged pointers are the way to go.

The Common Language Specification

One of the greatest draws of .NET is the wide variety of syntaxes for expressing functionality within .NET applications. Official .NET languages coming from Microsoft include managed C++, C#, and Visual Basic .NET. However, other companies are producing .NET-compatible languages. There's a version of PERL for .NET, and Fujitsu even has a COBOL compiler for .NET!

As you've seen, the .NET Framework defines a pervasive type system that permeates all executable code running under the common language runtime. Remember that one of the key goals of .NET is to provide a high degree of interoperability among components—no matter what languages they were written in. The common type system guarantees consistent data typing between components. The CLS guarantees that languages follow the CTS.

The CLS is a set of rules defining the behavior of externally visible items. These rules are necessary for software to interoperate within the common language runtime. Remember that the runtime wants to treat all data and code in the same way. Types that adhere to the CLS are completely interoperable. You can mark types as CLS-compliant using the *System.CLSCompliantAttribute*.

Assemblies

All right, that's enough talk about types. The next question is: Where does all this wonderful common language runtime code live? Are there still DLLs in this new world? What do executables look like? DLLs and executables are still around in the .NET Framework. However, now they're called *assemblies* and they contain Intermediate Language (IL)—not native code.

We looked at normal executables, normal DLLs, and COM DLLs earlier in this book. When we compiled that code, the compiler turned the source code directly into some native machine code. .NET executables and DLLs work a bit differently. They're compiled into assemblies. Technically, an assembly is simply a collection of type definitions. Type definitions include all the examples we covered earlier—code encapsulated within classes, enumerations, user-defined types, and so forth. Assemblies can also contain resources, such as bitmaps, JPEG files, and resource files.

Classic Windows development draws a strong distinction between DLLs and EXEs. A .NET assembly can be either a DLL or an EXE. Assemblies are the fundamental unit of deployment and include code that the runtime executes. All .NET code executed by the runtime must live within an assembly. Assemblies have only one entry point: *DllMain*, *WinMain*, or *Main*.

Every type within a .NET application must appear in an assembly somewhere. It is denoted by both the name of the assembly and the name of the type. However, once you get down to working with a type within a development environment like managed C++, the development environment usually takes care of managing the assembly name.

The native .NET types we've discussed already (such as *System.Object* and *System.ValueType*) are contained within the *System* assembly. Because assemblies define the type boundary within .NET, a type within the scope of one assembly is not the same as a type loaded in the scope of another assembly—even if it shares the same name.

The assembly is the smallest versionable unit in the common language runtime. Assemblies include type information and a section called the *manifest*, which describes the version information and dependencies on other assemblies.

Built-in Type Information

Built-in type information was one of the most important contributions that COM made to Windows programming. This is also known as *reflection*. DLLs or executables that have type information included with them become self-describing, enabling both tools and runtime environments to know and understand the contents of the module. For example, as you fill out a COM function call into Visual C++'s edit window, IntelliSense immediately comes up, showing you the function signature. IntelliSense works because there's type information included with the component. The MTS and COM+ runtimes use type information to manufacture proxy stubs on the fly.

When you're programming COM using C++, the way to get type information into the executable or the DLL is to include some IDL with the project. The IDL is compiled into a binary type library, and the type library is attached to the module as a resource. .NET includes the same facility, but the type information is automatically included within the assembly. There's no more need for an intermediate IDL file—when a .NET compiler compiles your code, it generates type information and adds it to the assembly.

The Manifest

In addition to the built-in type information, every assembly includes a section named the manifest. .NET assembly manifests can include dependencies on other assemblies, versioning information, and information relating to the culture and language for which the assembly was intended. An assembly's manifest is like a top-level directory for the assembly.

Like type information, manifests are integral to .NET development. The information within the manifest tells the loader which assemblies to load when loading an application, which version of an assembly to load, and so on. Manifests are generated automatically—no intermediate steps are involved in creating a manifest.

By including the dependency information, .NET solves a long-standing issue with COM. With COM, there's no easy way to figure out DLL dependencies. The Platform SDK includes a tool named Depends.exe that examines the import list of a DLL or EXE file to find out DLL dependencies. However, because COM exposes its functionality through interfaces (rather than standard DLL entry points) and because COM DLL loading information is mostly contained within the registry, there's no way to easily deduce DLL dependencies. .NET manifests do include the dependencies of assemblies. Because the assembly includes dependency information, the common language runtime loader makes sure all required assemblies are loaded before executing the code within an assembly.

Private vs. Public Assemblies

In COM's heyday, one of the most widely touted features of *IUnknown* was that it was supposed to enable component versioning. A dynamically evolving software project cannot be hardwired together. There must be some flexibility in the way the components connect. COM forces applications to ask their components for interfaces (rather than assuming the interfaces are there). When a new version of a component is dropped into an application (or perhaps an older version of a component is inadvertently installed), the application gets fair warning of the change. The problem with COM versioning is that despite the tremendous flexibility in how components are connected together, the versioning mechanism still fails from time to time. For example, if you install an old version of a component, clients expecting the new component will be mighty disappointed.

The main reason for this versioning failure is that COM components are visible to every application on the PC—they're global in nature. That means that replacing a component affects all the applications that depend on the component, in a ripple effect. All COM components are referenced in the registry—and the registry is available to all applications. The common language runtime solves this problem by distinguishing between public and private assemblies.

The .NET component model prefers private assemblies. When you confine functionality to a specific component and make it visible only to the client that needs it, you get rid of the ripple effect when you replace the component. Only clients of that particular assembly are affected. One main goal of .NET is to make deploying an application as easy as picking up the contents of a directory and using a copying mechanism (such as *XCOPY* or FTP) to move the contents to a new directory or machine. Because COM components rely so heavily on the registry, installing and uninstalling components is a major issue.

.NET component versioning works through an established directory structure. The directory containing the application is referred to as the AppBase directory of that application. The process of finding an assembly is called probing. The runtime performs several steps to locate an assembly. It first looks in the AppBase directory and then in a subdirectory under AppBase with the same name as the assembly, checking within the culture subdirectory if it does not find the assembly immediately. The runtime searches for DLLs first and EXEs second. It stops searching after it finds the first match. .NET provides a good amount of flexibility when probing—you can modify the probe mechanism by modifying the application's configuration file (an XML file accompanying the application that is used for tweaking your application).

.NET also includes provisions for sharing components between applications. Shared components are installed in the global assembly cache (GAC). The GAC is a special directory on your machine that holds shared assemblies. The GAC can hold multiple versions of the same DLL, thereby solving the versioning problem.

In COM, you name components uniquely using GUIDs.When you ask for a component via its GUID, you'll get the most current version of the component. In .NET, components are named uniquely through *strong naming*.

A common language runtime assembly name consists of four parts: a simple text name, a version number, culture information, and a strong name. A strong name is based on a pair of keys—one public and one private. The unique name of an assembly is the conjunction of the text name and the public key. You'll see an example of signing an assembly in Chapter 32.

.NET Versioning

As you just saw, .NET prefers private components to public components. However, sharing a component is sometimes essential. When you share code, versioning is very important. COM didn't quite get it right. Rather than hoping that the latest version of a component is available on a machine, .NET allows multiple versions of a single component to reside on the same machine. Naturally, this arrangement implies some form of versioning. .NET assemblies deployed in the GAC require version information in the manifest. This is simple enough—you just make sure the correct attributes are applied in the source code. Assembly references used by client code contain the version number of the assembly that the client expects to see. You'll see this when we look at some assemblies using a tool named ILDASM in Chapter 32. The runtime uses version numbers when binding to shared assemblies. Rather than hoping that a DLL is compatible by name, .NET builds the version number into the name of the DLL. Clients latch onto a specific DLL by binding to a specific version number.

Living Within the Common Language Runtime

We spent the first part of this book looking at how to write native-code Windows applications. Programming native-code applications offers performance advantages and flexibility. However, along with the freedom and flexibility comes a great deal of programmer responsibility and hygiene when it comes to resource management and type safety. Writing code to run under the common language runtime relieves you of many of the responsibilities normally associated with native-code programming. For example, the common language runtime takes care of programming responsibilities from array-bound checking to managing memory, avoiding thread deadlocks, and securing components programmatically. This is a benefit that Visual Basic developers have enjoyed for years. Now the convenience of having your code managed for you is available to C++ developers as well.

Intermediate Language and Just-in-Time Compiling

The traditional Windows-based applications we've been building throughout this book compile down to native Intel code and run right on the chip. .NET and the common language runtime work a bit differently—.NET assemblies compile down to IL. The common language runtime's execution engine (Mscoree.dll) compiles the IL into machine code immediately before its execution in a process known as *just-in-time (JIT) compiling*. It adds one more layer of indirection between the human-created source code and the chip the code is to run on. This layer of indirection carries many advantages with it.

One of the primary advantages of using IL is that multiple syntaxes can be used for writing .NET code. As long as the compiler can turn source code into IL, it does not matter which programming language or environment you use. In this book, we're using managed C++. However, many .NET languages are available: C# and Visual Basic .NET from Microsoft and even a version of COBOL.

Another advantage of using IL is type safety. How many times have you chased down pointer bugs, array indexing bugs, or parameter-passing bugs because of mismatched data types or incorrect type casting? It happens less in C++, but this sort of bug ran rampant in older C-style coding. If you use IL between the source code and the final native executable, the runtime can verify the code within an assembly during the final JIT compilation down to machine code. The common language runtime verifies the code to make sure that it does not do anything dangerous such as accessing memory directly. Adding IL between the source code and the final native code allows a higher degree of protection than having pure native-code applications around.

The final advantage of using IL is that it inherently decouples your EXEs and DLLs from the operating system and hardware platform. When an EXE or DLL consists of intermediate code (not native code), it is truly platform-independent. Right now, Microsoft has a version of the common language runtime that runs on Windows 2000, Windows NT, and Windows 98. IL allows for the possibility of deploying the runtime on other platforms that are not running Windows or not running Intel processors.

.NET Garbage Collection

Living under the common language runtime means that code doesn't have to look after itself. Developers who use native C++ must track their resources vigilantly in order to not cause leaks. .NET developers don't have to pay attention to that—.NET uses garbage collection.

You can find more comprehensive discussions of .NET garbage collection out there, including *Applied Microsoft .NET Framework Programming* by Jeffrey Richter (Microsoft Press, 2002). However, I'll give you a rundown of how memory lives within the common language runtime.

As a C++ developer, you're aware of how a program allocates and manages memory because you're the one doing it. You allocate an object using the *new* operator and delete it when you're done with it. You're probably also aware of some of the other kinds of memory used within your applications—

those kinds of memory taken up by global and static variables. Finally, many programs have local variables that live for a short time on the stack. .NET applications also use all these types of memory allocation.

The difference with .NET is that the common language runtime keeps track of all these resource allocations. All the memory allocation types mentioned earlier are referred to as an application's roots. The common language garbage collector watches all these memory allocations and determines when they're no longer referenced. When memory is no longer referenced, it's collected. This greatly simplifies programming.

One advantage of IL is that the JIT compiler knows about these references to the application's roots. The JIT compiler builds a list of root references and maintains it (with the help of the common language runtime) as the program executes. When the garbage collector has to figure out what memory is no longer referenced, the list of roots is the starting point.

While the program is running, garbage collection can occur in several situations: when an allocation fails, during calls to the *GC.Collect* method, and at otherwise regular intervals. When a garbage collection occurs, the common language runtime suspends all threads within the process during specific safe points (a location in the executable code where the runtime can safely suspend a thread), frees unreferenced objects, and collapses the managed heap.

While the threads are suspended, the garbage collector starts with application roots and walks the object graphs within the system, figuring out which objects are referenced and which are not. The runtime garbage collector is efficient and smart enough to detect cyclical references using internal lists that track references.

After figuring out which objects can be removed, the garbage collector moves nongarbage objects to the bottom of the heap to make room at the top. This makes subsequent memory allocations very fast because the top of the runtime heap is always clear. By contrast, the C++ memory manager often creates a fragmented heap while allocating and deallocating blocks of varying sizes.

The runtime then resumes the threads, and they're returned to the original calling program. The garbage collector updates any references to nongarbage objects if they've been moved. The application will be unaware of any relocations once the threads resume. For the most part, it's very hard to detect when garbage collection happens.

Most of this memory allocation and deallocation happens behind the scenes, and you don't have to worry too much about it. Even if you deeply nest references, the garbage collector will take good care of you and you can live a carefree existence as far as memory allocation is concerned.

Finalization

In C++, we're used to placing clean-up code within a destructor because we basically know that an object will be destroyed when it's no longer needed—the programmer is responsible for deleting objects. However, in .NET the garbage collector is responsible for getting rid of objects—and it often does so on its own schedule. You don't know when (or sometimes even if) an object will be freed. So instead of destructors, the common language runtime supports finalizers. If an object needs to be notified before it's being collected, a class can override the virtual *Finalize* method (which is inherited from System.Object). When the collector classifies an object as garbage, the runtime invokes the object's *Finalize* method before moving the memory back to the heap.

The garbage collector has been tightly tuned by Microsoft. When the garbage collector is left to its own devices, you'll barely notice anything when garbage is collected. However, if you end up overriding Finalize too often, you'll impede the garbage collector. Whenever the garbage collector finds an object with *Finalize*, it records the reference for consultation during collection, thereby slowing the allocation. The garbage collector has to check the finalization list and wait until *Finalize* is called to release the memory, thereby slowing collections. Remember that you need to override *Finalize* only when an object holds on to unmanaged resources. The common language runtime will manage nested references to managed objects for you. Finalization is really there to help classes manage non-.NET resources such as file references or other unmanaged resources.

Threading and the Common Language Runtime

Preemptive threading has been around since the earliest versions of Windows NT. Of course, the common language runtime would be an incomplete platform if it were missing the preemptive multitasking feature. Threading in the common language runtime is more straightforward than when you use the raw API. The common language runtime includes types for starting, stopping, and suspending threads.

AppDomains

The basic execution and resource boundary is the process space. Processes maintain their own heaps and other resources, and Windows processes define a security and execution boundary. The process space still exists for applications running under the common language runtime. However, process spaces can be further divided into AppDomains, which also serves as a security and execution boundary.

AppDomains are like logical process spaces within a real process space. Assemblies serve as the logical (rather than physical) deployment model. A physical process can host separate logical AppDomains to form separate fault-tolerance boundaries within a single process. That way, it can protect parts of your application from each other (for example, if you don't completely trust a component). An AppDomain gives you many of the same advantages that you get when you put your code into a separate process, but without the overhead of a process. Figure 31-3 shows several common language runtime components distributed between two AppDomains within a single process.

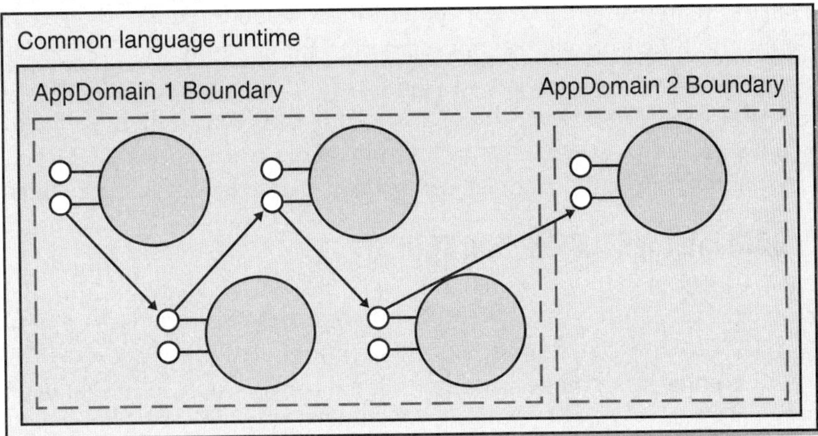

Figure 31-3 Common language runtime components distributed between multiple AppDomains.

Interoperability

One hard lesson we've all learned is the importance of backward compatibility and being able to link to older ("legacy") code bases. In fact, Windows owes much of its own success to backward compatibility. When people invest lots of money into applications, they're not going to simply toss them away just because a new operating system is available. Windows has always fully supported older versions of applications. Keeping the old code running is very important—just ask any COO or CTO. Companies are not going to rewrite all their code just because of .NET. Often the most critical part of an application is a very old component that nobody's touched for years. So getting new code to work with older code is an extremely important feature of .NET.

.NET provides three basic mechanisms to facilitate interoperability between new code and old code: platform invoke (P/Invoke) , COM-callable wrappers for calling from COM code to common language runtime code, and runtime-callable wrappers for calling from the runtime to COM components.

Platform Invoke

As you've seen, client applications need a way to load library code dynamically and get to the entry points. In Windows, these functions are *LoadLibrary* and *GetProcAddress*. If you find yourself needing to call entry points within a specific legacy DLL, P/Invoke is the way to go.

To use P/Invoke, you prototype functions within your managed code and mark them using the DllImport attribute. When the code compiles to an assembly, the functions will be understood to be living in an external DLL. The common language runtime will call *LoadLibrary/GetProcAddress* automatically. Using the *DllImport* attribute, you can specify the calling convention, you can alias the method so it has a different name from the real DLL function within your program, and you can control the character set that the function uses.

COM Interop: TLBIMP and TLBEXP

Of course, much of the code out there is COM code, so it's important to be able to call back and forth between COM code and common language runtime code. .NET provides facilities for both situations: calling a legacy COM class from the common language runtime and calling a common language runtime class from some existing COM code. The .NET Framework provides two utilities to accommodate these situations: the Type Library Importer (Tlbimp.exe) and the Type Library Exporter (Tlbexp.exe.). The Type Library Importer reads a COM type library, emits common language runtime metadata, and creates a runtime-callable wrapper. The Type Library Exporter reads common language runtime metadata and creates a type library and a COM-callable wrapper. These utilities are fairly straightforward to use.

32

Managed C++

In the previous chapter, we looked at the heart of Microsoft .NET: the common language runtime. A major goal of the common language runtime is to wipe away the boundaries we've been dealing with throughout the history of the Microsoft platform. Writing code to run on .NET means writing managed code that compiles down to Intermediate Language (IL) and is later compiled to native code. In this chapter, you'll learn what it takes to get code running under the common language runtime using Managed Extensions for C++.

The Common Language Runtime Is Your Friend

When Microsoft first started showing off its plans for .NET and for the common language runtime, a good many developers from the C++ camp responded with raised eyebrows. All right—so here we are, C++ developers, trained from the beginning to wring the most performance possible from the platform. We also want the greatest control possible. To do that, we manage our own memory, and we can program close to the hardware when we need to. At first glance, the common language runtime looks as though it will rip us from our foundations as C++ developers! That perspective definitely makes sense from the point of view of developers whose eyes are trained on shipping solid, shrink-wrapped-quality applications (either commercially or for the enterprise)—including the modern C++ Windows developer.

However, another software development perspective is at play here: that of developers who create software with high churn rates, fast deployment, and constant uptime as the primary objectives. That describes today's Web application market accurately, doesn't it? Modern Web-oriented software is supposed to evolve quickly, be ready to deploy after very short business cycles (a couple months at most), and is supposed to run 24/7. You could create such applications using C++, but perhaps there's a better way. With .NET, the better way is the common language runtime.

Having a runtime execution engine manage your code is a lifestyle that Visual Basic developers have enjoyed for years. We C++ developers often look at the Visual Basic crowd longingly (as they go home on time) or with disdain ("They wouldn't know what real software development is all about"). But think of the advantages a runtime engine gives you. First of all, no lost pointers. Someone else keeps track of them and cleans them up for you. How about mis-shapen pointers (for example, when you think a pointer is pointing at one kind of structure and it's really pointing to another kind of thing)? Having a runtime manage your code ensures that all pointers are compatible. A managed run-time also gives your code the ability to reflect on itself through the metadata. In C++, you need to use *<dynamic_cast>*. In the common language runtime, you just call *GetType* on any object whose type you want to know—a service of *System.Object*.

These types of services are just the ticket for writing quickly evolving soft-ware that needs to remain deployed constantly. We tried to write that kind of software for the Web using COM, but COM doesn't quite fit the bill for the rea-sons we looked at in the previous chapter. One reason is the disparate data typ-ing between COM development environments. Another reason that COM doesn't work completely is because of the involved process of managing com-ponents within the system. Finally, if you've ever tried to maintain a Web site using COM components, you know that the Web site must often come down when you want to change components because the DLLs are in use by the Web site. The common language runtime solves all these issues.

The advantage we have as C++ developers over the Visual Basic crowd is that while we're perfectly capable of writing common language runtime–compliant code (as we'll see in a minute), we always have the option of drop-ping down to normal C++ (unmanaged code) at any point for performance or control reasons.

The bottom line here is that the common language runtime is your friend, not your enemy—particularly because by writing code to run under the run-time, you can also write code that runs outside the runtime and mix the two freely

Why Use C++?

You saw in the last chapter that .NET introduces the notion of IL. As long you use a syntax for which there is an IL compiler, you're good to go in the .NET arena. The introduction of IL means that a multiplicity of programming syntaxes can coexist easily on the same platform. Of course, we'll see in this chapter that C++ is a perfectly decent way to write code for .NET. However, you have other choices as well. You've no doubt heard of something called C#. C# is a curly-brace-oriented syntax that offers the conciseness of C++ and the convenience of the nonpointer syntax of Visual Basic. Visual Basic is also a perfectly good way to write .NET software. With such an abundance of syntax choices, why would you ever decide to write .NET software in C++? There are actually a number of reasons, as we'll see here.

We'll see Managed Extensions for C++ up close in a minute. From far away, they're mostly special declarations and keywords that tell the compiler to emit IL instead of native code. Here's why you might want to use Managed Extensions for C++:

- **To move unmanaged C++ applications to the .NET Framework ASAP** Most highest-performing Windows-based applications these days are written in C++—and it's all unmanaged C++. Managed Extensions for C++ are easy to type into your code using the keyboard, and they provide a seamless transition to the .NET Framework. Unmanaged and managed code can easily exist in the same application—even in the same file. Once you have the application running under .NET, you can take your time to reimplement the code to take advantage of the .NET Framework. Another option is to keep your code running as normal unmanaged C++ and use managed wrappers to make your C++ code callable from common language runtime code.
- **To access .NET classes from unmanaged code** With Managed Extensions, you can directly create, and call, a .NET Framework class from your C++ code. You can also write C++ code that treats a .NET Framework component like any other managed C++ class.
- **To access a C++ component from a common language runtime–compatible language** Managed Extensions support calling a C++ class from any .NET Framework–compatible language. This is made possible by writing a simple wrapper class using Managed Extensions that exposes your C++ class and methods as a managed class. The wrapper is a fully managed class and can be called from any .NET Framework–compatible language. The wrapper class acts as a mapping layer between the managed class and the unmanaged C++ class—it simply passes method calls directly into the unmanaged class. Managed Extensions support calls to any unmanaged DLL or library, as well as unmanaged classes.

- **To access common language runtime code from COM** C++ is also useful for calling common language runtime code from COM components. You can use either the unmanaged COM support or the Managed Extensions to access common language runtime components.
- **To use managed and unmanaged code in one executable file** The Visual C++ .NET compiler translates data, pointers, exceptions, and instruction flow between managed and unmanaged contexts automatically and transparently. This process allows managed code to interoperate seamlessly with unmanaged C++ code.

Managed Extensions for C++ are quite flexible, and you can apply them in many ways. For example, you can apply managed extensions on an element-by-element basis (such as a class-by-class basis).

Managed C++ Extensions

The common language runtime defines two types of managed elements: *managed code* and *managed data*. Managed code cooperates closely with the common language runtime. This means simply that managed code provides the necessary metadata so the runtime can provide its services. Remember that the runtime provides memory management services, cross-language integration services, code access security services, and automatic lifetime control for objects. The runtime needs to know everything about the code it's hosting so it can provide these services.

The common language runtime also manages your application's data; that is, the runtime manages object layout. It also manages object references within your applications, releasing them when they're no longer being used. These objects are known as managed data.

So how do you write managed code? A handful of new keywords, applied judiciously, get rid of all the headaches associated with tracking pointers and memory and with mismatching types accidentally.

Writing .NET code using C++ turns out to be fairly straightforward. All it takes is a few new keywords and symbols placed in the correct place. Table 32-1 describes Managed Extensions for C++.

Table 32-1 Managed Extensions for C++

Extension Keyword	Functionality
__abstract	Types declared as *__abstract* cannot be instantiated directly.
__box	*__value* classes that apply the *__box* extension have a copy created on the common language runtime heap.
__delegate	Types declared as *__delegate* reference a unique method of a managed class (like a function pointer).
__event	Types declared using *__event* define an event method of a managed class.
__finally	Code within a *__finally* block becomes associated with the previous *try* block.
__gc	Types declared using *__gc* live on the managed heap.
__identifier	Tokens that apply the *__identifier* extension allow C++ keywords to be used as identifiers.
__interface	Types that apply the *__interface* keyword are declared as managed interfaces.
__nogc	Native C++ classes that apply the *__nogc* extension are not garbage-collected.
__pin	Objects that apply the *__pin* extension are prevented from being moved by the common language runtime during garbage collection.
__property	Fields that use the *__property* extension declare a property member for a managed class.
public, *protected*, and *private*	Types that apply these extensions define their visibility outside of an assembly. Fields (member variables and member functions) that use these extensions define their visibility within an assembly.
__sealed	*__gc* classes that use the *__sealed* extension cannot be used as a base class. This extension also prevents methods from being overridden in a derived class.
__try_cast	Using the *__try_cast* extension attempts the specified cast. The cast throws an exception on failure.
__typeof	This extension gets the *System::Type* of an instance of a type.
__value	Types that apply the *__value* extension are of the value type.

Visual C++ .NET and the Managed Extensions

You could create assemblies by hand using Notepad and makefiles, but Visual Studio .NET provides a much more streamlined approach to creating projects using wizards. When you open a new project, Visual Studio presents four templates for generating Managed C++ applications:

- **Managed C++ Application** Generates source code for producing a standalone C++ application with support for Managed Extensions. (For example, the correct command-line switches are flipped on to support Managed C++.) You use this project type for applications that run on the client, such as Windows Forms applications.
- **Managed C++ Class Library** Generates code that supports a C++ DLL using Managed Extensions. Use this option for creating managed components within .NET Framework applications.
- **Managed C++ Empty Project** Generates an empty project with the compiler and linker switches set correctly for supporting Managed C++ Extensions. This is an excellent option for moving existing C++ source files to a managed environment.
- **Managed C++ Web Service** Generates a Managed C++ Web service. (Web services provide programmatic access to a Web site.)

The samples from the SDK provide two additional Managed C++ wizards: one for generating Managed C++ Windows Forms applications and one for generating Managed C++ console applications. Chapter 4 presented a wizard for creating ASP.NET applications using Managed C++.

The Ex32a Example: A Managed C++ DLL Assembly

To give you a feel for how Managed C++ types work, this chapter includes an example with a potpourri of managed types. The example is Ex32a, which is generated using the Managed C++ Class Library project template. In keeping with C++ style, the project wizard generates a header file named Ex32a.h and a C++ implementation file named Ex32a.cpp. Even though the wizard emits a C++ file, this example shows all of the managed functionality inline in the header file. Here's the source code showing the managed types expressed using C++. The library includes a managed interface, a managed class, a managed structure, a managed enumeration, and a managed delegate.

```
// Ex32a.h
#pragma once
```

```
#using <System.DLL>
#using <System.Drawing.DLL>
#using <System.Windows.Forms.DLL>
#using <System.Runtime.Remoting.DLL>

using namespace System;
using namespace System::Collections;

namespace Ex32a
{

// C++ Assembly full of managed types...
public __value enum DaysOfTheWeek {
    Monday,
    Tuesday,
    Wednesday,
    Thursday,
    Friday,
    Saturday,
    Sunday
};

public __value struct AManagedValueStruct {
    int m_n;
    double m_x;
    String* m_str;

    AManagedValueStruct() {
        m_n = 0;
        m_x = 1.1;
        m_str=new String("Hi there from AManagedValueStruct");
    }

    void Method1() {
        Console::WriteLine("Called AManagedValueStruct::Method1()");
    }
};

public __gc struct AManagedGcStruct {
    AManagedGcStruct() {
        m_str=new String("Hi there from AManagedGcStruct");
    }
    ~AManagedGcStruct() {
        System::Console::WriteLine("AManagedStruct Going Away\n");
    }
    void Method1() {
```

(continued)

```
        Console::WriteLine("Called AManagedGcStruct::Method1()");
    }
    int m_n;
    double m_x;
    String* m_str;
};

public __gc __interface IPerson {
    void Eat();
    void Sleep();
    void Work();
};

public __gc class SoftwareDeveloper : public IPerson{
    ~SoftwareDeveloper() {
        System::Console::WriteLine
            ("Finalize called for SoftwareDeveloper");
    }
    void Eat() {
        System::Console::WriteLine("Eat pizza");
    }
    void Sleep() {
        System::Console::WriteLine("Sleep during the day");
    }
    void Work() {
        System::Console::WriteLine("Work during the night");
    }
};

public __gc class DotCOMVP : public IPerson {
    ~DotCOMVP() {
        System::Console::WriteLine("Finalize called for DotCOMVP");
    }
    void Eat() {
        System::Console::WriteLine("Eat to Schmooze");
    }
    void Sleep() {
        System::Console::WriteLine("Never sleep");
    }
    void Work() {
        System::Console::WriteLine("Work to get Venture Capital");
    }
};

public __gc class Bum : public IPerson {
    ~Bum() {
        System::Console::WriteLine("Finalize called for Bum");
    }
    void Eat() {
```

```
        System::Console::WriteLine("Eat sporadically");
    }
    void Sleep() {
        System::Console::WriteLine("Sleep whenever possible");
    }
    void Work() {
        System::Console::WriteLine("Work?");
    }
};
public __delegate void AManagedDelegate(String* strMessage);
public __gc __interface IAManagedInterface {
    void MethodA();
    int MethodB();
};

public __gc class AManagedClass : public IAManagedInterface {

    int m_n;
    int m_nSize;
    double m_f;
    String *m_str;

    DaysOfTheWeek m_DayOfWeek;
    ArrayList *m_rgManagedArray;

public:
    AManagedClass() {
        m_str = new String("This is AManagedClass\n");
        m_DayOfWeek = Friday;
    }

    ~AManagedClass() {
        System::Console::WriteLine("AManagedClass Going Away\n");
    }

    __property int  get_Size() {
        return m_nSize;
    }

    __property void set_Size(int value) {
        m_nSize = value;
    }

    void MethodA() {
        Console::WriteLine
            ("Here's some managed C++ code. This is MethodA.");
    }
```

(continued)

```
    int MethodB()  {
        Console::WriteLine
            ("Here's some managed C++ code. This is MethodB.");
        return 0;
    }

    void FillArray() {
        m_rgManagedArray = new ArrayList();

        Console::WriteLine("Creating a DotCOMVP");
        m_rgManagedArray->Add(new DotCOMVP());
        Console::WriteLine("Creating a Bum");
        m_rgManagedArray->Add(new Bum());
        Console::WriteLine("Creating a Software Developer");
        m_rgManagedArray->Add(new SoftwareDeveloper());
    }

    void ShowArray() {
        Console::WriteLine();
        if(m_rgManagedArray) {
            for(int i = 0; i < m_rgManagedArray->Count; i++) {
                Console::Write("Type: ");
                Console::WriteLine(
            (m_rgManagedArray->get_Item(i))->GetType()->ToString());
                IPerson* person;
                person = __try_cast<IPerson*>
                    (m_rgManagedArray->get_Item(i));
                person->Eat();
                person->Work();
                person->Sleep();
                Console::WriteLine();
            }
        }
    }

    void UseDelegate(AManagedDelegate *d) {
        d->Invoke("This is called through the delegate...");
    }

};

}
```

The result of building this project is an assembly that contains the managed types. The .NET Framework SDK provides a tool called the Intermediate Language Disassembler (ILDASM). When you open an assembly using ILDASM, ILDASM shows you the contents of the assembly. Figure 32-1 shows the Ex32a.dll assembly as viewed through ILDASM.

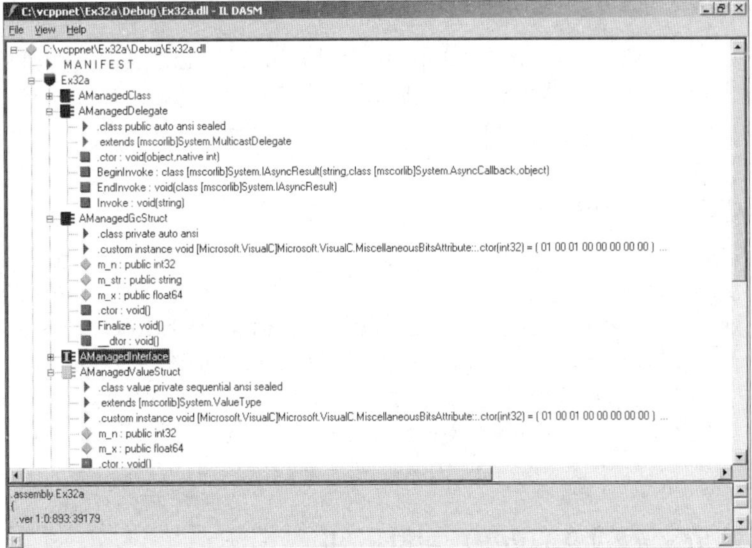

Figure 32-1 The Ex32a assembly as viewed through ILDASM.

ILDASM shows the internals of an assembly. Remember that all the type information for an assembly is available. The common language runtime library includes classes and methods for iterating through the contents of an assembly, which is actually very straightforward to do. Writing an ILDASM-type browser also isn't that hard to do. (It's much simpler using .NET than using COM's *ITypeLibrary* and *ITypeInfo* interfaces, for example.) In the following sections, we'll look at the types available through Ex32a.

DaysOfTheWeek

C and C++ have always provided the *enum* keyword for naming the types of a collection (such as months of the year or suits in a card deck), but the underlying structure behind the C and C++ *enum* has simply been an integer. That means you can write source code that mixes enumeration types (Monday, Tuesday, Wednesday, and so on) with raw integers. The managed types of the common language runtime allow you to specify the enumeration as a type, and the compiler enforces that typing, as shown in the following listing:

```
Void Afunction() {
    DaysOfTheWeek dow;
    dow = 3; // Would work in C and C++, but not
             // under Managed C++
    dow = Wednesday; // This is the only syntax
                     // that works under Managed C++
}
```

AManagedValueStruct and *AManagedGcStruct*

AManagedValueStruct is a value struct that lives on the stack and more or less describes formatted memory. *AManagedGcStruct* is a reference struct that describes a structure living on the garbage-collected heap.

IAManagedInterface and *IPerson*

IAManagedInterface and *IPerson* describe two managed interfaces. *IAManagedInterface* has two methods, *MethodA* and *MethodB*. *IPerson* describes a person type that eats, sleeps, and works. Interfaces are useful for describing basic, abstract functionality. The *DotComVP*, *SoftwareDeveloper*, and *Bum* classes (described shortly) implement the *IPerson* interfaces. Managed interfaces are different from COM interfaces in that they don't have the *IUnknown* functions preceding them, and the interfaces are managed by the runtime.

DotCOMVP, *SoftwareDeveloper*, and *Bum*

The *DotCOMVP*, *SoftwareDeveloper*, and *Bum* classes all implement the *IPerson* interface. However, they all do so in different ways. By expressing the functionality of these classes as an interface, you can use them wherever a person can be used. (These classes are type-compatible with *IPerson*.) You'll see this in the *FillArray* method of *AManagedClass*.

AManagedDelegate

AManagedDelegate represents a function signature that can be passed around as a type. You've seen examples of this throughout the C and C++ programming examples in this book. However, in the common language runtime, these function pointers (delegates) are managed types. Because the compiler enforces strict type checking, the possibility of a program error due to passing an incorrect function signature or passing the wrong arguments in the function goes away.

AManagedClass

The last type described in the Ex32a header file is *AManagedClass*, which implements *IAManagedInterface*. Notice that *AManagedClass* has several member variables (a couple of integers, a float type, a *String*, a *DayOfTheWeek* type, and an *ArrayList*). In addition, *AManagedClass* implements *IAManagedInterface* and exercises the *DotCOMVP*, *SoftwareDeveloper*, and *Bum* classes. Finally, notice the *UseDelegate* method, which passes around a delegate (a function signature type).

Making the Assembly Usable

Once the assembly is compiled, it will include all the types listed in the source code. You can use the assembly in a couple of ways. The first way is to deploy it as a private assembly. That means any client application that wants to use the assembly gets its own copy of the assembly (which will appear somewhere in the *AppBase* directory structure). To use Ex32a as a private assembly, you need to do nothing else. Just make sure the client applications have access to it.

The second way to use the assembly is to deploy it as a global assembly. To do this, you need to sign the assembly and then put it in the Global Assembly Cache (GAC). To sign the assembly, you run the program named SN.exe using the following command line:

```
sn -k InsideVCNET.snk
```

Running the SN program generates a signature key file that includes private and public keys that give the assembly a strong name (hence the name SN.exe). To include the signature in the assembly, you include this line in the Assembly.cpp source code:

```
[assembly:AssemblyKeyFileAttribute("InsideVCNET.snk")];
```

The line adds the public and private keys to the assembly. You can then add the assembly to the cache using the GACUTIL utility:

```
gacutil -i ex32a.dll
```

The final point regarding Ex32a is that the default source code generated by wizard updates the version number over the assembly each time it's compiled. The following line in AssemblyInfo.cpp is responsible:

```
// You can specify all the values or you can default the Revision
// and Build numbers by using the '*' as shown below:
[assembly:AssemblyVersionAttribute("1.0.*")];
```

You can change this directive to use a specific version number, or you can let the compiler build new versions with new numbers. Placing asterisks in the Build and Revision fields of the version signature (the third and fourth places of the build signature) causes the compiler to use date and time stamps for the build and revision numbers.

The Ex32b Example: A Managed Client Executable

Let's write a managed C++ executable to exercise the library. As you'll see from this example, writing C++ client code that uses managed types is fairly straightforward and nearly seamless. The following listing, Ex32b, shows a simple console application that exercises the types found in Ex32a:

```
// This is the main project file for a Visual C++ application
// generated using an application wizard.

#include "stdafx.h"

#using <mscorlib.dll>
#using <..\Ex32a\debug\ex32a.dll>
#include <tchar.h>

using namespace System;
using namespace Ex32a;

__gc class CDelegateHolder {
public:
    static void DelegateFn(String* str) {
        Console::WriteLine(str);
    }
};

void UseValueStruct() {
    Console::WriteLine("Working with AManagedValueStruct");
    AManagedValueStruct amvs;
    Console::WriteLine(amvs.m_str);
    amvs.Method1();

}

void UseGcStruct() {
    Console::WriteLine("Working with AManagedGcStruct");
    AManagedGcStruct *amgcs;
    amgcs = new AManagedGcStruct();
    Console::WriteLine(amgcs->m_str);
    amgcs->Method1();
}

// This is the entry point for this application
int _tmain(void)
{
    Console::WriteLine(
        "Creating and exercising an instance of AManagedClass");
    AManagedClass *amc = new AManagedClass();
    Console::WriteLine("Filling array");
    amc->FillArray();
    amc->ShowArray();
```

```
    Console::WriteLine();

    Console::WriteLine("Creating and using a Delegate");
    CDelegateHolder *dh;
    dh = new CDelegateHolder();
    AManagedDelegate *amd;
    amd = new AManagedDelegate(dh, dh->DelegateFn);
    amc->UseDelegate(amd);
    Console::WriteLine();

    Console::WriteLine(
            "Talking to the object through IAManagedInterface");
    IAManagedInterface *ami;
    ami = amc;
    ami->MethodA();
    ami->MethodB();

    Console::WriteLine();
    UseGcStruct();

    Console::WriteLine();
    UseValueStruct();

    GC::Collect();

    return 0;
}
```

Before getting into the details of the code, take a look at the top of the previous listing. There's an *include* statement for stdafx.h. That's normal, of course. The stdafx.h file includes a reference to mscorlib.dll. Immediately following the *include* statement are a couple of *#using* directives. The first one brings in a reference to the core runtime library. The second one brings in a reference to the Ex32a assembly. The reference to Ex32a makes Ex32a's types available to the application. Following the *#using* compiler directives are two *using* statements for specifying namespaces. These are for your convenience—you don't have to completely scope out every variable and object you use.

The structure of all console applications within the common language runtime is similar. The assembly needs to include a single class. (You can call it anything you want.) The class needs to include a single static method named *Main*. This is the entry point to the application.

The main thread to the application then instantiates various types living within Ex32a.dll and exercises them. The first object is an instance of *AManagedClass*. Notice the calls to *FillArray* and *ShowArray*. These methods fill an *ArrayList* (a data member within *AManagedClass*), which is an array of *IPerson* implementations. *ShowArray* pulls each object out of the array and asks the object what type it is and what exercises the *IPerson Eat*, *Work*, and *Sleep* methods.

Notice the *UseDelegate* class near the top of the file. This class holds a function of the same signature type declared by *AManagedDelegate*. The Ex32b application passes an instance of this method to the *AManagedClass UseDelegate* method to illustrate using delegates.

Ex32b then casts the *AManagedClass* object to *IAManagedInterface* and talks to the object through the interface. This shows how you can pare an object instance down to one of its interfaces and use the class through the interface type.

Finally, the main thread creates instances of *AManagedGcStruct* and *AManagedValueStruct* to show how managed versus reference types work. Notice that the value structure simply sits on the stack, while the reference types live on the garbage-collected heap. (They're instantiated using the *new* operator.)

The final act of Ex32b is to execute the garbage collector by calling *GC::Collect*. Notice how finalizers are called on the objects as they're garbage collected.

Figure 32-2 shows the results of executing the Ex32b application.

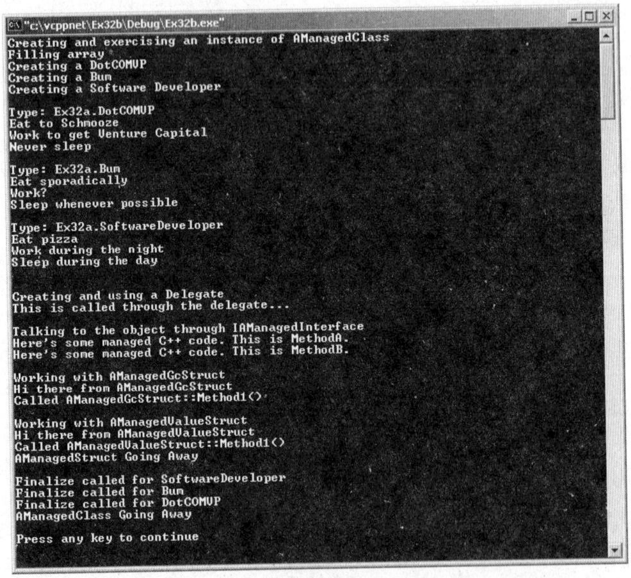

```
"c:\vcppnet\Ex32b\Debug\Ex32b.exe"
Creating and exercising an instance of AManagedClass
Filling array
Creating a DotCOMVP
Creating a Bum
Creating a Software Developer

Type: Ex32a.DotCOMVP
Eat to Schmooze
Work to get Venture Capital
Never sleep

Type: Ex32a.Bum
Eat sporadically
Work?
Sleep whenever possible

Type: Ex32a.SoftwareDeveloper
Eat pizza
Work during the night
Sleep during the day


Creating and using a Delegate
This is called through the delegate...

Talking to the object through IAManagedInterface
Here's some managed C++ code. This is MethodA.
Here's some managed C++ code. This is MethodB.

Working with AManagedGcStruct
Hi there from AManagedGcStruct
Called AManagedGcStruct::Method1()

Working with AManagedValueStruct
Hi there from AManagedValueStruct
Called AManagedValueStruct::Method1()
AManagedStruct Going Away

Finalize called for SoftwareDeveloper
Finalize called for Bum
Finalize called for DotCOMVP
AManagedClass Going Away

Press any key to continue
```

Figure 32-2 Running the Ex32b console application.

Adding Managed Extension Support

As you can see from the preceding examples, using managed types within C++ is quite easy. Managed types look, taste, and feel very like normal C++ types. However, they're a lot less hassle to use.

Building managed C++ assemblies from scratch is a breeze using the Visual C++ project wizards. However, sometimes you might need to add managed C++ support to your existing C++ applications. Let's look at how you go about converting a normal C++ application to a managed C++ application.

First, you modify the project settings. Standard C++ applications don't have the correct compiler and linker settings to compile down to the common language runtime. You must add the */clr* option, which enables support for Managed Extensions and forces a link to the proper library. To modify the project settings, right-click on the project node in Solution Explorer and choose Properties. Click on the C/C++ folder in the left pane of the Property Pages dialog box. Then click on the General folder under C/C++. Set the Compile As Managed property to *Assembly Support (/clr)*. If your application is an MFC application, you might need to tweak some of the other options, such as turning off the Program Database For Edit & Continue option (*/ZI*).

By default, the */clr* compiler option is not in effect. When it is switched on, metadata is generated for all code (wow!). Any code that can be compiled to managed code will be. Naturally, some C++ constructs can be compiled to managed code. The following kinds of unmanaged code will be generated automatically:

- *__asm* blocks.
- Functions that use any form of variant *args* in their parameter list.
- Compiler-generated thunks or helper functions. Native thunks are generated for any function call through a function pointer, including virtual function calls.
- Functions that call *setjmp*.
- Functions that directly manipulate machine resources. For example, *__enable*/*__disable* and *_ReturnAddress*/*_AddressOfReturnAddress* cause a function to be compiled as unmanaged native code.
- Code that appears after a *#pragma unmanaged* directive.
- Functions that reference aligned types (types declared using *__declspec(align(...))*

Using the */clr* compiler option requires that the */MT* compiler option be enabled. This causes the compiler and linker to use the multi-threaded versions of the CRT runtime functions. This is necessary because the common language runtime garbage-collects and calls object finalizers on a thread that runs independently from the main execution thread.

Once the target application has been built with Managed Extensions support, you can access all .NET Framework features, including your own managed types and the .NET common library. Notice that the example code for this chapter uses predefined system types (such as *String*, *ArrayList*, and *Console*) as well as types defined within a custom assembly.

Of course, there are some caveats about using managed types with unmanaged types. You are forbidden to nest managed types within unmanaged types. This makes sense—how should the destructor of a class holding a managed type behave? You cannot derive a managed type from an unmanaged type—a class has to be managed from the beginning. This means that it's generally impractical to use the Managed Extensions from within an MFC application. You cannot keep a managed type as a member variable for a class. However, you can create an instance of a managed type for the duration of a method call. For example, the following line creates a managed *ArrayList* within some unmanaged code:

```
void UseAManagedType() {
    ArrayList* al;
    al = new ArrayList();
}
```

Remember that MFC redefines the *new* operator within the debug version of MFC to track memory usage. That means you can't use the managed version of *new*. You'll get error C3828: "Placement arguments not allowed while creating instances of managed classes." To get rid of this error, use the following pragmas to undefine the *new* operator temporarily:

```
void UseAManagedType() {
#pragma push_macro("new")
#undef new
    ArrayList* al;
    al = new ArrayList();
#pragma pop_macro("new")
}
```

This lets you use managed types within an unmanaged application. However, most modern rich-client applications will be written using Windows Forms and ASP.NET, which we'll look at in the next two chapters.

33

Programming Windows Forms Using Managed C++

In the previous chapter, we looked at the fundamentals of writing managed code using the Managed Extensions for C++. Now we can do something practical with that information. The common language runtime provides many features and services. Two of the most prevalent features include Windows Forms for creating desktop applications and ASP.NET for writing Web applications. We'll start off with Windows Forms. Another feature is managed data access. We'll look at managed data access using ADO.NET in Chapter 35.

Windows Forms

Earlier sections of this book covered classic Microsoft Windows development. We looked at the Microsoft Foundation Classes (MFC) as the quickest way to write high-performance Windows-based applications. For years, the best way to get the highest-performing, most feature-filled desktop application was to use MFC. Microsoft .NET includes a desktop application development framework named Windows Forms.

Although the .NET initiative emphasizes Internet-based development, normal client applications will always be popular. The Windows user interface has been around a long time, and the underpinnings are not likely to go away soon. Under the hood, Windows applications will probably remain the same for the foreseeable future. You'll probably always be able to write Windows-based applications using *WndProc* functions and Petzold-style coding or using MFC. Windows Forms provides the highest-level abstractions available for Windows developers. They take a forms-based approach to development, much like Microsoft Visual Basic. However, Windows Forms makes available to all developers (including those using managed C++) the user interface facilities that Visual Basic developers have enjoyed for years.

Beneath the Veneer

As an MFC programmer, you're used to a single class library that works only under C++. The .NET Windows Forms library is a bit different. The Windows Forms classes are built into the .NET common language runtime. Earlier we looked at how MFC is basically a thin layer above API-level programming. If you look through the MFC source code, you'll find a *WinMain* function and some message loops—the heart of any Windows-based program. In fact, under the hood all Windows-based applications essentially work the same way. Windows-based applications register window classes that tie a *WndProc* to a default window style. Windows-based applications use the window classes to create instances of Windows user interface elements. Windows has some basic window classes defined under the hood (such as the *BUTTON* and the *COMBOBOX* classes).

In the earliest days of Windows programming, all applications were created from scratch, and a large part of the developer's time was spent getting the boilerplate code to work correctly. Once the boilerplate code worked, you could add event handlers gradually to develop an application by adding cases to a *switch* statement. MFC did away with requiring developers to carve out all their own *WinMain* and *WndProc* functions. Windows Forms continues the trend of eliminating programming details so you don't have to spend as much time writing grunge code.

The Windows Forms Structure

Windows Forms applications are structured much like Visual Basic applications, and Windows Forms development is similar to standard Visual Basic forms-based development. SDK-style applications interact directly with the Windows API. We saw earlier that MFC is only a very thin veneer between the API and the C++ source code. Windows Forms programming hides even more of the boilerplate details of Windows programming than MFC did. Windows Forms applications have all the same general features of normal Windows-based applications. They respond to the usual events, such as mouse movements and menu selections. Windows Forms can also render within the client area. However, the syntax for managing these features is more abstract than the syntax in a program you write with the SDK or even with MFC.

Windows Forms technology is useful for creating all the standard Windows applications we've seen so far: Single Document Interface (SDI) applications, Multiple Document Interface (MDI) applications, and dialog box applications. Much of Windows Forms development involves managing a form (or forms) and defining a user interface in terms of controls (combo boxes, labels, text boxes, and so forth). All these controls are found in the common language runtime. Windows Forms aren't limited to just form-based applications. Windows Forms include a canvas on which you can draw anything you want—just as you're able to do with the standard GDI device context.

Windows Forms simplifies desktop user interface programming in many ways. For example, Windows Forms define their appearance through properties. To move a Windows Form on the screen programmatically, you set the Windows Form's *Location* property. Remember that, when programming in MFC, moving a window involved calling *CWnd::MoveWindow*. Windows Forms manage their behavior with methods, and they also respond to events to define their interaction with the user.

The classes comprising Windows Forms applications are found in the common language runtime. The fundamental class behind a Windows Forms application is the *System::Windows::Forms::Form* class. Writing a Windows Forms application is a matter of tweaking its properties to get the windows to look the way you want them to look, and setting up event handlers for mouse movements, menus, and command. Because a Windows Form is a regular common language runtime–based class that fully supports inheritance, you can build hierarchies of Windows Forms–based classes in a standard, object-oriented way. Right now, the common language runtime contains only the most rudimentary classes for creating applications. However, third parties are rapidly building Windows Forms components and controls.

A Windows Forms Wizard

Microsoft Visual Studio .NET includes a wizard called the Managed C Windows Forms Wizard for generating a Windows Forms application. You can find the wizard by searching on "Custom Wizard Samples" in the Visual Studio online help. Click the ManagedCWinFormWiz link and follow the instructions for installing the wizard. We'll use the wizard to create a simple Window Forms application so we can examine how Window Forms work.

The Ex33a Example: A Basic Windows Forms Application with a Menu and a Status Bar

You can look through the copy of Ex33a that comes with the companion CD, or you can use the Managed C Windows Forms Wizard to generate the example.

To use the wizard, be sure it's installed. (You can get information about installing the wizard when you download it.) Choose New, Project from the File menu and then select the Managed C++ Windows Forms project. Type **Ex33a** in the Name text box and click OK. Here's the code produced by the wizard:

Source.cpp

```
#using <mscorlib.dll>
using namespace System;

// required dlls for WinForms
#using "System.dll"
#using "System.Windows.Forms.dll"
#using "System.Drawing.dll"

// required namespaces for WinForms
using namespace System::ComponentModel;
using namespace System::Windows::Forms;
using namespace System::Drawing;

__gc class WinForm: public Form
{
private:
    StatusBar  *statusBar;
    Button     *closeButton;
    MainMenu   *mainMenu;
    MenuItem   *fileMenu;
    Label      *todoLabel;

    String     *caption;   // Caption of the WinForm
    int        width;     // width of the WinForm
    int        height;    // height of the WinForm


public:
    WinForm()
    {
        // Set caption and size of the WinForm
        caption = "Default WinForm Example";
        width = 400;
        height = 500;

        InitForm();
    }

    void Dispose(bool disposing)
    {
        // Form is being destroyed.  Do any
```

```
    //  necessary clean-up here.
    Form::Dispose(disposing);
}

void InitForm()
{
    // Setup controls here

    // Basic WinForm Settings
    Text = caption;
    Size = Drawing::Size(width, height);

    // Setup Menu
    mainMenu = new MainMenu();
    fileMenu = new MenuItem("&File");
    mainMenu->MenuItems->Add(fileMenu);
    fileMenu->MenuItems->Add(new MenuItem("E&xit",
            new EventHandler(this, &WinForm::OnFileExit)));
    Menu = mainMenu;

    // Label
    todoLabel = new Label();
    todoLabel->Text = "TODO: Place your controls here.";
    todoLabel->Size = Drawing::Size(150, 100);
    todoLabel->Location = Point (50, 50);
    Controls->Add(todoLabel);

    // Set status bar
    statusBar = new StatusBar();
    statusBar->Text = "Status Bar is Here";
    Controls->Add(statusBar);

    // Setup Close Button
    closeButton = new Button();
    closeButton->Text = "&Close";
    closeButton->Size = Drawing::Size(75, 23);
    closeButton->TabIndex = 0;
    closeButton->Location =
         Drawing::Point(width/2 - (75/2), height - 23 - 75);
    closeButton->Click +=
         (new EventHandler(this, &WinForm::OnCloseButtonClick));
    Controls->Add(closeButton);
}


void OnCloseButtonClick(Object *sender, EventArgs *e)
{
```

(continued)

```
            Close();
        }

        void OnFileExit(Object *sender, EventArgs *e)
        {
            Close();
        }

};

void main()
{
    // ds
    // This line creates an instance of WinForm, and
    // uses it as the Main Window of the application.
    Application::Run(new WinForm());
}
```

The code listed above has been changed slightly. By default, the "todo:" comments generated by the wizard cover up the Close button generated by the wizard. The code listed above draws these comments a bit smaller. We'll look at the *Form* class in detail in a moment.

Figure 33-1 shows the Ex33a Windows Forms application in action.

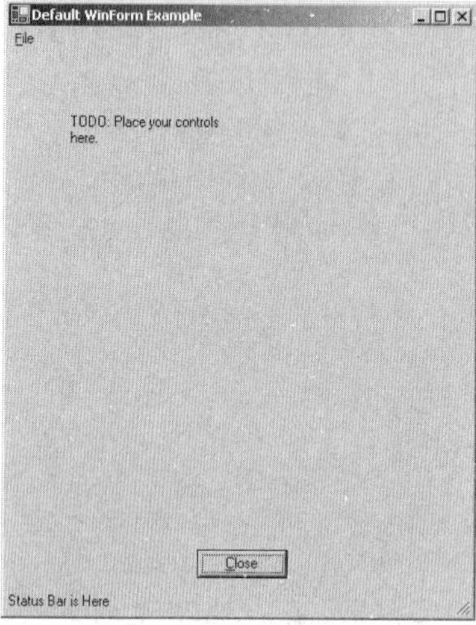

Figure 33-1 The Ex33a sample in action.

The *Form* Class

Windows Forms applications are based upon a class derived from the common language runtime *Form* class. Just as MFC used a C++ class library to hide the details necessary to manage a Windows application, the common language runtime classes hide the same details. That means no more defining *WndProc* functions, registering window classes, and running message loops.

Note the *#using* directive at the top of the Ex33a Source.cpp listing. This directive brings in the common language runtime, housed within mscorlib.dll. The *namespace* statements make coding more convenient—they eliminate the necessity of scoping every single variable.

Because this example is written in managed C++, the *Form* class is preceded by the *__gc* declaration. Remember that Windows Forms are common language runtime–based applications and are therefore required to live on the garbage-collected heap.

Any standard window can be represented by the *Form* class. You just need to make sure you use the correct form class (for example, there's an *MdiClient* class for supporting MDI applications) and set the properties to get the window to look the way you want it to look. It's generally much simpler than using the raw Windows SDK or even MFC. You can manage all these form properties at design time through the Visual Studio .NET Properties window, or you can manage them programmatically at run time.

Windows Forms applications bring the simplicity of Visual Basic–style development to developers who are using the common language runtime. Eventually we'll start seeing a great deal more consistency between applications because developers will be using the same framework. This means no more differences between MFC-based applications, Visual Basic–based applications, Windows SDK–based applications, and so on.

Handling Events

Windows is an event-driven operating system. Consequently, the main purpose of any Windows user interface program is to handle the various Windows events. We've been writing MFC code to handle all kinds of events, including mouse movement, mouse button presses, and key presses. Windows Forms handle most events by plugging in an event handler for each event that a program will handle. Notice how the earlier Ex33a Source.cpp program listing intercepts the events generated by the File, Exit menu command and the Close button control created on the fly by the program. By contrast, recall how MFC-based applications intercept/receive their events and pipe them through a command-handling architecture using message maps. Windows Forms use the same eventing mechanism for both commands and Window messages: The *Form* class intercepts these events, and if there's a handler plugged in for that particular event, the form directs execution flow there.

Drawing

Any Windows programming framework requires you to draw on the screen. The *Form* class defines an event named *OnPaint* that traps the *WM_PAINT* message. The *Form* class intercepts the *Paint* event, and you can add a handler to draw on the form. Drawing on a Windows Form is generally simpler than using the raw GDI. The drawing operations are encapsulated in the *Graphics* object passed in *OnPaint*'s arguments.

The Ex33a sample application listed earlier simply places a Label control and a Button control on the form. However, in the next example we'll see how the Windows Forms painting model supports many of the graphics primitives that Windows developers are used to.

The Ex33b Example: Handling the *Paint* Event

Ex33b illustrates handling the *Paint* event. The core code for this example was generated by the Managed C Windows Forms Wizard mentioned earlier. Here's the listing for Ex33b:

Source.cpp

```
#using <mscorlib.dll>
using namespace System;

// required dlls for WinForms
#using "System.dll"
#using "System.Windows.Forms.dll"
#using "System.Drawing.dll"

// required namespaces for WinForms
using namespace System::ComponentModel;
using namespace System::Windows::Forms;
using namespace System::Drawing;

__gc class Shape
{
public:
    Rectangle m_rect;
    Color m_PenColor;

    Shape()
    {
        m_rect.set_X(0);
        m_rect.set_Y(0);
        m_rect.set_Height(0);
        m_rect.set_Width(0);

        m_PenColor = Color::Black;
```

```
    }
    Shape(Rectangle r)
    {
        m_rect=r;
        m_PenColor = Color::Black;
    }
    virtual void Draw(System::Drawing::Graphics* g)
    {
    }
};

__gc class Line : public Shape
{
public:
    Line(Rectangle r) :
        Shape(r)
    {
        m_rect=r;
    }
    Line():
        Shape()
    {
    }
    void Draw(System::Drawing::Graphics* g)
    {
        g->DrawLine(new Pen(m_PenColor), m_rect.Left,
            m_rect.Top, m_rect.Right, m_rect.Bottom);
    }
};

__gc class Circle : public Shape
{
public:
    Circle(Rectangle r) :
        Shape(r)
    {
        m_rect=r;
    }
    Circle():
        Shape()
    {
    }
    void Draw(System::Drawing::Graphics* g)
    {
        g->DrawEllipse(new Pen(m_PenColor), m_rect.Left,
            m_rect.Top, m_rect.Right, m_rect.Bottom);
    }
};
```

(continued)

```
__gc class Rect : public Shape
{
public:
    Rect(Rectangle r) :
        Shape(r)
    {
        m_rect=r;
    }
    Rect():
        Shape()
    {
    }
    void Draw(System::Drawing::Graphics* g)
    {
        g->DrawRectangle(new Pen(m_PenColor),
            m_rect.Left, m_rect.Top,
            m_rect.Right, m_rect.Bottom);
    }
};

__gc class WinForm: public Form
{
private:
    MainMenu  *mainMenu;
    MenuItem  *fileMenu;

    String    *caption;  // Caption of the WinForm
    int       width;     // width of the WinForm
    int       height;    // height of the WinForm

    Shape*     l; // line
    Shape*     c; // circle
    Shape*     r; // rectangle

    Shape*     l2; // line
    Shape*     c2; // circle
    Shape*     r2; // rectangle

public:
    WinForm()
    {
        // Set caption and size of the WinForm
        caption = "Default WinForm Example";
        width = 400;
        height = 500;

        InitForm();
    }
```

```
void Dispose(bool disposing)
{
    // Form is being destroyed.  Do any necessary clean-up here.
    Form::Dispose(disposing);
}

void CreateShapes()
{
    int x = 10;
    int y = 30;

    l = new Line(Rectangle(x, y, 30, 60));
    x = x + 50;

    c = new Circle(Rectangle(x, y, 30, 60));
    x = x + 170;

    r = new Rect(Rectangle(x, y, 60, 60));

    y = 160;
    x = 10;
    l2 = new Line(Rectangle(x, y, 30, 60));
    l2->m_PenColor = Color::Red;
    x = x + 50;

    c2 = new Circle(Rectangle(x, y, 30, 60));
    c2->m_PenColor = Color::Blue;
    x = x + 170;

    r2 = new Rect(Rectangle(x, y, 60, 60));
    r2->m_PenColor = Color::Green;
}

void DrawShapes(System::Drawing::Graphics* g)
{
    l->Draw(g);
    c->Draw(g);
    r->Draw(g);

    l2->Draw(g);
    c2->Draw(g);
    r2->Draw(g);
}

void InitForm()
{
```

(continued)

```
            CreateShapes();

            // Setup controls here

            // Basic WinForm Settings
            Text = caption;
            Size = Drawing::Size(width, height);

            // Setup Menu
            mainMenu = new MainMenu();
            fileMenu = new MenuItem("&File");
            mainMenu->MenuItems->Add(fileMenu);
            fileMenu->MenuItems->Add(new MenuItem("E&xit",
                new EventHandler(this, &WinForm::OnFileExit)));
            Menu = mainMenu;

            //Paint Handler
            Paint += new PaintEventHandler(this, OnPaint);

        }

        void OnPaint(Object* sender, PaintEventArgs* e)
        {
            SolidBrush* b;
            b = new SolidBrush(Color::Black);

            e->Graphics->DrawString("Hello World",
                this->Font, b, System::Drawing::PointF(10, 10));
            DrawShapes(e->Graphics);
        }

        void OnFileExit(Object *sender, EventArgs *e)
        {
            Close();
        }

};

void main()
{
    // This line creates an instance of WinForm, and
    // uses it as the Main Window of the application.
    Application::Run(new WinForm());
}
```

Graphical Output The sample code produced by the wizard didn't do much in the way of handling graphics. Ex33b *does* include some graphics-rendering code. The rendering code in Ex33b uses GDI+, an enhancement of the normal

GDI we've already seen while working with MFC. Notice near the top of Source.cpp the class hierarchy defining three shape objects—a line, a square, and a circle—derived from a class named *Shape*. The *Shape* class has some attributes (a color and a bounding rectangle) and a *Draw* method.

The *Shape* class and its descendents are all defined as *__gc* classes, so they live on the garbage-collected heap. The *Draw* method takes an argument of type *System::Drawing::Graphics*. This type wraps the GDI's device context handle and manages calls such as *LineTo*, *Ellipse*, and *Rectangle*.

The *Form* class has an event named *Paint* to which you can attach a handler. The form attaches its *Paint* event handler in the *InitForm* method. Notice that *InitForm* creates several instances of the *Shape*-derived classes. When Windows rerenders the form, the *Paint* handler runs through the *Shape* objects and asks each one to render itself by calling the *Draw* method.

The *Draw* method extracts the *Graphics* object from the painting arguments and then draws each shape appropriately using a GDI+ call on the *Graphics* object. The *Line* object uses *Graphics::DrawLine*, the rectangle uses *Graphics::DrawRectangle*, and the circle uses *Graphics::DrawEllipse*. It's generally simpler to use GDI+ to render an object than it is to use GDI to render an object.

Figure 33-2 shows Ex33b in action.

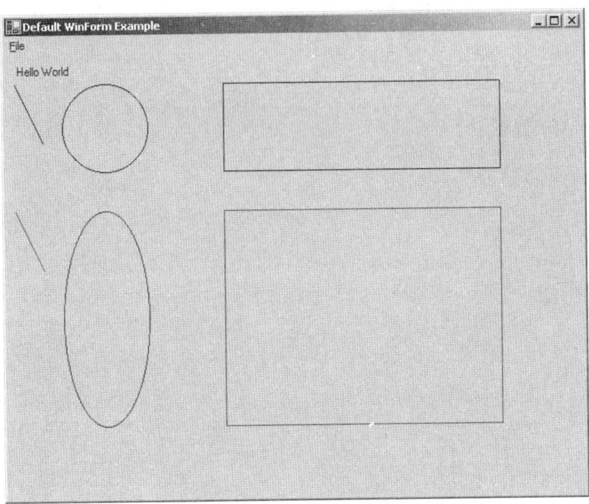

Figure 33-2 The Ex33b sample in action.

The Ex33c Example: An Interactive Drawing Program

To fully illustrate how Windows Forms works, let's take a look at a drawing program that interactively draws the shape objects listed earlier—a line, a square, and a circle. Ex33c is a slight variant of Ex33b. However, Ex33c handles mouse movement events and performs some custom tweaking of device context within the *Graphics* object.

As with Ex33a and Ex33b, Ex33c was created using the Managed C Windows Forms Wizard. I removed the "todo:" label and the Close button. Otherwise, it's a stock Windows Forms application. Here's the listing for Ex33c:

Source.cpp

```
#include "stdafx.h"
#include "math.h"

#using <mscorlib.dll>
using namespace System;

// required dlls for WinForms
#using "System.dll"
#using "System.Windows.Forms.dll"
#using "System.Drawing.dll"

// required namespaces for WinForms
using namespace System::ComponentModel;
using namespace System::Collections;
using namespace System::Windows::Forms;
using namespace System::Drawing;
using namespace System::Drawing::Drawing2D;

using namespace System::Diagnostics;

__value enum DrawingTypes
{
    None, Line, Circle, Rect
};
//
//
// shape hierarchy shown later…
//
//
__gc class WinForm: public Form
{
private:
    StatusBar  *statusBar;
    MainMenu  *mainMenu;
    MenuItem  *fileMenu;
    MenuItem  *drawingMenu;
    MenuItem  *circleMenu;
    MenuItem  *lineMenu;
    MenuItem  *rectMenu;
```

```
    MenuItem  *helpMenu;

    DrawingTypes drawingtype;

    ArrayList   *shapes;

    String      *caption;   // Caption of the WinForm
    int         width;     // width of the WinForm
    int         height;    // height of the WinForm

    Shape       *currentShape;

public:
    WinForm()
    {
        // Set caption and size of the WinForm
        caption = "Default WinForm Example";
        width = 600;
        height = 500;

        InitForm();
    }

    void Dispose(bool disposing)
    {
        // Form is being destroyed.  Do any
        // necessary clean-up here.
        Form::Dispose(disposing);
    }

    void InitForm()
    {
        // Setup controls here

        // Basic WinForm Settings
        this->set_BackColor(Color::White);

        Text = caption;
        Size = Drawing::Size(width, height);

        drawingtype = DrawingTypes::Line;

        // Setup Menu
        mainMenu = new MainMenu();
        fileMenu = new MenuItem("&File");
        mainMenu->MenuItems->Add(fileMenu);
        fileMenu->MenuItems->Add(
```

(continued)

```
        new MenuItem("E&xit",
            new EventHandler(this, &WinForm::OnFileExit)));
    Menu = mainMenu;

    drawingMenu = new MenuItem("&Drawing");
    circleMenu =
        new MenuItem("&Circle",
            new EventHandler(this, OnDrawCircle));
    lineMenu = new MenuItem("&Line",
        new EventHandler(this, OnDrawLine));
    rectMenu =
        new MenuItem("&Rectangle",
            new EventHandler(this, OnDrawRect));
    drawingMenu->MenuItems->Add(lineMenu);
    drawingMenu->MenuItems->Add(circleMenu);
    drawingMenu->MenuItems->Add(rectMenu);
    mainMenu->MenuItems->Add(drawingMenu);

    helpMenu = new MenuItem("&Help");
    mainMenu->MenuItems->Add(helpMenu);
    helpMenu->MenuItems->Add(
        new MenuItem("&About",
            new EventHandler(this, OnHelpAbout)));

    // Set status bar
    statusBar = new StatusBar();
    statusBar->Text = "Status Bar is Here";
    Controls->Add(statusBar);

    MouseDown += new MouseEventHandler(this,
        MouseDownHandler);
    MouseMove += new MouseEventHandler(this,
        MouseMoveHandler);
    MouseUp += new MouseEventHandler(this,
        MouseUpHandler);

    Paint += new PaintEventHandler(this, OnPaint);

    shapes = new ArrayList();
    UIUpdate();
}

void UIUpdate()
{
    // uncheck all items
    lineMenu->Checked = false;
    rectMenu->Checked = false;
    circleMenu->Checked = false;
```

```
    switch(drawingtype)
    {
    case DrawingTypes::Line:
        lineMenu->Checked = true;
        break;
    case DrawingTypes::Rect:
        rectMenu->Checked = true;
        break;
    case DrawingTypes::Circle:
        circleMenu->Checked = true;
        break;
    }
}

void OnDrawLine(Object* sender, EventArgs* e)
{
    drawingtype = DrawingTypes::Line;
    UIUpdate();
}

void OnDrawCircle(Object* sender, EventArgs* e)
{
    drawingtype = DrawingTypes::Circle;
    UIUpdate();
}

void OnDrawRect(Object* sender, EventArgs* e)
{
    drawingtype = DrawingTypes::Rect;
    UIUpdate();
}

void OnFileExit(Object *sender, EventArgs *e)
{
    Close();
}

void OnHelpAbout(Object* sender, EventArgs* e)
{
    ::MessageBox(NULL,
       "WinForms Drawing Example",
       "About WinForms Drawing Example", MB_OK);
}

void MouseDownHandler(Object* sender, MouseEventArgs* e)
{
```

(continued)

```
        if(!this->Capture)
            return;

        switch(drawingtype)
        {
        case DrawingTypes::Line :
            currentShape = new Line();
            break;
        case DrawingTypes::Circle:
            currentShape = new Circle();
            break;
        case DrawingTypes::Rect:
            currentShape = new Rect();
            break;
        default:
            return;
        };

        try{
            currentShape->m_topLeft.X = e->X;
            currentShape->m_topLeft.Y = e->Y;
            currentShape->m_bottomRight.X = e->X;
            currentShape->m_bottomRight.Y = e->Y;

            this->Capture = true; // Capture the mouse
                                  //  until button up
        }
        catch(Exception* ex) {
            Debug::WriteLine(ex->ToString());
        }

    }


    void MouseMoveHandler(Object* sender, MouseEventArgs* e)
    {
        if(!this->Capture)
            return;

        try{
            Graphics* g = CreateGraphics();

            Pen *p = new Pen(this->BackColor);
            currentShape->Erase(g);

            currentShape->m_bottomRight.X = e->X;
            currentShape->m_bottomRight.Y = e->Y;
```

```
            currentShape->Draw(g);
        }
        catch (Exception* ex) {
            Debug::WriteLine(ex->ToString());
        }
    }


    void MouseUpHandler(Object* sender, MouseEventArgs* e)
    {
        if(!currentShape)
                return;
        try{
            shapes->Add(currentShape);
            currentShape = 0;
            this->Invalidate();
            Capture = false;
            }
        catch (Exception* ex) {
            Debug::WriteLine(ex->ToString());
        }

    }

    void DrawShapes(System::Drawing::Graphics* g)
    {
        for(int i = 0; i < shapes->Count; i++)
        {
            Shape* s = dynamic_cast<Shape*>(shapes->get_Item(i));
            s->Draw(g);
        }
    }

    void OnPaint(Object* sender, PaintEventArgs* e)
    {
        Graphics* g = e->Graphics;
        DrawShapes(g);
    }


};

void main()
{
    TextWriterTraceListener * myWriter = new
        TextWriterTraceListener(System::Console::Out);
    Debug::Listeners->Add(myWriter);
```

(continued)

```
    // This line creates an instance of WinForm, and
    // uses it as the main window of the application.
    Application::Run(new WinForm());
}
```

To draw a shape, select a shape from the Drawing menu, click and hold the left mouse button inside the form's client area, and then drag the mouse to a new location and release the mouse button. The shape is continually redrawn smaller or larger as you drag the mouse.

This application uses a variant of the shape hierarchy from Ex33b. The application manages a list of *Shape* objects in an *ArrayList* (which you'll notice declared within the Windows Form). There are also a number of *MenuItem* objects declared and used. Let's start by hooking up the menu commands.

Intercepting Commands In MFC, window messages are mapped to handlers in C++ classes using a message map. The Windows Forms model uses delegates to expose events. The first kind of event we'll look at is a command event—one that comes from a push button or a menu command.

This application builds the menu manually, adding each menu command separately. Unfortunately, the current version of Visual Studio .NET doesn't include the high level of wizard integration for Windows Forms and managed C++ that we're used to with MFC applications. Each main menu command (File, Draw, and Help) is added to the top-level menu structure, and then individual commands are added to the main menus. We need only supply the string that appears on the menu, as well as a reference to a method that handles the menu event.

This application includes a File menu for exiting the application, a Drawing menu for selecting which shape to draw, and a Help menu. The Drawing menu sets an internal variable to indicate the current shape (the shape that will be drawn next). Notice that the drawing handlers also set the state of the menu commands with check marks to indicate which shape is about to be drawn (a task we accomplished using MFC's command architecture).

Intercepting Move Messages In addition to intercepting command messages, Windows Forms applications usually intercept other messages such as mouse movement. The *Form* class exposes the typical mouse events, such as mouse down, mouse move, and mouse up.

Ex33c handles the mouse down event by capturing the mouse and creating an instance of the current shape type. Once the mouse is captured by the application, all mouse messages are sent to the captured form. Ex33c's mouse move handler erases the current shape (more on that in the next section) and then resets the coordinates of the current shape using the screen coordinates passed to the handler as arguments. Finally, the mouse up handler completes the shape and adds the shape object to its internal list of objects.

Advanced Graphics Rendering If you look at the code for the shape hierarchy from Ex33c, you'll notice that it's a bit different from the shape hierarchy from Ex33b. The reason for this difference is that Ex33b's shapes don't continually redraw themselves as you drag the mouse. Ex33c handles the mouse movement by constantly erasing and redrawing the shape at its new coordinates—certainly a reasonable approach for a drawing program. When you release the mouse button, the residue lines have to be cleared up. Here's the shape hierarchy from Ex33c that accomplishes this cleaning:

```
__gc class Shape
{
public:
    Point m_topLeft;
    Point m_bottomRight;

    Color m_PenColor;

    Shape()
    {
        m_topLeft.X = 0;
        m_topLeft.Y = 0;
        m_bottomRight.X = 0;
        m_bottomRight.Y = 0;

        m_PenColor = Color::Black;
    }
    Shape(Point topLeft, Point bottomRight)
    {
        m_topLeft = topLeft;
        m_bottomRight = bottomRight;
        m_PenColor = Color::Black;
    }
    virtual void Draw(System::Drawing::Graphics* g)
    {
    }
    virtual void Erase(System::Drawing::Graphics* g)
    {
    }

    int SetROP(HDC hdc)
    {
```

(continued)

```
        int nOldRop = ::SetROP2(hdc, R2_NOTXORPEN);
        return nOldRop;
    }

    void ResetROP(HDC hdc, int nOldRop)
    {
        ::SetROP2(hdc, nOldRop);
    }
};

__gc class Line : public Shape
{
public:
    Line(Point topLeft, Point bottomRight) :
        Shape(topLeft, bottomRight)
    {
    }
    Line():
        Shape()
    {
    }
    void Draw(System::Drawing::Graphics* g)
    {
        System:IntPtr hdc;
        hdc = g->GetHdc();

        ::MoveToEx((HDC)hdc.ToInt32(), m_topLeft.X,
            m_topLeft.Y, NULL);
        LineTo((HDC)hdc.ToInt32(), m_bottomRight.X,
            m_bottomRight.Y);
        g->ReleaseHdc(hdc);
    }

    void Erase(System::Drawing::Graphics* g)
    {
        System:IntPtr hdc;
        hdc = g->GetHdc();

        int nOldROP = SetROP((HDC)hdc.ToInt32());
        ::MoveToEx((HDC)hdc.ToInt32(), m_topLeft.X,
            m_topLeft.Y, NULL);
        LineTo((HDC)hdc.ToInt32(), m_bottomRight.X,
            m_bottomRight.Y);
        ResetROP((HDC)hdc.ToInt32(), nOldROP);
        g->ReleaseHdc(hdc);
    }
};

__gc class Circle : public Shape
```

```
{
public:
    Circle(Point topLeft, Point bottomRight) :
      Shape(topLeft, bottomRight)
    {

    }
    Circle():
        Shape()
    {
    }
    void Draw(System::Drawing::Graphics* g)
    {
        // These are absolute coordiantes, so fixup

        System:IntPtr hdc;
        hdc = g->GetHdc();

        ::Ellipse((HDC)hdc.ToInt32(),
            m_topLeft.X,
            m_topLeft.Y,
            m_bottomRight.X,
            m_bottomRight.Y);
        g->ReleaseHdc(hdc);

    }
    void Erase(System::Drawing::Graphics* g)
    {
        System:IntPtr hdc;
        hdc = g->GetHdc();

        int nOldROP = SetROP((HDC)hdc.ToInt32());
        ::Ellipse((HDC)hdc.ToInt32(),
            m_topLeft.X, m_topLeft.Y,
            m_bottomRight.X,
            m_bottomRight.Y);
        ResetROP((HDC)hdc.ToInt32(), nOldROP);
        g->ReleaseHdc(hdc);
    }
};
__gc class Rect : public Shape
{
public:
    Rect(Point topLeft, Point bottomRight) :
      Shape(topLeft, bottomRight)
    {
```

(continued)

```
    }
    Rect():
        Shape()
    {
    }
    void Draw(System::Drawing::Graphics* g)
    {
        System:IntPtr hdc;
        hdc = g->GetHdc();

        ::Rectangle((HDC)hdc.ToInt32(), m_topLeft.X,
            m_topLeft.Y, m_bottomRight.X, m_bottomRight.Y);
        g->ReleaseHdc(hdc);
    }
    void Erase(System::Drawing::Graphics* g)
    {
        System:IntPtr hdc;
        hdc = g->GetHdc();

        int nOldROP = SetROP((HDC)hdc.ToInt32());
        ::Rectangle((HDC)hdc.ToInt32(), m_topLeft.X, m_topLeft.Y,
            m_bottomRight.X, m_bottomRight.Y);
        ResetROP((HDC)hdc.ToInt32(), nOldROP);
        g->ReleaseHdc(hdc);
    }
};
```

To make the rubber-banding work within the application (*rubber-banding* is the effect of stretching the shape as you move the mouse), you must make some standard GDI calls that aren't available within GDI+. Specifically, you need to call *SetROP2* to set the binary raster operations. When you drag one shape over another, by default Windows simply brute-forces the pen to draw. Using the raster operations, you can set up the device context so it doesn't erase the current contents of the screen (drawn by a previous pen) as you draw new shapes.

Each *Shape* class (the line, the circle, and the rectangle) has an *Erase* method as well as a *Draw* method. The *Erase* method uses the device context buried within the *System::Drawing::Graphics* object to set the raster operations. Calling *Graphics::GetHdc* gives you the same raw device context you get by calling the Win32 API method *GetDC*. The result you get from *Graphics::GetHdc* is a managed system type (an *Int32Ptr*). To get the actual device context, you must get the integer value (by calling *ToInt32*). You can then pass the device context to any function that needs it (such as the *SetROP2* method).

Finally, if you look at the *Draw* methods of each of the shapes, you'll notice that they call the standard Win32 API methods for drawing lines, ellipses, and rectangles. Mixing GDI+ with classic GDI sometimes results in unpredictable side effects. In the case of setting up the raster operations, the drawing code doesn't erase the old lines correctly.

Figure 33-3 shows Ex33c in action.

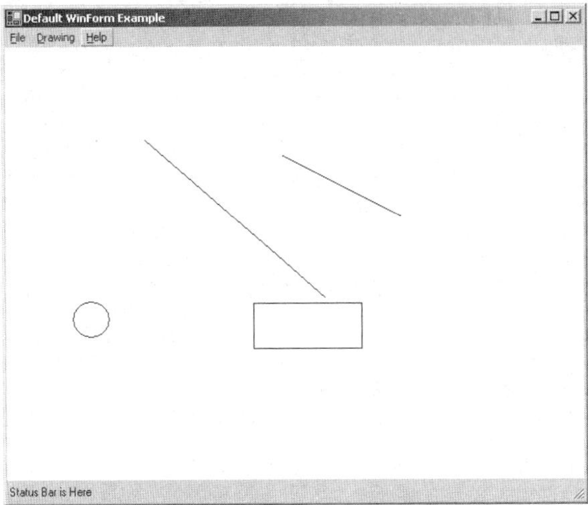

Figure 33-3 The Ex33c sample in action.

What's Missing from Windows Forms

Windows Forms is still very much in its infancy. While the basic tools necessary to create a Forms-based application using the common language runtime are all there, some of the niceties we're used to as MFC developers are missing. Windows Forms provides toolbar and status bar support, but you have to wire them up by hand (just as we did with the menus in the examples from this chapter).

Another missing piece is some sort of document/view architecture. We've got one as part of the MFC library, but it's not part of the common language runtime. However, writing some document/view components is fairly straightforward. To get an idea of what's involved, take a look at the Managed C++ Windows Forms Scribble sample from Visual Studio .NET.

34

Programming ASP.NET Using Managed C++

Since Microsoft .NET was released to the world at large (and even a bit before), its adoption rate has been staggering. Judging from seminar attendance, feedback on the .NET lists, and the size of the community growing up around it, .NET is going to be huge. One of the most compelling reasons to buy into the .NET movement is that it offers one of the easiest ways to get a Web site up and running quickly.

One of the most important parts of .NET is ASP.NET, which consists of a set of common language runtime classes. Chapter 28 and Chapter 30 introduced Microsoft Windows as a viable Internet server platform using the sockets API and the WinInet API and using ATL Server to write ISAPI DLLs. ASP.NET represents another way to intercept and process HTTP requests. In this chapter, we'll look at the ASP.NET architecture. The ASP.NET features we'll look at include the path a request takes from the time Microsoft Internet Information Services (IIS) passes it to ASP.NET to the time the ASP.NET application renders its content. You'll also see examples of writing ASP.NET Web sites using managed C++ components.

The Internet as a Development Platform

When you look at how software distribution technology has evolved, it's obvious that the next development platform will be the Internet itself. In the 1970s, most computing occurred between terminals and a mainframe. During the PC revolution of the 1980s, PC-to-PC networks connected offices together, allowing rich clients to share their files and resources. During the 1990s, DCOM promised to make real distributed processing possible.

The Web revolution of the late 1990s connected computer users between enterprises via human-oriented Web sites. However, while offices and companies (enterprises) were able to connect their computers together, there was no way to connect computers between enterprises programmatically. The main problem preventing DCOM from becoming a universal connection protocol is that the DCOM protocol and wire format are not shared by all computers. (DCOM is not the only network protocol/wire format out there.) However, there is a connection protocol shared the world over: HTTP. In addition, XML is a wire format that's widely available and understood.

Getting the Internet working as a development platform has required both a standard, reliable distributed user interface model and a widely used connection protocol to support programmatic Web sites. The Web-based user interface model—HTML over HTTP—has proven to be reliable and well-understood. Getting computers to work over the Internet programmatically will involve sending XML over HTTP using a format called SOAP. The latter protocol is often referred to as Web services.

Both of these communication standards and protocols (HTML and XML over HTTP) are agreed upon. All that's missing is a practical means of implementing these standards. This is where ASP.NET comes in. It offers a practical way to do both Web-based user interface and Web-based method calls.

The Evolution of ASP.NET

We covered the essentials of Internet connectivity and some development strategies in previous chapters. To fully understand the impact of ASP.NET, you need a sense of the evolution of the Web in the past few years. The Web of 1993 was very different from the Web of today. In the earliest days, most Web sites were simply hyperlinked files and graphics. These days, the Web represents a fully capable interactive computing platform.

As people began to get tired of looking at each other's photo albums over the Web, HTML began to develop into a markup language that could describe controls and interactive user interface elements, not just simple formatting. This paved the way for dynamic content—Web site content that changed at run time based on factors such as user selections, information in a database, and so on.

The first dynamic Web sites were written using the Common Gateway Interface (CGI). CGI launches a new process in response to each incoming HTTP request. The process emits some customized HTML based on the request. CGI was fairly effective, but one major drawback was the fact that each incoming HTTP request had to beget a new process, creating a huge burden on the server. (Creating a new process for each request is pretty expensive.)

To make things more efficient for Microsoft Windows–based Web servers, Microsoft implemented a programming interface named the Internet Server Application Programming Interface (ISAPI), which you saw briefly in Chapter 30. As learned in that chapter, IIS fires up a new instance of an ISAPI DLL that's been mapped to a specific file extension. The DLL renders specific HTML based on the incoming request. Unfortunately, when ISAPI DLLs were introduced, the only effective way to write them was using C++. Microsoft introduced Active Server Pages (ASP) to help developers develop Web pages more quickly.

Classic ASP is driven by a single DLL named Asp.dll. Asp.dll reads ASP files that combine script and HTML and renders markup language back to the client. The code within the scripting blocks controls the content coming from an ASP page. The script blocks usually drive COM objects that perform such operations as accessing databases and processing transactions. The ASP object model provides easily-accessed objects representing HTTP requests and responses. For example, to emit the string *Hello World* to the browser connected to your server, you just call *Response.Write("Hello World")* from within a server-side script block.

When ASP came out in the late 1990s, it made Web-site development available to non-C++ developers. No longer were ISAPI DLLs the only way to get content out to a client browser. However, classic ASP started showing some warts after developers began exercising it extensively. First, many ASP pages ended up being very disorganized. ASP let you wantonly mix user interface code and execution code in the same page, so many ASP pages end up looking like spaghetti code.

Second, the ASP object model is fairly unstructured. ASP has numerous intrinsic, or global, objects that seem to come out of nowhere. For example, when you write script code to generate the content of an HTTP request, the *Response* object includes the methods for writing text out to the client. Unfortunately, ASP doesn't support state management very well. These are just a couple of the issues faced by ASP developers—there are others. For example, classic ASP code tends to mix user interface code with executable code, making the page hard to maintain. If you want to run an ASP Web site over a Web farm, you need to manage application state between each of the servers yourself. Managing the state of your application's user interface involves lots of mundane code to check the state of the user interface between posts. ASP.NET has evolved to solve some of the most common problems facing Web site developers.

Most of the improvement ASP.NET makes over classic ASP is evolutionary. For example, ASP.NET includes similarly named objects (*Response*, *Request*, and *Server*) for managing requests. ASP.NET provides an architecture for these objects—they don't come out of nowhere. (ASP intrinsic objects are attached to a thread's context.) The syntactic similarity between ASP and ASP.NET means that many ASP pages can easily be run as ASP.NET pages if you rename them using the ASPX extension. (ASP.NET installs several file types in IIS (ASPX, ASMX, ASCX, and ASHX) that redirect processing to ASP.NET.

However, ASP.NET is more than a simple evolution of classic ASP. Whereas classic ASP leverages many features from IIS, ASP.NET generally uses IIS only to intercept the HTTP request. Features generally provided by IIS and the Web Application Manager (WAM), including such features as process isolation and security, are provided by the ASP.NET infrastructure and by classes within the common language runtime.

Rather than being interpreted (as classic ASP applications are), ASP.NET applications are compiled into common language runtime assemblies. Because ASP.NET applications are compiled, you can use any .NET language to write the executable part of a page. Also, because ASP.NET applications are compiled for the runtime, component integration within a .NET application is much easier than with classic ASP applications (which use COM as the component integration technology).

ASP.NET also includes some features completely absent from classic ASP, including server-side controls, data binding, and Web services. Server-side controls vastly simplify Web user interface programming by handling the mundane details of user interface state management between postbacks. Data binding also simplifies user interface programming by managing the details of rendering such collection-oriented user interface elements as combo boxes, list boxes, and grids. Finally, ASP.NET represents a framework for intercepting and mapping SOAP requests to individual methods written into your application.

The Role of IIS

Web programming involves processing HTTP requests, interpreting them, and delivering responses. ASP.NET is just a tool for processing HTTP requests. Its main purpose is to service HTTP requests and provide responses. Both ASP and ASP.NET process HTTP requests and deliver responses, but ASP.NET relies much less on IIS than ASP does. The IIS architecture has been around for a while, and it's not going to disappear soon. IIS still fields the HTTP request. However, if IIS detects an ASP.NET file extension in the request, it simply routes the request to ASP.NET's ISAPI DLL (Aspnet_isapi.dll) rather than the regular

ASP DLL (Asp.dll). We'll get a closer look at how this works in a moment when we look at the HTTP pipeline.

ASP.NET's Compilation Model

When IIS maps an HTTP request to ASP.NET, the ASP.NET runtime compiles the file into an assembly and shadow-copies the assembly into a temporary directory. (On Windows 2000, the directory is \Winnt\Microsoft.NET\Framework\v1.0.3705\Temporary ASP.NET Files.) Whenever ASP.NET detects that the source files are newer than the already-compiled assembly, it recompiles the assembly.

If you've ever worked with classic ASP, you might have come across a situation in which you've had to shut down the entire site to replace components because the components were in use. By performing the shadow copy described above, ASP.NET solves this problem. You can simply copy new source code and components over the old code and components because the files in your deployment directory are not locked. ASP.NET will recompile the new source code into a new assembly, copy the assembly to the temporary directory, and use the new assembly to service new requests.

Next, we'll take a look at the most common kind of request: one for a file with an ASPX extension.

The *Page* Class

Most requests to an ASP.NET page start out as a URL that includes an ASPX extension in the filename. The common language runtime class that handles this type of a request is *System::Web::UI::Page*. To start, here's the simplest "Hello World"-style ASP.NET page in a file named HelloWorld.aspx:

```
<%@ Page %>

Hello World from ASP.NET
```

There's not too much going on with this page—all it does is print out "Hello World from ASP.NET" to the browser requesting the file. However, it illustrates the fundamental page architecture behind ASP.NET. If you put this file in a virtual directory somewhere and then surf to it using a browser, ASP.NET will generate an assembly based on the ASP.NET syntax. If you start up ILDASM, you can find the assembly generated by ASP.NET. On Windows 2000, the assembly lands in the Winnt\Microsoft.NET\Framework\v1.0.3705\Temporary ASP.NET Files directory. If you hunt around for the virtual directory hosting the file, you'll see something like \vcppnet\cc541602\245fc247\uiya6evk.dll. This is the assembly generated by ASP.NET when a request is made for the page. Figure 34-1 shows ILDASM reflecting the page.

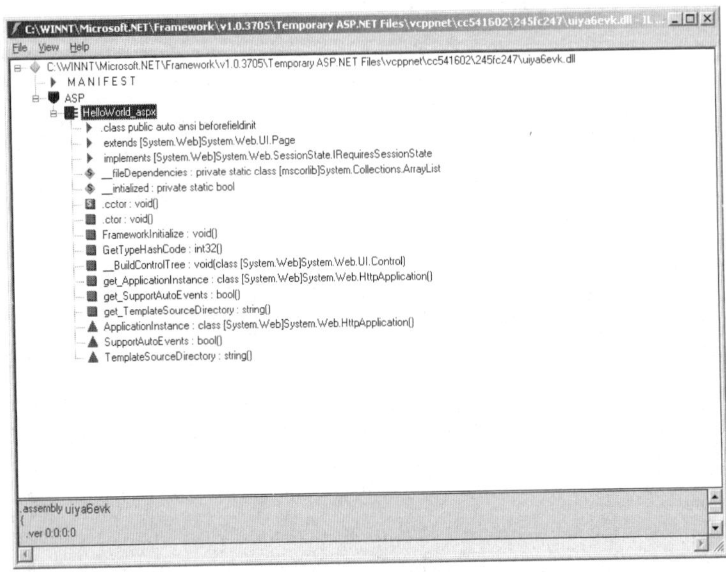

Figure 34-1 A very simple ASPX page reflected by ILDASM.

When you pop open the nodes within ILDASM, you'll notice that the assembly includes a namespace called *ASP* and a class named *HelloWorld_aspx*. If you look even closer, you'll see that the class extends *System::Web::UI::Page* and includes various member functions that are obviously necessary for rendering the page.

This exercise shows that when you surf to an ASPX page, ASP.NET automatically creates an assembly for you and generates a class for you—and that class derives from *System::Web::UI::Page*. The class is responsible for rendering HTML to the client. So, if ASP.NET inserts the class for you, is there any way you can replace the *System::Web::UI::Page* class with one of your own so you can provide your own processing? Yes, you can—and the technique is known formally as the *code-behind technique*.

Code-Behind

Every ASPX file generates a corresponding assembly when a request is made for the file. The ASP.NET page syntax includes a directive for defining the class that an ASPX page will use. You've seen that by default an ASPX page uses a class derived from *System::Web::UI::Page*. However, you can write your own page-derived class and insert it into the hierarchy.

The Ex34a Example: Defining an ASP.NET Code-Behind Page

This example project contains the code to define an ASP.NET code-behind page. To create the project, choose New, Project from the File menu and select Managed C++ Class Library from the list of project templates. (You can also use the wizard from Chapter 4, which generates a simple ASPX file and a code-behind page class.) The application wizard generates a class library project that will compile into an assembly that is similar to the assemblies we looked at in Chapter 32. Here is the code produced by the wizard:

Ex34a.h

```
// Ex34a.h

#pragma once

#using <system.dll>
#using <system.web.dll>
using namespace System;
using namespace System::Web;
using namespace System::Web::UI;
using namespace System::Collections;

namespace Ex34a
{
    public __gc class ManagedCPPPage : public Page
    {
    protected:
        ArrayList* m_arrayList;

        void AssembleChoices()
        {
            m_arrayList = new ArrayList();
            String* str = "Just-in-time Compiling";
            m_arrayList->Add(str);
            str = "Common runtime environment";
            m_arrayList->Add(str);
            str = "Multiple language support";
            m_arrayList->Add(str);
            str = "Simplified component model";
            m_arrayList->Add(str);
            str = "Excellent backwards compatibility";
            m_arrayList->Add(str);
            str = "ASP.NET";
            m_arrayList->Add(str);
        }
        void DisplayFeatures()
        {
```

(continued)

```
            for(int i = 0; i < m_arrayList->Count; i++)
            {
                Response->Write("<li>");
                Response->Write(m_arrayList->get_Item(i));
                Response->Write("</li>");
                Response->Write("</br>");
            }
        }

        void Page_Load(Object* o, EventArgs* ea)
        {
            AssembleChoices();
        }
        :
    };
}
```

Recall that .NET managed code needs to live on the garbage-collected heap. The class listed above is defined as a *__gc* class, and it derives from *System::Web::UI::Page*. The page handles the *Page_Load* event by assembling a list of favorite .NET features into an *ArrayList* (which is also a common language runtime class). Also notice the *DisplayFeatures* function, which simply cycles through the array of features and directs the list of choices to the browser that's making the request through the *Page.Response.Write* method.

> **Important** The code-behind assembly must live in the \bin directory beneath the virtual directory hosting the page.

To use the code-behind assembly, you simply refer to the assembly within the *Inherits* directive on the page. Here's the ASP.NET page that uses the *ManagedCPPPage* class:

```
<%@ Page Language="c#" Inherits="Ex34a.ManagedCPPPage" %>

<html>
<body>

<h3> Favorite .NET Features </h3>

<% DisplayFeatures(); %>

</body>
</html>
```

Figure 34-2 shows the output to the browser.

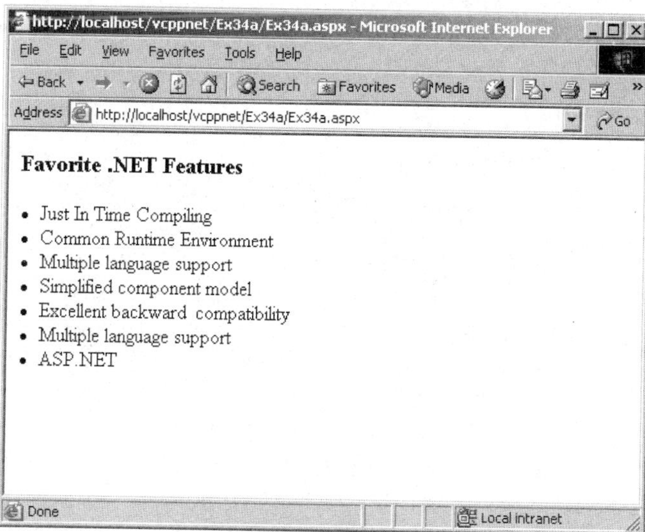

Figure 34-2 Output generated by the code-behind page.

To confirm that ASP.NET brought your class in, you can look at the resulting assembly within the Temporary ASP.NET Files directory. Figure 34-3 shows ILDASM reflecting the assembly generated by ASP.NET. Notice that the class used to define the page derives from Ex34a.ManagedCPPPage.

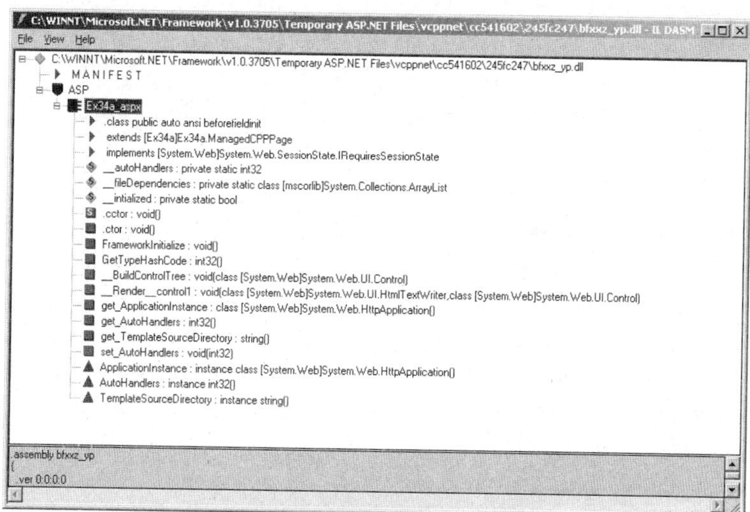

Figure 34-3 The code-behind DLL as reflected by ILDASM.

We cannot cover the entire scope of the *Page* class here. However, you should know that the *Page* class is the basis for two of the most powerful and convenient features of ASP.NET: Web Forms and server-side controls.

Web Forms

Traditionally, ASP development has involved a great deal of grunge code for coding a user interface. The primary difficulty in getting a user interface to work correctly over the Web is keeping track of the state of the user interfaces between posts. As an MFC developer, you're used to having all the user interface code for an application reside within a single process space. That means, for example, that when you define a combo box in a window or dialog box, the combo box will always show its correct state. For instance, if you select Oregon from a combo box that lists states, the combo box will continue to show Oregon until you select something else. (The combo box won't pop back and show Alabama). Windows itself keeps track of the state of the control.

The Web does not work this way. HTTP is a connectionless protocol, which means that once a response is sent from the server back to the client, the connection (and any state associated with that connection) disappears. (In a Windows-based desktop application, the state does not disappear.) The bottom line is that a browser only ever sees a snapshot of the state of the server. So user interface programming over the Web becomes problematic because it involves sending some HTML out to the client browser over a connection that doesn't stick around. The HTML that was sent to the browser can contain tags that will eventually render as Windows-style controls (such as combo boxes and list boxes). However, the state of the control (for example, which item in a combo box was selected) has to be handled manually.

The following listing is an example of some typical classic ASP-style code that maintains the state of a combo box on a Web page. The file is in Ex34a and is named Raw.asp.

```
<%@ Language="javascript" %>

<html>
    <body>
    Feature: <select name="Feature">
      <option
        <% if (Request("Feature") == "Garbage collection") {
        Response.Write("selected");
        }%> >Garbage collection</option>
      <option
        <% if (Request("Feature") == "Multiple languages") {
             Response.Write("selected");
```

```
        }%> >Multiple languages</option>
    <option
        <% if (Request("Feature") == "No more GUIDS") {
             Response.Write("selected");
        }%> >No more GUIDS</option>

    </select>

  </body>
</html>
```

This code checks the request coming from the client, finds out which item in the combo box was selected, and makes sure that it's the item appearing in the combo box by including *selected* with that option. When the browser gets the HTML back from the server, the browser will render a combo box with the correct selection showing. This is just a simple example, but it shows the kinds of machinations that ASP developers have had to go through to make even simple user interfaces work.

It turns out that most of the code necessary to keep a user interface consistent over a disconnected protocol can be pushed down into the runtime. That's exactly what ASP.NET Web Forms is designed to do—to handle control state management for you using server-side controls.

In terms of ASP.NET syntax, the easiest way to use server-side controls is to include the *runat=server* attribute in the tag, as shown in the following listing:

```
<html><body>
<form runat=server>
    Feature: <select name="Feature" runat=server>
      <option>Garbage collection</option>
      <option>Multiple languages</option>
      <option>No more GUIDS</option>
   </select>
</form>
</body></html>
```

There are two other important points here. First, the *select* tag that runs at the server is included between a *form* tag that also runs at the server. Second, the file includes an ASPX extension. This file is named SelectMe.aspx in the Ex34a directory on the companion CD.

When ASP.NET processes the ASPX page, it creates an instance of the .NET Framework class *System::Web::UI::HtmlControls::HtmlSelect*. The *HtmlSelect* control keeps track of the state of the combo box between posts. (You can look up the class in the help system, and you'll see it's just another .NET Framework class.) Two kinds of server-side controls ship with ASP.NET: HTML controls and Web controls. We'll look more closely at Web controls here because they're more consistent and flexible. Keep in mind, though, that the only thing the browser ever really sees is some HTML. The HTML controls and Web controls are classes that live on the server and are responsible for rendering HTML to the client. The *Page* architecture and the server-side controls are known collectively as Web Forms.

With the Web Forms model of programming, you feel like you're building a local user interface (as you might when using MFC). However, in reality you're programming a widely distributed user interface that's generated almost entirely by pushing HTML tags from the server to the client browser. ASP.NET keeps track of the state of the controls for you.

The following listing shows the Ex34a.aspx enhanced to use some server-side controls:

```
<%@ Page Language="c#" Inherits="Ex34a.ManagedCPPPage" %>

<html>
<body>
<form runat=server>

<h3> Favorite .NET Features </h3>

<% DisplayFeatures(); %>

  </br>
  <asp:Label text="Type your name:" runat=server />
  <asp:TextBox id="m_name" runat=server/> </br> </br>
  <asp:Label Text="Select your favorite .NET feature:" runat=server /> </br>
  <asp:CheckBoxList id="m_cblFeatureList" runat=server/> </br></br>
  <asp:Button id="Submit" OnClick="SubmitInfo" Text="Submit" runat=server />
  </br>
  <asp:Label id="m_labelInfo" runat=server />

</form>
</body>
</html>
```

The page includes several Web controls: three *asp:Label* controls, an *asp:TextBox* control, an *asp:CheckBoxList* control, and an *asp:Button* control. Notice that all the controls run at the server, and that the button seems to be wired up to some sort of handler. Here's the Ex34a code-behind class modified to handle the new controls on the form:

```
// Ex34a.h
#pragma once

#using <system.dll>
#using <system.web.dll>
using namespace System;
using namespace System::Web;
using namespace System::Web::UI;
using namespace System::Web::UI::WebControls;
using namespace System::Collections;
using namespace System::ComponentModel;

namespace Ex34a
{
    public __gc class ManagedCPPPage : public Page
    {
    protected:
        ArrayList* m_arrayList;
        CheckBoxList* m_cblFeatureList;
        Label* m_labelInfo;
        TextBox* m_name;

        void AssembleChoices()
        {
            m_arrayList = new ArrayList();
            String* str = "Just-in-time compiling";
            m_arrayList->Add(str);
            str = "Common runtime environment";
            m_arrayList->Add(str);
            str = "Multiple language support";
            m_arrayList->Add(str);
            str = "Simplified component model";
            m_arrayList->Add(str);
            str = "Excellent backwards compatibility";
            m_arrayList->Add(str);
            str = "ASP.NET";
            m_arrayList->Add(str);
        }
        void DisplayFeatures()
        {
            for(int i = 0; i < m_arrayList->Count; i++)
            {
                Response->Write("<li>");
                Response->Write(m_arrayList->get_Item(i));
                Response->Write("</li>");
```

(continued)

```
            }
        }

        void Page_Load(Object* o, EventArgs* ea)
        {
            AssembleChoices();
            if(!this->IsPostBack)
            {
                m_cblFeatureList->DataSource = m_arrayList;
                m_cblFeatureList->DataBind();

            }
        }
        void SubmitInfo(Object* o, EventArgs* ea)
        {
            String* s;

            s = s->Concat(S"Hello ", m_name->Text);
            s = s->Concat(s, S". You selected ");
            for(Int32 i = 0;
                i < m_cblFeatureList->Items->get_Count(); i++)
            {
                if(m_cblFeatureList->Items->get_Item(i)->get_Selected())
                {
                    s = s->Concat(s, S"<li>");
                    s = s->Concat(s, m_cblFeatureList->Items->
                        get_Item(i)->get_Text());
                    s = s->Concat(s, S"</li>");
                }
            }
            s = s->Concat(s, S"</br>");
            s = s->Concat(s, S" as your favorite .NET feature");
            m_labelInfo->Text=s;
        }
    };
}
```

The same list of features is displayed as with the earlier version of this example. However, notice that there's now a check box list from which to select your favorite feature, and a button to submit your choice back to the server. The check box list (*m_cblFeatureList*) is populated during the *Page_Load* event. Notice that the *m_cblFeatureList* includes a member named *DataSource* to which is assigned the *ArrayList* containing the feature list. This is an example of a data binding control. The check box list will render a check box tag for each element in the data source. This cuts down on a great deal of coding.

The HTML rendered by this ASPX page places raw text, a text input box, some check box tags, and a button on the browser. Clicking the Submit button causes a postback to the server, and execution is routed to the *SubmitInfo* method on the page. (*SubmitInfo* is a member of the code-behind page.) Figure 34-4 shows the Web page in action.

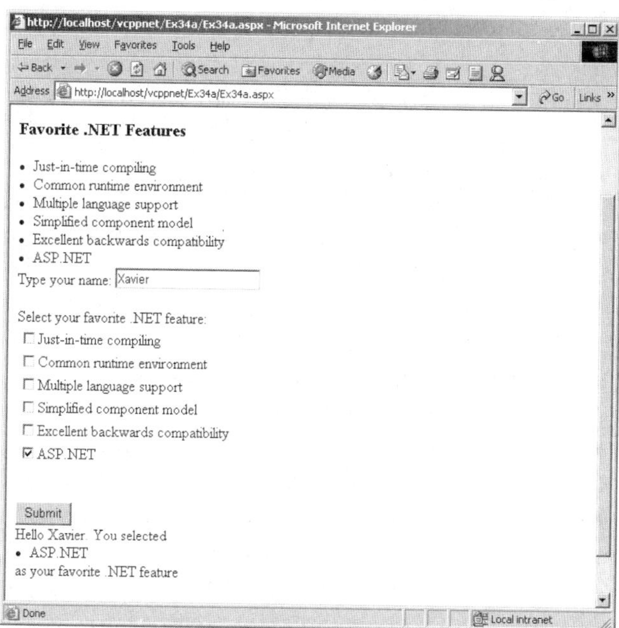

Figure 34-4 Ex34a with server-side controls.

What Happened to ActiveX?

At this point, many people will ask, "Why is all this processing being pushed back to the server? Won't this severely restrict my ability to create rich interactive sites?" This question is often followed by another one: "What happened to ActiveX?" The answers to these questions lie in understanding the problem that ASP.NET is trying to solve: how to get software out to as many people as possible using the wire that's already there.

First, consider where rich user interfaces came from—the desktop. Users are accustomed to rich GUI interfaces. A sophisticated user interface is almost a requirement for any site. One of the most valuable assets consumers can provide for a company is their attention to the company's Web site. Naturally, companies want to create compelling, useful Web sites. Therefore, Web users need sophisticated controls with which they can interact with the site.

Most browsers support standard controls such as buttons and list boxes. However, the standard controls can take you only so far. The earliest attempts to create sophisticated browser-centric applications were centered around ActiveX controls on the Microsoft platform.

When the user hits a page containing an ActiveX control, the browser proceeds to download an ActiveX DLL. You saw how ActiveX controls work in Chapter 9 and Chapter 26. The browser calls *CoCreateInstance* on the object, negotiates some interfaces, and renders the control in the host application. (In the case of the Internet, the host program is a browser.)

The ActiveX control approach has some specific advantages. The most significant advantage is that you can provide much more natural and intuitive ways for the user and Web site to talk to one another.

However, there's a problem with extending the browser to enrich the user interface using client-side technologies such as ActiveX: Client browsers have to support that technology. For example, if you want the browser to use an ActiveX control to interact with the site, that browser must have the infrastructure to support ActiveX controls, which is complex.

Ensuring that specific user interface technology (the COM infrastructure) is available on the client machine is impossible, especially with the advent of Web-enabled personal digital assistants (PDA)s and Web phones. A huge number of browsers are out there, and some might not support a special user interface infrastructure required by your site. If you make ActiveX controls integral to your Web site, you cannot reach certain clients.

This is why ASP.NET moves user interface's generation to the server—to increase the audience of your Web site by helping you manage (or eliminate) your Web site's dependence on a specific browser. The server can look out at the browser, figure out what kind of browser it is, and send out the appropriate HTML based on information coming from the browser's headers. It's also becoming much easier to develop sophisticated user interfaces based on HTML tags.

Next, we'll take a look at the HTTP pipeline and the lifetime of a request. Along the way, you'll see a couple of very useful extensibility points provided by ASP.NET.

The HTTP Pipeline

As with most HTTP requests handled by the Microsoft platform, the first stop for an ASP.NET request is IIS. IIS intercepts the request and examines the file extension of the request. IIS keeps a list of file extensions and the ISAPI DLLs that are supposed to handle the associated files. When an extension such as ASPX shows up, IIS routes the request to a DLL named Aspnet_isapi.dll. This DLL simply takes the request and pipes it into the ASP.NET worker process Aspnet_wp.exe. ASP.NET examines the file and figures out whether the file needs to be compiled (and, of course, compiles the file if necessary).

The *HttpContext* Object

Next, ASP.NET cooks up an instance of a .NET Framework class named *HttpContext*. *HttpContext* represents the current request and includes almost anything you'd ever want to know about the request. Inside *HttpContext* you'll find the URL used to surf to the page, the file path of the physical file, whether the user has been authenticated, whether the connection is secure, and so on. The context also includes a reference to the *Request* and *Response* objects. We'll look at how the context is useful in a moment.

The *HttpApplication* Object

After wrapping up the information about the request in a context object, ASP.NET passes the request through an instance of *HttpApplication*. Remember MFC's *CWinApp*? *CWinApp* plays the role of the singleton within an MFC application. It's a rendezvous point for global application-wide data and events. *HttpApplication* serves the same role within an ASP.NET application. As the request is being processed, the *HttpApplication* object fires events to any number of waiting HTTP modules.

The *HttpModule* Object

HTTP modules provide an opportunity for pre- and post-processing requests. Events fired by the application object include *BeginRequest*, *EndRequest*, *AuthenticateRequest*, and *AuthorizeRequest*. Any Web application that wants to intercept these events can install an HTTP module. An HTTP module attaches itself to the application object and listens for these various events.

The Ex34b Example: Creating an HTTP Module

Ex34b listens for the *BeginRequest* event and dumps some of the context information at the beginning of every request. The module also rejects every other request, which of course is not useful in real life. However, you can see how it might be useful to intercept some of these events to do your own authentication or something like that. Here's the listing for Ex34b:

Ex34b.h

```
// Ex34b.h
#pragma once

#using <system.dll>
#using <system.web.dll>
using namespace System;
using namespace System::Web;

namespace Ex34b
{
public __gc class RejectRequestModule :
    public IHttpModule
    {
        bool m_bRejectRequest;
    public:
        RejectRequestModule()
        {
            m_bRejectRequest = false;
        }
        void Init(HttpApplication* httpApp) {
            httpApp->
                add_BeginRequest(new EventHandler(this, OnBeginRequest));
            httpApp->
                add_EndRequest(new EventHandler(this, OnEndRequest));
        }

        void Dispose() {
            // Usually, nothing has to happen here. However, if
            // there's any clean up you need to take care of here,
            // Dispose is called before the module goes away.
        }

        // Event handlers
        void OnBeginRequest(Object* o, EventArgs* ea) {
            // showing how to get a reference to the application
            HttpApplication* httpApp = dynamic_cast<HttpApplication*>(o);
            // Getting the current context
```

```
            HttpContext* ctx;
            ctx = HttpContext::Current;
            ctx->Response->Write("Beginning Request <br>");
            ctx->Response->Write("URL Used to surf here: ");
            ctx->Response->Write(ctx->Request->Url);
            ctx->Response->Write("<br>");
            ctx->Response->Write("Authenticated? ");
            ctx->Response->Write
                (ctx->Request->IsAuthenticated.ToString());
            ctx->Response->Write("<br>");
            ctx->Response->Write("Using secure connection? ");
            ctx->Response->Write
                (ctx->Request->IsSecureConnection.ToString());
            ctx->Response->Write("<br>");
            if(m_bRejectRequest) {
                ctx->Response->Write
                    ("<br>Stopping every other request...<br>");
                httpApp->CompleteRequest();
                ctx->Response->StatusCode = 500;
                ctx->Response->StatusDescription = "Server Error";
            }
            m_bRejectRequest = !m_bRejectRequest;
        }

        void OnEndRequest(Object* o, EventArgs* ea) {
            HttpApplication* httpApp = dynamic_cast<HttpApplication*>(o);
            HttpContext* ctx = HttpContext::Current;

            ctx->Response->Write("<br>");
            ctx->Response->Write("Ending Request <br>");
        }
    };
}
```

Modules implement *IHttpModule*, an interface the ASP.NET infrastructure uses to tell the modules to initialize themselves. Modules are listed in the Web.config file that accompanies the application, as shown in the following listing:

```
<configuration>
    <system.web>
        <httpModules>
            <add type="Ex34b.RejectRequestModule, Ex34b"
                name="RejectRequestModule" />
        </httpModules>
    </system.web>
</configuration>
```

This configuration file tells ASP.NET to look for an implementation of *IHttpModule*. The file should be put in the virtual directory hosting the site. The name of the module class is *Ex34b.RejectRequestModule*, and the module should be found in the assembly Ex34b.dll. Finally, the system name by which the module will be known is *RejectRequestModule*. Modules are useful for implementing pre- and post-processing for various phases of an application. In fact, ASP.NET's session state, output caching, and various forms of authentication are already built into ASP.NET via *HttpModule*. Figure 34-5 shows the *HttpModule* in action.

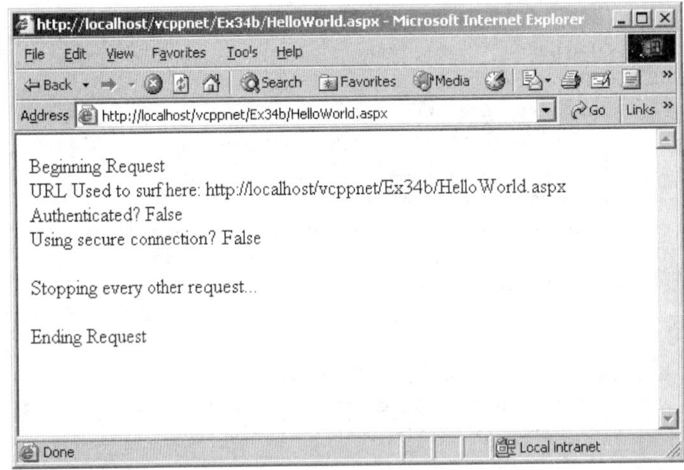

Figure 34-5 The Ex34b module dumping context information and stopping every other request.

After a request is routed through a pipeline of HTTP modules, it is ultimately routed to an HTTP handler.

The *HttpHandler* Object

You've seen the *System::Web::UI::Page* class, which contains the infrastructure for rendering normal Web pages with the help of server-side controls. However, ASP.NET is flexible enough to provide other ways of handling requests.

Imagine, for example, that you have a small file (such as a log file or a source code file) whose contents you want to make available to patrons of your Web site. However, you're also concerned about the performance and scalability of your application. If you look at the *System::Web::UI::Page* class, you'll notice that it's crammed with stuff. It's not a very lightweight class to instantiate and run. One option is to write a lightweight handler to process the request.

HttpHandler is simply a common language runtime class that implements *IHttpHandler*. It's listed in the application's Web.config file (just as *HttpModule* is).

The Ex34c Example: Implementing a Lightweight HTTP Handler

This example implements a lightweight handler for printing out files with the CPP extension. Here's the listing:

Ex34c.h

```
// Ex34c.h

#pragma once

#using <system.dll>
#using <system.web.dll>
using namespace System;
using namespace System::Web;
using namespace System::IO;
namespace Ex34c
{
public __gc class SourceCodeHandler :
    public IHttpHandler
    {
        void ProcessRequest(HttpContext* context)
        {
            context->Response->Write("Viewing file: ");
            context->Response->Write(context->Request->PhysicalPath);
            context->Response->Write("<br>");
            try
            {
                StreamReader* sr;
                sr = new StreamReader(context->Request->PhysicalPath);
                String* str;
                do
                {
                    str = sr->ReadLine();
                    context->Response->Write("<p>");
                    context->Response->Write(str);
                    context->Response->Write("</p>");
                } while (str != 0);
            }
            catch (FileNotFoundException* )
            {
                context->Response->Write("<h2>Sorry -");
                context->Response->Write("the file you ");
```

(continued)

```
                context->Response->Write("requested is not");
                context->Response->Write(" available</h2>");
            }
        }

        __property bool get_IsReusable()
        {
            return true;
        }
    };
}
```

When a request comes into ASP.NET, ASP.NET looks in the application's Web.config file to figure out which component should handle the request. If the file type is not listed within the application's Web.config file, ASP.NET looks in the machine-wide Machine.config file. If ASP.NET is successful in matching a file extension to a specific handler, it loads the handler and implements *IHttpHandler::ProcessRequest*. This handler processes the request by opening the requested file and dumping its contents for the browser on the other end.

When this source code is compiled and assembled, it must be installed in the \bin directory of the virtual directory hosting the site and listed in Web.config, as shown in the next listing. Look at the *httpHandlers* section in this file. The *add* element adds a handler to the list of handlers for the application. *Verb* defines what kind of HTTP request (*GET*, *PUT*, *POST*, or *) is processed by the handler. Notice that the *path* attribute specifies the file extension to match to the handler and the *type* attribute lists the common language runtime type representing the handler and the name of the assembly in which to find the class:

```
<configuration>
    <system.web>
        <httpHandlers>
            <add verb="*" path="*.cpp"
                type="Ex34c.SourceCodeHandler, Ex34c" />
        </httpHandlers>
    </system.web>
</configuration>
```

The last task to get this handler working is to let IIS know about the file extension for the source code files you want to view. Right-click on the virtual directory within IIS and choose Properties. Click the Configuration button to get a list of file mappings, as shown in Figure 34-6.

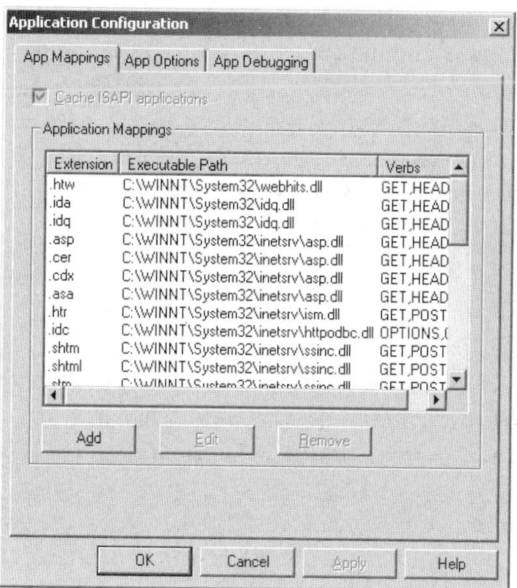

Figure 34-6 The Application Configuration property sheet within IIS showing the list of file-to-ISAPI DLL mappings.

Click the Add button to add a new extension. You'll see a dialog box, as shown in Figure 34-7.

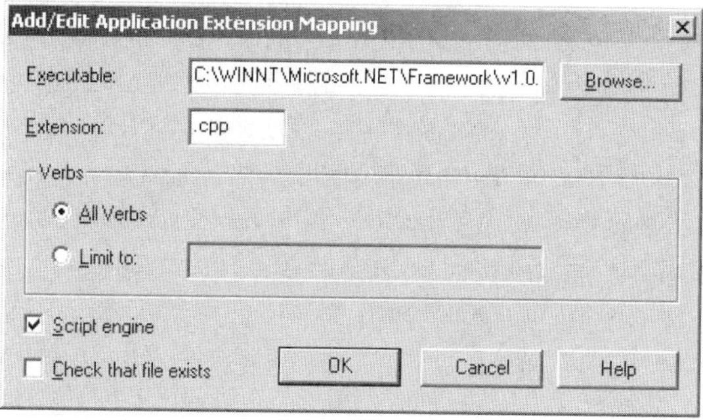

Figure 34-7 Adding a new file extension to the list of file-to-ISAPI DLL mappings.

Add **.cpp** as the extension, and point the executable to Aspnet_isapi.dll. (In Windows 2000, it's at \Winnt\Microsoft.net\Framework\v1.0.3705.) Now, when you surf to a file with a .cpp extension within that virtual directory, ASP.NET will load the handler. The handler will open the file and send the contents out to the client browser.

ASP.NET uses a handler to manage application-wide tracing. If you look inside the master Machine.config file on your host and search for *httpHandlers*, you'll see a file designation Trace.axd that's mapped to a system-provided class named *System.Web.Handlers.TraceHandler*.

Web Services

Most of this chapter has focused on using .NET as a tool for creating user-interface-based Web sites for human consumption. However, there's another use for the Internet on the horizon: programmable Web sites, also known as Web services.

COM and the Common Object Request Broker Architecture (CORBA) failed to connect the world together because DCOM and CORBA use very specialized connection protocols. As the Internet has evolved, it's become obvious that HTTP is a ubiquitous connection protocol, available on almost any device from desktop PCs to laptop computers, phones, and PDAs. The idea behind Web services is that a Web site can intercept more than just requests for HTML snapshots—it should be able to receive a SOAP request (specially formatted XML), map the contents of the request to a call stack, and execute the specified methods.

Web services will be big in the coming decade because they'll streamline business communication using common standards. Previous attempts at automating business communications and services (most notably Electronic Data Interchange, or EDI) failed for various reasons. One of the most problematic issues facing classic business communication automation was agreeing on the format for exchanging data. Web services rely on XML, which is widely understood by many computing platforms. When businesses need to communicate programmatically (to order supplies, for example), they can send a SOAP request to a Web site run by one of their suppliers. ASP.NET is probably the easiest way to create a programmable Web site.

Web Services Using Managed C++

Visual Studio .NET offers a wizard for generating managed C++ Web services. Example Ex34d shows how a managed C++ Web service provides calculator services over the Internet. Visual Studio .NET generates the required source code and sets up a virtual directory for your Web service.

There are three main parts to a managed C++ Web service: a header file, a source code file, and an ASMX file. Let's take a look at the header file first. Here's the listing for the default class (named *Class1*) generated by the wizard, with *Add* and *Subtract* methods included:

```
// Ex34d.h

#pragma once

#using <System.Web.Services.dll>

using namespace System;
using namespace System::Web;
using namespace System::Web::Services;

namespace Ex34d
{
    public __gc
        class Class1 : public WebService
    {

    public:
        [System::Web::Services::WebMethod]
        String __gc* HelloWorld();
        [System::Web::Services::WebMethod]
        int Add(int x, int y);
        [System::Web::Services::WebMethod]
        int Subtract(int x, int y);
    };
}
```

The most important part of this listing is the *WebMethod* attribute that precedes the function definitions. *HelloWorld* (added by the wizard) and *Add* and *Subtract* are all declared as *WebMethods*, which means they'll be exposed to the outside world as Web services. Here's the listing for the implementation file for *Class1*:

```
#include "stdafx.h"
#include "Ex34d.h"
#include "Global.asax.h"
```

(continued)

```
namespace Ex34d
{

    String __gc* Class1::HelloWorld()
    {

        // TODO: Add the implementation of your Web Service here

        return S"Hello World!";

    }

    int Class1::Add(int x, int y)
    {
        return x+y;
    }

    int Class1::Subtract(int x, int y)
    {
        return x-y;
    }

};
```

While these methods are admittedly simplistic functions, they'll do nicely to illustrate how Web services work. Notice that at this point, programming Web services is much like writing a component that will run on your desktop. The last piece of the ASP.NET Web service is the ASMX file (*M* standing for method). In this case, the listing is very short. It's only job is to tie the Web service to the *Class1* listed earlier:

```
<%@ WebService Class=Ex34d.Class1 %>
```

The *WebService* directive directs ASP.NET to use *Class1* to run the Web service. Now that the Web service is available, how do you call it? By finding out the capabilities of the Web service through Web Services Description Language (WSDL).

WSDL and ASP.NET

Clients understand the services available from a Web service by reading WSDL. To get a copy of a Web service's WSDL code, an ASP.NET client requests the service's file (the ASMX file) and passes *WSDL* in the query string. Figure 34-8 shows a browser surfing to Ex34d and asking the service for its description.

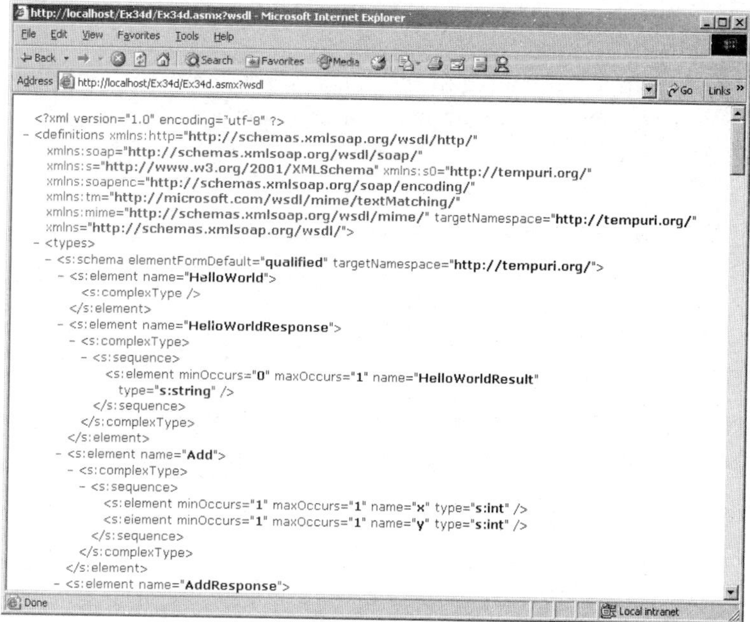

Figure 34-8 WSDL code generated by Ex34d.

Once you get the WSDL for a Web service, it's easy to write a client proxy to call the Web service.

Invoking Web Methods

There are a couple of ways to create a client-side proxy for a Web service. One way is to create a Web reference using Visual Studio .NET. When you create an application using Visual Basic .NET or C# (which is beyond the scope of this book), you can right-mouse-click on the project in Visual Studio Solution Explorer and then choose Add Web Reference from the shortcut menu. You basically point Visual Studio to the URL that's hosting the Web service you're interested in, and Visual Studio will create a proxy for you that hides all the details behind the underlying SOAP call.

The other way to create a proxy is to use the WSDL command-line tool and feed it the WSDL for the service you're interested in. Here's the command line for generating a proxy for the Ex34d Web service:

```
WSDL /language:CS Ex34d.wsdl
```

The WSDL tool generates C# code. (You can ask it to generate JScript or Visual Basic .NET source code as well.) You can compile the source code into an assembly and start calling the Web service right away. Because the resulting assembly is a common language runtime assembly, you can easily call it from some managed C++ code.

35

Programming ADO.NET Using Managed C++

Over the last few years, the Microsoft platform has accommodated an alphabet soup of acronyms representing various data access technologies, including ODBC (Open Database Connectivity), DAO (Data Access Objects), OLE DB (OLE Database), and ADO (ActiveX Data Objects), which until a few years ago was the preferred data access technology for the Microsoft platform. .NET has changed that.

ADO.NET will undoubtedly be the data access technology of choice for modern applications running under .NET. ADO.NET is the managed code alternative to traditional ADO. This chapter is all about data access under .NET. We'll look at connecting to databases, issuing commands to databases, reading data out of databases, and managing data sets using ADO.NET.

Managed Providers

As you saw in Chapter 31, .NET is based on a common runtime engine for all software running on the platform. The common language runtime takes good care of your code. It manages memory for you, provides interop services for you, and makes your code execute safely and securely.

The runtime doesn't provide native data access functionality, but .NET ships with a pair of managed database providers. The managed providers are represented by several classes that are members of the common runtime class library. The data access classes are known collectively as ADO.NET.

The ADO.NET *DataReader* class enables you to retrieve a forward-only and read-only stream of data from a database. The *DataSet* class provides an in-memory copy of data retrieved from a database. You can think of a *DataSet* object as a disconnected recordset in ADO. ADO.NET currently has no provision for server-side cursors. Some applications don't need this capability. Any applications that require server-side cursors can use the classic ADO recordset through the COM interop layer. The samples accompanying Visual Studio .NET include an ADO interop example. The example is included in the Microsoft Visual Studio .NET \FrameworkSDK\Samples\Technologies\Interop\Basic\ASPXToADO directory.

.NET Managed Providers

As far as ADO.NET is concerned, there are basically two kinds of databases: Microsoft SQL Server databases and all other databases that implement OLEDB. The SQL Server managed provider classes run within the common language runtime; the OLEDB managed provider uses native OLEDB and the COM interop layer to establish a connection to a data store.

ADO.NET includes the following basic functionality for working with databases: creating datasets, connecting to databases, issuing commands, reading data streams, and using data adapters to exchange data between a data source and a dataset. ADO.NET divides the functionality into interfaces and implementations. That is, there's a single connection interface, a single command interface, and a single data adapter interface. However, ADO.NET furnishes separate implementations of each of these interfaces. The managed data providers are generally divided into the *System::Data::SqlClient* namespace and the *System::Data::OleDb* namespace. Table 35-1 shows the ADO.NET interfaces and their separate implementations.

Table 35-1 ADO.NET Interfaces and Their Implementations

Interface	SQL Server Implementation	OLEDB Implementation
IDbConnection	*SqlConnection*	*OleDbConnection*
IDataAdapter	*SqlDataAdapter*	*OleDbDataAdapter*
IDbCommand	*SqlCommand*	*OleDbCommand*
IDataReader	*SqlDataReader*	*OleDbDataReader*
IDataRecord	*SqlDataRecord*	*OleDbDataRecord*
IDataParameter	*SqlDataParameter*	*OleDbDataParameter*

Figure 35-1 shows the relationship between the ADO.NET managed providers, SQL Server, OLEDB providers, and COM.

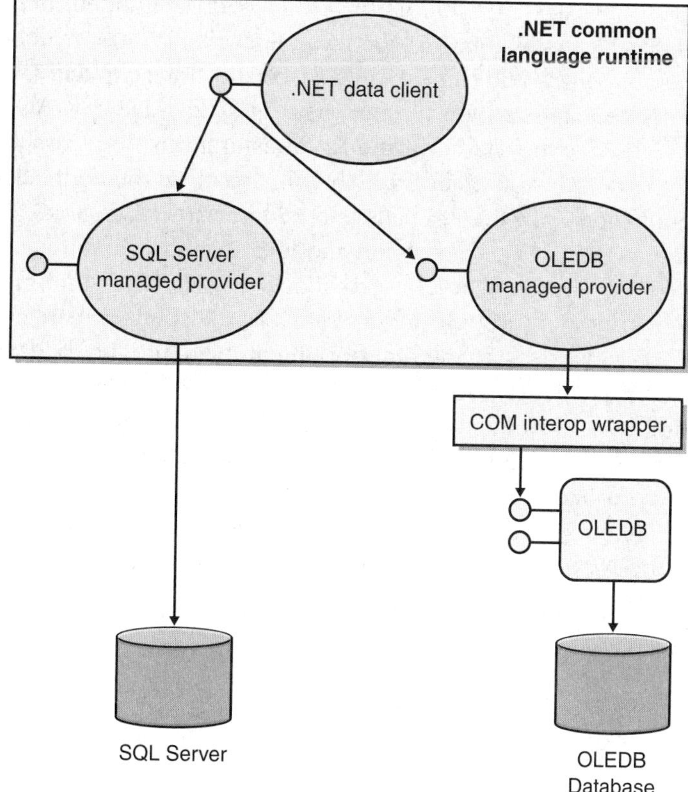

Figure 35-1 The relationship between the ADO.NET managed providers, SQL Server, OLEDB providers, and COM.

Working with the Providers

Let's take a look at what it takes to connect to a database and execute some code using ADO.NET and managed C++. The general operating mode for ADO.NET is to connect to a database, issue a command, and then examine the results. We'll examine connecting to a database first.

Connecting to the Database

The *SqlConnection* class and the *OleDbConnection* class implement *IDbConnection*, which provides methods for opening a database connection and for starting local transactions programmatically.

You saw in Chapter 31 that garbage collection is nondeterministic, which means you don't know when (or even if) a memory allocation will be collected. For that reason, you should close ADO.NET connections explicitly when they're no longer needed (rather then closing them in a destructor somewhere). *IDb-Connection::Close* is the method for accomplishing this task. You can also call *Dispose* on the connection object, which will also close the connection. Usually the *Open* and *Close* (or *Dispose*) calls live within a try/catch block.

The managed providers support modern database features such as connection pooling. The OLEDB data provider uses OLEDB's built-in connection pooling, which works through the classic COM+ dispenser manager. The SQL Server data provider uses an internal pooling architecture that behaves similarly to COM+ services' object-pooling feature.

The following listing shows a simple console program that connects to a database and issues a simple selection command. This example assumes that SQL Server is installed on the machine and that a database named *CompanyDB* is available. The example also assumes that there's a table named *Employees* containing the *Name* and *DeptID* columns within the database.

```
// This is the main project file for VC++ application project
// generated using an Application Wizard.

#include "stdafx.h"

#using <mscorlib.dll>
#using <system.dll>
#using <system.data.dll>
#include <tchar.h>

using namespace System;
using namespace System::Data;
using namespace System::Data::SqlClient;
using namespace System::ComponentModel;

// This is the entry point for this application
int _tmain(void)
{
    // Create a connection object
    SqlConnection* conn;
    conn = new SqlConnection
        (S"server=localhost;uid=sa;pwd=;database=CompanyDB");

    SqlCommand* command;
    command = new SqlCommand("select * from Employees", conn);
    IDataReader* rdr;
```

```
    try
    {
        conn->Open();
        rdr = command->ExecuteReader();

        while(rdr->Read())
        {
            Console::Write("Name: ");
            Console::Write(rdr->get_Item("Name"));
            Console::Write("Dept: ");
            Console::WriteLine(rdr->get_Item("DeptID"));
        }
    }
    catch (Exception* e)
    {
        System::Console::WriteLine(e->ToString());
    }
    __finally
    {
        conn->Dispose();
    }
    return 0;
}
```

Notice that the code creates an instance of the *SqlConnection* class and an instance of the *SqlCommand* class. Also notice that the code initializes the instance of the *SqlCommand* class with the connection object and a simple selection statement.

As long as the connection object and the command object work correctly, you can create a data reader by calling *SqlCommand::ExecuteReader*. The data reader reads through each row. You can use the data reader's *get_Item* method to find a value within a specific column for that row. (We'll discuss data readers in detail later in this chapter.)

The connection is opened and the command is executed within a try block to catch any errors. Errors that can occur include:

- Invalid connection string (wrong account or password or a bad database name)
- Wrong table name
- Wrong column names

If any errors occur during the process of connecting to the database and executing the query, ADO.NET will throw an exception. In the previous listing, the exception information is simply printed to the screen.

Issuing Commands

Connecting to a database and issuing a simple query is pretty straightforward. However, in real-world situations, collecting data is often much more involved. The command classes (*SqlCommand* and *OleDbCommand*) included with the managed providers are fairly sophisticated. You can use them to submit any valid SQL action statement or query to the database (or you can use another command language supported by an OLEDB provider).

SqlCommand and *OleDbCommand* both implement the *IDbCommand* interface. You might specify the command when you construct the command object, or you might set the command by using the *CommandText* property. The command object is associated with a specific connection object (as shown in the previous listing). The following listing shows how to initialize an *SqlCommand* from an existing connection. Notice that this approach emphasizes programming to the interfaces rather than to the actual classes.

```
IDbConnection* conn = dynamic_cast<IDbConnection*>(new SqlConnection(
    "server=localhost;uid=sa;pwd=;database=CompanyDB"));
IDbCommand* cmd2 = new SqlCommand(
    "select * from Depts",
    dynamic_cast<SqlConnection*>(conn));
```

You saw earlier that *IDbCommand::ExecuteReader* submits the command and retrieves results through a *DataReader* class. *IDbCommand* also includes a method named *ExecuteNonQuery* that returns only the number of rows affected.

When applying commands to a command object, an application can set the *CommandText* property to a SQL command (or perhaps some other command language supported by an OLEDB database) or a stored procedure name. The *CommandType* property indicates the meaning of *CommandText*—whether it's a plain-text command or a stored procedure.

Using Stored Procedures with a Command

You can use a command object to call stored procedures to perform database manipulation. *SqlCommand* and *OleDbComnand* implement *IDbCommand* and support parameterized statements through the *Parameters* property. The *SqlParameter* and the *OleDbParameter* classes encapsulate the parameter functionality necessary for stored procedures. Both the *OleDbCommand* and the *SqlCommand* include collections of parameters—*OleDbParameterCollection* and *SqlParameterCollection*, respectively. The following listing shows how to open an *SqlConnection* and associate it with an *SqlCommand* that executes a parameterized stored procedure. This listing expects a database named *CompanyDB* to be available, which includes a stored procedure named *getByDeptID* that takes a single string parameter (designating the department ID).

```
void RunStoredProc()
{
    // Execute a stored procedure
    SqlConnection* conn = new SqlConnection(
        "server=localhost;uid=sa;pwd=;database=CompanyDB");
    SqlCommand* cmd = new SqlCommand("getByDeptID", conn);
    IDataReader* reader;

    try
    {
        conn->Open();
        cmd->Parameters->Add(
            new SqlParameter("@dept_id", SqlDbType::VarChar, 11));
        cmd->Parameters->get_Item("@dept_id")->Value = S"Engineering";

        cmd->CommandType = CommandType::StoredProcedure;
        reader = cmd->ExecuteReader();

        // Use the reader to examine result set
    }

    catch(Exception* e)
    {
        Console::WriteLine(e->ToString());
    }
     __finally
    {
        conn->Dispose();
    }

}
```

As you set up parameters, you can designate the direction of each parameter to be *input*, *output*, *inout*, or *return*. Of course, the parameters you set up programmatically will need to match the format of the parameters in the actual stored procedure (although strict type checking for the parameters isn't enforced).

Using Data Readers to Retrieve Data

You can use data readers to retrieve read-only, forward-only data streams. As mentioned, after you create a command object, you can call *IDbCommand::ExecuteReader* to create a data reader for retrieving rows from a data source. Most SQL commands and stored procedures produce rectangular results. For example, when you issue *Select * from Employees*, you're asking to see everything within the Employees table. The result set you get back is a collection of homogenous rows that you can examine with an implementation of *IDataReader*. Columns within rows can contain only primitive data types, in accordance with the relational model.

Earlier, you saw an example of using a data reader to parse through a result set. The example got only a single result set back. The *IDataReader* implementations in ADO.NET (*SqlDataReader* and *OleDbDataReader*) provide forward-reading access to the result set. As you read through the result set using the reader, the reader always looks at the current row. Each time you call *Read* on a reader, you get a new row. *Read* returns false when there are no more rows to be read. The data readers in ADO.NET support multiple result sets. *IDataReader::NextResult* advances the data reader to the next result set. Here's an example of getting multiple result sets back from a single query:

```
void MultipleResultSets()
{
    SqlConnection* conn = new SqlConnection(
        "server=localhost;uid=sa;pwd=;database=CompanyDB");
    SqlCommand* cmd = new SqlCommand(
        "select * from Employees;select * from Depts", conn);
    IDataReader* rdr;

    try
    {
        conn->Open();
        rdr = cmd->ExecuteReader();

        bool more = true;
        while (more)
        {
            while (rdr->Read())
            {
                Console::Write("Column 0 = ");
                // Get the first column
                Console::WriteLine(rdr->get_Item(0));
                // Get the second column
                Console::Write("Column 1 = ");
                Console::WriteLine(rdr->get_Item(1));
            }
            Console::WriteLine("End of result set");
            more = rdr->NextResult();
        }
    }
    catch(Exception* e)
    {
```

```
            e->ToString();
        }
        __finally
        {
            conn->Dispose();
        }
    }
```

Error Handling

The data access code you've seen so far has been wrapped in try/catch blocks. For simple error handling, this is often sufficient. General errors will be caught by the generic exception class. However, sometimes databases return additional error information or even a collection of errors. To accommodate multiple errors, both SQL Server and OLEDB managed data providers subclass their own exception class, which can return a collection of errors.

The OLEDB data provider's *OleDbException* exposes an *Errors* collection that is similar to the ADO's *Errors* collection (which can be accessed through the OLEDB's *IErrorRecord* interface). Each error contains an error message, the provider's native error, and an optional *SQLState*. The *OleDbException* is derived from *ExternalException*.

The SQL Server data provider exposes an *SqlException* derived from *SystemException*. It encapsulates a *SqlErrorCollection* collection that exposes a superset of ADO's error information. This includes SQL Server–specific error information. *SqlError* is created by the SQL Server provider when an error occurs. It contains the SQL Server instance, the error severity, and an optional stored procedure name and line number.

One problem with classic ADO is that severe errors (showstoppers) and SQL warning messages (not showstoppers) are combined in the *Errors* collection. For example, one of these messages might indicate that a database language has changed. The combination might affect your result set, but it won't stop the query from running. The ADO.NET architecture exposes warnings as events, not as showstopping errors. You can watch the warnings or ignore them.

ADO.NET Datasets

A forward-reading stream can be useful for collecting moderate amounts of data, but it's not always the best data access method—especially in high-volume situations or when you need random access to the contents of a database. ADO.NET's dataset answers these needs. The ADO.NET *DataSet* class manages a collection of in-memory tables that represent a result set. The dataset is similar to the classic ADO disconnected recordset, but provides more functionality.

The dataset basically represents a snapshot of a result set (or possibly several result sets). A dataset is not associated with a specific physical database. It contains one or more instances of the *DataTable* class, and each table can be from a different data source. The dataset can acquire data tables from several sources, including physical databases and XML files. You can also create and fill data tables and data sets programmatically, as you'll see in the following section. Figure 35-2 shows the architecture of the ADO.NET *DataSet*.

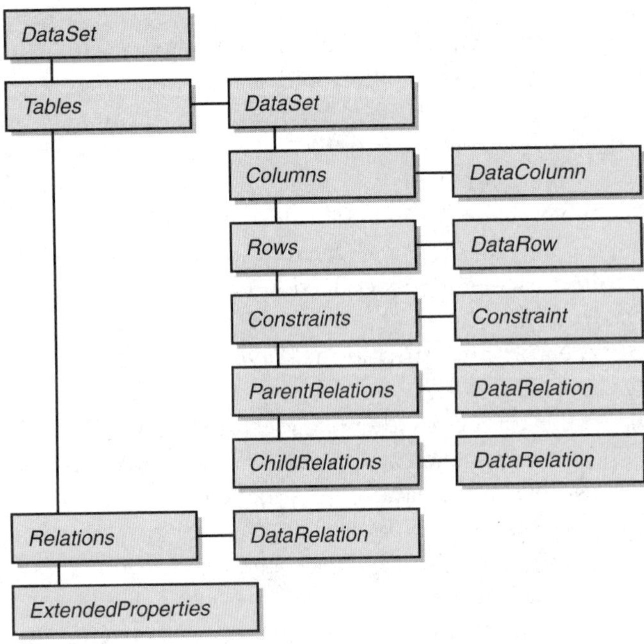

Figure 35-2 The architecture of the ADO.NET *DataSet*.

To access a dataset's tables, columns, and rows, you use a fairly regular collection syntax involving iterative calls to the *get_Item* method of the *DataTableCollection*, the *DataColumnCollection*, and the *DataRowCollection*. You can access any part of a dataset either by name or by ordinal.

Using the Data Adapter to Populate Datasets

ADO.NET includes classes that implement *IDataAdapter*, which is useful for loading datasets. The data adapter classes encapsulate a connection object and a set of command objects and take on the task of connecting to the database and constructing a dataset for you. The following listing shows how to use the *SqlDataAdapter* to fill a dataset.

```
void UseDataAdapter()
{
    SqlDataAdapter* da = new SqlDataAdapter(
        "select * from Employees",
        "server=localhost;uid=sa;database=CompanyDB");
    DataSet* ds = new DataSet();
    da->Fill(ds, "Employees");
}
```

This listing assumes that a database named *CompanyDB* is available through SQL Server and that there's a table named Employees. The *SqlDataAdapter* will select every row and every column from the Employees table and construct a dataset. The dataset will include a single table named Employees. Once the dataset has been loaded, you can easily enumerate the tables within the dataset and examine the contents of each row, as shown in the following listing:

```
void EnumDataSet(DataSet* ds)
{
    Console::WriteLine("Enumerating Tables in DataSet:");
    for(int i = 0; i < ds->Tables->Count; i++)
    {
        Console::Write("Table Name: ");
        DataTable* dt = ds->Tables->get_Item(i);
        Console::WriteLine(dt->TableName);

        for(int j = 0; j < dt->Rows->Count; j++)
        {
            DataRow* dr = dt->Rows->get_Item(j);
            Console::Write("Column 1: ");
            Console::Write(dr->get_Item(0)->ToString());
            Console::Write("  Column 2: ");
            Console::WriteLine(dr->get_Item(1)->ToString());
        }
    }
}
```

Data adapters aren't the only way to construct datasets. You can also create datasets in memory.

Creating In-Memory Datasets

Most of the data your application will work with probably live in a database somewhere, but sometimes it's useful to cook up datasets on the fly. For example, perhaps you have a small test scenario or you don't have a database available. Datasets are simply in-memory instances of table, row, and column collections, and you can construct them manually. The following listing shows how to create an in-memory dataset manually without going out to a database:

```
DataSet* ManufactureDataSet()
{
    DataSet* ds;
    ds = new DataSet();
    DataTable* dt = new DataTable();

    String* strType = S"Name";
    Int32 n = 0;
    __box Int32* int32Type = __box(n);

    dt->Columns->Add("Name", strType->GetType());
    dt->Columns->Add("DeptID", int32Type->GetType());

    ds->Tables->Add(dt);

    DataRow* dr = dt->NewRow();
    dr->set_Item(0, S"George Shepherd");
    n = 132;
    int32Type = __box(n);
    dr->set_Item(1, int32Type);
    dt->Rows->Add(dr);

    dr = dt->NewRow();
    dr->set_Item(0, S"Helge Hoeing");
    n = 132;
    int32Type = __box(n);
    dr->set_Item(1, int32Type);
    dt->Rows->Add(dr);

    dr = dt->NewRow();
    dr->set_Item(0, S"Lisa Jacobson");
    n = 115;
    int32Type = __box(n);
    dr->set_Item(1, int32Type);
    dt->Rows->Add(dr);

    dr = dt->NewRow();
    dr->set_Item(0, S"Brian Burk");
    n = 115;
    int32Type = __box(n);
    dr->set_Item(1, int32Type);
    dt->Rows->Add(dr);

    dr = dt->NewRow();
    dr->set_Item(0, S"Michael Allen");
    n = 115;
```

```
    int32Type = __box(n);
    dr->set_Item(1, int32Type);
    dt->Rows->Add(dr);

    return ds;
}
```

The code constructs a new dataset in the normal fashion. At this point, the dataset is empty. Datasets are collections of data tables, and the first thing the dataset needs is to have a table added to it. The data table is constructed in the normal fashion and added to the dataset's table collection. Once the table is added to the dataset, the code adds two columns to the table. These data columns are constructed with a column name and a data type. Managed C++ is finicky about how *GetType* is called (even though it is a static method). The previous code listing works around the problem by creating actual instances of the types that are supposed to make up the column. The rest of the code adds several rows to the table in the dataset.

Once the dataset has been constructed, you can march through its contents—just as you would any other dataset, as shown in the following listing:

```
void UseDataSet()
{
    DataSet* ds = ManufactureDataSet();

    Console::WriteLine("Enumerating Tables in DataSet:");
    for(int i = 0; i < ds->Tables->Count; i++)
    {
        Console::Write("Table Name: ");
        DataTable* dt = ds->Tables->get_Item(i);
        Console::WriteLine(dt->TableName);

        for(int j = 0; j < dt->Rows->Count; j++)
        {
            DataRow* dr = dt->Rows->get_Item(j);
            Console::Write("Column 1: ");
            Console::Write(dr->get_Item(0)->ToString());
            Console::Write("  Column 2: ");
            Console::WriteLine(dr->get_Item(1)->ToString());
        }
    }

}
```

Writing XML from Datasets

Fetching data from a database is one of the most common operations within modern applications, but at times you'll need to export your data for consumption by other applications. In the late 1980s and the early 1990s, the way to import and export data was through comma-delimited files. Comma-delimited files expressed their contents as lines of text whose embedded elements were separated by commas.

But soon comma-delimited files were out and XML files were in. XML has become the standard for expressing data in an interoperable format. ADO.NET's dataset marshals (serializes) as well-formed XML files and optionally as XML schema. To export a dataset's contents as XML, you simply call the *DataSet*'s *WriteXML* method, as shown in the following listing:

```
void UseDataSet()
{
    DataSet* ds = ManufactureDataSet();

    ds->WriteXml(S"C:\\CompanyDB.xml", XmlWriteMode::IgnoreSchema);
    ds->WriteXmlSchema(S"C:\\CompanyDB.xsd");
}
```

Dumping a dataset as XML yields the following XML file, given the in-memory dataset constructed in the previous section:

```
<?xml version="1.0" standalone="yes"?>
<NewDataSet>
    <Table1>
        <Name>George Shepherd</Name>
        <DeptID>132</DeptID>
    </Table1>
    <Table1>
        <Name>Helge Hoeing</Name>
        <DeptID>132</DeptID>
    </Table1>
    <Table1>
        <Name>Lisa Jacobson</Name>
        <DeptID>115</DeptID>
    </Table1>
    <Table1>
        <Name>Brian Burk</Name>
        <DeptID>115</DeptID>
    </Table1>
    <Table1>
        <Name>Michael Allen</Name>
        <DeptID>115</DeptID>
    </Table1>
</NewDataSet>
```

In addition to writing out XML files, the ADO.NET *DataSet* also serializes the schema so you (or some data consumer) can understand what types the tables in the dataset are composed of.

```
<?xml version="1.0" standalone="yes"?>
<xs:schema id="NewDataSet" xmlns=""
    xmlns:xs="http://www.w3.org/2001/XMLSchema"
    xmlns:msdata="urn:schemas-microsoft-com:xml-msdata">
    <xs:element name="NewDataSet" msdata:IsDataSet="true">
        <xs:complexType>
            <xs:choice maxOccurs="unbounded">
                <xs:element name="Table1">
                    <xs:complexType>
                        <xs:sequence>
                            <xs:element name="Name"
                                type="xs:string" minOccurs="0" />
                            <xs:element name="DeptID"
                                type="xs:int" minOccurs="0" />
                        </xs:sequence>
                    </xs:complexType>
                </xs:element>
            </xs:choice>
        </xs:complexType>
    </xs:element>
</xs:schema>
```

We've only scratched the surface of ADO.NET in this chapter. ADO.NET offers tremendous data access capabilities for any application written for the .NET platform. For a complete discussion of ADO.NET, see *Microsoft ADO.NET (Core Reference)* by David Sceppa (Microsoft Press, 2002).

Appendix A

Message Map Functions in the MFC Library

MFC now uses a *static_cast* within the message map macros to improve type checking. The type checking enforces return and parameter types. The stricter type checking produces error messages when potentially unsafe message handlers are used. For example, here's the *ON_COMMAND* macro:

```
#define ON_COMMAND(id, memberFxn) \
    { WM_COMMAND, CN_COMMAND, (WORD)id, (WORD)id, AfxSigCmd_v, \
       static_cast<AFX_PMSG> (memberFxn) }
```

The following tables list the message map functions in the MFC library, including the handlers for *WM_COMMAND* messages, child window notification messages, window notification messages, and user-defined message codes.

Handlers for *WM_COMMAND* Messages

Map Entry	Function Prototype
ON_COMMAND (<id>, <memberFxn>)	*afx_msg void memberFxn();*
ON_COMMAND_EX (<id>, <memberFxn>)	*afx_msg BOOL memberFxn(UINT);*
ON_COMMAND_EX_RANGE (<id>,<idLast>, <memberFxn>)	*afx_msg BOOL memberFxn(UINT);*
ON_COMMAND_RANGE (<id>, <idLast>, <memberFxn>)	*afx_msg void memberFxn(UINT);*
ON_UPDATE_COMMAND_UI (<id>, <memberFxn>)	*afx_msg void memberFxn(CCmdUI*);*

(continued)

Handlers for *WM_COMMAND* Messages

Map Entry	Function Prototype
ON_UPDATE_COMMAND_UI_RANGE (<id>, <idLast>, <memberFxn>)	afx_msg void memberFxn(CCmdUI*);
ON_UPDATE_COMMAND_UI_REFLECT (<memberFxn>)	afx_msg void memberFxn(CCmdUI*);

Handlers for Child Window Notification Messages

Map Entry	Function Prototype
Generic Control Notification Codes	
ON_CONTROL(<wNotifyCode>, <id>, <memberFxn>)	afx_msg void memberFxn();
ON_CONTROL_RANGE(<wNotifyCode>, <id>, <idLast>, <memberFxn>)	afx_msg void memberFxn(UINT);
ON_CONTROL_REFLECT(<wNotifyCode>, <memberFxn>)	afx_msg void memberFxn();
ON_CONTROL_REFLECT_EX (<wNotifyCode>, <memberFxn>)	afx_msg BOOL memberFxn();
ON_NOTIFY(<wNotifyCode>, <id>, <memberFxn>)	afx_msg void memberFxn(NMHDR*, LRESULT*);
ON_NOTIFY_EX(<wNotifyCode>, <id>, <memberFxn>)	afx_msg BOOL memberFxn(UINT, NMHDR*, LRESULT*);
ON_NOTIFY_EX_RANGE(<wNotifyCode>, <id>, <idLast>, <memberFxn>)	afx_msg BOOL memberFxn(UINT, NMHDR*, LRESULT*);
ON_NOTIFY_RANGE(<wNotifyCode>, <id>, <idLast>, <memberFxn>)	afx_msg void memberFxn(UINT, NMHDR*, LRESULT*);
ON_NOTIFY_REFLECT(<wNotifyCode>, <memberFxn>)	afx_msg void memberFxn(NMHDR*, LRESULT*);
ON_NOTIFY_REFLECT_EX(<wNotifyCode>, <memberFxn>)	afx_msg BOOL memberFxn(NMHDR*, LRESULT*);
User Button Notification Codes	
ON_BN_CLICKED(<id>, <memberFxn>)	afx_msg void memberFxn();
ON_BN_DOUBLECLICKED(<id>, <memberFxn>)	afx_msg void memberFxn();
ON_BN_KILLFOCUS(<id>, <memberFxn>)	afx_msg void memberFxn();
ON_BN_SETFOCUS(<id>, <memberFxn>)	afx_msg void memberFxn();

Handlers for Child Window Notification Messages

Map Entry	Function Prototype
Combo Box Notification Codes	
ON_CBN_CLOSEUP(<id>, <memberFxn>)	*afx_msg void memberFxn();*
ON_CBN_DBLCLK(<id>, <memberFxn>)	*afx_msg void memberFxn();*
ON_CBN_DROPDOWN(<id>, <memberFxn>)	*afx_msg void memberFxn();*
ON_CBN_EDITCHANGE(<id>, <memberFxn>)	*afx_msg void memberFxn();*
ON_CBN_EDITUPDATE(<id>, <memberFxn>)	*afx_msg void memberFxn();*
ON_CBN_ERRSPACE(<id>, <memberFxn>)	*afx_msg void memberFxn();*
ON_CBN_KILLFOCUS(<id>, <memberFxn>)	*afx_msg void memberFxn();*
ON_CBN_SELCHANGE(<id>, <memberFxn>)	*afx_msg void memberFxn();*
ON_CBN_SELENDCANCEL(<id>, <memberFxn>)	*afx_msg void memberFxn();*
ON_CBN_SELENDOK(<id>, <memberFxn>)	*afx_msg void memberFxn();*
ON_CBN_SETFOCUS(<id>, <memberFxn>)	*afx_msg void memberFxn();*
Check List Box Notification Codes	
ON_CLBN_CHKCHANGE(<id>, <memberFxn>)	*afx_msg void memberFxn();*
Edit Control Notification Codes	
ON_EN_CHANGE(<id>, <memberFxn>)	*afx_msg void memberFxn();*
ON_EN_ERRSPACE(<id>, <memberFxn>)	*afx_msg void memberFxn();*
ON_EN_HSCROLL(<id>, <memberFxn>)	*afx_msg void memberFxn();*
ON_EN_KILLFOCUS(<id>, <memberFxn>)	*afx_msg void memberFxn();*
ON_EN_MAXTEXT(<id>, <memberFxn>)	*afx_msg void memberFxn();*
ON_EN_SETFOCUS(<id>, <memberFxn>)	*afx_msg void memberFxn();*
ON_EN_UPDATE(<id>, <memberFxn>)	*afx_msg void memberFxn();*
ON_EN_VSCROLL(<id>, <memberFxn>)	*afx_msg void memberFxn();*
List Box Notification Codes	
ON_LBN_DBLCLK(<id>, <memberFxn>)	*afx_msg void memberFxn();*
ON_LBN_ERRSPACE(<id>, <memberFxn>)	*afx_msg void memberFxn();*
ON_LBN_KILLFOCUS(<id>, <memberFxn>)	*afx_msg void memberFxn();*
ON_LBN_SELCANCEL(<id>, <memberFxn>)	*afx_msg void memberFxn();*
ON_LBN_SELCHANGE(<id>, <memberFxn>)	*afx_msg void memberFxn();*
ON_LBN_SETFOCUS(<id>, <memberFxn>)	*afx_msg void memberFxn();*

(continued)

Handlers for Child Window Notification Messages

Map Entry	Function Prototype
Static Control Notification Codes	
ON_STN_CLICKED(<id>, <memberFxn>)	*afx_msg void memberFxn();*
ON_STN_DBLCLK(<id>, <memberFxn>)	*afx_msg void memberFxn();*
ON_STN_DISABLE(<id>, <memberFxn>)	*afx_msg void memberFxn();*
ON_STN_ENABLE(<id>, <memberFxn>)	*afx_msg void memberFxn();*

Handlers for Window Notification Messages

Map Entry	Function Prototype
ON_WM_ACTIVATE()	*afx_msg void OnActivate(UINT, CWnd*, BOOL);*
ON_WM_ACTIVATEAPP()	*afx_msg void OnActivateApp(BOOL, HTASK);*
ON_WM_ASKCBFORMATNAME()	*afx_msg void OnAskCbFormatName(UINT, LPTSTR);*
ON_WM_CANCELMODE()	*afx_msg void OnCancelMode();*
ON_WM_CAPTURECHANGED()	*afx_msg void OnCaptureChanged(CWnd*);*
ON_WM_CHANGECBCHAIN()	*afx_msg void OnChangeCbChain(HWND, HWND);*
ON_WM_CHAR()	*afx_msg void OnChar(UINT, UINT, UINT);*
ON_WM_CHARTOITEM()	*afx_msg int OnCharToItem(UINT, CListBox*, UINT);*
ON_WM_CHARTOITEM_REFLECT()	*afx_msg int CharToItem(UINT, UINT);*
ON_WM_CHILDACTIVATE()	*afx_msg void OnChildActivate();*
ON_WM_CLOSE()	*afx_msg void OnClose();*
ON_WM_COMPACTING()	*afx_msg void OnCompacting(UINT);*
ON_WM_COMPAREITEM()	*afx_msg int OnCompareItem(int, LPCOMPAREITEMSTRUCT);*
ON_WM_COMPAREITEM_REFLECT()	*afx_msg int CompareItem (LPCOMPAREITEM STRUCT);*
ON_WM_CONTEXTMENU()	*afx_msg void OnContextMenu(CWnd*, CPoint);*
ON_WM_COPYDATA()	*afx_msg BOOL OnCopyData(CWnd*, COPYDATASTRUCT*);*
ON_WM_CREATE()	*afx_msg int OnCreate(LPCREATESTRUCT);*
ON_WM_CTLCOLOR()	*afx_msg HBRUSH OnCtlColor(CDC*, CWnd*, UINT);*
ON_WM_CTLCOLOR_REFLECT()	*afx_msg HBRUSH CtlColor(CDC*, UINT);*
ON_WM_DEADCHAR()	*afx_msg void OnDeadChar(UINT, UINT, UINT);*

Handlers for Window Notification Messages

Map Entry	Function Prototype
ON_WM_DELETEITEM()	*afx_msg void OnDeleteItem(int, LPDELETEITEMSTRUCT);*
ON_WM_DELETEITEM_REFLECT()	*afx_msg void DeleteItem (LPDELETEITEMSTRUCT);*
ON_WM_DESTROY()	*afx_msg void OnDestroy();*
ON_WM_DESTROYCLIPBOARD()	*afx_msg void OnDestroyClipboard();*
ON_WM_DEVICECHANGE()	*afx_msg BOOL OnDeviceChange(UINT, DWORD);*
ON_WM_DEVMODECHANGE()	*afx_msg void OnDevModeChange(LPTSTR);*
ON_WM_DRAWCLIPBOARD()	*afx_msg void OnDrawClipboard();*
ON_WM_DRAWITEM()	*afx_msg void OnDrawItem(int, LPDRAWITEMSTRUCT);*
ON_WM_DRAWITEM_REFLECT()	*afx_msg void DrawItem (LPDRAWITEMSTRUCT);*
ON_WM_DROPFILES()	*afx_msg void OnDropFiles(HDROP);*
ON_WM_ENABLE()	*afx_msg void OnEnable(BOOL);*
ON_WM_ENDSESSION()	*afx_msg void OnEndSession(BOOL);*
ON_WM_ENTERIDLE()	*afx_msg void OnEnterIdle(UINT, CWnd*);*
ON_WM_ENTERMENULOOP()	*afx_msg void OnEnterMenuLoop(BOOL);*
ON_WM_ERASEBKGND()	*afx_msg BOOL OnEraseBkgnd(CDC*);*
ON_WM_EXITMENULOOP()	*afx_msg void OnExitMenuLoop(BOOL);*
ON_WM_FONTCHANGE()	*afx_msg void OnFontChange();*
ON_WM_GETDLGCODE()	*afx_msg UINT OnGetDlgCode();*
ON_WM_GETMINMAXINFO()	*afx_msg void OnGetMinMaxInfo (MINMAXINFO*);*
ON_WM_HELPINFO()	*afx_msg BOOL OnHelpInfo(HELPINFO*);*
ON_WM_HSCROLL()	*afx_msg void OnHScroll(UINT, UINT, CScrollBar*);*
ON_WM_HSCROLL_REFLECT()	*afx_msg void HScroll(UINT, UINT);*
ON_WM_HSCROLLCLIPBOARD()	*afx_msg void OnHScrollClipboard(CWnd*, UINT, UINT);*
ON_WM_ICONERASEBKGND()	*afx_msg void OnIconEraseBkgnd(CDC*);*
ON_WM_INITMENU()	*afx_msg void OnInitMenu(CMenu*);*
ON_WM_INITMENUPOPUP()	*afx_msg void OnInitMenuPopup(CMenu*, UINT, BOOL);*
ON_WM_KEYDOWN()	*afx_msg void OnKeyDown(UINT, UINT, UINT);*
ON_WM_KEYUP()	*afx_msg void OnKeyUp(UINT, UINT, UINT);*
ON_WM_KILLFOCUS()	*afx_msg void OnKillFocus(CWnd*);*

(continued)

Handlers for Window Notification Messages

Map Entry	Function Prototype
ON_WM_LBUTTONDBLCLK()	*afx_msg void OnLButtonDblClk(UINT, CPoint);*
ON_WM_LBUTTONDOWN()	*afx_msg void OnLButtonDown(UINT, CPoint);*
ON_WM_LBUTTONUP()	*afx_msg void OnLButtonUp(UINT, CPoint);*
ON_WM_MBUTTONDBLCLK()	*afx_msg void OnMButtonDblClk(UINT, CPoint);*
ON_WM_MBUTTONDOWN()	*afx_msg void OnMButtonDown(UINT, CPoint);*
ON_WM_MBUTTONUP()	*afx_msg void OnMButtonUp(UINT, CPoint);*
ON_WM_MDIACTIVATE()	*afx_msg void OnMDIActivate(BOOL, CWnd*, CWnd*);*
ON_WM_MEASUREITEM()	*afx_msg void OnMeasureItem(int, LPMEASUREITEMSTRUCT);*
ON_WM_MEASUREITEM_REFLECT()	*afx_msg void MeasureItem (LPMEASUREITEMSTRUCT);*
ON_WM_MENUCHAR()	*afx_msg LRESULT OnMenuChar(UINT, UINT, CMenu*);*
ON_WM_MENUSELECT()	*afx_msg void OnMenuSelect(UINT, UINT, HMENU);*
ON_WM_MOUSEACTIVATE()	*afx_msg int OnMouseActivate(CWnd*, UINT, UINT);*
ON_WM_MOUSEMOVE()	*afx_msg void OnMouseMove(UINT, CPoint);*
ON_WM_MOUSEWHEEL()	*afx_msg BOOL OnMouseWheel(UINT, short, CPoint);*
ON_WM_MOVE()	*afx_msg void OnMove(int, int);*
ON_WM_MOVING()	*afx_msg void OnMoving(UINT, LPRECT);*
ON_WM_NCACTIVATE()	*afx_msg BOOL OnNcActivate(BOOL);*
ON_WM_NCCALCSIZE()	*afx_msg void OnNcCalcSize(BOOL, NCCALCSIZE_PARAMS*);*
ON_WM_NCCREATE()	*afx_msg BOOL OnNcCreate (LPCREATESTRUCT);*
ON_WM_NCDESTROY()	*afx_msg void OnNcDestroy();*
ON_WM_NCHITTEST()	*afx_msg UINT OnNcHitTest(CPoint);*
ON_WM_NCLBUTTONDBLCLK()	*afx_msg void OnNcLButtonDblClk(UINT, CPoint);*
ON_WM_NCLBUTTONDOWN()	*afx_msg void OnNcLButtonDown(UINT, CPoint);*
ON_WM_NCLBUTTONUP()	*afx_msg void OnNcLButtonUp(UINT, CPoint);*
ON_WM_NCMBUTTONDBLCLK()	*afx_msg void OnNcMButtonDblClk(UINT, CPoint);*
ON_WM_NCMBUTTONDOWN()	*afx_msg void OnNcMButtonDown(UINT, CPoint);*
ON_WM_NCMBUTTONUP()	*afx_msg void OnNcMButtonUp(UINT, CPoint);*
ON_WM_NCMOUSEMOVE()	*afx_msg void OnNcMouseMove(UINT, CPoint);*

Handlers for Window Notification Messages

Map Entry	Function Prototype
ON_WM_NCPAINT()	*afx_msg void OnNcPaint();*
ON_WM_NCRBUTTONDBLCLK()	*afx_msg void OnNcRButtonDblClk(UINT, CPoint);*
ON_WM_NCRBUTTONDOWN()	*afx_msg void OnNcRButtonDown(UINT, CPoint);*
ON_WM_NCRBUTTONUP()	*afx_msg void OnNcRButtonUp(UINT, CPoint);*
ON_WM_PAINT()	*afx_msg void OnPaint();*
ON_WM_PAINTCLIPBOARD()	*afx_msg void OnPaintClipboard(CWnd*, HGLOBAL);*
ON_WM_PALETTECHANGED()	*afx_msg void OnPaletteChanged(CWnd*);*
ON_WM_PALETTEISCHANGING()	*afx_msg void OnPaletteIsChanging(CWnd*);*
ON_WM_PARENTNOTIFY()	*afx_msg void OnParentNotify(UINT, LPARAM);*
ON_WM_PARENTNOTIFY_REFLECT()	*afx_msg void ParentNotify(UINT, LPARAM);*
ON_WM_QUERYDRAGICON()	*afx_msg HCURSOR OnQueryDragIcon();*
ON_WM_QUERYENDSESSION()	*afx_msg BOOL OnQueryEndSession();*
ON_WM_QUERYNEWPALETTE()	*afx_msg BOOL OnQueryNewPalette();*
ON_WM_QUERYOPEN()	*afx_msg BOOL OnQueryOpen();*
ON_WM_RBUTTONDBLCLK()	*afx_msg void OnRButtonDblClk(UINT, CPoint);*
ON_WM_RBUTTONDOWN()	*afx_msg void OnRButtonDown(UINT, CPoint);*
ON_WM_RBUTTONUP()	*afx_msg void OnRButtonUp(UINT, CPoint);*
ON_WM_RENDERALLFORMATS()	*afx_msg void OnRenderAllFormats();*
ON_WM_RENDERFORMAT()	*afx_msg void OnRenderFormat(UINT);*
ON_WM_SETCURSOR()	*afx_msg BOOL OnSetCursor(CWnd*, UINT, UINT);*
ON_WM_SETFOCUS()	*afx_msg void OnSetFocus(CWnd*);*
ON_WM_SETTINGCHANGE()	*afx_msg void OnSettingChange(UINT, LPCTSTR);*
ON_WM_SHOWWINDOW()	*afx_msg void OnShowWindow(BOOL, UINT);*
ON_WM_SIZE()	*afx_msg void OnSize(UINT, int, int);*
ON_WM_SIZECLIPBOARD()	*afx_msg void OnSizeClipboard(CWnd*, HGLOBAL);*
ON_WM_SIZING()	*afx_msg void OnSizing(UINT, LPRECT);*
ON_WM_SPOOLERSTATUS()	*afx_msg void OnSpoolerStatus(UINT, UINT);*
ON_WM_STYLECHANGED()	*afx_msg void OnStyleChanged(int, LPSTYLESTRUCT);*
ON_WM_STYLECHANGING()	*afx_msg void OnStyleChanging(int, LPSTYLESTRUCT);*
ON_WM_SYSCHAR()	*afx_msg void OnSysChar(UINT, UINT, UINT);*

(continued)

Handlers for Window Notification Messages

Map Entry	Function Prototype
ON_WM_SYSCOLORCHANGE()	*afx_msg void OnSysColorChange();*
ON_WM_SYSCOMMAND()	*afx_msg void OnSysCommand(UINT, LPARAM);*
ON_WM_SYSDEADCHAR()	*afx_msg void OnSysDeadChar(UINT, UINT, UINT);*
ON_WM_SYSKEYDOWN()	*afx_msg void OnSysKeyDown(UINT, UINT, UINT);*
ON_WM_SYSKEYUP()	*afx_msg void OnSysKeyUp(UINT, UINT, UINT);*
ON_WM_TCARD()	*afx_msg void OnTCard(UINT, DWORD);*
ON_WM_TIMECHANGE()	*afx_msg void OnTimeChange();*
ON_WM_TIMER()	*afx_msg void OnTimer(UINT);*
ON_WM_VKEYTOITEM()	*afx_msg int OnVKeyToItem(UINT, CListBox*, UINT);*
ON_WM_VKEYTOITEM_REFLECT()	*afx_msg int VKeyToItem(UINT, UINT);*
ON_WM_VSCROLL()	*afx_msg void OnVScroll(UINT, UINT, CScrollBar*);*
ON_WM_VSCROLL_REFLECT()	*afx_msg void VScroll(UINT, UINT);*
ON_WM_VSCROLLCLIPBOARD()	*afx_msg void OnVScrollClipboard(CWnd*, UINT, UINT);*
ON_WM_WINDOWPOSCHANGED()	*afx_msg void OnWindowPosChanged (WINDOWPOS*);*
ON_WM_WINDOWPOSCHANGING()	*afx_msg void OnWindowPosChanging (WINDOWPOS*);*
ON_WM_WININICHANGE()	*afx_msg void OnWinIniChange(LPCTSTR);*

User-Defined Message Codes

Map Entry	Function Prototype
ON_MESSAGE(<message>,<memberFxn>)	*afx_msg LRESULT memberFxn(WPARAM, LPARAM);*
ON_REGISTERED_MESSAGE (<nMessageVariable>,<memberFxn>)	*afx_msg LRESULT memberFxn(WPARAM, LPARAM);*
ON_REGISTERED_THREAD MESSAGE (<nMessageVariable>, <memberFxn>)	*afx_msg void memberFxn(WPARAM, LPARAM);*
ON_THREAD_MESSAGE (<message>, <memberFxn>)	*afx_msg void memberFxn(WPARAM, LPARAM);*

Appendix B

MFC Library Runtime Class Identification and Dynamic Object Creation

Long before runtime type information (RTTI) was added to the C++ language specification, the MFC library designers realized that they needed runtime access to an object's class name and to the position of the class in the hierarchy. Also, the document-view architecture (and, later, COM class factories) demanded that objects be constructed from a class specified at run time. So the MFC team created an integrated macro-based class identification and dynamic creation system that depends on the universal *CObject* base class. And in spite of the fact that the Visual C++ .NET compiler supports the ANSI RTTI syntax, the MFC library continues to use the original system, which actually has more features.

This appendix explains how the MFC library implements the class identification and dynamic creation features. You'll see how the *DECLARE_DYNAMIC*, *DECLARE_DYNCREATE*, and associated macros work, and you'll learn about the *RUNTIME_CLASS* macro and the *CRuntimeClass* structure.

Getting an Object's Class Name at Run Time

If you want only an object's class name, you'll have an easy time, assuming that all your classes are derived from a common base class, *CObject*. (Note that this example does *not* use the real MFC *CObject* class.) Here's how you get the class name:

```
class CObject
{
public:
    virtual char* GetClassName() const { return NULL; }
};

class CMyClass : public CObject
{
public:
    static char s_lpszClassName[];
    virtual char* GetClassName() const { return s_lpszClassName; }
};
char CMyClass::s_szClassName[] = "CMyClass";
```

Each derived class overrides the virtual *GetClassName* function, which returns a static string. You get an object's actual class name even if you use a *CObject* pointer to call *GetClassName*. If you need the class name feature in many classes, you can save yourself some work by writing macros. A *DECLARE_CLASSNAME* macro might insert the static data member and the *GetClassName* function in the class declaration, and an *IMPLEMENT_CLASSNAME* macro might define the class name string in the implementation file.

The MFC *CRuntimeClass* Structure and the *RUNTIME_CLASS* Macro

In a real MFC program, an instance of the *CRuntimeClass* structure replaces the static *s_lpszClassName* data member shown above. This structure has data members for the class name and the object size; it also contains a pointer to a special static function, *CreateObject*, that's supposed to be implemented in the target class. Here's a simplified version of *CRuntimeClass*:

```
struct CRuntimeClass
{
    // Attributes
    LPCSTR m_lpszClassName;
    int m_nObjectSize;
```

```
    UINT m_wSchema; // Schema number of the loaded class
    CObject* (PASCAL* m_pfnCreateObject)(); // NULL => abstract class
#ifdef _AFXDLL
    CRuntimeClass* (PASCAL* m_pfnGetBaseClass)();
#else
    CRuntimeClass* m_pBaseClass;
#endif

    // Operations
    CObject* CreateObject();
    BOOL IsDerivedFrom(const CRuntimeClass* pBaseClass) const;

    // Dynamic name lookup and creation
    static CRuntimeClass* PASCAL FromName(LPCSTR lpszClassName);
    static CRuntimeClass* PASCAL FromName(LPCWSTR lpszClassName);
    static CObject* PASCAL CreateObject(LPCSTR lpszClassName);
    static CObject* PASCAL CreateObject(LPCWSTR lpszClassName);

    // Implementation
    void Store(CArchive& ar) const;
    static CRuntimeClass* PASCAL Load(CArchive& ar, UINT* pwSchemaNum);

    // CRuntimeClass objects linked together in simple list
    CRuntimeClass* m_pNextClass;    // Linked list of registered classes
    const AFX_CLASSINIT* m_pClassInit;
};
```

> **Note** The real MFC *CRuntimeClass* structure has additional data members and functions that navigate through the class's hierarchy. This navigation feature is not supported by the official C++ RTTI implementation.

This structure supports not only class name retrieval but also dynamic creation. Each class you derive from *CObject* has a static *CRuntimeClass* data member, provided you use the MFC *DECLARE_DYNAMIC*, *DECLARE_DYNCREATE*, or *DECLARE_SERIAL* macro in the declaration and the corresponding *IMPLEMENT* macro in the implementation file. The name of the static data member is, by convention, *class<class_name>*. If your class were named *CMyClass*, the *CRuntimeClass* data member would be named *classCMyClass*.

If you want a pointer to a class's static *CRuntimeClass* object, you use the MFC *RUNTIME_CLASS* macro, defined as follows:

```
#define _RUNTIME_CLASS(class_name)\
((CRuntimeClass*)(&class_name::class##class_name))
#ifdef _AFXDLL
#define RUNTIME_CLASS(class_name) (class_name::GetThisClass())
#else
#define RUNTIME_CLASS(class_name) _RUNTIME_CLASS(class_name)
#endif
```

Here's how you use the macro to get the name string from a class name:

```
ASSERT(RUNTIME_CLASS(CMyClass)->m_lpszClassName == "CMyClass");
```

If you want the class name string from an object, you call the virtual *CObject::GetRuntimeClass* function. The function simply returns a pointer to the class's static *CRuntimeClass* object, just as earlier the *GetClassName* function returned the name string. Here's the function for *CMyClass*:

```
virtual CRuntimeClass* GetRuntimeClass()
    const { return &classCMyClass; }
```

And here's how you call it:

```
ASSERT(pMyObject->GetRuntimeClass()->m_lpszClassName == "CMyClass");
```

Dynamic Creation

You've learned that the *DECLARE* and *IMPLEMENT* macros add a static *CRuntimeClass* object to a class. If you use the *DECLARE_DYNCREATE* or *DECLARE_SERIAL* macro (and the corresponding *IMPLEMENT* macro), you get an additional static member function *CreateObject* (which is distinct from *CRuntimeClass::CreateObject*) in your class. Here's an example:

```
CObject* CMyClass::CreateObject()
{
    return new CMyClass;
}
```

Obviously, *CMyClass* needs a default constructor. This constructor is declared protected in wizard-generated classes that support dynamic creation.

Now look at the (slightly abbreviated) code for the *CRuntimeClass::CreateObject* function:

```
CObject* CRuntimeClass::CreateObject()
{
    return (*m_pfnCreateObject)();
}
```

This function makes an indirect call to the *CreateObject* function in the target class. Here's how you dynamically construct an object of class *CMyClass*:

```
CRuntimeClass* pRTC = RUNTIME_CLASS(CMyObject);
CMyClass* pMyObject = (CMyClass*)pRTC->CreateObject();
```

Now you know how document templates work. A document template object has three *CRuntimeClass** data members initialized at construction to point to the static *CRuntimeClass* data members for the document, frame, and view classes. When *CWinApp::OnFileNew* is called, the framework calls the *CreateObject* functions for the three stored pointers.

A Sample Program

Here's the code for a command-line program that dynamically constructs objects of two classes. This isn't real MFC code—the *CObject* class is a simplified version of the MFC library *CObject* class. You can find this code in the dyncreat.cpp file in the \vcppnet\appendb folder on the companion CD.

```
// dyncreat.cpp : Defines the entry point for the console application.
//

#include "stdafx.h"

#include <stdio.h>

#define RUNTIME_CLASS(class_name) (&class_name::class##class_name)

class CObject;

struct CRuntimeClass
{
    char m_lpszClassName[21];
    int m_nObjectSize;
    CObject* (*m_pfnCreateObject)();
    CObject* CreateObject();
};

// Not a true abstract class because there are no pure
//  virtual functions, but user can't create CObject objects
//  because of the protected constructor
class CObject
{
public:
```

(continued)

```
    // not pure because derived classes don't necessarily
    // implement it
    virtual CRuntimeClass* GetRuntimeClass() const { return NULL; }

    // We never construct objects of class CObject, but in MFC we
    //  use this to get class hierarchy information.
    static CRuntimeClass classCObject;        // DYNAMIC
    virtual ~CObject() {};  // gotta have it
protected:
    CObject() { printf("CObject constructor\n"); }
};

CRuntimeClass CObject::classCObject = { "CObject",
    sizeof(CObject), NULL };

CObject* CRuntimeClass::CreateObject()
{
    return (*m_pfnCreateObject)(); // indirect function call
}

class CAlpha : public CObject
{
public:
    virtual CRuntimeClass* GetRuntimeClass()
        const { return &classCAlpha; }
    static CRuntimeClass classCAlpha;        // DYNAMIC
    static CObject* CreateObject();          // DYNCREATE
protected:
    CAlpha() { printf("CAlpha constructor\n"); }
};

CRuntimeClass CAlpha::classCAlpha = { "CAlpha",
    sizeof(CAlpha), CAlpha::CreateObject };

CObject* CAlpha::CreateObject() // static function
{
    return new CAlpha;
}

class CBeta : public CObject
{
public:
    virtual CRuntimeClass* GetRuntimeClass()
        const { return &classCBeta; }
    static CRuntimeClass classCBeta;         // DYNAMIC
    static CObject* CreateObject();          // DYNCREATE
protected:
    CBeta() { printf("CBeta constructor\n"); }
};
```

```
CRuntimeClass CBeta::classCBeta = { "CBeta",
    sizeof(CBeta), CBeta::CreateObject };

CObject* CBeta::CreateObject() // static function
{
    return new CBeta;
}

int main()
{
    printf("Entering dyncreate main\n");

    CRuntimeClass* pRTCAlpha = RUNTIME_CLASS(CAlpha);
    CObject* pObj1 = pRTCAlpha->CreateObject();
    printf("class of pObj1 = %s\n",
        pObj1->GetRuntimeClass()->m_lpszClassName);

    CRuntimeClass* pRTCBeta = RUNTIME_CLASS(CBeta);
    CObject* pObj2 = pRTCBeta->CreateObject();
    printf("class of pObj2 = %s\n",
        pObj2->GetRuntimeClass()->m_lpszClassName);

    delete pObj1;
    delete pObj2;
    return 0;
}
```

Index

Send feedback about this index to *msppindex@microsoft.com*.

E

F

G

H

J

K

L

M

N

O

P

Q

R

T

W

X

George Shepherd

When George Shepherd isn't writing .NET components for Syncfusion (*http://www.syncfusion.com*), he teaches short courses with DevelopMentor (*http://www.develop.com*). George is a contributing editor for MSDN magazine, and the coauthor of several other books on working with Microsoft technologies. George now prefers to play his Hamer Artist between compiles (although .NET's new JIT compiling doesn't leave as much time for that).

Drill Bit

The year was 1914, and the electric motor was still newfangled. Along came two bright young fellows, S. Duncan Black and Alonzo G. Decker, who saw its possibilities. They hooked one of the new motors up to a **drill bit**—a circular piece of metal with a chisel edge and cutting lips—and the world's first electric drill was born. It had a pistol grip and a trigger switch, and it made boring holes a snap, but it didn't really catch on until 20 years later when, in 1946, Black and Decker designed a model for consumers, and the tool took off. As usual, necessity was the mother of invention and the father of a highly successful company—a bit of wisdom you can drill home time and time again.*

At Microsoft Press, we use tools to illustrate our books for software developers and IT professionals. Tools very simply and powerfully symbolize human inventiveness. They're a metaphor for people extending their capabilities, precision, and reach. From simple calipers and pliers to digital micrometers and lasers, these stylized illustrations give each book a visual identity, and a personality to the series. With tools and knowledge, there's no limit to creativity and innovation. Our tag line says it all: *The tools you need to put technology to work.*

* From The Great Tool Emporium by David X. Manners (published by E.P. Dutton/Times Mirror Magazines, Inc., 1979)

The manuscript for this book was prepared and galleyed using Microsoft Word. Pages were composed by Microsoft Press using Adobe FrameMaker+SGML for Windows, with text in Garamond and display type in Helvetica Condensed. Composed pages were delivered to the printer as electronic prepress files.

Cover Designer:	Methodologie, Inc.
Interior Graphic Designer:	James D. Kramer
Principal Compositor:	Gina Cassill
Interior Artist:	Joel Panchot
Principal Proofreader:	Ina Chang
Indexer:	Julie Kawabata

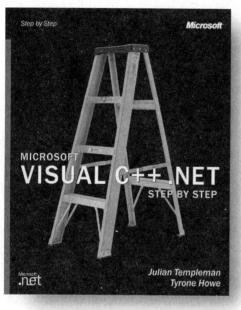

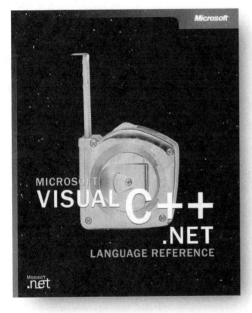

MICROSOFT LICENSE AGREEMENT

Book Companion CD

IMPORTANT—READ CAREFULLY: This Microsoft End-User License Agreement ("EULA") is a legal agreement between you (either an individual or an entity) and Microsoft Corporation for the Microsoft product identified above, which includes computer software and may include associated media, printed materials, and "online" or electronic documentation ("SOFTWARE PRODUCT"). Any component included within the SOFTWARE PRODUCT that is accompanied by a separate End-User License Agreement shall be governed by such agreement and not the terms set forth below. By installing, copying, or otherwise using the SOFTWARE PRODUCT, you agree to be bound by the terms of this EULA. If you do not agree to the terms of this EULA, you are not authorized to install, copy, or otherwise use the SOFTWARE PRODUCT; you may, however, return the SOFTWARE PRODUCT, along with all printed materials and other items that form a part of the Microsoft product that includes the SOFTWARE PRODUCT, to the place you obtained them for a full refund.

SOFTWARE PRODUCT LICENSE

The SOFTWARE PRODUCT is protected by United States copyright laws and international copyright treaties, as well as other intellectual property laws and treaties. The SOFTWARE PRODUCT is licensed, not sold.

1. **GRANT OF LICENSE.** This EULA grants you the following rights:
   - a. **Software Product.** You may install and use one copy of the SOFTWARE PRODUCT on a single computer. The primary user of the computer on which the SOFTWARE PRODUCT is installed may make a second copy for his or her exclusive use on a portable computer.
   - b. **Storage/Network Use.** You may also store or install a copy of the SOFTWARE PRODUCT on a storage device, such as a network server, used only to install or run the SOFTWARE PRODUCT on your other computers over an internal network; however, you must acquire and dedicate a license for each separate computer on which the SOFTWARE PRODUCT is installed or run from the storage device. A license for the SOFTWARE PRODUCT may not be shared or used concurrently on different computers.
   - c. **License Pak.** If you have acquired this EULA in a Microsoft License Pak, you may make the number of additional copies of the computer software portion of the SOFTWARE PRODUCT authorized on the printed copy of this EULA, and you may use each copy in the manner specified above. You are also entitled to make a corresponding number of secondary copies for portable computer use as specified above.
   - d. **Sample Code.** Solely with respect to portions, if any, of the SOFTWARE PRODUCT that are identified within the SOFTWARE PRODUCT as sample code (the "SAMPLE CODE"):
     - i. **Use and Modification.** Microsoft grants you the right to use and modify the source code version of the SAMPLE CODE, *provided* you comply with subsection (d)(iii) below. You may not distribute the SAMPLE CODE, or any modified version of the SAMPLE CODE, in source code form.
     - ii. **Redistributable Files.** Provided you comply with subsection (d)(iii) below, Microsoft grants you a nonexclusive, royalty-free right to reproduce and distribute the object code version of the SAMPLE CODE and of any modified SAMPLE CODE, other than SAMPLE CODE, or any modified version thereof, designated as not redistributable in the Readme file that forms a part of the SOFTWARE PRODUCT (the "Non-Redistributable Sample Code"). All SAMPLE CODE other than the Non-Redistributable Sample Code is collectively referred to as the "REDISTRIBUTABLES."
     - iii. **Redistribution Requirements.** If you redistribute the REDISTRIBUTABLES, you agree to: (i) distribute the REDISTRIBUTABLES in object code form only in conjunction with and as a part of your software application product; (ii) not use Microsoft's name, logo, or trademarks to market your software application product; (iii) include a valid copyright notice on your software application product; (iv) indemnify, hold harmless, and defend Microsoft from and against any claims or lawsuits, including attorney's fees, that arise or result from the use or distribution of your software application product; and (v) not permit further distribution of the REDISTRIBUTABLES by your end user. Contact Microsoft for the applicable royalties due and other licensing terms for all other uses and/or distribution of the REDISTRIBUTABLES.

2. **DESCRIPTION OF OTHER RIGHTS AND LIMITATIONS.**
   - **Limitations on Reverse Engineering, Decompilation, and Disassembly.** You may not reverse engineer, decompile, or disassemble the SOFTWARE PRODUCT, except and only to the extent that such activity is expressly permitted by applicable law notwithstanding this limitation.
   - **Separation of Components.** The SOFTWARE PRODUCT is licensed as a single product. Its component parts may not be separated for use on more than one computer.
   - **Rental.** You may not rent, lease, or lend the SOFTWARE PRODUCT.
   - **Support Services.** Microsoft may, but is not obligated to, provide you with support services related to the SOFTWARE PRODUCT ("Support Services"). Use of Support Services is governed by the Microsoft policies and programs described in the

user manual, in "online" documentation, and/or in other Microsoft-provided materials. Any supplemental software code provided to you as part of the Support Services shall be considered part of the SOFTWARE PRODUCT and subject to the terms and conditions of this EULA. With respect to technical information you provide to Microsoft as part of the Support Services, Microsoft may use such information for its business purposes, including for product support and development. Microsoft will not utilize such technical information in a form that personally identifies you.

- **Software Transfer.** You may permanently transfer all of your rights under this EULA, provided you retain no copies, you transfer all of the SOFTWARE PRODUCT (including all component parts, the media and printed materials, any upgrades, this EULA, and, if applicable, the Certificate of Authenticity), **and** the recipient agrees to the terms of this EULA.
- **Termination.** Without prejudice to any other rights, Microsoft may terminate this EULA if you fail to comply with the terms and conditions of this EULA. In such event, you must destroy all copies of the SOFTWARE PRODUCT and all of its component parts.

3. **COPYRIGHT.** All title and copyrights in and to the SOFTWARE PRODUCT (including but not limited to any images, photographs, animations, video, audio, music, text, SAMPLE CODE, REDISTRIBUTABLES, and "applets" incorporated into the SOFTWARE PRODUCT) and any copies of the SOFTWARE PRODUCT are owned by Microsoft or its suppliers. The SOFTWARE PRODUCT is protected by copyright laws and international treaty provisions. Therefore, you must treat the SOFTWARE PRODUCT like any other copyrighted material **except** that you may install the SOFTWARE PRODUCT on a single computer provided you keep the original solely for backup or archival purposes. You may not copy the printed materials accompanying the SOFTWARE PRODUCT.

4. **U.S. GOVERNMENT RESTRICTED RIGHTS.** The SOFTWARE PRODUCT and documentation are provided with RESTRICTED RIGHTS. Use, duplication, or disclosure by the Government is subject to restrictions as set forth in subparagraph (c)(1)(ii) of the Rights in Technical Data and Computer Software clause at DFARS 252.227-7013 or subparagraphs (c)(1) and (2) of the Commercial Computer Software—Restricted Rights at 48 CFR 52.227-19, as applicable. Manufacturer is Microsoft Corporation/One Microsoft Way/Redmond, WA 98052-6399.

5. **EXPORT RESTRICTIONS.** You agree that you will not export or re-export the SOFTWARE PRODUCT, any part thereof, or any process or service that is the direct product of the SOFTWARE PRODUCT (the foregoing collectively referred to as the "Restricted Components"), to any country, person, entity, or end user subject to U.S. export restrictions. You specifically agree not to export or re-export any of the Restricted Components (i) to any country to which the U.S. has embargoed or restricted the export of goods or services, which currently include, but are not necessarily limited to, Cuba, Iran, Iraq, Libya, North Korea, Sudan, and Syria, or to any national of any such country, wherever located, who intends to transmit or transport the Restricted Components back to such country; (ii) to any end user who you know or have reason to know will utilize the Restricted Components in the design, development, or production of nuclear, chemical, or biological weapons; or (iii) to any end user who has been prohibited from participating in U.S. export transactions by any federal agency of the U.S. government. You warrant and represent that neither the BXA nor any other U.S. federal agency has suspended, revoked, or denied your export privileges.

DISCLAIMER OF WARRANTY

NO WARRANTIES OR CONDITIONS. MICROSOFT EXPRESSLY DISCLAIMS ANY WARRANTY OR CONDITION FOR THE SOFTWARE PRODUCT. THE SOFTWARE PRODUCT AND ANY RELATED DOCUMENTATION ARE PROVIDED "AS IS" WITHOUT WARRANTY OR CONDITION OF ANY KIND, EITHER EXPRESS OR IMPLIED, INCLUDING, WITHOUT LIMITATION, THE IMPLIED WARRANTIES OF MERCHANTABILITY, FITNESS FOR A PARTICULAR PURPOSE, OR NONINFRINGEMENT. THE ENTIRE RISK ARISING OUT OF USE OR PERFORMANCE OF THE SOFTWARE PRODUCT REMAINS WITH YOU.

LIMITATION OF LIABILITY. TO THE MAXIMUM EXTENT PERMITTED BY APPLICABLE LAW, IN NO EVENT SHALL MICROSOFT OR ITS SUPPLIERS BE LIABLE FOR ANY SPECIAL, INCIDENTAL, INDIRECT, OR CONSEQUENTIAL DAMAGES WHATSOEVER (INCLUDING, WITHOUT LIMITATION, DAMAGES FOR LOSS OF BUSINESS PROFITS, BUSINESS INTERRUPTION, LOSS OF BUSINESS INFORMATION, OR ANY OTHER PECUNIARY LOSS) ARISING OUT OF THE USE OF OR INABILITY TO USE THE SOFTWARE PRODUCT OR THE PROVISION OF OR FAILURE TO PROVIDE SUPPORT SERVICES, EVEN IF MICROSOFT HAS BEEN ADVISED OF THE POSSIBILITY OF SUCH DAMAGES. IN ANY CASE, MICROSOFT'S ENTIRE LIABILITY UNDER ANY PROVISION OF THIS EULA SHALL BE LIMITED TO THE GREATER OF THE AMOUNT ACTUALLY PAID BY YOU FOR THE SOFTWARE PRODUCT OR US$5.00; PROVIDED, HOWEVER, IF YOU HAVE ENTERED INTO A MICROSOFT SUPPORT SERVICES AGREEMENT, MICROSOFT'S ENTIRE LIABILITY REGARDING SUPPORT SERVICES SHALL BE GOVERNED BY THE TERMS OF THAT AGREEMENT. BECAUSE SOME STATES AND JURISDICTIONS DO NOT ALLOW THE EXCLUSION OR LIMITATION OF LIABILITY, THE ABOVE LIMITATION MAY NOT APPLY TO YOU.

MISCELLANEOUS

This EULA is governed by the laws of the State of Washington USA, except and only to the extent that applicable law mandates governing law of a different jurisdiction.

Should you have any questions concerning this EULA, or if you desire to contact Microsoft for any reason, please contact the Microsoft subsidiary serving your country, or write: Microsoft Sales Information Center/One Microsoft Way/Redmond, WA 98052-6399.

PN 097-0002296

Proof of Purchase

Use this page as proof of purchase if participating in a promotion or rebate offer on this title. Proof of purchase must be used in conjunction with other proof(s) of payment such as your dated sales receipt—see offer details.

Programming with Microsoft® Visual C++® .NET, Sixth Edition (Core Reference)

0-7356-1549-7

____

CUSTOMER NAME

Microsoft Press, PO Box 97017, Redmond, WA 98073-9830